D0533601

Roger's Profanisaurus
DAS KRAPITAL

★★★ DAS ★★★
KRAPITAL
ROGER'S PROFANISAURUS

First published September 2010 by
Dennis Publishing Ltd.,
30 Cleveland Street,
London W1T 4JD.

Distributed by Pan Macmillan Ltd.

ISBN 978-1-907232-90-9

Copyright © 2010 Fulchester Industries/
Dennis Publishing.

The right of Fulchester Industries to be
identified as the authors of this work has
been asserted by them in accordance with
the Copyright, Designs and Patents Act
1988.

All rights reserved. No part of this
publication may be reproduced, stored in
or introduced into a retrieval system, or
transmitted, in any form, or by any means
(electronic, mechanical, photocopying,
recording or otherwise) without the prior
written permission of the publisher. Any
person who does any unauthorised act in
relation to this publication may be liable
to criminal prosecution and civil claims
for damages. So stick that in your pipe
and smoke it.

A CIP catalogue record for this book
is available from the British Library.

Compiled, edited and illustrated
by Graham Dury, Davey Jones &
Simon Thorp.

Production managed by Stevie Glover.

Designed by Wayne Gamble.

Printed by Printer Industria Gráfica
Newco, Barcelona.

CONTENTS

FOREWORD BY TV FUNNYMAN

letter

RICHARD HERRING

THERE is nothing big or clever about swearing.

Well, that's a load of cock porridge! As *Roger's Profanisaurus* proves more than adequately.

Big. Look at this thing. It's massive. Have you ever held something as thick as this in your hands? No you haven't. And what is more remarkable is this King Dong of a book is filled with thousands and thousands of definitions of only about twelve basic things. Other dictionaries get to write down the meanings of anything they fancy, but the *Profanisaurus* is just piss, shit, sperm, cocks, bums, fannies, farts, sex, wanking and…. No just nine basic things. Incredible.

And clever. By Jesus' spunk stained shroud (it takes a good three days of wanking to actually create an image of yourself) it's clever. The inventiveness on display here astonishes me and I am a comedian so it is my 9 to 5 job to come up with euphemisms for the penis (the Honourable Member for Fuckinghamshire is my own personal best).

It's a fair bet that cavemen only came up with the notion of language so that one of them could say to the others "Look at my cock!" And ever since then man has struggled to come up with ever more elaborate words for bodily effluent and that little bit of skin between the genital and anus. So to invent something worthy of inclusion in this shitbrick of a book after so many years of civilization shows intelligence of the highest order. The contributors are true poets of the gutters and occasionally of the sewers and even more occasionally of the graveyards. Let's not encourage those last ones though.

It's big and clever and it will help you pass the time whilst you're having a shit. Let's see the *Oxford English Dictionary* nick that tagline.

Richard Herring

SWEARING THROUGH THE AGES

IT **IS** believed that our prehistoric ancestors discovered swear words over two million years ago, shortly after the first tools were invented. When Stone-Age man accidentally hit his thumb with a primitive flint-headed hammer, he found that a stream of profanity poured out of his mouth and turned the Paleolithic air blue. The age of bad language had begun.

THE ancient Egyptians believed swearing to be a sign of great power and wisdom – and the most potty-mouthed of all the Pharaohs was Tutankhamen. The boy-king ordered a message of breathtaking rudeness to be inscribed in hieroglyphics upon the door to his burial chamber. Indeed, when Egyptologist Howard Carter excavated the tomb and deciphered this expletive-ridden message – the famous 'Curse of Tutankhamen' - his aunt, who was accompanying him on the expedition, was so shocked that she suffered a fatal heart attack and died on the spot.

SWEARING THROUGH THE AGES

IN 1517, German theologian Martin Luther nailed a parchment to the door of the Castle Church in Wittenberg. On this parchment was written a list of 95 swear words, including 'twat', 'ringpiece' and 'fuckpuddle'. Luther was challenging the medieval orthodoxy, which permitted foul language to be spoken or written only in Latin, thus making it the preserve of the rich and educated classes. Luther argued that swearing should be accessible to the masses, and expressed in the language of the ordinary people.

WHEN Walter Raleigh sailed to the New World in the late sixteenth Century, the Native Americans he met introduced him to several exotic new expletives, such as 'motherfucker' and 'goddam limey sonofabitch.' Raleigh brought the swear words back to England with him, and they caused a sensation at the Royal Court. Indeed, so impressed was Queen Elizabeth by the word 'asswipe' that she bestowed upon Raleigh a knighthood for his services to gutter language.

SWEARING THROUGH THE AGES

THE spiritual father of the Profanisaurus was Dr Samuel Johnson, author of the first Dictionary of the English Language, which was published in 1755. Although he omitted all rude words from his magnum opus, Johnson himself suffered from Tourette's syndrome. He would regularly shock fellow patrons of coffee houses, taverns and literary salons by shouting out profane utterances, followed by pithy definitions of their meaning and examples of their usage from classic works of the past.

1829 proved to be a landmark year in the annals of swearing. For on July 4th a coachbuilder named George Shillibeer introduced the first public omnibuses to London - and along with them, the first bus shelters. Within minutes of the new shelters being erected, urchins had covered them with scrawled vulgarities and gratuitous bad language. The defacement of bus shelters swiftly became the most popular means of communicating obscenities to the general public.

SWEARING THROUGH THE AGES

THE reign of Queen Victoria heralded a dark period for
rude words in Britain. For the prim and proper monarch
was distinctly not amused by even the mildest forms of
profanity. On one occasion she ordered that Prime Minister
William Gladstone's mouth be washed out with soap after he
inadvisably said 'toilet' whilst in conversation with her. So strait-
laced was the Queen that she refused to believe even in the
existence of the word 'fitbin'.

THE invention of the television marked a new era for swearing. But early innovators of the medium were highly sensitive to the use of rude words. When dour Presbyterian Scot Lord Reith founded the British Broadcasting Corporation in 1927, he imposed strict standards on the language that could be used in transmissions. Guidelines issued to producers at Alexandra Palace specified the substitution of swearwords with acceptable synonyms, such us 'Fubbing cund', 'cogsugger' and 'soapy tid-wank'.

aard on *n.* A gentleman's erection that resembles nothing so much as the twitching snout of a hungry anteater, eager to get stuck into a mound.

aard vark *exclam.* How somebody with a gobful of hot chips might say "hard work".

aardvark's nose *n.* A *kindling limb* with an intact *fiveskin.* An *anteater, tickle tackle, windsock. 'Then God spake unto Abraham in a loud voice, saying, Any uncircumcised male, who has still got an aardvark's nose, will be cut off from his people; he has broken my covenant.'* (*Genesis*, Ch. 17 v 14).

AA, with the *euph.* Said of a lady who, for whatever reason, relies on battery power to furnish her with conjugal entertainment.

abattoir floor *n.* A particularly untidy *snatch.* Slightly *grimmer than a butcher's dustbin;* much grimmer than a *butcher's window.*

ABC *abbrev.* The Anus Bollock Connector or perineum. See *barse, tintis, notcher, Finsbury Bridge, taint etc.*

Abdul's special sauce *n.* A thin, red, oddly metallic-tasting liquid occasionally found in *badly-packed kebabs,* which usually ends up smeared round the mouths of hungry gents after closing time on Saturday nights.

Aberdare tic-tac *n.* An anabolic steroid tablet. Named after the South Wales town where every young man between the ages of nineteen and twenty-four eats them like sweets.

ABFAB/abfab *1. abbrev.* Common contraction of the title of the TV comedy show *Absolutely Fabulous. 2. n. acronym.* A lady who has such a *lovely personality* that, when she is viewed from the waist down, it is impossible to tell which way she is facing. Unless you can see her feet. Arse Both Front And Back.

a bit more choke and she would have started *exclam.* Humorous expression to be used after one has just launched a particularly loud and/or prolonged *air biscuit.* Also *a confident appeal by the Australians there.*

abnormal load *n.* An *arse* so large it necessitates a motorcycle outrider.

abra-kebabra *n.* A magical illusion performed after a night on the *piss,* whereby a traditional Turkish delicacy is made to disappear down the performer's throat, only to reappear a short time later on the back of a taxi driver's head.

abrowsal *n.* Embarrassing state of penile semi-hardness seen in the trousers of gentlemen casually flicking through *jazz mags* whilst ironically laughing and shaking their heads or when browsing the top shelf *art department* in a newsagents or motorway services.

abseiling *n.* The act of masturbating whilst using a *dildo* in one's *anus.* From the similar coordinated two-handed action which is apparently required, not to mention the fact that there is a good chance the emergency services may have to be called out to rescue you at any moment.

absolute discharge *1. n.* Legal procedure whereby the defendant is found guilty, but no further action is deemed necessary by the court. *2. n.* In sex, the situation that obtains when a beastly male is able to *empty his nuts* up a lady without lett or hindrance, because she is on the pill or already pregnant or similar.

ACAB/acab *acronym.* All Coppers Are Bastards. Popular knuckle and forehead tattoo amongst members of the urban underclasses.

acafella *adj.* Descriptive of an unaccompanied act of personal entertainment. *'No groupies in tonight, lads. We'll just have to go acafella.'* (The Flying Pickets, overheard in the dressing room, Ebbw Vale Leisure Centre, 1983).

accessories *n. Tits. 'Miss Jolie's outfit is set off with a lovely set of accessories.'*

access time *1. n.* In computing, the time taken between requesting and receiving data. *2. n.* In foreplay, the time taken for a woman's *blip tap* to produce sufficient *moip* to allow a gentleman to penetrate her smoothly without feeling like he is scraping his *giggling stick* on the Great Barrier Reef.

accident brown spot *n.* A health & safety hazard where one is quite likely to *crap* oneself, *eg.* Turn 13 of the Olympic bobsleigh track at Whistler Sliding Centre, Vancouver.

accordian, the *n.* Playfully slapping one's better half's buttock cheeks into each other whilst scuttling her from behind. And collecting loose change from passers-by.

ace *1. n.* In tennis, a powerful point-winning serve that the receiver's racquet does not touch, of the sort that Boris Becker used to hit, and thus *2. n.* A sexual encounter that is over in one stroke, *eg.* Boris Becker's broom cupboard dalliance with Angela Ermakova in 1999.

ace of arse *n.* The patch of dark skin around the *anus*, frequently shaped like the ace of spades symbol, which forms the target of cosmetic bleaching. The *arisola*.

ace of hearts *n.* An alarming sheet of used *bumwad* that informs the wipee that his *nauticals* have been ruptured by an excessively large or firm *Bungle's finger.*

acid splashback *n.* The subject of a fleeting, paranoid sensation experienced by a person sitting on a recently disinfected *khazi*, fearful that a sudden spout of *turd*-propelled bleach might dissolve their *nipsy.*

Acker Bilk *1. n.* Neatly-goateed, Jimmy Hill-lookalike yokel clarinettist who rose to prominence during the trad boom of the 1960s, releasing eleven Top 50 singles, including the plaintive, chart-topping *Stranger on the Shore. 2. n.* A meticulously well-kept *minge* of the sort often seen in *jazz mags.* A *fanny* that is trimmed to a sharp point and wears a striped waistcoat and bowler hat.

Acker Bilk's beard *n.* An anonymously-deposited, above-the-waterline mini *skidmark*, where an *ocean-going lobster* has nudged the porcelain on his way to *Shanks Bay.* A *stranger on the shore.*

acne carriage *n.* The preferred conveyance of the sort of spotty-complexioned gentlemen who effect backward-facing caps. Usually a Vauxhall Corsa or Citroen Saxo. An *estate car.*

a confident appeal by the Australians there *exclam.* Phrase which should be amusingly delivered in the voice of Richie Benaud following a raucous *shout from down under.* An antipodean twist on *a bit more choke and she would have started; speech!, you're only supposed to blow the bloody doors off.*

acorn *n.* A little *bell end* nestling forlornly in the *pubage* of a fat German naturist, that looks unlikely to ever grow into a mighty oak.

acrotwat *n.* One who, after copious consumption of *giggle water*, becomes possessed by the spirit of The Great Wallenda and is compelled to attempt feats of derring-do upon scaffolding, public statuary *etc*. Usually with comically fatal results.

AC Slatering *n*. The act of taking a *crap* whilst facing the wrong way round on the *chod bin*, presumably after taking off your underwear. From the character AC Slater in utterly, utterly *crap* 1980s US teen sitcom *Saved by the Bell*, who always had to turn his chair round the wrong way before sitting on it, though presumably without taking off his underwear.

action man eyes *n*. The surreptitious sideways glance - initiated by a small, well-concealed lever - which an eagle-eyed gentleman gives to the top shelf of the magazine section as he leaves a newsagent or petrol station.

action man's hand *n*. *medic*. A condition symptomised by manual paralysis, brought about by excessive or prolonged masturbation.

activity *n*. A "hands on" style of *mammary management*. *Come in Tokyo, finding Radio Hilversum*.

Adam Ant, give her an 1. *v*. To inscribe a white line across a lady's face using one's *naughty paintbrush*, in a style reminiscent of the briefly-popular eighties pistol-waving dandy highwayman's makeup. To *lob ropes* over the bridge of a *bird's* nose. 2. *v*. To lob a car starter motor through her front window.

Adam's bridge *n*. The bit of skin between a lady's *gash* and her *freckle*. The *tinter, carse, taint, twernt etc*.

additional feature *euph*. A *bongo vid*. From the discreet way in which pay-per-view *stick flicks* were described on the hilarious parliamentary expenses claims submitted by the former Home Secretary.

address the speaker of the house *v*. To *suck off* the *honourable member for Pantchester*. To engage in *horatio*.

add-to-basket bride *n*. A lifelong partner and soul-mate acquired via a touchingly romantic and secure internet transaction. *'Have you met my add-to-basket bride, vicar? Her name escapes me for the moment, but I'm pretty sure it begins with a vowel.'*

ADIDAS/adidas *acronym*. Conditioned Pavlovian response of those who were potty-trained the old fashioned way. After Dinner I Do A Shit. Also, for those of a lexicographical bent, the letters may be reversed to spell *SADIDA*, *ie*. Soon After Dinner I Do Another.

admiral's in port, the *exclam*. Phrase shouted aloud when one finds that someone has left an unattended *dreadnought* at anchor in the *chod bin*.

Adrian Chiles 1. *n*. *prop*. Cushion-faced former presenter of *The One Show*. 2. *n*. *rhym*. *slang*. Haemorrhoids.

adult *adj*. Something to have *one off the wrist* at, on or over *eg*. Adult channel, adult magazine, adult phoneline, adult text messages.

ADW *abbrev*. All Day Wank. A 24-hour trip to the *Billy Mill Roundabout* with no hand signals. Something to do if you're a lighthouse keeper or Apollo Command Module pilot at a loose end, when trapped under a collapsed building following an earthquake or after an elderly and much-loved member of the royal family dies and they put the telly off.

aerial assault *n*. An act of *horatio* given to a man whilst he is standing on a chair, due to the lady being unable to kneel down, *eg.* When she is wearing party clothes, a wedding dress, a spinal brace *etc.*

aero-dynamic *adj.* Used when referring to a chocolate-chomping *bird*'s body that would not fare particularly well in a wind tunnel test.

aeroplane blonde *n.* A dark-haired female who bleaches her *barnet*, *ie.* She is equipped with a "black box".

Afghan 1. *n.* A long, silky-haired *fanny.* Named after the long, silky-haired dog which was briefly fashionable in the 1970s. 2. *n.* A mouldy, tangled *fanny.* Named after the mouldy, tangled coat which was briefly fashionable in the 1970s.

A for apple *n.* A *Thora Hird* that splashes down in the water, resulting in a wet *bomb-bay.* Named after the scene in the film *Dambusters* when the eponymous Lancaster releases a bomb that bounces too high and brings down the plane. Although that was bollocks because the real A for Apple successfully caused a small breach in the Mohne dam before being shot down over the Dutch coast on its return flight. An *own goal.*

afterburner *n.* A pyroflatulatory *anal announcement.* A *blue streak, St. George's ruin, go for throttle up.*

after dinner bint *n.* A *bird* who only lets you *fuck* her after you have taken her out for a meal.

after dinner speech *n.* A hearty bout of flatulence following a particularly large repast. Delivering an *after dinner speech* is considered good etiquette in some cultures, such as Humberside.

after froth *n.* The dazzling remnants of ejaculation which are still to be found

lingering in the *hog's eye* fifteen minutes after the main event.

afternoon wood *n.* The equivalent of *morning wood* for students, people who are actively seeking employment, professional musicians and members of the royal family. Post-meridian priapism.

aginda *n.* A clearly set out plan to stay in on your own and drink three quarters of a bottle of Tanqueray, before laughing and crying yourself to sleep on the floor. And doing *any other business* in your pants.

aggrophobic *n.* One who is afraid of fighting.

ah, bisto! *exclam.* A witty interjection uttered by a *beneficiary* when he detects the aroma of a warm *meat feast* at an *air buffet.*

ahead on pints *adj.* In an advanced state of inebriation but still standing, just. When you are *ahead on pints*, the previous ten rounds have taken their toll to such an extent that the next glass of *knock out punch* could well send you to the canvas and out for the count.

AHIAO *abbrev.* Used in reference to an exceptionally accommodating young lady. Any Holes In Any Order.

Agatha Christie *n.* A silent, putrid *fart* committed by someone in this very room, and only one person knows whodunnit.

aim Archie at the Armitage *euph.* To *point Percy at the porcelain.*

airbag *n.* A budget airline stewardess who looks like she's parachuted out of the ugly plane and hit every cloud on the way down. See also *trolley tubby.*

air bags *n.* Huge breasts which can leave you temporarily deaf. *Oomlaaters.*

air biscuit *n. Fart, botty burp.* A floating body of *trouser gas* that could ruin your appetite.

airborne toxic event *1. n.* Five-piece US rock band from Los Feliz, Los Angeles. *2. n.* A *Ming the merciless*, following which one would be well advised to keep all doors and windows tightly shut until the all-clear has sounded.

airbrakes, disengage the *v.* To discharge the first *horse & cart* of the morning.

air buffet *n.* A lingering, gaseous meal which is more nourishing than an *air biscuit*, and to which one may make several visits.

airburst *n.* A *Jedi knight* that explodes on contact with the atmosphere, leaving the *pan* with the texture of a Wall's Feast ice lolly. A *flock of pigeons*, a *space shuttle*.

airhorn *n.* When you can just pull up your *trolleys* and walk away. The eighteenth *Barclay's* of the morning.

air lingus *n.* A sexual position adopted by soft porn *jazz mag* lesbians, where one of them is just about to lick the other one's *twat*. Not to be confused with cunnilingus, which is the Irish national airline.

air onion *n.* A *Lionel Bart* that makes the eyes water.

air sitar *n.* A twangy *trouser cough* with a distinct Bollywood influence.

air tulip *n.* A delightfully fragrant *gut*, of the sort that would be *dropped* by Lady Di, Audrey Hepburn or Grace Kelly. But not Jocky Wilson.

airwolf *1. n.* Helicopter-based TV series indistinguishable from helicopter-based TV series *Blue Thunder*. *2. n.* A terrible howling sound heard after a night *on the pop*. A particularly predatory *jam tart*.

air your guts *v.* To *puke*. To *shout soup*.

AKAWKFA *abbrev.* A gobshite who is always spouting off in the pub on subjects of which he has no discernible comprehension or expertise. A Know All Who Knows Fuck All. *'Today's birthdays: William Roache, actor, 1932; Al Pacino, versatile actor, 1940; Robert Peston, BBC AKAWKFA, 1960.'*

Alan Johnston's vegetable patch *n.* A *ladygarden* that isn't as bad as *Terry Waite's allotment* by any means, but would nevertheless benefit from an afternoon's work with the shears to bring it up to snuff. From the BBC journalist who was kidnapped in the Gaza Strip and spent several months chained to a radiator while his parsnips went to seed.

alans *rhym. slang.* Ladies' *undercrackers*. From Alan Whickers = knickers. *'Come on, love, fair's fair. I bought you six pints of Younger's and a bag of scratchings, so get your alans off.'*

alarm cock *n.* Apparatus which springs into action first thing every morning, and can be used by a man to wake up his spouse. Usually by sticking it up her *arse*.

albatross *1. n.* A large seabird with a 12-foot wingspan that is said to bring good luck to sailors. *2. n.* A *grumble flick* sexual position featuring five men and one woman flapping about, which was the inspiration for a Fleetwood Mac instrumental in 1968.

Albers pitstop *n.* Leaving the toilet with your *cock* still hanging out of your trousers. From the farcical episode halfway through the 2007 French Grand Prix at Magny-Cours when Spyker driver Christijan Albers exited the pit lane with half the fuel rig hanging off his car.

alcofrolic *n.* A frivolous yet ultimately

regrettable act of *carnival knowledge* which is embarked upon whilst *heavily refreshed*. *'I'm sorry, love. She meant nothing to me. It was just an alcofrolic.'*

alcoholiday *n.* A sojourn from which one doesn't bring back any memories.

alcohologram *n.* A fascinating multi-dimensional optical illusion which usually occurs round about the eleventh pint of *wifebeater*.

alcohorlicks *n.* A series of warming, malty beverages drunk during the morning that aid restful sleep during the afternoon.

alcopocalypse *n.* The morning after a smashing night *on the pop* when one feels like one has just been strafed by helicopter gunships.

alcopoop *n.* The loud, smelly, life-affirming *shit* you have the next morning after a heavy night *on the razz*, which quite often contains your hangover. An *escape sub*.

alcopopscotch *n.* The nimble pavement-hopping required to avoid stepping in brightly-hued vomit when proceeding down Preston Road, Hull, or similar streets throughout the land, on a Friday night.

alcotroll *n.* A woman who looks *fugly* even through high-powered *beer goggles*.

alcozheimers *n. medic.* State of advanced mental befuddlement occasioned by excessive and/or prolonged *top shelf drinking*, which is typically symptomised by forgetting what you are doing, aimlessly wandering up and down and periodically soiling yourself.

al dente *1. adj.* From the Italian, meaning "to the tooth" or "to the bite". A poncy way of saying "just so", when referring to the precise way that one likes to cook one's pasta. Not a problem that arises, of course, if one gets one's spaghetti out of a dented tin, and eats it cold with a spoon because one's gas has been cut off. *2. adj.* Middle class, but well hard.

Aldi TT *n.* Any ageing coupe, usually of Korean manufacture, bought by folk whose motoring aspirations sadly outstrip their modest budget by a considerable margin. A two-door *estate car* or *Lidl red Corvette*.

ale force winds *n.* The toxic sciroccos which blow through *cack canyon* the morning after a night spent getting *hammered* on brown beer. Ale force winds which measure highly on the *Beaufart scale* may occasionally be accompanied by an unexpected fall of *ale stones*.

alehouse ball *n. sport.* In Sunday League football, a mindless punt which is lumped vaguely forward with no clear idea as to its purpose or intended recipient. *'And a right alehouse ball from Ronaldinho, there. A complete waste of... Fuck me! The buck-toothed cunt has scored!'* (John Motson, June 2002).

alehouse tan *n.* The healthy, florid complexion and broken facial veins sported by the dedicated *turps nudger, eg.* Tramps, regional newsreaders and sundry eminent Premiership football club managers.

alements *n. medic.* Any lacerations, abrasions and contusions discovered following an evening *on the pop. Binjuries.*

alesheimer's disease *n. medic.* Premature senility and memory loss of memory brought about by intemperate imbibition of *bed glue*. See also *alcozheimers*.

ale stones *n.* A downpour of marble-sized *tods* after a night spent quaffing Younger's Scotch Bitter.

Alfred *n.* An itchy *cock*. Named after the "master of suspense" film director Alfred Hitchcock, who was well known in Hollywood for having an itchy *cock*.

Alf's nose *euph.* Term used to describe the state of a fellow's *giggle stick* following prolonged immersion in water. From the sad, wrinkled proboscis of the TV alien puppet. *'I've got a right Alf's nose after that swim, I can tell you.'* (Captain Matthew Webb, Calais, 25th August 1875).

Ali *n.* A *dropped gut* of the *silent-but-deadly* variety, named in honour of the erstwhile pugilist because it "floats like a butterfly and stings like a bee".

alien *n.* The sort of *tom tit* that rips you apart in an attempt to get out, in a similar style to the space monster that exits John Hurt half way through his pudding in the film of the same name. Though not through your chest, obviously. The opposite of a *lager log.*

A-list *1. n.* An index of top celebrities, *eg.* Kylie Minogue. *2. n.* Mental catalogue of people you would like to *do up the shitter, eg.* Kylie Minogue.

alisthair darling *n.* A *bird* with mismatched plumage, *viz.* One whose *barnet* colour contrasts with her *pube* colour, in a style reminiscent of the unsettling eyebrow/hair hue combination of the former ventriloquist's dummy-esque Chancellor of the Exchequer and Member of Parliament for Edinburgh South West. An *aeroplane blonde.*

Alka-Seltzer *n.* The involuntary fizzing of a female's *parts* when she becomes aroused.

all at sixes and fours *adj.* Descriptive of a mixed up chap who is equally happy with *rice or chips.* Bisexual, derived from the scoring opportunities available to a snooker player who doesn't really care whether he pots the *pink* or the *brown.*

all-black *n.* A woman who, when performing an act of *horatio*, starts off impressively but invariably loses her nerve and chokes at the finish, in the style of the well-known New Zealand national rugby team, who are notoriously bad at sucking *cocks.*

all cisterns go *exclam.* A hearty cry from the toilet cubicle after the launch of a particularly hefty *escape sub.* Often to be heard the day following a heavy session *on the hoy.*

allotment *n.* Anywhere that isn't the allotment, *eg.* The pub, the bookies, the dog track. *'I'm off to the allotment, love. Have you done me a clean shirt?'*

all porned out *adj.* Of a male who is *working from home*, suffering from overexposure to internet *grot* and therefore unable to summon sufficient enthusiasm to continue his research. A temporary situation.

alloy welder *n.* A *happy shopper, switch hitter* or *half rice half chips* fellow. A bisexual who happily *drinks from both taps.* Derived from the AC/DC welding machine which is required when welding aluminium alloys, as opposed to the fully-heterosexual DC-only equipment typically employed when joining ferrous metals.

all quiet on the breast an' cunt *phr.* Somewhat contrived exclamation which is, nevertheless, descriptive of a lady who has retreated from the front line in the *sex war. 'Seen that Germaine Greer recently?' 'Aye mate, it's definitely all quiet on the breast an' cunt there.'*

all quiet on the western front *1. n.* Title of a famous Oscar-winning film, depicting the horrors of trench life in the 1914-1918 War, *based on a novel originally published in Germany*, which is a bit rich because they probably started it. *2. phr.* Something to say when a chap fails to *rise to the occasion*. *'How's that, Pele? Owt stirring yet?' 'Sorry, Mrs Pele. It's all quiet on the western front, I'm afraid. I'd best have another handful of them Bongo Bill's banjo pills.'*

all rib and dick *adj.* Of a male, decidedly thin. *'I never took to that David Tennant as Dr Who you know, Mother Superior. He's all rib and dick if you ask me.'*

all the shit *n.* See *shit, all the.* Go on, you're not going to get the definition here, you'll have to flick half way through the fucking book for this one.

all threes *n.* Naturally-assumed *self abuse* position, balanced on one hand and two knees, adopted when one's *noddy book* is placed on the edge of a bed or sideboard.

almond *1. rhym. slang.* Penis. From almond rock = cock. *2. rhym. slang.* Socks. *3. n.* An imperial measure of *sailor's ale*, approximately one stomach full. Derivation unknown. *4. n.* A lightweight drinker, *ie.* One who has to be rushed to hospital for a stomach pump after necking a pint-and-a-half. Derivation also unknown.

almond flakes *n. Mandruff, dried taddies.* Also *mammary dandruff.*

almond smoothie *n.* A generous (approximately a pint and a half) serving of *man milk*. Derivation unknown.

almosturbate *v.* To stop halfway through an act of sinful *self-pollution*, either to avoid being caught or as part of an attempt to summon up a modicum of enthusiasm for a *poke* when one really isn't in the mood. To practise *wankus interruptus*, to *stir the tanks.*

alternative, the *n.* The *arse. 'And David sent messengers, and took Bath-Sheba: and she came in unto him, and it was her unclean time so he done her up the alternative.'* (from *2 Sam.* 11:3).

amateur night *n.* See *Black Eye Friday.*

amateur juggler *n.* A person who is prone to occasional flatulence, from the fact that he or she "drops one every now and then".

ambassador's hedge *n.* An immaculately-trimmed *bush.*

ambassador's reception *euph.* A visit to the toilet involving the expulsion of a pyramidal pile of small, nutty *rabbit tods*, similar in appearance to the famous all-night-garage-gift chocolates which were popular with visiting foreign dignitaries in the 1980s.

ambisextrous *adj.* Descriptive of a happy shopper, that Is to say one who is able to *bat for both teams. Half rice half chips.*

American tip *1. n.* A piece of handy advice given by someone from the USA. *2. n.* A short *rubber johnny* that just covers the *herman gelmet* and prevents the *wanked-up spunk* going on the hotel sheets.

American trombone *n.* A *spit roast.* A horny trio of two men - usually Premiership footballers - and one woman, who plays the *pink oboe* of one of the men, whilst the other strikes up the *double bass.*

amidships *euph.* A polite term used by cricket commentators, vicars and public school nurses to describe the *knackers* and *cock. 'Ooh, Aggers! That delivery* *was pitched long, swung back in from middle and off and caught him squarely amidships.'* 'Yes, Johnners. The poor cunt must be in fucking agony. More cake?' (*Test Match Special*, Radio 3).

amnesic dysentery *n. medic.* A hangover. *'Oliver Reed, the British actor who appeared in Tommy, Women in Love and the Mike Aspel Show, died today following a long battle with amnesic dysentery. He was 61.'*

amsterdamage *n.* Serious destruction or impairment of one's mental, physical, marital and financial faculties that inevitably begins five minutes into a no-frills flight with your mates to the Dutch debauchery capital, and persists for an inordinate number of days after your ignominious deportation back to Blighty.

anal announcement *n. Fart, chuff, beefy eggo, trouser cough.* A rousing *rumpet voluntary.*

anal boot *n. milit.* An army barracks forfeit whereby members of a platoon spit into a glass of beer before another stirs it with his *cock*, after which it is poured down the cleft of another's *arse* into the mouth of the unlucky loser of a bet.

anal delight *1. n.* A soft, light, fluffy chocolate or butterscotch-coloured pudding served in a large porcelain bowl. *2. n.* Pleasures taken in *tradesman's practices.*

analog *n.* A written record of every time the missus lets you up the *wrong 'un.*

analogue to digital conversion *1. n.* The electronic process by which a current or voltage is changed from a continuous, varying signal into a series of discrete numbers. *2. n.* An unwanted consequence of using insufficiently robust

bathroom tissue, *viz.* Getting all *shit* on your fingers when wiping your *arse.*

analogy *n.* The comparison of a lady's bottom to another thing, such as a peach or the back end of a bus.

analversary *n.* Once-a-year bash at the wife's *freckle.* Something a married man never forgets, bizarrely.

anchor man *1. n.* A puce-faced, be-wigged alcoholic who reads the news from behind a desk because he is in no fit state to leave the studio and file a report whilst standing up. *2. n.* The first link in a multi-person *bum chain.*

anchovy's fanny *n.* The *fishiest* of all possible *suppers.*

and Bully's special prize *exclam.* Comical preamble to announce the impending arrival of something that sounds more like a motorboat than it does a caravan. Also *gentlemen start your engines.*

and if you've just joined us *exclam.* Said as if addressing an unseen camera on a topical chatshow. A convenient phrase which can be used to fill in awkward conversational silences, for example during a tea party to which Chrissie Hind, Bernard Matthews, Simon Weisenthal, David Irving, Germaine Greer and John McCririck have been invited.

andrexia nervosa *n. medic. psych.* The state of mild, ironically bowel-loosening panic that sets in after one has imprudently sat down on the *chod bin* and opened up the *clackervalve* before checking if there is any *arse paper* left on the roll.

Andrex index *n.* Rating system that graphically indicates the artistic merits or otherwise of a particular *grumble flick.* '*The plot is, at best, contrived, the direction, dialogue and camerawork are, to put it* *kindly, barely adequate and the acting is wooden to the point where I feared that several of the leading characters could at any moment succumb to an attack of Dutch Elm disease. Nevertheless, these shortcomings are more than made up for by the frequent, graphic, hardcore sex sequences where you really can see it going right in, not to mention out and off. It earned a stonking five on the Andrex index, and that's why Double Facial Cum Guzzling Anal Sluts 8 is my Movie of the Week.'* (Jonathan Ross, *Film 2009*, BBC1).

Andrex runway *n.* The long strip of *arsewipe* stretching from *pubes* to throat on a *relaxing gentleman's* prone body that provides a convenient landing strip for his airborne *jizz.* A *wank runway.*

Andrex sandwich *n.* The horizontally-stratified result of two successive bouts of defecation, the second occurring directly after the toiletee has wiped himself clean but before he has had the opportunity to flush. Prevalent in the lavatories of East Coast Main Line trains and domestic post-*cuzza* situations but, inexplicably, rarely depicted in TV adverts involving labrador puppies.

and that's raced away to the cover boundary *exclam.* Spoken in the manner of a Test Match Special pundit, preferably John Arlott, Henry Blofeld or Brian Johnston, when someone *slips one through* at the *gasworks end.* See *another brutal forehand there by Sharapova.*

and there goes Nigel Mansell *exclam.* Post-flatulatory announcement, ideally to be delivered in the excitable style of former Formula 1 commentator Murray Walker.

Andy Dufresne *n. prop.* An odourless *guff;* a *dropped gut* that does not smell. From the escaping convict character played by Tim Robbins in *The Shawshank Redemption*, who crept through a tunnel of *shit* and came out nipping clean at the end.

an excellent theory, Dr Watson *exclam.* Another humorous quip which can be used immediately after someone has *dropped* a very loud *Exchange & Mart.* Also *a confident appeal by the Australians there; you'll have to buy that now, you've ripped it.*

angel *1. n.* Spin-off series from *Buffy the Vampire Slayer.* *2. n.* A passive *puddle jumper.* A fellow who bends over whilst another is *good with colours* up his *arse.*

anger jam *n.* The sticky substance ejected from the *slag hammer* whilst watching a German *art film* with one clenched fist, a red face and gritted teeth.

angle grinder *n.* A multiple-participant circular *bum chain*; a challenging yet rewarding sexual position engaged in by public schoolboys in their dormitories, monks in the cloisters of the Monastery at Zakynthos and leather-capped *book readers* in Richard Littlejohn's fevered imagination. Also known as *Pierre's delight, the pink spider, the Dutch cartwheel* or *monkey cuddle.* It is believed that seasoned experts can perform the *angle grinder* with as few as three practitioners, when it is apparently called a *tricorn.*

angry *adj.* Of a gentleman, to be aroused into a state of tumescence. To have a *bone on.* *'Exhausted by writing of the Great Fire of London, I decid'd to retire early to my bedchamber, whenceforth I perchanced upon Flossy the maid, bent* *over the counterpane of my four poster bed. The sight of her thus did inflame the most base of my passions, and I fast became as angry as a rolling pin.'* (*The Diary of Samuel Pepys*, 1666).

angry pirate *n*. An unlikely sounding and quite possibly illegal sexual act whereby a fellow *shoots his mess* into his lady-friend's eye and then kicks her in the shin. For some reason.

ankle chaingang *n*. A crowd of middle-aged ladies out on the town.

ankle spanker *1. n*. An extremely long *cock*. *2. n*. A normal-sized *cock* on a man with extremely short legs.

Annabels *rhym. slang. Chalfonts, Adrians,* haemorrhoids. From thin former semi-personality Annabel Giles = farmers. *'Jesus your holiness, I'm getting some gyp off me Annabels today, I can tell you.'*

Anne Frank *rhym. slang*. To masturbate. Whilst hiding in a cupboard for five years.

Anne Frank's drumkit *sim*. Used to describe something utterly useless that merely takes up space. *'That (insert name of current England manager here) is about as much use as Anne Frank's drumkit. They should never have got rid of (insert name of last-but-one England football manager here).'*

annual sex *n*. That special time of year when one's better half forgets herself and consents to intercourse. Your *fanny-versary*.

another brutal forehand there by Sharapova *exclam*. Humorous phrase that can be employed, expressed in the style of a Wimbledon tennis commentator, when someone's rear end serves up an unnecessarily loud grunt. Depending on the precise pitch and timbre of the said *heart to heart*, the expression *another brutal forehand there by Venus Williams/Elena Dementieva* or even, in extreme circumstances, *Michelle Larcher de Brito etc.* may be substituted. See also *a bit more choke and she would have started; answer the door, Lurch.*

answer the door, Lurch *exclam*. A phrase which can be usefully uttered after someone exorcises a voluble *food's ghost* from the *devil's kitchen*. From *The Addams Family*. Or possibly *The Munsters*.

Ant & Dec *euph*. The phenomenon of one *clockweight* looking slightly bigger than the other, especially on a Saturday night. The *oddball couple*.

Ant & Decs *1. n*. Popular *art pamphlet* photographic studies, wherein the model displays her well-trimmed *minge* and *anus, ie*. A half-bald *twat* and a little arsehole. *'Right love, that's the hamburger shots finished. Now roll over and I'll take a couple of Ant & Decs to finish off the film.' 2. n. prop. rhym. slang. Dunghampers, undercrackers, poop-catchers, kicksies, thunderbags, squirrel covers, tacklebags, scads, scuns, shreddies etc.* Underpants. From Ant & Decs = Bill Grundies. *'Oi, Maggie! Throw us up another pair of Ant & Decs, will you? I've shat this one.'*

antanddecstrous *adj*. Of a fellow, blessed with the miraculous ability to feel two *cunts* at the same time. *Firky-bifoodlidacious. 'Look at Lembit with the Cheeky Girls. How does he do it, Vince?' 'The bent-faced josser's antanddecstrous, Nick.'*

anteater *n*. See *aard on*.

anticibation *n*. The hopeful, *half-a-teacaked* wait of an excitable young man whilst he is watching a late night foreign film on BBC2 or Film 4, in the knowledge that these minority channels aren't averse to showing *tits, bums* and *fannies* as long as they are integral to the plot and there's subtitles to make it look all meaningful and artistic.

anti-cockwise *adj.* Descriptive of the changed sexual orientation of a previously heterosexual woman who has gone a bit *lezzy*. *Off solids*. *'I see that Samantha Fox has went and turned all anti-cockwise, then.'*

anti fatter *n.* A woman with such *big bones* that even necking a pint of medical disinfectant alcohol won't make her seem attractive. An *alcotroll* with a *lovely personality*.

anus *n.* An offensive term for the *council gritter, brass eye or nipsy.*

anus horribilis *n.* An *arse* that looks like it hasn't been wiped for a year, *eg.* HM The Queen's, during the notorious twelve-month butlers' strike of 1992.

anybody injured? *exclam. interrog.* Humorous interjection following a particularly loud *horse and cart*. See also *an excellent theory, Dr Watson; what's that, Sweep?*

Anzac biscuit *n. Aus.* A *turd* full of disturbingly-recognisable lumps of food, slightly less appetising than the oat comestible of the same name.

apache *1. n.* Sex without a condom, riding *bare-back*. *2. n.* Popular instrumental hit by 60s guitar combo The Shadows.

apeshit *1. n.* That which is flung at your granny in a zoo. *2. adj.* In a state of mental perturbation. *Fucking radgy.*

Apollo 13 *n.* An unexpected and disastrous venting of gas, which necessitates the abandoning of all plans, and an emergency return trip home. An *Apollo 13* crisis is only averted once a safe *splashdown* has been achieved. And one's trousers and underpants have been put out for the binman. From the ill-fated Moon mission starring Tom Hanks.

appendix tickler *n.* A *kidney stroker*. A bout of *backdoor work* up the missus's *chamber of horrors*. *'Turn over, love. I fancy an appendix tickler tonight. You'll like it. Not a lot, but you'll like it.'*

apple catchers *n.* Generously-proportioned *dunghampers* for the more generously-arsed lady.

apple daft *adj.* Descriptive of the state of cerebral confusion achieved by *Harry Ramps* following *al fresco* consumption of cheap white cider.

apple grumble *n.* American *tug pamphletry.*

appointment *n.* A euphemistic drinking opportunity. *'I know I promised to put those shelves up tonight, love, but I've got an urgent appointment at eight.'*

approach Dresden *v.* To experience a strong feeling in the *back body* that one will shortly be opening the *bomb bay doors*, in the style of a World War II pilot flying a fully-loaded Avro Lancaster towards the popular RAF target city. Possibly accompanied by the ominous sound of ack-ack, warning sirens and a certain amount of shrapnel.

Aquafresh *1. n.* A *skidmark* created on the inside of the trousers of someone wearing a G-string, *ie.* Three stripes of two different colours. *2. n.* The thin, breath-freshening red stripe down the length of a *tom tit*, caused by a bleeding *clackervalve.*

Arabians *rhym. slang.* To have the *Gladyses*. From Arabian nights =

Earthas. The *Brad Pitts*.

Arab stallion, hung like a *sim. Donkey-rigged, well-endowed*.

archaeologist *n*. A curious gentleman with a preference for poking his *tool* about in historical *trenches* belonging to women of a certain age. One who is not averse to *meating the ancestors*. A *biddy fiddler*.

archer fish *n*. A *brown trout* which, upon impact, generates a high-speed jet of water that accurately strikes the still-closing sphincter. Or knocks a fly off an overhanging branch.

are you in there, Mr Hill? *exclam*. A jocular remark made to put people at their ease when someone has *launched an air biscuit* which smells like the late Benny Hill's flat did after the police broke down the door.

Argos biro, hung like an *sim*. Of a gentleman, to be furnished with a *gut stick* the size and shape of one of the famous catalogue shop's customer-insulting ball-point pens. Descriptive of a chap who has a *cock like a bookie's pencil. eg. The Rt Hon Jack Straw MP*.

Argos it *v*. After splitting up with one's significant other, to mentally leaf through one's back catalogue of past sexual relationships because you simply can't be *arsed* to go out *on the pull*. From the advertising slogan of the endlessly-depressing high street store; "Don't shop for it, Argos it."

argosm *n*. A joyless, spirit-sapping orgasm achieved using a catalogue.

argue with the colonel *v*. To suffer from gastric complications following a visit to a famous Kentucky-based fried chicken restaurant. *'Are you okay, love? You've been in there nearly three hours.' 'I'll be*

fine. I'm just arguing with the colonel.'

aris *rhym. slang*. Convoluted rhyming slang for *anus*. From Aristotle = bottle, bottle and glarse = arse.

arisola *n*. The darker patch of skin which forms a decorative escutcheon around the *rusty bullet hole*. The *ace of arse*.

Ark Royal landing deck *n*. Descriptive of the state of the U-bend in a student house *crapper*. *The starting line at Brands Hatch*.

Arkwright *n*. A lady of easy affections and loose knicker elastic. One whose *twat*, like the South Yorkshire/Lancashire corner shop in the popular situation comedy, is "open all hours".

Arkwright's till *euph*. Descriptive of an unpredictable and over-aggressive woman, who snaps at the slightest provocation and takes all one's money. Named after Ronnie Barker's dangerous-looking prop in *Open All Hours*.

arm and hammer 1. *n*. Trade name of a brand of inexplicably expensive toothpaste which contains baking powder in case you want to make some fluoride-flavoured muffins. 2. *n*. The two components required by a *wanksmith* before he gives a length of hot *pink steel* what-for on his scrotal anvil.

Armani & Navy *n*. Poorly-made imitation designer clothes purchased from a scouser in a street market.

armbreaker *euph*. A particularly vicious *hand crank*. *'What with excellent browsing and sluicing and a couple of armbreakers and what-not, my afternoon passed quite happily.'* (from *Wooster Wanks Himself Daft*, by PG Wodehouse).

armchair angler *n*. One who gets his *tackle* out in order to enjoy a spot of *indoor fly fishing.*

armtits *n. Bingo wings, dinner lady's arms.*

army and navy *adj.* Descriptive of one who likes his *bread buttered both sides. Half rice, half chips.* 'Birthdays: Elvis Presley, swivel-hipped toilet-death rocker, 69; Shirley Bassey, fling-titted entertainer, 67; David Bowie, wonky-eyed army and navy pop star, 57.' (*The Times*, Jan 8th 2004).

Arnie *n.* A *tom tit* that is, for whatever reason, cut short and thus leaves one with the chilling impression that, like the sinister, right wing Austrian muscle man, it'll "be back".

around the world *n.* Sexual practice which lasts considerably less than eighty days and costs about £25. *Anilingus, back-dooral* or *rimming.*

arrange the orchestra *v.* To make adjustments to one's *horn, woodwind, string* and *brass* sections. To rearrange your *fruitbowl* through your trouser pockets. *Wind the clock, nip and roll, sort out the boys, tune the banjo, stir the stew, pop the mouse back in the house.*

arse 1. *n.* The *Gary Glitter*, the *chuff*, the *nick*, the *tradesman's*, the *chamber of horrors.* The *an∗s.* 2. *exclam.* A negative reply, expressing denial. *'Did you or did you not, on or about the night of June the twelfth 1994, feloniously and with malice aforethought murder Nicole Brown Simpson and Ronald Goldman?' 'Did I arse'.* 3. *v.* To *do*, up the *arse. 'Have you seen the new girl in accounts? I'd give her a right good arsing, I would.'*

arse about *v.* To have a bit laugh and carry on.

arse about tit *adj.* Somewhat muddled. *'Ladies and gentlemen, this is your cap-*

tain speaking. I'd like to apologise for that slightly bumpy landing, only I've been drinking since we took off and I got the controls all arse about tit on the final approach.'

arse angel *n.* The dark, spreadwinged patch of perspiration on the back of a jogger's shorts, or a driving instructor's trousers.

arse antlers *n.* That Celtic tattoo that dodgy *birds* seem to think is a classy thing to have growing out of the top of their *bum crack.*

arse baby *n.* A *ring ripper*, a *dreadnought.* A huge *turd.*

arse bar *n.* Unappetising *bum toffee* confection following which you would be well advised not to lick your fingers clean.

arse barnacles *n.* Unremovable *winnets* on which the fingers of the right hand can be keelhauled. *Miniature heroes.*

arse biscuit *n.* A *turd* that is suitable for dunking.

arse bra *n.* A pair of heavily-elasticated ladies' *dunghampers. Harvest festivals* which exhibit a high coefficient of isotropic homogeneity.

arse candle *n.* A *shirt raiser* which is so protracted and gaseous that, were one to apply a lighted match, it would sustain a flickering, votive-like flame.

arse confetti *n.* The mixed assortment of small, curly hairs and, apparently, grit that is typically left scattered across the toilet seat by a previous occupant. *Bumdruff.*

arsecons *n.* Of e-mails and phone texting, resourceful use of punctuation to illustrate the condition of someone's *jacksie, eg.* Normal *arse* (-!-) lard *arse* (-!-) tight *arse* (!) sore *arse* (-∗-) slack *arse* (-0-)

etc. Arse icons.

arse crackers *1. n.* Unnaturally pendulous *clockweights* that belabour the *farting clappers* when one is forced to run in loose shorts. *2. n.* Notably unsuccessful brand of crispbreads, launched by McVitie's in 1975.

arse cress *n.* Spindly anal vegetation that doesn't get much light. The hairs that attach the *winnets* to *Dot Cotton's mouth*.

arse curtains *n. Under-crackers* as worn by a well-upholstered female whose glands have eaten all the pies.

arsed *adj.* The state of being bothered. '*CEDRIC: Come onto the balcony, Lavinia. The moon is so terribly, terribly enchanting this evening. The stars are twinkling like the lights in your eyes when you laugh. LAVINIA: (off stage) In a bit. I can't be arsed at the minute.*' (from *Don't Put your Daughter on the Game, Mrs Worthington* by Noel Coward).

arse de triomphe *n.* A particularly impressive *derriere*, with a load of red-faced Frenchmen driving round it in circles, honking their car horns.

arse fairy *n.* A bit like the tooth fairy, only instead of removing milk teeth from under your pillow and leaving small amounts of cash wrapped in toilet paper behind, she miraculously changes the missus's smashing, firm bottom into a flabby, wide one when you're not looking. '*Bloody hell, love. The arse fairy's been, so I'm leaving you.*'

arse feta *n.* The barely-edible cheese that forms inside Clive James's trousers on hot days.

arse fuse *n.* The first tab of the morning, the lighting of which precipitates a sudden and breath-taking pyrotechnic display.

arse glue *n.* A particularly spicy *cuzza* that, once eaten, has the unique property of sticking one's buttocks to the *chod bin* for most of the following day.

arse grapes *n.* Haemorrhoids, *farmers, Chalfonts, Emmas, ceramics*.

arsehole *1. n.* The *dirtbox*, the *tea towel holder. 2. sim.* Measure of the roughness of someone or something. '*That Jordan is as rough as arseholes without her make-up on. Mind you, when she's got it on she's as rough as fuck.*' *3. n.* Descriptive of a person with a character comparable to that of Jimmy Carr or Dave Lee Travis.

arseholed *adj.* Completely *wankered. Shit-faced.*

arsehole farm *n.* A golf course.

arse juggler *n.* A chap who prefers to travel on an alternative means of municipal public transport to the one that might otherwise have been expected. A *book reader* or *puddle jumper*.

arse Karcher *n.* A bidet.

arse ker-plunk, play *v.* To squeeze an *Exchange & Mart* out when you know there is a danger of *following through* at any moment. To *pull out a straw* and hope you don't *drop a marble*.

arse labour *v.* The agonising cramps which indicate it is time to give birth to *Meatloaf's daughter*. '*Was I really going that fast, officer? I'm terribly sorry, only we've been out for a couple of arse glues at a well-known Newcastle upon Tyne curry restaurant, and my wife has gone into arse labour.*'

arse like a brake light *sim.* Of one's *ringpiece*, to be enjoying the benefits of last night's *Ruby Murray*. '*Come to the*

Curry Capital, Bigg Market, Newcastle upon Tyne. You'll get a warm welcome, a hot curry and an arse like a brake light the next morning - or your money back!' (Speech to the United Nations, the late Abdul Latif, Lord of Harpole).

arse like a Tetley tea bag *sim.* Descriptive of a *ringpiece* the morning after sinking a powerful vindaloo. From the old television advert in which, to the accompaniment of a voiceover by Barnsley's greatest son Brian Glover, a tea bag was suspended in mid-air, boiling water was poured onto it, and red hot, steaming brown liquid flooded out. An *arsehole* that feels like it's got two thousand perforations.

arse like a wind sock *sim.* A well-*bummed shitter*.

arse like the top of a sauce bottle *sim.* A less-than-clean rectum. A *nipsy* where slight spillages and leaks have dried *in situ*, and which will have to be picked clean.

arse mail *n.* A miasmatic special delivery which may take two or three minutes to reach each person in the room. The contents of one's *whiffy bags*.

arse man *n.* One whose *boat* is *floated* by ladies' *buttocks* in preference to their *gams* or *thruppennies*.

Arsenal are at home *euph.* Of a *bird*, to be *up on blocks*, *chasing the cotton mouse*, *dropping clots*, *smoking short cigars etc*. Arsenal can be replaced by any football team who play in red.

Arsenal sock, fanny like a *sim.* Descriptive of one of those 2-foot long, bright red, knitted vaginas that smell of feet and liniment.

arseology *n.* The scientific study of the bottoms of comely female undergradu-ate archaeologists who dig trenches for ventriloquist's dummy-faced *shortarse* Tony Robinson on *Time Team*; a rigorously academic discipline principally undertaken by middle-aged gentleman amateur enthusiasts on Sunday afternoons.

arse on, to have a *v.* To have a *monk on*. To be in a huff or bad mood. *'There once was a man with an arse on / Who went to take tea with the parson / He was in such a mood / He refused all his food / That stroppy old cunt with an arse on.'* (from *The Book of Fucking Nonsense* by Edward Lear).

arseovoir *n.* The little indent just above a builder's *arse* that holds about half a pint of sweat. The *bum cruet*.

arse pips *n. Winnets, tagnuts, dangleberries*.

arse piss *n.* Diarrhoea, *rusty water, anal fire water, Jap flag juice*.

arse-ritis *n. medic.* Affliction affecting long-term jobseekers which is characterised by stiffness in the buttocks and legs. Usually caused by sitting down all day watching *American Chopper, Mega Machines, Monster Garage* and *Massive Engines* on the Discovery Channel. And then again an hour later on Discovery +1.

arse spider *n.* A tenacious, well-knotted *winnet* that cannot be removed without bringing eight spindly hairs with it.

arsetex *n.* Public lavatory bowl render. Also known as fartex.

arse Tourette's *n. medic.* Comedy disorder of the lower alimentary canal characterised by sudden, repeated bowel movements and uncontrollable, involuntary anal vocalisations. Particularly prevalent amongst the elderly, the infirm, and recent visitors to the Curry Capital, Bigg Market, Newcastle upon Tyne.

arse tramp *n.* A *cleft*-dwelling vagrant who hangs around in the bushes long after his pals have been moved on by the prudent use of *bumwad*. A tenacious *dangleberry*.

arse vinegar *n.* The acidic contents of the *arseovoir*.

arse wasps *n.* A swarm of aggressive, imaginary insects that attack and sting your *anus* after a particularly spicy meal. *Indian killer bees*.

arse weasel *n.* A long, flowing *cack* that tickles the *nipsy*.

arse whisperer *n.* One who has the magical and rare ability to quieten down a lift full of people by silently *dropping a gut*.

arse wig *n.* The *tagnutty* halo of hair around the *gammon ring*.

arsewipe 1. *n.* Bathroom tissue, *bumwad*, *shit scrape*. 2. *n. pej. US.* Contumelious epithet for a *tosser*. Often pronounced as "asswipe", because they're not very good at English.

arsicle *n.* A frozen *turd* hanging out of the bottom, discovered upon waking up at the conclusion of a refreshing, post-pub, drunken snooze on the toilet. A *stalacshite*.

art department *n.* The newsagent's top shelf, where the proprietor keeps magazines which are of particular interest to connoisseurs of the undraped female form.

artful as a supermarket butcher *sim.* Descriptive of a woman who makes the best of her limited visible assets by presenting herself in an appealingly packaged manner whilst simultaneously concealing what lies beneath. From the similar skills of a superstore meat ven-dor, who takes a slab of old mutton and, with careful manipulation, disguises the fat, hairy bits and gristle so that it looks like an unblemished morsel of tasty lean fillet.

art pamphlet *n.* A *jazz magazine*, *bongo periodical* or *noddy book*. Any one-handed reading material.

artichoke *n. Aus.* Ugly *slapper*.

asbolut *n.* Generic name for spirit-based boozes of the sort typically shoplifted by lively, hooded youngsters from their local offy.

asbopolis *n.* A claimant-rich conurbation such as Liverpool or Manchester, which boasts a vibrant youthful culture of non-comformist behaviour.

asburb *n.* Any housing estate which embraces a dissentient lifestyle.

Asda rollback *n.* A crafty *self-harm* opportunity taken advantage of by a *tescosexual* during the *wank window* whilst his missus is out at the supermarket buying his tea.

Asdas, legs like *sim.* Expression which can be used waspishly when referring to a lady who is generous with her favours, *ie.* One whose legs, like those of the sexually promiscuous supermarket, are "open twenty-four hours".

Aslan *n.* Typically sexist, male description of a woman who has the hair of a lion, the face of a witch and the body of a wardrobe, *eg. Fugly*, frightening, feminist icon the late Andrea Dworkin.

Aslan is on the move 1. *exclam.* A popular line from one of them Narnia books, in which the presence of a big lion is announced. 2. *exclam.* Something to say the day after a big curry, when your stomach emits a huge roar and you have to run to the *crapper* before your entire digestive system ends up in your underpants like a big steaming pile of wildebeest entrails.

ass *n. US.* That part of the body the *whupping* of which indicates a comprehensive victory, which is often altruistically put on the line by police commanders and of which the invitation to kiss is often rhetorically made.

assess for flesh *v.* To perform a high-speed visual scan across a page of online photo album thumbnails, such as like what might be found on the internet, in order to identify and locate surreptitious *t & a*. And *c.* What BBC News 24 presenters are doing when you think they're checking their laptops for the latest developments in a breaking story.

assets *n. journ. Charms.*

asstrash *n. US.* Rectal garbage.

asstrocity *n.* A *shit* so unpleasant as to constitute a breach of the Geneva Convention. *'I wouldn't go in there for ten minutes or so if I was you, Mr Boutros Boutros-Ghali, me nan's just committed a terrible asstrocity.'*

ASWAD/aswad *1. n.* Lightweight 80s reggae band formed by Doughnut or somebody off *The Double Deckers. 2. acronym.* A Slash, Wank And Dump. A multi-tasking *chod bin* visit. *3. n.* A woman who is, architectuarally speaking, far more attractive when viewed from a rear elevation than a frontal one. A *back beauty.* From the previously-mentioned poor quality novelty reggae band's only chart-topping hit single *Don't Turn Around.*

at a loose end *adj.* Descriptive of a fellow who is *relaxing in a gentleman's way. 'Why is there spunk all over the walls, floor and ceiling, Jeffrey?' 'Sorry Mary, I was at a loose end.'*

at it *adj.* To be engaged in copulation like knives. The use of this term is restricted to disapproving neighbours. *'Tssch. Sounds like those two next door are at it like knives again.'*

Atkinson diet, the *n.* English food, eaten in preference to any of that bloody foreign muck. Named after robustly-opinionated former television football pundit Ron.

ATM *1. abbrev.* A cashpoint. Probably an abbreviation of Automatic Till Machine or something like that. *2. abbrev.* Anal To Mouth. A self-explanatory activity apparently much-favoured by aficionados of the sort of *grumble flicks* which rarely get shown on Channel Five. *3. abbrev.* Similarly, a dirty lady. From Arse Then Mouth. *'Blimey. That Fiona's a right ATM, isn't she?'*

atomic mutton *n.* A mature woman trying to look younger than she obviously is and ending up looking like a *tart* in the process, *eg.* Liz McDonald out of *Coronation Street* or Floella Henshaw in *Two Pints of Lager and a Packet of Crisps.*

atomic tortoise *n.* Any superficially innocent-looking pastry product which conceals a filling hotter than the sun. For example, a meat pie bought from a particular pie shop which, bizarrely, we are unable to name due to legal restrictions in Cardiff. The pie shop's in Cardiff, not the legal restrictions.

Attenborough's passport, fanny like *sim.* Description of a lady's *bodily treasure* which is distinctly dog-eared and well-thumbed, in the style, one would imagine, of the erstwhile globe-hopping naturalist's travel documents. *'Christ almighty,*

I knew she'd been around the block a few times, but when I got down there she had a fanny like Attenborough's passport.' (wedding day speech by HRH the Prince Andrew, Duke of York).

auditioning the finger puppets *n.* A single act, one woman show which is not suitable for children. *Gusset typing, Kit-Kat shuffling.*

Augustus *n.* A homosexual. A *botter.* From *Charlie and the Chocolate Factory*, where Augustus Gloop got stuck up the chocolate pipe.

auld lang syne *n.* A frankly unlikely crossed-hands *circle jerk* in a porn cinema.

auntie *1. n.* Affectionate term for the BBC coined by the BBC. *2. n.* An elderly *gentleman who is good with colours.*

auntie matter *n. Olive oil, Mabel syrup, olden syrup.*

auntie's round *exclam.* Euphemistic reference to *a visit from Aunt Flo.*

aunt Mary *n.* A lady's hairy *fadge. A Judith.*

aurora tandoorialis *n.* The brightly-coloured, incandescent halo visible around the *bomb-bay doors* of a curry enthusiast. A *Hawaiian sunrise, proctologist's bonus.*

Aussie kiss *n.* Similar to a *French kiss* but performed *down under.*

Austen Tourette's *n. medic.* Male psychological condition characterised by the involuntary making of sarcastic and disparaging comments whilst sat with one's wife/spouse/girlfriend watching a *Pride and Prejudice*-style costume drama on the television. Treatment usually consists of the sufferer being walloped with a scatter cushion and sent from the room until the poncey bonnet-wearing non-sense has finished.

autoglass repairman *n.* A peripatetic tradesman who spends his days injecting his *special resin* at high pressure into dubious *cracks* of various shapes and sizes.

autograph the gusset *v.* To allow the newly-born *turtle's head* to countersign one's *bills.*

avril *n.* The lavatory. Named after the popular singer Avril Latrine.

awaken the bacon *v.* To sexually arouse a lady's *puh-seh.* To turn on the *blip tap* prior to a sizzlesome *Dutch breakfast.*

away win *n.* An adulterous episode which happily goes undetected.

AWOL *1. abbrev. milit.* Absent Without Leave. Even though the O is right in the middle of the word "without". *2. abbrev.* A Wank On my Lonesome. Difficult to imagine how it might be used, but at least the O stands for a proper word on its own.

axle grease *n.* A budget lubricant used in *grumble flicks. Hockle flobbed* onto a *herman gelmet* before it gets pushed in.

Axminster Annie *n.* Affectionate nickname for a woman who prefers carpet to sausages.

Ayers Rock *n. rhym. slang. Aus.* Something large, red and *in the South.* *'Oi, Germaine. When you've finished burning your bra, come over here and have a nosh on me Ayers Rock.'*

Aztec two-step *n.* Diarrhoea dance along the lines of the *Tijuana cha-cha* or *Turkish two-step. Sour apple quickstep. 'Tonight, Bruce, Anton will be performing the Aztec two-step, as he bought some dodgy boil-in-the-bag prawn chimichangas at a car boot and he had them for his lunch.'*

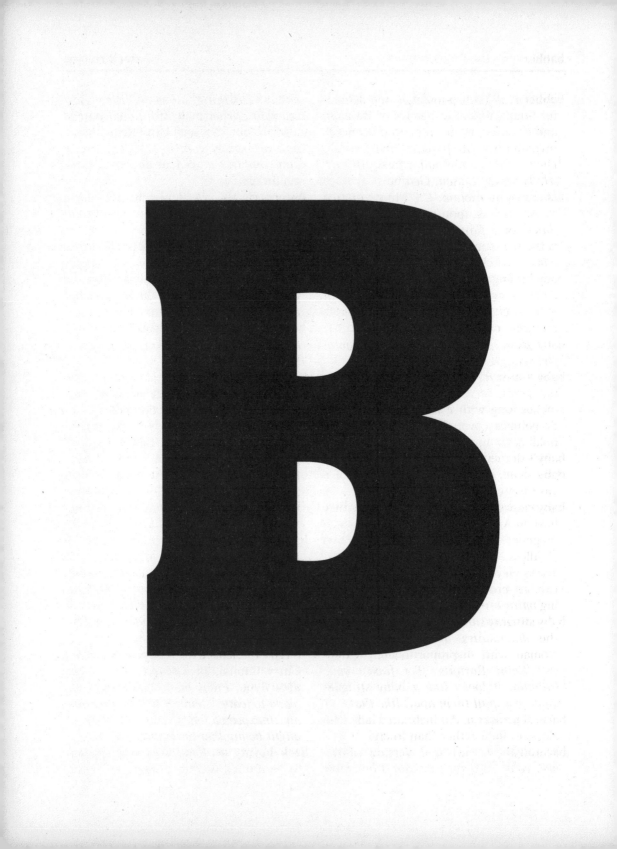

babber *v.* A term popular in the delightful South Yorkshire hamlet of Barnsley and its environs, meaning to *shit* oneself involuntarily. To *papper*. *'Ayup, why's Dickie in his football shorts, Brian?' 'He babbered hissen, Geoffrey.'*

babia majora *exclam.* *US.* Phrase uttered by Americans upon sighting a gaggle of *flange* or a *flange* of *quim* at a public gathering, such as a senior prom, clambake or lynching party.

baby birding *n.* In the world of *grumbular* cinematography, the jostling of two or more *stick vid* starlets hungry to get a mouthful of the same tasty *worm*.

baby gravy *n.* Spaff, speff, spongle, spungle, spangle, heir gel.

baby's arm *n.* Descriptive of a substantial penis, *ie.* One that is a good ten inches long with a bend in the middle. Sometimes covered in jam and usually holding an apple.

baby's dinners *n.* Assets, air bags, norks.

baby-sham *n.* The weedy ejaculate of a vasectomy victim. *Decaff jitler.*

baby shower 1. *n.* Some sort of party they have in American sitcoms, during which pregnant women are given gifts and childless, needy thirty-something characters played by actresses like Courtney Cox get broody. 2. *n.* The act of splashing *bairn brine* onto a ladyfriend.

baby stingray *sim.* A term used to describe the *downstairs accoutrements* of a woman with disproportionately extensive *Keith Burtons*. *'For fuck's sake Camilla, it looks like a baby stingray when you pull them apart like that.'*

bacardi bruiser *n.* An inebriated lady who elects to fight rather than to cry.

bacardigan *n.* *Tart fuel* version of the *beer coat*. *'Are you sure you'll be warm enough walking along Whitley Bay seafront during a blizzard in November wearing just those skimpy Kylie shorts and a spangly boob tube?' 'Oh yes. I don't notice the cold when I've got me bacardigan on.'*

Bacardi geezer *n.* A bloke who quite inexplicably chooses to quaff *tart fuel* as his favourite tipple.

bacca wrapper *n.* A particularly long, loud, wet, rattling *heart-to-heart*. Origin unknown, but a term apparently in common usage in the Gornal area of the Black Country. *'Open the window, mother, and put the budgie's cover on. I've got a bacca wrapper brewing up here.'*

Baccus Marsh *n.* *Aus.* A *dobber* or *lazy lob-on*. From the spongy area halfway between *Melbourne* and *Ballarat*.

baccy pouch *n.* An overgrown *mapatasi*. A *pant moustache*, a *St. Bruno*.

bachelor's boomerang *n.* A rock-hard sock found under the bed or sofa cushion of a gentleman who is not in a steady relationship. *A midget's surfboard, Mother Shipton's sock.*

bachelor's collar *n.* Unbroken ring of *cheese* round the neck of the *bell end*, indicative of enforced sexual continence, poor genital hygiene, or most likely a combination of both. *Cliff's ruff.*

bachelor's newsletter *n.* A *tug pamphlet*.

backbench rebellion *n.* A rectal revolt, often experienced following a night at the Curry Capital, Bigg Market, Newcastle upon Tyne. *'I thought you said you were ready to leave.' 'Sorry love, I've just had an unexpected backbench rebellion. I might be another ten minutes.'*

back beauty *n.* A woman who appears to be attractive from behind, but when seen from the front is a bit of a horse. *Back beauties* form a staple joke in Benny Hill's humorous televisual oeuvre. A *backstabber, golden deceiver.*

back brace *1. n. medic.* A *Meatloaf's daughter* of such length, girth and consistency that, prior to its delivery, you are unable to bend or flex your spine and are forced to adopt a standing posture and facial expression reminiscent of an outraged Frankie Howerd. *2. n. medic.* Gentleman's orthopaedic device employed in order to rectify the debilitating effects of over-optimistically attempting a *thirty-four-and-a-halfer*. *'Excuse me, do you have any back braces in stock?' 'I'll just go and have a look, Lord Archer.'*

back catalogue *n.* Material which one has brought out before. And is plastered all over the bowl of one's *chod bin* with loads of flies buzzing round it.

backdooral *n.* A type of unhygienic behaviour involving bottoms and mouths. *Around the world, rimming.*

back door boogie *1. n.* In heterosexual relationships, the ritual dance which accompanies a game of *hide the salami* when observing *canine rules*. *2. n.* In *book-reading* relationships, the theme tune for *Pot Brown*.

backeye *n.* The *brown eye, red eye* or *brass eye*.

backfire *v.* To *fart* with sufficient volume to startle a police horse.

back garden *n.* That place, situated at the rear of the premises, where the more vertiginously-inclined horticulturalist may till the soil, sow his seed and keep a selection of rusty bicycles. The *podex* or *council gritter*.

back gwats *n.* See *back tits*. It's only

another eleven definitions from here.

back on 3s and 4s *adj. medic.* Assessment of one who has returned to a state of defecatory normality following a (possibly curry-induced) period of gastric upset. This is based on the Bristol Stool Form Scale, which doctors use to fit *Brads* into one of seven categories. 3 and 4 are considered healthy and normal.

back on solids *1.euph.* Descriptive of a woman who has recently been *drinking from the hairy goblet*, but who is now back eating *beef on the bone*. A cured *lezza*, like that *piece* Chris Huhne chucked his missus for. *2. euph.* Descriptive of a *fan of musical theatre* who has taken a brief excursion into the world of heterosexual relations, but is now happily *uphill gardening* again.

back one out *v.* To *reverse park your breakfast*, a tricky process which usually involves much looking over the shoulder, grunting and sweating.

back passage *n.* A rear exit and/or entrance through which tradesmen are encouraged to pass.

back pocket rocket *n.* A *turd* that shoots out of your *arse* at speed and disappears round the bend, leaving no trace whatsoever and making you wonder whether you did a *crap* at all or if you just imagined the whole thing. A *ghost shit*. See *bang! And the dirt is gone!*.

back scuttle *1. v.* To *scuttle* from the back. *2. n.* A *scuttle* from the back. *3. n.* A crematorium receptacle in which vertebrae are kept.

back seat driver *1. n.* Car passenger who offers useful advice and helpful tips to the driver. *2. n.* Gentleman who puts his *sixth gearstick* up someone else's *exhaust pipe*. A *botter* rather than a *bottee*.

backstabber *n*. A *stegular* woman who practices a cruel deception on innocent men. A *back beauty.*

backstage pass *1. n*. In the showbiz world, a token which allows one privileged access to the behind-the-scenes areas of a theatre or similar place of entertainment, usually obtained by *sucking off* a fat, bearded man in a Hawkwind T-shirt. *2. n*. Permission from one's ladyfriend to give her an *appendix tickler. 'I don't know why she's got the hump. The way she was acting, I was sure I had a backstage pass.'*

backter *rhym. slang*. A lady's *front bottom*. From back to front = cunt. *'Oi, Fatty. Careful near me backter with that champagne bottle.'*

back tits *n*. On the more pie-loving lady, the folds of fat which spill over the rear panels and fastenings of her bra, giving her the appearance of having *knockers* on her back. *Back gwats.*

back to handcranking *phr*. Expressive of the unfortunate situation whereby a chap is forced to *fall back on his own resources. 'It's a terrible business. The missus is on life support after getting dragged into the works of that escalator on the London Underground, so it's back to handcranking for me.'*

backwards burp *n*. *Fart, air dump, tree monkey.*

backwards compatible *1. adj*. In the world of computers, a term guaranteeing that one bit of equipment or software will work with another, older piece of equipment or software. Not that it will. *2. adj*. In the world of *anabatic geoponics*, prepared to be the wheelbarrow rather than the earthy chap pushing it from behind.

back wheels *n*. *Bollocks, balls. 'What a gob, Your Royal Highness. You've even managed to get my back wheels in.'* (Peter Sellers overheard behind a hedge at Kensington Palace).

backwoodsman *1. n*. An unkempt, feral type with a Davy Crockett hat and a blunderbuss, who subsists on a diet of gophers. *2. n*. A *woodsman* with a natural bent towards the *exhibition position.*

backyard fireworks *n*. An exciting display of *rear end affection* after dark. *'I made her jump last night with some backyard fireworks.'*

bacne *n. medic*. Dorsal pustules, spinal zits. *'Excuse me, Lord Archer. Would you like me to scrub your bacne for you?' 'No thank you, Mr Big.'*

bacon bazooka *n. Pork sword, spam javelin, mutton musket*. The penis.

bacon belt *n*. The perennially unstylish lardy spare tyre visible between the fashionable hipster jeans and modish crop top of a fat *bird. Muffin tops.*

bacon mudguards *n*. The lateral escutcheons on a woman's *spam hatch.*

bacon powder *n*. Illicit, particulate condiment much favoured in the cruets of media types. Also known as *showbiz sherbet, charlie, dickhead dust, Bolivian marching powder, Keith Richards' dandruff, sniff. 'The ambulance has just pulled up outside. Quick, hide the bacon powder.'*

bacon strips *n*. Female external genitalia, presumably with the word 'DANISH' printed on in blue ink. A *ragman's coat. Bliffage.*

badass *1. adj*. A street term descriptive of the sort of splendid moves made by an accomplished dancer. *2. adj*. A street term descriptive of the excellence of a *motherfucker. 3. n.* Street term describing a *freckle* which is afflicted with *farmers.*

Bader *v. medic.* To suffer temporary legular paralysis brought on by sitting reading the *Autotrader* on the *chod bin* for an excessive time. A complaint named after the tin-legged World War II fighter pilot Sir Douglas Bader. Often accompanied by *Bombay birthmarks.*

Bader's balance *n.* The semi-leaning, stiff-legged stance adopted by a *relaxing gentleman* as he approaches the successful climax of a *Hilary.*

badger *n.* A *minge* you could pluck and make into shaving brushes.

badger loose *euph. RAF.* An air force issue *air biscuit.* "I say, Ginger,' cautioned Biggles, sniffing the air. 'Smells like number two engine is on fire.' 'No, that's me,' confessed Algie. 'I've just let a badger loose.'" (from *Biggles Follows Through,* by Capt. WE Johns).

badger the witness *v.* To *wank.* During a recess in court.

badger's ballbag, face like a *sim.* Phrase used to describe something or someone not very attractive. *'I wouldn't say my wife's ugly, ladies and gentlemen, but when they were designing the Royal Wedding stamps, the Post Office accidentally printed a picture of a badger's ballbag on them instead of her portrait, and no-one noticed.'* (HRH the Prince of Wales addressing the Royal Institution of British Architects Annual Dinner, Mansion House 2005).

badger's drift *n.* The *smelly bridge, notcher* or *taint.*

badly-packed kebab *n.* An untidy vagina that only starts to look appetising after 10 pints. A *butcher's window, ripped*

sofa or *full Turkish.*

bad thrower *n.* A *puddle jumper,* one who is *good with colours, not the marrying kind.* A *heemasex.*

badunkadunk *n. onomat.* A big *arse.*

bag ladies' period *sim.* Unpalatable. *'Don't buy Mrs Timpkin's home made jam, vicar. I've tasted nicer bag ladies' period.'*

bag *n.* Slapper, boot.

bagbird *n.* An attractive young *bag lady.*

bag for life *1. n.* A revolutionary twenty-first century device for carrying your organic groceries out of the supermarket and hoisting them into the boot of your hybrid-powered Lexus 4x4; similar to an old-fashioned shopping bag but with the added advantage that it combats global warming, reverses El Ninos and thus prevents polar bear cubs from drowning in the Gulf Stream. *2. n.* What a gentleman receives after his wedding vows. The strange phenomenon of instantaneous female personality change that occurs the moment that matrimonial formalities are successfully completed. *3. n. rhym. slang.* The wife.

baggage boy *n.* Of *pooves* and *poovery,* the opposite of a *pillow biter.* A *backseat driver.*

baggage handler *n.* Unpleasantly sexist term for a fellow who is not too fussy about the quality of his *cockwash* arrangements. Also *dog handler.*

baggage handler's arm, cock like a *sim.* To have a *chafed chap* due to excessive *self discipline* or sexual intercourse. From the similarity to the injuries suffered by airport luggage operatives as they poke their forearms through the zips of partly-opened suitcases feeling for cigarettes, booze, cameras, wallets, porn, ladies' underwear *etc.*

bagging *v.* Discreet public lavatory *cottaging* technique involving one participant standing in a shopping bag to mislead any *tit-head* peering under the cubicle door looking for *botters*.

Baghdad, she's been shot over more times than *sim.* Humorously said of a lady with a *glazed expression*.

bag it up *v.* To perform the preliminary preparations for a *posh wank* on one's *old fella*; that is to say, to don a *jubber ray* or *American tip*.

bag of slapped twats, ugly as a *sim.* Not conventionally attractive, facially inept. Descriptive of one who looks like *she's fallen off the bells at Notre Dame*.

bag of slugs *n.* A particularly slimy *mingepiece*. *'Jeeves answered on the first ring. 'What-ho, old chap,' I said. 'Fish out those French letters from my dressing table, there's a fellow. I'm out with the Duchess of Worcester and I've just got my fingers off her. By Jove, it was like putting my hand in a bag of slugs.''* (from *I'm Coming, Jeeves!* by PG Wodehouse).

bagpeel *n. medic.* The condition suffered by men on hot days, symptomised by the *ball bag* glueing itself to the inner thigh, necessitating awkward, Jack Douglas-style leg spasms to separate the two.

bagpipe *v.* To ignore the *pink* and the *brown*, and instead shove the cue straight into the top corner pocket. To have armpit sex, or engage in an *Hawaiian muscle fuck*.

bagpuss *n.* An old, fat, furry *cunt*.

bagsy *v. legal.* An make an assertion of claim upon something, based solely upon the legal precedent that the one who speaks first has primary rights of ownership. *'Right. Bagsy me the Sinai. Yous lot of had it since the Six Day War in 1967. It's not fair.'* (Anwar Sadat, Israeli-Egyptian Summit, 1978).

bahdumb bahdish *1. n. onomat.* The sound of a drummer pointing out where the jokes are in Jay Leno's script on the *Tonight Show*. *2. n. onomat.* The sound of a *Sir Douglas Hurd* leaving your *nipsy* and momentarily later hitting the water in the *pan*.

bahookie *n. Scot.* Arse. *'Jings, crivens, maw! A've got a braw thistle stuck in ma bahookie.'*

baibhe *n. Gaelic.* A rough old *slapper*. Bag.

Bailey's mouthwash *n.* Of a lady, to *horate* a gentleman friend with her gob full of ice cubes.

Bailey's moment *n.* A situation whereby an otherwise straight gentleman chooses to indulge in an act of *puddle jumpery*.

bairn brine *n.* Baby gravy.

bairn's sock, it's like trying to get a roll of carpet into a *sim.* Gentleman's generally somewhat hyperbolic excuse for not wearing a *jubber ray*.

bake one *v.* To not go for a *shit* when you really ought to. *'How was Glastonbury, dear?' 'I'll tell you when I come out the shitter, mum. Only I've been baking one since last Wednesday'.*

Bakerloo breeze *1. n.* The pungent wind that precedes the London underground train moments before it exits the tunnel. *2. n.* The pungent *wind* that precedes the *cocoamotive* moments before it exits the *bonus tunnel*.

baker's ache *n. medic.* Chronic stomach cramps resulting from keeping an *arse cake* in one's *dirty oven* for too long. *'We had been digging through the hot* *sand day and night for almost a whole week before we finally reached the door of Tutankhamun's tomb. Amidst all the excitement, there had been no opportunity for me to attend to my most basic human needs and as a result I had the baker's ache something chronic. Putting aside my discomfort, with trembling hands I made a tiny breach in the upper left hand corner of the entrance. Widening the hole a little, I inserted the candle and peered in. At first I could see nothing, the hot air escaping from the chamber causing the candle to flicker. Presently, details of the room emerged slowly from the mist, strange animals, statues and gold - everywhere the glint of gold. Jesus though, I didn't half need a shit, I can tell you.'* (Howard Carter, November 26th 1922).

baker's impatience *n*. See *potter's wheel*.

Bakewell *rhym. slang.* A *dropped hat*. From Bakewell tart = Exchange & Mart.

bald-headed hermit *n*. A long-winded way of saying *cock*. Also *bald man*.

bald man *n*. *Kojak, Captain Picard, Spurt Reynolds etc*. The penis, the *old man*, the *chap*.

bald man in a boat 1. *n*. A lady's *clematis*. The *wail switch*. 2. *n*. A hairless fellow esconced in a waterborne craft.

baldy hof incha *n*. *Glasweg*. Literally "hairless half incher", a phrase much used when Celtic and Rangers fans convene to discuss Keith Chegwin's penis.

Balham ballet *n*. The intricate, yet graceful movements of an inebriated tramp on any South London high street.

Balkans *n*. In British *Carry On* films, a vague euphemism for the testicles, *bollocks*. Also the *Urals*, the *Balearics*.

ball *v*. *US*. To *poke, nob, bang*.

ballacks *exclam*. Mild curse which can be used when everything in life is set up perfectly, only for it all to turn to *shit* at the last minute. Named after the eponymous German football captain and Chelsea midfielder, who contrived to achieve runner-up status in three major footballing competitions within the space of a mere five weeks.

Ballarat *n*. *Aus*. A fully-erect penis. See also *Lake Wendouree, Baccus Marsh*. *'Are you ready yet Bruce?' 'Almost there, Sheila. I'm nearly at Ballarat.'*

ball bag *n*. Bag in which *balls* are kept. The *nadsack, knackersack* or scrotum.

ballbearings in a condom *sim*. Descriptive of an older woman's saggy *knee shooters* whilst she's on top.

ball bumpers *n*. Cosmetically enhanced lips, as worn by Brian's late mum off *Coronation Street* and, less attractively, by former Homebase ad queen Leslie Ash.

ball buster 1. *n*. Unpleasant neighbour who puts a garden fork through your football when you kick it over the fence. 2. *n*. A sexually-aggressive female. A *cock chomper*.

ball glaze *n*. *medic*. The clear, colourless solution secreted by the *clockweights* which gives the tadpoles something to swim in. Also *guardsman's gloss, perseverance soup, dew on the lily*.

balloon animal boobs *n*. Amusing, squeaky, odd-shaped breasts.

balloon knot *n*. *Ringpiece, chocolate starfish, Dot Cotton's mouth*. A puckered *gazoo*.

ballrooms *rhym. slang*. Diarrhoea. From the Sweet song Ballroom Blitz = Brads. *'Over to you Esther.' 'Actually Cyril, can* *you do the next bit with the potato that looks like a cock as well? Only I've got the ballrooms.'*

balls *1. n.* Testicles, those miniature, spherical *spunk* factories a gentleman keeps in his *chicken skin handbag. 2. n.* Courage, guts. *'I like him. He's got balls.' 3. exclam.* Denial. *'Has he balls got balls!' 4. exclam.* Rubbish, nonsense, poppycock. *'Balls! Of course he's got balls.' 5. n.* Round things you play football with.

balls deep *adj.* Of a *pork sword,* buried up to the hilt. The maximum *length* which it is possible to *slip* someone. In a *sausage and doughnut situation,* the greatest extent to which the *sausage* can *fuck* the *doughnut. In up to the apricots, in up to the maker's nameplate etc.* In Jack Straw's case, that's about an inch and a half in.

ballseye *exclam.* Director's cry of approbation heard on pornographic film sets, coinciding with the starring male thespian managing to successfully *chuck his muck* directly into the eyeball of his lady counterpart. *'Well done, Gunther. Ballseye!'*

balls like bats' wings *sim. medic.* Descriptive of deflated, leathery testicles, a condition often accompanied by insanity, blindness and stunted growth. *Knackers* that have been *wanked* flat.

balls-on *advb.* Used primarily as the adverbial function of adjective modifier, usually in the superlative, eg. *'My Porsche is balls-on fast.'* or *'Have you tried Red Bull? Man, that shit is balls-on!'*

ball swipe *n.* While *dogging,* the act of resting your *cods* on a fellow *dogger's* windscreen and requesting that they turn on their wipers at high speed to smack them from side to side whilst you pleasure yourself. It is, apparently, recommended that the dogger should receive a jet of cold screenwash every five minutes or so to soothe irritation.

ballsworth *n.* An imperial measurement of *spunk* volume, approximately half an ejaculation or one-fortieth of an *almond* avoirdupois.

ball tampering *1. n.* Evil, despcable act performed upon the seam of a cricket ball which could well lead to the downfall of civilization. *2. n.* Evil, despicable act performed upon the seam of a scrotum which could well lead to being placed on the sex offenders' register.

bally heck *exclam.* Wartime form of *bloody hell used* when swearing was rationed. Strong expletives and eggs were reserved for soldiers on the front line. *'Bally heck. A doodlbug's just blown Mother's head off. What rotten luck.'*

balm before the storm *n.* The clear seminal secretion that heralds, to the observant *merchant,* the imminent onset of a full-on *yoghurt drop. Guardsman's gloss, pre-cum, perseverance soup, ball glaze, Winner's hors d'oeuvres.*

baloobas *n.* See *bazoomas.*

balsa *n.* A semi-erect penis, resembling the soft texture of the popular model aeroplane construction material, opposite of *hickory dick.*

bampot *n. Scot.* Survivor of the mental health system. A *mentalist,* a *head-banger,* a *heed-the-baall.*

banana *rhym. slang.* Hampshire rhyming slang for *feeshus.* From banana split = shit.

banana hammock *n.* Skimpy *undercrackers* or swimming trunks. The male equivalent of *genital floss.*

banana yoghurt *n*. Not particularly healthy breakfast alternative to *porridge*, to either *swallow* or *spit*. Rich in *Vitamin S*.

B&B bungee jump *n*. An accident caused by the parting of two single beds at a crucial moment during a night of boarding house passion, causing one of the participants to plunge to the floor, restrained only by an insecure, rubbery connection. *'Andrew Flintoff has withdrawn from the third Test against Pakistan at Edgbaston after suffering a groin strain in a B&B bungee jump accident at a guest house in Ramsbottom. A local woman is in Intensive Care.'*

B&Q *n*. A hurried act of furtive intercourse enjoyed in the spare room of one's girlfriend's parents' house. A *B&Q* is performed with a sock inserted in the lady's mouth, with a view to maintaining radio silence during the entire sorry, sordid business. From Brief and Quiet.

B & T *abbrev*. Cheap thrills which may be taken with a slice of lemon. *Bum* and *Tit*.

bandy *adj*. Of a female, to have a bit of a *froth on*. *'That Issey Miyake after-shave stinks like shite, but it knocks the birds bandy, I can tell you.'*

bang *v*. To copulate like a *shithouse* door in the wind.

bang! and the dirt is gone! *exclam*. What Barry Scott shouts when he done a *ghost shit* on the toilet.

banger hangar *n*. *Sausage wallet, cock wash*.

bangers *1*. *n*. Things you stick up cats' *arses*. *2*. *n*. *Carry On*-style *tits*.

bangers and mash *1*. *n*. The flushed heaps of half-dissolved bumwad, human excrement, used *fanny nannies* and whathave-you which are often to be seen adorning the tracks at railway stations. Not, as a passenger, that you get the impression that anyone has ever managed to successfully flush a train toilet. *Rat's banquets, Radcliffe's sleepers*. *2*. *n*. The contents of a well-used but badly-flushed *bog*, the *bangers* being the *turds* and the mash being the *bumwad*. Usually found in the public conveniences of pubs, campsites and non-stop coaches to Spain. *"Cinders and ashes, Thomas, your coaches are a disgrace,' cried the Fat Controller. 'There are used tickets on the floor, soot all over the windows and Clarabelle's cludgy is full of bangers and mash."* (from *Thomas and the Dyno-Rod Man* by Rev W Awdrey).

Bangladeshi bagpipes *n*. A musical instrument played in curry house toilets throughout the land. Also *Bombay bagpipes*.

bangles *1*. *n*. All female pop group consisting of one *fox* and a pack of *hounds*. *2*. *n*. Particularly delicate parts of the *crown jewels*. The *orbs*, rather than the *sceptre*. *'Ooh, doctor. I've caught me bangles on some barbed wire.'*

bangover *1*. *n*. The post-*piss-up* headache that, temporarily vanquished by the act of love, returns with all its mates at the moment of *stackblow*. *2*. *n*. Those morning feelings of sluggishness, listlessness and lethargy induced by an over-exuberant bout of *horizontal jogging* (that's *fucking a lady* up the *cunt*) the night before.

banjo *1*. *n*. US. Musical instrument played by inbreds in the deep south, that makes a twanging sound when plucked. *2*. *n*. The thin ridge of skin on the penis connecting *Kojak's roll-neck* to the *bobby's helmet*, that makes a twanging sound when plucked. The *guy-rope.*

banjo cleaner *n.* Of ladies' dentition, that gap between the two upper front incisors which effectively scrapes detritus from a gentleman's *banjo* during *horatio.* Guy Ritchie used to be renowned for having one of the cleanest *banjos* in showbusiness.

banjoed *adj. Pissed-up, wankered, arseholed, shitfaced, rat-arsed.*

banjo pills *n. medic.* Viagra. *Cock drops, mycoxafloppin.* Also *blueys, Bongo Bill's banjo pills.*

banker *n.* A lady, spotted upon entry to a nightclub, who one thinks will be a certainty should all other attempts to *pull* fail.

banker's draught *n.* Eminently-civilised flatulence emitted from the bottom of a pinstriped city gent. A *dropped bowler hat.*

bannistered *adj.* To be in a state of extreme *refreshment,* to the extent that one has to be carried home by two friends. Derived from the state that record-breaking athlete Roger Bannister got himself into after crossing the finish line after running the world's first sub four-minute mile.

bannocks *1. n.* Unappetising Scottish bread buns. *2. n.* Unappetising Scottish *knackers. 3. exclam.* Expression of anger or frustration. *'Aw Bannocks! A've just dropped a fuckin' ha'penny doon the drain. Bang goes oor dinner, children.'* (Cartoon by Phil May, *Punch,* 1896).

banshee *n.* A terrifying, wailing act of flatulence with Steve Severin on bass and Budgie on the drums.

BANT/bant *acronym.* Big Arse No Tits.

banty *n.* One who nods at *stoats.*

bapdog *n.* An ugly *bird* with a cracking pair of *tits, ie.* One who has *hefferlumps.*

bap happy *adj.* The stunned, bemused state that one enters having overdosed on *meat vids, bongo mags* or the Bravo Channel.

bapjism *n.* The very first *pearl necklace* that a young lady receives.

baps *1. n.* Soft bread rolls that you could stick a sausage in. *2. n. Tits* with a similar aptitude.

bapset *n.* A lady's matching underwear outfit. A useful term for those who are unsure of the correct pronunciation of the word "lingerie". *'I like your bapset, Dita. Get that in Matalan, did you?'*

baptism *1. n. Chestular rope-lobbing.* The act of sprinkling *holy water* across a pair of lady's *bazongers. 2 . n.* Psychological term for a defining stage in the development of a chap's *headlamp* fixation. *'Patient Z first developed his taste for large breasts during lactation, and has thenceforth gained excitation throughout his life from both seeing, sucking and fondling large breasts. I call this moment his 'baptism' as a bubby man or bap-fancier.'* (from *Das Psykologikken Geprinkipelschaft auf den Stonkenjubblies* by Sigmund Freud).

barbecue sauce *n.* Cheap, yet strangely potent bottled lager swilled down by the man of the house in order to keep cool when bending over a tray of blazing charcoal lumps in the back garden, whilst wearing a humorous apron with a cartoon drawing of *tits* on it. *'Ooh, me guts are rotten this morning, love. I don't know whether it's all them half-cremated, half-frozen chicken thighs and raw sausages I ate last night or* *the twenty bottles of barbecue sauce I necked while I was cooking them.'*

barber's bin *n.* A particularly badly-kempt and unruly *snatch*. *'I'm sorry but I'm not doing that again, your worship. It was like sticking my head in a barber's bin.'*

Barber's Bridge *1. n.* A small town in Gloucestershire that was the site of the first intermediate station north of Gloucester on the old Ledbury & Gloucester Railway, as is well known. *2. n.* The small tuft of hair left on a lady's nethers after a *Brazilian* wax.

barber's floor *n.* A particularly hairy *quim*, with a glum, sixteen-year-old on the minimum wage disinterestedly pushing a brush round it.

barber's lather pot *sim.* A generously-filled *snatch*. Also a *billposter's bucket*, a *St. Bernard's chin*. A very, very, very *well-buttered bun*. *'My daughter is a groupie for So Solid Crew.' 'Good heavens! She must have a twat like a barber's lather pot.'*

barber's lolly *1. n.* In childhood, a reward given for sitting still whilst one's hair is cut. *2. n.* In adulthood, a reward given in return for performing any unpleasant task. *'Suck that? Alright, but you'll have to buy me an expensive barber's lolly afterwards, your Grace.'*

barber's pole *n.* The stripy result of *parting the whiskers* while the *painters are in*. An *eggy soldier*.

barber's sandwich *n.* A badly-pruned *muff*, from its resemblance to a buttered bap inadvertently dropped onto the unswept lino in a hairdresser's.

Barclay's *rhym. slang.* A *J. Arthur*. From Barclay's Bank = ham shank.

Barclay's premier league *n.* Notional society of top-ranking, record-breakingly prolific masturbators. *'He's Barclay's premier league material, he is. No wonder the BBC used to pay him six million quid a year.'*

barf *v.* To *vomit, huey, puke, bowk, yoff.*

barf bag *n.* Sick bag, as found on an aeroplane. Also a useful alliterative insult.

bargain *rhym. slang.* A *cuntish* fellow. From the popular daytime TV show, *Bargain Hunt*, which was originally hosted by popular orange *bargain* David Dickinson although it's now hosted by that spivvish *cunt* with a bow tie.

bargain bucket *n.* An over-employed and overstretched *clopper*. A *Mary* like a *welly top*.

bargain cunt *n.* Upon purchasing a new item, for example a television set, ipod or washing machine, that acquaintace who always maintains that you should have come to him first as he could have got it for you for half what you just paid. However, when put to the test, the *bargain cunt* is invariably unable to obtain anything on the cheap because their "mate is away" or some such similar lie.

bargain munter *n.* Term for a lady who is yours for as little as one or two drinks, *ie.* One who is literally "cheap as chips".

barge-arse *n.* A lady of rotund posterior aspect.

bargoyles *n.* Hideously ugly female pub fixtures.

bark at the ants *v.* To *yoff*.

barker's egg *n.* Poodle *shit*. A dog *turd* so old that it has gone white.

barker's truffles *n.* Pedigree *dog eggs* of the type you might expect to step in on such thoroughfares as Mayfair or Pall Mall, but would rarely encounter on Botchergate in Carlisle.

bark carrots *adj.* To *park a tiger*, to *vomit, puke, sing a rainbow, barf.*

barking spider *n.* The *ringpiece, freckle, chocolate starfish, rusty sheriff's badge, nipsy.*

barmaid on her first shift, like a *sim.* Disparaging description of a sexually inexperienced lady clumsily attempting to furnish a gentleman with a *hand shandy*. *'Fucking hell love, what are you doing down there? You're like a barmaid on her first shift.'*

barn door gentleman *1. n. Aus.* Term used by early antipodean settlers to describe clumsy fellows. *'In Sydney, the idea of some barn door gentleman, an untutored hayseed, big-booting nervously about the drawing-room and breaking the china, filled the matrons with horror.'* (from *The Fatal Shore* by Robert Hughes). *2. n.* A *heavily refreshed* gent who dispenses with the customary niceties on his return home, braying through the letterbox, punching walls, throwing his tea at the wall, *pissing* in the sink *etc.*

Barnes Wallis *n.* The type of *turd* released from the *bomb bay* which sends a splash of water onto your *undercarriage*. A *panbuster*.

barney *n.* An instant *diamond cutter*. Named after the not-at-all-*Colwyn Bay* children's dinosaur that grows from something small and harmless into a large purple-headed monster in the blink of an eye.

barney rubble *n.* That which, during the course of a good-natured exchange of political viewpoints, is torn up from pavements, walls *etc.*, and *hoyed* at the *tit-heads*.

Barney Rubble's car *n.* An enormous pile of *logs*.

Barnsley *n.* An unexpected *semi*. From the eponymous South Yorkshire football team's surprising performance in the 2008 FA Cup, when they made it into the final four. *'Eeh by gum. Yon forward defensive prod from young Ernie Sheepshanks were textbook, weren't it Geoffrey?' 'Aye, Dickie. It were that good I've got a Barnsley.'*

Barnsley blow job *n.* During sexual congress in the *missionary position*, when the lady *drops a gut* with sufficient gusto to blast her suitor's *balls* up his *arsehole*.

Barnsley briefcase *n.* A Netto, Aldi or Kwiksave carrier bag carried into work each day by one who is employed as a professional call-centre operative in the salubrious South Riding metropolis. The typical contents of a Barnsley briefcase include a triangular, pre-packed sandwich, a bottle of Oasis, a copy of the *Sun* and a biro which pokes out the bottom of the bag. Not to be confused with a *Basingstoke briefcase*, which is a carrier from Waitrose, Sainsbury's or some other upper class establishment.

Barnsley chop *n.* Type of lamb cutlet served to guests at the Brooklands Hotel in the salubrious Yorkshire resort.

Barnsley moustache *n.* A tide mark of *fanny batter* resembling the facial hair sported by youths of the eponymous northern beauty spot. Caused by an accumulation of *blip* during vigorous *cumulonimbus*.

Barnsley shag *n.* An act of sexual intercourse which climaxes not with an orgasm, but with the bloke falling asleep *on the job* due to a surfeit of Younger's Scotch bitter.

Barry Gibb *n.* The *centre console* or *carse.* Because it used to be situated between a *cunt* and an *arsehole.* Before the one with the beard and the hat died.

barryjuana *n.* Bargain basement variety of cannabis, which comes in a browny-green lump containing additives such as rubber. Smoked in large quantities by the tracksuited inhabitants of Barry - the delightful South Wales beauty spot made famous in the television series *Gavin and Stacey.*

barrymored *adj. naut.* Catastrophically holed below the waterline. Derivation unknown. *'It's no good, Captain. We struck that iceberg at a speed of nearly thirty knots. There is a breach in the starboard hull almost three hundred feet long and five of the watertight compartments are filling with water as we speak. The Titanic is barrymored. We have no option but to abandon ship.'*

Barry Scott! *exclam.* A humorous rejoinder issued after either passing wind or doing a great big *shit.* Named in honour of the shouty Cillit Bang ad personality's accidentally kitsch catchphrase "Bang! And the dirt is gone!"

barse *n.* The little bit of skin between a chap's *bannocks* and his *freckle.* The *great.*

barse broth *n.* One part *wet fart* and a generous portion of hot *wedding vegetables* mixed well in the *undercrackers* results in a family size helping of *barse broth.* Serve with or without croutons, according to taste.

barse mallow *n.* A light, pink fluffy substance that forms spontaneously in a *salad dodger's tintis.* A sweet-toothed counterpart to the more savoury *arse feta.*

bar stool *n.* An habitual drinker's *turd,* typically a thin, sickly *arse weasel* that slides out and lies forlornly in the water feeling very sorry for itself.

Barthez *1. n.* Former Manchester United goalkeeper. *2. n.* A bald *twat.*

Bartlett's dilemma *n.* A gentleman's happy bedtime conundrum. From the scene in *The Great Escape* when Bartlett (played by Richard Attenborough) has to decide which of the three tunnels to send his chaps down.

barumph *v.* To sniff a lady's bicycle seat. To *snurgle.*

base pissing *n.* The extreme sport of urinating from a great height for the purposes of entertainment, *eg.* Off a cliff into the sea, off a bridge into a river or out of a tree onto a cow.

bash *n.* A woman's *fanny.*

bashing booth *n.* A small room or cubicle where a gentleman may sit in quiet, solitary contemplation of a live *jazz* performance. The working environs of a *jizz mopper.*

bash the bishop *v.* To *pull the Pope's cap off,* to *box the Jesuit.* To *bank with Barclay's.*

Basil *n. rhym. slang.* A lady's *George.* From TV fox puppet Basil Brush = bush.

Basildon bagpipe *n.* An Essex-based development of the *trombone,* whereby the lady sucks the gentleman's *clockweights* whilst *tossing* his *charlie* with one hand and fingering his *freckle* with the other, causing him to emit a series of shrill squeaks and an unpleasant droning sound.

Basildon Brazilian *n.* An economical bikini wax technique espoused by Essex maidens prior to vacationing in sunnier climes, which involves a box of Tesco Chablis, a wooden tent peg to bite on and a roll of duct tape.

Basildon water feature *n.* A skip half full of rusty water.

basket making *v. arch.* Medieval sexual intercourse. *Coccupational therapy.*

bastard *n.* A football referee.

baste *v.* Of a professional sportsman, to pull out mid-*roast* and *tip his filthy concrete* up the lady's back.

baste the turkey *v.* Of dirty ladies, to squeeze men's *bulbs* so that *hot fat* shoots out the end of their *cocks.*

bateau mouche *n. Fr.* A *dreadnought* that is so satisfyingly large one could easily imagine it being used to to take tourists along the Seine. A *pleasure steamer.*

bath bomb *1. n.* A ball of effervescent salts which fizzes when dropped into the water. *2. n.* An unfortunately-timed *evacuation* which can quite take the shine off an otherwise pleasant soak in the tub.

bathroom broadband *n.* The installation of a lengthy and unsightly dark brown or black *cable* in the bottom of the toilet bowl. A substantial *download.*

bathroom origami *n.* The ancient and beautiful oriental art of folding *bumwad* into complex geometric folds, pleats and creases in order to avoid getting all *shit* on one's fingers.

bathturbate *v.* To *polish the lighthouse, wax the dolphin,* play *up periscope.* To masturbate in the bath. Derivation unknown.

bat in the cave *n.* A precariously-suspended *bogie* that hangs upsettingly in someone's nostril.

Batman on the side of the Palace, like *sim.* Descriptive of something which sticks

out a mile, such as Sharron Davies's splendid nipples during the Athens 2004 Olympic coverage.

batman's cave *euph.* A lady's *secret entrance* which is difficult to locate due to an over-abundance of *bush.*

batmobile *n.* Descriptive of the state of one's *brass eye* after a particularly hot *Ruby Murray.* '*I had a real ring stinger at the Curry Capital last night. My arse is like the back end of the fucking batmobile this morning. Five stars.*' (*Guardian* food critic Victor Lewis-Smith, 2005).

bat on a sticky wicket *v.* To not be *the first man in*; to stir another gentleman's *porridge.* To partake of a *buttered bun* or have *sloppy seconds.* Also *bat on a wet wicket.*

baton rouge *n.* After a visit to the *deep south* when the *levees have broken*, the resultant state of one's *Dr John.* A step further than a *gypsy week*, but probably not as far as a *scrapheap challenge Barber's pole, vampire wick end, blood sausage.*

bats at dusk, to come out like *sim.* Of loose stools, to exit the *clay pit* at a ferocious rate. Descriptive of a *flock of pigeons* or the *splatters.*

batter catcher *n.* That small tuft of hair tucked under the bottom lip, for example the one sported by Sir Trevor McDonald or Tom Waits, which enables its owner to trap some of that pungent fishy juice for later.

battered kipper *n.* A frothsome *gash* on your old *trout.* A *blippy mackerel.*

battery tits *n.* Affectionate epithet for a *bird* with tiny *knockers.* From the battery and comedy bra size AA.

batting for both sides *euph. Bowling*

from both ends, as opposed to just the *gasworks end*.

batting for Darrington *euph. Good with colours*. From Ambridge's perennial opponents in the Whit Monday Single Wicket Competition for the Mark Hebden Memorial Trophy in *The Archers*. *'Your George still not got himself a nice girl-friend, then, Mrs Michael?' 'No, he's batting for Darrington these days.'*

battlecry *n.* A loud and stirring *rumpet voluntary*, signalling a declaration of war against a particularly troublesome *Thora*.

battleship rivets *n. Chapel hat pegs, JCB starter buttons, blind cobblers' thumbs.*

battleshit *n.* A large, steaming *dread-naught* that creates a menacing block-ade, and thus prevents the passage of any further ocean-going vessels.

batty-boy *n. W. Indies.* A *tail-ender* who habitually serves his balls up from the *pavilion end*.

batty crease *n.* The line of whiting or chalk on a cricket pitch which defines the position of the batsman.

batulence *n.* Extremely high-pitched *fart-ing*, which only creatures of the order *Chiroptra* are able to hear. Also known as Galton's whistle, named after the ultra high-pitched device used by dog football referees on *That's Life*.

bat wing *n.* When *John Wayne's hairy saddlebag* is stuck to the inner thigh and forms a stretched, leathery bracket not dissimilar to the veiny aeronautical appendage of the flying titmouse.

bat wings *n.* Thin, leathery, nocturnal flaps. *Beef curtains* that Ozzy Osbourne might inadvertently take a bite out of.

baw bag *n. Scot.* Oor Wullie's scrotum. A tartan *chicken skin sporran*.

bawd *n. arch.* Old fashioned term for a *rub-a-tug shop* proprietress.

bawhair 1. *n. Scot.* A single pubic hair. 2. *n. Scot.* A *de minimis* unit of measure-ment. *'A quick look oer the shoulder a'fore ye pull awa frae the kerb, indicate tae pull oot, let the clutch oot a bawhair an' awa' ye go.'*

bay window over a tripe shop *n.* The *gunt*.

bazongers *n.* Gravity-defying, surgically-enhanced, hemispherical breasts that explode in aeroplanes. *'Look out the window, Alex. The people on the ground look like ants. Oh shit, me bazongers of blown up.'*

bazoomas *n.* See *begonias*.

BBBA *abbrev. medic.* The Bit Between the Bollocks and the Arse. The *barse*, the *ploughman's*, the *scruttock*, the *ABC*, the *great*.

BBC *abbrev.* Big Brother Contestant. A person who appears pleasant enough at first, but who quickly turns out to be a right *spastard*.

BBLB 1. *abbrev.* Big Brother's Little Brother. Television show fronted by George "Shabba" Lamb, designed to wring the last dregs of phoneline money out of Channel 4's bovine reality show viewers. 2. *abbrev. medic.* The painful result of sitting cross-legged in tight-fit-ting trousers for a significant time whilst fantasising about noshing the *tits/bush* off Orlaith from *Big Brother 6*, to pick an example entirely at random.

BDF *abbrev.* A festive *own goal*, brought about by excessive consumption of rich foodstuffs, a surfeit of sprouts and too much ale. A Boxing Day Fart with all the trimmings.

bead *v.* To exude pre-ejaculate during

moments of arousal. *To perspire out of one's hog's eye. 'I tell you, Alan, I was that excited I was beading before I'd even parked the car.'* (Stan Collymore, Radio 5Live).

bead curtains *n. Dangleberries, toffee strings, mud-buttons, tagnuts.* Also *beaded curtain.*

Beadle *1. n.* A *cunt* with a neatly-cropped bikini line. A *bushell*, a *Californian wax*. *2. v.* To fondle a pair of *Kelly Brooks*.

Beadlehands *exclam.* Alternative exclamation to *butterfingers.*

Beadle pint *n.* A half. Also known as a *Jeremy* of lager.

Beadle's fist *n.* A tightly-shrivelled or retracted scrotum.

beagle break *n.* A five-minute recreational interval at one's place of work which is spent on the *cancer verandah*.

Beaker's mouth *n.* The involuntary movement of a *bird's* vaginal lips when she is being taken up the *bonus tunnel*, as seen in many a *grumble flick*. Reminiscent of the movements of the Muppet character Beaker "me-mo-ing".

beanbagging *n.* A very specific form of *teabagging*, in which either Sean Bean or Rowan Atkinson lower their *beans* into the mouth of a recumbent lucky lady.

bum worm *n.* A tiny *poo* poking its head out between your cheeks to take the air.

beanfeast *1. n.* A "delicious alternative to meat" made by Batchelors. *2. n. Lesbo* group carryings-on, a televisual spectacle much enjoyed by bachelors. A sapphic orgy. A *carpet munchers'* all-you-can-eat buffet.

bean flicker *n.* A lady of lesbicious tendencies. A wearer of *comfortable shoes, tennis fan, lady golfer.*

beans on toast *1. n.* A quick and yet satisfying snack. *2. n.* A quick and yet satisfying *tug*. *'I'm just going to nip home for beans on toast.'*

bear bile *n.* Descriptive of any food or drink that is particularly unpalatable. *'Betty, this hotpot is like fucking bear bile, I said bear bile.'*

bear claw *n.* Late night, drunken, clumsy pawing at a ladyfriend's *honey pot*, possibly resulting in torn garments.

beard *1. n. arch.* Fulsome *twat-thatch, mapatasi. 2. n.* A woman who is married to a *batty-boy* in order to conceal his true sexuality. See *whiff of lavender. 'Do you reckon that Sophie's a beard then, or what?'*

bearded bank robber *n.* A lass with a particularly hairy *biffer* who wears nylon tights but no *undercrackers*.

bearded clam *1. n.* An edible mollusc. *2. n. Aus.* An edible *fish mitten*.

bearded squid *n.* A *fanny* that will bite your face off.

bear trap *n.* A big *cludge*, strong enough to snap a man's ankle if he put his foot into it. One might imagine that Pat Butcher out of *EastEnders* has a bear trap in her knickers, for example.

bear trapper's hat *n.* An excessively hairy *front bottom*. A *biffer*, a *Davy Crockett hat. 'Put my ladder up to the flat / Saw a nun with bear trapper's hat / I get a wank out of things like that / When I'm cleaning windows.'* (from *The George Formby Song Book*, 1945).

beast with one back, make the *v.* To perform an act of sexual intercourse whilst experiencing a fifty percent personnel shortfall.

beast with two backs *n.* A strange, grunting animal with two heads and four legs, commonly found in Newcastle bus shelters, back alleys and taxi queues after midnight.

beast with two cracks, the *euph.* An unconvincing display of feigned *girl-on-girl action.*

beat a donkey out of a bog *sim. Ulst.* A Northern Irish expression useful when describing something with roughly similar dimensions and proportions to a shillelagh. *'Have ye seen the size of the Pastor's cock? You could beat a donkey out of a bog with that fucker, so ye could.'*

beaten like a ginger step-child *adj.* Descriptive of a particularly ferocious and merciless thrashing, for example, off a bouncer at a nightclub, a policeman in a cell, or Bjork at Bangkok Airport. *'This is dreadful. I don't think Hawking can take much more of this punishment. Bruno's raining the blows down now, left right left right. I can't look, this is terrible. Hawking's being beaten like a ginger step-child.'* (Harry Carpenter, commentating on charity boxing match, *BBC Children in Need*, 1998).

beat the buzzer *v.* To impregnate one's wife in the week prior to the divorce coming through.

beat the meat *v.* To avail oneself of a *ham shank*, perform the *five-knuckle shuffle, pull your pud, fire the one o'clock gun etc.*

beaver 1. *n. US.* Female pubic hair. *Gorilla salad.* 2. *n. coll. US.* An offensively sexist term used when referring to a group of *birds.* Also *blart, mackerel, fanny.* *'Heavens to Murgatroyd. Check out the beaver in here, dudes.'*

beaverage *n.* That which is quaffed from a *hairy goblet.*

beaver cleaver *n.* Primitive male wooden weapon for splaying *beaver.*

beaver dam 1. *n.* Ladies' personal feminine hygiene requisite. *Jam rag, fanny nanny, blobstopper,* large pile of tree trunks. 2. *n.* A bath plughole, when blocked up with the flotsam and jetsam of the wife's *minge.*

beaver lever *n.* A *flapjack.*

beaver paddle *n.* Bizarre act performed by a man mid-way through committing sexual intercourse with a lady, when he unexpectedly pulls out his *meat flute,* grips it in his hand and then slaps it repeatedly against his partner's *bodily treasure.* From the similarity to the way that the eponymous Dodd-toothed tree-noshing rodent of the genus *Castor* slaps its scaly tail against the water for a cheap sexual thrill.

beaver's guts *n.* In the world of *art pamphlet* photography, that which is visible in a *close up pink* study. A *ripped sofa.*

beaver tails *n.* Long, flat *thrupenny bits* which resemble the unerotic, scaly tails of the eponymous wood-chomping animals. Also known as *socktits, spaniels' ears, NGTs.*

because you're worth it *exclam.* Waggish phrase to be used by a gentleman as he rubs his recently dropped *spooge* into his ladyfriend's hair.

Beckham, do a *v.* To fail to *score,* despite being given every opportunity to do so.

Beckham penalty *n.* A *piss* which combines high speed and inaccuracy, hitting everywhere except its intended target. Often results in a *Queen Mum's smile.*

becksfart *n.* Brand-specific lager hangover flatulence. Has an aroma a bit like egg mayonnaise.

bed *v.* A tabloid term, to *fuck. 'I went*

out with Tracey last night and ended up bedding her up the arse in the bus shelter.'

bed bellows *n*. The action of a semi-somnolent *guffer*, who lifts and lowers his leg in order to flap the quilt up and down and thus bring the benefits of his rectal largesse to the attention of his *bird*. Or bloke if he is a she, or indeed *one of them*.

Bedford diff *euph*. A female rear end that has succumbed to the ravages of time. *'Bloody hell Fred, did you see that lass's arse? It was hanging down like a Bedford diff.'*

bed flute *n*. Woodwind instrument closely related to the *pink oboe* that responds well to double tonguing.

bed glue *n*. Liquid that adheres people firmly to their mattresses, especially students. Beer.

bedknobs and broomsticks *1. n*. Film starring her out of *Murder She Wrote* and that bloke out of *Mary Poppins* who looks like her out of *Murder She Wrote* wearing a false moustache, which stirs up Pavlovian feelings of boredom, resentment and uninterest in anyone who ever sat through an episode of fucking *Screen Test* in the 1970s. *2. n*. The early morning result of a low fibre diet.

bed muscle *n*. The *old fella*.

bedroom popadoms *n*. Large, dried *wankerchiefs. Porn crackers, wankers' crisps*.

bedruggled *adj*. Describes the appearance of one who has aged beyond their years due to an heroic intake of illicit pharmaceuticals and/or booze, *eg*. Ozzie Osbourne, Keith Richards, Amy Winehouse.

Bee Gees bite *n*. The first mouthful of an extremely hot foodstuff, such as a Pop Tart or McDonald's apple pie, that causes the eater to involuntarily perform the falsetto "ah-ha-ha-ha-" intro to *Stayin' Alive*.

Bee Gee Tips *n*. A cup of scalding hot tea.

beef *n*. A hearty *brew*. A *beefy eggo*.

beef baubles *n*. Testicles. *'The bad news, Evel, is that you failed to clear the row of 16 double decker buses. The good news, however, is that one of your beef baubles did.'*

beef bayonet *n. Bacon bazooka, mutton musket, lamb cannon, luncheon meat howitzer*.

beef box *n*. A container into which *sausages* are put.

beef cloud *n*. A *fart* that smells like one has just opened a very old tin of Butcher's Tripe Mix dogfood or a fresh packet of Bernard Matthews' honey roast ham.

beef curtains *n. medic*. Of women's genitalias, those folds of skin known as the *labia majorcas*, or big lips. Or indeed *piss flaps*.

beef dripping *n*. The spreadable extract found in a *butcher's window*, traditionally used in the preparation of *fish suppers*.

beef encounter *1. n*. A romantic, one-off *bang*. A *hit and run*, a *none night stand*. *2. n*. In a public place, for example on a railway platform; a short-lived romantic dalliance of the sort that Trevor Howard and Celia Johnson are unlikely ever to have experienced.

beef or salmon *1. n*. Name of the much-fancied horse which nevertheless ran a nightmare in the 2006 Cheltenham Gold Cup. *2. n*. Question asked of a person of indeterminate alignment in order to ascertain whether they eat *meat* or *fish*.

beef teabag *n.* A set of *knackers* dipped in meaty stock and then popped into a lucky recipient's mouth. *'We boiled up snow and ice to make hot, beefy Bovril, then gave Sherpa Tensing a beef teabag.'*

beef wellington *1. n.* Popular dish originally popularised by 19th century military hero the Duke of Beef. *2. n.* A rubber prophylactic device placed over a gentleman's *meat flute* to prevent babies and/or *the clap*. *3. n.* A *wizard's sleeve*, a *clown's pocket*. A voluminous *mimsy* of such epic proportions that one might wonder whether one's entire lower leg might comfortably fit in it.

beefy eggo *n.* A pungently carnivorous *Exchange & Mart*.

beerache *n. medic.* The painful afliction of the eardrum usually experienced after returning home *pissed* and late. Like tinitus, but with an annoying woman's voice instead of bells.

beer angel *n.* The unseen guiding force that watches over and keeps safe the inebriated as they stagger across all six lanes of the North Circular at chucking out time.

beer armour *n.* The invisible protective clothing that prevents injury on the way home from the pub by shielding the body from all sensation of damage on contact with the pavement.

beer baby *n.* A large booze-induced gut. A *Foster's child, verandah over the toyshop.*

beer badly *adj.* A popular turn of phrase in the Barnsley area. Suffering the malign after-effects of *refreshment*. *'What's up wi' thee?' 'Shut it, ah'm beer badly, tha knows.'*

beer bollocks *n.* Courage-filled *cojones* grown by a usually timid man after he has imbibed several pints of strong lager. *'Where's Terry?' 'He's lying down on the pavement outside. He grew some beer bollocks and decided to take on all four of the bouncers.'*

beer buggy *n.* A shopping trolley, *esp.* one found abandoned at the side of the road.

bump start *n. An invigorating, pre-breakfast bout of self-pollution.*

beer callipers *n.* Miraculous leg splints which enable *wankered* stragglers to make their way home at closing time.

beer cancer *n. medic.* The sort of hangover that not only makes you feel utterly *shit*, but lasts so long that you suspect you may be genuinely ill. Shane McGowan has now been fighting a brave battle against terminal beer cancer for over twenty years.

beer coat *n.* An invisible, yet warm outer garment worn when walking back from a club at three in the morning.

beer compass *n.* A homing device that ensures your inexplicably safe arrival home after a night *on the pop.*

beer cones *n.* Invisible contraflow system surrounding a drunkard meandering up the road, allowing traffic to move freely around him.

beer degree *n.* A qualification attained after a sufficient intake of alcohol, which enables one to talk at length and with complete authority on any given topic.

beer facelift *n.* Subjective cosmetic surgical procedure which is only visible to *pissed up* men. *'Have you seen Bazza's new bird? He met her when she had a beer facelift and now he can't shake her off.'*

beer goggles *n*. Booze-fuelled optical aids which make *hounds* look like *foxes*.

beer graduate *n*. One who has moved onwards and upwards in the beverage world. A gentleman who drinks such strong ales that his wife wakes up with two black eyes and a headache as well.

beer halo *n*. Alcohol-induced self-righteousness.

beer hunter *1. n*. A jolly drinking game whereby Chris Evans's employees are forced to open cans of beer into their ears from a six-pack, one tin of which has been shaken vigorously. *2. n*. A demented person who searches the house for a drop of booze in the early hours, *eg*. As Chris Evans has been known to do.

beeriod *n*. Twice-weekly malady suffered by men after a night *on the lash*. Symptoms include headache, mood swings and a bloated stomach. *'Leave me alone, woman, me beeriod started this morning.'*

beer lag *n*. The disruption to human sleep patterns encountered after intense lunchtime drinking which leaves one unable to keep one's eyes open for *Wild at Heart*, but wide awake at two in the morning.

beerlarious *n*. Amusing only when drunk; specifically, putting a traffic cone on a statue's head.

beerloom *n*. Any item that one wouldn't ordinarily touch with a bargepole, but which suddenly seems irresistible when you go on eBay *pissed* out of your skull in the wee small hours. *'A Madness fruit machine? What on earth possessed you? How much did you pay?' 'Nearly three hundred quid. It's a fucking beerloom.'*

beer miles *n*. Easy, cheap, long-distance travel made possible by the consumption of large quantities of ale.

beer monkey *n*. A mythical simian creature which, during a drunken slumber, sneaks into your bed, ruffles your hair, steals your money and *shits* in your mouth.

beer muffs *n*. Invisible ear defenders that attach themselves to a man's head after several pints, rendering him unable to hold a conversation without shouting or to watch TV at anything but full volume.

beer mugger *n*. The unseen assailant you discover has hit you over the head and taken £35 out of your wallet the morning after you "nip out for a couple of pints".

beero *n*. One who, fortified by several pints, is prepared to engage in acts of incredible heroism, *eg*. Squaring up to doormen on the other side of the street, gesticulating at others in an abusive manner from inside a car travelling at speed.

beer plugs *n*. Alcoholic sound level inhibitors which occasion a total lack of response to any form of auditory stimulus. *Beer plugs* allow a *pissed* individual to remain happily and soundly asleep in the midst of such high volume disturbances as nightclub PA systems, burglar/ fire alarm sirens and rozzers with dogs kicking his door in.

beer pressure *n*. A benevolent psychological influence applied by drinking companions, encouraging one to consume more alcohol than one feels comfortable drinking.

beer queer *1. adj*. Of a normally heterosexual person, to be tempted to go *half rice half chips* when fuelled by sufficient quantities of *dizzyade*. Booze bent. *2. n*.

One who takes his drink the other way. A *teapot sucker*. A teetotaller.

beer scooter *n*. Miraculous method of transport employed when leaving the pub after drinking an elegant sufficiency of alcohol. So-called because one returns home seemingly in no time and at incredible velocity.

beer shoes *n*. Gloves

beer sniper *n*. An invisible marksman who silently "takes out" drunkards causing them to unexpectedly collapse in the street, fall off bar stools, go arse over tit half-way through singing *Rehab etc*.

beer stretcher *n*. A magical post-pub St John's Ambulance service. When *fully-refreshed* and lying down in the *Scotsman's lounge*, ditch or on the pub toilet floor, one is immediately whisked home on the *beer stretcher* to the comfort of one's own bed, to awaken in the morning with absolutely no memory of the journey. *'I came home on the beer stretcher, only I must have stopped off at the all-night garage because when I woke up there was a 50+ wank mag and an empty packet of scotch eggs on the bed.'*

beer thinners *n*. The pint of water one forgets to consume at the end of a long evening *on the pop*.

beer tent *n*. Jocky Wilson's shirt.

beer whistle *n*. At a football match, the signal given 10 minutes before half time that causes a mass exodus of gentlemen going for a pint, a pie, a *piss* or any simultaneous combination of the three.

beerwolf *n*. One who wakes up in unfamiliar surroundings with torn clothes, aching limbs, the taste of blood in his mouth and suffering from nightmarish flashbacks to terrible events which occurred the previous evening.

beer wood *n*. The thing that feels like an erection, but isn't, whilst attempting sexual congress under the influence of alcohol.

bee's dick *n*. The incredibly small distance, or period of time, which is needed in order to achieve an important outcome. *'I nearly finished the exam. I was a bee's dick short of finishing the last eight questions.'*

bee stings *n*. Small *tits*. *Chestnuts, stits, tisn'ts*.

Beethoven's fifth *n*. A large, stirring movement of the bowel which may leave the performer deaf.

beetle bonnet *n*. The female pubic mound as viewed through tight garments. From the design of the VW car. *Camel's foot, camel's lip,* visible *knicker sausages*.

begging Jock *n*. A tired, weathered cludge resembling nothing so much as the cupped, beseeching hands of a middle-aged Scottish *gentleman of the road*.

Begone, Demon Lord of Karanga! *exclam*. Powerful oath which is invoked when attempting to flush away a particularly obstinate *shite*. Taken from the fantasy novel *Demon Lord of Karanga* by David Eddings.

begonias *n*. See *bejonkers*.

behind with the rent *euph*. A polite way of explaining that one is a *good listener*. *'Mum, dad, I've got something to tell you. There's no easy way of saying this, so I'm just going to come straight out with it. I've had an idea for a television programme - It's a Royal Knockout. Oh yeah, and I'm behind with the rent.'*

bejonkers *n*. See *bouncers*.

Bela Lugosi's gob *n*. An *axe wound* which drips with fresh blood on a regular basis. A *jam sandwich*.

Belfast taxi *n*. Battery-powered shopping scooter for old people too fat or idle to walk. A *Disneyworld dragster* or *Frinton Ferrari*.

Belfast tickle stick *n*. A baseball bat, iron bar, length of four-by-two, *etc*.

Belgian *1. adj*. Of chocolates, twice as expensive as normal. *2. n*. In the world of sex, a spot of *ESD* or *ATM*. *Hot karl*.

Belgian biscuit *n*. Sexual practice of Flemish origin and costing over £100. Not to be confused with *Belgian bun*.

Belisha beacon *n*. Flashing orange globe on a black and white pole, named after the British Transport Minister in 1934.

Belgian bun *n*. Walloon-based deviant behaviour which comes in at about £75. Not to be confused with *Belgian biscuit*.

belgrano *n*. A lady who looks irresistably *fuckable* from behind.

bell *n*. A lady's *clit*. The *devil's doorbell*, found just above the *snail's doorstep*.

bell clapper *n*. An humungous dangling *turd* that tolls the *bummocks* as one tries to swing it loose.

bellefire *1. n*. A crappy manufactured girl group. *2. n. medic*. A *herman*-based symptom of *cock rot*.

bell end *1. n*. An amusingly-named tent. *2. n. medic*. The *bobby's helmet, bobby splithead*. The glans of the penis. Also *bellend, bellender*.

bell end brie *n*. Brimula, *fromunder, knacker barrel*.

belle of the dole *n*. A recently-dumped thirty-something mother who gets all done up to the nines to sign on, in order to demonstrate that she is better than all the other single mums who she has spent years berating.

bell housing *1. n. mech*. The flywheel/clutch cover on a car. *2. n*. The *fiveskin* on a gentile's genital.

bellooning *n*. The gentlemanly art of pinching the tip of the *prepuce* whilst having a piss in order to give the *bellend* a good wash.

bell rag *n*. A cloth with the specific designated purpose of removing *spodge* from *under the bridge*. The raw material from which *bedroom poppadoms* are forged by *wanksmiths*.

bell-swagged *adj*. To be endowed with a large *bishop's hat* on a contrastingly-small *Jesuit*. *Mushroom-rigged*.

bell tower *n*. *Knob* shaft. *Bean stalk*.

bell wringing *v*. A harmless pastime that builds up the arm muscles, and has been popular with monks for the last two thousand years.

belly flopper *n*. A clumsy *brown trout* whose graceless entry into the water causes splashing of the *arse*.

belly full of swimmers *n*. Delightfully alluring phrase used by the charming ladies of Bristol when planning to start a family. *'Come home with me and give I a belly full of swimmers.'*

belly warmers *n*. Big, droopy *tits*. *Overblaaters*.

belongings *n*. Word used in the badly-translated subtitles of an un-named Dutch/German *bongo vid* to describe the leading gentleman thespian's nether parts. *'That's right you whore. Take his belongings and put them in your mouth.'*

belt-fed mortar *sim. milit*. A measure of the sexual enthusiasm of a lady. See also *shithouse door in the wind, kangaroo shagging a space hopper. 'I bet she bangs like a belt-fed mortar.'*

Ben Jones *euph.* An act of *horatio*. A *chewie*, a *BJ*. Named after the Absolute Radio presenter. Also *Billy Joel, Boris Johnson.*

bender 1. *n.* A prolonged drinking spree. An *all-dayer*, or *Leo Sayer*. 2. *n.* A crustie's tent. 3. *n.* A *pinch of snuff.*

bender like Beckham *n.* A fellow who tries to emulate the fashionably androgynous mien of the publicity-hungry LA Galaxy midfielder, *eg.* Wearing ladies' earrings, sarongs, makeup *etc.*, but who merely ends up making himself look like a right *puff*. A bit like David Beckham does.

bend one in *v.* To manage to commit sexual intercourse up a lady. *'She sounds well fit. I'd like to bend one into her, Cilla.'*

bend the elbow *v.* To go for a *beer goggles* fitting.

benefactor *n.* Of *farts* and *farting*, the selfless altruist who supplies it. Also known as the *donor*.

beneficiaries *n.* Those who benefit from the smelly largesse of a *benefactor's custard*.

benefit buddies *n.* The group of lonely OAPs and unemployable misfits who gather outside the Post Office half an hour before it opens in the morning just to talk to one another.

benefit buffet *n.* In supermarkets, the shelves situated close to checkouts that bear a mouth-watering array of dented tins, loaves of bread with torn packaging, crushed crisps and almost out of date meat.

Ben Hur *v.* To *take a lady from behind* whilst using her arms as chariot reins. Also *Ben her, the charioteer.*

Benny Hill *rhym. slang.* A form of oral contraception. *'It's nothing to do with me, Mrs Gamp. You told me you was on the Benny Hill.'* (from *Nicholas Nickelby*, by Charles Dickens).

bent 1. *adj.* Descriptive of a fellow who prefers not to walk through puddles. *Good with colours as a nine bob note.* 2. *adj.* Descriptive of a dishonest *scuffer.*

bentertainment *n.* The sort of TV programmes that only girls and *botters* watch, *eg. What Not to Wear, Sex & the City, Coronation Street etc.*

bepalmed *adj.* Of a jobseeker or student, to be marooned in that awkward hour or so when he's already *wanked* his *knackers* flat as a pancake, but it's too early for a drink. *In colimbo.*

Beppe's beard *n.* A severely but neatly-trimmed *bush*, named after the severely but neatly-trimmed chin growth of the former *EastEnders* character. A *clitler, Mugabe muff.*

Berk *n.* See *Berkeley Hunt.*

Berkeley Hunt *rhym. slang. Cunt.*

Berlin Wall 1. *n.* Heavily-policed strip of no-man's land formerly dividing the forbidden East and free West halves of the German city. 2. *n.* The *taint, tinter, notcher, carse, biffon, scran, twernt, Humber Bridge etc.*

Bermuda triangle *n.* A mysterious area where *skin boats* full of semen seem to disappear. For two or three minutes.

berry 1. *n.* A sexual deviant, a kinky person. A goddam prevoit. 2. *n.* One who has *carnival knowledge* of animals. *'Today's birthdays: Bruce Forsyth, big-chinned tap-dancer, 1928; Sir John Mills, iconic film and stage actor, 1902; Eric Gill, artist and berry, 1882.'* 3. *n.* A lady with a great body, but a less-than-pleasing face, *ie.* One who has the body of Halle, but the face of Chuck. *eg.* Sarah Jessica Parker. A *bobfoc*.

bertie *1. n.* A male homosexual. *2. n.* A *charlie*. *3. adj.* Of a woman, to be blessed with morals as *slack as a brewer's cock*. From the spoonerism Bertie Ditch = dirty bitch. '*...or should he go for saucy number three, who sounds well bertie and takes it up the council?*' (Graham Skidmore, voiceover on *Cilla's Blind Date*, LWT).

Bertie Bassett's hat *n.* The small, unsatisfying, sticky nugget of dark excrement that drops to the bottom of an otherwise empty toilet bowl. *'No sign of Bertie, but he's dropped his hat.'*

Berwick Rangers' goalmouth *1. n.* The badly churned-up sea of mud between the posts at Shielfield Park. *2. n.* The badly churned-up sea of mud in the back of a pair of badly-*shitted undercrackers*.

bespectable *adj.* Respectable in glasses, *eg.* The late Richard Wattis. You remember him, he was Eric and Hattie's neighbour in *Sykes*.

bet middler *n.* A woman who looks like an odds-on favourite "from a distance", but is *minging* close up.

bet she can shit! *exclam.* Uttered to your mate under your breath as you pass a particularly keen *avoider of leaf vegetables*.

better an eviction than a bad tenant *exclam.* Amusing, aphoristic Wildean apophthegm, proffered as a riposte to someone launching a particularly crusty *air biscuit*. See also *a bit more choke and she would have started; a confident appeal by the Australians there; an excellent theory, Dr Watson; anybody injured?; don't tear it, I'll take the whole piece; how much?; keep shout-*

ing sir, we'll find you; more tea vicar?; someone let him in; someone's tinkered with Herbie; speak on, sweet lips that never told a lie; speak up caller, you're through; taxi for Brown; that's working, now try your lights; well struck sir!; what's that, Sweep?; you'll have to buy that now, you've ripped it; sew a button on that; catch that one and paint it blue; good health!; pin a tail on that; you're only supposed to blow the bloody doors off and *there goes the elephant*.

Betty Both *n.* A *happy shopper*, a *switch hitter*. '*Yes, he is. I've heard he's a Betty Both and so is his wife.*' (Paul Lavers, unintentional live broadcast, Friendly TV, 2003).

Betty Swollocks *n.* Polite term for *knacker* discomfort. '*Forgive me, Your Majesty, whilst I adjust my doublet and hose. I have sailed the seven oceans these last six months and have not changed my codpiece since we left the New World. I fear I have the most awful Betties.*' (Sir Walter Raleigh, Audience with Queen Elizabeth I, 1584).

Beverley *n. rhym. slang.* A lady's rigorously-depilated *bush*. Named after the formerly popular singer Beverley Craven = shaven haven. '*I couldn't believe my luck, nan. When I stuck my hand up her dress she wasn't wearing any knickers. And she'd got a Beverley.*'

Beverly Hills *n.* Ridiculous, Californian-style silicon-stuffed *churns*.

bevvy *1. n.* A portion of *booze*. A quantity of drink. *2. n.* A number of beauties, although that might be spelled differently, come to think of it.

bezzing *1. n.* Vigorous chewing of the face after taking one too many *disco biscuits*. '*Shit, these beans are good. I'm bezzing* *me tits off!'* 2. *n.* The act of dancing like a drunken gibbon, in a similar fashion to Mr Bez (real name The Hon. Beswick Ffitzherbert-Cholmondeley) out of the Happy Mondays pop group.

biddeos *n. Scud videos* in which the actresses look somewhat younger on the packaging than they do in the film itself.

biddy fiddler *n.* A fellow who prefers the company of ladies who are of sufficient maturity that they can ride the bus for free during off-peak periods. A *granny magnet*.

biff *n.* Poetic epithet for a lady's *bodily treasure*. *'Cross your legs again, will you Sharon. The camera missed your biff that time.'*

biffer *n.* A particularly hairy *minge*. *'Gaw, you've got a right old biffer on you there, Mother Superior.'*

biffie *n. Bog, shitter, dunny, cludgy. 'I'd give the biffie ten minutes if I was you, nan.'*

biffin *n.* Perspiration which condenses in the *biffin bridge* area during coitus.

biffin bridge *n.* See *barse*.

biffing plate 1. *n. Beetle bonnet, monkey's forehead.* 2. *sim.* That which is flat. *'Christ! This lager's as flat as Kate Moss's biffing plate.'*

biffon *n.* That part of the female anatomy between the *council gritter* and the *fadge*, which the man's *clockweights* "biff on" during intercourse. The *taint.*

bi-furious *adj.* A man who flies into a rage at the slightest suggestion that he may be tempted to occasionally travel a couple of stops *on the other bus.*

big bamboo 1. *n.* A chap's *old man.* 2. *n.* In the film *Chitty Chitty Bang Bang,* a rousing, knockabout song performed by Dick Van Dyke. About his cock.

Big Ben 1. *n.* A large bell in St. Steven's Tower, London. 2. *n.* An enormous *erection,* possibly with Robert Powell hanging off it.

big boned 1. *adj.* Of thin people with corpulent skeletons, suffering from an unfortunate medical condition that makes it look like they eat forty cakes a day. *Glands.* 2. *adj.* What *donkey-rigged* men are, when they've got a *horse's handbrake.*

big brother is watching you *phr.* The *wood*-felling realisation, whilst watching a *scruff* video, that there is a photo of a grinning sibling on top of the TV set which must be laid face down before one can continue *relaxing in a gentleman's way.*

big cock day *n.* A day, quite possibly in spring, the arrival of which is greeted with the *dawn horn,* and throughout which the sap continues to rise. *'As he wrestled himself into his shreddies, D'Arcy knew it was going to be a big cock day.'* (from *Pride And Prejudice* by Jane Austen).

biggie smalls *n.* Fat lasses' knickers.

big mac 1. *n.* A disappointing *hamburger,* consisting of two tired, grey pieces of meat, random, sorry-looking vegetation and traces of unidentified mayonnaise-like liquid. 2. *n.* A high street fast food that looks and tastes like 1. 3. *n.* A carefully chosen, artfully lit and meticulously composed photograph of the sort used by a rough female on a social networking site to ensure that her image is as misleadingly attractive to the eye as possible. Named after the laughably-unrealistic burger photographs displayed above the counters of certain litigious fast food restaurants, that bear scant resemblance to the dishevelled objects their customers find in the box after purchase.

Bi Jovi *n*. A *Bone Jovi*, unexpectedly encountered in somewhat *puddle-jumpy* circumstances, which might surprise a fellow to the extent that his monocle falls out.

bike *n*. A frequently-*ridden* woman, one who has had thousands of gentlemen swing their legs over her. Often prefixed with a location. *'You don't want to go near her, mate. She's the office/factory/London Symphony Orchestra and Festival Chorus bike.'*

biker's highway code, thin as a *sim*. Reference to something which is notably slight. *'Strewth Marvin, I saw Tim Henman's grand slam record today, and it is as thin as a biker's highway code.'*

bikini burger *n*. A *vertical bacon sandwich*. See *hairy pie*.

Bilbo Baggins' foot *n*. An hirsute vagina, resembling the hairy toes of a hobbit.

bile mile *n*. The finishing straight of a marathon *spewing* session, where one's gallbladder is going flat out to produce something worth *yoffing*, but is frankly fighting a losing battle.

bilge tanks *n*. The "double gut" effect caused by an overly-tight belt on an overly-large belly.

bilious fog *n*. Any cloud of dense, sulphurous, boiled-egg-and-Brussels-sprout-induced vapour emanated from *cack canyon*, so thick that a safe passage may only be negotiated through it by means of a machete or chainsaw.

Bill Grundies *rhym. slang*. Undies, trolleys, dunghampers.

Billingsgate banjo *n*. Something that a lady strums and which smells of fish.

That'll be her *twat*, then.

Billingsgate box *n*. Minge. Based on a comparison between the smell of a cockney seafood market and a cockney *fadge*.

billposter's bucket *sim*. Large paste-filled *snatch*. *'I was stationed in Scutari Hospital for six months, the only woman amongst thousands of soldiers. By the end of my first shift I had a twat like a billposter's bucket.'* (from *My Poor Cunt - The Crimean Wartime Memoirs of Florence Nightingale*).

bills *n*. *Shreddies, bills, dunghampers*.

Bill Wyman *rhym. slang*. A lady's *virgin string*. From Bill Wyman = hymen.

Billy Connolly's beard *n*. A *ragweek fanny*.

Billy Dainty *n*. The awkward, foward-leaning posture that a chap has to adopt in order to mask a *bone on* when making his way, for example, to the pub bogs. Named after the priapismic Happy Shopper Max Wall who played the brown-coated cameraman on *Emu's Broadcasting Company*.

billy goat's mouth *n*. An exceptionally loose vagina. With bits of the Mayor's hat sticking out of it.

Billy Mill roundabout *n*. Climactic point of a bout of masturbation. From the climactic point of the A1058 Coast Road near Newcastle. The *vinegar strokes*. *'My mum walked in just as I was coming up to the Billy Mill roundabout.'*

Billy no mates *1. n*. A lonely little buoyant *turd* that remains hanging around in the *chod bin* after all the others have gone to the beach. *2. n*. A person bereft of close acquaintances.

Billy Smart *n. rhym. slang*. A *Bakewell* equipped with a top hat and a red tailcoat.

Billy Two-Mirrors *n.* Affectionate nickname for one whose bones are so big that they need two mirrors in order to fully encompass their reflection. Also *Bessie Two-Mirrors*. *'Oi, Billy Two-Mirrors. You forgot my McFlurry, you fat cunt.'*

Billy Wright *n.* Legendary Wolverhamtpon Wanderers footballer who married Vera Lynn or the Andrews Sisters or someone, latterly immortalised as rhyming slang for *shite*. *'Aw. Who's done a Billy Wright in my shoe?'*

bilp *n. Blip.*

biltrum *n.* The *chin rest*. See *wannocks*.

bimbo *n.* The likes of Jordan, Jodie Marsh or Joanne Guest. A *tit-for-brains*.

bimboid *adj.* Appertaining to the likes of Jordan, Jodie Marsh or Joanne Guest.

binge wanker *n.* A fellow who concentrates his week's quota of masturbation into the period between 6pm on a Friday and 10pm on a Sunday, but "never on a school night".

bingo armour *n.* The excessive amounts of tawdry jewellery worn by flabby-armed ladies enjoying a night frantically crossing out numbers in a former cinema. *Blingo, bingo clink.*

bingo bongo *1. exclam. zool.* The mating call of the male silverback western lowland gorilla *(Gorilla gorilla gorilla)*. *2. n.* Granny porn. *'Oi, mister. Give me a pack of Scotch eggs and a bingo bongo mag, will you? I'm off me face.'*

bingo dabbers *n.* The enlarged nipples of a pregnant lady. *'They used to look like raspberries, but ever since she's been up the duff, they've looked more like bingo dabbers.'*

bingo partner *n.* A man who is engaging in a romantic dalliance with a somewhat more mature lady.

bingo top *n.* A lady's upper body garment, cut in such a way as to encourage men to cast their "eyes down" in the hope of a glimpse of *nork* and/or *Bristol Channel*. *'I couldn't help it, love. She was wearing her bingo top.'*

bingo wings *n.* Upper-arm adipose underhang found on post-menopausal ladies of a common bent. *Arm tits.*

binjuries *n.* Ailments acquired whilst in a drunken stupor, *eg.* Griddle burns on the *arse* cheeks caused by falling onto an electric fire on Anglesey, to pick an example entirely at random.

Bin Laden's beard *n.* A particularly luxuriant, yet unruly *stoat*. The antithesis of a *Hitler tash*.

bin lid penny *euph.* A more extreme version of *half a crown thru'penny bit* for the more anally-flexible frightened person. *'I bet it was bin lid penny for Nick Ross every time the doorbell rang until they arrested Barry George. And after that too.'*

bin lids *n.* The areolae round a lady's nippular bits.

binorkulars *n.* Sunglasses as worn by an observant fellow at the beach. *Perv windows.*

bin ripper *n.* An *alcoholic womble*. One who finds his treasure amongst the things everyday folk leave behind. A *Harold Ramp.*

bint *n.* Derogatory term for a daft *slapper*, *eg.* Jordan, Jodie Marsh or Joanne Guest.

bintage year *n.* A period of twelve months frittered away *putting it about* with ladies of easy virtue.

binternet *n.* The world-wide electronic network which can apparently be used to view titillating pictures of young ladies

'*NORFOLK: She has the most agreeable butfer. BISHOP: The butfer, sir? Wherefore is it called thus? NORFOLK: Sir, butfer that, thou wouldst be in the shit.*' ~ from *The Merry Readers' Wives of Windsor* by William Shakespeare.

in various states of undress.

bint imperials *n. Rocks* so hard that your *bird* could break her molars on them. But without the breath-freshening qualities of their confectionery almost-namesakes.

bint sauce *n.* Any beverage which is particularly appealing to a bar's distaff clientelle. *Tart fuel, knicker oil, bitch piss. 'Pint of Exhibition, three bags of scratchings and half a dozen pickled eggs for me and a small bint sauce for the missus, please.'*

bio bling *n. Jelly jewellery. Pearl necklaces, spunky earrings* and the like. Also *Jizzie Duke.*

bi-pod *n.* The MP3 player of someone with unaccountably diverse and eclectic musical tastes, where a predominantly macho selection of music (*eg.* Heavy metal, punk, brass bands *etc.*) is inexplicably intertwined with tracks such as *It's Raining Men, YMCA* and *Kay Why* by Brothers Butch.

bips *n.* Fucking enormous hips, like those you see on the American monsters in the queue for the turkey legs at Disneyworld. From beast + hips. *'Oi, Steve! Come through here and check out this woman's bips on Jerry Springer!'*

bird *n.* Outdated, offensively sexist way of referring to a woman. *'Phoar! Is this your new bird? She's a bit of alright, ain't she. Fantastic tits. What does she go like, then?'*

bird flu *n. medic.* Ante-*women's things* irritability. *Pre-rag radge, strawberry mivvie.*

birdie dance *n.* Arm-flapping terpsichorean routine performed whilst hovering above the *crapper*, trying to lay an *egg.*

bird on the wire *1. n.* Title of a track on Leonard Cohen's 1969 album *Songs from a Room*, which was later re-recorded by Judy Collins. *2. n.* A female who is highly strung due to *a visit from aunt Flo.*

bird sanctuary *n.* A place where women of the opposite gender can congregate, safe from the reaches of male gentlemen, *eg.* The bingo, the hairdressing salon, the cleaning products aisle at Tesco's.

bird scarer *n.* A particularly long or girthsome, or long and girthsome, *stench hammer.*

birds' custard *1. n.* A sweet, gloopy substance that comes out of a tin. *2. n.* A savoury, gloopy substance that comes out of a lady's *clout. Blip, bilp, fanny batter, moip.*

birds' nest *1. n.* In nature, where chicks hang around open-mouthed, eager to be fed a fat worm. *2. n.* In pornography, and the real life of the lead singer of Saxon, much the same thing. Only without Bill Oddie watching through binoculars, you would hope.

birdseed *n. derog.* Nickname for a henpecked fellow.

bird's trifle *1. n.* Popular proles' pudding containing several fingers and a lot of jelly, topped with custard and cream but frequently missing the cherry. *2. n.* A dirty lady's *letterbox.*

birdstrike *1. n.* In aeronautical circles, a high altitude pigeon or similar avian hitting the whirring fanblades of a jet engine, leaving everything covered with blood, minced guts and feathers. *2. n.* One's wife or girlfriend's monthly *moon juice* session, when she wheels her *fanny* into the hangar for a week's essential *flap* maintenance.

Birkenhead confetti *n.* Gravel.

birminger n. A Brummie bird who is a minger. From Birmingham + minger.

Birmingham botox n. Budget cosmetic procedure, available in most Black Country pubs, which leaves one's face looking not unlike that of Sylvester Stallone's mum. A sound pasting.

biroglyphics n. The mysterious and generally unattributed ideographs which are commonly found adorning overused lecture hall tables, telephone kiosks and public lavatory cubicle walls, where they offer fascinating insights into more primitive cultures. 'I can't read a word of this on the cludgy door. Something about George Michael, then what looks like a phone number.' 'Let me have a look, I can read biroglyphics.'

birth marks n. The two red welts atop a male's knees after he has been sat on the crapper for a long period reading the Autotrader whilst dropping a box of shoes from the attic.

biscuit n. A turd.

biscuits 1. n. UK. the contents of the stomach after a heavy night's drinking. 'Get me a bucket, quick, Your Honour, I'm gonna chuck me biscuits.' 2. n. US. Tight buns. Attractive ass cheeks.

bishop rage n. A monkey spanking performed with such vigour that one takes on the appearance of one of Francis Bacon's famous screaming Popes.

bishop's dick, stiff as a sim. Descriptive of the muscular and joint rigidity experienced after a 20-mile walk. 'With Striding Edge safely negotiated, I wearily descended the Victorian pony track down Birkhouse Moor with its fine views across to St. Sunday Crag. At the foot of the slope I crossed Grisedale Beck and joined the tarred road for the difficult last eight miles, finally entering Patterdale as stiff as a bishop's dick.' (from Coast to Coast the Miserable Way by Alfred Wainwright).

bishop's licence n. That which is granted to a man left home alone by his wife, enabling him to wank himself blind at his leisure.

bishop's mitre n. A bobby's helmet.

bishop's waltz n. The practice of keeping one's threadbare old t-shirt held up over the chest with the chin and one's soiled tracksuit bottoms held out at the waist with the thumb of one hand, the other wrist dripping with fresh kebab fat, whilst waddling awkwardly to the toilet following an act of mid-morning self pollution. Also known as a spangle dash.

bismarking n. An act of love where a man strikes a lucky lady repeatedly around the chops with his cock for their mutual pleasure. Also colting, salami slap.

bisto skids n. The beefy stains left down the back of the pan after a night on the sauce. Toilet snail trails.

bit, a 1. n. An imperial unit of the other, slightly less than an entire portion. 2. n. Unspecified quantity of sex, usually partaken on the side.

bitch piss n. Alcopops. 'A pint of Timothy Taylor's Landlord please, barman, and a bottle of bitch piss for the missus.'

bitch tits n. Large, flabby breasts found on overweight males of any age. Particularly amusing when sported by obese American children on Oprah. Triple-hearters, dog udders, moomlaaters.

bitchwhore n. A woman who is not only a bitch, but is also a whore.

bite the mango v. To chomp on a particularly moist flange, such that the juice dribbles down the muncher's chin. One of your five-a-day.

biting point *n*. The first tingly inklings down amongst the loins that a prolonged bout of *self help* might just possibly be about to prove worthwhile after all. *Fringles*.

biting the butter *n*. Going down to commit an act of *cumulonimbus* on a *plumper's clunge*, only to find the experience akin to that of biting into a warm, salty slab of Lurpak.

bit of fluff *n*. A singular piece of *totty*.

bit of grey *euph*. Davina McCall's mother's *badger*.

bit of rough *n*. A sexual partner, usually male, from a lower social echelon. One who wouldn't think twice about wiping his *cock* on a *bird's* curtains, *eg*. Mellors in *Lady Chatterley's Lover*, or HM The Queen's *tit*-feeling bedtime interloper Michael Fagan.

bitten by the brewer's horse *euph*. To be as *refreshed* as a Space Shuttle pilot.

bitterflies *n*. Mythical intestinal insects that flutter in the stomach when it's knocking off time and one can almost taste the first pint.

BJLs *abbrev*. Blow Job Lips. See *DSLs*

blaaters *n*. *Oomlaaters*.

black and blue menstrual show *n*. An unprovoked assault accompanying a particularly disputatious *tammy huff*. A bruising *blobstrop* encounter of noteworthy pugnacity, tempestuousness or excitability.

Blackbeard's ghost *n*. A triangular, white, spooky apparition occasionally glimpsed by the *one-eyed lookout* in one's *crow's nest*. A mature lady's once-raven *mapatasi*. A *fanny badger*.

black country urgency *n*. The performance of a task with dizzying slowness and ineptitude, in the style of a denizen of the West Midlands.

Black Eye Friday *n*. *N. Ir*. The Friday immediately preceeding Christmas, on which Ulsterfolk of all sexes, ages and mental capabilities descend upon drinking establishments to celebrate with each other the anniversary of the birth of Our Lord Jesus Christ. The traditional end result of this festive gathering incorporates (in no particular order of preference) violence, molestation, vomiting, crying, marital breakdown and pregnancy. Also known as *Amateur Night*.

black forest gateau *n*. A particularly daunting *hairy pie*.

black forest shateau *n*. An overly-rich mountain of *feeshus* of the sort produced the morning after an evening out on the Guinness.

black mamba *n*. The horrifically toxic *chod-bowl* aftermath of a night spent knocking back something that is supposed to be good for you.

Blackpool cock *n*. A pink, sticky erection upon which one's *bird* could break her teeth. And which would make her feel sick before she was even half way through eating it.

blacksmith's apron *n*. A lady's substantial, leathery *front bottom*.

bladdered *adj*. See *blitzed*.

bladdertorial combat *n*. Vicious man-to-man duel, whereby a man attempts to drink more pints of booze than his comrades before having to relieve himself.

bladdiator *n*. A fellow who engages in *bladdertorial combat*.

blamestorming session *n*. A round-the-pub-table discussion which incorporates forcefully-expressed opinions.

bland job *n*. Being *tossed off* by a lass

whilst so *pissed* that one can hardly feel it. See *no job*

blanket drill *n. Milit.* An early morning *mutton musket* practice that results in the loss of the *officer's mess.*

blanket ripper *n.* Back-draught in a *Dutch oven.*

blanket welding *n.* Under-the-covers heavy manual work involving *pink steel*, which may lead to blindness.

blart *1. n.* Vagina. *2. n. coll.* Women, *totty.* '*Golly gosh! This nunnery is heaving with blart*'.

blart attack *euph.* A strange feeling, starting in the *pills* and spreading down the right arm, upon finding oneself surrounded by a large quantity of top flight *cabbage. Acute vangina.*

blart gallery *n.* A pub containing wall-to-wall *totty.*

blarticulate *adj.* Silver-tongued; able to charm the *dunghampers* off the ladies. '*Blimey, that Russell Brand isn't half blarticulate. He stopped to ask me granny for directions and her knickers fell off.*'

blartist *n.* One who demonstrates unrivalled skills in the field of *blartistry.* '*Titian remains among the foremost blartists of his era, and few would dispute that the sublime nudes of his oeuvre constitute an unrivalled array of proper little minge winkers.*' (Brian Sewell, *Titian's Tiffins*, Evening Standard, August 2002).

blazing saddles *1. n.* Title of Mel Brooks's spoof Western, one scene of which involved a great deal of farting. *2. n.* The *ringpieces* of a group of men who have enjoyed a surfeit of *Edwina* the previous night, and consequently do a lot of farting. And *shitting* blood.

bleachy head *n.* The unmistakable post-ejaculatory miasma of ammonia coming off of one's *old man.*

bleed the lizard *v.* See *siphon the python.*

bleed the radiator *v.* To commit an act of flatulation in which one would be well advised to hold a rag over one's *brass eye* to prevent sludge going all over the wall. A bit like when you have to sort out your central heating, only you don't have to spend twenty minutes emptying out the kitchen drawer looking for that little brass key.

Bleep & Booster *1. n.* Vaguely- remembered black and white *Blue Peter* science fiction series, voiced by the same bloke who did *Captain Pugwash. 2. n.* The *ringpiece.*

bletherskate *n. Scot. Shit-for-brains, fuckwit, twat.* Literally meaning *bag of shite.*

blick *n.* Pubic scurf, *muffdruff.*

bliff mag *n.* Rhythm journal, art pamphlet, noddy book. A pornographic magazine.

bliff *n. Minge, front bottom.*

bliffage *n.* Very generously-cut *bacon strips.* Also *gruffage, quimmage.*

blimp *v.* To surreptitiously ogle ladies' breasts and *arses* from behind a pair of mirrored sunglasses.

blimplants *n. Knockers*, surgically-enhanced to comic proportions, as sported by the likes of Jordan and the late Lolo Ferrari. *Bazongers.*

blimp my ride *phr.* Rueful expression descriptive of the process whereby the missus undergoes rapid and frighteningly-unpredictable ballooning as soon as she feels the coast is clear, *viz.* Straight after the ink is dry on the marriage certificate.

blind cobbler's thumbs *n*. Large, well-hammered *nipples*. *Pygmies' cocks, chapel hat pegs, fighter pilots' thumbs.*

blind dirt snake *n*. A malodorous, legless lizard inhabiting *cak canyon*, which migrates south every morning. A *Richard the Third*.

blind man's buffet *n*. A *fanny* that can be located by the olfactory senses alone. *Blind man's muff.* A stanksome *snatch*.

blind man's porn *n*. Explicit sexual noises, usually coming from an adjacent room or house. A *horn chorus*.

blind skateboarder's elbow, cock like a *sim*. *'But you must believe me when I tell you that I have found it impossible to carry the heavy burden of responsibility and to discharge my duties as King as I would wish to do without the help and support of the woman I love. And I tell you what, I've loved her that much recently I've got a cock like a blind skateboarder's elbow.'* (Abdication speech of King Edward VIII carried live on the *Ed Stewpot Stewart Show*, BBC Home Service, December 11th 1936).

blinglish *n*. Street language spoken by rappers and bishop's son DJ Tim Westwood.

blinkered *adj*. Wearing one's *trolleys* back to front in order to deliberately impair the *beast's* vision.

blip. *n*. The watery substance of female love. *Fish cream, nog juice, moip, bilp.*

blip fountain *n*. *medic*. The Bartholin's gland that secretes vaginal lubrications. The *batter tap*.

blistered pisspot, face like a *sim*. Useful phrase to describe the appearance of a woman who has fallen out of the ugly tree and hit every branch on the way down. And then landed in a pile of broken glass, *eg*. Sonia from *EastEnders*. *'Ladies and gentlemen, here to perform her latest single is a singer who needs no introduction. Her debut single Lost in France went straight into the Top Ten; her follow up, Total Eclipse of the Heart, went platinum in eight countries. Ladies and gentlemen, she sings like a cat having barbed wire pulled out of its arse and she's got a face like a blistered pisspot so let's give a big Summertime Special welcome to Bonnie Tyler.'*

blistering barnacles *1. exclam*. Mild oath ejaculated by Captain Haddock in the popular *Tintin* stories. *2. n*. Badly-scalded *clockweights*, caused by showering in foreign hotels with unfathomable tap operation systems. *3. n*. Sun-dried *love tomatoes* as found on British nudists who have fallen asleep on a Mediterranean beach and also on spivvish TV rag & bone man David Dickinson. *Dry roasted nuts.*

blit *n*. See *blivvet*.

blitzed *adj*. See *wankered*.

blivvet *n*. coll. *Mackerel, blart, fanny, tussage.*

bloatee *n*. The type of carefully-toped beard favoured by the chubbier male, in the vain hope that it will demarcate his chin from his neck and thus indicate where his face stops. As sported by hopelessly optimistic *pie shifters* such as Chris Moyles, Johnny Vegas, Rik Waller, Lisa Riley *etc*.

blob *1. n*. Condom, *French safe, French letter, rubber Johnny*. *2. v*. To inadvertently make pregnant. *"You look a little green around the lemon, old chap. Bad news is it?' I asked as Jeeves continued to study the letter. 'I'm afraid so Sir,' he replied. 'I attended a party of the* *downstairs staff of Brokenbury Manor, and I am afraid things got a little out of hand. To cut a long story short, Sir, it appears that I have blobbed the cook."* (from *Use the Back Door, Jeeves* by PG Wodehouse).

blob blimp *n*. A post-coital cabaret in which a used *jubber ray* is inflated and knotted for the amusement of one's ladyfriend.

blob it *v*. To oversleep. *'Jesus, Phil, look at the time. Get up, quick! I'm being coronated in half an hour and we've blobbed it.'*

blob jockey *n*. A gentleman with a penchant for the fuller-figured, Rubenesque lady. A *chubby chaser.*

blobsleigh *n*. Unexpected barefoot skid on last night's discarded prophylactic. The *spunky-footed luge.*

blobstopper *n*. A *fanny mouse*, a *slim fanatella* or *jam rag*. Put crudely, a feminine hygiene product.

blobstradamus *n*. A woman who look into the future to predict the state of her *things* during a particular date range. *'So are you and your piece off to Ayia Napa the first week in June, then Dave?' 'No. Blobstradamus says she'll be up on blocks that week.'*

Blofeld brunette *n*. A natural blonde who dyes her hair dark to feign intelligence. However, inspection of her lap reveals a white *pussy*. And draft plans for world domination.

Blofeld's kiss *n*. The tell-tale facial pillow scar left by a shaken but unstirred, drunken night's sleep. *'"And for God's sake wash your face, 007," added M. "You can't meet the Swedish Ambassador sporting a Blofeld's kiss."'* (from *James Bond and the Blustery Day*

by Ian Fleming).

blonde bombsite *n*. The distressing prospect that often greets a chap upon waking after a night of loud *banging* in the dark. The very antithesis of a blonde bombshell; more Marilyn Manson than Marilyn Monroe, if you will.

blonde herring *n*. A woman who looks like she ought to be a nice bit of *mackerel* from the back, but who turns out to be an *old trout* from the front. A *golden deceiver.*

blongle *n. medic*. Seminal fluid containing traces of blood. *Blunk, blism, blimphet.*

blood and custard *1. n*. Humorous, sexcase/train-spotter parlance for the cream and maroon livery in which British Railways coaching stock was painted in the 1950s and 1960s. *2. n*. The sort of curse that a soft pirate like Captain Pugwash might have uttered when he discovered that Cut-throat Jake had beaten him to the treasure of the San Fandango. *3. n*. The evidence left on the sheets after one has *done* it with a lady during her *unclean time.*

blood bachelor *n*. Married man undergoing the monthly interruption to his rightful conjugal privileges whilst his missus is *on the mop.*

blood diamond *n*. A particularly painful *turd.*

bloodhound's jowls *1. n*. Oversized *beef curtains* which could track an escaped convict across Dartmoor. *2. n*. A mature *bird's funbags* during the later stages of collapse.

blood in your undies, here's *exclam*. Heart-warming oath in the style of "bottoms up" or "cheers" which can be used when raising a glass amongst company.

A simple way of toasting the health and future happiness of those about whom we care. *'And now I would like to propose a toast: To the President of the Arab Republic of Egypt, Anwar al-Sadat, and to the Prime Minister of the State of Israel, Menahem Begin; to the great peoples they serve, the people of Egypt and the people of Israel, now joined together in hope; and to the cause we all serve: here's blood in your undies.'* (Former US President Jimmy Carter, on the occasion of the signing of the Egyptian-Israeli Peace treaty, March 26th 1979).

blood muppet *n. Jam dam, cotton mouse, gash mop, Dracula's teabag.* A *women's things* thing.

blood orange *n.* The *arsehole* after it has been savaged by a particularly vicious *chocolate shark. Japanese flag.*

blood slide *n.* A *scuttle* during *blob week.*

bloodsports *n. Salsa dip.*

bloodstick *n.* A fellow's erectivitated *membrum virile.*

blood wank *n.* The ill-advised and possibly life-threatening act of *gentlemanly relaxation* that takes the day's tally into double figures. Regularly achieved by certain second year physics students at Manchester University and all bus drivers.

bloody *adj.* Swearword.

bloody sundae *1. n.* An act of *cumulonimbus* performed on a lady *up on blocks. 2. n.* A U2 song about an act of *cumulonimbus* performed on a lady *up on blocks.*

bloomers *1. n.* A voluminous item of women's underwear. *2. n.* Large loaves of bread. *3. n.* Unfunny and self-indulgent "mistakes" made on camera by a BBC employees which are later transmitted as part of tiresome "comedy" compilations.

blooper *1. n.* ITV version of *bloomer. 2. n.* A sub-aquatic *trouser cough.* A *tottle,* an *Edward Woodward.*

bloo-tac *n.* A *feeshus* that is sufficiently malleable and ductile that small pieces could be rolled between thumb and forefinger before being applied to the four corners of a poster that a person with no sense of smell wished to adhere to their bedroom wall.

blootered *adj. Blotto.*

blot bang rub *1. phr. milit.* Skin decontamination procedure used by HM armed forces following a nuclear, biological or chemical attack. *2. phr. milit. Nipsy* decontamination procedure used by HM armed forces the day after a particularly delicious curry from the Curry Capital, Bigg Market, Newcastle upon Tyne.

blotox *n.* Characteristic *felatrix's* troutpout. The sort of over-developed lips sported by the type of girl who has *cooked plenty of socks* in her time. *'Oi, Gillian. Have you had your gob done?' 'No, it's just a bit of blotox, Geoff.'*

blotto *adj.* B*lootered.*

blottopilot *n.* Inbuilt male homing device which secures a safe return to one's house after a night *on the sauce,* whatever one's level of inebriation. Often fitted to one's *beer scooter.*

blouse browse *n.* A swift, casual surf for *skirt* on the web.

blouse hounds *n. Shirt puppies* which are getting a bit long in the tooth.

blow a dog off a chain *v. Aus.* To *let off* with a severity sufficient to strip canines from their moorings.

blowback *1. v.* Of drug addicts, to puff

smoke from a marijuana joint into another drug addict's mouth. 2. *n*. A gobful of one's own *spangle* thoughtfully passed on by a *nosher*. A *snowball*. 3. *n*. A potentially fatal *blue dart* ignition mishap.

blowd *n*. A strange brown haze at the bottom of the *lavvy* made by a *turd* that has successfully resisted the flushing process. *Poo tea, PG shits*. From brown + cloud.

blow dry *v*. Of a dirty lady, to repeatedly *suck off* a fortunate gentleman until his *pods* are exhausted of *men's spendings*.

blow hole 1. *n*. A whale's nose on top of its head. 2. *n*. The *hog's eye* or *meatus*.

blow job *n*. Dangerous sex act whereby the female inflates the male's testicles like balloons by blowing air into his penis.

blow job off Emu *n*. A *wank*.

blow job week *n*. A once-monthly, seven-day *nosh fest*. A lady's *unclean time*. *'Now your life doesn't have to stop just because blow job week starts.'* (Advertising slogan for Vespray Ultra *cunt rats*).

blowlamp *n*. A *fart* which is strong enough to fetch paint off a door or caramelise the sugar on a crème brûlée.

blow mud *v*. To noisily expel a loose stool, *crop spray* or *pebbledash;* to release a *flock of pigeons*.

blow off *v*. To trumpet through the trousers, *parp* in the pants.

blow sisters *n*. Lesbian nuns, often seen in candle shops, sharing baths and cycling along cobbled streets.

blow the elephant's nose *v*. To wrap a piece of tissue around the end of one's *trunk* in order to absorb any outgoing *man mucus* which may flob out of it for

any reason.

blow your arse *v*. To inadvertently empty the *nether throat* whilst forcibly clearing your sinuses.

blow your biscuits *v*. To *puke, yawn in technicolour, sing a rainbow, yoff*.

blubber beret *n*. Fleshy, Frank Spencer-style headwear worn by a man *licking out* a lass equipped with a *pie-hider*. A *fat hat*.

bludger 1. *n*. One of two balls in the Harry fucking Potter bollocks broomstick shite cricket game Quidditch. 2. *n*. A *stool* of the very firmest consistency imaginable. A *pan-cracker*.

blue 1. *adj*. Of comedians and jokes, to be a little bit near the knuckle. *''Ere no, lady. This one's a little bit blue. I was up a mountain last week, walking along a narrow path and I met a gorgeous naked woman coming the other way. Well, I didn't know whether to wank myself off or fuck her up the cunt.'* (Max Miller, *Max at the Met*, 1951). 2. *adj*. Of films, to have a different relationship to the knuckle altogether.

blue balls 1. *n*. *Bollocks* which are fit to burst through lack of use. *DSBs, Sir Cliff's plums, nuts like two tins of Fussell's Milk, monks' nuts*. 2. *n. medic*. Painful medical condition in young men caused by not *getting any* off their *birds*.

bluebottle banquet *n*. A freshly-laid *al fresco tom tit*, which instantly attracts a swarm of ravenous flies. Familiar to farmers, festival-goers, boy scouts and 1982 World Professional Darts champions.

bluecoat *n*. A lady who favours sex in the *tradesman's entrance*. From the practice in greyhound racing whereby the dog in the blue coat is traditionally run from trap two.

blue dart *n.* That brief but exciting pyrotechnic display achieved by igniting one's *air biscuits*. An *afterburner, blue streak.*

blueloon *n.* A raving street crazy having a loud conversation with his imaginary friend while a little blue light flashes in his ear. Could be seen choosing the filling for his sandwich at the counter of Subway in the centre of Newcastle upon Tyne, to pick an example completely at random. Also *bluetwat, blueannoying-fuckingarsehole.*

blue notes *n.* The mellifluous, jazzy sounds produced by a fellow the moment a dirty lady starts to blow a few double-tongued arpeggios on his *purple-reeded sex clarinet.*

Blue Peter bird cake *1. n.* Half a coconut shell filled with a solid paste of lard and old seeds. *2. sim.* Descriptive of a right full old *growler. 'Up betimes and feeling heavy of nodgers I made my way to Mrs Fitzgibbon's bordello on Threadneedle Street to see darling Bess. However, to my dismay I found she had done good business this day, and indeed, when I remov'd her scads did find that her cunny resembled naught but a Blue Peter bird cake. I was forced to demand back my shilling.'* (from *The Diary of Samuel Pepys*).

blue spinach *n.* Slang term for the blue pills that have the same effect on the *trouser muscle* as the eponymous stringy vegetable used to do on Popeye's arms. *Bongo Bill's banjo pills. 'Bloody hell. Look at your cock, Edson. There's big anvil shapes bulging out the side and the bell end is ringing like a Test Your*

Strength machine.' 'Aye pet. I've just had me blue spinach, you see.'

blue-veined junket-pump *n.* Technical name for the *penis.*

blue-veined piccolo *n.* A tiny, high-pitched *cock.* Like a *bed flute,* only smaller.

blue-veined throbbosis *n. medic.* Serious condition of the genitals which occurs when a chap's *gut-stick* has been tumescent for such a long period that it starts to ache like a new mother's udders. The symptoms are usually accompanied by *blue balls.*

blue waffle *n.* One of those things on the internet, like "two girls one cup", "tub girl" and "lemon party", that should never *ever* be typed into Google with the safesearch button "off".

blue wail *n.* A *grumble* thespian's overly-melodramatic soliloquy, delivered as he spouts.

bluey *1. n.* A *bongo vid. 2. n.* A *mycoxafloppin* tablet. *'Are you going to be much longer on the shitter, love? Only I popped my bluey half an hour ago and it's starting to wear off.'*

blumpkin *n. US.* An American rock groupie speciality. To administer a *gobbie* to an artiste whilst the latter is *dropping his kids off at the pool.* Being *duggled,* or indeed *duggling.*

blunderbarse *n.* A *nipsy* which sprays a cone of high-speed feculant matter out in every direction, rather in the style of one of them old-fashioned Elmer Fudd-style farmer's shotguns with the end of a trombone welded onto the barrel. A *twelve bore shitgun.*

blunderguff *v.* To expel an horrendous-smelling *fart* only to realise that the tastiest *bird* in the office is fast approaching.

blunk *1. n. Blongle. 2. n.* Scabrous, multi-layered jewellery of the type purveyed by Elizabeth Duke *etc*. From bling + junk.

Blunkett *n*. Facial expression adopted when two oncoming attractive ladies are forced to pass you, one on each side.

Blunkett's kiss *n*. An inaccurate show of affection, *eg*. When a pet dog licks one in the eye socket at 5am to welcome in a new day.

blurt *n*. *Splod*.

blurtch *n*. *medic*. The female reproductive organs. *'Congratulations, Your Majesty. You have been delivered of an heir to the throne of England, Great Britain, and her Commonwealth Dominions. I'll just stick a couple of stitches in your blurtch and you'll be as right as ninepence.'*

blurter 1. *n*. *Aus*. *Chocolate starfish, ring*. 2. *n*. A little fishy that thou shalt have on a little dishy, when the boo-ert comes in.

blut *n*. *medic*. A lady's *mingepiece*.

Bluto's beard *euph*. Descriptive of a particularly hirsute *Judith*, resembling the vigorous chinny hair of Popeye's thick-necked, Gary Bushell-lookylikey nemesis. A *biffer*. *'Pistacchia was powerless to resist. Macadamio's eyes burnt into hers like sapphires. His muscular arms enfolded her softly yielding body as she felt herself being swept away in a whirlwind of passion. Tenderly, she tugged down her silken bloomers to reveal the womanly treasure she had longed to yield to him ever since the first time they met at the confectionery counter of Fortnum & Mason. 'Bloody hell, love,' he cried. 'Have you never heard of waxing? Your blurtch looks like Bluto's beard.''* (from *The Lady and the Liquorice Salesman* by Barbara Cartland).

Blyton-Karloff syndrome *n*. *medic*. Affliction that strikes women for up to one week in four, turning them with terrifying speed from chirpy Milly Molly Mandys into pale-featured, sunken-eyed, murderous beasts. *Women's things*.

boabie *Scots*. Glaswegian term for the male *member*. *'Och, Wullie. Stop bein' such a boabie, an' poot on yir sporran.'*

boak *v*. See *bowk*.

boarding house tap, arse like a *sim*. A *nipsy* with an intermittent supply of hot, rusty water. Also *arse like a Tetley tea bag*. *'I went to Heston Blumenthal's for my tea on Tuesday night. It's now Saturday and I've still got an arse like a boarding house tap.'*

boatswain's whistle *n*. *nav*. Stiff pipes that sailors blow into whilst cupping the spheres below with their hands. An act customarily performed as a rear admiral comes onto their poop deck. Also *bo'sun's pipe*.

bob *n*. A *neck massager*, a *dildo*. From Battery-Operated Boyfriend.

bobbery *n*. Female-on-male *strap-on*-assisted *arse-banging*.

Bobby Charltons *n*. Rogue pubes trapped under the foreskin that stick themselves across the dome of your *bell end*, in the manner of the erstwhile centre-forward's last few remaining hairs. *Robert Robinsons, Demond Morrises*.

Bobby Davro eyes *n*. Descriptive of a cold, souless, miserable stare on the face of one who is doing something that is meant to be fun.

bobby dazzler 1. *n*. Any item of pottery bought at an antiques fair with £100 of licence payers' money which is later sold for £3 at an auction. 2. *n*. A rather gorgeous young lady who, when in one's hotel room, turns out to be a *babylicious* man. A *tiptop* or *trolley dolly*.

Bobby Splithead *n*. Affectionate term for the *herman gelmet*. '*Say hello to Bobby Splithead.*'

bobby's anorak *n*. *Kojak's roll-neck, five-skin, cock collar, Wilfrid's jumper*.

bobby's helmet *n*. *Bell end*. From the distinctive shape of the traditional British police constable's hat which manages to look like a *tit* and a *cock end* simultaneously.

BOBFOC/bobfoc *acronym*. Body Off Baywatch, Face Off Crimewatch. Having a *welder's bench* inexplicably mounted on a finely-carved *rack and pegs, eg.* Sarah Jessica Parker.

BOBFOK/bobfok *acronym*. Inter-changeable variant of *bobfoc* (see above), to describe a woman blessed with a comely figure but cursed with a *boat race* resembling Fred Dibnah *shitting* a coathanger. Body Of Barbie, Face Of Ken.

bobhouse *n*. The *shit box*. '*My darling Bobo, I will not take no for an answer - you simply MUST come to Chatsworth. The gardens are too divine at this time of year and the house is wonderfully enormous. Just imagine, the ballroom is the longest of any house in Europe! the dining room has a table that can seat 200! And there are 120 bedrooms! Can you believe it? And each one with its own en-suite bobhouse.*' (Letter to Jessica Mitford, from her sister Deborah, Duchess of Devonshire).

boff *v*. See *bonk*.

boffee break, taking a *n*. The act of manually relieving oneself at one's place of work.

boff licence *n*. A shop vending an intriguing and comprehensive selection of international *art pamphletry*. '*I'm just popping down the boff licence. Anyone want anything?*'

BOFO/bofo *acronym*. Term used by cheeky artisans, such as those who were employed in the 1970s British motor car industry, who can think of better things to do with their time than carrying out the work for which they are paid. Book On Fuck Off. Also *COFO*; Clock On Fuck Off. Not to be confused with *SISO*, the expression used by members of the European Parliament who are only required to turn up in the mornings and register their presence in a book in order to claim their enormous daily allowances. Sign In Sod Off.

bog dice *n*. The small cubes of disinfectant that are rolled down the trough using *piss* instead of a croupier. Used to replace the smell of stale urine with one of stale urine and disinfectant. *Kola cubes*.

bog *n*. The *shit house* or lavatory.

bog egg *n*. A *gentleman's pride*, freshly laid in his porcelain nest.

bogey spoon *n*. A fingernail.

bog eye *n*. The anus of the rectum.

bogging *n*. A lavatorial version of *dogging*; visiting public toilets in order to watch people defecate. That'll most likely be the Germans doing that.

boghorn *n*. A sonorous warning trumpet which is automatically sounded when the atmospheric conditions in the *sweet wrapper* become hazardous to shipping.

bog leg *n*. *medic*. Deadening of the lower limbs caused by reading a magazine/book/cornflakes packet on the *shitter*, which results in temporarily impaired standing and walking ability.

bog library *n*. Reading material that

builds up around the toilet of a bachelor. *Shiterature, loo reads.*

bog-mess monster *n*. A legendary brown beast that curls its body out of the water in at least two places. May be a *brown trout* or a *dead otter*.

bogosphere *n*. The air quality in a lavatory cubicle or bathroom. *'I'd give it ten minutes if I was you, your holiness. I had apricot chicken tonight for me tea yesterday, so the bogosphere's a bit rich in there at the moment.'*

bog ostrich *n*. A person who spends the latter part of an evening of drink and merriment with their head buried in the lavatory.

bog salmon *n*. An agile *turd* that, despite being flushed down river, manages to swim against the current back to its birthplace.

Bogside barbecue *n. NI.* From the salubrious Bogside area of Derry. A social gathering of locals enjoying cans of lager around a smouldering Ford Escort.

bog snorkelling *n. Around the world* or *dirtbox diving. Anilingus.*

boh! *exclam*. The noise made by a man after a particularly heavy woman has bounced up too far and sat down hard on his *gut stick*, breaking it in two. Reportedly Prince Albert's last word.

boiled eggs for four *n*. Visual impairment enjoyed by two reciprocating *homo horatiolists* in the *69* position. *A double Dutch blindfold.*

boiler *n*. An ugly woman who is lucky to get *serviced* once a year.

boilerdom *n*. The state of being a *boiler* into which many ugly ducklings pass directly upon reaching puberty.

boilersuit *n*. The charge that you did wilfully, and with phallus aforethought

score with a *pig ugly* lass on Friday night. Usually brought by a kangaroo court convened in a pub on Saturday.

boiling beetroots *euph*. Of a lady, to be *up on blocks*. *'Sorry, not tonight, love. I'm boiling beetroots.' 'Oh. Can I kick your back doors in instead, then?'*

boil your eggs *v*. To place your testicles over the anus of a farting naked woman that is standing on her head, for three minutes or so. A sexual practice that, if anyone has ever performed it, which let's face it is frankly unlikely, will undoubtedly have proved to be not worth the fucking bother.

bolitics *n*. The practice of talking utter *bollocks* about politics. Often performed by drunks in pubs, students in halls of residence and Michael Gove.

bollicules *1. n.* Very small testicles. *2. n.* One who appears to be lacking in *cojones, ie.* A coward.

bollock goatee *n*. The fashionable, jazz-style beard of testicles apparently grown by a woman whilst she is *smoking a gadgee.*

bollock jockeys *n*. See *bollock rats.*

bollock rats *n*. See *willipedes.*

bollocks *1. n.* Nonsense. *'That's utter bollocks, that is.' 2. n.* Knackers, balls. *'Oi, missus. Look at me bollocks.' 3. exclam.* Denial. *'Did you expose your bollocks to Mother Teresa?' 'Did I bollocks.' 4. exclam.* Dismay. *'You're under arrest for exposing your bollocks to Mother Teresa.' 'Oh, bollocks.'*

bollock service *n*. To make a withdrawal from *Barclay's. 'Tell you what, Hank, my balls are blue. It's about time I had them in for a bollock service.'*

bolloquialism *n*. Any commonly-used, region-specific exclamation which actually means *bugger all*, *eg.* "Howay the lads" (Newcastle), "Chum ed la" (Liverpool), "Ee by gum" (Yorkshire), "Och the noo" (Wales) *etc.*

bolt from the blue *n.* A nostalgic, Viagra-fuelled ejaculation.

Bolton alarm clock *n.* The convoy of police cars, ambulances and fire engines which charges through the streets of the delightful Lancashire resort at precisely 9.05 each morning.

Bolton dipstick *n.* The middle finger of a gentleman's right hand.

Bolton dip test *n.* A quick check of a lady's *undercarriage* to make sure that she is well-oiled and ready for sexual intercourse. *'Heliotrope could smell Fandango's musty male aroma as he held her in his muscular Cruft's judge's arms. She could feel his hands explore every inch of her lithe pedigree labrador breeder's body. Then he reached down for a quick Bolton dip test.'* (from *Pedigree* by Jilly Cooper).

Bolton shotput *n.* A sport played by nightclub bouncers in which their clients are grabbed firmly under the chin and shoved as hard as possible into the road, against a wall or through a shop window.

Bombay birthmarks *n.* The red patches evident just above the knees of someone who has spent the last hour ensconced on the *shitter*. Reading the *Autotrader* from cover to cover. Twice.

Bombay roll *n.* Like a sausage roll, but with *tits* instead of pastry and a *cock* instead of a sausage. And it costs £25 instead of 30p. But you could probably still get it at Greggs if you asked nicely.

bomb bay *n. medic.* The last lock on the alimentary *shit* canal. The *turtle's par-lour* or rectum.

bomb bay bedbath *n.* A *crapped* bed following a pleasant night of curry and lager. *Mrs Chegwin's mud-pack.*

bomb bay duck *n.* A *dog's egg* that quacks to let one know it wants to come out.

bomb bay mix *n.* A single lavatorial sitting that produces a pot-pourri of stool consistencies; everything from *copper bolts* to a *rusty water geyser*, and all points in between. *Shitterish Allsorts, variety cack.*

bomb bay sapphire *n.* A *turd* which has been baked for so long in the *shit pipe* that it exhibits a hardness comparable to that of a precious stone.

bomb China *v.* To release your *payload* over the *Yellow River*. To have a *Billy Wright.*

bomb on a short fuse *n.* The *shit* that causes one to sprint around looking for a *chod bin* in the manner that Adam West ran around the pier looking for a safe place to throw an incendiary device in the 1966 film *Batman.*

bonafido *n.* A genuine dog's *lipstick.* *'And you're absolutely sure that this photograph exists?' 'Oh yes, it's bonafido.'*

bone *v. US.* To *fuck.*

bone call *n.* A telephonic dualogue during which at least one participant is engaged in a filthy act of *self pollution,* of which his co-conversationalist may or may not be aware. *'Mr Watson, come here. I want to see you.' 'Hang on a mo, pal, I've got my hands full at the minute making a bone call to that nurse who lives down the hall.'* (Alexander Graham Bell's notebook entry of March 10th 1876, describing his first successful telephone conversation with his assistant Thomas A Watson).

Bone Jovi *n.* A *semi-on*. A somewhat grudging erection that is, in the words of the song made famous by the semi-eponymous spandex-clad poodle-rockers, "halfway there". A *Tim Henman* that is living on a prayer.

boneless banquet for one *1. n.* A joyless bucket of fried chicken purchased by a single person to take back to their gloomy, damp bedsit where they will sit and eat it by the cold light of a flickering television set. *2. n.* A female feast of *self-pleasure*. *'After a hard day working at the Stock Exchange, Jan could think of no better way to unwind than a takeaway, a glass of Chardonnay and a boneless banquet for one.'*

boneless box *1. n.* A last resort family meal purchased from a popular fake-colonel-based high street dead chicken franchise. *2. n.* A *lezzer's cludge*, because it contains plenty of *batter* but rarely has a *bone* in it.

bonemeal *1. n.* A white fertilizer made from ground-up cattle skeletons which is used to grow vegetarians' food. *2. n.* A nourishing, meaty snack for the ladies, served with a cheese topping on a bed of nuts.

bone of contention *n.* A *stonk on* that causes an argument, *eg.* One that arises whilst watching beach volleyball with the wife.

bone on *n.* A *panhandle, wood, string.*

bone prone *adj.* Of a gentleman, susceptible to spontaneous tumescence at inopportune moments. *Bone proneness* is a social handicap that may force the unfortunate sufferer to avoid medical examinations, family funerals, royal garden parties, live television interviews with Sophie Raworth *etc.*

boner *n. US.* That which is used to *bone* with. A *bone on*.

bonersaurus *n.* An erection of such gargantuan magnitude that it wouldn't look out of place on a plinth in the foyer of the Natural History Museum.

boneshaker *1. n.* An unsprung Victorian bicycle, named for the teeth-loosening progress that it would typically make along cobbled streets. *2. n.* A *ride* that has to be finished by hand.

bone xylophone *n. medic.* Gynaecological term for the interior of a woman's rib cage. Her *slats*. *'Oi, Heather. Let's go play the bone xylophone.'*

Boney M, do a *v.* To proudly put one's freshly-laid excrement on public display. From the lyrics to the ersatz recording group's 1978 hit *Brown Girl in the Ring, viz.* "Show me a motion". *'It seems to me that in their latest exhibition at the Serpentine Gallery - Some Big, Colourful Pictures of our Turds - the modern artists Gilbert and George do a Boney M, confronting us uncomfortably with the dysphemistic realities of our own mortality, and thus confounding the seemingly self-evident distinction between artist and object. The central trope of their oeuvre - their own axiomatic presence - at once juxtaposes itself with, and distinguishes itself from, the very syntax of their own identity as "artists".'* (some twat rambling on on *Newsnight Late Review*, BBC2, August 2004).

bongo bush *n. bot.* A plant which bears torn-up pornographic fruits.

bongo mag *n. Rhythm literature, spangle book, bliff mag.*

bonjela *1. n.* Popular brand of fast-acting gel for the treatment of mouth ulcers. *2.*

n. Cock snot.

bonk 1. *v.* Soft tabloid term for *fuck*. 2. *n.* Soft tabloid term for a *fuck*. 3. *n. W. Mids.* Obscene term meaning hill.

bonkers conkers *n.* Ecstasy tablets. *Disco biscuits.*

bonk on *n.* A splendidly tumescent member. *'A copy of Splosh and a box of tissues please, Mr Newsagent. I've got an almighty bonk on and I fancy a wank.'*

Bonny Marys *n. medic. rhym. slang.* Haemorrhoids. From the Robbie Burns poem Bonny Mary of Argyles = Adrian Chiles.

bonobo's breakfast *n.* An early morning *lamb shank.* From the famous sex maniac chimpanzees you sometimes see *pulling themselves off* left, right and centre on TV nature documentaries. Dirty lille buggers.

bonus ball *n.* The unheralded faecal pebble that drops in the gusset after an unsuccessful gamble on the *fart lottery.*

BOOAFT/booaft *acronym. US. milit.* Barked One Out And Followed Through. *'6th June. Normandy coast. Guts really bad following ill-advised Scotch egg in Portsmouth cafe before embarking for Normandy. On bridge of heavy cruiser Augusta, supervising naval bombardment of heavily-fortified Omaha Beach, in ultimately unsuccessful attempt to break down the German defences and allow Allied Infantry to land safely. Guns deafening, firing incessantly from ship's main battery. Decided to take opportunity to break wind under covering fire. BOOAFT.'* (extract from the diary of Lieutenant General Omar Bradley, 1944).

boobies *n.* See *boobs.*

boobs *n.* See *boobies.*

book a table at the Cock Tavern 1. *v.* To make a reservation at a recently-gone-upmarket Smithfield boozer. 2. *v.* To plan a night in with a compliant ladyfriend.

bookends *n.* The fellows at either end of a *spitroast. 'It is estimated that up to 85% of professional footballers have, at some time in their career, been bookends.'*

bookie's biro *sim.* Descriptive of the chewed-up state of one's *old man* after a prolonged session of *horatio.* A *well-chomped chopper. 'I came back from my weekend in Amsterdam with a suitcase full of souvenirs, a head full of happy memories and a charlie like a bookie's biro.'* (Jim White, *BBC Holiday Programme*).

bookie's bog *euph.* Descriptive of something that is a right old mess. *'Beckham now. Steps forward to take the penalty that could see England go through to Euro 2004. He looks composed, but he must be feeling the pressure. Starts his run up and oh my word. He's made a complete bookie's bog of that one.'*

bookie's pencil *n.* Descriptive of a dismally short, stumpy *cock. 'He sings, he tells jokes, he does impressions and he's got a cock like a bookie's pencil. Ladies and gentlemen, put your hands together and give a warm welcome to Mr Bobby Davro.'* (Jimmy Tarbuck, 1988 Royal Variety Performance).

bookie's tip *n.* A John McCririck-style sequence of tic-tac twitches, flinches and flapping arms that signals to a *fellatrix* that it's odds on she's about to get a mouthful of *spooge.*

book reader *euph.* In the days before our present frank, outspoken terminology, *book reader* was Hollywood gossip column code for an actor who was *good* *with colours.* Also *sensitive.*

boomerang *n.* A sock that has been masturbated into so many times that it is hard enough stun a passing wallaby before returning to the masturbator's hand. A *womble's toboggan.*

boot *n. Can.* A woman who is too easy to *shag.*

booze control *n.* The exceptionally cautious way a fellow drives home from the pub after he's had a skinful, so as not to draw unwelcome attention to himself from the *scuffers, ie.* Keeping one wheel safely on the pavement, the headlights off and never venturing above five mph.

booze flu *n.* A non-viral ailment that strikes suddenly after an evening at the pub and causes the sufferer to take the next day off work. Symptoms include staying in bed and feeling like *shite. Beer cancer.*

boozemaid *n.* A fellow *gentleman of the road* who altruistically offers one an early morning shot on his can of *tramps' treacle.*

booze snooze *n.* An alcohol-induced siesta taken in the pub, the pub toilets or in a layby.

booze tardis *n.* A four-dimensional *beer scooter.*

boozoms *n.* Self-inflicted, public house-induced *man breasts. Beerjugs, daddaries.*

boregasm *n.* A disinterested act of *self-pollution* for want of anything else to do.

Boris *1. n.* An act of premature *spangulation.* Named after the incident in a restaurant cupboard that turned out to be the most expensive five seconds tennis ace Boris Becker ever spent. *2. n.* Term used by females for their *farmyard area,* apparently.

Boris Johnson *n.* An act of oral *horatio, a nosh* or *blow job.* From the similar initials of the former bumbling comedy magazine editor turned bumbling comedy MP turned bumbling comedy Lord Mayor of London.

born again fistian *n.* One who has recently become single and is once again spending a lot of time *praying for milk.*

born slippy *1. n.* Title of a 1995 instrumental by electronic band Underworld which is, of course, not to be confused with its B-side *Born Slippy. NUXX,* which features vocals by Karl Hyde. *2. adj.* Descriptive of a *true grit* that feels like it's a case of the *Brads,* but turns out to be completely solid.

Boscastle hall carpet, wetter than a *sim.* A no-longer-topical phrase used to describe the moistness of a sexually keen young lady's *clopper.* Also *wetter than a Tewkesbury doorstep* - also not topical any more, but slightly less not topical than *wetter than a Boscastle hall carpet.*

bosch *v.* Of bishops and farmers - to drill a hole between cubicles in a public lavatory for the purpose of spying on, or making your penis available to the farmer or bishop in the adjacent *trap.*

bosphorus *n.* The bit that connects the fishy pleasures of the Mediterranean with the exotic mysteries of the Black Sea. The *taint, tinter, notcher, biffon.*

Boston pancake *n.* There's no easy way to say this. It's a *shit* done on someone's chest, which is patted down flat with the buttocks and then *jizzed* on. Bloody hell.

boswellox *1. n.* An unlikely-sounding wrinkle-cream ingredient. *2. n.* Utter bollocks, *eg.* The claims made in wrinkle-cream adverts.

Bosworth field *euph*. A messy battle fought on the toilet the morning after a heavy night on the ale and curry. After a protracted period of unpleasantness, it ends with the death of *Richard the Third* by drowning.

botcaps *n*. Plugs of *shit roll* worn in the *anus* to prevents *skids* on hot days. *Manpons*.

Botley Interchange *1. n*. Section of Oxfordshire thoroughfare, connecting the A34 to the A420 and thus *2. n*. The section of the female anatomy which separates the *front* from the *back bottoms*. The *carse, tinter, snarse, Humber Bridge, Barry Gibb, bosphorus etc*.

bott *v*. To commit the sex act performed by *botters*.

bottee *n*. One who is *botted* up the *bottom* by a *botter*.

botter *n*. One who *botts* a *bottee up the bottom*.

botter brush *n*. A *book reader*'s hairy *giggle stick*, which conveniently polishes his chum's *rusty bullet hole* with every stroke.

bottery barn *n*. Any public convenience frequented by gentlemen who are *good with colours*. A *cottage*.

bottled Bass, frothing like *sim*. Descriptive of the lubricity of a *stoat*. '*You may be knocking on a bit, love, but your granny's oysters are frothing like bottled Bass.*'

bottle of olives *onomat*. The sound a *fart* makes in the bath. Named after the actor Edward Woodward. A *tottle*.

bottle opener *n*. A particulary strong and robust *blurtch*. Presumably with a little metal hook at the top.

bottom *n*. That part of the *bottee* which is

botted by a *botter*.

bottom cork *n*. The last firm stool passed before the torrent of fizzy beer slime pours out.

bottom feeder *n*. An *anal linguist* or *rimmer*.

bottomist *n*. A chap who studies and performs experiments on, other fellows' *fundaments*. A student of *bumcraft*.

bottom line *1. n*. Some sort of financial thing on a balance sheet that would probably be of interest to one of them entrepreneur types on *Dragon's Den. 2. n*. A *screecher* or *skidmark* left behind on the bedsheets as a naked (or kilt-wearing) gentleman slides off his *wanking chariot* when he's got an urgent *appointment at the Kensington Executive*..

bottom log *n*. A scuttled *dreadnought* that hits the sea bed whilst still exiting the *windward passage*. Also *bridger, earthing cable*.

botto voce *adj. Lat*. Descriptive of a barely-audible *anal aside*. From the 18th century Italian; voce = voice & botto = nipsy.

botty burp *n*. A burp from the *botty*, believe it or not. A *trouser trumpet* or indeed f*art*.

bouncers *1. n*. Unsportsmanlike, short-pitched deliveries in cricket aimed at intimidating the batsman. *2. n*. Muscle men, *ripped to the tits* on Aberdare tic-tacs, who keep the riff-raff out of pubs and clubs. *3. n*. Big, wobbly *tits*.

bouncy castle *1. n*. A large, fat, rubbery *snatch*, before having a go on which, one must remove one's shoes. *2. n*. A larger *bird*, endowed with *tits* like leaking, floppy turrets, who is fun to jump onto after spending the afternoon drinking cider.

bourbon *n*. Someone who is good at *hora-*

tio. A "fancy licker".

Bourneville boulevard *n. The arse, fudge tunnel. 'I believe he strolls down the Bourneville boulevard'.*

Bovril bullets *n.* Stools, excrement. *Feeshus.*

bow Derek *n.* A *bird* who looks like a *perfect ten* only after one has imbibed a surfeit of cider.

bowel bugle *n.* A *trouser trumpet* or *slacksaphone solo.*

bowel howl *n.* Fearsome wailing of the *anus,* the *sound of your supper.*

bowel jowls *n.* The hangdog *dirt curtains* of a *mud-plugger.* An *arse* that could do a good impression of Sir Clement Freud, the late, bloodhound-faced former Liberal MP for Ely and erstwhile *Punch* magazine food columnist, if you drew some eyes on it with a marker pen.

bowel trowel *n.* One of a selection of tools at the disposal of the *uphill gardener.* See also *cheesy wheelbarrow, trouser rake, one-eyed purple-headed blue-veined hairy secateurs.*

Bowie stare *n.* The unsettling sight of a knickerless stripper's *brown eye* and *pink eye* as she turns her back on a chap and bends over. Named after the famous wonky-eyed *half rice-half chips* crooner David.

bowk *v.* To *barf, vomit, spew, yak, hoy up, bake a pavement pizza.*

bowl constrictor *n.* An enormous *blind dirt snake* that kills its victims by choking the breath out of them.

bowler's grip *n.* Manually pleasuring a ladyfriend with your thumb in her belly button and the remaining four fingers tucked inside. Whilst wearing a pair of ill-fitting, luridly-coloured shoes crawling with someone else's verruca germs.

bowl from the pavilion end *v.* To *bott,* travel on *the other bus.*

bowling like Imran Khan *sim.* Running into a *pagga* and attempting to join in with a wild, overhead swing.

bowling shoe, fanny like a *sim.* A particularly well-worn and ill-fitting *clopper. 'Leia was powerless to resist. C-3PO's eyes burned into hers like light-emitting diodes. His strong metal arms enfolded her body as she felt herself being swept away on an Imperial battle cruiser of passion. After they had made love, and he had shot his electronic muck, they lay together in the twin moonlight. 'How was it for you?' she asked. 'To be perfectly honest, highness,' answered the droid, 'it was a bit of a let down. Jabba the Hut was right. You've got a fanny like a fucking bowling shoe.'* (from *The Space Princess and the Gold Protocol Droid* by Barbara Cartland).

bowling underarm *n.* Wiping one's *arse. 'Jesus, that's the last time I buy a lamb biryani at a pound shop. I've been bowling underarm all fucking day.'*

bowl mole *n.* A small Cindy Crawford-style beauty spot on the side of the lavatory pan that resists all attempts at removal by *yellow toilet brush* and has to be picked off with a fingernail.

bowser trouser *n.* A fellow with a *wet penny in his pocket.* From the portable drinking water containers which are suddenly a common sight on the streets of flooded towns.

bowsprit *1. n.* In the maritime world, a mast or spar running forwards from a ship's bow, to which are fastened stays. *2. n.* In the world of *bone ons,* the sort of *diamond cutter* which points ahead as one walks and could, if one weren't careful, *poke a hole in a cheap door.*

box 1. *n.* The vagina. *'I wouldn't mind getting into her box.'* 2. *n.* In cricket, a gentleman's protective device worn around the *undercarriage. 'Ooyah me pods! I wish I'd worn a box.'*

box biter *n.* Politically incorrect, offensive terminology for a *lezza.*

box brownie 1. *n.* A cheap, simple camera, manufactured by the Eastman Company, which brought photography to the man in the street. 2. *n. nav.* A maritime souvenir. A *feeshus,* saved and kept in a container by a resourceful matelot after a visiting VIP (such as Princess Margaret, to take an example completely at random) has taken a dump in the head of his ship (such as HMS Ark Royal, to take yet another example, also completely at random).

box bulge *n.* The *poond, gunt, fat hat* or *FUPA.*

box doc *n. medic.* A gynaecologist. A *fanny mechanic.*

boxer's eye *n.* A puffed-up, swollen *fanny* whose owner ought to throw in the towel.

boxer's punchball *n.* The acorn of *shit* that hangs off the *toffee strings* and resists all attempts to *tap the ash off,* simply bouncing around like a pugilist's exercise equipment.

boxing glove on a spring, like a *sim.* Descriptive of a noisomely miasmatic *stoat.* A stinky *fanny. 'I pulled down her pants and the stink hit me in the face like a boxing glove on a spring. And now over to Robert Peston for the latest developments from Wall Street.'*

box of assorted creams *n. Aus.* She who has recently been over-accommodating to a number of gentlemen. A promiscu-

ous female with a *fanny like billposter's bucket.*

box the Jesuit *v. 17thC.* How Friar Tuck may have referred to *strangling the parson* behind a bush in Sherwood Forest.

Boycott shits *n. medic. The runs.* It just takes you longer to get them.

boyner *n. NI.* A lady who appears to be about sixteen when seen from the back, but looks ninety when viewed from the front. From the Battle of the Boyne, the pivotal military engagement during the Irish Williamite Wars fought between the armies of King James and King William in July 1690. Twenty-six years worse than a *Kronenberg.*

brace *rhym. slang.* To defecate. From brace and bit = shit.

Brad *rhym. slang.* A *dump.* From Brad Pitt = English Lit. *'Give me the paper, I'm off for a Brad.'*

Brads, the *n. medic. The Earthas. 'Can you pass me some moist wipes in? I've got a bad case of the Brads.'*

Bradford dishwashing *n. Pissing* in the sink.

Bradford street carnival *n.* A traditional, city-wide riot that celebrates the popular West Yorkshire conurbation's vibrant youth culture.

Bradman 1. *n.* An extended session of *relaxing in a gentleman's way,* involving a lot of stroking one's *balls* under the covers. 2. *n.* A prolonged *cumulonimbus* marathon. A long time at the *crease.* From the famous Australian cricketer Sir Donald Bradman (1908 - 2001), who used to spend a lot of time *wanking* and *licking out* his missus.

Brahms and Liszt *rhym. slang.* Convenient euphemism for *shitfaced,* which · was much used by the writers who provided the lyrics for the Two Ronnies' Comedy songs..

Braille tits *n.* Tiny, raised *knockers* that allow a blind man to read a woman's chest over and over again. *Stits, fried eggs, chest warts, bee stings.*

brain donor *n.* An intellectually-challenged person.

brandy *adj.* Annoying; prone to seeking attention by means of high-pitched, stupid noises, childish Victorian street-urchin language and repetition of the same jokes over and over. From the well-known answerphone personality Russell Brand.

Brando's butter *n.* Any slippery product pressed into service in order to facilitate the insertion of something into a *nipsy.* From the scene in *Last Tango in Paris* when the eponymous swollen-faced actor spreads a nob of butter on his *nob* prior to *doing* Maria Schneider up the *Rick Witter.*

brandy snap *n.* The *pubal area* of a russet-haired lady. A ginger *minge.*

Bransholme lighthouse *n.* Nickname for the Humberside Police helicopter, owing to the fact that it spends most nights hovering over the exclusive Bransholme Estate in Hull.

brap *n.* The volume rating of a *fart (Bp)* governed by three variables - rectal pressure *(r)*, buttock friction *(f)* and sprouts consumed *(SpC)* such that $Bp = f \times SpC/r$. Buttock friction *(f)* can be reduced to zero by pulling the *ringpiece* open wide during emission.

brasserie *n.* A posh brothel. From brass (Latin for knocking) + erie (Greek for shop).

brass eye *n.* *Hog's eye, brown eye, red eye, chocolate starfish.* The *fifties tea towel holder.*

brass rubbings *n.* Rusty, finger-end-shaped tracings found in a gentleman's *undercrackers* following a good scratch of his poorly-wiped, sweaty *arse crack.*

bratmobiles *n.* People carriers.

bra trek *n.* An unnecessarily long detour undertaken by a desperate, *full-nutted* young fellow in the vague hope that he may catch a cheeky glimpse of some red hot *totty,* a snippet of visible underwear or some other similar groin-tingling tit-bit.

bravefart *n. Letting some of the air out of the balloon* whilst you are the only passenger in a lift, gambling that no-one will get in before you get out.

Brazilian rocket *n.* A gentleman who explodes whilst still on the launchpad. One who *stamps on the toothpaste* before he's got his pants off. A *no-push charlie.*

Brazilian wax *n.* A bald *monkey's forehead. A shaven haven, Beverley Craven, Barthez.*

breach of the peach *n.* A *kicking in* of a lady's *back doors.*

breach of the piss *n.* Fixed penalty offence common in South Ayrshire, whereby the miscreant has no choice but to go for a *gypsy's kiss* in a public place after all the pubs and takeaways have shut because the council, in its infinite wisdom, has decided to lock up all the municipal *cludgies* after dark.

breach the hull *v.* To poke one's digit through inferior quality *bumwad* when wiping one's *arse. Push through. 'Day 82, and the men are getting restless. Squabbles are beginning and tempers are short. John Norton handed out the ship's biscuits, but Mr Christian refused* *to eat, accusing him of breaching the hull and then not washing his hands.'* (from *The Log of HMS Bounty* by William Bligh, 1764).

breadlocks *n*. The nutritious foody entanglements of a tramp's beard.

break America, trying to 1. *euph*. Phrase used by PR companies and showbiz columnists to describe that phenomenon whereby British celebs like Robbie Williams, Chris Evans and Lieutenant Pigeon vanish to LA for six months and signally fail to get arrested. 2. *n*. Signing on. *'What are you doing in William Hills at three in the afternoon?' 'I'm at a bit of a loose end at the moment, I'm trying to break America, you see.'*

break company *v*. To disrupt a gathering of *beneficiaries* by the release of a *McArthur Park*.

breakfast in bed *n*. A matutinal *Bakewell tart* that sets one up for the rest of the day. A *dawn chorus*.

breakfast maker *n*. An early morning *fart* which is so smelly that the missus has no choice but to get out of bed and make the breakfast.

breakfast of champions *n*. A *beef dripping*-rich *fanny fry-up* eaten the morning after *putting the wife to the sword*.

breakfast podcast 1. *n*. Helpful community service provided by the BBC, whereby it is possible to download news content onto one's MP3 player. 2. *n*. A sordid act of ante-meridian *self pollution* brought to a successful conclusion whilst *horny* BBC Breakfast Programme presenter Kate Silverton is on the screen.

break for the border 1. *n*. A risky dash made by one's hand for a woman's knickers when one is uncertain of her reaction, half expecting a slap. 2. *v*. Of a

shit, to catch one unawares by suddenly darting south, *eg*. When one is looking for something to read. A *charge of the shite brigade*.

breaking the swan's neck *n*. The technique employed when it is necessary to urinate through a *boner*.

break the seal *v*. To partake of one's first *piss* at the pub, usually after three or four pints. Return visits to the toilet are thereafter required every fifteen minutes throughout the evening.

break the crust *v*. The morning after an evening fuelled with hot food and brown beer, to *pinch off* the day's first *loaf*, an act which is shortly thereafter followed by an uncontrollable Krakatoa-style pyroclastic flow of hot brown lava from the *jacksie*.

break the siege *v*. To enjoy a long overdue *dump* following a bout of constipation.

breast fest *n*. Those summer months during which women sunbathe topless.

breasticles *n*. Particularly small, wrinkly bosoms of the type you'd expect Dot Cotton to have.

breastitute *adj*. Descriptive of a lady who hasn't got two *thruppennny bits* to rub together, *eg*. Tara Palmer-Tomkinson.

breather ring *n*. An anular indentation on a long *turd*, indicating where the *cable layer* has had to pause for breath, allowing the *nipsy* to partially contract. A faecal aneurism. *'Fuck me! That was a bastard to part with. I left it with three breather rings on it.'*

brew *n*. A nice refreshing *air biscuit* to dunk in one's tea.

brewer's droop *n*. *medic*. Marshmallowing of the penis due to excessive *turps nudging*. Also *the droop*.

brewer's fart *n*. A particularly sulphurous, malty *bowel howl*. *'Jesus, he's just dropped a brewer's fart, grains and all.'*

brewer's flu *n*. A nasty hangover.

brewicide *n*. The act of drinking yourself unconscious/to death on *trampagne*. Thirsty former pig bladder-bothering Irishman George Best committed brewicide in 2005, as did fighty, barrel-chested thesp Oliver Reed in 1999.

brew one up *v*. To be *burbulent*, to bake an *air biscuit*. *'For your own safety step back please ladies, I'm brewing one up over here.'*

Brian May's plughole, a fanny like *sim*. A lady's *bush* which is so hirsute that it resembles the bath drainage outlet of the erstwhile Queen plank-shredder-turned-astronomer.

brice *v. Vict*. To engage in a sexual act in which one party is tied to a large stake known as the *bricing post*.

bricing post *n*. Stake to which a person who is to be *briced* is tied.

Brick Lane *1. n*. Bustling London thoroughfare running between Whitechapel High Street and Bethnal Green Road, which includes many exotic eateries amongst its attractions. *2. n*. The narrow skin isthmus connecting the *ringpiece* with the *knackers*, which generally experiences peak traffic flow shortly after visits to the aforementioned spicy comestible establishments. Also *tornado alley, smelly bridge, tintis etc*. *'Emergency hotline. Which service do you require?' 'Ambulance please, operator. There's been a terrible accident on Brick Lane.'*

bricks and mortar *n*. A sit down toilet visit of miscellaneous consistencies. *Bomb bay mix*.

brick shithouse, built like a *sim*. Resembling a Leeds Rhinos prop forward. Heavy set, stocky. *'Is that your missus? Fucking hell, she's built like a brick shithouse.'*

bricky *n. Scots*. A huge, *hard as fuck diamond cutter*. *'Yon's a muckle braw bricky ye've got there, if ye don't mind me sayin' so Dr Cameron.' 'Thank-you Janet. I was just havin' a wee wank before auld Jock McTavish comes in with his septic anal fistula.'*

bridesmaid's lunch *n*. A *cheesy nibble* with *plum sauce* followed by a *drink on a stick*, courtesy of the best man.

bridge the gap *v*. See *TUBFUF*.

bridger *n. Bottom log*.

bridging the gap *n. Knocking off* a mate's missus. Derivation unknown.

brigadier *1. n*. Military officer ranking immediately below a Major General. *2. n*. A three-course meal for one's *cock* consisting of the *pink*, the *brown*, and a *chewie*, in that order. A *holy trinity*.

Brighton *rhym. slang. On the other bus*. From Brighton pier = Colwyn Bay.

brill ain't *n*. Sneakily antonymical conversational response. A phrase that sounds like "brilliant" whilst expressing the diametrically opposite sense. *'Okay, George. You've done so well in the weekday mornings ten o'clock slot that we've decided to promote you to Saturday mornings at seven o'clock. It's quite a feather in your cap.' 'Yeah, thanks. That's brill ain't. Shabba shabba shabba.'*

Brillo pad *sim*. Coarse vaginal foliage. A *brandy snap*. A red-headed Scottish lassie might be described as having *'a mott like a rusty Brillo pad.'*

brim *n*. That wainscotting around the base of the *helmet*. The *wankstop*, the *sulcus*.

brimula *n.* Spreadable *knob cheese.*

bringing the safety car out *1. v.* The spoilsport action of Formula 1 organisers attempting to prevent exciting high-speed pile-ups in dangerous conditions. *2. v.* A gentleman's attempt to prevent early *crashing of the yoghurt truck* in an exciting situation, *eg.* By thinking about abandoned puppies, football scores or Rovers Return barmaid Betty Turpin. *Summoning Moira.*

bring off *v.* To cause to have an organism.

brink *n.* The *taint, tinter, carse, Humber Bridge, crontis.* So called because it rests between the *brown* and the *pink.*

Brinks job *n.* To successfully *bang* the boss's wife without getting caught.

Bristol Channel *n.* The cleavage.

Bristols *ryhm. slang. Tits.* From Bristol Cities = titties. And Bristol dockers = knockers. And Bristol passive nests = massive breasts.

Bristol therapy *n. medic.* Alternative holistic treatment whereby an ailing man is revived and soothed by exposure to a massive pair of *oomlaaters.*

Britney's chuff *euph.* A situation when a much-anticipated reality in no way matches up to what you'd imagined it would be like, to the point that you begin to wish you'd never seen it. *'I got the Sky Sports so I could watch the Ashes series. A right Britney's chuff that turned out to be.'*

broadband blister *n.* A callus that appears on a chap's *stench hammer* shortly after his internet download speed increases.

broat *n.* See *vurp.*

brobs *n.* Overwhelmingly large *tits.* From the giant Brobdingnabians in *Gulliver's Travels.* Opposite of *lils.*

broken heart *n. rhym. slang.* An *air biscuit.* From broken heart = Exchange & Mart.

broken ice cream machine, arse like a *sim.* Symptom of major gastro-intestinal meltdown which results in a day spent off work, sitting on the *chod bin* reading the local *Autotrader* and moaning.

broken washer *n.* The bit of a gent's plumbing that inevitably deteriorates with age, leading to intermittent dripping that keeps him up at night.

bromance *n.* A special, completely manly relationship between a pair of one hundred percent heterosexual men that involves a lot of hugging and intimate conversations, and which baffles and discomfits their other friends, wives and girlfriends.

Bronx cheer *n. arch.* Obsolete term for a *fart* used exclusively by Whoopee Cushion manufacturers.

broomstick *n.* Any small runaround car aimed specifically at the ladies' market, *eg.* Renault Clio, Ford Fiesta, Nissan Micra.

broon baboon *n. Scots.* A *skid mark* in the stygian depths of a Hibernian *gurgler. 'Frae Stornaway tae Ullapool, Kingussie an' Dunoon / The rain fell a' the mornin' and it was michty foggie / I borrow'd next door's lavatory brush tae clean a broon baboon / That ma darlin' Mary hod left theer in ma boggie.'* (from *Ode tae a Haggis Bought frae the Auchtermuchty Rugby Club Car Boot* by Rabbie Burns).

brothel sprouts *n. medic.* An attack of genital herpes following a visit to a house of ill repute. *'What's that on your cock, Lord Archer?' 'Oh that? It's nothing, just a few brothel sprouts, that's all.*

I've got them all up my back as well, you know. And I'm a thief.'

brother *n. Bean flicker, tuppence licker, carpet muncher.* A lesbian.

brother, email my *euph.* To masturbate. From the US baseball player Carlos Zambrano, who was put on the Chicago Cubs injured list because of a wrist injury caused by spending four hours a day on the internet "emailing his brother".

brown admiral *n. zoo.* The common and far from beautiful butterfly that can be found in the pants of someone who has failed to *draw an ace.* A *gusset moth* or *wind sketch..*

brown ballerina *n.* The "tutu" effect achieved when one's index finger pierces cheap bathroom tissue whilst wiping one's *ringpiece. Also Kermit's collar.*

Brownbeard's hammock *n.* A useful, suspended cotton receptacle in which to place a roll of *arsewipe* whilst *dropping the kids off at the pool, ie.* Your *underkegs* round your ankles.

brown bear's nose *n.* A cute little round *turd* that hibernates at the bottom of the *grizzly bear pit.*

brown Betty *n.* The mess that can result from *back door love* with someone with a full or disturbed bowel.

Brown bounce *1. n.* Journalistic catchphrase describing the surprising resurgence in popularity of the former government following the Prime Minister's level-headed response to the global financial crisis. *2. n.* When a *bird* sticks your *cock* up her *arse* and rides it like she's on a spacehopper. That is to say, halfway up the path at the side of your house before falling off and grazing one of her knees. *3. n.* Upon dropping a rather large *brown trout* into the *Rick*

Witter, the phenomenon of it disappearing reassuringly from view, only for it to disconcertingly bob back up to the surface. Usually happens when *laying a cable* at someone else's house.

brown brakelight *n.* A visible warning that the person in front of you may have slammed the *anal anchors* on slightly too late, and that as a consequence it may be best to steer a wide berth around them.

brown bullet-hole *n. Bumhole, barking spider.*

brown daisy *n.* An unpleasantly-scented flower which attracts flies instead of bees and butterflies. A *bronze eye.*

brown drought *n. medic.* Constipation.

brown dwarf *n.* The tiny, superdense, hard-to-find nugget of highly-compressed *barker's egg* hiding somewhere on the sole of one's shoe.

brown extender *n.* At B&Q, a device for raising the height of an existing fence.

brown eye *n.* The *ring* through which the *brown trouts* jump on their daily migration to the sea.

browneye lashes *n.* Glamorous hairs that surround the *balloon knot.* Often caked in a brown, mascara-like substance.

browneye points *n.* Favour accumulated in one's better half's eyes by means of doing chores, putting up shelves, not *crapping* in the kitchen sink *etc.,* thus increasing the chance of her letting you do her up the *shitter.*

brown finger poncho *n.* The square of *arsewipe* through which the digit pushes when one *breaches the hull.*

brown flower in the window, have a *euph.* Expression of one's need to defecate. *'Sorry, love, I'll get a fire engine off to you as soon as I can, but I've got a* *brown flower here and it needs to be put in some water.'*

brown hatter *n*. A *bottsman* with *shit* on his helmet.

brown helmet *n*. An award presented to a man by his girlfriend or wife to commemorate the day she leaves him, *ie*. Metaphorically *shits* on his head. *'And it came to pass that Naboth had journeyed to the shops and his wife Bathsheba was left alone in his tent. And David came unto her in the tent of Naboth and knew her twice. And she took up her chatels and went to live in the tent of David amongst the Gibeonites. And Naboth did return to his tent and found that Bathsheba was gone. And he went to the inn with his mates Mephibosheth and Jonadab son of Shimeah, and he wailed and gnashed his teeth saying, I always did my best for her, no man could have done more. Yet she gives me the brown helmet. And great was his sorrow, even unto the twelfth pint.'* (from *Epidydimis*, Ch. 6 vv12-16).

brown herring *n*. Alarming intestinal rumblings, pops and gurgles that imply the urgent need to *drop anchor in Shanks Bay*, but once one is seated on the *porcelain throne* reveal themselves to be nothing more substantial than a soggy *air biscuit*.

brownhouse gases *n*. Environmentally harmful emissions from a *tail pipe*.

brownian motion *1. n.* The apparently random movements of minute particles immersed in a fluid, discovered by physicist Richard Brown. *2. n.* The frequent and painful visits to the *throne room* experienced by one who has recently enjoyed a delicious meal at the Curry Capital.

Brownington-on-Sea *euph. Vict.* Name of a mythical town used by discreet nineteenth century types when broaching the embarrassing subject of *snipping off a length of dirty spine* in polite company. *'Pray kindly excuse me, your majesty. I most earnestly crave your indulgence while I take my leave, for I have a somewhat pressing engagement in Brownington-on-Sea.' 'I quite understand, Mr Disraeli, but check the maid's left a new roll of shitscrape in the crapper before you park your breakfast, won't you. Only I had to use the fucking cardboard tube to wipe my arse when I went this morning.'*

brown jack *n*. World War II artillery expression for what comes out of your *nipsy* when confronted by World War II Germans.

brown jewels *n*. The monarch's *winnets*. The *dangleberries* of state.

brown laser *n*. A beam of hot, liquid *shite* that exits the *brass eye* at the speed of light, and which could easily cut a secret agent in two.

brown light's flashing *euph*. Emergency warning sign of a toiletry nature. *Umber alert. 'Can you hang the washing out for me, dear?' 'Sorry love. Brown light's flashing, with you in five.'*

brown lilo *n*. A buoyant *tom tit* that, left alone, will eventually float out to sea and be eaten by a cod.

brown maverick *n*. The stooling stage which comes immediately prior to *touching cloth*. The *turtle's head, winking at Calvin, Yoffy's finger*. From the lyrics to the Rodgers & Hammerstein standard *Oh, What a Beautiful Mornin', viz*. "Oh the cattle are standin' like statues / Oh the cattle are standin' like statues / They don't raise their heads as they see me ride by / But a little brown maverick is winkin' her eye."

brown men on swings *n*. See *miniature heroes*.

brownout *n*. After a heavy night on the tiles, the distinctly unpleasant consequence that is one stage further than a blackout. *'Aw, bloody hell Maggie. The dog must've climbed in the bed and done a dirt in my pyjama bottoms last night, look. Again.' 'You can't fool me, Keith. We haven't even got a dog. You've had another one of your brownouts, haven't you.'*

brown owl *n*. A sizeable *log*. *Meatloaf's daughter*, a *dead otter*.

brown party *n*. See *yellow party* and make the imaginative leap yourself.

brown ping pong ball *n*. A remarkably natatorial *plop* which refuses to go to the beach, no matter how many times you flush it. One of them really annoying ones that raises your hopes by going round the U-bend, only to dash them when it bobs back to the surface a few seconds later. A *brown zombie*.

brown pipe engineer *n*. An *arse mechanic* who always calls at the *tradesman's entrance*.

brown pocket *n*. A smuggler's receptacle that allows him to spirit contraband through customs. *'Did you bring anything back from Amsterdam, Phil?' 'Yes. I've got some clogs and cheese in my suitcase and a lump of squidgy black in my brown pocket.'*

brown roulette *n*. A game of chance with potentially disastrous consequences whereby one *shoots rabbits* through an *arse* over which one has little control. To risk a *fart* whilst suffering with the squits. *Twisting on nineteen.*

Brown's dilemma *euph*. The uncomfortable scenario whereby one enters a befouled public *bog* and is forced to decide whether to clear all the *shit* up or leave it for somebody else. *'What are you going to do, Tony? It's a real Brown's dilemma.' 'I think I'll just leave it for Gordon, Cherie.'*

brown sunrise *n*. Whilst ensconced on the *throne*, the majestic sight of a *Thora Hird* gradually emerging from behind the knackers as one watches with the head between the knees. A sign that it's time to buy some Bill Tidy books to keep on the cistern.

brown-tak *n*. A pliable, adhesive compound used by prisoners to stick posters to the wall. Also known as *scat-tak* and *bloo-tak*.

brown tap *n*. A particularly non-viscid bout of the *Mexican screamers*. The *gravy rocket*.

brown ticket *n*. Secret prize hidden inside certain Cadbury's chocolate bars several years ago. The lucky winner of a *brown ticket* received a day-long trip to the *chocolate factory*. *Salmonella serovar Montevideo*.

brown tie *n*. The dirty mark left between a lady's *jugs* by a man having a *sausage sandwich* immediately after taking her up the *council gritter*. *Shit tie*.

brown trout *n*. A *turd*, big job, shite.

brown trout pond *n*. The lavatory bowl.

brown wings *n*. The honour bestowed on who has performed *bumilingus* on a lady Hell's Angel.

brown zombie *n*. A *Douglas* that refuses to be flushed away and keeps on coming back.

Brummie orgasm *n*. A plangent, discordant and ultimately deafening sound. *'As the giant iceberg tore through the mighty liner's hull, in that same dread moment the ship's cat was tipped into a pan of boiling cooking fat and the palm court orchestra was caught in the deadly whiplash of the broken cables. It sounded like a Brummie orgasm.'*

Bruce Lees *n.* Firm nipples. A frankly racist and inaccurate reference to the San Francisco-born kung fu master of Chinese descent. *Hard nips.*

Brucie *n.* A *fart* which is performed whilst adopting the silhouetted "Thinker" stance made famous by Bruce Forsyth on *The Generation Game*, followed by a camp little kick forwards.

brush up on one's Punjabi *v.* To lick a lady's *bodily treasure*. *'Virginia looked resplendent as she descended from the Sao Paolo steamer, quite bronzed and elegant in the London mist. After taking tea at Claridge's we took the charabanc to my rooms at Oxford, where I relished the opportunity to brush up on my Punjabi.'* (from *The Diaries of Evelyn Waugh*).

brut *1. n.* Great-smelling man musk peddled by an unlikely alliance of bald former prize-fighters, motorcycle racers and unstable future football managers who found themselves sharing a bathroom mirror in the 1970s. *2. n.* The predictable end scene of a *grumble flick* when the lady participant encourages her male co-star to "splash it all over". And she's not talking about his aftershave. She's talking about his spunk.

BS *abbrev. US.* Booooool-shee-it.

BSH *abbrev.* British Standard Handful. The Imperial unit by which *knockers* were measured in the good old days of

Confessions films.

bubble and squeak *1. n.* A budget meal usually cooked and eaten by students, consisting of ageing mashed potatoes, cabbage and various other unappetising plate-scrapings. *2. n.* An *apple tart* emitted following a meal constaining a high proportion of re-heated, left-over brassicas.

bubbies *n.* Coy term for *breasts*, much beloved of writers of cod-Victorian pornography. *"Ooh, zur! What does you think of moi bubbies, then?' asked Molly the Milkmaid, as she unzipped the Squire's heaving breeches.'* (from *A Roll in the Hay*, by Jeffrey Archer).

bubble poo *n. Fizzy gravy.*

bubblebum *n.* An unfortunate release of *burbulent gas* through moist *buttocks*, the resulting sound being eerily reminiscent of Leonardo di Caprio's final words in *the film Titanic*.

bubblyduck *n.* A particularly loud, prolonged and wet *fart*. Named because the sound is identical to that of an agitated mallard being drowned in a bucket of custard.

bucket fanny *n.* A spacious or roomy vagina. *Tardis twat, cathedral, welly top.*

Buckfast bravery *n.* Instances of incredible courage manifested by ruddy-faced Caledonian outdoorsmen, *eg.* Strolling across four lanes of traffic without looking left or right, sleeping on a railway level crossing, fighting a police horse *etc.*

Buckfast breakfast *n.* The first meal of the day for many a heather-dwelling *Angus McRamp.*

buckie *n. Scots.* Affectionate nickname given to the tonic wine traditionally produced for Glaswegian tramps by the monks of Buckfast Abbey, Devon.

buckle bunny *n*. US. A *cock*-hungry *bird*.

Buddha's earlobes *euph*. A particular type of *beef curtains* that dangle around a lady's thighs and resemble nothing so much as the pendulous lower pinnae of the popular pot-bellied spiritual leader. Often found on Australian females. *'Fuck me, Daphne. I never noticed how low your piss flaps hang. They're like Buddha's fucking earlobes.'* (Des Clarke, *Neighbours*, 1988).

buddy breathing 1. *n*. In SCUBA diving, of two divers to share a mouthpiece in an emergency situation, taking it in turns to suck on the same oxygen supply. 2. *n*. In *jazzular cinematography*, of two actresses to share a genital, taking it in turns to suck on the same *spongle* supply. *Baby birding*.

budget spunk *n. medic*. The fluids that a gentleman expels after undergoing a *walnut whip*. *Decaff spaff*.

budgie smugglers *n*. Extremely tight gentlemen's bathing trunks. *Noodle benders*.

budgie's tongue, dry as a *sim*. Said of a *tart* that turns out to be slightly less moist inside than one might have hoped. *'She was cheap, I'll give her that. But she was as dry as a budgie's tongue.'*

budgie supping *v*. The act of pitiful beer drinking performed by men who aren't used to it, *eg*. A terrified Tony Blair pecking at a pint for the benefit of TV cameras in Sedgefield Labour Club.

budgie's tongue *n*. Descriptive of the female erectile bit, particularly when her *fanny* has climbed a little plastic ladder to ring a bell.

budmiser *n*. The unusually quiet member of a lad's night out who waits until he has downed four rounds of drinks before revealing that he has come out without any cash.

buff, to *v*. To engage in the removal of the *poo*/sweat mix which accumulates in a chap's *arse cleft* during a long drinking session, or perhaps whilst moving filing cabinets down a fire escape on a hot and humid day, by the vigorous application of copious amounts of *bumwad*.

buffage *n*. US. Highly offensive and sexist term used by women to describe men. *'Hey girls, check out the buffage in here.'*

buffeting *n*. The disturbing half-gulping, half-choking carry-on that precedes a *psychedelic yawn*. A *frogs' chorus*.

buffet on Jeremy Kyle, like the *sim*. Descriptive of any offering of foodstuffs that is supposed to provide diners with a well-balanced meal, but instead presents them with an artery-hardening array of comestibles which are stuffed with vast amounts of sugar, salt, pig fat and cocoa solids, *ie*. The menu on offer at any student refectory or school canteen when Jamie Oliver isn't there filming it.

buffet slayer *n*. A female *lard of the manor*. A lady with a penchant for eating more than her fair share of free food.

buffing *n*. *Gusset typing*. The act of female masturbation.

buffty *n*. Scot. A gay fellow. A *Gordon*.

BUFFY/buffy 1. *n. prop*. That tasty piece of young *blart* who fights vampires on Sky One. 2. *acronym*. The complete opposite of 1. A Big Ugly Fat Fucking Yeti. A lady who's been beaten senseless with the *nice personality stick*.

bugger 1. *n*. He who pokes animals, *arse-*

holes or animals' *arseholes*. A *berry*. 2. *v*. To break or damage. To *fuck*. 3. *exclam*. A cry of dismay. *'PC World phoned up while you were out. They said they'd managed to get your laptop going again, and you can pick it up any time tomorrow from the Police Station.' 'Bugger.'*

bugger all *n*. *Nowt, fuck all*.

bugger's grips *n*. Sideburns. Any tufts of facial hair on the cheeks. *Bugger's handles, face fannies*.

Bugner's eye *n*. Flapless female genitalia, resembling boxer Joe Bugner's closed-up eye in every fight he had.

build a log cabin *v*. To pass a series of sturdy stools.

builder *n*. A sexually unresponsive lady-friend, *ie*. One that "never *comes*". Also *plumber, gasman, Initial City-Link van driver*.

builder's breakfast *n*. A hearty, choles-terol-laden, no-nonsense vagina that services the early-morning nourishment needs of the nations's bricklayers, chippies and plasterers.

builder's bum *n*. The protrusion of fat, sweaty *arse* cheeks above the sagging waist of the jeans. Common amongst bricklayers, council workmen and top fashion designer Alexander McQueen. *Bricky's crack, Dagenham smile*.

builder's piss *n*. A quick trip to the toilet for a *number one* which suddenly, without warning, develops into a far bigger job than was originally anticipated.

bukhaki *n*. *milit*. Nocturnal military manoeuvre involving a billetful of other ranks masturbating onto the face of their sleeping brother in arms, who has returned to his barracks in a state of critical *refreshment*. *'Bukhaki's happened in the night / The soldier wakens in his bunk / His eyes don't open to the light / They're all gummed up with squaddies' spunk.'* (from *Conscious* by Wilfred Owen).

bukkake 1. *n*. Saucy carry-on whereby a load of randy blokes *tip their filthy concrete* onto a delighted *plasterer's radio*. From the noun form of the Japanese verb *bukkakeru*, meaning "to dash water". 2. *adj*. *Jap*. Descriptive of dishes, such as bukkake-udon and bukkake-soba, where fresh soup-like toppings are poured on top of noodles. 3. *adj*. In Britain, descriptive of dishes about to be served to *Sunday Times* food critic Michael Winner, such as soup and macaroni cheese, onto which a group of kitchen employees - not to mention other customers - *empty their nuts*.

bulimia amnesiac *n*. *medic*. One suffering from a condition whereby they binge eat, then forget to throw up. A *salad dodger, lard arse*, one who is a martyr to their glands.

bull *abbrev*. *US. BS*.

bulldog chewing a wasp *sim*. Descriptive of a lady's face that does not conform to conventional ideals of beauty. Also *bulldog licking piss off a nettle, welder's bench, stripper's clit*.

bulldog eating porridge *sim*. Poetic term describing a *lady's bodily treasure* in the aftermath of an act of love. *'When I'd finished with her, she had a fanny like a bulldog eating porridge, I can tell you.'*

bulldog's tail *n*. A *turtle's head*.

bulldyke *n*. A butch, masculine or aggressive *lezza*. *Diesel dyke*.

bullet-proof vest 1. *n*. *milit*. Armoured clothing designed to minimise injury from incoming gunfire. Usually worn by TV reporters trying to look butch in conflict zones. *2. n.* Reinforced clothing designed to minimise the impact of outgoing nipples. Usually worn by females in cold conditions.

bullet train *n.* A *ride* that is over far too quickly.

bullet wound *n.* The unfortunate situation whereby a *relaxing* man *empties his clip* into his navel and then proceeds to scuttle to the lavatory to sort himself out a bit whilst hunched over, clutching his stomach and thus, to a casual bystander, creating the impression that he has been shot.

bullfrogging *1. n.* A specialised variation on the act of *horatio*, whereby the *nosher* takes not only the *noshee*'s *tallywhacker* but also both his *magic beans* into his or her mouth, thus creating the effect of the state amphibian of Missouri (*Lithobates catesbeianus*) complete with its swollen throat and guttural retching call. *2. n.* The act of *farting* against a closed door from the outside, so that the occupants of the room believe that a large bullfrog is about to enter.

bullfruit *n.* A *tailgunner* who is a bit *rock*. A canny hard *puff*.

Bullimore *n. prop.* An extremely buoyant bit of *cack,* which refuses to drown. Named after extremely buoyant round-the-world yachtsman Tony Bullimore, who spent three days being lashed by storms under his capsized boat.

bull queen *n.* A large, butterfingered prison inmate who cannot keep hold of the soap in the shower, and who instructs other, smaller, prisoners to bend over and pick it up for him. Then he sticks his *cock* up their *arse.*

bull's dick, thick as a *sim.* Somewhat unintelligent, *fuckwitted.* '*That turd serving me in McDonald's was as thick as a bull's dick.'*

bullseye *n.* Successfully going *straight for the kill* in the bedroom, without foreplay or any of that mullarkey.

bullshit *1. n. Feeshus* of male cattle. *2. n.* Rubbish, nonsense, *bollocks. 3. v.* To lie, deliberately mislead, talk rubbish to. '*Don't you bullshit me now, you hear, bitch, or I'll cut yo' jive-ass face wide open.'* (Sir Neville Chamberlain to his wife, after she informed him that Hitler had invaded Poland).

Bully's Prize Board *1. n.* Part of the popular darts gameshow *Bullseye,* where guests could win various prizes announced by Tony Green in the following distinctive manner: "*HHHHIN One!...HHHHIN Two!..."* etc., and thus *2. n.* An ultimately unsatisfying and prolonged toilet visit whilst suffering from a *log jam,* when it would be a good idea to settle down, find your rhythm *etc.* '*Sorry I'm late, ladies and gentlemen. I've been stuck on Bully's Prize Board.'* (HRH Prince Charles, addressing the Board of Architecture and National Heritage, 1987).

Bully's special prize *1. n.* A speedboat. *2. n.* An extra large, beefy *shit.* '*I'd give it ten minutes before you go in there, Your Majesty. I've just won Bully's special prize.'*

bum *1. n.* Arse, bottom, poop-chute. *2. n. US. Harold Ramp, pan handler.* A homeless person. *3. v.* Of cigarettes, to scrounge, scavenge. *4. v.* To *bott. 5. adj. US. legal.* Of *raps,* to be unjust, unfair. *6. n.* Trebor mint preservation apparatus. *7. adj.* Of steers, misleading or inaccurate.

bumanizer *n.* A fellow who boasts an impressive tally of conquests in the field of *countergradient horticulture.*

bum bandit *n.* A robber, outlaw or highwayman who steals people's bottoms.

bum bar *n.* A richly-textured item of *arse chocolate. 'Take the helm, Captain Hardy, I'm off down the poop deck for a bum bar.'*

bum baubles *n. medic.* Big, round, shiny *farmers* that your missus and the doctor can see their faces in.

bum beater *n.* A chap's *membrum virile. 'And Onan knew that the seed should not be his; and it came to pass, when he went in unto his brother's wife, that he spilled it on the ground, lest that he should give seed to his brother. And the thing which Onan had done with his bum beater displeased the LORD: wherefore he slew him also.'* (from Genesis 38:9).

bum beaver *n.* An *arse* where the *cress* has grown out of control. A *botty beard,* a *DLT.*

bumbilical cord *1. n.* A length of *cable* that is so firmly attached to the bottom that one's partner has to fetch a pair of scissors to complete the birthing process. *2. n. Uphill gardening string.*

bumblebee dance *1. n.* Action performed by bees in which they shake their abdomens to indicate to other members of the hive in which direction the pollen lies. *2. n.* The waggling of the buttocks in order to dislodge a reluctant *geetle* from the *dot.* A *logarhythm.*

bumboozled *1. adj.* Innocently beguiled into a state of mental disorientation by a passing, shapely *peach pie. 2. adj.* Of an otherwise resolutely heterosexual fellow, like a rugby player for instance, to be drunkenly tricked into a spot of *puddle jumpery.*

bum brake *n.* The *cigar cutter* or *nipsy.*

bum brusher *n. Vict.* A schoolmaster. From the good old days before political correctness when there was nothing wrong with a spot of wholesome, *arse*-based corporal punishment which never did red-faced ex-military men who write to the *Daily Telegraph* any harm. A phrase which is quite possibly still in current usage on the Isle of Man.

bum chain *n.* A rather intimate version of the Conga, danced around the streets at the end of a *brightly-coloured* party.

bum chums *n.* Primary school term for any two boys who always sit next to each other.

bum cigar *n.* In after dinner conversation, a stool. *'Well, if you'll excuse me ladies, I think I shall retire to the bathroom and light a bum cigar.'*

bum conkers *n.* Shiny, brown, spherical agglomerations which hang off the *arse strings,* and can be baked in the oven or soaked in vinegar.

bumcraft *n. Uphill gardening, cable laying, stepping on ducks.* The wholesome enjoyment of all things *bumular.*

bum crumbs *n. Kling-ons* which have ceased to cling on. Usually found in the bed or in the gusset of the *trolleys.*

bumdruff *n.* The *anal scurfage* and general buttock effluvium left on the back of the *bog* seat after one has been for a *digestive transit. Arse confetti.*

bum drummer *n.* A *bad thrower.*

bum fluff *n.* Risible pubescent attempt to grow a moustache.

bumfoolery *n.* Light-hearted action centred loosely around the *Bleep & Booster. Carry On* film-style *good-with-coloursness.*

bum goblin *n.* A gnarled, malevolent *turd*

that jumps out from behind you, casting a painful spell on your *ringpiece*.

bum grapes *n*. Agonising, juice-filled, seedless, purple fruits which grow well in the moist, shady regions of the *Khyber Pass*.

bum gravel *n*. A scree-like accumulation of anal detritus found in the bed after one has *raked one's arse out*.

bum gravy *n*. Diarrhoea, *rusty water*.

bum jumble *n*. Bits and bobs of excrement. *'Fucking hell, Brendan. Paula's left some bum jumble in the road again.'*

bum lungs *n*. Additional, apparently rectally-situated, breathing apparatus which allows members of the fairer sex to speak continuously without pausing for breath.

bummange *n*. A light, fluffy *arse* dessert. *Anal delight*.

bummer 1. *n*. One who *bums*. 2. *n*. A disappointing situation. Such as being stuck on a beach for the whole summer, after missing a charabanc.

bummocks *n*. The buttocks of the *bum*.

bummy mummy *n*. A *milf* who could well benefit from having her *back doors* kicked in. A *milb*.

bumnugget *n*. A *number two*, consisting of an accretion of many smaller *number twos*.

bump *v*. To *bum* your *bird* immediately prior to dumping her. From bum + dump.

bumpies *rhym. slang. Fun bags*. From bumpy bits = tits.

bump the kerb *v*. Of a *heavily-refreshed* gentleman, to make a series of ineffectual attempts to get his *cock* into the *hairy parking space*. A repeated failure to score a *hole-in-one*. 2. *v*. To deliberately on purpose nudge the wife's *wrong*

'un with the *pit prop*. *'Sorry love. I seem to have bumped the kerb there.'*

bum puppy *n*. A friendly, over-eager *Bakewell tart* that leaps and gambols around you, and licks your face.

bum rope *n*. *Shit*. *'Has anybody seen the Autotrader? I'm just going to cut some bum rope.'*

bum rudder *n*. Richly poetic description of a fellow engaged in a spot of *back door work*. *'I scored with Eliza the other night. What a filthy cow, she even let me put it in her ass. You should've seen me, I was hanging out the back of her like a bum rudder, Professor Higgins.'*

bumscare *n*. Severe pressure in the lower abdominal region prior to a controlled explosion.

bumshee *n*. A blood-curdling howl of anguish coming from a lavatory cubicle.

bum sink *n*. The toilet.

bumsong *n*. A long, tuneful and mellifluous *botty bugle*.

bum spuds *n*. Faecal tubers. Human stools.

bumtags *n*. *Dangleberries*.

bum tongue *n*. A large piece of *shit* hanging from *Dot Cotton's mouth* just before it licks the bowl.

bum-uppance *n*. Like comeuppance, but reserved for those people who, in the process of hanging curtains in their kitchens whilst wearing loose-fitting dressing gowns, somehow slip and end up with a foreign object, such as a potato or a milk bottle, stuck up their *arse*. Various well known people have famously got their bum-uppance, including (name removed on legal advice), (name removed on legal advice) and Lord Archer of Weston Super Mare.

bum vinegar *n*. The sweat found between

the *arse* cheeks in general, and in particular during or after exercise. A condiment that goes well with *arse feta*. *Sarsehole*.

bumwad *n*. Lavatory tissue, *shitscrape*.

bun-chukas *n*. Saggy *lils* that can be swung around the waist and shoulders, and used *in extremis* as offensive weapons. Extra-mobile *knee shooters. Socktits* with a billiard ball in the end.

bung hole *n*. The vagina, at which a dirty lady *fizzes*.

bunglasses *n*. Like *binorkulars*, but pointing slightly lower down.

Bungle's finger *n*. A short, stocky *turd*, named after the ursine simpleton from the 70s children's show *Rainbow*.

bun in the oven, to have a *v*. To be pregnant, *up the stick, in the club, in trouble, up the pasture. 'Guess what, love. I've got a bun in the oven.' 'That's nice. Is my tea ready yet?'*

bunion ring *n*. An old lady's *jacksie*.

bunko booth *n*. Paul Daniels's *shithouse*. A water closet cubicle.

bunk up *1. n*. A utility poke. *'Darling, you look beautiful tonight. Any chance of a bunk up?' 2. n*. Assistance in climbing. *'Shit. I'm so pissed I can't get onto the bed. Any chance of a bunk up?'*

bunk-up badge *n*. A love bite, usually found on really ugly people's necks to prove they have a love life. Or a at least access to a bicycle pump. A *hickie*, a *bub*, a *shag-tag*.

bunnet brie *n. Scot. McHelmetdale. 'Whit's yon stink, maw?' 'Och, Wullie. It's jist Granpaw's bunnet brie, son.'*

bunnet cheese *n. Glasweg*. The piquant, cheesy deposits which accumulate around the brim of the *haggis farmer's hat*.

bunny-boiler *n*. A determined woman who misinterprets a one-off drunken *scuttle* as the overture to a deep and lasting relationship, then tries to win your affections when you go back to the missus by boiling your kids' pets and in the end you have to drown her in the bath but she's not even dead. *A pork 'n' stalk*.

bunny rub *n*. A *tit wank, diddy ride, Bombay roll*.

buns *1. n*. Regional variation of *baps*. *2. n. US. Ass* cheeks.

bunt *1. n*. A disease of wheat caused by the *Tilletia* fungus. *2. n*. The bulging part of a fishing net or a ship's sail. *3. v*. To block a ball with a bat. *4. v*. To greedily steal hampers of tuck from one's fellow public schoolboys. *5. n*. On a *salad dodging* lady, where the stomach seamlessly merges into the pudendums. From belly + cunt. Also known as the *super-poond* or *gunt*.

bunting *n*. Church fete-style strings of *jizz* looped around a *grumble flick* actress's face.

bunty or twinkle? *exclam. interrog*. A polite question, ostensibly alluding to the titles of girls' comics from the 1970s, asked in order to ascertain whether a lady acquaintance who is off to powder her nose will be *dropping the kids off at the pool* or *splashing her boots*.

buppy fat *n. Cheb*-fuelled *teacaking* of the *giggle stick*.

Burberry apes *n*. Designer-clad football hooligans.

Burberry shitbomb *n*. The delightful smell of perfume in the water closet after one's girlfriend or wife has been in to *drop the kids off at the pool*. Air freshener on lead guitar and vocals with excrement on bass and drums.

burbulence *n*. The uncomfortable alimentary rumbling which precedes the breakage of wind. *'Over Nova Scotia I finished the last of my egg sandwiches. Half an hour later I hit a pocket of burbulence, and had to fasten my seat belt and extinguish all lights.'* (from *My Flight Across the Atlantic* by Amelia Earhart).

burglar's dollop *n*. An episode of trouser-soiling through fear or nerves. *'David Cameron takes the stand for his keynote address to the Blackpool Conference. It's a real burglar's dollop moment for the embattled Tory leader.'* (Nick Robinson, BBC News 24).

burial at sea *n*. The dignified delivery of a stool, without *splashback*. The opposite of a *depth charge* or *belly flopper*.

burly *n*. *Bum wipe*, toilet paper, *chocolate shark bait, turd tokens, shit tickets*.

BURMA/burma *acronym*. Secret code used on military correspondence - Be Upstairs Ready My Angel.

burn bad powder *v. arch. milit*. Of *trouser trumpetry*, to *light a tyre*, emit a *fyst*.

burning bush *n*. Cystitis.

Burnley taxi *n*. A police car.

Burnley wallet *n*. Rough and ready Lancashire street punishment technique, referred to in *Phoenix Nights*, which involves pulling the victim's scrotum up under his chin before performing some sort of horizontal cut across his *Sir Cliff's neck*.

burnout *1. n*. In the world of dragster racing, a short burst of wheelspin on the starting line which is intended to warm up the racing slicks and which leaves impressive, black, smoking stripes on the tarmac. *2. n*. In the world of

diddy-riding, an unfortunately exposed *arse crayon* which leaves a thick stripe of brown residue on one's ladyfriend's torso. And a strong smell of burning tyres.

burn out the arse clutch *v*. To fail to avoid defecating into one's *hoggers* whilst standing up having a *piss*.

burnside drawer *n*. The bottom drawer in the office desk, which contains contraband material, *ie*. Alcohol, cigarettes and pornography. Named after no-nonsense, good old-fashioned copper Detective Chief Inspector Frank Burnside out of off of *The Bill*.

burnt tyre *n*. An acrid, black, semi-vulcanised *Peter O'Toole* passed through the *back body* following a night on the Guinness.

burp the worm *v*. To *choke the chicken*.

burtains *n. medic. Labia majorcas. Gammon flaps, Keith Burtons*. From the contraction of beef + curtains.

bury a quaker *v*. To dispense with the contents of one's rectum. *To crimp one off, lay a cable*, release a payload from the *bomb bay*.

bury bad news *v*. From the government's cheeky habit of releasing bad figures and/or unpopular legislation on days when the headlines are dominated by other, more dramatic news, to disguise one's flatulent emissions by making clever use of one's environment. For example, to *pump* out a vile, sulphurous *trouser cough* just after you start the car so that the miasma is masked by the eggy whiff from the catalytic converter; to *drive over cats' eyes* whilst driving over cats' eyes; to open a packet of ham whilst *opening a packet of ham*; to *cut the cheese* whilst cutting cheese. To *cover one's tracks.*

bury the hobbit *v.* To lose *Bilbo Bellend* in the *wizard's sleeve.*

bus bender *n.* A *bird* who is so *well-nourished* that, if she were to be involved in a road traffic accident, she would cause more damage to the vehicle that ran into her than she would incur herself.

bus driver's knob *n. medic.* A state of almost permanent semi-priapism suffered by corporation omnibus operators who sit on a vibrating seat all day, eyeing up their *horny* female passengers. A long lasting *semi-on, Varney's teacake.*

bush *n. Gorilla salad, ladygarden, mapatasi.* Female pubic hair.

bushcraft *1. n.* Survival techniques employed in the Australian Outback. *2. n.* Recreational techniques employed in the *Tasmanian Outfront.*

bush meat *n.* Meat found under *bushes.* Usually *vertical bacon.*

bush pig *n.* A slightly more polite term for a *swamp hog.*

bush tents *n.* Ladies' *applecatchers.*

bushell *1. n.* An imperial measure of grain equivalent to 2219.36 cubic inches, under which one can hide one's light. *2. n.* A hairy *cunt.*

bushman's hankie *n. Aus.* Term given to the process whereby mucus is expelled from the nose by placing a finger over one nostril and blowing. Popular amongst professional footballers. A *single barrelled snot gun, oyster.*

bushmonk *n.* A saucy chap who hides or secretes himself in an item of shrubbery for the purposes of *boxing the Jesuit,* especially near the bowling green in Heaton Park, Newcastle upon Tyne.

bushtucker *n.* Anything on the menu when *eating out* in Tasmania.

bushtucker challenge. *n.* Particularly unpalatable *hairy fish and chips.*

business lacumen *n.* A singular display of poor decision making ability. *'Oh yeah, I've got great business lacumen. After my disastrous foray into the Video 2000 system, I sank what remained of my family fortune into the Rabbit CT2, Mercury Callpoint and Zonephone telephone networks. Anyway, as I was saying, have you got ten pence for a cup of tea, pal?'*

busker's hat *n.* The pocketful of change left over from a night *on the lash,* that feels like about twelve quid, but when emptying it into one's hand to buy a bottle of blue Powerade the next morning, turns out to be about thirty-six pence worth of one and two pees.

bus knob *n. medic.* Involuntary *lob on* brought about by the gentle, but insistent, vibration provided by the engine of a passenger service vehicle, transmitted to the sufferer's *lunchbox* through his seat. Especially if he's wearing loose trousers and sitting next to a fat-*titted* Swiss back-packer.

busman's jollyday *n.* The habit of public transport drivers to pair up at the depot so that they can give each other *blow jobs* at the end of their journeys. Particularly enjoyed, it says here, by those gentlemen working the 170 Roehampton to Victoria route.

busted sofa *n.* A *shaven haven* with very plump lips. *Pete Burns's gob.*

busted wheelbearing on a '63 DAF truck, moaning like a *sim.* Descriptive of the sounds made by a particularly vocal *piece* enjoying a *length.* From the characteristic orgasmic-lady-style sound produced by troublesome Swedish HGV wheelhubs which is well known to vintage lorry mechanics. *'Lady Chatterley was powerless to resist. Mellors's eyes burnt into hers like created tanzanites. His strong gamekeeper's arms enfolded her tender body as she felt herself being swept away on a supercellular mesocyclone of passion. Before long, they were in the throes of passion on the floor of his rude hut, and Connie couldn't stop herself moaning like a busted wheelbearing on a '63 DAF truck every time he pushed his working class gut stick up her frothing upper class cludge.'* (from *The Lady and the Gamekeeper* by DH Lawrence).

busting low *1. n.* This modern, mysterious fashion whereby young fancy Dans walk about with their trousers hanging off their *arses*, held up only by a polio victim-style crooked arm. *2. n.* Reaching the final, desperate stages prior to a full-scale *crapping* of the *apple catchers*. See also *growing a tail, the turtle's head, riding a brown pony along a bumpy track, kettling*.

bustman's holiday *n.* A topless beach.

bust off *v.* To masturbate.

busy *adj.* Of a gentleman, *light on his feet*. *'How come your eldest lad's not got himself a nice girlfriend yet then?' 'Oh, he's got no time for girls, my Colin; he's always so busy, see. Cottaging and bumming, mainly.'*

butch as a fitter's dog, as *sim.* Phrase descriptive of a particularly masculine-looking *tuppence-licker*.

butcher's daughter *1. n.* A woman who has had unlimited access to the pastie counter. A *salad dodger. 2. n.* A woman who has had more than her fair share of *sausages, eg.* Her late Royal Highness, Princess Margaret. A *slapper*.

butcher's dishcloth *sim.* A delightful expression, descriptive of the *sump* of a lady's knickers when *the fleet is in*.

butcher's dog, to lie like a *sim.* Descriptive of the bedtime arrangements of a married man. To sleep within reach of the *beef* whilst forbidden to touch it.

butcher's dustbin *n.* A sight grimmer than a *butcher's window*.

butcher's kiss *n.* Evidence left on the bedsheet that a fellow has been *doing it* to his wife during *cricket week*.

butcher's string *n.* Skimpy underwear on a fat lass.

butcher's turd *sim.* Descriptive of the richness of something. *'Do have some more gateau, Mr D'Arcy.' 'Well perhaps just a little slice, Mrs Bennet. It's as rich as a butcher's turd.'* (from *Pride and Prejudice* by Jane Austen).

butcher's window *n.* An appetizing display of raw female genitalia.

butfer *n.* An amusing term for the female perineum. The *carse*, the *tinter*. *'NORFOLK: She has the most agreeable butfer. BISHOP: The butfer, sir? Wherefore is it called thus? NORFOLK: Sir, butfer that, thou wouldst be in the shit.'* (from *The Merry Readers' Wives of Windsor* by William Shakespeare).

butler in the pantry *n.* A polite *Brad* which knows its place, remaining below stairs, occasionally coughing discreetly until summoned.

butler's cuff *n.* A tightly-buttoned vagina, the opposite of a *wizard's sleeve*. A *fanny like a mouse's ear*.

butler's revenge *n.* A silent but deadly *fart. SBD.*

butler's ringpiece *adj.* Descriptive of something that is nipping clean. *"What* *can you see, Holmes?' I expostulated, as the great detective peered into his microscope. (I need not remind you of how in the past, he had solved the mystery of the Pope's cap when he found gibbon's tooth marks on the cardinal's walking stick.) 'I'm examining the handle of this dagger of unusual oriental design in the hope of finding a speck of tobacco, only available from one shop in London, or a hair from a rare species of Patagonian chinchilla,' he replied. 'However, I fear our murderer has wiped it as clean as a butler's ringpiece.''* (from *The Brown Hatted League* by Sir Arthur Conan-Doyle).

butt cutlet *n.* A wholesome organic *loaf* cooked up in the *dirt bakery*. A vegetarian's *turd*.

butter balls *n.* Pejorative epithet used to describe a young man who is clumsy or lacking in due diligence when using his *gonads; one* whose careless behaviour often leads to accidents and thus to DNA tests on the *Jeremy Kyle Show*. Also known as a *butter bollocks* or *pram filler*.

buttered bun *n.* A well-used *snatch*. A *box of assorted creams*.

butterface *n.* A woman with a great figure, but the physiognomy of a darts player's wife. From the phrase "A good body, but her face..." A *bobfoc*.

butterfly with tits *euph.* Hyperbolic figure of speech pertaining to a particularly unlikely state of events. *'You'll never guess who come in the Dog and Duck for the meat draw on Friday, Dave. That Stella McCartney.' 'Oh yeah? Well I was in the park yesterday and I seen a butterfly with tits.'*

butter your cheeks *v.* To *fart* and *follow through*.

buttflood *n.* The *squirts*, the *Earthas*.

Buttfuck Egypt *euph.* US. Any rural area which exhibits a paucity of standard amenities, such as shops, pubs and potential partners who are not already betrothed to members of their own families, *eg.* Various English Fenland towns, or certain estuarine villages in north and mid-Essex. *'We hope you have enjoyed your flight with us today. We will shortly be landing at Peterborough Sibson Airport. Welcome to Buttfuck Egypt.'*

butt nuggets *n. Annabels*.

buttock *n.* Fifty percent of an *arse*.

buttock broker *n.* A controller of prostitutes, a pimp. A *titty farmer, pussy farmer, gash baron*.

buttock hall *n. Meat market*. A pub or club frequented by *slappers*.

buttock jig *n.* A close, horizontal dance that takes place after chucking out time. *Making the beast with two backs*.

button *n.* A lady's *clematis*. The *devil's doorbell, wail switch, bald man in a boat*.

button groove *n. Hairy axe wound*, the *snapper*. The vulva.

button view *n.* The tantalising *sneak-peek* of a woman's *ta tas* and/or *tit pants* viewed through the gap in between the buttons of her shirt or blouse.

butt plug *n.* A medical appliance used to prevent water from the bath going up your *arse*.

buttress *n.* A *grumble flick* actress who makes a speciality of performing in *back door action* productions.

butt slammers *n.* US. Members of the gay community, who tend to accidentally catch their bottoms in the door in their eagerness to go out and be homosexual.

butt sneeze *n. US. Fart.*

butt's fizz *n.* Celebratory *bubble poo.*

buy a headache *v.* To purchase a strong alcoholic beverage.

buying your better half an anniversary present *euph. Flogging on* to the *binternet* whilst the missus is out of the house. From the subtle "eight second demos" television advert for Windows 7, *viz.* "Buying your better half an anniversary present and you don't want her to find out? Turn on Private Browsing. Do your thing, clickety-click and no-one knows what you've been up to." See also *do your thing, clickety-click.*

buysexual *n.* A fellow who pays for *it.* Buysexuals in their natural habitat can commonly be observed in the Zeedyjk area of Amsterdam. And again two weeks later, sitting on uncomfortable plastic chairs outside the GUM clinic of their local hospital.

BVH *abbrev.* Blue Veined Hooligan. A hard, six-inch tall, one-eyed, purple-faced skinhead.

BWR *abbrev.* Beeps When Reversing. Code used between considerate men to identify, yet save the feelings of, a lady who has failed to achieve an acceptable level of thinness. A *barge arse,* a *double sucker.*

Byker button *n.* A safety pin. Named after the exclusive Newcastle millionaires' playground made famous by TV's PJ and Duncan, Ant and Dec.

Byker plug *n.* An anally-inserted wad of *bog paper* reputedly favoured by habitual drinkers of Newcastle Brown as a means of preventing spontaneous bowel evacuations.

Byker tea cake *n.* A *Glasgow kiss.* A headbutt. *'Fuck me! Did you see that? Fucking Zidane just give fucking Materazzi a fucking Byker tea cake!'* (John Motson, commenting on the 2006 FIFA World Cup Final).

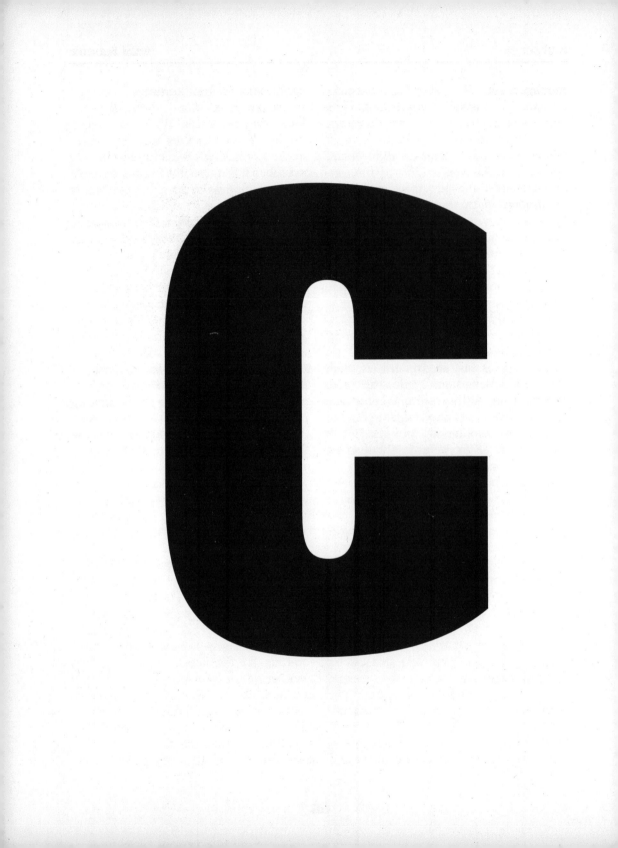

cabbage *n. coll.* Girls, *totty, blart, tussage.* *"What-ho, Jeeves!' I ejaculated. 'I've just been down to the Pink Flamingo club. Never seen so much cabbage in all my born pecker."* (from *Achtung, Jeeves!* by PG Wodehouse).

cabbage fart *n.* An *old dog's alarm clock.* A *dropped back* that smells of rotting vegetation.

cabbage gas *n.* Naturally-occurring renewable fuel which powers *Dutch ovens.*

cabbie's doorbell *n.* A car horn, used to inform a street that their neighbour's 3.00 am taxi has arrived.

cab hookers *n.* Taxi drivers who walk the streets outside nightclubs in the early hours, soliciting for business.

cabin crew doors to manual *exclam.* Phrase shouted as you run to the toilet upon sensing the onset of a severe attack of diarrhoea. From standard aircraft taxiing procedure (British Airways Pilot's Manual Section 4: What to shout when the pilot's about to shit his trousers).

cabinet re-shuffle, carry out a *v.* To rearrange one's *honourable members, wind the clock. 'Your honour, my client was merely carrying out a cabinet re-shuffle when he was caught in the bushes behind the nurses' home.'*

cable laying *n.* The excretion of lengths of *copper bolt.*

cable stitch *1. n.* A knitting term describing yarn which has been looped to resemble a twisted rope. *2. n.* A sharp, stabbing pain in the side caused by excessive exertion whilst trying to expel a recalcitrant length of *dirty rope.*

cable water *n.* The *piss* you suddenly realise you need after *dropping a copper bolt,* even though you've already zipped up your trousers, put your coat on and

are halfway back to the bar.

cab man's rests *rhym. slang.* Bristols, thrupenny bits.

caboose *n.* The *anchor man* in a *bum train.* *Lucky Pierre's* rear attendant.

cacafeugo *1. n. prop.* A Spanish ship captured by Sir Francis Drake on March 1st 1579. *2. n. Shit fire.* Red hot *squirts,* often experienced following a deliciously spicy repast at the Curry Capital, Bigg Market, Newcastle upon Tyne.

cack *1. n. Shit,* excrement, *feeshus. 2. v.* To *papper,* usually one's *trolleys.* Also *cacka, cak. 3. exclam.* Expression of disappointment. *'Mr President. The House Judiciary Committee has instigated articles of impeachment against you for obstruction of justice, abuse of power and contempt of Congress.' 'Oh cack.'*

cack shack *n.* The *crapper* or *shit house.* *'The throne room is out of order, Your Majesty. Her Royal Highness Princess Michael of Kent done a Meatloaf's daughter in it earlier on and then His Royal Highness Prince Michael of Kent blocked it with bangers and mash trying to flush it away for her, the daft twat. I'm afraid you'll have to use Camilla's cack shack instead.'*

Cadbury alley *n. Bourneville Boulevard.*

cafe hag *1. n.* A popular brand of decaffeinated coffee. *2. n.* A *fit* woman whom, upon returning to your flat for coffee following a night out, under the harsh fluorescent lights of your kitchen whilst waiting for the kettle to boil, appears neither *fit* nor womanly.

cafetiere, the *n.* The ethically dubious motion of pushing a lady's head *south* against a certain amount of resistance.

cajooblies *n. Oomlaaters.*

cake detector *n.* A portly person. One

who does need to ask directions to the bakery. A *salad dodger*, a *piabetic*, a *double fare*, a *barge arse*.

cakeover *n*. That staple of daytime television where they take a plain, fat lass, give her new clothes, make-up and hair, and she comes out at the end of the show looking like a plain, fat lass with new clothes, make-up and hair.

cakey *n*. A slightly larger woman, complete with *bingo wings, cankles etc*. Named for her self-evident love of baked confections.

Calcutta rinse *n*. The act of using an inverted showerhead to cleanse one's *rusty bullethole* when bereft of *shit tickets*.

Calcutta splutter *n*. A rousing, Neddy Seagoon-style *ringpiece raspberry* blown the morning after an inadvisably piquant *cuzza*. Also *Bombay spray*.

California tan *n*. An extreme, scatalogical sexual peccadillo practised by those for whom *Cleveland steamers, Boston pancakes* and *Belgian biscuits* have become a little mundane, not to say jejune, if you will. Without going into too much detail, you will need a supply of laxatives, a sieve and a new carpet.

call down for more mayo *v*. To *jack the beanstalk*.

call Huey *v*. To vomit, *puke*. Also *call Ralph, call Ruth, call God on the great white telephone etc*.

calling for cock *n*. Of a lady, yawning.

call in the bomb squad *v*. To successfully defuse a particularly dangerous *false start* at an awkward social event.

call Radcliffe *n*. To leave halfway through something you know you won't be finishing, *eg*. A crap pint, a bad relationship, an Olympic long distance race. '*How*

did you like Vera Drake?' 'Jesus Christ. I called Radcliffe on it after the first half hour, mate. Went to see Spongebob instead.'

call to prayer *n*. An early morning, wailing *horse and cart* which indicates that it is time to rise. A *breakfast mecca*.

calve *v*. To have a difficult delivery on the toilet. To attempt to pass an exceptionally toublesome stool where, in extreme cases, it may be necessary to tie a rope around it and get someone to pull it out. A *Herriot turd*.

camel's foot *n*. *Twix lips. Beetle bonnet*. The pediments of the *toblerone tunnel*.

Camillas *n*. The bowels. Named after equine-featured former Prince's *spunkbucket*, now her Royal Highness the Duchess of Cornwall and Queen-in-waiting Camilla Parker-Bowels.

camp *adj*. As butch as Kenneth Williams.

Campbell *v*. To inadvertently utter the *c-word* in inappropriate circumstances, such as whilst hosting an early morning programme on a national radio station. A term coined by Andrew Collins and Richard Herring, which refers to eponymous presenter Nicky's habit of repeatedly saying the *c-word* whilst presenting his early morning programmes on a national radio station.

Campbell's condensed *n*. A small volume, double-strength *brew* which, when diluted with air, can feed a whole room.

camper's kebab *n*. A *dump* taken in one's hat when one would rather not leave the tent. '*It was blowing a terrible blizzard last night. Indeed, it was so cold that when nature called, Bowers decided not to risk exposing himself to the risk of frostbite and instead ordered a camper's kebab. After living on nothing save* *penguin fat, rancid pemmican and seal blubber for six months, the smell was too much for Oates, who called him a dirty cunt and went outside to get some fresh air. He ventured out into the blizzard and we have not seen him since.'* (from the handwritten entry for March 18th, 1912, found in a *Lett's Antarctic Explorer's Diary* on the body of captain Robert Falcon Scott).

can *1. n. US.* Bottom. *2. n. US.* A quantity of *Bob Hope, marijuana. 3. n. US.* Prison. *4. n. US.* Toilet, *shithouse. 'They put me in the can after I was caught in the can sticking a can up my can.'*

canary killer *n.* A *fart* that smells like a 60s cokeworks.

canary, send in the *exclam.* Old mining term now appropriated by folk who have just befouled the air in the bobhouse. *'Fuck me. Send in the canary before you use that shitter, your Holiness. I just done a right smelly dump in there.'*

cancer shop *1. n.* A charitable retail outlet selling corpses' trousers, Mantovani records and damp, mouldy copies of *Readers' Digest. 2. n.* A high street tanning studio.

cancer veranda *n.* The *al fresco* area around an office door to which *snoutcasts* are exiled.

c and c *abbrev. Clips and cunts.* Generic term for any television programme consisting of nothing but clips from other televison shows/films/ads/videos interspersed with hilarious, insightful and profound comments from assorted *cunts* whose only reason for existing appears to be appearing on *c and c shows.*

candy floss *1. n.* A large, fluffy fairground snack which is impossible to finish, damages the teeth and invariably leaves one feeling slightly nauseous. *2. n.* A large, fluffy *bush* which is impossible to finish, damages the teeth and invariably *etc., etc.*

can I quote you on that? *exclam. interrog. rhet.* Another one of those useful phrases to drop into the awkward silence which follows a voluble *botty burp.* See also *my, that duck's got bad breath.*

cankle *n.* On a lady with a lovely personality, where the calf is indistinguishable from the ankle.

cannonball *v.* Of a fortunately flexible gentleman who never leaves the house, to perform a *thirty-four-and-a-halfer.* To administer *self-horatio.*

cannonball express *n.* A big *turd* that comes "a-steamin' and a-rollin'" out of the brown engine shed, before jumping the points and de-railing into the porcelain buffers. Or something. From the rollicking theme tune to the 1960s children's programme *Casey Jones.*

cannon wheels *n.* The testicles. *'Have you got the end in yet?' 'Aye, I'm in up to me cannon wheels you cheeky cow.'*

canoe *n.* A streamlined *poo* which is shaped perfectly to ensure anal comfort throughout its expulsion from the *dirt bakery; ie.* One that tapers to a point at both ends like a shuttle off a powerloom.

can tan *n.* The healthy, bronzed skin tone achieved by gentlemen who sit on the *shandy sunbed* all day, supping from tins of 9% lager. *Tramp's tan.*

can't understand new technology *exclam. acronym.* Phrase which can be usefully dropped into the conversation during meetings with patronising IT personnel, or encounters with smart-arsed salesmen in electrical stores, when you are being bombarded with technical bullshit. *'Yeah, the Canon EX-t 677 has nine million pixels. That's with the super hybrid aspheric inkjet CCD of course. Now the Bang and Olufsen B3 X-Z66 has a signal to noise ratio of three hundred, so obviously you're going to see a fall off in your midrange transients on your hard disk especially since its only got an ISO range of 100-1600kHz. This button toggles through the various modes; shuffle play, flatscreen DVD, wireless bluetooth. Obviously, it's your money, but if it was me I'd go for the Samsung GR 88X-Z23232323b, because it's got the tiltable USB. Do you want to take out the five year extended warranty?' 'Eeh, sorry. Can't understand new technology.'*

canvas cashpoint *n.* On a festival campsite, an illicit source of money, cameras, mobile phones, car keys, iPods *etc.* Someone else's tent.

can you leave the fat on mine? *exclam.* Humorous response to a particularly meaty *anal announcement* from the *trouser grill.*

cappuccino fanny *n.* When the *furry cup* has reached its maximum froth.

captain *n.* The penis. *'Don't be shy, love. Pop your head below decks and say hello to the captain.'*

captain, do a *v.* To display one's *buttocks* through the back window of a coach, usually to a couple of nuns in a Morris Minor. To do a *moonie.*

Captain Caveman *n.* A yodelling *biffer.*

Captain Hogseye *n.* Curly-bearded seafarer with a shiny, bald, purple head who trawls in *cod cove.* And spits a lot.

Captain Hook *n.* A fellow proficient in the gentle art of using his crooked index fin-ger to haul the gusset of his ladyfriend's *bills* safely out of the way, for whatever reason.

Captain Oates, to do a *v.* To altruistically leave the pub early when struggling with the pace, so as not to hold your more manly fellow drinkers back.

Captain's pie *1. n.* Tasty *slice* caught fresh by Captain *Hogseye. Haddock pastie. 2. n. milit.* Of naval catering, that pie which belongs to the captain.

caramel keg *1. n.* A much-loved, self-explanatory chocolate in a box of Cadbury's Roses. *2. n.* A lady with a *pint glass figure, eg.* Her with the red face and the glasses who used to show off at the front of Les Dawson's Roly Polys tap-dancing troupe.

caravanner *n.* A slender gentleman hitched to a distinctly more sizeable spouse, *ie.* One who is used to towing a large, ungainly *load* around. *'Today's Birthdays: George Ellery Hale, American astronomer, 1868; Giacomo Leopardi, Italian poet, 1798; Christos Papakryiakopoulos, Greek mathematician, 1914; Ben Ofoedu, Celebrity Wife Swap caravanner, 1972.'*

carbon arseprint *n.* A measure of an individual's contribution to global warming (or climate change, in the event of a shit summer), caused by a release of *brownhouse gases* so powerful that it leaves a sooty residue in the *dunghampers.*

carbon cockprint *n.* The amount of CO2, greenhouse gases, fossil fuels and what-have-you produced, emitted and consumed by a chap in search of sexual gratification. *'What? You're going all the way to Stockholm just to shag that bird? Your carbon cockprint will be massive.'*

carbon dating *n.* Of a young gentleman,

the act of going out with a somewhat more mature lady friend.

carbon dibaxide *n*. Chemical name for *arse gas*.

car bootylicious *adj*. Descriptive of those rough *bints* one sees in *saggy-arsed* velour tracksuits and *bingo clink*. Also *aldilicious*.

car crash flash *n*. When a woman with *big bones* sits down in a very short skirt. Something you really don't want to look at, but nevertheless feel strangely compelled to.

cardie muffins *n*. *Tits* of the sort you would expect a spinster librarian to have.

Cardiff grandmother *n*. A lady whose own children have left the nest and who is now, at the age of twenty-eight or so, out *on the pull* again.

cardinal's cap *n*. *medic*. A swelling and reddening of the *herman* brought on by chronic *bishop rage*. *Fireman's helmet*.

cardington *n*. A vast bra for the storage of vast *knockers*. Named after the Bedfordshire airfield where two enormous airship hangars were constructed side by side in 1917. *'Lot 456. Substantial Playtex cardington, formerly the property of the television impressionist Faith Brown. May be of interest to circus freakshow exhibitors, or could possibly be cut down and used to carry oversized piles of loose coal, roadstone or sharp sand. Estimate £30-£35.'* (extract from Christie's Showbiz Memorobilia Auction Catalogue, October 2003).

cardswipe *n*. The groove on a *bird's* frontage.

card table *n*. A position whereby a lady engages in simultaneous oral/vaginal pleasures with two gentlemen who, should they wish, could play a game of cards on her back. Admittedly an unlikely scenario. A *spit roast*.

cargle *v*. Of a *dirty lady*, to gargle with a gentleman's *erotic spendings*. Like they do. From cum + gargle.

cargoyle *n*. A lady with such *a lovely personality* that all dates with her are spent in the car to avoid the possiblity of being spotted in her company.

Carling darling *n*. A lady whose attractiveness only becomes apparent after one has had a few. A *ten pinter, gallon girl*.

carnival *n*. A sexual game where a woman sits on a man's face and he has to guess her weight.

carnival knowledge *n*. Biblical phrase meaning to have sex. *'And it came to pass that Mary was up the spout, yea though Joseph had not lain with her, and certainly had not carnival knowledge of her.'* (from *St. Paul's Letters to the Gas Board*, Chapter 6, *v*. 3-5).

carniwhore *n*. A speciality film actress with a real taste for meat.

Carolgees' cuff *n*. Having one's *wanking spanner* wrist deep in a hairy *biffer*.

Carol Vorderman, do a *v*. To sit on the *Rick Witter* doing what the eponymous *Countdown* mathematician is good at, *viz*. "Working one out". *Do the numbers round*.

car park, to *v*. To kick the *Brad* out of someone. To *take them outside*.

car park karaoke *n*. A post-drink entertainment where women *pissed up* on bacardi breezers take turns on the *purple-headed microphone*.

carpark sutra *n*. The ancient mystical art of gymnastic *screwing* on the back seat of an Astra. Usually whilst parked

'Miss Pollard bent down to pick up the chalk and gave William his cheapies.' ~ from *William Stirs Below* by Richmal Crompton.

round the back of Shire Oak Miners' Welfare and surrounded by a crowd of enthusiastic onanists staring through the windows.

carpenter's dream *n.* A sexually promiscuous woman. From the fact that she is "flat as a board and easy to screw". A *boot*.

carpet duster *n.* A dense, heavier-than-air cloud of *carbon dibaxide* which forms a thin layer over the whole floor surface.

carpet muncher *n.* A lady who enjoys *gorilla salad*, but turns her nose up at *meat and two veg.*

carpet tiles *rhym. slang. Bumgrapes. Adrian Chiles.*

carrot bladder *n. medic.* Secret internal organ situated just beside the pyloric sphincter from where diced carrots magically appear when you vomit. (© Billy Connolly Ltd. 1978).

carrot knackers *n.* Affectionate term for a ginger-haired fellow. *'Oi, carrot knackers. There's a picture of you in a nazi armband on the front of the Sun.'*

carrot snapper *n.* A lady with the sort of protruding front teeth that would do a rabbit proud. A *bunny girl. 'Famous people born on the 27th December: Johannes Kepler, astronomer who correctly explained planetary motion, thereby becoming the founder of the science of celestial mechanics, 1571. Louis Pasteur, scientist and discoverer of the theory that infectious diseases are caused by germs, whose pioneering work became the foundation of the science of microbiology, and hence a cornerstone of modern medicine, 1822. Janet Street Porter, screeching carrot snapper, 1946.'* (from *Schott's Oh Fucking Hell, What Am I Going to Put in it This Year Book, 2006*).

carry out, to have a *v.* To *cack* oneself and have to walk to the nearest convenient spot for a *scrape out.*

carry your bat *1. v.* In the world of cricket, to return to the pavilion, having remained at the crease throughout the team's entire innings without getting out. *2. v.* In the world of *having it off*, to abandon a drunken act of sexual intercourse after failing to *drop your filthy yoghurt* up a lady due to the effects of strong liquor.

carse *n.* The female equivalent of the *barse. Biffon.*

Carsten Janker *rhym. slang.* A *wanker.* From the bullet-headed footballing kraut who taunted the crowd after putting Germany 1-0 ahead at the start of their 5-1 trouncing by En-ger-lernd, En-ger-ernd, En-ger-lernd! En-ger-lernd, En-ger-lernd, En-ger-lerrr-ernd! We beat them in 1966 too.

cartman *n. medic.* A small *stool.* From the little shit in the popular children's cartoon series *South Park.*

carwash *n.* View of the vagina whilst performing *cumulonimbus.* The hair of the *muff* looking like them big whirly brush things that knock your wing mirrors off.

Casanova's rubber sock *n.* Condom, *blob, dunky, French letter, Coney Island whitefish.*

cashanova *n.* One who doesn't waste his money, but spends it wisely on prostitutes. A chap who pays for his love. A *punter,* a *John,* a *buysexual.*

cash crash *n.* A deliberate car accident intended to enrich the perpetrator by insurance and injury claims.

cash for gash *euph.* A stop at the bank machine on the way out *on the pull.*

cash in the attic *1. n.* Vile daytime TV programme in which gullible homeowners are bullied into selling their worthless heirlooms for the entertainment of semi-comatose students, professional comedians and the unemployed. *2. v.* To perform a *money shot* into a *bird's* mouth.

cashpoint cripple *n.* See *video cripple*.

cassoulet anglais *n. Fr.* A *can* full of sausage and beans. How a modern languages undergraduate might refer to the state of a blocked *shite house pan* in shared student accommodation.

casting Churchill's reflection *euph.* A political impression involving a porcelain bowl with water in the bottom, your *arse* and a *bum cigar*.

castle on the queen side *1. v.* In chess, to perform the risky strategy of castling on the opposite side of the board from the usual default manoeuvre of castling on the king's side. Whatever that means. *2. v.* Of a man, to be prone to a spot of *airborne puddle avoidance*. *'You see him over there? That bloke with the bushy moustache and the leather motorcycle cap, grinning from ear to ear in the middle of that writhing, sweaty, naked homosexual bumchain? Well, I have it on very good authority that he castles on the queen's side, if you know what I mean.'*

Casualty moment *n.* The identification during the course of your everyday activities that the action you are performing resembles the sort of thing typically seen in the opening sequences of the hospital-based BBC tea-time calamity-fest, *eg.* Carrying a pan of hot fat through a room full of toddlers playing marbles, preparing to perform an unrehearsed fire-breathing act at the opening of a posionous snake zoo, cutting the hedge with an electric circular saw whilst drunk and standing on a swivel chair, deciding to change into your swimming trunks whilst driving at high speed into a fogbank near Beachy Head.

Catalan custard *n.* Strange, viscous deposit found in the gusset of one's *grundies* after a heavy night *on the piss* in Barcelona. A discovery which is accompanied by unnerving, nightmarish flashbacks to an unpleasant interlude set on a seedy strip club stage which involves a blindfold, a man dressed in a monkey suit and a cheering crowd. *'What's up, Bill?' 'I've found some Catalan custard in my gusset, Marge.'*

Catalina lob on *n.* An unexpected increase in girth discovered when going for a *slash* during the ad break in *My Name is Earl*.

catbab *n.* An exotic snack containing unidentifiable meat of questionable provenance, usually sold out of the window of an old ambulance.

catcher's mitt *n.* A contraceptive diaphragm, a *fuck-plug*, *babe roof*.

catering for cyclists *adj.* A scene often found in parks during the summer when a generously-proportioned lady lies on her back to sunbathe and thus unwittingly creates an ample facility in which to trap the front wheel of one's velocipede.

cat five *1. abbrev. RAF.* Classification of an aircraft that is considered beyond repair following a crash, which you would assume would be most aircraft that have had a crash. *2. abbrev. RAF.* Classification of a *chod bin* that is considered beyond use following a *dirty bomb*.

cat flaps *1. n.* Means by which a cute little pussy can enter the house. *2. n.* Means by which a *cock* can enter a cute little *pussy.* Labia minora, *Keith Burtons.*

Catford bunch *n.* An inexpensive floral offering to a ladyfriend, hand made from the flowers taped to the railings and lamp-posts of South London in memory of the recently-stabbed.

cathedral *sim.* Describing an oversized vagina which is too echo-y for a satisfactory *organ recital.* A *bucket fanny.*

catholic tastes *1. n.* Wide-ranging interests, from the word "catholic" meaning "universal". *2. n.* Narrowly-focused interests, specifically those pursued by certain members of the left-footed clergy which revolve principally around the contents of their prepubescent choirboys' surplices.

cat on the bed *euph.* Descriptive of the sensations transmitted through the mattress that a gentleman feels when his fellow bedlady is *playing the invisible banjo.* *'Can you feel something, Your Majesty?' 'It's just a cat on the bed, Mr Fagan. Now go back to sleep.'*

cat scarer *n.* An unsuccessful haircut. A coiffure so bad that the victim's own moggy doesn't recognise them and runs off.

cat's face *n.* Mrs Slocombe's *cunt.*

cattle *rhym. slang.* To engage in coitus. From cattle truck = fuck. Also *trolley* (& truck), *Friar* (Tuck) or *Russian* (duck).

cat with a strawberry-flavoured arse, like a *sim.* Descriptive of the happy demeanour of those who cannot believe the extent to which Heaven appears to have smiled upon them, *eg.* A rollover lottery winner, a dog with two *cocks* or whichever ne'er-do-well is presently *banging*

Charlotte Church.

cat with its throat cut, like a *sim.* Humorous term used to describe an extremely alarming, hirsute *front bottom.* Also *like a cat with its head cut off.* *'Put your applecatchers back on will you, Germaine. We can't print a picture of that bloody thing. It's like a cat with its throat cut.'*

caught white handed, to be *v.* To lose a game of *rushin' roulette.*

cauliflower *1. n.* Sex. *'Hey! Your missus gave me a bit of cauliflower while you were at work last night.'* *2. n. 18thC.* Lettuce.

cauliflower beanbag *n.* The *hanging brain.* *'Excuse me officer, I wonder if you'd be so good as to direct me to the nearest casualty department, only I appear to have inadvertantly caught my cauliflower beanbag in the nozzle of this Hoover Dustette vacuum cleaner.'*

cauliflower biff *n. medic.* A *clout* that has had a right good *banging.* A *blurtch* that looks like one of Bill Beaumot's ears.

cauliflower cheese *n.* Smegma.

cavalier *n.* An uncircumcised penis. With a wide *brim*, a big smile and a feather stuck in the top.

cavalry caviar *n.* A highly-prized, piquantly-flavoured salty delicacy, traditionally served in armed forces circles on a digestive biscuit or cream cracker. *Officer's Mess.*

cave paintings *1. n.* Mysterious and multicoloured daubings of dinosaurs, which date from the upper Palaeolithic period after the last ice age. Found extensively decorating the inside walls of limestone caves in France and Spain during the 19th century. *2. n.* Mysterious and multicoloured daubings dating from a night after protracted consumption of draught Bass. Found comprehensively decorating the insides of *undercrackers* and bed linen the length and breadth of the UK on most weekend mornings.

caviar *1. n.* Expensive delicacy made from fish periods. *2. n.* Web-speak for scatalogical *grumble,* apparently.

cedar burp *n.* A small outbreak of *chocolate thunder*.

celeberating *n.* The practice, typically espoused by the denizens of the gutter press, of featuring so-called celebrities in their pages in order to attack and generally humiliate them. Famous people who have been widely and unfairly celeberated include pointy-titted scrawnbag Madonna and baldy-quimmed mentalist Britney Spears.

cellulike *n.* A *chubby chaser*. *'Today's birthdays: Charlie Parker, American jazz musician, 1920; James Hunt, British racing driver, 1947; Lenny Henry, former cellulike, 1958.'*

cellulite's on but theres no-one at home, the *exclam.* Phrase which can be usefully employed to describe a thick, fat-thighed lady. Were the occasion to arise.

cemetery gates *n.* An old lady's *muff minders. Granny's oysters.*

centre console *1. n.* On an aeroplane, the control panel situated between the pilot's and the co-pilot's seats. *2. n.* How airline personnel refer to the *butfer, gooch, barse etc.,* from the punchline to a joke which is popular amongst trolley dollies, *viz.* "What do you call the bit between the cunt and the arsehole? The centre console." *'When his plane the Spirit of St Louis landed at Le Bourget Field at the end of his epoch-making trans-Atlantic solo flight, Lindbergh had been tightly strapped into his cramped, pressed-steel pilot's seat in the unheated cockpit of the Ryan monoplane for more than thirty-three hours. He later recalled that it was not until two days later that he finally regained some feeling in his centre console.'*

centre parting *n.* Highly enjoyable form of solo *balloon knot* sport whereby the practitioner sits on a sturdy, solid chair or bench and then forcibly breaks wind whilst leaning forward at an angle of forty-five degrees, thus causing the emitted *trouser cough* to shoot straight up the middle of his or her back, like a sort of gaseous Evel Kneivel going up a ramp. HRH the Duchess of York is said to be an enthusiastic *centre parter* and, during Christmas dinners at Balmoral often demonstrates her skills by knocking a paper crown off the top of her own head.

cervix charge *n.* The hidden costs incurred in the *getting over of one's leg, eg.* Flowers, meal, taxi home, changing locks *etc.*

CF Bundy *abbrev. medic.* Doctors' shorthand written on the charts of terminally ill patients. Completely Fucked But Not Dead Yet.

CFN *abbrev.* A *ringpiece* which flies in the face of the Kyoto agreement, and burns at tremendous temperatures, belching out toxic fumes and clouds of particulates which are harmful to the ozone layer and one's underpants. A *heavy smoker,* an *arse* with a huge *carbon dibaxide* footprint. Coal Fired Nipsy.

CGI *1. abbrev.* The City and Guilds Institute. *2. abbrev.* Cunt Gap Index. A measurement on a scale of finger widths of the size of a woman's *Toblerone tunnel*.

chain reaction *n*. Upon rising from the *chod bin* and prior to flushing, the involuntary act of retching and/or, *in extremis*, the *blowing* of one's *chunks* as a result of the aromatic miasma of one's own foetid *digestive transits*.

Chalfonts *rhym. slang*. Piles, *bum grapes*. From the town of Chalfont St. Gemerroids, Buckinghamshire.

challenge oneself *v*. To engage in a spot of *five against one*. To *knock yourself about a bit*.

champagga *n*. A fight fuelled by expensive beverages, as opposed to Special Brew. A brawl one may see once in a blue moon outside a brasserie.

champagne corks *n*. Bullet-hard *nipples* that pop out of the *tit pants* with enough force to take your eye out. *Organ stops*.

champagne shit *n*. A sit-down toilet visit where one strains for some time to *pop a cork*, but once it goes it is followed by a magnum of fizzy brown liquid. A *champoo*.

Chanel No.2 *euph*. The distinctive, delicate perfume of the alimentary canal. Hopefully not sniffed off your wrist. *Oh de toilette*.

change ammo *v. milit*. To empty one chamber of the *mutton musket*, readying the firing piece for the next shot. To take a last minute *gypsy's kiss* prior to a *poke*.

change at Baker Street *v*. During intercourse, to decide to *play the B-side*. From the only station on the London Underground where it is possible to change from the Pink line (Hammersmith & City) to the Brown line (Bakerloo).

change at Oxford Circus *v*. Similar usage to *change at Baker Street*, but for monthly ticket holders. *Going from red to brown*.

change lanes *v*. To switch, mid-romp, from vaginal to anal penetration or vice versa. *'Just like when on the road, when on the job it is good practice to signal one's intentions before changing lanes so as not to take anyone by surprise.'* (from *The Joy of Sex* by Dr Alex Comfort).

change rain *n*. A shower of coins which falls from the trouser pockets when a gentleman is attempting to undress quietly and not wake his slumbering wife.

changing the guard *n*. *Women's thing* replacement, a ceremony occurring shortly after *trooping the colour*.

changing the washer *n*. Remedial action required to address the issue of post-curry *ring* leakage. In the event of the *balloon knot* failing to keep one's *rusty water* sufficiently at bay, furtive trips to the water closet are required to make good the faulty orifice using an index finger swathed in toilet tissue.

Chan it *v*. To take unnecessary risks in mundane situations whilst under the delusion that if the shortarsed 80s martial arts hero Jackie can do it, then so can you. Examples include running between two buses, escaping an attacker on your bicycle and fending someone off with an umbrella *etc*.

chanson *n*. Any tacky trinket or ornament adorning an elderly person's mantelpiece. From the Manhattan Transfer song, which seemed to be performed on *The Two Ronnies* every week for about fifteen years, whose lyrics went; "Chanson d'amour / Tat! Tat! Tat! Tat! Tat!"

chap 1. *n*. The *charlie*. 2. *v*. To gently slap your *chap* in the face of your sleeping wife, girlfriend or party guest, take a photograph and leave it in a place where they are bound to come across it, *eg.* On a fridge door, car windscreen, the internet.

chapel hat pegs *sim.* Large, erect *nips.* *Pygmy's cocks, Scammell wheel nuts, JCB starter buttons.*

chapel of rest *n.* The snug bar of the Northumberland Hussar pub on Sackville Road, Heaton, Newcastle upon Tyne.

chapkin *n.* A protective cloth placed over a fellow's stomach and chest in order to soak up any salty spillages which may accidentally occur for any reason whilst he is lying on his back.

chappatio *n.* The flattish remains of a very good night out on a section of path outside the front of one's house, *ie.* An Indian-themed pavement pizza.

chap's eye *n.* A politically correct alternative to the outdated, offensive term *Jap's eye*, which can be used to describe the male urethral opening when in polite, right-on company. Usefully, in the event of an outraged reaction to an accidental slip, the speaker can claim to have said "chap's eye" in the first place, thus making his accusers feel like racials.

chapstick *n.* An implement with which a lady moistens her dry lips.

charge of the light ale brigade *n.* The Friday 2pm stampede of builders, roofers and scaffolders to the pub. Or any other day that a drop of rain has fallen. Or it looks like it might rain later. Somewhere in the British Isles.

charging the brush *n.* The act of sneakily dampening the finger just south of a lady's *devil's doorbell* prior to (and in order to achieve better-lubricated) re-touching of same.

charge the skin dynamo *n.* To pull oneself off. *'What are you doing in there, Richard?' 'Just charging my skin dynamo, Jacqui.'*

charioteer, the *n.* Self explanatory sexual position involving a woman with long hair who's down on all fours and a man with very short legs pretending to be Charlton Heston. A *ben her.* Also *attempting to enter the gates of Rome.*

charity work *n.* The altruistic act of buying a drink for, or flirting with, an aesthetically-challenged woman out of pity. *'Where are you off to, John?' 'I'm just going to go on the dance floor to do a bit of charity work with fat Lisa from accounts.'*

charlie 1. *rhym. slang. Cunt.* From "Charlie Hunt". *'You look a right charlie'.* 2. *n. Showbiz sherbet.* 3. *n. Hampton Wick,* the penis.

Charlie Cairoli's hat *n.* A lady's *minge,* brimful of *spoff.* From the erstwhile clown's blancmange-filled bowler.

Charlie Dimmock's nipples *n.* Term used by vicars to describe the hat-pegs in their chapels.

charlie in the chocolate factory *n. Bolivian marching powder* snorted in a public *shithouse eg.* The *crappers* at the Groucho Club.

Charlie Potatoes *n.* One who labours under the misapprehension that he all that when he ain't. Someone who thinks he's the *bollocks, eg.* Patrick Kielty, Chris Moyles. *'Look at that cunt swaggering about like he's Charlie Potatoes.'*

charlies *n.* 1970s *assets.*

charlies' angels 1. *n.* See *tit fairies.* 2. *n.* Women who appear attractive to a man as a consequence of him having taken a quantity of *showbiz sherbet* on board. A Class-A variation on the term *five pinter.*

Charlie two-dinners *n.* A gentleman whose glands eschew salads in favour of pies, sausages and more pies. A *double sucker.*

charlimingus *n.* Technical term for *double bassing.*

charms *n.* In British tabloid journalism, a coy way of referring to the breasts. Usually prefixed "ample". *'Lovely Lisa, 21, who hails from Hyde in Cheshire, loves detective stories, but it would be a criminal waste to "hide" away her ample charms! Not to mention her pink nipples and the areolae which radially delineate the extent of the lactiferous ducts in her mammary tissue.'*

charm the snake *1. v.* To perform a public entertainment act whereby your *Ophiophagus hannah* is encouraged to rise and dance mesmerically before eventually spitting its venom. *2. v.* To perform a personal entertainment act whereby your *membrum virile* is encouraged to rise and dance mesmerically before eventually spitting its venom.

charva *n. Charver, chav.* A *scratter.*

charva cava *n.* Substandard *trampagne.* White cider.

charver *1. v. US.* To have sex, *shag. 2. n.* Boy, lad, adolescent. *3. n.* Aerosol-snorting, be-tracksuited *twocker, borstal boy, car radio removal mechanic. 4. n.* A 10-year-old mother of several *pastie babies.* Also, *charva, chav.*

chasbo *n.* A *burberry ape, scratter* etc. The proud owner of a legal document awarded for bad conduct and anti-social behaviour. And five As at A-level, these days.

chase the dragon *1. v.* To "snort" a syringe full of marijuana cigarettes up your bottom through a burnt spoon. *2. n.* To attempt to get a good whiff of one's own *dropped back* in an attempt to acheive the ultimate high.

chase the cotton mouse *v.* To have the *painters in, flags out,* to *surf the crimson wave,* be *up on blocks.*

chastity patch *n.* A small smear of excrement surreptitiously wiped on the back of one's girlfriend's neck before she goes on a lasses' night out, the aim of which is to deter any would-be suitors.

Chatham crow *n.* The classy corvoid tattoo that ladies of the eponymous Kent Olympic village typically sport on their lower backs just above their *arse cracks. Chatham crows* are usually displayed to best advantage by a pair of jeans or sweatpants that are three sizes too small. *Arse antlers.*

chauffeur's glove *n.* A tight-fitting *flunkey.* Possibly with three buttons on the back.

chav *n.* A member of the lower orders. The sort of person who would have been unlikely to turn up on *Ask the Family* in the 1970s. *Also charver, charva.*

chavalanche *n.* A terrifying Burberry-clad cascade of *scratters.*

chavalcade *1. n.* A town centre procession of souped-out, clapped-up Astras, Corsas and XR3is driven by a motley assortment of *scratters, neds, pogs, ratboys* and *Burberry apes. 2. n.* A pram-pushing convoy of the above on their way to Greggs.

chavalry *1. n.* Mobile units of these halfwit *ratboys* on toddlers' BMX bicycles you get on the pavements these days, easily recognised by their uniform of shellsuit trousers, hoopy pullovers, leather gloves and peaked caps. *2. n.* Members of the *scratting* classes who have for some unfathomable reason taken up equestrian pursuits, *eg.* Jordan with her fucking pink horsebox.

chavatar *n.* A cyberspace representation of an autochthon of the lower social strata. *'Aw bloody hell, some fucking chavatar's nicked me quest point cape.'*

chav bible *n.* The Argos catalogue.

chavelin *n.* Semi-olympian sport played by denizens of the urban underclass. Darts.

chavel inn *n.* A low quality hotel, with its bar populated by *burberry apes,* aggressive manual workers and, unfortunately for themselves, peripatetic sales managers working for *tight-arsed* companies.

chavellers' cheques *n.* Giros.

chavenue *n.* A boulevard favoured by promenading *scruburbanites.* A *cul-de-scrat.* From charming + avenue.

chaviar *n.* Supermarket own-brand "value" baked beans.

chavity *n.* Donations requested by *asbopolitan* burghers for drink, drugs *etc.* *'Hey mate, have you got fifty pence for chavity? I'm desperate for a cup of tea. And a fix.'*

chav laptop *n.* An offensive, mocking term for an open takeaway pizza box. Also *scouser's laptop.*

chavrolet *n.* A *scratter's* motor vehicle, normally an uninsured, lower-end production model souped up to *bloody fuck* with alloy wheels, blue downlights, spoilers, tinted glass, laughably loud sound systems *etc.*

chaviot of fire *n.* A burnt out Clio, Astra or Citroen AX on a rough estate. A *fourth party insurance* write-off.

chav-nav *n.* Ankle-mounted hi-tech electronic device which ensures that *scratters* can find their way home before 8pm

each evening.

chavrons *n.* The trendy, angular shapes cut into the Action Man-style hair on a young ASBO laureate's head.

chav years *n.* The bizarre, accelerated ageing effect often exhibited by the denizens of the less elevated layers of society. *'Did you see her mum on the news? She's only thirty-two but she looks about fifty.' 'Oh yeah. She's ageing in chav years.'*

cheapies *n.* Schoolboy sexual thrills. *'Miss Pollard bent down to pick up the chalk and gave William his cheapies.'* (from *William Stirs Below* by Richmal Crompton).

cheating nipsy *euph. medic.* Haemorrhoids. *'Darling, I'm just taking the dog for a walk. Do you fancy coming along?' 'Sorry, I can't, darling. My nipsy's cheating on me.' 'How can you be sure?' 'I found lipstick on my gusset.'*

chebs *n.* Tits, norks, headlamps. Breasts.

check the oil *v.* To put one's *cock* in some *bird's dirtbox* before pulling it out, inspecting, it and wiping it with a cloth.

check the roast *v.* To see whether what you've been baking is ready to come out. To go for a *shit.*

check one's emails *v.* To search for *grumble* on the interweb, for the purpose of fuelling a sordid and shameful act of *self harm.* *'Hurry up there, son. I want to check my emails. Into a sock.' 'Alright dad. Can I just finish off my homework first, though? Into a sock.'*

check on the scones *v.* To *turn one's bike around,* have a *Chinese singing lesson, strain the potatoes, see a man about a dog.* To relieve oneself, *have a slash.*

checkout time *n.* The period that elapses whilst the heady aroma of an *air biscuit* permeates its way out through the layers of one's clothing.

cheddar apple *n*. A very large, cheesy *bell end*.

cheek flapper *n*. A *fart* which registers highly on the *brap scale*. A *clapper rattler*, a *drive on the cats' eyes*.

Cheeseboard Charlie *n*. Amusing pejorative term used to describe an individual who is excessively accustomed to big restaurant sessions. *'Oi, Cheeseboard Charlie, shut your fucking pie hole. Let Shirley Maclaine get a fucking word in edgeways, will you, you fat twat.'* (Michael Parkinson interviewing Peter Ustinov, BBC TV, 1978).

cheese cracker *n*. A savoury, pungent *custard tart*. An *air snack* rather than a *buffet*.

cheese cutter *n*. *medic*. A rogue *pube* caught in the *fiveskin*, whilst still attached to the body. Results in two-fold agony; simultaneously cutting into *Captain Picard's head* whilst trying to tear itself out at the root. A *Bobby Charlton*.

cheesegrater special *n*. An aggressive *wank* carried out using nails as a punishment. Samuel Pepys records in his diary entry for March 18th 1668: *'At noon home to dinner, where my wife still in a melancholy fusty humour, and crying; and doth not tell me plainly what it is, but I by little words find that she hath heard of my going to plays and carrying on with darling Deb every day in her absence; and that I cannot help. After supper, we retired to bed where I felt decidedly amorous and got the mummy's arm. However, my wife's cantankerous humour was decidedly not improved at all and although I did kiss her and touch her thing she was against it and laboured with much earnestness, and yet at last I did make her take me in her hand but the rotten cow gave me a cheesegrater special.'* (from *The Diary of Samuel Pepys*, March 18th 1668).

cheese map *n*. Protein-based staining often to be found on the front of a young man's lower nightwear. *'Mums know that new Azox 2-in-1 will remove 99% of all household stains even on the cold water cycle. Dried-on food on the baby's bib, grass and mud on Janet's hockey skirt, oil and grease on dad's overalls or cheese maps on Jimmy's pyjama bottoms ... none of them can stand up to Azox's magic new non-bio formula.'*

cheesepipe *n*. The tubular organ that secretes *chucky cheese*.

cheesepipe clingfilm *n*. Condom, *rubber johnny*.

cheese ridge *n*. The fertile area of the *cheesepipe* where *knob cheese* is matured for weeks and months. The *brim* of the *lid*. Your sulcus.

cheese whistle *n*. The marvellous musical instrument kept in a fellow's tweeds. The *pink oboe* or *bed flute*.

cheesy wheelbarrow *n*. A self-explanatory sexual position utilised by two *uphill gardeners* during sports day.

cheezer *n*. That which is a cross between a *chick* and a *geezer*, *eg*. Julian Clary or Richard Branson.

chef's apron *euph*. A pair of particularly large and sanguine ladies' *dung-hampers*. *Ashley's shopcoat*.

chef's arse *n*. An uncomfortable, perspiring, smelly *bum cleft*. From the condition's prevalence amongst catering professionals, *eg*. Gordon Ramsay, Anthony Worrall-Thompson and Nigella Lawson.

chef's special sauce *n. Spunk. 'Here is your steak, Mr Winner. And chef wanted you to know that he enjoys your Esure adverts so much, he's put you an extra helping of his special sauce on there.'*

cheggered *adj. Pissed* as an *Exchange & Mart*. Derivation unknown.

Chelmsley Wood foreplay *n.* Any form of domestic violence or spousal abuse. Named after the Chelmsley Wood area of Solihull, West Midlands, which is known to be somewhat rough.

Chelmsley Wood lie detector *n.* A West Midlands Police Force truncheon.

Chelmsley Wood pill *n.* Anal sex. *UTBNB.* One up the bum, no harm done. A *Colchester condom*.

chemi-khazi *n.* What one commits when entering a portable lavatory cubicle at a music festival. *Pooicide.*

cheps *n. Chebs.*

Cherie Blair *n.* A mouth conducive to group fellatio. A *Carly Simon*, a *three-dick gob*, *Wallace*.

Cherie Blair's cake hole *n.* A strangely convoluted and, frankly, frightening *fanny*.

Cherie's smile *n.* Scary-lipped part of the anatomy of a lady who's been around a bit, for example one of those not-particularly-good time girls commonly to be seen disporting themselves in windows near the Holiday Inn, Nuremburg.

cherknobyl *n.* A *love-length* that accidentally blows up with little or no warning.

Chernobyl *euph.* The situation that obtains when cleaning up your *nipsy* takes significantly longer than the split-second explosion that necessitated such a course of action.

cherry 1. *n.* An intact *virgin string*. One that has not been *popped*. 2. *n.* One's virginity generally.

cherry boy *n.* A crimson, hormone-filled adolescent male with an intact *virgin string*, on whom a dampened finger will sizzle.

chess champion *n.* A socially maladroit person who is so gifted and special that they are still, at the age of thirty-seven, living at home and allowing their mum to choose their wardrobe, thus killing any hope they may have once harboured of ever *popping their cherry*.

chest dogs *n.* Fully grown *chest puppies*.

chest furniture *n. Tits, hooters, sweater-meat.*

chestnuts *n. Stits, juglets.*

chest pillows *n. Chebs* again.

chest tuners *n.* The symmetrical dials on a lady's *frontage* that enable a gentleman to find Radio Luxembourg. *Nips.*

Chewbacca after a fight *sim.* Descriptive of a particularly untidy *biffer*.

Chewbacca's calling *exclam.* A long, protracted *fart* similar to the strangulated guttural mewings of the famous *Star Wars* dog.

Chewbacca's growl *n.* The involuntary shrieks and groans released when one passes a *bum spud* as *wide as a footballer's tie knot*.

chewie *n.* An act of *horatio*, a *sucking off*, *gobbie, nosh.* A *Boris Johnson*.

chewing a toffee *n.* The unpleasant sensation of anal chafing and squelching when walking out of the *bog* following insufficient wiping of the *freckle*.

chewing on a brick *n.* Of *logs* and *logging*, that desperate point when the *turtle's head*, and indeed its *shoulders* protrude, and the *arse* is left gumming away at a *dirt*.

Chicago shuffle *n.* An entirely imaginary

sexual act whereby a lady traps a gentleman's *member* under her arm before shuffling a pack of cards. A *Las Vegas bagpipe*, a *Monte Carlo musclefuck*.

chichis *n. Mex. Tits*, breasts.

chicken *n.* Young gay male. A *botter's apprentice*.

chicken breasts 1. *n.* A big, fat, alluringly-shaved *snatch*. 2. *n. Blimplants*.

chickenhawk *n.* The time-served *botter*, to whom several *botter's apprentices* are apprenticed.

chicken skin handbag *n.* The scrot, *nadbag*.

chicken wings *n. medic.* The anatomical spare skin underneath the upper arms of a *Duchess of Giblets*, so called as they resemble the contents of a KFC Zinger burger. *Bingo wings, dinner ladies' arms*.

chill the husband's salad *v.* Of a lady, to position herself such that a cold blast from the air conditioning goes up her skirt, thus keeping her *lettuce* crisp and fresh. The opposite of *warming the husband's supper*.

chimbonda *n.* A lady with oversized *pins* wearing leggings that are far too tight. Named after the diminutive, muscly-legged, Guadeloupe-born Blackburn Rovers right back Pascal Chimbonda, who has a penchant for wearing tights under his shorts. *Two pounds of shit in a one pound bag*.

chimney sweep 1. *n.* A soot-covered man who cleans your chimney. 2. *n.* A soot-covered man who *bangs* you up the *dirtbox*.

chimney sweep's brush *n.* Dick Van Dyke's penis.

chimping 1. *n. Spanking the monkey* whilst grinning from ear to ear. And hav-ing a cup of PG Tips. 2. *n.* The frankly unlikely (though you wouldn't put it past the Germans) act of shitting into your hands and throwing it at your partner, for your mutual pleasure. *'Mature professional gentleman, married, 52, seeks discreet, elegant, educated lady, 35-45, for long walks in the country, fine wine and food, trips to the theatre and sophisticated classical music concerts. Must be into chimping.'*

chimp oneself red *v.* To furiously *relax in a gentleman's way*, to have *one off the flipper*.

CHIMPS/chimps *acronym.* Somewhat ungenerous police station terminology referring to Community Support Officers. Completely Hopeless In Most Policing Situations. *'Hello, is that the Emergency Services? There's a naked, blood-soaked, axe-wielding lunatic screaming and masturbating in my living room.' 'Unfortunately there are no proper policemen available to help you due to health and safety stroke public liability insurance issues. We're sending a couple of chimps over, but their mum says they've got to be home for their tea no later than six.'*

chimps' fingers *n.* Particularly dry, thin stools, often with distinct knuckles. *'Twenty six days at sea, and the men are wracked with stomach cramps. Regular bowel motions are naught but a memory. I myself have not passed solids for nigh on two weeks, and that was but a couple of chimps' fingers 200 miles SSE of Christmas Island.'* (from *The Journal of William Bligh*, 1765).

chin airbag *n.* A phantom double chin on a non-fatty. Usually associated with *pissed*, impromptu group photographs on a night out, especially common late on during wedding receptions when wearing a collar and tie and leaning slightly backwards. A *pelican's beak*. *'Fucking hell! It's a great photo of everybody, but look at me! Looks like my chin airbag has gone off.'*

Chinese algebra, harder than *sim.* Descriptive of the magnificent tumescence of a right *diamond cutter*. *'You're a lucky lady tonight, love. This bugger's harder than Chinese algebra.'*

Chinese fire drill *n.* A scene of utter disorder and pandemonium. *'Emergency services were today called out to the Dover branch of Netto after staff reduced to price of own brand baked beans to 1p a tin. In the Chinese fire drill that followed, 17 people were trampled to death and another 68 were detained in hospital, suffering crush injuries'.* (BBC News 24, Jan 3rd 2003).

Chinese firework *n.* The *cock* of a *one pump chump*, ie. One that *goes off* almost instantaneously.

Chinese gravy *n.* Something with a foul flavour. *'I was dining at the Y the other night and my fish supper tasted worse than Chinese gravy.'*

Chinese helicopter pilot *sim.* A bloke sitting up and operating his *chopper*.

Chinese junk *rhym. slang. Jitler, pineapple.*

Chinese mouse, hung like a *sim.* Opposite of *hung like an Arab stallion*.

Chinese singing lesson *n.* A *gypsy's kiss*. A *piss*.

Chinese tool *n.* A feeble penis, ie. One that is barely up to the job in hand.

Chinese wicketkeeper *euph.* One who gamely adopts the bending stance of a stumpsman whilst grimacing. A *pil-*

lowbiter, an *uphill gardener's cheesy wheelbarrow*.

Chinese wordsearch, hard as a *sim.* A good way to describe a particularly tumescent erectipulation of the *gentleman's parts;* that is to say, when one's *on* is very *hard* indeed. *'I woke up this morning and I was as hard as a Chinese wordsearch, Your Majesty.'*

chin music, play a little *v.* To give some wiseguy a fourpenny one up the bracket.

chinook position *n.* Coital congress arrangement often practised behind skips, up back alleys and round by the wheelie bins at the back of the kebab house, wherein the female participant is supported betwixt her partner's virile member and a wall. So called because it involves being lifted off the ground by a powerful *chopper*. Also known as a *fork lift truck* or *flying buttress*.

chinook, the *n.* When two gents simultaneously *willycopter* a lady in the face. Named after the dual-rotored vehicle used by the RAF to safely transport Princes William and Harry to stag parties on the Isle of Wight.

chin rest *n. Duffy's bridge.*

chinstrap *n.* The small piece of skin which holds the *German helmet* safely in place. The *banjo* or *guyrope*.

chin splash *n.* Condition caused by trying on a *pearl necklace* in a clumsy manner.

chin tinsel *n. Sloom*-based decorations dangling from the mandibles of a *messy eater*.

chin varnish *n. Perseverance soup.*

chinwag *n.* The side-to-side use of one's lower mandible, preferably with a few days' growth of stubble, in the style of a ruminating heffer, to stimulate a lady's *barnyard foliage.*

chipnosis *n. psych.* A state of mind brought about by a night *on the sauce*, whereby you find yourself in a takeaway restaurant craving food that has been fried in a suspicious brown liquid of dubious origin.

Chip Pan Alley *n.* The sort of High Street which only contains chip shops interspersed with the occasional tattoo parlour.

Chipperfield *n.* A proper leathering you get off a bouncer for no good reason.

chippie's toolbag *n.* Of women's *bodily treasures*, the *labia majorcas*. The *beef curtains, mutton shutters, Deputy Dawg's ears.*

chippopotamus *n.* A generously-proportioned lady who honestly just eats like a mouse but whose glands scoff vast quantities of deep-fried spuds.

chippy lippy *n.* Tell-tale traces of tomato sauce on one's face and clothing after a night on the town. *'Me missus went nuts because she thought I'd been gobbing off with some bird. Turns out it was just chippy lippy.'*

chip shop, taken up the *euph. Done up the wrong 'un.*

chip shovels *n.* The hands of a fat lass.

chips & gravy *euph.* Tickety boo. *'From here on in, treacle, it's all fucking chips & gravy.'* (HRH the Duke of Windsor to his new bride, Mrs Wallis Simpson on the occasion of their marriage, June 3rd 1937).

chips 'n' hame *phr. Scot.* The observed state of someone's failure to *score* and their resulting departure from the pub or club. *'Wee Angus has had nae luck the neet.' 'Aye, Hamish. It's chips 'n' hame for him.'*

chips that pass in the night *n.* A post-pub takeaway that makes its presence felt in one's bed several hours later.

chipwreck *n.* A person who has unaccountably failed to lose weight despite clearly putting a lot of time and energy into nimbly *dodging salad.* Ironically, chipwrecks typically adhere to the government's healthy eating injunction to eat five or more portions of fruit or veg each day, concentrating particularly on regular portions of the vegetable *Solanum tuberosum.*

chirp on *n.* The sort of good-natured, non-threatening erection that Kenneth Connor would have got in *Carry On Cruising* when Liz Fraser bent over to pick up a quoit. A *stiffy* that causes one to slap the back of one's neck and pull one's collar out whilst rubbing one's right leg up and down one's left calf.

chirpy scouser, as popular as a *sim.* Very unpopular indeed. *'Houston, I have a problem. I just dropped a really bad fart in my spacesuit, and let me tell you it's about as popular as a chirpy scouser. Oh yeah, the oxygen tank's just exploded and all.'* (Commander James A Lovell, transmission to Mission Control from onboard Apollo 13, April 13th 1970).

chisel a gargoyle *v.* To *hammer your nail* into a *ten pinter* in the grounds of a religious establishment such as Salisbury Cathedral, York Minster or St George's Church, Unsworth, Bury. To pick a location entirely at random.

choad *n.* A *cock*, specifically one that is wider than it is long.

chocnose *v.* A traditional end of party trick whereby a guest drops his trousers and rubs his *arse* on the nose of a comatose friend for the amusement of the other guests. *'August 3rd. Opening night party for Cavalcade at The Savoy. Kit (Hassall), Gerty (Lawrence) and Fanny (Brice) were all in attendance. Ivor (Novello) passed out on the chaise longue after drinking far too much Bolly, and Jimmy (Clitheroe) chocnosed him, poor dear. How we laughed!'* (from *The Diary of Noel Coward*).

chocolate cha-cha *n*. Unlikely- sounding rooftop dance in the style of Dick Van Dyke, but performed by *chimney sweeps* of the *chocolate* variety.

chocolate chimney sweep *n*. A soot-covered man who is not interested in *rodding out* ladies' flues.

chocolate chip *n*. Special type of dark, shiny residue which is only found spattered on the bowls of the lavatories at international airports. *Chocolate chip* can only be removed using products which are so astringent that they can not be sold to the general public.

chocolate eclair *n*. A *Cleveland steamer*.

chocolate eye *n*. The *bronze eye, brass eye, red eye, brown eye*. The *bumhole*.

chocolate fountain *n*. A spectacular anal, upside-down firework ignited in the lavatory to celebrate having a belly full of beer and a dodgy curry the night before.

chocolate iceberg *n*. Giant *turd* sitting in the pan, nine tenths of which remains below the surface. A *growler*.

chocolate knob, to have a *v*. Of a fortunate fellow, to experience little or no difficulty in persuading ladies to perform *horatio*.

chocolate quilting *n*. The considerate public lavatory practice of covering a floating *Bullimore* with a duvet of toilet tissue so as to avoid startling the next occupant.

chocolate sandwich *n*. A sexual act performed in the presence of Arthur Lowe in the film *Oh Lucky Man!* involving a black man and two white lady strippers.

chocolate speedway *n*. *Bumhole, poop chute*.

chocolate speedway rider *n*. Purple-helmeted star of the *dirt track*.

chocolate starfish *n*. *Rusty sheriff's badge, Bovril bullet hole*. The *clackervalve*.

chocolate thunder *n*. *Tail winds*, a *trouser typhoon*. Also *under thunder*.

chocolate wink *n*. A gentleman's cheeky treat for the special lady in his life whereby, when exiting the shower, he bends forward, reaches back and parts his buttocks, momentarily exposing his *bronze eye*.

chod bin *n*. The lavatory bowl.

chodder *n*. *Knob cheese*. Also *helmetdale, brimula, fromunda, Fred Leicester, Lymeswold* etc.

chod hop *v*. To move with increasing desperation from cubicle to cubicle in a municipal *crapper*, searching for an acceptable toilet to use, *ie*. One which is not covered in diarrhoea, has no *piss* on the seat, has a lock on the door *etc*.

chod's law *n*. The immutable axiomatic principle which states that, after you have waited in eight hours for a home delivery, the driver is guaranteed knock on the door at the precise moment you sit down and start to *drop the kids off at the pool*. Unless he's from Initial City-Link, in which case he won't bother knocking. Or even leaving a card.

choir of angels *n*. A cloud-parting zephyr of heavenly *wind* that rises in pitch, timbre and volume, bringing a lump to the throat and a tear to the eye.

choke a brown dog *v*. To apply the *bum brake* too early. To nip a *shite* halfway through.

choke out, got the *euph.* Slow to sparkle the morning after a night of unseemly alcohol consumption. *Flooded.* *'You won't get much sense out of Judy this morning. She's still got the choke out.'*

choke the chicken *v.* To masturbate.

choke the goose *v.* To masturbate again.

cholesterol special *n.* A Byronic breakfast, *ie.* One that is "swimming in grease".

chommie *n.* The *barse.*

chooza *n.* NZ. A *choad.*

choozies *n.* Aus. Breasts.

chop *v.* To *wallop your wood*, practise karate whilst holding a weapon in the hand. To *turn Japanese.*

chopper 1. *n.* Penis. *'That (insert name of striker currently having a run of bad form) couldn't score in a brothel with a £50 note wrapped round his chopper.'* 2. *n.* Fancy orange bike that fat kids owned in the 1970s. 3. *n.* Helicopter. 4. *n.* Axe. 5. *n.* Nickname of anyone with the surname Harris.

choreplay *n.* Tiresome pre-sex ritual required by selfish women. *Frigmarole.*

chortlies *n.* The sort of *Confessions* film-style *top bollocks* that are guaranteed to bring a smile to a passing chap's face, result in a vicar/hedge cycling incident or cause an ambulance driver to spit out his pastie.

chorus from Mama Jo's bongos *n.* An early morning *fart* that sounds like someone from *Scooby Doo* running on the spot before scarpering from the ghost. *Morning thunder.*

Christmas 1914 *euph.* A period of unnatural calm and tranquility between the beginning of something and the moment when the full horror of what has been set in motion becomes apparent. The *grace period* between the consumption of a hot meal and the inevitable bloody trauma that ensues.

Christmas spirit *n.* An essentially altruistic approach to oral sex adopted by generously-inclined ladies. *'Henry rather liked his new bird as she displayed the Christmas spirit in abundance, noshing him off three times a day and never asking for anything in return.'*

chrome-dome *n.* Slap head, baldy.

chubasaurus *n.* A large *pant pointer.* A mammoth *dobber.*

chubblies *n.* A fat *bird's choozies.*

chubby bullet, take the *v.* To distract and occupy the *lettuce-averse* mate of a fit *bird* your friend is attempting to chat up. To act selflessly, like a soldier who throws himself on a grenade to save his comrades, or a CIA agent who dives into the path of an assassin's bullet. *'Thanks for taking the chubby bullet, mate.'*

chubby checker *n.* A pornographic film-set technician responsible for monitoring and maintaining the leading man's state of penisular tumescence. A *fluffer.* *'Cut! Either we've got the wrong lens on or Gunther's losing string. Quick, somebody fetch the chubby checker out the bookies.'*

chubby dart, throw a *v.* To get a ladyfriend to drink several pints of beer and then *toss off* your *bendy bully* whilst kneeling in front of you. More accomplished *chubby dart* throwers can do it with a crafty thumb and three fingers just like Eric Bristow.

chuck flick *n.* An artistic cinematographic production that eschews plot and dialogue in favour of action, *eg. European Cum-Bath 26.* A *stick vid,* a *grumble flick.*

chuckle brother *1. n.* Either of the male participants in a *spit roast*. From the children's TV comedy northerners' catchphrase "To you, to me". *2. n.* Of two men engaged in a simultaneous romantic dalliance with a young lady, the act of passing her back and forth between them. *'Tell you what, Supersonic, let's phone Pat Coombs and see if she fancies a quick chuckle brother in the Blue Peter Italian Sunken garden.'*

chuckle vision n. The stirring view of rolling *cuntryside* experienced whilst taking a breather during an act of *cumulonimbus* on a fat lass.

chuck out special *n.* Large quantities of leftover fried chicken that have been sweating all day, which are available for next to no money from USA Fried Chicken in Witney, Oxfordshire at around 2am.

chuck salt *v.* The consequences of masturbating again, after already masturbating oneself dry.

chuck up *v.* To vomit, *honk up, barf.*

chuck your muck *v.* To *lose your mess, spend your wad, tip your filthy concrete.* To ejaculate.

chuckies *n.* Balls.

chucky cheese *n.* Vomit-inducing tangy cheddar matured in unwashed *brims.*

chudleighs *n. Chuds, chebs, charlies, charms, chichis, choozies.* Ladies' *tits.*

chuff *1. v.* To *pass wind, shoot a bunny rabbit.* *'Oops! Best open a window vicar. I'm about to chuff.'* *2. n.* Vagina, lady's *front bottom.* *3. n. zoo.* A parsimonious *anus,* usually of a gnat.

chuffage *n.* coll. A *rats' banquet, bangers and mash, Radcliffe's sleepers.* Railway track faecal detritus.

chuff chowder *n.* A pungent soup served

as a first course when *dining at the Y.* Hopefully without croutons.

chuff mountain *n.* A surfeit of *cabbage* at a party.

chuff muncher *n.* A *woman in comfortable shoes* with a penchant for chowing down on other ladies' *Jacky Dannies.*

chuff-nuts *n. Dangleberries.*

chuffdruff *n. Muffdruff.* Residual flakes of desiccated *mess* and *fanny batter* found on the *mapatasi.* Pubic equivalent of *mammary dandruff.*

chufflink *n.* A piece of over-elaborate *clitoral* ironmongery of the sort often sported by loose women in *bongo vids.*

chuftie plug *n. Cotton pony.* Tampon.

chug *v.* To *choke the chicken, spank the monkey, burp the worm.*

chugg boots *n.* Ersatz sheepskin-style footwear as worn by members of the lower orders.

chugger *n.* A clipboard-wielding charity collector who stalks Britain's pavements wearing a luminous bib and relieving passers by of their valuables, loose change, spare time *etc.* From charity + mugger.

chugnuts *n.* Extremely big piles. *'A cushion, Mrs Bennet, a cushion! I fear the frivolities at Lady Marchmain's ball have brought down my chugnuts no end.'* (from *Pride and Predudice,* by Jane Austen).

chumbawumbas *onomat.* A rather predictable use of a pop group's name as slang for breasts. Other examples of this phenomenon are; *Bananaramas* (penises), *Wurzels* (testicles) and *Bee Gees* (hairy twats).

chumblies *n. medic. Nuts, knackers, clockweights.*

chum bucket *1. n.* Underwater burger restaurant in the children's cartoon series *Spongebob Squarepants*, which is in competition with Bikini Bottom's other sub-aquatic fast food outlet the Krusty Krab. 2. *n.* A lady's *snatch* with all the aromatic qualities of a pail of live fish bait.

chumley warning 1. *n.* The signal a gentleman gives to a fussy *nosher* to tell her that *Elvis is about to leave the building.* 2. *n.* The signal a lady gives to a *nosher* to warn him that she is about to *step on a frog.*

chunder *v. Aus.* To *chunk, shout soup.*

chunderbirds *n.* Binge-drinking teenage girls full to the brim with *tart fuel* and screwtop wine, who stagger around parks and town centres vomiting and crying. *'It's seven pm on a Friday and Chunderbirds are GO!'* (voiceover from Police surveillance video footage of Chappelfield Park, Norwich on Fair night).

chunk *v.* To vomit. Also chunder, *blow chunks.*

Churchill *n.* A *bum cigar* of such monstrous dimensions that, when it finally makes its way through the London sewage system and proceeds to travel down the River Thames at funereal pace, it causes all the cranes in the East End to lower their arms in sorrow at its passing.

Churchill bulldog 1. *n.* An ugly, overweight *10-pinter.* After her resemblance to the TV insurance advert canine. 2. *n.* A girl who loves to say "Oh, yus" in the back of a car.

churchilling *n.* Nodding in agreement and pleasure whilst shouting the phrase "yus!" like a cross between Arthur Mullard and Derek Guyler, for example

whilst being *ministered to* by the missus. From the loose-necked motor insurance company advert computer-generated parcel shelf pitbull.

churns 1. *n.* Breasts. 2. *n.* Testicles. 3. *n.* Seemingly any vessel containing white fluid.

chutney Chuckle brother *n.* A *dirty Sanchez.* Also *Stinky Selleck.*

chutney ferret *n.* A *chocolate speedway rider.*

chutney locker *n. medic.* The *bomb bay*, the rectum. Also *date locker.*

cidercafe *n.* A town centre bench or war memorial from which *ciderspace* can be accessed.

ciderdown *n.* A *piss*-stained duvet used to keep an *apple-happy* gentleman of the road or bag lady warm in a shop doorway.

cidersense *n.* Superhuman state of enhanced mental acuity experienced as a consequence of drinking White Lightning or Frosty Jack.

ciderspace *n.* A virtual multidimensional world inhabited by tramps.

cider terrorism *n.* Unlawful attacks and threats of attack against fellow drinkers at the end of a long sesh on the 'bow.

cider visor *n.* Fruit-based *beer goggles* for the younger street drinker.

cigarbutts *n.* JCB starter buttons, blind cobblers' thumbs, Bruce Lees.

cigar clipper 1. *n.* An exceptionally tight *clopper.* A *mouse's ear*, a *paper cut.* 2. *n.* The *nipsy.*

circle jerk *n.* A communal *hand shandy* session. A *milk race, daisy chain, auld lang syne.*

cistern chapel *n.* The porcelain font where *Meatloaf's daughter* is baptised.

clabby *adj.* Exceptionally pink. Used to

describe *bacon strips*. '*Fuck me, love. You've got some clabby bacon strips on you, I'll give you that. And I've seen a few cunts in my time, what with being a consultant gynaecologist and obstetrician.*'

clacker 1. *n*. One half of a dangerous, finger-breaking 1970s toy. 2. *n*. The *fanny*. 3. *n. coll. Blart, tussage, mackerel*. 4. *n*. Fifty percent of the contents of the *clackerbag*.

clackerbag *n*. A leathery receptacle for *clockweights*.

clacker lacquer *n. medic*. Shameful secretion from the *blip tap* up a lady's *snapper. Love juice, moip, fanny lube, bilp, parsley sauce*.

clackervalve *n*. The *nipsy*, the *ringpiece*, the *arsehole*. '*Porphyria was powerless to resist. His eyes burned into hers like sapphires. His muscular arms enfolded her body as she felt herself being swept away in a whirlwind of passion. Tenderly, Sven lay her down on the ottoman, whipped off her scads and stuck his thumb up her clackervalve.*' (from *The Lady and the Football Manager* by Barbara Cartland).

clacker whacker *n*. Any hand-held, anatomically-formed object used by a woman to relieve stress. A *neck massager*.

clackweed *n*. Perennial pubic hair.

Clacton chinwag *n*. The oral intercourse that takes place between a man and a kneeling woman who has had a couple of bottles of *tart fuel*. A *blow job*.

clad the impaler *v*. To don a *jubber ray*.

clagnet *n*. A net-like tangle of *arse cress* which forms over the *freckle*, leading to a sensation similar to that felt when one defecates through a pair of fishnet tights. One would imagine.

clagnuts *n. Dangleberries, tagnuts. Miniature heroes*.

Claire Goosebumps *n*. Smashing *Gert Stonkers* of the type sported by the popular former *Casualty* actress. *Tits* which are capable of "*Waking the Dead*".

clamateur *n*. A clumsy, naive male who is inexperienced in the workings of the fairer sex's *farmyard apparatus*. A *batterfingers*. '*Honestly Jet, it was nothing. He had no idea what he was doing down there. He was a total clamateur.*'

clam bunting *n*. Ladies' lacy intimate apparel. '*Oh bugger. Someone's nicked me clam bunting off the line again.*'

clamchop *n*. The tasty cut of fish-like mutton found in a lady's knickers.

clamdruff *n*. The dried *jitler, fanny batter* and general downstairs effluvium and detritus that accumulates around the *bodily treasure* of a lady who is less than attentive in the ablutionary department. *Pornflakes, chuffdruff*.

clam dunk *n*. A spectacular shot at the *furry hoop*. A *break for the border*.

clamembert *n*. Female equivalent of *helmetdale. Fanny cheese*.

clam jousting *n*. A *fur-bumping* encounter between two *scissor sisters* afflicted with lesbism. Also *velcro fastening*.

clamouflage *n*. Thick, impenetrable *bush* which makes the target impossibly hard to spot at first glance. The *pubes* on a *biffer*.

clam ram *n*. A *gut stick, cock, cheesepipe*.

clam shandy *n*. A lady's version of a *hand shandy*. A few scales on the *invisible banjo*.

clam smacker *n*. A *bean flicker*.

clank *v*. To *relax in a gentleman's way* over a *site of special interest* along the information superhighway. From click + wank. *'Gaw! That sounds fucking filthy. Three jizz-hungry birds going good on one guy, I'm gonna go clank that, just as soon as I can find my credit card. Meanwhile, over to Daniel Corbett for tomorrow's weather.'*

clankers *n. onomat.* The same as *clinkers*, only louder.

clap, the *n. medic.* Any sexually transmitted disease, but usually gonorrhoea. Or syphilis. *Cock rot.*

clapometer *n.* Imaginary medical instrument used by doctors to diagnose the *clap. 'Don't touch her. I hear she scores ten on the clapometer.'*

clap oneself in on the home straight *v.* To spurt to victory by a short neck in a *milk race.*

clappers 1. *n.* In *farting*, the buttocks. *'Christ! That one didn't half rattle the clappers.'* 2. *n.* That part of a bell like which a sexually enthusiastic lady *goes.*

clapping fish *n.* Female genitalias.

Clapton *n.* A nicely-paced *Jodrell*, such as a gent might enjoy when his wife is out for the evening, or in hospital. After eponymous plank-spanker Eric's nickname "Slowhand". *'It was a normal Thursday night, your Honour. The missus had gone out with the girls so I put Jenna Jameson on the video, opened the hand cream and settled down for a Clapton.'*

Clara Dawes *n.* An extremely hairy *mott.* A *Judith*. From the *parts* of the actress playing the part of Clara Dawes in the recent TV adaptation of *Sons and Lovers.*

claret mouse *n.* A *Dracula's tea bag.* A spent *jamrag.*

Clarkson's cock *n.* Anything small, based on the commonly-held assumption that men, such as the out-spokenly irreverent, curly-topped motorhead petrol-mouth *Top Gear* presenter, only feel the need to drive round in big-engined sports cars in order to mask some deficiency in their *trouser departments. 'You couldn't even swing Clarkson's cock in here.'*

clarts *n.* Tacky excrement, such as would cling to the lavatory bowl above the water line rather than slip below the surface.

clarty goalmouth *n.* A *muff* one could lose a boot in.

Clattenburg *n.* Heavily-edited hardcore pornography *ie.* Where it obviously *goes in*, but you don't see it. Named after the hapless referee in the famous 2005 Mendes goal incident, where it obviously went in, but he didn't see it. Also known, since the 2010 World Cup Finals, as a *Mauricio Espinosa*, after the hapless linesman in the England/Germany match.

clatter *v.* To *pleasure* a lady, esp. from behind. *'I'd love to spend a minute or two clattering into the back of that.'*

claw, the *n.* The bizarre contortions of a semen-covered hand that a fellow is forced to employ in order to avoid spilling any *splinkle* onto his mum's soft furnishings whilst making his way to the toilet following a successful bout of *self help.*

claypit *n.* Source of the raw material for making *coil pots.* The *arse.*

cleach *n.* The small strip of skin between a *bird's front bottom* and her *back bottom*. Scientifically referred to as the *taint, tinter, carse, snarse, Niftkin's bridge, clutch* or *biffon,* but more crudely called the perineum.

clean and jerk *1. n.* Standard sort of weightlifting method, also sometimes known as the clean and press. *2. n.* Seizing the opportunity for a spot of *self improvement* whilst taking a bath. *Waxing the dolphin, polishing the lighthouse, up periscope, burping the sea slug.*

clean behind the curtains *v.* To perform thorough *cumulonimbus* on a young lady's floppy *bits and pieces*.

clean the au pair's teeth *v.* To receive the oral sex.

clean the guttering *v.* Following a post-*Ruby Murray* downpour, to pay extra attention to the process of wiping the *nipsy*.

cocoa channel *n.* The *wrong 'un*.

clean up on aisle two *exclam.* That second visit to the *shitter*, about ten minutes after a somewhat softish *download*, when you realise that more wiping of the *marmite pot* is needed. A situation that is often announced over the tannoy in supermarkets.

clean workspace *n.* A shaven *fanny*.

clear the custard *v.* To have a long overdue *hand shandy*. *'I've got ten minutes before I have to take mass. I'll just nip upstairs and clear the custard.'*

clear your scroat *v.* To relieve oneself of a viscous build-up by means of a tactical *wank*. *'What are you doing in there Cliff? You're going to be late for Una.' 'I'll be out in a moment, Bruce. I'm just clearing my scroat.'*

cleaverage *n.* A self-advancement strategy utilised by *well-qualified* women; the use of their *competitive advantages* to put themselves into more advanageous positions. *'Having suffered a downturn in her finances, Carol used her considerable powers of cleaverage to negotiate a drink at the bar.'*

clems *n.* The *clockweights, swingers, nads, cods.* Testicles.

Cleveland steamer *1. n.* A merchant cargo vessel operating on Lake Erie. *2. n.* A sexual act much favoured by your average Teuton that doesn't bear thinking about. A *chocolate eclair.*

cliffclangers *n.* Heavy, swollen *bollocks, eg.* The sort that might be owned by an ageing Christian rock and roll singer who has yet to find the right girl. *Cliffhangers.*

cliff Richard *n.* An *al fresco turd* which is discreetly deposited over the edge of a bank.

climb on *v.* The culmination of a romantic evening. *'Lavinia was powerless to resist. His eyes burned into hers like rubies. His strong arms enfolded her tender body as she felt herself being swept away on a tidal wave of passion. Then he dropped his trolleys and climbed on.'* (from *The Lady and the Gentleman* by Barbara Cartland).

clinkers *n. onomat. Aus.* Tenacious particles of feculant welded onto the *arse spider's* legs; *toffee strings, winnets, kling-ons, dangleberries, bum conkers.*

clint *n.* The fibrous flotsam, jetsam, effluvium and detritus that inevitably gets caught in the labyrinthine recesses of a lady's *clown's pocket.*

clit bang *n.* Generic feminine hygiene product, *eg.* Sprunt, Febreze, Toilet Duck *etc.*

clit car *n.* A once desirable motor vehicle that has been rendered undesirable as a consequence of its own popularity, *eg.* The Subaru Impreza, them Minis or the Fiat 500. From the fact that, like a *clematis*, "every *cunt's* got one".

clit and run *n.* A light-hearted indecent assault whereby one makes a playful grab for *Captain Caveman's nose* followed by a swift getaway into the crowd.

cliterati *n.* A dazzling array of *grumble vid* starlets. Perhaps attending some sort of *bongo* convention on the Bravo channel.

cliterature *n.* One-handed reading matter.

clitler *n.* A fashionable *downstairs* moustache, as seen on female *grumble* artistes who leave a daft little tuft. A *toothbrush muff, mufftache, muffgabe.*

clitmus test *n.* The various fondlings, fiddlements and gropages undertaken by a conscientious chap in order to establish whether his ladyfriend is ready for him to *slam in the lamb*. A *Bolton dip test.*

clitoris allsorts *n.* The array of delicacies on display in the windows along a typical Amsterdam street.

clitty litter *n.* Vaginal flotsam and jetsam in the *drip tray* of a lady's *dunghampers*.

clivanus anvaclit technique *n.* The semi-skilled action of tonguing a lady's *clematis, bodily treasure* and *back body* in one smooth, continuous motion, and then performing the same erotic trifecta in reverse. *'Make £££s performing the clivanus anvaclit technique on bored housewives. I can show you how!'* (advertisement for the Buster Bloodvessel School of Oral Sex, Margate in the *International Herald Tribune*, August 1986).

cloacal chords *n.* The organs of anal speech which are located in the *nether throat* and occasionally, particularly after a visit to the Curry Capital, Bigg Market, Newcastle upon Tyne, manage to achieve a high falsetto which could shatter a crystal wine glass or drive a collie dog mad.

clock *n.* One who swings like a pendulum do. A *happy shopper*, a *switch hitter*, one who is *half rice half chips*. *'Birthdays: David Bowie - musician, artist, film actor and right fucking clock, 55.'* (*The Times*, 8th Jan 2002).

clock springs *n.* Very strong, curly pubic hairs usually spotted on the *clockweights* or coiled tightly around the top of the *belltower*. Often found stuck onto bars of soap.

clockweights *n.* Large, metal, adjustable testicles that have to be *cranked* at least once every eight days.

clodge *n.* The *spadger*.

clodger *n.* A female tenant who defrays part of her rent by sub-letting her *clodge* to her landlord. Or, for that matter, in these modern times of lesbians and equal opportunities and what-not, her landlady.

clogmaker's hammer, arse like a *sim.* Descriptive of the buttocks of a 33rpm gentleman who appears to be *banging* his *old boot* at 78.

clopper *n.* A romantic term for the female genitalia. *'Ocarina was powerless to resist. His eyes burned into hers like topazzes. His strong arms enfolded her body as she felt herself being swept away on a hailstorm of passion. 'Take me, Abdul, take me', she gasped. 'I'm fizzing at the clopper''.* (from *The Dowager and the Sheik* by Barbara Cartland).

clop slop *n. Moip, blip, fanny batter, sloom, trawler's bilge, parsley sauce, clacker lacquer, crème de la femme, girlpop, jungle juice, vagoline, beef dripping etc.*

close the deal *v.* To *scuttle* a *bird*.

close to his mother *euph.* Of a fellow, *sensitive, good with his hands* or *style conscious*. Not to put too fine a point on it, *light on his feet*.

close-up pink *n.* Medically-explicit *clabby cliterature*. Erotica that wouldn't look out of place in a gynaecology textbook.

closing time donner *n.* A well-worn *grotter* that looks like a rushed and messily-prepared Turkish cat sandwich. *'Lady Emma was powerless to resist. His eye burned into hers like a marble. His muscular arm enfolded her body as she felt herself being swept away in a gale of passion which measured a good five on the Beaufort wind force scale. She felt a thrill of forbidden pleasure as the Admiral pulled down her bloomers. 'Take me, Fellatio,' she cried. 'Take me now!' 'Bloody hell, love,' said Lord Nelson, peering at her fanny through the wrong end of his brass telescope. 'What have you been up to whilst I've been away at sea engaging Napoleon's war fleet at Aboukir Bay in the Battle of the Nile? Your blurtch looks like a closing time donner.''* (from *The Wife of the Ageing British Envoy and the 18th century Naval Hero* by Barbara Cartland).

clot mops *n.* Feminine napkins. *Dangermice.*

cloth tit *n.* The least far a gentleman can get in a sexual encounter with a lady. *Outside tops. 'Did you fuck her?' 'No, I only got my cloth tit.'*

clout *1. n. Clunge. 2. n.* South African lesbian rock band.

cloven hoof *n. Camel's foot, camel's mouth, camel's lips.* In fact, any part of a camel. *'Did you see Madonna at Live Earth? I was right at the back of the sta-*dium and I couldn't get a view of the big screen, but even I could see her cloven hoof. And I've got cataracts.'*

clown car *n.* Stuffing your *Johnson and the boys* into your ladyfriend's mouth, so that steam comes out of her nose and her ears fall off.

clowns' buckets, spunk *v.* Of single gentlemen who have spent the day *challenging themselves* repeatedly, to eventually conjure forth nothing more than a wince upon ejaculation.

clown's flower *n.* Amusing phenomenon that occasionally occurs when a fruity gentleman ventures *down south* for a spot of *funny fingers* and *cumulonimbus on his ladyfriend* and he accidentally stimulates her *magic bean*, causing her to *piss* in his face in the style of a circus funnyman's booby-trapped buttonhole.

clown's hat *n.* A *bald man in a boat*. A *clematis* with all wallpaper paste shooting out of the top of it.

clown's pie *n.* A very, very wet *clodge. 'Finding ourselves alone in the shooting lodge at Balmoral, Her Majesty bade me descend to her ladygarden. After fifty years of widowhood, I found her to be be considerably aroused. It was like being hit in the face with a clown's pie.'* (from *The Memoirs of Queen Victoria's Ghillie* by John Brown).

clown's pocket *sim.* To describe the bigger, baggier and perhaps yellow and red checkered vagina. *'May I introduce my wife, Your Worship? She has a fanny like a clown's pocket.'*

clown's smile *n.* Facial make-up donned when performing at the *red ring circus. Mexican lipstick, pasata grin.*

clubbed seal, raw as a *sim.* The state of a

bird's nether pelt after she's been *banged* senseless with a substantial *giggle stick*.

cludger *n.* A lower class lady from the north west of England, specifically Bolton.

cludgy *n. Shite house*, lavatory, *thunderbox*.

clump *n. coll. Blart, fanny, tussage. 'I tell you what, Mother Superior, this place is absolutely fucking crawling with clump.'*

clumper *n.* The *nipsy, clackervalve, cigar cutter*.

clumsy beekeeper, face like a *sim.* Descriptive of a lady with a *lovely personality*. She who has a mug like a *stripper's clit*.

clunge *n.* A *clout*, a *furry hoop, hairy goblet*.

clusterfuck *1. n.* A group of people unable to make a simple decision, *eg.* Friends standing on a pavement outside a pub wondering where to eat, or a group of PC World salesmen on a team-building course trying to construct a raft out of oil drums, planks and rope. *2. n.* A *gang bang*.

clutch *n.* The piece of skin between the anus and the vagina. So called because it works like its namesake component on a car, *ie.* It helps you to hit the right *hole*. The *carse, tinter, notcher, Humber Bridge etc*.

clutteris *n.* A lady's *on-switch* surrounded by so much knotted hair that you can't find it when you want it.

coal hole *n.* Any grubby little aperture around the back of something. A popular entry point for burglars and tradesmen.

coal scuttle, polish the *v.* To indulge in a foul act of *self-pollution, bleed the hydraulic system, stab the cat etc.* To have a *wank. 'Bless me holy father, for I have sinned. On Friday, I committed the sin of envy when my brother bought himself some new shoes. On Saturday I committed the sin of sloth when I fell asleep during the qualifying session for the Grand Prix. Then this morning I'm ashamed to say I had impure thoughts about polishing the coal scuttle over the bra pages of the Freeman catalogue.' 'Sorry my son, what was that again? I was just busy polishing the coal scuttle over the bra pages of the Freeman catalogue.'*

coat hangers *n.* Large erect *nipples* that can double up as an emergency car aerial.

cob on *n.* A foul temper, usually displayed by *werecows*. A *blob strop*.

cobblers *ryhm. slang. Bollocks.* From cobbler's awls = balls.

cobs *n. Nads, pills, pods.* Testicles. *'Ooyah! Go and fetch a cloth our Ashley. I've caught me cobs, I say me cobs, in the bacon slicer again.'*

coccupied *adj.* Of a desirable woman, to already have a boyfriend. *'Phwooar, I really fancy that Sienna Miller. If she wasn't already coccupied and if I didn't have another 60 hours of my community service nightshift at the offal plant to go, I'd be up her like a rat up a drainpipe, I'm telling you.'*

cock *1. n.* Penis, *willy, knob. 2. n.* A person to whom a chirpy cockney wishes to speak, often prefixed by "Wotcha..." *3. n.* A gentleman chicken. *4. v.* Something that you can do to a snook. *5. n. Yorks.* The hardest kid in the school, usually a self-appointed position.

cock-a-doodle-poo *n.* The *shit* that, needing to come out, wakes you up in the morning. *Alarm cack.*

cock-a-fanny *n.* The act of hiding one's *wedding tackle* between one's legs to give the appearance of having female genitals. Popularised by Captain Sensible, the murderer out of *The Silence of the Lambs* and East German female shotputters of the 1970's.

cock-a-hoop 1. *adj.* The metaphysical state of mind produced by advantageous circumstances. *'I just won a million on a scratchcard. I'm cock-a-hoop.'* 2. *adj.* The state of one fellow who is engaged in an act of *brown love* with another. *'I just managed to get my glans up your nipsy. Frankly, I'm cock-a-hoop.'*

cock block *n. Shag slab, wanking chariot,* bed. *'I wouldn't mind lying that on me cock block.'*

cock book *n.* Literature which encourages a chap to whip up a quick *cheese-based white sauce.*

cockbuster *n.* A video shop, or indeed work colleague, specialising in the commercial hiring of *grumble vids.*

cockchops *n. pej.* A pernicious, malicious, seditious fool. A *fuckwit,* an idiot. *'Armstrong: 'That's one small step for man, one giant leap for mankind.' (Beep) Aldrin: 'Oi, cockchops. That should have been "one small step for A man." I knew they should of let me go fog out the rocket.''* (from NASA transcript of Apollo 11 mission, 1969).

cock clamp *n.* A *'v' clamp,* a *mouse's ear.* A tight *muff.*

cock collar *n.* The *fiveskin.*

cock doily *n.* Something worn as a fashion accessory by an over-dressed, affected, foppish twat, *eg.* Them flouncy cuffs that dangle out the end of Laurence Llewellyn-Bowen's sleeves.

cock drops *n. Blueys.* Viagras.

cock duster *n.* A handlebar moustache sported by the sort of leather-clad *Village People*-style *bad throwers* who people Richard Littlejohn's explicitly graphic nightmares each night. Also *scrotum tickler.*

cock eggs *n. medic. Clems, swingers, clockweights. Testicles.* Also *knob eggs.* *'Vasectomy is a simple, routine procedure. The surgeon makes a small inscision in the scrotal sac, through which he severs the cock eggs from their clacker strings. All this is carried out under a local anaesthetic.'* (Family Planning Leaflet, The Marie Stopes Foundation).

cockfest *n.* A pornographic film featuring quantities of *skinclad tube.*

cockfoster *v.* To lovingly nurture *half a teacake* until it becomes a full *stonk on,* perhaps whilst travelling in a crowded London Underground carriage.

cock had been caught by a fisherman, like his *sim.* Description of the buttock-clenched, pelvis-thrust-forwards way a chap sprints to the khazi during a sudden *shit rush.* *"Heathcliffe must have the runs again,' sighed Cathy. 'Only this morning I saw him running to the crapper like his cock had been caught by a fisherman."* (from *Wuthering Shites* by Charlotte Bronte).

cock hair *n.* Imperial unit of measurement used in engineering, equivalent to 2.32 *gnat's cods. 'It seems that the O-ring failed 45 seconds after take off, allowing a jet of superheated gas just a cock hair wide to penetrate the main solid fuel booster, leading to the loss of the Challenger.'* (NASA Official Accident Inquiry Report, 1987).

cock harp *n. medic.* Condition of the male

wedding vegetables whereby two or more pubic hairs become trapped in the brim of the *farmer's hat,* resulting in a tightly-strung scrotal guitar which plays at a pitch only audible to dogs and bats. Also known as a *foreharp* or *Frodo's banjo.* See also *Bobby Charltons.*

cock heavy *adj.* Descriptive of a drinking establishment blighted with a serious lack of *buffage.* Also *sword heavy.*

cock holster *n.* A romantic term for a lady's mouth. *'Felicity was powerless to resist. His eyes burned into hers like amethysts. His strong arms enfolded her tender body as she felt herself being swept away in a whirlwind of passion. Then, she knelt before him and he stuck his eight-inch charlie into her cock holster.'* (from *The Officer and the Gypsy Duchess* by Barbara Cartland).

cockidex *n.* Gloopy adhesive in a handy pump dispenser, which is nevertheless difficult to apply neatly. *Pyjama glue, sement, jazz glue, Aphrodite's evostick, gonad glue, prick stick, man mastic.*

cock in a top hat, sticking one's *v.* Unfulfilling *futtering* up a slack *snapper.* *'How was it for you, Mr Deayton?' 'Like sticking my cock in a top hat, you whore. Now slag off.'*

cocking her into it *v.* The gentleman's art of cajoling a lady with whom he is sharing a bed into coitus by means of persistent and relentless nudging and frottering. To annoy a woman with one's genitals so much that she eventually lets one *on the nest.* *'The missus told me she had a headache, but I managed to cock her into it anyway.'*

cockjaw *n.* The open-mouthed expression adopted by porn queens after they've quaffed a gobful of *manpop.*

cock knocker *n.* A gentleman who *bangs* at the *back door.*

cock knot *n.* The machine head of the *one stringed banjo,* the *frenum.*

cockless pair *n.* A particularly athletic-looking lesbian couple.

cock lodger *n.* An idle man who persuades a gullible single mum to let him move in and sit on her sofa all day watching DVDs in exchange for the odd *scuttling.*

cock mess monster *1. n.* A *grumble flick* actress, transformed by a small fortune in *money shots.* A *plasterer's radio. 2. n.* A cryptozoological beast occasionally sighted floating round the bath after *playing up periscope.*

cock monkey *1. n.* A lady who does a lot of jumping about, squealing and general circus-like activity in the *fart sack,* especially when presented with a banana. *2 n.* A film set technician who keeps the gentleman lead thespian erect during set changes, drug runs, *spunk* mopping *etc.* A *fluffer.*

cock moss *n.* The cobwebby bryophytes which slowly grow on fallow, fallen *wood.*

cockney *1. n.* A pearly-buttoned, colourfully-opinionated person born within the sound of Big Ben, who either drives a taxi or sells fruit on a market. *2. n.* A person of indeterminate gender. From cock + fanny.

cock nostril *n.* A term for the *Jap's eye* which can be used by the more politically correct.

cocknuckle *n.* The sixth knuckle, that always comes at the top of the deck in a *five knuckle shuffle.* The *glans.*

cockofadge *n.* A very butch woman, or possibly a slightly effeminate man. *'Did* *you see that, Tommy? Couldn't tell if it had a cock or fadge.'*

cock off *v.* To suspend one's working day in order to enjoy a protracted recess of *gentlemanly relaxation*. *'Fiona, where's Huw gone? He's supposed to be reading the closing headlines in three minutes.' 'I'm sorry, Sophie. I think he cocked off during the local news.'*

cockoholic *n.* One who is addicted to cockohol. *'Mate of mine used to work as a roadie for Abba. Reckoned that blonde bird was a fucking cockoholic.'*

cock or ball? *n.* Name of a game, similar to Hangman or I Spy, which can be used to pass the time during long train journeys, dull wedding services or interminable funerals, whereby the interlocutor requires their neighbour to identify a flap of nondescript skin poking through his trouser fly.

cock patience *n.* A solitary pursuit whereby one whiles away the hours with one's favourite *Gash 'n' Gary* mags arranged in a circle around oneself.

cockpit *n.* The piece of skin between the *devil's bagpipes* and the *German shepherd's winkhole*. The *barse*.

cock porridge *n.* A messy load of oats fired from the *porridge gun*.

cock puppet *n.* A petite lady. A *throwabout*.

cock rock *1. n.* A variety of popular music performed by *rock poodles* such as *Whitesnake, Van Halen etc. 2. n.* The substance that *knobs* are made of that is able to go from marshmallow limp to diamond hard at the thought of a pair of *tits*.

cock rot *n. medic.* VD, a *dose*.

cocksmith *1. n.* A tradesman skilled in the forging of lengths of *pink steel*. A

pornographic thespian. *'Today's birthdays: Boris Volynov, Soviet cosmonaut, 75; Robson Green, actor, 45; Benjamin Dover, cocksmith, 55.' 2. n.* One who is prone to *pulling his wire*. A *wanker*. *'Today's birthdays: Boris Volynov, Soviet cosmonaut, 75; Benjamin Dover, actor, 55; Robson Green, cocksmith, 45.'*

cocks in hands, put *phr.* An expression used by film directors and magazine editors hoping to widen their products' appeal to the male market. *'Okay Miss Cruz, Miss Johannsen, that's a wrap on the lez-up. Right, people, that ought to put cocks in hands. I suppose we'd better start working on a plot or something.'*

cock smock *n.* An old T-shirt laid across the stomach while *hand-jiving*, in order to catch any passing *spunks*. A *chapkin*.

cock smoker *n.* A lady who doesn't mind a puff on one's *Whitehouse cigar*. A *fellatrix*.

cock snot *n.* Semen, sneezed out of the *cock nostril*.

cock sucker *n.* A motorist who cuts you up.

cocksucker's doormat *n.* Facial hair growth favoured by the ageing male attempting to hide his jowls. A goatee beard, *bloatee*.

cock tease *n.* A woman who wears *fuck me shoes* and then changes into *fuck off slippers* when you get back to her place.

cocktoberfest *n.* Pejorative epithet that can be given to any *sausage-heavy* gathering. *'Fuck me, Dr Williams. This General Synod's a bit light on pussy, isn't it.' 'You can say that again, Bishop. It's like cocktoberfest in here.'*

cockumentary *n.* A serious-minded factual film exploring issues surrounding the adult entertainment industry broadcast at 11 o'clock on Bravo in order to educate and inform the viewers. While they *wank*. The sort of programme that should be sponsored by Kleenex. A *masturmentary, sockumentary, rudimentary*.

cockusoap *n*. A television serial drama, the cast of which contains a disproportionate amount of high quality *tussage, eg. Hollyoaks* but not *Last of the Summer Wine*.

cock venom *n*. *Spaff, spodge, spooge, etc. Spunk*.

cockwash *n*. The *punani*. See also *token for the cockwash, municipal cockwash. 'My charlie's absolutely filthy. I think I'll stick it through the cockwash on Sunday morning.'*

cockwasher *n*. A *fellatrix* who takes it *up to the back wheels*. A *deep throater*, a *pork sword* swallower. A woman with a *bollock goatee*.

cockwomble *n*. An easily-pleased male who is prone to wander, particularly around the common end of the market, in order that he might mingle with "the things that the everyday folks leave behind".

cockwood *euph*. Building trade argot for a six-inch length of timber which is customarily offered to the lady of the house by a labourer in the hope of gaining her favour. *'Where's Gary disappeared to?' 'Don't know, boss. Last time I seen him he was down by the skip gathering cockwood to light Mrs Clopper's fire.'*

cocoa channel? *phr. interrog*. Asked with one eyebrow raised. Ostensibly the sort of query that a charmer like Nigel Havers, Peter Bowles or Dean Gaffney might put to his ladyfriend about her perfume preferences, but which is in fact a subtle enquiry as to whether she takes it up the *council gritter*.

cocoa sombrero *n*. A Mexican *brown hatter*.

coco plops *n*. Pieces of post-curry *bowl fodder* that are "so chocolatey they turn the water brown". See also *rusty copper bolts*.

coco-pops *n*. *Winnets*, known briefly as Choco Krispies.

coconut husk *n*. In erotic photography and nude police work, the soft mound of *clocksprings* which becomes visible when a lady *assumes the position*.

coconut minge-mat *n*. Pubic hair you could wipe your feet on. A *welcome twat*.

cod *adj*. Extremely *Swiss*. Fucking rubbish. *Mouse*.

cod cove *n*. A *fish mitten*.

cods *n*. *Balls*. Often prefixed "a kick in the...".

cod's mouth *n*. The shaven *part* of a mature lady who is attempting to ape the appearance of a younger *piece down there*, such that it looks like the mouth off the lead singer of Aerosmith has been transplanted between her legs. See also *trout's mouth*.

cod's wetsuit, wetter than a *sim*. Descriptive of a woman's *bits and bobs* when she's *dripping like a fucked fridge*. Also *otter's pocket*.

coffee bean *n*. The back view of a dirty lady's *Gareth* as she bends over on all fours. *Coconut husk*.

coffee turtle *n*. The first *turd* of the day, powered on its way by the first cup of Nescafe of the day.

coffin-dodger *n*. Affectionate term for an

incontinent, elderly relative. An *oxygen thief*.

coilus interruptus *n. Lat.* Method employed by God to prevent the birth of *Meatloaf's daughter* whereby the Jehovah's Witnesses ring the doorbell just as you are laying the foundations of a *log cabin*.

coins of the realm *n.* Trouseral *piss spots* of various sizes sported by gentlemen leaving public house lavatories.

coitus binterruptus *n. Lat.* Any act of congress which is disturbed half-way through by the unexpected return of the *bag for life*.

Colchester condom *euph. milit.* Anal sex, *one up the bonus tunnel*, a phrase used by squaddies in the garrison town. *'Please be careful, Field Marshal'. 'Don't worry, sweet tits, I'll be using a Colchester condom when I meet you behind the skip.'*

cold starter *n.* When several abortive attempts must be made to have a *tom tit* before a satisfactory *cable* can be laid.

cold tea bag *n.* The feeling one gets in one's underpants a couple of minutes after a badly-diagnosed *trouser cough*.

colimbo *n.* That desolate time of day occurring in the afternoon and heralded by the appearance onscreen of Peter Falk's squint-eyed, dirty-raincoated supersleuth, when the jobseeker/person *working from home* realises that not only is there nothing new worth watching on Sky, but it's also as yet still too early to start drinking.

collagen biospheres *n. Knockers* which miraculously iron the wrinkles out of a fellow's *twig*.

collanders *n.* Ill-fitting underpants that may *strain one's vegetables*.

collar and cuffs *euph.* Matching hair colour, up top and down below. *'See that blonde? Do you reckon her collar matches her cuffs?'*

collect a debt *v.* To *beat your meat* like it owes you money.

collie's chest, fanny like a *sim.* Descriptive of the more hirsute ladygarden. *'This is the tale of Bertha Boot / Who's bought a brand new bathing suit / When she wears it in the water / You see things you didn't oughta / On the beach at Whitley Bay / Her knockers show up clear as day / But down below the view is best / Her fanny's like a collie's chest.'* (from *Odd Odes* by Cyril Fletcher).

colly wobbles *n.* The strange, unnerving feeling that one is being watched whilst having sex. Possibly by a *wanking* ex-Premiership footballer.

colon burger *n.* A *shit* weighing in at a quarter of a pound uncooked.

Colonel's revenge, the *euph.* Painful condition of the alimentary tract occasioning multiple visits to the *khazi* taken at extremely short notice. Usually experienced following consumption of one or more of the "KFC Zinger"-branded products which are offered on the menu of the popular high street fried chicken outlet.

colonsequences *n.* Blanket term for lower alimentary tract-related problems experienced as a result of over-indulgence. *'Christ, I had a skinful the night before the wedding. Tell you what, though, I was suffering the colonsequences the next day. I had to run off to the bog three times during the wedding service or else I would've shat meself. Sometimes I wonder if I'm really cut out to be a vicar, you know.'*

Columbian flush *n.* Tell-tale double or triple toilet evacuation procedure used by *showbiz sherbet* enthusiasts to conceal the preparation and consumption of their favourite powdery foodstuffs.

Columbian hay fever *n. medic.* Specific form of allergic rhinitis triggered by sensitivity to the pollen of the *Erythroxylum coca* plant. *Columbian hay fever* is chiefly characterised by symptoms such as red eyes and a runny nose, and is suffered to a disproportionate degree by people working in the advertising, music and children's television businesses.

Columbian oranges *n.* A refreshing line of *showbiz sherbet* enjoyed in the *bogs* at half time.

Columbo's coat *n.* A tatty and creased-up *fanny* that looks like an aged basset hound might use it for a bed. Not to be confused with a *Columbo's mac* which is, of course, a tatty and creased-up *fiveskin* that looks like an aged basset hound has spent the morning chewing it behind the sofa. *'Oops. I think my Columbo's mac has got caught in your Columbo's coat.'*

Columbo's mac *n.* A rumpled prepuce that is much too long for the *one-eyed bobby* it covers. *Delaney's overcoat.*

Colwyn Bay *1. n.* Welsh seaside resort famous for its multi-storey Morrisons and its elephant-less zoo. *2. rhym. slang.* Homosexual. *'This is your cellmate, Lord Archer. Try not to drop anything on the floor, only he's a bit Colwyn.'*

combo *n. One* in the *goo*, then *one* in the *poo*. To *pot the brown* after the *pink*, though not at the Crucible.

combover *n.* A *swope*.

combustoflatulation *n.* Anal flame-throwing. *Pyroflatulation, blue streak.*

come *1. v. Cum. 2. n. Cum.*

comedy Dave *n.* Vituperative epithet applied to someone or something who signally fails to radiate humour, *eg.* Fecal vomiting, IT consultants, photocopier repair men, Lord Sebastian Coe. Named after the assistant to Radio 1 fat *cunt* Chris Moyles. *'I was listening to that fat cunt Chris Moyles's radio show the other morning and I must say, his assistant comedy Dave is a right comedy Dave.'*

come in Tokyo *n.* Manipulating both a lady's breasts at the same time in the manner of a World War II radio operator. *Finding Radio Luxembourg.*

come like a bishop *sim.* Of a man, to ejaculate in an explosive style, as one would imagine a long-term celibate does every now and again.

come to bed pies *n.* Pastry-based foodstuffs presented to a fat lass in exchange for a *bunk up. Pork for pork.*

come to bunkbed eyes *n.* Miscollimated ocular organs; one of which is looking at you, whilst the other is looking for you.

comforts *n.* Casual visitors, because they just "come for t'day".

comfort wipe *n.* Having a quick *bumwad* swab at the *gammon ring* during a *stand up visit* to the water closet, just in case an earlier *Exchange & Mart* was *loaded*. An act that brings a certain peace of mind to the anxious wipee.

commercial shake *n.* An act of *self harm* carried out by a TV viewer during the ads, so as not to interrupt his appreciation of the programme. The volume of the transmission is helpfully increased during the adverts so that they can be heard from the toilet.

commercial sex *n.* An act of penetrative

congress enjoyed during the advertisement break in a television programme, usually the three-minute long intermission halfway through *Coronation Street.*

commission a ship *v.* To take a *dump,* from the spectacular splash caused when the prow of a freshly-launched *battleshit* hits the water.

committee shitty *n.* A *motion* that is seconded after the paperwork is complete. A *council dump.*

commodore *n.* A *bird* who is blessed with a *lovely personality,* but cursed with ravenous glands. From the fact that, in the words of the chart-topping 1978 song by Lionel Richie's semi-eponymous pop group, she is "once, twice, three times a lady".

community chest *n.* A pair of *charlies* that the whole estate has had a go on.

communting *n.* Choosing to live in an area within a convenient distance of a place where one confidently expects to find ugly women to *tup.* *'We are delighted to welcome to the market this deceptively delightful 1 bedroom studio flat which would make an ideal starter home for the single, semi-skilled gentleman, and is deceptively delightfully situated within easy communting distance of the Bigg Market. £95,000 ono.'*

competitive advantage *euph.* Big *tits, first impressions, qualifications,* high capacity *juggage. 'I know her criminal record, history of drug use and non-existent educational attainments perhaps count against her, but I felt as soon as she walked into the room that she had a competitive advantage over the other candidates.'*

compliments to the chef *n.* The drunken, unintelligible, Marlon Brando-style ramblings of a lucky woman immediately after she has completed a successful act of *horatio* on an accommodating gentleman friend.

compliment the chef *v.* To *drop one's guts* after a meal. Good manners in some countries and Humberside, but if in any doubt, it's probably best to check first with your host.

compose one's thoughts *euph.* Polite phrase often used by snooker commentators to describe the actions of players who leave the table in between frames. To defecate, take a *shit, drop the kids off at the pool, light a bum cigar, crimp one off etc. 'It's all square in the Embassy World Snooker Championship finals and you could cut the atmosphere here at the Crucible with a knife. And as referee Len Ganley prepares the table for the all-important deciding frame, Ray Reardon's just leaving the arena for a moment to compose his thoughts. Let's hope he washes his hands after he wipes his arse.'*

con *n. Fr.* Cunt, *fanoir.*

Conanism 1. *n.* The act of *wanking* oneself *off* so frequently that one develops a right arm like right wing, muscle-bound shit actor, execution-happy California State Governor and right *wanker* Arnold Schwarzenegger. 2. *n.* Pleasuring yourself, in an unspeakably barbaric way, *eg.* Whilst wearing a butcher's chain mail glove.

command module *n. Bell end,* glans, *bishop's mitre.*

con artiste *n. Fr.* A *cunning linguist, muff diver,* a *Jacky Danny Cousteau,* a *puba diver.*

concraptions *n.* The agonising stomach twinges experienced before giving birth to an *arse baby*. *'I'd best get to the khazi, love. My concraptions are only a minute apart and I'm three centimetres dilated.'*

concrete donkey *n*. A *horse's handbrake*, a *diamond cutter*.

conduct the ragtime band *v*. To wave one's *baton* in a rousing performance of the Russian national anthem when *Arsenal are playing at home*.

cones *n*. Pointy, orange, dayglo breasts found alongside the M25 or in Madonna's vest.

cones are out *euph*. A warning that there is only one lane in use. *Blow job week*.

conflatulations *n. interj*. A term of praise accorded one by one's friends after one has *stepped on* a spectacular *duck*.

congrafellation *n*. The act of giving a lucky lady an appreciative pat on the head after she has performed a decent *blowjob*.

congress tart *n*. Pastry-based confection with a layer of raspberry jam and a moist coconut topping.

conjaptivitis *n. medic*. Occlusion of the male urethral opening due to a deposit of ossified *spangle*.

conkers *n*. See *hairy conkers*.

conkers deep *adj*. To be in a state of total intromission. *In up to the back wheels, in up to the maker's nameplate*.

conker water *n*. *Spangle, spooge, spadge, gunk*.

consider it licked *exclam*. A *sotto voce* compliment paid to an attractive young lady one has just clapped eyes on in the street, nightclub or a railway carriage *etc*.

constipation constellation *n*. The situation whereby one has to bear down with such force on a breached *dreadnought* that one sees stars.

continental breakfast *n. milit*. The humorous squaddie's pastime of having a dig around in his *Marmite pot* before inscribing a *dirty Sanchez*-style moustache onto the top lip of a slumbering comrade. *'Quadrangle trench was somewhat shallow and left us exposed to enfilade fire from the woods to the South. Boothby had found a German shovel and spent the afternoon digging for all he was worth. By dusk he was exhausted by his efforts and fell thankfully into a deep sleep. Lieutenant Cholmondeley took the opportunity to give the poor fellow a splendid handlebar continental breakfast.'* (from *Memoirs of an Infantry Officer* by Siegfried Sassoon).

continental shelf *n*. Feature of foreigners' barbarian design *jobby engines*, providing a place in the *throne room* where one's *royal decrees* can pile up to be admired before being flushed away.

contraflow *n*. A spot of *backdoor work*, *ie*. Going against the prevailing traffic.

control alt delete *phr*. The amusing way in which an IT worker announces that he is about to *log out*. *'Where are you going, Iain?' 'I'm off to control alt delete.'*

convent porridge *n*. Hot, steaming *spunk* ladled out of a cauldron by a smiling Mother Superior. *Nuns' porridge, jizz*.

convict lenses *1. n*. Particularly high-powered version of *beer goggles*, as commonly worn by men who have recently been released following a prolonged period of incarceration at Her Majesty's Pleasure. Or, conversely, *2. n*. Metaphorical astigmatic optical apparatus sported by the sort of woman who sees a conviction for armed robbery or murder as an attractive secondary sexual characteristic in a suitor.

convict's shuffle *n*. The "chaingang"-style gait one adopts when looking for *bumwad* whilst manacled round the ankles by one's lowered *grundies*.

convoy cock *n*. *milit*. A squaddie's *travel fat*.

conulingus *n*. *Licking out* a ladyfriend on the spurious assumption that she will later reciprocate on a *quid pro quo* basis, only to be left with dangerously *blue balls*.

cooch *n*. US. A Yankee *poon*.

cooint *n*. A variation on the popular rude word *cunt,* used in the quaint picture-postcard village of Barnsley, South Yorkshire.

cooking at both ends *adj*. Of the eater of a spicy *cuzza*, descriptive of the burning sensations experienced first in his throat and then, about an hour later, when his *bottom hob* gets lit. *'Come to the Curry Capital, Bigg Market, Newcastle upon Tyne, where we'll prepare you a meal that will have you cooking at both ends in no time.'*

cooking lager *n*. Utility pub booze, as drunk by Selwyn Froggatt. *Wallop*. Also *cookin'*.

cooking on gash 1. *phr*. Turn of phrase employed by a gentleman who is confident that he has a cast iron guarantee of getting *on the nest*. *'I couldn't wait for the Remembrance Day ceremony to get finished so I could get that bird from the office back to my Grace & Favour apartment in Whitehall. "John, you'll be cooking on gash this afternoon," I thought to myself with a smile before puking up my dinner.'* (extract from Rt Hon John Prescott MP's autobiography, serialised in the *Sunday Sport*). 2. *n*. A

fellow who is enjoying an extremely good run pulling the ladies, in the style of Robin Askwith in the *Confessions* films, viz. *'Hey Mick, I heard you were out shagging again last night.' 'Yes, Keith. I'm cooking on gash at the moment. As indeed I have been pretty much constantly since about 1963.'*

cook off 1. *v*. *milit*. Of ammunition, to detonate spontaneously due to excessive heat. 2. *v*. Of a bachelor, to detonate spontaneously in his trousers due to excessive lap-dancing.

cooter 1. *n*. *prop*. US. A character from *The Dukes of Hazzard*. 2. *n*. The visible contents of Daisy Duke's shorts in the *Dukes of Hazzard*.

cooter cutters *n*. US. The type of shorts worn by Daisy Duke in *The Dukes of Hazzard*, in which she kept her *cooter*.

cop a feel *v*. To get one's *tops* or *fingers*. Or *tops and fingers*.

copperation *n*. A nerve-shredding game whereby a fellow opportunistically *cops a feel* of his sleeping partner's *bodily treasures* in the hope that he won't set her buzzer off and make her nose flash.

copper bolt *v*. A very heavy or dense *sweaty morph*. With a clockwise thread.

copper's torch *n*. A large, heavy, *bellswagged schlong* dangling disturbingly between the legs of a skinny old man. A *schlepper*. *'What's the matter, your holiness? Are you wrestling with an intractable theological conundrum, such as the concept of original sin?' 'No, cardinal. I've just went for a slash and I've been and caught me copper's torch in me zip.'*

copper wire *n*. A stray pube appearing, somewhat embarrassingly, in a handful of loose change.

copy twat *n*. An acquaintance that always gets the same clothes, car, phone, *bird etc*. as oneself.

cordless bone *n*. A *bobby's helmet* without the *roll-neck* and *cheese-slicer* apparatus.

cordon bleugh *n*. The sophisticated sort of food whizzed up on their bedsit minihobs by sad bachelors, *eg*. A pot noodle sandwich, bubble and squeak made from the remains of an uneaten pot noodle sandwich, a bubble and squeak leftovers sandwich, cornflakes and lager.

corgi *1. n*. A high class hound, such as those that accompany the Queen. *2. n*. A high class *hound*, such as the one that accompanies Prince Charles.

corgi registered *euph*. Humorous description of a man who is fully qualified at *servicing boilers*.

Cornish internet *n*. Ceefax, teletext. The *skinternet*.

corpsing *1. n*. Of an actor, getting the giggles. *2. n*. Of a *wanker*, *pulling himself off* with freezing cold hands.

corridor of uncertainty *n*. The no-man's land encountered during a drunken act of congress, when one is unsure of where *John Thomas* is a-roaming. *'Hang on a minute, love, I've just entered the corridor of uncertainty. Stick us in the front door, would you?'* (from *The Night After We Won the Ashes* by Frederick "Andy" Flintoff).

corked *1. adj*. Of wine, to be contaminated with bits which render it unpalatable. *'Mr Winner's sent his 1978 Montrachet back. He says it's corked.'* *2. adj*. Of *spaff*, to be contaminated with bits which render it unpalatable. *'Mr Winner's sent his soup back. He says the spunk in it is corked.'*

corks *1. n*. Nipples. *2. exclam*. 1950s schoolboy cry of surprise. *"Corks!', cried Darbishire. 'I've just seen Matron's corks. Anyone for a daisychain?"* (from *Jennings and the Sticky Sheets* by Anthony Buckeridge).

corn *rhym. slang*. The *chopper*. From corn on the cob = knob.

cornbeef cudgel *n*. Short, thick *trouser stick* the "taking up" of which relieves *gentlemanly tensions*, and so aids restful sleep. The *spam baseball bat*.

cornbeef gash *n*. A *fanny* that has quite clearly been pulverised to a gristly shadow of its former glory but is, nevertheless, a cheap, sure thing. With plenty of batter.

cornbeef lighthouse *n*. Big thing that flashes to attract sailors' attention.

cornbeef sandwich *n*. The contents of Daisy Duke's *cooter cutters*.

cornhole *1. n*. US. Brass eye, ring, balloon knot. *2. v*. To shove one's *cock* up the same.

Cornish chuff *1. n*. A wrongly-spelled crow-like bird (*Pyrrhocorax pyrrhocorax*) which is native to the Cornish coast and characterised by its red beak, red legs and high-pitched, excitable "chiow" call, it says here. *2. n*. Pastie-powered act of flatulation which could cause a stampede in a tin mine.

Cornish payrise *n*. An increase in remuneration vouchsafed with one hand whilst being simultaneously taken away with the other. *'In his budget speech, Mr Osborne confirmed that he would be offering pensioners an index-linked Cornish payrise of 0.03%, on top of the 1p a week he had already promised them in his Autumn statement.'*

corn on the cob *n*. A *spitroast*, where two

gentleman revolve a hot lady in a shallow dish of melted butter.

corn on the nob *n*. A niblet on a *bottsman's lid*.

corn on the swab *n*. Telltale *shitscrape* evidence of previous sweetcorn consumption.

cornucopia *n*. A horn of plenty. A *cock* with all grapes, wine and fruit coming out of the end. *'Look at the size of the norks on that one, Dr Spillsbury. She's given me the cornucopia.'*

coroner's cloth *n*. A piece of lavatory tissue tactfully placed over *skidmarks*, *pebbledashing* or any other discomfiting debris one has left in the toilet bowl, in the same way that Police scene-of-crime officers would cover up a dead body or other such unpleasantness from the gaze of passers-by. *Chocolate quilting, papering over the cacks, Turin shroud.*

corporate dogging *n*. Watching your workmates getting *shafted* by the management.

corpy *adj*. Of household fittings and suchlike, a bit *council. 'Ooh, I wouldn't buy one of them onyx-effect dessert trolleys, your royal highness. They're a bit corpy.'*

cortina, the *euph*. The deeply erotic, although physically improbable, act of inserting both fists into a partner's anal or vaginal orifice before "turning the wheel" left and right as if negotiating a slippy road after mixing crossply and radial tyres on the same axle of a 1970s Ford saloon car. Also known as the *fist and twist* or *steering into the skids.*

corybungo *n*. Arse, *fundament*, backside. *'The tomato boat's just docked, so you'll have to do me up the corybungo.'*

cosif *n*. *medic*. The *tinter*, the *taint*. The perineum. '"Cos if" it wasn't there, her guts would fall out.

cossie fog light, arse like a *sim*. One's *nipsy*, following a difficult digestive transit. *'Come to the Curry Capital, Bigg Market, Newcastle upon Tyne for a night out you'll never forget and a morning in with an arse like a cossie foglight.'*

costume drama *n*. The frantic behaviour of an hysterical woman who cannot decide what to wear for a party.

cottage *v*. To visit a thatched public lavatory with climbing roses round the door looking for a bit of *Colwyn Bay* action.

cottage cheese pastie *n*. A well-*shagged hairy pie*

cottage kex *n*. Type of gentlemen's trousers with an elasticated waist, enabling them to be lowered or raised at extremely short notice and with the minimum of fuss. Favoured by men who are *good with colours*, for some inexplicable reason.

cottage spy *n*. An inquisitive gentleman in a rain mac who stands uncomfortably close by whilst one is taking a *Chinese singing lesson* in a public lavatory. A *willy watcher*.

cotton bullet *n*. A cotton mouse.

cotton eclipse *n*. The rare, fleeting opportunity for a *sneaky peek* that a fellow gets when a woman sitting opposite him sits down or crosses her legs. A *brief encounter*.

cotton mouse *n*. A *cotton pony*.

cotton pony *n*. A *cotton bullet*.

cougar *n*. *US*. Sexist and offensive American slang term for an older woman in pursuit of a younger man, *eg*. Mrs Robinson in the film *The Graduate* and Mrs Robinson in the House of Commons and Northern Ireland Assembly.

cough a dead rat *v*. To *drop a gut*, to s*tep on a duck*. To flatulate.

cough and drop nurse *n*. A comprehensive school health visitor who checks whether or not adolescent schoolboys' *nuts* wobble whilst they are clearing their throats.

cough cabbage water *v*. To tread on the *gloy bottle*.

cough your filthy yoghurt *euph*. A romantic expression for ejaculation. To do a *money shot*. '*Ursula was powerless to resist. His eyes burned into hers like sapphires. His strong arms enfolded her tender body as she felt herself being swept away in a whirlwind of passion. Then he dropped his trolleys and coughed his filthy yoghurt in her hair.*' (from *The Gentleman and the Lady* by Barbara Cartland).

coughy morning *n*. The result of an occasional smoker having too many *Harry Rags* the night before.

council *1. rhym. slang. The bumhole*. From council gritter = shitter. *2. adj*. General purpose dismissive term for anything or anyone deemed somewhat lacking in class. '*Mummy, can I go and play with Jade and Kylie?*' '*No, sweetheart, you can't. They're a bit council.*'

council catwalk *n*. A public place in which *fugly birds* congregate or otherwise disport themselves, normally wearing skimpy tops two sizes too small, the better to show off their collections of prison *tats*.

council cock *n*. A genital which is unemployed and living on handouts.

council diamonds *n*. Sparkling pavement residue found, for example, following a collision between a *Vauxhall Chavalier* and a telephone box.

council fm *n*. The medley of *shite* music that is played at extreme volume levels out of the windows of low income homes, mainly during the summer.

council futon *n*. Piece of dual-purpose street furniture which is used for sitting on during the day and sleeping on at night. A park bench.

council gritter *rhym. slang. Gary Glitter, apple fritter, pint of bitter, shitter*. The anal aperture, is what it is.

council pop *n*. Water. Also *tapoline*.

council Sky *euph*. Free-to-air digital television.

council suitcase *n*. A binliner.

council tax *n*. A weekly levy paid in manageable £1 installments over the fag counter at the newsagent, which funds the Royal Ballet. Lottery ticket money.

council twat *n*. A scraggy, utility *clout*. Not very good quality, but it does the job.

Countdown shuffle *n*. Solitary afternoon game played by housebound bachelors, the unemployed and those who "work from home", the aim being to *chuck your muck* over pulchritudinous mathematician Rachel Riley before the eponymous gameshow timer reaches zero.

country air *n*. The smell of a *fart* dropped whilst driving past a field. '*Mmmm. Just smell that country air, children.*'

countryfile *1. n*. Title of a BBC programme about trees and shit. *2. n*. Person with a perverted desire to indulge in sexual activity in the open air.

coup de tat *n. Fr*. A sudden and unexpected takeover of a previously-classy high street by pound shops, Wilkinson's and *scratter*-filled amusement arcades. '*Head for the hills, everyone. There's been a coup de tat in Leamington Spa.*'

course I loves thee, fucks thee dunn I? *n*. West Country gent's riposte to the question put by his girlfriend: "Do you love me?"

court Madam Knuckle *v*. To woo your right hand. See *Madam Palm and her five daughters*.

Covent Garden nun *n*. A *fuckstress*. A *Fulham virgin*. A *ho'*.

covered wagon *1 n*. The method of holding the *tassel* in which the thumb is on the underside of the *shaft* and the fingers form a canopy like the top of a cowboy's wagon. A style much favoured by the street-urinating drunkard. *2 n*. To drive your old cow under canvas after you've had a bellyful of beans. A *Dutch oven*.

covering fire *n*. The act of waiting for someone in a public toilet to turn on the taps or hand-driers before defecating in order to conceal the appalling cacophony that accompanies the release of one's *bumload*.

cowboy walk *n*. Broad, rolling, John Wayne-style gait required when walking to the *bog* with the *turtle's head*.

Cowell movement *n*. A cod-musical, tuneless, screeching *arse ballad* involving a surfeit of ostentatious, Mariah Carey-style arpeggiation and faux-soulful grimacing, which brings tears to the eyes of anyone unlucky enough to hear it.

cowelloke *n*. Plastic singing, as practised by the sort of talent-free *cunts* who appear on pleb-fleecing primetime telly *shitfests*.

cowgirl *n*. A sexual position popular with the choreographers of American *grumble flicks*, involving a lazy man and a bow-legged woman. A *fucking bronco*.

cow parsley *n*. The salad first course eaten by a *barge arse* as an antidote to the three-cake blowout she will shovel down her fat face for dessert.

cow's cunt, flatter than a *1. sim*. Perfectly horizontal or otherwise free of contours. *'It occurred to me that if it were possible to flow a ribbon of liquid glass freely onto a bath of molten tin, the resulting sheet of continuous "float glass", once cooled with sufficient care, would be flatter than a cow's cunt.'* (from *Alastair Looking Through the Glass - My Life in the Wonderland of Transparent Silica-based Amorphous Solids* by Sir Alastair Pilkington). *2. sim*. Exhausted or otherwise bereft of vim or vigour. *'You couldn't give me a jump start off your Popemobile could you, your holiness? Only the battery on me Bedford Rascal's flatter than a cow's cunt.'*

cow's stomachs *n*. the effect of an ill-fitting bra on an over-endowed lady, giving the appearance of four udders instead of two.

coyote *euph*. A woman who you would chew your own arm off to get away from in the morning.

coyote gulch *n*. A searingly hot and dry *wizard's sleeve*.

crabalanche *n*. Sudden outpouring of latero-perambulatory seafood from a dirty *bird's drip tray*.

crabe *n*. A measure of *shite*, thought to equal about two crates full.

crab ladder *1. n*. The *gut stick*, penis. *2. n*. The hairy line that links the top of the pubes to the belly button. *Crab trellis, pubic footpath*.

crab paste *n*. A deposit of *fanny batter*, especially on a cucumber.

crabs *n*. *Bollock jockeys, mechanical dandruff*, pubic lice.

crack 1. *n. Minge, fanny. 'Close your legs honey, folks will see your crack.'* (Ronald Reagan at his presidential inauguration, 1980). 2. *n.* Pointless *bollocks* spoken after four pints of Guinness in Irish theme pubs. 3. *n.* The cleft of the *arse* cheeks. The *bottom line*.

crack a boiling egg *euph.* Descriptive of the aftermath of a bathtime act of mono-manual pleasure, whereby the bather is surrounded by bobbing white flotsam, similar to the stringy albumen leaked by a cracked egg into a pan of water.

crack a fat *v.* To achieve a *bone on*.

crack a moistie *v. Aus.* Of a *rude lady*, to become aroused in the *downstairs department*. To get a *wide on*.

crack and bone man *n.* A bisexual gentleman. A *happy shopper*.

crack a stiffy *v.* To *crack a fat*.

crackerjacks *n.* Testicles. *'It's Friday, it's five to five, and I'm off upstairs to whack me crackerjacks.'*

crack hanger *n.* The inverted coat hanger-shaped triangle of thong visible on women bending over in hipster jeans. Also *top triangle*.

crackler *n.* A particularly satisfying *dump* that crackles like somebody gently crumpling a crisp bag as it exits the *nipsy*.

crackling *n.* Appetising *totty, talent*.

crack maggot *n.* See *man overboard*.

crack one's back *v.* To commence a long overdue *Ingrid, ie.* Where one's spinal column sounds like it is breaking up and is about to emerge through one's *clackervalve*.

crack one's nuts *v.* To *break one's eggs*.

cracksuit *n.* Convenient form of leisure clothing favoured amongst chemically dependant members of the urban underclasses. A *smacksuit*.

crack the flags *v.* A vigorous, no nonsense *gut drop* that makes a fresh, crisp sound.

cradock 1. *n.* A *cock-a-fanny.* 2. *n.* An old *cunt* with wonky, bright red lips. Named after the famous TV chef of the 1960s and 1970s, Fanny Cradock, who was an old *cunt* with wonky, bright red lips.

CRAFT/craft 1. *acronym. medic.* Doctor's notes terminology for a geriatric patient exhibiting symptoms of the onset of senile dementia. Can't Remember A Fucking Thing. 2. *acronym.* Term used by educationalists to describe the learning potential of their less academically-gifted pupils on school records.

crafty ant *n.* Awkward instantaneous occurrence of *ringpiece* itchiness which happens at the exact moment when it would be most unsuitable to give it a good scratch. Generally occurs the morning after eating a mixed kebab from Abdul's, Manchester.

crafty butcher *n.* A male homosexualist, *ie.* A man who likes to "take his meat around the back."

crafty fisherman *n.* An hermaphrodite, *ie.* One who carries around a spare set of *tackle*.

cranberry dip *n.* A special sauce for sausages only available during *rag week. Tomato boat ketchup*.

crane operator *n.* A *stick vid* actress with a *joy stick* in each hand, the motion of which gives the appearance that she is positioning a crane or wrecking ball. Also *Madam two-swords, downhill skier*.

crank 1. *n.* Penis. 2. *rhym. slang.* To have a *wank* in the style of someone attempting to start a vintage car. A *ham shank*.

3. n. A bathroom multi-tasking exercise. A *crap* and a *wank* performed simultaneously by someone with an extremely busy schedule. *4. v.* To cry and *wank* at the same time.

crap *1. n. Shit. 2. v.* To *shit. 3. adj. Shit. 4. exclam. Shit.*

craps *n. US.* A shit game with dice.

craparazzi *n.* Photographers assigned to the *shitterati, eg.* Snapping former *Big Brother* contestant Cameron Stout leaving a launderette in Arbroath for a six page spread in *Heat* magazine.

crap flaps *n.* The doorstep of the *nipsy*. The insides of the cheeks of buttocks of the *arse*.

crapidation *n.* In a public lavatory, the fear of the appalling horrors about to be exposed when lifting the lid. *'With a trembling hand and much crapidation, Roderick made to lift the lid. What he saw plastered in the bowl made the blood freeze in his veins. It was a sight that was to cast a black shadow over his soul for the rest of his life.'* (from *The Fall of the Shithouse of Usher* by Edgar Allan Poe).

crapier mache *n.* Those little bits of *bumwad* that gather around one's *dot* after a severe wiping. A *wasps' nest.*

crapitus *n. Lat. medic.* The creaking noise emitted by overstretched or broken *farting strings* as a *Meatloaf's daughter* forces its way out of the *chamber of horrors,* sounding similar to the noises made in days of yore by a galleon at anchor.

crapkins *n.* Fast food restaurant paper serviettes which, when pilfered in handfuls, act as free toilet paper. Popular amongst cash-strapped students.

crap nap *n.* An alcohol-induced siesta taken in a pub gents cubicle, when one is overcome with sudden tiredness at the effort of pulling down one's trousers and sitting on the *throne. Shitwinks.*

crapper *1. n.* The lavatory. Named after the inventor of the self-cleaning water closet, Thomas Shitehouse. *2. n.* A *crap rapper.* From crap + rapper. *'Today's birthdays: Lev Demin, Soviet cosmonaut, 1926; Mohammed Abed Elhai, Sudanese writer and academic, 1944; Daz Sampson, British crapper, 1974.'*

crappetite *1. n.* An insatiable hunger for the *jobby engine. 'That Mexican/Thai sausage curry from the Chinese last night has given me a fierce crappetite this morning, I can tell you.' 2. n.* A penchant for more proletarian comestibles, such as Scotch eggs, Pot Noodles, KFC chicken poppers, Rustler's burgers, pickled onion Space Raiders and Angel Delight.

crappling hook *n.* Any convenient tool, usually one's fingers if truth be told, used to fish out the floating remnants of a recently-chopped *dead otter* to avoid the embarrassment of your host/colleagues/cellmates discovering any telltale evidence of your recent, unflushable efforts.

crappuccino *n.* A particularly frothy form of diarrhoea which one only gets whilst abroad. See *kexpresso.*

crappy ending *1. n.* In a British massage parlour, a disappointing conclusion to proceedings. *2. n.* In a German massage parlour, a thoroughly successful conclusion to proceedings.

crappy salad *n. Scots.* Leafy foodstuffs, including lettuce and that. *"Whit's the matter, Wullie? Ye look like ye've seen a ghostie.' 'Jings, hoots and crivens* *m'boab, Angus! Some bampot's left a wee bit o' crappy salad in the box next tae ma deep-fried pizza.'*

craptain Webb *n.* A long *turd* that "dips its toe" in the water before diving in and embarking for France. A *bridger* or *bottom log.*

craptivating *adj.* Descriptive of something completely *shit*, yet strangely fascinating, *eg. All New TV's Naughtiest Blunders*, (2004), presented by Steve Penk.

craptop *n.* The temporary replacement computer that you are forced to use whilst your usual machine is at the menders or being examined by the police.

crash land the helicopter *v.* To engage in a particularly stressful, two-handed battle with your *chopper* that ends messily.

crash mat *n.* A *pap baffle*, a *turd raft*, *pilo.*

crash one's pants *v.* To momentarily lose control of one's *motions* leading to a *pile up* in one's *garnies*. *'I was so scared when Derek went into his trance, I nearly crashed my pants, I can tell you.'* (Yvette Fielding, *Most Haunted Live*, Living TV, Oct 31st 2003).

crash the yoghurt truck *v.* To *shed one's load* at the *Billy Mill roundabout. Empty the wank tanks.*

cravate de notaire *n. Fr.* Literally, a *solicitor's tie*. Version of *pearl necklace* from France, where lawyers in courtrooms have all *spunk* down their shirt fronts.

crazy log *n.* A little *shit* that produces an annoying crescendo of high-pitched *ringtones.*

cream *v.* To *drop your yop*, esp. in your pants. To *milm.*

cream, over-whisking the *n.* Excessive indulgence of one's *egg white cannon*. *'You've got a distinctive hobble in your step, Watson. You've not been over-whisking the cream since the missus left, have you?'*

cream pie *n.* In the world of erotic cinematography or photogravures, a *blurtch* or *freckle* with all *spoff* up it.

cream rinse *n.* A bubbly hair-care product that is often provided gratis with a *facial*. A *spermanent wave.*

cream tea *n.* A couple of generously - proportioned *nipplecakes*, topped off with a healthy dollop of *squirty cream. Iced baps.*

cream tea *n.* A posh *bird's* cuppa into which one has *jaffed*. Over the back of a spoon.

credit crunch *1. n.* An international economic meltdown which has caused the price of Tesco's 26p oranges to go up to 29p. *2. n.* In masturbatory management, the critical point when a man who has been single for a prolonged period finds that he has insufficient collateral in his *wank bank* to fund his increasingly impoverished efforts at *self abuse.*

credit cruncher *n.* An opportunistic *Max Planck* enjoyed as a result of the present fiscal downturn, *eg.* Whilst at home due to reduced hours, being laid off or made redundant, or perhaps during a leisurely visit to the *bogs* at work because it is quiet.

credit munch *n.* A *drink on a stick* or *vertical bacon sandwich* enjoyed whilst temporarily mired in reduced circumstances.

creme de la femme *n. Moip.*

creme de month *n.* Bi-fortnightly *egg nog* that tastes anything but refreshingly minty.

creosort *n*. A woman who has overdone it with the fake tan.

crepitate *v*. To discharge a noxious fluid accompanied by a slight explosive sound. How Stephen Fry would describe *following through*.

crescent wank *n*. To arrange one's favourite *jazz periodicals* in a half-moon display, before kneeling down to perform a five finger exercise on the *spunk trumpet*.

cricketer's tea *n*. A liquid lunch of the sort formerly favoured by brittle Ashes hero Freddie "Andrew" Flintoff.

cricket week *n*. A five day test, when a gentleman must *bowl from the pavilion end* while his wife is *padded up*.

crimping off a length *n*. *milit*. Naval slang for *dropping a depth charge, laying a cable*.

crimson wave *n*. Also *crimson tide*. See *surfing the crimson wave*.

crinkle cuts *n*. *medic*. The large, crenellated *scallop lips* that protrude from a salty *bag*. *Real McCoy's, Nicki Lauda's lugs, turkey's wattles*. A *doctor's signature*.

cripple crapper *n*. A *chod bin* designated for the exclusive use of persons of restricted mobility. '*Fuck it. Look at the queue for the shitters. I'll just nip into the cripple crapper.*'

crone bone *n*. A state of somewhat unsettling sexual arousal brought on by an unlikely stimulus, *eg*. A picture of Camilla Parker-Bowels in jodhpurs.

crop spraying *v*. See *pebble dashing*.

crosswind *n*. A violent or angry *trouser cough* which could make steering difficult.

crossword, teeth like a *sim*. Descriptive of the off-putting appearance of horrendous dentition, liberally strewn with gaps and cavities. Along with a sexy *bird* taking off her sunglasses to reveal that she was cross-eyed, and another one turning round and revealing herself to be Henry McGee with a bubble perm, a girl smiling and having teeth like a crossword was the third situation that Bob Todd encountered whilst trying to chat up women in unrealistic speeded-up discotheques on the *Benny Hill Show*. *English teeth*.

crotch broth *n*. *Scots*. Semen, *manfat etc*. '*Och, help m'boab, Morag. Oor Wullie's got all crotch broth matted in his sporran again.*'

crotch crickets *n*. *Crabs*.

crotch eggs *n*. Hairy *knackers*.

crotch gremlins *n*. *medic*. Any genital ill humour of the sort which is typically contracted from dodgy foreign *pieces* or Skegness toilet seats. *Pox, cock rot, clap*, the *Val Doonican*.

Crouch's leg *n*. A long, thin, pale, pastie, sorry-looking penis with which its owner, contrary to all outward impressions, just keeps on *scoring*. Also *Crouch's calf*.

crouching tiger, hidden dragon *n*. Ancient Chinese sexual position. *Doggy-style* sex with a woman so *fugly* that one can't bring oneself to look her in the face.

crouton *n*. An erection that floats in one's soup.

crow *1*. *n*. *US*. That *muck* which has been *chucked*, esp. onto the *mapatasi*. Post-*porking* residue on the *hairy clam*. *Muffdruff*. 2. *n*. Nostril carrion. A *bogie, greb, greenie*, particularly when wiped on a wall.

crowbar *n*. An erection which is hard enought to force a sash window with. A *jemmy-on*.

crowd pleaser *n.* Unusual or noteworthy stool which one feels an urge to show to someone before flushing it away.

crown jowls *n.* The baggy bit of excess skin that hangs off the end of the *grub screw. Kenny's hood.* The *fiveskin.*

Crown St. Princess *n.* A scrawny *good time girl* who works on Crown Street, which is apparently the red light district of Liverpool. A Scouse *mattressback, Covent Garden nun.*

crow's nest *n.* A particularly ramshackle *snatch* in which a *one-eyed pirate* might feel at home.

Croydon national anthem *n.* The sound of sirens, which causes the denizens of the popular Surrey town to stand. A *Bolton alarm clock.*

Croydon plaque *n.* A temporary police notice commemorating a recent newsworthy event, and appealing for witnesses to come forward. Named after the bullet-riddled South London beauty spot, where such lively street furniture is a commonplace addition to the lively urban *aceldama.*

cruiser and tug *n.* The common phenomenon of a stunning female who is always accompanied by an ugly little fat friend.

crumpa lumpa *n.* A tubby, *cake-worrying* lady with an orange hue that suggests that she frequents a cheap tanning salon or, alternatively, that she is exhibting the symptoms of a beta carotene overdose.

crumpet *1. n.* A traditional Scottish cake made of soft, light dough, eaten toasted and buttered, and much craved by the late Sid James. *2. n.* 1970s *blart.*

crumpet batter *n.* Gentleman's erotic spendings.

crumpeteer *n.* A fellow who has a way with the ladies. An expert in the science of *crumpetology.* 'Birthdays: Curtis Mayfield, soul musician and corpse, 58; Charles R Drew, physician and blood plasma pioneer, 96; Allen Ginsberg, beardy poet, 74; Tony Curtis, actor and veteran crumpeteer, 75.' (from *The Times,* June 3rd 2000).

crumpet trumpet *n.* An involuntary release of air from a young lady's *front bottom.* A *vulvuzela, forward hat drop, queef, snatchaphone* or *Lawley kazoo.*

crunchie *1. n.* A tasty confectionary snack. *2. n.* A brittle sock worn on the foot the day after one has *wanked* into it.

crunk *n.* The *taint, barse, tintis, tinter.*

crusties *1. n.* Dog-on-a-string-owning soapophobes. *2. n.* Over-worn *bills* somewhat lacking in "April freshness". *Dunghampers* with a dirty *drip tray.*

Crystal Gayle *1. n. prop.* Long-haired, lightweight US country performer of the 1970s. *2. n.* A prison-based sexual act which may (in fact, almost certainly will) "make your *brown eye* blue". '*He walked into the shower block / Of Reading's dreadful gaol / And stooping to pick up the soap / The prisoner's face turned pale / As a voice behind him whispered / 'How about a Crystal Gayle?''* (from *The Ballad of Reading Gaol* by Oscar Wilde).

crystal maze, go *v.* To find oneself unable to perform a simple task due to pressure, *eg.* A learner driver being unable to get the car out of reverse gear during a test, Eamonn Holmes being unable to competently present a television programme when the cameras are on. To go all *cunty booby.*

CSB *abbrev.* Default hairstyle setting for young lady *scratters.* From Chav Scrape Back.

CT scan *n*. Act performed by men in public areas. A quick glance at passing ladies' *Toblerone tunnel* areas to check for the presence of *camels' toes*.

Cuban wank *n*. A *diddy-ride*, a *Bombay roll*. A *tit-wank*.

cubism 1. *n*. A French school of painting typified by the works of Picasso and Braque which amalgamated multiple viewpoints into a complex surface of geometrical planes. 2. *n*. A harmless gentleman's hobby which involves sneaking into a cubicle in the female toilets of a pub, club or department store and listening in to the action in the neighbouring "cubes".

cuckold *n*. A man whose wife allows another man to lay his *cock eggs* in her.

cuckoo *n*. A scoundrel who moves in on a *bird's nest* when someone else has nipped to the bar after doing all the groundwork.

cuckoo fart *n*. The act of *dropping one's hat* in the presence of another person in such a manner that they believe the resulting miasma to be their own dirty work.

cuddle *n. rhym. slang*. A *slash*. From cuddle and kiss = *piss*. *'Excuse me, vicar. Do help yourself to another rich tea. I'm off to the shitter for a quick cuddle.'*

Cuddles's mouth *n*. A particularly free-moving set of lady lips, framed by an enormous clump of gingery fuzz. Named after Keith "Orville the Duck" Harris's less successful, though equally annoying, *gobshite* monkey companion.

cuff the dummy *v. US. milit*. To *wank*, *scrub the cook, box the Jesuit*.

cuff stinks *n*. The malodorous end result of an unfortunate sleeve mishap suffered when wiping one's *nipsy* following a messy *Brad*.

cum 1. *v*. A sexiness-enhancing mis-spelling of *come* used by the authors of *bongular* literature to describe male ejaculation. 2. *n*. A sexiness-enhancing mis-spelling of *come* used by the authors of *bongular* literature to describe male ejaculate. 3. *n*. A sexiness-enhancing mis-spelling of *come* used by Noddy Holder in the title of his band Slade's 1972 hit *Cum On Feel the Noize*.

cumbalina *n*. A female of diminutive stature who demonstrates a marked penchant for *pork lollies*. A *throwabout*, *laptop*.

cumbeard *n*. A white, coagulated sperminiferous goatee worn by a lady who has helped herself to a double portion of *spangle*.

Cumberland 1. *n*. A long *turd* which forms a spiral in the *pan*, in the style of the popular helical pub grub sausage. 2. *n*. A gentleman's *porky banger*.

Cumberland curl 1. *n*. A somewhat off-puttingly designed Wetherspoon's pub sausage which presents a convincing simulacrum of a *shite*. 2. *n*. A somewhat off-puttingly designed *shite* which presents a convincing simulacrum of a Wetherspoon's pub sausage.

Cumberland gap 1. *n*. A repetitive, annoying skiffle song by the late Lonnie Donegan which topped the hit parade in 1957. 2. *n*. The triangular gap at the top of a lady's thighs which arouses curiosity as to whether the old *Cumberland* could fit through. The *Toblerone tunnel*.

cumbleweed *n*. Crispy, crinkly-leafed flora which proliferates under the beds of teenage boys, bachelors, students and jobseekers, becoming particularly abundant immediately after the new issue of *Nuts* comes out. *Cumcabbage, bedroom popadoms, porn crackers.*

cumbrella *n*. A *dunky*.

cumchugger *n*. A *bird* who enjoys guzzling *spadge*.

cumdown *n*. That feeling of soul-crushing worthlessness that follows a *Sherman* as inevitably as night follows day. See also *wangst* and *wank hangover*.

cumjunctivitis *n*. *medic*. Unpleasant, sticky eye infection which is an unavoidable complication following careless *telescoping*.

cumster *n*. A small hamster-like female who fills her cheeks with your *nuts*.

cum on one's faggots *v*. To put one's future prospects in jeopardy as the result of a foolhardy action. To *piss on one's chips* or *fart on one's Weetabix. eg*. A jewellery firm boss jocularly referring to his company's products as "crap, or a butcher being exposed in his local paper for masturbating on his rissoles;

cum to mind *v*. Of a person or favoured memory, to appear as a mental image in the imagination of one embarking on the *vinegar strokes*. *'These days I find it's often Kylie Minogue who cums to mind when I'm poking the missus.'*

cum to one's senses *v*. To experience feelings of self loathing and disgust immediately upon ejaculation when, all of a sudden, one experiences a Damascene conversion and wearing the girlfriend's lingerie, *poking* a Bangkok *ladyboy* or *wanking* into Carol Decker's wardrobe *etc*., no longer seem a such a good idea.

cumulonimbecile *n*. Someone who is ignorant of how to pay *lip service* to a lady.

cumulonimbus *n*. *Lat*. Oral sex. Tongular

stimulation of a lady's *wail switch*.

cumcrete *n*. A naturally-occurring *rock*-based aggregate which, once set, has sufficient tensile strength to bond hairs together in a vice-like manner. *'Oi, Eric. What's this stuff all up the dog's back? I can't get his brush through it.' 'Cumcrete, Ethel.'*

cum whip *n*. The act of grasping one's *todger* at a critical point during a bout of *self harm* and enhancing the *muck chucking* experience with a rapid, Indiana Jones-style snap of the wrist.

cunch *n*. A satisfying midday snack furnished by, or comprising of, the secret *girly parts* of an obliging ladyfriend. Derivation unknown.

cunker *n*. Romantic term for one of a lady's *bodily treasures*. The *snatch*.

cunnifungus *n*. *Lat*. Female equivalent of *knob cheese 'n' mushroom*.

cunnimingus *v*. The act of orally pleasuring a lady with personal hygiene issues. *Licking a nine volter*.

cunny *n*. *Lat. Fadge*, vagina. From the Latin cunnus = shagpipe.

cunnylicious *adj*. Descriptie of any woman, or part thereof, demanding to be eaten.

cunshine *n*. The frustrating reflections which invariably hinder full enjoyment of the glossy *whacknicolour* photographs in *art pamphlets*. Also *porn glare, razzle dazzle*.

cunt 1. *n*. *14thC. medic*. Polite term for lady's genitals. 2. *n*. *21stC*. Impolite term for lady's genitals. 3. *n*. How a person in the Cotswolds might refer to a mole. *'The cunts have dug up the lawn again, the little cunts.'* 4. *n*. A traffic warden.

cuntbitten *adj*. Of a gentleman, to have

contracted *VD* from a dirty lady. To be struck down with a *dose* of clappage.

cunt book *n.* The *dog house.* '*16th August 1945. Went down the Feathers with Joe and Dwight to celebrate winning the War. Back to Downing Street 4am. Lost keys. Climbed up drainpipe and fell into bins. Woke kids up. Clementine came down to let me in. I reckon I'm in the cunt book for at least a fortnight.*' (from The Diary of Sir Winston Churchill).

cunt bread *n.* A yeast infection on a lady's *ninja's toe.*

cunt bubble *1. n.* An air lock up the *blurtch*, often leading to a *Lawley kazoo.* *2. n.* A traffic warden.

cunt buster *1. n.* An enormous erection. A *diamond cutter.* '*Olivia was powerless to resist. His eyes burned into hers like sapphires. His strong arms enfolded her softly yielding body as she felt herself being swept away in a whirlwind of passion. Then he dropped his trolleys revealing a right cunt buster.*' (from The Lady and the Gypsy by Barbara Cartland). *2. n.* A large baby.

cunt candle *n.* An outstanding idiot amongst men, one who stands out like a shining beacon of utter imbecility, *eg.* The Rt Rev Graham Dow, former Bishop of Carlisle, to pick an example entirely at random.

cunt corks *n.* A term used in chemist's shops when one is too embarrassed to ask for a box of *women's things.*

cunt dentist *n.* A gynaecologist.

cunteen *n.* A number which is larger than twelve but smaller than twenty, and is used to describe the size of a group of something one dislikes, *eg.* '*There were cunteen fucking TV chefs.*'

cunt flump *n.* A monthly feminine requisite, named after the furry, absorbent, wooly-hat-wearing, garden-loving children's television characters of the 1970s. '*I would be quite happy - as, I am sure, would other honourable members - if the Government regarded women's wotsits as being free of VAT. Cunt flumps are not a luxury; they are essential items in a lady's budget.*' (Stephen Pound MP, reported in *Hansard*).

cunt guff *n.* The *dropping forwards of a lady's hat.*

cunt grunt *n.* A politer term for a *fanny fart.* Also a *queef*, a *hat dropped forward*, a *Lawley kazoo, Seagoon's last raspberry, cunt guff, vulvuzela.*

cunt hook *n.* Any stylish car such as a VW Lupo or Daewoo Matiz with oversized wheels, blacked-out windows and rear spoilers, which impresses discerning ladies. A *fanny magnet.* '*Fiesta XR2, red, D reg, 312k, 1 new tyre, some history, MOT October, a real cunt hook £120 ono. First to see will buy. No tyre kickers.*'

cuntinental *n.* Anyone who sits outside a cafe in Britain drinking coffee and eating croissants whenever the drizzle lets up for ten minutes.

cuntinental breakfast *n.* An insubstantial early morning *meal at the Y* which leaves the diner wanting more.

cunting *n.* A lady's bestest knickers, brought out to decorate the *hairy goblet* on special occasions.

cuntingency plan *n.* An emergency arrangement for the provision of alternative *fanny* in case the usual supply dries up for any reason. *Plan C.* '*Colonel Hepscott-Whyte? I'm afraid*

"I say, Jeeves. Could you take these trousers to my tailor and have him replace the zip fastenings with good old fashioned buttons?' I croaked. 'I only bought them last week and I've grated the cheddar four times. My poor cock end is ripped to pip, don't you know.'' ~ *Swallow it All, Jeeves* by PG Wodehouse.

I've got some bad news for you. Your wife has been run over by a steam roller and killed. Is there anybody who could come over to stay with you tonight? Would you like me to get in touch with someone?' 'No, I'll be fine, officer. I've got a cuntingency plan. The wife's sister's a bit of a goer.'

cuntispiece *n.* The explicitly-illustrated leaf which precedes the title page of a *bongo book*.

cuntitude *n.* A *cuntish* attitude.

cuntlashed *adj.* Twice as drunk as *shit-faced*.

cuntlery *n.* Any utensil or digit used to assist when *dining at the Y*. For example, fingers, lolly sticks, clothes pegs or spoons *etc.* used to hold back the *beef curtains*.

cuntlifters *n.* An elderly lady's *dung-hampers. Granny's bills*.

cunt mumps *n. medic.* That condition which causes a female to instantly reject the conversational gambits of a potential suitor.

cuntrified *adj.* Of a public house, to have been turned into a ritzy wine bar by the addition of a DJ, bowls of olives on the bar and a bunch of *twattish*, braying media types.

cunt ruffler *n.* A man who enjoys provoking ladies who have *fallen to the communists* because he finds their mood swings amusing. Easily recognised by his black eyes, missing teeth and stab wounds.

cunt rug *n.* A *muff*, a *merkin*. A pubic *syrup*.

cunt scratchers *n.* Humorous term for hands. *Wanking spanners, dick skinners*.

cuntsman *n.* US. A *cocksman, stickman,*

crumpeteer. A Don Juan type, highly skilled in the pursuit of *poontang*. *'Today's birthdays. Rod Stewart, singer, songwriter, cuntsman, 73.'*

cuntstruck *adj.* Besotted, hopelessly in love.

cuntuppance *n.* Well-deserved humiliation following some sort of *fanny*-related behaviour. *Lust desserts. 'I see Darren Day's got his cuntuppance in the News of the World again.'*

cuntwank *n.* A one-sided, loveless, no-nonsense bout of intercourse. A *hands free. 'I've just seen that Victorian lesbo drama on the telly. Phwooar! So I'm off upstairs for a cuntwank off the missus.'*

cuntweep *n.* The *bird's custard* found in a lady's *alans* after she has sat in the office all day chatting about Robert Pattinson, whoever he is.

cunty booby *adj.* To be in a state of confusion. *'I don't pretend to understand the universe - when I start thinking about it I go all cunty booby, me.'* (from *Latterday Pamphlets Number 6*, by Thomas Carlyle).

cupcake *n.* A small quantity of *fart* gas caught between the palms of the hands and released in a person's face. An *amuse nez*.

Cupid's measles *n. medic.* Victorian terminology for *cock rot*.

Cupid's toothpaste *n.* Oral *gunk*.

cup cracker *n.* A *cabman's rest* which is too large for the *titpant* to which it has been allotted.

curd *n.* Jizz.

curl one in *v.* To achieve a particularly skillful *fuck* from an impressively difficult starting position. *'Victoria Adams, the former Spice Girl, today refused to* *comment on allegations that her hus-band, transvestite advert star David Beckham, had curled one into his personal assistant, TV pig wanker Rebecca Loos.'* (BBC News 24).

curl one off *v.* To carefully deliver a *mudchild*.

curler 1. *n.* A lump of excrement. 2. *n.* Something in Olive off of *On the Buses*'s hair. 3. *n.* A lump of excrement in Olive off of *On the Buses*'s hair.

curry hurry *n.* The increasingly-hasty homeward bound trot of one who has recently partaken of some sort of exotic foodstuffs which are already *touching cloth* in high-temperature, quasi-viscous form.

curry McFlurry *n.* A soft, whipped-up delight with chili and chicken sprinkles, conjured forth from the *back end of the Batmobile* by the previous night's feast of brown booze and piquantly-spiced Asiatic sweetmeats.

curryoakie *n.* An enthusiastic but tuneless *fart* performed after a gallon of bitter and an Indian meal. A *blanket ripper.*

curry slurry *n.* The mixture of semi-liquified excrement, intestines and internal organs left in the pan of the *chod bin* the morning after a particularly hot Madras. *'I'd give it ten minutes if I was you, dear. I just did a bit of a curry slurry in there. Oh, and can you call an ambulance. And a priest.'*

curtain *n.* Jason Donovan's foreskin. From his 1992 song about *wanking* entitled *Any Dream Will Do*, which contained the lines "I close my eyes / Draw back the curtain (ah-ah-ahh)".

curtain call *n.* A return to the lavatory for an *encore dump.* A *second sitting.*

curtain drop *n.* *Cat flap* length. The size of a woman's *beef curtains.*

curtain rings *n.* Labial ironmongery.

curtain twitchers *n.* *Tennis fans, lady golfers.*

curvy *adj.* UK. *journ.* Of women, to have large breasts and/or *arses.* *'Curvy Nigella Lawson cooked a right royal supper of cod and green-ended chips for foreign dictator George W Bush when he recently visited the Queen and her brood of bisexual children.'* (*BBC Good Food Magazine*, November 2003).

cushion creeper *n.* An upholstery-muffled *Exchange & Mart.*

custard 1. *n.* A sweet sauce made from eggs and milk that goes well with rhubarbs. 2. *n.* Someone who is simultaneously a bit of a *cunt* and a bit of a *bastard,* eg. Tim Henman, Danny Dyer. 3. *Rhym. Slang.* A *Bakewell.*

custard cannon *n.* *Lamb cannon, mutton musket, pork sword, beef bazooka, spam blunderbuss, etc, etc, et fucking cetera.*

custard cousin *n.* The relationship a fellow has with others who have shared the same *slice* of *pie. eg.* Bryan Ferry and Mick Jagger are *custard cousins,* as are Liam Gallagher, Ally McCoist, Jim Kerr and the 14th Batallion of the Royal Scots Dragoon Guards.

custard muscle *n.* Subcutaneous body fat. *'You cheeky cow. That's solid custard muscle is that.'*

custard pie *n.* A pre-*spoffed fadge.* Referred to in various blues songs, including 1947's *Custard Pie Blues* by Brown McGhee. Also forms the basis of the Led Zeppelin song *Custard Pie* which opens their 1975 double album *Physical Graffiti* in which Robert Plant exclaims: "Save me a slice of your cus-tard pie", apparently implying that he would later like to re-*poke*, and indeed *nosh* on, his *bird's* aforementioned *jitler*-filled *clopper*.

custody tart *n*. An arrested woman who *sucks off* the duty sergeant, or performs similar act in lieu of bail.

customer service 69 aisle x *exclam*. Phrase called out over supermarket tan-noys to alert male staff of the presence of a fit *bird* in aisle x, so they can go over and *sneak a peek* whilst pretend-ing to run a price check or look at some tins or something.

cut and paste *1. n*. In the world of educa-tion, a process used by students when "researching" their essays and disserta-tions on Wikipedia. *2. n*. A method used by internet-surfing politicians when compiling telling dossiers in order to justify taking a country to war. *3. n*. In the world of motion picture *grumble* drama, the act of withdrawing from a lady's *minge* in order to deposit the contents of one's *clackerbag* on her face or *thrupenny bits*. *'Hurry up Gunther, we're running out of tape. It's time for a cut and paste.'*

cut a rug *1. v*. In World War II, to take to the dancefloor and impress onlookers by jitterbugging energetically, especially with an American airman. *2. v*. To *split a kipper, part the whiskers etc*. To make penetrative love to a lady.

cut 'n' shut *1. n*. A second hand car, skillfully engineered from the front and back of two insurance writeoffs. *2. n*. A woman, seemingly constructed of two ill-matched donor women, *eg*. A fantas-tic body, but a *minger;* a cutie, but built like a bus; or a flat-chested bonebag sat

on a big *arse* and tree trunk legs.

cut price spice *n*. A lady who models her-self on Victoria Beckham, but does so on a much tighter budget. Accompanies *David Peckham* on trips in his *estate car*.

cut the cheese *v*. To *drop some back*. Also *cut the brie, open the ham*.

cut the cord *v*. To break the link between one's *arsehole* and an invisible, yet high-ly noticeable cloud of recently expelled *gut gas* by means of rapid, short wafting motions of the hand.

cut through the red tape *v*. To ignore received wisdom and *swim when the red flags are flying*.

cutty sark *n*. A large *floater* that burns on its way out.

cuzza *n*. A *Ruby Murray*.

cyber clap *n*. The embarrassing situation whereby your home computer becomes riddled with viruses as a result of *buy-ing your better half an anniversary present*.

cybertranny *n*. Man or woman who pre-tends to be of the opposite sex in inter-net chat rooms, *eg*. 16-year-old Brenda turns out to be a 35-stone tattooed American man called Jim-Bob. With his dead mother in a fridge.

Cyclops *n*. A legendary purple-headed monster with a single *hog's eye*. And two big hairy *bollocks* underneath.

Cyclops' hoof *1. n*. The ungulate toe of an Homeric monster as imagined by Ray Harryhausen in the popular *Sinbad* films. *2. n*. A Cinerama *camel's foot*, as often seen in Nottingham city centre on Friday and Saturday nights.

Cyprus manoeuvre *n*. Removing the penis during *doggy sex* and re-entering "accidentally" up the *bonus tunnel*.

The *Limasol slip*. Invented in 1972 by Greek scientists.

Cyril Sneer's sneck, cock like *sim*. A man's wrinkly, bedraggled *tackle* following a no-nonsense bout of penetrative affection. Named after the miserly, pink humanoid's flaccid nose in the 1980s cartoon *The Raccoons*.

Czech book *n*. A *twatalogue* featuring undraped studies of sultry young ladies from the former East European state. *'I fancy banking at Barclay's, but I can't find me Czech book anywhere, mum.' 'Have you looked on top of your wardrobe? That's where your dad keeps his noddy mags.'*

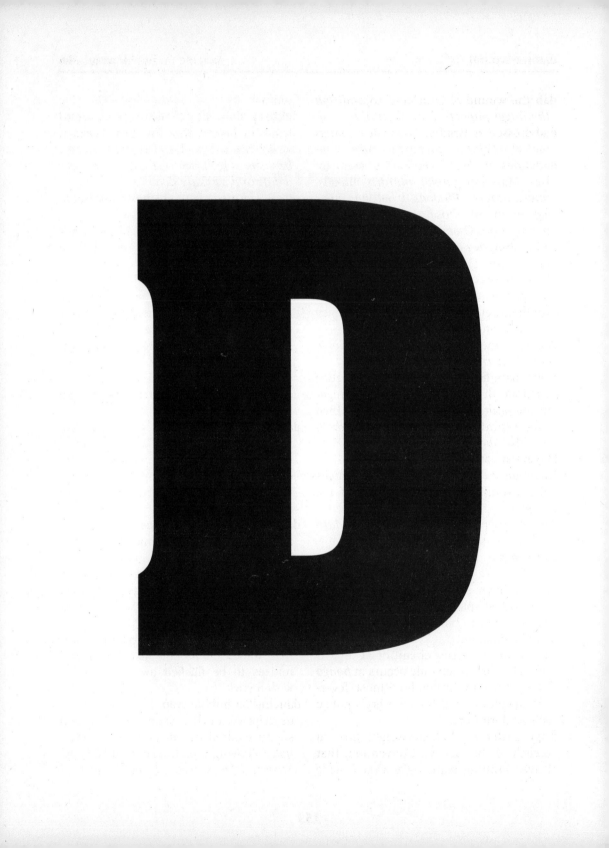

dab the wound *v*. Of a lady, to *audition the finger puppets, dial Australia*.

dad dressed as Brad *n*. The male counterpart of a *Whitney dressed as Britney*.

daddaries *n*. Male version of mammaries. *Mannery glands, mantits, moobs, moomlaaters. 'Phwoar. I bet you don't get many of those daddaries to the pound, Lord Owen.'*

daddy long-legs squatting on a wasp, like a *sim*. Descriptive of a sexual act between two participants of vastly differing heights, *eg*. Sophie Dahl and Jamie Cullum, Peter Crouch and Abby Clancy or Ian Krankie and Wee Jimmy.

daddy's sauce *n*. *Baby gravy, pineapple chunk, heir gel*.

Dagenham handshake *n*. Sexual practice whereby the gentleman inserts a finger in the *pink*, a finger in the *brown*, then uses a third to ring the *devil's doorbell*. See also *shocker*.

Dagenham smile *n*. *Builder's bum*.

Dagenite *n*. A *Bakewell tart* that smells like a dropped Ford car battery of the 1970s.

dags *n*. Shepherd-speak for sheep's *dangleberries*.

dairy bags *n*. Proper old-fashioned *churns* of the sort Nurse Gladys Emmanuel would have stuck in Ronnie Barker's face whilst plumping up his pillows, causing him to blow his cheeks out and blink amusingly.

daisy chain *n*. Series circuit of *AC* or *DC* sex. The sort which only occurs in *bongo films*, Richard Littlejohn's most feverish imaginings and Stephen Fry's public school dormitory.

daisy cutter *n*. A heavyweight *fart*, in breach of the Geneva Convention, that leaves nothing standing within a wide radius.

dakkery doo *n*. A relaxing concurrent *shit* and a *Harry Rag*. From the German word Dak = cigarette. *'His Holiness will be with us presently, Cardinal. He's just went for a dakkery doo.'*

dalek *n*. An erection which is reminiscent of a forehead-mounted sink-plunger, with bollocks made out of Morris Minor indicators, which is best viewed from behind the sofa.

dalhoonies *n*. *Gazungas*.

daltons *n*. The *nuts*. *'Ooh, me daltons!'*

damaging gusts 1. *n*. *met*. In weather forecasting circles, a warning of wind likely to cause harm to buildings. 2. *n*. In curry-loving circles, the onset of the sort of *nipsy* turbulence which could easily dislodge a nearby chimney pot or take the roof off the shed.

dance of the seven ales *n*. Unbalanced, faux-seductive terpsichorean moves essayed in nightclubs by *pissed* revellers of either gender in a misguided attempt to secure some *floor sweepings* before the *ugly lights* come on.

dance the blanket hornpipe *v*. To perform a sailor's jig in one's hammock. To have *all hands on dick*.

dancer's lance *n*. An unwelcome *dalek* that appears when dancing closely with a lady. A *Saturday night lever, St. Vitus pants*.

dancing bear *n*. A grizzly brown monster that stands on its end in the *pan* and refuses to be flushed away unless hit with a stick.

dancing on bubblewrap, like *sim*. Phrase descriptive of the snap, crackle, pop sound emitted by one's *chocolate starfish* following a particularly fruity *Ruby Murray*. *'Jesus man. I spent most of* *last night sat on the bog sounding like S-Club 7 dancing on bubblewrap. I'm never going to Curry Capital, the Bigg Market, Newcastle upon Tyne again. Till Friday.'*

dancing with the captain *n.* Masturbation. Wearing a bowler hat. See *grandma's party*.

dang *1. n.* Penis. *2. exclam. US.* Expression of annoyance. *'Dang them pesky Al Qaeda varmints.'* (George W Bush, State of the Nation Address, 2002). *3. n.* A word which, together with ding and dong, features prominently in the lyrics of Eurovision Song Contest entries.

dangermouse *n.* A tampon or *slim fanatella*.

danger wank *n. Self-abuse* technique whereby you shout your parents from downstairs, and then try to *blow your tanks* before they get to your bedroom. A *dangerous spurt* for an adrenaline *jizz-junky*.

dangleberries *n. Winnets*; excrement adhering to the *arse cress* around an inefficiently-wiped *ringpiece. Fartleberries, toffee strings, bead curtains, kling-ons, clinkers, miniature heroes*.

dangler *n.* A dangling *donger, a copper's* torch. *'Oi missus, look at me dangler.'*

danglers *n.* Hairy conkers. *'Oi missus, look at me me danglers.'*

dangly ham *n. Beef curtains, bacon strips*.

Danny Fishcharge *n.* Spooneristic vaginal *gleet*.

Danny's delay *euph.* The sensation of thinking that you are fully ready to pay a fruitful visit to the *Rick Witter*, only to find that your *cable* is not quite ready to quit the *nipsy* just yet, thus prolonging your time *on the throne*. Named

after Flt. Lt. Danny Velinski, played by Charles Bronson in the film *The Great Escape*, who suffered a sudden bout of claustrophobia which held up his exit from the dirt tunnel for a few minutes.

Dan Pallet *1. n. prop.* Charismatic and erudite sports reporter on BBC Midlands News. *2. n.* Pieces of wood roughly nailed together to form a platform on which Daniels can be stacked for ease of transport or storage. *3. n.* A *double penetration* or *DP*, if you will. Also *man at C&A, Dorothy Perkins, double decker. 'Hello-o. Fancy a quick Dan Pallet with me and Barry, love?'*

DAPPAG/dappag *acronym.* A reference to a peanut-bladdered fellow, such as a Premiership footballer or Bobby Davro, for example. Drink A Pint, Piss A Gallon.

darb *v.* To *shag, bonk, bang*.

dark end of the street *1. n.* Soul ballad written by William "Spooner" Oldham and covered by a succession of deeply misled white singers, usually following in the footsteps of Joe Cocker. *2. euph.* The *tradesman's entrance. 'And just exactly where do you think you're going with that, Charles? You've got the wrong one.' 'Actually, one fancied a walk to the dark end of the street, Camilla.'*

dark fart *n.* A *dropped gut* that contains a spot of unexpected *shopping*.

dark star *n.* Black, or rather brown hole from which the *pink Darth Vader* might emerge wearing a *shitty* helmet. *Uranus*.

darned hole in a jumper *sim.* Descriptive of a tightly-gathered *ringpiece*.

darted animal *n.* A *heavily refreshed* fellow who is reeling along and staggering from side to side, just prior to falling over in the gutter, in a style strongly reminiscent of a rogue rhinoceros which has just been shot with a tranquiliser gun.

Darth Vader's hat stand *n*. A sinister, six foot tall, wheezing *cock*.

Darth vulva *n*. The act of eating a *fish supper* with such gusto that it makes a sound not unlike Luke Sywalker's evil nemesis/long lost father trying to eat a squid without taking his helmet off.

dash for gash *n*. The desperate last half hour before chucking out at a night club. The *two am bin rake*.

date locker *n*. Rectum, *bomb bay*.

Dave Narey *rhym. slang. Scot*. A woman who would benefit from a major *waxing session, eg*. Anne Robinson and her who did *99 Red Balloons*. Named after the Dundee United footballer who famously scored with a 25-yard toe-poke against Brazil in the 1982 World Cup.

David Coulthard's chin *euph*. A gentleman's disturbing experience of glancing in the mirror midway through an *act of personal delight* and noticing that his lower mandible is stuck out in a style reminiscent of the box-faced ex-Formula One never-quite-was-been's.

David Peckham *n*. A young man who aspires to look like the England captain, but lives a very different lifestyle. ie, he has bleached, slicked-up hair, but wears *Armani and Navy* and drives a G-Reg Astra.

dawn horn *n*. An early morning *tent pole, bed flute. Morning wood*. See also *big cock day*.

dawn lumberjack *n*. A *woodsman* who is partial to taking his *chopper* in his hand early in the morning.

dawn patrol *1. n*. The somnambulant truckers, amphetamine-crazed taxi drivers and insomniac *Daily Mail* readers who tune in to thirsty presenter Sarah Kennedy's surreal, early hours ramblings on Radio 2. *2. n*. In the world of *gentlemen's entertainment* venues, the collection of circus sideshow freak strippers who take over from the *A-team* at about half past four in the morning. Named, appropriately enough, after the marching group of elephants in Disney's *Jungle Book*.

day in the wife, a *n*. A long-awaited Sunday afternoon *scuttle*. *'Can't come down to the boozer, lads. I'm spending a day in the wife.'*

daylighting *1. n*. Construction industry term describing the appearance of a tunnelling machine or driven pipe emerging from a soil face. *2. n. Touching cloth, turtle's head*.

Daz moment *n*. The exact time that a *MILF* reaches her sexual peak. From the washing powder advertisement slogan: "Get out the dirty, even at thirty".

DCAF *abbrev*. Pronounced "de-caff" like the pointless coffee, a term used to describe a woman walking in front of you whose rear aspect is so sexually attractive that you would be prepared to enjoy *carnival liaisons* with her regardless of how *fugly* her mug may turn out to be. Don't Care About the Face.

dead cat bounce *1. phr*. In stockmarket and economic parlance, an unexpected improvement in prospects which is swiftly followed by a further fiscal downturn. *2. phr*. Following a heavy night *on the sauce*, waking up feeling improbably chipper, only for your condition to inevitably and rapidly go downhill as the morning progresses.

dead heat *n.* The situation whereby the urge to defecate comes to glorious fruition at the exact moment when the buttocks touch the *bog seat*.

dead heat in a Zeppelin race *sim.* Large *tits, knockers, bazookas, oomlaaters, Gert Stonkers* that cause you to shout "Oh, the humanity!".

dead herring *n.* A female woman in a pub or club who looks as filthy as a pornstar but turns out to be as frigid as a deceased fish.

dead man's handle *n.* The life-saving "Stop" button on a DVD remote control, over which a gentleman's left thumb constantly hovers whilst he is enjoying an artistic videographic presentation.

dead man's wellies *n.* The often colourful but highly-repulsive used prophylactics which pepper festival campsites and pub car parks following bank holiday discos.

dead otter *n.* A single stool of immense proportions.

dealer's choice *1. n.* In card games, the situation whereby the player controlling the pack is permitted to dictate the rules of the game and the specific variant that is played. *2. n.* In a relationship, the situation whereby the gentleman is privileged to choose the favours that he requires of his ladyfriend as a consequence of some propitious circumstance, such it being his birthday or her wanting something. *'I'm sorry, love, but if you want that new kettle it's up the wrong 'un and no buts. I'm calling dealer's choice.'*

deal or no deal *n.* Gentleman's nightclub quandary; whether to turn down the offer of a certain *legover* from a below-par *boiler* early in the evening in the hope that he can get a higher calibre *box* later on, and thus risking ending up with *fuck all* at the end of the night. From the popular TV show for the housebound, where the constant question posed by tidy-bearded not-at-all-sinister host Noel Edmonds is: "Well, deal or no deal? Do you want to open the box?" *'Ayup. That scutter with the home-made tattoos is really giving you the glad eye, but there's some real quality blart over there. It's make your mind up time, is it deal or no deal?'*

dealt a Beadle, to be *v.* Whilst playing cards, to receive a totally *shit* hand.

Deansgate tornado *n.* Invisible yet severe, alcohol-fuelled, destructive cyclone which invariably strikes Manchester town centre between 11pm and 3am on Friday and Saturday nights. So named because it leaves irreparable carnage throughout the area, with people staggering about in torn clothes and clinging to lampposts to retain their balance. A *Whitley Bay whirlwind.*

dearotica *n.* Type of DVD ordered from a Nigerian porn site that costs the hapless purchaser the entire contents of his bank account. And his marriage.

death by chocolate starfish *1. n.* An incredibly disgusting *McArthur Park.* *2. n.* A chronic attack of the *Earthas.*

death nest *n.* Estate agent speak for the smaller house that elderly people buy late in life.

death row *1. n. US.* A section of a prison where the Texan authorities keep simpleminded black men prior to their execution for crimes which they have usually not committed. *2. n.* A retirement home or sheltered housing complex.

death star *n.* The *nipsy.*

debtors' dish *n.* Satellite television broadcast receiving apparatus. Term used by bailiffs and debt collectors who know that their indolent quarry will be at home watching advertisements for loan companies on the *shit pump.*

decadong *n.* A male *membrum virile* which, when roused to anger, achieves a length of ten inches in the old money.

decafathon *n.* A gruelling day-long test of stamina, consuming only things that are good for you. *'Battered sausage, chips and soapy peas please love, and a big bottle of Tizer. I'm doing a decafathon tomorrow.'*

declaration to the house *n.* When living in shared premises, the statement delivered to other tennants who might enter a *dumping shed* which you have recently vacated, explaining that you have nothing to do with the foul stench within.

decorate the downstairs loo *v.* To *plaster the toilet. 'Where's Esther? She's supposed to be on Luton High Street patronising some plebs for the Six O'Clock News cameras.' ' She's just decorating the downstairs loo.'*

decrapitation *n.* The act of cutting the head off a *Richard the Third,* in order to answer the door, get the phone or present *Thought for the Day* on Radio 4.

deep vein throbnosis *n. medic.* An uncomfortable *chob-on* that is worryingly difficult to shift.

deerstalker *n.* A lady's *bodily treasure* with tweedy *flaps* and a pipe stuck in it. Also known as a *Basil Rathbone.*

defarture lounge *n.* The vestibule of the *dirt bakery,* where *exhaust gases* gather in order to build up to maximum pressure. *'Fuck me, Your Majesty. I've got a right beauty brewing up in the defarture lounge, I don't mind telling you.'*

deflate *v.* To *suck off. 'Oi, Gillian. Deflate this for me, will you?'*

de-icer *1. n.* Motorists' windscreen-clearing solution, typically a bottle containing a poisonous-looking blue mixture of ethyl alcohol and low molecular weight glycol. *2. n.* Any drink bought for a woman by a man in the hope of de-frosting her *snatch,* typically a bottle containing a poisonous-looking blue mixture of ethyl alcohol and low molecular weight glycol.

de-ice the flaps *1. v.* In aeronautical circles, to carry out various procedures on an aeroplane which ensure that ice deposits on the wings do not impair the operation of the control surfaces and mechanisms. *2. v.* Of a frigid lady, to make use of her *muff* after a substantial lay-off.

Deirdre's neck *n.* The knotted strings supporting the *nadbag* that are under immense tension.

deja poo *1. n. Fr.* The peculiar feeling that you've had a particular *shite* before, or in a dream or something. Usually happens on a Sunday, if that's any help. *2. n. Fr.* An eerily familiar *copper bolt* that reappears after the first flush. A *poomerang.*

delete some cookies *v.* To nip upstairs for a sly *Max Planck. 'Evening, love. I've had a very busy day, so I'm just off upstairs to delete some cookies.'*

Delhi belly *n.* Delicate stomach condition leading to the *Eartha Kitts.*

Delia *n.* At a social engagement, the cringeworthy performance of an embarrassingly loud and drunken partner. From tired and emotional TV chef Delia Smith's motivational half-time address at the Norwich versus Man City game on

February 28th 2005. *'Oh Christ. She's had half a dozen Bacardi Breezers on an empty stomach. Give it ten minutes and she'll be doing a Delia on me.'*

Delilahs *n.* Stickily sweatsome *plums* which attach themselves to the side of the leg, and require hip-swivelling moves of the sort favoured by leather-faced, leather-trousered Welsh *scads* magnet Tom Jones to dislodge.

delivery from the coalman, take a *v.* To have a grubby chap empty his *sack* in your *back passage* on a regular basis.

dell 1. *n. 16thC.* Prostitute, *tom.* 2. *n.* Original Hampshire venue of Southampton F.C.'s annual relegation battle.

Denis Norden, do a *v.* To chat up a piece of *clump* in an unnecessarily long-winded and tiresome way instead of just asking for a *poke*. From the way that the erstwhile, antediluvian *It'll be Alright on the Night* host used to bore the liver out of everyone for ten minutes before each batch of funny clips.

Dennis Wise *n. prop.* In golfing circles, a short yet daunting putt. A nasty little five-footer.

dented tin *n.* A *bargain basement babe*; a woman who, at first glance, appears to be a total stunner but who is rendered affordable by a subtle fault, *eg.* Bad breath, an obsessive compulsive disorder, a small prehensile tail *etc.*

dentist, pretended she was at *euph.* Of an accommodating lady, to put her head back and open wide, though possibly not to spit afterwards. *'Good date, Mike?' 'Oh aye. She pretended she was at the dentist.'*

Deptford wives *n.* An *ankle chaingang* of women of uncertain breeding, stagger-ing under the weight of their *bingo clink* on a night out. Often to be seen lifting their tops to expose their *noinkers* for the cameras of Bravo TV's hard-hitting documentary series *Booze Britain*.

depth charge *n.* A large or heavy stool; a *copper bolt*. Also *belly flopper, Admiral Browning, Maxwell.*

derection *n.* The opposite of an erection, usually obtained by thinking about something unerotic. See *summoning Moira*.

derren *adj. medic.* Of a man, to be sterile. From the mentalist magician Derren Brown who, in a TV Russian Roulette stunt, was found to be *firing blanks*. *'No, we don't need a blob, love, I'm derren. But if you're really worried, I'll slip it in your brown pocket.'*

designer vagina *n.* Any *muff* which has been trimmed into an unusual shape, *eg.* A heart, a *Hitler tash*, the Netto logo or Craig David's beard. *Armani fanny, Versnatche.*

desk lifter *n.* An attractive lady teacher who, on bending over to pick up some chalk can cause 30 desklids to be raised simultaneously.

desktop dusting *n.* A fellow's daily ritual of deleting the numerous *male interest* images and thirty-second video clips from his desktop, recent documents and internet history folders, and thus leaving his computer as *clean as a gay bloke's flat.*

desktop dykes *n.* The sort of aesthetically-pleasing *lipstick lesbians* found in huge quantities on a healthy young man's hard disk, but exceedingly rarely, if ever, encountered in real life.

detesticles *n.* Like regular *clockweights*, but hateful to look at. Just like regular *clockweights*, then.

Dettori, do a *v.* Of a bloke, to leave the scene preveniently following the successful conclusion to an act of congress. Named after the "flying dismount" made famous by jockey Frankie Dettori MBE who, whenever he's ridden a winner, immediately jumps off, smiling.

devil's bagpipes *n.* A chap's *meat and two veg.*

devil's chimney *1. n.* Geological tourist attraction in the absence of anything else to look at on the Isle of Wight. *2. n.* The *shitter.*

devil's dumplings *n.* The *chesty substances* found on ladies' fronts.

devil's evacuate *n.* Piping hot *bum slurry* fermented in the depths of Hell. Diarrhoea.

devil's handshake *n.* A Roman Catholic *wank.* A means of reserving oneself a place in the eternal lake of fire.

devil's inkwell *n.* A gentleman's post *bust off* navel, brim-full with his onanistic yield.

devil's kiss *n.* A *fart* released during sex in the *69* position. *Hell's mouth.* On the plus side, it's probably not quite as bad as a *Satan's banquet.*

devil's kitchen *n.* The *chamber of horrors* or *dirt bakery.*

devil's playground *n.* A sulphurous pit. The *arse* or *wrong 'un.*

devil's whisper *n.* The absolutely last *Exchange & Mart* it is possible to let out before you really have to go for a *shit.*

dewing up *n.* Of a dirty woman, *creaming her bills.* 'Bless me father, for I have committed the sin of impure thought. I got front row tickets for Michael Bolton at the Arena and I was dewing up before he even come on the stage.'

dew on the lily *1. euph.* A lubricat-ed *flange. 2. n. Knob glaze, pre-cum. Perseverance soup, knuckle varnish.*

dew south *n.* The condition of a young lady's *parts* when she is in a state of arousal, for example whilst watching Preston scratch his *nuts* on *Celebrity Big Brother.*

dexys, do a *v.* Of a sexist male, to sober up in the night and realise that the dolly *bird* he thought he'd pulled has turned into a right *hound.* To do a *midnight runner.*

DFKDFC *abbrev. medic.* Used in patients' notes during diagnosis - Don't Fucking Know, Don't Fucking Care. *'Patient: Female. Age: 72. Presented: Hot flushes, swollen tongue, racing heart, low blood pressure, tingling down right side, loose finger nails. Diagnosis: DFKDFC. Treatment: Amoxyl 3 times a day.'*

dial Australia *v.* Of a lady, to *reach down under* using her digits. To *gusset type* or do the *front bum shimmy.*

diamond cutter *n.* The hardest erection known to man. *Pink steel.*

diamond in the muff *n.* A genuinely attractive woman in a *grumble flick.*

Diana, to do a *v.* To collide at a spot between two *tunnels* when having sex. To hit the *taint* with one's *bell end.*

Diana's dashboard *euph.* A *Kurt Cobain's ceiling.* A tasteless turn of phrase used to describe a messy pair of ladies' *scrods* during *rag week.*

dibble *1. v. 14thC.* To *shag. 2. n.* Cartoon police officer in Top Cat. *3. v.* To playfully prod around at the *hangar doors.*

Dibnah dick *n.* A sudden loss of erectile strength causing the *skin chimney* to collapse as if its foundations have been destroyed by the late eponymous Bolton steeplejack. Can be brought on by catching a whiff of badly-wiped *arse* when *changing at Baker Street.*

dick *1. n. US.* Penis, *pud, plonker. 2. n.* Idiot, *plonker.* '*Rodney, you fucking dick.*' (*Only Fools and Horses' Christmas Special,* 1955) *3. v.* To *fuck.*

dick and dom *euph.* A perfect bachelor's night in, *viz.* A *wank* followed by a pizza.

dick-do *n. US.* Light-hearted epithet used to describe a *salad-dodger.* Based on the assumption that "their gut probably sticks out more than their dick do". '*Deaths; Peter Ustinov, polyglot dick-do, 82.*' (from *The International Herald Tribune,* March 29th 2004).

dick docker *n.* A rabbi.

dick duster *n.* A hairy top lip on a lady. '*Anne, we'll have to do the wink again. You've got something on your dick duster.*'

Dickens cider *euph.* Saucily humorous phrase with a very specific usage, in that it can only really be used effectively in response to a very narrow range of questions, preferably posed by a red-nosed man in a pub on a garishly-illustrated seaside postcard, *eg.* '*What'll your missus be having tonight, Dave?*' '*Hopefully she'll have a Dickens cider, Bob.*'

dickhead *n.* Fool, *joskin, shit-for-brains.* An idiotic fellow.

dickhead dust *n.* White powder which, when snorted through a rolled-up banknote, turns even the nicest individual into a complete *twat.* Cocaine, *showbiz sherbert, Bolivian marching powder etc.* '*One of the Sunday newspapers reported that a Blue Peter presenter had been seen taking dickhead dust. I believe that he has not only let himself and the Blue Peter team down,*

including the dogs and tortoises and the Italian sunken garden, but he's also let all of you down badly. He himself agrees with me that, in the circumstances, he can no longer continue as a presenter on the programme. However, he'll be back in a couple of years doing phone-ins on Radio 5 and then he'll get Simon Mayo's gig.' (On-air apology by Lorraine Heggessey, head of BBC Children's Television, 1999).

dickie dido *n.* Something on a lady, the hairs on which come down to her knees.

Dickinson holiday *n.* A bottle of fake tan which makes the wearer look like a fucking satsuma. Named after bright orange cheeky ex-con TV auction wideboy David Dickinson.

dickling *n.* Sympathetic term descriptive of a fellow believed to have been short-sold in the *trouser department.* '*Today's birthdays: 1903; Habib Bourguiba, Tunisian politician: 1934; Jonas Savimbi, Angolan politician: 1946; Jack Straw, British dickling.*'

dick phlegm *n. Cock hockle.*

dick skinner *1. n. prop.* British disc jockey who used to be on Radio 1 but now he's on XFM. *2. n. medic. US. Wanking spanner, cunt scratcher.* Hand.

dick splash *1. n.* Urine on trousers or suede shoes caused by shakage or *splashback.* See also *forget-me-nots. 2. n. US.* Contumelious epithet for an unworthy person. Named after Senator Richard Splash, Vice President under Jimmy Carter.

Dick Turpin's hat *n.* A good old-fashioned three-cornered hairy *blurtch.*

dick van dyke *n.* A strap-on cockney. A lesbotic *twat* rattler, a dildo. A *Mary pop-in.*

dick weed *n. US.* A goldang *melon farming fuckwit.*

dick wheat *n.* Male pubic hair.

dickwit *1. n.* Probably a character from a Charles Dickens novel. *2. n.* A bloke who thinks with his *charlie*. *3. n.* A foolish person.

diddies *n. Scot.* Ladies' *tits.*

diddy man *1. n.* A jam butty miner. *2. n.* A *sausage sandwich* enthusiast.

diddy ride *n. Scot.* A deep-fried *sausage sandwich.*

Dierdres *n.* The stringy tendons, ligaments and sinews that pop out of a fellow's neck as he reaches the *vinegar strokes.* Named after the high-tension, harp-like structures which anchor Ken Barlow's missus's head onto her shoulders in *Corrie.*

diesel dyke *n. US.* A butch or masculine lesbian. Also *bulldyke, fanny nosher.*

diet choke *n.* A refreshing, low-calorie drink which is rich in *vitamin S.*

diet fart *n.* A loud clearing of the *nether throat* that sounds dangerous but actually has no smell and is harmless. *'No need to open the window, Your Majesty. It was just a diet fart.'*

difficult brown *n.* Tricky option in *bum games.* See also *Irish, snookered behind the red. 'I'd rather take the easy pink than the difficult brown.'*

difficult child *n.* One who, once *dropped off at the pool,* refuses to go into the water and clings onto the side.

digby *n.* A big, ugly woman. From the 70s children's film *Digby, the Biggest Ugly Woman in the World.*

Digby's collar *euph.* A *wizard's sleeve,* named in honour of the capacious, leathery neck restraint worn by the famous *Screen Test* sheepdog. Also *Clifford's collar.*

digestive transit *1. n.* Advert-speak for a big, steaming *crap. 2. n.* Lightweight commercial vehicle which delivers biscuits.

dig in the whiskers *n. Aus.* A spot of *beard-splitting. 'Fuck me, look at that Sheila. She's worth a dig in the whiskers, wouldn't you say, Rolf?'*

dig up a badger and bum it *exclam.* Phrase used when in a state of extreme sexual frustration. *'I tell you what, Una. I'm that horny I'd happily dig up a badger and bum it.'*

dildo *n.* Practice version of the *pork sword.* A *bob, neck massager, dolly dagger.*

dill *1. n.* An unpleasant thing put in burgers by the staff at McDonald's. *2. n.* A type of pickle.

dillberries *n. Dangleberries, wufflenuts.*

DILLIGAF/dilligaf *abbrev.* Disinterested rhetorical response to a question or enquiry. Do I Look Like I Give A Fuck.

dilm *n.* Unpleasant-tasting spermicidal lubricant on a *dunky.*

dilmah *n. Aus.* An amusing party entertainment whereby the performer of the trick bounces his *knackers* on the forehead of the first person to fall asleep. Named after an Australian brand of tea bag and the similar dunking action associated with them.

dimmock *1. v.* Of a lady, to create a *water feature.* See *squat 'n' squirt. 2. v.* Of a lady's nipples, to pop out like a car cigarette lighter.

dine at the Marriott's buffet *v.* To succumb to a bout of alimentary unpleasantness. Named after Tottenham Hotspur's meek last-match-of-the-season capitulation to West Ham in 2006, after the team's players were (our lawyer wishes to make clear) definitely not poisoned by dodgy comestibles consumed at the plush five-star hotel the previous evening. *'Uh-oh, and if our helicopter camera high above Tower Bridge could just zoom in there.... yes, it looks like Radcliffe's been dining at the Marriott's buffet again, Sue.' 'Yes, Steve. She's definitely shat herself alright.'*

ding-a-ling *n*. Chuck Berry's *cock*. With two silver bells hanging off it on a string.

ding! dong! *exclam. arch*. Caddish expression of delight when Terry-Thomas spotted a woman with *dunce's hats*, or when a cat fell down a well.

dingleberry roast *n*. A lighted *fart*, an *afterburner, a blue streak*.

dingo's breakfast *n. Aus*. A *piss* and a bit of a look around.

dining with the Askwiths *euph*. Illicit or surreptitious *puddle jumping*. From the deliberately misleading excuse offered to his missus by flamboyant Victorian playwright Oscar Wilde when he was late home for his tea; *viz*. That he was going for a meal with *Confessions* film actor and Patricia Hayes-lookalike Robin Askwith and his family.

dinner lady's arms 1. *n. medic*. Bingo wings. 2. *sim*. Large, but nonetheless unhealthy-looking *cocks*. A lardy penis that looks like it might have a heart attack at any moment.

dinner masher *n*. A *botter*.

dipping a worm in a bucket *v*. Engaging in unsatisfying sexual congress. *The last hot dog in the tin*.

dip 'n' dazzle *n*. A humourous epithet used to describe one whose ocular organs are so far out of whack as to be reminiscent of badly-adjusted headlights. An *Isaiah*. *eg*. The late Marty Feldman or that Kit Williams who done the book with the rabbit.

DIPS/dips *acronym*. Paris Hilton's car wing mirrors. Drunken Impact Protection System.

dip your nib in the office ink *euph*. To partake in a romantic liaison with a female work colleague. To *shit on your own doorstep*. *'What am I going to do, Tony? The News of the World's caught me dipping me nib in the office ink again.'*

dip your wick *v*. To slip your vinegary *dill* into the *hamburger*.

director's commentary *n*. The disconnected, self-obsessed *sotto voce* ramblings of bitter-sodden tramps.

director's cut *n*. The point in an 18th generation *jazz video* where a previous *Chinese helicopter pilot* has inadvertently pressed "Record" instead of "Pause", leaving the viewer with a four-second clip of *Panorama* circa 1994.

dirt bakery *n*. That part of the human anatomy where *holemeal loaves* are freshly manufactured around the clock. The *chamber of horrors*.

dirtbox *n. Date locker*, rectum. Source of delights for devotees of *bumcraft*.

dirty Beppe *n*. A *dirty Sanchez*, but with coverage extended to the chin.

dirty bomb 1. *n*. A crude explosive device containing radioactive material designed to contaminate an area, making it uninhabitable. 2. *n*. A *dropped back*, the fallout from which makes the immediate vicinity uninhabitable for the foreseeable future, *eg*. One detonated by Jocky Wilson at a cocktail party. 3. *n*. A *shit explosion* that peppers the bowl with bio-hazard shrapnel.

dirty Bristow *n.* A sexual act performed by a lady whereby she kneels behind a standing gentleman and licks his *anus* whilst reaching through his legs to stimulate his penis. Occasionally stopping to swig a pint of lager. *Tromboning.*

dirty chips *n.* One distinctly unappetizing result of not pulling your string vest up properly when going for a *sit-down lavatory adventure* (© G Coren, 2008). You'll be needing that string vest washed and all.

dirty dentist *n. Fanny mechanic, snatch doc, box doc, cunt dentist.* A consultant gynaecologist. *'I'm having a bit of bother with me clopper, love, so I'm off to the dirty dentist for a scrape.'*

dirty devil *n.* An under-duvet *dropped gut* that tests one's relationship to breaking point. *'Sorry about that dirty devil, love. Anyway, it's your turn on top, isn't it? Then you can stick the kettle on.'*

dirty fart *n.* A *Lionel Bart* with delusions of grandeur. A *follow through.*

dirty lolly *n.* A girl whom one is tempted to *pick up* and lick, but who is probably covered in germs.

dirty onion *n.* The overture to an act of *backdoor romance* that is performed with such unexpected vigour by the *bummer* that it brings an involuntary tear to the eye of his *bummee.*

dirty penguin, walk the *v.* To waddle in a shameful, short-stepping manner designed to ameliorate the unpleasant consequences of *gambling and losing* whilst out and about.

dirty protest *n.* The result of placing a bowl of baked beans in the microwave without covering it up, creating - in miniature - the *shit*-smeared decor of a late

1970s Northern Irish prison cell.

dirty Sanchez *1. n.* Television programe in which a group of educationally subnormal Welshmen dare each other to drink *piss*, set fire to their *bell ends*, nail their scrotums to double decker buses *etc. 2. n.* Sticking one's finger up a lady's *back bottom* during *doggy-style* sex. Then drawing a moustache on her top lip, apparently.

dirty secret *n.* A pungent *back biscuit* left by a surreptitious *benefactor* as he innocently sidles away from a group. *'I knew they weren't going to offer me the job. Mind you, at least I managed to leave a dirty secret as I got up to leave.'*

dirty spine, snip a length of *v.* To *lay a cable, drop a copper bolt.*

dirty Stilgoe *n.* A variation on the *dirty Sanchez*, but this time with the full beard drawn on, in order to create the effect of the erstwhile *Nationwide* topical songsmith Archie Slogdirt *(anag).*

dirty ticket *n.* A very easy lady. *'I must say, when I first met Sarah at Klosters, I thought she was a bit of a dirty ticket. However, she's put all that behind her now, and I think she's going to make an excellent Duchess.'* (Prince Philip, wedding reception speech, 1986).

dirty Titchmarsh, do a *v.* To perform a rudimentary garden makeover without the owner's knowledge, a process that typically involves adding a used *jubber* and a pair of discarded *scads* to the existing landscaping arrangement. See *incapability brown.* *'You know that lass I was talking to in the pub? The one who was feeling sick so I took her outside for some fresh air? After she spewed up we got talking, and to cut a long story short, we ended up doing a* *dirty Titchmarsh in a garden round the corner.'*

dirty U-boat *n.* The (probably non-existent, though if it does exist, it'll be very popular in Germany) act of doing a *poo* in the bath for sexual gratification.

dirty waffle *n.* A *shit* placed in a sock and then inserted into your hotel trouser press in order to fill the air with the aroma of hot, baking *turd*.

dirty water *n. medic.* A medical term for seminal fluid. *Bollock bile.*

disabilitits *n.* Funbags which are so large that they become a hindrance. Faith Brown is apparently entitled to a parking permit because of her terrible *disabilitits.*

disco fanny *adj.* The full strength flavour achieved by a vigorous evening of giving it *six nowt* on the dance floor.

disco light beauty *n.* A woman who looks cracking when viewed from the DJ booth, but is revealed in all her hideous glory when the *ugly lights* go on.

disco nap *n.* A spot of mid-afternoon shut-eye that ensures you will be able to stay awake whilst clubbing until the early hours.

disfabled *adj.* To be claiming invalidity benefit on dubious grounds, *eg.* That copper who was off work with stress, but bravely managed to referee a Premiership football match.

dishonourable discharge *1. n. milit.* The shameful result of knocking the *little general's helmet* off. *2. n.* An act of *self delight* performed in a morally questionable location, *eg.* In the toilets of your nan's nursing home, at a funeral parlour or into a knicker drawer belonging to the un-named vocalist of a late 1980s power-pop combo while she is on stage. Singing *China in Your Hand.*

disneyland *n.* A woman who takes an inordinate amount of time and a large amount of money to get into, although once you do, all the *rides* are free. Also *legoverland.*

display model *n.* A bit of *morning wood* that's just for show and, despite everyone's best efforts, refuses to *go off.*

ditch one in the Hudson *v.* On the way home from the pub, curry house or Fat Duck, to suddenly get the *two minute warning* whilst still a considerable distance from the safety of one's own *dumper* and be forced to make an emergency *final approach* and *splash landing* in a nearby quiet thoroughfare. To suffer a *turd strike.*

ditch pig *n.* An affectionate, lighthearted epithet for an ugly fat girl.

dive on the barbed wire *v.* Of an heroic member of a predatory group of males encountering a similarly-sized cohort of females, to bravely volunteer to establish an early foothold by approaching the least attractive (and therefore, in all likelihood, the most receptive) of the counterpart group, thereby allowing his comrades to clamber across behind him. To *take the chubby bullet.*

diving bell *n.* A notably cold, hard *muff* which clangs when you bang it.

diving for pearls *n. Post-poke* truffling in the *bearded clam.*

divot *n.* A particularly hairy *placket.*

dixy's midnight runs *n. medic.* The overwhelming urge to empty one's *Camillas* during the penultimate hour of the day, felt shortly after consuming any form of vaguely poultry-based sustenance prepared at the popular north-western fast food franchise.

DIY *euph*. A single-handed job done around the house at the weekend using one *tool* and a bag of *nuts*.

dizzyade *n*. Beer. Also *dizzy pop*.

Dizzy Gilespie *n*. A formidable blast on the *spunk trumpet* where the lady's cheeks puff out like a bullfrog's, and it would be a good idea for the man to stick a mute up his *arse* to keep the noise down.

do *v*. To give someone *one*. *'No kissing, just cold, hard sex. And absolutely no simulation - these birds are really being done.'* (from an advertisement for erotic videos in the *Daily Express*).

do a West Ham *sim*. To *score* and *stay up* when you haven't really got it in you. Formerly *do a Southampton*.

dobber 1. *n*. A *rubber johnny*. 2. *n*. A semi-erect *dill*. A lazy *lob on*. 3. *v*. To cheat someone out of something, to rip off. From a bloke called Dobber Bailey from Coventry who famously, twenty years ago, got ripped off buying an engine for his Triumph TR7. *'I tried to buy a genuine Nigerian Breitling off the internet but I got dobbered.'*

dobgob *v*. To *spooge up* when only half *stonked*. Also *dobglob*.

Doc Brown, do a *v*. To delete all the *left-handed websites* from one's computer's history file, an act usually carried out between 12.30am and 1.00am, after the wife has gone to bed. Named after the eccentric inventor in the *Back to the Future* films, who was not averse to meddling with the past when the need arose.

dock 1. *n*. Arse. The polite term by which horsey types refer to their steeds' *fudge tunnels*. 2. *v*. To *shag*. Up a horse's *arse*. Possibly whilst standing on your motor-cycle helmet.

docker's omelette *n*. A glistening gobbet of rubbery phlegm with remarkable anti-traction properties. A *gold watch*, a *Rolex prairie oyster*.

docker's tea break *sim*. Descriptive of something very long. *"Oh, what a tiny little man,' laughed Verruca Salt as she saw the Oompah Loompah with his bright orange skin and green hair. 'He may be small,' cautioned Mr Wonka as he turned briskly on his heel, 'but he'll have a cock as long as a docker's tea break."* (from *Charlie and the Chocolate Sandwich* by Roald Dahl).

docker's thumbs *n*. Nipples so hard one could hang a soaking wet duffle coat off them. *Scammell wheelnuts, JCB starter buttons, Dimmocks, chapel hat pegs*.

docking *n*. The rolling of one's *fiveskin* over another chap's hat. A *clash of heads*.

docking station *n*. A *puddle jumpers'* hostelry where copious amounts of *fairy liquid* are quaffed.

dockyard cat, fanny like a *sim*. Descriptive of a particularly unkempt, semi-feral *snatch*. *Terry Waite's allotment, Alan Johnston's vegetable patch*.

dockyard rivets *n*. *Cigarbutts, pygmies' cocks*.

doctor's signature *n*. A particulary wiggly pair of *beef curtains* resembling a GP's illegible scrawl at the bottom of a prescription.

Dodd finger *n*. An exploratory digit that tickles a lady's *tradesman's entrance* during the *warm-up exercises*, in order to ascertain whether she's up for a spot of *rearguard action*. From the dentally-challenged scouse jam butty magnate's famous between-the-legs tickling stick.

'I say. What a lovely day, madam, what a lovely day for sticking my Dodd finger up your arse and saying, "How's that for something to bring Tears to your eyes?"'

Dodd job *n.* A *nosh* administered by the more toothsome lady, or perhaps one who likes to bite. *'Fancy another Dodd job, Normski?' 'No thanks, Janet. By the way, have you seen the TCP anywhere?'*

dodd *v.* To *shit* oneself in public. Named after a certain James Dodd who *shit* himself on the way to work and then phoned in to say he couldn't come in because he had *shit himself.*

dodger's conscience *n.* The ridiculous purchase of a diet drink after a *Duke* or *Duchess of Giblets* has ordered a large pie and chips, two pickled eggs, a battered sausage and "a saveloy while I'm waiting".

doesn't play poker *euph.* Said of a fellow who *knows what's in his flowerbeds.* *'You know him who does the weather on the BBC? He doesn't play poker, you know. I seen it in the Daily Mail.'*

doesn't really follow football *euph.* Descriptive of a chap who *is doesn't play poker.* Also *not really interested in cars. 'See that bloke over there getting banged up the shitter off the big hairy man in leather shorts? Well, apparently he doesn't really follow football, if you get my drift.'*

dog 1. *n.* A woman who fails to reach an acceptable standard of attractiveness. A *steg, hound.* 2. *n.* A male prostitute. 3. *v.* To hang around in car parks at night, in the pretence of walking a dog, in order to spy on courting couples and watch it *go in* whilst *searching for loose change* in one's pockets.

dog at broth, like a *sim.* Descriptive of a desperate sexual act, usually *cumulonimbus. 'After returning from war service, Prince Philip was like a dog at broth when introduced to Her Majesty's front bum.'*

dog beers *n.* Any ale drunk by one who is unable to handle their beer. Drinking one *dog beer* leaves the average *two pot screamer* feeling and looking like he has drunk seven.

dog catcher *n.* A man who goes looking for unwanted *hounds* in a nightclub after all the pedigree *blart* has been collared. A *munter hunter, rat-trapper.*

dog deaf *n. medic.* Selective hardness of hearing which affects *shit machine* owners, rendering them unable to hear their beloved pets barking all day and night, and also leaves them aurally insensate to desperate entreaties from their neighbours to keep the bastard things quiet.

dog eating hot chips *sim.* A crude and voracious, yet effective, *horatio* technique. *'Lusitania was powerless to resist. His eyes burned into hers like garnets. His muscular arms enfolded her body as she felt herself being swept away in a force 10 gale of passion. Slowly, she fell to her knees and unzipped Giuseppe's breeches and went at his cock like a dog eating hot chips.'* (from *The Countess and the Lion Tamer* by Barbara Cartland).

dog eggs *n. Turds*, often laid on the pavement. *Lawn sausages.*

dog egg theory *n.* Scientific *blart* hypothesis; *viz.* The older it is, the easier it is to pick up.

doggie chalks *n.* White canine excrements. *Poodle shit.*

doggies *n.* Intercourse performed in the

position favoured by *hounds*, usually near some dustbins.

dogging *n*. The saucy behaviour of one who *dogs*.

doggy style *adj*. From the back. Or up against a visitor's trouser leg.

dog handler *n*. Offensively sexist term for a man who is prepared to go out with a right *fugly* old *ditch pig*.

dog in a bath *n*. A bedroom game like *rodeo sex*. *'The missus was setting the video last night and I was on me vinegar strokes when I called her by her sister's name. It was like trying to keep a dog in a bath.'*

dogler effect *n*. The scientific phenomenon of a woman who looks attractive from a distance who, as she get nearer is revealed to be a bit of a *hound* but then, as she walks away again, gradually gets more attractive again. Also known as *dogler shift*.

dog lime *n*. *Dog eggs*, canine feculant.

dog-locked *adj*. Stuck in a compromising position due to an unlikely muscular spasm, usually in the back of a car in a *Confessions* film. Also, *dog's lock-in*.

dognose *v*. To disturb one's slumbering wife following a *slash* in the small hours by touching her on the leg or buttocks with a cold, wet *bell end*.

dog section 1. *n*. Division of the constabulary that uses highly-trained alsatians to apprehend people who run around with quilts tied to their right arm, firing starter pistols into the air. 2. *n*. Sexist and offensive police station slang for the corner of the canteen where the pig-ugliest and *lesbo* WPCs (*ie*. the ones who least resemble strippagrams) congregate to eat.

dog slobber *n*. *Electric spaghetti*.

dog slug *n*. The act of licking around, and indeed inside, another person's *rusty sherrif's badge*. A *trip round the world*, a *rim job*.

dog toffee *n*. Tacky pavement deposit that readily adheres to the sole of a shoe or supports an upright lollipop stick.

dog toss *n*. Grinding against a woman's leg in an over-eager fashion whilst dancing at a night club, school disco, or wedding reception.

dog track *n*. The song (usually *Lady in Red*) played at ten to two in a nightclub, that precipitates a last-attempt mad dash onto the dancefloor by all remaining *hounds* on the premises. A *desperate dance*.

dog with two dicks, like a *sim*. Descriptive of a *tomcat with three balls*. To be incredibly pleased with oneself. *'That's one small step for man, one giant leap for mankind. I'm on the Moon and I'm as happy as a dog with two dicks, me.'* (Neil Armstrong, July 1969).

dog's arse *adj*. To be troubled with wind. *'Excuse the wife. I'm afraid she's got a dog's arse today, Your Holiness.'*

dog's back *n*. See *Bilbo Baggins' foot*.

dog's bollocks *n*. Bee's knees, *donkey's knob, monkey's nuts, cat's knackers etc*.

dog's legs *n*. *medic*. Temporary weakness in the male thighs following a spot of *back-scuttling* with a *dirty lady*.

dog's lipstick *n*. A shimmery pink, retractable cosmetic favoured by magicians' assistants.

dog's marriage *n*. A twenty-minute *al fresco back scuttle* that ends when the neighbours throw a bucket of water over you.

dog's match *n*. A sexual encounter in a

public place, *eg*. In a bush, doorway, taxi queue or hospital casualty cubicle.

Doherty's kitten *euph*. Not to be confused with Delaney's donkey, a person of either gender who regularly partakes in a spot of *cumulonimbus*. '*I tell you what, our vicar's licked more crack than Doherty's kitten.*'

dole pole *n*. A walking stick used as a prop by an enterprising able-bodied person whilst attempting to claim extra social security benefits. See also *social sticks*. '*Eeh. Look at the time. I'll have to run or I'll be late for my appointment at the DSS.*' '*Don't forget your dole pole.*'

dolesmith *n*. One who makes a living by practising the traditional British craft of collecting state benefits.

doley's blackout *n*. A mid-afternoon session of *self-abuse* snatched during a lull in daytime television. Achieved by shutting the curtains after *Quincy* for a quick *tug*.

Dolita *n*. A young *piece* who will never have to work a day in her life.

dolly dagger *n*. A *bob*, *dildo*.

dollymop *n*. An amateur or inexperienced prostitute.

dolmio day *n*. The first seventh of *rag week*.

dolphin skin *n. medic*. The epidermis of the *herman gelmet*.

Don King in a headlock *sim*. Descriptive of a foreign lady's armpits.

Donald 1. *n. rhym. slang. Fuck*. From Donald Duck. 2. *adj. rhym. slang*. Irretrievably broken or ruined, a term derived from the name of the erstwhile speech-impaired, bad-tempered Disney cartoon fowl. From Donald Ducked = fucked. '*What's up, Cliff?*' '*I snapped me banjo string and now me cock's Donald, Hank.*'

Donald Campbell *n. prop*. At the end of a long and unproductive visit to the toilet, the eventual arrival of some sort of relief. From the famous last words of the speed ace as his motorboat Bluebird K7 flipped over at approximately 300mph during a world record attempt on Coniston Water in 1967, and he *shat* himself, *viz*. "I'm going, I'm going, I've gone!"

donger *n. Whanger, pork sword, dill.*

dongloids *n*. Telltale globlets of *jizz* found on the marital duvet following a *game of singles.*

donkey 1. *n*. A clod-hopping footballer, such as Titus Bramble off of Wigan Athletic or St Johnstone's Michael Duberry. 2. *n*. A male prostitute, derived from the onomatopoetic fact that he is a "he-whore".

donkey kisser *n*. An inexperienced osculatrix. A lady who *snogs* like a burro chewing an apple.

donkey punch *n*. Of *bum games*, to knock your partner out cold with a blow to the back of the head whilst in the *vinegar strokes*. Has the same aphrodisiacal effect as slamming a goose's neck in a drawer whilst committing bestiality. Results in inceased orgasmic intensity and a custodial sentence.

donkey rigged *adj*. Of a man, blessed with a sizeable *stick of rock*.

donkey's earhole *n*. A particularly large, flappy, twitching vagina. A *hippo's mouth*, a *clown's pocket*.

Donkey style, do it *v*. To copulate up the *wrong 'un*. ie, in the *ass*.

donkified *adj*. To have a *horse's handbrake*, to be in a state of *tumescence*. To be *on the bonk.*

donner *n*. An unattractive woman, a *ten*

pinter, ie. Someone one wouldn't fancy too much when sober.

donny burns *n.* The tan achieved when standing in the away end at Doncaster Rovers on a hot day, when only half of your body is exposed to the rays of the scorching South Yorkshire sun.

donor *n.* One who believes it is better to give than to receive. See *benefactor.*

don't tear it, I'll take the whole piece *exclam.* Ancient, humorous, rag trade-based phrase used in response to an extremely dry, raspy *trouser cough. See also anybody injured?; well struck Sir!*

doodlebugs *n.* Heavy *Gert Stonkers* which, when released from their restraining *tit pants,* dive earthwards suddenly and without any warning, leaving smoking craters where they strike the ground. *Metatarsal breakers.*

doofa *n.* A *ten-to-two-er.* From the phrase "She'll do for me".

dooking for fritters, looks like he's been *sim.* Amusing Caledonian expression used to describe a youth with a *plooky* face, who looks like he might have been *bobbing for chips in a deep fat fryer.*

doomsday book *n. Toilet literature* perused between sobs whilst suffering an apocalyptic rectal breakdown. Usually the *Autotrader.*

Doonicans *n.* Assorted *claps,* NSUs and *doses.* From the initials of the bejumpered Irish rocking chair croonster Val.

doorbell *n.* A small button above the *snail's doorstep* that is so difficult to find, that it is often easier to use the *knockers.* The *clematis.* Also *devil's doorbell.*

doorman, have a word with the *v.* To butter up the *bald headed bouncer* in order to be allowed into the premises he is guarding. To *cumulously nimbate* the *clematis.*

doormat basher *1. n.* One who whacks their partner's *fanny* on the back yard wall to get the dust off it, whatever that means. *2. n.* A *lesbo.*

doos *n. Tits.*

doppelbanger *1. n.* A cheeky bloke who gets to *shag* a girl because she is so drunk that she thinks she is being *shagged* by her boyfriend. Being a *doppelbanger* is something of a legal and moral grey area, and may result in a substantial prison term. *2. n.* A *porkswordsman* who has, somewhat disconcertingly, elected to *do the dirties* on a regular basis with a female who looks exactly like himself.

doppelganger dick *n.* A *hard on* of such intensity, that one's own face is seen reflected in the shiny head, affording it the appearance of a miniature double. A *mini me.*

dopper *n.* A *dork.*

Doppler shit *n.* A *twintone bum siren* that gradually changes in pitch and clarity, before suddenly - and alarmingly - dropping an octave.

doris *adj. rhym. slang. On the other bus.* From the name of the famous Hollywood musical actress who, in the 1950s and 60s, starred in a series of light romantic comedies with *doris* actor Rock Hudson; Doris Domosexual.

doritoes *n.* Exceptionally cheesy feet.

dork *n.* A *dopper.*

Dorothy Perkins *n.* DP, double penetration. Of a lady, to simultaneously have *gentlemen callers* at her front and back doors. Also a *man at C&A,* a *double decker. 'In the cinema, one so-called film featured a man using disgusting sexual language. Another showed a* *lady baring her bosoms in the most provocative manner. A third film showed two well-hung men giving a woman a right Dorothy Perkins whilst she repeatedly took the Lord's name in vain. I was so disgusted that I vomited into my handbag. I think Mr Muggeridge next to me felt ill too, as he was groaning and rummaging frantically in his trouser pockets for a handkerchief.'* (Mary Whitehouse's report on a fact-finding trip to Amsterdam's Red Light District, 1968).

Dorothy Porker *1. n.* A white lie told to his wife by a man who, although he's not *good with colours*, is not averse to occasionally *helping out the other side* when they're a bit short. *2. n.* Unkind epithet for a comedienne who thinks she's funny because she has *big bones*.

dorsal fin *n.* The sharp ridge or crest, consisting of raw cornflakes, which painfully slices lengthways down the *clackervalve* during a *sit down visit* to the water closet to *park one's breakfast*.

do the decent thing *v.* Of a lady who is *up on blocks*, to dutifully empty her husband's *bins* by means of an act of *horatio*.

do the rubbish *v.* To *take it up the wrong 'un*. Named, aparently, after a girl working in an Italian restaurant in Glasgow who not only took out the refuse but also happily took it up the *council gritter*. *'That bird last night was a right dirty cow, mam. She did the rubbish.'*

double adapter *euph.* *AC/DC* man equipped with a *one pin plug* at the front but also having the benefit of a fully-functioning *single pin socket* at the back. A *switch hitter*.

double Barker *n.* A woman blessed with the body of Sue, but cursed with the face of Ronnie. A *bobfoc*.

double bassing *v.* To have sex from behind, fiddling with the lady's left nipple with your left hand and twanging away at her *clematis* with your right - a position similar to the one adopted when playing the upright bass, although the sound is completely different. To perform *charlimingus*.

double booked *adj.* Of a lady, to be romantically entertaining two gentlemen at the same time. A *man at C & A*.

double bouncers *n.* Value for money *tits* that resonate at twice the frequency of the woman's gait. *ie.* Two bounces per step taken.

double cuffs *n.* The excessively-large *chinstraps* on a *bear trapper's hat*.

double dipper *1. n.* One who, unable to decide between *rice and chips*, has half a portion of each. A *switch hitter*, a *happy shopper*. A bisexual. *2. n.* One who does a bit of *double dipping*.

double dipping *1. n.* The social faux pas of returning a previously bitten tortilla chip, for instance, into a communal bowl for a second portion of sauce, as seen in the *Seinfeld* episode *The Implant*. *2. n.* The social faux pas of tramping your *naughty boot* through all the *muck* in your ladyfriend's *back yard* before waltzing in through her *front door* and leaving *shit* on the *snail's doorstep*.

double doors *n.* Beef curtains, cat flaps, hangar doors.

double dragback *1. n.* The Marseille turn. An impressive football trick as perfected by the likes of headbutt-happy Frenchman Zinédene Zidane. *2. n.* A painful *wanking* accident whereby an inexperienced masturbatrix loses rhythm, resulting in one downward stroke being immediately followed by another, thus causing severe *one string banjo* trauma. An ineptly-syncopated *Barclay's*.

double fare *n.* One whose fat *arse* takes up two seats on a train or bus. A *salad dodger, barge-arse, fat fuck*.

double glazing *n.* Something that the late Ted Moult would almost certainly not have approved of or, indeed, endorsed in a long-running television advertising campaign. Two blokes *blowing their beans* over one *bird* at the same time.

double header *n.* Of a *grumble flick* thespienne, the intriguing act of performing simultaneous *horatio* on two *gut sticks*.

double the melt *v.* To give a lady not one, but two portions of hot stringy cheese in her *hambuger*. To squirt a second portion of filling into a *vertical bacon sandwich* with one's *cheddar apple*.

double velvet *n.* A particularly keen *ginger beer, ie.* Someone who "loves your bum".

double yolker *n.* A pornographic actor blessed with the elusive ability to fire off two consecutive *pop shots* without pausing for a sit down and a cup of tea in between. It is not known whether this happens in civilian life.

Dougal *1. n.* The agitated, easily-animated, Tony Hancock-soundalike cylindrical dog from The *Magic Roundabout. 2. n.* A hairy *fanny* that has really gone to seed.

doughnut puncher *n.* A *dinner masher.*

doughy hood *1. n.* Character in *The Archers* played by Arnold Ridley, better known as Private Godfrey in *Dad's Army. 2. n.* A *women's thing* that can probably be fixed with a tub of natural yoghurt.

dowel *1. n.* In carpentry, a piece of wood that fits exactly into a hole. *2. n.* In sex, a piece of *wood* that fits exactly into an *a-hole.*

Dow Jones *n.* A fellow who is expert in the art of *footsie.*

downhill skier *n.* See *skiing position.* A *crane operator.*

downtime *n.* The period which elapses between ejaculation and rearousal. In most men, downtime is around 20 minutes, though in the case of Cliff Richard it is now 41 years and counting.

down to the viscounts *euph.* Descriptive of a chap who is bereft of *spangle* and thus scraping the bottom of his *biscuit barrels.* A reference to the apparently unpopular foil-wrapped minty confections which are only eaten when all other snack options have been exhausted. *'Quick Horace, shoot it on my belly.' 'I can't, love, sorry. I'm down to the viscounts.'*

dowsing rod *n.* A *twig* that involuntarily twitches when approaching an area of great wetness.

doxy *n. arch.* Whore, *slag.*

D'Oyly *rhym. slang.* From D'Oyly Carte = heart to heart.

do your thing, clickety-click *euph.* To have a *wank* over internet pornography. See also *buying your better half an anniversary present.*

DP *acronym.* Double Penetration. Especially *one up the arse, one up the fanny.* Often leads to a *Newton's cradle.*

Dracula's tea bags *n.* Used *dangermice.*

drag and drop *1. phr.* In computing, the ingenious method whereby, thanks to the use of a graphical user interface, PC users can move icons between folders or create shortcuts on their desktop. 2. *phr.* The first cigarette of the day which, when combined with coffee, can lead to a cataclysmic opening of the *Camillas*.

dragging a wardrobe up a concrete ramp, like *sim.* A phrase descriptive of a particularly cavernous and rasping act of flatulation.

dragging like a seal's ringpiece *sim.* Descriptive of something that seems to last forever, *eg.* Being chained to a radiator next to Brian Keenan in Beirut, waiting for a Pink Floyd song to reach a bit of tune you recognise, watching an *Only Fools and Horses* Christmas Special.

dragon food *n.* Chocolates bought for *her indoors* when one is in the *cunt book*. *'Shit, I've been out on the piss for three days. I'd better stop by the garage and pick up some dragon food before I get home.'*

dragon's nostril *n.* The state of the ring-piece after a hot *Ruby Murray* or a vigorous *St George.*

dragon's snout *n.* A particularly grotesque *turtle's head* which is accompanied by blasts of fiery breath, and may cause damsels to become distressed.

drain your spuds *v.* To micturate. To have a *gypsy's kiss, slash.*

drat strap *n.* A G-string worn underneath the sheer outer garmentry of a young, nubile bit of *crackling*. Named after the cry of frustration and disappointment it elicits from the intending pervert.

draw a cock over it *v.* To do a shoddy job or *cunt* something *off*. *'England certainly didn't turn in a particularly impressive performance against Germany this afternoon, eh Alan?' 'No Gary. They pretty much drew a cock over the entire game.'*

draw an ace *v.* On wiping one's *arse* thoroughly, to eventually have an unsoiled piece of paper which indicates that the process has been successfully completed.

draw mud from the well *v.* To *follow through*. *'I've just drawn mud from the well, so it's back to Jeremy in the studio.' 'Thank-you Kirsty.'*

drawn-on durex *n.* A biro line sketched around the base of the penile shaft which fools a drunken lady into thinking one has taken sensible precautions.

drayhorse's bottom lip *sim.* A big, floppy, whiskery *snatch*. Full of carrots.

dread logs *n. Winnets* you could use to batter down a door.

down to one's last bead *adj.* Having an empty *sack, balls like bats' wings.* Bereft of *men's spendings, wankrupt.*

dreadnought *n.* Even bigger than a *dead otter.*

dreamboat body, shipwreck face *n.* A jaunty, nautical alternative to *bobfoc* when describing your local Sarah Jessica Parker.

dream topping *n.* Night *spongle*, whipped up in the *farmer's hat* during pornographic REM sleep.

dress-messer *n.* A gentleman with a *hair trigger*.

drink from both taps *v.* To be bisexual, to *bend both ways*. See *double adapter.*

drinking cap on *euph.* Descriptive of one whose thought processes have been severely disrupted as a result of taking alcoholic beverages on board. *'Powell, who clearly had his drinking cap on, was arrested at the motorway service station shortly after 5.30am.'*

drink my kids *exclam*. Informal variant of *"suck my penis"*, usually used in a declamatory sense, rather than a genuinely sexual one.

drink on a stick *n*. A *nosh*. *'Pull over in this layby, Geoff. I fancy a drink on a stick.'*

drinks under the dartboard, looks like she *sim*. Of a lady who possesses a face that does not conform to classical standards of beauty.

drips in the tap, a few more *phr*. Excuse given by a gentleman who is returning from the pub *bogs* with a *wet penny in his pocket*. *'Look at that. I put it away too early when there was still a few more drips in the tap. Anyway, where was I? Oh yes, your grandad's operation. Well, I'm afraid there were complications during surgery. I think you should prepare yourselves for some bad news.'*

drip tray *n*. The often crusty sump in a pair of lady's *dunghampers*.

dripping like a fucked fridge *sim*. Of a lady, to be sexually aroused. *'I'm in the mood for love / Simply because you're near me / and whenever you're near me / I drip like a fucked fridge.'* (Song lyric, *The Mood for Love* by Cole Porter).

dripping like a George Foreman grill *sim*. Descriptive of a *bird* who is *fizzing at the bunghole* or *dripping like a fucked fridge*.

drive from the ladies' tee *v*. Of a man, to sit down in order to have a *slash*.

drive stick *1. v. US*. To be capable of driving a motor car equipped with a manual gearbox. *2. v. US*. To be a lady in uncomfortable shoes, to not *like tennis*. To be a non-*lezza*.

drive the porcelain bus *v*. To pay a kneel-down visit to the lavatory during which one holds the rim like a Routemaster steering wheel and does some *psychedelic yodelling*.

driving on the cats' eyes *v*. To emit a long, low, rumbling *fart* that sounds like it's going to damage one's suspension.

driving range *n*. The perineum. Where one hits one's *balls* when practising with one's *wood*.

drop a clot *v. medic*. To menstruate. *'It was D'Arcy who spoke first. 'Your disdain takes me somewhat aback, Miss Bennet. I fear I might have acted in some way inappropriately to cause you such offence.' 'No, Mr D'Arcy, your behaviour has been impeccable, and the fault lies with me. I am dropping clots at the moment and find myself in the foulest of humours,' she replied.'* (from *Pride and Prejudice* by Jane Austen).

drop a deuce *euph*. *Lay a cable*, do a *number two*, *do a duty*, defecate. Phrase popularised in the US comedy show *My Name is Earl*.

drop a dress size *v*. Of a lady, to do a really big *digestive transit*. *'Fern, you're looking well this morning. Have you had your hair done or something?' 'No, Eamonn. I just dropped a dress size I've been baking for a couple of weeks, that's all.'*

drop a gut *v*. To *step on a duck*.

drop a link *v. milit*. To *do a duty*. From the practice of armoured units, who apparently sometimes have to remove a short section from their tank tracks when they become slack. *'Field Marshal Montgomery, we're ready to start the battle of El Alamein. Are you coming out?' 'With you in a minute. I'm just dropping a link.'*

drop a pebble *v*. To erroneously emit a

rabbit tod whilst attempting to *shoot a bunny*. See also *follow through*.

drop a tadpole in her beer *v. Aus.* To make a lady pregnant. *'Her Majesty the Queen is pleased to announce that after several years of trying, HRH Prince Edward, the Duke of Wessex has finally succeeded in dropping a tadpole in the Rt Hon Sophie, Countess of Wessex's beer.'* (Official notice, Buckingham Palace Gates, May 2003).

drop anchor in bum bay *v.* To arrive at the *rear admiral's* favourite port of call. To wash up on *spice island*.

drop fudge *v.* To *pinch a loaf, crimp one off*.

drop her yoghurt *v.* Of a lady, to have an orgasm in her *parts* for whatever reason.

drop one *v. Let off, drop your hat, step on a duck, float an air biscuit*.

drop one's back *v.* To enflatulise the atmosphere around one's *gammon ring*.

drop one's revels *v.* To suffer an unfortunate chocolate-based *follow through* experience whilst *clearing one's nether throat*. *'It's no good. I can't finish this Olympic Marathon, I've dropped me Revels.'*

drop one's yop *v.* To ejaculate messily in a manner reminiscent of a bottle of the popular drinkable yoghurt being dropped onto the tiled floor of a petrol station. *'What's the matter, Cliff?' 'I just dropped my yop, Sue. Best get the Vax out.'*

dropout *n.* Underpant condition whereby a *knacker* protrudes from the bottom of the *shreddies*, or famously in Peter Beardsley's case, football shorts.

dropped pie, face like a *sim.* To resemble one who has been bobbing for chips in a deep fat fryer.

dropping a weight division 1. *n.* In boxing, the act of a fighter losing sufficient poundage so as to be able to compete in a lower weight category, thus enabling him to take on a larger number of opponents in the ring. 2. *n.* In *shitting*, the act of expelling such an impressive quantity of *feeshus* that you could conceivably make the move from heavy to cruiserweight or, if you really go for it, even middleweight.

dropping the shopping *euph.* See *drop the kids off at the pool*.

drop the kids off at the pool *euph.* To defecate out of your bottom into the toilet.

drop your guts *v.* To break wind. *"Fossilised fish hooks,' croaked Venables. 'Which one of you beanfeasters has dropped his guts?"* (from *Jennings Makes a Daisy Chain* by Anthony Buckeridge).

drop your hat *v.* To *fart*. Also *drop a bomb, drop your handbag, drop a gut*.

drop your hat forwards *v.* To *fanny fart, muff chuff, queef*. To play the *Lawley kazoo*, blow a *Harry Ramsden's raspberry*. *'Just as I was donning the beard, she dropped her hat forwards'*.

drop your tank 1. *n.* Term which is apparently used by firefighters when they need to empty four hundred gallons of fluid quickly from their pump. 2. *n.* Successfully concluding a romantic encounter by quickly emptying a large quantity of fluid. *'(ALEX pulls DAN towards her and starts pulling at his flies.) ALEX: Come on, Dan. Make love to me now, here in the elevator. You know you want to. You've wanted to since the first time you saw me. DAN: No, you're alright love. I've already dropped me tank, thanks.'* (from the screenplay for *Fatal Attraction*, 1987.).

drown a copper *v*. To sink a *dreadnought*, give birth to a *dead otter*.

drown a duck *v*. To float an *air biscuit* whilst in the shower. Descriptive of the noise produced by a quivering *ringpiece* in the presence of flowing water.

drowning motorbike *n*. A particularly wet *Exchange and Mart*. A *bubbly duck, gargling custard*.

drown some kittens *n*. To pass a litter of small stools which nobody wants to give a home to. Then throw them off a canal bridge in a sack.

drown the chocolate slugs *v*. Alternative to *lighting a bum cigar* for those anticipating a looser stool.

drug smuggler's wait *n*. An interminable period of lavatorial pandiculation which involves sitting on the *bog* waiting for one of them *shits* that take ages to come down, like when you've ate too much meat or tons of eggs.

drugs bust *n*. Simultaneous entry of two *bobbies' truncheons* through the front and back doors. Also *police raid, SVSA*.

druncle *n*. A male relative who generally stinks of *refreshment*. '*Do something, dear. Your Druncle George has just dropped the baby onto the barbecue again.*'

drunk's piss, as clear as *sim*. Descriptive of something which is perfectly transparent. From the fact that a *heavily-refreshed* fellow's urinary emissions are often so dilute that he can get away without rinsing the sink clean after he's done a spot of *Bradford dishwashing*.

dry bob 1. *n*. A public schoolboy who doesn't row. 2. *v*. Fully-clothed sex, leading to *milmed kex*. 3. *n*. A bankrupt *money shot*, a *spaffless stack blow*.

dry docked *adj*. Lack of lubrication situation where a low tide of *blip* prevents the *skin boat* sailing smoothly into *tuna town*.

dry run *n*. A trip to the toilet cubicle, complete with a fifteen minute sit-down with the trousers and *grundies* round the ankles, taken with no intention whatsoever of *laying a cable*. A half holiday enjoyed during the working day which has all the benefits of a lavatory break with none of the *nipsy*-based aggravation that usually accompanies such a visit.

DSB *abbrev*. Dangerous Sperm Build-up. To have two tins of *Fussell's Milk*. '*I'm sorry, Sir Cliff, but you are suffering from DSB. As your doctor, the only course of treatment I can prescribe is an ADW.*'

DSL *abbrev*. Dick Sucking Lips.

DSSneyland *n*. The Gurnos Estate, Merthyr Tydfil. See also *giropractor*.

dub *n*. Duck in Flowerpot Men language. See *flub*.

duck bread *n*. A girl who is past her prime.

duck butter *n*. *Aus*. Assorted smegmalogical effluviums accumulating under the *fiveskins* of the unclean.

ducking *n*. Aquatic version of the popular erotic hobby known as *dogging*, which takes place not in a car park, but in a boatyard, harbour or along a quayside. A practice which presumably involves a scandal-ridden Premiership footballer in a raincoat walking along the side of a river accompanied by a duck on a lead, waiting for the opportunity to watch a pair of tabloid newspaper reporters pretending to *have it off* in a cabin cruiser whilst he *tosses himself off* inside his trousers for the benefit of a nearby photographer with a long lens.

duck sandwich *n.* Prominent *pudenders* visible through the tight leggings of fat-thighed ladies. *Knicker sausages.*

duck sausage *n.* A filling gourmet meal which is best eaten in a crouched position. *'I'm glad you got to meet Val Doonican after the concert, nan.' 'Aye, but I had to have three portions of duck sausage off the roadies to get backstage.'*

duck's breakfast *1. n. Welsh.* Early morning *sausage* and *split kippers.* Accompanied by gentle quacking and a flurry of feathers. *2. n.* Phrase used to describe how poor people, for example students, start their day. That is to say "a drink of water and a shit."

duck smuggler *n.* A *Glen Miller,* one who produces a *string of pearls*, as if trying to smuggle a duck past customs by hiding it up his *arse*. One who lets out a sequence of quacks whilst walking.

ducks on the stairs! *exclam.* Something a person might usefully shout to clear a path whilst charging towards the *crappers* in Tesco whilst suffering from a bout of explosive diarrhoea.

duck soup *n.* The products of a *follow through.* The sixth Marx Brother, *Skiddo.*

duckwalk *1. n.* A unique dance pioneered by virtuoso guitarist Chuck Berry. *2. n.* In *farting,* the process of letting out little pockets of gas in time with each step. An *ugly duckling,* a *string of pearls.*

duel fuel *n. Fighting water.*

duel with the pink Darth Vader *n.* A *Hand Solo.*

duelling banjos *1. n.* A female dormitory *wank race. 2. n.* The vigorous *Scruggs-*style double-tug motion of a *meat vid crane operator. 3. n.* The situation that occasionally obtains when two uncircumcised males are having sex with the same woman, and the undersides of their shafts catch on each other.

duff *1. n. Bum, arse. 2. n. Fadge, minge, twat, clopper.*

duffy's bridge *n.* The *biffin bridge, tinter, taint, barse.* The perineum of either gender.

DUFTO/dufto *acronym.* Any old *bird* at a film premier with a whiff of mothballs around her, *eg. Carry On Breathing* star Barbara Windsor. Dug Up For The Occasion.

duggle *v.* To receive or perform an act of oral *horatio* whilst *crimping off a loaf.* To take part in a *blumpkin.*

dugs *n. Baps, paps.* Olde worlde version of *jugs,* still in use amongst yokel folk.

Duke of giblets *n.* A *salad dodger.*

Dukes *rhym. slang.* Haemorrhoids. From Duke of Argyles = piles.

dump *1. n.* A 40-minute reading session in the *dunny. 2. v.* To *curl one off.*

dump and burn *1. v. milit.* RAF term for the act of jettisoning fuel behind engines on afterburn, resulting in a spectacular display of rumbling noise and flames. *2. n.* Going for a *tom tit* after consuming unhealthy levels of spicy food, resulting in rumbling noise and flames.

dump dew *n.* The glistening pool of sweat left on the *bog* seat after *laying* a particularly troublesome *cable.*

dumpling *1. n.* A solitary, suety *turd* floating in a pan of *bum stew. 2. n.* A woman who is blessed with such a *lovely personality* that you would have to roll her in flour to find her wet bits.

dumplings *1. n.* Baby *dumps. 2. n.*

Particularly filling breasts that go well with *meat and two veg*.

dump station *n*. The *chod bin*.

dump valve *1. n*. A thing that a reader of *Max Power* might attempt to somehow fasten to his car engine. *2. n*. The *nipsy*.

duncan *n*. A *floater*. From buoyant former Olympic sportsman Duncan Goodhew.

dunce's hats *n*. Them conical pointed *tits* found underneath woollen sweaters in 1950's America. *Twin peaks*.

Dundee cake, like half a *sim*. Term used when describing a particularly large *trophy* left in the bottom of the *shitter* by the previous user. *'I would avoid trap two if I was you, your Majesty. The Archbishop of Canterbury was in there just now. He flushed it twice but it still looks like half a Dundee cake down there.'*

dung dreadlocks *n*. Haile Selassie's *beaded curtains*. Laid-back *tagnuts*.

dung funnel *n. medic*. *Fudge tunnel*.

dunghampers *n*. *Undercrackers, trolleys, bills*.

dung lung *n. medic*. Descriptive of one who has been *necking turds*. A halitosis sufferer.

dung puncher *n*. A gentleman homosexualist. A *doughnut puncher* or *spud fumbler*.

dunk *1. n*. To dip a biscuit in a cup of tea. *2. n*. To dip one's *wick* into a *billposter's bucket*.

dunky *n*. Protective sheath to prevent the penis going soggy and falling off into the *hairy goblet* during dunking.

dunny *n. Aus*. Toilet, *netty, cludgy, shite house*.

dunny budgie *n. Aus*. A fly buzzing round an Australian *bog*.

dunnylingus *1. n. Aus*. A romantic *nosh*

at a *vertical bacon sandwich* enjoyed in a public lavatory cubicle. *2. n*. A *trip around the world*.

dusk tusk *n*. Twilight counterpart of *dawn horn*, a cause of insomnia which can usually be remedied by loosening off one's *nuts* with a suitably-sized *wanking spanner*.

dustette *n*. Obsolete hand-held Hoover vacuum cleaner which proved very popular with bachelors who needed to suck the dust off sausages.

dustman's library *n*. An archive of vintage, recycled *niff mags* usually found in the cabins of dustcarts, or the portacabin at the local civic amenity site.

dust mite *n*. An habitual cocaine user. *'Today's birthdays: Gustav Kirchhoff, German physicist, 1824; Wally Schirra, American astronaut, 1923; Pete Doherty, English twat and dust mite, 1979.'*

dust the duvet *v*. To *hitchhike under the big top*, to *starch the sheets*.

dusty klatt *1. n. prop*. Young Canadian motorcycle racer. *2. n*. A lady's *parts of shame* that have never done anything to be ashamed of. A *furry hoop* that has seen less use than Jeffrey Archer's honesty box. *3. n*. A redundant *fanny* that won the West 125cc Motorcycle Championship in 2005.

Dutch *n*. *Sausage sandwich, tit wank, diddy ride*. Also *Dutch fuck*.

Dutch afterburner *n*. The romantic act of having your girlfriend *fart* in your mouth, then blowing it up her nose. That's going to take some arranging.

Dutch Alps *n*. Small breasts, *fried eggs, stits, patsies, bee stings*. Also *Lincolnshire Cairngorms*. As scaled by a *Dutch mountaineer*.

Dutch arrow *n*. A *woody shaft* shot up

the *bonus tunnel*.

Dutch bellows *n*. A *blanket ripper*.

Dutch blast *n*. Accordian-like effect achieved at the open end of the duvet when one wants to sample or indeed share the fragrant fruits of a bedtime solo on the *botty bugle*.

Dutch blindfold *n*. In the *69* position, with the woman underneath and the gentleman's *clockweights* fitting nicely in her eye sockets. All things considered, it's probably just as well she can't see anything.

Dutch boy *n*. A lady in *comfortable shoes*, a *tennis fan*, a lesbian, *ie*. One who always has their finger in a *dyke*.

Dutch Breakfast *n*. Something you have after *awakening the bacon* that will set you up for the day.

Dutch brylcreem *n*. A glutinous product that you don't particularly want in your hair. *Gunk, heir gel*.

Dutch canal *n*. That nameless bit between a chap's *balls* and his *arsehole*, variously known as the *scrincter, stinker's bridge, scran, gisp, barse, tintis, great, notcher, ABC, gooch, Finsbury bridge, isnae, scruttock, Perry Como's lip, tornado alley, scranus, smelly bridge, Brick Lane* or *crunk*.

Dutch cap *n*. An extremely tight-fitting rubber hat worn in Holland.

Dutch conclave *n*. A particularly impressive form of *Dutch oven* in which a foul-smelling smoke is emitted from the end of the quilt, reminiscent of the moment when the College of Cardinals announces the election of a new Pope by farting up the Vatican chimney.

Dutch door *n*. A *bird* who *swings both ways*.

Dutch floor polish *n*. *Spunk*.

Dutch gasmask *n*. The heroic and selfless act of a fellow who prepares a *Dutch hand grenade*, only to clasp his hand over his own mouth in order to spare the nasal sensibilities of all nearby.

Dutch hand grenade *n*. A *beefy eggo*, caught in the hand and then detonated under an unsuspecting person's nose. A *cupcake*.

Dutch Marathon *n*. The hasty, yet seemingly never-ending walk home after purchasing a new selection of *fleshmags* from a specialist newsagent.

Dutch miracle *n*. The magical appearance of *art pamphlets* under a mattress or on top of a wardrobe in a hotel bedroom.

Dutch oven *n*. The act of cooking one's partner's head beneath the bedclothes using *cabbage gas*.

Dutch oyster *n*. An exotic mouthful of the contents of one's own *winkle*. One probable consequence of a *Swiss kiss*.

Dutch rudder *n*. For want of anything better to do, having someone complete your act of masturbation for you by pulling up and down on your forearm whilst you hold your own penis.

Dutch salute *n*. *Irish toothache*. An erection.

Dutch satay *n*. The epilogue of a *stick vid* where the starlet sucks on the leading man's rapidly softening phallus after she's been *front* and *back fucked* with it, and had it smear *spunk* all over her *tits*.

Dutch sauna *n*. *Drowning a duck* whilst sharing a hot shower cubicle with one's spouse. An aquatic *Dutch oven*.

Dutch souvenir *n*. A little something brought back in the urethra to surprise the wife and help you remember Amsterdam.

Dutch strawberry *n*. The *herman gelmet*.

With all pips stuck on it.

Dutch teabreak *n.* The act of *relaxing in a gentleman's way* whilst at work. Taking a *monkey's fag break*.

Dutch tug *n.* A no-nonsense paid-for *hand-job*. Do not pay more than £10.

Dutch welcome mat *n.* A stain on the carpet which indicates where a *feeshus* has been inefficiently expunged from the weft at some point in the past.

Dutch wink *n.* The flashing of the *bacon rasher* when crossing and uncrossing the legs. *'The film has action, drama, suspense and a superb Dutch wink from Sharon Stone.'* (Barry Norman, reviewing *Basic Instinct*).

DVDA *abbrev.* Double Vaginal, Double Anal. The Holy Grail of *bongo video* acts, presumably involving four India-rubber men and one uncomfortable woman.

dyke *n.* Lesbian, *tuppence licker, carpet muncher, three wheeler*, a *woman on the other bus*. See also *diesel dyke, bulldyke*.

dyke differential *n.* The notable discrepancy between the attractiveness of the sort of lesbians depicted in *grumble vids, seed catalogues etc.*, and the sort actually encountered in real life.

dykey likey *n.* A straight man who is befriended by *ladies in comfortable shoes*. The male version of a *fag hag*.

Dylan *n.* A tangled, matted, unkempt mess of a *bush,* resembling the hairstyle of grizzled singer-songwriter Bob. A *Terry Waite's allotment.*

Dyson *n.* A *bird* with a right good suck on her.

dysparpsia *n. medic.* A gastric dysfunction that manifests itself in a series of strident anal announcements. *'Listen to that. there must be a circus in the next field. I can hear a troupe of performing seals tuning up their car-horns whilst the brass band practises clown music on a selection of trombones, euphoniums and sousaphones.' 'No, that's me. I'm suffering from a spot of dysparpsia. Oh no, the caravan door's jammed shut.'*

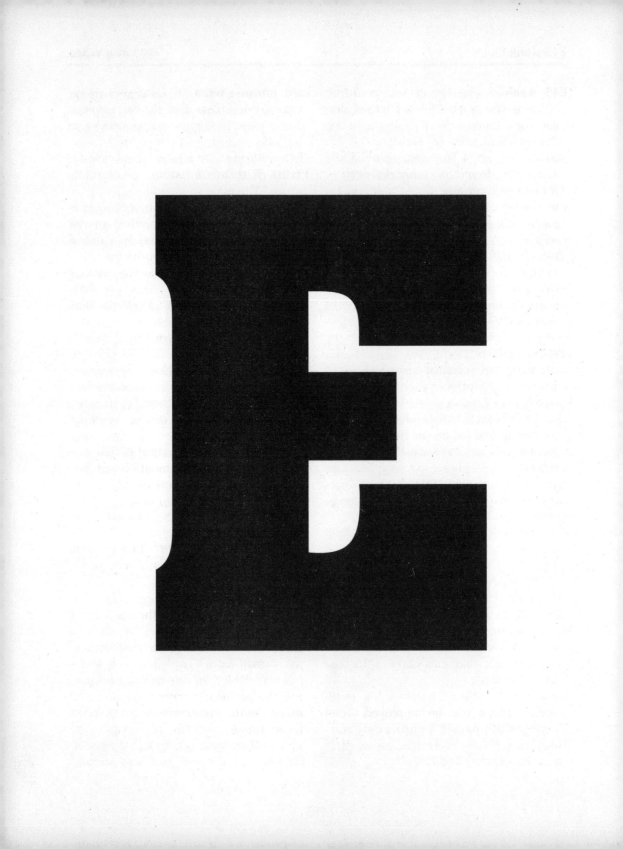

E45 wank *n.* An act of *self pollution* utilising the popular low-friction dermatological unguent. An *E45 wank* has the added benefit of moisturising the *pink oboe,* especially important if one is suffering from a dry, chapped *cock* or eczema on or around the *farmer's hat.*

ear chafers *n.* Ladies' stocking tops, *giggle bands.*

ear pie *n.* A right *bollocking* a woman gives a man when he stays too long in the pub, forgets her birthday, *fucks* her sisters, *etc.*

earlids *n.* Invisible, soundproof flaps of skin which descend over a gentleman's ears when he is being conversed at by his lady wife.

early barf *n.* A premature end to a night of drinking, caused by an individual's inability to hold his or her *sauce, eg.* Former US President George Bush, who spewed up and fell on the floor after just half a pint of weak shandy when out on a pub crawl with Japanese Prime Minister Kiichi Miyazawa in 1992.

early day motion *n.* A *turd* break taken as soon as one arrives at work.

early gurning centre *n.* A place to which one can go in order to view under-age revellers displaying the characteristic facial tics and spasms associated with consumption of *disco biscuits, eg.* The Pier, Cleethorpes.

early morning dip *n.* To make love to a woman whilst she is still asleep. A romantic act that can carry a 15-year prison sentence.

early taxi? *exclam. interrog.* A witty riposte which can be employed when someone has passed a particularly noxious wind. *'Will you be needing an early taxi, Archbishop Williams?'*

earn brownie points *v.* Of a gentleman, to perform selfless acts of kindness, like doing the dishes or a spot of ironing in the hope that one's partner will express her gratitude with a game of *mud darts.*

Eartha Kitts *rhym. slang. Shits,* diarrhoea. Also *Brads.*

earthing cable *n.* An elongated *copper bolt* that touches down safely in the *chod bin* water before it has fully exited the *nipsy.* A *bridger* or *bottom log.*

Easter Island statue with an arse full of razor blades *sim. Aus.* A permanently grave, sour expression. A phrase that describes Jimmy Nail to a T.

Easyjet seat pocket, fanny like a *sim.* A *wizard's sleeve.* From the fact that the seats of the older models of jet departing from Luton have huge, overstretched flaps on the back of them, from years of accommodating all manner of bulky goods.

eat *v.* To perform a "despicable" (© *The Sun* newspaper, 2008) mouth-based sexual act on the *pudenders* of another. To *nosh* someone, either *off* or *out.*

eat breakfast backwards *v.* To *drive the porcelain bus, yoff, barf.*

eat cockroaches *v. 18thC.* To engage in the filthy, disgusting act of *self-pollution.*

eat fancy cakes *v.* Of a gentleman, to have a tendency towards the craftier end of *butchery.* To *jump puddles,* to be a *ginger beer. 'It's a disgrace that the perfectly-good word "gay" has been taken from us. Well I for one will not be joining the politically correct brigade and using polite euphemisms to describe these people and the things they get up to. There's no getting away from it, they eat fancy cakes, pure and simple.'*

(letter from a Colonel in *the Daily Telegraph*, 2010).

eat humble cock *v*. Of a lady who has been involved in a disagreement with a gentleman friend, to acknowledge in the time-honoured manner that she may not have been right after all.

eating catfood by seven *phr*. A humorous way of describing the often embarrassing and regrettable outcome of acting on ill-thought-out *highdea*s entertained during the early hours of a chemically-deranged social evening.

eating sushi off a barbershop floor *sim*. Performing *cumulonimbus*.

eatin' me's spinach, I's *exclam*. Useful phrase which can be uttered out of the side of the mouth whilst passing a *Thora* of such a massive circumference that one's face takes on the assymetrical physognomial mien of squint-eyed, steroid-abusing, pipe-smoking cartoon sailor Popeye for the duration of the process. *'Are you alright, Holly? You've been in there a long time.' 'It's okay, Phil. I's eatin' me's spinach.'*

eat one's greens *v*. To do something one would really rather not do just to earn *brownie points* from a female partner, *eg*. Listen to her go on about her day, putting some shelves up.

eat out *v*. To *lap fanny*, to *dive muff*, to *cumulonimbulate*. To *lick out*, *dine at the Y*.

eau de colon *n*. *Rusty water, fizzy gravy*.

ebdon slide *1. n*. In snooker, the careful positioning of the fingers on the table whilst cueing. *2. n*. In sex, the careful positioning of the fingers on the lady's *bits* in order to expose the *clematis*.

EC flag *n*. Nipple.

Eccles cake *n*. A casually discarded

Eartha. Named after local newspaper hack (name removed following legal advice) of the *Sussex Express* who, after a night on the strong cider, *shat* himself in the pub and shook it out of his trousers before ordering another pint of Biddenden's 9-percenter.

eccles snake *n*. A penis with warts.

eclipse girl *n*. A female lady in a pornographic film or magazine who, if you stare at her for too long, will make you go blind.

econnoisseur *n*. A budget-conscious erotic epicurean, who appreciates the benefits of the Freeman's catalogue bra pages and Smartprice tissues.

Ecosser *n*. A patriotic Scottish person who proudly displays his national identity by affixing a sticker to the back of his Japanese car. In French.

Eddie *n*. See *Stobart*.

Edinburgh *rhym. slang*. A deep-fried *fur burger*. From Edinburgh Fringe = minge.

editing suite *n*. The part of a man's brain that is able to instantly store and arrange stock sexual imagery for future use. *'Look at the jugs on that filly, Hudson.' 'Yes Sir, that's certainly one for the editing suite.'*

e-dophile *n*. A world wide web chat room *nonce*. An internet *diddler*.

Edward II *euph*. A fiery, post-*Edwina ringpiece*, combined with severe stomach cramps, internal haemorrhaging and ice cold sweats. From the similar experience of the famous historical king, who was *bummed* with a red-hot poker by his wife's boyfriend, a situation which led, not long thereafter, to his demise.

Edward Woodward *onomat*. A bathtime *fart*. A *bottle of olives, tottle*.

Edwina *n*. A curry that is a real pain in the *arse*.

eel out of a welly, like shaking an *sim*. Phrase which can be used to describe the experience of having a *shit* that takes very little effort. *'How was it, Mother Teresa?' 'Like shaking an eel out of a welly, your Holiness.'*

e-gasm *n*. A *web-grumble*-assisted *stack blow*.

egg-bound *adj*. Blocked of *dung-funnel*, constipated.

egg drop soup *n*. Home-made version of the classic Chinese dish, prepared by gentlemen in the bath.

egg in the nest *n*. A bald *noggin* which is still surrounded by a halo of hair, *eg*. The hemispherical pate of comedy scientist Professor Heinz Wolff.

egg Mcwhiff *n*. A particularly sulphurous mid-morning *air buffet* produced after breakfasting at a fast food restaurant.

egg white cannon *n*. A 4-inch *blue-veined blunderbuss* loaded with two *balls*.

eggy pop *n*. Any beer that has a proven impact on one's *Camillas, eg*. Robinson's Unicorn Best Bitter.

eggy soldier *n*. The result of taking a *dip* whilst the *red flag is flying*.

e-gret *adj*. A feeling of self-reproach experienced following any ill-considered internet transaction. *'E-grets, I've had a few.'* (Pete Townshend, song lyric).

e-gypsy *n*. One who can't make up their mind which ISP to use, resulting in one's e-mails to them always being returned. A wandering nomad on the information superhighway.

Egyptian PT *1. n. milit*. Sleep. *2. n*. Masturbation.

Eiffel Tower, do the *v*. Of a pair of professional footballers engaged in a *spitroast* with a lucky young lady, to make eye contact and exchange a high five, thus creating the characteristic outline of the famous Parisian pylon.

eighteen spoker *n*. A particularly hairy woman's *arsehole* resembling a tiny bicycle wheel, hopefully without a derailleur gear in the middle.

eighteen wheeler *n*. A *turd* of such length that it runs a significant risk of jack-knifing in the *pan*. A *Stobart*.

ejamulation *n*. The inadvertent release of a sudden, premature spurt of jam when biting into a doughnut.

elbow bender *n*. A *bar fly*, a *boozer*.

Eleanor Rigby's funeral *euph*. A mutually unsatisfying sexual encounter, *ie*. One at which, in the words of the famous Beatles song, "nobody came".

electric chair *1. n*. A device used to keep the number of educationally subnormal black men in Texas at a manageable level. *2. n*. The last resort seat in a pub next to the most crashing bore in the establishment.

electric lemonade *n*. A hallucinogenic, West-country scrumpy cider. Also known locally as *Tone Vale Tonic,* after the former mental institute that housed many of its devotees.

electric spaghetti *n. Spunky string.*

electric twitch *n*. Involuntary jerk of the head displayed by *grumble flick* starlets upon receiving a faceful of *jitler*. Named after the similar reflexive spasm which can be achieved by stroking the bars of an electric fire.

elepants *n*. Jumbo-sized ladies' trunks.

elephant gun, the *n*. When a *horatiee* has manfully managed to abstain from firing off his *single-barrelled snot gun* for a week prior to an amorous engagement, the redoubtable blast of fermented, cheesy *spluff* that hits his lucky *horatier* squarely between the eyes shortly after - or, indeed, just before - she begins operations.

Elephant Man's hat *sim*. Descriptive of a very spacious *fanny*. A *clown's pocket*, a *hippo's yawn*.

elephant nudging a tree, like an *sim*. Phrase used to describe the act of doggedly persisting with sexual relations despite suffering from *brewer's droop*.

elephants *adj. rhym. slang*. Drunk. From elephant's trunk.

elephant's ears *n*. Enormous, grey, flappy flaps. Huge *Keith Burtons*.

elephant's kneecap, fanny like an *sim*. Useful phrase that can be used when describing the *pudenda* of a female who has attained the twilight years of her life. *'Fucking hell, Esther. No offence, like, but you've got a fanny like an elephant's kneecap.'*

elephant, the *n*. Penile puppetry diversion. An amusing and charming simulacrum of the popular grey-skinned, gampstand-footed pachyderm achieved using a chap's generative member and his pocket linings pulled inside out. A great way to break the ice at parties or, indeed, to get yourself placed on the sex offenders' register.

Elevenerife *n. prop*. The fictitious holiday destination of the sort of *twat* who always has to go one better than everyone else. *'Been on your holidays, Nick? Where'd you go, then?' 'We had a week in Tenerife, Sir Alan.' 'Oh yeah? I just flew back from a fortnight in Elevenerife. In a solid gold jumbo jet. And my suitcases are made of diamonds.'*

eleven-pointer *n*. An altogether successful date. Red, pink, brown (mouth, *fanny*, *freckle*).

Ellen MacNomates *n. prop*. Female version of *Billy no mates*, a girl without any friends. Named after popular lone round-the-world yachtsperson Dame Ellen MacNomates.

Elton John *n*. A *Dutch oven*. From the lyrics to the erstwhile Mr Dwight's 1983 single *I Guess That's Why They Call it the Blues*, *viz*. "Rolling like thunder / Under the covers".

Elton John with a fanny, he's like *sim*. Descriptive of someone who obviously doesn't know what they are doing. *'Have you seen that (insert name of unpopular footballer here)? He's like Elton John with a fanny.'*

Elvis *n*. A *shit* that requires so much effort to force out that one almost has a stroke. The oppposite of a *life affirmer*. *'Are you okay? You look terrible, Your Majesty.' 'I'll be fine, Bishop. That Boxing Day Elvis just took it out of me, though.'*

Elvis's leg *n*. The onset of the *vinegar strokes* whilst *fucking* upright in a doorway, bus shelter or taxi queue. Often accompanied by an "Uh-huh-huh" vocalisation and involuntary curling of the lip.

embalmer, the *n*. Specialised wrestling move whereby one's good lady's stomach gets covered with *sex wee*.

Embassy No. 2 *1. n*. A cigarette/excrement combination performed in workplace toilets up and down the country. *'Keep an eye on runways six to fourteen for me, will you, Mrs Depledge? I'm just nipping out for an Embassy No. 2.' 2. n*. An urgent *shit*, usually prompted by the first puff one takes on the first cigarette of the day.

embuggerance *n*. Anything that causes obstruction or annoyance. *'And Peter Sallis's underpowered Austin A30 is going to be a real embuggerance for Jenson Button as the Mercedes driver attempts to put in a quick lap to get his car on the front row in tomorrow's race.'*

emergency handbrake *n*. The act of suddenly bringing an act of frenzied *relaxation* to a halt whilst watching such programmes as *Hollyoaks* or *Neighbours*, when the shot cuts from a *fit* piece of *tussage* to a *vinegar Joe* such as Jack from the Dog in the Pond, or Harold from the General Store.

emergency stop *1. n*. In a driving test, the moment when the candidate is required to bring his vehicle to a sudden halt whilst maintaining full control at all times. *2. n*. The act of suddenly pressing the *dead man's handle* upon hearing the missus entering the lounge whilst watching a *noddy film*. It would be a good idea to pull your trousers up too, if sufficient time is available.

emergency strop *n*. An unexpected fit of menstrual temper. A *tammy huff, tamtrum* or *blobstrop*. *'Jesus, Dave, how did you get your black eyes, broken nose, missing teeth, stitches and whiplash?' 'The missus done an emergency strop when I wasn't expecting it.'*

emissionary position *n*. A coital arrangement which is guaranteed to bring things to some sort of conclusion when all else has failed and both participants are starting to get bored. *'It's no good, June, me spigot's starting to go soft again. And I think me back's about to give out.' 'Okay Terry. My old lobster pot's had enough too. Let's just switch to the good old emissionary position so you can tip your filthy concrete and we can get off to sleep.'*

Emmas *rhym. slang.* Nobbies, farmers, ceramics, lever arches. From Emma Freud, Clement's chimp-eared daughter, who's got terrible haemorrhoids.

emotional crotch *n*. A girlfriend.

empathy flush *n*. A rare and touching gesture of solidarity amongst men ensconced in adjoining lavatory cubicles, whereby a fellow responds to a courteously-applied *sympathy flush* with one of his own, to indicate support for the original flusher in his time of difficulty.

emptying the handbag *n*. A particularly satisfying rectal clear-out following a prolonged bout of constipation. Named after the television laxative advert in which a *backed-up* young lady smilingly tips a load of food out of her reticule before heading off to a party.

empty one's back *v*. To *crimp off a tail*, to *lay Al Jolson to rest*.

empty one's beer sack *v*. To go for a *piss* in a pub.

empty the bins *v*. To ejaculate. *'The Holy Father condemns as anathema all artificial forms of contraception. The only means of birth control allowable within the Roman church is the practice of ejaculatio extra-vagio. That is, to whip the charlie out at the vinegar strokes and empty the bins onto the gunt.'* (Papal Edict, 1988).

empty the caboose *v*. To excrete, pass motions, *drop the kids off at the pool etc*.

empty threat *n*. A terrifyingly loud *fart* that mysteriously fails to assault one's nasal passages. The opposite of an *SBD*.

Emu's beak *n*. A *bird's snapper* that can

suddenly, and unexpectedly, turn ugly. And make your shoe fall off.

Ena Sharples' mouth *n.* A disapproving, puckered *rusty bullet hole.* Commonly seen on *grumble mag* models bending over a snooker table. Also *Dot Cotton's mouth,* the *tea towel holder.*

enamel bucket *n.* A big, dry, cold, rattly *fanny.*

end-of-level wank *n.* An act of filthy *self pollution* undertaken in order to calm the nerves sufficiently to proceed past a particularly tricky portion of a console game. *'I must have tried a hundred times to complete that section, but as soon as I had an end-of-level wank it was like taking candy from a baby.'*

end of terrace *n.* A less-than-partial *pan-handle.* An erection that shares many of the attributes of a *semi,* but lacks some of its credibility.

end of that bottle of HP, well that's the *exclam.* Phrase to be used following the production of an exceptionally squirty-sounding *Heart to Heart,* that may or may not have resulted in a *follow through.* So called from its audible resemblance to the noises made by the final dregs of a heavily-depleted sauce bottle being squeezed over a *cholesterol special.*

end of the Morning Fresh, sounds like the 1. *exclam.* Phrase used when running out of the eponymous cheapo washing up liquid, as one squeezes the final dregs of nasty yellow stuff through the nozzle. 2. *euph.* Phrase used typically following a visit to Newcastle's world-famous Curry Capital restaurant, as one forces the last drops of nasty yellow liquid through one's *nozzle.* Unlikely to be accompanied by a wholesome aroma of

lemony freshness.

enemy at the gate *n.* A particularly insistent *copper bolt* which makes its presence felt at a somewhat inconvenient time, *eg.* When one is getting married, going in for a job interview or about to lay siege to Stalingrad in 1942. *'Do you, Diana Frances take Charles Philip Arthur George as your lawfully wedded husband, to have and to hold from this day forward, for better, for worse, in sickness and in health, to love and to cherish, till suspicious death do you part in about sixteen years or so?' 'Sorry bish, got to dash. I've got an enemy at the gate.'*

Engelberts *rhym. slang. Eartha Kitts, squirts.*

English batsman *n. Aus.* Someone who doesn't spend very long at the *crease.* A *two push Charlie,* a *two stroke joke,* a *one pump chump.*

English disease, the *n.* Homosexuality, as defined by the French.

English lit *n. rhym. slang.* A *shit. 'I'm off for an English. Here's Garry with the sport.'*

English overcoat *n.* The French equivalent of the English *French letter.* A *Coney Island whitefish, cheesepipe clingfilm.*

engorgement ring *n.* A mythical item of *betrothal jewellery* promised to a lady in return for getting one's *nuts* emptied.

engrossed in the ladies' tennis final, I'm *exclam.* An urgent, panic-infused rejoinder to the wife/children/in-laws/neighbours/fire brigade that they must not, under any circumstances, enter the room in which a fellow is currently ensconced. An injunction that is typically delivered in a rather high-pitched, strained voice and is often accompanied by the muffled sound of trousers being pulled back up and frantic wrestling with a zip. A variation on *enjoying the Hollyoaks Omnibus*. *'Darling, where are you? I want to show you my new Manolos.' 'I'm in my study, darling. But don't come in, I'm engrossed in the ladies' tennis final.' 'Is that all? For a moment there I thought you were having a wank.'*

Enochs *rhym. slang*. The guts, hopefully not suffering from rivers of blood. From the horrible pensioners' favourite Tory MP Enoch Bowel.

enormity of the situation *euph*. A *pan handle*. *'Come on, love. Why can't you grasp the enormity of the situation?'*

'Enry's 'ammer *n*. A *diamond-cutting* erection of such proportions that it deprives the brain of blood and leaves the owner in a semi-comatose state, as if he had been hit around the head by OAP boxing champ and widescale aftershave distribution champion Henry Cooper's trademark left hook. About forty years ago.

ENT *1. abbrev*. Hospital department specialising in audiometry, tympanonometry, electronystamography, mastoid disease treatments and sinus problems. *2. n*. A *shit* or *fart* that attacks the ears, nose and throat.

Enterprise transporter accident *euph*. A nice looking *bird* with lousy *knockers* accompanied by a ugly *bird* with great *knockers*.

entertainment system *n*. One's ladyfriend's *tits*, *arse* and *fanny*. *'What's that in your bag, Dr Von Hagens?' 'Just an entertainment system. I'm taking it home for the weekend.'*

entrance exam *n*. The general prodding, rubbing, squeezing, poking, pinching, sniffing *and what-have-you* that a fussy lady carries out on a prospective paramour's *giggle stick* before eventually allowing him *on the nest*.

epilog *1. n*. Just when you think you've finished *dropping the kids off the pool* and cleaned up after them, then another one emerges as if from nowhere: that's the *epilog*. A *second sitting*. *2. n*. A large calibre, late night *flashing light* that feels like it may induce a seizure.

equipment *n*. Either a lady's *headlamps* or a gentleman's *unmentionables*, and occasionally both. *'Would it be it alright if I stuck my equipment between your equipment, love?' 'No you can't stick your equipment between my equipment. Now, you've already got your eight favourite records, the Bible and the complete works of Shakespeare. Which other book are you going to take to your Desert Island?'*

erectile vomiting *n*. *Shooting* your *load*, a lot.

erection section *n*. The top shelf of a newsagents.

erector scale *n*. Scientific system for the measurement and classification of the intensity of male arousal. Similar to the Richter scale but with *bone ons* instead of earthquakes. *'And finally, an appearance by that Lily Allen on How to Look Good Naked could only manage five on the erector scale.'* (Trevor McDonald, ITV *News at Ten*).

Eric *n*. Schoolboy alternative to a *Jake*.

Eric Liddle's home straight *euph*. The final, agonising moments of the *vinegar strokes*, when a *self harmer* throws back his head and opens his mouth wide in a style which is eerily reminiscent of the

1924 Olympic 400 metres Champion, as immortalised in the film *Chariots of Fire*.

Ernie *n*. A lucky chap blessed with the ability to ejaculate within seconds of commencing sexual intercourse. Coined in honour of Benny Hill's famous comedy song about "the fastest milkman in the West".

Eros *n*. The pose that must be struck when *pissing* in a toilet with no lock on the door, precariously balancing on one leg with the other holding the door shut.

escape from alcotramp *v*. To suddenly spot something fascinating in a shop window across the street when approaching an animated *Harold Ramp*.

escape sub *n*. A technologically-advanced brown, sea-going vessel in which an evil hangover makes its getaway. An *alco-poop*.

ESD *abbrev*. Eat Shitty Dick. To *smoke a pink cigar* fresh from *kak canyon*. *Hot karl*.

eskimoing *n*. *Ice docking*.

eskimo's glove *n*. Warm, furry mitten that smells of fish and can accommodate one's whole hand. Not unlike a large vagina.

eskimo's hotpot *n*. A steaming, freshly-baked *shit* in deep snow. *'I'm just going outside for an eskimo's hotpot. I may be some time.'*

espresso *n*. A *quickie* gratefully received from a stranger in a lay-by or motorway service station, which wakes up a fatigued lorry driver, traffic policeman or commercial traveller so that he can continue his journey with a smile on his face.

Essex tartan *n*. Burberry.

estate car *n*. *Acne carriage*.

estimate the bith girth *v*. To perform the first act of coitus following childbirth. *Stirring the paint with a toothpick*, postnatal *last hotdog in the tin*.

etch-a-sketch *v*. To attempt to draw a smile on a woman's face by simultaneously twiddling both of her nipples. *Finding Radio Luxembourg, come in Tokyo*.

eternity leave *n*. The sack. *'My boss caught me photocopying some woman's arse on the office Xerox machine, and sent me on eternity leave. What's more, he says he's going to make sure I never get a job in a mortuary ever again.'*

Ethel 1. *n. rhym. slng*. An act of *self abuse*. From Ethel Merman = Sherman tank = wank. *'Where is he? He's due on the balcony to bless the crowds in thirty seconds.' 'Don't worry, Cardinal. He's just went in the bog for a quick Ethel over the letters in the Daily Sport.'* 2. *euph*. A person in your circle of friends who is known to be under-endowed in the *trouser department*. From the *EastEnders* character of the same name, who never stopped going on about her "little willy". Until she died in 2005, obviously. *'Today's birthdays: Haystacks Calhoun, American wrestler, 75; Sir Terry Wogan, Irish radio and television presenter, 71; Jack Straw MP, Parliamentary Ethel, 63.'*

Ethelbrown the Ready *n*. A pretender to the *porcelain throne*. A *King Richard* in waiting.

ethics girl *n*. The kind of girl who doesn't *fuck* on a first date, won't *do it* in a car or shop doorway and wouldn't *swallow* even if one could get her to suck it in the first place. The antithesis of an Essex girl.

eticlit *n*. The observance of rules of correct decorum when *dining at the Captain's table*.

Eton leapfrog *n*. *Bottery*.

euphemersity *n*. An educational institution which has been promoted beyond its abilities, *eg*. The University of Glamorgan which, let's face it, is really Treforest Tech.

euphijism *n*. A word so laden with erotic potency that it has a young gentleman's Harry Monk up and over like a pan of milk left on a high flame. For example, the word "blow" when Lauren Bacall done it in *To Have and Have Not* (1944).

everlasting gobstoppers *n*. Something that your *babe* could easily choke to death on. The *clockweights*, *knackers*.

every dark clout has a silver lining *prov*. An optimistic phrase that reflects on the fact that the most hirsute beaver can nevertheless prove bountiful.

everything but the girl 1. *n*. Hull-based 90s duo featuring a woman with a face like a Nicholas Lyndhurst who's been hit with pan. 2. *n*. A sophisticated *wank* incorporating low lights, soft music and a bottle of wine.

excalibird *n*. A magnificent *piece* that a chap manages to *pull* successfully, against all the odds.

excalibur *n*. A magic *turd* of legendary proportions that rises eerily out of the water in a mist-shrouded toilet.

excalibut *n*. Gentleman's Mach 3 razor clogged up with his girlfriend's *trouser twiglets*.

Exchange & Mart 1. *rhym. slang*. To *drop a gut*. 2. *rhym. slang*. A *dropped gut*.

excremation marks *n*. The tell-tale *skid-mata* left on one's gusset following a

spot of extra-*grundular moonraking*.

ex files *n*. A *wank bank* folder containing the most filthy memories of sexual depravities enjoyed with previous partners.

exhaust pipe engineer *n*. One who tinkers with *exhaust pipes*.

exhaust pipe *n*. The *Bumhole*, *fudge tunnel*, *back box*. Also *tailpipe*.

exhibition position *n*. Variation on *doggy-style* sex. The man takes the kneeling position from behind, places one hand on the lady's back and the other jauntily on his hip. Then turns and smiles at an imaginary audience, pretending to be a moustachioed German *Frankie Vaughan* star.

exit wound *n*. The state of the *freckle* after a particularly fierce *Ruby Murray*.

exorcist *n*. One who is gifted with the power to rid a place of spirits, especially the top shelf behind the bar. *'Today's birthdays: Stuart Hall, loquacious presenter, 80; Annie Lennox, Scotch song-strangler, 55; Shane MacGowan, plastic Paddy exorcist, 52.'*

expecting a harsh winter *euph*. Of a *bird*, to be putting on weight or over-eating. *'She's stuffing her face with eclairs. She must be expecting a harsh winter.'*

expresso bongo 1. *n*. A *crap* film from the 60s starring Sir Cliff Richard. 2. *n*. The fast forwarding through the uninteresting bits of films which almost certainly do not star Sir Cliff Richard.

extras *n*. Something one tentatively asks for whilst winking at a masseuse or osteopath. The *tugging* as opposed to the *rubbing* in a *rub-a-tug shop*.

eyeburns *n*. Where the eyebrow on an hirsute chap continues seamlessly into his sideburn. Also *sidebrows*.

eye cabbage *n.* The opposite of *eye candy.* An ugly girl you leave at the side of your plate.

eyeful of both ends, an *n.* A *sneaky peek* down a ladyfriend's *tit pants* and up her skirt, all accomplished during the same swift movement, *eg.* When she bends to tie her shoelaces, falls down an escalator *etc.*

eye magnets *n.* Lovely *tits* at which any red-blooded man could not resist the temptation to *sneak a peek.*

eye of Sauron *1. n.* In JRR Tolkein's *Lord of the Rings*, a "lidless eye wreathed with flame" with which the Lord Sauron watched over Middle Earth, and thus *2. n.* A lidless eye wreathed in flame which is the inevitable consequence of dining at the Curry Capital, Newcastle upon Tyne. A *Johnny Cash, Japanese flag, Wigan rosette.*

eye of the fart *n.* The region of uncannily fresh air which can be found at the centre of a strong *Exchange & Mart.* Also *eye of the storm.* 'Fuck me, your Holiness, was that you? It fucking stinks.' 'Sorry, Cardinal. I can't smell anything because I'm sitting in the eye of the fart.'

eyes like a shithouse rat *sim.* Descriptive of one with extraordinary visual acuity. 'Check my collar for lipstick will you, Edwina. Only my Norma's got eyes like a fucking shithouse rat.'

eyes like sheep's cunts *n. medic.* Self-explanatory symptom of an extremely bad hangover. See *feel Welsh.*

'Aw. He must like you, Dr Watson,' expostulated the great
detective, sucking on his pipe thoughtfully and adjusting the
brim of his deerstalker with the handle of his magnifying glass
whilst playing his violin. 'He's trying to lippie your leg, look.''
~ from *The Hound of the Baskervilles* by Arthur Conan Doyle.

F1 finish *euph*. Fitting climax to a piece of cinematographic *grumble*. Three sweating guys shaking their *bottles* and spraying frothy liquid all over each other after a long hard afternoon.

FAB/fab *1. n*. Expression meaning "yes" made famous in the string-heavy children's series *Thunderbirds*. *2. acronym*. Standardised weighting order for assessing the quality of a piece of *crumpet*, *viz*. Face; Arse; Baps. *3. acronym*. The unpleasant olfactory combination of Feet, Arse and Balls encountered when entering a young man's bedroom, a prison cell or a monastery. *'This room smells FAB, Brother Dominic.' 'Yeah, sorry about that. I haven't washed my feet, arse or balls for a month.'*

Faberge egg *n*. A large oval *dump* which comes out encrusted in red jewels as a result of *famers* or a ripped *nipsy*. A *limited edition*.

face fannies *n*. *Bugger's grips*, sideburns. As sported by the singer out of Supergrass and Anne Robinson.

face, front and forks *euph. milit*. A *whore's bath*, taken when there's no time, opportunity or inclination for a shower. Flannelling the face, chest, groin and armpits. *'You're due on set in five minutes, Miss Collins.' 'Right you are. I'm just doing me face, front and forks.'*

face grating *n*. Performing the act of *cumulonimbus* upon a woman with advanced *five o'clock fanny*.

face painting *v*. To adorn one's spouse with *jelly jewellery*.

face saver *n*. An early morning taxi which removes a less-than-attractive female from one's house before the neighbours awaken.

face the fast bowlers *v*. To increase the strength of your drinks in order to attain your target of getting *pissed* more quickly.

face the spinners *v*. To turn to a more ladylike-strength drink in an attempt to stop getting *pissed* quite so quickly.

factory AIDS *n*. The miscellany of invisible, yet ever present, bits of dirt, snot, *spunk* and *turd* which is present on all new culinary purchases. *'Trevor, can you pass me one of those new lunchboxes so I can pack the kids' turkey twizzlers?' 'Hang on, luv. I'm just washing the factory AIDS off them.'*

fadge *1. n*. A cross between a *fanny* and a vagina. *2. n*. How the Queen pronounces the word "fudge".

FADS/fads *acronym*. From the motor trade, descriptive of something worthless, *eg*. The trade-in value of any Citroen over 3-months old. Fuck All Divided by Six.

faecal position *n*. The delicate, round-shouldered and slightly curled posture adopted by someone who has been caught short some distance from lavatory facilities.

faecal touch *n*. Opposite of the Midas touch, *ie*. Everything this person touches turns to *shit*, *eg*. Sir Clive Sinclair.

FAFCAM/fafcam *acronym*. Fit As Fuck, Common As Muck, *eg*. Denise Van Outen, Suzanne out of Hear'Say.

faff *1. n*. A lady's *front bottom*. *2. v*. To *fart about*.

faffro *n*. An overly-fussy hairstyle of the sort effected by drainpipe-legged *crumpeteer* Russell Brand, for example, which has clearly entailed a great expenditure of effort and expense by the hairee whilst yielding *shite* results.

FAFTAF/faftaf *acronym*. A woman who

is extremely attractive but who unfortunately failed her rocket science exams. Fit As Fuck, Thick As Fuck.

fag 1. *n.* An 8-year-old boy at a public school who has to fetch tea, fetch toast and *fetch off* a prefect. 2. *n. Tab, ciggie, a cancer stick.* 3. *n. US.* One who is *good with colours.*

fag fireworks *n.* The brief, but nonetheless impressive night-time pyrotechnic display given to motorists following behind vans.

fag hag *n.* A wizened old woman who prefers the company of homosexuals.

fagnet *n.* A man who, when out clubbing, only manages to attract *botters.*

fagnolia *adj.* The yellowy-creamy-brown colour which used to be found on the interior walls of betting shops and pubs but is now restricted to the houses of chain smokers.

fagnostic *n.* One who either doesn't know or hasn't quite made his mind up which way he wants to swing.

fagriculture *n. Uphill gardening* and its associated lifestyle.

fail one's driving test 1. *v.* To prove unable to reach a required level of ability when driving a motor vehicle. 2. *v.* To prove unable to steer a *fart* around a *brown obstacle.* To *gamble and lose, follow through.*

faint on *n. medic.* A devastating condition affecting certain males who are *hung like rogue elephants.* When a *fat is cracked*, the shaft drains the body of its blood, causing the patient to become light-headed.

fairy goblet *n.* Bronzed chalice favoured by the more *style-conscious* gentleman about town. *Spice island.*

fairy hammock *n.* A *tart's dunghampers.*

fairy liquid *n. Tart fuel.* Drinks such as WKD and Bacardi Breezers for homos and girls.

fairy wings *n.* The gossamer tracery of *arse* sweat left on the seat when a lardy chap gets up off the *bog* on a warm day.

fajita 1. *n.* Mexican stuff piled on a flour or corn tortilla. 2. *n.* A discreet way to refer to a *lady in comfortable shoes.* 'Today's birthdays: Charlie Parker, American jazz musician, 1920; James Hunt, British racing driver, 1947; Jeanette Winterson, Yorkshire fajita, 1959.'

fakeon 1. *n.* A bacon substitute eaten by *Guardian*-reading types. 2. *n.* A Community Support Officer or Happy Shopper copper. 'Don't worry, man. They is not real pigs, they can't even arrest you. They is just fakeon.'

fall at Beecher's *v.* To *come off* before reaching the finishing post. To suffer from premature ejaculation.

fallen off her bike *euph.* A monthly *cycle accident* leaving a woman bleeding from the *saddle area.*

fallen to the communists *euph.* Of a woman, to have *fallen off her bike.* 'Any luck last night?' 'No. She's fallen to the communists.'

falling down juice *n.* Beer. Also *fighting water, bed glue, dizzyade.*

fall of soot *n.* The messy result of a failed *driving test.* A *follow through*, a *lost gamble.*

fall out the officers *exclam.* Piece of light-hearted badinage which traditionally greets a loud blast on the *botty bugle.*

family jewels *n.* Priceless heirloom *knackers.*

famous five go to Brighton 1. *n.* Title of an Enid Blyton bedtime story, probably. 2. *n.* Allowing one's digits to venture

South for an adventure after lights out.

fancy wank *v.* To use an ugly *bird's blurtch* to save wear and tear on your wrist. *Hands free.*

fandruff *n. Fanny* dandruff. *Muff-druff, scurf 'n' turf.*

fanic *n.* State of alarm when one is about to *step on a frog* whilst scared that one's flatulence may contain a *free gift,* for example after drinking several pints of beer and eating a big curry. This problem may be alleviated by retiring to a convenient *fanic room* and taking suitably sensible precautions prior to *dropping one's guts.*

fanjita *n.* A *tuppence.*

fankle *n.* The bit on a fat lass's leg that comes between the calf and the foot. From fat + ankle. Also *cankle.*

fannanigans *n.* Women's things. From fanny + shenanigans.

fannicure *n.* A pampering of the *bush.* A *quim-trim, eg.* A *Hitler tash.*

fanny *1. n.* UK. *Snatch, snapper, quim, cunt, puh-seh.* Female genitals, ladies' *pudenders. 2. n.* US. *Arse, backside. 3. n.* Fictitious Great Aunt. *4. adj.* Like a fan.

Fanny Adams, sweet *phr. Fuck all.*

fanny apple *n.* A neonate. A new born baby. *'Births: Smith. At the Portland Hospital. To Evadne and Captain George Everard, a boy, Spartacus, brother to Troy and Elgin. Mother and fanny apple doing well. Deo Gracias.'* (*The Times* Feb 12th 2004).

fannyarse *n.* A *crafty butcher* whose *dirt-star* has been *lubbocked* to the extent that it resembles a lady's *quim.*

fanny badger *n.* See *Blackbeard's ghost.*

fanny batter *n.* The substance which leaves one's chin greasy after a *fish sup-*

per. *Sloom.*

fanny battering ram *n.* A stout length of *wood* used to burst *Mary Hinges.* A *crowbar.*

fanny bib *n.* A sanitary towel.

fanny bomb *n.* The female organism. *'How was it for you, pet? Did the old fanny bomb go off?'*

fanny by gaslight *1. n.* Post-discotheque, back-alley coitus, *chinook.* A *fork lift truck,* if you will. *2. n.* Title of a 1944 Gainsborough Studios melodrama starring Phyllis Calvert as the daughter of a Cabinet Minister who is unknowingly employed by her father, Lord Manderstoke (James Mason), as a servant, and gets *fucked* in a back alley by Harry Somerford (Stewart Grainger) shortly after chucking out time.

fanny famine *n.* A period of time during which a chap leaves his genitals fallow. *Fanny famines* of varying durations are typically experienced by divorcees, catholic clergymen and Peter Pans of pop.

fannyfare *n.* A brassy *flap raspberry* that could make a room full of Chelsea Pensioners rise to their feet and salute.

fanny farm *n.* A *knocking shop.* A brothel, *trollbooth* or *maison de tolerance.*

fanny filter *n.* The "safe content" option on an internet search engine which prevents teenage boys and office workers locating pictures of the one thing they would like to find on the worldwide information superhighway.

fanny fit *n.* A *bird's* unnecessary histrionic episode. A *tammy huff, blob strop* or *showing off.*

fanny flange *n.* The vaginal escutcheon.

fanny footprint, reducing your *n.* Deleting text messages, pictures and call logs, in order to prevent the world collapsing round you.

fanny fright *n. medic.* Nervous condition affecting some macho men who suddenly find themselves unable to have *a bit* when presented with an opportunity. *Lack of composure in front of goal.*

fanny full *euph.* A building site term used to describe a small quantity of something, for example casting plaster mixed up in a margarine tub to fill the gaps between sections of coving. *'How much plaster do you want, dad?' 'Just a fanny full.'*

fanny gallops *n.* In a lady, the early rumblings of sexual excitement at the sight of a Calvin Klein Y-fronts poster. *The hots.*

fanny hammer *n.* A *bob.*

fanny hockle *n.* The product of a post-coital *fadge cough.*

fanny hopper *1. n.* A 2-foot diameter inflatable orange vagina with handles at the top. *2. n.* A springy *crumpeteer* who hops from one *fanny* to another like a cricket. A *stickman*, a *skippy, eg.* Darren Day, Mick Jagger, John Prescott.

fanny licker *n.* A small dog, such as a Yorkshire Terrier or Pekingese, which is best-suited to sitting on a lady's lap. *"Oh God. Tricky-Woo's got worms,' wailed Tristram as he put down the phone. 'Tricky-Woo?' I said. 'Who, or indeed what, is Tricky-Woo?' 'My dear James, it's Mrs Pomfrey's fanny licker,' laughed Siegfried, as he stuck his arm up yet another cow's arse."* (from *Some Vets Do 'Ave 'Em* by James Herriot).

fanny magnate *n.* A commercial purveyor of ladies' favours. A *pimp, fanny farmer.*

fanny magnet *n.* Something or someone to which top drawer *blart* is inexplicably drawn, *eg.* A Ferrari, Rolex watch, Mick Hucknall.

fanny mechanic *n. medic.* One who performs *MOTT tests*, a *box doc, a snatch quack, a scrape doctor.* A gynaecologist.

fanny nanny *n.* A feminine napkin, fanny bib.

fanny nosher *n.* A *woman in comfortable shoes* who takes the *other bus* to *dine at the Y.* A *tennis fan*, a *lady golfer*, a *carpet muncher.*

fanny paddy *n.* A *muff huff*, a *blob strop.* A *monty.*

fanny rat *n.* A sexually promiscuous male. A *skippy*, a *bed hopper. 'Today's birthdays: David Mellor QC, former Conservative politician and fanny rat, 58.'*

fanny swill *n.* The frothy, post-coital substance exuded by a lady after a good session.

fannytastic *1. adj.* Anything wonderful to do with the female genitals. *2. adj.* Descriptive of a thing which is so excellent that it can only be compared with a *fanny. 'Have you been watching the X-Factor this year?' 'No, I've got cataracts and burst eardrums and it's been fannytastic.'*

fanny tax *n.* Surcharge paid on drinks in a bar staffed by top class *blart.*

fanny turd *n.* A child. *'Births: Chocmonockly-Ffeatherstonehaugh. On February 17th, at the Portland Hospital. To Rupert and Rowenta (nee Ponfrit-Cake), a 6lb 8oz fanny turd, Parkinson Cowan. A brother for Tefal, Moulinex and Tarpaulin. Deo Gracias.'* (from *The Times*, Feb 12th 2004).

fannyversary *n.* The single once-a-year *fuck* off his missus to which a husband is legally entitled. *Annual sex.*

fanoir *n. Fr.* French insult. *'Vous etes une fucking grand fanoir, M. D'Artagnan.'* (from *The Three Musketeers* by Alexander Dumas).

fanoose *n.* The *tinter, taint, twitter, Humber Bridge, twernt* etc.

FANTA/fanta *acronym.* A one night stand. Fuck And Never Touch Again.

fanta pants *n.* A light-hearted term used to describe a woman with an orange *bush. 'The Red Shoes (UK, 1948) Ground-breaking expressionist fantasy directed by Michael Powell and Emeric Pressburger, starring fanta pants ballerina Moira Shearer.'* (from *Halliwell's Film Guide 2001*).

fan your arse *v.* To perform a male courtship display; masculine showing off. *'Well you can tell by the way I fan my arse / I'm a woman's man, with a sweaty barse.'* (Song lyric, *Stayin' Alive* by The Bee Gees).

FAP/fap *1. acronym.* The Portuguese Air Force or *Força Aérea Portuguesa. 2. acronym.* The Peruvian Air Force or *Fuerza Aérea del Peru. 3. n. onomat.* A term apparently popularised on the internet for the sound made by a single stroke of gentlemanly *self improvement.* Also *fap fap fap,* an exclamation of red-blooded approval for the pulchritudinousness of a female. *'Romeo: See, how she leans her cheek upon her hand! O that I were a glove upon that hand, that I might touch that cheek! Fap fap fap!'* (from *Juliet does Verona and Mantua* by William Shakespeare).

farce *1. n.* A play which involves Brian Rix hiding in a wardrobe and his trousers falling down in front of the vicar. *2. n.* The *snot, tinter, snotter* etc. Also *farse.*

farm bent *adj.* Descriptive of a *berry* who finds himself inclined to quadruped romance as a consequence of enforced rural remoteness. *'GRAMS: Wine bar. Int. Day. FX: Door opens. EDDIE GRUNDY: Nelson! Come quickly! There's trouble in 5 Acre field! NELSON GABRIEL: What on earth? EDDIE GRUNDY: It's your dad, Nelson. He's gone farm bent. NELSON GABRIEL: Oh no, not again. GRAMS: Dissolve to ext. day. FX: Distressed cow. WALTER GABRIEL: Ooh, yeah. Take that Daisy. You know you want it right up you, you dirty bitch. FX: Particularly loud moo.'* (from *The Archers*, BBC Radio 4, October 2nd 1983).

farmers *rhym. slang. Emmas.* From Farmer Giles = piles.

farmer sutra *n.* The ancient Dutch treatise on the art of erotic *barnyard love.* With a comedy soundtrack.

farmer's breakfast *n.* A *shit* and a drink of water.

farmer's broth *n. Spiff, spodge, sprangle* etc.

farmer's protest *n.* An outbreak of chronic *ooh-aarrhoea* which pebbledashes the *chod bin* bowl with semi-liquid *shit.* From the universal habit of agricultural types who register their objections to unfair bank service charges by spraying thousands of gallons of cow *crap* all over the front of their local branch.

farn't *n.* An *air biscuit* that, no matter how hard one tries, cannot be *floated.* A *fart* that can't.

FARO/faro *acronym.* A gentleman's post-coital afterplay. Fart And Roll Over.

farse *n.* The narrow isthmus of skin that separates a lady's *fanny* from her *arse.* Derivation unknown.

fart *1. n.* A *bottom burp*, an expulsion of foul air from the *chamber of horrors* that causes the *clappers* to vibrate musically like a tuning fork. A *beefy eggo*, a *poot*, an *air biscuit*. *2. v.* To *drop* one of the above, *step on a duck*.

fart about *v.* See *faff*.

Fartacus *n. prop.* A hero who takes responsibility for a *duck* they didn't *step on*. From the Roman slave Spartacus who was crucified on the Appian way for *letting off* in the presence of Julius Caesar.

fart blanche *n. Fr.* The opportunity to freely *drop a Tommy Squeaker* without fear of detection, *eg.* In a noisy hampacking factory, in the pits at a stock car race, or when nursing one's great uncle back to health from a near-death diarrhoea mishap.

fartbreak ridge *n.* The rugged, windswept anatomical scarp that runs from the *anus* to the *nutsack* or *fanny*, upon which *farts* sometimes break. The *biffin bridge*.

fart buffer *n.* The methane safety cushion which presages the *turd* and allows one a little extra time to reach the lavatory. The *turtle's breath*. *'I'm afraid I must dash, Your Majesty. I've used up my fart buffer and I'm touching cloth.'*

fart catcher *1. n.* Male homeosexualist. *2. n.* Derogatory term for one who waits on another person, *eg.* A valet or footman. *3. n.* A fawning BBC News "royal correspondent" like Nicholas Witchell.

farter *n. Aus. milit.* A sleeping bag. *'Tuesday, December 18th, 1912. Ate last of the pemmican in the night. Heavy snow again. Found Bowers dead in his farter. There is no hope for us now.'* (from *The Journal of Captain Scott*).

fartex *n.* Trade name of that tasteless swirly material with lumpy bits which is loudly pebbledashed by the *tradesman's* round the inside of one's lavatory, and which can adversely affect the value of one's property. *Fartex* is applied by means of a portable high-pressure spray system and is available in a wide range of brown shades. Or black if you've been eating liquorice or have intestinal bleeding. Also *arsetex*.

fart funnel *n.* The *rumpet*.

fart higher than your arse *euph.* To have an inflated opinion of oneself. To think one all that when one ain't, *eg.* Talentless fat *fuck* Chris Moyles.

farticles *n.* The crumbs of an *air biscuit*, often found in the sheets after *breakfast in bed*.

fartificial *adj.* Said of something that sounds like someone *stepping on a duck*, whilst having an altogether different explanation. *'Did you just step on a duck, Chris?' 'No, that noise was fartificial, Kate. I actually just stepped on a duck.'*

farting against thunder *met. meteorog.* Descriptive of a hopeless task that will inevitably end in failure, *eg.* Attempting to pay by cheque in McDonald's, saying "no" to a Pennine Windows telesales person, trying to get Theresa May MP to give you a straight answer to a question, *etc. Pissing into the wind.*

farting around the poo *phr.* An expression which describes someone who isn't doing a job properly, in the style of someone who really needs a *shit* but is putting it off and instead simply passing gas around the *turd* in their *bomb-bay*. *'Mr President, I can assure you that this company is certainly not farting around the poo here. We recognise the urgency* *of the situation in the Gulf only too well. On Monday afternoon, we intend to have a meeting to discuss a possible plan to plug the break in the pipeline with old table tennis balls, shredded Wellington boots, broken fountain pens and discarded tea-bags.'*

farting bracket *n.* A device to the left of the brake pedal found in luxury motor vehicles equipped with automatic transmission, which enables the driver to lift one buttock and *let one go* without taking his attention off the road. *'Once again, the Mercedes E Class has an extensive range of dealer-fit options. But at this price range, things like air conditioning, farting bracket and CD autochanger really should come as standard.'* (Jeremy Clarkson, *Sunday Times* July 2003).

farting clappers *n. medic.* Small, fragile, castanet-like bones up one's *nick* that resonate at particular frequencies, producing an unexpectedly loud "braaap!" sound in polite company.

farting crackers *n.* Trousers. *'When invited to a black tie function, the correct mode of attire for gentlemen would be; white dress shirt and collar, cummerbund, black shoes, black dinner jacket and corresponding farting crackers.'* (from *Debrett's Guide to Etiquette* by Buckridge Pottinger).

farting on eggshells *n.* Carefully *letting one off* when one fears that there is a distinct possibility of *following through*.

farting point, the *n.* The inevitable stage in any relationship at which the male partner brings an end to the practice of *farting* covertly and begins *blowing off* in an audible and olfactorily detectable manner.

farting sideways *v.* To have a bad case of *Badminton Trials*. *"Do please sit down, Mr Willoughby,' Lady Marchmaine invited. 'Thank you, madam,' he replied, 'but if it is all the same with you, I shall remain standing. I rode a fox to earth over three counties yesterday and I fear I am farting sideways."* (from *Sense and Sensibility* by Jane Austen).

farting strings *n. medic.* Tendons or ligaments in the *lisks* which are prone to snapping during periods of excessive mirth. *'In a landmark court case, a Birmingham pensioner with an IQ of 6 is suing the BBC after snapping her farting strings laughing at the sitcom My Family.'*

fart juggler *n.* One gifted with the ability to hold and queue *dropped hats* when in a potentially embarrassing situation, for example in a lift, and then fire off a *repeater* when at a safe distance. An *air traffic controller, stacker.*

fart knocker 1. *n. Bum bandit, fudge nudger.* 2. *n.* One who criticises another's *air biscuits.*

fartleberries *n. Dangleberries, winnets, chocolate raisins.*

fart on one's weetabix *euph.* To spoil one's chances. A less vulgar version of *piss on one's chips.*

fartoodeetoo *n.* An amusing, burbling, polyphonic *gut drop* that sounds not unlike the indecipherable burblings of the *Star Wars* Dusty-Bin-a-like droid.

fart sack *n.* The bed. *'Malaria was powerless to resist. His eyes burned into hers like Swarovski crystals. His strong arms enfolded her body as she felt herself being swept away on a monsoon of passion. Roughly, Pablo took her by her* *heaving shoulders, pushed her down and did her on his king-sized fart sack.'* (from *The Countess and the Matador* by Barbara Cartland).

fart sauce *n.* A *raspberry coulis* that is served with *arse cress.* The rancid juice accompanying a wet *poot.*

fart scissors *n.* Imaginary implement which would prove useful when a chap has retired to a discreet antechamber to *cut the cheese,* only to discover that the piquant aroma of his expelled *flatus* is following him back into the room like an over-affectionate stray puppy.

fart sucker *n.* A sycophantic *arse licker* or *shirt fly, eg.* Any member of Steve Wright's fucking "afternoon posse" on Radio 2.

fart to a shit fight, bring a *v.* In a competitive situation, to be seriously overmatched.

fartwa *n.* A never-ending sentence which was issued against his customers by the late Abdul Latif, Lord of Harpole.

fart wire *n.* The rear string of a thong which bisects the buttocks and, like a cheese-wire cutting through cheddar, will effortlessly slice through the densest *trouser cough. Officer's laces. 'Smile over here for the Daily Star, Miss Katona! Hang on... fuck me... hold the front page. I can see her fart wire!'*

fart with a skin on it, face like a *sim. Aus.* Useful expression which can be used when referring to a person with looks which do not conform to our society's conventional standards of attractiveness.

farty winks *n.* A flatulent and refreshing post-prandial nap usually taken on a Sunday afternoon in order to let one's guts settle after a big dinner. *'Jesus. Is the dog ill?' 'No, it's your dad. He's just having farty winks in front of the Grand Prix.'*

fast roping *n.* Unlikely-sounding masturbation technique which involves poking your *arse* with your left thumb whilst *tugging yourself off* with the other hand. So named as it is evidently not dissimilar to the method employed by the military for getting down a crag quickly. *Abseiling.*

fasturbation *n.* Emergency, hurried *self abuse.*

fat bird's armpit, wetter than a *sim.* An expression used by meteorologists when talking about excessive precipitation. *'Northern areas, which we have represented on this weather map at an angle so that the distance from Nottingham to Aberdeen occupies the same amount of screen space as the gap between Exeter to Plymouth, can expect a mild, dry morning, with scattered sunshine. However, don't organise any barbecues just yet, because during the early afternoon, this large area of wet air moving in from the Atlantic will meet this high pressure front over the Pennines, and by teatime the whole fucking country will be wetter than a fat bird's armpit.'*

fat bird's shoe, full as a *sim.* Descriptive of a something or someone which is stuffed to bursting point, *eg.* A former glam-rock star's hard disk, a postman's wardrobe, Jim Davidson's skin. *'More spooge, Marc?' 'No thanks, lads. I'm as full as a fat bird's shoe.'*

fat food *n.* The sort of lipid-heavy *scrote cuisine* favoured by the sort of folk who prefer to eschew such frankly bourgeois dining accoutrements as cutlery, tables, plates, vegetables *etc. 'They say fat* *food's not healthy but my dad ate nowt but pies all his life and he lived to be seventy-eight stone. He died when he were twenty-six.'*

fat hat *n.* *Blubber beret.*

fathletics *n.* Darts, snooker, pool *etc.* The less physically-demanding sports, as enjoyed by the *big-boned*. From fat + hletics.

fat lass sarnie *n.* A shameful, yet hugely satisfying sandwich that must be consumed out of the view of one's mates on account of its embarrassing nature, *eg.* A crisp, mayonnaise and tomato ketchup bap.

fat lollies *n.* The sort of high denomination seventies-style *thrupenny bits* often to be seen on a cockney criminal's *bird* when he is being arrested mid-*shag* on *the Sweeney*. *Fat lollies* were also the default *jug* setting on negligee-clad women who typically answered the door to milkman/plumber/mobile gynaecologist Robin Askwith in the *Confessions* films.

fat man's salad *n.* Pouring a bag of nuts into a bag of crisps to make an additional side dish accompaniment for a pint of lager. That'll be two of your five-a-day right there, then.

fat nav *n.* The inbuilt homing system which allows the more copiously-skeletoned to find their nearest branch of Greggs.

fat rascals *n.* Playful *titties*.

fat rash *n. medic.* An area of inner thigh soreness on a *salad dodger,* caused by the severe chafing which occurs when running to the pie shop as closing time approaches.

fattitude *n.* That which is used by *big-boned* ladies in Halifax Yates's when turning down the mock advances of groups of twenty-something males on Fridays.

fattle *n.* Collective term for women whose glands are well versed in lettuce avoidance techniques.

fatty *n.* Something that causes much hilarity in the school showers. An erection. Unless it's the PE teacher's.

fatty clappers *n.* Good old-fashioned no-nonsense *knockers*. The sort of *devil's dumplings* that would make Kenneth Connor have a sort of minor epileptic fit. *Fat lollies, milky swingers, bouncers.*

faunacation *n.* Sinful acts of congress with members of the animal kingdom. Like octopii, rhinocerii or platypii.

faux-caine *n.* Particularly poor quality *marching powder,* of the sort that a cash-strapped local television personality might snort up his or her nose through a rolled scratchcard or bus ticket.

faux parp *n.* The passing of gas in a sophisticated social setting. *'I'll never forget the first time I had to serve Her Majesty with a cup of tea in her Balmoral quarters. I was so nervous that I committed an horrendous faux parp while I was bending over her bed to get the bag out the cup and she nearly spewed.'* (from *She Told Me I Could Have Them Dresses, Honest - The Memoirs of a Royal Butler* by Paul Burrell).

faux-pwa *n.* A slip of lap-dancing club etiquette. To *milm* one's *kex* when fishing for a tenner to stuff in a bored dancer's *dunghampers.*

fauxtrot *n.* Of a woman crossing the street, the act of escalating the frequency of her footsteps whilst not actually increasing her velocity, with the purpose of creating the illusion that she is getting a *fucking* move on.

fawn *v*. To *come*, to *reach the Billy Mill Roundabout*. *'The Russian Queen was powerless to resist. Rasputin's eyes burned into hers like sapphires. His muscular arms enfolded her body as she felt herself being swept away in a whirlwind of passion. Then he whipped out his charlie and fawned all down her dress.'* (from *The Lady and the Cossack* by Barbara Cartland).

fawnication *n*. Sex (possibly illicit) with a young deer.

f-duct *1. n*. An aerodynamic channel between the legs of a Formula One racing driver. *2. n*. An aerodynamic channel between the legs of a woman.

feasting with panthers *n*. Doing a bit of *the love that dare not speak its name.* See *zorba*.

feather spitter *n*. An over-enthusiastic *pillow biter*.

Featherstone wedding cake *n*. A pork pie, a post-matrimonial delicacy which is popular amongst the denizens of the delightful West Riding beauty spot.

fecal treacle *n*. The sort of ultra-adhesive *bum toffee* that clings tenaciously to the side of the *shit pot* with the same force as No More Nails. *Pooperglue, fartex, ploppydex*.

feck *1. exclam. Ir. Fuck*. Popularised by Fathers Ted and Jack. *2. n*. That quality which a feckless person is lacking.

feckfast *n. Ir*. An act of ante-matitudinal congress involving *cumulonimbus*, which delays the perpetrator to such an extent that he is forced to forgo his morning muesli and subsist until his elevenses on the nourishment he can obtain from the *fanny batter* in his beard.

fecorations *n*. Useful conflation of "fuck-ing" and "decorations" which can be muttered by one not wholly imbued with a spirit of seasonal goodwill when venturing into the attic in early December in search of a damp box of knotted green wire, broken glass and spiders.

feeders' wives *n*. The specialist section of a *bongo mag* which is devoted to amateur photographs of *pillow-smuggling* beauties.

feeding me rabbits *euph*. Having a *wank*. From the character Lucien in Liverpudlian sitcom *The Liver Birds*, who would stay home alone all day and answer the door looking dishevelled, explaining *"I was just feeding me rabbits"*, in Ringo Starr's voice.

feed it a bun *phr*. Term used to emphasise the enormousness of a male member. *'I didn't know whether to suck it or feed it a bun.'*

feed the beavers *v*. To *drop a log* into the *yellow river*.

feed the cat *euph*. An excuse used when popping out for a spot of extra curricular activity. *'Sorry Fizz, I can't see you tonight. I've got to feed the cat. Have you seen my blobs anywhere?'*

feed the ducks *v*. To *wank*. From an apparent similarity in hand movements to a man on a park bench *wanking*.

feed the fish *v. nav*. To vomit over the side of a ship, *bury one's biscuits* at sea. A nautical *honk*.

feed the pony *v*. To *frig* a lady's *front bottom*.

feel like Andy Warhol looks *v*. To *feel Welsh*.

feel Welsh *v*. To be hungover, to feel none too chipper. To have *eyes like sheep's cunts*.

feeshus *n*. Excrement. *'Who's left a fee-*

shus in the pan?'

feet seeking pissile *n*. A wayward *gypsy's kiss*, typically but not exclusively the first one of the day, that goes everywhere but into the lavatory bowl. Wearers of suede shoes are particularly vulnerable to *feet seeking pissile* attack.

felation *n*. The feeling of sublime joy a gentleman feels when having the immoral act of *horatio* performed upon his turgid person.

feastender *n*. A fat cockney *piece*.

felch *v*. The tender act whereby a gentleman orally retrieves his *spoff* from his partner's *arsehole*. Also *feltch*. *'Birds do it / Bees do it / Even educated fleas do it / Let's do it / Let's felch some spunk.'* (Song lyric *Let's Do It* by Cole Porter).

felchmeister *n*. *Ger*. A man in lederhosen with a shaving brush in his hat who is particularly adept at *felching*.

fellowship of the ring *n*. A highly improbable circular formation involving an unknown number of *bad throwers*. A felicitous consequence of such an unlikely happenstance is that every participant would be a *lucky Pierre*.

felmet *n*. *medic*. The point where the *five-skin* is connected to the *bell end*. The *bobby's chinstrap*, the *banjo*.

felt tip *n*. A marker pen *stool* that protrudes from the *nipsy* and keeps drawing lines on one's *bumwad*.

fem *n*. A highly photogenic species of *lady golfer*. Commonly found sitting in pairs on the sofa on TV porn channels. Also *femme*.

femtex *n*. Hormone-based explosive which becomes dangerously unstable once a month.

fenchested *adj*. Of a lady, to be sadly lacking where it counts. To have *Dutch Alps*.

Named after the horribly flat, unsexy fenland area of eastern England.

feng shit *n*. Mystical process in which everything in the smallest room must be just right to ensure the most auspicious energy flow through one's nether channels. The routine undertaken by a defecator to ensure that a big *turd* comes out and doesn't go back up again. *'Answer the doorbell will you, love. I'm having me crap and the interruption ain't half upsetting me feng shit.'*

fent *n*. The erotic perfume of a woman's *clout*. If a worn pair of ladies' pants is draped over a steaming kettle, the room will soon be filled with the alluring aroma of *fent*.

fent-a-ghost *n*. The strange aroma of *fent* left in your duvet, which lingers no matter how many times you change the bedding, normally experienced after *shafting* a regular *pie eater*. Humorously named after the utterly *shit* 1970s children's television programme *Rent-A-Ghost*, starring Nadia Popov from *Coronation Street* who is Gail Tilsley's gold-digging mum Audrey who used to be married to Alf Roberts who fell off the car park in *Get Carter*.

fentilator *n*. A pair of *birds'* used *grundies* worn on the head whilst *boxing the Jesuit*. A *musk mask*.

Fergie frown *n*. The milk-curdling expression assumed by a bloke's betrothed when he returns home *blind refreshed* after being unavoidably detained at a licensed tavern. From the side-splitting repertoire of comedy faces utilised by Manchester United supremo Sir Alex Ferguson when his team are being comprehensively outplayed, like when they got dumped out of the FA Cup by Leeds United.

ferning *1. n.* Of a man, adopting an unctuously empathetic attitude when trying to get into a good-looking bird's *dung-hampers*. Effecting an insincere interest in such feminine interests as shoes, dresses, flower-arranging, periods and that. *2. n.* The simpering interview technique adopted by Ryvita-chomping former daytime TV gastric-bandolero Fern Britton whereby she feels everybody's pain.

fernougle *n. Scots.* A Scotsman's *heated handrail* of humungous proportions. A *sporran splasher*. *'Just got in from the Isle of Skye / My fernougle's lang but my kilt's cut high / The ladies shout as I go by / 'Donald where's yer troosers?''* (Sir Harry Lauder, traditional Scottish song).

Ferrari pitstop *n.* An ill-judged *splash and dash*, in which a gentleman leaves the *bogs* with his *cock* still hanging out and spilling fuel along the floor.

Ferris Bueller, the *n.* Self-satisfied pose adopted by a fellow whilst his *handy shandular* needs are being manually administered to by another. From the eponymous *wanker*'s picture, grinning smugly with his hands behind his head, on the poster for the film *Ferris Bueller's Day Off*.

fertle *v.* To *feed a lady's pony* through her *bills*.

festival flange *n.* Extra premium strength *minge. Disco fanny* that has been baked in the sun and hasn't been washed for two days. The Special Brew of *twats*.

festival hot dog *n.* A hand-held *pap baffle*. As used by the artists Gilbert & George in the preparation of their shitty pictures.

festival knickers *1. n.* The undergarmentry effected by young ladies at open air pop concerts, *ie.* Crispy *shreddies* with a long weekend's worth of excitement evident in the gusset. *2. n.* The undergarmentry effected by young ladies at open air pop concerts, *ie.* none at all.

fetching off *n.* The gentle art of *tipping your concrete* into a lady's knicker drawer whilst she's out of the room. *'Hurry up fetching yourselves off, you lot. Carol Decker out of T'Pau's just finishing her encore and she'll be back any moment.'*

fetch the shovel, Mildred! *exclam.* Cry of mock panic upon rising from the *chod bin* and being confronted with the horrors one's *nipsy* has wrought. Also *go get the mongoose!, alert the coastguard!*

FFTBBB *abbrev.* The inevitable converse of a *bobfoc*. A girl who possesses a face pretty enough to be rendered by a Renaissance great, but who has a body resembling a medieval vision of Hell. Face From Titian, Body By Bosch.

fib tits *n.* Breasts that cause disappointment when removed from their enhancing *tit pants*, when they prove to have been lying about their proportions and/ or pertness all along. *'How did you get on with that cracker with the great tits from the Feathers?' 'Crap mate. Turns out she had fuckin' fib tits.'*

fidl *n.* A budget-conscious *strum* over a cheap'n'cheerful *bongo mag*, such as *Razzle*.

fiddler crab *1. n.* In the world of human *relaxation*, a gentleman who has *relaxed* so much that one forearm is the size of Popeye's whilst the other has practically withered away. *2. n.* In the world of marine biology, the South eastern Atlantic crustacean *Uca pugnax, Uca* *pugilator* or *Uca minax,* distinguished by the fact that one of its arm nipper things is much larger than the other, possibly as a result of too much *wanking.*

field trip *n.* The inevitable consequences of any *al fresco* sojourn which involves the consumption of psilocybin mushrooms or other illicit narcotic comestibles. Usually whilst one's pupils are occupied filling in worksheets that will later be shredded and used as bedding for the school gerbils.

fiery surprise *n.* To receive a brand spanking new electric fire that one never knew about.

fifth Marx brother *n.* Faecal residue left on the gusset of the *undercrackers* as a result of insufficient wiping. From Ginger Marx. *Skiddo Marx, duck soup.*

fifty-fifty, go 1. *v.* On a popular television quiz programme, to have the computer "randomly" and unerringly remove the two less likely answers, leaving the contestant puzzling over the same pair of possibilities they originally suspected may have been correct. 2. *v.* To risk releasing a *Bakewell tart* into one's trolleys, despite the fact that there is a very real possibility that it will be accompanied by half a cup of tea and a chocolate eclair.

fig *n.* A lady's pudendum.

fight a turkey *v. Choke a chicken.*

fighter pilot's thumbs *n. Chapel hat pegs, pygmies' cocks.*

fight fire with fire *v.* Of a bearded fellow, to perform *cumolonimbus* on an hirsute *flange* in the style of that bloke in *The Joy of Sex* who looks like he's got his chin stuck in Jeremy Beadle's disguise box.

fighting a boozing battle *n.* A familiar sight outside late bars and nightclubs, *viz.* Young men wearing white, short-sleeved shirts, exchanging blows whilst under the influence of alcohol. *'Where's Harry?' 'Last time I saw him he was outside on the steps fighting a boozing battle with a photographer, Wills. He said he'd see you back at the Chinook.'*

fighting dog's ear, fanny like a *sim.* A phrase that could be used in polite company when referring to the state of a female's *bits* after a right good *hammering. 'Arachnaphobia was powerless to resist. His eyes burned into hers like hot toast. His muscular arms enfolded her body as she felt herself being swept away in a dual cyclone of passion which reached every nook and crevice of her being and which seemed to last for hours. When he had finished doing her, he rolled off, dropped his guts and lit a Woodbine. 'How was it for you, darling?' he whispered. 'Did the earth move for you?' 'Not half,' she replied. 'You've left me with a fanny like a fighting dog's ear here."* (from *The Egyptian Concubine and the Cheesemonger* by Barbara Cartland).

fighting water *n. Falling down juice, wreck the hoose juice, Spesh.*

fight or flight turd *n.* A monster lurking in your lower *Simon Cowell* that is of such proportions that you can't make your mind up whether to run away and hide, or face it like a man.

FIGJAM *abbrev. Aus.* Antipodean phrase used when referring to a colleague who believes himself to be the *dog's bollocks* when he is, in reality, a *tosser.* Fuck I'm Good. Just Ask Me.

file under W *euph.* To store in one's *mammary banks* an erotic image which is later referred to for a nefarious purpose. *'Crikey, she's got enormous norks. File under W.'*

FILF/filf 1. *n. acronym.* The object of a *chubby chaser's* affections, a *bird* that gives a gentleman *Victoria wood.* Fatty I'd Love to Fuck. 2. *n. acronym.* The gay or bisexual equivalent of *milf.* 3. *n. acronym.* A *gilf* that has gone off a bit but still manages to get a standing ovation from one's *orchestra stalls, ie.* Shirley off *EastEnders*, Liz McDonald off *Corrie* or HM Queen Elizabeth II off the stamps and pound notes. Fossil I'd Love to Fuck.

filfy *adj. 'That Rt Hon Diane Abbott MP's well filfy.'*

fill in *v.* Of a gentleman, to pass on the benefits of things he has discovered whilst browsing the internet to his significant other. *'Goodness gracious me. I had no idea that Lindsay Lohan's figure was quite so Junoesque. I'd better go and fill in the missus.'*

fill your boots *v.* To make the most of a sexual opportunity. Often prefaced "go on son".

fillet-o-fish *n.* A *haddock pastie* that is on the menu, but for which one has to wait four minutes whilst it is prepared.

film four *n.* The act of having to stay awake till four in the morning in order to *enjoy* a meaningful French art film on the obscure *wankers'* movie channel.

filth machine *n.* An old computer which is kept purely for the purpose of surfing porn.

filthy Ned *n. Dirty Sanchez's* brother.

final whistle *n.* A *fart* that comes in three loud, controlled blasts, causing half the assembled crowd to jump up and cheer.

final word *n.* Lavatorially speaking, the short, sharp blast on the *botty bugle* that announces to anyone in the vicinity that a bloke's *python* has been well and truly *syphoned.*

finding a peanut in a kebab *euph.* Descriptive of the difficulty encountered when a gentleman attempts to locate the *wail switch* during foreplay.

finding nemo *n.* The performing of an act of oral *cumulonimbus. Dining at the Y, licking out.*

find the key to the pie cabinet *v.* Of a lady, usually, to become significantly larger than in former years. *'That Claire out of off of Steps appears to have found the key to the pie cabinet. Still would, though. Meanwhile, over to Daniel Corbett for tomorrow's weather.'*

finger blessing *v. Firkyfoodling* sans *dunghampers.*

finger food *n.* Something small and delightful you pick up at a party, but which leaves your fingers smelling of fish.

finger of fudge *n.* The consequences of *breaching the hull.* A *taxi driver's tan.*

finger pie *n.* A *handful of sprats*, a *pony feeding session.*

fingers *n.* Sucessfully gaining digital access to one's *bird's snatch.* *"Smell them!', cried Jennings 'Pwoar!'* sniffed Darbishire. *'What an ozard ronk. What have you been up to?'* Jennings grinned conspiratorily. *'I just got my fingers off Venables' sister in the prep room and I'm never going to wash my hand again."* (from *Jennings and the Strange Urges* by Anthony Buckeridge).

fingersmith 1. *n.* A disgusting *self-polluter* of either gender. 2. *n.* Piss-poor BBC costume drama about Victorian *carpet-munching*, which disappointed thousands of sofa-bound *fingersmiths* across the country.

fingertip grip *1. n.* In the world of snooker, holding the butt of one's cue with the very ends of one's digits in order to better control a tricky shot. *2. n.* In the world of somewhat desperate late-night-television-fuelled *gentleman's relaxation,* to *chalk your naughty cue* at the sight of BBC snooker presenter Hazel Irvine. Presumably whilst hoping against hope that the whole sordid, dismal transaction will be successfully completed before John Virgo appears on the screen and sets you back a good ten minutes.

finisher *n.* The favourite page of an *art pamphlet* saved for the climax of a *cat stabbing* session.

finishing the dishes *1. n.* That deflating experience when you discover that the fucking dishwasher has not cleaned its contents properly so you have to complete the fucking job yourself, wondering all the while what was the fucking point of getting the fucking bastard thing in the first place. *2. n.* Resorting, following a disappointing or regrettable act of coitus, to a dispiriting act of *monomanual labour.* *'When the Lord saw what Onan had wrought He was sore displeased and great was His anger, and he spake unto Onan in a loud voice saying Onan, you did lie in your tent with your wife Tamar and yet while she slept did you then take yourself in your hand and thus did spill your precious seed all upon the ground and everywhere which was exceedingly sinful in mine eyes. And Onan waxed sorrowful for he saw that he had indeed sinned before the Lord, begging forgiveness from Him saying, O Lord, I am sorely repentant*

for my wickedness but yea, I was only finishing the dishes.' (from *The Book of Mike and the Mechanics*).

Finnegan's wake *n.* Descriptive of one's face upon waking in the morning after a heavy session *on the turps* and a poor night's sleep. Characterised by grey pallor and puffyness around the eyes.

Finsbury bridge *n.* The *barse.*

fire cover *1. n.* What an heroic soldier requests from his comrades prior to single-handedly storming an enemy machine gun nest. *2. n.* A request made to the wife when on holiday and staying in a tiny hotel room, after you have consumed a dodgy paella and a plethora of *pedro's piss.* *'My guts are rotten, love. I've got to go to the bog. Put the telly on, will you? Give me some fire cover.'*

fire down below *exclam.* An announcement used by a gentleman signifying the discovery of a genuine redhead.

fire in the hole *exclam.* A somewhat plaintive warning shout issued from the water closet after a night on the pop and curry, possibly at the Curry Capital, Bigg Market, Newcastle upon Tyne.

fireman's blanket *n.* A precautionary *turd*-catching mat of *shit rag* laid on the *bog* water surface, with the intention of preventing noise and/or *splashback.* Also *crash mat, pap baffle, turd raft, pilo.*

fire off some arse chaff *v.* To *drop a gut* in order to get rid of someone who is following you around.

fire off some knuckle children *v.* Of a healthy young man, to *sow his wild oats* on the ground/into a tissue/into a sock/up the dog's back/into a lady's knicker drawer/onto Michael Winner's lunch.

fire one across the bows *v.* A *navel engagement* whereby the *pirate of men's* *pants* withdraws from the battlezone just before the *egg white cannon* shoots its payload into *cod cove*.

fire snakes *n.* Venomous post-curry or post-chilli stools that rattle out the *arse* at a fair old lick.

fire the early morning gun *v.* To *drop anchor, lay a cable, take a sounding*. To enjoy an ante-matidudinal *shit*.

fire, throw a log on the *v.* To *shit* oneself whilst attempting to light a *fart*.

firing blanks *v.* Post-*snip spoffing*. '*You can put the ticklers away love, I'm firing blanks.*'

firing on one cylinder *euph.* A deep, rumbling *trouser trumpet* with "put-put" noises at the end, reminiscent of a 1950s British motorbike being revved and then allowed to stall.

firing the one o'clock gun *1. n.* Act performed every day at around thirteen hundred hours from the parapets of Edinburgh Castle in order to make all the American tourists in Auld Reekie *shit* their tartan troosers. *2. n.* Act performed by a man upon returning home during a lunch-break whilst his flat-mates, kids *etc.* are out. '*Well, that's all the lunchtime news from me Martyn Lewis. I'll be back with the main headlines at six, but meanwhile I'm nipping off home to fire the one o'clock gun.*'

firing up the Quattro *euph.* Getting into something that may have looked and felt great in the eighties, but which has since lost some of its former allure. *Milfing.*

firkin *1. n. arch.* A measure of ale capacity, equal to nine gallons or half a kilderkin. *2. n.* The *firkwitted* epithet for half the *firkin* pubs in Britain.

firkyfoodling *n. arch.* Tudor foreplay. '*Dearest Maid Miriam. Until lately did my husband Henry be a most wonderful and caring lover. But forsooth I am most sad to relate that of recent times he wanteth naught but most hasty coupling with me. He spendeth no time on the firkyfoodling. Yea I fear that my tastes for the courses of love hath declined as a consequence. And now he hath vouchsafed to cut my head from my shoulders. Five wives hath he taken already before me, and of two hath he separated their heads from their shoulders. What am I to do? Pray, pray, pray help me. C. Parr, London.*' (Letter to *Daily Mirror*, 1545).

first impressions *n.* Breasts. *Competitive advantages, impressive CVs.*

first load *n.* That which is flushed down the *chod pan* prior to that second round of lower intestinal grumbling which heralds the arrival of a bonus *drop of shopping*.

first mud *n.* The *popping* of a *brown cherry*.

first on the dancefloor *euph.* Of a gentleman who *knows what's in his flowerbeds*; being *good with colours, sensitive*, prone to supra-puddular aerobatics and what-have-you. *Queer as a nine bob note.*

first two inches are cold, the *exclam.* A cry to indicate the urgency with which one requires a lavatory. '*I answered the urgent hammering on the door. It was Holmes, in the guise of a Greek Admiral, and possessed of a wild expression the likes of which I had never seen before. 'What is it, Holmes?' I expostulated. 'Why, it's three in the morning.' 'There is no time for explanations, Watson,' he gasped as he pushed past me towards my water closet. 'The first two inches* *are cold.'* (from *The Case of the Great Big Shit* by Sir Arthur Conan Doyle).

firtle *v.* To cut a hole in a poster of one's favourite pop star, film actress or politician, and *fuck* it.

fish 1. *n. prop.* Former lead singer out of Happy Shopper Genesis pop band Marillion, real name Derek Penis or some such. 2. *adj.* Not very good. *Crap, swiss, pants, mouse, fucking rubbish. 'That lead singer out of Marillion is fish'*

fish box *n.* A lady's *twat. Billingsgate box, fish mitten.*

fish drowner *n.* A *clown's pie.*

fisherman's jumper *n.* A damp, overly-hairy *cunker*, smelling not too dissimilar to a deep sea trawler captain's wool sweater after hauling in a net full of haddock. *'Having been accustomed all my life to ideals of a feminine nakedness gleaned from classical antiquities, I was somewhat taken aback on my wedding night to find that my young bride had a right old fisherman's jumper between her legs.'* (from *The Memoirs of John Ruskin*, 1819-1900).

fisherman's sock, pull her on like a *sim.* No-nonsense method of sexual intercourse. *'Concertina was powerless to resist. His eyes burned into hers like zirconium. His muscular arms enfolded her body as she felt herself being swept away on a tsunami of passion. They stood before each other naked, until he could wait no longer. Roughly, he grasped her by the waist and pulled her on like a fisherman's sock.'* (from *The Lady and the Independent Financial Adviser,* by Barbara Cartland).

fisherman's swig *n.* A well deserved sup from the *hairy goblet.*

fish from the other bank *v.* To be *on the other bus*, to *jump puddles*, to be *good with colours.*

fish fryer's cuff *sim.* Descriptive of a pair of well-worn knickers with a heavily-*battered* gusset.

fish-hook shit *n.* A *turd* containing a sharp object that snags the *nipsy, eg.* A peanut, a filling, the wife's *clit ring.*

fish mitten *n.* A *muff* that keeps the fingers and thumb of one hand warm.

fishmitten's bark *n.* An audible release of *clam gas.* A *queef.* A *fanny fart, hail Mary.*

fish peach *n.* A recently shaven *haven* with three days of stubble. Combines the texture of the eponymous furry fruit with the bracing zest of a bank holiday in Whitby.

fish slipper *n.* A more voluminous version of the *fish mitten*, into which a gentleman is wont to slip *half a foot* with not inconsiderable relief at the end of a trying day at work.

fish supper *euph.* 1. *n.* A Friday night feast with the tang of the sea and plenty of batter. 2. *n.* Fish and chips.

Fishwick 1. *n. prop.* A small Scottish village 4 miles west of Berwick upon Tweed. 2. *n.* The bit of braided string that hangs out of a *kipper* that has *fallen to the communists.* A *mouse's tail.*

fist 1. *v.* Of boxers, to punch someone in the ring. 2. *n.* Of *puddle jumpers*, to punch someone in the *ring*. 3. *n.* Of heterosexuals, to punch someone in the *quim.*

fist magnet *n.* Someone who attracts punches to his face, *eg.* Jimmy Carr.

fist of fury *n.* Of a gentleman with a restricted *wank window*, for example whilst his missus has just nipped next door for a cup of sugar, a mindlessly violent act of *self abuse* carried out in a sort of masturbatory red mist. An *arm-breaker, bishop rage, power wank.*

fist rape *n.* Taking advantage of your clenched hand after inviting it back to your place for a coffee and a flick through a *meat mag. Knuckle glazing.*

fist sitting *n.* The act of supporting the buttocks on one's clenched hand whilst engaging in a bathtime masturbation session, thus preventing the tell-tale splashing, squeaking noises that are unavoidable as the pace picks up towards the vinegar strokes.

fit *adj.* Attractive, worthy of *one.*

fitbin *interj.* The rudest word in the English language, so rude that its meaning has been encased in 500 tons of concrete and dumped in the Irish Sea.

five against one *n.* A very one-sided but nonetheless enjoyable game of wrestling in which *Madam Palm and her five sisters* attempt to *strangle Kojak.* The game ends when someone *makes the bald man cry.*

five day test *n.* A pointless *Ethel* that never really gets going and typically has no prospect of a satisfactory conclusion. *Strangling the coach.*

five finger spread *n.* Counter-productive attempt to suppress *a yoff* with the hand. A *chuckspreader, yawn sprinkler.*

five knuckle shuffle *n.* A *one-handed workout* to a Geri Halliwell yoga video.

five o'clock fanny *n.* A stubbly *ladygarden.* A *Flintstone fanny,* a *face grater.*

five o'clock fart *n.* The raucous and often terrifying consequence of sitting in an office all day unable to *let rip* until home-time.

five pee fifty pee *sim.* Anal/numismatical comparison descriptive of the rapidly-alternating diameter of one's rectal sphincter at moments of extreme nervousness. *Bin lid penny.* 'Did you see the match last night?' 'Yeah, the last ten minutes were proper five pee fifty pee.'

five-pinter *n.* A very ugly woman who one would only happily chat up after five pints of *dizzyade.* A *St. Ivel lass.*

five pint facelift *n.* A subjective improvement in one's partner's appearance brought about by the consumption of 62.5% of a gallon of booze.

fiver *n.* A diet-conscious individual, who sensibly foregoes the government-recommended "five a day" for the much more modest "five a year".

fiver in, a *1. phr.* Levy paid in order to gain entry to a public house or similar. *'How much is it to get into the Hare and Hounds on New Year's Eve?' 'It's a fiver in.'* 2. *n.* A *fisting.* 'Are you going to (name of formerly popular entertainer's name removed on legal advice)'s party after chucking-out time? It's a fiver in.'

fives *n.* A traditional Etonian game played with four fingers, a thumb and a *cock.*

fiveskin *n. Fourskin.*

five-to-two-er *n.* A *bird* who is desperate minutes uglier than a *ten-to-two-er.*

fizzing at the bung hole *adj.* Descriptive of effervescent sexual arousal in a woman. *Dripping like a fucked fridge, frothing like bottled Bass.*

fizzle *n.* A gentle or quiet *arse firework* to which it would be unwise to return.

fizz pan *n.* The *chod bin, poop tureen, asserole dish.*

fizzy gravy *n.* Diarrhoea, *rusty water. Champoo,* if you will.

fizzyjizz *n.* Aerated semen caused by over-enthusiastic *cat stabbing. Bubblecum.*

fizzy knickers *n.* A *wide on.*

flabia *n.* A fat *cunt.*

flabstinence *n.* The involuntarily celibate state forced upon the *salad-shy* by their physical condition.

flabulous *adj.* Term applied to *big-boned birds* who over-compensate for their excessive surface area by presenting to the world a raucously upbeat personality, *eg.* Liza Tarbuck, Lisa Reilly, anyone called Lisa, basically.

flabwank *n.* An act of personal satisfaction carried out into an area of soft tissue located somewhere on a *lettuce dodger's* capacious frame, *eg.* Into a *bingo wing,* the *under-gunt* or flabby upper-thigh mass.

flaccid flashback *n.* A ghastly, inappropriate, unerotic memory, *eg.* Nan burping after eating too much stuffing, topless uncle mowing the lawn, Olive off *On The Buses,* that bit in *Oh Lucky Man!* with the man's head sewn onto a pig's body, that pops into one's head during sex, causing one to deflate like one of Richard Branson's balloons.

flackets *n. medic.* Beef curtains.

fladge and padge *abbrev.* Of *rub-a-tug shop* services, getting a bit of *Mr Whippy* off a whore in a nurse's outfit. From flageantry and pageantry. *'Bit of fladge and padge today, I think.' 'That'll be fifty pounds, Lord Archer.'*

flag bravo *n. nav.* A large red pennant unfurled atop a ship's masty thing to warn others of any dangerous activity which may be taking place. *2. euph. nav.* A term used by female members of the Royal Navy to describe their monthly period of confinement. *'Ooh, Admiral. I wouldn't go munching on me oggie if I was you. I've got me flag bravo hauled up.'*

flags are out *exclam. Wet paint* warning when the fixture list shows *Arsenal are playing at home.*

FLAME *abbrev.* Fanny Like A Mouse's Ear. An expression typically accompanied by a workmanlike rubbing together of the hands and a Mike Reid-style Jack the lad neck-thrust.

Flamingoland *n.* A watering hole with a high density of *Yorkshire flamingos.*

flamingo's flip-flop *n.* A particularly *moist flange.* Also *otter's pocket, fish drowner, mermaid's flannel* or *clown's pie.*

flamingo up *n.* Like a *cock up,* only much, much bigger.

Flanders poppy *sim.* A *ringpiece* that has been through the wars, *ie.* One that is bright red and shot to pieces.

flange *1. n.* A *fish mitten. Muff, beaver, minge. 2. n. coll.* Not a word to describe a group of baboons. The correct term for a group of baboons is "troop" or "congress". So there. *3. n. coll. Fanny, blart, tush, buffage.*

flangepiece *n.* Slang term used when referring to someone as a dolt or buffoon. *'Oi, Menuhin, put your fucking bow down. This movement's supposed to be fucking pizzicato, you fucking flangepiece.'* (Sir Edward Elgar, 1927).

flangina *1. n. medic.* Any form of physical or emotional pain caused to a man by the nagging of his female partner. *'I know I said I'd be back by ten and now it's Tuesday, but for fuck's sake give it a rest will you, woman. You're bringing on my flangina.' 2. n. medic.* Women's things.

flannelled *adj.* The state of one's face after *going down* on a *fish drowner.*

flap a herring *v.* To *fart* in a wet and

audible manner, such that the *cheeks* of the buttocks clap together.

flap dabbling *n*. In the world of *masturbating* ladies, to *gusset type* in a disinterested fashion. From flap + dabbling.

flap dance *n*. A terpsichorean performance in a gentleman's club which involves a little more *close up pink* than is customary in the circumstances.

flap-flops 1. *n*. The shoes commonly worn by old ladies in naturist resorts. 2. *n*. The *tits* commonly worn by old ladies in naturist resorts.

flapjack 1. *n*. A dense, syrupy cake, a bit like concentrated guinea pig *shit* mixed with muesli, that has pretentions to healthiness. 2. *n. medic*. A *quim quack's* tool for jacking *flaps* apart. A speculum. 3. *n*. A device, usually in the form of a small gift, given by a suitor to his intended in the hope that it will help him *get some cabbage* off her. 4. *n*. The frankly unhealthy act of *freeing the tadpoles* over one's good lady's *parts of shame*.

flapjacking *n*. Two tasty ladies having a nibble at each other's *sticky bits*. '*Come and look at this, your Holiness. there's a new flapjacking vid on ScrewTube.*'

flapmates *n*. A pair of cohabiting *curtain twitchers*. *Tennis fans*.

flapmonger *n*. One who mongs *flaps*. A *tart farmer*, fanny farmer, *pimp*.

flappetite *n*. A healthy appetite for flaps. From flap + appetite.

flappocks *n*. The confusing yet strangely intriguing in-between-style genitalia of a *trolley dolly* who is half way through a programme of gender reassignment surgery, in either direction.

flap snack *n*. A quick *fish burger* or *bacon sandwich*. Elevenses at *the Y*. Token

cumulonimbus.

flapsnapper *n. medic*. In the world of gynaecology and obstetrics, a firstborn infant which weighs in at more than 9lbs in the old money. '*Births: Haystacks. On March 9th at Halifax Maternity Hospital. To Mavis and Horace, a bouncing, bearded 38lb flapsnapper, Giant.*' (from *The Yorkshire Post*, March 11th 1946).

flap snot *n. medic. Danny Fishcharge. Lizzie dripping, clam jam. Gleet.*

flap the kipper *n*. Practice indulged in by lady rowers. Probably not as entertaining as it sounds.

flaptulence *n*. The *dropping forwards* of a *lady's hat*. *Queefage, fanny farting*.

flapuccino *n*. A highly-aroused *quim* on a dirty lady, whereby a cocktail of sundry miscellaneous *below-stairs* fluids have been whisked up into a froth against her pubic hair. With a sprinkle of chocolate powder on the top and one of them little biscuits in a plastic bag.

FLARP/flarp *acronym*. That unfortunate situation whereby a young lady has allowed her *fusewire* to go the way of a neglected dog's fur. As is well known to viewers of daytime television programmes such as *Animal Rescue Live*, the only remedy in such situations is the application of agricultural shearing equipment in order to completely remove the hopelessly matted fleece. Fanny Like A Rescue Poodle. See *noodle knickers*.

flash *v*. To treat a lucky lady to a surprise private viewing of one's *fruitbowl*.

flasher *n*. A gentleman who frequents municipal parks wearing a mac, beret, little round glasses and trouser bottoms tied round the knees with string.

flash in the pan 1. *n*. A *spooge*-free male

orgasm. A cashless *money shot*. 2. *n.* The act for which George Michael was arrested in a Beverly Hills public lavatory on April 7th 1998.

flash the ash *exclam.* A gentle reminder of a person's social responsibility to share his cigarettes with others in his peer group. *'Oi, fuck face! Flash the ash, you tight-fisted cunt.'*

flash the upright grin *v.* To expose the female genitals, *flash the gash*.

flat as a kipper's dick *adj.* Bidimensionally homologous. Descriptive of unleavened *baps*.

flative *adj.* Of food, that which induces flatulence, *eg.* Cabbage, sprouts, *musical vegetables*.

flatliner *n.* A burst of numerous, regularly-spaced *air biscuits* of equal length and volume, followed by one long, sustained release of *brown air*. From this act's rhythmic similarity to the sound made by TV hospital drama heart monitors just before a fashionably-stubbled surgeon reluctantly stops pumping the patient's chest, looks at the clock, then pulls off his rubber gloves and flings them away.

flat slag *n.* A previously rotund lady who has lost a lot of weight, resulting in an excess of skin.

flat Stanley *n.* A sexual encounter involving a very large lady.

flat, straighten up the *v.* Of a closet *puddle-jumping* couple, to hang a *Hollyoaks* calendar on their wall in order to disguise the *whiff of lavender* in the air.

flatter than a plate of piss 1. *sim.* Topographically or otherwise planar, *eg.* Lincolnshire, Jemini's performance of the UK entry *Cry Baby* in the 2006 Eurovision Song Contest, Kate Moss's biffing plate. 2. *n.* Insufficiently effervescent. *'Oi, landlord. Get us another pint, will you. This fucker's flatter than a plate of piss.'*

flatty, crack a *v.* To suffer an unfortunate erectile dysfunction in the *trouser department*.

flatulence *n.* The whole kit and kiboodle of *farting*. From the Latin *flatus* = to start & *lentus* = a cold tractor.

flavour of the month *n.* The savoury tang of *moon juice*. The *twaste* left in the mouth following a *scrapheap challenge*.

fleahive *n.* A filthy approximation of a 1960s-style beehive haircut, which can make you start to itch if you so much as look at it. As worn by thirsty singer Amy Winehouse.

fleemail *n.* A rapidly-scribbled note of thanks, including a false name and address, left on the pillow of a *munter* by a long gone *fanny hopper* who woke up without his *beer goggles* on.

flembrandt *n.* A distinctive piece of pavement art seen adorning much of London's walkways. *Lung paint*.

fleshbombs *n.* Two large wads of *jubbly gelignite* packed in a woman's *tit pants*.

flesh lettuce *n.* Crinkly downstairs *lady bits*.

flesh tones *n.* The sweet music played on the *bed flute*. The lyric-free theme tune *to the old meat whistle test,* teased out of the *Devil's bagpipes* by a skilled *pink oboist*.

flesh wallet *n.* The *hairy cheque book, pubic purse*. Somewhere to put one's *money shots*.

fleshy flugelhorn *n.* Tuneful variation on the *bed flute, pink oboe, spunk trumpet, beef bassoon, pork euphonium*.

flex, to have a *v.* To *bust off*.

flicker book *n.* An *art pamphlet* for a lady, if indeed such a thing exists. Sheet music for an *invisible banjo* player.

flick finger *n. medic.* The finger with which a woman *flicks herself off.*

flies' dinner gong *n.* A entemologically Pavlovian *custard tart.*

flik *n.* Dried up *spoff* found on curtains, furniture, foreheads, shrouds *etc.* '*I felt so betrayed when the President denied we had had a relationship. Then my friend Linda Tripp reminded me that I still had the dress with his flik all over it in the cupboard.*' (Monika Lewinsky, Statement to the US Senate Impeachment Committee, 1999).

flinge *n. coll. Blart, tussage, flap.* From flange + minge. '*Come on. Let's go and find some flinge.*'

flingel *rhym. slang. Cunt.* From the instrumental hit *The Rise and Fall of Flingel Bunt* by The Shadows.

flinging in the rain *n.* The act of masturbating in the shower.

fling string *v.* To *jizz* via air mail. To *lob ropes.*

flip flop *1. n.* A poor quality shoe substitute worn by people who can't afford heels. *2. n.* A *tug* administered whilst one is so unenthusiastic about life that one can't even muster up a *semi-on.* A *flap.*

flipper *n.* A Taiwanese *ladyboy* that fools the gagging punter to the extent that he thinks: "Fuck it. I've paid me money, I'll just flip her over".

Flipper's beak *n.* A *shaven haven*, often to be seen poking out of the water and making a clicking sound before wrestling a pistol out of a bank robber's hand.

flipping pancakes *n.* The practice of loosening up one's *batter* prior to sending it arcing up into the sky. On a Tuesday.

float an air biscuit *v.* To release a *tree monkey* from captivity.

floater *1. n.* A *turd* in the pan which will not flush away. *2. n.* A member of the crap 70s soul band, *eg.* Larry (Cancer), who likes a woman that loves everything and everybody.

flock of pigeons *n.* The sound of a loose bowel movement.

flock of sparrows, coming out like *sim.* Descriptive of the more urgent *digestive transit.* '*I was on the toilet all night. It was coming out like a flock of sparrows. Cyril?*' '*Thank-you Esther.*'

flog'n'bog *v.* To multi-task by having a *shit* and a *wank* at the same time. To *shank.*

flog pocket *n.* The front flap of a pair of Y-fronts, useful when a fellow needs rapid access to his *old chap* for whatever reason.

flogging on *v.* Accessing the internet in search of *left-handed websites.*

flog the log *v.* To *whup one's wood, spank the plank.*

floor chimes *n.* The collection of empty cans and bottles under the driver's seat of a regional television presenter's Jag, which roll together, producing a soothing jingle-jangle sound when the car goes round a corner, up a kerb or over a bicycle.

floordrobe *n.* The clothing receptacle most used by students, teenagers and men home from the pub.

flop out *n.* Condition whereby the flaccid penis protrudes through the bottom of the underpants, this often occurring during the transfer from a sitting to a standing position.

floppy red cup *n.* The *Hairy goblet, furry cup.*

flop to pop *n.* A standard interval used to measure the quality of *horatio* techniques. The time taken to ejaculate from a flaccid start. *'Egbert was powerless to resist. Her eyes burned into his like sapphires. Her ladylike arms enfolded his masculine body as he felt himself being swept away in a whirlwind of passion. Then she knelt down in front of him and took him from flop to pop in three minutes flat.'* (from *The Officer and the Gypsy* by Barbara Cartland).

Florida fartbox *n. US.* An *abnormal load. Orlando dirtbox.*

florins *ryhm. slang.* The *shits.* From the pre-decimal coins known as *two bob bits.*

flossing the squirrel *v.* Of a lady, to be sporting a thong-styled underpant.

floury bap *n. rhym. slang. N. Ire.* How a Belfast baker would refer to a *crap. 'Hold the shop for me a while there, will you? I'm off in the back room for a floury bap into that bucket behind the raisins. And while I'm there, I may as well start them flapjacks.'*

floydian slip *n.* An inappropriate and unexpected remark made at a dinner party after indulging in one too many aperitifs. Named after the late, robustly-opinionated, deceased, drunken TV chef Keith.

flub *1. onomat.* The sound of a *fanny fart. 2. v. Fuck* in Flowerpot Men language. See *dub.*

fluff *n. nav.* A maritime *blow off.*

fluffer *n.* In a *bongo vid* studio, a professional *fellatrix* employed between takes to ensure the tumescence of the male actors.

fluffit *n.* The sweetest name in common use for the *cunt.*

flum *n. Ladygarden, snatch thatch, pubes.*

flump *1. n.* A cylindrical marshmallow sweet. *2. n.* An offensive and hurtful term used by sexist women to describe the flaccid penis of a man who, for all they know, may be suffering from serious medical problems. *3. v.* To thumb in a less than tumescent member when attempting sexual congress with some *tart* whilst completely *hammered.*

flunkey *1. n.* A Royal slave, one who fawns on a *nob, eg.* Nicholas Witchell. *2. n.* A *dunky.*

flush hour *n.* In a workplace, the period of time after morning coffee during which there is even a queue for the gents' *shitter.*

flushin' roulette *n.* The high stakes game played by festival-goers as they steel themselves to open the porta-loo door.

flush out the brown rabbit *v.* To introduce your *pink ferret* to the missus's *front warren* and thus elicit an evacuation from her *back warren.*

flush puppies *n.* Dalmatian-spotted suede shoes that have been standing too close to a urinal.

flushstration *n.* The sense of increasing annoyance felt when a *faecee* one has just excreted refuses to disappear down the U-bend, despite repeated cranks on the handle.

flute player's lips *n.* Descriptive of the *ringpiece* ejecting last night's curry and beer.

flutter *n.* Of a lady, to urinate charmingly, *viz.* Without *blowing off* like a backfiring Harley Davidson Fatboy halfway through.

flux capacitor *1. n.* The invention that allows a 35-year-old Michael J Fox to play a teenager in the *Back to the Future* trilogy. *2. n.* The Y-shaped vein on the shaft of the *tallywhacker*.

fly feast *n.* An *al fresco* act of *cable laying*, usually up an alleyway or behind some bushes.

fly sheet *n.* A *fiveskin*.

flying pastie *n.* Excrement wrapped in newspaper and thrown into a neighbour's yard for whatever reason. See *pyropastie*.

flying Scotsman *n.* A highly complicated sex act that doesn't sound like it's worth the bother.

flying squirrel *n.* Genital manipulation amusement. *Farmyard* animal impression involving the stretching of one's scrotal leather almost to breaking point, in the style of the wing-like membranes on the popular airborne rats of the genus *Pteromys*.

fly's eyes *n.* A gentleman's party trick whereby the shorts or bathers are pulled tight between the legs so that the *clockweights* bulge out on either side of the gusset. *'August 6th. We all go down to Cliveden for the weekend. Gerty (Laurence) and Fanny (Brice) were there as usual. Ivor (Novello) entertained us all by singing King's Rhapsody by the pool, and followed it by doing fly's eyes. How we all shrieked. Benjamin (Britten) laughed so much he shat himself, poor dear.'* (from *The Diaries of Noel Coward*, 1938).

fly's graveyard *n.* The *nutsack* netherworld situated on the dorsal side of the *chicken skin handbag* which to this day remains unseen by human eyes.

fly the flag *v.* NZ. To *zuffle*.

fly tipping *n.* The act of rewarding a fly for excellent service in a soup restaurant.

fnarr! fnarr! *exclam.* Suppressed childish exclamation of amusement uttered after a double entendre. Also *k-yak! k-yak!*

foaming at the bunghole *adj.* Frothing at the gash. Glistening.

fodder *n.* Collective term for the mental images of pulchritudinous young ladies that a gentleman files away in his *mammary banks*, to be retrospectively reviewed in those future moments when he needs to *relax*.

FOFFOF/foffof *acronym.* Fair Of Figure, Foul Of Face. *Bobfoc*.

fofo *n.* Acronymous game played by beastly males, preferably from the safety of a patrol car with the windows wound all the way up, and involving the instant answering of a paraphrased version of the following question, *viz.* "Would you care to partake in sexual relations with the indicated young lady, or would you rather prefer to request her instantaneous departure?" That is to say, somewhat more succinctly, "Fuck Or Fuck Off?"

FOG *abbrev.* The sort of stare that one gives to a senior citizen at a bus stop in order to avert the possibility of them attempting to strike up a conversation about the weather, the paucity of the old age pension or the size of these new five pence pieces. From Fuck Off Granny.

foggles *1. n.* R.A.F. Wrap-around glasses used in pilot instrument training, which are frosted except for a section at the bottom, so as to restrict the pilot's view to his instrument panel only. *2. n.* A phenomenon whereby, on meeting a lady, one's attention is focused on the lower features to the exclusion of anything above shoulder level. *'She was a blonde, or perhaps a brunette. She might have* been ginger. I can't remember, officer. I had my foggles on.'

fog up *adj.* Of *train pulling*, to be the driver, as opposed to the *porridge stirrer* in the *guard's van*. 'Bagsy me fog up. I don't want any of you lot's sloppy seconds again.'

folder *n.* One whose good breeding, manners and culture have instilled in them the proper way of preparing toilet paper for smudging the *chocolate starfish*.

follow through *v.* To accidentally soil one's *undercrackers* whilst attempting to release a bubble of *carbon dibaxide*. To create *russet gusset, drop a pebble*.

fomp *v. US.* To engage in sexual foreplay, to *firkyfoodle*.

fond of shopping *euph. Good with his hands.*

fond of walking holidays *euph.* A *woman in comfortable shoes*, a *tennis fan*, a *tuppence licker*.

fondleberries *n.* Testicles.

Fonz, the *n.* Sexual act involving a man being *noshed off* whilst his *nosher* simultaneously sticks both thumbs up his *sheriff's badge* and attempts to say "Heeeey".

food in the beard *euph.* A symptom of insufficient wiping after a *tom tit*. To have *winnets* in the *crackers*.

food's ghost *n.* An invisible, eerie presence accompanied by a low humming sound and the stench of death. A *McArthur Park*.

foop *n. onomat.* The sound of a penis being removed from an anal passage, presumably a bit like when you blow across the top of an empty milk bottle.

footballer's tie-knot, wide as a *sim.* An expression that describes something that is wider that it ought to be. 'Thank you,

Your Holiness, but I'd rather not sit down. I had a cack this morning and the bastard was as wide as a footballer's tie knot, believe me.'

foot high club *n.* A more affordable version of the *Mile High Club* for the lower orders. Usually involving a park bench, the back seat of a car, a shop doorway or the cage in a police van.

footstool *n. Pavement toffee, barkers' eggs* and the like, when trodden on.

footwell flavour *n.* The soul-destroying aroma of *footstool* that appears three minutes after turning on the car heater.

Forbsy drop, the *n.* The act of taking a full pint to the pub toilet and returning with it empty in an attempt to look like a hardened drinker. Named after a lawyer from St Albans who can't take his beer. 'Heavily made-up Prime Minister Tony Blair today visited the Labour Club at his Sedgefield constituency, and performed several Forbsy drops for the benefit of television news cameras, before announcing his intention to resign and leave Gordon Brown well and truly in the shit.'

force field *n.* A thick *fart* that clings to the warp and weft of one's *duds*, preventing anyone from coming within six feet for a good ten minutes. A *Velcro guff*.

FORD *abbrev. medic.* Casualty doctors' notes terminology. Found On Road Drunk.

foregasm *n.* A *stack* which is *blown* whilst still trying to *light the fire*. When a gentleman *spends his money* before he's even got *into the shop*. Going *up and over like a pan of milk* before the niceties of *frigmarole* have been satisfactorily completed. A *Pope-shot*.

forget the password *v.* To suffer from

constipation. To repeatedly fail in your attempts to to *log on*.

foreigner 1. *n.* A person from another country in this country. Or a person from this country in another country. Or a 1970s *poodle rock* band. 2. *n.* A private job unofficially done using the facilities of one's business. 3. *n.* A *dump* made uncomfortable due to the fact that it is being performed on someone else's *crapper*

file under W *v.* To download the image of a lady into one's *mammary banks*, with the intention of using it as *fodder* in the future.

foreploy *n.* Any gambit used to get a woman into bed, *eg.* Claiming to be an airline pilot, member of the SAS, employee of the month at McDonald's *etc.*

foreporn *n.* The token, exaggerated, wooden acting preceding the *spaff candy* of a *grumble vid*. Usually viewed on fast forward.

fore-skin conclusion *n.* Much like a foregone conclusion, but specifically applied to sexual situations; a turn of phrase which can be usefully employed in those circumstances when a chap is one hundred percent guaranteed to *get his end away*. '*Are you off to decorate that lass's house tonight then?*' '*Yep.*' '*Reckon you'll get a shag out of it?*' '*It's a foreskin conclusion, mate.*'

foreskin jogging *n.* The act of *bashing the bishop* at a leisurely, gentle pace so as not to get out of breath or peak too early. *Treading water.*

foreskinzola *n.* A pungent, unappetising, mature *knobcheese.*

forget-me-mott *n.* An unkempt bed of *gorilla salad*, which could do with a bit of judicious pruning.

forget-me-nots *n.* The final notes in a *Chinese singing lesson*. Droplets which form a tiny but embarrassing wet patch on your trousers. *Dicksplash.*

forgetiquette *n.* To inadvertently forget one's manners, *eg.* When taking a mobile phone call during Earl Spencer's speech at Lady Di's funeral, scratching one's *arse* and sniffing your fingers just prior to shaking the Queen's hand backstage at the Royal Variety Performance.

fork lift truck *n.* An exotic sexual position performed in back alleys and shop doorways, whereby the female participant is hoisted clear of the ground by the thighs in order to keep her *arse* clear of *piss*, vomit, broken glass and spent *jubbers*. A *chinook.*

form 1. *n.* Means of judging horses by statistics, before *pissing your money up the wall* at the bookies. 2. *n.* Means of judging *birds* by statistics. *Fitness, fuckability, prodworthiness.*

Forsyth 1. *n.* A rug worn across the lap to preserve one's modesty whilst vigorously *enjoying* art films in the presence of others. 2. *v.* To play the *generation game*; to have romantic liaisons with both mother and daughter. To *play one's cards right*, going "higher" (mother) and "lower" (daughter), if you will.

fort knockers *n.* Highly reinforced and practically impenetrable bras of the sort that nuns, librarians and Ann Widdecombe might wear.

Forth bridger *n.* An irritable and cantankerous woman who appears on *Newsnight Late Review* and seems to *have the painters in* all year round, *eg.* Germaine Greer, Bonnie Greer, any woman called Greer.

forty-eight volter *n*. Even more shocking than a *nine volter*. A *minge* which, when licked, generates an electrifying effect similar to that obtained by applying one's tongue to an array of forklift truck batteries wired up for maximum current.

forty wanks *n*. An impromptu and refreshing afternoon *shuffle*.

Fosbury plop *n*. An *arse baby* of such proportions that the delivery method involves arching the back in the style of the revolutionary 1960s Olympic high-jumper.

FOTBOAL shirt *n*. Any item of fashion-wear purchased from a street vendor at a significantly lower price point than which its manufacturer recommends, and consequently with little or no regard as to the legitimacy of its provenance. Fell Off The Back Of A Lorry.

fough *n*. An inadvertent *dropping of the guts* when clearing one's throat. Derivation unknown. Possibly from Frank + Bough.

fouled hand *1. n*. In poker, a selection of cards that is ruled unplayable because of an irregularity, *eg*. That it contains too many or too few cards. *2. n*. When an accidental rip in one's lavatory tissue results in *Linda Bellingham's fingertips*.

foul papers *1. n*. In the world of Shakespearean scholarship, manuscripts bearing abandoned drafts of the bard's work. *2. n*. In the world of *arse-wipe* studies, soiled *bumwad*.

foul Paulo *n*. An Italian *Dirty Sanchez*. A faecal moustache.

four-man bob *n*. A large, speedily-ejected *turd*. Possibly rocking backwards and forwards 2 or 3 times before coming out.

four minutes *rhym. slang*. Haemorrhoids. From four minute miles = piles.

fourth base *1. n. US*. Something to do with baseball or American football or something. *2. n*. The *anus*.

fourth party *adj*. The type of motor insurance favoured by the council *estate car* driver, *ie*. None. *'It's alright, mate. That'll just polish out. Anyway, I've got full fourth party insurance. You stand there and I'll just get back in my car to write down my details.'*

fox licking shit off a wire brush, face like a *sim*. Phrase which is useful when one is referring to someone of a notably miserable mien. *'Did you see John Prescott on the stand at the Labour Party Conference? He looked like a fucking fox licking shit off a wire brush.' 'Thank-you, Martha. And now back to Jeremy in the Newsnight studio.'*

foxymoron *n*. A lady whose incredible physical attractiveness is matched only by her marked lack of intellect. *'Famous people born on November 23rd: John Wallis, influential English mathematician, 1616; Franklin Pierce, 14th President of the United States, 1804; Manuel de Falla, greatest Spanish composer of the last century, 1876; Kelly Brook, wonky-titted foxymoron, 1979.'* (from *'Schott's Oh Fuck Oh Fuck Oh Fuck the Deadline's Tomorrow Book, 2005'*).

Foyston Gap *n*. The space at the top of a woman's thighs, a term peculiar to Greatfield, Kingston upon Hull, East Yorkshire. The *Toblerone tunnel*.

fraggle in the frazzle *n*. A penis hiding in a clump of unruly pubic hair.

Frampton *1. n. prop*. An overrated 1970s singer with a voice like Steven Hawking.

2. n. A *fanny fart.*

Francis *n. US.* A lady's *arse.*

franger *n. Dunky, English overcoat, blob, jubber ray.* A gentleman's prophylactic sheath.

frankenfiver *n.* A unit of currency which has been craftily customised by a previous handler, consisting of either a torn five pound note sellotaped back together, two torn five pound notes joined together to create a new one or, more spectacularly, a piece of genuine legal tender which has been hybridised by the skillful addition of Monopoly money. Usually issued as change from a larger denomination note, the *frankenfiver*'s status as legal tender is a source of lively debate and discussion, especially amongst the taxi drivers to whom it is subsequently proffered.

Frankenstein's feet *sim.* The illusion of having someone else's feet stiched onto one's legs caused by the serrated indentations left by tight socks on one's ankles.

frankentits *n. Knockers* which exhibit baseball-stitch-style scarring from their implant operations, leaving them looking like something knocked up by Peter Cushing in his laboratory. *Beverly hills* are usually revealed as *frankentits* when viewed from underneath.

frankfurter water *1. n.* Salty, meat-flavoured fluid in which a slippery sausage has been steeped. *2. n.* Salty, meat-flavoured fluid which has just come out the end of a *slippery sausage.*

Frankie *rhym. slang. Grumble, scud* material. From Frankie Vaughanography = pornography.

frap *v. onomat.* To *break company* through the *snippit valve.*

frappers *n. Fr. Knockers.* From the French word "frapper", meaning "to knock". *'Zut alors, tout le monde! Check out les frappers smashants on that oiseau at le bus-stop.'*

frappuccino *n. 1.* A pretentious and expensive cross between coffee and Angel Delight, a bit like a caffeine-enriched slush puppy, but costing about eight quid at Starbucks. *2. n.* The creamy head cooked up by a lady's *cabbage* when in a state of high arousal. *'I was on form last night, I'll tell you. By the time I got down for me fish supper, she was frothier than a frappuccino. And now over to Daniel Corbett for tomorrow's weather.''*

frazzle *n.* Any *bongo mag* catering exclusively for readers with a taste for old biddies.

freckle maggots *n.* Rolled-up pieces of 3-ply *shit ticket* which congregate around the *tea towel holder* after it has been given a right good wipe.

freckle *n. Aus. Arse, brown eye, chocolate starfish, dot.*

Fred *n. rhym. slang. Sprongle.* From the famous golfer Fred Funk, whose name rhymes with *spunk.*

freemason's handshake, fanny like a *sim.* A tight vagina, particularly one which applies unusual pressure to the second knuckle of one's right hand.

free the Middleton two *v.* To drive over speed bumps at an excessive velocity in the hope of getting one's ladyfriend's *Gert Stonkers* to bounce right out of her low-cut top. Named after the Leeds area which is richly-blessed with both traffic-calming street furniture and *big-titted* single mothers.

free the tadpoles *v.* To liberate the residents of one's *wank tanks.* To have a *tug.*

fred Leicester *n.* Pungent cheese cultivated in the *brim* of the *farmer's hat.*

Freeman's disgrace *euph.* The ignominious experience of *shitting* oneself whilst seated at a table in a curry house. Named after a certain Mr Neil (surname removed on legal advice), who shamefully soiled his tweeds after sampling one spoonful of Curry Hell, the world's hottest curry, at the Curry Capital Restaurant (formerly the Rupali), Bigg Market, Newcastle upon Tyne.

French *n.* Popular coital position whereby the man sits astride a bicycle selling onions while the woman perches on the handlebars and inflates his testicles.

French accordian player *n.* A gentleman inexperienced in the art of romancing a lady, who believes the best way to go about things is to press and squeeze everything he can find as quickly as possible. A *clamateur* musician.

French cough *n. medic.* The gagging, retching noise a woman makes when she has *sucked off* more than she can chew. *'Yes, you thought she was in a Range Rover parked in a layby near Wetherby, but she's travelled over two hundred miles to be with you tonight. It's the owner of that distinctive French cough ... Gillian Taylforth.'*

French cricket, play *1. v.* To improvise a simple, two participant ball game using a tennis ball and racquet. *2. v.* To improvise a simple, one participant ball game using the contents of one's underpants and one's right hand.

French cup *n.* In a gent's monomanual act of onanistic *self delight*, a cupped left *dick skinner* in which the *family jewels* rest whilst the sinful deed is undertaken. Or vice versa for a left-handed *Barclay's*, obviously. *'Jonathan, could you keep one hand on top of your desk at least while you're interviewing Dita Von Teese?' 'Sorry John, no can do. You'll just have to film me from the shoulders up, I'm afraid. I'm doing the French cup as well.'*

French horn *1. n.* Brass orchestral instrument, distinguished by its rotary valves, narrow conical bore and large, flared bell. *2. n.* Sexual position in which the female sits on the male's lap and he gets a mouthful of *tit* and four fingers in her *letterbox. 3. n.* A *bone on.*

French letter *n.* A *durex* or *English overcoat.*

French palm *n.* Secret sexual technique which quite possibly explains why our Gallic cousins are widely regarded as the world's greatest lovers. Not to put too fine a point on it, the use of a cupped hand on a lady's *front bottom*, rather in the style of those coarse youths at swimming pools who make *farting* noises under their armpits.

French polish, to *v.* To *buff up one's wood* till you can see your face in it. And all *spadge* comes out the end. To have a *Tom Hank.*

French safe *n.* A secure *box* that can be cracked open by fiddling with a little button at the top. Usually found behind a hinged oil painting on the front of a woman's *trolleys.*

French sickness *n.* Any *cock rot* caught from prostitutes advertising their services in phone boxes for £20 or less.

French snuff *n.* The pungent particles of *shit* which are inhaled from the end of the index finger after it has just scratched the *rusty bullet hole.*

French tickler *1. n.* Some sort of Ken

Dodd-style comedy prophylactic available from pub bogs vending machines in the 1970s. *'What a lovely day, madam, what a lovely day for rolling a contraceptive sheath equipped with wobbly protrusions ostensibly intended to heighten sexual pleasure onto Nicolas Sarkozy's erect penis and saying "How's that for a French tickler?"'* 2. *n.* A *cock* with a significant amount of stubble covering it.

French wank *n.* A *posh wank*.

French week *n.* A long and demanding day at work which is probably equal to the amount of effort expended by our gallic cousins from Monday to Friday. *'How was work today?' 'Crazy, I put in a French week.'*

frenchy *n.* Rubber carrying case for a *French horn*.

Freudian slip *n.* An inadvertent slip of the tongue revealing subconscious sexual desires. Named after crack-headed, *motherfucking* psychoanalyst Sigmund. *'Would you like a piece of my two foot black cock up your arse, Vicar? Oh, I'm sorry, I meant a piece of my home-made sponge cake.'*

friar's chin *n.* To tuck one's vest/shirt/jumper under one's chin to keep it out of harm's way whilst *pulling the Pope's cap off* over a *Tijuana bible*. See *bishop's waltz*.

friar's weeds *n.* A holy unkempt garden of *13 amp fusewire*.

Friar Tuck *rhym. slang.* An act of coition. A *Donald Duck*.

friction bairns *n.* The offspring of a homosexual. So called because the *lavender* father shoots his load solely as a result of friction. *'Ere, did you know that Julian Clary's missus has just had twins?' 'Friction bairns, them.' 'And that Graham Norton's got eight kids, you know.' 'Aye. Them lot's all friction bairns and all.'*

Friday foal *n.* One who, late on a Friday evening, proceeds to take on the ambulatory characteristics of a new-born baby deer. A *beer Bambi*.

Friday night gamble *n.* Rejecting the advances of a perfectly acceptable bit of *tussage* on the chance that one might pull something even better later on in the evening. *Twisting*.

fridge magnet *n.* A man whose successive girlfriends' sexual appetites are a source of disappointment to him. *'Trish won't take it fudgeways either. What am I, a fridge magnet?'*

fried chicken *n.* A sweaty, greasy, shaven *bargain bucket*, as seen on a drunken young lady who's been dancing all night.

fried eggs *n.* Small *baps, titterlings, stits*.

fried eggs and bacon *euph.* The inexplicable phenomenon of morbidly-obese women who still manage to somehow have no *shirt potatoes* whatsoever.

friend of Dorothy *n.* Politically correct terminology for a chap on whom *nature has played a cruel trick*.

friendly fire 1. *n. milit.* The actions of US armed forces against journalists, ambulances, wedding parties and anyone who fights alongside them. 2. *n.* An unexpectedly powerful *jizz bolt* that overshoots the belly and hits a *self-abuser* in the face. 3. *n.* Of a gentleman *jazz flick* actor, to be caught in the line of fire of a fellow thespian's *pop shot*. 4. *n.* Small residue of urine ejected from the penis when one is trying to put it back into one's flies following a *scoot*. Usually when wearing light-coloured trousers.

frig *v.* To *frotter, wank*, esp. a lady's *squidge*.

friggonometry *n.* The precise science involved in selecting and arranging one's fingers at the correct angle whilst *diddling* a rude lady's *devil's doorbell*. The *Ebdon slide*.

friggy pudding *n.* Any sort of post-*frotter* residue which a young chap might find on his fingers after giving a *friggonometry lesson* to a female accomplice.

fright *n. coll.* Collective term for a group of ugly women. *'Right, so that's agreed. Susanna's going to be the lead singer. Now we just need a fright of birds to stand behind her and play the instruments.'*

frightened skydivers *sim.* Descriptive of stools that are reluctant to exit the *bomb bay doors*. *'I think I'm going to have to try All Bran. My turds are like frightened skydivers.'*

frigmata *n.* Sanguinous marks on the hands of one who has been *flicking the bean* of a woman when *Aunt Flo is visiting*.

frigment of one's imagination *n.* A subject conjured up in the mind to oil the wheels of *self abuse*.

frigmarole *n.* Unnecessarily time-consuming foreplay performed on a missus. *Choreplay*.

frigor mortis *n. medic.* State of stiffness in one's *old chap*.

frigspawn *n. Cock eggs* in the bath.

friguratively *adv.* Descriptive of someone talking a load of *wank*. *'Did you see Robert Peston on the Ten O'Clock News? He explained how the whole economic system works, speaking figuratively of course.'*

fringe-parter *n.* A gusty *fanny fart* during a session of *cumulonimbus*. A *lip rattler*.

Frinton Ferrari *n.* A pensioner's mobility vehicle. *A Holland-on-Sea hotrod*.

frist *n.* The unique joint between the arm and hand of a lady who suffers from *cake retention*. From fat + wrist.

fritter *1. n. NZ.* A hot, *batter-coated morsel*. *2. n.* An item of food cooked in a frying pan.

fritzkreig *n.* The early morning nabbing of all every sunlounger on the premises by German hotel guests.

frock *n.* Cosmetic husband in a *lavender marriage*. The male equivalent of a *beard*.

Frodo *n.* An annoying little *turd* that clings to the *ring*. A *geetle* that forces one to *tap the ash*.

Frodo's banjo *n.* See *cock harp*.

frog, catching the *n.* The act following a successful *peel and polish*, whereby a lady cups her hands to collect her manfriend's expelled *baby gravy*.

frogging *n.* Towpath-specific form of *dogging*, practised by boggle-eyed men crouching next to moored canal boats with insufficiently tightly-drawn curtains. *Ducking*.

froggy style *n.* Type of sexual congress performed in the style of the popular warty green amphibians, *ie. Back-scuttling* their lass, then pulling out at the last moment and *spunking* up her back.

frog's chin *n.* The saggy *bag of tripe* that hangs over and obscures the *furry bike stand* of an unacceptably curvaceous lady. The *gunt, bunt, poond, fupa*.

frombie *n.* A lady who is blessed with such a *lovely personality* that the only way a gentleman could bring himself to do her would be "from behind".

from Devizes *euph.* Descriptive of a lady who either has one *nork* larger than the other or, alternatively, one *nork* smaller than the other. Or both. From the famous limerick by Poet Laureate John Masefield, *viz.* "There once was a girl from Devizes / who had knockers of differing sizes. / One breast was small, and of no use at all / but the other was large, and won prizes".

fromunder *n.* Type of pungent cheese cultivated by the less hygiene-conscious elements of male society. Also *helmetdale, brimula, knacker barrel.*

frontal forelimb *n.* A prehensile *dobber.* A *middle stump, third leg.*

front bottom *n.* Ladies' *parts of shame.*

front bummer *n.* A woman in *comfortable shoes* who is *fond of walking holidays.* And *quims.*

front bum trumpet pump *n.* A *cunt grunt, queef, kweef, cunt guff, muff chuff, Harry Ramsden's dinner gong, Seagoon's last raspberry, frampton, hat dropped forward, Lawley kazoo, muff chuff, crumpet trumpet* or *fanny fart.* See also *vulvuzela.*

front loaded date *n.* A social engagement where the male party's sophisticated and gallant veneer gradually slips away, until by the end of the evening he is revealed in all his boorish glory.

frostitute *n.* A lady of the night who gives her clients a service without a smile.

frothing at the gash *adj.* See *frothing at the South.*

frothing at the South *n.* Of a lady, being in a state of preternatural sexual excitement. Also *fizzing at the bung hole, gagging for it, frothing like bottled bass, dripping like a fucked fridge.*

frott *v.* To *frotter.*

frottage 1. *n.* The act of deriving pleasure by rubbing one's clothed genitals on any convenient surface, *eg.* A door jamb, a fridge, a woman's *arse* on a crowded tube train. 2. *n.* Of a pair of *book readers, frotting.*

frottage cheese *n.* The sticky end product of a successful act of *frottage.*

frotter 1. *v.* To *frott.* 2. *n.* One who *frotts* or *frotters.* A *frotterer.*

frotterer *n.* One who indulges in *frottage, ie.* One who *frotts.* A *frotter.*

frozen points *n.* The *Bruce Lees* of a sexually excitable woman.

frube *v.* After an act of *self harm,* to squeeze the remaining drops of *spodge* out the end of one's *giggle stick,* as one would the fromage frais from one of those yoghurt-filled tubes.

fruit *n.* A chap who is not particularly good at throwing.

fruit & flowers *euph.* How drugs are referred to on television production accounting sheets.

fruit bowl *n.* Two plums and a banana. The collective term for a gentleman's *wedding tackle.* The *orbs and sceptre.*

fruit feeler *n.* A gentleman who is *light on his feet,* and who tends to *fumble spuds.*

fruit fly *n. Fag hag.*

fruit machine Freddy *n.* A chap who is well known to the local damsels for his lack of *staying power.* From the fact that, like a one-armed bandit, "they would be lucky to get three nudges out of him". One who is *up and over like a pan of milk.* Also variously known as a *two push Charlie, speaking clock, Timmy two stroke, one pump chump, two stroke poke, Brazillian rocket, English* *batsman, two stroke joke, Ernie, minute man, point & squirt merchant, Peter two pumps* or *SISO.*

fruit salad *n.* A small lady blessed with a big *top bum, ie.* A small *peach* with a large *pair.* Works better spoken out loud than when written down.

fruit shoot *n.* The *spendings* of a fellow who is *good with colours.*

fruit up *v.* To *toss* someone else *off,* in a public school dormitory for example. *"What's going on in here?" thundered Mr Wilkins as he burst into the showers. 'Please, Sir,' announced Venables, 'I gave Jennings a ten shilling postal order to fruit me up. Now he says he's sprained his wrist during Latin prep, and he won't give it back."* (from *Suck THIS, Jennings* by Anthony Buckeridge).

frum *v.* To *frig* a *bum.*

frump *v.* To sniff your girlfriend's younger sister's *bills. 'Not going away with the bird's family, mate?' 'No, I'm looking after the house for them. Wouldn't miss out on all that frumping for a big clock.'*

fruttocks *n.* The cheeks of the spare *arse* that certain *salad dodging* ladies possess around the front. The *bilge tanks, front buttocks.*

frying chips *n.* The sound a lady makes when she is seated on a *thunderbox, splitting her whiskers* and *putting out a fire.*

FTSE *1. abbrev.* Financial Times Stock Exchange. An index of the performance of the top 100 companies that allows people with pension funds to work out how much they have lost that day. *2. abbrev.* A *pappering of the kex.* Follow Through, Shit Everywhere.

fubes *n.* 13 amp, usually ginger, *pubes.*

Contraction of fusewire + pubes.

fuck *1. n.* A single act of copulation. A *bang* or *poke. 2. v. intrans.* To *have it off. 3. v. trans.* To *poke, nob,* or *shag* someone, or something, up the *cunker,* up the *dirtbox* or in any other available orifice. *4. v.* To comprehensively beat someone in a bout of fisticuffs, esp. a member of the constabulary. *'Come on, let's fuck a copper!' 5. v.* To break or damage something beyond repair. *'Ah, Mr Knievel. I've examined your X-Ray and I'm sorry to tell you that every bone in your body is fucked. And that includes them really little ones in your ears.' 6. v.* To dismiss something with contempt, particularly for a game of soldiers. *'There's a Health & Safety presentation about using the photocopier starting in five minutes.' 'Fuck that for a game of soldiers. I'm off for a fag and a wank.' 7. interj.* An exclamation of disappointment. *'I've just won two tickets to see Syd Little's gospel show.' 'Oh, fuck!' 8. exclam. interrog.* Slightly stronger version of "on earth" when used in a question. *'What the fuck happened here?' 9. exclam. rhet.* A forceful refutation. *'Did you fuck my wife?' 'Did I fuck!'. 10. n.* That which is given by a person who cares. *'Isn't it dreadful about the Queen Mum dying?' 'Personally, I couldn't give a fuck'. 11. n.* The flying thing that one who doesn't care could not give to a rolling doughnut. *12. exclam.* When used reflexively as a purely rhetorical invitation, an expression of incredulity at a thing, such as an unexpected turn of events or a piece of news. *'Well madam, you may be pleasantly surprised to learn that if this vase, in its present condition, were to come to auction today, I am confident that it* *would fetch at least twenty-five thousand pounds. You should insure it for at least thirty thousand pounds, possibly forty thousand.' 'Fuck me!'*

fuckabulary *n.* Those twenty words which, skilfully combined and recombined, make up the entire dialogue of all the porn movies ever made. Also *cockabulary.*

fuckadillo *n.* A quirk or peccadillo in a person's sexual life. *'She always liked to do it with a Bourbon cream gripped between her knees. It was just a fuckadillo of hers.'* (Arthur Marshall being interviewed about the late Duchess of Argyll on the *Russell Harty Show,* LWT 1978).

fuck all *n.* Nowt. 'Did you fuck her last night at all?' 'Did I fuck. I got fuck all all night.'

fuck all in a five-year plan *adj. Can.* An attempt to justify an extravagant purchase. *'I know strictly speaking we don't need a subwoofer on the stereo, but 800 quid is fuck all in a five-year plan. Now put them scissors down, love.'*

fuck an air fanny *v.* To *relax in a gentleman's way.* To *have it off* with a *ghost rider.*

fuckanory *exclam.* An extension of the word *fuck,* used to express extreme shock, disappointment or annoyance.

fuckard *n. arch.* Someone who was no rocket scientist a full five hundred years before rockets were invented. Except in China. A 15th century *Johnny No-Stars.* A *dolt,* a *fuckwit.*

fuck butter *n.* KY jelly. *I can't believe it's not batter.*

fucker 1. *n.* A disagreeable, overweight person, often prefixed "big fat". 2. *n.* Anything at all. *'Fucking hell, look at*

the size of that fucker!' (Sir Christopher Wren on seeing the dome of Saint Peter's in Rome).

fuckfoods *n.* Any provocatively-shaped or saucily-textured comestibles that could, in an extreme emergency, be pressed into impromptu service by the enterprising shopper who finds him or herself feeling a bit frisky in Tescos. Examples include, but are not limited to, cucumbers, corncobs, oven-ready chickens, bananas, curly-wurlies, gourds and liver.

fucking the night *sim.* Copulating with a *yeti's welly. 'How was it for you, Andrew, darling?' 'It was like sticking my cock out the window and fucking the night, Sarah.'*

fuck juice *n. Jitler.*

fuck me shoes *n.* Footwear worn by a *boot.*

fuck off 1. *exclam.* A request for someone to leave. 2. *adj.* Of a price, quote or estimate for goods or services, an over-inflated figure intended to put the customer off when the supplier doesn't want the business. *'He wants me to clean his gutters out, but I don't fancy going up there. I'll give him a fuck off price.'* 3. *adj.* Descriptive of anything that is exceptionally large or intimidating. *'He came to clean me gutters out, and turned up with a big fuck off ladder. And he only charged £250. Well you wouldn't catch me going up there for that money.'* 4 *exclam.* An expression of incredulous stupefaction. *'Here, you'll never guess who come in here the other day and bought an Eccles cake and some rubber bands. Elton John! Stood right where you're stood he was, plain as day, in them big shoes he had in Tommy. Paid with a million pound* *note, he did, and told me to keep the change.' 'Fuck off!'*

fuck 'n' chuck *n*. A lady with whom a gentleman has had a *whirlwind one-night romance*, who does the decent thing by leaving you alone afterwards. The opposite of a *bunny boiler*. A *hump 'n' dump*.

fuckpond *n*. A little post-coital pool that forms in a depression on the bottom sheet, usually full of tadpoles. A *fuckpuddle*.

fuckpouch *n*. The overhanging lump of *ladyflesh* which casts a shadow over the main event. The *poond, blubber beret, fat hat*.

fuckshitfuckshitfuckshit *exclam*. Phrase uttered when driving a car through a particularly tight space at too high a speed.

fucksock *n*. The sort of condom one's granny would knit.

fuck stick *n*. A short, stout piece of *wood* used for *fucking* something. A penis.

fucksticks *exclam*. An expression of mild impatience. *'Fucksticks. I've left the communion wafers in the vestry.'*

fuckstrated *adj. US*. To have a severe case of *DSB*.

fuckstruck *adj. Cuntstruck*.

fuck the dog *1. v. Can*. To do absolutely nothing. *'Busy day at the office, dear?' 'Not really. Made a few calls in the morning, went to the pub at dinnertime, fucked the dog in the afternoon.' 2. v.* How the English Arts & Crafts sculptor, typeface designer and printmaker Eric Gill (1882-1940) occupied his spare time when he wasn't sculpting, designing typefaces or making prints. Well, you had to make your own entertainment in them days.

fuck trophy *n*. A baby. Usually applied to the progeny of ugly couples who need proof of their ability to achieve congress.

fuck truck *1. n*. A "UK Amateurs" film production that is unlikely to win the Best Cinematography prize at this year's Academy Awards. *2. n*. A filthy van with a mattress in the back, used for location filming in *1*.

fuckwit *n*. A simpleton, a fool, one of little intelligence, a *bollock brain, Johnny No-Stars*.

fuck with the cock you've got, you can only *exclam*. Useful get-out clause for men defending themselves against accusations of inadequacy. *'Well, we made the wrong tyre choice at the start of the weekend and our new rear diffuser package is still not delivering the downforce on the slower corners. Still. you can only fuck with the cock you've got, so eighth is quite a reasonable result at the end of the day.'*

fucky dip *n*. The randomized means of selecting oneself a *special friend* for the duration of a swingers night, *eg*. Picking a set of car keys from a bowl on a coffee table in a suburban semi with pampas grass in the front garden. In a 1970s film starring Linda Bellingham, Bob Todd, John Junkin and Cardew Robinson. Also *quimbola, twottery*.

fud *n. Scot. Berkeley Hunt*. A *flingel*.

fud slush *n*. Scottish *fanny batter*, usually smeared on the face whilst eating a *haddock pastie*.

fudge *v*. To lie in the spoons position with one's partner, and *fart* so that it vibrates onto their person.

fudge factor *n*. Scientific assessment of how much a chap is *au fait with Doris Day*.

fudge packer *n.* One who packs fudge for a living, for example in the despatch department of a fudge factory.

fudge tunnel *1. n.* A tunnel made out of, or for the underground transportation of, fudge. *2. n.* The *arsehole*.

fudgeways *euph. Up the council.*

fuggit *exclam.* Ancient Egyptian curse uttered when denied a British passport.

fugly *adj.* Fucking ugly.

fugly but juggly *euph.* A bird who was at the back of the line when looks were being given out, but who evidently pushed right to the front of the queue at the *knockers* counter.

FUKT/fukt *acronym.* Post Office acronym for any parcel marked "fragile", which has come open as a result of being kicked around by bored sorting office staff playing football. Failed Under Kinetic Testing.

Fulham handshake *n.* A friendly greeting exchanged between two gentlemen in a public lavatory cubicle. A *WC Handy*.

fullbeams *n.* Ladies' *headlamps* which really ought to be dipped in order to avoid dazzling oncoming males.

full Belgian *n.* the opposite of a full *Brazilian*. A large, untidy *muff*. A *Judith* or *Terry Waite's allotment*.

full cuntal lobotomy *n.* A loss of reason found in men when presented with open *pissflaps*. The nervous system shuts down and all actions are controlled by the *hairy brain*.

full English *1. n.* A particularly greasy early morning *bang*, often followed by a big *shit* and a cup of tea. *2. n.* The *undercrackers* of the doubly incontinent after they've been *given it with both barrels. 'Can you give these a wash please, Maggie? I'm afraid they're the full English.'*

full English breakfast *n.* A very untidy vagina that is frankly too much to face just after you get up. A big plateful of *knicker sausages, bacon strips*, fried mushrooms and baked beans.

full English, she/he eats a *1. euph.* Said of a person who shows a healthy appetite for a *Byronic breakfast*. *2. n.* Said of a person of either gender who likes their *bacon* as much as their *sausage*. Subtly descriptive of the proclivities of an *alloy welder*.

full frontal prudity *n.* A marked reluctance to appear *in the rik* in the bedroom or locker room. Common amongst *plumpers* and *needle dicks*.

full Nelson *n.* When *wrestling oneself*, a hold involving one hand, one eye, and a funny-shaped hat.

full Roger McGuinn, the *euph.* An extensive set of genital ironmongery that "jingle jangles" like the trademark Rickenbacker 12-string guitar played by the eponymous Byrds plank-spanker. See also *Sam Spoon's rhythm pole. 'Ooh, Evan. I didn't realise you had the full Roger McGuinn.'*

full service history *n.* A fellow's detailed knowledge of who has previously messed about under his wife's *beetle bonnet*.

full set of valves and sockets *euph.* Complimentary reference to a particularly nubile young lady, when she excites concupiscence in a passing gentleman. *'Gwooar, fuck me. I tell you what, that Konnie Huq's got a full set of valves and sockets. And now over to Daniel Corbett for tomorrow's weather.'*

full theatre tour *n.* Access to all parts of a ladyfriend, *ie.* Starting off in the *Upper Circle*, then moving into the *Lower Circle* before finishing off in her *Private Box* with a box of Maltesers. May also encompass a *backstage pass* and emptying one's *orchestra stalls*. In her hair.

full throttle for take off *exclam.* The only way of having a *gypsy's kiss* when in possession of a *diamond cutter*.

full Trumpton *n. onomat.* A lengthy recital on the *rear end trumpet* which sounds eerily reminiscent of Captain Flack calling his Fire Brigade register, *viz.* "Pugh! Pugh! Barey McGrew! Cuthbert! Dibble! Grubb!". A *full Trumpton* may also continue with the sound of a tappetty vintage Fire Engine being cranked into reluctant life with a starting handle.

fumble bags *n.* Good value *knockers*.

fumbling with your change *n.* Surreptitious act of *self pollution* achieved through the pockets of your trousers.

fun bags *n.* Breasts, *knockers*, *thru'pennies*.

funbagtastic *exclam.* Upon seeing a glorious pair of *fleshbombs*, one might utter: *'Funbagtastic!'*

fun boy three *1. n.* Novelty pop act of the early 1980s; a sort of Ska/New Wave Worzels. *2. n.* The *fruit bowl* of the male. The *meat and two veg, fishing tackle*.

funburn *n. medic.* Painful reddening on the skin around the elbows, knees and buttocks, after *having it off* on a cheap nylon carpet.

funch *n.* Sex during your lunch hour, from fuck + lunch. A *nooner*.

fun cushions *n. Dirty pillows*.

funderwear *n.* Erotic but impractical lingerie. Purchased at great psychological expense by red-faced husbands, only to be returned to the shop the next day by thunder-faced wives. *Gash garnish*, any clothing bought from Ann Summers.

fun extractor *n.* A sour-faced woman sitting in the corner of a room, sucking all the enjoyment out of the atmosphere. *'Jesus, we went round to Tez's but he had the fun extractor turned on and it was a shit night.'*

fun junction *n. medic.* The area in a young lady's *soft undercarriage* between the *front* and *rear bottoms*. Upon arrival, a fellow might exclaim: *'Which way along the fun junction today?'*

funky hammer juice *n.* The *clam bisque* which, it is rumoured, sometimes sprays from a *dirty lady's clopper* whilst she is being *nimbed* on her *cumulus*. *Oyster juice*.

funky spingers *n.* Spooneristic *knuckle glitter*.

funny bone *n.* An inexplicable erectivitation of the *membrum virile* that occurs during a comedic performance. *Stand up, heckler's lump*.

funny girl *n.* A *trolley dolly* who has that little bit extra. Often found in Thailand and unreliable anecdotes about a friend of a friend who went on holiday to Thailand. A *tiptop*.

fun size *n.* A very small *turd*. But bigger than a *miniature hero*.

funt *n.* The kind of advertising executive that came up with the recent "Do You Speak Micra" campaign.

funtan *n.* A short-lived, healthy glow in the face of a gentleman following a spot of *self-discipline*.

fun tube *n.* A *rubber johnny*. *'Three fun tubes please, chemist.' 'I'm afraid we only have extra small in stock, Mr Davro.' 'Oh, bugger. Don't you have anything smaller?'*

FUPA/fupa *abbrev.* Fat Upper Pussy Area. The bloated lower belly of a woman. See *gunt*.

fur burger n. Minge, *hairy pie, vertical bacon sandwich.*

furgle 1. *n. prop.* Christian name of the lead singer of the Undertones. 2. *v.* To copulate rudely, crudely or noisily.

fur on it, it's got *exclam.* Phrase used to describe a *grizzly* that has been maturing in the *chamber of horrors* for far too long. *'So, Audrey, that's a very generous offer from the banker. Is it deal or no deal?' 'I'll tell you in a minute, Noel. I'm just off to the shitters to strangle a Mars Bar. I've been baking this fucker in that long it's got fur on it.'*

furry bicycle stand n. A *hoop* set into concrete outside the library.

furry letterbox n. An eight inch wide, spring-loaded horizontal *clapping fish.* That traps the postman's fingers.

furt 1. *n.* A painful passing of wind, possibly following the consumption of several pints of Guinness and a quantity of pickled eggs. From fart + hurt. 2. *n.* A furtive fart. 3. *v.* To *step on a duck*, surreptitiously.

fur trapper's cabin n. A city centre dwelling, such as a flat or bedsit, which is retained by a married man solely for the purpose of midweek *beaver-hunting* expeditions. A *stabbin' cabin.* *'ARCHER OF WESTON-SUPER-MARE, Lord: 12(g) Controlling shareholdings: Andartis Limited (art dealers), Artdeal Limited (art dealers). 13(a) Significant shareholdings: Corporate Dynamics Limited (investment holding company/investment in golf centre operating company), Winner Land SL (Majorcan residential property investment), Albert Goodwin plc (Enterprise Investment Scheme, Fine Art), Between 5% and 30% share of profits in various theatrical productions: Grease, London; The Sound of Music, London; Flashdance The Musical; The new Grease on Broadway Limited Partnership; The Sound of Music (Canada) Inc. 13(b) Landholdings: Rented urban property in London, Tyne & Wear, North Shields; Fourth floor fur trapper's cabin in Shepherd Market, London W1.'* (from *House of Lords Register of Members' Interests*).

fusewire n. A ginger person's *thirteen amp gorilla salad. Fire down below.*

Fussell's Milk 1. *n.* A thick, sweet condensed milk. 2. *n.* The contents of the male *churns* after prolonged abstinence from sexual activity. *'A sackcloth shirt in place of silk / My nads like tins of Fussell's Milk.'* (from *The Ballad of Ford Open Prison* by Jonathan Aitken).

futtering n. A *trip to Hairyfordshire.* A bout of *front door work.*

futurehead 1. *n.* In popular music, any member of the eponymous Sunderland-based 4-piece beat combo. 2. *n.* The tungsten-tipped head of a *Thora* which announces its impending arrival by burrowing through the *nipsy* like the Mole out of Thunderbird 2.

futz n. US. The vagina.

fuzzbox 1. *n.* A guitar effects unit popular in the late seventies. A *big muff.* 2. *n.* A *minge.*

fyst n. *arch.* A 15th century, foul-smelling *fart.*

fysticuffs n. *arch.* Getting punched by one's beneficiaries after *scaring the cat.*

Gabrielle *n.* A semi-successful *Velma.* A *King Harold.* Occluding one of your ladyfriend's eyes with a well-aimed *jizz-bolt.* A *spoff monocle, German eye-bath.*

gag *1. n.* A pre-*spew* spasm, often cause by a blockage in the throat - what Mama Cass supposedly did on a sandwich but Linda Lovelace didn't do on a *cock. 2. v.* What women are doing *for it* when they want it up 'em.

gagfluff *n.* The little rolls of smegma and underpant fibres that a lady encounters under her chap's *fiveskin* whilst she is performing *horatio.* Also the fragments of *bogroll* and *dessicated blip* found amongst a lady's *flaps* by a fellow performing *cumulonimbus.*

gag hag *n.* An unfussy lady who is prepared to *have it off* with stand-up comics. A comedic groupie.

gak *n. Springle, sprongle, sprungle.*

gallagher *n.* The stylised *horatio* technique employed by one who is too vertically challenged to reach the *giggle stick* using conventional methods. Named after the distinctive stance taken by eponymous Oasis frontman Liam, whereby he tilts his head back and mouths upwards into the microphone.

gallic *n.* Stimulating a partner's *balloon knot* with the tongue. Doesn't do a lot for fresh breath confidence. *Rimming.*

gallon girl *n.* An Imperial-quantity-specific *gifwid.* An *eight-pinter.*

galloping knob rot *n. medic.* VD, any painful *Doonican* resulting in the production of *gleet* and the *pissing* of razor blades.

gallop the lizard *v.* To *relax* in a *gentlemanly manner.*

gam *1. n. US.* Lady's leg. *'Hot Diggety! Check out the gams on that broad, Bub.' 2. v. abbrev. Gamahuche.*

gamahuche *v.* To *cumulate* one's partner's *nimbus.*

gamble and lose *v. US.* The secret vice of a *man of the cloth.* To *fart* and *follow through.*

gammon and pineapple *n. Ham-on-ham.*

gammon flaps *1. n.* Hole in a farmhouse door through which pigs are able to come and go at will. *2. n. Beef curtains, gammon goalposts.* The saloon doors on a *bird's blurtch.*

gammon ring *n.* The *nipsy.*

gander's neck *n.* An extremely long, thick *gut stick* which hisses menacingly if one gets too close.

Gandalf's floppy hat *1. n.* The grey headwear favoured by Tolkein's heroic wizard. *2. n.* The lop-sided fungus that can flourish atop the *bell end* of a less-than-scrupulously-hygienic *lord of the ring.* Also *pith helmet.*

gang bang *1. n.* A *shit* song by Black Lace, which featured in the splendid film *Rita, Sue and Bob Too. 2. n.* A nightmarish sexual free-for-all in a tastelessly-decorated living room.

gap lapper *n.* A *tennis fan.* Or possibly one who runs repeated circuits around a clothes shop.

gaping gill *n.* The state of an unfortunate *grumble flick* actress's *ringpiece* just after the male lead has withdrawn his *slag hammer.* Named after the famous North Yorkshire pot hole, that is 50m across and 200m deep. But not full of *spunk.* Also *granny without her teeth in, gaper.*

garbonzas *n. Gazungas.*

garboon *n.* One who *barumphs.* A *snufty, snurglar.*

Gardener's Question Time *1. n.* Achingly dull Radio 4 programme on which middle-aged women from Harrogate ask Eric Robson whether their compost needs pruning if there's going to be a late frost or something. *2. n.* A series of discreet enquiries made of a certain type of street gentleman by a herb enthusiast in the hope of purchasing a certain type of home-grown foliage which is a popular filling for roll-up cigarettes.

garfunkel *1. v.* To cover a public lavatory seat with paper in order to avoid contamination of one's posterior. The late *Carry On* star Kenneth Williams was by all accounts a keen *garfunkellist* when forced to evacuate his troublesome bowels in a toilet other than his own. To *scump*. *2. n.* Any *ad hoc* protective paper structure created in or on a municipal *chod bin*, "like a bridge over troubled water".

garlogies *n. Bell end* bogies.

Garrity dance *n.* The action of moving straight to the landing, knees together, after taking a *Brad* and finding nothing to wipe your *balloon knot* with. Named after the stupid dance popularised by the now deceased lead singer of Freddy and the Dreamers, who was always running out of *shitscrape*.

Gary Glitter *rhym. slang. Shitter, anus.*

gaseous clay *n.* A bowel movement in which the sufferer passes flatulence-assisted stools which look like something from a school pottery lesson and which, upon hitting the pan, "'float like a butterfly". However, because of their high exit velocity, they also "sting like a bee".

gash *1. n. Hairy axe wound* between a woman's *lisks*. The vulva. *2. n. coll.* *Totty, blit, bush, talent, blart.*

gash and Gary *n.* Of *jazz periodicals*, a comprehensive *below stairs* photograph of a lady in which both her *front* and *back doors* are on display. *Close-up pink.*

gash back *1. n.* Reward points earned by buying flowers, chocolates *etc.*, which can be redeemed at the *fish counter*. As opposed to *brownie points*, which can be cashed in *up the arse. 2. n.* The spontaneous recollection of what you managed to *pull* at the weekend, which will result in a sudden urge to either nip to the bog for a quick *ham shank*, or accelerate into a tree on the drive to work. *3. n.* A *grumble* flashback, that is to say the experience of spotting a person you think you recognise, then realising it's because you've seen someone who looks like them in a bit of *Frankie* recently

gash baron *n.* A merchant trading in women of questionable repute. A *tart farmer*, flapmonger, pimp.

gash card *n.* A female only method of payment for goods and services. Accepted by taxi drivers, milkmen and pizza delivery boys. *Hairy cheques.*

gash crash *n.* A motor accident, usually in early spring, caused when drivers are distracted by appealingly-attired females. *Rear ender.*

gash feathers *n.* The plumage on a *bird's nest*. Female pubic hair.

gash in the attic *1. n.* Every dad's secret roofspace stash of 1970s *grumble. 2. n.* A fortuitous bundle of *bongo mags* found stashed in the loft of a newly-acquired property. *Ceiling whacks.*

gash mark six *n.* A state of feminine arousal. *'A lady's hairy oven must be heated to gash mark six before the* *gentleman slams in his lamb.'* (from *Bedroom Management* by Mrs Beeton).

gash mask *n.* A woman who sits atop a man's face in order to prevent him breathing in any harmful odours.

gash matter *n.* Remnants of a *fish supper* on the chins of a *diner at the Y*. An *11 o'clock shadow*, dried *sloom, scraps*.

gashmina *n.* A posh *jam rag*.

gash pastie *n.* A particularly flaky vagina. *'She was so dry down there it looked like a gash pastie.'*

gashpatcho *n. Spanish soup*, which is on the menu for a few days each month. Also *tomato boat ketchup, cranberry dip, moon juice, egg nog, lunar mess* or indeed *fanny jam*.

gash plaster *n.* A feminine napkin, a *jam rag, dangermouse*.

gash rash *1. n.* A light-hearted ladies' *downstairs thing*, eg. thrush. *2. n.* Gentleman's post *lick-out* irritation of the chops.

gash splash *n.* The distaff equivalent of a *gentleman's wash*. *'Bloody hell, Barbara. I just popped next door to borrow Jerry's watering can and I caught Margot having a gash splash in the kitchen sink.'*

gash station *n.* A nightclub or bar where less-than-discerning gentlemen are able to *cop off* with *welly-topped slappers*.

gashtray *n.* The *gusset* of a lady's *farting crackers*.

gashtronome *n.* A connoisseur of *haddock pasties*. A *fish supper* gourmand.

gas man *n.* In a *grumble flick* production, an actor whose responsibility is to look for potential leaks in an actress being *spit-roasted* and to plug them up, rendering the said lucky lady *gastight*.

gastight *adj.* Of a *stick vid* actress, to be simultaneously bunged up in all available orifices. *Corgi certified*.

gatekeeper *n.* An obstinate *turd*, firmly-ensconced across the *nipsy*, that bars the way and stubbornly prevents others from passing. Also *pace car, doorman*.

gaucho growler *n.* A short back and sides on a *velcro triangle*.

gay *1. adj.* Limp of wrist, tending to ask others to shut doors, critical of the "dust in here". *2. adj.* Of retired colonels who write to the *Daily Telegraph*, a perfectly good word for happy or brightly-coloured. *3. adj.* Synonym for bad, as used by gay disc jockey Chris Moyles.

gay by *n.* A road-side area where *fruit-feelers* can congregate to *look for badgers*.

gay church *n.* That which *puddle jumpers* attend religiously. The gym.

gaydar *n.* A remote imaging process developed during the war at Bletchley Park which is able to detect leather caps and Judy Garland records at substantial distances.

gaylord *n.* A good-natured term of homophobic abuse used by schoolboys to refer to anyone who is not gifted at sport or who wears glasses.

gazoo *n. Arse, bum*.

gazungas *n. Gert Stonkers*.

Gazza strip, the *n.* Gateshead/Low Fell. An area of historically-disputed territory situated between Newcastle and Sunderland, where a number of public houses are used by rival fans of both teams on derby days, leading to outbreaks of sporadic violence and damage.

gearbox *n.* The *anus*. *'Molly was powerless to resist. His eyes burned into hers like anthracites. His strong arms enfolded her body as she felt herself* *being swept away on a squall of passion. Then, in a single move Buzz pulled down her clouts, bent her over the ironing board and stuck his charlie up her gearbox.'* (From *The Cornish Milkmaid and the Astronaut* by Barbara Cartland).

gee gee *1. n.* Childish expression for horse used, usually in its plural declension, by gambling types. *'I'm going to put a few quid on the gee gees.' 2. n.* A girl who is pretty much definitely going to *suck you off*. A Guaranteed Gobble. *'Today's birthdays: 1625 - Francois de Harlay de Champvallon, Archbishop of Paris, who succeeded his uncle in the archiepiscopal see at the early age of twenty-six; 1857 - Max Wagenknecht, German composer of melodic organ music; 1955 - Gillian Taylforth, On Safari with Biggins cheesecake and gee gee.'*

geek *n.* Someone who knows too much about a subject that it isn't worth knowing anything about, *eg.* Computers, PlayStation cheat codes. A *human rhubarb*.

geek's sheath *n.* A nerd's means of preventing the transmission of viruses onto his computer whilst visiting sexual sites on the web. An internet prophylactic of the sort manufactured by McAfee, Norton Utilities *etc.*

geetle *n.* The little pointed bit of *shit* that hangs outside one's *nipsy* after one has had a *Gladys*. A *bumbob*.

geeze bag *n. Wind bag, fartpants.* A prolific *pump* artist.

geezerbird *n. Gadgy wife, half-a-gadge.* A butch-looking woman.

Geldof *v.* To impose a fairly woeful performance on an unwilling audience who feel it would be impolite not to indulge you. *'Go and find your grandad's mouth organ. He's allowed to Geldof on Christmas Day.'*

gender bender *n.* An effeminate, flowery male of indeterminate or obscure sexual orientation, *eg.* Boy George.

gender blender *n.* A person whose physical and facial appearance offer no clue as to which sex they belong to, *eg.* The man/woman who drove the 47 bus into Nottingham in the early 1980s.

gene pool *n.* The puddle of *heir tonic* that is wont to collect in a gentleman's navel following a supine act of *self respect.*

genie rub *n.* Buffing up a *skin lantern* until you are granted three sticky wishes.

genital floss *n.* A skimpy bikini bottom. *Arse floss.* A thong.

genitalia failure *n.* Marshmallowing of the *cock.* The *droop.* Something inexplicable that has never happened before, usually.

genitalman *n.* A chap who lets his *hanging brain* do his thinking for him. *'Today's birthdays: Sir Anthony Hopkins, Oscar-winning actor, 68; Sir Ben Kingsley, Oscar-winning actor, 62; Paul Ross, low-rent gameshow genitalman, 49.'*

gentertainment *n.* A gender-specific videographic *divertissement.* *'There's a bloke, walks right into a flat / Sees a bird, who is rubbing her twat / No need to guess, what comes after that / That's gentertainment!'* (from *That's Gentertainment!*, song by Howard Dietz and Arthur Schwartz).

gentle giant *n.* A *shit* so big that it brings tears to your eyes, but which gently kisses you on the cheek just before it leaves. A *French lodger.*

gentleman's excuse me *1. n.* A popular *meat flick* scenario in which several blokes take it in turns to *push a lady's guts in. 2. n.* The gallant post-nightclub practice of assisting a *plumper* with whom one has inadertently *copped off* into a taxi, gallantly shutting the door for her and then running like *fuck.*

gentleman's jacket *n.* A piece of toilet roll laid in the *pan*, Walter Raleigh-style, to prevent unnecessary *splash-back* when launching a *dreadnought.* Also *crash mat, pap baffle, turd raft, pilo.*

Gently Mentally *n.* An affectionate nickname bestowed upon a local Care in the Community-type *nutjob* who is not harmful to humans. *'It's Gently Mentally from down the road. He wants to know if he can borrow your chainsaw. And your ice hockey mask.'*

gentleman's gel *n.* A soothing facial/breast cream for ladies which doubles as a hair styling product. *Heir gel.*

gentleman's machinery *n.* Polite phraseology for a fellow's *rude mechanicals.*

gentleman's reading room *n.* The one room of the house where one may comfortably relax and peruse the *Autotrader* from cover to cover. The *shitter.*

gentleman's relish *n.* A polite term for *jizz*, such as what might be used by society folk at a Buckingham Palace Garden Party.

gentleman's toe pump *n.* The frantic but pleasurable wiggling of the toes, about 15 seconds after the *jester's shoes*, that helps out the last drops of *jitler.*

gentleman's wash *n.* A hurried washing of the male genitals (usually in a pub toilet sink) in anticipation of some forthcoming sex action.

gentlemen start your engines *exclam.* Witty preamble to the kick-starting of an un-silenced, high-revving, methane-powered lump.

Geordie Alka-Seltzer *n.* In former times, a popular hangover cure in north-eastern dockyards, now often used on budget flights back from Prague by young men who have over-imbibed. *A wank.*

Geordie curls *euph.* See *scouse dreadlocks.*

Geordie hummus *1. n.* Pease pudding. See also *Yorkshire caviar. 2. n. rhym. slang.* Phlegm. From George Lucas = mucus.

Geordie overcoat *n.* A vest or sleeveless T-shirt as donned by the entire male population of Newcastle-upon-Tyne during periods of particularly cold weather.

George *v. US.* To *roger.*

George Best undercoat *n.* The pint of milk drunk "to line the stomach" prior to going out on a drinking binge lasting several days. *'I can't be over the limit, officer. I may have necked 10 pints, but I had a George Best undercoat before I came out.'*

George Orwell *n.* A girl who looks "19" from behind but "84" from the front. Named after the eponymous author's famous book *The Road to Wigan Pier.* A *Kronenberg.*

German *n.* A sexy romp involving *shitting* on each other like pigs.

German ambassador *n.* A *pastry chef.* From the amusing fact that the German word for an ambassador is Botschafter.

German cornflake *n.* A herpes scab on one's *herman gelmet.*

German eyebath *n.* A *spoff monocle.* A *Gabrielle.*

German pit crew *euph.* The furry underarm area of a European *bird*, for example her who done that song about red balloons.

"Curiouser and curiouser' thought Alice, as the white rabbit came scampering past. 'I wonder where he's going in such a hurry.' 'Oh, my dear paws!' he cried. 'Oh my fur and whiskers, I'm loaded. If I don't reach the lavatory soon I shall surely papper my grundies.'' ~ *Alice's Adventures in Wonderland*, by Lewis Carroll.

German rigger *n.* Theatrical term for one who prefers his *rigging* done in the German fashion.

German's eye *n. Jap.* The frankly racist way the *Jap's eye* is referred to in Japan. So called because "it never smiles".

German wings *1. n.* A budget Teutonic airline which offers regular flights from Berlin, Stuttgart and Cologne. *2. n.* The first time you get *shat* on by a *good time girl* in one of Hamburg's more cosmopolitan tourist districts. The peer-reviewed honour bestowed on one has just had their debut *scat* experience. Not the bollocks Cleo Laine-style jazz singing kind, neither. *'Did you have a successful business trip, Jeffrey?' 'Yes Mary. I managed to catch the Hamburger Symphoniker performing Lohengrin at the Laeiszhalle Musikhalle, signed a seven-figure pan-European paperback deal for my new novel and, even better than that, I got my German wings too.'*

gerotica *n.* What one gets indelibly burned into one's hard disk the moment one logs onto www.hornygrannies.com. *'Honestly officer, it's just a little bit of harmless gerotica. Someone must have downloaded it onto my laptop as a joke.'*

gertie *1. n.* Fanny, minge. *2. n. coll.* Women, *blart*.

Gert Stonkers *n. Gonzagas.*

get *n. Bastard, twat.* Often applied to children, prefixed "You cheeky little..." and accompanied by a swipe to the back of the head.

get a click *v.* To score, pull, tap off, with a view to *getting boots*.

get boots *v. US.* To *get it on, get your end away*.

get it on *v.* To *get off, get it up* and/or get *your oats*.

get it up *v.* A significant part of *getting your end away* after *getting off*.

get off *v.* Of teenagers, to *get a click*, take the first step towards *getting your oats*.

get off at Edge Hill *v.* To do a *coitus interruptus*, to withdraw before *spangling*. From Edge Hill, which is the last railway station before Liverpool Lime Street. Similarly *Haymarket* (Edinburgh), *Gateshead* (Newcastle), *Marsh Lane* (Leeds) *etc.*

get on at Baker Street without a ticket *euph.* To do a spot of *caboose work* without first obtaining the necessary authority. From the fact that Baker Street is the main station on the brown Bakerloo line on the *shit-hole* London Underground.

get one's sovereigns on *v.* Whilst preparing for a *pagga*, to adorn one's hands with cheap *clink*, thereby creating a budget knuckle duster effect. To *put up your Lizzie Dukes*.

get some blood in it *v.* To have the early stages of a *bonk-on, half a teacake*.

get the key in the lock *v.* To manage, miraculously, to engage in some vague sort of penetrative intercourse with one's better half whilst in a state of *refreshment*.

get up them stairs *exclam.* A gentleman's instruction to his wife which indicates that he has finished eating, drinking and watching football, and now wishes to retire to the bedroom to make an ungainly and flatulent attempt at sexual intercourse.

get wood *v.* To attain a state of tumescence, *get string*. *'Quick, Heinz! Roll the camera. Gunther's got wood.'*

get your end away *v.* To *get it on*.

get your oats *v.* To *get your end away*.

get your own back *v.* To sup at the *furry*

cup after leaving some *hot fish yoghurt* inside the *snail's doorstep*, assuming you've not fallen asleep, that is.

GFS *abbrev. medic.* Doctor's notes terminology used to indicate that the patient may be talking out of their *arse*. Gesticulating From Sacrum.

Ghandi's flip flops 1. *adj.* Descriptive of the dryness of a nun's *cunt*. 2. *n. Spaniel's ears*.

ghee whizz *n.* A buttery, sludgy *piss* taken by a chap stricken with a urinary tract infection.

ghostbuster *n.* An eminently successful act of single-handed *exorjism*. From the lyrics of the theme song from the 1984 film starring Dan Ackroyd, Bill Murray and the other one who had glasses, *viz.* "Bustin' makes me feel good."

ghost jizz *n.* The non-existent result of a *flash in the pan*. A *map of Atlantis*.

ghost rider *n.* The beautiful, fictitious and weightless young lady that a prostrate young man imagines to be astride him during a bout of *self delight*. A *frigment* of a *tugster's* imagination.

ghost shit *n.* Stool or *dump* of which there is no trace when one stands up and turns to admire it. A *poogitive*.

gib 1. *v.* To *bullshit*. 2. *v.* To gatecrash. 3. *v.* To stick your *old man* up a goose's *arse* and slam its head in a drawer. As you do.

gibbon gristle *n.* A funky penis.

giblets *n.* A *club sandwich*, a *ragman's coat*.

Gibraltese backhand *n.* A masturbatory act carried out in the characteristic style of the monkeys on the famous Spanish rock. The *Gibraltese backhand* involves a lazily inverted reverse grip and is typically performed whilst sitting on the bonnet of your car with your tongue hanging out.

gick *n. Ir. Shit.*

gideon gumboot *n.* A used *blob* found pressed in a bible in your hotel/motel bedside cabinet.

gift to womankind *n.* An early morning *tent pole* in the *fart sack;* a phrase used by Ian Dury in the song *Let Me Hit Your Twat with My Rhythm Stick.*

GIFWID/gifwid *acronym.* A plain lass who becomes the object of a gentleman's affections when he has taken an elegant sufficiency of booze on board. Girl I Fancy When I'm Drunk.

gigglebiscuit *n.* Name given to the sort of irritatingly shallow woman who uses the pursuit of chocolate as the basis for her humour, *viz. 'Shall I have another chocolate biscuit? Oooh, shouldn't. Naughty! Giggle, giggle'.*

gigglers *n.* Suspender belt. *Giggle band.* 'Get past there and you're laughing'.

giggle stick *n.* The *twig, giggling pin.*

giggling pin *n. Mr Happy.*

gilbo *n.* The kind of phlegm eructated during a cold, after drinking cream soda, or when afflicted with a serious chronic disease of the bronchial tract. *Gold watch, dockers' omelette, greb.*

GILF/gilf *acronym.* Granny I'd Like to Fuck. A sexually-alluring older woman, *eg.* Marie Helvin, Kathleen Turner, Blanche off *Corrie, before she died.*

gilgai 1. *n. Geol.* In the world of earth science, micro-relief characterised by small hummocks separated by shallow troughs, and hence 2. *n.* A *diddy ride* on *Miss Lincolnshire.*

gillespie *n.* A diminutive male generative member. From the well-known graffito on the toilet wall in Wirral Grammar school depicting a small penis with the caption "Gillespie's dick x 4".

gimp *n*. A giant, masked *bummer* kept in a box in the basement of a gun shop.

gimp mask *n*. A tightly-fitting facial covering worn exclusively by giant *bummers* kept in a box in the basements of gun shops.

gin bin *n*. A lady who has imbibed more than her fair share of *the water of life* down the years, to the detriment of her physical appearance. *'Fuck me, camera two, the gin bin's got the shakes again. Best cut to Richard.'*

ginger beer *rhym. slang*. A *pinch of snuff*.

gingerbread man *n*. A rejuvenated fellow emerging from a lavatory cubicle with a spring in his step. From the lyrics of the Sammy Davis Junior song, *viz*. "Fresh out of the pan / Sweet gingerbread man".

gingle *adj*. The forlorn state of being ginger and single.

gink *n. Geek*. A short-sighted Colonel in a checked suit and bowler hat.

ginster *n*. A young lady who, at first sight, appears rather appetising but who leaves you feeling unsatisfied, disappointed, slightly nauseous and with a strange taste in your mouth. Derivation unknown.

Ginster's finest *n*. A *twat* that looks, smells and tastes like an out-of-date Cornish pastie. Often eaten by long distance lorry drivers.

gintellectual *n*. A barstool-dwelling philosopher, whose words of wisdom are typically prefixed "Apparently ... " or "I know a bloke who ... ". A *gobshite*.

gintelligence test *n*. A challenging general knowledge quiz administered after midnight by one's significant other, containing questions such as "What time do you call this?", "Where the hell have you been until four in the morning?" and "Why didn't you answer your phone?".

ginvalid *n*. One who has tragically lost the use of their legs following a long battle with the Gordon's.

gip *n*. The sensation at the back of the throat heralding the arrival of *Hughie and Ralph*.

gipper *1. n*. Legless American footballer played by former late US president Ronald Reagan (now deceased) in the inspirational film *Bedtime for Bonzo*. *2. n*. A *bird* who is as filthy as the bait bucket on a fishing boat.

gipsy week *n*. A *bird's* time of the month. *'DON JOHN: Marry, Borachio. How fared thee last night behind the tavern with thy wanton wench Margaret? Did'st thou fill thy boots? BORACHIO: I'faith, I did not the dirty deed. For by my troth, 'twas gipsy week. DON JOHN: Gipsy week, sayest thou? Wherefore is it called thus, sirra? BORACHIO: I'll vouchsafe you for wherefore 'tis called thus, my liege, for when I didst put my hand down her pants, I didst get my palm red.'* (from *Much Ado About Wanking* by William Shakespeare).

giraffe piss *n*. The standard method of urination when in possession of a *panhandle, ie*. To stand with one's legs wide apart and angle the *tent pole* down towards the bowl in the manner of a long-necked cameleopard drinking at a water hole. *Full throttle for take-off*.

giraffe shit *n*. Any stool passed, which causes one to stretch one's neck to get away from the smell.

giraffiti *n*. Vandalism which is spray-painted very, very high up.

girlfriend experience *n*. A chargeable extra service which is sometimes offered by *rub-a-tug-shop* masseuses, *ie*. A bit of kissing and tenderness prior to a short, low-esteem, guilt-ridden *bang* on a wipe-clean sheet.

girlpop *n*. *Moip, blip, fanny batter.* Secretions of the *Bartholin's* gland.

girly goatee *n*. A lady's pubic effusion, which can be rubbed and tugged at thoughtfully during moments of contemplation.

girobics *n*. The regular fortnightly exercise a long term jobseeker gets every other Thursday when he lifts his lazy fat *arse* off the sofa and ventures forth to collect his *beer tokens*.

giro jolly *adj*. Subject to the euphoric mental state attained by the unemployed on Thursdays.

giropractor *n*. One with a wealth of expertise in the manipulation of the state benefits applications system, available for consultation in the Gurnos Social Club, Merthyr Tydfil from 10.30am to 12.30pm Monday to Sunday.

giroscope *n*. A satellite dish. *Debtors' dish.*

girotica *n*. The restricted range of *relaxation* material which is affordable on the restricted budget of a chap who is searching for gainful employment, *eg*. Repeats of *Baywatch* on UK Gold, viewed from his foetid bed in the middle of the afternoon.

gisp *n*. *medic*. A term used by doctors in North Wales to describe the bit between the *balls* and the *arsehole*. *The barse, tintis, great, ABC.*

give Ronaldo a rub down *v*. Celebrity slaphead *wanking* terminology. *Strangle Kojak, take Captain Picard to warp speed, polish Telly Savalas up and down until spunk comes out of his head.*

give the dog a bone *v*. To sexually satisfy a female before one goes rolling home.

Give the sock drawer a good seeing-to *euph*. *milit*. To embark upon a sustained bout of frenzied masturbation whilst a member of the Household Cavalry.

giving it the gun *n*. The act of going down on one knee in front of your girlfriend, mate's wife, wife's sister, or occasionally the wife, whilst holding your hand like a Magnum 45 and pushing it in and out.

Gladys *rhym*. *slang*. To defecate. From Gladys Knight = shite.

gland grenades *n*. Hairy, wrinkled *spunk* bombs that have a tendency to *go off* in one's hand if they are not *tossed* far enough.

glandlord *n*. The owner of a property who prefers his tenants to pay the rent with their *hairy chequebook*.

gland national *n*. A *grumble flick* sequence featuring a *bit of bush* with a large number of sweating stallions *jumping* over it.

gland of hope and glory *n*. A magnificent *custard cannon* which, at the rousing climax to a performance, would bring the crowd to its feet at the Royal Albert Hall, just before you were bundled off the stage, sectioned under the Mental Health Act and put on the Sex Offenders Register.

glandscape *n*. The breathtaking *panhandloramic whacknicolour* vista that opens up before a chap's *hog's eye* whilst he is enjoying a *crescent wank*.

glandstand *n*. A Saturday afternoon erection, starting 5 minutes before *World of Spurt*.

glandular fervor *n. medic.* A disease affecting men which causes them to masturbate like nobody's business.

glans hatch *n.* How members of the motor racing fraternity refer to a lady's *clopper*. *'She needs more of ze punishment I zink. I'll smack her arse for a bit before sticking me floppy old frankfurter up her glans hatch. Then we'll have a nice cup of tea in the kitchen.'*

glarsefibre *n.* The badly-matted yet rust-proof *shite/arsecress* matting effect achieved on a catastrophically ineptly-wiped *freckle*. From the resultant disaster area's resemblance to a crudely-repaired body panel on a crashed vehicle.

Glasgow hankie *n.* Technique employed by professional footballers and gentlemen of the road, whereby one nostril is held closed whilst its companion is evacuated onto the pavement or turf by means of a sharp nasal exhalation. Also known as an *oyster* or *bushman's hankie*.

Glasgow marathon *n.* A walk to the chip shop, tobacconist or off licence in your pyjamas, slippers and a coat. *'Kerry Katona runs Glasgow Marathon!'* (headline from *International Herald Tribune*, June 8th 2008).

Glasgow postman *n.* A thief. After the remarkable frequency with which birthday cards, parcels and giros go missing in the Glaswegian postal sorting system.

Glasgow salad *n.* Chips.

Glasgow shower *n.* A quick swipe of underarm deodorant used as an alternative to washing when in a hurry or Glaswegian.

Glasgow toothpaste *n.* An extra-strong mint.

glassback *n.* A person with a poor health record at work. One whose constant illnesses keep them from work, but don't prevent them going to the pub at night or refereeing Premiership football matches at the weekend. A *sicknote*.

glassblower's pinch *n.* Final and desperate act of urine retention. Last ditch effort before turning your pantaloons into *tramp's trousers*.

Glastonbury main stage *euph.* The state of the *chod bin* following a harrowing post-Curry Capital visit, when it is left looking like the torrential-rain-soaked muddy fields of the popular alternative culture festival. Also *Ray Mears's dinner, Cheggers's mattress*.

Glastonbury tailback *n.* The uncanny ability of some fussy people, usually women, to *squeeze their fig* for five days when lavatorial conditions are not quite to their liking.

Glaswegian siesta *n.* A night in a police cell.

glaze a knuckle *v.* To *wank*.

glazed sexpression *n.* The facial qualities of a woman who, whilst wearing glasses, nevertheless manages to pull off the trick of looking like a *right goer, eg.* That Anastacia, Valerie Peron when she's being a librarian in a *Carry On* film and those *birds* in the SpecSavers ads. But not Olive out of *On the Buses*.

glebe end *n. Lincs.* A quaint colloquial expression for the *herman gelmet*, the origins of which are lost in the mists of time.

glee *n. Spoff, spadge, spunk.* *'Blimey, when that Konnie from Blue Peter comes on telly, I can hardly contain my glee.'*

gleet *n. medic.* Unpleasant mucopurulent discharge caused by *cock rot*. *'Blimey, when that Konnie from Blue Peter* *comes on telly, I can hardly contain my gleet.'*

Glenshane pass *n. rhym. slang.* Alternative to the *Khyber*, up which a *bumsex*-fixated Northern Ireland resident could take his missus. *'Don't take me up the Glenshane Pass tonight, Ian. It's giving me terrible piles.'*

gliffet *n.* The scrotal *oxter.* That warm, moist channel between a gentleman's *nadsack* and his inner thigh, where a particularly piquant variety of sweaty cheese matures in the dark.

Glist *1. n.* Julie Walters's favourite dishwasher tablet. *2. n. Ball glaze.*

glistening for it *adj.* Of a lady, sexually aroused, *fizzing at the bung hole. "And we know for a fact, that Lady Marchmaine could not have killed the Bishop,' added Miss Marple waspishly. 'She had ridden from Barnchester to the Manor House in twenty minutes. When she arrived she was glistening for it and spent the afternoon with Brigadier Lewerthwaite in his quarters. So YOU, Nurse Hatpin, must be the murderer!"* (from *Ten Pairs of Knickers* by Agatha Christie).

glitterati *n. coll.* Celebrity paedophiles.

glitter ball *n.* An under 16s' disco.

glob *v.* To emit a viscous fluid slowly and rhythmically out the end of the *giggling pin.*

globes *n.* Hanging objects of joy.

globstopper *n.* A mental image of a negatively attractive person or scenario that is summoned in order to *keep the wolf from the door*, so to speak.

gloke *n.* A woman who exhibits pseudo-blokish behaviour such as watching football, drinking beer, farting, smoking a pipe *etc*, in the mistaken belief that this will result in her being regarded as one of the lads, *eg.* Sara Cox. A *ladette.*

glorious goodwood *1. n.* Horse-racing meeting. *2. n.* A truly magnificent erection that impresses the passing populace with its magnitude, girth and lovely mane.

glory hole *n. US.* In a *cottage*, that hole made by *bosching*, through which the Bishop of Durham could touch a farmer's *cock* nearly 40 years ago.

glory wipe *n.* The token single sheet polish required after passing the rare but pleasant stool which slips out *like an otter off the bank*, leaving no trace of *Sir Douglas* on or around the *balloon knot.*

glovebox *n.* Another name for a lady's *parts of shame.* Usually containing bits of tissue, tampons, travel sweets *etc.*

glow-worm *1. n.* A long, thin, shiny *shite* produced after a really hot curry, that lights up the *pan. 2. n.* Someone who the boss reckons has got the sun shining out of their *arse.*

gloy *n. Mess*, semen. From the paper glue used in schools. *'Oops! I think I've just trod on the gloy bottle.'*

gluebook *n.* A well-read *art pamphlet* that is no longer openable.

glue gun *n.* Tool used to stick the pages of *niff* mags together.

glunk *n.* Improvised, viscuous adhesive used by students to stick torn wallpaper back in place in the minutes prior to a landlord's inspection. From glue + spunk.

Gnasher's loot *n.* A promiscuous woman's sexual history, *ie.* A long string of *big sausages.*

gnat's cock hair *n.* A standard Imperial measure equal to approximately one and a quarter eighty-eighths of a sixteenth of an inch. A phrase often used to describe any small distance. Often shortened to a *gnat's*. Also *bawhair*. *'How far do you want this filing cabinet moving?' 'Oh, just a gnat's cock hair towards the wall, that's all.'*

gnome's hat *n*. At the top of a toilet-dwelling heap of excrement, the drooping conical summit which pokes out above the surface of the water.

gnomon *1. n*. Obscure word known only to the likes of Stephen Fry and Robert Robinson, describing the little sticky-up bit which casts a shadow on a sundial. *2. n*. The little sticky-up bit which casts a shadow on an under-endowed man, *eg*. The Rt Hon Jack Straw MP.

gnosh *v*. To suck a penis in an enthusiastic and extremely noisy fashion.

go ahead London *exclam*. A humorous term used to break the ice when tweaking the nipple of a woman one has only just been introduced to. 6 months probation.

go all the way to Cockfosters *v*. To have a *full portion of greens* with plenty of *summer cabbage*. *'I thought I'd have to go home via the Billy Mill roundabout, but she took me all the way to Cockfosters.'*

goal hanger *n*. An annoying, predatory male friend who allows you to work your midfield magic on a girl in a nightclub before stealing your glory by nipping *in the box* for a simple tap in.

goalmouth scramble *n*. A hugely exciting, writhing mass of arms and legs which includes lots of intimate contact, but doesn't end up with anyone actually *scoring*. Frantic *heavy petting*.

gob *1. n*. The *North and South*. *2. v*. To spit, *hockle*. *3. n*. A body of *lung butter*

so propelled. A *greb*, a *greenie*.

go behind the red button *v*. To access a woman's *interactive features*.

gob job *n*. A *chewie*, a *sucking off*.

gobbie *n*. See *gob job*.

gobble *n*. Noise made by turkeys.

gobbler *n*. An eager *fellator/fellatrix*. One who frequents a particular Gulch on Hampstead Heath.

gobbler's cough *n. medic*. Condition arising from the build up of genital detritus in the throats of over eager *noshers*. *White owl pellets*.

gobshite *n*. Someone who talks *crap. eg*. Any contributor to *Thought for the Day*, but particularly Anne Atkins.

gock *n*. The male version of the *gunt*. Unsightly lower abdominal protuberance filled with residual beer, crisps and pies. From gut + cock. *'What's that on the top of your head, Gillian?' 'It's your gock, Geoff.'*

go commando *v*. To *freeball*. To go out *undercrackerless*.

go cunt up *adj. Arse over tit*. Pear-shaped, badly awry. *'Houston, Houston, we have a problem. There's blowback in Challenger's solid rocket boosters. It looks like things could go cunt-up.'* (Silus T Oysterburger, Mission Controller, KSC Florida).

Godfather Part 2 *1. euph*. When the second *wank* of the day unexpectedly turns out to be more enjoyable than the first. *2. n*. A highly-praised and critically-acclaimed second *bang* off the same *wood*.

God goggles *n*. The imaginary optical accessories created by decades of religiously-inspired celibacy, which cause a priest to get a raging *diamond cutter* when he sees a sixty-year-old nun with a moustache.

God's sleeping tablet *n.* The natural way to induce restful sleep. In men, *cracking one off*; in women, *strumming the invisible banjo. Wanker's cocoa, temazepalm, a knuckle nightcap.*

Godzilla *n.* A ferocious burp, accompanied by clawing motions with the hands.

go faster stripe *n.* A *fanny bush* shaved into a more aerodynamic design. *Pires's chin.*

go for poke *v.* To commit all one's available resources towards the sole aim of achieving some sort of sexual congress.

going down *1. v.* Doing the oral sex on someone, *giving head. 2. exclam.* Expression often used to describe the imminent movement of a lift.

going down on Hetty Wainthropp *n.* Horrific mental image summoned up in order to quell an untimely *bone on, eg.* When on the bus or tube, just as you have to stand up after being knighted by the Queen, or seconds before being called by Anne Robinson to make the Walk of Shame from behind your contestant's podium on *The Weakest Link.*

going for a McShit *v.* Visiting the bogs in fast food restaurants when one has no intention of buying the food. If challenged by a suspicious manager, the assurance of a food purchase after the toilet visit is known as a *McShit with lies.*

going for a thong *n.* The act of habitually manoeuvering oneself behind women who are sitting down and leaning forward such that there is a gap between their trousers and their underwear, in the vain hope of catching a glimpse of the tops of their *officers' laces.*

going live *1. n.* A former Saturday morning children's TV programme starring prostitute dungeon visitor Jamie Theakston. *2. n.* Sex performed without a prophylactic appliance. *Riding bareback,* a *bath without wellies, skinnydipping.*

going to Paul's *exclam.* Phrase used to excuse oneself when leaving polite company to go and do a great big *shit.*

going to the judges *euph.* An indeterminate end to a bout of drunken sex.

going to work for BT *n. Laying a cable. 'I'm just going to work for BT for ten minutes, love. Can you put the kettle on? And open the window?'*

go interactive *v.* To *tickle* a lady's *bean.* From the BBC teletext instruction to "press the red button".

gold watch *n.* A small clock or chronometer, made of precious metal which leaps from the throat after a cough. A *docker's omelette, greb, sheckle, prairie oyster.*

golden bogey *n.* A nose-stud.

golden deceiver *n.* A blonde *piece* who looks gorgeous from behind, but is actually a right *dog* from the front. A *backstabber,* a *back beauty.*

golden goal *1. n.* Highly popular innovation in football matches whereby, during extra time, the team that scores first immediately wins the match, thus leaving the opposition gutted. *2. n.* The act of *scoring* in extra time at the end of a night *on the razz,* thereby leaving your mates sick as parrots. After drawing a blank at the club and/or pub, pulling a stunner on the bus home or at the kebab shop.

golden globes *1. n.* Happy Shopper television version of the Oscars ceremony. *2. n.* Vintage *knockers,* which evoke fond remembrance of times past. *Old 'uns but* *good 'uns, lifetime achievement baftas.*

golden handshake *n.* A rather sloppy *gypsy's kiss.*

golden rivet *n. naval.* The *freckle*, the *dot*, the apple of the *captain's* eye for *rear admirals* who *swab the poop deck. Spice island, bottery bay.*

golden shower *n.* To be *pissed* on by a big German for a saucy treat. *Water sports.*

golden slumbers *1. n.* Title of a ballad written by the 16th/17th century English poet and dramatist Thomas Dekker. *2. n.* Song penned by Paul McCartney, using copyright-free lyrics from *1.*, featured as part of the sixteen-minute medley which ends side two of the Beatles *Abbey Road* album. *3. n.* Nocturnal micturition. *Pissing* the bed.

golden ticket *1. n.* In Roald Dahl's *Charlie and the Chocolate Factory*, the magical token which allowed Charlie Bucket and his aged grandfather to visit Willie Wonka's fantastic confectionery works, and thus *2. n.* In a sexual relationship, permission to enter the wife's mysterious and exciting *chocolate factory*, though preferably without an elderly relative in tow.

goldfrapp *n.* A *Jonathan* executed whilst wearing a *jubber ray*. A *posh wank, French wank, boil in the bag*. A *birthday bash.*

golf ball *n.* An oversized, pock-marked *clit* discovered lying in an area of rough.

golf ball arse *n. medic.* Condition of the *buttocks* after sitting for too long on a beaded car seat.

golf tees *n. Bruce Lees.*

golfer's divot *n.* A shapeless clump of *pubage* flying through the air.

gonad glue *n. Gloy, gunk.*

gone southporn *phr.* A reference to a gen-

tleman's decision to change his *relaxing* hand from right to left, perhaps when upgrading his broadband subscription. *'I just got 8Mb download speed and I was having a bit of trouble controlling the mouse, so I've gone southporn.'*

gone to Iceland *euph.* Crude, sexist expression used about a once more-or-less *satiscraptorily* attractive lady who has subsequently turned into a fat, ugly *minger, eg.* Former Atomic Kitten turned celebrity docusoap carcrash nightmare Kerry Katona.

gonga *n.* A *docker's omelette* that occasionally has to be swallowed rather than served up on the pavement.

gonk *1. n.* A *shit* fairground prize, made out of stolen cats, that looks like a miniature cross between Gail Tilsley and Don King. *2. n.* A *rub-a-tug shop* punter.

gonzagas *n. Guns of Navarone.*

Gonzo's nose *sim.* Descriptive of a gentleman's sorry-looking, unresponsive *trouser truncheon*. Named after the *Muppet Show* character. *'I'd love to give you one, darling, but I've had ten pints and I've got a cock like Gonzo's nose.'*

gonzo vid *n.* Low budget, unscripted pornography where the cast wait until the cameras start rolling before going to the toilet. An acquired taste.

goober *n. Aus.* Antipodean term for *cock venom*. *'Strewth, Rolf, what the billabong have you been doing? My underwear drawer's full of goober.'*

gooch *n.* The *barse, tintis, Finsbury bridge, great*. See also *goosh*.

good Charlotte *n.* The powerful early morning sexual frisson experienced when listening to sultry-voiced Radio 4 newsreader Charlotte Green on the *Today* programme. A *good Charlotte* can occasionally be somewhat disturbing; for example when she is reading out the death toll in some terrible disaster or the subtly-veiled details of the bizarre erotic adventures of a disgraced Liberal Democrat leadership candidate.

good cop, bad cop 1. *n.* Of two gentlemen, to be faced with the classic *cruiser and tug* combination at the bar; they must chat up both, knowing one will achieve a good "cop", the other a bad one. 2. *n. Cuffing the suspect*, but using both hands at different times.

good listener *n.* A man who is *good with colours, light on his feet.* One who *likes shopping.*

goodnight sweetheart 1. *n.* Woeful, ill-thought-out time travel *shitcom* featuring Nicholas "Rodney "Plonker" out off of *Only Fools and Horses"* Lyndhurst. 2. *n.* The final, affectionate *anal announcement* a married man delivers before drifting off to sleep.

good nintentions *n.* That which you meant to do, *eg.* Household chores, DIY, tax return *etc.*, once you had completed your current video game level - but which you never quite got round to doing, despite staying up till four in the morning.

goods to declare, have *v.* To take the *red channel* at customs.

good time *n.* Street prostitute parlance for a fucking awful time.

good with colours *adj.* Of a gentleman, to be adept at *jumping over puddles.*

gooey in the fork *n.* Of a lady, to be not far short of *dripping like fucked fridge.*

go off *v.* Of women, to pass their "best before" date. *'I tell you what, I wouldn't mind nobbing that Charlotte Church.' 'You'd best get your finger out and do her before she goes off, then.'*

Goofy's ears *n.* Dangling labia, particularly pendulous *gammon flaps.*

goo gargle *n.* A hot protein mouthwash, which is spat out as opposed to being swallowed.

google *n. Spunk* produced as a result of internet porn.

googlewhack *v.* To type a bit of *crumpet*'s name into the popular internet search engine with the specific intention of *relaxing in a gentleman's way* over the resulting "hits".

goo gun *n.* A *pocket paste dispenser, jizz stick.*

goolies *n.* The colloquialism for testicles least likely to offend a grandparent. *'Oi nan. Get your glasses on and I'll show you me shaved goolies.'*

goose *n.* A light-hearted sexual assault, often taken in bad spirit by po-faced lesbians.

goose, shit like a *v.* To suffer from a loose motion in the *back body. 'Don't drink that cloudy pint, Kirsty, or you'll be running off to shit like a goose all the way through Newsnight Late Review.'*

goosh *n.* Yet another word for a chap's *tintis.* Also *gooch*, named after the famous cricketer Graham Barse.

gooze *v.* Of a *bongo vid* actress, to make a big show of pretending to swallow her leading man's *milm* after a facial *money shot. 'That bint ain't swallowin', she's just goozin'.'*

gorblimey *adj.* A type of trouser popular among council tenants in the 1950s.

Gordon and Tony *euph.* Bitingly satirical way of referring to a lady's *pleasure holes* (until mid-2007 anyway), because it's a *cunt* next door to an *arsehole. George and Dave.*

gorilla autopsy *n.* A large, untidy and

hairy *clout,* such as the one on Lindsey from the Tartan Arms, Lloret de Mar, circa 2002.

gorilla biscuits *euph.* Descriptive of a lady with a *lovely personality.* '*I wouldn't say my wife's ugly, ladies and gentlemen, but she could get a job at the bakery pushing her face into the dough to make gorilla biscuits. My name's Tony Blair, I'm here all week.*'

gorilla salad *n.* Ladies' pubic hair. *Twat thatch, roughage.*

gorilla's armpit *n.* A *fanny* which would daunt all but David Attenborough.

gorilla's breakfast 1. *n.* A *shit* that smells good enough to turn around and eat again right out of the *pan,* as gorillas do in the wild on winter mornings. 2. *n.* An affectionate name for an early morning *pan cracker.*

gorillas in the mist 1. *n.* Boilers who, through an alcoholic fog, take on siren-like qualities. Can lead to *dances with wolves.* 2. *rhym. slang. Wankered.*

gorilla's knuckles *n.* The *camel's lips.* A cleft which is clearly visible through a lady's garmentry.

go the whole log *v.* When visiting a public toilet, to make the impromptu decision to avail oneself of the facilities to a fuller extent than one had originally intended. '*Sorry to keep you waiting. I only went in to cut the end off a bum cigar, but once I'd got me trousers off I thought fuck it, and decided to go the whole log. Anyway, where was I? Oh yes. How do you find the defendant, guilty or not guilty?*'

go through the gears *v.* To perform a *fart* of continuous melody, going up in pitch every few seconds, making a sound like a London Routemaster bus pulling away.

got it all to do 1. *phr.* Woefully-bullish statement of the situation from a football commentator or former manager when England concede a third goal in the eighty-fifth minute. 2. *phr.* A hopelessly-optimistic attempt to *take Captain Picard to warp speed* when you have a masturbatory mountain to climb, for example following ten pints of stout or over your granny's knitting catalogue.

got mice *adj.* Of a lady, to be *visited by Aunt Flo.* To be *up on blocks.*

go to Barnsley *v.* To *do* the *tradesman's entrance* of a lady. Named after the famous South Yorkshire *shit hole.*

got football at ten-thirty *phr.* Useful Sunday morning escape phrase to be used when your *beer goggles* demist to reveal that you didn't *cop off* with Maria off *Coronation Street* but with her late neighbour Blanche instead. Works especially well when the football season is actually in progress.

go through the motions *v.* To indulge in the filthy German habit of carefully examining one's stools on the *jobby shelf* before flushing.

gouch *n.* The *biffin bridge, chin rest, taint, tinter, notcher.*

go ugly early *v.* A nightclub or party gambit. To settle for a keen *swamp donkey* rather than chasing after something better and risking ending up with nothing. To *stick at 15.* '*Good piss up last week, Gaz. I saw you went ugly early.*'

Govan tumbleweed *n.* Those blue and white-striped bags made of the thinnest imaginable plastic, available from corner shops, cheap off-licences and vendors of deep fried foods, that end up blowing around the streets of the self-styled Glasgow borough of "exceptional opportunity". Govan tumbleweed that ends up stuck in a tree is known as *Govan bunting.*

gpg *abbrev.* A statutory sexist measure of how much *horatio* a young lady will provide proportionate to the amount of *tart fuel* that a gentleman has purchased for her. Gobbles Per Gallon. Also *spg* = swallows per gallon.

GPMG *abbrev. milit.* A lady who looks attractive at a distance but is not quite so alluring when viewed from nearby. Named after the army's General Purpose Machine Gun, which is "good at range but unbelievably messy close up".

grace period *n.* The few precious hours after a hot *cuzza* during which one can *tread on a duck* without the fear of *following through*. *'I tried Abdul Latif's Curry Hell, reputedly the hottest curry in the world. Upon the first taste, my eyes melted and my throat burst into flames, and with a grace period of just forty-five seconds I was straight off to the lavvy. On my 2-mile journey home I had to stop the car on 173 occasions, each time not knowing which end to point at the gutter.'* (Restaurant Review by Jonathan Meades, *The Times Magazine*).

Graham Norton's hair *n.* Descriptive of one's *barnet* after being *seagulled* by a gentleman, or after walking under Status Quo's hotel room balcony.

grampire *n.* An octogenarian whose shrunken gums have long ago given up the ghost and thrown in the towel in the battle to accommodate their vintage dentures. Often seen on buses vainly attempting to wrap their 1950s Nye Bevan pearlies round a Werther's original.

granbies *rhym. slang.* Term widely used in Leicestershire to describe the male testicles or *clockweights*. From the now-defunct concert venue Granby Halls = orchestras. *'He'll be alright in a couple of minutes, your Holiness. He's just had a kick in the granbies, that's all.'*

grandad erector *n.* A sight so sexually stimulating that it could raise the dead.

grandad's coin purse *n.* A *growler* with a pair of tightly-drawn *beef curtains*, which requires tough finger action at both ends in order to gain entry. Also variously known as a *butler's cuff, cigar clipper, mouse's ear* or *OJ's glove.* A *blurtch* that is tighter than a *worm's belt.*

grandalf *n.* An old *bird* with a *wizard's sleeve.*

grandchav *n.* One who is blessed with grandchildren whilst still young enough to fully enjoy the experience. A *Cardiff grandmother. 'Mum. Could you help me with my homework, please?' 'Go and ask your grandchav, I've not finished mine yet.' 'But she's still doing hers too.'*

Grandma *rhym. slang.* An act of defecation. From the dimly-remembered children's television character Grandma Flump = dump.

grandma's party *n.* A bout of masturbation. Wearing a bowler hat. See *reggae like it used to be.*

grandma's perfume *n.* The smell of *piss. Eau de toilette publique.*

grandmaster flash *n.* A tumescent mid-*Barclays membrum virile*, typically being pushed ever closer to the edge by his *furious five.*

grandma's Wolsley *n.* The greying *minnie-moo* of an old dear which hasn't given anyone a *ride* since the 60s. Something with a pool on the floor under it, that smells of leather, dried grease and perished rubber.

Grand Old Duke of York *n*. An unconvincing erection, a mix of duty and apathy, one that is "neither up nor down". A *lard on*, a *dobber*, *half a teacake*. A *Prince Andrew*.

grand slam *n*. In the world of *salad dodging*, the fabled achievement of enjoying the holy quartet of takeaway meals in one day, *viz*. McDonald's for breakfast, Kentucky Fried Chicken for lunch, Burger King for tea and a dodgy kebab on the way home from the pub.

gran flakes *n*. The contents of a nursing home Hoover bag.

granny batter *n*. KY jelly.

granny magnet *n*. A male who, having had no luck finding a ladyfriend of his own age, is forced to *cop off* with a right old *slapper*, *eg*. The *blotto* one with the incontinent laugh being held up by her mates in the kebab shop.

granny's attic *euph*. An unattractive lady, *ie*. One of whose cobwebby *clopper* it could humorously be said, "nobody's been up there in years".

granny's elbow *n*. An unpleasantly-elongated *ball sack*. A *rantallion*.

granny's flannel *euph*. An extremely dry *Cradock*. *'How did you get on fucking that bird last night, Russell?' 'I did me best, Jonathan, but her cunt was like a granny's flannel and I couldn't get me cock in. Anyway, just before Sally Traffic with the travel news, it's time for the Radio 2 Record of the Week - On a Little Street in Singapore by everybody's favourite, Manhattan Transfer.'*

granny's hat, muff like your *sim*. Descriptive of a particularly hairy *otter's pocket*, possibly smelling strongly of mothballs and damp.

granny's kiss *n*. From a gentleman's perspective, the experience of performing *cumulonimbus* on a badly-maintained *clopper*. Not unlike receiving a smacker from one's sloppy, pucker-lipped grandmother sporting a *Magnum PI* moustache and tasting like she's just eaten a gammon butty.

granny's mouth *n*. A saggy, loose-lipped, whiskery *cunker*.

granny's oysters *n*. Elderly female genitalia.

granny's purse *n*. The condition of one's *clappers* after a comprehensive bowel evacuation, *ie*. Firmly snapped shut.

Grantham's stalactites *n*. Vertical rivulets of dried *Melanie* on the back of a laptop computer. Named after the Dirty Den actor, amateur marksman and webcam exhibitionist Leslie.

grape smugglers *n*. Tight gentlemen's briefs, as worn by *grumble flick* stars in the 1970s. *Noodle benders*.

grappling hooks *n*. The unyielding fasteners on a lady's *tit pants*.

grass art *n*. The Tony Hart-like placing of garden seats, picnic tables *etc*. on the lawn, so that by the end of the Summer one has created a humorous image in the turf, such as a pair of rudimentary *tits*, a *meat and two veg* or simple expletive.

grassy knoll 1. *n*. Site where the second gunman stood during the assassination of JF Kennedy. 2. *n*. A *ladygarden*.

grated carrot *n*. Coarse, ginger-coloured *gorilla salad*, suitable for a *vagetarian* diet. Rusty *fusewire*.

grating the cheddar *n*. *medic*. To accidentally scrape one's *lid* along the zip of one's *flies*. *"I say, Jeeves. Could you* *take these trousers to my tailor and have him replace the zip fastenings with good old fashioned buttons?' I croaked. 'I only bought them last week and I've grated the cheddar four times. My poor cock end is ripped to pip, don't you know."* (from *Swallow it All, Jeeves* by PG Wodehouse).

grattan 1. *adj.* Descriptive of a state of ill-health. *'Shut the curtains will you, love? I must have had a bad pint last night and I feel right grattan.'* 2. *v.* To masturbate over desperate material in the absence of anything better to masturbate over. See *grattanification.*

grattanification *n.* A young man's use of the bra pages of his mum's catalogue in order to fuel his single-handed progress towards an *argosm.*

grave-sniffer *n.* A senior citizen. A *coffin-dodger, oxygen thief.*

greasebox *n.* A *quim.*

greasy waistcoat pocket *n.* A shallow, well-oiled *fanny* large enough for a thumb to be inserted. Or a gold watch.

great escape *n.* A *breakout* that is planned well in advance and released surreptitiously over a period of time. And probably shaken nonchalantly from the bottom of the trouser legs whilst whistling.

greatest hits *rhym. slang.* The *shits. 'Bloody hell, Egon. You're a shadow of your former self. What happened?' I went for a delicious eight-course slap-up banquet at the Curry Capital, Bigg Market, Newcastle upon Tyne three weeks ago and I've had the greatest hits ever since. I tell you, I've a good mind to dock them a star in my next Good Food Guide.'*

great, the *n.* That bit of the male anatomy which is between the back of the *gooch* and the front of the *barking spider.* The *barse, tintis, notcher* or, more crudely, the p*rineum. So-called because any time one's missus goes anywhere near it, one exclaims: "Ooh, that's great!"

Great Yarmouth gnomes *n.* Washing machines, broken tellies and *pissed* mattresses used as garden ornaments in the *shit* Norfolk town.

greb *n.* Hockle.

Greek *n.* Any sex games in which the *rusty bullet hole* is centrally involved. *Swedish.*

Greek biscuit *n.* A sexual act in which one man kneads another man's *clacker-bag,* as though preparing the dough prior to a spot of baking. Icing optional.

Greek courage, full of *adj.* Kebab-fuelled. For example, a pair of blokes having a fight on the pavement outside the Paradise Grill, Newcastle-under-Lyme, to pick an example entirely at random, could be described as being *full of Greek courage.*

Greek sauna *n.* A *Dutch oven.*

Greek ship about, there must be a *exclam. nav.* Old merchant navy rejoinder to a matelot complaining of having an itchy *ring.*

Greek tip *n.* A stray pubic hair adhering to coinage that is handed over in shops, restaurants, *etc. Copper wire.*

green goddess 1. *n.* A middle-aged woman doing star jumps and running on the spot on breakfast telly in the 80s. 2. *n.* One of those laughably ancient-looking emergency tenders which were brought out of mothballs regularly during the 80s to take the place of proper fire engines during strikes. 3. *n.* A vintage, dumpy-looking *bird* who will *do the job* in the absence of a flashier, modern-looking model.

green wings *n*. An unwanted accolade. Sex with a *clappy slapper*.

Greggs baby *n*. The distended abdomen of a young lady, of whom it is difficult to determine whether she is with child or *with steak slice*.

Greggs dummy *n*. A chicken and mushroom-filled pacifier used by teenaged mums to soothe their teething infants.

Greggs dyke *n*. A big, fat, sweaty *lezzer*.

Greggs revenge *n*. Descriptive of the delightfully rich aroma produced when one *steps on a duck* after consuming a Steak Bake purchased at a popular high street bakery.

gregnant *adj*. Suddenly putting on weight as a result of a passionate relationship with the famous pie and pastie-based *fat food* retailer. *Up the pastry*.

grey flannel *n*. A pensioner's *opera curtains*. *Granny's oysters, biltong*.

Greyfriar's Bobby *n*. *Edinb. rhym. slang*. A *feeshus*.

greyhound *1. n*. A very short skirt, *ie*. One that is only one inch from the "hare". *2. n*. An hilarious heterosexual changing room impression involving an erect *chopper* and a champagne wire.

grey wings *n*. The honour awarded to someone who has indulged in a *rumpular pumpular* act with a ladyfriend of more mature aspect. A medal for a chap who has bravely faced up to a spot of *gash in the attic*.

grilled tomato *n*. An unappealing *bit of crumpet* that a gentleman puts off *having a go at* until all his other options are exhausted at the end of the evening. *'Shit. I fell over in the car park and broke both me hands so I can't even have a wank. I suppose I'll have to go and chat up that grilled tomato by the fag machine now.'*

grimble *n*. Glossy, American marshmallow-hard pornography, usually shown on Bravo on Friday nights.

grime bubble *n*. A *fart, air biscuit*.

grime capsule *n*. A stack of 1980s *jazz mags* left behind by builders and discovered years later under the floorboards whilst renovating a house. A *Dutch miracle, basement jacks*.

grimsby *n*. A mingsome *minge*.

Grimsby meal *n*. An unpleasant northern *fish supper*.

grimquims *n*. A collection of unsightly *butchers' dustbins, stamped bats, ripped sofas, ragman's coats* and *badly-packed kebabs*. *'Did you see last month's Razzle stack? What a bunch of grimquims.'*

grimshits *n*. A portmanteau term for faeces distinctly lacking in cohesion. *Fizzy gravy, bubblepoo* and *bicycle chains* are all *grimshits*.

grind *v*. To have sex with all the fervour of an old bus going up a steep hill in Lancashire. ie, If you stopped, you really wouldn't have it in you to start again.

grinding the cotton *n*. Committing the act of sexual congress without first taking the elementary precaution of removing one's clothing.

gripper *1. n*. More light-hearted heterosexual changing room horseplay, this time where somebody grabs hold of one's *arse cress* and gives it a great big yank. *2. n*. Unusual Christian name of a bully who featured in early series of the gritty school-based kids' soap *Grange Hill*. *3. n*. Midlands term for one who partakes of solitary hand-based pleasures.

gripping the lather *n*. The precise moment when a spot of innocently pleasurable bath-night self-soaping becomes an undeniable act of filthy beastliness. Again.

gristle thistle *n.* Persistent purple-headed weed, commonly occurring in *moss cottage* gardens. *Turning Japanese knotweed.*

grizzly bear pit *n.* The *pan* of a blocked *chod bin*, viewed from above.

groaner *n.* A *Thora* that is so big that it cannot be expelled without vocal assistance. A *U-blocker.*

grogan *n. Scot.* A *log*, a *Douglas.*

groinery *n.* The craft of *morning woodwork*, in which only one *handtool* is used.

groin grease *n.* The sweat that builds up around the inner thighs and *knackers* of a *salad dodger* on a hot day. *Arse feta.*

grolsch *n.* An under-lubricated *snatch*, ie. One that is "not ready yet" and needs another minute's brisk rubbing.

grommet *n.* 1950s *Totty.*

gronk *n. RAF.* To have a *shit*. *"Bandits at three O'clock!' ejaculated Algy. 'Great!' replied Biggles. 'I've got half an hour to have a big smelly gronk!'"* (from *Biggles Drops his Fudge* by Capt. WE Johns).

gronk board *n. milit.* A panel where photographs of the ugliest women *banged* by sailors are displayed for the amusement of the entire ship's crew.

groodies *n.* How *charms* are referred to in the film *A Clockwork Orange.*

groovy legs *n. med.* Post prolonged *doggystyle* sex wobbly numbness in the lower limbs. *'I wasn't sure how long I was back-scuttling her, but it must have been ages, because when I stopped I had my groovy legs on.'*

G-rope *n.* A *G-string* for the fatter lass.

grope fruits *n. Shirt potatoes, fat rascals.*

grot cotton *n.* Amusing nickname which can be applied to an actress/model who tends rather more towards the *bargain bucket* end of the erotic entertainment industry.

grotdog *n.* A lower-grade hotdog, of the sort which might be purchased at Walthamstow Dog Stadium, to pick a location entirely at random.

grot slot *n.* The married man's 30-minute long internet pornography download window which occurs whilst his wife is at the shops.

grotter *n.* The *snatch.*

groundhog lay *n.* A depressingly familiar intercourse routine between a man and his long term girlfriend.

groundhog wank *1. n.* A dismal attempt at *self abuse* which repeatedly peters out, leaving the *wanksmith* with no choice but to start again. *2. n.* The overly-familiar *tug* sequence of a *pornogamist* who only owns one *art pamphlet.*

ground zero *n.* The *freckle* the morning after an evening of heavy *refreshment.*

Grove Hill decking *n. Al fresco* horizontal timber structures typically adorning the front and rear gardens of homes in one of the less affluent estates in Middlesbrough. Pallets.

grow a tail *v.* To defecate, *build a log cabin. Snip a length of spine.*

growl at the badger *v. Scot.* To noisily *nosh* a *beaver*. To loudly *nod at a stoat.* To *gnosh.*

growler *1. n.* The sort of meat and potato pie sold from one of the various catering outlets inside the ground at Gigg Lane, Bury, in the mid-1980s. So-called because within 30 minutes of eating the pie, one's stomach would begin to growl. A *Cornish nasty. 2. n.* The *shithouse. 3. n.* A semi-submerged *dreadnought*, nine tenths of which lies hidden below the surface.

grown-up book *n. Self-help pamphlet, jazz mag, niff mag, noddy book, pop-up book.*

grub *n. Barse cheese.*

grubscrew *1. n.* An act of intercourse performed at work during a lunchbreak, perhaps in a store room or on a photocopier. *2. n.* A tiny, shrivelled *yang*, found on Egyptian mummies, Siberian nudists, Bobby Davro and the Rt Hon Jack Straw MP.

gruffalo *1. n.* A monstrous, hairy character from the children's book of the same name. *2. n.* A particularly hirsute, nasty-looking snatch. A *wolf pussy*. *3. n.* An unacceptable, unpleasant and misogynistic term which can be applied to a female who is blessed with a *lovely personality*. Other, similarly unacceptable, unpleasant and misogynistic terms include *pig in knickers, bush pig, ditch pig, swamp hog, swamp donkey, steg, hippocrocapig, rhinocerpig* and *sea monster.*

gruffle bag *n.* That strangely satisfying feeling of having *airy pillows* in your *undercrackers*, experienced just after you *cleave off* an *anal announcement*.

gruff nuts *n.* Them bits you can see hanging down between a woman's legs when she bends down to touch her toes. A somewhat less appetising-sounding version of the *reverse peach*.

grumbelows *n.* A retail purveyor of *seed catalogues*. A *bongo store*.

grumbilical cord *n.* The sturdy wire that links one's satellite dish to one's Sky box, allowing ladies' *grotters* to appear on one's television screen.

grumble *1. rhym. slang.* The vagina, *quaynt, placket, Berkeley.* From grumble and grunt = cunt. *2. n.* Any form of *Frankie Vaughan* featuring *tits, arses and grumbles.*

grumble bee *n.* A *tugster* who is unable to select a favourite *art pamphlet*, and so flits from one to another.

grumbled *1. adj.* Of *tescosexual* gentlemen, the state of being caught mid-way through an act of *jazz*-fuelled onanism, when their spouse returns unexpectedly early from a shopping expedition. *2. adj.* The unfortunate situation when one's mother/wife/cleaning lady stumbles across one's stash of *art pamphletry.* Caught in possession of pornography. *'Mr Baddiel, I was cleaning your room, and I found 56 tons of hard core anal pornography on top of the wardrobe.' 'Oh, no! I've been grumbled!'*

grumblehound *n.* A creature whose nose, upon entering the newsagent, can be seen twitching in the direction of the top shelf.

grumble in the jungle *n. Rhythmic cliterature* found whilst taking the dog for a walk in the woods. That which is found under the *bongo bush. Grummer.*

grumbler *1. n.* A whinger or nay-sayer, if you will. *2. n.* A purveyor of *adult* entertainment. *'Today's birthdays: 1770 - Thomas Johann Seebeck, German physicist and discoverer of the thermoelectric effect; 1806 - Isambard Kingdom Brunel, British engineer, railway pioneer and steamship builder; 1926 - Hugh Marston Hefner, pyjama-clad US grumbler.'*

grumble sale *1. n.* A mass sell-off of second hand *gentleman's relaxation pamphletry* due to relocation, marriage or death. *2. n.* Any offer of cut-price merchandise in the window of a retail purveyor of pornographic requisites.

grumbleweed *1. n.* A Syd Little lookalike,

usually the director's brother, who manages to poke a selection of *cliterati,* who would normally not even wipe their *arse* with him. *2. n.* A miraculous patch of undergrowth where discarded pornography can reliably be located. *3. n.* One who has masturbated so many times in a single session that he can no longer muster the strength to lift the pages of his *scud mag.* One who has *wanked* himself into enfeeblement. *4. n.* A token *fluff tuft* on an otherwise clean-shaven porn starlet's *snatch.* A *clitler. 5. n.* Any member of the geriatric West Yorkshire-based comedy combo, specialising in gasmask-related songs and disturbingly accurate impressions of Sir Jimmy Savile.

grumbleweeds *n.* The matted, sticky mess of *friar's weeds* which one is left with after surprising oneself with a startlingly copious payload of *spoo,* and which will require a good few yards of *shit scrape* to mop up.

grummer *n. abbrev. Biff mags, art pamphlets.*

grump on *n.* Reluctant *wood.* An erection that has to be cajoled to tumescence. Prevalent amongst *jazz* actors, *slag night* strippers and men married to Janet Street-Porter.

grumpy pumpy *n.* Getting your oats from a resentful conjugal partner.

grundle *n. US.* The *barse.*

grunge *1. n.* Style of rock music which emerged principally in the Seattle area during the 1980s, and is characterised by distorted guitars, quiet bits followed by loud bits, and the singer shooting himself through the mouth in mysterious circumstances. *2. n.* To put it crudely, a fat, hairy *lezzer's twat.* '*Oi, Courtney. Put your fucking grunge away or I'll shoot meself.*'

grunter *n.* A much loved and well respected senior citizen who fought in two world wars *etc.,* but who now cannot get off the sofa without grunting.

grunties *n. Jobbies,* faeces, *poo.*

grunts *n.* The type of *fugly boots* whose blurred Polaroid pictures appear on the readers' wives pages of *tijuana bibles.*

guard dogs *n.* A pack of fierce hounds that accompany their attractive friend, preventing any bloke from trying his luck. *Tugs.*

guardsman's hat, fanny like a *sim.* Descriptive of an enormous black, hairy *snatch* that could, if one wasn't careful, slip down over one's eyes. Also, *busby berkeley.*

guard's parcel *n.* A present that turns out to be a disappointment. Derived from the advice given to those who live near a railway line frequented by freight trains, *ie.* Never pick up what looks like a discarded package near the tracks, it may contain the guard's excrement if he's been taken short. '*Pulling up Beattock, the guard needs a shite / But there's no bogs till Glasgow, much later tonight. / In time-honoured fashion he empties his arsehole / Into brown paper to make a guard's parcel.*' (from *The Shite Train* by WH Auden).

guard's van *n.* When *pulling a train,* the least desirable position in the queue. The last *pink carriage* into *fanny* station. '*Bagsy I'm not in the guard's van fellas.*'

Guatemalan taco *n.* A sexual act which makes a *Cleveland steamer* seem positively salubrious.

gubbed *adj. Trousered, wankered, shitfaced, arseholed.*

gubbs *n. Thru'penny bits.*

guck *n. Muck, spod, gunk, mess, filthy concrete.*

guff *v.* To *let one go, step on a frog.*

guff cloud *n.* The noxious, green vapour produced by *dropping one's hat. Carbon dibaxide.*

guff grenade *n.* A handful of flatus, grabbed from the gusset area and lobbed over-arm in the direction of an enemy combatant.

guide dog *n.* A woman, leading a man round the shops on a Saturday afternoon, who is so ugly that she calls into question his powers of visual acuity.

guide dogging *n.* The act of *dogging*, but involving a car with tinted windows, so it's difficult to *see it going in.*

guided muscle *n.* The *veiny bang stick.*

guiltimatum *n.* An offer a chap can't refuse, whereby he is coerced by his significant other into shopping for children's shoes, attending a tedious family gathering or cleaning out the drains by being reminded of previous misjudgements he may have committed in the course of his relationship. *'Eeh. I never thought I'd see Chris de Burgh going round Ikea on a Bank Holiday Monday.' 'Yeah, apparently his missus gave him a guiltimatum when she caught him fucking the nanny.'*

Guinness elbow *n. medic.* Repetitive strain injury which principally afflicts keen imbibers of the popular Irish stout. *'What's afflicting you there, Michael?' 'Sure it's nothing. Just a touch of the old Guinness elbow, Patrick. Well, that and my usual alcohol-induced cirrhosis of the liver.'*

Guinness pig *n.* Sexist terminology referring to an unattractive *bit of crack* pulled after a heavy night knocking back Ireland's popular altruistic stout.

Guinness rope *n.* A length of dense *cable* which blocks the *pan* after a heavy feed of the black stuff. It takes 119 seconds to lay the perfect length of *Guinness rope.*

guinnets *n.* Jet black *dangleberries* that cling to the *arse* after a night drinking the famed stout. *Buoys from the black stuff.*

gummy mix, drop one's *euph.* To accidentally do a little bit of inadvertent *shopping*, for example whilst out shopping.

gums around me plums, get your *exclam.* An irresistible romantic overture made by a male to a female.

guns of Navarone *n. Whoppers, tits, flesh-bombs, milky swingers.*

gunt *n. Can. Bunt.*

GUPO/gupo *acronym.* Abbreviation used by women who work in professions where their male co-workers are often *friends of Dorothy* (*eg.* airline in-flight attendants, members of the Royal Ballet and what-have-you), to prevent them making utter *twats* of themselves at the works Christmas party by making a pass at their one male colleague who has acted straight all year. Gay Until Proven Otherwise.

gurgler *n.* The toilet, *shite pipe,* drain. *'Have you got a coat hanger? Only I was spewin' up last night an' I coughed me fuckin' falsies down the gurgler.'*

gurk *1. v.* To burp. *2. v. Aus.* To *guff.*

gurkha's sword *n.* A *hard on* which has to be used before it can be put away. From the not necessarily true belief that a member of the tough Nepalese regiment must draw blood with his kukri before he is allowed to return it to its sheath.

gurning chimp *n.* A particularly expressive *fanny*.

gurniture *n*. Orthodontic bracery.

gurnturd *n*. A troublesome and stubborn *digestive transit*, the successful passing of which necessitates the pulling of a Popeye-style grimace. From the comedy facial gymnastics practised by toothless West Cumbrian drunks sticking their heads through horsecollars during patronising "local colour" pieces on *Nationwide*.

guru Palm and the five pillars of wisdom *n*. *Madam Palm and her five lovely daughters*. A *wanking spanner*.

gusset *1. n*. The bottom of the *hoggers* area of a woman, the *fairy hammock's drip tray*. *2. n. coll*. Flange, totty, fanny, blart.

gusset graze *n. medic*. The friction burn on the side of one's *old man* incurred when administering *a bit of the other* to a young lady whilst tenderly riving her nethergarmentry to one side.

gusset icing *n*. The decorative crust which has fallen off a *bird's clown's pie*, giving her a *gusset like a fish fryer's cuff*. *Fanny batter*.

gusset nuzzler *n*. A *fanny nosher*, a *lady golfer*, a *lesbian*.

gusset pianist *n*. *Invisible banjo* player. *'I've heard she plays the gusset piano.'*

gusset shot *n*. The thrilling glimpse of a young lady's *drip tray* with which an observant fellow is occasionally rewarded when watching *birds* dismounting from their bicycles. Perhaps whilst hiding in the bushes outside the nurses' home or a hall of residence. A *sneaky peek*.

gusset sugar *n*. Tooth-rotting *muffdruff*. *Batter bits*.

gusset typist *n*. A *bean flicker*, female merchant, *gusset piano virtuoso, touch typist*.

gustatory athlete *n*. One who sprints past the salad. Coined by the commentators on nightmarish US TV show *Gluttonbowl* to describe the parade of disgusting, big-boned inbreds taking part in their vile, yet extremely entertaining, eating competition.

gustbin *n*. A rather charming term used to describe the nether regions of a rather large lady.

gut grunt *n*. A burbulent rumbling in the viscera, or any subsequent anal emission.

gut spuds *n*. Spheroid *bum shrapnel*. *'Sorry mam. I dropped my gummy mix when I was out shopping so there's a few gut spuds in me kegs.'*

gutted hamster *n*. *Gutted possum, gutted rabbit, giblets, roadkill*.

gutters *n*. An unattractive female. *'Have you seen the bird on page 3 today? Jesus Christ, what a fucking gutters.'* (former *Daily Mirror* editor Piers Morgan reviewing the papers on BBC News 24, 2002).

gutter's shed *1. n*. A dockside building where fish are filleted. *2. n*. A particularly mingsome *minge*.

gut instinct *n*. The timely sixth sense which enables a man to accurately predict that something bad is about to happen. *'My gut instinct is telling me it's time to open the window, love.'*

Gutierrez's Spider-Man mask, seen as much action as *sim*. Description of someone who rarely *scores*. Derived from Argentinian Newcastle United winger Jonas Gutierrez's famous goal celebration, whereby he apparently whips out the aforementioned superhero facial disguise on the vanishingly rare occasions when one of his shots hits the back of the net. *'Hank: What's up with you, Cliff? You've got a face like a wet weekend in Weston Super Mare. Cliff: I suppose I'm just feeling a bit blue, Hank, that's all. Here we are travelling across Europe in a double decker bus full of fanny, and my poor old cock's seen about as much action as Gutierrez's Spider-Man mask. Hank: Say, that's just given me a great idea for a song! (starts picking tune out on guitar)'* (extract from screenplay for *Summer Holiday*, 1963).

guttocks *n.* The rolls of fat that obese women get on their stomachs which, when turned through 90°, look remarkably like their *arse. Fruttocks.*

guy dye *n.* Technique by which a fellow achieves a subtly psychedelic pattern on the front of his T-shirt over the course of a relaxing Sunday afternoon.

guyrope *n.* The flap of skin connecting the *flysheet* to the *tentpole.* The *banjo, Tarzan cord.*

guzunda *n.* A potty or *pisspot.*

gwank *n.* A girlie *wank.* A bout of *auditioning the finger puppets.*

Gwendolen *n. prop.* A superficially-alluring *bird* who is packing a little bit extra in the *nest* department. A *rotten peach.* Named after the bar-room *bobby dazzler* inadvertently acquired by Crocodile Dundee in that film he done. A *flipper, shim, ladyboy, tiptop* or *trolley dolly.*

gwibble *n.* A dribbly, underpowered ejaculation, opposite of a *pwa.*

gymbo *n.* Those conniving, make-up-encrusted, marriage-wrecking *boilers* who are apparently frequently to be found lurking in posh health and racquet clubs, where they do little or no training in case the perspiration ruins their *warpaint.* From gym + bimbo.

gym buddah *n.* An overweight woman in sportswear, with *overblaaters* and a huge *gunt.*

gymsniff *n. prop.* A gentleman who attends the gym and who prefers to use the apparatus directly after sweaty *birds* in order to sniff the seat.

gynaecolumnist *n.* Any female journalist who uses her newspaper column to bang on about *women's things, eg.* Julie Burchill.

gypsy clit *n.* A nomadic *clematis.* One which, despite a fellow's best efforts to find it, never seems to be in the same place two nights running. A *Flying Dutchman*, a *Scarlet Pimpernel.*

gypsy's curse *n.* The loss of *wood* before insertion, as a result of failing to buy some pegs at some point in the past 20 years.

gypsy's dog, like a *sim.* Descriptive of someone who looks like he could do with a square meal. *'Feargal Sharky? He's like a gypsy's dog, him. All ribs and bollocks.'*

gypsy's eyelash *n.* The rogue *clockspring* in the *Jap's eye* that causes the *piss* to go everywhere but in the *bog.* Common cause of *pan smile* or *Queen Mum's grin.*

gypsy's kiss *rhym. slang. Piss.* Usually abbreviated to gypsy's. *'Keep a look out for icebergs, will you? I'm just off below decks for a gypsy's.'*

habeas porcus *n*. Latin legal term, which literally means *getting off* with the fattest *bird* in the pub.

Hackney air show *n*. The nightly, and often daily, helicopter aerobatics performed by the Old Bill as they hunt for burglars, rapists and terrorists in the eponymous metropolitan garden village.

Hackney bunting *n*. Police crime scene cordon tape, which is commonly used to decorate the streets of the delightful London borough.

hack off a lump *v*. To *crimp off a length*. To defeculate.

haddock pastie *n*. *Hairy pie*, a *Grimsby meal*.

Hadley job *n*. An act of *horatio* during which the *noshatrix* handles your *tassel* in the foppish, effete manner that the lead singer of *Spandau Ballet* used to handle his microphone.

had the dick *adj*. Descriptive of something which is broken beyond repair. *"What-ho, Jeeves,' I exclaimed. 'Fetch the Frazer-Nash round to the front door, there's a good chap. I feel like taking a spin.' 'I'm afraid that may not be possible, Sir,' he replied. 'Your Aunt Millicent drove it to Ascot and back with the handbrake on, and I fear it has had the dick."* (from *For Fuck's Sake, Jeeves!* by PG Wodehouse).

haemogobbling *n*. *Dining at the Y* when the house wine is *moon juice*.

haemogoblin *n*. A gentleman who has a fish supper at the *all-night sushi bar*, despite the fact that it is closed for redecoration.

hag *n*. An ugly woman, *boiler, boot, steg, swamp donkey, ditch pig*.

hag do *n*. Linguistically speaking, a cross between a hen night and a stag do.

Either way, it's a nightmarish booze-fuelled gathering of people you would rather not *have it off* with.

haggis *1. n*. Unappetising object consisting of meat and oats stuffed into a veiny skin bag. *2. n*. Unappetising object consisting of meat and oats stuffed into a veiny skin bag.

haggis rag *n*. A small piece of fabric, esp. towelling, used for wiping clean or drying the *haggis* after a bout of exercise.

hagnetism *n*. The mysterious, invisible force that makes certain men attract only ladies with *lovely personalities*.

hail damage *n*. The vile, unsightly, dimpled skin found on the thighs of middle-aged celebrity women and brought to the world's attention by gleeful paparazzi. Cellulite.

hairache *n*. The mother of all hangovers. *'I can't go on, Richard. You'll have to do the programme on your own. I've got hairache.'*

hair of the dogging *n*. Any attempt to relieve residual feelings of guilt felt by an habitual car park *perv* who assuages his angst by habitually going out and doing it again the next day. *'Where are you off to, Stan?' 'Just popping out for some hair of the dogging, love.'*

hair trousers, to be wearing *v*. To be naked from the waist down.

hairy axe wound *n*. Vertical *gash*. The *mingepiece, quim, cock socket*.

hairy beanbags *n*. Pink 1970s style seating provided within the underpants for the exclusive use of the *bald man, Spurt Reynolds, Kojak, Captain Picard, etc.* Testicles.

hairy brain *n. medic*. The small wrinkled organ, about the size of two plums, that governs a gentleman's thought processes. Also *hanging brain*.

hairy cheque book *n*. *Gash card, furry purse*.

hairy conkers *n*. *Knackers, clockweights*.

hairy cornflake 1. *n*. An affectionate name for *shit* DJ Dave Lee Travis, coined and used exclusively by himself. 2. *n*. Affectionate name for a small, dried crust of *poo* stuck firmly to the *arsecress*. 3. *n*. An hirsute breakfast cereal that was expensively launched by Kellog's in 1976, but inexplicably failed to find favour with the public.

hairy cup *n*. *Hairy goblet, furry hoop*.

hairy doughnut *n*. An occasionally jam-filled confection, often dusted with *gusset sugar*.

hairy goblet *n*. *Hairy cup, front bottom, bodily treasure, parts of shame*.

hairy handshake *n*. A firm five-fingered greeting that costs £10 from a woman behind a skip, after which there are no hard feelings.

hairy harmonica *n*. Any organ that can be played without using the hands, producing a sequence of rising tones.

hairy knickers *n*. Descriptive of that situation when a lady removes her *farting crackers* and her unruly *minge* makes it appear that she has yet to do so. An extremely well-carpeted *barber's floor*, a *Terry Waite's allotment*. An extreme *biffer*.

hairy mits *rhym. slang*. Tits. 'Look at the hairy mits on that! I could do her through a hedge backwards.'

hairy muff *exclam*. A light-hearted alternative to saying "fair enough", used by the same sort of people who make a point of asking "anyone fuck offy?".

hairy pants *n*. See *hairy knickers*.

hairy pie *n*. *Haddock pastie*.

hairy pint *n*. An unsuspecting person's alcoholic beverage that has been discreetly spiked for the amusement of onlookers with a small quantity of *pubes*.

hairy raisins *n*. *Hunchback spiders*.

hairy saddlebags 1. *n*. *Knackers* 2. *n*. *Pissflaps*.

hairy scallops *n*. The furry shellfish eaten when *bearded clams* are out of season.

hairy swingers *n*. Hirsute *man-sacks* containing the *hairy conkers*.

hairy toffee *n*. *Dangleberries, kling-ons*.

hairy window *n*. That semi-translucent panel in the front portion of a pair of ladies' *scads*, through which it is just possible to make out her *gorilla salad*, though not her *curtains*.

half a crown thru'penny bit *sim*. Pre-decimal version of *five pee fifty pee*, used to describe the rapid flexing of the *nipsy* during moments of severe anxiety. *Bin lid penny*.

half a jaffa *n*. That which may be glimpsed in the crotch area of a young lady wearing tight jeans. *Twix lips*.

half a lemon *n*. A paradoxical form of *lady golfer* who only fancies women who look like blokes.

half a nasty *n*. A *podge-on, dobber, grump on*.

half a teacake *n*. Not quite a *fatty*, the beginings of an erection. The state you would like your *fruitbowl* to be in when a new woman sees it for the first time.

half babies *n*. *Spuff, spingler, sprodd, spoddle, heir gel*.

half blood prince 1. *n*. A chap's *member* after he's *had it off* with a woman during *rag week*. A *barber's pole*. 2. *n*. A *cock* that is so floppy it would struggle to get into a *wizard's sleeve*.

half caff *n*. The strength of a fellow's

spooch immediately post-vasectomy, *ie.* Before he's *crashed his yoghurt truck* the requisite twenty times to ensure he's completely *decaff.*

half Elvis, to do a *v.* To fall asleep, but not quite die, whilst having a *shit* on the toilet. Usually done by one in an advanced state of *refreshment.*

half leapfrog *n.* Having sex in the *doggie position, setting the video.*

Halfords hero *n.* Motorist behind the wheel of a *noughtomobile*, who has kitted out his bottom-of-the-range hatchback with several hundredweight of expensive tat, including alloy wheels, ludicrous spoilers, an extremely loud stereo and an exhaust pipe like a fucking coal scuttle.

half rice half chips *adj.* Descriptive of a *switch hitter, alloy welder* or *happy shopper*; one who *drinks from both taps/ bowls from both ends. AC/DC.*

half time talk *n.* In a *spitroast grumble flick*, the token dialogue which occurs between the two leading men whilst they change ends, eat orange segments *etc.*

halopecia *n. medic.* Baldness caused by over-use of the XBox headset.

hamburger *n.* Of the female anatomy, that which can be seen in a *hamburger shot.* Something that really ought to have a *dill* stuck into it.

hamburger hill *n.* The large tor that frequently casts *stoat valley* into shadow on ladies of advancing years. A *gunt, fupa.*

hamburger shot *n.* A rear view in a *scud mag* displaying a *vertical bacon sandwich.* A *reverse peach.*

ham fisted *euph. Mid-wank.* 'My mum came in and caught me ham fisted the other night. I didn't know where to look.'

ham howitzer *n.* A *lamb cannon, beef blunderbuss, spam magnum*, any sort of meat + any sort of firearm.

Hamish blue *n.* Ripe, azure-tinted *knobcheese*, found north of the border and south of the sporran.

hamlet *n.* A half-hearted grade of erection, which can be found somewhere mid-way between a *flop on* and a *diamond cutter* on the universal scale of penile harditude. "2B or not 2B".

hammock *n.* Panty liner, *jam rag, sanitary towel, fanny napkin.*

Hammond's hat *n.* A *helmet* covered in *skidmarks.*

ham-on-ham *n.* Descriptive of the delightful sight of two ladies going at it *hammer and tongues. Gammon and pineapple.*

Hampton *rhym. slang. Dick.* From Hampton Weenis, a village in Essex with all wiggly blue veins up the side.

ham shank *rhym. slang.* A *Barclay's, J Arthur, Max Planck.*

ham slices *n.* Peeling the *chicken skin handbag* away from the inner leg on a particularly hot day. From the similarity to the process of peeling apart the layers of sweaty meat when opening a packet of Bernard Matthews Honey Roast Ham. *Bagpeel.*

hamshank redemption *n.* A discreet bout of *male pleasure* enjoyed whilst desperately trying not to waken up one's cellmate.

hamster's mouthful *n.* A man's *ballsack camel's toe*, caused by comedically tight trousers, as demonstrated by Jamie Redknapp on *Sky Sports Super Sunday.* 'Redknapp's looking very uncomfortable in the final third, Andy.' 'Yes Martin. What a hamster's mouthful. Take a bow, son.'

handbrake n. An unwanted and inexplicable thought or image that pops into a fellow's mind, bringing a sudden stop to an act of *self pollution, eg.* His late grandmother looking at him and tutting, his dead budgie lying on the bottom of its cage, the bit of the Zapruder footage where Kennedy's brains fall out the side of his head and his cranium goes skidding across the top of his car's boot, Germaine Greer's *Oz* magazine *hamburger shot etc.*

hand Chandon n. A high class *hand shandy* off a posh *bird*, who *pops your cork* with her thumbs under the *brim* of your *lid.*

hand cock's half hour n. "Thirty minutes? That's very nearly an armful."

handful of sprats n. *1950s.* A fistful of *fish fingers, finger food.*

hand grenade n. Somewhat unpleasantly, you would imagine, for all concerned, an act of *fisting* which culminates in an opening of the hand.

hand job n. Manual relief, one of the cheaper *extras* available at the *rub-a-tug shop,* or in the pub car park.

hand love n. The sordid act of *self-pollution.*

hand pump n. *milit. Wanker, nut juggler etc.* 'Oi! Windsor, you fucking hand pump. Get them fucking boots back on, Your Royal Highness.'

handruff n. Flaky deposits consisting of an amalgam of dried *potato fat, perseverance soup* and *helmetdale* found on the palms, thighs and soft furnishings of bachelors who have been watching a few episodes too many of *Desperate Housewives* without occasionally pausing to give the inside of the *farmer's hat* a wash.

hands free wank n. See *fancy wank.*

hand shandroid n. A mechanical, robotic *wanking* device, such as one might build out of a shop dummy and a lawnmower engine.

hands like cows' tits sim. Descriptive of one who is dextrously inept. An alternative to "butterfingers". *'I'm terribly sorry, Mrs Johnson, but I accidentally cut through a major blood vessel near your husband's heart and he didn't survive the surgery. I'm afraid I was on the pop last night and I've got hands like cows' tits this morning. My bill will be in the post. The nurse will show you out. Good day.'*

hand shandy n. A frothy one, pulled *off the wrist.*

hand solo n. A solitary interlude of *self improvement.*

hand to gland combat n. A three-minute, one-man gladiatorial combat bout involving a *spam javelin.*

handycrap n. A *shit* taken by an able-bodied person who goes into *arse labour* only to discover that all the other toilets are occupied, out of order or blocked with *bangers and mash,* and is forced to avail himself in the disabled facilities.

handy pandy n. A high risk *sherman,* taken over a particularly fetching children's TV presenter.

hang a rat v. To go to the lavatory for a *number two.* 'Where is he? He's supposed to be on the balcony blessing the multitude.' 'Keep your fucking hair on. He's just went to the khazi to hang a rat.'

hang a roll of flock wallpaper euph. A somewhat hyperbolic description of what one could do with a copious amount of thick *spoff. ''I say, Jeeves,'*

I expostulated. 'There's always capital fun to be had down at the Drones Club with old Fink-Nottle and the chaps, but hang it all if one doesn't sometimes hanker after a spot of female company.' 'Indeed sir,' rejoindered the stalwart gentleman's gentleman. 'The fragrant tenderness of the fairer sex is as balm to the soul. Who would deny that she is God's sublime creation, able to express more in a sigh than can a man in a sermon.' 'Yes, there is that, Jeeves old chap,' I replied at length after pondering the sage retainer's wise words. 'Plus which, you could hang a roll of flock wallpaper with what's brewing in my nads." (from *Stick it up your Hoop, Jeeves!* by PG Wodehouse).

hanging bacon *n*. A *club sandwich* which hopefully isn't held together with a cocktail stick.

hanging baskets *1. n*. Dangling areas of foliage which can look nice when properly tended but attract flies if allowed to run to seed. *2. n*. Blooming marvellous *tits* which sway in the breeze and look like they've been assiduously cultivated.

hanging brain *n*. A *coffin dodger's clockweights*, dangling out the leg of his shorts.

hanging chod *n*. A semi-detached *turd*.

hanging gardens, the *n*. The horrific rear elevation of a naked man bending over. Definitely not one of the Seven Wonders of the World.

hanging out the back of *adj*. Engaged in *doggy-style* sex with someone.

hanging salad *n*. *Wedding tackle, fruit bowl, family jewels*.

hanging the Mona Lisa in the North point Arcade, like *sim*. A particularly Humberside-centric apophthegm, wittily referring to a good pair of *top bollocks* which are wasted on an ugly woman, from the fact that the situation is metaphorically akin to hanging a priceless Renaissance work of art in the cultural desert which is the North Point Shopping Arcade, Bransholme, Hull.

hang in the balance *v*. Of a fellow's *chap*, to float at the exact mid-point between a *lazy* and a *full lob*.

hangman's noose *n*. A capacious vagina, big enough to push your head into. A *wizard's sleeve*, a *clown's pocket*.

hangover Holmes *n*. A chap who uses all the evidence available to him about his person (*eg*. Bus tickets, cash machine receipts, stains, wedding rings, bruises, lovebites, *crabs*) in order to deduce what he got up to the previous night.

hang ten *1. v*. In surfing slang, to stand on the front of the board with all of one's toes curling over the edge. *2. v*. To be *masturbatricized* by one's partner using her feet rather than the more traditional *wanking spanners*. *'Riding waves is really sweet / Catching tubes a real good treat / But best of all is hanging ten / With me knob between the missus's feet.'* (from *Wankin' USA* by the Beach Boys).

hangunder *n*. A feeling of generalised debility in an inveterate drinker, caused by underindulgence the previous night. *'Giz a shot on that white lightning, pal. I've got a terrible hangunder and I just can't seem to shift it.'*

hang up the wank sock *v*. To get married. *'In 1848, at the age of twenty-nine, Ruskin met Euphemia Chalmers Gray and decided to hang up his wank sock.'*

hang your hole *v*. To *moon* or *do a cap-*

tain. At two nuns in a Morris Minor, as previously noted.

hanky panky *n. Slap and tickle, a bit of the other, nookie, how's your father.* Light-hearted *fucking.*

Hannibal Lecter's breakfast *n.* The feast which awaits a man performing *cumulonimbus* on *Billy Connolly's beard,* and the ensuing *pasata grin* it leaves on his face.

ha'penny *n.* Vagina. A *tuppence.*

happy camper *n.* One on whom *nature has played a cruel trick*, yet treats their predicament light-heartedly, *eg.* Graham Norton, Duncan Norvelle, Peter Tatchell.

happy Christmas Heather *euph.* The sinister half-grimace, half-smile worn on the face of one whose prolonged bout of constipation has just reached an agonising, *ring*-bursting climax. Named after the even more pained half-grimace, half-smile allegedly worn by Stella McCartney when she was forced to greet her unidextrous ex-wicked-stepmother at family events.

happy ending *1. n.* In a film or novel, for example, a narrative denouement in which the various strands of the plot are drawn together in a satisfyingly felicitous manner, leaving the viewer or reader with a warm glow of pleasure. *2. n.* In a massage parlour, a denouement in which the customer gets *tossed off*, leaving him doing his flies back up with a feeling of dejection, despair and self-loathing while the masseuse disinterestedly wipes his grey *spunk* off her hand with some Tesco Discount Brand kitchen roll.

happy Harry *n.* A semi-erect penis. A *dobber*, a *lard on*, *half a teacake.*

happy Havana *n.* A firm, rectilinear *bum cigar* of such pleasing proportions that it could almost have been rolled on the thigh of a sultry temptress, and requires little or no wiping to boot.

happy lamp *n.* The *sixth gear stick. 'I'm horny. Think I'll give my happy lamp a quick genie rub.'*

happy paper *n.* Beer tokens, folding money.

happyrash *n. medic.* A light-hearted dose of the *pox*. A *Doonican.* Any non-fatal *STD.*

happy sack *n.* The scrotum, clackerbag, chicken skin handbag, *hairy saddlebags.*

Happy Shopper *1. n. prop.* A cheap 'n' cheerless grocery brand. *2. n.* A bisexual - one who *shops on both sides of the street. A half rice half chips person.*

Happy Shopper copper *n.* A community police support officer. *'I was too young to get a job as a lollipop man so I became a happy shopper copper instead.'*

Happy Shopper knockers *n.* No-frills *jugs.* Like proper *tits*, but with less filling. *Skimmed milkers.*

harbouring a known criminal *n.* Holding in a noisome *bottom burp* or suppressing a *baby's arm* whilst in an enclosed area or in close proximity to a lady.

harbour master *n.* A man who has piloted the course of a few *tugboats* in his time, he can tell you. A *stickman, fanny hopper, crumpeteer.*

hardbore *n. Grumble* that promises to be a real *meat vid* on the box, but when you get it home you find it's got Robin Askwith, Bill Maynard and Doris Hare in it. And Tony Blair's father-in-law.

hard hat *n.* A *stiffy*, or erection of the male parts. *'Fancy a spot of potholing under the bridge?' 'Not until I've got my* *hard hat on, love.'*

hardly on *n.* A barely-leavened *teacake*. Not quite three quarters of *half a soft on.*

hard off *n.* Something of a disappointment. *'After all the excitement of our last-gasp comebacks in the quarter and semi-final stages, I've got to admit that our four-nil defeat to Seville in the UEFA cup final in Eindhoven was something of a hard off, Adrian.'* (Then Middlesbrough manager Steve McClaren speaking on BBC Radio 5, May 10th 2006).

hard on *n. Wood*, a *bone on*, a *bonk-on.* A fully-tumescent gentleman's part.

hard work *exclam.* How somebody with a gobful of hot chips might say "aardvark".

hariolae *n.* The hairs that foreign ladies cultivate around their *hunchback spiders.*

Harlem shuffle *n.* The facial gurning and involuntary neck spasms that beset a gentleman during the *vinegar strokes*, making him look like septuagenarian *harbour master* Sir Mickolas Jagger strutting about on stage. *'Quick, camera two, a close up of Gunther's cock. He's doing the Harlem shuffle.'*

harlet *n.* A young *slapper.*

Harley Davidson *n.* An act of lavatoryless defecation, in which the dumper is forced to cling to trees or railings in order to steady himself, thus adopting a position similar to that used when riding an impractical American motorcycle. A *fatboy, soft-tail.*

harlot *n.* A scarlet woman, a wicked lady.

Harlow pub quiz *n.* Entertainment regularly held at the Essex town's popular nightspots. The quizmaster usually asks one of two questions: "What the fuck are you looking at?" or "Do you fucking want some?", to which all the possible answers are wrong. *West Yorkshire Mastermind.*

Harmison loosener *n.* An explosive delivery first thing in the morning which ends up anywhere but near to its intended target. *'Last night's chicken jalfrezi resulted in Derek sending down a ferocious Harmison loosener.'*

harpooning *n. Having it off* with a blubbery *bird.*

Harry *1. rhym. slang. Jizz.* From Harry Monk = spunk. *2. rhym. slang.* Hobo. From Harry Ramp = tramp *3. rhym. slang.* Cigarette. From Harry Rag = fag. *4. rhym. slang.* Cheese sandwich. From Harry Rees-Bandwich.

Harry Hill *n. rhym. slang.* The contraceptive pill. *'It's alright Boris, I'm on the Harry Hill.'*

Harry Rampsdens *n.* Discarded fish and chips, as feasted upon by cheery gentlemen of the road. *Tramps' truffles.*

Harry Ramsden's raspberry *n.* The combination of smell and sound to be endured during a dirty girl's *fanny fart.*

Harry Redknapp's eyelids *sim.* Descriptive of particularly hang-dog *beef curtains*, that look like they've been sat up all night playing on a Nintendo DS.

Harry's challenge *n.* A daunting *fish supper* that is too much for one man. A big *kipper.* From the menu at the Yardley branch of Harry Ramsden's which offered a meal of that name, and where one was granted a certificate if the portion was finished.

Hartlepool baguette *n.* Unpalatable, trouser-based, cheese-heavy *al fresco* snack which is popular with young ladies in the picturesque northern resort, particularly at chucking out time.

Harvest Festival *n.* Domestic state of play for the bachelor gentleman when, following a fortnight *on the lash*, he is reduced to living on out-of-date tinned food from the back of the cupboard.

harvest festivals 1. *n.* One-night stands, *ie.* Ploughing the field before scattering. 2. *n.* A pair of well-fitting but comfortable underpants where "all is safely gathered in".

hasbian *n.* A past-it *lesbian* whose *carpet munching* days are over.

hatchback *n.* A woman with prominent buttocks. *'Jesus. Look at the arse on that that Mother Superior over there by Guercini's altarpiece of the Burial of St Petronilla, your Holiness. What a hatchback. You could stand your pint on her parcel shelf.'*

hatch eggs *v.* To remain seated on the *chod bin* long after the last *turd* has been dropped. *'What are you doing in there? I've got the turtle's breath and a new Autotrader.' 'I'm hatching eggs.'*

hat rack *n.* Someone whose head is only of any use for the storage of hats. A *Johnny No-Stars*, a *shit-for-brains*. *eg.* Bez out of The Happy Mondays, Universities Minister The Rt Hon David Willetts MP.

hatstand *adj.* Descriptive of one who has mental health issues.

hatties *rhym. slang.* Delirium tremens. A *turps nudger*'s shakes. From *big-boned Carry On* actress Hattie Jelirium-Tremens.

have a go at oneself *v.* To *stab the cat, feed the ducks, stab the ducks, feed the cat.*

have it off *v.* To get *a bit*, have a *portion*, give somebody *one*. To get one's *leg over.*

have one's arse in one's hand *euph.* To be in a bad mood, to have a strop on. *'Arnie's BACK!... and this time he's got his arse in his hand!'* (Advertising poster for *Terminator 3*).

Havers, on the *adj.* Descriptive of the way certain blokes smarm up to members of the opposite sex in an overly charming way, *eg.* Kissing their hands, listening to them *etc.*, in the style of middle-aged charmer Nigel Havers.

have the painters in *v.* To menstruate, be *on the blob. To fall to the communists.*

having a Wilkie *n.* Sitting on the toilet with your hands cupped together and clenched, your face a picture of concentration, whilst trying to will your *brown ball* between the white porcelain posts of the *bum sink*. A somewhat contrived reference to the characteristic kicking stance of heavily-constipated part-time England rugby *glassback* Jonny Wilkinson.

Hawaiian muscle fuck *n.* The act of *bagpiping.*

Hawaiian sunrise *n.* A glorious and uncomfortable orange, red, blue and purple aurora, which can be seen around one's *ringpiece* early in the morning after consuming spicesome comestibles.

Hawaiian waft *n.* To disperse the aroma after *stepping on a duck*, using an exotic hula-hula motion.

Hawick *onomat.* To *puke.* After the Scottish border town. *'I think I'm going to Hawick.'*

hay fever *n. medic.* A seasonal illness, whose sufferers are forced to convalesce at home during the summer months, with the windows and curtains shut to prevent "pollen" getting in. And also so that the neighbours/postman *etc.*, don't see them sat on the sofa *wanking* over the Wimbledon Ladies' heats.

HD ready *1. adj.* Of large, flatscreen television sets in electrical shops, descriptive of the fact that they are capable of displaying impressively detailed pictures of yachts, the Changing of the Guard and tropical fish. *2. adj.* A gentleman's assessment that his current feminine companion is sexually amenable, *ie.* That she is "ready for his Hot Dog".

he-dam *n. Knobcheese, helmetdale, purple Leicester, brimula, Lymeswold etc.*

head *n.* Something which is given by women to men, and is afterwards described as "good" by the recipient when talking to friends. A *chewie, nosh, gobbie.* Not to be confused with the Monkees' film of the same name, which was anything but good.

head and breakfast *n.* A place where one can get a *Thai at night*, and a *full English* in the morning.

head for the hills *exclam.* To be forced to hide your *soldier* in the *Dutch alps*, because the *redcoats are in the valley*.

head in one's top pocket, to have *v.* To be so copiously-*refreshed* that one's head cannot balance on one's neck any more and seems to be falling into the top pocket of one's shirt. An extreme form of *nodding.*

headlamps *n. Bristols, jugs, charlies, assets. 'Phewf! I wouldn't mind giving her headlamps a rub.'*

head off a nun, like trying to get *met.* Descriptive of something very difficult to achieve. *Finding a pube in an afro. 'And I fully intend to bring in legislation on asylum that will make getting*

British citizenship like getting head off a nun before the next parliament.' (David Blunkett addressing the Labour Party Conference, 2003).

headwind *n. Trouser cough* emitted right under the nose of a fellatrix. *Devil's kiss, Hell's mouth.*

Heather Mills! *exclam.* Incredulous declamatory response uttered when a third party makes a claim which is so outrageous and unlikely that a reasoned rejoinder is almost impossible. Named after Macca's hyperbole-prone, assymetrically-limbed ex-missus. *'I reckon Derby could still do it, you know. Man United are only sixty points ahead.' 'Heather Mills!' 2. n.* A descriptive exclamation used by players of ball sports such as pool or golf when a ball falls short of its target, because "it hasn't got the legs".

health stick *n.* A fruity penis, packed with the goodness of nuts and nourishing *Vitamin S.*

heavage *n.* A *Bristol Channel* that is only there thanks to cleverly engineered *tit pants.*

heave *v.* To vomit, *make a pavement pizza*, release a loud *technicolour yawn.*

heave a Havana *v. Grow a tail*, take a *dump, light a bum cigar, cast Churchill's reflection.*

heave-ho *1. n.* The arse. *'She threw me out on my heave-ho.' 2. n.* The *Spanish archer. 'She gave me the heave-ho on my arse.'*

heavy dick *n.* The very first stirrings of erectivation. The beginnings of a *semi-on.* For example, that situation which occurs when one is on holiday abroad, whereby a combination of warm weather and semi-naked women leaves you feeling like you've got a sock full of sand in your pants. *'Hey, I don't like admitting it, boys, but that tranny off There's Something About Miriam has given me a bit of a heavy dick.'*

heavy shooter *n.* One whose *money shots* tend to be *pwas* rather than *gwibbles.*

heavy wetter *n.* An extravagant *spender;* a gentleman who produces an unfeasibly large amount of *heir gel* when he *goes off.* Also known as a *milkman.*

hedge coke *n.* Plastic bottles filled with fluid too pale to be true cola, discarded on roadside verges by lorry drivers in order to tempt thirsty runners or cyclists in need of refreshment. *Trucker's tizer, kidney cider, Scania scotch.*

hedge funds *n.* The substantial deposits of crumpled *grumble* stashed in the hedgerows of suburban alleyways or scrublands by canny young *merchant bankers. Ray Mears's library.*

hedgehog *n.* A *ladygarden that was mowed* five days ago. A *face grater.*

hee *1. n. Thai. Minge, hairy cheque book.* *2. interj.* A noise made by laughing gnomes/laughing policemen.

hefty-clefty *n.* A *welly top,* a *horse's collar,* a *melted welly, spla welly.* A very wide *Mary.*

Heinz jacuzzi *n.* The luxurious, self-indulgent pleasure to be had in any bath, courtesy of an earlier consumption of baked beans. *'I'd give it ten minutes if I was you, dear. I've just had a Heinz jacuzzi. And probably best not to light any tea-lights in there for a few hours, neither.'*

heirbags *n.* The containers where *liquid kids* are stored, and which handily prevent injury to the *barse* when you are kicked between the legs. The *testicles.*

heir gel *n.* See *heir spray.*

heir spray *n.* A man's volatile *baby juice. Spooge, spoff, spaff, spiff, jitler. Merry monk.*

Helena Bonham *euph.* The *anus.* From the charming English rose actress Helena Bonham-Farter.

helicopters, attack of the *n.* Drunken spinning of the head, a sudden reminder that you need to make an urgent call on the *great white telephone.* The *whirlies, wall of death.*

helium balloon *n.* The unfortunate situation that sometimes obtains during a spot of *backdoor action,* when the woman *blows off* and inflates the gentleman's *chicken skin handbag,* causing him, at the very least, to talk like Joe Pasquale or, in extreme cases, to float helplessly out of the window and be pointed at by passing children.

hello Cleveland *exclam.* Phrase uttered by a gentleman who is *doing* a lady from behind and inadvertently *pots the brown* rather than the *pink.* From the scene in *Spinal Tap* when the band find themselves in the wrong tunnel.

helmet *1. n.* The *bell end, glans, bishop's mitre, purple pearler. 2. n.* A quantity of *fellatio.* An amount of *blow jobs. 'My nan wanted to meet Roger Whitaker, and she had to give the roadies some helmet to get backstage.'*

helmetdale *n.* A strong-smelling, mature *knob cheese.*

helmet mag *n.* A *stroke periodical, art pamphlet, noddy book.*

helmet pelmet *n.* The *fiveskin, Kojak's roll-neck.*

helmetscale *n.* Fully-ossified *Lymeswold* that has to be chipped off the *Pope's cap* using a toothpick or, in serious cases, a Dremel. Found only on the most determined opponents of genital hygiene of the sort you might find hanging around in Maplin's.

helmet, to give it some *v.* To engage in an activity with some gusto. To give it *rice*, give it *welly*, give it *six-nowt, go at it three cocks to the cunt. 'It may be necessary to apply a considerable amount of torque in order to loosen the wheel studs. Indeed, you may have to give the wheel brace quite a bit of helmet before they begin to yield.'* (from the *Austin Maxi Haynes Manual*, 1978).

helter skelter *n.* The urgent, churning sensation in the lower bowel which indicates the imminent arrival of a high-speed *mudchild* sitting on a metaphorical doormat with its boots sticking out forwards.

Hemingway sphinx *n.* A breed of hairless cat.

hen don't *n.* The sight which, when a chap walks into a bar in which are ensconced 15 *pissed-up* women wearing pink cowboy hats, causes him to turn on his heel and immediately walk straight back out again.

Hendrix on the high notes *sim.* Descriptive of the facial contortions of a gentleman in the final throes of coitus, reminiscent of the late plank-spanker in full axe frenzy. The *vinegar strokes*.

Henman *n.* An impotent fellow. Named after the former British tennis sensation Tim, who never managed to make it past the *semi* stage.

Henrietta Street *1. n.* An old, narrow, twisty thoroughfare in Whitby and thus *2. n.* An ageing, serpentine *clunge* with a strong aroma of kippers and haddock.

Henry Moore *1. n.* A large pile of *shit* in a public place. *2. n.* A large reclining dog

turd on the pavement.

Henry the Eighth *n.* A king amongst *farts*, that is to say one which will do in the wife.

he-nut butter *n.* Put crudely, the viscid liquid which contains spermatazoa, the male gametes or germ cells. In more scientific terms, *spaff, jitler, chalaza, baby batter etc.*

Herbert Pocket *n.* The pocket that the *herbert* slips into. The *arsehole*. From the name of the character in *Great Expectations*, played in the film by Sir Alec Guinness, and the one that he gave to police upon his arrest for *cottaging*.

Herbie's bonnet *n.* The *beetle bonnet, camel's lips.* A *twat* with the number 53 stuck to it.

herbievore *n.* A lady - or man - who only eats *beetle bonnets*.

hernobyl *n.* A bout of *rag week* meltdown, resulting in widespread, catastrophic damage to property, health and the environment.

Hershey highway *n.* *US.* Transatlantic *Bourneville boulevard, Cadbury alley.*

Hershey highwayman *n.* *US.* An *ass bandit.*

Heskey *n.* A girl who *goes down* at the slightest touch.

he's lost a lot of blood *1. exclam.* Staple quote of many 1980s action movies, supposedly throwing into question whether or not the severely-injured lead actor will pull through to the end of the film, whereas the whole audience knows perfectly well that of course he fucking will, on account of he's featured prominently on the posters. *2. exclam.* Something a gentleman might ruefully say to an unimpressed female companion, immediately preceding "this has never happened before".

hettython *n*. The act of taking the day off work, closing the curtains and watching all five series of *Hetty Wainthrop Investigates.*

hibernating grizzly *n*. A big, hairy, brown *shit* asleep in the *claypit* that one would be foolish to rouse from its slumbers.

hickies *n*. *Slapper*-speak for love bites, *shag tags*.

hickory dick *n*. A *cock* so hard it would bend any nails one attempted to drive into it.

hide the salami *n*. A bedtime game for two players, one *sausage* and a *hairy pie*. Also *sink the salami, bury the bratwurst, conceal the Cumberland.*

hiding policemen's helmets *adj*. Of a lady, to be *nipping out, smuggling peanuts.*

highdea *n*. A brilliant plan or scheme that is conceived whilst under the influence of stupefying intoxicants that, when viewed in the cold, sober light of day, is revealed to be a load of old *cack*, *eg*. Writing a sitcom about the funny things students say when stoned, building a floating city in the sky using helium-filled girders, or Fleetwood Mac's *Tusk* album. A West country equivalent is the term *cidea*.

high miler *n*. An *old banger* who looks like she's been round the clock a few times, but is still running, *eg*. Joan Collins, Shirley Bassey.

high pressure vein cane *n*. Short for the penis, *prick, tallywhacker, Hector the meat injector*.

high speed rinse *n*. An act of *self pollution* committed in the shower. *Flinging in the rain.*

high street harpy *n*. The opposite of a *high street honey*, whatever that might be. A *chavtastic, scratter* woman of the sort that lurk in gangs in town centres, waiting for easily-embarrassed, middle-aged men to pass, before yelling at them to show them their *cocks*.

high velocity trifle *n*. A soft *feeshus* fired from the *chocolate starfish* at great speed, which is instantly aerated into a smooth, frothy confection when it meets the outer atmosphere. The resultant fluffy material is ideal for pebble-dashing porcelain and has powerful adhesive properties when brought into contact with blankets, sleeping bags and quilts.

Hilary *n*. *rhym. slang*. A *five knuckle shuffle*. From US actress Hilary Swank. *'I just seen that Carol Vorderman flogging loans on the satellite and I knocked out a quick Hilary there and then.'*

hillbilly's hat *n*. A particularly dishevelled *cock socket*. A *Clampett.*

hill start *n*. The painstaking task of pleasuring oneself after a heavy drinking session, when reaching *biting point* can take hours.

Hilton breakfast *n*. A product or service which combines substandard quality with a premium price, facts which become apparent only when it is too late to change your mind and run away. Examples of *Hilton breakfasts* include poncy salon haircuts, Galloway pony treks and early morning meals at certain international hotel chains which will remain nameless for legal reasons.

Himalayas *n*. Gentlemen who *till the soil* on very steep inclines.

himbledon *n*. Fortnight long festival of *men's singles* enjoyed by sofa-bound bachelors whilst watching the famous All-England women's tennis tournament on television. With the curtains pulled tightly shut.

hindsight *n*. The reflex action of a man turning swiftly in order to track an outstanding *arse* as it makes its way across the room or along the pavement. Hindsight is estimated to be the cause of 95% of low-speed rear-end collisions on British high streets, and up to 99% of accidents involving straw-hatted vicars riding their bicycles into hedges.

hingoot *n*. *Scot*. A lady of easy virtue, a *slapper*, a *prossie*, a *good time girl*. Literally, a woman who has enjoyed so much *cock* that her fanny is "hinging oot".

hippobotamus *n*. A large, out of proportion lady's rear end, of the sort viewed when following Kerry Katona down the desserts aisle at Iceland.

hippocrocapig *n*. Ann Widdecombe if you set her head on fire and put it out with a shovel. A *rhinocerpig*.

hippo's ear *n*. A *hippo's mouth*. A *donkey's yawn*. A *fanny* like a *bucket*.

hippo's mouth *n*. Another large, unsightly, gaping vagina.

hippo's saddle *n*. Something big, grey and leathery in a lady's *knickers*.

hipposuction *n*. Optimistic cosmetic surgical procedure carried out on the larger lady.

hipsies *n*. Tree-hugging new-age travellers who, despite being in love with the planet, nevertheless contrive to leave a big pile of dog *crap*, *johnnies* and *shit*-filled carrier bags behind when they tow their clapped-out, smoke-churning Transit vans off the site.

hip tits *n*. The large pair of flabby rolls of stomach blubber that hang down around the waists of those unbelievably fat Americans you see waddling around Disneyland. *Bilge tanks, jerry cans*.

hissing Sid *n*. One's *one-eyed trouser snake*.

hit and miss *rhym. slang. Piss*.

hit and run *v*. To indulge in sexual intercourse with a *boiler* despite one's better judgement, then leg it before she wakes up.

hitch-hiking under the big top *n*. Early morning *blanket drill, starching the sheets, polishing the tent pole*.

hitching to heaven *n*. More thumb-based *hand to gland* combat.

Hitler piss *n*. A braced, Nazi salute position from which to have a drunken *Chinese singing lesson* at the pub toilet trough.

Hitler tash *n*. A *clitler*, a *Lamborghini*.

Hitler wank *n*. An act of *self-pollution* performed in a shower with the left arm lodged firmly against the cubicle wall to prevent loss of balance.

HMP *abbrev*. A lady for whom only the finest things in life will do. High Maintenance Pussy.

hobbit *n*. A small hairy thing.

hobbit dick *n*. A *penis* that is wider than it is long. A *tuna can cock, Welshman's cock, choad, chooza*.

hobble squat *n*. The locomotive technique employed by one who has just *released the chocolate hostage*, only to discover that there is a marked dearth of *shit tickets* in his *chod booth*. Also known as the *convict's shuffle, jailbreak, paperchase* or *the penguin*.

hobgoblin *n*. A *bumgoblin*.

hobnail boots, that one wore *exclam*. A phrase shouted loudly in order to make the most of a volubly-*dropped gut*. *'In polite company, following another's audible act of flatulence, it is permissible to offer a comment. If the wind* *breaker was the wife of a Governor General, one might say 'One-nil to you, your Excellency'. If the younger son of a Duke has farted, a comment such as 'Fuck me, that one wore hobnail boots, my Lord, would be perfectly acceptable.'* (from *Debrett's Etiquette*, 1928).

hobnob 1. *n.* A big, dirty *ringpiece*, barnacled with such an excess of *winnetry* that it takes on the appearance of the much-loved, family biscuit. *'Oi, Moyles. Put your trousers back on, will you. I don't want to look at your fly-ridden hobnnob, you fat cunt.'* 2. *n.* A particularly more-ish biscuit. *'Oi, Moyles. Have you eaten the whole packet of hobnobs again, you fat cunt? And ten big cakes and four stones of sausages.'* 3. *v.* To associate with one's social superiors. *'Oi, Moyles. Have you been hob-nobbing with Rose West again? You fat cunt.'* 4. *v.* To engage in sexual congress on a kitchen work surface, especially the top of the cooker. To have a *cillit bang. 'That Chris Moyles is a fat cunt, isn't he?'*

Ho Chi Minge *euph.* A straggly, unkempt *nether beard* on a female lady. From its likeness to the straggly, unkempt-*fanny*-like *face fungus* of the popular North Vietnamese leader. *'And our final guest on Question Time tonight is former transport minister Glenda Jackson, who is the only Oscar-winner ever to hold a high office of state in this country, having won the 1969 Best Actress Academy Award for her performance in Women in Love. However, she is probably better known to filmgoers in this country for her part in Ken Russell's Tschaikovsky bio-pic The Music Lovers, where you could see her Ho Chi Minge. Eeurgh.'*

hockmagandy *n.* The one day of the year when Scotsmen *fuck* their wives. *McFannyversary.*

hoeing the HP *v. Uphill gardening* on the *brown sauce allotment.*

HOFNAR 1. *n.* prop. A mid-nineties Seattle-based college band. 2. *acron.* US. Hard On For No Apparent Reason.

hog's eye *n.* The serving hatch through which *perseverance soup* arrives.

hog's eye hairpiece *n. Aus.* That long, piss-combed tuft of hair that seems to grow out the end of a dog's *unit.* Like on the top of Woody Woodpecker's head.

hogans *n. US. Heroic charlies, Gert Stonkers, Norma Snockers.*

hold your nerve *v.* To bravely *step on a duck* when suffering from a bout of the *runs.* To *twist on nineteen.*

hole 1. *n.* Anything you can stick something up. 2. *n.* The next category of sexual attainment up the scale after *cloth tit; tops* and *fingers.*

hole in one *n.* Successful penile intromission without using the hand for guidance.

holiday money *n.* Male genitalia, the *family jewels, meat and two veg,* the *fruit bowl.*

holiday on rice *n.* Any trip to a foreign locale where the exotic cuisine sampled enthusiastically on the first day leaves one with such a bad case of the *shits* that one only dares eat boiled rice, or something equally bland, for the rest of one's stay. *'Oh yes, Sid had the tom yam goong as his starter and I had the pla nueng manao. For the main course he had chu chi pla kraphong, and I went for the suea rong hai and kaeng khae. For pudding, we both had the khanom bua loi. It really was absolutely deli-*

cious. *The rest of the fortnight was a holiday on rice.'*

Hollyoats *n.* A leisurely Sunday afternoon bout of *personal pollution* enjoyed whilst watching the omnibus edition of the blonde-heavy Chester-based soap. Careful control is required to avoid emptying one's *saddlebags* as Mr Cunningham appears on screen, or when it cuts back to Nick Grimshaw in the *T4* studio.

Hollywood wax *n.* A completely depilated *mingepiece*. A *Barthez.*

Hollywood ending 1. *n.* A satisfying cinematic denouement in which good triumphs over evil and everyone goes home happy. 2. *n.* A *tom tit* that necessitates no wiping.

Hollywood loaf *n.* A *podge-on, half a teacake.* So named because of its popularity with male actors called upon to perform in the nude.

holmaphobe *n.* A person with an entirely rational hatred of fat *fuck* Eamonn Holmes.

holy trinity 1. *n.* A scene in a *bongo movie* where a triumvirate of male thespians simultaneously enter a single actress via the three main access portals thoughtfully provided by Mother Nature. 2. *n.* One twenty pound note, one tenner and one fiver destined for a quiet night down the pub. 3. *n.* A *shit*, a shower and a shave, though not necessarily in that order. 4. *n.* Engaging in anal, oral and vaginal sex in one session.

homburger *n.* A vegetarian fast food option for *good listeners.*

home baking aisle 1. *n.* The least popular section of the supermarket. 2. *n.* The *arse crack*, where *air biscuits, chocolate logs* and *fudge loaf* are prepared.

home brew *n.* Laser-print quality *grumble mags* made from *cyber scud.*

hominous *adj.* Of events, about to turn gay with tragic consequences. *'I've just been invited back to a swimming pool party at the home of a popular comedian, all-round entertainer and quiz-show host.' 'That sounds hominous.'*

hommage *n.* Act of devotion performed in a kneeling position.

homnambulist *n.* Chap who gets an inexplicable urge to go walking about on Hampstead Heath in the wee small hours.

homoclaustrophobia *n.* Mainly irrational fear of being trapped in an enclosed space with a *bad thrower.*

homosexual *n.* A man or woman who is attracted to members of his or her own gender. Often at bus stops. From the Greek homos = lifter, sexualos = togas.

homversation *n.* Of males, the discussion of anything at all except cars and football, but particularly *Coronation Street*, clothes, hair and cottaging anecdotes.

honesty box bargain *n.* A *five fingered discount* available to the value-conscious shopper at railway station newsagents. Named after the express counter which used to be thoughtfully provided for the use of passengers who were in a hurry not to pay.

honey altar *n.* The sunken treasure that the *muff diver* goes in search of.

honeymoon period *n.* For a bloke, the happy, short-lived period between his bird's *rag weeks.*

honeypot *n.* A waxy *fanny* surrounded by bees.

Hong Kong Pooey *n.* A process of deduction undertaken whilst ensconced on the *throne* with a bad dose of the *Brads*, whereby the previous day's meals are pondered over in the style of the eponymous cheaply-animated *shite* 1970s martial arts/janitor/dog/crimefighter cartoon series. "Was it the binding four-egg omelette for breakfast? No. Was it the cheese pastie and Scotch egg lunch? No. Was it the gallon of Guinness and chicken Madras supper? Could be!"

honkies *n*. Big *muckspreader* round back.

honk up *v*. To *hoy up, bowk*.

honour the crowd *v*. To *let rip* with such an evil smell that innocent bystanders are forced to stand and applaud. *'And Henman honours the crowd as he bends down to pick up his kit for his annual Wimbledon early exit, and gracious me, judging by the stains on his shorts, the poor fellow must have followed through.'* (Dan Maskell (deceased) BBC TV commentary).

hooberstank *n*. The first, and usually biggest, *fart* of the morning. *Morning thunder, reveille, dawn chorus*. A *breakfast maker*.

hoobs 1. *n*. A bizarre set of Muppet aliens which appear on Channel 4 in the mornings. 2. *n*. A particularly impressive set of *funbags* which, if they made a sound, which they do not, would make a sound not unlike blowing across the top of a jeroboam. From huge + boobs. Also *hoobies*.

hoodwink 1. *v*. To deceive, or mislead by falsehood, *eg*. When selling endowment mortgages or pension schemes. 2. *v*. The act of squeezing the *fiveskin* over the *Dutch strawberry* in order to encourage the last few drops of *piss* to exit the *blow hole*.

hoofpaste *n*. A feminine hygiene product,

eg. *Vagisil, Canestan* or *Sprunt*.

hooker 1. *n*. US. A *ho'*, a *pro*. 2. *n*. A bloke in a rugby scrum who performs sexual favours in return for money.

hooker's toothpaste *n*. *Slag hammer yoghurt*.

hooking fish *v*. *Feeding the ducks, stabbing the cat*.

hoop *n*. That aperture into which a man might slam a *dunky*.

hoopage *n*. A spot of the old *bum sex*. *'The lotus floats upon the lake in the moonlight / Knickers off love and bend over / I fancy a bit of hoopage for a change.'* (from *Up the Bum No Babies - a Haiku Collection* by Matsunaga Teitoku).

hoop flogger *n*. A lady who is *on the batter*.

hoop, furry *n*. *Sweep's brush*.

hoop soup *n*. *medic*. The *runs, trots, squits etc*. Galloping diarrhoea. *'Sorry I had to rush off while you were talking to me just then, only I've had this terrible hoop soup for weeks, and I felt another burst coming on. Anyway, I'm back now. Can I finish taking your order?' I can particularly recommend the caramel mousse.'*

hoop stretcher *n*. A *crafty butcher* who hides his *salami* in a *tea towel holder*.

hootchie *n*. US. *Totty, blit, muff*.

hootchie cootchie *n*. *Hanky panky, how's your father*.

hooter *n*. Conk, *neb, sneck*. Nose. Not the singular of *hooters*.

hootermammy *n*. A former *Miss Lincolnshire* who receives a visit from the *titty fairy* during pregnancy. One who has *collected the baby bonus*.

hooters *n*. Bazookas, baps, headlamps. Not the plural of *hooter*.

Hoover's disease *n*. *medic*. Condition

contracted by all women shortly after they get married, where they make a continual whining sound but don't suck any more. Also *Dyson's syndrome.*

hoover up *v.* To try, usually unsuccessfully, to "sniff up" the smell of a recently dropped *fart* when one sees an attractive woman approaching.

HOP/hop *acronym.* Hang Over Poo. Giant, exceedingly loose stool, the noisy passing of which is a significant milestone in the recovery from a hangover. An *alcopoop*, an *escape sub.* *'Ahh! I feel much better after that hop. Anyone fancy a pint?'*

hop into the horse's collar *v.* Nip to the *municipal cock wash.*

hopper arse *n.* A *forty guts*, *salad dodger.* A *big-boned* person, with really fat *glands.*

hoptical illusion *n.* A ropey *piece* who appears beautiful when viewed through *beer goggles.*

horatio *n.* Posh Latin term used by doctors, lawyers and police to describe a *chewie.*

horizontal jogging *n.* Hilarious euphemism for sexual intercourse, esp. "a bit of the old...".

horizontally accessible *adj.* Describing a young lady with *yoyo knickers.*

horn chorus *n.* A very loud, early morning wakeup call from an adjacent hotel or halls of residence room, usually at around three am or, failing that, about half an hour after the local nightclubs kick out. The *horn chorus* is typically accompanied by the sound of squeaking bedsprings and/or a rhythmic thumping noise on the connecting wall.

hornbag 1. *n.* A bag for keeping horns in. 2. *n.* An extremely attractive woman, *ie.*

One who gives you *the horn.*

horndog *n.* An extremely unattractive woman, *ie.* One who loses you the *horn.* A *derection.*

horn, the *n.* Ceremonial symbol of a man's affection for a woman, paradoxically given by the woman to the man.

horny 1. *adj.* The state of a man whilst in possession of *the horn*, or indeed a woman who fancies a shot on it. 2. *adj.* Descriptive of a woman who gives a man *the horn.* *'Hey, that Kate Silverton on BBC News 24 is well horny.'*

horse eating oats *sim.* Feeding the pony. *'And David went unto the house of Bathsheba and she had not known her husband Naboth for ages. And David did put his hand down her knickers and lo, it was like a horse eating oats.'* (*Deuteronomy 6:23*).

horse's collar 1. *n.* Vagina. 2. *sim.* Comparison implying generous *farmyard* proportions. *Cathedral, clown's pocket, hippo's mouth. 'I wouldn't say my wife's got a tight minge, ladies and gentlemen. That's because she's got a fanny like a horse's collar.'*

horse's doofers *n.* Superlative *mutt's nuts, dog's bollocks*, bee's knees. The *donkey's knob.*

horse's handbrake *n.* A *diamond cutter*, a *concrete donkey*, a raging *bone on* wrought from *pink steel.*

horseshoe, the *n.* The act of arranging one's favourite *technical manuals* in a semicircular fashion, each one opened at its most alluring double-page spread, before indulging in a session of frenzied *self pollution.* A *Dutch rainbow, crescent wank.*

horse's head, sitting on a *n.* Of people queueing for the *dunny*, to be suffering from a more extreme case of the *turtle's head*. *'Hurry up will you, I'm sitting on a horse's head out here.'*

horse's nose *n.* The early stages of a *Beverley Craven* being allowed to grow out. Noticeable when *feeding the pony. Five o'clock fanny.*

hosebag *n.* Woman of loose morals. She with a *twat* like a *paper hanger's bucket. A boot, slapper.*

hose job *n. Blow job, chewie, horatio.*

hose monster *n.* An ugly woman who cannot get enough hosepipes.

hospital button *n.* A particularly unhealthy looking *gold watch. 'Call 999 love. I've just howked up a hospital button.'*

hot *adj.* Condition which, in conjunction with *horny*, is often used to describe ugly, fat, bored women eating crisps and doing the *Take a Break* crossword on the end of expensive telephone sex lines, *eg. 'Hot and horny bitches thirsty for your love seed. £1.80/min.'*

HOTBOT/hotbot *acronym.* The expression of one's desire for a *dog's marriage.* Hang Out The Back Of That.

hot circle *n.* Letting go of a particularly rancid *Exchange & Mart* and then walking round a (seated or standing) group of unsuspecting friends, thus imprisoning them in an invisible, sulphurous stockade from which there is no escape.

hot cross bunning *n.* The act of *icing* one's ladyfriend's face in two perpendicular sweeps, with the intention of creating a physiognomical effect eerily remniscent of the popular glazed Easter-time confectionery sweetmeat.

hot cup of tea with two lumps *n.* The practice of *teabagging*, but this time with the lady's mouth full of hot water. *Warming the pod, PG lips, dick brew.*

hot dog *1. n.* An egg delicacy famously enjoyed by the cult actor Divine in the film *Pink Flamingoes* (Children's Film Foundation, 1977). *2. v.* To eat said morsel, freshly laid by a poodle. *3. v.* To slap one's *sausage* into a lady's *buns*, with plenty of onions.

hot-dog end *n.* The *turtle's head*. From the similarity to how a hot-dog sausage looks when poking out of the end of a bread roll. *'Hurry up in the shit house, gran. I've got a hot dog end here.'*

hotel toast *euph.* Descriptive of a girl who's not as *hot* as she once was.

hot fish yoghurt *n.* Cream sauce filling for a *hairy pie.*

hot hello *n.* The warm trickle down her leg that reminds a lady of the deposit that was recently made into her *special bank.*

hot karl *n.* Post-anal sex *horatio.*

hot lunch *n.* See *Cleveland steamer.* Or better still, don't.

hot meat injection *n.* An inoculation with the *spam syringe.*

hot monocle *n.* Half a *Velma.* A facial ejaculation which reduces one's *bird's* ability to see by fifty percent. Also *Gabrielle, King Harold.*

hots, the *n.* What *birds* get for Spanish waiters.

hotty *n. US. Totty, blart.*

hot water bottle *n.* An unattactive woman who is taken into a bloke's bed purely in order to keep it warm. *'I don't know what he sees in her.' 'She's a hot water bottle. He'll chuck her in the Spring.'*

hound *n.* Offensively sexist term for a *dog, steg, boiler.*

hound cable *n. Barker's rope, footstool. Dog shite.*

housewarming gift, leave a *v.* To make a

deposit in the toilet of a friend's house, but not pull the chain.

hovis *n.* A particularly tight *snapper*. A *butler's cuff*. From the bread advertising slogan "White with all the goodness of brown."

Howard *n.* When an altruistic chap has *blown his beans* up his ladyfriend, but takes advantage of his last few seconds of penile hardness to generously give her a couple of extra pushes for good luck. A "little Xtra", named after bespectacled building society mouthpiece Howard off of the Halifax adverts. If the pushes are administered up the *bird's dirtbox*, it is called a *Howard brown*, thus using the poor fellow's full name for a cheap comic effect.

Howard's Way *rhym. slang. Colwyn Bay.* From the shit BBC TV drama of the same name. *'Mum, Dad, I've got something to tell you. I'm Howard's Way.'*

how much? *exclam.* Amusing mock-shocked utterance from one who has just *broken wind. Don't tear it, I'll take the whole piece; that's working, now try your lights.*

how's your father *n.* Sex. Often prefixed "Fancy a quick bit of... ahem...?"

hoy *v.* To throw, lob, chuck, esp. beer down one's neck.

hoy up *v.* To *spew up, barf,* esp. beer up one's neck.

HPS *abbrev.* Horizontal Payment Scheme. Female method of remuneration favoured by taxi drivers, traffic wardens and drug dealers. Also *hairy cheque book, gash card.*

HP sauce *n.* Viscous fluid found in the *dunghampers* of excitable *birds.* A savoury condiment product of the *haddock pastie.*

HR department *1. n.* The Human Resources section of a business, whatever that means. *2. n.* An impressive set of *competitive advantages.* A *Huge Rack. 'Phwooar! You've got a very impressive HR department there, Lord Owen. I bet you don't get many of them to the pound.'*

HRTV *abbrev.* Any daytime television programe which is primarily aimed at bored, middle-aged housewives, *eg. This Morning, Loose Women, Des and Mel, Biker Buildoff etc.*

huby *n.* A semi-erect penis, a *dobber, half a teacake,* a lazy *lob on.*

huffle *v.* To *bagpipe.* To take part in an *Hawaiian muscle-fuck.*

Hughie Green *n.* A swift *wank* taken when "opportunity knocks". *'Mr Pickwick closed the door behind Mrs Fezzyfelt, sat down behind his old oak desk, and took the turnip watch from his waistcoat pocket. 'Odds bodkins,' he shouted. 'Five minutes until Mr Sticklebrick arrives. Time enough for a swift Hughie Green.''* (from *The Pickwick Papers* by Charles Dickens).

Hugo Boss *n.* The act of holding the wife's or girlfriend's head under one's quilt after *farting.* A *Dutch oven.* From the male perfume advertising slogan "Your fragrance. Your rules".

hulk on *n.* An instant and unstoppably enthusiastic erection, that refuses to be calmed and threatens to burst through the slacks.

hulk spunk *n.* Snot.

hum *1. v.* To *ming,* stink. *2. v.* To sing with the lips closed, or as near to closed as possible during a *hum job. 3. n.* A Bad smell.

hum job *n.* Vegetarian oral sex involving

no meat, just *two veg.* accompanied by simultaneous humming of the musical variety.

Humber Bridge *1. n.* Suspended estuary crossing which connects Grimsby to Hull and thus *2. n.* The thing on a lady which links the *fishy bit* to the *shitty bit.* The *taint, tinter, carse.*

humble grumble *n.* Poor man's porn, *eg.* Women's Health Week leaflets pressed into service as *monomanual literature. Paupernography.*

humdinger *n.* A *fart* which makes the wallpaper peel.

hummer *1. n.* A large, butch military vehicle favoured by Californian hairdressers and Arnold Schwarzenegger. *2. n.* Arse, *bum. 3. n.* A *humdinger.*

hummersexual *n.* One who finds himself so deficient in the *trouser department* that neither a sports car nor a vast Harley Davidson motorbike can furnish sufficient compensation, and so he is forced to climb behind the wheel of an absurdly large and comically butch 4x4 vehicle. *'Born on This Day in History: Honzhi, Emperor of China, 1470; Henry Ford, Motor Industry Pioneer, 1863; Emily Bronte, Novelist, 1818; Vladimir Zworykin, Russian Physicist, 1889; Arnold Schwarzenegger, Hummersexual Actor, 1947.'*

hummingbird, hung like a *adj.* Having a *cock* like a *Chinese mouse.*

hummingbird's wing *sim.* Descriptive of the speed of a naughy lady's fingers whilst interfering with her *bodily treasure. 'I come home from the pub last night and caught the missus playing her banjo to an Enrique Iglesias video. Her fingers were going like a fucking hummingbird's wing, I can tell you.'*

hump *1. v.* To *shag*, have sex in the style of an old Labrador with its *lipstick* out. *2. v.* To carry heavy amplification equipment to and from a live music venue whilst one's *arse* sticks out the back of one's jeans.

hump and dump *1. v.* To behave in an ungentlemanly manner towards a young lady who you've picked up. See also *FANTA. 2. n.* Unkind name for the young lady concerned.

Humphrey *n.* An artistic U-bend *skidmark*, named after the late actor Humphrey Bogart.

humpty *n.* The act of *humping.*

hunchback spiders *n.* Ladies' hairy nipples.

hunchie *n.* A particularly difficult *mudchild*, that leaves one contorted like a constipated labrador in the park.

hungry arse *n.* Condition afflicting women whereby their *bills* disappear up the *crack* of their *hummer* as they walk.

hungry hippos *1. n.* Frantic and quickly-broken 1970s board game for children. *2. euph.* Affectionate collective epithet for a herd of salivating, *salad-dodging* lasses in the queue for one's local *kebabulance* after a night on the *tart fuel.*

hunt for brown October *n.* The act of seeking out and destroying a *U-bend U-boat.* With a bog brush, stick or barbecue utensil.

hurl *1. v.* To *hoy. 2. v.* To *hoy up.*

hurt yourself *v.* To vigorously *relax in a gentleman's way. 'Thanks for that new porn, mate. I'm going to go home now and hurt myself.'*

hush puppies *n. Blouse hounds* so cute that all red-blooded men are rendered speechless in their presence.

hussy *n.* A shameless woman, a drunk

and an unfit mother.

hymen climbin' *n.* The act of being the first felow to plant his *flagpole* up *Mount Venus*. Plucking a *bird's virgin string*.

hyperfentilation *n.* Mild dizzyness caused by deep breathing whilst wearing a *musk mask*.

hypnotits *n.* Export strength *hush puppies*.

"I am the Spirit of Christmas Past."

'Quite satisfied, Scrooge closed the door and locked himself in; double-locked himself in, which was his custom on these occasions. Thus secured against surprise, he took off his cravat; put on his dressing-gown and slippers, and his nightcap; and sat down before the fire with a copy of *Razzle* for a quick one o'er the thumb.' ~ *A Christmas Carol* by Charles Dickens.

I bet that holds some shit! *exclam*. A compliment proffered to a *bird* with a big *arse*.

Ibiza itch *n. medic*. Any *happyrash* or minor *Doonican* caught by one's *downstairs unmentionables* whilst holidaying on the popular nsu-kissed Mediterranean island. *'He's the man, the man with the Midas...Sorry Mr Broccoli, I've got to go and put some ointment on me clopper. I've got Ibiza itch something rotten.' 'I know, love. We could hear you scratching at it over the French horns.'*

IBM *1. n. prop*. A large computer company. *2. abbrev*. Itty Bitty Meat. A small *hampton*. *3. abbrev*. Inches Below Muff. The units in which a *greyhound skirt* is measured.

IBS *1. abbrev. medic*. Irritable Bowel Syndrome, a condition of the *Camillas* chiefly characterised by abdominal pain, urgent bowel movements and diarrhoea, the cause of which remains fundamentally unknown. *2. abbrev. medic*. Irrational Bitter Skitters, a condition of the *Camillas* chiefly characterised by abdominal pain, urgent bowel movements and diarrhoea, the cause of which is *necking* too much brown beer. The *cask ale can-can* or *real ale rumba*.

I can't believe it's not batter *n*. KY Jelly, *granny batter*.

I can't believe it's nut butter *exclam*. *'Oi, waiter. What's this funny-tasting stuff spread on my bread rolls?' 'It's I can't believe it's nut butter, Mr Winner. And all the chefs have wanked into your soup too, you fat cunt.'*

ICBM *acronym*. Of modern day state-of-the-art trouser weaponry, an Inter Cuntinental Ballistic Missile.

iced fingers *n*. Bakers' confectionery-speak for the results of *glazing the knuckle*.

ice docking *n*. The saucy practice of titilating a lady using a *dildo* carved from a frozen *turd*.

ice the cake *v*. To decorate a *tart* with *cream*. Often seen in European *grumble flicks*. *'Gunther! There's only thirty seconds of tape left in the camera. Quick, ice that cake!'*

ice the log *n*. An environmentally-sound toilet visit where one has a *wank* after a *shit*, thereby saving water on the flush and halting global warming.

I closed my eyes and she slipped away *Phr*. A phrase best employed when reflecting on a lengthy and emotional relationship with, and subsequent painful splitting-up from, a *power ballad* of monstrous proportions. From the 1976 Boston hit *More than a Feeling*.

i-fart *n*. A *crowd pleaser* released whilst listening to a portable MP3 player on earphones which, in the *benefactor*'s head was a stealthy, undercover *one cheek sneak* but which, to the other occupants of the carriage, was a veritable *call to prayer*.

if that's not out I'm not playing *exclam*. A Wildean post-flatulatory aphorism.

if you're selling that bike saddle... *exclam*. A light-hearted phrase shouted out by a jolly van driver to help boost the self-esteem of a comely female velocipedist.

Iggy popshot *n. Whacking* off on a *TV*'s ass.

ignoranus *n*. One who is not only incredibly thick, but an *arsehole* to boot.

Ikea bulb *n*. A lady that *blows* first time one *turns her on*.

I know a good cure for that *exclam*. A slightly unsympathetic reply given by a dispenser of *man medicine* to his girlfriend when she complains about an ailment of some sort.

I'll bet he doesn't eat his crusts *exclam.* Said of a chap who, it would appear, is unlikely to wade his way through small bodies of standing water, has a penchant for taking his peas minted and who rarely, if ever, encounters significant difficulty when dealing with colours.

I'll give it five *1. exclam.* Brummishly-accented catchphrase coined by diminutive Wednesbury minx Janice Nicholls on *Thank Your Lucky Stars* in the 1960s. *2. exclam.* Catchphrase used in countless West Midlands homes on a Sunday morning, when the lady of the house wants to use the *bog* after her man.

I'll name that tune in one *1. exclam.* Said after a warm up on the *trouser trumpet*, especially if Tom O'Connor's round. *2. n.* A game that can be played when listening to a new Oasis single. *'I'll name that tune in one - it's Jean Genie mixed with Subterranean Homesick Blues.'*

I'm not right *exclam.* Recognition that the noisome miasma from one's alimentary canal has eventually proved too rich for one's olfactory senses. A reaction to the fact that the speaker has delivered a *stinker* that not even its own mother can love. *'Are you happiness, my dear Albert?' 'Nein my leibchen Victoria, I'm not right. It must of been them French eggs I had at the Great Exhibition.'*

Imperial barge *n.* The male member. A particularly majestic *skin boat*. *'You should have seen how Mrs Eisenhower's eyes lit up when my nine-inch imperial barge heaved into view.'* (from *The Memoirs of Winston Churchill*).

impersonate Stalin *v.* To perform oral sex on a woman, *don the beard, eat hairy pie*. *'Hold tight up there love, I'm just gonna do a quick impersonation of Stalin.'*

in-box *1. n.* A deskbound office receptacle for messages, communiques, unpaid bills and the like. *2. n.* A lady's *furry hoop*. *'What shall I do with this, Miss Pleasurecraft?' 'Oh, just stick it in my in-box.'*

incapability brown *n.* A *shit* in the garden, left by a passing drunkard.

Indian mustard *n.* Diarrhoea.

Indian rope trick *1. n.* An impressive erection attained under seemingly impossible circumstances, *eg.* After twelve pints and/or six *wanks. 2. n.* The process of having a*n Ingrid Pitt* whilst standing on one's head, the object being to see how high you can raise your magical *cable* without it breaking up into individual *Bungle's fingers.*

indoor fishing *v.* A coarse form of *angling for tadpoles.*

indoor hobo *n.* One who lives inside, but looks like they should be living in a doorway, *eg.* Johnny Vegas, Ricky Tomlinson, Tracey Emin. A *tramp's mate.*

indoor sports *n.* Exercise; specifically a workout for the right arm and wrist.

infellation *n.* The rising cost of *Boris Johnsons.* *'Ooh, this infellation is terrible. I remember the days when you could get the bus into town, a slap up tea at the Lyon's Corner House and a whore to suck you off in a doorway afterwards, and you'd still have change from half a crown.'*

Ingrid *1. rhym. slang.* An act of anal excretion. Named after the luscious "tits out" *Hammer Horror* actress Ingrid Pitt. *2. rhym. slang. A lady's jubbly.* Named after the luscious *"Ingrids* out*" Hammer Horror* actress Ingrid Pitt.

inheritance *n.* A miasmatic bequest bequeathed to a toilet-goer by the previous occupant.

injury time *1. n.* The dying seconds of a football match where the losing side throw caution to the wind and take a shot at anything in a desperate attempt to score. *2. n.* The last song of the evening in a nightclub.

Inman's twitch *n.* The brisk, staccato, buttock-clenched walk to the toilet when one is attempting to prevent *turtle* egress. From the gait adopted by late 1970s sitcom actor John Inman.

in off *1. n.* In billiards and snooker, the potting of an intended ball following a felicitous ricochet. *2. n.* Also in billiards and snooker, the potting of an unintended ball following an infelicitous ricochet. *3. n.* In sexual relations the potting of a supposedly unintended *difficult brown* caused by a suspiciously felicitous ricochet whilst aiming for an *easy pink. 'Sorry dear. I must have got an in off there.'*

in receivership *adj.* Involved in a toilet situation which necessitates a sudden complete *clearout of stock*. A *dump* where "everything must go". *'I'm afraid Sir Clive can't come to the phone right now as he is in receivership. If you're phoning to complain about the shitty rubber keys on your ZX81 computer, please press one. If you're phoning because your C5 has run out of battery power after less than a hundred yards, please press two. For all other enquiries, please press three.'*

inside burns *n. Thighbrows, judge's eyebrows, Rhodes Boysons.* Effusive lateral *pubage* out the sides of a young lady's *dunghampers. 'I'm with you all the way on burning your bra and everything, Germaine. But could you do something about your inside burns? They're putting me off my stroke.'*

inside job *n.* A game of *pocket billiards.* Vigorously and rhythmically looking for change in your front pockets at a sophisticated lap-dancing establishment. An *IPW.*

installing Windows *n.* Excuse given to the missus when one intends to lock oneself in the spare room and *wank* one's *plums* flatter than Tara Palmer-Tompkinson's chest over a series of hardcore internet *grumble* websites. *'What are you doing in there, Jerry? Tom and Barbara are waiting downstairs with a birthday cake for you.' 'Nothing Margot, just installing Windows. Could you push some more tissues under the door, please?'*

interior decorating *n.* Slapping a bit of white emulsion about the womb using the *naughty paintbrush.*

international breeding programme *1. n.* Zoological project whereby examples of endangered species are paired with overseas counterparts in order to maintain a healthy gene pool. *2. n.* A cheap holiday in Tenerife.

internectuals *n.* Those people who consider themselves part of the academic elite as a consequence of their ability to look stuff up on Wikipedia.

internet ready *adj.* Descriptive of one who already *paddles the skin canoe* with their left hand.

internetty *n.* A lavatory cubicle which is within laptop wireless network range, allowing a computer literate toilet-user to browse the worldwide web for antiquarian books, to pick an example at random, whilst he is seated on the *thunder box* masturbating furiously.

interrogate the prisoner *v.* To *box the Jesuit, strangle the parson, choke the chicken, bash the bishop, pull the Pope's cap off, have a five knuckle shuffle, pull your pud, spank the monkey etc.* To interfere with oneself in the *farmyard area*. *'Richard, come down and get your tea.' 'I'll be right down, Judy. I'm just interrogating the prisoner. Into your shoe.'*

in the club *adj.* Up the duff, pregnant, preggers. From *in the pudding club*.

in the hockey team *adj.* Descriptive of a lesbidaceous woman. Or *lady golfer*.

in there like swimwear *euph.* Descriptive of one who ingratiates himself with ease. A reference to the way bathing togs have a marked tendency to go straight up your *arsehole*. *'Did you see Ronnie Wood with that busload of Eastern European waitresses who are young enough to be his daughters? He was in there like swimwear.'*

in through the out door *1. n.* Title of Led Zeppelin's not very good final album. *2. n.* How Robert "Percy" Plant might refer to a spot of *back door action*.

investigating kung fu gangs *euph.* The deadly act of bizarre auto-erotic asphyxiation, in the course of which a fellow *chokes his chicken* furiously whilst strung up like a choked chicken in a butcher's window. After David Carradine's family's frankly unconvincing explanation for how the late actor met his grisly fate in a hotel wardrobe.

in vino fertilisation *n.* The usual manner in which babies are conceived.

iplod *n.* A speed camera.

ipod earphones *n.* Particular type of *jelly jewellery* furnished simultaneously by two generous gentlemen engaged in an act of *double glazing*. Stereophonic streams of *jitler* dribbling down from a lady's ears. *Shot by both sides.*

iprod *n.* Small portable device that annoys other passengers on crowded buses and trains.

Ipswich smile *n.* A *pasata grin*.

iPud *n.* A portable, self-contained source of cheap entertainment which can be accessed via the trouser pockets and which keeps commuters smiling on crowded tube trains.

IPW *acronym.* The act of rummaging for change in one's trousers whilst in a lapdancing establishment. In-Pocket Wank, an *inside job*.

Irish *1. n.* Heterosexual anal sex, supposedly as a means of contraception. *UTBNB. 2. rhym. slang.* Hairpiece. From Irish coupe = toupee.

Irish alarm clock *n.* Ten pints of Guinness. From the fact that a night on the black stuff more often than not leads to horrific, involuntary bowel movements which cause one to wake early the next morning. *'I hope you don't sleep in tomorrow. You're piloting a Space Shuttle up to the International Space Station, remember?' 'Don't worry, dear. I've set my Irish alarm clock.'*

Irish bhaji *n.* The sort of black, spicy, onion-smelling *Thora* which emerges from the *back body* the morning after one takes on board an excessive amount of stout.

irish luggage *n.* Politically incorrect phrase used to describe the life's accumulations of a *paraffin*, traditionally carted about in a picturesque knotted hankerchief on the end of a stick slung over his shoulder, but more usually in an old supermarket trolley filled with *shitty* bundles of carrier bags.

Irish shave *n*. A *dump*.

Irish toothache 1. *n*. An erection, *bone on*. *'Is that a gun in your pocket, or have you just got Irish toothache?'* 2. *n*. Pregnancy. *'Is that a spacehopper in your smock, or have you just got Irish toothache?'*

iron *rhym. slang*. A *crafty butcher*. From Iron hoof = poof.

IRS 1. *abbrev. US*. The yankee taxman. 2. *abbrev*. Itchy Ring Syndrome. Irritating anal affliction caused by insufficient wiping of the *chocolate starfish*, or by inflammation of the *farmers*.

I say! *interj*. Caddish expression of delight upon seeing a pair of *dunces' hats*. See also *ding! dong!*

I shot the sheriff *exclam*. A humorous rhetorical apopthegm uttered upon leaving the crapper after dropping a *U-bend straightener*. From the line in the eponymous Bob Marley song, *viz*. "One day the bottom will drop out".

Isle of Wight 1. *n*. A UK holiday destination made popular by Queen Victoria. 2. *rhym. slang*. A load of rubbish. From Isle of Wight = pile of shite. *'That holiday we had on the Isle of Wight last summer was a complete Isle of Wight. We're going to Wales this year.'*

i-shuffle *n*. The self-harming behaviour of a fellow watching a *pudcast* on his ipod. An *i-wank*.

isnae *n. Scot*. The *taint, tintis, ABC, scruttock*.

issues with tissues *phr*. Euphemistical term used when speaking about someone believed to be a serial masturbator.

'Why can't we give him a knighthood, your Majesty? He presents one of the country's most popular box-based television quizzes, after all.' 'Issues with tissues, Lord Chancellor. Issues with tissues.'

is that Ziggy? *exclam*. Expression which can be used to lighten the mood when one has just *stepped on a duck* in polite company. A reference to the question commonly asked by cigar-chomping holographic sidekick Al when speaking into his multi-dimensional walkie-talkie in an attempt to get in touch with his 1999-based employer in the retrospectively bizarre TV series *Quantum Leap*.

Italian chipper *n*. A filthy dirty masturbating woman. From the fact that the Italian word for a deep-fat fryer is apparently *friggatrice*.

itch *n*. The feeling of mild sexual attraction towards his wife which a married man gets on average once every 7 years.

Itchypoo Park *n*. The area around *spice island* during a bout of *IRS*.

it's a buoy! *exclam*. Useful expression which can be employed following the delivery of a sizeable, floating *Meatloaf's daughter*.

it's a knockout *n*. An amusing pub game where an individual with *legs like snapped candles* has to attempt to carry three brim-full pint glasses through a jostling, crowded hostelry from bar to table without spilling any.

it's his stag *exclam*. Phrase shouted by a merry fellow's intoxicated friends as he is roughly half-nelsoned into the back of a police van the night before his wedding. Possibly not acknowledged as a plea of mitigation in a court of law.

it's the beer talking *exclam*. Phrase offered

by way of an excuse when those killer *ale force winds* start blowing the morning after a night spent swilling *pop*.

I've farted, so I'll finish *exclam*. Humorous riposte to the question, "How much longer are you going to be in there?".

I've lost R2 *exclam*. Said following a particularly vigorous expulsion of faecal matter, which leaves the *shitter* traumatised by a wave of aftershocks. Taken from the destruction of the Death Star scene in the little known 1977 film *Star Wars*.

I've loved in it *exclam*. Humorous staff version of the popular fast food advertising jingle, usually sung whilst preparing or serving *McDonald's special sauce* on the minimum wage.

ivory tower *n*. A night-time erectitivation of the *membrum virile*. A *dreaming spire*, a somnolent *dusk tusk*.

i-wank *n*. A bout of frantic self abuse fuelled by erotic images uploaded onto a portable video player or mobile phone. An *i-wank* is typically followed by a period of soul-destoying guilt and invariably concludes with the hasty deletion of all pornographic material from the aforementioned media device. Also *i-shuffle*.

I want to do a poo at Paul's *phr*. Humorous expression of a desire to engage in a penetrative romance with another fellow's ladyfriend.

I was in Baghdad when you were in your dad's bag *exclam*. A more witty version of "I was doing this when you were still in short trousers", overheard in a warehouse in Warrington.

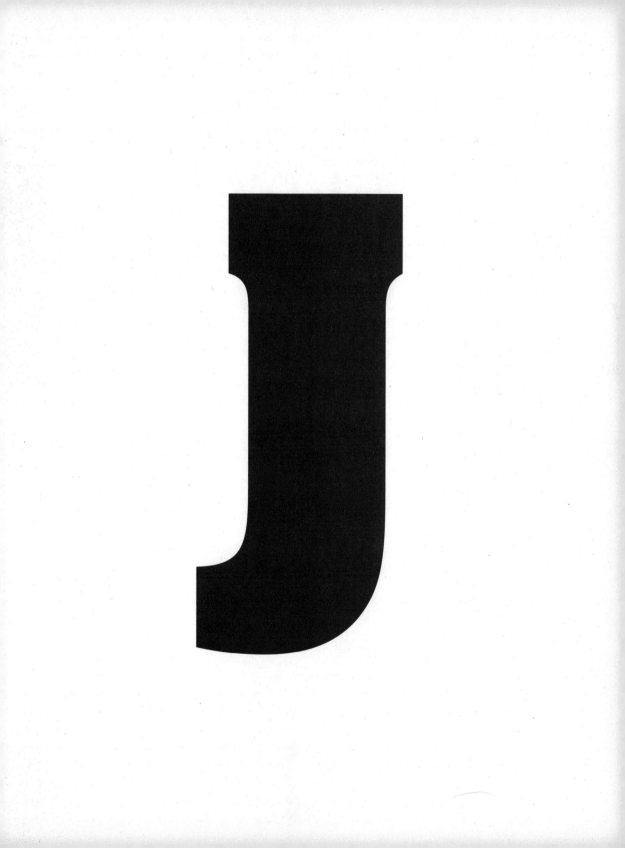

jackage *n. coll.* Any materials used by a fellow for the purposes of *jacking off to, at, on* or *over. Jazz, grumble, grummer, Frankie Vaughan etc.*

jackal, the *1. n.* The mysterious assassin hired to bump off Charles de Gaulle in the novel by Frederick Forsyth, later played by Edward the Eighth in the film of the same name. *2. n.* The moustachioed seventies pornstar lookalike international terrorist from the days back when you didn't have to be scared of terrorists. Him with the sunglasses off the front of the Black Grape album. *3. n.* A gentleman's covert delight; crouching down and sneaking forwards in order to gain proximity to a passing lady's bottom in order to catch a whiff of her *particulars.* An act characteristically accompanied by bared teeth and clawing motions with the hands.

Jack Douglas *1. n. prop.* British film and television performer notable for wearing dungarees and a cap, whose Alf Ippatitimuss character was prone to sudden, spasmodic physical tics and hence *2. n.* Any violent, involuntary recoil from something, *eg.* A pint of milk which has gone off, a blocked train lavatory swimming in urine and faeces, or Shane MacGowan's breath.

jacked up *1. adj.* To be celibate whilst suffering from a *dose. 2. adj.* Of a woman, to be *up on axle stands.*

jack-in-a-box *n.* A thirsty-pet-frightening, Aristotle-confounding *digestive transit* that is, inexplicably, less dense than water, no matter how many flushes are thrown at it.

jack off *v.* To *whack off, choke the chicken, jerk the gherkin.*

jack roll *1. n. SA.* A gang bang. *2. n. US.* A mugging.

jack shit *n. Bugger all, sweet FA,* zero, zilch.* Nowt.

jacksie *n.* Polite word for *arse,* especially in the recepticular context. '*You can stick your fucking knighthood up your jacksie, mate. I paid for a peerage.*'

jacksie rabbit *n. Muddy funster.*

Jackson *n.* A truly disappointing breast. From the infamous "wardrobe malfunction" incident which occurred during the 2004 Super Bowl XXXVIII halftime show, when one of Janet Jackson's rubbishy *knockers* fell out when she was doing some sort of dance routine with Justin Timberlake.

Jackson Bollock *n.* That square of carpet situated between a bachelor's computer chair and his monitor which, were it to be illuminated using an ultraviolet lamp, would resemble nothing so much as a monochrome painting by the more-or-less eponymous American Abstract Expressionist painter.

jacksydent *n.* A trouser mishap, a *follow through.* From jacksie + accident. '*Paula Radcliffe has pulled out of the 10,000 metres final, after suffering a nasty jacksydent during the Marathon.*'

jack the beanstalk *v.* To attempt to pull up the *purple-headed gristle thistle* by the roots.

Jack the ripper *n.* A hard, thick, blood-thirsty *turd* that is *wider than a footballer's tie-knot,* which does its evil work in one's *back passage.* A *ring splitter.*

Jacky Danny *rhym. slang. James Hunt.*

Jacobs *rhym. slang.* Testicles. From Jacobs crackers = bollocks. Generally stored close to the cheese.

Jade yawning, a fanny like *sim.* A tragic *clown's pocket*, an extreme *hippo's mouth*.

Jafaican *n*. The sort of ludicrous artificial Caribbean accent effected by middle class youths.

jaff *v*. To *wank*. In Norfolk. There's nothing else to do in Norfolk. *'Ooh, I just jaffed behind the slaughterhouse. It was boodiful, really boodiful.'*

jaffas *n*. The *nuts* of the *fruit bowl. Family jewels.* *'Ooh, peck me jaffas. That's boodiful, really boodiful.'*

jail bait *n*. Worms dug up by tunnelling prisoners and later, after their escape, used for fishing.

jailbird *1. n*. An habitual criminal, who accepts arrest as an occupational hazard, and presumably accepts imprisonment in the same casual manner, *eg*. "Lord" Jeffrey Archer. *2. n*. An unattractive lady of whom it might be said: "Christ. I'd rather do time than do her." *eg*. That grim *pro* with whom "Lord" Jeffrey Archer *had it off* before giving her two grand in a brown envelope.

jailbreak *n*. Upon discovering that you have run out of *arse paper*, shambling out of the *bog* and across the landing in search of fresh supplies, with your trousers round your ankles like shackles. Also known as *the penguin, convict's shuffle* or *paperchase*.

jake *1. n*. A columnar monument erected in memory of a nice pair of *jamboree bags* one once saw, or a notable scene from a *meat vid*. *2. n. Scot*. An ugly woman, *horndog, lumberjill*.

jamboree bags *n*. Funbags, fat rascals.

jambush *n*. A *blobstrop* that comes out of nowhere.

James *rhym. slang*. A *twat* in the pejorative rather than the gynaecological sense. From the inexplicably popular helium-voiced singer/songwriter James Blunt = fucking cunt.

James Browns *n*. The deeply upsetting noises which emanate from a row of office toilet cubicles during the daily 10.00am works *turd off*. From their similarity to the rambling squeals, incoherent grunts and random vocalisations which passed for lyrics in the songs of the hardest working corpse in showbiz.

James Cameron's camera *euph*. A subaquatic *Thora* which, despite repeated flushing, continues to inhabit the haunting depths of one's U-bend. Named after the deep-sea video equipment submersible that was used to provide footage of the sunken RMS Titanic and which, every time it landed on the wreck or sea-bed, caused a cloud of brown rust particles to swirl about. An *Alvin*.

James Hunt *rhym. slang. Jacky Danny*. Named after the late Formula 1 racing driver and *crumpeteer*.

jammer *n. Carib*. A *pud*. See also *windjammer*.

jammet *n. Carib*. A West Indian term for a *slapper*.

jamming device *1. n*. James Bond-style Cold War espionage contraption, which is designed to prevent radio signals from reaching the enemy. *2. n*. Something rarely if ever encountered by agent 007; a feminine hygiene requisite. Also colloquially known as a *blobstopper, fanny mouse* or *Dracula's teabag*.

jammy dodger *n*. A lady who uses the fact that the *tomato boat has docked* to avoid performing her wifely duty.

jammy todger *n*. Something you wouldn't get off a *jammy dodger*. A *barber's pole*.

jampax *n*. A *clot mop, cotton pony*.

jam rag *n*. A tampon, *fanny mouse*, *chuftie plug*.

jam raid *n*. *Crimson tidal* movement which leaves *tuna town* inaccessible by *skin boat* at certain times of the month.

jam sandwich 1. *n*. A *tomato saucy* three-some featuring two strong-stomached men and a lady who is *reading Cosmo*. 2. *n*. A *rag week snatch*, ie. One with two layers of crust and a sticky red filling. 3. *n*. Unamusing CB-lingo for a police car, used by lorry drivers who think they are behind the wheel of a chrome-laden eighteen-wheeler running moonshine in *Smokey and the Bandit*, but are in fact driving a grimy 1988 Foden loaded with rancid chicken guts along the A515 between Sudbury and Yoxall looking for a *fat-titted* hitch-hiker to grope and possibly murder.

jam session *n*. An improvised ragtime duet.

Jane 1. *n*. A ladies' lavatory. 2. *n*. A *Mary*.

jang *n*. Dong. *'Fuckanory. I've caught me jang in me zip. Court is adjourned.'*

janitorial pleat *n*. An unexpected *stiffy* or *tent pole*, named after the unique and unusually-positioned design feature found only in the work trousers supplied to lecherous old school caretakers.

Japanese flag *n*. Appearance of the *arse-hole* when blighted by *ring sting*. *Arse of the rising sun, Hawaiian sunrise.*

Japanese teardrop *n*. An unexpected single drop of *merry monk* that turns up ten minutes after the *bolt* has been shot, regardless of how thoroughly one mops the *herman*. The *missing fish*.

Jap's eye *n*. Politically incorrect, border-line racist male urethral opening, *hog's eye*, *chap's eye*.

jarred *adj*. Pissed, sloshed, wankered.

J Arthur *rhym. slang*. Wank. From the erstwhile British film distributor J Arthur Rasturbation.

Jason Donovan moment *n*. The *point of no return* when you are about to *cumu-lo* the *nimbus* of a less-than-pleasant *bird*. From the *Joseph and his Amazing Technicolour Dreamcoat* song lyric, as popularised by the eponymous former *Neighbours* hunk and Kylie beau, *viz.* "I close my eyes, pull back the curtains, a-a-aaaargh!"

jaywank *v*. To cross the *Billy Mill Roundabout* without due care and attention. To *change up into sixth gear* without regard to the sticky consequences.

jazz 1. *n*. Improvised music characterised by syncopated rhythms. 2. *n*. The *fadge, mott*. 3. *n*. Sex, intercourse, *the other*. 4. *n*. Frankie Vaughanography.

jazz drummer, go at it like a *sim*. To hunch over one's plate and shovel food into one's mouth at an unseemly speed, in a style reminiscent of Gene Krupa or Buddy Rich giving it *three cocks to the cunt*.

jazz egg *n*. A little *spodge* of *spadge*. A *spoff* of *spuff*, *jot* of *jit*.

jazz festival *n*. The purchase of two or more *Noddy books* at one time.

jazz fusion *n*. The process by which the pages of a *scud mag* are cemented together.

jazz mag *n*. A published pamphlet of artistic material, a gentleman's interest journal. Printed in *whacknicolour*.

jazz magnate 1. *n*. A porn millionaire, one who who has benefited from a series of wristy investments. 2. *n*. A short, blind, hairy-palmed lunatic who owns a substantial stash of *scud mags*.

jazz oyster *n.* A *bongo book snapper*, prised open to reveal the *clematis* within.

jazz potatoes *n.* Spuds which have been *salted* at the kitchen staff's discretion. *Winner's dinners.*

jazz stash *n.* A fellow's library of monomanual reference works. Usually kept on top of a wardrobe, but in Frank Skinner's case kept in several large warehouses on an industrial estate.

jazz talc *n. Bolivian marching powder, showbiz sherbet, Keith Richards' dandruff.*

jazz trumpeter's cheeks *sim.* Descriptive of a lady's well-rounded *arse*. Dizzy Gillespie's-face-style buttocks.

jazz vocalist *n.* One who encourages himself with erotic one-sided *acafella* conversations ("ooh, baby, yeah!" *etc.*) with the girls in his *biff mags* whilst practising *self-pollution.*

JB *n.* See *Jodrell.*

j-cloth *n.* A teenager's phenomenally-absorbent underbed sock, used for cleaning up adolescent spillages.

jebbs *1. n.* Manufacturer of crash helmets and hence *2. n.* Big round *knockers* which carry a BSI kitemark and comply with BS 6658.

Jedi *rhym. slang.* A *turd.* From Jedi knight = shite.

jeeving *n.* The act of *touching a lass up* under her clothing but over her underwear. *Tickling the pony's nose* while it's still got its nosebag on, if you will.

Jehovah's stiffness *n.* An unwelcome erection which arrives at the most inconvenient times and then refuses to leave. A *tiffter, Jake, Eric.*

Jehovah's wetness *n.* In ladies, autonomic dampness *under the bridge* experienced at inopportune moments.

jelly bag *n.* The wrinkled retainer where a gentleman keeps his *Egyptian Halls.* The scrotum. *'How's that, DPM?' 'Sorry, Tracey, nowt's happening yet. Try tickling me jelly bag for a bit. And make it snappy, will you. I'm speaking at a memorial service for the dead of two world wars in twenty minutes.'*

jelly hammock *n.* Drip tray.

jelly jewellery *n.* The earrings, nose studs, fancy spectacles and other facial adornments a lady sometimes receives when she was expecting her partner to give her a *pearl necklace.*

jelly roll *1. n. US. Snatch, muff, totty. 2. n.* Getting *fucked* by a jazz pianist who died in 1941.

jelly water mangos *n.* Large *knockers, gazunkas.*

Jenny *n. US. Boris, minge.*

Jeremy Beadle's thumb, hung like *sim.* An unacceptably tasteless and offensive way of referring to a fellow who is somewhat under-endowed *down there. Hung like a Chinese mouse.*

jerk *n.* A stupid, dim or dull person.

jerking from home *n.* Failing to watch any daytime television due to multiple sessions of *self delight.*

jerkin' the gherkin *n.* Jiggling a small cucumber round on the end of a string.

jerk off *1. v. Jack off. 2. n. US. A goddam dicksplash, asswipe.*

jerkolator *n.* An extremely noisy *blow job*, performed by someone who comes back for coffee.

jerk station *n.* An old computer of limited function and nominal value, used principally to browse the web in search of erotica. A *filth machine* or *dirty mac.*

jerkwad *n. US. Tosser, fuckwit, wankip-*

ants. A person to whom one might show the elevated second finger of one's right hand before rhetorically inviting them to swivel thereupon.

jerry in the trench *euph*. Phrase used when describing an itchy *ringpiece* when one is in polite company. Useful when one finds oneself suffering from an attack of *arse wasps* or *wire spiders* at Glyndebourne, the Hay-on-Wye Literary Festival or the Queen Mother's funeral, for example.

Jersey Royals *euph*. Smallish, but pert and firm, *shirt potatoes* which are particularly good boiled with a bit of butter on. *Sara Cox's orange pippins*.

jester's shoes *n. medic*. The involuntary upward curling movements of the toes that herald the onset of the *vinegar strokes*, whilst lying on one's back *wanking*. *'Zoom in on Gunther for the money shot, camera two. He's got the jester's shoes.'*

jeweller *n*. A gifted manufacturer of *jelly jewellery* and *pearl necklaces*.

jewels *n*. The *family jewels* which are kept in the *fruit bowl*.

jibble *n*. The final, sad, leaking tears of *spangle* which drip out of one's *hog's eye* in those *wangst*-ridden moments of spiralling despair and self-loathing which apparently follow a bout of *self help*. From jizz + dribble.

jig-a-jig *n*. It, *how's your father*.

jigger *n*. *18thC*. That tool with which a man commits *jiggery pokery*. The *fuck stick*.

jiggered *1. adj*. In a state of fatigue. *Buggered, knackered, shagged out. 2. adj*. Something that a surprised person is confident that they will be.

jiggery pokery *n. Shenanigans*, assorted sexual goings-on. *'I'll have no jiggery pokery going on under my roof.'*

jiggle ring *n*. The larger lady's *muffin top* lifebelt, shaken to attract the attention of prospective partners. *'Don't look now, but that munter at the bar is offering you her jiggle ring.'*

jiggle show *n*. A titillating, but *chest tuner*-free early evening television show, *eg. Baywatch, Charlie's Angels.*

jiggle the jewellery *v*. To *box the jesuit, rough up the suspect.*

jigglypuff *n*. A man who watches female television programmes, such as *EastEnders* and *Emmerdale*, of his own free will.

jill off *v*. Female equivalent of *jack off*, to *paddle the pink canoe*. Until it leaks.

Jimmy hat *1. n*. A latex prophylactic device designed to keep the head of the penis dry during intercourse. *2. n*. A piece of headwear designed for or worn by someone called Jimmy.

Jimmy Edwards *n*. Tufts of *pubage* protruding either side of a bikini bottom, resembling the handlebar moustache of the late *Whacko!* star. *Thighbrows*.

Jimmy Riddle *rhym. slang*. Vicar-friendly term for *turning your bike around*. *'I'm just going for a Jimmy Riddle, vicar.' 'Well don't forget to shake the end of your cock to get the last few drops off it.'*

Jimmy sack *n*. School lavatory high jinks. During an act of urination, the *fiveskin* is pinched shut, creating a high-pressure bag of *piss* at the end of the penis. This can be used to chase people as, when released, a *Jimmy sack* can be explosive.

Jimmy Savile *1. n*. Yorkshire-born ex-coal miner, who went on to become a founding Radio 1 DJ, and hosted the first edition of *Top of the Pops* as well as *Jim'll Fix It*. (The rest of this definition has been cut in anticipation of a substantial amount of legal advice.) 2. *n*. A *bum cigar* of such humungous proportions that it forces involuntary high-pitched warbling noises to issue from its begetter's mouth, in the style made popular by the erstwhile ennobled *Jim'll Fix It* presenter when fixing it for his young guests to mow the lawn in the *Blue Peter* garden, or some other such bit of low-budget BBC tomfoolery.

Jimmy White's brother *n*. The most boring member of any group of lads who turns up every night at the pub to sit in abject, oppressive silence. From the urban legend that when Jimmy White's brother died, his friends broke into the undertakers to take the corpse out for one last *piss-up*.

Jimmy Wonkle *n*. The gentleman's *widdle tap*.

Jim Royle's beard *n*. A *Dylan*.

jism *n*. Semen. Also *gism, jissom, jizz, jizzom*.

jitbag *n*. A *dunky, jubber ray*.

jit gel *n*. US. The contents of a used *jitbag* once it has floated across the Atlantic.

jit gel rag *n*. US. Any available object upon which you wipe your *cock* after sex, *eg*. Tissues, underpants, curtains, tramp's beard.

jitlag *n*. The slimy, post-coital *jazz egg* that drops out the end of one's *charlie* about 20 minutes after *stack blow*. The *post bolt*, the *missing fish*.

jitler *n*. *Spunk*.

jizlas *n*. Thin sheets of paper used to mop up *tugwax*.

jizz 1. *n*. *Jism*. 2. *v*. To *shoot one's load*, lose one's mess.

jizzabyte *n*. A unit of computer memory equivalent to approximately 1 million million gigabytes. 1 jizzabyte is defined as the approximate amount of hard drive space occupied by the pornography downloaded by an average teenage youth in a single calendar month.

jizzard *n*. A swirling blizzard of the wrong sort of *snow*, sufficient to stop a *train being pulled* in a *grumble flick*.

jizzaster *n*. The leaving of incriminating masturbatory evidence behind. '*That wad of spunk on the carpet was a fucking jizzaster. Not to mention the Fuck Truck tape in the video, or the circle of open wank mags on the living room floor. Or me lying unconscious in the middle of it all with my trousers round my ankles and my red-raw cock in my hand.*'

jizzbags *n*. The scrotum, *John Wayne's hairy saddlebags*.

jizz bib 1. *n*. A sacrificial T-shirt placed over the stomach and chest to prevent seminal claggage of the chest hair during a horizontal *wank*. 2. *n*. A *shirtlifter*'s goatee beard.

jizzbolt *n*. A glob of ejaculate that leaves the *hog's eye* with enough force to put the television screen through. A *golden shot, Bernie the bolt*.

jizzbolt jury *n*. Any group of men watching and discussing the merits of a *stick vid*.

jizz drive *n*. An external storage medium for *left-handed website* downloads.

jizz funk *n*. The musical genre of which the soundtracks to 1980s *stick vids* are principally constituted.

jizziotherapy *n*. A three-minute, one-handed massage that relieves stiffness for up to half an hour.

jizz jar *n*. Girlfriend. Probably considered derogatory, although one would think they'd take it as a compliment.

jizz juggler 1. *n*. An enthusiastic *wankatrix*. 2. *n*. One of the less successful variety acts to audition for *Britain's Got Talent*.

jizzle *v*. To drizzle *jizz*. Derivation unknown. *'Just think, son, Status Quo are staying on the top floor of this hotel. Ooh, I think it's starting to jizzle.'*

jizzmopper *n*. A member of the honourable profession of peep show *wank booth* hygienist.

jizzmopper's cloth 1. *n*. An absorbent rag used by a *jizzmopper* in the performance of their daily duties. 2. *sim*. Descriptive of a *cockoholic*'s knickers.

jizzness *n*. Tiring occupation of well-*whoreganised* peripatetic executive/commercial traveller types. *'I have just been to Amsterdam for the weekend on jizzness. My next jizzness trip is planned for Estonia.'*

judge the sludge *v*. To lean over to one side on the *chod bin* in order to look down and assess the prodigiousness and quality of your rectal wares. *'I'll be out in a minute Tracey, I'm just judging the sludge. Christ almighty, this one looks like King Kong's cock.'*

jizzn't *n*. The *spunk* of a man who's either had a vasectomy or whose *tadpoles* aren't very good at swimming. *'I'm sorry, Mr Dawson. I've had a look at your sample under the microscope and I'm afraid it's jizzn't.'*

jizz off a porn queen's face *sim*. A hardcore version of "water off a duck's back". *'Frankly, Clare Short's criticisms of Tony Blair's presidential style of gov-*ernment are like jizz off a porn queen's face to the Prime Minister.'* (Andrew Marr, Radio 4 *Today* programme, May 2003).

jizzy rascal *n*. A cheeky chap who *starches the sheets* at every available opportunity.

J-lower *n*. A girl blessed with a substantially bigger and even more gravitationally-challenged *council gritter* than Miss Lopez. See also *Sharon sixteen stone*.

J-No *n. prop*. A self-deluded *bird* with a horrible fat *arse* who believes she looks good in tight jeans or hipsters.

Joan Collins' knickers See *tart's window box*.

Joanie *n*. A voluminous, tight, curly-permed *front bottom* of the sort that one might imagine finding on Richie Cunningham's sister in *Happy Days*.

job *n*. A *feeshus*.

jobby, a big *n*. *Scot*. A *dreadnought*. That which is wheeked.

jobbycentre *n*. A municipal toilet. *'Where are you off to, George?' 'I'm just off down the jobbycentre, Andrew.'*

jobby engine *n*. The lavatory or water closet. The *shit pot, bum sink*.

jobby jouster *n*. A Knight of *King Richard the Third*.

jocaine *n*. *Showbiz sherbet* that's been mixed with baking powder or talc, and thus fails to come up with the goods when snorted through a rolled ten pound note in a lavatory by a sweating children's television presenter. *Salted sniff, faux-caine*.

jockanory *n*. A tale of woe proffered by a ruddily-complexionned Scotsman who finds himself perennially short of just fifty pence for the train fare he requires to take him back to the rolling heather of his homeland. Pal.

jockeys *rhym. slang.* Nipples. From jockeys' whips = nips.

jockey's coffin *n.* An exceptionally small and snug-fitting *fluffit.* A *mouse's ear,* a *paper cut.* *'And so it was that Mary was pure and had not known a man and had a snatch like a jockey's coffin, yet she was great with child.'* (*Luke* 1:4).

jockey's starting position *n.* The well-braced *arse*-in-the-air stance adopted by one who is shortly anticipating a *shot from the starter's gun.*

jockey yoghurt *1. n.* Brand of sweet-tasting fermented dairy produce which is popular in Europe. *2. n.* The *milm* decorating the insides of an eager fellow's *scads* after an evening of *searching for loose change* at a lap-dancing establishment, whilst travelling on a crowded tube train or hiding in the branches of a tree overlooking the local nurses' home.

jockflap *1. n.* A Scottish panic. *'Tommy, dinnae get yersel in such a jockflap. I'm sure they cannae prove it.'* *2. n.* Scottish *ladyparts.*

Jodrell *rhym. slang.* A *J Arthur.* From the UMIST radio telescope Jodrell Wank.

Jodrell banquet *n.* Having a *wank* whilst sitting on one's knees with all one's *jazz mags* laid out on the floor in the style of a parabolic array of radio telescopes. Also known as a *pornorama, wank crescent* or *glandscape.*

Joe Strummer *1. n. prop.* Legendary deceased singer/songwriter of the Clash popular music combo. *2. n.* Nickname given to an individual who is prone to engage in spontaneous bouts of onanism.

joff *v.* To *milm* one's *grundies* without even being *tumescent.* Derived from Jizz On Flop. *'I joffed when I found my dad's bootleg Night in Paris vid behind some tins of paint in the garage.'*

jog for yoghurt *v.* To take a mild bit of manly exercise.

jogging behind a gritter *sim.* Descriptive of the face of a woman with a less than peach-like complexion, *eg.* Susan Tully, Frances de la Tour, Kate O'Mara. *'Jesus Christ! She's got a face like she's been jogging behind a gritter. Where did you find her?' 'She was jogging behind a gritter.'*

John *1. n. Percy, Willie, John Thomas.* A *cock.* *2. n.* A *pro's* client, a *Hillman Hunter.* *3. n. US.* A *crapper.*

John Craven *1. rhym. slang.* A *shaven haven.* A *Beverley.* *2. n.* The act of drinking five pints of beer or lager without going to the toilet for a *piss* until the third pint is finished. Derivation unknown, but possibly a reference to a "spoof" article about newsreaders' drinking capacity in issue 28 of the downmarket magazine *Viz* which enjoyed a brief vogue in the last century. A three pint total is known as a *Jan Leeming,* from the same supposedly "humorous" article.

John Holmes *n.* A massive marijuana cigarette, named after the legendary saucy actor of the same name who reputedly had a large *tassel.* (Not to be confused with a *Luke Jackson* - a rather small and unsatisfying marijuana cigarette named after Luke Jackson from Sutton Coldfield).

John Lees *rhym. slang. Scots. Tits.* From noted dead blues groaner John Lee Hooker = sooker.

John Merrick's cap *n.* A vast, out of

shape *fanny*.

Johnny *n*. A *dunky*, a *jubber ray*. *'Eurgh! I just found a Johnny in my Big Mac.'*

Johnny cache *n*. The bedside drawer in which prophylactics are stored.

Johnny Cash 1. *n*. £2 for 3. 2. *n*. A *Wigan rosette*. A *burning ring of fire*.

Johnny in the Shining, like *sim*. Desperate to get into the bathroom. *'What have you done to my bloody bog door, Barry?' 'Sorry Paul, I had the turtle's head so bad I was like Johnny in the Shining.'*

Johnny jibber *n*. To lose *wood* upon opening the *flunkey*. Premature ejaculation and *Johnny jibber* are thought to affect 1 in 4 males at some time in their life.

johnnylingus *n*. Oral stimulation of a *jubbered-up* member, for example off a fussy lady when one has a dose of *cock rot*.

Johnny no-stars *n*. A *dolt*. From the "star rating" system on the badges displayed by staff at McDonald's. One who occupies a place on the lower end of the evolutionary fast food chain.

John O'Scrotes *euph*. Any seaside town characterised by a seasonal influx of pill-popping, lager-swilling, fornicating *ratboys* and *slappers*, *eg*. Salou, Magaluf, Ibiza or Frinton.

John Sargent 1. *n*. A *fry-up face*. Refers to anyone with features resembling the former BBC Chief Political Correspondent. 2. *n*. A great British fried breakfast of which, before commencing, one might say "Now over to BBC Chief Political Correspondent John Sargent".

John the Baptist 1. *n*. prop. Biblical character, a sort of Happy Shopper Jesus who got his head cut off at the request of some New Testament pole dancer or other. 2. *n*. A pungently prophetic *air biscuit*; one that speaks of a greater one

to come (probably in solid form).

John Thomas *n*. How gamekeeper David Mellors referred to his *slag hammer* in the controversial novel *Lady Chatterley's Lover*.

John Wayne's hairy saddle bags 1. *n*. *Jizzbags*. 2. *n*. *Saloon doors*.

John Wayne's safety catch, more time off than *sim*. In an office or workplace, descriptive of employees who are constantly ill. *Glassbacks*.

John Waynes *n*. Walking like Mrs Thatcher, George Bush or Tony Blair when he was visiting George Bush, *ie*. That gait adopted after *giving birth to Meatloaf's daughter*. Makes the walker look like they've been sitting on a horse for three days.

John Wayne toilet paper *n*. The shiny, ineffective school bog *bumwad* remembered with scant affection from childhood days, and still employed in public lavatories. From the fact that "it's rough, tough and don't take shit from no man".

join Dutch's unit *v*. To have a *wank*. From the scene in the film *Predator* when Arnie (Dutch) says: "General, my team works alone, you know that".

joiner's bag *n*. A battered, capacious *blurtch* with all hammers and spirit levels falling out of it.

join giblets *v*. To do *thingy* with a bare lady.

join in the applause *v*. To make a lady *airtight*. *'I went into my flatmate's room to borrow his weights. He was doing his bird from behind so I joined in the applause.'*

jollies 1. *n*. *Police*. In constabulary terms, trips to scenes of crimes. 2. *n*. Women's breasts. *'Look at the jollies on that nun, Your Holiness.'*

jollup *n.* A dollop of *jizz*. From the Greek jollopus = dollop of jizz.

jollyrancher *n. US.* One blessed with the cat-like ability to *cannonball, ie.* A man who never leaves the house but orders in a lot of breath-fresheners.

Jonathan *rhym. slang.* A *Sherman tank,* a *Barclay's,* from the masturbating TV presenter Jonathan Ross OBE = toss OBE.

jonk *v.* To *jizz, spaff, spunk up, spuff, spill the Brasso, tip one's filthy concrete, lose one's mess, shoot one's load, shoot one's bolt, shoot one's stack, shoot one's wad, drop one's yop, discharge the mutton musket, slime, chuck one's muck* or *empty the bins. 'What's the matter, Carol?' 'Someone's been in me dressing room again and jonked in me undercracker drawer.'*

joombye *n. Scot. Jism, jizz, Mc-Spunk,* deep-fried *vitamin S.*

Jordan's toppers *1. n.* Wholesome breakfast bars, full of natural ingredients. *2. n.* The ludicrously-proportioned *chestular assets* of Mrs Andre, full of artificial ingredients, E-numbers and synthetic additives.

Joseph's balls *n. medic. Nuts* that have not been evacuated for a long time. From the supernaturally cuckolded biblical carpenter's testicles. *'How's tricks, Cliff?' 'To tell you the truth, Hank, I've not had any since the late fifties, and it feels like I've got Joseph's balls in my pants.'*

joskin *n.* A country bumpkin, a rustic dolt, a *sheep shagger.*

josser *n. 19thC. Fuckwit* or parasite. The ideal name for someone who is both.

jostle the chosen one *v.* To *pull the Pope's cap off,* to *box the Jesuit.*

jotter *n.* The *teatowel holder, loon pipe, council gritter, gazoo, balloon knot, raisin, chocolate starfish, Gary, rusty sheriff's badge, freckle, clacker valve, kakpipe, corn dot, ringpiece, crapper, aris, quoit, poop chute, panda's eye etc.* The *arsehole. 'Palmolive was powerless to resist. His eyes burnt into hers like malachites. His muscular arms enfolded her body as she felt herself being swept away in a mistral of passion. "I love you, Alfonso,' she gasped. 'Take me now, I'm yours.' 'Drop your grundies and bend over then, love,' said Alfonso, unzipping his heaving slacks. 'I'll slip you a quick length up the jotter."* (from *The Lady and the Travel Rep* by Barbara Cartland).

joy division *1. n.* Seminal indie band whose lead singer hanged himself in Macclesfield. Well, you had to make your own entertainment in them days. *2. n.* The *notcher, carse, barse, Humber Bridge, tinter, taint, tisnae, tissent etc. 3. n. medic. Banjo* trauma, that is to say the unthinkable consequences of an accident wherein "love has torn us apart".

joy plug *n.* The congealed remnant of a successful *wank* that causes a slight pause at the start of a *hit and miss.*

joyrider's moustache *n.* The light growth of fluffy top lip *bum fluff* popular with teenage delinquents.

joystick *n.* Of *choppers,* the cockpit instrument or *knob,* which gets throttled. *Trouser toy, pant plaything.*

joy valve *n.* A lady's *bodily treasure.*

J-pig *n.* An internet *porn monster.*

jubblies *n.* Lovely breasts, *funbags, milky swingers, fat rascals.*

jubnuts *n. Bead curtains, dangleberries,*

dags.

judges' eyebrows *n. Spiders' legs.*

Judi Dench *n. rhym. slang.* A stench.

Judith *n.* A very dense, dark *fadge,* as sported by the character Judith in *Monty Python's Life of Brian.* *'Bloody hell, love, you've got a right Judith on you. It looks like you've been hit between the legs with a bag of soot.'*

juggage *n.* Collective term for a lady's assets. *'Phwooar. Your missus carries a lot of juggage, don't she.'*

jugged-mare *n.* An aesthetically-challenged woman who is nevertheless worth a go due to her large *tits.* A *bapdog.*

jugged up *1. adj.* Of a happy fellow, to find himself well catered for in the *headlamps* department. *'Dave doesn't come out much since he met Double-D Denise. He's jugged up.' 2. adj.* Of a lady, to be generously endowed in terms of chestular glandage. *'Blimey, she's jugged up. She must have been re-racked, surely.'*

juggernaut juice *n.* Roadside *rusty cola* found in lay-bys, discarded alongside rolls of carpet containing strangled hitch-hikers. *Truckers' tizer, kidney cider, hedge coke, Scania scotch, wagon wine.*

juggernorks *n.* A huge pair of *Gert Stonkers* that come bearing down on you well ahead of their owner. *Stobarts, mammoets, norberts.*

jumble grumble *n.* Car boot sale-quality *self-help* material, *eg. Razzle, Nuts,* the bra pages of the Freemans catalogue. *Poornography, paupernography.*

juggery pokery *n.* An act of penile love performed amongst a woman's secondary sexual characteristics. A well-sprung *tit fuck,* if you will.

juggler's doughnuts *1. n. prop.* A popular themed fast food store at Alton Towers.

2. n. Shirt potatoes when handled in the style of a circus performer tossing balls from hand to hand.

juggstaposition *n.* The visual mismatch of two contrastingly-sized pairs of *oomlaters* in close proximity, Trinny Woodall standing next to former Foreign Secretary Baron Owen of the City of Plymouth, for example.

juggsy malone *n.* A tiny woman with massive *tits.*

jug jousting *v.* A *bunny rub.*

jugly *adj.* Ugly, but with big *knockers, eg.* Anna Ryder Richardson, Erica Rowe, Johnny Vegas.

jugs *n.* A lady's *top bum.*

juice of hazard *n.* Any over-strong, export strength alcoholic beverage, *eg.* Methylated spirits, metal polish, Carlsberg Special Brew *etc.,* the prolonged consumption of which may lead to unruly and erratic driving, especially when attempting to outrun the police.

juices are running clear, the *1. phr.* Of a bird which has been removed from the oven, a check made to ensure that it is fully cooked and ready to be boned and eaten. *2. phr.* Of a *bird,* when the *painters* have left, and she is ready to be *boned* or *eaten.*

juicy flute *n.* A chewy, salty snack for the ladies. The *gut stick.*

JULF/julf *acronym.* Jumped Up Little Fucker, a pushy *twat.*

jullet *n. medic.* The phenomenon of the breasts, upper chest and chins of a *salad-dodging* lady all being merged into the same wobbling mass of flesh. The antipode of the *gunt.* From jugs + gullet.

jumble sale lawn sprinkler *n.* The first *piss* of the day, which sprays absolutely anywhere except in its intended direction.

jump *v.* To have sex with someone's bones off the top of a wardrobe.

jump on the grenade *v.* Of a man, to perform the noble and selfless act whereby he *cops off* with an ugly *bird* solely to enable his friend to *pull* her fit mate. From the slightly less impressive story from World War I where a Private threw himself on a grenade to protect his comrades from the blast.

junction nine *n.* A ribald term for a folically-challenged fellow. From the similarly named interchange on the M25, which *goes to Leatherhead*. *'Famous people who were born on February 22nd: George Washington, first president of the United States of America, 1732; Lord Robert Stephenson Smythe Baden-Powell, hero of the siege of Mafeking and founder of the Boy Scout movement, 1857; Kenneth Williams, raconteur, diarist and film, stage, television and radio actor, 1926; Bruce Forsyth, chinny junction nine, 1928.'* (from *Schott's Oh Fuck it, That'll Have to Do, I'm Off Down the Pub Book, 2006*).

jungle juice *n. Blip, moip, fanny batter.*

jungle VIP *n.* A woman with pendulous breasts. From the apposite lines of the song performed by Louis, the orangutan "King of the swingers" in Disney's *Jungle Book* on *Screen Test* every fucking week.

junior *n. US.* Penis, usually used in reference to one's own.*'Could I have an appointment with the doctor, please? Junior's had an accident with the Hoover.'*

junior scrabble, easier than *sim.* Phrase which can be used when referring to an accommodating lady who is quite prepared to allow gentlemen to have penetrative sexual intercourse up her without requiring the poor sods to jump through hoops first.

junk *1. n. coll.* The contents of the *fruit bowl.* "I say, Jeeves. Drat these new fangled flies in my plus-fours,' I blustered. 'Haven't I just caught all my junk in the bally zipper mechanism." (from *Ooh, Yes! Just There! Don't Stop, Jeeves* by PG Wodehouse). *2. n.* The *ejaculate* that lobs out the end of the *cock* part of the *junk.* "Launder these plus fours, Jeeves, there's a fellow,' I said. *'I'm meeting Aunt Agatha for tea, and there's dried junk down the front from where Dulcie Wegg-Prosser gave my old chap a strop in the back of the Lagonda."* (from *Fetch Some Tissues, Jeeves* by PG Wodehouse).

junk mail *n.* Any mis-aimed *pop shot* from the *spam javelin, eg.* In the eyes, up the nose, over the computer keyboard, into a fellow commuter's pocket *etc.*

jurassic parp *n.* A bubble of fossilized *carbon dibaxide* from the *tar pit* that could bring tears to the eye of a brontosaurus.

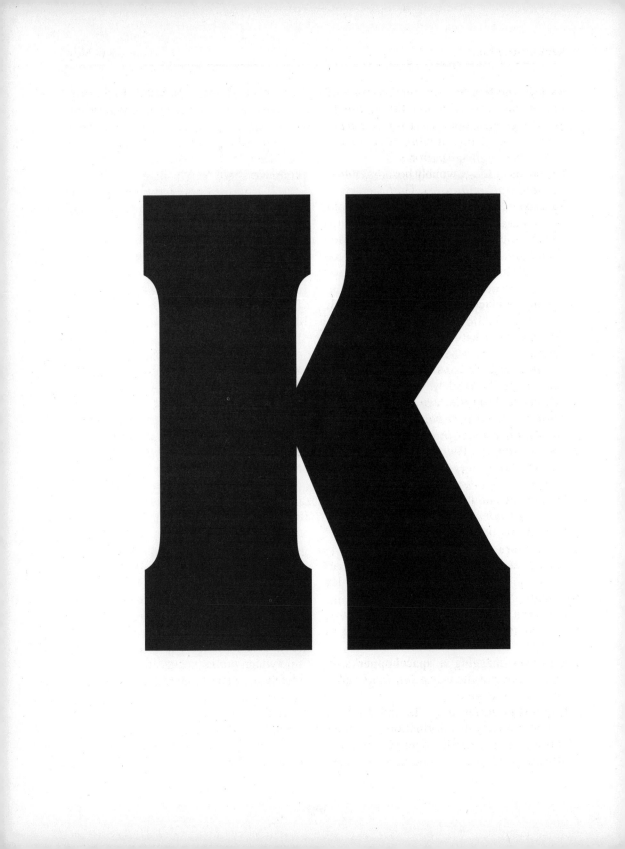

kack-in-the-box *n*. An unpleasant surprise encountered upon lifting the lid of the *gurgler*, such as a floating *teddy bear's arm*, a pile of *bangers and mash* or a *flock of dirty sparrows*.

kahoonas *n*. Large wobbly bosoms, *golden bodangers, kermungers, Gert Stonkers*.

kakatoa *n*. An earth-shattering anal explosion that can be heard half way round the world and which causes tidal waves and *poonamis* to sweep through the *chod bin*, devastating everything that lies in their path. Also *crackatoa, cackatoa*.

kak in the black *n*. A *number two* which, unsettlingly, has to be dropped in the pitch dark because the *bog* lights don't work.

kak *n*. *Keech, kaka, shite*. Feculant matter, to put it crudely. '*These ads with Esther fucking Rantzen in are the final straw. Fetch a jiffy bag, dear, I'm going to send her a kak in the post.*'

kak klaxon *n*. The *rectal hooter* from which loud anal honks are emitted, together with the occasional *bonus ball*.

kakpipe cosmonaut *n*. He who prefers to *dock* his *command module* in the *rear unloading bay*.

kama slutra *n*. Exotic repertoire of sexual positions practised in cars, in shop doorways and behind skips *etc*. on Saturday nights.

kangaroo pouch *n*. A large *granny fanny*, big enough to fit your head in. A *horse's collar*.

kangaroo shagging a spacehopper *sim*. Descriptive of the way a *shit house* door blows in the wind.

Kaplinsky, suffer a *v*. To fail to hear some important information as one's attention is entirely focused upon the thighs or cleavage of the person speaking. Named after Natasha Kaplinsky, whose thighs and cleavage historically drowned out the news on BBC TV's Breakfast Programme.

Karl Denver *1. n*. Famous singer, now desceased, whose voice ranged from a dark baritone to a powerful high-pitched yodel. Best known for singing the song *Wimoweh*. *2. n*. A chromatic *clapper rattler* produced whilst standing up from a chair. The *Karl Denver* begins in a lower key, but rises up the scale as the buttocks close, eventually achieving a powerful falsetto for the finale.

Karl marks *n*. Patches of reddened skin on the inner thighs of a lady who has spent the day being *licked out* by a bearded fellow. Or a bearded lady, if she's a lesbian who works in a circus. To each according to their needs and all that.

Kate Bush *n*. A gargantuan *Vince* which proves so difficult to pass that it causes even the deepest-voiced male to cry out in a glass-shattering falsetto reminiscent of the eponymous Bexleyheath-born chanteuse at full chat. A *wuthering shite*.

Kate Nash *n. rhym. slang*. *Gash*, named after the Happy Shopper Lily Allen singer-songwriter. '*Get your Y-fronts off, Germaine, and I'll get a shot of your Kate Nash.*'

Katie Swunt *n*. Spooneristically cryptic ladies' expression; a refined, feminine version of *Betty Swollocks*.

kazoo *1. n*. A tissue paper-covered aperture which *hums* tunelessly. *2. n*. A completely unmusical musical instrument. A *swannee whistle*.

KD lady *n*. A *lezza*. Named after comfortably-shod Canadian chanteuse KD Lang, who has yet to find the right young man.

Keats *n*. A bout of *self abuse* that one embarks upon, despite being physically debilitated. Named after the romantic poet John Keats who, struck down in his early years with galloping consumption, still managed a couple of *tugs* a day.

kebabble *n*. The incoherent mumblings and inept attempts at ordering food endured by the staff of greasy takeaway outlets after the pubs have closed.

kebabe *n*. A woman who looks incredibly tasty when one is *pissed* at two in the morning, but the thought of whom turns one's stomach in the sober light of day.

kebabulance *n*. Late night emergency vehicle, such as the one parked on Christchurch Road, Reading or Link Road, Sawston.

keck cackler *n*. One with an easily-amused *kazoo*. A person who exhibits *canned laughter*.

keck cougher *n*. He who *burps backwards*, or emits *under thunder* when *clearing his nether throat*.

kecks *n*. See *kegs*.

keech *n*. *Crap, kak, kaka, keek*.

keel haul *v*. To drag one's tongue underneath a woman from *lip* to *ring*.

keema naan *n*. A shaved *fanny* with the very tip of the *bacon* sticking out.

keeping it on the clutch *n*. When watching an erotic televisual broadcast, skillfully working a *wank* just below *boiling point* to see one through the adverts. *Treading water*, holding it at *the biting point*.

keep one's powder dry *v*. To feign disinterest in a bout of sex with the wife to ensure one can give it to the girlfriend with both barrels in a later engagement.

keeps his coins in his wallet, he *euph*. Phrase which can be used when referring to a fellow who is *good with colours, sensitive, good with his hands, stylish, a good listener etc. 'See that chap in the bushes with the big moustache?' 'Who, the one bumming the bloke in the leather chaps whilst listening to Judy Garland records on his walkman?' 'Aye. well him, right. Keep it under your hat, but I have it on very good authority that he keeps his coins in his wallet.'*

keep shouting Sir, we'll find you *exclam. milit*. Humorous phrase uttered after someone has *dropped* a particularly loud *gut*. See also *how much?; taxi for Brown* and many more.

keep the change *v*. Of a lady, to imbibe the issue of an act of *horatio*, as opposed to expectorating it. To *swallow*.

keepy-uppy 1. *n*. A marathon ball control game practised by schoolboys in the park. 2. *n*. A marathon *ball* control game practised by Sting in his wife. Tantric sex.

kegs *n*. See *kex*.

keister *n*. *Nipsy, kazoo*.

Keith Burtons *n*. Spooneristic *beef curtains*.

Keith Harris, do a *v*. To get your hand so far up a *bird's hole* you could make her mouth move. From the formerly popular flightless duck ventriloquist. Also *do a Rod Hull, give it some Orville*.

Kelly Brooks *n*. An ill-matched pair of wonky *jugs*.

Kemal *n*. A sexual act performed in a sordid or dirty location. Named after the *Big Brother 6* contestant who confessed on camera to *sucking someone off* in a skip. Not even behind a skip. IN a skip, for fuck's sake.

Ken Dodd *v*. To masturbate into your partner's hair whilst they are asleep, such that they awaken next morning with a hairstyle similar to that of the scouse comic.

Ken Dodd's hairbrush *n.* A particularly unkempt lady's *clunge.* From the fact that the erstwhile dentally-challenged taxophobe gagsmith's hairbrush probably looks like a scraggy *twat,* with all bits of unusually-coloured hair stuck out of it at funny angles. *Terry Waite's allotment.*

Kennedy *n.* A sexual session which incorporates penetration in all orifices except the ears and nose. From the sex-mad American president John F. Kennedy who once said "you haven't finished with a woman until you've had her three ways".

Kennedy flu *n. medic.* Early morning ailment with a variety of symptoms including slurred speech, confusion and extreme right wing opinions.

Kennedys, the *n. prop.* The male genitalia; the *fruit bowl, meat and two veg, the boys.* Named after the famously ill-fated US political dynasty, *ie.* Jack and Bobby, and Ted in the middle with his big head.

kennel maid *n.* The hostess of an inexpensive massage parlour.

Kent quake *n.* A gentle rumble followed by the release of an unimpressive amount of *arse gas* through one's *fissure.* A flatulent event which is low on the *sphincter scale,* but which could nevertheless cause a small amount of structural damage.

Keown surgery *n.* A piece of maxillofacial reconstruction (commonly a broken nose) performed by a no-nonsense centre-half during a Sunday League football match.

kerbside quiche *n.* A *pavement pizza.*

Kermits, the *n.* Of a gentleman, the unwelcome situation of being constantly stalked and chatted up by a *pig* he would never wish to *fuck* in a million years.

kerrangatang *n.* A large, hairy, heavy metal enthusiast.

Kestrel manoeuvres in the dark *n.* The wayward shuffle of a *Harold Ramp* who has spent the whole day on the *wifebeater.*

kettling *1. adj.* Descriptive of the state of being in dire, immediate need of a *shit.* From the fact that a metal lid placed over one's *clackervalve* in such circumstances would rattle urgently, and possibly emit a high-pitched whistle to boot. *2. adj.* Of a sexually excited woman's *mingepiece, frothing* so vigorously that one could, if one were sufficiently ingenious and in possession of a length of suitable pressure hose, use it to power a "Mamod" traction engine across the bedroom floor or a small steam launch across Lake Windermere. *3. n.* Technique of high pressure demonstration control used by the Metropolitan Police which is intended to provoke anger in the crowd, thus giving the *scuffers* an excuse to crack some heads.

kex *1. n. Shreddies, trolleys,* underpants. *2. n. Round-the-houses, kegs.*

kexorcism *n.* The act of driving out an evil, demonic *food's ghost* from one's *chamber of horrors.*

kexpresso *n.* A type of diarrhoea produced by one who needed a *crappuccino,* but couldn't get to the toilet on time.

key dropper *n.* A *bottee.*

keyboard hero *n.* One who is bravely prepared to engage in prodigious acts of personal courage that would normally entail the risk of a thorough kicking if he were not protected by the anonymity of an internet message board.

keyhole surgery *n.* The act of having a vigorous and satisfying dig around a particularly itchy *teatowel holder*.

keystone *1. n.* In architecture, the wedge-shaped stone at the apex of an arch upon which the integrity of the entire structure is dependent. *2. n.* In multiple-participant-based sexual shenanigans, the crucial 5th or 6th man without whom a *daisy chain* is doomed to failure. *3. adj.* Of massed policemen, prone to falling over, hopping whilst rounding corners and being dragged along dusty roads behind charabancs whilst holding their hats on with one hand.

KFC *1. abbrev.* Something quick, spicy and filling involving a bit of greasy old *cock* and a *bucket of batter*. Knob Filled Cunt. *'I thought we'd stay in tonight, love. Fancy a KFC?' 2. n.* A girl who will cheaply provide a bit of breast, a bit of leg and a *box* to put your *bone* in.

khaki buttonhole *n.* The *chocolate starfish, rusty bullet hole*.

khazi *n. Shitter, bog, cludgie. NB.* For best effect, this word should be spoken in the style of Wilfred Brambell.

Khyber *rhym. slang. Arse.* From Khyber Parse.

kick start the motorbike *v.* To lift one's leg prior to popping an anal wheelie.

kick the knackers out of *v.* To complete the majority of a piece of work. *'By the February of 1498, and after two full years of work in the refectory of St Maria delle Grazie in Milan, Leonardo had just about kicked the knackers out of his Last Supper fresco. Accordingly, in March of that year he embarked for Florence in order to start inventing the helicopter.'*

(from Vasari's *Lives of the Painters*).

kick with the left foot *v.* What players who arrive on the *other bus* tend to do, a football equivalent of *bowling from the pavilion end*.

kid juice *n.* Baby gravy, heir spray.

kid's piss *n.* A nightclub toilet act of urination whereby the *kex* and *bills* are lowered onto the shoes at the urinal by someone too *pissed* to attempt a penile extraction through the flies.

kidney cider *n.* A discarded drinks container at the side of the road containing lorry driver's urine. *Trucker's tizer, Scania scotch*.

kidney fizzer *n.* Uncomfortably biological hangover after a particularly heavy night of binge *refreshment*, characterised by bubbling sensations in the lower back. *Alcoseltzer*.

kidney prodder *n.* During an act of sexual congress, a particularly impressive thrust.

kidneys, shit one's *v.* To experience a traumatic *digestive transit* as a result of severe alarm or a particularly hot *Ruby Murray*. *'Come for a meal at the Curry Capital, Bigg Market, Newcastle upon Tyne, and if you don't shit your kidneys, I'll give you your money back'.* (Abdul Latif, Lord of Harpole, short-lived Tyne Tees Television advertising campaign, 1996).

kidney wiper *n. Slat rattler.* See also *purple headed womb broom*.

kid with an ice-cream, like a *sim.* Descriptive of the face of a lucky *grumble flick* starlet after a series of well-aimed *pop shots*. Descriptive of a *plasterer's radio*.

kife *1. n. coll. Blart, totty, tussage, buffage. 2. n. The other.*

kilt *1. n. coll.* Skirt. *2. n. coll. Scot.* Blokes.

kilt lifter *n.* A Scottish fellow who is *good with colours,* a *McQueen,* a *gay Gordon.*

King Alfred's cakes *n.* Severely overcooked products of the *dirt bakery.*

kingbast *n.* A sweary term that can be shouted in front of grannies, vicars, nuns *etc.* without causing offence. Contraction of *fucking bastard.*

King Canute *n.* An enormous *Richard the Third* that blocks the bend and holds back the tide of the flush, causing the toilet to overflow.

King for a day *euph.* To have a bad case of the *Brads, ie.* To spend all day on the *throne.*

King Kong's finger *n.* A *turd* large enough to flatten a car or bring down a bi-plane. An *Elvis killer.*

King of the elephants *exclam.* An affectionate chorus, sung humorously in the street whilst pointing at someone with *big bones.*

King of the mountains *1. n.* In bicycle racing, the competitor who is the best at riding his bike up hills. In the Tour de France, the king of the mountains can be recognised by the fact that he wears a distinctive polka-dot jersey. *2. n.* A smug gentleman whose ladyfriend is blessed in the *headlamp* department. Can be recognised by the fact that he's usually to be seen on the front of *OK!* magazine, getting married, renewing his vows, having a christening, releasing a *shit* record, lounging in a swimming pool, recovering from a critical illness, bravely facing up to his divorce, battling for custody of his kids *etc.*

kinky! *exclam.* See also *can you leave the fat on mine?* and *ten points to Gryffindor.*

kipling triple *euph.* An exceedingly good *threes up* when a lady has an *eclair* in her mouth, a *cream horn* in the *gazunder* and something "ruddy 'ard" up the *shitter.* '*To Cliveden for the weekend with dear Johnny (Geilgud), Ivor (Novello), and darling Kit (Hassall). Ivor brought a crate of terrifically good Bolly down in the dicky seat of his laundalette and I'm afraid we all got a little tipsy over a plate of rather fine Whitstable oysters. Anyway, one thing led to another, the high jinks got a little out of hand and the four of us ended up doing a kipling triple on the croquet lawn.'* (from the Wartime Diaries of Hylda Baker).

kipper *1. n.* The *Billingsgate box, minge, captain's pie. 2. n.* That useful bit of skin that keeps the *plums* safely out of the *arse's* reach. The *barse, tintis, notcher. Perry Como's lip.*

kipper basting *v.* Shagging.

kipper carriage *n.* Any battery-powered contrivance employed by *old trouts* who are bent on terrorising pedestrians and sneering at children who dare to cycle on the footpath between their home and the cat-food shop.

kipper for breakfast *n.* To rise early and go for a *horizontal jog*; an ideal cure for *dawn horn.*

kipper's cunt *n.* Even more pungent than an *anchovy's fanny.* The *ne plus ultra* of fish-smellyness.

kiss for granny *n.* The hermetically-sealed, tightly-pursed peck one gives one's girlfriend after *crashing the yoghurt truck* in her gob. A *nun's kiss.*

kissing tackle *n.* The north and south, *cakehole.*

kissing the tortoise *n*. Some sort of activity that doesn't bear thinking about, as performed by Ian McCulloch out of Echo and the Bunnymen, and subsequently sung about in that band's song *Seven Seas* on the 1987 album *Ocean Rain*.

kiss of light *n*. A pre-breakfast *Boris Johnson*. From the lyric of the 1977 Be Bop Deluxe song of the same name, which includes the line "Mine is to be her taste of the sea this morning".

kiss the Amish *v*. To perform oral sex upon a particularly *Dave Narey* pair of *catflaps*. To *lick out* a *bear trapper's hat*, *eat sushi off a barbershop floor*.

kiss the frog *v*. Of a lady, to perform *horatio*.

kiss the porcelain god *v*. To *talk on the great white telephone, drive the porcelain bus*.

Kit-Kat *v*. To stimulate a lady with four fingers at once, using a swift, forward thrusting, karate chop-type motion.

Kit-Kat shuffler *n*. *A masturbatress, weasel buffer, gusset typist*.

kitten eyes *n*. Of a lucky lady who has just received a hefty load of hot *fish yoghurt* in her face, to have difficulty peeling her eyelids apart, in a manner reminiscent of a three-day-old baby cat opening its *minces* for the first time. *'Aw bless. She's got kitten eyes, look.' 'Quick. Freeze the frame, your Holiness. I'm nearly there.'*

kitten hammer *n*. A penis. From the scientific fact well known amongst twelve-year-olds that every time they masturbate, a kitten dies.

kitten hammock *n*. *Tit pants*.

kitten purse *n*. Charming, feminine term for a lady's *cludge*.

kittens' noses *n*. *Puppies' noses, jockeys*. Nipples.

kiwi fruit *n*. A particularly hirsute *nadsack*. Named after the Chinese gooseberry, a fruit which exhibits a marked similarity to a hairy scrotum in both appearance and indeed flavour.

klatch *n*. Drip tray flotsam, *jelly hammock* jetsam. *Gusset effluvium*.

kleeneczema *n*. *medic*. The skin condition contracted when a tissue sticks to a *wedding-milky* hand.

kling-ons 1. *n*. One of numerous races of *Star Trek* alien with Cornish pastie foreheads. 2. *n*. *Winnets, dangleberries*, assorted anal hangers-on.

klutz *n*. A thickhead. From the German *for fuckwit*.

knack 1. *v*. To break. 2. *v*. To hit. 3. *v*. To hurt. *'He knacked me with a baseball bat and knacked my shin. It fucking knacks, doctor.'*

knackatoa *n*. An unpredictable eruption of sticky magma from a fissure set above hot *rocks*.

knacker 1. *n*. A single testicle. 2. *n*. A *knobhead*. 3. *v*. To tire out. 4. *v*. To break.

knacker barrel *n*. Attractively-packaged *smegma*.

knackernits *n*. *medic*. Crabs, *pissnits, mechanical dandruff*.

knackers *n*. Balls, *nuts*, plural testicles. *'Mmmm. Just taste that re-formed mixture of gristle, seagull shit and ground-up turkey knackers. Boodiful, really boodiful.'*

knacker tea *n*. That dark yellow urine which has been mashing all night, becoming so concentrated that it could dissolve porcelain.

knackrobatics *n*. The vigorous and often spectacular manoeuvring of a gentleman's *John Thomas* during a bout of *bedroom gymnastics*, usually attempted after being inspired whilst watching an educational *bongo vid* such as *Lovers' Guide 1, Lovers' Guide 2, Lovers' Guide 3* or *Anal Assault 7*.

knee shooters *n*. Large breasts with downward-pointing *jockeys*.

knee trembler *n*. Frightening intercourse while both parties are standing up. Often in a shop doorway.

knicker bacon *n*. Labial rashers.

knicker bandit *n*. A raider of washing lines, *Daz back doorstep challenger*.

knickerdropper glory *1. n*. A fruit-based treat served to a lady as an aid to a beautifully romantic evening, *eg*. Half a bottle of orange *tart fuel* topped up with neat vodka. *2. n*. The best of all possible chat-up lines. Vouchsafed by God to to such *polyamorous* chaps as Mick Jagger, Rod Stewart and, evidently, Tiger Woods.

knicker oil *n*. Alcopops, *tart fuel*.

knicker sausages *n*. Large *fanny lips*. Often found in *frying pants*.

knickers like Jack the Ripper's hankie *sim*. Descriptive of the *dunghampers* of a lady who failed to *pad up* properly during *cricket week*.

knickers like Curt Cobain's ceiling *sim*. Telling phrase descriptive of the situation that sometimes obtains when a lady has taken insufficient precautions to protect her *fairy hammock* whilst she's *got the painters in*.

knickertine stains *n*. *Skid marks* off an *arse* that is a *heavy smoker*. See also *wind sketch*.

knight *v*. To reward a lady with one's *pork sword* in recognition of her outstanding service in the kitchen. To *put to the sword*, to *fuck*.

knob *1. n*. The penis, *prick, John Thomas*.

Also *nob*. *2. v*. To engage in the romantic courses of physical love. *'I knobbed the arse off her.'* *3. n*. About a *cock*'s worth of butter.

knobbledygook *n*. The incoherent gibberish spoken by a young lady at the height of sexual pleasure. Or perhaps while her mouth is full.

knobbysox *n*. Relaxing and absorbent items of hosiery suited to accommodating the more sensitive portions of the male anatomy.

knob cheese *n*. *Smegma. Foreskin feta* found underneath *Kojak's roll-neck* and around the *banjo* or *cheese ridge*. Also *knob Stilton, knob yoghurt, Helmetdale, bell end brie, Lymeswold, brimula, fromunder*.

knob chopper *n*. Precariously-balanced lavatory seat which falls down while one is having a *piss* and therefore must be held up manually. A *penis fly trap*.

knob clocker *n*. An inveterately curious fellow standing at a public urinal who takes the opportunity to surreptitiously eye up the opposition. A *willy watcher*.

knobelisk *n*. A square-sectioned genital column that is thick at the base and tapers towards the top. *Cleopatra's needle*.

knob end *1. n*. The *herman gelmet*. *2. n*. The extremity of a door handle. *3. n*. A *knobhead, jerk wad*.

knob fodder *n*. *Blart, flange, tussage, fanny*.

knobhead *n*. A *fuckwit*, thickhead, oaf.

knob hinge *n*. *anat*. The point on the male anatomy where the lower abdomen meets the top of the *giggling pin*; the fulcrum point of a *bone on*, if you will.

knob jockey *n*. Someone who sits on a door handle whilst the door is in motion for sexual gratification.

knob of butter *n. medic.* Softness in the *trouser department. Brewer's droop. Pele's cock.* Impotence.

knob scoffer *n.* Pejorative epithet implying that an individual likes to *smoke the white owl.*

knobseeker's allowance *n.* Funds self-allocated by proactive single females specifically for the provision of makeup, slutty clothing, *boob jobs* and other items intended to make them more attractive to members of the opposite sex.

knob shiner *n.* Someone who is always prepared to polish a *pink oboe.*

knob snot *n. Cock hockle.*

knob socket *n.* Any orifice that a penis could be put into, *eg.* The neck of an oven ready chicken, a hole in a tree, a Hoover dustette, the wife's *fanny, etc.*

knobstacle course *n.* Attempting sex with a *bird* whilst in a drunken stupor. See *labiarinth, Hampton Maze.*

knob throb *n.* The pulsating surge of blood to the genital region which heralds the onset of a raging *diamond cutter.*

knobtical illusion *n.* An excuse given by a man for the apparently pitiful size of his *manhood. 'It only looks small because of the way the bathwater's bending the light. It's a knobtical illusion. It's making the ruler you're holding next to it look bigger too. That proves it.'*

knob toffee *n.* Sperm that could pull your missus's fillings out.

knobwebs *n.* Symptoms of a prolonged period of sexual abstinence, when fluff, dust and spider webs gather around a chap's *cock. 'He said son, you are a bachelor boy / And that's the way to stay / Dusting the knobwebs off yo-ur old man / Until your dying day.'* (Song

lyric by Cliff Richard, 1962).

knocker hoppers *n. Tit pants, rascal sacks.*

knocker jockey *n.* A small woman with very big *tits.* A *midget gem.*

knocker nest *n.* A bra. See also *over the shoulder boulder holder, kitten hammock.*

knockers 1. *n.* Devices for banging on doors. 2. *n.* Breasts. *'What a lovely pair of knockers, Lord Owen.'* 3. *n.* Of football punditry, those who have criticised a player in the past. *'Well Brian, the lad has certainly had his fair share of knockers.'*

knocking shop 1. *n.* Brothel, *rub-a-tug parlour.* 2. *n.* A pub or club where women go to be picked up. A *meat mart.*

knockin' on Heaven's door 1. *n.* Title of a bad record by not-quite-*poodle rockers* Guns 'n' Roses, based loosely on quite a good song by Bob Dylan. 2. *n.* The act of trying to penetrate a lady up her *tradesman's.*

knock off the bobby's helmet *v.* To engage in a fistfight with one's *little Kojak.*

knock one in *v.* The female version of *knock one out.* To *play the invisible banjo.*

knock one on *v.* To have it off. *'I've got five minutes before the wife picks me up, love. Do you fancy nipping into the stationery cupboard and knocking one on?'*

knock one out *v.* To have *one off the wrist. 'I've got five minutes before the wife picks me up, love. Do you fancy keeping lookout while I nip into the stationery cupaord and knock one out?'*

knock the back out of her *v.* Of a man, to have a very energetic *romp* up a lady.

knock the bottom out of *v.* To *bang the*

arse off someone. *'How did you get on with that pissed up slapper you pulled last night, constable?' 'Great. I took her into the back of the van and knocked the bottom out of her, sarge.'*

knock the lid off the ark *v.* To release an *arse banshee* of biblical proportions that causes everyone in the room to disintegrate. From the climatic scene of the first *Indiana Jones* movie.

Knorr stockpot *euph.* A fat, meaty, ill-kempt *ladygarden*. So-called as it looks a bit like fat, meaty, ill-kempt chef Marco-Pierre White and, in the words of the advert, "you can really smell the beef".

knot splitter *n.* A *toilet baby* of impressive, *nipsy*-challenging girth. *'Gerry (alarmed): What was that scream, Margot? Are you alright in there? (Flush sounds. Toilet door opens. Margot appears, holding doorframe to steady herself) Margot: Get me a gin and tonic, Gerry, and make it a large one. Gerry (pouring drink): What's happened? Margot: That's the last time I eat a slice of Tom and Barbara's Broad Bean Flan. I've just done a knot splitter in there that's probably blocked the drains from Surbiton to Thames Ditton. (Tom appears at the French windows in wellingtons.) Tom: Have you just started the extractor fan in your bathroom, Margot? Margot: Yes. Why? Tom: Well, three of my pigs have just fainted. FX: 10 seconds of canned laughter. Cue theme music and end titles.'* (Extract from script of *The Good Life Christmas Special*, BBC TV 1978).

know, in the Biblical sense *v.* To have *carnival knowledge* of or to *bang* someone. *'Last year at Club 18-30 I knew about*
forty birds in the Biblical sense, in eight days! And another six sucked me off.'*

Knowle facelift *n.* Budget cosmetic surgery, whereby bags under the eyes, wrinkles and even eyelids are flattened by the over-enthusiastic application of hair scrunchies.

knows what's in his flowerbeds, he *euph.* *Good with colours. 'You know that bloke at number thirty-one? Well I was talking to Edna in the butchers and, well, not to put too fine a point on it, let's just say he knows what's in his flowerbeds, I'll put it no stronger than that.'*

knows what's in his wardrobe *euph.* Said of a young man who *knows what's in his flowerbeds* too.

knuckle glitter *n. Funky spingers.*

knuckle nightcap *n.* A late-night *Sherman* which aids restful sleep. *Forty wanks.*

knuckles, as blurry as a wanker's *sim.* Descriptive of something that is very out of focus. *'Despite intensive, round-the-clock investigations, police been unable to identify any suspects. Unfortunately, although the build up to the murder, the hit itself and the gunman's escape through Fulham in a speeding car were all captured on numerous CCTV cameras, all the footage turned out to be as blurry as a wanker's knuckles.'* (Nick Ross, *Crimewatch UK*, 1998).

koala bear's ears 1. *n.* Tufts of female *puberage* sticking out the sides of *dunghampers. Judges' eyebrows, thighbrows.* 2. *n. Aus.* The *man flaps* that protrude round the sides of over-tight *noodle benders.*

Kojak's moneybox *n.* The *herman gelmet.*

Kojak's roll-neck *n. Foreskin.* Based on

the slap-headed lolly-sucking 1970s TV detective who always wore a cheesy-necked pullover.

KOKO/koko *acronym*. An exclamation coined by the Central Office of Information during World War II for the use of armed services personnel. Knickers Off, Knockers Out.

konz *n*. How a native Cornish speaker would refer to a *cunt*. *'Oi, fetch us some more clotted cream and jam for my fucking cream tea, you konz.'*

kosher dill *n*. A circumcised *gherkin*.

Kronenberg *n*. A lady who appears from behind to be about "16", but reveals herself to be about "64" when she turns round. From the famous "Young Bird Old Bag" lager made by the Kronenberg brewery.

Kruger *n*. A scary *hand job* from a woman with extremely long fingernails.

A *Freddy*.

kumikaze attack *n*. A ruthless close-range facial assault waged by the *Jap's eye*. *Cum bombing*.

kung food *n*. Chinese comestibles.

kung-foolery *n*. Alcohol-induced martial art, the practice of which involves much flailing of limbs and falling over, often resulting in broken bones.

Kursk *n*. A giant *dreadnought* mouldering at the bottom of the *pan*.

Kuwaiti tanker *rhym. slang*. A *merchant banker*.

kweef *n*. *US*. A *pump* from the *front bottom*, a *drop of the hat, forwards*, a *Lawley kazoo, vulvuzela*.

KY jelly *n*. Your pudding after a *fish supper* at *granny's oyster bar*.

Kyle style *n*. The fashions worn by denizens of the urban underclasses. *Scrote couture, Armani & Navy, Primani*.

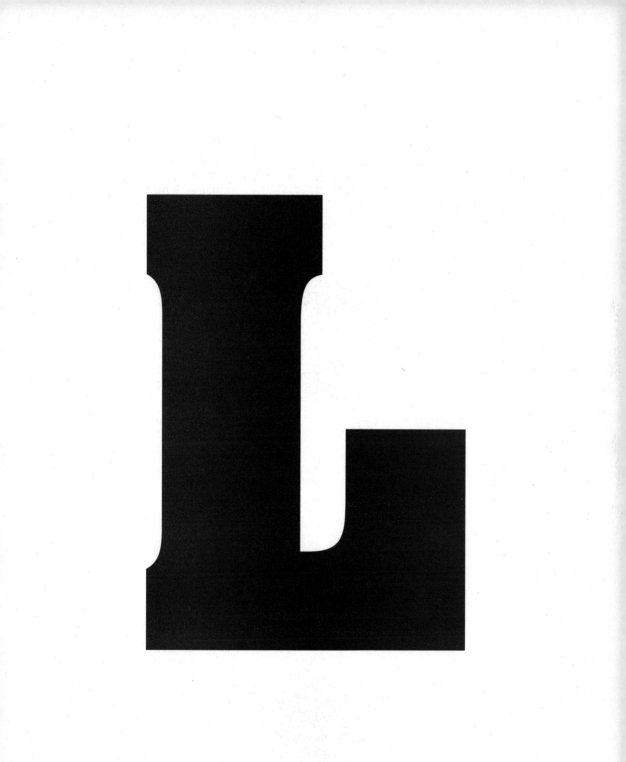

labia lard *n*. *Fanny batter, blip, beef dripping.*

labia majorca *n*. *medic*. A cheap and popular destination for lads on holiday. *Mutton shutters, Ibiza curtains.*

labia minorca *n*. *medic*. A slightly smaller holiday destination, though just as popular.

labiarinth *n*. A term describing the unnecessarily complex design of a woman's *Hampton Maze.*

labiathan *n*. A dauntingly large and unwieldy *fanny. John Merrick's cap.*

lab kebab *n*. Ladies' donner labiums. The *vertical bacon sandwich, fur burger.* Looks quite appetising when you've had a *skinful.*

labrador lipstick *n*. A dayglo pink *stalk on.*

lab technician *n*. Someone with a workmanlike attitude to handling *knicker bacon.*

lace curtain *1. n*. An exceptionally long *fiveskin, Serge Gainsbourg's mouth. 2. n*. A delicate gossamer fretwork of *helmetdale.*

lack of composure in front of goal *1. n*. Syndrome suffered by footballers who fail to score when presented with a gilt-edged opportunity. *2. n*. A sudden lack of penile composure whereby one's *midfield playmaker* fails to rise to the occasion. *Falling at the final hurdle.* '*Pele there, suffering from a rare lack of composure in front of goal, Brian.*'

lactose intolerant *adj*. Said of a frigid woman who refuses to imbibe the *milk of human kindness*. '*My missus never swallows. She's lactose intolerant.*'

ladyboy *n. ornith*. A confusing species of *cock bird* with female plumage and *tits*. A *chickboy*. Native to Bangkok and Iggy Pop's hotel room. A *shim, tiptop, trolley dolly, bobby dazzler.*

Lady Chalk of Billingsgate *n*. Thrush, a yeast infection of the vagina. '*I regret to announce that Lady Chalk of Billingsgate is visiting at this present time, Bishop. Could you pass the yoghurt?*'

Lady Ga Ga's cock *euph*. Descriptive of something that is plainly obvious to everyone, but is never openly admitted to. Like the fact that Cliff R(the rest of this entry has been omitted on legal advice).

ladygarden *n*. The fertile patch where a *downhill gardener* plants his seeds.

ladyglue *n*. Clear, viscous fluid exuded by ladies of the female variety before, during and after moments of peak sexual excitement, such as seeing Enrique Iglesias, Barry Manilow or Michael Bolton in concert.

lady golfer *n*. A *wearer of comfortable shoes*. A *carpet muncher, tennis fan, KD lady.*

lady in waiting *1. n*. Actress in a *meat movie* threesome who, temporarily, has nothing to do. A *grumble gooseberry*, a *ballflower. 2. n*. A reclining *grumble flick* actress anticipating the imminent arrival of several short flights from the *Greek Island of Testos. 3 n*. The lady in a *flesh mag*, who is sure to "do the job", but is held in reserve until the rest of the publication has been thoroughly investigated. A *finisher.*

lady killer *n*. A penis of such extreme length or girth that it could prove fatal. A *cunt buster*, a *kipper ripper, kidney wiper.*

lady marmalade *n*. Patti Labelle's *labia lard. Fanny batter* with bits of orange peel in it.

Lady Penelope's minge *n.* A *snatch* that is *boiling beetroots, ie.* One with "a string attached".

ladypetals *n.* A demure and winsome soubriquet for the *pissflaps* of the *cunt.*

lady petrol *n.* Four star *tart fuel, unleaded bitch piss.* White wine.

lady's bridge *1. n.* See *varse. 2. n.* Title of a Richard Hawley album about his missus's *varse.*

lady's low toupee *n.* A *merkin,* a *cunt rug.* An all-weather *ladygarden.*

lady-tramp *n.* A woman of deceptively sophisticated appearance who lets herself down the moment she opens her mouth, *eg.* Denise Van Outen, Hilda Baker.

lager bomb *n.* A strong-smelling *becksfart,* a symptom of *brewer's flu.*

lagerlepsy *n. medic.* Falling asleep suddenly when you have had one beer too many. *'My client would contend, your honour, that he was not drunk whilst in charge of his vehicle. Tragically, he suffers from a rare medical condition which is exacerbated by sitting down between the hours of 11.00pm and 5.00am, and had merely sunk into a lagerleptic coma whilst driving home from the pub.'*

lager log *n.* A sleek and smooth morning-after *feeshus* that slips into the water *like an otter off the bank.* The opposite of an *alien.*

lager top *n.* A market-bought polo shirt which is unsubtly decorated with the logotype of a leading designer who is unlikely to have benefitted financially from the few pounds its owner spent on it. As worn by the kind of young men who are typically seen drinking loudly outside pubs or on public transport. A *Ted Faker.*

lairy-focals *n.* Aids to double vision which make a bloke feel hard as nails whilst rendering all the ugly women he sees beauty queens. Particularly fighty *beer glasses.*

Lake Wendouree *n. Aus.* Ejaculation. From the very, very small, sticky lake at *Ballarat,* Australia.

lamb cannon *n.* A high-calibre arms development dating somewhere between the *mutton musket* and the *bacon bazooka.*

lamb hangings *n.* A none-too- appetising *butcher's window* display. *Mutton shutters, beef curtains, gammon goalposts, steak drapes, bacon strips, flackets.* A lady's *labia majorcas.*

Lamborghini *n.* A *cunt 'tache.* A small, pointless tufty outcrop of pubage remaining on a *shaven haven.* A *jazz fanny* or *clitler.*

lamp a champion *v.* To squeeze out a much larger *shit* than you thought possible. To *punch way over your weight* in the lavatory.

Lance Harmstrong *n.* Nickname given to a *scratter* who acts dead hard despite riding round on a toddler's mountain bicycle, tucking his tracky bottoms into girl's white socks and wearing an *Essex tartan* hat.

land ahoy! *exclam.* Another of the growing list of witty remarks to be uttered after *the wind changes.* Also *good point well presented, they have a range now Captain* and *ah, the mating call of the mallard.*

landing *n.* The area between the bedroom and the lavatory, or between the *shitter* and the *sack.* The *barse, ABC,* the perineum. A place where it's probably best to leave the light off, all things considered.

landlady's forearm *n. medic.* Ailment closely linked to *bingo wings*, suffered by fat, dumpy women, *eg.* Star Psychic Sally Morgan, her off *Wife Swap* and all dinnerladies.

landmine *n.* A fresh *dog's egg* hidden in a suburban lawn, which is often detonated by a lawnmower, leading to untold misery.

Lando *n.* A *clag, dangleberry* or *winnit.* Named after the *Star Wars* rebel character who was caught on the edge of the Sarlak pit and was thus forced to hang near its foul-smelling and gaping mouth until either picked clear by Han Solo or blasted off with the shower.

land on your nads *phr.* To experience the opposite of landing on your feet. *'Did you hear about Trevor? He accidentally knocked up fat Annie from the Dog and Trumpet. Now he's had to marry her and take a job as a giblet puller's assistant in his father-in-law's abattoir.' 'Fuck me. He sure landed on his nads there, didn't he?'*

landslide victory *n.* A huge vote of confidence for a sitting party.

langball *n.* Type of *dangleberry* which attaches itself to *John Wayne's hairy saddlebags.*

langer *n.* Penis.

langered *adj. Wankered. Refreshed.*

language Timothy! *exclam.* Yet another humorous rejoinder to a person *letting some air out of the balloon,* spoken in the style of Ronnie Corbett's screen father Sydney Lumsden in *Sorry* - better known as *Coronation Street*'s Betty Driver, alias Betty Turpin's late fictional husband Cyril, who was, in real life, married to the late Mrs Slocombe out of *Are You Being Served?,* real name the late Mollie Sugden - William Moore (1916-2000).

lank *adj.* Late, as a result of going for a *wank. 'Sorry I'm lank. Now here are the main headlines.'*

lapdog *n.* A Spearmint Rhino dancer with a *lovely personality.* A *4am girl.*

LAPOS/lapos *acronym.* A *knob* sported by the less generously-endowed gentleman. Like A Penis Only Smaller. *'STRAW, Jack, Lab., Blackburn (1979) b. 3 Aug. 1946. Ed. Brentwood Sch.; Leeds Univ.: Inns of Court Sch. of Law. Parliamentary Career: Contested Tonbridge and Malling 1974, succeeded Barbara Castle in this seat, Foreign Secretary (2001 - 2006),* Lord High Chancellor of Great Britain and Secretary of State for Justice (2007 - 2010), Shadow Deputy Prime Minister (2010 -). *Chairman All Party Lapos Group (1979 -).'* (from *Who's Who With a Really Really Small Cock*).

lapper *n.* Hairy pie eater, *bacon sandwich* connoisseur.

lap poodle *n.* A gently-bouffanted *minge,* much in fashion in the 1970s. A *Judith, Jackson, muffro.*

laptop *n.* A light, compact, perfectly-formed piece of kit that can be booted up on your lap or table as desired. A *throwabout.*

larder lout *n.* A person *with a lovely personality* who can't stop grazing. Fridge clearances a speciality.

lardigan *n.* A woollen outer garment worn knotted around the waist by larger ladies in a futile attempt to hide their big, fat *arses.*

lardi gras *n.* A Lizzie Duke-heavy festival of *cracksuit-wearing, big-boned scrat-*

ters which takes place every Saturday afternoon outside the golden arches at a precinct near you.

Lard of the flies *n.* The male *membrum virile,* just fattening up nicely in the trousers.

lard of the manor *n.* The *piabetic* bloke who lives on your estate. A *Duke of Giblets.*

lard on *1.n.* A porn star's perfunctory *hard on* which does the job, but only just. A *satiscraptory bonk on.* 2. *n.* The state of non-sexual excitement felt by a *bigger-boned* gentleman when approaching a Ginster's display. 3. *n.* The sort of small erection experienced when looking at a *filfy plumper.*

lard wimple *n.* A *pelican's beak, chin airbag.*

lardy dah 1. *adj.* Of a gunner with small round glasses, bald, thin and able to play the piano. 2. *n.* A lady *with a lovely personality* who has ideas above her social station.

large hadron collider, like shooting electrons in a *sim.* Unsatisfying coital congress with a *bucket-fannied slapper. Also throwing a Woodbine up Northumberland Street* (Tyneside), *throwing a sausage up Briggate* (Leeds), *chucking a fag down Parliament Street* (Nottingham). *'I fucking tell you what, right, some of the birds I've fucked have twats so big it's like shooting electrons in a large hadron collider.'* (Russell Brand sitting in for Ken Bruce, BBC Radio 2).

large hard-on collider *n.* A fat lass who is capable of generating vast amounts of kinetic energy with her pelvis, possibly leading to a pair of bruised *Higgs bosons.* And a broken *cock.*

lark rise to camel foot *euph.* Waking up with a *stiffy* and getting *stuck in* straight away.

larse *n. medic.* The lateral point of the upper thigh where the leg becomes the *arse.* The bit seen in *jazz mags* that remains white even though the model has spent many hours on a sunbed. *'... the femoral vein ascends behind the semi-tendinosus, where it joins the great saphenous vein just behind the larse and continues on to meet inferior vena cava half way between the tits and the fanny...'* (from *Andy Gray's Anatomy*).

lasagne turd *n.* A *tom tit* topped with a layer of *arsewipe,* followed by an unexpected bonus layer of *bum mince,* then finished off with an extra stratum of *shit tokens.* Parmesan optional. *Bangers and mash, Viennetta.*

lashing strap *n.* In the haulage industry, a 3-inch-wide strap and buckle arrangement with a breaking strain of 5 tons, used by lorry drivers to tie down heavy loads onto the backs of their trucks. 2. *n.* The choice of thong or *tit pants* strap for the fatter lass, *eg.* Michelle MacManus off *Pop Idol.*

lash on, get a bit *v.* To find some female company. *'Howay, let's gan oot an' get a bit lash on.' 'Very well, your Grace.'*

Lassie, buried more bones than *sim.* Of a woman, to be velocipedically inclined, municipally speaking. *'Paris Hilton? Nice looking chick, but she's buried more bones than Lassie, your Holiness.'*

last drag on a rollup *euph.* The pained, one-eyed expression pulled by a guitarist hitting a high note or by a *grumble* actor going for the *money shot.*

last hotdog in the tin *sim.* Descriptive of penetrative sex with a lady possessed of a *wizard's sleeve. Wall of death*, dipping a worm in a bucket.

last meat supper *n*. Final fling before marriage. It's all *fish suppers* thereafter.

last minute bookings *n*. The desperate and desperately unattractive *blart* that one is free to pull at 1.59 am after the *ugly lights* come up in a nightclub. *Floor sweepings*, *sediment*.

last night's pizza *n*. A woman that was hot when you picked her up, but doesn't seem quite so hot the next morning. *Hotel toast*.

last of the shampoo, that's the *exclam*. What a lady says to cover up her embarrassment when she *drops a gut* in the shower. Or when she runs out of shampoo.

last orders *n*. The ring of an *arse bell* that causes a stampede of similar magnitude to that experienced at 10.50 pm in pubs up and down the land. *'Stand back, your holiness. I had three scotch eggs and a pint of Bass for lunch, and I've just called last orders.'*

last orders at the pink bar *euph*. Announcements heralding the onset of the *vinegar strokes. 'Are you on the pill, love, 'cos it's last orders at the pink bar?'* (Wilfred Hyde-White quoted in the *Memoirs of Joyce Grenfell*).

last pearl, piss out the *v*. Following ejaculation, to visit a lavatory/sink/bath/telephone kiosk/bank doorway in order to urinate and thus scour out any remaining *jelly jewellery* which may be nestling inside the brim of the *farmer's hat*. To have a *pipecleaner*.

last pint in the barrel *n*. A particularly wet, sticky and unsatisfactory *shite*.

last post *n*. Ceremonial act of *standing to attention* whilst lowering one's *bird's*

knickers last thing at night.

last resort *n*. A light-hearted pet name for the *bag for life, ie*. That which one reluctantly returns to after a failed night *on the pull*.

last turkey in the shop *n*. Yet another bit of *ad hoc* genital vaudeville that never fails to impress the ladies, although it typically finds somewhat less favour with one's probation officer. See *the elephant*.

last week's lettuce *n*. An unappetising lady's *cludge*, from its similarity to an out-of-date salad, *ie*. Brown, limp, sweaty, and sticking to the side of the bag. *'Fancy a lick of last week's lettuce, Charlie?' 'No thanks, Camilla.'*

last whoreders *n*. The chaotic rush for *rashgash* in a meat market at ten to two. *The witching hour, two o'clock binrake*.

last year's hanging basket *n*. An untidy, straggly *mott. Kenn Dodd's hairbrush, Terry Waite's allotment*.

latch lifter *n*. A borrowed fiver which enables one to enter a public house. *'Lend us a latch lifter till I get my giro, will you?'*

lathered *adj*. Pissed, plastered, langered.

LATTOT/lattot *exclam. acronym*. Derogatory term used towards a man who sports bigger breasts than most women. Look At The Tits On That. *'You join us at the State Opening of Parliament, just as the Liberal Democrat peer Lord Owen of Plymouth takes his oath of allegiance. And as he steps forward... Fuck me! Lattot!'*

laugh at the carpet *v*. To *park a tiger*. To vomit.

laugh at the grass *v. Aus*. An *al fresco* liquid guffaw at a particularly amusing bit of floor. *'Where's Bruce, Bruce?' 'He's outside laughing at the grass, Bruce.'*

launch your lunch *v.* To *hurl one's biscuits.*

lava lamp *1. n.* A kitsch electrical appliance that was all the rage in the 1960s and again now, especially in the Gadget Shop. *2. n.* The appearance of the bath after one has *waxed the dolphin* in it.

lava lamp, guts like a *sim.* The unpleasant sensation that big, glowing, waxy bubbles of gas are backing up one's large intestine. Possibly following a night on the pop or a delicious meal enjoyed at the Curry Capital, Bigg Market, Newcastle upon Tyne.

lavatory *n.* The smallest room, little house, *loo*, water closet, convenience, place of easement, *shithouse, crapper, privy, bog*, latrine, *cackatorium, temple of cloacina*, toilet, *khazi, thunder box, comfort station, meditation room, library, gentleman's reading room*, shitter.

lav child *n.* A *turd.* Arse baby.

lavender *adj.* Pertaining to *good listeners.*

Lavender Lodge, they live in *euph.* Coded reference to women who are *fans of walking holidays.* Named after the *lady golfer* residents of the eponymous address in in the village of Fawcett Magna, near Ambridge, in Radio 4 serial *The Archers.* See also *batting for Darrington.*

lavender marriage *n.* Any matrimonial coupling about which there is a whiff of *lavender.*

lavender milk *n.* The ejaculate of a fellow who prefers to skip across small areas of standing water.

lavitation *n.* The yogic exercise performed when hovering over a public lavatory seat so as to avoid direct contact when having a *shit.*

lav train *n.* The swarm of ladies that all go to the toilet together in pubs.

Lawley kazoo *n.* A *hat dropped forwards. Harry Secombe's last raspberry.* A *kweef.* Derivation known, but subject to legal restrictions.

lawn monkey *n.* The possible consequences of a *split jubber ray.* Also *yard ape, turf chimp, fanny turd.*

lawn sausages *n. Park links, dog's eggs, dog toffee, hound cable.*

Lawrence *n.* Somewhat contrived epithet for a fellow who is in single-minded pursuit of his *summer cabbage.* From "Lawrence of a labia".

lay *1. n.* Prospective or past sexual partner. *'I knew your wife many years ago. She was a terrific lay.' 2. v.* To *fuck* a woman with a small amount of cement and a trowel.

lay a cable *v.* To *build a log cabin, grow a tail, drop a copper bolt.*

lay a cuckoo's egg *1. v.* A party trick where a foreign *bogie* is introduced into an unconscious reveller's nostril for the amusement of the other guests. *2. v.* To get someone else's missus *up the duff. 'Have you seen him? Nowt like his brother or his dad. He's fucking ginger. Somebody's laid a cuckoo's egg there, if you ask me?'* (*Nigel Dempster's Diary,* 1984).

lay-and-display *n.* A type of European lavatory where the *twinkie* lands on a dry porcelain surface for inspection prior to being flushed away.

laying the tarmac *n.* A *Boston pancake* that ends up costing much more than the original estimate.

lazy lob on *n.* A semi-erect penis, a *dobber, half a teacake.*

lazy man's wee *n.* A gentleman's sit-down *piss*, usually taken in the middle of the night when his aim cannot be trusted. A *she-pee*.

lead in your pencil, to have *v.* To be *on the stonk*. Not like one of those floppy, leadless pencils.

lead the children of Israel to safety *v.* To commit an act of *rag week cumulonimbus*. To *part the red sea*.

lead the llama to the lift shaft *v.* To point *Percy* at the vagina.

leaker *n. Aus.* A sexually alluring female, that is to say, one who "has holes that need to be plugged up".

leap of filth *n.* The feeling of blind trust needed when buying *grumble* online. 'He told us: '*I feel badly let down. I made a twenty quid leap of filth and you can't even see it going in.*' Cyril...' 'Thank-you Esther.'

leap round *n.* A round of drinks purchased by the slower drinker in the group, in which he does not buy a drink for himself, to prevent himself falling behind. Similar in concept to a leap year, only with a pint less rather than a day more.

learn *v.* Of a man, to make love to his sweetheart. '*Get on that bed. I'll fucking learn you, you dirty bitch.*'

leather on willow, like the sound of *sim.* A very pleasing *crack*. '*Was her topiary in good order?*' '*Leather on willow, mate. Leather on willow.*'

leave her on charge *v.* To deliberately keep the missus in a state of sexual anticipation. '*Me and the wife are going away for a lovely weekend without the kids tomorrow, so I'm not sure whether to give her a good seeing-to tonight or to just leave her on charge. What do the panel think?*' '*Bob Flowerdew?*'

leave negative feedback *v.* To *fart* and walk away.

lecher's nightmare *n.* A grisly underwear display given by Stilton-thighed elderly ladies when they sit in deck chairs. *Next month's washing.*

lechfast *n.* A young East European man's morning meal enjoyed straight out of the tin. From Lech - the name of a popular premium strength lager which is popular in Poland.

left footer *n.* A gay or Catholic person, but ideally one who is both.

left hand down, a bit *adj. Good with colours.* '*Have you met Quentin? You'll like him, he's a bit left hand down a bit.*'

left-handed batsman *n.* Someone who prefers his balls delivered from the *pavilion end.*

left-handed web site *n.* An internet website specialising in *cyberscud*, causing visitors to use the mouse with the wrong hand.

left legger *n.* A lady who particularly enjoys being *sorted out* on the front passenger seat of a car. Derived from the technique of hanging her left leg out the window, thus affording the driver unhindered access to her *cunker*, assuming he can avoid getting the gear lever stuck up his *arse..*

left luggage *n.* Traces of *feeshus* left in the toilet bowl even after flushing.

left the lid off the gluepot? who's *interrog.* Rhetorical device implying that someone smells of *merry monk*. '*Jesus, Your Majesty! Who's left the lid off the gluepot?*'

legacy *1. n.* The glorious bequest to the nation of a highly-popular and successful Prime Minister. *2. n.* A stinksome *Thora* left by the previous incumbent of a water closet who couldn't be *arsed* to flush. *'Gordon, can you bring the plunger up, please? Tony's left a legacy in the upstairs cludgie.'*

leg bye *n.* When a *Harmison loosener* trickles down leg-side for some unexpected *runs.*

leg elvising *n.* The frantic *Ed Sullivan Show*-style gyrations performed whilst trying to shake a bit of *follow through* out the bottom of one's trouser leg.

leg iron shuffle *n.* The gait adopted by one with the *turtle's head,* trying to make it to the *crapper* without *signing his bills.*

leg lifter *n. Benefactor.* Somebody who *breaks company.*

leg man *n.* One who prefers ladies' *gams* to their *tits* or *arses.*

leg necklace *n.* An act of *cumulonimbus.*

lego hand *n. medic.* A tertiary form of *wanker's cramp.* A condition afflicting the hand of one who has overindulged in *self-pollution.* From the similarity to the rigid, empty grasp of the Danish toy figures.

leg over *n.* A *sausage and doughnut situation. 'Did you get your leg over?' 'No, but I got tops and three fingers.'*

leg tensing *n.* The act of tensing one's leg when having a *toss. 'This wank is going nowhere. I'd better get a bit of leg tensing in.'*

leg warmer *n.* The *fiveskin* or *peparami wrapper.*

Lehman's wank *n.* Example of masturbatory meltdown. The collapse of an act of filthy *self abuse* mid-way through trading due to a lack of interest.

leisure facilities *n. medic.* Breasts, com-petitive advantages, impressive CVs.

leisure trove *n.* A veritable Aladdin's cave of *relaxation-oriented literature,* such as might be discovered in the study of a recently-deceased vicar by his startled family.

lemon party *n.* A term that it isn't wise to type into Google Image Search with the Safesearch function set to "Off". See also *blue waffle.* Or rather, don't.

Lemsip and a wank *n.* A cure for whatever ails you. A p*anhandle-acea.* After listening to one's tale of woe, divorce, sacking *etc.,* a mate might reply, *'Have a Lemsip and a wank and you'll soon feel better.'*

Lemmy's warts *n.* Off-puttingly big nipples.

lend *v.* To give, in the *sausage* sense. *'Phwoar! Your mum's a bit of alright. I wouldn't mind lending her one'.'*

length *n.* An Imperial saucy postcard unit of *the other,* as *slipped* to a woman by a man who works in a lino factory.

Lenny, do a *v.* To exhibit the symptoms of a *morning glory, ie.* To be "up at the crack of dawn". An amusing reference to the popular light entertainer Lenny Henry, whose penis used to be occasionally erect near the vaginal entrance of his ex-wife, the actress Dawn French.

Leonardo *n.* An annoying little piece of *shit* that refuses to go down the *pan* after the main *dreadnought* has sunk. Named after the little actor who annoyingly floated around, refusing to die quickly at the end of *Titanic.*

Leons *n. medic.* The *trots.* From Leon Trotsky (1879-1940), the Russian revolutionary and Marxist theorist who famously got an ice-pick that made his ears burn, and also suffered something rotten with the *Mexican screamers*.

leopard's back *n*. Worse than a *tiger's back*; a *chod bin* that has been peppered with *arse shrapnel*.

Leo Sayer *rhym. slang*. All dayer. *Bender*, a prolonged drinking session, all day party.

lesbian *n*. A *tennis fan*.

lesbiany *adj*. Appertaining to lesbism. *'Any chance of you and your mate doing something lesbiany?' 'Okay, we'll put some more comfortable shoes on, how about that?'*

lesbionage *n*. The furtive act of watching a couple of *carpet munchers* as they *munch* each others's *carpets*, perhaps whilst up a ladder and wearing infra-red night vision goggles.

lesbo *n*. A *tuppence licker, bean flicker, carpet muncher, lickalotopus, dyke*.

lesbology *n*. The scientific study of lesbian activity. A branch of feminism studied almost exclusively by males which involves much scrutiny of video footage.

lesbro *n*. A heterosexual man who prefers the company of women who prefer the company of women. The male equivalent of a *fag hag*. A *rug hugger*.

lesidue *n*. Pronounced "lezzy dew". The moisture that remains on the morning bedsheets of those ladies who choose to eschew cramped footwear.

Leslie gash *n*. A luscious-lipped trout-pouting *fanny*. After the Ivy Tilsley-gobbed former Homebase ad star.

let off *v*. To *let rip, blow off, launch an air biscuit*.

let off some steam, Bennett *exclam*. Humorous preamble to a *gaseous emission*, to be delivered in the style of Arnold Scharzenegger in the film *Commando*. Or any other of his films, for that matter.

let one go *v*. To *let off*.

let Percy in the playpen *n*. Of a woman, to consent to intercourse.

let rip *v*. Let one go.

let's get rrrrready for grumble! *exclam*. An ear-piercing shout, similar to that made by a boxing match announcer, uttered by a man when his wife has left the house and gone to her mother's for the weekend, thus affording him a rare opportunity to enjoy a period of uninterrupted quality time with his *art pamphlet* collection.

letter from Mr Shit, a *euph*. An advance announcement that a visit from a long-awaited guest is imminent. A *custard tart*.

let the dog out *v*. To nip home at lunchtime and *feed the ducks* after a frustrating morning surrounded by *office beaver*. Fire the one o'clock gun. *'Hold all my calls, Miss Jones. I'm just nipping home to let the dog out.'*

let the twins out *euph*. Of a lady, to remove her brassiere.

lettuce *n*. The crinkly leaves underneath the *gorilla salad*. The *piss flaps*.

lettuce licker *n*. A *lezza*.

lever arches *rhym. slang*. Haemorrhoids. From lever arch files = Chalfonts.

lezza *n*. A woman who is *fond of walking holidays*.

lezzo boots *n*. Any clumpy, unfeminine footwear worn by women. The opposite of *fuck me shoes*. *Fuck off slippers*.

Liam Gallagher, the *n*. The swaggering, reclined, semi-horizontal walking style that a man adopts during his customary midnight stroll from bedroom to bathroom in search of toilet roll; his laid-back gait adopted in order to negate the effects of gravity upon his nocturnal emissions, and thus protect the pile of his landing carpet. Also known as an *Ian Brown*.

lib dem loafers *n.* Unsightly open-toed sandals of the sort typically worn with socks by balding *euphemersity* lecturers.

libratory *n.* A *crapper* which is well stocked with *shiterature*. From library + lavatory.

lick a bus battery *v.* To commit *cumulonimbus* on a lady who is 2.66 times skankier than a *nine- volter*.

lickalotopus *n.* Scientific name for an experienced *carpet muncher*.

lick both sides of the stamp *v.* To be *AC/DC*, a *happy shopper*, a switch hitter, *half rice half chips*.

licker licence *n.* Permission to have a drink from the *hairy goblet*.

licking a nine-volter *n.* The act of *cumulonimbus* on a particularly skanky *snatch*, the eye-watering effect being the same as placing your tongue across the terminals of a PP3 battery.

lick of paint *n. Mexican lipstick. Pasata grin.* Consequence of a late *licker licence.*

lick one's arse and call it chocolate *phr.* Expression used to bring a deludedly optimistic person down to earth. *'Mr Speaker, my Right Honourable friend the Chancellor has told the house that thanks to his prudent fiscal policies the economy is in a stronger position now than ever. He is entitled to take that view, of course, and he is likewise entitled, should he wish, to lick his arse and call it chocolate.'*

lick out *1. v.* That which is done by a small child to a bowl of cake mix. *2. v.* That which is done by a moustachioed

grumble star to a *haddock pastie.*

lick-twat *n. prop.* One who has the gift of tongues. A *cumulonimbalist.*

lid *n.* The bit above the *brim.* The *herman gelmet.*

Lidled *adj.* Descriptive of a town or district that is in decline, evidenced by the opening of a branch of Lidls. Also *Nettoed, Aldied. 'Dover, once the gateway to Europe, home of the White Cliffs, now sadly Lidled.'*

life affirmer *n. Shit* taken during the worst depths of a hangover or other depression which is of such magnitude that it restores one's vital signs. A *crap* which would make the late Fred Astaire dance down the street, occasionally bouncing his silver-topped cane off the kerb.

lifting the cheek *n.* The sly behaviour of a *cushion creeper.*

light curry supper *n.* A vast, Chernobyl-strength vindaloo consumed at the end of a heroic night's drinking.

lighthouse cat, rank as a *sim.* Descriptive of a gentleman who has experienced an excessively long period without getting his hands on a *bird. 'Giz a shot on your clopper, Una. I feel as rank as a lighthouse cat.'*

lightning in a bottle *n.* A photographic *art study* which captures the moment a gentleman *expels his custard* in a shot arcing majestically towards the face of a beautiful young lady. Named after the equally tricky task of photographing a high-voltage meteorological discharge.

light the afterburners *v.* In honour of short-arsed scientologist Tom Cruise's fly-by of the aircraft carrier control tower in the movie *Top Gun*, to release an enormously powerful *ass blast* which results in rattling windows, disorientated friends, spilled coffee, a bollocking from the boss and possibly, some time later, the death of a close friend.

lilies on the pond *n*. The artistic practice popularised by impressionist painter Claude Monet of laying sheets of toilet tissue on the water surface before giving birth to *Meatloaf's daughter*. A *pap baffle*.

lils 1. *n*. 1950s/60s *Tits*. 2. *n*. *Stits*. From Liliputians.

lime water *n*. Semen, spunk, spooge, spangle, tweedle.

limpeting *n*. The dirty ladies' version of *teabagging*.

Linda Bellingham's fingertips *n*. The result of *breeching the hull* as a consequence of either over-zealous wiping of the *rusty sheriff's badge* or the purchase of insufficiently robust *arse paper*. Or a combination of the two. From the state of the erstwhile gravel-voiced Oxo mum's digits after a day spent crumbling her favourite stock-cubes into casseroles for her fictitious family's tea. Also known as *taxi driver's tan, mechanic's nails, finger of fudge, filter tip*.

lineman's pastie *n*. A very full disposable nappy thrown from a train window at loafing, orange-clad track workers.

lingam *n*. Hindu. Penis. From ancient *grumble book The Karma Sutra*.

links effect, the *euph*. The aromatic toilet visit which is enjoyed the morning after a night on the beer and *Ruby Murray*, when one's *arse* resembles a sausage machine as operated by a cack-handed contestant on *The Generation Game*.

lino munching *n*. The correct term for *rug munching* when the munchee's *pile* has been waxed off.

lion *n*. More *chod bin* contents terminol-

ogy. A magnificent two-tone *poo*, in gold and brown. Often makes its appearance accompanied by a loud roar and a pride of smaller cubs.

Lionel Bart *n. rhym. slang*. A particularly musical *custard tart* that gets you out of bed and forces you to swing the windows open and take a deep breath.

lion tamer's corpse *sim*. Descriptive of the sorry state of one's *chap* after a *rag week romp*. *Barber's pole*.

lippie *v*. Of a dog, to *frotter* on one's leg with its *lipstick* out. *'Aw. He must like you, Dr Watson,' expostulated the great detective, sucking on his pipe thoughtfully and adjusting the brim of his deerstalker with the handle of his magnifying glass whilst playing his violin. 'He's trying to lippie your leg, look.''* (from *The Hound of the Baskervilles* by Arthur Conan Doyle).

lip reading *n*. Observing women in tight pants who have the *camel's foot*. *'If she bends over any more I'll be able to read her lips from here.'*

lip ring *n*. A lipstick line around the circumference of one's *sword* which enables one to gauge how far it has been *swallowed* whilst one's wife is in the next room being sick.

lip ripper *n*. A magnificently girthsome *charlie*.

lip service *n*. A lacklustre act of *horatio* performed by a timid or blocked-nosed *nosher*.

lip sink *n*. The wash basin in the ladies' toilet of a pub in which *birds* have the female equivalent of a *gentleman's wash* when they have *pulled*.

lipstick *n*. A dog's *cock*, available in a variety of shimmery colours.

lipstick lesbian *n*. Glamorous, feminine

female homosexual, commonly found on the Adult Channel but rarely down the pub.

lip stretcher *n.* A particularly girthsome *choad.* A *Pringle tube.* A challenge to a pair of *DSLs.*

liquid allsorts *n.* The non-viscous feculant miscellany that results from an ill-advised binge on the Bertie Bassetts or Pontefract cakes.

liquid bookmark *n.* A homemade means of marking one's place in the pages of a gentlemen's *art pamphlet.*

liquid gold *n.* A cup of tea in Betty's tearooms.

liquid kids *n. Spooge, spunk,* heir gel, baby gravy.

liquid laughter *n. Puke, psychedelic yodelling.*

liquid pretzel *n.* A salty, refreshing snack. A somewhat tangled *lobbed rope.*

liquid rage *n. Fred.*

liquorice allsort *n.* A dark haired woman who frequents both the tanning salon and the tooth-whitening clinic. From her resemblance to the popular Bertie Bassett confectionery homunculus.

liquor portal *n.* The hole in the space/time continuum found outside pubs which transports the inebriated to the safety of their hallways in the blink of an eye. A science fiction *beer scooter.*

little & large show *1. n.* Early evening BBC1 series featuring the eponymous, contrastingly-sized double act, which unaccountably ran from 1978 to 1991. *2. n.* A pair of *Kelly Brooks* in a low-cut top or bikini.

Little Ben *n.* A small *Big Ben.*

little death *n. Fr.* In a male, the post-coital feeling of *shagged outity* which is symptomised by the opposite of rigor mortis.

liverdance *n.* The involuntarily rhythmic terpsichorean movements of an extremely heavily *refreshed* reveller. A *dance of the seven ales.*

liver lapels *n. Beef curtains, labia majorcas,* especially when used on Ed Gein's home-made suit.

live rounds in a training exercise, use *v.* To fire potentially dangerous *spammunition* into the field of battle when it might have been more sensible to keep your *bacon bazooka* safely muzzled, *eg.* Whilst having a final *bang* with a departing ex or whilst enjoying a drunken penetrative *romp* up a chubby waitress with big *tits. 'Why the long face, Boris?' 'Ich bin caught auf using live rounds in ein training exercise, Des.'*

liver sock *1. n.* The *fanny. 2. n.* A *butcher's favourite.*

livin' alright, that's *exclam.* Verbal accompaniment to the act of *spaffing* onto the missus's *poond.* From the Joe Fagin-performed theme tune to 1980s comedy drama *Auf Wiedersehen Pet,* in which he exhorted listeners to "send a little back to the wife".

Livingstone daisies *1. n. Bot.* Attractive flowers that come out when the sun shines. *2. n.* Attractive *knockers* that come out when the sun shines, causing taxi drivers to mount the pavement, milkmen to fall down manholes and straw-hatted vicars to ride their bicycles into fruit barrows.

lizard rag *n. Aus.* A scaly piece of bedside cloth used for wiping excess *spoff* and *moip* from one's *bloodstick* after *popping the turkey in the oven.*

lizard's lick *n.* A feeble ejaculation that barely clears the *hog's eye,* the unimpressive result of excessive *beauty shivering.*

A bankrupt *money shot*. A *gwibble*.

Llewellyn-Bowen's cuff *n*. An over-elaborate vagina. A foppish *ragman's coat*.

load *1*. *n*. 1996 Metallica album. *2*. *n*. The quantity of *cock hockle* blown, chucked or shot at the point of orgasm. *3*. *n*. That which is shed by a lorry driver, whilst *wanking* in a layby.

loaded *adj*. *Aus*. To be in need of a great big *shit*. To be *touching cloth*. *"Curiouser and curiouser' thought Alice, as the white rabbit came scampering past. 'I wonder where he's going in such a hurry.' 'Oh, my dear paws!' he cried. 'Oh my fur and whiskers, I'm loaded. If I don't reach the lavatory soon I shall surely papper my grundies."* (from *Alice's Adventures in Wonderland,* by Lewis Carroll).

loaded for bear *1*. *adj*. Hunting term, indicating that one is packing particularly impressive ammunition. *2*. *adj*. *Fucking* term, indicating that one is packing particularly impressive ammunition.

loading the mag *euph*. *milit*. *Thumbing in a slacky*. The act of easing a *lard-on* into a *fanny* in a porn film.

load of old shoes falling out a loft, like a *sim*. Descriptive of a heavy bout of loose, lively diarrhoea. A *flock of pigeons*.

load rage *n*. A violent confrontation in which a purple-faced *bald man* is struck viciously with a *wanking spanner*.

lobcock *n*. A large, flaccid penis such as could be *lobbed* onto a pub table by its drunken owner the way that Michael Elphick hits the fish on the bar in *Withnail and I*.

lob on, lazy *n*. *Half a teacake*.

lobotomy bay *n*. Semi-mythical destination of any serious drinking binge.

lob ropes *v*. To *jizz* onto something through thin air, *eg*. A face, some hair, some *tits etc*.

location, location, location *n*. To make a visit to all three aspects a lady's property in one visit, *ie*. *Upstairs*, *downstairs* and *round the back*. *'And now on Channel 4, Location, Location, Location.' 'Hey, I tell you what love, no offence but I wouldn't mind going location, location, location with that Kirstie Allsopp.'*

locked out, Mrs Brown is *euph*. Having *followed through*. *'Apologies, Your Excellency, but I really must be excused. I've just opened the back doors and it appears Mrs Brown is locked out again.'*

lock'n'load *1*. *phr*. Expression used in innumerable action movies as the hero leaps into action and cocks his weapon. *2*. *phr*. Expression used by a saucy *slapper* as she primes a chap's *custard cannon* with a practised snap of the wrist. *3*. *phr*. Expression used by a jobseeker as he pulls the curtains prior to his fifteenth *tug* of the morning.

locksmith *n*. A girl who has an impressive working knowledge of *knobs* and their operation.

log *n*. *Bum cigar, brown trout*.

logacy *n*. The long-lasting stench in a toilet cubicle, left by a generous *benefactor* for future generations to enjoy.

logarhythm *1*. *n*. In mathematics, a word that sounds like the exponent of the power to which a base number must be raised in order to equal a given number. Something like that, anyway. *2*. *n*. In shitting, the regularity of one's motions. *3*. *n*. The shaking of one's *arse* in an attempt to break the neck of a dangling *turtle*. The working out of a *simple harmonic motion*.

'When Elizabeth was near, D'Arcy's heart raced, and he got a panhandle that could poke holes in a cheap door.' ~ Pride and Prejudice by Jane Austen.

log cabin *n*. A wendy house for *Meatloaf's daughter*.

log fire *n*. The pain experienced in the *back body* the morning after eating a particularly spicy *Ruby Murray*. *Ring sting, Johnny Cash*.

log flume *1. n*. Simultaneously defecating and urinating down the same leg of one's kex. *2. n*. A *turd* in a pub *pissing* trough. *3. n*. A *Thora* splashing down into the pan.

log in *v*. To arrive at work, switch on one's computer, then disappear for a paid *shit*.

log splitter *1. n*. A rugged device consisting of hydraulic rams and a sharpened wedge, used to simplify and expedite the process of preparing firewood. *2. n*. An ossified mat of congealed *winnets*. *Rhino horn*.

lollipop lady *n*. A woman who is partial to the occasional *slice of cheesecake*.

lolly bag *n*. The scrotum.

lolly stick *n*. Anything pointlessly, but intentionally added to a pile of *shite*. A *turd's barnacle*. *'Has anyone seen that Big Brother's Little Brother? What a fucking lolly stick that is.'*

long ball game *1. n*. In football, a series of aimless pokes in the direction of the box in the hope of scoring. *2. n*. In bed, a series of aimless *pokes* in the direction of the *box* in the hope of *scoring*.

long distance Clara *1. n*. Wholesome female lorry driver in BBC children's series *Pigeon Street*. *2. n*. A *lorry driver's lunchbreak*, ie. Having a *crap* in a lay-by. *'Come in Steady Eddie. When are you expected back at the depot?' 'Control, this is Steady Eddie. I'm currently on the A66 but I had a wick Ginsters for breakfast at Abingdon Services, so I'm going to need ten minutes for a long distance Clara in the Barnard Castle lay-by.'*

long haul fanny *n. medic*. Condition of the female *farmyard area* caused by prolonged sitting in a cramped, crowded space, chief symptom of which is a distinctly malodorous *quiff*. Also known as *frequent flyer fent* or *cattle class crotch*.

longshanks *n*. One who is blessed/cursed with a very low-swinging *chicken skin handbag*. A *rantallion*.

lonk *v. German*. To *shit* oneself on orgasm.

look at *v*. Euphemism for masturbation. *'Did you look at that porn film I lent you yesterday?' 'Yeah, I had a quick look.'*

look for badgers *v*. To cruise for gay sex. Also *stretch one's legs*. *'I'm just going to stretch my legs. In a bush with a Tory MP.'*

looking for change in the hairy purse *n*. Deep, middle finger coin-sorting movement popular with *gusset-typing* old ladies at supermarket checkouts.

loon pipe *n. Anus*.

looniform *n*. Characteristic garb of one who favours screaming at the traffic as an occupation, usually consisting of a 1970s jacket and trousers that clear the ankles by a good three inches.

loop the loop *v*. To order a *vertical bacon sandwich* to *eat out* and a *drink on a stick* for the lady, *No.69* on the menu.

loo read *n*. Any book or magazine best perused whilst defecating. *Shiterature*.

loose at the hilt *adj*. Having diarrhoea, *the Brads*.

loose clacker *n. coll*. A herd of *ten-to-two-ers*. Ropey *cabbage*. The group of girls remaining unspoken for at night club chucking out time.

loose fries in the bag *euph.* Descriptive of a feeling of serendipitous sexual jubilation on discovering the *bird* one is *copping off* with has hidden extras, *eg.* She has a shaved *snatch*, is wearing stockings, is a *swallower.* From the joyous feeling experienced when, on finishing one's McDonald's, one finds extra chips in the bottom of the bag.

loose lips *n.* Affectionate description of a woman who has been *cocked* more times than Davy Crockett's rifle.

loose, on the *adj.* Of a *dirty lady, frothing like bottled Bass.* Having a *wide on.*

loose sausage meat *n.* A flaccid penis which cannot be funnelled into a condom. *Stuffing the marshmallow.* 'Sorry love, my sausage meat seems a bit loose.'

loose shunting *n.* A *dog's marriage* with a *clown's pocket.*

looviathan *n.* A *sea biscuit* of such gargantuan proportions that, once flushed, it forms the subject of myriad breathlessly-recounted legends amongst grizzled sewermen.

Lord Foulbowel *n.* One whose lower chamber is a rich source of *brownhouse gases, eg.* A Coventry City fan who spends 72 hours farting in a car accompanied by 4 friends as they attempt to visit all 92 football league grounds to raise money for charity.

Lord of the Pies *n.* A *salad dodger*, a *double sucker.* One whose *big bones* and *glands* are always dragging him into Greggs.

Lord Winston's moustache *n.* A particularly hairy and poorly-trimmed *biffer,* named after the exuberant face fungus

of the popular ennobled telly boffin, test-tube *fanny apple* pioneer and former leading *twat mechanic* Dr Robert Winston. Also *Rhodes Boysons, whackos.*

lorry driver's breakfast, fanny like a *sim.* Descriptive of a *clopper* which is cheap, greasy and requires plenty of sauce before consumption.

lorry driver's lunchbreak *n.* A *crap* in a layby, a *long distance Clara.*

loser cruiser *n.* Any form of public transport used predominantly by members of the urban underclass, *eg.* The Number 585 Otara to Central bus in Aukland, New Zealand. S*cum shovel.*

lose some weight *v.* To perform a *digestive transit. 'Sorry, Your Majesty. I need to lose some weight. Could you point me at the nearest shitter, love?'*

lose the marathon *v.* To take a long time to complete an act of *excreeshus.* Derivation unknown. *'That crap took me so long I would've lost the marathon.'*

lose your darts *v.* To become inexplicably impotent, or otherwise unable to *raise your throwing arm. 'I don't quite know how to put this, doctor, but I seem to have lost my darts, if you know what I mean.' 'There's no need to worry, Mr Brown. I'll put you on a course of Bongo Bill's Banjo Pills.'*

lose your manners *v.* To *shoot a bunny* whilst in polite company.

lose your mess *v.* To ejaculate, *shoot your load.*

losing ten seconds *adj.* Descriptive of one who has a *mole at the counter.* From Paula Radcliffe's 2005 London marathon run, during which she experienced controversial *traffic calming measure* difficulties that slowed her down by the specified time interval whenever a "violent stomach cramp" wracked her scrawny frame.

LOTIMTO/lotimoto *acronym*. Lovely On The Inside, Minging On The Outside.

lotties *n*. *Lils*, *dugs*.

loudmouth soup *n*. Beer.

Louis *v*. To force out a stubborn *turd* with such strain that one pulls a face like Satchmo going for a top E, and then has to mop the top of one's head with a handkerchief.

lounge with the furniture removed, like a *sim*. A spacious *liver sock* into which one could fancy fitting a table tennis table.

love bat *n*. During a game of sexual intercourse, the short, stout implement with which the man strikes his wife's *cunker*. See also *slag bat*.

love beads *n*. *milit*. Road surface farm animal containment provision which provides exceedingly fleeting and intermittent sexual stimulation for squaddies in the backs of "rumpety-pumpety" army trucks. A cattle grid.

love bumps *n*. *Funbags, guns of Navarone*.

love cough *n*. The *dropping forwards* of a *lady's hat*. A *queef*, a *Lawley kazoo*, a *frampton*. A *fanny fart*.

love juice *n*. That liquid produced in the *Billingsgate box* upon which the *skin boat* sails. Often referred to as *luv jooz* in illiterate 1970s *scud literature*. *Blip, moip*.

love lane *euph*. Poetic euphemism for a *bird's clopper*.

lovely personality, she's got a *euph*. Said of a woman who is not conventionally attractive for whatever reason.

love palace *n*. Coarse version of *cunt*.

love puff *n*. Gentle, romantic *air biscuit* launched in the direction of one's partner in bed, often the morning after a *Ruby*, in an attempt to cement the intimacy of the moment.

love sausage *n*. Big pink *banger* served with *hairy love spuds*.

love socket *n*. Vagina, entry point for the *main cable*. Also *rocket socket, serpent socket, spam socket*.

love spuds *n*. Starch-filled root vegetables found in the *shreddies*.

love torpedo *n*. *Rumpleforeskin*.

love tripe *n*. The savoury folds of tender flesh around a *bird's goalmouth*. The *labia majorcas* and *minorcas*.

love truncheon *n*. *Copper's torch*.

love tunnel *n*. That place in which *Percy* the small pink engine shunts his *load*. For about three minutes before he *blows his stack* and his *back wheels come off*.

lower decking *n*. The act of deliberately not flushing away a *dreadnought* in one's work toilets, then hiding in the adjoining cubicle to savour the next occupant's reaction.

low hanging fruit 1. *n*. *polit*. Funding which can be cut back easily during a belt-tightening budget. 2. *n*. *Nads* that hang out of badly-designed shorts.

low loaders *n*. Saggy breasts with a minimal amount of ground clearance. *Ulrikas*.

lowthario 1. *n*. A *fanny rat* who will *cattle* any old *boiler*. 2. *n*. An amorous midget.

LRF *abbrev*. Low Resolution Fox - a female who appears to be attractive from a long distance, but is in fact unbelievably ugly close up.

lucky dip *n*. The fortunate, final wipe of

one's *ring* which reveals a hidden *clod,* thus preventing *pappered pants* and an *autographed gusset.*

lucky Pierre *n.* In *botting* circles, the busiest *botting* link in a three man *bum chain*; the filling in a *shirt lifter* sandwich. A *botter* who is simultaneously a *bottee.*

lullage *n.* The overhanging flab seen on fat lasses wearing trousers they fully intend slimming into. A *gunt,* a *poond,* a *muffin top.*

lulu *n.* A lady who is getting on a bit, but is still worthy of *lengthage.* A *gilf.*

lumber 1. *n.* A raft of tightly-packed *turds* occluding the toilet water surface in a *chod bin* after an afternoon testing the "all you can eat" buffet at an Aberdeen Steak House. 2. *n.* A unspecified quantity of erect penii.

lumberjack's homework *euph.* The act of waiting till you get back from work before *dropping your logs.* '*I'm dying for a shit, Dave. But I knock off in five so I may as well bake it a bit longer and do a spot of lumberjack's homework.*'

lumberjill *n.* A hatchet-faced woman that fells one's *mighty redwood.*

lunchbox lancer *n. arch.* Medieval term for a *cocoa shunter.* '*Fear not the French, for their knights are without heart, and their King without wisdom. But keep thine backs as to the wall, for amongst their number thou shalt find more than a few lunchbox lancers, I can tell thou.*' (from *Henry V part III* by William Shakespeare).

lunchbox *n.* In British tabloid journalism, that conspicuous bulge in athlete Linford Christie's shorts, where he used to keep his sandwiches, a carton of Ribena, a Twix and an apple.

lunchboxing *n.* Unbelievably perverse sexual practice which makes a *Cleveland Steamer* sound about as rude as getting a peck on the cheek off Julie Andrews.

lunching at the Lazy Y *v. Dining out* cowboy style, on *hairy pie,* beans and coffee.

lunchtime recital *n.* When a pair of *book readers* retire to the works lavvies for a prandial *pink oboe* duet.

lung butter *n.* Phlegm, *green smoking oysters.*

lungry *adj.* Having an appetite for cigarettes. '*Giz a drag on that, your Excellency. I gave up for new year and now I'm proper fucking lungry.*'

lung warts *n. Stits, fried eggs. Parisian breasts.*

lurpy *n. Can.* Heterosexual *horatio.*

lush puppies *n.* Those grey slip-on brogues or loafers worn with white socks by middle-aged, *turps-nudging* "oldest swinger in town" types. '*Oi, Ho-Chi Minh or whatever your fucking name is. Where've you put me lush puppies?*'

Luton, a *n.* Pubic hairstyle named after the popular Bedfordshire airport. An amateurish attempt at a *landing strip,* but with patches of different length *bush* everywhere.

LVC *abbrev.* Used in reference to a particularly impressive *Bristol Channel.* From the name of the famous Harry Fowler-lookylikey Spaghetti western actor Lee Van Cleavage.

lychees *n.* A sweeter, more exotic *knacker*-speak alternative to *plums.*

Lymeswold *n.* Mild, blue, soft *knobcheese. Full fat fromunder, knacker barrel, Fred Leicester.*

Mabel *adj. rhym. slang.* Epithet bestowed upon an excitable and/or unpredictable female. From Mabel = mentally fucking unstable. *'Hey Dave, I hear you're going out with the barmaid from the Railwayman's Club. Watch out for her, mate, she's Mabel.'*

Mabel syrup *n.* Old *bird's flange juice. Olive oil, OAP soup, olden syrup.*

macbeth *n.* Whilst sitting on the *bog* straining, the release of an apparently ferocious *Exchange & Mart* that comes to naught. A *dropped gut* that is "full of sound and fury, signifying nothing", as William Shakespeare had it in the famous toilet soliloquy from the Scottish Play. *Macbeth*, that is.

mac in the bath, I wouldn't wear my exclam. Expression of a gentleman's unwillingness to don a prophylactic sheath on his *cock end.* Also *I wouldn't wear my wellies on the beach.*

machelor *n.* A married bachelor, *viz.* A chap who plays the field, but keeps a little something at home for when all else fails. *'Today's birthdays: Maximilian Hell, Slovakian astronomer, 1720; Maria Reiche, German mathematician and archaeologist, 1903; Jeffrey Archer, athlete, author, politician, machelor, 1940.'*

mack *n.* Penis, *tadger.*

mackerel *1. n.* Pimp, controller of prostitutes. A *tart farmer, flapmonger. 2. n.* The *tarts* he farms. *3. n. coll.* Cabbage, *crumpet, blart.*

mackerel microphone *n.* The bit of a lady that a fellow presses his lower face against, horse-racing-commentator-style, whilst carefully adjusting the settings on her *Bruce Lees* when he is attempting to *call Radio Tokyo.* The *cleft, quacker* or *furry hoop.*

Madam Palm and her five sisters *n.* A hand when used for five minutes of harmless fun that will certainly result in its owner being cast into a lake of fire by our infinitely merciful God. A *dick skinner.* Also *Palmela Handerson. 'I'm nipping off to bed with Madam Palm and her five sisters.'*

madam's apple *n.* A warning sign that the stunning Thai temptress you have picked up in a Bangkok bar may turn out to be equipped with *plums* and a *tummy banana* as well as a *large pear.*

Madam Twoswords *n.* A multitasking actress in a *stick vid* or *art pamphlet* who has a gentleman's waxy *charlie* in each hand. A *crane operator*, a *downhill skier.*

mad as a lorry *adj.* About as *radge* as it is possible to be.

mad cow disease *1. n.* Viral disease caught off cheap pies. *2. n. medic.* A monthly hormonal condition causing distress to men's ears. *Rag rage, tammy huff, blob strop.*

Madeley *n.* A bloke who feels comfortable talking about relationships, star signs, *Sex and the City, Ally McBeal* and *shit* like that.

Madeline Allbright *rhym. slang. US.* An *excreeshus*, a *pop.*

madman's arse *euph.* Descriptive of an extremely unruly hairstyle, *eg.* That barnet sported by erstwhile gun-toting "Wall of Sound" murderer Phil Spector.

mad woman's shit, all over like *sim.* Descriptive of something extremely disorganised and chaotic. *"I really must apologise for the most dreadfully untidy state of my study, Mrs Fezzypeg,' said Mr Pickwick as he anxiously cleared a* *bundle of papers off the chair nearest to the fire, motioning at his visitor to be seated. 'Only my Tax Return's supposed to be in tomorrow and as usual, my bank statements are all over the room like mad woman's shit."* (from *The Pickwick Papers* by Charles Dickens).

magic carpet *n.* A small layer of cloth which prevents any distasteful *ball-on-ball action* from occuring when a fellow is *double teaming.*

magic circle *1. n.* A group of conjurors who never reveal their secrets. *2. n.* Paul Daniels's *nipsy.*

magic Harpic ride *n.* A mysterious journey of Oriental delight, sponsored by your local curry house. *'Come to the Curry Capital (formerly the Rupali), Bigg Market, Newcastle upon Tyne, and we promise you a magic Harpic ride which will last all night.'*

magician *euph.* A pal who *knows what's in his flowerbeds.* From the fact that, on a night out, he will often "disappear with a poof".

magician's hankie *1. n.* A *shite* that just keeps on going and going, like the endless knotted cloths pulled out of conjurors' hats. *2. n.* A *botty burp* which, to the surprise of the assembled audience, continues to emerge over an astounding length of time, and in several audibly discrete segments.

magician's knickers *n.* Pants that keep disappearing up one's *arse.*

magicking the beans *v.* The late Gareth Hunt's *wanking* action.

magic sheet *n.* An enchanted blanket, often seen in American TV movies which clings to an actress through some invisible force, covering her *fission chips.*

magnificent seven *n.* The frankly unlikely scenario of getting the opportunity to unload one's *weapon* in every available orifice on a woman.

magnificent six *n.* The same act as above, but performed on Daniella Westbrook.

magnifiscent *adj.* Miasmatically splendid, specifically used when referring to a notably potent *dropped hat. 'I say, your majesty. That Bakewell you just done was fucking magnifiscent. Now would you let me out of the sleeping bag?'*

magnify *v.* Of a gentleman, to trim back his pubic foliage in order to create the illusion that his *endowment* is more substantial than it actually is. *'Did you see the chopper on that stripper tonight, Ada?' 'Aye I did, Dolly. But don't be too impressed - it was tied off and magnified.'*

magnolia *1. n.* A neutral, inoffensive wall-covering. *2. n.* A lady who "goes with anything".

mahogany chair leg *n.* An unusually wide, closely grained and uncomfortable *stool,* which appears to have been turned on a lathe by a Victorian craftsman in the days when things were built to last.

mailed and sent *rhym. slang.* On *the other bus.*

main cable *n.* One's live AC feed into the *love socket.*

maison de tolerance *n. Fr.* A brothel. Also *boutique frappante, magasin de frottage et remorqueur, ferme de Francoise.*

Major Morgan *1. n.* Early electronic hand-held game which, if its grittily realistic television advertising was anything to go by, would cause an unpopular child to instantly become a sort of playground Pied Piper. *2. n. rhym. slang.* A gentleman's generative member. *'Oi Shirl, go and fetch the death and disasters.*

I've only been and caught me bleedin' major morgan in the Thousand Island dip on me Cliff Bennett and the Rabble Rousers again.'

make a bald man cry *v.* To masturbate. *'Have you seen Kylie's arse on the front page of the FT today? It's enough to make a bald man cry.'*

make a clog *v.* At the climax to an act of onanistic *self delight,* to discharge one's *custard rifle* into a sock. From the fact that, after being left for a few days, said item of hosiery becomes as hard as a piece of traditional Dutch wooden footwear. *'What are you doing in the shed, Ruud?' 'Making a clog, dear.'*

make babies *v.* To go *bone jumping,* to fornicate with the object of *dropping a tadpole in a young lady's beer.*

make like a Chinese helicopter pilot *v.* To indulge in an act of *self delight,* to *grin like a wanking Jap* whilst *polishing the joystick.*

make the rounds *v.* To have one final grope of all one's ladyfriend's *treasures* before falling asleep.

make the weigh-in *v.* To enter the toilet as a middleweight and come out half an hour later as a welterweight. To do a really big *poo.*

make your shit hang sideways *v.* To be annoying. *'That Matthew Kelly really makes my shit hang sideways.'* (Bernard Levin, TV Review in *The Times*).

making nylon *v.* An experiment in the bath resulting in the creation of viscous, stringy threads that stick to the hairs of one's legs.

making way for the lady *n.* An example of *toiletiquette.* The innate sense of courtesy that seems to exist between urine and excrement whereby, during a *sit-down lavatory adventure, piss* invariably halts its stream to politely make way for the lady-like *Thora Hird,* before resuming its steady flow thereafter. *Crapping manners,* the *pisso doble.*

malapriapism *n.* A mistaken penile intrusion into an orifice which is close by, but not the same as, another one, leading to an unintentionally amusing effect. A *cock up.*

male varnish *n.* Viscid fluid which is worn all over the hand, across the chest, and on one's ladyfriend's face. Like nail varnish, but harder to remove from clothing. *Vitamin S.*

MALLAM/mallam *acronym.* Middle Aged Loser Living At Mummy's.

malt loaf *n.* Pungently sweet-smelling *feeshus,* as dropped by a vegetarian or one whose diet substantially eschews Haribos, sausage rolls and Ginster's pasties.

mambas *n.* Mammaries, *mumbas.*

Mambo number five *1. n.* An annoyingly catchy novelty hit record which contains an instrumental line that sounds like a repetitive *fart. 2. n.* A repetitive *fart* that has all the makings of an instrumental line in an annoyingly catchy novelty hit record. A *Rotterdam Termination Source.*

mamfest *1. n.* The stirring sight of a lot of ladies' breasts *en masse, eg.* At the beach, in a nightclub, through a hole drilled in the wall of a ladies' changing room. Contraction of mammary festival. *2. n.* A particularly fine and well presented pair of *bangers.*

mammaries *n.* Mammary glands, *tits, swinging pink milk churns, knockers.*

mammary dandruff *n.* Morning-after residue from a *sausage sandwich,* the dusty remnants of a *pearl necklace*.

mammary stick *n.* Convenient, pocket-sized electronic device for the storage of one's cybertronic *Frankie Vaughan* collection. A *sly-pod*.

mammogram *n.* An item of mail containing a few saucy snaps of his missus's bare *norks*, which is hopefully sent to a member of Her Majesty's armed forces by his good lady and not the milkman.

mamnesia *n. medic.* A highly specific form of male memory loss. Upon seeing a fantastic pair of *norks*, the sufferer forgets key facts about himself, *eg.* That he is married, that he has four children, or that he is the presenter of a topical quiz show. Also *penile dementia*.

mam sandwich *n.* Two amply-proportioned *milkers* with the head of a happy gentleman wedged snugly between them.

manaesthetic *n.* Dextrous manual self-manipulation of a fellow's nether regions that brings on a state of pain-free slumber at the end of each day.

managlypta *n.* Peculiar raised relief effect observed on the walls of a gentleman who is prone to acts of *self harm*, but who cannot be *arsed* to find a tissue, sock, pet *etc.* on which to deposit his *erotic spendings. Managlypta* is most commonly found decorating the surfaces immediately adjacent to a long term bachelor's computer desk.

man at C&A 1. *n.* A *DP* or *Dorothy Perkins*. 2. *n.* A chap who *enjoys shopping in both departments*, that is to say a bisexualist.

manbag 1. *n.* A practical and fashionable portmanteau which can be slung across the shoulders, an accoutrement typically favoured by Europeans and creative media types. Not in any sense a handbag, despite all appearances to the contrary. 2. *n.* The *sack* in which a chap retains his *two veg*. The scrotum.

manberries *n.* Coarse term for the *clockweights, John Wayne's hairy saddlebags, knackers etc*. Testicles, *yongles*.

manberry sauce *n. Gentleman's spendings*.

mancakes *n. Heirbags* that have been *wanked* flat.

mancumber *n.* A male member of such cucurbitaceous dimensions as to satisfy the most capacious lady's *nugget bucket*.

Manc wag 1. *n.* A spooneristic *bongo book*. 2. *n.* A north-western footballer's doxy.

mancy *n.* A very girly fellow. One who is as *good with colours* as a nine bob note.

mandle *n.* A gentleman's *handle. 'Oi, love. Have a crank on me mandle, see if you can get me bollocks started.'*

mandruff *n.* Flakes of dried *lovepiss* found on one's wife's head and shoulders.

mands *n.* The large, shovel-like hands which are often the only warning to a holidaying lothario that he may be about to bite off more than he bargained for, so to speak, when he gets his latest conquest back to his hotel. From man + hands.

manecdote *n.* A dissembular vocalised narrative involving fighting, drinking, driving or sexual derring-do that is intended to enhance a fellow's standing amongst his peers.

manflesh, you shall taste 1. *exclam.* The words uttered by Saruman to his prized fighting Orc as he is sent to hunt down the Fellowship of the Ring. 2. *exclam.* A stirringly-worded promise made to a casual lady acquaintance as a fellow unzips his *kegs* behind a skip.

mangerine *n*. A fellow with sunbed-roasted skin. *'Todays birthdays: Heather Mills, altruistic unidexter, 42; Melanie Jism, ex-Spice Girl, 36; Des O'Connor, television mangerine, 78.'*

mange tout, Rodders, mange tout *exclam*. Simultaneous cry of offence and exhortation issued by a young lady when her gentleman paramour draws back from *cumulonimbus* on encountering her piquantly *clinker*-ridden *maiden hair*, best delivered in the style of Del Boy Trotter out of off of *Only Fools and Horses* and usually accompanied by an insistent thrusting of the poor chap's noggin back where it came from.

mangry *adj*. Sexually frustrated. From man + angry. *'I've not had any action for two weeks now and I'm starting to get really mangry.'*

manker *n*. A *wanker* from Manchester, eg. Liam Gallagher.

M & S turd *euph*. A *shite* which is worthy of special attention due to its exceptional quality. "This is not just a turd, this is a five-day matured, chicken vindaloo with garlic naan and eight bottles of Cobra turd."

man eggs *n*. Sperms, *taddies*.

man fanny *1. n*. A changing room entertainment whereby a bare gentleman impersonates a bare lady. A *cockafanny*. *2. n*. A risible goatee beard sported by polytechnic lecturers and 45-year-olds who have just bought a motor bike.

manfat *n*. Semen. Also *man milk, cock snot*.

manflaps *n*. The tiny flaps surrounding the *Jap's eye*, usually only visible when taking a much needed high pressure

piss. The *hog's eyelids*.

Manfred *rhym. slang. Jitler, jism, spaff*. From the not-particularly-famous-amongst-cockneys German philosopher Manfred Bunk = spunk.

Manfred Mann *1. n*. South African keyboards player and progenitor of the popular earthband of the 1960s. *2. n*. An amusing way to describe a male homosexual threesome; ideally one which features a man called Fred as *lucky Pierre*.

mange *n*. See *mangina*.

mangina *1. n*. The badly-sewn Cornish pastie-like seam running along the underside of the scrotum that stops one's *clockweights* falling out and rolling under the fridge. *2. n*. The *nipsy* of one who is *good with colours*. *3. n*. The hilarious men's locker room jape of sticking one's *meat and two veg* back between one's legs to create a convincing simulacrum of a lady's *clout*. *3. n*. *Old Greg's* downstairs mix-up in the *Mighty Boosh*.

manging *adj. Minging*.

mangos *n*. See *jelly water mangos*.

man handle *n*. The *bone on* that a store detective gets upon apprehending a female shop lifter in anticipation that she may offer to *talk to the judge* in the stock room.

manhood *n*. In British tabloid journalism, the penis.

man in the iron mask *n*. An extremely hirsute *snatch* trapped inside a pair of knickers. From the classic tale by Alexandre Dumas.

manjack *n*. A *poo* which is so rigid that it starts lifting you off the *bog* seat when it hits the bottom of the *pan*.

manky panky *n*. Sexual congress between tramps, crusties and sundry other unwashed sorts, usually attempted in a public park following the consumption of copious quantities of *spesh*, white cider and metal polish.

manmalade *n*. Sticky, tangy paste excreted from the business end of a gentleman's *fruit bowl*. Hopefully without any bits of peel floating round in it. *Anger jam*.

man mastic *n*. Sticky white substance used for sealing ladies' eyelids *etc*.

man mayonnaise *n*. *Gentleman's relish, hanging salad cream, semen mayo*.

man medicine *n*. *Vitamin S*, administered via a *spam syringe*.

man meringue *n*. A light, crumbly nest of dried *milm* found on the inside of a gentleman's well-worn *Bill Grundies*.

mannequim *n*. A *sailor's favourite* or similar ersatz *spouse*.

mannery glands *n*. A portly gentleman's dugs. *Bitch tits, moobs, moomlaaters*.

manny *n*. The convincing illusion of womanhood achieved when a gentleman tucks his *giggling stick* and *knackers* back behind his legs. A *cockafanny*. A contraction of man + fanny. See *man fanny, mangina*.

man of the cloth *n*. Our *farter*, who, despite fervent prayer, finds that he has besoiled his raiments. A *through-follower*.

man on the inside *euph*. The stage of a *digestive transit* just before the *turtle's head*. 'Why's Colin walking so funny?' 'He's got *a man on the inside*.'

manopause *n*. Male mid-life crisis, characterised by the acquisition of a sports car, a motorbike and/or a girlfriend young enough to be one's daughter.

man overboard *n*. A *bald man in a boat* whom you fear has become detatched from his mooring, but who turns out to be a pellet of compressed *shit scrape*.

man pop *n*. *Spooge, jitler, baby gravy*.

Mansfield motorcycle *euph*. Any form of assited mobility conveyance, *eg*. Shopping kart, electric scooter *etc*.

manshake *n*. A vigorous three-minute greeting for one's best friend.

manshee *n*. One who could conceivably be a man or a woman.

man's makeup *n*. The light brown stripe left on a light-coloured bath towel by a chap's vigorous drying of his *potty slot*. Often blamed on his missus's foundation or bronzer. '*Terry, you dirty bastard. Why can't you wipe your arse properly? You've left man's makeup all over the towel again.*' ' *I've not done that, June, you fucking cow. It was you taking your slap off when you were pissed last night.*'

manstruating *adj*. Of a male, being quick to lose one's rag at seemingly inoffensive comments regarding one's appearance, personality, behaviour or membership of Oasis. '*Take no notice of our Liam. He's manstruating this week.*'

mantanamo bay *n*. The place your missus sends you when you are in the *cunt book*, from where you never know when you might be allowed to return home, and where you can find yourself subject to intense, hostile barrages of questions at any hour of the night or day.

mantap *n*. A fellow's *cock*. '*What is it this time, June? Can't you see I've got a bad back and my boss is coming for dinner unexpectedly and I'm pretending to have forgotten our wedding anniversary?*' '*Really, Terry. Have you been running your mantap in the kitchen sink again? Only there's piss all over the fucking pots.*'

manties *n*. Women's underwear worn by a

bloke who is firmly in denial about his true proclivities. *'Nah, I'm not wearing a G-string, these're manties. There is a difference.'*

mantiliner *n.* See *mantipad*.

mantipad *n.* A folded piece of lavatory paper placed in a fellows underbreeches in order to absorb any excess drips. Also *mantiliner, swedge, manpon, botcap, toffee rizla*.

man trap *n.* The female genitals, the *hairy love pit*.

mantrum *n.* A hissy fit thrown by a man. For example, the bit off that Elton John fly-on-the-wall thing when he was in the south of France and the woman went "yoo-hoo" at him when he was playing tennis, remember, and he flounced back up to his hotel suite and started packing his suitcase? That was a mantrum.

manwich *n.* The lucky chap filling pressed between two slices of ladies.

man with nice nails *n.* One who is *good with colours*.

mapatasi *n. Aus. Minge.* From "Map of Tasmania", the small hairy island that smells of fish off the south east coast of Australia.

map of Africa *n.* The cartographical stain left on the bed sheet and often the mattress below after an exchange of bodily fluids. A splodge of *splooge*. Also *map of Ireland, map of Hawaii*.

marabou stork *n.* A *fixed bayonet, the old Adam*. An erection.

maracas *n. Knackers, clackers,* those things that swing beneath *tallywhackers* making a rattling sound.

marble cake *n.* The swirly, variegated *excreeshus* of a lady just after she's had her *back doors kicked in*. Also *Swiss roll*.

marge *n.* A loose woman. From margarine, which "spreads easily". Also *Flora*.

margold *n.* The common male ability to do five *pop shots* in two hours. To do a margold. After a boast by *grumble* thespian Bill Margold on Channel 4's *After Dark* programme many years ago.

Marianas trench *1. n.* The deepest recorded sub-marinal depression on Earth, found in the Pacific ocean and reaching a depth of 35,839 feet below sea level. *2. n.* A *fanny* like a fucking bucket.

marine ply *n.* Pages of a favoured *bongo book*, stuck together with salty *pyjama glue* to form a tough, hard-wearing laminate.

Mario Kart piss *n.* A hurried *wazz* that must be successfully completed within a very short space of time. From the online game Mario Kart, where players must nip into the back garden and get their *scoot* in before the next race starts.

marks of Mecca *n.* Carpet burns on the knees caused by excessive worship at the *hairy temple*.

marks out of two? *interrog.* From one ogling male to another, to cue the reply "I'd give her one."

mark your territory *v.* To *drop your guts* and walk away. To *leave negative feedback*.

Marley arse *n.* Accumulated *winnetage*, leading to *anal dreadlocks. Tagnuts* that have gone to pot.

Marley's chains *euph.* Breasts that, despite having headed south in a big way, must still be carried about by their owner. From the chain-dragging ghost of his former business partner that visits Scrooge in Charles Dickens's *A Christmas Carol*. Also *Ulrikas*.

marmalade madam *n. 17thC. Tom, doxy,*

flapper, laced mutton. A *ho'*.

Marmite driller *n*. One who *jumps over puddles* on the *Marmite motorway*.

Marmite kofte *n*. The sort of viscous black *shite* that, instead of dropping into the *chod bin* pan in the traditional manner, chooses to smear itself around the *nipsy* like so much axle grease. The resulting Augean Stables-style cleaning session only ever happens when one is in a hurry to catch a plane, train, last orders or read the closing headlines at the end of the *BBC Six O'Clock News*.

Marmite motorway *n*. *A-road, arse, back passage*.

Marmite pot, arse like a *sim*. A *ringpiece* which, after a particularly sticky *Brad Pitt*, seems to have a never ending supply of *shit* and the wiping of which will never *draw an ace*.

Marmite stripe *n*. Brown stain or *skidmark* found on unwashed *shreddies*. *Russet gusset*.

Mars bar *1. n*. A caramel, nougat and chocolate confection, which when eaten daily is a scientifically proven aid to work, rest and recreation. *2. n*. A substantial and impressive *burnout*.

mars bra *n*. The common practice (in Germany anyway) of *dropping a length of dirty spine* onto your ladyfriend's *dirty pillows*.

Martin! Martin! Martin! *exclam*. Phrase which can be shouted when standing next to someone whose repeated *gut dropping* implies that they may imminently *curl one off* all over the floor. From the zookeeper on *Blue Peter* who persistently called the name of his off-screen helper when Lulu the elephant tried to *shite* all over John Noakes' left foot.

Marty Feldmans *n*. On certain ladies, the lop-sided *tits*, where the nipples point up, down and all around. Named after the late comedian Marty Feldman, whose distinctive nipples pointed in different directions.

Mary *1. n. Sponge, pillow biter, angel. 2. n. Bean flicker, carpet muncher. 3. n*. A *liver sock*.

Mary Chipperfield *n*. A *wank ie*. A *monkey spamking* session. From the famous circus chimp dominatrix of the same name.

Mary Hinge *n*. Spooneristic *biffer*.

Mary Poppins' bag *n*. A surprisingly roomy *fanny*. A *clown's pocket* out of which it would be possible to pull a mirror, a lamp and a large potted plant.

mash *v*. To fondle a lady's *shirt potatoes* as if testing them to destruction.

massage parlour wank *1. sim*. Something that is performed quickly and efficiently. *'And the wheel change and refuelling was performed like a massage parlour wank by the Ferrari mechanics and Schumacher should exit the pit lane still in the lead.'* (Murray Walker). *2. sim*. Something that is expensive and over too quickly, *eg*. The Pepsi Max ride at Blackpool.

masterfaece *n*. A *humming bird* of such epoch-defining magnificence that you briefly consider fishing it out of the bowl, putting it in a frame and hanging it in the nearest art gallery. Mind you, if you did you'd probably win the fucking Turner Prize. We're going to hell in a handcart, you couldn't make it up.

master of ceremonies *1. n*. In this modern "hippy-hoppy" style of so-called music, a fellow in an ill-adjusted baseball hat who shouts about how super he is into a microphone. *2. n.* A red-faced, tail-coated man at a formal dinner who hits a wine glass with a spoon to get everyone's attention, before introducing some mercenary *cunt* like Jimmy Carr who then gets up and makes a few lame cracks about the managing director's golf handicap in return for several thousand pounds and a free tea. *3. n.* One's *knob, todger, old man etc*. The male penis.

masturbatabase *n.* A gentleman's computerised repository of *relaxing* imagery. *'What's this folder here on your desktop, Terry? I can't open it. It seems to be password protected.' 'Oh that? It's nothing, June. Just some boring figures, that's all. It's my masturbatabase.'*

masturmentary *n.* TV programme with a high *tit* and *fanny* count with a token bit of information thrown in to justify its showing, *eg*. A behind-the-scenes look at the pornographic film industry. The staple fare of late night satellite telly.

matelot's matress *n. nav.* A thick piece of bedding material provided to keep *Jack Tars* jolly in their bunks. A Wren.

Mather & Platt *rhym. Lancs. Manc.* A lady's *bodily treasure*. Named after an old established Mancunian engineering company. *'I wouldn't mind getting me hands on her Mather & Platt, our Liam.'*

mathsturbate *v.* To have a vowel and three consonants whilst thinking about Carol Vorderman. To practise one's *six-nowt times table*.

mating call *n.* The activation of pub toilet hand-driers as a deliberate attempt to impress any *birds* within earshot.

Matteson's *euph.* In grumbular cinematography, the unfortunate outcome of a female protagonist missing her target by a centimetre or two when squatting down on her male co-star's *cock*, causing it to bend into a shape which is disturbingly remniscent of the popular cheap sausage.

mattress back *n.* A polyamorous lady who is generous with her romantic favours.

MAWBAB/mawbab *acronym.* A woman who refuses to make the effort and effects short hair, corduroy trousers, comfortable shoes *etc*. Might As Well Be A Bloke.

may contain nuts *phr.* Notice which really should be displayed on the outside of a Thai *bird's underkegs*, serving as a warning that there is a pretty good chance that she may turn out to be a *trolley dolly*.

mayor's hat *n.* A *howzat* often eaten by goats.

McArthur park *1. n.* A 1970's maudlin ballad by Richard Harris. *2. n.* A particularly evil *dropped gut* that gives the impression that "something inside has died".

McCoys *n.* Flakes of dried, salty, starchy material found on a bachelor's bed linen, socks, carpet *etc*. Named after the popular snack's advertising slogan, because they are "man crisps". See also *prawn crackers, porn crackers, popshottadoms, singlie rosettes* and *wanker's crisps*.

McDonald's farmyard *n.* The restaurant area of a high street fast food outlet, filled with sundry dullards, *scratters* and fatties grazing on burgers and fries whilst snorting appreciatively.

McEwan's Exports *n.* Fiercely nationalistic Scottish people who take every opportunity to proudly declaim their love for their homeland, despite choosing to live in America. Or Australia. Or

Spain. Or anywhere except Scotland, *eg*. Veteran syrupped former milkman turned spy Sir Sean Connery.

McFadden transfer *n*. Upgrading to a better model, such as from Kerry Katona to Delta Goodrun, to pick an example entirely at random.

McGregor *n*. *A Mary* that is "torn between two lovers". *A Joy Division*.

McKeith *n*. A textbook *dump*. Named after excrement-obsessed TV gerbil Gillian McKeith.

McKeith's handbag, smells like *sim*. Anything that *ronks* of *shit*, as one imagines the previously-mentioned comedy PhD-ed *turd*-tamperer's accessories must. Also *Oaten's briefcase*.

McSplurry *n*. The type of *grimshit* one experiences after dining for a week solely at a fast food restaurant. *Bubblepoo*.

McSquirter twins *n*. A gentleman's *clockweights*. Named after the identically-dead, unconscionably right-wing pair of blazered *Record Breakers* co-hosts. The *gonk-faced Mother Teresa sisters*.

McSuck *n*. An *horatio* delivered with a force equivalent to that required to drink a newly poured McDonald's Thick Shake.

MDF *abbrev*. A *dobber*. Medium Density Flop-on. Not quite *wood*.

me *n*. Personal pronoun used at the end of a sentence to emphasise preference. *'For all these wenches are beauteous fair, and I doth admire them all, me.'* (from *Romeo and Juliet* by William Shakespeare).

meat and two vag *n*. A *threesome* involving two ladies and a smiling man who keeps pinching himself.

meat and two veg *n*. A gentleman's *undercarriage*. A *pork sausage* and a couple of love spuds.

meat balloons *n*. Older boys' playthings, which do not stick to the wall even after protracted rubbing on a jumper. *Mumbas, large tits*.

meat flower *n*. Delightful, poetic term for a lady's *bodily treasure*.

meat flute *n*. *Pink oboe*.

meat harp *n*. A vaguely fan-shaped instrument that a lady may choose to strum angelically from time to time. A *bird's fly-trap*.

meat injection *n*. An inoculation against virginity.

Meatloaf, doing a *n*. Being denied a spot of *backdoor work* whilst being granted access to her other orifices by a young lady. From the lyric of the song made famous by the fat, sweaty singer, *viz*. "Two out of three ain't bad." Or, if you prefer, "I'll do anything for love, but I won't do that."

Meatloaf's daughter *n*. A big boned *mudchild*. A *dreadnought*.

meat market *n*. Bar or club where *birds* with short skirts and blotchy legs dance round their handbags, waiting for a *pull*. A *meat rack, buttock hall*.

meat microphone *n*. Sensitive device on a very short lead into which drunken *car park karaoke* participants need little encouragement to vocalise.

meat moth *n*. A *spam butterfly* commonly attracted to the bright lights of a *grot mag* photographer's flashgun.

meat movie *n*. A *grumble flick*.

meat paste *1. n*. Something your mum puts on your sandwiches at school. *2. n*. Something disgruntled chefs put on Michael Winner's sandwiches.

meat petite *n*. Descriptive of a *Little Richard*.

meat platter *1. n.* An unappetizing raffle prize on offer in a working men's club. *2. n.* An unappetizing *clopper* on offer behind a skip a working men's club car park.

meat stub *1. n.* A rudimentary Wikipedia entry about some sort of butcher's produce, for example the article about haslet. *2. n.* A rudimentary male *pudender*, of the sort boasted by Bobby Davro or Jack Straw.

meat tenderiser *1. n.* A wooden mallet of the sort used by people who cook food on the television, but which has sat gathering dust in that pot of on your kitchen worktop for years now. *2. n.* A chap who *pounds his pork* with life-threatening ferocity, though hopefully not with a wooden mallet.

meat tie *n.* Formal pink neckwear for topless ladies. Tied with a shiny purple knot. With all *spunk* coming out the end. The sausage in a *sausage sandwich*.

meatus *n. medic.* The proper name for the *hog's eye*, apparently. *'Hello, doctor? This is Mr J Brown from Notting Hill. I'd like a confidential word about my meatus. I stuck a propelling pencil lead down it for an experiment and I think it's snapped.' 'I'm terribly sorry, you must have dialled the wrong number. This is Midday Money on Good Morning with Phil and Holly. You're live on air.'*

mechanic's bulge *n.* Arm muscle unavoidably cultivated by a chap who lies on his back *tightening his nuts* all day.

mechanic's nails *n.* Finger-end condition cause by *bumwad pushthrough. Taxidriver's tan.*

mechanical dandruff *n.* Royal Air Force *crabs, willipedes.*

medieval fireplace *sim.* A vast, gothic vagina with a big piece of pork slowly revolving in it.

Mediterranean Tetley *n.* When on one's holiday, suffering from a dose of the *squitters* and not minded to locate a lavatory, going for a paddle with the intention of letting the bowels go through the perforated netting lining of one's swimming shorts. "Letting the flavour flood out" like one of the eponymous teabags.

medophile *n.* One who has become so accustomed to participating in *saucy mesomes* that it has become his preferred form of sexual activity. One who is no longer *master of his own domain.*

meeting with the big man *n.* A session of *self-indulgence* whilst at work. *'Coming onto the cancer verandah, Dave?' 'No can do. I've got a meeting with the big man.'*

megraine *n.* Intermittent illness afflicting ladies and footballers when they realise they are no longer the centre of attention.

Mekon *1. n. prop.* The chief villain and leader of the Treens featured in Dan Dare's *Eagle* adventures of the 1950s, distinguished by his enormous cranium and little body, and hence *2. n.* A badly-poured pint which is "all head and fuck all else".

Melanie *n. prop. Gentleman's spendings.* From the name of the famous shellsuited singer and cartwheelist Melanie Jism. *Spurty spice.*

Melanied *adj.* Drunk, battered, *blatted.* From the surname of All Saints popsie Melanie Blatt. *'I'm sorry Moira, but I can't let you go on air and read the news in that state. You're absolutely Melanied.'*

Melbourne *n.* A soft *cock.*

melching *v.* Minge *felching.*

melon farmer *exclam.* The BBC-autho-rised, poorly-dubbed version of *moth-erfucker* used in films such as *Die Hard* and the entire *Beverly Hills Cop* series. Also *ever-loving, muddy funster.*

melons *n.* Female breasts. A large "pear".

melted welly *n.* A poetic term describing a lady's *bodily treasure.* *'Spatula was powerless to resist. His eyes burnt into hers like mamellated chalcedony. His muscular arms enfolded her body as she felt herself being swept away on a noctilucent cloud of passion. 'Am I the first?' whispered Dartanyan. 'Sort of,' she vouchsafed in return, her voice quivering with unrequited passion. 'I've not let the other two have a shot on me melted welly yet.'"* (from *The Lady & the 3 Musketeers* by Barbara Cartland).

Melvin *v.* To grab by the *balls.*

Melvyn 1. *rhym. slang.* A cigarette. From Melvyn Bragg = fag. 2. *rhym slang.* Sexual intercourse. From Melvyn Bragg = shag. *'Me and the missus always light up a nice Melvyn after we've had a quick Melvyn.'*

member for trousers north, the right honourable *n.* One's *cock*; the *MP for Pantchester.*

menage à moi *n. Fr.* A three-in-a-bed romp where the two ladies fail to turn up. A *wank.*

menage artois *n.* An unconventional, yet loving, relationship struck up betwixt a gentleman and a well known brand of imported lager.

menage à un *n. Fr.* A saucy *mesome.*

men in the rigging *n. naval.* Small *tag-nuts* trapped in the hairs of sailors' arses. *'Six months since leaving Tahiti and no sign of land. We ate the last of the breadfruit weeks ago. Water and toi-let paper strictly rationed. Crew growing restless, complaining of scrofula, scurvy and men in the rigging. Lord help us.'* (from *The Diary of Fletcher Christian*, 1789).

menoporn *n.* Faux middle brow, often historically-set literary works aimed at ladies of a certain age, which feature phrases such as "She took him to her secret hidden place". *'Come on, love. We're going to miss the flight.' 'Hang on. I'm just getting myself a bit of meno-porn to read by the pool.'*

men's spendings *n. arch.* Withdrawals from the *clackerbag.*

men-stool cycle *n.* The short, yet happy period of a man's life when his *shit* appears at the same time every day.

menstrual arithmetic *n.* The reliably accu-rate calculations performed by a clued-up *left-footer* to decide whether it is safe to *shoot his load* up his missus, who is also the mother of his eighteen children.

menstrual cycle display team *n.* Any group of *birds* consisting of a moody one, a happy one, a normal one and a randy one.

merchant *rhym. slang. Kuwaiti tanker.*

merkin *n.* Man-made *mapatasi,* a *stoat syrup, pubic Irish.*

mermaid 1. *n.* A fat *bird* with a pretty face, but nothing worth bothering with below the *tits.* 2. *n.* A woman who is good to look at, but just won't open her legs.

mermaids *n. pej. Aus.* Australian truck-ers' slang for Department of Transport compliance officers who check that their lorries are not overladen by means of portable weighing machines which they set up at the roadside. So-called because they are "cunts with scales".

mermaid's flannel, wet as a *sim.* Descriptive of a very, very, very wet *fanny*. Also *otter's pocket, clown's pie, fish drowner.*

merry monk *rhym. slang.* The happy result of *pulling the Pope's cap off.*

Mersey trout *n.* A sweetcorn-eyed brown scouse fish.

Merthyr socialite *n.* A South Wales man-about-town who is often spotted in a giddy social whirl flitting between William Hills, The Windham and The DSS offices.

mesome *n.* A *one-in-a-bed romp, menage a un.* A wank. *'I'm off upstairs for a mesome.'*

mertis *n.* Gereral term for any unpleasant substance, such as an accumulation of white residue at the corners of an overweight cruise liner chef's mouth, something your dog lies in on a vet's back room floor whilst recovering from a general anaesthetic, or that sticky sediment you get between the fingers of a sweaty man who moves filing cabinets up and down fire escapes for a living. *'Montellimar supreme. A frothy concoction of delicious milk chocolate, with a tempting vanilla praline mertis filling, topped off with chopped hazelnuts and a dead bluebottle which must of fell in the machine at the factory.'* (Description from *Netto Chocolates Belgian Assortment*).

MESS/mess *acronym. Spunk.* Named after the chef's secret ingredient in McDonald's Extra Special Sauce.

mess *n.* Semen, *gunk, cock hockle.* That which is lost when one *chucks one's muck.*

Messerschmitt knickers *n.* An easy lady's

scads, *ie.* Ones which "come down without much of a fight".

metabollock rate *n.* Scientific assessment of the speed of a chap's recuperation; specifically a measure of the time it takes for him to recover his ardour after *tipping his filthy concrete. 'Don't put your knickers back on yet, love, I'll be back on in five. I've got a very high metabollock rate, me.'*

Metal Mickey/Minnie *n.* One who wears an inordinate amount of cheap *bling* in the forlorn hope that it will somehow help them look classy.

meta-phwoars *n.* Those peculiar, coy words beloved of tabloid journalists when they are writing about *tits* but scared to use the word *tits, eg.* "Assets", "charms", "pink-tipped jelly earmuffs" *etc.*

metatarsal breakers *n. Headlamps* that look fantastic in their current *titpants*, but which, once unclipped and subjected to the full force of gravity, fly to the floor where their impact may result in fractures to the footbones of their owner or innocent bystanders.

metime *n.* The temporal period which a *gentlewoman* puts aside for the purpose of *relaxation.*

metrobone *1. n.* The infectious, rhythmic, slapping disco beat created by the impact of buttocks and thighs during the act of *doggy-style* intercourse. *2. n.* An involuntary public transport tumescence.

Mexican aftershave *n.* The acrid tang of chilli and garlic left in the *bog* after a rather nasty night of beer and spicy food.

Mexican picnic *n.* SVSA, a *drugs bust.*

Mexican barbecue *n.* SVSASO. A *Mexican pinic* with a *cock* in the mouth for good measure.

Mexican lipstick *n.* The embarrassing *Thompson's tide marks* often found after *eating out* with a lady who was *up on blocks*. A *pasata grin*.

Mexican omelette *n.* Alternative to a *Boston pancake*, but with extra salsa and a nice nap afterwards.

Mexican screamers *n. medic.* A gastro-enterological disorder characterised by fiery liquid excrement. *Tijuana brass-eye, Mexican shat dance.*

Mexican suicide *n.* To die peacefully in one's sleep. *'It is announced with deep regret and sadness that Her Royal Highness Princess Margaret committed Mexican suicide at 6.32 this morning at St George's Hospital.'*

Mexican wave *n.* The act of getting up off the *thunderbox* and then having to sit back down again for a further, unexpected evacuation of the *Enochs*. From the similarity to the eponymous transverse, laterally-displaced, periodical motion exhibited by bored sports crowds. A *second sitting*.

mezoomas *n. Pink velvet cushions* on which the *family jeweller* prefers to display a *pearl necklace*.

MFI *n.* A massive everything-must-go weekend *shit* enjoyed on a Sunday morning after downing eight or nine pints and a curry on Saturday evening.

Michael Owen's knee, a dick like *sim.* Something that goes pop within a minute.

Michaels *rhym. slang.* Piles. From the 1970s TV game show host Michael Miles. *'These nylon trolleys don't half chafe me Michaels.'*

Michael McIntyre *euph.* A high velocity *Boris Johnson*. From the perceived similarity of a rapid fellator's head to the vibrating, blurred noggin of the eponymous high-pitched TV comedy panel show stalwart during one of his side-splittingly hilarious (to him at least), acutely-observed routines.

Mickey 1. *n. Irish. Dick.* 2. *adj. Mouse.* *'Sarah was a bit Mickey this morning. I think she was pissed again.'*

Mick Jagger smoking a cigar, like *sim.* A mid-way point during the launch of a *bum torpedo*, when it is neither in the tube nor heading for the beach, but is somewhere in between. *Casting Churchill's reflection. 'If I leaned forward now, Jeeves, it would look like Mick Jagger smoking a cigar.'*

middle leg *n.* The penis. Also *middle stump, third leg.*

middle order collapse 1. *n.* Historically, an all too typical performance of the England cricket team when faced with the prospect of a victory or a draw in a test match. Or even just the slight possibility of not losing by an innings and six hundred runs for once. 2. *n.* A sudden want of tumescence halfway through a bout of penetrative affection.

Middlesbrough accent *n. medic.* A severe cough. *'The patient typically presents complaining of headache, high temperature, a productive Middlesbrough accent and nausea. Treatment - 200mg Amoxyl, three times a day'* (*Tuberculosis - a Guide for Doctors* - Health Department leaflet).

Middlesbrough salad, as lonely as a *sim.* Particularly isolated, like a forlorn green garnish sat untouched on a plate next to a parmo. *'Alone, alone, all, all alone / Alone on a wide wide sea! / No Middlesbrough salad there's ever been*

/ Has been as lonely as me.' (from *The Rime of the Ancient Mariner* by Samuel Taylor Coleridge).

midfield playmaker *1. n.* In football, an overpaid, prancing, centrally-positioned player, *eg.* A *knob* like Glenn Hoddle. *2. n.* A *knob*.

midge's bawhair *n.* A metric division of length that can only be measured using an electron microscope and a magnifying glass at the same time. A hundred times smaller than a *bee's dick*. *'Fuck me, Henri. You'd better let me drive for a bit. I've had less than you and we were a midge's bawhair from hitting that white Fiat Uno, you know.'*

midget gems *n.* Small, petite but perfectly-formed *teats*, such as the delights found on Keira Knightley or Amanda Holden. *Melting moments.*

midget porn *1. n. Grumble* thoughtfully provided by publishers for keen masturbators who are, ironically as a result of their hobby, too vertically challenged to reach the newsagent's top shelf. Examples of midget porn include *Ice, Nuts* and *Front. 2. n. Art pamphletry,* videographic *grumblery* and interwebular erotica featuring the saucy carryings-on of little people, and usually featuring a coked-up woman dressed in a distinctly half-arsed Snow White costume, one would imagine.

midget's surfboard *n.* A bachelor/teenager/priest's *spongle*-hardened sock which has become petrified by a plethora of *emissions* and which is on the Home Office's list of approved weapons which can be used against household intruders. Also *Womble's toboggan, Mother Shipton's sock, bachelor's boomerang.*

mid-loaf crisis *n.* Anything that spoils the enjoyment of a good *tom tit, eg.* A doorbell or telephone ringing, a dawning realisation that there is no *bumwad,* or a policeman approaching the shop doorway.

midnight mouth organ *n.* A high- cholesterol instrument played with relish around kicking out time in town centres across the land. A kebab.

midruff *n.* The exposed area of torso between a young lady's cropped top and her low-cut jeans which may have been toned, tanned and firm a couple of years ago, but which now hangs over her waistband like so much uncooked bread dough. *Muffin tops,* the *jiggle ring..*

midstool *v.* Act of a chap who is so hopelessly lost in love that he would happily kiss the *clackervalve* of the object of his desire whilst they are half way through *dropping anchor* at *bum bay. 'FREDDY: You know what, Professor Higgins? Miss Doolittle's the one for me. I'm head over heels in love with the girl and I don't care who knows it. Dash it, old man, I think I'd even midstool Eliza if she asked.'* (from *Pygmalion* by George Bernard Shaw).

mighty mouse *1. n.* A Superman-style cartoon rodent, feebly animated by Paul Terry Studios from the 1940s onwards, and occasionally broadcast on British television in the 1970s and 1980s in the interests of disappointing and depressing the nation's children, who were hoping for a Tom & Jerry. *2. n.* Put politely, a *feminine hygiene requisite* of a sort suitable for the larger-*cunted* lady. A *tampaximum.*

mighty Wurlitzer *1. n.* An enormous organ. *2. n.* Reginald Dixon's *cock.*

mild astegmatism *n. medic.* Bizarre ophthalmological phenomenon whereby the subjective attractiveness of a young lady decreases at a rate proportional to the amount of light ale one has imbibed. Like *beer goggles*, but in reverse.

mile high club *n*. Glamorous society of jet-setters who have had an uncomfortable, unsatisfactory *scuttle* in the *crappers* on an airliner.

mile high DIY *n*. An act of *self delight* carried out in the aeroplane *bogs* on the return flight from Corfu, for example. *'Captain, you're needed in the cockpit. Engine two is on fire and we've lost all aileron and elevator control. And the co-pilot's gone mad and is screaming about God.' 'With you in a tick, treacle. I'm just doing a spot of mile high DIY.'*

mile high grub *n*. An *art pamphlet* purchased at an airport newsagent.

mile 'I' club *n*. Similar to the *Mile High Club*, but for the solitary traveller. *Mile high DIY.*

MILF/milf *acronym*. Mum I'd Like to Fuck. *Yummy mummy*.

MILILF/mililf *acronym*. A situation that was presumably unknown to the late great Les Dawson; that rare occasion when a fellow's *bag for life's* mum could also be doing with a good *seeing to*. Mother-In-Law I'd Like to Fuck.

milf float *n*. A pretend sports car, such as the Peugeot 206CC, driven by an attractive young mother in an effort to recapture the carefree spirit of her lost youth.

milf grand prix *n*. The impressive grid line-up of gleaming four-wheel-drive sports utility vehicles which takes place on the pavements outside the gates of every posh secondary school in the country at 3.30pm.

MILK/milk *acronym*. A step down from a milf. Mum I'd Like to Know. A mature lady you like, but she isn't worth a *shag*.

milkers *n*. *Dairy bags*.

milking the thistle *n*. *Scots. Wanking*.

milkman *n*. That whistling chap who comes in the early morning, leaving *yoghurt* in the back passage.

milkman's bonus *n*. An unexpected gift after delivering the *cream* to *Mrs Brown*. A *winnet on a stick, shitty dick*.

milkman's gait *n*. The walk adopted by someone who has *overshagged*.

milk of human kindness *n*. See *liquid rage*.

milk race *1. n*. Adolescent *wanking* game for two or more public school children. *2. n*. A barrack room *toss-up* to decide who eats the last cream cracker.

milk shake *1. n*. The uncontrollable quaking caused by imminent *stack blow*. *Elvis's leg, Cecil Parkinson's disease*. *2. n*. The combination of wobbles, undulations and simple harmonic motions that a middle-aged woman's *bits* perform while she's riding her bloke. *3. n*. A dance favoured by *birds* who are past the first flush of youth, involving an excess of alcohol and much swaying of the hips.

milk shower *n*. A form of soft-core dairy-based *watersports* that may be engaged in by a man and his lactating missus whilst she is enjoying a ride on his *solicitor general*.

milk the cow with one udder *v*. To be the only hand in the *farmyard area*.

milk the snake *v*. To practise *self abuse*.

millennium domes *n*. The contents of a Wonderbra, *ie*. Very impressive when viewed from the outside, but there's actually *fuck all* in there worth seeing.

Disappointing *tits*. See *heavage*.

Millennium Falcon *n*. Epithet used when referring to a dodgy *bird* which your mate has been *banging*. From the *Star Wars* film dialogue referring to Han Solo's spaceship; "You came in that thing? Wow, you're braver than I thought."

Mills & Bone *n*. Erotic literature with plot pretensions for the red-blooded bachelor.

milm *v*. To cover something in *jism*. 'Oy, mum, I've milmed me kex.'

mimsy 1. *adj*. Descriptive of the state of the borogoves. 2. *n*. A *clopper*.

minotaur 1. *n*. In Greek mythology, a monster with a man's body and a bull's head. 2. *n*. In nightclubs, a monster with a woman's body and a face like a cow's *arse*.

mince medallions *n*. *Dangleberries, klingons*.

mince morsel *n*. An exceptionally pungent *Exchange & Mart* released in a confined area by an anonymous assailant.

mincident *n*. An unplanned and unnerving encounter with a gentleman adept at *jumping over puddles, eg*. Whilst bending over for the soap in a communal shower, failing to stand with one's back to the wall as a Gay Pride march comes past or when inadvertently sticking one's *cock* through a hole in a public lavatory cubicle wall.

miner's face, as filthy as a *sim*. Descriptive of a very accommodating lady who is eager to please in the bedroom. Right dirty.

miner's snot *n*. The liquid, stringy black *lav children* that can result from a night spent *sniffing the barmaid's apron*.

miner's sock *n*. A perspiring, debris-laden *clopper* after a hard day's graft.

minesweeping *n*. Behaviour which is widely practised at the conclusion of wedding receptions, funeral teas, parties and the like, whereby the band, waiters, undertakers and other sundry hangers-on comb the venue and consume any left-over food, booze, bridesmaids *etc*.

ming 1. *v*. *Scot*. To emit a foul smell, to *hum*. 'Hoots mon, it's minging in here!' 2. *n*. A foulsome miasma. 'Gaw, blimey! What's that blooming ming?' 'I'm afraid Jocky Wilson has done a shit in your shoe, Mr Bristow.' 3. *v*. To exude ugliness. 'That bellringer is minging.' 4. *n*. The bill, the *scuffers*, the *bizzies*. 5. *n*. A new marijuana cigarette made up from discarded ends. A tramp's *spliff*. 6. *n. prop*. The evil Emperor of Mongo in *Flash Gordon*. 7. *n. coll*. A quantity of ugly women. 'Don't bother going to Simbas tonight. The place is heaving with fucking ming.'

Ming the merciless *n*. An exceptionally foul-smelling *horse and cart*.

minge *n*. *Snatch, cludge, clopper, blurtch, quim*.

minge benefits *n*. The *snatch*-related rewards received by a man as a result of a selfless act performed for a loved one, *eg*. Cooking dinner, buying flowers or sitting through *EastEnders* without complaining.

minge binge *n*. The frantic fish-eating spree of the *gash gannet*.

minge fringe *n*. The hairiest part of a lady's *growler*, that a fellow is forced to brush out of the way repeatedly whilst he is enjoying a libation at the *blip tap*.

minge hinge *n. medic*. The female childbearing pelvic area. 'This is the tale of Dora Duckett / Who had a minge hinge like a bucket / Her hubbie swore it was *so wide / His charlie never touched the side / Despite her Albert Hall-like muff / He somehow got her up the duff / One night she cried out "Wake up Sid! / I think I'm going to have the kid!" / "Don't panic dear," her husband said / "I'll call the doctor from his bed" / The quack said "How d'you do" to Dora / And slipped his hand in to explore 'er / He stuck his arm right up her clout / As anxiously he felt about / "What's up?" Mr Duckett said / "Can you feel the baby's head?" / "Fuck the sprog," the doctor cried / "There's room for octuplets inside! / I've got my hand up your wife's crotch / Because I've lost my fucking watch."'* (from *Odd Odes* by Cyril Fletcher).

mingelicious *adj*. A *front bottom* alternative to the more *fat-arse*-centric term of approbation *bootylicious*. *'That Kylie Minogue is right mingelicious isn't she, Cardinal?'*

minge mat *n. Mapatasi, velcro triangle.*

minge miner *n*. A gynaecologist. Also *box doc, snatch doc, snatch quack, fanny mechanic, cunt dentist, dirty dentist* or *mingineer.*

mingeneering *n*. The science of *fanny mechanics. Snatch patching,* gynaecology.

mingerling *n*. To move and socialise amongst the less obviously attractive ladies in a nightclub after resigning oneself to the fact that one isn't going to pull a *looker. 'Well, looks like all the class blart has been snaffled. Better start mingerling, I suppose.'*

minge syringe *n. Pork sword;* a further addition in the *minge* rhyming series.

minge winker 1. *n*. A striptease artiste. 2. *n*. She who flashes her *gash, eg.* Whilst folding her legs. *'Today's birthdays - Sharon Stone, minge winker, 49'.*

mingicles *n*. Frozen *piss* stalactites dangling off *birds' snappers,* which form in northern climes when short-skirted young ladies go for a *gypsy's kiss* and then venture out into the freezing weather without first pausing in the *bogs* to *shake the lettuce.* Also known as *slicicles.*

mingineering *n*. Gynaecology. *'Today's birthdays: Rembrandt van Rijn, Dutch artist, 1606; Ian Curtis, British musician, 1956; Robert Winston, British mingineer, 1940.'*

minglewank *n*. A surreptitious *tug* performed through the trouser pocket in a crowded place, *eg*. On a tube train, in a supermarket, at a funeral.

miniature heroes 1. *n*. Small *fudge nuggets* which, even in the face of vigorous wiping, cling tenaciously to the *arse cress.* 2. *n*. Tiny *arse bars.*

minihughie *n*. A mouthful of *spew* that can be discreetly swallowed back down. The *vurp's* slightly bigger brother.

mini series 1. *n*. A troublesome *log* that requires several flushes to see it off. 2. *n*. A pile of *shite* starring Jane Seymour or Jenny Seagrove.

minjury *n*. An accident that occurs to a lady's *foofoo. 'Careful with that champagne bottle, Fatty, you'll do someone a minjury.'*

mink *n*. A more up-market name for the wife's *beaver.*

minkle *n*. Hampshire term for a lady's *front pocket. 'Fuck me, vicar. You can see her minkle.'* Can also be used as a friendly greeting. *'Hallo vicar, you fucking minkle.'*

mink's minge, soft as a *sim*. Descriptive

of something which is very soft, *eg*. Fine velvet, silk pyjamas or Keith Flint out of The Prodigy. *'New Andrex Ultra. 50% longer, 50% stronger, but still as soft as a mink's minge.'* (Ad Campaign, Bartle Bogle Heggarty BBD DDP Needham Buggery Bollocks).

minky 1. *n*. A French monkey. 2. *n*. A species of whale. 3. *n*. A *hornbag*. An attractive female.

minnie moo *n*. *Foofoo, fluffit*.

minute man *n*. *medic*. One afflicted with the hilarious and shameful condition of premature ejaculation. A *two push Charlie*, a *point and squirt merchant*.

misanthropissed *adj*. Drunk to a state of curmudgeonliness, like one of those blokes you see in your local Wetherspoon boozer, drinking heavily in silence.

miserbation *n*. The practice of *wanking* over free underwear catalogues, travel brochures and other sundry *humble grumble*, as indulged in by parsimonious bachelors who consider shelling out good money on a copy of *Razzle* to be a frivolous waste of money. *Ebenezer spooging*.

miser's shite *n*. A miraculous bowel movement, the wiping of which causes no soiling of the first sheet.

Miss Chesterfield *n*. A buxom young lady. A well-upholstered *piece* with buttons on the ends of her *tits*.

Miss Hastings *n*. An ugly woman who is in fact the least ugly woman in one's environs. From the heavily be-uglywomanned Sussex seaside town.

missionary impossible *n*. A lady with a *lovely personality* who can only be *poked* in the *doggy position*. A *lumberjill*, a *bobfoc*, a *frombie*.

missionary position *n*. Sexual intercourse

enjoyed when ensconced in a large cooking pot suspended over an open fire, whils immersed up to shoulder level by bubbling water with all carrots in it.

Miss Lincolnshire *n*. Any woman with *spaniel's ears*. *'And this year's Miss Lincolnshire is Patsy Kensit.'*

Miss Pwllheli *n*. The ugliest female in any locale who could, should she wish, move to the north Wales town and win its annual beauty pageant by default.

Miss Selfridge shuffle *n*. The embarrassed, self-conscious little dance performed by a man left waiting in the lingerie department of a department store whilst his wife is in the changing rooms.

missus button *n*. The control on the front of a PC (often labelled "reset") which can be hit to remove all the vile, hardcore *grumble* from the screen when one's wife or partner returns home unexpectedly. The *top shelf destruct button*.

misterectomy *n*. *medic*. Radical surgical procedure. The removal of a gent's *matrimonial components*. *'Come over here, Tiger. Me mum wants to give you a misterectomy.'*

Mitchells *n*. Huge pairs of *tits*. Termed after their resemblance to the bald heads of erstwhile *EastEnders* hard boys Phil and Grant. *'Dear Miriam, I found a lump in my left Mitchell and I'm scared to go to my doctor in case she gives me bad news.'* (Problem page, *Daily Mirror*, June 2002).

mixed grill *n*. A particularly unappetising *Fred Kite* of varying consistencies, colours and constitution. A *full German*.

Mobe *n*. Abbreviation of Moby Dick. An epic *turd*, longer than a *mini series*, which may require harpooning with the lavatory brush to see it off.

mobile throne *n*. A portable *shit house* that everyone avoids at pop festivals because the floor is two inches deep in *mocking birds*.

mocking birds *rhym. slang.* *Douglas Hurds*.

mock turtle *1. n.* A character in *Alice in Wonderland* by antique kiddie diddler Lewis Carroll. *2. n.* Something that feels like a *shit,* but turns out to be a *fart*.

model T fart *n*. A *wind breakage* that sounds like one is about to be run over by Laurel and Hardy.

mod's parka *n*. A young lady's *clopper* of a particularly unattractive mien, resembling a sort of floppy funnel with a bit of flea-bitten fur stuck round the collar. Possibly encountered on Brighton beach whilst a youth in a leather jacket strikes it repeatedly using a length of metal pipe.

mofo *n. abbrev.* Abbreviation for *monkey feather*.

Mogwai's eye, fanny like *sim.* Descriptive of particularly bulbous *Keith Burtons*. Named after the eyelids of the famous 1980s Gremlin, which resembled particularly bulbous *Keith Burtons*.

mohair knickers *n*. Large, unruly *minnie moo*; one with *spider's legs*. A *biffer*.

moip *n*. Female genital lubrication. *Froth, fanny grease, vagoline, beef dripping, blip, bilp, sloom*.

moip mop *n*. A gentleman's beard used to soak up *sloom*, in the same way one would use a slice of bread to soak up gravy. *'Short back and sides, please. And could you trim the stray bits off my moip mop.'*

moist and meaty *adj.* Alliterating adjectives used extensively to describe the female and male genitals respectively, as well as dog food.

mole at the counter *euph.* A mammalian *turtle's head*. *"From the imprint of his shoes, Watson, I deduce that our quarry is a left-handed doctor of unusually short stature, who has known prosperity but has lately fallen on hard times. And by the short, irregular length of his stride, it is apparent that he has a mole at the counter,' said Holmes.'* (from *The Case of the Speckled Bowl* by Sir Arthur Conan Doyle).

mole in the back garden *n*. Small, brown animal that pops its head out for a second, leaving an unpleasant mound of soft dirt around the edge of its burrow.

mole's eye *n*. A *fanny* which makes a *mouse's ear* look like a *horse's collar*. *'Consignia was powerless to resist. His eyes burnt into hers like ambers. His muscular arms enfolded her body as she felt herself being swept away on tradewind of passion. "Now, Fernando,' she gasped. 'Take me now. All these years in the convent I've been saving myself for the right man, and now I've found you.' 'Fucking get in," breathed Fernando. 'You must have a snatch like a mole's eye."* (from *The Nun and the Windowcleaner* by Barbara Cartland).

molten brown *euph.* An unpleasant, morning-after-Vindaloo-style *digestive transit,* which melts the *balloon knot*. Named in direct contrast to the rather pleasant bathroom cosmetics manufacturer. A *rogan splosh, dump and burn*.

moment of clarity *n*. The instant following *stackblow,* when a *self-polluter* is assailed by intense feelings of disgust and self-loathing, and vows never to touch himself *down there* again. Just like he did an hour previously. *Wangst, wanguish.*

Monday roast *n.* Following a substantial meal on the Sabbath, the next day's hearty morning *sit-down visit*, complete with *air biscuits* and gravy.

Monet bird *n.* A lady who, in reference to the painted works of the renowned French impressionist painter Claude Monet (1840-1926), "looks good from a distance". A *low resolution fox.*

moneymoon *n.* The magical, but all too short period of financial stability which one enjoys after a win on the horses or taking out a Payday Loan.

money shit, the *1. n.* The main event during a visit to the *Rick Witter*, usually preceded by the dropping of several, less satisfying *rabbit pellets. 'Aaah. That's the money shit alright.'* 2. *n.* The climactic scene in a German *grumble* film.

money shot *n.* The moment in a *bongo flick* where the leading man makes a small deposit from *Kojak's money box*, usually into the leading lady's face. A *pop shot.*

money tits *n.* The sort of smashing *Davy Jones's lockers* any man worth his salt would happily hand over his hard-earned wages to see unfettered, *eg.* The *fat rascals* fastened to the chest of leek-chomping warbler Charlotte Church.

mongrel *n.* A *dobber*, a *semi*, *half a teacake.* A *cock* in a state of semi-turgidity that is neither one thing nor the other. A *knob* which is *on the bounce.*

monkey *n.* Vagina. A *toothless gibbon.*

monkeybagging *n.* A man's means of heightening his pleasure whilst an act of oral *horatio* is being performed on his *tummy banana. Monkeybagging* involves the simple act of tugging one's

partner's ears away from, and perpendicular to their head, thus modifying the shape of their mouth and lips.

monkey bath *n.* A bath so hot, that when lowering yourself in, you go: "Oo! Oo! Oo! Aa! Aa! Aa!"

monkey cum *n.* Any cream-based *tart fuel, eg.* Bailey's.

monkey feather *exclam.* Bizarre substitute for *m*******f****** dubbed into Eddie Murphy films on BBC1 to avoid offending some stupid old cunt. Also *mother father, money farmer, melon farmer, muddy funster.*

monkey pie *1. n.* A chip shop delicacy heated to the temperature of the earth's core which, upon taking the first *Bee Gees bite*, causes its purchaser to cry out in a series of inarticulate, high-pitched simian shrieks. *2. n.* A hairy, ill-mannered *clopper* that keeps blowing raspberries.

monkey run *n.* The awkward act of half-sprinting, half-hobbling from the computer to the bathroom, performed by a web *grumble* enthusiast with the *jester's shoes* who has realised too late that all the socks are in the wash. A gait which brings to mind that of Clint Eastwood's ginger simian sidekick Clyde in the *Every Which Way but Loose* movie series. A *wounded soldier's walk, bishop's waltz.*

monkey's chin *n. Twix lips, beetle bonnet*, a prominent *mound of Venus.*

monkey's fag break *n.* Like slipping out for five minutes for a fag, but for a *ham shank* instead of a *Harry Rag*. A *wank* at work.

monkey's fist *n.* A small, brown *Richard the Third.* Found by a cockney vicar on the pavement.

monkey's forehead *1. n. velcro triangle, mapatasi.*

monkey's kneecap *n.* A scabby *quim* one could spend all day picking the fleas out of.

monkey's tail *n.* A small lick of *turd* on the rear of the seat caused by sitting too far back whilst *dropping the kids off at the pool.*

monkey's toe *1. n.* A nipple big enough to peel a banana. A *Westminster Abbey hatpeg. 2. n.* The *turtle's head.*

monkey wank *n.* To masturbate oneself or another person using the feet. Whilst swinging in a tyre.

Monkhouse's Syndrome *n. medic.* To vomit into the mouth and swallow with a tortoise-like gulp and hand gesture, reminiscent of the late Bob Monkhouse introducing a punchline. *Bob's Full Mouth.*

monk's chain *n. eccles.* A circle or line of friars, public schoolboys or BBC football commentors interfering with each other's *parts of shame.* A *daisy chain,* a *circle jerk.*

monk's chunks *n.* The excess *smeg* build-up of a man who has given up caring any more.

monk's cowl *n.* A *wizard's sleeve.*

monk's hood *n.* A voluminous *Jacky Danny.* A *wizard's sleeve,* a *hippo's mouth, Jade yawning.*

monks' trunks *n.* Underpants that are crunchy with dried *spunk.*

monster munch *n. Cunnimingus.* From the comparable olfactory experience of sticking one's face in a bag of the popular pickled onion snack and breathing deeply.

Montezuma's revenge *n. medic. Mexican screamers,* the *shits. Tijuana cha-cha.*

Named after the Aztec ruler Montezuma (1466-1520) who, following the conquest of his homeland by the Spaniard Hernán Cortés, vowed to exact his vengeance by giving a thousand generations of Europeans mild diarrhoea.

monthly wrench *n.* The variably-sized *tool* which a chap employs in order to *tighten his nuts* whilst his *ride* is *up on blocks. Wanking spanner, dick skinner.*

Monty *n.* A *blopstrop, tammy huff.* From the mood swings of Ryder Cup winner and perennial *moan-arse* Colin Montgomerie.

moo *n.* A name to call the wife when one thinks the word "cow" is too offensive. *'Where's me bladdy tea, eh? You fucking stupid old moo.'*

moobs *n.* Flabby breast-like structures sported by non-sporting gentlemen whose only form of daily exercise is to jog past the salad in the works canteen. From man + boobs. *Man breasts, mannery glands, bitch tits.*

mooey *n.* A *sausage wallet, minnie moo.*

moomlaaters *n.* Traffic-stopping *moobs.*

moomph *1. v. Aus.* To sniff a lady's bicycle seat. *Barumph, snurgle. 2. n. Aus.* One who *moomphs.* A *garboon, snufty, snurglar.*

moon *v.* A rugby move, where the prop forward sprints around the defending back four to the rear of the bus and presses his naked *arse* up to the back window.

moon grease *n.* Sweaty *barse* juice. *Driving instructor's suet.*

moonie *1. n. prop.* A follower of the Rev Ying Tong Yiddel-I Moon. *2. n.* An act of *mooning. Hanging your hole.*

moon juice *n.* The liquid product of a lady's monthly discomfort. The cargo of the *tomato boat*. *Lunar mess, fanny jam.*

moonraker 1. *n*. One who is prone to the vigorous and blatant scratching of their *ringpiece*. 2. *n*. Space-based James Bond film in which, for the purposes of a particularly off-colour Christmas afternoon pun, a weightless Roger Moore apparently attempts to *thumb in a slacky* after already losing his *mess* up a scientist who is named to imply that she is a talented *cock-sucker*.

moonwalk *n*. The optical illusion of walking without moving achieved by someone trying to wipe a *dog's egg* off their shoes onto the grass.

moose *n*. *Boiler, steg*. Often a feminist who's got *Don King in a headlock*.

moose knuckles *n*. *Can. Camel's foot, Ninja's toe*.

moosetrap *n*. The protracted, often expensive, and frankly unnecessary efforts expended when attempting to seduce a right *boot* of a lass when, in reality, a simple "Fancy a bang?" would probably achieve the same outcome. Inspired by the popular charity shop 1970s children's boardgame *Mousetrap*, which featured an overly-complicated contrivance for the purpose of entrapping a small plastic rodent that was frankly going nowhere.

moped *n*. A fat woman. Fun to *ride*, but you wouldn't want your mates to know.

Mordor march past *n*. The parade of spinsters that forms between a club and a kebab shop at closing time.

More Four whore *n*. One of those crappy presenters, usually of property programmes, who is never off Channel Four's endless bloody channels, and sells him/herself constantly with increasingly tawdry and desperate trailers, ads *etc*.

Also *mo'fo'ho'* for short.

more Ginster than gangster *adj*. Descriptive of the sort of portly *twat* with a shaved head, tracky pants, white polo shirt, lots of expensively cheap jewellery, and who has to use the roof of his ageing BMW in order to haul himself out onto the pavement before strutting off like an overweight Al Capone. '*The guy thought he was some kind of toughnut, but actually he was more Ginster than gangster.*' (from *The Pram in the Lake* by Raymond Chandler).

more lip than a cow's got cunt, you've got *exclam*. Something to say to someone with a cheeky disposition, *eg*. A double glazing salesman, a potty-mouthed Radio 2 presenter on the telephone or an overly-insistent Jehovah's Witness on the doorstep. Also, for the more poetically inclined, *more front than a cow's got cunt*.

more tea vicar? *phr*. Faux-farcical attempt to distract a clergyman after the launch of an *air biscuit*, now widely used to diffuse post-*fart* tension. See also *keep shouting Sir, we'll find you; speak up caller, you're through*.

morgan *rhym slang*. *Arse*. From Morgan Stanley Dean Witter = shitter.

morgue cheater *n*. A senior citizen. A *coffin dodger*, an *oxygen thief*.

mornflakes *n*. Residue found in one's *pubes* after carelessly *relaxing in a gentleman's way* several times the previous evening.

morning glory *n*. The appearance of a *tent pole* first thing in the morning. A *dawn horn, jake*.

morning level crossing *euph*. The first *piss* of the day. From the fact that you have to wait for the barrier to go down before you can proceed. Even though, on a real level crossing, you have to wait for the barrier to go up before you can proceed, obviously. Unless you're a train driver.

morning line, the 1. *n.* Channel 4 horse-racing programme hosted by Happy Shopper Steve Rider Derek Thompson and celebrity nose-picker John McCririck. 2. *n.* The results left in one of them back to front German *shitters* when one *releases the chocolate hostage* after a breakfast of schnitzels, boiled cabbage and lager.

morning thickness *n.* A post-slumber state of erectivitation. Also *morning wood, morning glory.*

morning thunder *n.* The first, usually very powerful *fart* of the day. A *breakfast maker.*

morning wood *n.* Ante-meridian tumescence.

Morrissey's stag night, like *sim.* Descriptive of a public house peopled entirely by broken men of indeterminate age staring silently at their half-empty pint glasses. *'Shall we go to Yates's instead? It's like Morrissey's stag night in here.'*

mortal *adj. Refreshed* within an inch of one's life.

mortal combat *n.* Fighting between intoxicated fellows. Or occasionally, in the case of certain self-sufficient *Harold Ramps*, between a single intoxicated fellow.

Moses effect *n.* What a seatbelt or bag strap does to a lady's *baps, ie.* Causing them to part like the Red Sea.

mosquito's tear *n.* An unimpressive quantity of ejaculate produced by a young man or bachelor at the conclusion of his ninth *pull* of the day, when the amount of *spuzz* issuing from his *hog's eye* is roughly equivalent to the quantity of liquid which drips onto the cheek of an insect of the family *culicidae* during the final scenes of *Love Story,* when Ali McGraw pegs it.

Moss Bros hire trousers, more cocks in her than a pair of *sim.* Descriptive of a loose-moralled lady who boasts an impressively extensive sexual back catalogue. *'I tell you what, I wouldn't say she's easy, ladies and gentlemen, but she's had more cocks in her than a pair of Moss Bros hire trousers. So in conclusion, can we all raise our glasses and toast the bride and groom?' 'Thank-you, vicar. And now it's time for the best man's speech.'*

moss cottage *n.* The ideal home for *John Thomas,* with all pubes round the door.

mosstril *n.* A single nasal aperture of the sort sported by celebrity types (*eg.* Daniella Westbrook) who find *Keith Richard's dandruff* a bit moreish.

mothball diver *n.* One who savours *granny's oysters.* A *biddy fiddler.*

moth boy *n.* The member of a drinking party who, upon entering a pub, proceeds directly to the bandits, attracted by the flashing lights. *Fruit fly.*

mother and child reunion *n.* Having a massive *feeshus* which is immediately followed in the same sitting by a much smaller counterpart. From the eponymous song, containing the apposite lines "The mother and child reunion / is only a motion away", which was written after Paul Simon experienced just such an eventuality in the bogs at Widnes Railway Station.

motherfucker *n.* In films directed by

Quentin Tarrantino, an unpopular gentleman. A polite term which can be used in the place of obscene terms such as *melon farmer, monkey feather, money farmer etc.*

Mother Hubbard's dog *sim.* Descriptive of an underused *minge, ie,* Drooling and *gagging for a bone. 'It's noo a score and seven years since her beloved Bonny Prince Albert passed awa'. Today, whilst oot aside the loch, Her Majesty confided in me that she missed his big wullie affy bad, and that most o' the time, her wee royal badger was akin tae Mother Hubbard's dog.'*

mother ship and a fleet of shuttles *euph.* In the world of defecation terminology, another way of describing that phenomenon whereby a large *dreadnought* is immediately followed by a flotilla of smaller vessels which have been queuing behind it like nippy hatchbacks behind a tractor on a country road. A *pace car* situation.

mother's love *n.* The quality which alows one to re-enter the *cludgie* after *laying a cable* when others have deemed the *ming* too evil to tolerate.

Mother Teresa's finger *n.* The opposite of a *Bungle's finger.* A pale, sickly, insipid *copper bolt* which resembles nothing so much as a digit from the hand of the erstwhile saintly Albanian bauble-hoarding nun. *'Best call the doctor and see if I can get an emergency appointment, love. I just done a Mother Teresa's finger.'*

moth sandwich, dry as a *sim.* Descriptive of something which is extremely deficient in the moisture department. *'What's the matter down there, Mr Elliott? Why have you stopped?' 'I'm going to have to go in the kitchen, I say the kitchen, for a glass of water, I say a glass of water, Mrs Bishop. Yon twat's as dry as a moth sandwich, I say a moth sandwich.'*

motion sickness *n.* Nausea caused by doing a *dump* so foul that it makes one gag.

motion thickness *n. Travel fat.*

motorboat, the *n.* The act of placing one's face between a lady's *baps* and pushing them together from either side whilst making the noise of an outboard motor. A woman can thus be described as *motorboatable* if she possesses sufficient *motorboatability.* A *two-stroke man sandwich.*

motorcycle kick stand *n.* The morning erection that manifests itself whilst one is asleep on one's side, preventing one from rolling over onto one's stomach.

motorhead *1. n.* A famous heavily metallic popular music combo, famous for their jaunty ditties, including *Ace of Spades* and *Killed by Death. 2. n.* An urgent *blowjob* delivered at breakneck speed behind a sleazy burger bar, cinema or skip.

mott *1. n.* A lady from Cumbria. *2. n.* Part of a Norman fort from GCSE history. *3. n.* A *minge, mapatasi.*

mottaging *n.* The female version of *cottaging,* if such a thing exists.

mottzerella *n.* A stringy, warm substance with the appearance of melted cheese, found on a *smeesh* which has been somewhat neglected in hygiene terms. *Voodoo butter, chodder.*

mound of Venus *n.* The craggy outcrop above *salmon canyon* usually hidden by a dense covering of *bush.* A *beetle bonnet, monkey's forehead, grassy knoll.*

mount *v.* To *hop on* for *a bit.*

Mountbattens *n*. Small fragments of shattered *turds* found floating in the toilet.

Mount Fujis *n*. Uncannily conical tits as seen in 1950s American B films. *Twin peaks, sweatermeat, dunce's hats.*

mouse *adj*. Descriptive of someone who is poor at what they do. *Swiss. 'That Eamonn Holmes is a bit fucking mouse, isn't he?'*

mouse meat *n*. Cheese.

mouser *n*. A bird who, when called upon to *do the decent thing*, nibbles rather than sucks. One would imagine that Mavis Riley, during her short, ill-fated marriage to Derek Wilton, was probably a *mouser*.

mouse's ear, fanny like a *sim*. Descriptive of a tight *minnie moo*, a *butler's cuff*.

mouse's tongue *sim*. Descriptive of a very small penis. With cheese on the end.

mousetrap *1. n*. Agatha Christie play which performs a sort of Care in the Community role for bad actors. *2. n*. A bin found in the ladies' restrooms where women may discreetly dispose of their feminine hygiene products, such as *jamrags, fanny nannies*, and *chuftie plugs*. *3. n*. One's wife's *minge* for the week or so each month when she is *dropping clots*. *4. n*. A poorly-balanced *chod hopper* lid that guillotines down onto the top of a fellow's *twig* while he's *straining his greens*, causing him to let go and make a grab for it and resulting in *piss* going everywhere. Also *pivotal moment, golden handshake, Newton's curse.*

moustaka *n*. A female lady's pubic hair which has been neatly parted down the centre in the style of a Wild West saloon bartender's moustache.

mouth muff *n*. A goatee beard normally sported by someone who mans an IT help desk and likes T'Pau. A *cocksucker's doormat.*

mouth-to-muff *n*. Lesbotic resuscitation technique. Also *quimlich manoeuvre.*

moving Blackbeard's eyepatch *n*. The time-saving practice of riving the gusset of a lady's *applecatchers* to one side in order to gain a swift entry to her *James Blunt*. Also *using the catflap, playing the violin. 'Lift your legs up, love. I can't get your knickers off.' 'Aw bloody hell. I'm really tired. can't you just move Blackbeard's eyepatch while I catch forty winks?'*

moving heavy furniture *euph*. An especially awkward and protracted evacuation of the *Denis Howells* which leaves the victim out of breath and sweating.

moy *1. n*. Helmet cheese. *Smegma. 2. adj*. Shit. esp. *dog's moy. 'Waterworld (1995. Dir. Kevin Costner) starring Kevin Costner and Dennis Hopper. A visually-striking, futuristic pile of high budget dog's moy.' (Halliwell's Film Guide).*

moylaise *n*. Sense of deep and lingering existential gloom which descends upon one when contemplating the inexplicable popularity of the Radio One breakfast host.

Mr Benn, to do a *v*. To get so *mullered* that one goes into a toilet in a pub, and the next thing one remembers is exiting the toilet of another pub, suspecting one has had a little adventure inbetween.

Mr Blobby *1. n*. Tidy-bearded annoying *cunt* Noel Edmonds's rubber-suited annoying *cunt* side kick. *2. n*. A gentleman during the one week in four when he has to do without, due to his wife being *Mrs. Blobby. 3. n*. A fellow who is currently *manstruating*.

Mr Bond *n*. A particularly buoyant *turd* that returns to the surface of the water even after flushing. *'Ah, so we meet again, Mr Bond.'*

Mr Brown is at the window *euph*. To have the *turtle's head*. First used by Queen Victoria. *'Pray forgive us, Mr Gladstone, but we cannot receive you at the moment. Mr Brown is at the window, and we fear we may papper our kex.'*

Mr Bum has his hand up *exclam*. A phrase used in polite company when one is forced to interrupt proceedings in order to *see a man about a brown horse*. *'Doctor Hawley Harvey Crippen. You have been found guilty by this court of the charge that you did, with malice aforethought, murder your wife Cora on or about the thirty-first of January in the year of our Lord nineteen hundred and ten. Do you have anything to say before I pass sentence?' 'Indeed I do. As God is my witness, I am confident that if, in the future, haplotypes from the genetic material found buried under my cellar are compared with the mitochondrial DNA of my wife's relatives, it will be conclusively proven that ... actually, could I please be excused for a moment, your honour? Mister Bum has his hand up.'*

Mr Flitcroft's woes *n*. Constant reminders that one's relationship is on the rocks, *eg*. A piece of music, a photograph, a fifty-thousand strong jeering football crowd.

Mr Happy's business suit *n*. An *English overcoat*.

Mr Hyde *1. n*. The uncontrollable, throbbing, dribbling, twitching, hairy beast into which Dr Jekyll transforms in the famous book and Russ Abbott sketch by Robert Louis Stevenson. *2. n*. The uncontrollable, throbbing, dribbling, twitching, hairy beast into which one's *knob* transforms when a particularly *fit bird* walks past.

Mr Jones *1. n. 19thC*. Penis. *2. n*. A butcher who frequently purports that "they don't like it up 'em".

Mr Sausage *n*. The excitable trouser man. Title of a *Mr Men* book that was hastily withdrawn from shops within an hour of going on sale in 1976.

Mr Trebus's yard *sim*. Descriptive of a much-neglected, unhygienic and rat-infested *clopper*. With a couple of mopeds buried in it. From the late *Life of Grime* star's *shit*-filled garden.

Mr Whippy *1. n*. Semi-viscous ice-cream that comes out of a tap in a van. Invented by Margaret Thatcher, interestingly enough. 99p. *2. n*. Flagellation, corporal punishment dished out at *rub-a-tug shops*. From £25. *3. n*. Semi-viscous *feeshus* that comes out of a tap in your underpants. 15 Deutschmarks.

Mr Whippy's in town *exclam*. Declaration that all is not well in the *chamber of horrors*.

M32 *n*. A *tit fuck*, *ie*. The most direct route for *coming* into the *Bristol* area.

muck *1. n*. Mess, *baby bouillon*, *load*, *bolt*. That which is *shot*. *2. n*. *'Have a look on Bravo, vicar. There's usually a bit of muck on there at this time of night.'*

mucksavage *n*. A *bumpkin*, a *buffle*, a *cabbagehead*. A *joskin*.

muck spreader *n*. Arse, bum.

muck truck *n*. A late night emergency food vehicle parked at the side of the road near a pub or club at chucking out time, where the cuisine is often somewhat less than haute, but looks smashing after a gallon or so of *pop*. *A kebabulance.*

muck trumpet *n*. A tunefully farty *brass eye*.

mucky dip *n*. A *scuttle* up the *coal hole*.

mucky *n*. Any item of a pornographic nature, book, video, *etc*. *'Have you got any mucky I can borrow?' 'Yes, but don't get any spragg on it this time.'*

mud *1*. *n*. Excrement. *2*. *n*. Excrement 1970s pop group.

mud button *n*. Winnet, dangleberry, tagnut, clinker, etc.

mudchild *n*. A *sweaty Morph*. Also *mud child*.

mud darts *n*. Anal love. Bum sex.

mudeye *n*. Arse, ringpiece, one's old-fashioned *fifties tea towel holder*.

muddy funster *1*. *n*. A *botter*. *2*. *n*. A *melon farmer*.

muddy welly *n*. A soiled prophylactic sheath which is best left by the *back door*.

Mudgee mailbags *sim*. Great big *norks*. Named after the remote Australian outback town of Mudgee, which gets its post delivered twice a year, apparently receiving it in large *tit*-shaped sacks. *'Christ, you've got knockers like Mudgee mailbags, your Majesty.'*

mud hole *n*. That *hole* from which one *blows mud*. The *crop sprayer, cable layer, nipsy*.

mudlark *1*. *n*. A horse which enjoys heavy ground. A *mudder*. *2*. *n*. The sort of goings-on enjoyed by foreign sex perverts on the internet.

mud oven *n*. The rectum of the *anus*. *'Mitochondria was powerless to resist. His eyes burned into hers like haema-* *tites. His muscular arms enfolded her body as she felt herself being swept away in a pyroclastic flow of passion. Then he said those words of which she had dreamed so long, yet never dared hope to hear. 'How much to give you one in the mud oven, then love?'* (from *The Aged Prostitute and the Scouse Football Star who Got Signed by Manchester United for Twenty-Eight Million Quid* by Barbara Cartland).

mudpussy *n*. The *arse*, when used by heathens for purposes for which the Lord did not intend it.

mud valve mechanic *n*. A *brown pipe engineer, exhaust fitter*.

mudweiser *n*. A glass of warm, American *piss*-like lager consumed at Glastonbury, which contains dried *cowshit* flakes that have fallen off your *crap*-caked face, but which you drink down anyway because it was three pound *fucking* forty and you can't be *arsed* to start queuing all over again.

mudwife *n*. One who assists another during the delivery of a particularly large, or breech, *Meatloaf's daughter*. *'Bobby Brown admitted on television last night that he has had occasion to act as a mudwife to his constipated missus Whitney Houston.'*

mud wrestling *n*. A long and messy battle on the toilet, involving much grunting and groaning, which usually ends in either a knock-out, a fall or a submission.

muesli *n*. A sub-*pink* genre of close-up glamour photograph, depicting a tight-lipped *fish mitten*. From the description on at least two supermarket own brand boxes of muesli which state: "To open, slide finger under flap".

muff *1. n. Minge, fanny. 2. v.* To *shag*, have intercourse with. *3. v.* To fluff, miss an easy goal-scoring opportunity. *'Oh fuck! Emile Heskey has muffed it.'* *4. n.* Stevie Winwood's brother, who played bass in the Spencer Daviis Group. *5. v.* To *lick out. 6. acronym. coll.* Mums Up For Fucking.

muff diva *n.* A histrionic lady of sapphic inclination.

muff diver *n.* A footballer who misses an easy goal scoring opportunity, then falls over in an attempt to win a penalty kick.

muff diver's dental floss *n.* Female pubic hair.

muff huff *n.* Menstruational moodiness or PMT. A *period drama*, a *blob strop*.

muffia *n.* A collection of criminal women, or women who are married to criminals.

muffin *1. n.* Flour-based bakery product. *2. n.* 1960s TV mule whose name remains a source of perpetual hilarity among the elderly and infirm.

muffin tops *n.* The pastry-like midriff overhang achieved by lasses wearing tight, low-slung *kex*.

muffle *v.* The female equivalent of *zuffle*.

muffled *adj.* Of ambient noise, subjectively abated as a consequence of a lady's thighs clamped tightly around the sides of a *cumulonimbalist*'s head, thus occluding his ears. Or, indeed, her ears in these days of lesbians and what-not.

mufflinks *n.* Female genital jewellery. Pierced fanular silversmithery. *Curtain rings*.

muff nudge *n.* The light brushing of a female hairdresser's *beetle bonnet* against one's elbows when she leans forward to cut one's hair.

muffocation *n.* Inability to breathe when a *dirty lady* is sitting on your face.

muff riders *n. Birds' crabs.*

muffro *n.* Female pubic coiffure that resembles nothing so much as the popular hairdo which was famously sported by Jermaine Jackson in the seventies. On his head, of course, not his *cunt*.

mufftash *n.* The stylish, Kevin Webster-style furry residue which adorns the upper lips of those who have but recently been *licking out* a lady's *mimsy*. A *Barnsley moustache*.

muff trumpet *n.* A *fanny fart* that would have a troop of soldiers standing by their beds.

mug stains *n.* Large, dark, flat *jockeys* that often appear during pregnancy.

Mugabe *n.* The frankly silly postage stamp-sized tuft of *muff turf* left above the *wuwus* of certain porn actresses and *jazz mag* models. A *muffgabe, clitler*.

mule's lip *n.* A large foreskin, like a sulky Frenchman's mouth.

muller *v.* To perform *horatio*. From the advertising slogan of the popular yoghurt, *viz.* "Lick the lid of life".

mullered *adj. Langered*.

muller love *n.* The temporary amorous feelings one has towards a right *pig* as a result of being *mullered*. Finding someone attractive when looking at them through *beer goggles*.

mullet *n.* Inbreds' haircut favoured by country and western singers, the verminous trailer-trash guests on the *Jerry Springer* show and 1980s footballers.

mulligan *n. Aus.* Penis.

mumbas *onomat.* Breasts. If *oomlaaters* made a noise, they would say "mumbas" in a deep, fruity baritone.

mumble in the jungle *n. Cunnibungalus*.

mumblers *n.* Tight women's bicycle shorts

through which you "see the lips move but can't understand a word".

mummy returns *n*. A *brown zombie* that comes back wrapped in *shit tickets*.

mumph *onamat*. See *flub*.

Mumrah's cock *n*. The tissue wrappings placed around *Pharaoh's flute* to prevent any spillages of *kid juice* onto ceremonial robes *etc*. Particularly handy whilst re-enacting the ancient Egyptian creation myth of Atum, who had a swift *one off the wrist* on the Primordial Mound in the Void of Nu, and was surprised to discover that the first *wad* of supernatural *jitler* out of his *hog's eye* contained both the god Shu and the goddess Tefnut, who became the parents of all the other elements of the world. From the bandage-wrapped mummy in *Thundercats*™.

mumrar *n*. The act of sneaking up behind your mother and shouting "RAR!"

munch bunch *n*. A gang of *dykes* in a carpet warehouse.

mung 1. *n*. Type of bean which is popular with *Guardian* readers. 2. *n*. A particularly runny type of *arse feta*. 3. *n*. That smell which emanates from within the fleshsome rolls of a *Duke of giblets*. *'Rik – I like what you did with the song, but I'm not sure that your interlude of vigorous breakdancing during the middle eight was such a good idea. There was a right fucking mung in here by the time you reached the last chorus. Dr Fox has had to open the window.'*

Mungos *n*. Great big sideburns as worn by Jerry Dorsey, lead singer of Mungo Jerry. *Bugger's grips, face fannies.*

municipal cockwash *n*. A lady who is indiscriminate with her affections.*Town bike, box of assorted creams, buttered bun.*

munter gatherer *n*. A fellow who appreciates the company of women with *lovely personalities.*

munter punter *n*. A revoltingly chauvinistic, politically incorrect and unacceptably sexist term for a chap who habitually squires *women with lovely personalities*. A *dog handler*.

munts *n*. Particularly butch, though not necessarily *lesbotic* ladies, often found amongst the sailing community. From men + cunts.

muppet's mouth *n*. A *fanny* whose lips don't exactly follow the words its owner is speaking.

murray walker *n*. One who enjoys an *al fresco Ruby* whilst meandering back from the pub. Named after the excitable Formula 1 motor-racing commentator Martin Brundle.

muscle mary *n*. An extremely well-built *ginger beer*. A *canny hard puff*.

mush in the bush *n*. The kind of sex act that Dick Van Dyke might perform on Julie Andrews. *Cockney cumulonimbus*.

musical vegetables *n*. Baked beans, as eaten by cowboys and *trouser trumpeteers*.

musical wank *n*. A *strum* undertaken to the rhythm of some music, such as the "We buy any car dot com" jingle.

musk mask *n*. To wear a lady's *undercrackers* as a balaclava whilst having a right good *wank*.

mustang *n*. Of *shitty arses*, that stubborn *dangleberry* which cannot be shaken off.

mute button *n*. In a public lavatory, for example, the invisible remote control that you apparently operate upon entering, which renders any *trap* occupant completely silent until they have heard you wash your hands and leave the room.

Mutley chunter *n.* The act of voicing disapproval under one's breath when forced to perform an act under duress, in the style of Dick Dastardly's dog. Usually involves muttering "ratting, dratting," *etc.* through tightly-clenched teeth.

muttered Pooh *exclam.* An amusing way for a literate fellow to round off a bit of *back chat.* Likewise *grumbled Eeyore,* or *said Thomas.*

mutton dressed as kebab *sim.* Ugly women who doll themselves up and make themselves look even worse, *eg.* Julie Goodyear. Also *mutton dressed as spam.*

mutton musket *n.* A smaller, more portable field weapon than the *lamb cannon.* Also *mutton bayonet, mutton dagger.*

mutton tugger *n.* In a slaughterhouse, one whose job it is to pull the meat off the bones of old sheep.

mutt's nuts *adj.* Descriptive of something which is very good. The *dog's bollocks, the vicar's cock.*

mycoxafloppin *n. medic.* The principal active ingredient in Viagra.

Myleene *rhym. slang.* The *anus.* From the fat-titted former Hear'Say-songstress-turned-not-very-good-television-presenter Myleene Klarsehole.

mystic smeg *n. Erectoplasm.*

mystic steg *n.* A malevolently *fugly* presence which haunts you, asking you what your fucking star sign is.

Nadal rally *n.* A noisily energetic marathon bout of lovemaking, characterised by the loud grunts which accompany each stroke.

nadbag *n.* The *nut sack, pod pouch, scrot sling, chicken skin handbag.*

nadger *n.* A testicle which has been battered black and blue. *'I tell you what, she loves it rough. She's left me with a right pair of nadgers, Mother Superior.'*

nadgina *n.* A *cockney's pod purse*, which has been refashioned into a *cludge* at the skilled hands of a dextrous surgeon. *'Day forty-four in the house, and Nadia's giving her nadgina a quick rinse in the sink.'*

nad nogg *n. Splod.*

nadpoles *n. Jizzbag taddies. Spunks*, spermatozoan humunculi.

nads *n. Knackers*, testicles, *plums.*

Nagasaki tan *n.* A sunbed-induced glow of such ferocity that it appears that one was present an the detonation of an atom bomb, *eg.* One sported by Judith Chalmers, Des O'Connor, Jodie Marsh, Dale Winton or David Dickinson.

NAKED!!!!! *adj.* Not in any real sense naked. A variation on the original word, used on the cover of lads' mags in order to hype up pictures of some *bird* who is either not naked at all or is strategically covering up her bits, so you can't see them and she may as well be wearing a big jumper. Also NUDE!!!!!, STARKERS!!!!!, WE ALREADY RAN THESE PICTURES SIX MONTHS AGO & WE HOPE YOU DON'T NOTICE!!!!!

name that tune *exclam.* A humorous exclamation called out to draw attention to an amusing breaking of wind at a middle class dinner party.

nam-pla *1. n.* Fish sauce, an essential Thai cooking ingredient. *2. n. Knob cheese*, an essential ingredient when cooking for Michael Winner.

nana Kournikova *n.* A *bird* who appears to be fit from the back, but who on turning round is revealed to be a pensioner. A *Kronenberg*, a *Toyah*, a *boyner.*

nan bread *n. Bingo wings, dinner ladies' arms, arm tits.*

nanbretta *n.* A mobility scooter.

nangerine *adj.* The characteristic orange skin tone of *biddies* who over-winter in Tenerife.

nan's grin *n.* A toothless *Beverley Craven.*

nan's mattress, as pissed as your *sim.* To be in an extreme state of *refreshment. 'Ladies and gentlemen, welcome aboard flight BA103 from Oslo. We would advise you to keep your safety belts fastened throughout the flight as it looks like it could be quite a bumpy ride. We're not expecting any turbulence, it's just that the captain is as pissed as your nan's mattress.'*

Narnia, so far in the closet he's in *euph.* Of a man, to be in denial over how chromatically adept he is.

NASCUA/nascua *acronym.* Unpleasantly sexist way that a less politically correct man might refer a somewhat uptight lady. Needs A Stiff Cock Up Arse.

nastonbury *n. Festival fanny.* The ripe *fent* coming off a *clout* that hasn't been cleaned for four days.

national grottery, win the *v.* To be the lucky discoverer of a massive deposit of porn hidden under a *bongo bush*, in a skip or a recently-deceased vicar's study. To scoop the *jack-off pot.*

nature's make-up *n.* A range of black and

blue eye cosmetics favoured by the wives of certain British sportsmen and actors.

naughty Nazi salute *n*. A *herman gelmet* standing to attention.

nauticals *rhym. slang*. Piles. From nautical miles.

navigator of the windward pass *n*. A *rear admiral*.

Navy cake *n. milit*. Army and Air Force term for the *arse*.

Navy gravy *n*. The salty spume found in a jolly Jack Tar's beard. *Sailor's ale*.

NBR *abbrev*. No Beers Required. A good-looking woman. Opposite of a *five pinter*.

NCP yoghurt *n*. The viscous off-white fluid spilled onto their *grot mags* by car park attendants *relaxing* in their booths. *'Excuse me, mate. Have you got any change for the ticket machine...? Eurgh. What's all that stuff on your hands, trousers and splashed across the open pages of your bongo book?' 'It's NCP yoghurt, that's all. And no, I don't have any change for the machine. Fuck off.'*

NDL *abbrev*. Nipples Don't Lie. Body language phenomenon that gives anthropologists an insight into how they are getting on when chatting up *birds* in the pub.

Neapolitan knickers *n*. The disgusting state of a proper old *slapper's gusset*. Vanilla, strawberry, chocolate, the lot.

Neapolitan shit *n*. Three different levels of excremental viscosity in a single sitting.

neckbreaker *n*. A *log* of such length, rigidity and tensile strength that it lifts the *shitter* vertically off the *pot*, crushing his or her neck against the ceiling. It is a little-known fact that Queen Victoria's death certificate gives her cause of death as "a neckbreaker occasioned by eating a plethora of black pudding, fruitcake and milk stout for her tea the day before."

necking turds *v*. Accusation made against one suffering from halitosis. *'Excuse me, madam, I don't wish to appear rude, but have you been necking turds?'*

neck tripe *n*. The unappetizing hanging flesh that adorns the throats of ageing ladies.

ned *n*. A Glaswegian *scratter*.

neddies *n*. Nellies.

needle dick *n*. Light-hearted, affectionate term of locker room abuse/ridicule describing a fellow with a small penis. *'Oi, we're one man short for the five-a-side here. Where's needle dick?' 'Didn't you hear? He's killed himself.'*

nellies *n*. Knockers, tits, neddies, melbas.

Nelson Mandela *rhym. slang*. Wreck the hoose juice, wifebeater. Stella.

Nelson's column, a *n*. A profound tumescence. Something that is tall, hard as rock, has one eye at the top, and attracts filthy *birds*. And Japanese tourists with cameras.

Nemissus, the *n*. The wife. From the ancient Greek legends, a vengeful harpy who harries an individual to his fate. *'It's alright, love,' spake the mighty Zeuss, appearing to the Nymph in the form of a swan. 'We can use my place up Mount Olympus. The Nemissus is out with the girls tonight.'* (from Hesiod's *Theogony*).

Neptune's kiss *n*. A cold, wet smacker on the *old fashioned fifties tea towel holder* caused by *splashback*.

Nescafe handshake *n*. An act of masturbation. A reference to the adverts where coffee granules used to appear in deceased *New Avengers* star Gareth Hunt's right hand after he pretended to have a *wank*. Also *magicking the beans*.

nesting *n*. Installing a floating mat of *bumwad* into the *pan* prior to taking a *dump,* in order to reduce the noise of the *cable* hitting the water and also to minimise the risk of any splashback up the *nipsy*. *Fireman's blanket*.

net curtains *n*. Old ladies' *drapes,* which tend to twitch over to one side when the neighbours come out.

nether eye *n*. That single *unseeing eye,* situated in the *nether region,* which cries brown, lumpy tears.

nether throat *n*. In *farting,* the *poot chute* or *botty bugle*. *'Pardon me while I clear my nether throat.'*

nettie *n*. Outside loo, *clart cabin, shite house. Dunny, cludgie, growler, khazi*.

nettiquette *n*. Code of polite behaviour followed by lavatory users. From nettie + Rosanna Arquette.

net pet *n*. Amongst the sort of people who habituate internet chatrooms such as Second Life and the like, a boyfriend or girlfriend with whom many hours are spent flirting without actually ever meeting in the flesh. A useful rule of thumb is that a sexually-adventurous blonde, 18-year-old *net pet* from the Home Counties will, more often than not, turn out to be a toothless 50-year-old Tennessee hillbilly with his dead mum in the fridge and a suit made of *fannies*.

Netto fabulous *adj*. Descriptive of one who eschews posh jewellers such as Tiffany's and Asprey's in favour of down market *blingmongers* like Price-drop.TV and Argos.

Netto ghetto *n*. A bijou shopping arcade consisting entirely of discount stores, *eg*. The Loreburn Centre, Dumfries.

neuticles *n*. Trade name for an American brand of artificial *knackers* for castrated dogs.

never had time for a wife *euph*. *Not the marrying kind*. From the lyrics to the Billy Joel song *Piano Man,* which refer to Paul "the real estate novelist" who, despite being too busy working to get married, apparently has plenty of time to hang around in bars talking to sailors.

new age traveller's cheque *n*. A giro.

Newcastle cup run *euph*. Descriptive of that wistful feeling experienced by gentlemen looking down at their own erections and wishing they could *suck* themselves *off*. From the fact that they know "it's within reach, but it's never going to happen".

new sheriff in town, there's a *exclam*. Phrase used when someone visiting one's home delivers an *air biscuit* which achieves hitherto unprecedented levels of pungency.

Newton effect *n*. When struggling to pass a three *breather ring dreadnought,* the pleasing sensation as the force of gravity finally takes over.

Newton's cradle *1. n.* A still fashionable, chromed executive toy which, by means of colliding, suspended balls demonstrates Newton's third law of motion. *2. n.* The off-putting and often *timber-felling* image of two *grumble flick* actors banging their *knackers* together as they perform a *DP.*

Newton's revenge *n*. The cruel effect of gravity upon aged *tits*.

next one's through the goods *phr*. British Rail-based *farting* terminology, signifying that the next toot on the whistle heralds the arrival of the cargo.

next sale *n.* Twice-yearly incident where one is awoken at some ungodly hour to clear out a pile of unwanted *shit*.

NFF FFN *abbrev. Nice From Far, Far From Nice.* Descriptive of a lady who looks alright from a distance, but is a right *steg* close up. A *Thora bird*, a *golden deciever, lrf.*

NGTs *abbrev.* National Geographic Tits. Flat, pendulous breasts as sported by old tribeswomen in the aforesaid school library *jazz mag. Spaniel's ears.*

niags *rhym. slang. Nuts.* From Niagara Festicles = testicles.

nice hair, she's got *euph.* Description of a lady with a *lovely personality*, but without the *lovely personality.* *'That Right Honourable Ann Widdecombe MP, she's got nice hair, hasn't she.'*

nicely poised *adj.* Of a gentleman, to be prone to *jumping puddles.* To be *good with colours, on the other bus.*

nice piece of glass *n.* Comestible ordered by humorous males at the bar. *'I'll have a nice piece of glass in a Stella sauce, please.'*

nichter scale *n.* Tabulated rating system used to articulate how much one would prefer not to *do* someone. *'Have a look at the fucking state of that. Christ on a fucking bike. She must register at least 9.5 on the nichter scale.'* (Sir Terry Wogan, introducing the Serbian entry to the 2007 Eurovision Song Contest).

nick bent *adj.* Temporarily travelling on the *other bus* whilst staying at Her Majesty's pleasure.

nickles and dimes 1. *n.* Low denomination US currency. 2. *n.* A low denomination *grumble vid money shot.* A *stick flick lizard's lick.* *'Goddammit, Gunther.*

That was goddamn nickles and dimes.' *'What do you expect? It's the fifth pop-shot I've done in two hours.'*

nick one to the wicketkeeper *v.* To fail to avoid the *follow-on* whilst wearing white trousers.

niff mag *n. Bongo comic.*

niftkin's bridge *n.* Female equivalent of the *biffin bridge* or *barse.*

Nigella *n.* A feature of a person or thing that distracts you from its supposed purpose, *eg.* A hairy mole on a teacher, ridiculous graphics on telly news programmes (*vide* BBC Arts Correspondent Razia Iqbal introducing an item on a Pop Art Exhibition as an array of brightly-coloured Andy Warhol silkscreen prints hung on the wall as the camera pans round the exhibition, for *fuck*'s sake), or a pair of splendid *knockers* housed in a low-cut dress sported by an absurdly flirtatious television chef.

Nigella express *n.* Nipping downstairs in the middle of the night for a quick *wank* by the light of the fridge.

Nigella shites *n.* The aftermath of eating upper class fodder.

night bus 1. *n.* A cheap ride home after a night *on the sauce.* Usually stinks of fags and puke, and costs about two quid. 2. *n.* A cheap *ride* at home after a night on the sauce. Usually stinks of fags and puke, and costs a Bacardi Breezer.

nightclub bouncers *n.* Pairs of burly *knockers* that are exposed to the public on Friday and Saturday nights. *'Fancy your chances with those nightclub bouncers, Dave?' 'Not really. To tell you the truth I think I'd rather get my head kicked in by those two big doormen instead.'*

night watchman *n.* A nocturnal *copper*

bolt that has failed to flush away and is discovered guarding the U-bend the next morning.

nikey pikey *n*. A white-baseball-capped, Saxo-driving, Reebok Classic-wearing self-unemployed gentleman, as found on the Central Avenue area of Hayes, Middlesex.

NILF/nilf *acronym*. Nannies I'd Like to Fuck. Tasteless term used by sexist beasts to describe those eastern European beauties who look after middle class brats 22 hours per day in return for significantly less than the minimum wage and a company pram.

nillionaires' row *n*. Name given to any run-down street in one of the country's less salubrious residential areas.

NIN *acronym*. *medic*. Normal in Norfolk. Doctor's shorthand implying that your physical and mental characteristics indicate that there is every chance that your mother is possibly also your sister, cousin, aunt and perhaps even your father.

nine-bob-note, as bent as a *sim*. *Colwyn Bay*.

nine dart leg *1. n*. The successful completion of a game of darts using the minimum number of throws possible, a feat achieved notably on TV by Phil "The Power" Taylor during the 2002 World Matchplay Championship. *2. n*. The successful completion of a sexual encounter in the shortest possible time, usually achieved by a *two push Charlie*.

ninety-nine *n*. After over-enthusiastic *nesting* on the *Morgan Stanley Dean Witter*, a *Sir Douglas Hurd* that sticks upright out of the paper at a jaunty angle, thus resembling the popular chocolate ice cream decoration. Hopefully without the monkey blood.

ninety-nine flake *n*. A particularly off-colour hybrid of *felching* and *ice docking* which frankly doesn't bear thinking about.

ninety-sixing *n*. A spot of *sixty-nining* that goes a bit wrong. For example, when one's partner farts directly up one's nose, spoiling everything for ever.

ninja shit *n*. Upon entering a public lavatory cubicle for a *sit down visit,* to be met with a smell so foul that one has to pull one's jumper up over one's nose and mouth, in the style of the eponymous incognito Japanese fighters, before one can continue.

ninja's toe *n*. A *camel's foot*.

ninth finger *n*. The *cock*.

nip and tuck *n*. The act of *nipping off* one of *Bungle's fingers* at the knuckle, with the result that the stump is retracted cleanly into the *bomb bay*. The correct response to a *mid-loaf crisis*.

nip 'n' roll *n*. The dextrous art of relieving an itch in *John Wayne's hairy saddlebags. Sorting out the boys*.

nipnosis *n*. Trance-like state induced by concentrating one's gaze on a pair of bobbing *milkers*. Often only ends when the *nipnotised* subject drives through a red light and broadsides a police car. *Titnosis*.

nipping Christian *n*. A cutpurse, a thief.

nipping the turtle *n*. *Crimping off a length, shutting the bomb bay doors*.

nipplecakes *n*. Appetising breasts that one wouldn't mind *icing. Baps*.

nipples in the fridge *phr*. Turn of phrase which can be usefully employed when referring to a person who has, to use Ann Widdecombe's telling comment about Michael Howard, "something of the night" about them. *'That Ann*

Widdecombe's a funny fish, I reckon she's got nipples in the fridge, me.'

nippodrome *n.* Any place where a chap can go to enjoy a lively display of *milkers, eg.* A lap-dancing establishment, a nudist beach, the male squash court changing rooms at Newcastle Polytechnic where there used to be a *Carry On Camping/ Sex Offenders Register*-style hole drilled through into the ladies', apparently.

nip on *n.* A nippular erectivation. A *chapel hat peg hard on*.

nipotism *n.* In the world of business, the discriminatory practice of hiring and promoting ladies on the basis of *first impressions*, to the detriment of the careers of their more flat-chested counterparts.

nipsy *n. medic.* The pincer-like muscle just around *Ena Sharples' mouth* that cuts one's *Bungle's finger* to length when contracted. The blade of the *cigar cutter*.

nip/tuck *euph.* A lady who is not only blessed with *nipples like pygmies' cocks*, but also has a *front tuck like a camel's hoof*.

nitby *n.* Semi-acronymous term describing a *chav* baby. Corruption of "Not in the Baby Book", from the unusual names given to *Greggs dummy*-sucking nippers, *eg.* Tiaamiii, Chardonnay, Beyonce, Scratchcard *etc.*

NIYMFO/niymfo *acronym.* See *moped.* Not If Your Mates Found Out.

Noah's arse *n.* In the world of adult videography, a delightfully erotic scene involving double anal penetration. From the fact that in the flood/boat fairy story detailed in the biblical book Genesis, the animals "went in two by two".

nob *1. n.* A hay clarse, hoity-toity person.

A toff. *2. n.* A small piece of butter. *3. v.* To *fuck*, to penetrate with the *knob*.

Nobbies *rhym. slang.* Haemorrhoids. From 1966 toothless footballer Sir Norbert Staemorrhoids.

nobgoblins *n.* Those mythical creatures that make one's *meat and two veg* itch the second one is in polite company.

nobsessed *adj.* Of a girl, infatuated with a thoroughly unsuitable man who is, moreover, a bit of a *wanker. 'I don't know what it is about Kate Moss and Pete Doherty. She's just nobsessed with him.'*

nob snog *n.* A genteel term for an act of *horatio*.

nob snot *n. Cock hockle.*

nob Tarzans *n. medic. Genital guests* who swing from *pube* to *pube* through one's underpant jungle. *Crabs.*

nob turban *n.* A crest of Kleenex adorning one's post-*wank helmet. Mumrah's cock.*

nocturnal emission *n. medic.* The end result of a *wet dream*.

noddies *n.* The bikini overflow of an unwaxed lady, from its similarity to the effusive *bugger's grips* worn by 1970s rock legend Noddy Holder. *'Cor, look at the noddies on that Bulgarian lass.'*

nodding donkey *1. n.* A type of mechanical hacksaw used in metalwork. *2. n.* An ugly *bird*, usually with big teeth and ears, who doesn't often turn down the chance to *chew on a carrot*.

noddy *n.* Condom, *French letter*, a cock "holder".

noddy book *n. Bongo mag.*

noddy holder *n.* An expression hailing from the English Midlands and meaning, quite simply, a brassiere.

Noddy Holder's sideburns *sim.* Descriptive

of a particularly luxuriant ginger *bush*, the kind that Charlie Dimmock probably has.

no deal Noel *exclam*. Humorous idiomatic locution uttered in response to a loudly *dropped hat*. See also *you're only supposed to blow the bloody doors off, I'll give it five, what's that Sooty? etc.*

nodge *v*. To observe the sexual activity of others. To *voy*, to *dog*.

nodger *n*. A *peeping Tom*, voyeur. A *merchant* who prefers "live" *grumble* rather than the recorded variety.

Noely *1. n*. Affectionate self-coined nickname for TV and radio un-personality Noel Edmonds. *2. n*. A *cunt* which is so small and tight that no-one can get any enjoyment out of it. Derivation unknown.

no glans land *n*. The nether regions of a lady's nether regions. The *carse, taint, tinter, notcher, twitter, snarse* or whatever.

noinkers *n*. *Jubblies, kahunas, shirt potatoes, boobs, sweater fruit, knockers, cab man's rests, baps, funbags, bumpies, neddies, chichis, mambas, dirty pillows, chebs, charlies, diddies, doos, cajooblies, jugs, bubbies, zeps, bazongers, headlamps, whammies, norks, bangers, tits, dumplings, hogans, thrupennies, assets, churns, whammers, yoinkahs, begonias, mumbas, pink pillows, top bollocks, melons, oomlaaters, nellies, choozies, chubblies, chumbawumbas, blimps, charms, baby's dinners, fun cushions, paps, bojangles, garbonzas, airbags, Gert Stonkers, puppies, Bristols*. A lady's b*soms.

no job *n*. Being *sucked off* by a lady whilst so *pissed* one can hardly feel it. See also *bland job*.

nolita *n*. A woman who looks to be in her mid-teens from the back, but who turns out to be in her mid-50s from the front. A *Kronenberg, boyner* or *back beauty*.

nollies *n*. Word used by posh southern ladies when referring to a gentleman's testicles. From nuts + bollocks + goolies. *'The Archbishop of Canterbury's shoes were so shiny that when he lifted his arms up to crown me Queen of Great Britain and all her Commonwealth Dominions, I could see his big hairy nollies reflected in them.'* (HM the Queen, interviewed by Matthew Wright on *The Wright Stuff*, Channel 5).

nollocks *exclam*. A curse which can be used in polite company without causing offence. *'Don't talk fucking nollocks, vicar. Of course you want another cup of tea.'*

no man's land *n*. The disputed zone between a gentleman's *arsehole* and his *balls*, that is to say his perineum. Also *ABC, BBBA, great, gisp, gooch, Finsbury bridge, duffy's bridge, notcher, joy division, Perry Como's lip, kipper, the landing, stinky Mervin, tornado alley, twitter, wannocks, chommie, cockpit, grundle, scran, stinker's bridge, ploughman's, quiche, biffin bridge, taint, barse, tintis, scruttock, crunk* and *scranus*.

nonads *1. n*. A fellow who is bereft of knackers, *eg*. A eunuch guarding a harem, a *castrato* in a nineteenth century Italian opera company, a member of the apocalyptic, phenobarbital-quaffing Heaven's Gate sect or Evel Kneivel following one of his less successful motorcycle stunt attempts in the 1970s. *2. n*. A chap who is fighty at the back of a crowd when he's *pissed* but who keeps well fucking quiet when he's on his own.

'Excuse me, barman. But have you got pork scratchings?' 'Yes. I got them when I fucked your missus under the pier last week.' ~ Bamforth's *Seaside Chuckles* postcard by Donald McGill, 1926.

nonce jotter *n*. The sex offenders' register. *'Just sign the nonce jotter here please, Mr Glitter. And then could you autograph this LP for my auntie Jean?'*

nonebrity *n*. A pointless media figure who would love to rise up high enough to scrape onto the bottom end of the D-list. For example, that bloke off that thing with her who used to be in *Big Brother*, him who always seems to appear in those things with her off *Celebrity Love Island*, you know, that one who's living with her with the big *tits* off the adverts who used to go out with him out of Boyzone or was it Westlife.

non-mover at number two *n*. How Noel Edmonds might refer to a *floater* bobbing about in one of his hundreds of toilets.

noodle benders *n. Aus*. Close-fitting Speedo-style swimming trunks. Also *dick stickers, meat hangers*.

noodle knickers *n*. Affectionate epithet which can be applied to the *downstairs areas* of the more pubically rampant lady. Also *tank driver's hat, Taz, wookiee hole, mary hinge, yak, superfuzz bigmuff deluxe edition, Judith, eskimo's glove, muff like your granny's hat, gruffalo, wolf pussy, fanny like a guardsman's hat, busby berkeley, hairy knickers, Lord Winston's moustache, Paddy McGinty's goat, Percy Thrower's lawn, Terry Waite's allotment, radar trap, barber's floor, beartrapper's hat, biffer, Bilbo Baggins's foot, black forest gateau, bushell, Clara Dawes, divot, Dougal* and *gorilla autopsy*. See also *FLARP*.

nookie *1. n*. Sex, only a *bit* of which it is advisable to have at any one time. *2. n. prop*. A humorous name for a ventriloquist's bear.

nooner *n*. See *funch*.

noose massoose *n*. A young lady skilled in *triggernobetry, viz*. One who can perform the *walnut manoeuvre. 'Have you met the Countess? She's a noose massoose, don't you know.'*

Norfolk *n*. A man-sized measure of vodka, *ie*. Six fingers. From the flat area of England where the folks keep themselves to themselves, if you know what they mean.

norkelling *v*. When on holiday, the act of wandering along the beach to examine the wares on display. Preferably from behind a pair of *perv windows*.

norkestra *n*. A gathering of *well-qualified* ladies that deserves a standing ovation. A *string section*.

nork hammock *n*. Of female fashions, a halter neck top.

norkolepsy *n. medic*. A trance-like state in men caught in the beam of a fantastic pair of *headlamps, eg*. In the office, swimming pool, night club, church *etc. Titnotism*.

norks *n*. Knockers. Also *norkers, norgs, norgers*.

norks and mingey *euph*. The feminine triumvirate. A pointlessly laboured pun on the title of hyperactive lycanthropic funnyman Robin Williams's 1978-1982 US sitcom *Mork and Mindy*.

norks north *euph. Tits up. 'Put simply, Huw, the fucking economy's gone norks north.'* (Robert Peston, *BBC 6 O'Clock News*, every night for the last 18 months).

Norman Cook *n*. A measure of alcohol which after being drunk can make a *Fat Bird Slim*. Approximately two *St. Ivels*.

Norma Snockers *n*. Wieldy *bojangles*. See

also *Gert Stonkers*.

Norris *rhym. slang*. One of these dirty women who says she can ejaculate. From the late right wing *Record Breakers* presenter Norris McWhirter = squirter.

Northern Rock hard *adj*. Descriptive of a chap who suddenly and unexpectedly suffers a catastrophic slump in his ability to maintain an acceptably large *endowment. Sub prime. 'I don't know what happened. Everything was going along fine, then suddenly I was Northern Rock hard. It was as though Michelle MacManus had walked into the room.'*

Northern Rock moment *n*. The point at last orders, when you realise that you forgot to visit the cashpoint before you came out and are thus bereft of *liquid funds*, and are therefore reduced to grovelling round the pub, seeking a "lender of last resort".

north face *1. n*. Brand name of a clothes manufacturer which seems suspiciously popular amongst BBC personnel. *2. n*. Mountain climber's euphemism for the more difficult route up a lady. *'Gladys had the painters in the South Col, so Alf decided to attempt the tricky north face.'*

norton *n*. A *bearded clam*.

Norwegian's lunchbox *sim*. Descriptive of a *clopper* that smells like half a stone of whale blubber marinated in roll-mop herrings and sour milk.

Norwegian wood *1. n*. An erection achieved in a sauna. *2. n*. Title of a Beatles song, which John Lennon wrote after getting an erection in a sauna.

NORWICH *acronym. milit*. Cipher used on military correspondence - Knickers Off Ready When I Come Home. First used during World War I, when Norwich was known as Korwich.

no score drawers *n*. Unflattering ladies' undergarments worn when the *pools panel is sitting* and the dividend forecast is low.

nosebleed *n*. A *fart* that is *fuck off* strong. An *air onion*.

nose, blow one's *v*. To wipe away the post-ejaculation *sprongle* from one's *hog's eye. 'I had to blow my nose on the back of her dress before pulling my pants back up.'*

nose fruit *n*. Bogies.

nose jizz *n*. Snot.

nosh *n*. An act of *oral affection* which, according to Bill Clinton but perhaps not his wife, does not constitute sexual relations.

noshferatu *n*. The sort of chap who doesn't mind *dining at the Y* whilst *the painters are in*. One who likes his *tuna* with plenty of *tomato sauce*.

nosh off *v*. To perform *philately* on a man.

nosh out *v*. To perform *cumulonimbus* on a woman. To *lick out*.

noshtalgia *n*. Fond remembrance of particularly good tunes played on one's *pink oboe* in days gone by.

notcher *n*. *Biffin bridge*. The area of skin between the *clockweights* and the *starfish*, so called because it's "notcher" *bollocks* and it's "notcher" *arse. The great*.

not the marrying kind *adj*. Descriptive of a fellow who is *nicely poised* or *good with colours. 'Has your Cedric found himself a nice girl and settled down yet?' 'No, well you know my Cedric. He's not the marrying kind.' 'Still a male prostitute then?' 'Yes.'*

not now, Cato *exclam*. Phrase made popular in the Peter Sellers *'Pink Panther'* films, which can be used by a gentleman who is affected by an unwanted bout of priapism, *eg.* On a bus, whilst looking at the frozen foods in the Heaton, Newcastle branch of Safeway's in about 1990, or whilst blessing the masses from an open-topped Range Rover.

nought and a one, a *euph.* Obsolete beardy-weirdy computer operator slang for a *gypsy's kiss.* From the fact that when operating an old fashioned ICL card-punching machine, pressing the nought and the one buttons at the same time encoded a *slash. 'Where are you going, Mr Babbage?' 'I'm just off for a nought and a one whilst my difference engine reboots.'*

noughtomobile *n.* A vehicle that occupies the lowest possible position on the *fanny-magnetism* scale, *eg.* A souped-up Daewoo Matiz with *Max Power* stickers.

nought to sixty *1. n.* Measure of acceleration time by which men in pubs judge the relative merits of various Lamborghinis, Ferraris and Aston Martins which they have never even seen, let alone driven. *2. euph.* An incredibly rapid erection which takes everyone around it by surprise. A *viagra sunrise.*

now back to Davina *exclam.* A humorous interjection or quip, to be made immediately prior to *letting off.* See also *gentlemen start your engines.*

now I'm no expert on cricket, but I'm pretty sure that's out *exclam.* Yet another post-*fart* quip to add to the collection.

NSFW *1. abbrev.* Internet warning that the content being linked to is Not Safe For Work. *2. abbrev.* Internet warning that the content being linked to is safe for work. Not Suitable For Wanking.

NTL *n.* An excessively long stay on the toilet reading the paper, philosophising *etc.* After the telecommunications company who spend months *laying* just one *cable.*

nubility, the *n.* A clique of high class young ladies that give a bit of *blue blood* to anyone driving past.

nudger *1. n.* A *Colwyn Bay* male. *2. n.* What a *fudge nudger* uses to *nudge fudge.*

nuggets *1. n.* Testicles. *2. n.* Any inedible part of a chicken or turkey, when coated in batter or breadcrumbs. *eg.* Its *nuggets.*

number one *euph.* A *penny, tinkle.*

number one wood *1. n.* A top-rated distance club for golfers. *2. n.* A rare, *diamond-cutting hard on. Pink steel. 'Call the doctor, will you love. I got a number one wood when I was watching Barbarella and I've burst all the stitches in me bellend.'*

number threes *n.* Vomit.

number two *euph.* A *sit down, tuppence,* a *duty.*

nummghh *exclam.* The insulting noise made by pushing the tongue into the lower lip, usually directed at a person of low sense, or one who has inadvertently asked a foolish question. Regionally accentuated by either loose wristed hand waggles or transverse elbow-crested ear slaps.

numpty dumpty *n.* One who is both overweight and who lacks intelligence. An epithet coined by one or other of the sweary Scotch blokes in the film *In the Loop.*

numpy pumpy *n.* Penetrative sexual

intercourse engaged in by members of the lower orders, of the sort that keeps the Jeremy Kyle programme supplied with *scratters* who want DNA tests.

nunga munching *v.* The ganneting of *hairy pie, licking out* a lady's *clunker* with relish.

nunnery *n.* Elizabethan name for a *rub-a-tug shop* from an age when nuns were widely believed to wear *yo-yo knickers*.

nun's fanny 1. *sim.* Descriptive of something that is extremely dry, *eg.* The Sahara desert, Amy Winehouse's throat. 2. *euph.* Anything that is particularly tight, *eg.* Any space a lady attempts to park a car in, the glove that OJ Simpson didn't wear when he wasn't murdering his wife.

nun's rug *euph.* A vintage item which is nevertheless in absolutely mint, unused condition. *'For sale. L-registered Morris Marina in magnificent muconium beige livery with mouseback vinyl roof. This car has covered just 6 miles since new and has been kept in a dry, heated garage for the last thirty-two years, only being taken out once by its careful lady owner for a short run to the shops and back in 1973, after which it broke down and refused to restart. It still bears the original polythene seat-covers and has not even been run in yet. A real nun's rug of a classic which can only appreciate in value in the coming years. £18,500 ono.'*

nun's tits, pale as a *sim.* Descriptive of skin that doesn't get much exposure to sunlight. *'After answering his latest set of drugs charges, crack-guzzling Babyshambles frontman Pete Doherty stumbled down the courtroom steps looking pale as a nun's tits.'* (Report,

BBC Radio 6Music News, every fucking half hour).

nun's tits, useful as a *sim.* Phrase used in reference to something, or someone, of no obvious utility whatsoever. *'Have you seen that (insert name of a newly-signed expensive football player here)? he's about as useful as a nun's tits.'*

Nurembergs *rhym. slang.* Haemorrhoids. From Nuremberg Trials = piles. Also *Seig Heils, four minute miles.*

nurfing *n.* Barumphing, snurgling, moomphing, quumfing.

nurse! *phr.* Melodramatic exclamation made following a vicious *Exchange & Mart* that may, one fears, have necessitated a change of plus-fours.

nut allergy *n. medic.* Potentially serious medical condition suffered by frigid women which, if left untreated, can lead to a severe *Vitamin S* deficiency.

nut butter *n.* A lightly-salted dairy product served hot from the male *churns* onto *baps.*

nut chokers *n.* Gentlemen's tight *shreddies, budgie smugglers, noodle benders.*

nutcrackers *n.* Unfeasibly tight "spray-on" *round the houses* sported by *rock poodles* such as Justin Hawkins out of now-defunct comedy band The Darkness and Sachs maniac Russell Brand.

nut custard *n. Banana yoghurt.*

nut dust *n.* All that is left for a fellow to *jonk* after he has *relaxed in a gentleman's way* all day until his *knackers* are as *flat as bats' wings* and he is *chucking salt.* See also *weeze.*

nut fangle *n.* Pre-*wank* prep work.

nuthard *n.* A *Bruce Lee* which sticks out as a result of inclement meteorological conditions.

Nutkin *n.* Of a man, the worst hairstyle

it is possible to have, *eg*. Those worn by Phil Harding (*Time Team* yokel archaeologist), Bill Bailey (troll-like comedian) and Terry Mancini (has-been QPR footballer). Named after TV animal trainer and former sealion's dinner Terry Nutkin.

nutmegs *n*. *Balls* that hang down right between a footballer's legs.

nuts 1. *n*. A fellow's *pods*. 2. *n*. Things your missus only eats as a special treat at Christmas. That'll be your *pods* again, then. 3. *adj*. Mental. *'You should meet my brother, he's absolutely nuts. Seriously, he made a skin suit from his landlady and got sectioned under the 1971 Mental Health Act.'*

nut sack *n*. The scrotum, *nadbag*.

nymph 1. *n*. The caterpillar of a dragonfly. 2. *n*. A sexy young *bird*.

nympho *n*. Sex-crazed *bird* that's *gagging* for it 24 hours a day, 7 days a week. The sort who would *shag* a pneumatic drill and blow up the generator. Usually works on a premium-rate telephone *wank* line.

nymphomaniac *n*. One who can't get enough of premium-rate telephone *wank* lines. A short, blind, insane man living in a sleeping bag on a shop doorstep.

nymphomation *n*. The insider data shared between a group of males about an unusually accommodating girl that one of them has *shagged*. *'Russell just gave me some great nymphomation about Georgina. I'm going to ring up her grandad and tell him straight away.'*

NYPD blue *n*. A *poke*, where the *pokee* assumes the position of someone being frisked by New York's finest, against the wall or across the bonnet of a car. A *dog's marriage*.

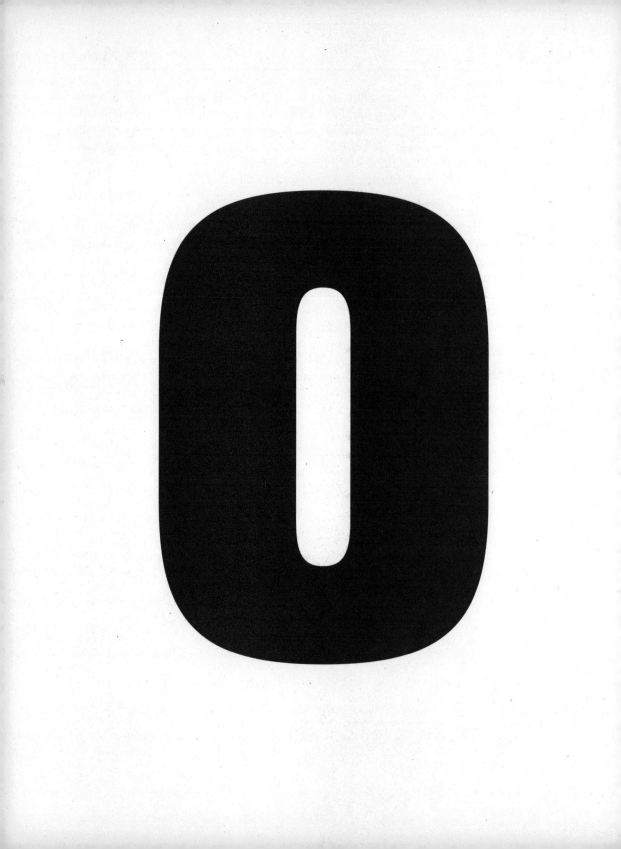

oakhampton *n*. A sturdy bit of *wood*. A *hard-on* you could mount on a lathe and turn the leg of a slate bed snooker table out of. Not to be confused with the Devon town of Okehampton, which is spelled differently and doesn't have all wiggly veins going up the side.

OAP-dophile *1. n*. A *biddy fiddler* or *granny magnet*. *2. n*. A young woman who is inexplicably attracted to a (usually extremely wealthy) elderly man, *eg*. (Long list of names deleted on legal advice).

Oaten's briefcase, it smells like *sim*. Descriptive of a particularly unpleasant miasma. Derivation unknown. *'Did you have second helpings of that twenty-two bean casserole last night? It smells like Oaten's briefcase in here this morning.'*

oats *n*. A *portion* of that which one gets during sex with a Quaker. *Tiffin, crumpet*.

OBE *1 abbrev*. A memorable token of one's evening out, awarded by a nightclub bouncer as one is ejected from his establishment. One Behind the Ear. *2. abbrev*. Order of the Brown Entrance. An honour bestowed on a gentleman for services to his *bird's shitter. Brown wings*.

obesetiality *n*. The ethically questionable act of performing an act of penetrative intercourse on a *right plumper*.

Obi-Wan's cape *euph*. Phrase used to describe the unfortunate occurrence of extreme flaccidity inside a chap's *grundies* (for example following immersion in cold water) to the extent that his *old man* completely vanishes, leaving in its stead an empty crumpled, pile of skin resembling nothing so much as a small, pink walnut whip. With the wrinkly nuts dangling underneath it rather than perched on the top. *Shrinkage*. From the scene in *Star Wars* where erstwhile Jedi Knight Sir Alec Guinness gets whacked with a neon tube by the Green Cross Man. Also the *Wicked Witch of the West*. *'Not tonight, Josephine, I've just got out of the swimming pool and I've got Obi-Wan's cape.'*

occupy the crease *1. v*. In cricket, to build a long innings without worrying unduly about anyone else's best interests. *'Boycott is a selfish cricketer, regularly occupying the crease with scant consideration for the needs of his team.' 2. v*. To pleasure one's missus orally. *'Boycott is a selfish lover, seldom occupying the crease and showing scant consideration for the needs of his ladyfriend.'*

odds are good but the goods are odd *exclam*. Phrase which may be usefully employed on a Friday night when *picking up* women on Teesside.

offer a Jaffa cake *v*. To instigate a homosexual courting ritual involving the popular orange-flavoured biscuit/cake confection. If any male accepts another's offer of a Jaffa cake, then they are tacitly agreeing to partake in an act of anal romance.

office meerkats *n*. Groups of infantile male workers who repeatedly stand up and sit down between the hours of 11.00am and 1.00pm, in order to peer throught their windows at attractive females going on their lunch.

officers' laces *n*. Ladies' string-like thongs buffed brown between their *arse cheeks*.

off-piste *euph*. Sexual term whereby a gentleman ventures away from the officially-sanctioned area into more rugged and challenging terrain. *'Come on, love. I've cooked dinner and even helped with the washing up. How many more brownie points do I need before I can go off-piste?'*

off-shore wanking business *euph.* An oil rig, upon which only male workers are permitted. *'Our Derek earns good money. He works in the off-shore wanking business, you know.'*

off the meaten track *euph.* Descriptive of a woman who is *off solids* or *on the turn*. In the early stages of *lesbitis*.

off the team *adj.* To be forbidden from playing on the *furry turf*. To be in your missus's *cunt book*.

off your face *adj. Ripped to the tits* on the demon drink, *disco biscuits* or *plant fertiliser*.

off your trolley *adj.* Hatstand, nuts, mental.

oil of goolay *n.* A white, sticky-type foundation cream which reduces the signs of ageing when applied to ladies' faces out the end of one's *cock. Vitamin S-*enriched facial emollient unguent produced by a chap's *clockweights*.

on crutches *euph.* Of a heavily-inebriated person, supported on either side by a pair of marginally less *pissed* companions. *'I'm afraid the groom's going to be a bit late for the service, vicar. He's had a bit of a heavy morning and, to cut a long story short, he's on crutches.'*

oil spill *n.* An *Eartha* that constitutes a health threat to marine life.

oil tanker *rhym. slang.* An *onanist, merchant*.

oil the bat *v.* To *polish the pork sword, wax the dolphin*.

oil the truncheon *v.* To buff up the *bobby's helmet, collect kindling, wank*.

oily loaf *n.* A well-baked *turd*.

oily rags *n. rhym. slang.* Cigarettes. *'Finish stitching up the patient will you, nurse? I'm just off outside for an oily rag.'*

OJ's glove 1. *n.* The state of the hand after *finger banging* a lady during *ragweek*. 2. *n.* An extremely tight-fitting *liver sock*.

okra 1. *n.* Tropical plant of the mallow family, *Hibiscus esculentus*, colloquially called lady's fingers, and hence 2. *n.* A dirty woman's act of *self pollution*.

okay kids, runaround! *exclam.* A humorous quip to be used following a *windy pop*. Best delivered in gruff, cockney tones reminiscent of the late Mike Reid, but while he was alive. See also *you should put that on Ebay*.

old Adam *n.* Onan's partner in Biblical crime.

Old Bailey bird *n.* An embarrassingly unattractive ladyfriend who you would ideally like to smuggle into the house under a blanket, in a style reminiscent of the way that the police bundle particularly unpopular murderers into court buildings on the news.

old dog's nose, dry as an *sim.* Descriptive of a *pink wafer*. A *moipless muff*. *'What's up love? I've been tickling your wotsit for a good three minutes and you're still as dry as an old dog's nose.'*

olden doubloons *n.* The *dunghampers* of a young lady who eschews *clackerfloss* preferring instead *bills* of a more matronly cut. *Elepants*.

oldest toad in the pond *n.* A particularly low, vociferous, grumbling *mariner's chart*, usually after eight pints of stout and a bar of Bourneville.

old faithful 1. *n.* A spectacular eruption of hot steam from a hole in the ground in Yellowstone National Park, USA. *2. n*. A spectacular eruption of hot *spooge* from the mouth of an inexperienced *cock nosher*, particularly one lying on her back.

old fellow yellow *n*. A senior citizen's saffron-hued *baby gravy*. *Gold top, mellow yellow*.

Old Holborn *n*. The frayed edges of the *velcro triangle*, a *pant moustache*. *Spiders' legs*.

oldie horn *n*. See *prunetang*.

Old Leigh oyster *n*. A particularly viscous phlegm delicacy which requires a sight more chewing than its bivalve namesake. A *docker's omelette*.

old man *n*. Penis. Also *the old fella*. *'The old man's been out of work for six months. Most days we play pocket billiards to keep him occupied.'*

Old McDonald's combover *n*. Stray *pubage* agonisingly trapped under the brim of the *farmer's hat*. *Bobby Charltons*.

old shocker, the *n*. To surprise one's sexual partner by poking a cheeky *pinkie* up their *chuff* during intercourse. *"I say, Bertie. You'll never guess what,' gasped Piggy excitedly. 'I've just been in a clinch with Marjorie in the rose garden. Just as I got to the vinegar strokes, she popped me the old shocker. Quite took me aback, don't you know."* (from *Now Start Humming, Jeeves* by PG Wodehouse).

Olive oil *n*. *Mabel syrup*.

Oliver *rhym. slang*. Inebriated. From Oliver Twist = pissed. *'Please Sir, can I have some more?' 'Fuck off, you're Oliver.'*

Olympic village *n*. Any urban area with a disproportionate number of fat, unhealthy inhabitants wearing shitty, polyester-based sportswear.

omelette maker *n*. A lesbian, *lady golfer*.

Omo *euph*. Available for sex. From the habit of housewives who leave a box of the eponymous washing powder on their windowsill in order to advertise the fact that they are "On My Own" to passing tradesmen. A secret signal, similar in intention to, but slightly less elaborate than, that time when Lady Di got herself photographed in front of the Taj Mahal.

omosexual *n*. Any man who *has it off* with bored women whose husbands are out at work/on an oil rig/in prison for greivous bodily harm, *eg*. All plumbers, milkmen, door-to-door brush salesmen *etc*.

onanism *1. n*. Incomplete sexual intercourse. *Vatican roulette*. *2. n*. What the biblical *wanker* Onan the Barbarian did when he *spilled his seed* on the wainscotting. *Cuffing the dummy*.

one *n*. A *poking*. The SI unit of sex, given to a woman by a man and measured from the moment it *goes in* to to moment it *goes off*. Equivalent to six tenths of a *portion*, 180% of *some*, and 2.36 *bits of the other*.

one-armed Scouse *n*. A feloniously-adjusted fruit machine.

one-armed taxi driver with crabs, busier than *sim*. Phrase used to describe a person who is rushed off their feet. *'That Michael McIntyre's never off the fucking telly these days is he? He's busier than a one-armed taxi driver with crabs.'*

one cartridge, ignition off, clear out the cylinder *exclam*. Phrase used when performing a particular sort of explosive, underpant-wrecking *Exchange & Mart*. From the scene in the classic Sunday tea-time film *Flight of the Phoenix*, when pilot James Stewart uses up a precious ignition cartridge to clear engine debris, much to the annoyance of kraut modelmaker Hardy Kruger.

one cheek sneak *n*. The stealthy approach to *shooting bunnies*. From a sitting position, lifting one *buttock* in order to slide out an aurally-undetectable *air biscuit*. A *cushion creeper, leg lifter.*

one-eared spacehopper *n*. Cliff Richard's genitals. A *panhandle* on someone with *DSB.*

one-eyed pant python *n*. A *cock* that could crush a pig to death.

one-eyed trouser snake *n*. A *spitting cobra.*

one-eyed Willie *n*. *Pirate of men's pants.*

one-eyed Willie's eye patch *n*. A condom, *English sou'wester and full-length kagoule.*

one-eyed zipper fish *n*. A *Cyclops, trouser trout.*

one for Esther *1. n*. A *cock* shaped like a vegetable. *2. n*. A vegetable shaped like a *cock.*

one four seven *1. n*. In snooker, a complete clearance in which the player empties the table in a single visit, scoring maximum points in the process. *2. n*. In toiletry, a complete clearance in which the toiletee empties his *Camillas* in a single sitting, finishing with a black. *'Watch my pint, boys. I'm going for a one four seven.' 2. euch.* After *dropping the kids off at the pool*, finding that the first sheet of *arsewipe* is completely pristine after use, *ie*. A *high break.*

one-handed mag *n*. *Jazz magazine, rhythm read, art pamphlet, a grumbular* periodical.

one-holed flute *n*. A *pink oboe*, a *blue-veined piccolo*, a *purple headed* (insert name of vaguely-cylindrical woodwind

instrument here).

one in - one out *phr*. The direct, causal relationship that exists between drags on the day's first *Harry rag* and *farts.*

one in the pump, to have *1. v*. To have the *hots* for a female. *'Phoar! I've got one in the pump for her, I can tell you.' 2. n.* Drinking parlance for a pint paid for but not yet poured.

one man and his log *n*. A Sunday afternoon entertainment following a heavy lunch, whereby a gent tries to force a large *flock* through a very narrow gate whilst whistling and emitting guttural cries.

one-man orgy *n*. A long-lasting and elaborate *cat stabbing* session involving assorted stimuli, speeds and positions. *Everything but the girl.*

one oar in the water *n*. Descriptive of someone unlikely to forge a successful career in rocket science, but who may find gainful employment chasing trolleys round Sainsbury's carpark. *'Doctors feared that after his near fatal quadbike accident, Mayall could have been left with one oar in the water. Amazingly, he made a full recovery, although he will remain on fit pills for the rest of his life.'* (Profile of Rik Mayall, *The Guardian*, Sept. 2001).

one o'er the thumb *n*. A *five knuckle shuffle. 'Quite satisfied, Scrooge closed the door and locked himself in; double-locked himself in, which was his custom on these occasions. Thus secured against surprise, he took off his cravat; put on his dressing-gown and slippers, and his nightcap; and sat down before the fire with a copy of Razzle for a quick one o'er the thumb.'* (from *A Christmas Carol* by Charles Dickens).

one off the crossbar *n*. To be just not quick enough in dropping one's *scads* after being caught short by an unexpected visit from *Mr Whippy*. To *beskid* the waistband of your *shreddies*.

one off the wrist *n*. *Five knuckle shuffle, wank, hand shandy*.

onepack *n*. A *beergut, party seven*.

one pint Winehouse *n*. A woman who quickly becomes aggressively inebriated, thinks she can sing and then staggers about a bit on her heels before falling flat on her face.

oneplay *n*. Pre-masturbatory arousal techniques.

one point five *n*. A toiletry visit product that falls somewhere between a *number one* and a *number two*. A runny *shit*. Or more rarely a lumpy *piss*. A *bicycle chain*.

one pump chump *n*. One who *goes off* on the first push. Twice as fast as a *two push Charlie*.

oner *n*. The line of condensed *arse cleft* perspiration left on a plastic seat after it has been sat on in the summer months. Upon exiting a taxi and preparing to pay, one might point to the seat and say, *'There's a oner, keep the change.'*

one shit wonder *n*. A popular musician or beat combo who has a brief, singular moment in the charts sun, despite being *crap, eg.* Falco, Chesney Hawkes, Vanilla Ice *etc*.

one string banjo *n*. A skin-covered instrument upon which a man might *strum* to his heart's content.

one-stroke cylinder engine *n*. A *Bakewell* released whilst walking that lasts for several paces. A *string of pearls, duck-walk*.

one under the Metro *n*. A discreet gentleman's surreptitious means of relieving tension beneath a strategically-placed free newspaper whilst travelling on public transport.

one yank Frank *n*. A solo version of a *fruit machine Freddy*. An over-excitable masturbator.

oneymoon *n*. A romantic week's break from the missus which affords the married gentleman a welcome opportunity to enjoy an uninterrupted seven day period of luxurious *self abuse*.

oneymoon suite *n*. In an hotel, a room set aside for unaccompanied commercial travellers who do not wish to be disturbed; must include at least two *Frankie Vaughan* channels and a copious supply of quilted toilet tissue.

on golden pond 1. *n*. Title of a crushingly dull-looking film featuring, as far as you could tell, a lot of shots of Jane and Henry Fonda squinting in floppy hats. And Katharine Hepburn. 2. *euph*. Waking up on a tiled floor and realising that one has relieved oneself in the night without the benefit of plumbing. *Golden slumbers*.

on her dabs *adj*. Of a lady, to be menstruiferous. *Boiling beetroots, serving strawberry jam for tea*.

onk, on the *adj*. Of the male generative member, up and fighting. *'I popped a bluey, and half an hour later I was on the onk for the first time in twenty years.'*

only shit with the arse you've got *phr*. Civil engineering expression bemoaning the provision of substandard tools and/ or materials. *'Fuck knows if we'll ever get the 2012 Olympic complex finished. Then again, you can only shit with the arse you've got.'*

on the batter *adj*. Of a lady, to be involved in the practice of showing successive gentlemen good times behind a skip for £5.

on the bench *adj*. After being *off the team*, to be optimistic that you may be given a late chance to *score*. To be in your missus's slightly better books. *'After the shameful episode with the exotic dancer I have alas been off the team these last six weeks. Today I bought my darling Victoria a bunch of flowers from the all-night garage, and I think I am on the bench.'* (from *The Journal of Prince Albert*).

on the blob *adj*. *Riding the menstrual cycle, up on blocks, fallen to the communists.*

on the bonk *adj*. *Sergeant Sausage* when saluting.

on the bus to Hebden Bridge *adj*. Descriptive of a *woman in comfortable shoes*, or *tennis fan*. From the unusually large amount of *lesbitious* women living in the Yorkshire mill town.

on the hoy *adj*. *On the piss, on the razz, hoying* it down one's neck, and then back up again onto one's shoes.

on the job *adj*. *At it*. Busying oneself with one's partner's plumbing.

on the mop *adj*. Of a lady, to be suffering from *women's things*.

on the musical side *adj*. *Light on one's feet.*

on the nest *adj*. To be treating your *bird* to a big juicy *worm*.

on the number 73 bus *adj*. Term descriptive of a *lady golfer*. From the TV personality Sandi Toksvig, who is one, and who presented the 1980s show *Number 73*.

on the other bus *adj*. Homosexual, *bowling from the Pavilion end*.

on the pull *adj*. Fishing for *kipper, on the salmon, on the sniff*.

on the slipway *adj*. Of stools and stool movement, having the *turtle's head*. *'Get out of that fucking bathroom will you, I've got a dreadnought on the slipway.'*

on the sniff *adj*. On the pull, on the tap, getting *a bit lash on*.

on tow *adj*. Of a woman, to be *up on blocks*. From the visible rope.

ooglewhack *v*. To have a much-needed *whack*, after having *oogled* an attractive lady.

ooh-aarrhoea *n. medic*. Farmer's *squirts*.

oomlaaters *n*. Very large *chumbawumbas, mumbas*.

oomph! *n*. Sex appeal. *'By crikey, that Norma Major, she hasn't half got some oomph!'*

oor wullie *n. Scots*. A communal double-ended *neck massager* kept in a drawer at the but 'n' ben.

oot on the tap *adj. NE*. Out *on the pull*, as opposed to *on the hoy*.

OPE *abbrev*. A dazed and other-worldly sensation brought on by a visit to a mechanic, dentist, solicitor *etc*. Out-of-Pocket Experience.

open a packet of ham *v*. To *let off* a *beefy eggo*. From the practice of ham production line workers who *fart* into the packages of ham before sealing them. *'Who's opened a packet of ham?'*

open clam shots *n*. *Full-on oysters, close-up pink*. Artistic/medical *adult* camera work.

open Dracula's coffin *v*. An act involving a protracted creaking noise, accompanied by an ungodly stench. To *drop a McArthur Park*.

Openshaw rush-hour *n*. Weekdays

between noon and 1pm, when all the *tax dodgers* finally get their fat *arses* out of bed, jump into their people carriers and go into town to spend their benefits at Primark.

open the bloodgates *v*. Of a woman, to shed the first tears that herald the commencement of *rag week*.

open the hangar doors *v*. Of an experienced lady, to prepare herself for sexual intercourse. *'Wisteria was powerless to resist. His eyes burned into hers like amethysts. His muscular arms enfolded her body as she felt herself being swept away in a hurricane of passion. Gently, Renaldo laid her down on the silken ottoman in front of the roaring fire. Then, as he pulled her knickers off, she lifted her legs and opened the hangar doors.'* (from *The Lady and the South American Footballer* by Barbara Cartland).

open your lunchbox *v*. To float an *air biscuit* reminiscent in aroma of yesterday's egg sandwiches.

opera house *n*. A large vagina with heavy pink safety curtains and great acoustics.

operate the spangle pump *v*. To express oneself onanistically. *'Oh bugger. The plumber's operated the spangle pump into my knicker drawer again.'*

Operation Chariot *n*. The act of ramming your *skin boat* into a ladyfriend's *dry dock*. A technique used, for example, when it's ten minutes till *Match of the Day* is on. Named after the famous British seaborne raid on St Nazaire, on the night of March 28th 1942, when HMS Campbeltown was loaded with explosives and steered at high speed into the port's *piss flaps*, ten minutes before *Match of the Day* started.

orangina *1. n*. Refreshing continental citrus beverage, made with real orange pieces. *2. n*. A particularly untidy ginger *clopper*, which wouldn't look out of place between the legs of Clint Eastwood's monkey's missus.

oranguman *n*. A colour-blind sun-worshipper with a healthy glow that registers 165 on the Pantone scale. *'Today's birthdays: 1813 - Richard Wagner, German composer; 1844 - Mary Cassatt - American artist; 1907 - Laurence Olivier, British actor; 1978 - Katie Price, tit model; 1955 - Dale Winton, oranguman TV presenter.'*

orang utan salad *n*. Ginger *gorilla salad*. *Fusewire, grated carrot.*

orang utan's forehead, fanny like an *sim*. Charming turn of phrase which can be usefully employed when referring to a *brandy snap* which is liberally adorned with ginger *fubes*. *'Bloody hell, Mrs Waterman. You've got a fanny like an orang utan's forehead. Oh yeah, congratulations, it's a girl.'*

orchestras *rhym. slang*. The testicles. From orchestra stollocks = bollocks.

oreo *n*. An inverse *chocolate sandwich*.

organzola *n*. *Helmetdale*.

orgasm *1. n*. A *fanny bomb*, a *stack blow*. *2. v*. To *ring the bell*, *shoot one's load*, *chuck one's muck*.

Oscar *n*. US. *Dick*, penis.

Oscars night *n*. An unpredicted bout of heavy *women's things*, which leaves a red carpet from the front door to the *crapper*.

osteopornosis *n*. medic. Degenerate condition symptomised by skeletal atrophy, progressive hypermetropia, early-onset pre-senile dementia and hairy palms.

other, a bit of the *n*. Some.

other place, the *1. n.* In parliamentary terminology, how Honourable Members refer to the chamber they eventually hope to end up in. *2. n.* In sexual shenaniganism, the *chamber* that dishonourable fellows hope their *members* will eventually end up in.

otter *1. n.* An aquatic mammal. *2. n.* A bald male gentleman who isn't interested in *beavers*.

otter's nose *n.* When getting *tops and fingers*, that which is felt by the latter. Something wet *under the bridge* that smells of fish. *'I got a result last night. I touched the otter's nose.'*

otter off the bank, like an *sim.* Phrase used to describe a *turd* of particularly fine composition, which slips into the water from one's *bumhole* with a certain amount of panache.

our survey said *exclam.* Just for a change, something you can say *before* you *drop your hat*.

outer bull *n.* A *piss* into a toilet which hits only the porcelain around the puddle, thus keeping the noise down. The opposite of a *dad's piss*, named after the dartboard location that scores 25.

out of botty experience *n.* A *dump*.

outrigger *1. n.* A thin, supplementary float that is rigidly fixed parallel and to one side of the main hull of a canoe, in order to minimise the risk of capsizing when filming the opening title sequence for *Hawaii Five-0*, for example. *2. n.* Prior to a routine, middle-of-the-night *tug*, a leg which a chap swings out of bed and uses to brace himself firmly against the floor in order to ensure that his *bag for life* isn't disturbed by any rhythmic mattress turbulence that may ensue.

out to the wing *exclam.* Comment typically made by older gentlemen before they *break wind*. So used because of the characteristic noise made by an old leather football when it was hoofed with a sturdy boot. *'Out to the wing.' 'Indeed your holiness. Shall I get a nun to open the window?'*

overblaaters *n.* Pendulous *oomlaaters* which rest on a big round gut.

overclubbed *1. adj.* In golf, descriptive of an approach shot chipped towards the green which misses its intended target and tangles itself in the rough, eliciting groans from disappointed spectators. *2. adj.* In a *meat flick*, descriptive of a *pop shot* loosed off towards an actress's face which misses its intended target and instead tangles itself in her hair, eliciting groans from disappointed spectators.

over Niagara in a barrel *phr.* The situation which occurs when flushing a blocked toilet, for example in a train lavatory, causing the water level to rise up to the rim, thus causing any floating *Thoras* to risk taking a death-defying plunge over the edge.

overnight bag *n.* An aesthetically unimpressive *one night stand*.

over the lines, colour in *v.* To spray a lady with semen after withdrawing from an orifice. To *crash the yoghurt truck* outside the delivery bay.

over the shoulder boulder holder *n.* An industrial-strength bra; heavy lifting apparatus for *jelly water mangos*.

owl movement *n.* A *greyfriars bobby* that is of much greater girth than is comfortable, thereby causing its progenitor's head to spin through 360 degrees and their eyes to widen in the manner of the eponymous nocturnal, mouse-skeleton-hockling bird of prey.

owner operator *n*. A lorry driver who *sheds his load* wherever the fancy takes him.

own goal *1. n.* A blast from the *kazoo* which is so obnoxious that even he who dealt it cannot stay in its presence. *2. n.* A trouser-bound *guff* which involves a brown *follow through*. From the Bomb Disposal Squad parlance for the premature detonation of a terrorist's bomb. At which point, presumably, said terrorist *shits* himself. If he's got time.

own up *v*. In a *breaking company* situation, to identify oneself as the *benefactor*. *Read the will.*

Oxford John *n*. A slow-braised *lamb shank*.

OXO *n*. Inserting one's thumb into a lady's *back bottom* and a finger into her *front bottom*, before rubbing the two digits together as if crumbling the eponymous stock cube.

oxygen thief *n*. A senior citizen, a *coffin dodger.*

oyster *n*. A *bushman's hankie.*

oyster catcher *n*. A lady of *lesbitious* tendencies. From the fact that she is, like her ornithological namesake *Haematopus palliatus*, a *bird* which spends a great deal of time in pursuit of *bearded clams.*

oyster shot *n*. In the world of glamour photography, a carefully composed, lit and framed shot of a model's *clam* as she bends over, viewed from behind.

Ozzy ramble *n*. The shuffling, confused gait adopted by a man with a *horse's handbrake* and his trousers round his ankles, as he tries to manoeuvre around the sofa in order to secure a better angle to gain entrance to his good lady's *coconut husk*. From the shuffling, confused gait characteristic of shuffling, confused heavy metal pipistrelle gourmand Ozzy Osbourne, real name Oswestry Ostrichbourne.

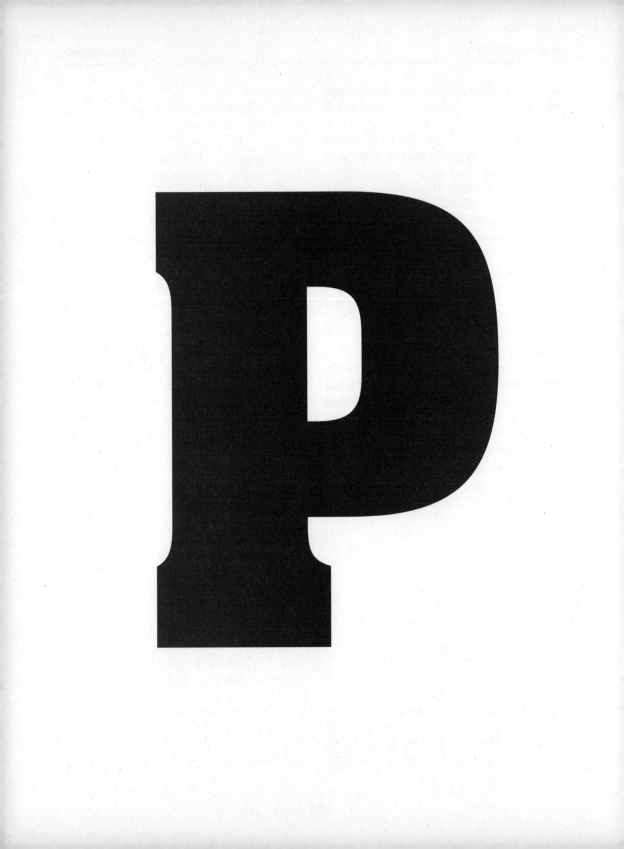

pace car *n*. When paying a *sit down visit*, the slow, unaerodynamic leading *turd* that once out of the way, allows the fast, souped-up *botrods* behind it to put their foot down into the first bend.

packet *n*. The contents of the *kecks* visible in relief at the front of the *trolleys*. Male equivalent of the *camel's foot*. *Darcy Bussell's footrest*, the *lunchbox*.

packing string *adj*. Of a lady, *up on blocks*. Also *chasing the cotton mouse, dropping clots, smoking short cigars, boiling beetroots, on the blob, fallen to the communists, riding the menstrual cycle, on her rags, reading Cosmo. On tow*.

paddle one's own canoe *v*. To enjoy a leisurely punt using a short pink pole. With all veins up the side. *'Dysphagia was powerless to resist. His eyes burnt into hers like soldering irons. His muscular arms enfolded her naked body as she felt herself being whisked away on a meringue of passion. 'Ravish me now,' she gasped. 'Take me here on the chaise longue, I'm all yours.' 'Sorry ma cherie, I'd love to oblige,' replied Toulouse-Lautrec. 'But I've just spent all afternoon paddling my own canoe in sniffer's row at the Moulin Rouge, and now my clockweights are flat as a crepe suzette.''* (from *The Artist's Model and the Short-arsed Post-Impressionist Painter* by Barbara Cartland).

paddle the pink canoe *v*. To *friggify*. Weekend recreational pursuit of the *gusset typist*.

paddling pool *n*. Male showertime entertainment whereby the *fiveskin* is pulled apart and the *charlie* is aimed up at the showerhead, causing it to fill up with water to the satisfaction of the *pool attendant*.

Paddy McGinty's goat *1. n*. Hilarious song made famous by twinkle-toothed, sweater-wearing, sedentary crooner Val Doonican. *2. n*. Pungent, hairy *snatch* that could eat a mayor's hat. Also *Delaney's donkey*.

Paddy's hankie *n*. The hand.

paddywhack *v*. To *bang* a young lady who *has a lovely personality*. From the famous nursery rhyme chorus about an old man engaging in penetrative sexual intercourse with an ugly *bird*, *viz*. "Nick-nack paddywhack, give the dog a bone".

padlocks *n*. *Tits* that would be better off in socks than in bras.

paedophile's door *euph*. Anyone who combines a low income with constant high expenditure. *'MRS ALLONBY: They say, Lady Hunstanton, that Lord Illingworth finds himself perpetually penurious. Indeed, in that respect he is not dissimilar to a paedophile's door. LADY HUNSTANTON: Indeed Mrs Allonby? And why, pray tell, would that be? MRS ALLONBY: Because, Lady Hunstanton, he is always broke.'* (from *The Importance of Being Bummed by Jockeys* by Oscar Wilde).

paedo lumps *n*. Raised areas of tarmac in the carriageway that cause motorists to drive slowly past primary schools.

paedo pellets *n*. Werther's originals.

paedophiladelphia *n. Frottage cheese*.

paedorinal *n*. In a public lavatory, the urinal which is situated alongside the shorter, small boys' version.

paedoscopes *n*. Those thick-rimmed National Health Service spectacles exclusively worn by trainspotters, scout masters and other assorted sex cases. *Paedospecs*.

paedosmile *n*. A particularly sinister grin, the type a *kiddie fiddler* might have.

PAFO *acron. medic.* Term used by consultants in Accident and Emergency departments to explain random cuts and bruises. Pissed And Fell Over.

page three Stannah *n*. A scantily-clad lady of advancing years, who nevertheless provides one with a bit of a lift.

pagga *n*. A free-for-all combat between anyone who wants to join in.

pagga starter *n*. A strong beer which breaks the ice at fights. *Supermarket smack, spesh.*

painting the ceiling *n*. Having a go with the *naughty paintbrush* and some *guardsman's gloss* whilst in a supine position.

paint the baby's bedroom *v*. To slap a bit of *managlypta* around the vaginal walls.

paint the back door *v*. To drop a wet *fart, follow through.*

paint the town beige *v*. To indulge in an unambitious, lacklustre night out with one's mates.

Paisley jogger *n*. A thief or shoplifter beating a hasty retreat through the streets of the popular Glasgow garden suburb.

pantomime horse dilemma *n*. Conundrum facing a pair of *chuckle brothers* when faced with a *man at C&A* situation after picking up a right mucky *scratter* outside a Leeds pub late on a Friday, *viz*. "Which end of the beast to take?"

paisley removal *n*. Pointing *Percy* directly at an area of *pebble dashing* in order to amuse oneself during a *Chinese singing lesson*. See also *piss polo*.

palace gates *n*. *Fanny lips, beef curtains.*

palmageddon *n*. A disastrous act of *self delight* which leaves the perpetrator wishing the ground would open up and swallow him. For example, the one indulged in by Dirty Den actor Leslie Grantham in his *EastEnders* dressing room in May 2004, and witnessed on the internet by a Sunday newspaper reporter calling herself "Halo Polisher".

palma sutra *n*. An exotic selection of positions in which a gentleman may enjoy solitary congress with his *dick skinner*, *eg*. The dying swan, the swooping dove, the *sticky belly flap cock*.

Palmela and her five sisters *n. prop*. The right *cunt scratcher*.

Palmela Handerson *n*. One's dream date to go out for a cruise in the *wanking chariot*.

palmesan *n*. The result of *pulling the Pope's hat off* repeatedly and excessively without pausing to perform the occasional spot of basic genital maintenance in between. Particularly rife amongst those presently seeking gainful employment. Also *dolecelatte*.

palm fruit *n*. A lady's *chestular* offerings. Two of your five a day.

palmistry *n*. A mystic art involving the flat of the hand and the *cock*. The skilled *palmist* is able to look a few minutes into the future and foresee a period of mopping up *jizz*.

palmouflage *n*. Any form of *grumbular* disguise utilized when approaching the tills at the newsagent, *eg*. A copy of *The Economist* wrapped round *Razzle* or a copy of *Razzle* wrapped round *New Cunts 85*. Or a copy of *New Cunts 85* wrapped round *Viz*.

palmorama *n*. A late night "investigative" report into the American porn industry or similar, eagerly watched by single men who have a penchant for hard news. A *masturmentary, rudimentary, sockumentary.*

palm Sunday *n.* A relaxing *day of wrist* spent in one's own company in the absence of other weekend commitments.

palm ticklers *n.* Small, flat *lils* with protruding nipples. *Empire biscuits.*

palpootations *n.* Involuntary and unnerving contractions of the *nipsy* which make the heart beat faster the morning after a night *on the pop.*

pamper day *1. n.* An outpatient-style visit to an over-priced country hotel where big girls go to feel special, get their nails cut, sit in some mud *etc. 2. n.* Following ten pints of Guinness and a curry the previous night, a day spent wearing an emergency underpant lining, such as an old sock, woolly hat or similar, as a precaution.

panaconda *n.* A South American *dirt snake* of enormous length, that suffocates its victims if they get too close.

panavision *1. n.* Cinematographic company founded in 1953. *2. n.* The vertiginous, anamorphic vista across the porcelain expanses of *Shanks Bay* afforded to a fellow whilst he is attempting to cough up eight pints of stout, six bags of semi-digested pork scratchings and a *catbab* with *all the shit* which he swallowed less than half an hour ago without chewing.

panda's eye *n.* A *ringpiece.*

pander *1. v.* To act as a go-between in an act of sexual intrigue, *eg.* To go and buy a hamster and some parcel tape for that odd couple in the flat below. *2. n.* A large, impotent, bamboo-eating mammal.

panderer *n.* One who *panders.*

P and O *euph.* A quick, perfunctory act of intercourse. A *roll on, roll off.*

panhandle *n.* An erect penis, *wood, stalk*; a *bonk on.*

panhandle pipes *n.* A Peruvian sex act, whereby a woman blows across the top of several men's *cocks* of differing length side by side. Presumably in a shopping precinct.

panjammer *n.* A stool that laughs in the face of the flush. A *U-blocker,* a *plumber's bonus,* a *crowd pleaser.*

pankled *adj.* Having one's pants pulled down to one's ankles. Derivation unknown.

pan of burnt chips *n. orthodont.* Descriptive of dentition that leaves a lot to be desired. *'So in she comes with another fucking fishbone stuck in her craw. So she opens her mouth and it's like a pan of burnt chips in there. I know she's 102, but for Christ's sake, she should have had them out years ago.'* (from *The Memoirs of Doctor Gladstone Gamble, Balmoral GP in Residence*).

pan pipes *n.* A simple wind instrument that plays haunting music in the *shit house.*

pan scourer *n.* A vagina covered in a coarser grade of *muff swarf. Brillo fanny.*

pan smile *n.* The crescent-shaped *piss*-bleached patch of carpet that grins yellowly around the base of the toilet. The *Queen Mum's smile.*

pant anchors *n.* Your *bollocks,* specifically when they are placed above the elastic waistband of your *scads* to enable you to *piss* hands free without soaking your *kegs.* Used in pub toilets when texting, reading whilst standing up or propping yourself up to avoid falling over *etc.*

pantballing *n.* An involuntary, messy but exciting sport, usually played on Saturday and Sunday mornings by men who were copiously *refreshed* on dark beers and a *Ruby Murray* the previous evening.

pant hamster *n*. Natural prey of the *one-eyed trouser snake*.

pantilever *n*. The *piss handle*.

pantler *n*. An inexpedient *stonk on* which looks like an accident-prone reindeer has run into a washing line.

pant moustache *n*. Effect achieved when the *mapatasi* extends symmetrically beyond either side of the *shreddies*. *Thigh brows, whack-os, Rhoydes Boysons*.

pants 1. *interj*. Exclamation of dismay. 2. *adj & n*. Rubbish, *shit, pig's arse, bollocks*. '*You're talking pants!*'

pant stripper *n*. Any fancy alcoholic drink that more or less guarantees free access to the *hairy pie. Knicker oil, WD69*.

pantymonium *n*. A flatulent charivari. A loud volley of *farts* causing havoc in the *undercrackers*.

pap baffle *n*. The scrunched-up piece of *shit scrape* placed in the *pan* which makes the person in the next cubicle genuinely believe that your *crap* doesn't make a "plop" when it hits the water.

paperchase 1. *n*. The athletic pursuit of *bumwad* from cubicle to cubicle with trousers and *grundies* around one's ankles. 2. *n*. The manic sprint around the house trying to pick up all the incriminating soiled tissues and *grot mags* one has strewn about before the wife returns from her shopping expedition.

paper cut *n*. Opposite of a *wizard's sleeve*. A *fanny* tighter than an *OJ's glove*.

paper hanger's bucket *n*. A big sloppy *twat* full of wallpaper paste.

paper over the cacks *v*. To discreetly drape an unflushable, floating *Richard the Third* with toilet tissue in a vain attempt to mask its identity.

paper saver *n*. A bowel movement that leaves the paper clean straight off the tee.

PAPFAP/papfap *acronym*. Pretty As a Picture, Fat As a Pig, *eg*. Sophie Dahl before she's went on her diet. A *lardy lovely, pillow smuggler, filf*.

Papillon's purse *euph*. The rectal orifice when used as a repository for valuables, *eg*. When in a prison, boarding school or whilst negotiating the "Nothing to Declare" channel of a Turkish airport. From the film starring Steve McQueen in which the convicts stashed their cash "up the pipe".

pappalonia *exclam*. Outburst of appreciation for a woman with a massive set of *gazongers*.

papper *v*. To *shit*. '*Oh no, I think I just pappered me trolleys. So it's over to John Kettley for the weather whilst I have a look.*'

paps 1. *n*. Celebrity-hungry photographers who murdered our Princess of Hearts. 2. *n. arch*. Olde Worlde *Tittes*.

papsack *n*. A pair of *tit pants*, a *knocker hopper*. A *brassiere*.

parade ground poo *n*. A *turd* of such magnitude that the only fitting response is to hang a *bumrag* flag on it and salute as it passes out of the *chod-bin*.

paradise pie 1. *n*. A very succulent pudding served in restaurants. 2. *n*. A *puh-seh* that is mouth-watering to the eye.

paraffin *n. rhym. slang*. A gentleman of the road. A hobo. From paraffin lamp = Harold Ramp.

paraffinalia *n*. The tools of the trade accumulated by a professional *hobo, eg*. Dozens of bags containing rubbish, an old pram, a greasy anorak and a family-size plastic bottle of white cider.

parallel parked *adj.* In bed together, having sex. *'Were you parallel parked with her last night?' 'Not half! I was in up to the bumper mate.'*

paralytically incorrect *n.* A consequence of heavy intoxication where one's easy-going, tolerant views are discarded in favour of a rather more robust manifesto.

parcel force *n.* Means of making *chod's law* work for you. Going to the toilet and pretending to have a *shit*, in order to fool the fates and cause the postman to make a package delivery at a time of your choosing.

parcel shelf *n.* The viewing platform provided in a German *jobby engine*, where one's *Thoras* can be inspected at leisure prior to being flushed away.

parfume de plop *n.* Acrid odour which accompanies a *twin tone* and heralds the arrival in the *bomb bay* of a *Peter O'Toole*.

Paris-chute *euph.* Something that rarely fails to open, as sported by the well known hotel-named socialite, chihuahua enthusiast and scrawny twilit internet *grumble* star.

Parisian breasts *n.* See *lung warts*.

Paris Stilton *euph.* A lady who, from a distance and hidden behind her large sunglasses, make-up and handbag, looks reasonably appetizing - but who, on closer inspection turns out to be pock-marked, blue-veined and stinky. Also *lrf*.

park and ride *1. n.* Scheme run by one's local council. *2. n.* Scheme run by one's local prostitutes. *3. n.* Hurried intercourse in the back seat of a stationary car. A *rear-end shunt*.

park the custard *v.* To *laugh at the carpet*.

park the fudge *v.* To *shit*, pass a stool, crimp off a length.

park the pink bus *v.* To *slip* a lady a length. *'Time for bed. Come on, let's park the pink bus in the furry garage.' 'Okay. Then we can have a fuck.'*

park the tiger *v.* To puke, *yodel*, let out a *technicolour yawn*.

park your breakfast *v.* Light a *bum cigar*, lay a cable.

parlour *n.* Place where one is only allowed on special occasions. The *bonus tunnel*.

parp *1. onomat.* A romantic foreplay technique whereby one squeezes a breast in the same way that a clown would honk a car horn. *2. n. onomat.* A *fart*.

parrot dyke *n.* A *lezzer* who has occasionally slipped out of her *comfortable shoes* and *done it* with a man. From the fact that she has "enjoyed a 'cockatoo' in her time".

parson's sack *n.* The swollen state of a *scrotbag* which is as *full as a fat bird's shoe* following an enforced period of celibacy and/or masturbatory abstinence. *'Testicular pressure. The greatest internal pressure sustained in a pair of testicles is one of 65 atmospheres (995lb/sq.in) or approximately 49,400mm of mercury at sea level, in the parson's sack of the pop singer Sir Cliff Richard (GB), following a 45-year build up of seminal fluid'.* (from *The Viz Sexist Book of Records*, Boxtree £4.99 or 3 copies for 10p at car boot sales).

particulars *n.* Of low budget British sex comedies involving police officers, ladies' *bills*, knickers. *'Excuse me, madam, but I may need to take down your particulars. And have a look at your snatch.'*

parts of shame *n.* A God botherer's genitals.

party popper *n.* When a chap's wife or mistress struts around the house naked with the tail of her *fanny mouse* hanging out of her *skirting board,* and he feels the urge to pull it and see if her *arse* flies off. See *time bomb fuse.*

pasata grin *n. Mexican lipstick, clown's smile.*

passion cosh *n.* A stout, six-inch, hand-held weapon. With all veins up the side. A *love truncheon.*

passion fingers *n. Aus. milit.* An Australian army term for a clumsy fellow, *ie.* Everything he touches he *fucks.*

passion flaps *n.* A more romantic alternative to *piss flaps.*

passion pit *n.* Bed, *fart sack, scratcher, wanking chariot.*

passion wagon *n.* Clapped-out van, usually a Ford Transit, with blacked-out windows and a *piss*-stained mattress and several empty beer cans in the back. Also *shaggin' wagon, spambulance, fuck truck.*

pass the hat round *1. v.* To collect money for the driver on a coach trip. *2. n.* To take part in a *gang bang.* *'On their tour bus going from gig to gig, the members of Motley Crue like to pass the hat around.'*

pass the mic *1. n.* A section from the woeful TV show *The Hitman and Her,* where a couple of *slappers* took it in turns to wail into a microphone. *2. v.* A scene in all decent *grumble flicks* where a couple of *slappers* take it in turns to suck the leading man's *charlie.*

pastie baby *n.* An ear-ringed neonate sucking on a *Greggs dummy.*

pastie spumante *n.* A cheap, yet pleasingly effervescent, *quim.*

pastietute *n.* A *good time girl* whose idea

of a good time involves a couple of Steak Bakes and a custard slice. A prostitute who is a good deal heavier than her *slagboard postcard* picture might suggest.

pastifier *n.* A savoury item stuffed into a baby's mouth to stop it crying during a Saturday morning trip to Primark. A *Greggs dummy.*

pathfinder *1. n. milit.* A lone soldier who is sent ahead of his platoon in search of enemy activity or pockets of resistance. *2. n.* The first, brave finger to venture into the gusset region of a young lady's *dunghampers* in order to check whether the *Russians have invaded. 3. n.* An *air biscuit* that lets one know in no uncertain terms that it's time for a *tom tit.*

Patrick Moore *n. rhym. slang.* How a cockney astronomer might refer to the door of his observatory. *'Fackin' nora, Sir Bernard. Shut the bleedin' Patrick Moore, will yer? I'm bent over me eighteen inch catadioptric Cassegrain trying to get a look at a large Magellanic cloud in the Crab's Head Nebula and there's a terrible Robert Kraft going right up me Willem de Sitter.'*

Patrick, pull a *v.* Of a man who is about to *tip his filthy concrete,* to contort his face such that it resembles that of the famous Selsey-based stargazer, comedy glockenspiel player and *Sky at Night* presenter, with one eye half open and the other scrunched shut. *'Gunther, we're running out of tape here. Just pull a Patrick so we can all go home, will you.'*

patty *n.* A posh lady's *snatch, ie.* What her majesty the Queen calls her *cunt.*

Paul Daniels' hankie *sim.* Descriptive of a flaccid *member* being manually encouraged into a lady's opening. From the "hankie in the fist" trick performed by the eponymous suddenly-bald magician. *Playing snooker with a piece of string, pushing marshmallows into a moneybox.*

Paula, have a *v.* 1. *v.* To relieve oneself in a public place. From Olympic marathon live TV *shitter* and London marathon live TV *pisser* Paula Radcliffe. Also *do a Radcliffe.* 2. v. To interrupt an important task in order to have a "wee". *'Dr Barnard, we're ready for you to put in the new heart.' 'Hang on a tick. I'm just off for a quick Paula.'*

Pauline *rhym. slang.* A *minge.* From late former *EastEnders* misery-guts Pauline Fowler = growler.

Paulsgrove street party *n.* A lively all day *al fresco* celebration which involves looting, drug runners, prostitutes, police armed response units, surveillance helicopters and general rioting. Named after one of the popular *shit hole* estates in Portsmouth.

Paul's house, go to *v.* To embark on a visit to the *smallest room* in order to do a *number two.* A reference to the popular Glade air freshener advert, *viz.* "I'm going to do a poo at Paul's".

pavement pizza *n.* The contents of your stomach as they appear after *barfing* in the street. A *parked tiger.*

pavement skating *n.* Sliding, Torville & Dean-style, on a moist *barker's egg* whilst running for a bus.

Pavlov's log 1. *n. medic.* Conditioned reflex action causing one's *bomb bay doors* to start opening upon seeing a toilet. From the famous experiments of Russian psychologist Professor Ernst Pavlov, who rang a bell every time his dog done a *shit.* 2. *n. medic.* The onset of defecatory cramps caused by the aroma of ground coffee.

pay and display 1. *n.* Type of automated car park ticketing system whereby, typically, if it's forty pee an hour and you've only got a pound coin, it fucking gives you two hours instead of the two and a half fucking hours you've fucking paid for. 2. *n.* A high quality female escort, often sourced from eastern Europe, who is available at rates of between £1000-£2500 per evening to accompany gentlemen to social events, providing decorative companionship and thus impressing friends, colleagues and family friends.

payday weekender *n.* After getting your wages on the Friday, the *shit* which you have on the Sunday, which resembles chocolate Angel Delight, has the texture of fresh tarmac, and smells like a Falaraki skip during a Greek heatwave.

pay in installments *v.* To be forced to make multiple lavatory visits to relieve the *Camillas* after a night of *Ruby Murray* and brown ales.

peach stone *n.* An hibernal scrotum, clenched tightly like a Scotsman's fist round his change.

peanut brittle *n. medic.* Condition of a hardened drinker whose only solid intake for some days has been items available at the bar. Symptoms include mental fragility and uncontrolled shaking. *'Harry froze as they spotted an unshaven Mr Snape slumped at the bar of the Black Cauldron. 'We're done for now', he cried. 'No we're not,' replied Hermione. 'He's been drinking all weekend and he's completely peanut brittle.''* (from *Harry Potter and the Wizard's Sleeve* by JK Rowling).

Pearl & Dean necklace *n.* A frankly unlikely sexual scenario, where one *jizzes* onto one's girlfriend in the pictures, presumably whilst shouting: "Pa-paa...pa-paa...pa-paa...pa-paa...pa-pa-pa...pa-paa...pa-paa...pa-paa...pa-paaaaa...paaaaow!"

pearl divers' lungs *sim.* Descriptive of the impressive ability of a man to *go down* for prolonged periods without the need to come up for fresh air.

pearl drops *n.* Scumbled *spunky* deposits found on the walls of gents' toilets, particularly in the south. Also known as *Wham juice.*

pearl grey tea *n.* Effeminate beverage which is customarily sipped in the afternoon with the little finger cocked elegantly. The taste, smell and texture of *pearl grey tea* are the subject of much heated debate; some people guzzle it down hungrily whilst others prefer to spit it out. *Spunk, spooge, spaff, spoff, springle.*

Pearl Harbour *n. prop.* A place where one's *Jap's eye* commits atrocities.

pearl necklace *n.* Those globular consequences of having a *sausage sandwich* at the *Billy Mill Roundabout* that so delight the ladies.

pearly gates *1. n.* What you knock on when you die. *2. n.* The sloppy *cat flaps* of a woman with multiple piercings in the *farmyard area.*

pebbledash *v.* To *crop spray* the toilet bowl with *clarts*, thus negatively affecting the value of your home.

pecker *1. n. US.* Penis. *2. n. UK.* Nose.

pecker wreckers *n.* A *bird*'s corrective orthodontical scaffolding.

pecking *v.* The head-nodding motion exhibited by one in such a *state of refreshment* that they can hardly keep awake.

pedal *rhym. slang.* To commit an act of *self-pollution.* From pedal and crank = Jodrell Bank.

pedalophile *n.* One who hires an item of holiday boating equipment, the better to practise a spot of ocean-bound *hornithology* whilst *cleaning his glasses.* A very specific epithet which you don't really get the opportunity to drop casually into the conversation very often, to be frank.

pedigree chum *n.* Unpleasantly sexist term describing the *salad-dodging ditch pig* one you always seem to get in the middle of a bunch of *fit birds.*

pedro's piss *n.* Bland Spanish lager such as San Miguel, served lukewarm in plastic cups on the Costa del Sol. *'Eggo and chippos, please mate, plenty-o ketchup and another pint of pedro's piss, por favor.'*

pee *1. v.* To *piss.* *2. n.* Some *piss.*

peel *1. v.* To strip, pose nude. *2. v.* When so doing, to draw back the *beef curtains.* *'Crikey, have you seen Razzle? I never knew Joanne Guest was a peeler.'*

peel and polish *n.* A swiftly-administered, no frills *blow job.* *'Ten quid for full sex, fifteen for anal, three quid for a quick peel and polish.'*

peeling the carrot *v.* Spanking *the monkey.*

peeling the midnight spud *n.* The semisomnolent act of scratching one's sweaty *knackers* red raw. Also *boiling the midnight potato.*

peel session *euph.* Mark E Smith having *one off the wrist.*

peel the eel *v.* What Ray Mears does when he's all alone in the wilderness.

peel the furry prawn *v.* To manually attend to the *pudenders* of a young lady who is disinclined to wash.

peemale *n*. A man who urinates sitting down, possibly as a means of expressing solidarity with women, but more likely through alcoholic exhaustion. One who *drives from the ladies' tee*.

peep over the garden fence *v*. To attempt to conceal an unwanted erection by flattening it upwards against the stomach and tucking the *helmet* behind the waistband of the underpants. A *Kilroy*, a *Chad*.

peesouper *n*. The eye-watering, choking experience of having to use a train toilet several hours after the water for flushing has run out. That is to say, every time you use the toilet on a train. Even if you're the first person to use it when it has just rolled out of the fucking factory.

peg *v*. Of a modern lady, to do a gentleman up the *council gritter* with a *strap-on*.

PEGOOMHS *abbrev*. The sudden psychological condition which manifests itself upon completion of coitus. Post Ejaculatory Get Out Of My House Syndrome.

Pele's cock *n. medic*. An inability to attain an erection, with reference to the Brazilian goal ace's *cock drop* ads. Male sexual impotence.

pelican's beak *n*. A flappy double chin that is unpleasant to look at, *eg*. That of the late Thora Hird, or Hugh Lloyd.

pelican's yawn *sim*. A *fanny* big enough to hold 50lb of fish. A *hippo's mouth*.

pelt lapper *n*. A lady in *comfortable shoes*, a *tennis fan, a lady golfer*.

penalty pox *n*. A *clap* contracted from a bout of adulterous *futtery*.

pendolino *n*. An exceptionally large *brown trout*. Named after one of them technically-advanced, state-of-the-art Class 390 tilting trains currently operated by Virgin Rail on their West Coast Main Line route, because it doesn't go roung the bends as well as it should and it makes you an hour late for work.

Penfold has drowned *exclam*. A witty warning made to one's housemates that there is a mole-like substance floating in the *shit pan*. From 1970s cartoon vermin Dangermouse's annoying *turd* of a sidekick.

penguin *1. v*. Act performed by a prostitute whereby, upon receiving payment but before providing service, she pulls the gentleman's trousers around his ankles and runs off down the alley. From the resemblance of the client's gait to that of the flightless Arctic bird as he attempts to give chase, much to the amusement of onlookers. *2. n*. The trouser-ankled, cheeks-apart waddle adopted by one who has been surprised after *dropping the kids off at the pool* by a lack of *bumwad*.

penile dementia *n. medic*. The effect a *panhandle* has on its owner in the company of a *hornbag*, causing him to temporarily forget about his wife and children.

penis *n*. A man's *old man*, a chap's *chap*, a gentleman's *gentleman*. The *veiny bang stick, slag hammer*.

penis de milo *n. medic*. Total debilitating paralysis in both arms, caused by excessive chipping away at one's *stonker*. Named after the famous armless Greek sculpture.

penis fly trap *n*. A precariously balanced toilet seat which stays vertical for a few moments before dropping upon unsuspecting *helmets* in its path. A *knob chopper*.

penny dreadful 1. *n*. A cheap, third-rate novel picked up when nothing else is available. 2. *n*. A cheap, third-rate woman picked up when nothing else is available.

penny farthing 1. *n*. An enormous bike, which is somewhat difficult to mount due to its enormous size, though surprisingly easy to ride once you get going. 2. *n*. An enormous *bike*, who is somewhat difficult to *mount* due to her enormous size, though surprisingly easy to *ride* once you get going.

penny farthings *n*. *Kelly Brooks*. A comically mismatched set of breasts. With a man in a top hat bouncing up and down on top of them.

penny stamp *n*. *rhym. slang*. A happy-go-lucky, nomadic gentleman of the road, who answers to no-one as he takes his carefree pleasures where he may, merrily wandering the highways and byways of the land. *'Aw bloody Nora. A penny stamp's been and left a great big shit on the fucking steps again.' 'Can't you just step over it, Your Majesty?'*

pensioner falling downstairs *sim*. Descriptive of the noises made by a series of solid motions hitting the water in quick succession. A *load of old shoes falling out of a loft*.

pensioner's banquet *n*. Free food samples in supermarkets, *eg*. Bits of cheese that they've accidentally bought in far too much of *etc*.

pensioner's leg *n*. A thin, pale, knobbly, varicose-veiny penis.

pensioner's tits, as low as a *sim*. Descriptive of something that is lower than one would reasonably expect. *'The ball pitched on middle and off and stayed as low as a pensioner's tits all the way to the stumps. A terrific delivery.'* (Bob Willis commentating on England v Zimbabwe, BBC Radio *Test Match Special*, Summer 2003).

people porridge *n*. *Heir gel, baby gravy, population paste, pram fat*.

peperami wrapper *n*. The *fiveskin* or *leg warmer*.

Percy 1. *n*. *UK*. Penis, especially Robert Plant's penis. *'I'm just off to point Percy at the porcelain.'* 2. *n*. A small green 0-6-0 saddle tank steam train named after the late Rev W Awdrey's small, green penis.

Percy Thrower's lawn *n*. A *muff* that has been allowed to go to seed. A hairy, unkempt *fanny. Terry Waite's allotment*.

perform Alkan's trois etudes op. 76 1. *v*. In the world of classical piano music, to play the three studies written by Charles Valentin Alkan in which the first movement is designated for the left hand alone, the second for the right hand alone, and the climactic finale is achieved with both hands working together. 2. *v*. A virtuoso *Sherman* using first the left hand, then the right hand and finally both hands at once.

period drama *n*. Moody and erratic behaviour of women at times of menstruation. A *blobstrop, tammy huff, showing off*.

period features 1. *n*. Blocked fireplaces, draughty sash windows, warped panelled doors, paint-encrusted decorative mouldings and other sundry desirable architectural bits and pieces which allow thieving estate agents to bump up the prices of houses. 2. *n*. In women, short temper, sore nipples, irrational behaviour and the propensity to throw sharp objects violently across the room.

period pain *n. medic.* A dull, cramping ache in the ears and brain of an adult man which recurrs regularly every twenty-eight days when the missus is *on the blob.*

perousal *n.* The frisson of sexual arousal attained whilst flicking through a prospective purchase in *Grumbelows.*

perpetual motion *n.* A seemingly endless *shit.*

Perry Como *rhym. slang.* An easy-listening *crafty butcher.*

perseverance soup *n.* The tiny tears from the *hog's eye* which precede ejaculation. The clear secretion which lubricates the glans. That which comes out of the kitchen before the main course. *Dew on the lily, ball glaze, guardsman's gloss, knuckle varnish.*

Persian shampoo *n.* The act of ejaculating into your partner's hair and rubbing it in. Then rinse and repeat.

persil *n.* A gentleman homosexualist of the *Colwyn Bay* persuasion. One who is *good with his hands.*

personal best *n.* A chap's proudest individual achievement; his tally of the greatest number of *wanks* in a day he's ever managed during his life. Since his twelfth birthday, comedian David Baddiel's *personal best* has consistently also been the World Record.

personalities *n.* Tabloid euphemism for breasts. *Charms, assets, terrible arthritis. 'My, you've got a lovely pair of personalities. What are they, double-Ds?'*

pertigo *n. medic. psych.* Feeling of mild giddiness, light-headedness or generalised wobbliness experienced by a gentleman who is faced with a neat *tush* in a nightclub, office, at a funeral *etc.*

Peruvian num-nums *n.* The involuntary chewing noises emitted whilst turning over in one's sleep during the early hours of the morning.

perveillance *n.* Surreptitiously surveying an area for local *talent. Perveillance* is most effectively carried out whilst strolling along a beach wearing mirrored sunglasses.

perv windows *n.* Sunglasses.

petal dick *n.* A gentleman drinker who requires the toilet before his fifth pint. A *shandy pants, shandy pandy.*

Pete feet *n.* Name given to a *bird* who arouses suspicion because of her abnormally proportioned lower pedal extremities. Named after *Celebrity Big Brother* contestant, Colobos-monkey-coat-wearing, comedy-rubber-lipped, scouse *trolley dolly* and former Dead or Alive front-person Pete Burns. *'I only realised she was a Pete feet after I'd handed me cash over. After you with the anusol there, mate.'*

Peter O'Toole *rhym. slang.* A *Thora Hird.*

Peter two pumps *n.* An inexperienced *swordsman. A two push Charlie, two pump chump.*

petit filou *n.* A *hairy yoghurt pot* so small that the *naughty spoon* has trouble getting in. A *mouse's ear.*

petrol pump *n.* A post-curry *follow through* after which one would be well advised to avoid naked lights. A *ring-stinging* four star *backfire* from a fellow's *tailpipe* that would fail even the most cursory emissions test.

petting zoo *n.* A low quality night club where it is nevertheless a racing certainty that you will manage to get your *tops and fingers.*

pezzle *n.* How a Cornish farmer probably

refers to his *slag hammer.*

PG tits *n.* Comically conical brassieres of the sort worn by Madonna, which give the impression that the wearer has two pyramids growing out of their chest. *Witches' hats.*

phalitosis *n. medic.* Post-*horatio* breath.

phallicopter, the *n.* A rotational exhibition of genital gymnastics, performed upon his *chopper* by a gentleman in a vain attempt to impress his ladyfriend.

phallucy *n.* Any statement made by a man about the size of his *third leg, eg.* In the readers' letters page of a *grumble book* or a small ad in a *greet & meat* mag.

phantom farter *n.* An anonymous *benefactor.*

phantom of the opera *n.* Appearance of a *stick flick* actress after her co-star has *crashed his yoghurt truck* copiously down the side of her face.

pharoah's tomb *1. sim.* Descriptive of a post-argument atmosphere. *2. rhym. slang.* The spare room.

phat *adj.* A modern "street" term used to denote excellence. Also *bad, badass, kickass. 'Shnizzle my pizzle, vicar, this new Flemish double manual harpsichord of yours is really phat.'*

philanthropissed *adj.* Drunk on someone else's money.

Phil Collins *1. euph.* An act of genital copulation committed without the use of a *jubber ray.* From the title of the annoying, rubbish, short-arsed, shiny-topped songster's 1985 album *No Jacket Required. 2. n. prop. Making the bald man cry,* that is, in the words of the eponymous crying, bald *wanker,* when one "can feel it, coming in the air tonight".

philosopher's stone *n.* A *turd* that emerg-

es after a couple of hours' intense concentration.

phlegm brûlée *n.* A particularly creamy *docker's omelette* with a hard crust. Usually hocked up during a hangover.

Phoney Soprano *n.* One who has watched the eponymous New Jersey-based organised crime drama too many times and, as a result, believes himself to be a leading character thereof, despite actually working in Cash Converters, sellotaping the front covers of tattered, second-hand CDs back together.

phonography *n.* The sort of saucy mobile telephone video-clips which are popular with skint, squniting, *one-handed texters.*

photo finish *1. n.* A session of *horizontal jogging* in which both contestants break the tape at the same time. Also *dead heat. 2. n.* The frantic action of trying to leaf through your *jazz mag* to find your *finisher* when you're at the *point of no return,* desperately trying not to accidentally *spunk up* over an article about vintage cars.

photon torpedo *n. Star Trek* convention terminology for a *tom tit* expelled with such force that it completely destroys any *klingons* in the area.

phuq *n. & v.* Ingenious alternative to the word *fuck* which, whilst perfectly understandable, is able to evade the attentions of over-solicitous business e-mail censoring systems.

phwoarberries *n.* Big, ripe, juicy *tits.* With cream all over them. Breasts which, even when covered up, elicit a strangulated cry of "phwoar!" in the style of Kenneth Connor spotting Joan Sims in the shower in *Carry On Up the Jungle.*

piabetic *n.* A larger-boned fellow who

risks falling into a coma if not kept regularly supplied with pastry-based products.

Picasso arse *n*. A lady's *chuff* in knickers so tight that she appears to have four buttocks.

Picasso face *n*. Descriptive of a *bird* who is certainly no oil painting.

picket line copper *n*. The front man in a *bum chain*. From the way he is jostled about from behind, and has to hold onto his hat to stop it falling off, one would imagine.

picking the seam *1. n*. In cricket, the illegal activity whereby a fielder lifts the stitching on the ball in order to give his side an unfair advantage over their opponents. *2. n*. Thumb and forefinger method of relieving an itch present in a gentleman's *chicken skin handbag. Ball tampering*.

pick it up and run with it *1. exclam*. Desperate expression commonly used by ex-public school *rugger buggers* who have screwed up their lives by becoming media sales managers. *2. v*. To *cop off* with a *right howler* and get her out of the nightclub before any of your mates see her.

pickle tray *1. n*. An appetiser taken before an Indian meal, eaten with popadoms, whilst you decide what to have for starters, main course, and something nice to finish off with. *2. n. Cloth tit, outside tops, inside tops and fingers*. But not *your hole. 'How did you get on with Big Marge from the typing pool?' 'She's frigid, that one. I didn't get past the pickle tray.'*

picture but no sound *euph*. Descriptive of the wife's mood when one rolls in from the pub as *refreshed as a newt* with one's *earlids* pulled firmly down.

piddle *1. v*. To *pee*. *2. n*. Some *pee*.

piddle paddle *n*. An unconvincing and unathletic "quick dip in the ocean" taken whilst at the seaside, where one ventures in only waist deep and emerges shortly thereafter with a refreshingly empty bladder. A *seawee*.

piddling pool *n*. Shallow area of water where small children can happily play for hours without, for some strange reason, demanding the toilet every five minutes.

pie & drive *phr*. A useful phrase when describing the hasty purchase and consumption of a hangover-killing Gregg's pasty on the way to work the morning after a heavy night's drinking. *'You look like shit, love. Are you sure you'll be alright for work? You've got a dozen cataract operations to do today, remember.' 'I'll be cool. I'll just pie & drive.'*

pie blight *n. Muff druff*.

pie chart *1. n*. A circular diagram divided into sectors, the various sizes of which represent different quantities or amounts of pie. *2. n*. The centrefold pages of a gentleman's *artistic periodical*.

pie curious *adj*. Descriptive of a person who, whilst not a full blown *Duke of Giblets*, is nevertheless not averse to a spot of sly *salad-dodging* from time to time.

pie-hider *n*. A *gunt, bilge tank, muff pelmet*. The kind of overhanging gut that allows a lady to strip from the waist down whilst still retaining her modesty.

pie-liner *n*. A femidom.

piesexual *adj*. Of a fellow with a romantic penchant for the more voluminously-skeletonned lady.

pie shifter *n*. A *big-boned* person who can single-handedly clear the Ginster's display in their local petrol station. *'Famous people who have died on 11th February: Pietro Cataldi, mathematician, in Bologna, Italy, 1626; Rene Descartes, mathematician, in Stock-holm, Sweden, 1650; Willhelm Killing, math-ematician, in Munster, Germany, 1923; Egbert van Kampen, mathematician, in Baltimore, Maryland, 1942; Vladimir Smirnov, mathematician, Lenin-grad, USSR, 1974; William Conrad, pie shift-er, in Hollywood, California, 1994.'* (from *Schott's Increasingly Desperate Christmas Gift Book*, 2004).

piece of piss *n.* An easy thing. *'Hey, this show jumping thing is a piece of piss.'* (Christopher Reeve), *'Hey, adjusting television aerials is a piece of piss.'* (Rod Hull), *'Hey, fighting stingrays is a piece of piss.'* (Steve Irwin).

pieceps *n.* Bulging stomach muscles made famous by former Everton goalkeeper Neville Southall.

pieman's wig *1. n.* An artificial hairpiece worn by a purveyor of pastry-enveloped foodstuffs. *2. n.* An untidy *cunt-rug*.

Piers Morgan *n. rhym. slang.* An inef-fectual *cock*. From the name of former *Daily Mirror* editor and ineffectual cock Piers Morgan = organ.

pig at a tatty, going at it like a *sim. Yorks.* To engage in an act of oral pleasure with uninhibited gusto in Yorkshire. *"Eeh, by gum, Cathy lass. Slow tha' sen down a bit', said Heathcliffe. 'Appen tha's going at it like a pig at a tatty."* (from *Wuthering Heights* by Charlotte Bronte).

pig at the gate *euph.* A *mole at the coun-ter, Mr Brown at the window.*

pig bite *n.* A poetic term for the vagina. *'A daughter of the Gods, divinely tall /*

And with a pig bite like a horse's collar.' (from *A Dream of Fair Women* by Alfred Lord Tennyson).

pigboard *n.* The rear wall of a metropoli-tan phonebox.

pigbox *n.* A Nissan Micra full of rough women, driving round a provincial town playing Destiny's Child and hunting for *cock*.

pigeon's breakfast *n.* Some sick. A *pave-ment pizza*.

pigeon's chest *n.* The female swimsuit *lunchbox*. The *beetle bonnet, shark's fin*.

pig fart *n.* The erotic sound a *bit of crackling's* intimate parts may occasion-ally make whilst she is in the process of getting a good *stuffing*. A *queef*.

pigpenning *n.* Sitting surrounded by, and stewing In, your own filthy, foetid smells because you simply can't be *arsed* to get up and move to safety. Named after the character in the long-running *Peanuts* cartoon strip who was constantly envel-oped in a cloud of his own scribbled flatus.

pig's tits *rhym. slang.* The *shits*. *'After you've been to the rub a dub, climb the apples and pears to the Curry Capital, Bigg Market, Newcastle upon Tyne, for a Ruby Murray that will give you the pig's tits, or your money back.'* (Advert in *Country Life* magazine).

pig's toe *n.* The *pig's trotter*.

pig's trotter, the *euph.* Prominent and well-defined labial *moundage* which is visible through a lady's leggings. A phe-nomenon also sometimes referred to as a *camel's foot, twix lips* or *knicker sau-sages*. *'You'd best sit behind the desk to read the news tonight, Kirsty. You've got a right pig's trotter in them kecks.'*

PIK *acronym*. Pig In Knickers. An extremely unattractive, fleshy woman.

pikea *n*. Open air broken furniture showroom. Usually set up in Essex laybys after the travellers have moved on.

pikey bollards *n*. Large rocks and boulders placed along roadsides in areas where the local inhabitants already have plenty of pegs.

pikeydegradable *adj*. Descriptive of any item that magically disappears when left out by the bin or in a skip, *eg*. Old tellies, knackered computers, broken furniture, washing machines. *'Hey, neighbour! You can't just leave that broken TV out on the pavement.' 'Don't worry, it'll be gone by the morning. It's pikeydegradable.'*

pikey sauna *n*. A lingeringly warm *dirty cough* that hangs around in the trousers, making one's *bollocks* sweat.

pikey's banquet *n*. The sort of dodgy-looking and hideously-overpriced burgers and hotdogs which are sold at fairgrounds and festivals.

pikey's bonus *n*. A *grumble flick* found inside a stolen video recorder. A *scouser's jackpot*.

pikey's pit stop *n*. A visit to a garage forecourt to refuel one's car when one has neither the means nor inclination to pay. A *splash 'n' dash*.

pikeys' wedding *n*. A *pagga*, a fierce fight. *'January 18th, 1915. This morning some of the chaps went over the top. The German guns were merciless, cutting them down like wheat stalks before the scythe. I have never witnessed such a pikeys' wedding and I'm sure it will haunt me for the rest of my days.'* (from *The Diary of Rupert Brooke*).

pile high club *1. n*. The notional society of fellows who have distinguished themselves by *pappering their trolleys* whilst seated. *2. n*. Exclusive brotherhood of those who have earned their *brown wings*. *3. n*. The selection of chavs, scratters and poor people who attend a once-in-a-lifetime free wedding buffet and, as a consequence, abuse their hosts' generosity to the maximum.

pile of dead fannies, smells like a *sim*. Descriptive of something which gives off a foul, fishy odour. *'Bloody hell, Dr Von Hagens. What have you got in your garage? It smells like a pile of dead fannies.' 'It's a pile of dead fannies, mein dear chap.'*

PILF/pilf *acronym*. An alluringly glamorous female television personality. Presenter I'd Like to Fuck.

poo pourri *n. Fr*. A pile of irregularly-shaped, brown organic material, often found lying in a bowl and stinking the room out.

pilgrim's pocket *n*. A particularly dry *clout*. *'Edwina was powerless to resist. John's eyes burned into hers like semi-precious lapis lazulis. His strong arms enfolded her body as she felt herself being swept away on a mistral of passion. She gasped as she felt his powerful, but gentle fingers teasing at the moist flower of her secret sanctum. 'Fuck me, your minge is sopping,' he exclaimed. 'Norma's twat's always dry as a pilgrim's pocket.''* (from *The Junior Health Minister and The Chief Whip*, by Barbara Cartland).

pillicock *n. arch*. A *tummy banana*. From the pig's *pizzle* used in an early form of badminton.

pillock *n*. Tame, TV sitcom-friendly insult. Possibly derived from *pillicock*.

pillow biter *n*. One who bites their pillow, often in a moment of steeply-raked horticultural delight. Also *mattress muncher, feather spitter*.

pillow mint *1. n*. Small, inexpensive chocolate treat left on a guest's bed in better hotels in order to create the illusion that customer satisfaction is of the slightest importance to the management. *2. n*. A hefty *feeshus* left in the *pan* with the express intention of offending the next occupant of the *shithouse*.

pills *n*. Pods, knackers, niags.

pilot error *n*. A misjudged *joystick* move that causes an immediate tailspin.

pilot light *n*. An ex-socialite now restrained by the *pink handcuffs, ie*. One who "never goes out".

pilot's poke *n*. An emergency jettison of surplus fuel. *Roger and out*.

pilot the submarine *v*. To urinate nocturnally whilst too refreshed to find the light switch in the bathroom, thus being forced to direct one's stream solely by the sound it makes upon impact with the water/carpet/walls/dog/your feet. *Pissing by sonar*.

pimp my ride *1. n*. Television programme in which knackered old *bangers* are given a new lease of life. *'Please, MTV, pimp my ride.' 2. v.* Surgical programme in which knackered old bangers are given a new lease of life. *'Please, doctor, pimp my ride. Paying special attention to her saggy tits, triple chin, beergut and flabby arse.'*

pinballing *v*. To make progress home from the boozer by a series of ricochets from one item of street furniture to the next. Accompanied by the ringing of bells and clunking noises.

pinch a loaf *v*. To *curl one off*.

pinch of snuff *rhym. slang*. A *crafty butcher*.

Pinder's tits *euph*. Descriptive of something that you are not really bothered about any more. From the fact that glamour model Lucy Pinder is never going to get her *nips* out and what's more, after waiting this long, no-one particularly cares. *'You going to get Kate Bush's new album, then?' 'No. It's Pinder's tits, that.'*

pineapple *rhym. slang*. Semen. From pineapple chunk = spunk.

pinhole *n*. A *Mary* that makes a *mouse's ear* look like a *hippo's mouth*.

pink *v*. Of a lady, to make a *fanny slug* on a window for the amusement and edification of passers by.

pink, the *n*. A really good eyeful of the female genitals, esp. in a *meat mag*. See *close-up pink*.

pink bat's face *n*. A nocturnal, high-pitched *spam butterfly* that eats *meat moths* for breakfast.

pink berets *n*. Large, flat breasts with stiff *nips*.

pink breathalyser *n*. The alternative drink-driving test offered to inebriated lady motorists by the more resourceful *scuffer*. *'Could I ask you to blow into this pink breathalyser please, madam? I'll tell you when to stop.'*

pink cigar *n*. Penis. Not to be confused with *bum cigar*, except in Germany. *'Tell me madam, do you perchance smoke the pink cigar?'*

pink Darth Vader *n*. Knob. From the *Star Wars* character with a *bell end* helmet.

Pink Floyd *euph*. The act of entering the dark side of a lady's *moon*. *'Fedora was powerless to resist. His eyes burned into hers like diamonites. His strong arms* *enfolded her body as she felt herself being swept away on a 930 millibar sea surge of passion. Suddenly, she felt Jalfrezi's hot breath on her cheek as he whispered in her ear. 'Can I put Pink Floyd on tonight, love?' he asked. 'Alright then,' she replied. 'But only if you promise not to play any of your shit prog rock records while your cock's up my arse."* (from *The Woman Named After a Type of Hat and the Man Named After a Chicken Dish* by Barbara Cartland).

pink mist *n.* The priapismic haze that descends to cloud a man's better judgement. Also *penile dementia*. *'Well, at the end of the day, Brian, I just seen Wayne's bird over there and the pink mist came down, basically.'*

pink oboe *n. Bed flute. 'Tell me madam, do you perchance play the pink oboe?'*

pink pillows *n.* Ladies' *love cushions*, bosoms.

pink shit, have a *v.* The end of a romantic evening of *back door work*. The termination of the process of anal intercourse.

pinksmith *n.* One who is expert in *fannycraft*. A *crumpeteer*.

pink steel *n.* Even harder than *wood*. Material used to forge *diamond cutters*.

pink ticket *n.* Imaginary *vadge* visa issued to a husband when he spends the night apart from his wife. *'Eureka! I've got my pink ticket for the conference on Tuesday.'*

pink velvet sausage wallet *n.* Short for *quim*.

pink wafer *n.* A *blurtch* which resolutely refuses to exude *fanny batter* even after being lovingly coerced for several minutes.

Pinocchio *euph.* A *book reader*. One who

is *good with colours, not the marrying kind, bent as a nine bob note etc.* Named after the famous theatrical puppet out of off of the eponymous Disney film, because "he wasn't a real boy".

pinot grigio pashmina *n.* Like a *bacardigan*, but for posh *birds* in Wilmslow or Alderley Edge; a warm yet invisible shawl consisting of several glasses of white wine.

pint glass figure *n.* Like an hour-glass figure, but with very little narrowing in the middle, *eg.* Vanessa Feltz.

pintle *n.* Olde Worlde *Chopper*. *Pipe cleaner, pizzle*.

pip *n.* An upper class *hat* of the kind one might imagine Penelope Keith *dropping*.

pipe 1. *n. Fr.* An act of oral love. A *nosh, chewie, blow-job*. 2. *n. Cock*.

pipe bomb *n.* An explosive *shit* that goes off without warning in the *pan*, causing massive collateral damage.

pipecleaner 1. *n.* Furry wire used by children to make models in playschool. 2. *n.* The first *piss* taken after committing an act of *self-pollution*. 3. *n.* A *blood sausage*.

pipe of peace, smoke the *v.* Of a woman, to *do the decent thing* following an argument with her significant other.

piper at the gates of dawn 1. *n.* An early Pink Floyd album. 2. *n.* An early morning *turtle's head*. *Cock-a-doodle-poo*.

piper at the gates of porn *n.* The anticipatory semi-erection achieved involuntarily by a chap entering a newsagent with the intention of purchasing a *gentleman's rhythm pamphlet*.

pipe smoker 1. *n. US. Botter* . 2. *n.* A person who smokes a pipe.

pips have gone, the *euph.* Inevitable situation that brings about a swift conclusion to any bout of telephone sex. *'Sorry love, got to go. The pips have gone.'*

pirate *n.* A *breastitute* lady, *ie.* One with a "sunken chest".

pirate of men's pants *n.* Swashbuckling term for your *jolly rogerer, cock, one-eyed willie.*

pirate's piss *n.* The *piss* you have with one eye shut to improve targetting after a long night *on the pop.*

Pires penalty *n.* An unsatisfying and embarrassing *dribble* instead of a *shot* which hits the *back of the net.* A *money shot* that's down to its last couple of coppers; a *gwibble.*

pishap *n.* A minor, urination-related mishap, such as carelessly splashing one's shoes, dribbling a dewdrop down the front of one's tweeds or accidentally catching one's penis whilst removing it from the the letterbox of BBC Director General Mark Thompson.

piss *1. v.* To micturate. *2. n.* Some micturition. *3. adv.* Extremely. *'That driving test was piss easy'. 'Your three-point turn was piss poor.'*

pissabled *adj.* A state of drunken infirmity whereby one is unable to walk upstairs, park one's car properly *etc.* Also *shandycapped.*

piss bib *n.* See *piss catcher.*

piss bliss *n.* The moment just before a long-awaited *scoot,* when a gentleman keeps it in for a couple of seconds longer, primarily for a cheap thrill.

piss catcher *n.* The absorbent, magnet-shaped furry rug which was installed around the plinth of many a typical home lavatory during the 1970s. Also known as a *pan smile* or, after it had been in place for a few months, the *Queen Mum's grin.*

piss chase *1. n.* Excuse for an *ad hoc* pub crawl, especially during cold weather. A game of *piss chase* involves going into a pub for a much needed *wazz,* and whilst there feeling morally obliged to have a pint. This results in one again being in urgent need of the lavatory a quarter of a mile further down the high street, and so on and so forth until closing time. Or indeed until death from old age, now that the pubs never shut. *2. n.* Popular playground game in Germany.

piss chisel *n.* A high-powered stream of *wazz* used to chip *skidmarks* of one's lavatory bowl. The *yellow toilet brush.*

pissed *1. adj.* UK. Soused, potted, refreshed. *2 adj.* US. Annoyed. *'That cotton-pickin' Osama Bin Laden has gotten me real pissed, bub.'*

pissed as a tramp *adj.* To be so *refreshed* as to not care where one sleeps.

pissed up *adj.* Descriptive of a fellow who is comprehensively *wankered.*

piss factory *n.* Vict. A public house.

piss flaps *1. n.* Labia, *beef curtains.* *2. interj.* Exclamation of disappointment. *'Oh piss flaps! I never win the Lottery!'*

piss fork *n.* A post-coital bidirectional urine flow. *Twin jets.*

pisshead's labourer *n.* A barman.

pissinfectant *n.* The use of a stream of forcibly-directed *slash* in order to remove from the *bog* an area of stubborn *pebbledashery* left by the previous occupant, thus killing two birds with one stone. Also known as the *yellow toilet brush, piss chisel.*

pissing in the wind *v.* Wasting one's time, attempting the impossible.

pissing tic-tacs *n.* The peculiar sensation of urinating whilst suffering from a nasty dose of *knob rot.* Not quite as bad as *pissing razor blades.*

piss it up the wall *v.* To fritter away something, *eg.* Money, talent, urine.

piss it *v.* To do something *piss* simple, *piss* easily.

piss kitten *n.* The completely redundant spare woman who follows her friend to the toilet, for no other reason than to increase the length of the queue.

piss like an American fighter pilot *v.* When extremely *Brahms*, to micturate in a haphazard and inaccurate fashion, *ie.* Spraying urine all over the floor, seat, shoes, John Simpson, *etc.*

piss mist *n.* The fine mist that forms around a urinal trough at shin level when having a *gypsy's kiss*. Only noticeable when wearing shorts. *Wee fret.*

piss off *1. exclam.* A polite form of *fuck off. 2. v.* To annoy. *'The graphics on the BBC news really piss me off.'*

piss on your chips *v.* To put yourself at a long-term disadvantage through a foolhardy short-term action. *Fart on your Weetabix, cum on your faggots.*

piss, piece of *n.* A portion of easiness. *'Hey, flying this Concorde out of Charles De Gaulle Airport is a piece of piss.'*

pisspint *n.* A drink purchased "because it's only fair, isn't it", when calling in at a public house for the sole purpose of making use of the *bogs*.

piss polo *1. n.* Game of skill whereby disinfectant tablets are pointlessly manoeuvred in a urinal trough by the participants' *wazz* streams. *2. n.* A very unsuccessful flavour of sweet.

piss porch *n.* The skin awning which protects a lady's *bald man in a boat* from the weather.

piss pot *1. n.* Lavatory bowl. *2. n.* Idiot, fool. *3. n.* Old-fashioned motorcyclist's helmet.

pisspotical *adj.* A state of confusion, disarray or disharmony, *ie.* That which apparently exists at Houghton-le-Spring Housing Benefit Office.

piss pregnant *adj.* Suffering from a desperate need to micturate, for example on a tube train or whilst reading the news, as a consequence of earlier sinking nine pints of *neck oil*. *'Sorry about the state of my trousers, by the way. I was piss pregnant on the bus, and my waters broke just before I reached my stop. But to get back to your question; what qualities do I think I could bring to this position?'*

piss proud *adj.* To be the owner of a *dawn horn*, a *morning glory*, motorcycle kick stand.

piss rusty water *v.* To pass liquid *feeshus*.

piss sauna *n.* The all-enveloping fog of urine steam in an outside pub lavatory on a cold winter's evening.

pissterical *adj.* In a state of uncontrolled alcohol-induced panic, anger or excitement. *'I would request that the members of the jury should pay no attention to Miss Winehouse's pissterical outburst.'*

piss through a stiffy *v.* To attempt the impossible. *''I say, Jeeves old chap,' I ejaculated, 'It really is dashed annoying. I mean, what's a bally chap supposed to do? I've been trying to catch the Hon. Celia Hunt-Fosbury's eye all week, but she always seems to have that dumpy chum of hers from Roedean in tow.' 'I take it, sir,' replied the sage retainer, 'that you are referring to the cigar-smoking young lady in tweeds...?' 'That's the one,' I cried. 'You've got her bang on the pip. What shall I* *do, Jeeves?' 'I incline to the view, sir,' the inestimable manservant continued, 'that, in the circumstances, you should withdraw gracefully. I fear you may be trying to piss through a stiffy there."* (from *Fuck Me Sideways, Jeeves!* by PG Wodehouse).

piss up *n.* An ale soirée; a social gathering of boozing companions.

piss whip *n.* The effect created by drunkenly waving one's *pezzle* up and down whilst having a *gypsy's kiss.*

piss whistle *n.* A *bed flute,* a *pink oboe.*

piss with the lid down *v.* To do something very foolish, to make a schoolboy error. *"Mr Paravicini's murderer is in this very room, and I'm afraid it is you, Brigadier Lewerthwaite!' cried Miss Marple. The room fell silent. 'After murdering him, you dressed him in his pyjamas and carefully put his cufflinks on the dressing table to give the impression that the crime had been committed after bedtime, when you were playing bridge with myself and the Bishop. However, I'm afraid you pissed with the lid down, Brigadier,' she said. 'What the deuce do you mean?' Lewerthwaite blustered. 'Simply this,' she continued. 'You placed the cufflinks on the right hand side of the dressing table when the position of the inkwell on his Davenport clearly showed him to have been left handed.'* (from *Ten Little Black and White Minstrels,* by Agatha Christie).

piss wicks *n.* One's shoelaces in a urine-flooded pub toilet.

pissy fit *n.* The kind of foul-tempered strop that can only be achieved when one is *blind refreshed.*

pisticuffs *n.* A comical, drunken attempt at combat.

pisto *n.* Nasally-abusive miasma prevalent in tower block lifts, multi-storey car park stairs or around gentlemen of the road. "Ah, pisto."

piston slap 1. *n.* On a 1980s/90s Nissan or Ford motor vehicle, for example, when the mileage reaches a point such that the pistons have worn down so they slap the sides of the cylinder bores. 2. *n.* An unsatisfactory act of coitus during which one's *tallywhacker* doesn't touch the sides. Caused by a overly capacious vaginal cylinder bore rather than an undersized piston, obviously.

pistorectomy *n. medic.* The act of vomiting up one's own internal organs whilst life-threateningly *merry.*

pistory *n.* The oral anthology of dubious recollections and downright lies recounted by a young man after a night out *on the lash, eg.* "I'd already had thirteen pints when that bird started giving me the eye" and similar tosh.

pit bull *n.* A stocky, tenacious *Thora,* usually the final one of a visit, that hangs onto the *ringpiece* like grim death. An *angry monkey,* a *Harold Lloyd,* a *Robert Powell.*

pit cat *euph.* A little-used *clopper.* A *pussy* that never sees the light of day.

pitch a tent *v.* To get *wood* either beneath the bed linen, or conspicuously in your trousers.

pitch inspection *n.* The checking of one's *bills* for any sign of a *bonus ball* after a risky *Exchange & Mart.*

pitch invasion 1. *n.* Entertaining 1970s football match behaviour in which the crowd unexpectedly leaves the stands and makes its way onto the field of play. 2. *n.* Entertaining *farty-arse* behaviour in which a quantity of *feeshus* unexpectedly leaves the *arse* and makes its way onto the *gusset* of the *trolleys*. A *follow through*.

pit clit *n. coll.* Gorgeous lycra-clad *blart* that stand around holding umbrellas on the starting grid of F1 races.

pit fillers *n.* Massive *thru'penny bits* which emigrate towards a *bird's* oxters when she's lying on her back.

pit prop *n.* Strategic structural member found in a *passion pit*. A *tent pole*, a *dawn horn*.

pitta tits *n.* Unleavened *baps* on a lady's chest. From their similarity to the unappetising Greek flatbreads seen in cosmopolitan retail emporia such as the Spar.

pizzle *n. medic.* A sorry-looking *penis*, like one would imagine the Pope has. *Gonzo's nose.*

placket *n. arch.* A Medieval maiden's *cunt.*

plamff *n. Scot.* One who, apparently bored of sniffing bicycle seats, opts to cut out the middle man and sniffs the gussets of ladies' soiled *bills* instead, *eg.* Jonathan Ross OBE.

plank *n.* A planned *wank.* From planned + wank. A useful entry in a stressed executive's diary for when his wife or girlfriend is absent which, during any subsequent inquisition into his scheduled assignations, can be explained away as a highly improbable trip to a local timber merchants to peruse their selection of stout battens.

Planter's hum *n.* The nauseating smell of *air croutons.* From the aroma of a freshly-opened bag of dry-roasted peanuts.

plap *1. n. onomat.* The sound a *digestive transit* makes when it hits the *chod pan* water, particularly if it's one of them ones with the consistency of warm plas-

ticine. *2. n. onomat.* An alternative to a *Peruvian num-num. 3. onomat.* Upon waking, the noise made whilst testing that one's mouth still works first thing in the morning. *4. onomat.* Lip-based vocalisation indicative that one could murder a pint.

plasterer's radio *sim.* Descriptive of a lucky lady who is heavily adorned with *jelly jewellery.* Frequently found on Japanese and American cyber-scud.

plastic cockney *n.* A *mockney.* A posh person who affects to be an Eastender, *eg.* Ben Elton, Nigel Kennedy, Shane MacGowan.

plasticine hammer, knocking a nail in with a *sim.* Descriptive of the difficulty experienced when trying to *bang* a young lady who has signally failed to provoke a sufficient level of tumescence in one's *chap. Playing snooker with a piece of string.*

plastic paddy *n.* A posh person who affects to be Irish, *eg.* Shane MacGowan.

plate *1. n. arch.* Horatio. *2. n. arch.* Cumulonimbus. *3. n. arch.* A general purpose term for any sort of oral/genital shenanigans performed behind a Victorian skip. *'How much, love?' 'A penny for full, a farthing for hand or a ha'penny for plate, your grace.'*

play a tune on the devil's clarinet *1. v.* To masturbate. *2. v.* To borrow a woodwind instrument from the Lord of Hades, before knocking out a jazz standard on it.

playaway *n.* Masturbatory technique of chaps not overly-endowed in the trouser department, *eg.* Pygmies, Jamie Theakston, the Rt Hon Jack Straw MP. From the song lyrics: "One finger, one thumb, keep moving".

play Drake *euph*. In a sexual engagement, to delay until the very last possible moment before *joining in the fray*. From the no doubt apocryphal story of olden days sailor Sir Francis Drake who, in 1588, waited until he had finished his game of bowls on Plymouth Hoe before addressing the imminent threat of the Spanish Armada. And then waited until he had defeated this waterborne invasion force before performing an act of penetrative vaginal intercourse up Queen Elizabeth I.

play dough *n*. Disposable income, *beer tokens*.

play good cock/bad cock *v*. A popular method of *self-interrogation* in which alternate violent and gentle strokes are employed to get the suspect to *spill his guts*.

playing Buckaroo with Muhammad Ali, like *sim*. Descriptive of a situation where one cannot lose, *eg*. Racing Eddie Large up Mount Snowdon, running a premium rate phone-in competition on GMTV, or standing for election against John Redwood.

playing chopsticks *n*. A beginners' duet. Mutual masturbating.

playing snooker with a piece of string *sim*. Trying to *sink a pink* with a *marshmallow cue*.

playing the accordian *v*. To alternately pull apart and squeeze together the cheeks of one's *arse* when perched on the *choddy hopper* in an effort to encourage the last bit of *shit* to drop off before polishing one's *nipsy*.

playing the bone-a-phone *v*. *Wanking*, pulling oneself a *hand shandy*.

playing the invisible banjo *v*. George Formby-esque female masturbation technique. *Scruggs style*.

playing the upside-down piano *sim*. The overture to the second movement of *hiding the sausage*. *Firkyfoodling*.

play statues *v*. To stop suddenly in the street with a pensive look upon one's face as one tries to determine whether one has just done a *guff* or a *poo*.

playsturbation *n*. Portmanteau term describing the activities of a single gentleman or temporarily home-alone husband who spends his time alternately playing action adventure games and *pulling himself off*.

play the Atari *v*. To waggle one's *joystick* furiously, whilst poking one's tongue out with concentration and excitement, in the style of an 80s computer console gamer having a *wank*.

play the B-side *v*. To swap from the *Missionary position* to the *doggie position*. '*I got fed up with looking at her face while I was giving her one, so I flipped her over and played the B-side.*'

play the back nine *v*. *Irish golf*. To use one's *wood* to play into the bunker, *get the dog in the bathtub*.

play the bacon kazoo *v*. To *nosh* noisily on a *lab kebab*.

play the pink oboe *v*. To perform oral sex on a man, presumably with a thin reed sticking out of his *hog's eye*. Often used to denote homosexuality. '*I didn't know Michael Barrymore played the pink oboe.*'

play the violin *v*. To scrape your *bow* against a lady's *G-string*. To make sweet music with a lady after merely pushing the *jelly hammock* of her *dunghampers* to one side.

play the whale *v*. To *spew*.

play your arse right *n*. Game which can

be played by two men sitting outside a health club or swimming pool, *eg.* Policemen in their patrol car, plumbers in a van or emeritus professors of moral philosophy sitting in the window of a teashop. Based on the formerly popular Bruce Forsyth TV vehicle *Play Your Cards Right*; in this variant contestants have to predict whether the *muck spreader* of the next lady who emerges through the front door will be bigger or smaller than the last.

pleasure *v.* Tabloidese, to *suck* or *wank off*. To perform a lewd act on oneself or on someone else.

pleasure trove *n.* A dazzling collection of *niff mags* found under a hedge or on top of an older brother's wardrobe.

plinth *v.* Of males *on the job*, to manoeuvre oneself into a comfortable position for penetration.

plod *n.* A *half-on.*

plod fodder *n. coll.* Highly arrestable individuals, usually found hanging round outside off-licences on dodgy estates.

plonker 1. *n.* Penis. 2. *n.* Crap put-down line from Britain's favourite tedious TV sitcom.

plop corn *n.* Thrill-seeking undigested yellow foodstuff which rides one's *log flume.*

ploughing the sand 1. *v.* A seemingly never ending and unrewarding job, *eg.* Painting the Forth Rail Bridge, working as BBC Radio 6Music's Pete Doherty or Amy Winehouse news correspondent. 2. *n.* Being *on the job* whilst far too *wankered* to *shoot one's stack.*

ploughman's *n.* The *barse, taint, notcher etc.* 'Mr Kneivel's motorbike hit the last bus at an approximate speed of 120mph, before careering into several *fruit machines and a tuppenny waterfall. He suffered severe internal injuries including fractured ribs, two broken legs and a fractured skull. He also ripped his ploughman's wide open on the petrol tank.'* (Attending physician's report, Las Vegas County General Hospital Accident & Emergency Department, 1978).

ploughman's lunch *euph.* A dirty *bird's all day breakfast,* from the fact that it "looks like beef, smells like cheese and tastes like a pickled onion".

pluke *n.* A facial spot. A *zit, plook.*

plumbago *n. medic.* Painful ache in the *Gladstones* caused by over-revving the *spunk* engines without releasing the *horse's handbrake. Lover's nuts, blue balls.*

plumber's bonus *n.* A *U-blocker* of such proportions that it has to be dealt with by someone who has served an apprenticeship. A *windfall* or *shitty & guilds.*

plumber's lung *n.* A violent *arse bark.*

plumber's mate *n.* A bored housewife who entertains herself during the day by watching repeats of *Flog It* and *sucking off* sundry tradesmen who have called to fix the washing machine.

plumber's privilege *n.* The ancient right granted to plumbers, which entitles them to relieve themselves into whichever appliance they have just installed, *eg.* Sink, bath, dishwasher *etc.*

plumber's toolbag *n. Furry bicycle stand, mott.*

plumber's wipe *n.* The art of shoving one's hand into a lady's *driptray,* and rubbing backwards and forwards, in the same way that a plumber would wipe a recently-soldered joint.

plum duff *rhym. slang.* A *book reader.*

plumpa-lumpa *n.* A short fat *bird* with a

bright orange face.

plumper *n*. A *Buffet slayer*. A lady of ample proportions.

plums *n*. *Knackers, balls*, testicles.

plum sauce *n*. Ejaculate.

plums to prunes *euph*. The before and after states of a chap's *hairy saddlebags*. *'Jonathan was powerless to resist. His eyes burned into the centrefold's minge like quartzes. His hairy hand enfolded his battered charlie as he felt himself once again being swept away on an onanistic whirlwind of passion. Then, all too soon it was over and he felt his ardour subsiding. 'Bloody hell, that was fast,' he panted as he wiped his hand on the curtains. 'I went from plums to prunes in less than a minute.'* (from *The Film 2005 Presenter and the Japanese Jazz Mag* by Barbara Cartland).

plum tomatoes *n*. The state of a chap's *knackers* after he's done it with a lady who's *on the blob*.

plunker *n*. *US*. *Johnny*, a *spunk*-proof jumpsuit for a *plonker*. A *Trojan, jubber*.

Plymouth Argyles *rhym. slang*. Piles.

poacher's folly *1*. *n*. In traditional countryside parlance, the act of shooting at rabbits and thereby scaring away the big game. *2*. *n*. In nightclub parlance, the act of chatting up the first rough *bird* one sees in a club and thereby scaring away the decent *tussage*. *Going ugly early*.

poacher's pocket *1*. *n*. A fashion accessory favoured by illicit hunters and shoplifting television celebrities. *2*. *n*. A very large *fanny* with a jar of coffee and some batteries stowed up it.

poaching an egg *n*. The correct manner of defecation when in earshot or noseshot of polite company. Dropping anchor into an already flushing toilet, thus whisking away all potential noises, miasmas and stipplings. *'When taken short whilst on state visits, Her Majesty always poaches an egg in case she leaves a tiger's back on the skidpan and causes a diplomatic incident.'* (Nicholas Witchell, BBC News 24).

Pob lips *n*. The state of the *ringpiece* during an acute bout of diarrhoea. From the relentlessly low budget, spitting Welsh children's TV puppet of the same name.

pobolycwm *n*. *Welsh*. Literally "People who like quim".

pocket battleship *1*. *n*. A compact, heavily-armed warship, such as The Graff Spee. *2*. *n*. A short, yet aggressive *hard on*. A Bob Hoskins amongst erections. *3*. *n*. An ugly, short *bint, eg*. That fucking nightmare off *Wife Swap*.

pocket billiards *n*. A game for one player, two *balls*, and a *cock*.

pocket bonk-on *n*. Like pocket chess and pocket Scrabble, a genital erection that is for some reason smaller than usual, but still perfectly functional. Ideal for caravan holidays.

pocket fisherman *n*. He who plays with his *tackle* through his trouser pockets.

pocket frog *n*. A *fart, botty burp, anal announcement*.

pocket pinball *n*. A game where the testicles are fired up into the chest, where they ricochet from organ to organ whilst bells ring and one's eyes spin round.

pocket pinball wizard *n*. A fellow who may not be deaf or dumb, but is almost certainly blind.

pocket rocket *1*. *n*. A small, but powerful motorbike. *2*. *n*. A small, but powerful *knob*.

podcast 1. *n*. A broadcast of digital content played back on one's personal entertainment device. 2. *n*. A broadcast of the contents of the *pods* caused by using the digits to play with one's *personal entertainment device*. 3. *n*. A metric unit of *spaff* equal to approximately one fortieth of an *almond*.

podge-on *n*. A small *semi on* which presents one's *old man* in a more favourable light than it deserves. *Half a teacake, dobber.*

pod purse *n*. Where the loose change for a *money shot* is kept.

pod race *n*. To *crack one off* in a high-pressure situation where time is of the essence, *eg*. While the missus is out making a cup of tea or choking on a boiled sweet.

poe *n*. The *fadge*. From the Gothic author Edgar Allen Minge.

poe slap *n*. A *fanny nanny, dangermouse.*

POETS day *acronym*. Friday. From Piss Off Early, Tomorrow's Saturday.

poffle *v*. To *shart. Gamble and lose.*

pog *n*. Scratter.

pogie *n*. US. Where American *plonkers* go dressed in their *plunkers*.

pogue mahone *exclam. Gael*. Original name of the Pogues. An anglicisation of the Irish "pog mo thoin", meaning "kiss my arse". A reasonable request, given the state of Shane MacGowan's mouth.

pointer sisters *n*. A slightly perkier version of the *Winslet twins.*

point Percy at the porcelain *v*. To take Robert Plant to the toilet for a *wee wee.*

poke *v*. What *plonkers* do to *pogies.*

poke holes in a cheap door *phr*. Property of a *diamond cutter*. 'When Elizabeth was near, D'Arcy's heart raced, and he got a panhandle that could poke holes in a cheap door.' (from *Pride and Prejudice* by Jane Austen).

pokelore *n*. Mythical yarns of exciting sexual adventures spun to mates down the pub.

poker face 1. *n*. In poker, a blank, emotionless expression that does not reveal anything about the cards being held by a player to his opponents. 2. *n*. In *poking*, the frenzied, red-faced grimace of a chap who is on the point of *blowing his stack.*

poker hand *n*. A morning spent on the lavatory evacuating one's *Camillas*. A *running straight* followed by a flush; then a *full house* followed by a royal flush.

poke the spider's eye *v*. To dig at one's *claypit* through one's *farting crackers.*

pokey bott wank *n*. A two-handed act of *self gratification* which combines *wanking* with one hand whilst sticking a finger from the other one up your own *arse. Abseiling. 'Are you coming up to bed, Tony?' 'In a minute, Cherie. I'm just having a pokey bott wank.'*

pokies 1. *n*. Gambling machines, or one-armed bandits if you will. 2. *n*. Ladies' *nips* when visible through their clothing. Ringo Starr's sister-in-law Daisy Duke out of *The Dukes of Hazzard* was well known for her *pokies*. By a spooky coincidence, the pilot episode of *The Dukes of Hazzard* was entitled *One-Armed Bandits. Chapel hat pegs, pygmies' cocks, blind cobblers' thumbs etc.*

polestruck *adj*. A shallow lady who is erotically fascinated by firemen and their equipment.

pole tax *n*. A pecuniary sum or duty levied upon the patrons of *gentleman's entertainment* venues before the next performer deigns to appear on stage. Usually in the form of putting a quid in a pint glass, or a hat.

pole vault 1. *n*. Vagina, *stench trench*, strong room where the *spam sceptre* can be safely housed. For a couple of minutes. 2. *n*. The mental repository of erotic imagery which is relied upon by ladies, or indeed gentlemen who are *close to their mothers*, to get them *over the line* during bouts of onanistic *self indulgence*. Similar to, though also the opposite of, the heterosexual *mammary* or *spank bank*.

police horse fart *n*. A *change of heart* capable of dispersing an unruly mob.

policeman *n*. An amusing way of *dropping one's bait*, specifically the act of placing both hands behind the back and bending the knees out in a comical fashion as a prelude to the release of flatus. Can be accompanied by the words "'ello 'ello 'ello" or indeed "evenin' all", in the style of Dixon of Dock Green, according to personal preference.

policeman's dinner *n*. *US*. An *arsehole*.

policeman's knock, hard as a 1. *sim*. Descriptive of a ne'er-do-well, for example, perhaps ensconced in a public house bar. *'I wouldn't mess with him, mate. He's as hard as a policeman's knock.'* 2. *sim*. Descriptive of the physical resilience of an object. *'Lady Alexander caressed his thigh, slowly moving upwards and gasped. "My word, corporal. You're as hard as a policeman's knock!"'*

policewoman's treat *n*. A bobby's *bob*.

polish a turd *met*. To fruitlessly attempt to dress up something *shite*, *eg*. The relaunch of the Morris Marina as the Ital, or putting a baseball cap on William Hague.

polish one's spectacles *v*. To surreptitiously *masturbate* one's penis through one's pockets, *eg*. When looking for change in a strip club or when sexually aroused on a tube train.

polish the lighthouse *v*. To *throttle Captain Birdseye* in the bath.

POLO/polo *acronym*. *milit*. Code used on military correspondence prior to coming home from a posting abroad. Pants Off, Legs Open. See also *NORWICH*, *BURMA*.

polony party *n*. A social gathering of two or more consenting adults where party games include *hide the sausage*, *park the salami* and *split the kipper*. And one's party bag would contain a slice of cake and a dose of the *clap*. An orgy.

pommel horse, an army surplus *sim*. Descriptive of a woman who is slack in both the moral and vaginal senses. *'Or will lucky Benedict choose number three, the vivacious Mother Superior who loves to party and has had more jumps than an army surplus pommel horse?'*

Pompey pineapple *n*. The high tension raked-back hairstyle favoured by *bingo clink*-clad southern *slappers*.

pompom *n*. *Jam*. A furry thing waved by cheerleaders to entertain a crowd.

ponce 1. *n*. A *pimp*. 2. *n*. Brian Sewell soundalike. 3. *v*. To borrow something with no intention of giving it back, *eg*. Cigarettes, garden tools, the Elgin Marbles.

poncilitis 1. *n*. *medic*. Inflammation of the poncils. 2. *n*. *medic*. Inflammation of nothing whatsoever, but which nevertheless results in much pathetic whining from someone in rude health who is clearly a great big *ponce*.

pond skater *n.* A particularly tenacious *floater* held in place by *chod bin* surface tension, that resists all attempts at flushing it away.

pong *n.* The smell of a *poot.*

pony *rhym. slang. Shit.* From pony and trap = crap. *'Just wait in the back of the cab, mate. I'm off into the rub-a-dub sweet-wrappers for a pony. I'll be quick because I've left the meter running.'*

pony express *n.* An urgent *package* that always gets through.

poo 1. *exclam.* A word spoken with fingers on nostrils to describe an unpleasant odour. **2.** *n. Shit.* **3.** *v.* To do a *duty.*

pooaplegic *n. medic.* One who, having sat on the toilet for too long, has lost all feeling below the waist. A *crapple.*

pooch coning *n.* A decidedly risky sexual pursuit which involves smothering *nut butter* over your privates, it says here, and then getting your next door neighbour's dog to lick it off. Nice to know that it's got a name at last.

Poocomknockerphilication *n. Cleveland steaming,* as performed by Ken Dodd.

poo cradle *n.* The floating raft of toilet tissue placed in the bowl before *dropping the kids off at the pool* in order to minimise the risk of *splashback.* Also *crash mat, pap baffle* or *pilo.*

poocumber *n.* A long, green *pop.*

poodini *n.* One of those rare *turds* that magically escapes through the U-bend without any assistance whatsoever, even if you'd got a policeman to chain it up in a canvas bag first. A *ghost shit.*

poof *n.* A man who doesn't want another pint.

poo fairy *n.* Magical entity which regularly visits the female half of the population, resulting in the male half being under the handy illusion that ladies never need to *lay a cable.*

poof dust *n.* Phrase used by schoolboys to describe talcum powder in the days before there was such a thing as diversity training.

poof paw *n. medic.* Mysterious and debilitating physical condition whereby, upon waking, one experiences a lack of grip-strength and manual dexterity sufficient to open one's breakfast ales.

poof's pizza *n.* Quiche. Also *puff's pizza.*

poofter *n. Aus.* An Australian man who doesn't want another ten pints.

poogasm *n.* The shiver of satisfaction that a chap gets when he knows he's got a cup of tea in one hand, a new copy of the *Autotrader* in the other, and he's just about to unleash a *yard of ale* out of his *arse.*

poogle *v.* To look something up on an i-phone whilst ensconced on the *shit pot. 'What are you doing in there, dear?' 'Out in a minute, love. I'm just poogling the symptoms of irritable bowel syndrome.'*

poogina *n.* A lady's back *front bottom.*

poo horn *n.* The kitchen utensil kept by the *chod bin* for easing *pan-blocker*s round tight-fitting U-bends, *eg.* Bread knife, scissors, egg whisk. *'Nip upstairs and fetch the poo horn down, will you love? The kids want an omelette.'*

pooligan *n.* One who habitually *dumps his guts* in the *chod bins* of friends, family or casual acquaintences without giving a second's thought to the social embarrassment that the fallout from his actions will cause.

pools for stools *euph. medic.* Descriptive of a patient who is suffering from the *Engelberts.*

poolystyrene *n.* One of them eager little brown fragments of buoyant *crap* that has broken away from the *mother shit* of a previous *chod bin* occupant, and simply cannot be flushed away.

poomerang *n.* A *turd* which is able to return from the U-bend with twice the force with which it was flushed away in the first place.

poon *n.* *Fanny, crumpet, toosh.* '*I guess, this means my poon days are over.*' (Abraham Lincoln after his inauguration in May 1776). '*Knickers off, this is poon city!*' (Bill Clinton after his inauguration in June 1993).

poond *n.* A *gunt*, a *fupa.* From the Geordie "a poond o' tripe".

poonder *v.* To mull things over on the *throne*, perhaps whilst reading the *Autotrader.*

pooning *n.* The act of sniffing ladies' bicycle seats.

poontang 1. *n.* A *clopper.* 2. *n.* Some *clopper.*

poo packer *n.* A *stylish* chap.

poop catchers *n.* Knickers, dunghampers, bills.

poop chute *n.* *The bumhole, arse,* up which parking tickets can be rammed.

poop deck *n.* The floor of the house upon which the bathroom is situated.

poop hoop *n.* The back door of the *dirt bakery*, through which the *burnt chocolate cakes* are ejected.

pooping cough *n.* *medic.* A highly debilitating smoker's condition which, when coughing severely whilst *heavily refreshed*, causes one to *soil* one's own *rompers.* 2. *n.* Clearing one's throat melodramatically whilst ensconced in a public lavatory cubicle, in order to disguise the shameful fact that one is having a *shit.*

poo pourri *n.* The stench of feculant, masked by the use of cheap air freshener. A *Burberry shitbomb.*

poo preview *n.* An *air buffet*, a *mariner's chart.*

poornography *n.* *Grumble* of a core which is somewhat less than tumescent. The sort of soft-focus cotton wool-strength *grot* broadcast on Bravo, Virgin 1, or on Channel 5 in the old days before they started doing primetime *farmyard pig wanking.* (From poor + nography).

poor sense of direction, have a *v.* Of a man, to be *good with colours.*

poosex *n.* A charming word for *brown love.*

poosticks *n.* Game whereby lolly sticks are inserted into *barkers' eggs* by curious children. "*What are you doing?*" squeaked Piglet excitedly. '*I'm pushing a lolly stick into a dog shit,*' replied Christopher Robin.' (from *When we Were Alive* by AA Milne).

poot 1. *v.* To sound one's *botty bugle*, often after eating *musical vegetables.* 2. *n.* A *flies' dinner gong.*

poo tea *n.* An unrefreshing brown infusion made by allowing *logs* to brew in the pot for a long time. *PG shits.*

poot flute *n.* *Trouser trumpet, singing ring, cornhole cornet, swannee whistle.*

pooter *n.* The *bum* bellows with which you *poot.* The *poot flute.*

pootube *n.* The flue on a *Dutch oven.* A tunnel created by the strategic lifting of part of the duvet, the purpose of which is to control the flow of *carbon dibaxide* in whichever direction a *benefactor* wishes.

poove *n.* A *crafty butcher.*

poovert *n.* A poo pervert or *scat man.* A

"My God!' the boatswain cried. 'What has happened to the ship?' 'The Pequod has been stove in by a Leviathan, a Great White Whale!' replied the helmsman, scarce able to comprehend the enormity of his own words. 'Rat's cocks,' yelled Ahab. 'That's fucking torn it!'' ~ *Moby Dick* by Herman Melville.

crothers. Usually a German, if truth be told. From poo + pervert.

poovery *n.* *Bottery* and everything associated therewith. *Bumcraft.*

pop *n.* *Poo.* A word used to great effect by Adam & Joe off of the radio. *'Who's just walked this dog pop in on their shoes?'*

POP/pop *acronym.* Post Orgasmic Piss. *'Thanks for the fuck, your Majesty. I'm just nipping to the lavvy for a pop.'*

pop a knocker *v.* Of a lady, to overreact to a situation in a melodramatic fashion. *'Christ, love, it was only a chewie off your sister. There's no need to pop a knocker.'*

popazogalou *n.* A *chewie*, a *gobble*, a *blow job*. From the name of the landlord in the film *Personal Services* who accepted payment in kind.

popemobile *n.* Sexual position favoured by members of the *dogging* community. With the front seats folded fully flat, the man lies on his back and the woman sits atop him in the *reverse cowboy* position. Through the steamed-up National Health spectacles of the casual passer-by *wanking* in his trousers, her erotic gyrations resemble nothing so much as the pontiff waving to the adoring crowds from behind the two-inch-thick bullet-proof glass of his trademark automobile.

Pope's swear box, the *euph.* Something that has little or no contents. *'I can't come out this weekend, Paul. I've got less money than the Pope's swear box.'*

Popeye 1. *n.* Term used to describe the gagging noise a woman might make during a particularly vigorous *Boris Johnson*. 2. *n.* The state of a lady being airtight in all orifices. From the eponymous spinach-chomper's pre-punch-up catch-phrase "That's all I can stands and

I can't stands no more."

Popeye eating spinach *sim.* To engage in enthusiastic *cumulonimbus*. With a pipe in one's mouth. *'And the husband of Bathsheba did venture forth for Regal Super Kings that numbered two score and did leave Bathsheba alone in the tent. And David did enter the tent and did know Bathsheba. And David did kneel before Bathsheba, and lo, he did go at it like Popeye eating spinach.'* (from *The Book of Clive* 6:3-5).

Popeye's laugh *n.* The involuntary, guttural, gagging noise made by a *fellatrix* who has *bitten off more than she can chew.* Coined due to the sound's similarity to the one-eyed, pipe-chomping, grotesquely-distended-forearmed, spinach-powered cartoon sailor's trademark "uggugguggugg" guffaw. A *French cough.*

Popeye wipe *n.* The first, agonising attempt at a spot of *ringpiece* polishing after one has *dropped* a quantity of unruly, *screaming Mexican kids off at the pool.* From the resulting adoption of a facial expression resembling that of the popular spinach-chomping, one-eyed cartoon schizophrenic.

pop her cork *v.* To give a lady an organism. Presumably by shaking her up and down for twenty seconds and then pushing her *clit* up with your thumbs.

poppycock *exclam.* Nonsense, bollocks. *'I just seen Amy Winehouse at the bar buying a soft drink.' 'Poppycock.'*

pop shot *n.* Scene in a *grumble flick* in which a male actor is required to splash his *population paste* for the camera, after being suitably prepared by the *fluffer.* A *money shot.*

pop the brown champagne *v.* To uncork

one's *rusty bullet hole* the morning after a night spent over-indulging oneself on booze, 'babs and chilli sauce. *'I'm feeling a bit better now, but fuck me, the first visit after I got up was like popping a bottle of brown champagne, I tell you. Meanwhile, over to Daniel Corbett for tomorrow's weather.'*

pop the turkey in the oven *v.* To pluck the feathers from one's penis and put it in a vagina at gas mark six, prior to getting one's father-in-law to cut it into slices. To *fuck*.

population paste *n. Joy gloy*, semen, *spunk, Aphrodite's evostick, jazz glue, prick stick.*

pop-up book *n.* A special type of reading matter where things magically spring into three dimensions as one leafs through the pages. *A bongo mag, art pamphlet, DIY manual.*

pop-up box *1. n.* Something utterly *shit* which cannot be avoided on the internet. *2. n.* Something utterly smashing which can be seen on the internet. A prominent ladies' pubular mound. Also known as a *proud Mary, beetle bonnet or pigeon's chest.*

pop-up panic *n.* The bowel-loosening fear that comes from having to hurridly close down internet *grumble* sites one has been ogling due to the impending approach of a boss, spouse, parent or policeman, only to be suddenly assaulted by a barrage of obscene pop-ups that multiply the more one tries to delete them.

pop-up pirate *1. n.* A game where one wrong move could cause the *one-eyed fella* to spring up out of his *barrel. 2. n.* Likewise, a *stonk on.*

pop your cherry *v.* Lose your virginity, *break your duck.*

porcelain beard *n.* The stray *pubes* that befringe a public urinal.

porcelain tingle *n.* The cold shock that occurs when one's *bell end* touches the lavatory pan when sitting on the *throne.* A *harprick.*

pork *1. v. Aus.* To *fuck. 'I couldn't pork her because she had the painters in.' 2. n. Aus.* The *spam javelin.*

pork 'n' stalk *n.* A lady with whom one has had a whirlwind one-night romance, who continues to bombard one with texts, phone calls and cooked pets. A *bunny boiler.*

pork and beans *adj.* A term to describe a *happy shopper*, or *Betty Both*. One who *bowls from both the pavilion and the members' end. Half rice, half chips. 'Birthdays: David Bowie, formerly pork and beans, now just beans, singer, 56 today.' (The Times* Jan 8th, 2003).

pork pie jelly *n.* Any lubricant that is applied to the *meat* in order to ease its insertion into the *hairy pie, eg.* KY jelly.

pork pie that's been trodden on *euph.* An *untidy slice. A ripped sofa, stamped bat, butcher's window, ragman's coat.*

pork pills *n. pharm. Cock drops, blueys. Viagras, Bongo Bill's banjo pills.*

pork prescription *1. n.* A *bacon bazooka*, to be swallowed twice a day instead of meals. *2. n.* Doctor's authorisation for a *meat injection.*

pork scratchings *n. medic.* Irritation of the *old chap* as a result of a misguided liaison with a promiscuous lady. A *dose. 'Excuse me, barman. But have you got pork scratchings?' 'Yes. I got them when I fucked your missus under the pier last week'.* (Bamforth's *Seaside Chuckles* postcard by Donald McGill, 1926).

pork stork *n*. *'Dad, where do babies come from?' 'The pork stork, son.'*

pork sword *n*. Penis, *tallywhacker, lamb cannon*.

Porky Pig, do a *v*. In the spirit of the stuttering, porcine Warner Bros. cartoon character, to walk or drive around town wearing only a shirt - with no trousers or underwear of any kind.

pornado *n*. The situation where a computer user's desktop gets taken over by erotic pop-ups which are opening faster than he can close them.

pornbroker *n*. The man at work who can be relied upon to lend you a bit of *mucky* to see you through hard times. A *porn-meister*, a *jazz magnate*.

porn buddy *n*. A *cliterary executor*. A single fellow's best friend who, in the event of his untimely death, is charged with the important task of removing and disposing of the deceased's stash of *grumble* before his grieving parents arrive to search through his effects for touching mementoes and stuff to put on eBay. If former Poet Laureate and life-long jazz enthusiast Philip Larkin's *porn buddy* had managed to carry out the Hull University librarian's final wishes, it is estimated that the resulting bonfire of hardcore *art pamphlets* would have been visible from the Moon.

porn cocktail *1. n*. In certain "niche" areas of saucy film making, a beverage concocted from the mingled *tadpoles* and *man mayonnaise* of a number of male performers which is ingested with a limited amount of relish by the female lead. *2. n*. Residue found on the bed-sheets of frustrated teenagers.

porner shop *n*. A small retail establishment which, despite intense competition from the internet, continues to purvey paper-based masturbatory materials in defiance of all economic principles. *'I'm just off to the porner shop, Dave. Do you want anything?' 'Aye Morwenna. Get me twenty Benny Henny, a bag of Monster Munch and this month's Face Squatting Femmes.'*

porn flakes *n*. The crusty bits found on the sofa/sheets the morning after a late night *scruff video* session.

porn flour *n*. Any powdery substance used for the purpose of locating the wet parts on a larger lady. *'I'm off out with big Janice from accounts tonight.' 'Good luck, mate. Don't forget to take a bag of porn flour.'*

porn fuzz *n*. Characteristic picture quality of an 18th generation *bongo vid*. *Readybrek glow*.

porn glare *n*. The cruel, frustrating shaft of light which partially obscures the spreadeagled *bird* on the double page spread of an *art pamphlet* as the victim strives for *vinegar*. *Razzle dazzle*.

pornhography *n*. *Grumblular* entertainment featuring female participants of notably poor quality.

porn horn *n*. A three-quarters-hard erection regularly seen being fed into the models in *scud films*. An *Indian rope prick*.

pornithologist *n*. One who enjoys looking at pictures of *birds* rather than going out and looking at them in the flesh. A *cock twitcher*.

pornithology *n*. The scientific study of two *birds at it like fucking knives*. *Lesbology*.

porn mauve *n*. Distinctive colour assumed by all male genitalia in *grumble vids*, although rarely if ever seen in real life.

porn mirage *n.* A cruel trick of the light, whereby a *tug*-hungry adolescent spots some *grummer* under a hedge, which on closer inspection turns out to be an Argos catalogue or the *Sunday Mirror* TV guide.

pornogamy *n.* Amongst impoverished gentlemen, the practice of remaining continuously faithful to the same dog-eared *seed catalogue* for all their sexual and emotional needs.

pornoisseur *n.* A gentleman who appreciates only the finest things in one-handed life.

porno mouth *n.* A young lady whose coital utterances closely resemble the dialogue from *grumble flicks, eg.* "Split me in two with your big cock" *etc.*

porn on the fourth of July *sim.* Temporary Tom Cruise-style male lower body paralysis that occurs when attempting to stand up to turn off the video after loosing off several rounds from the *mutton musket.*

pornorama *n.* A magnificent, breathtaking array of *meat mags,* arranged in a vista to provide variety and spectacle whilst having a *tug.* A *wank crescent, glandscape.*

porno star, take it like a *phr.* Conciliatory and sympathetic expression uttered to one who has suffered poor luck, but needs to draw a line under it and carry on, *ie.* "Take it on the chin". *'Don't worry Gordon, some time we all have to take it like a porno star. There'll be other opinion polls.'*

pornowhack *n.* The act of entering an obviously filthy expression into Google, but unaccountably returning no "hits".

porn penguin *n.* A brisk, comical waddle across the living room in order to pause, rewind or fast forward through the plot-related bits of a *tug film* when the batteries have failed in your remote.

porn sacrifice *n.* A poorly-hidden stash of low-quality *grumble* designed to put your missus off the scent of the *export strength* stuff. A *blue herring, stalking horse.*

porn trauma *n.* Upon reaching the *vinegar strokes* whilst watching an *art film* and finding the screen suddenly filled by a big, sweaty bloke with large sideburns, being too late to stop, and *gwibbling* to a disappointing finish. See *vinegar Joe.*

pornucopia *n.* A seemingly endless supply of *jazz, eg.* On the top shelf of the magazine rack at Barton Park lorry services on the A1.

porn ultimatum *1. n.* The point at which the newsagent tells you to stop browsing and either buy a *bongo book* or get out of his shop. *2. n.* A pact made between two friends that each of them will clear his counterpart's house of any stashed adult material in the event of his death, in order to save the blushes of bereaved family members, ex-wives, the police *etc.*

porn vortex *n.* A whirling fifth dimension where time has no meaning, encountered when browsing the worldwide web for *left-handed websites.* One could fall into a *porn vortex* and emerge ten minutes later to discover that three days have elapsed.

porpoise nose *n.* Like a *turtle's head,* but a bit more urgent. And making a clicking sound.

porridge gun *n.* Tool for distributing *population paste* quickly and efficiently.

PORT/port *abbrev.* A politically correct term for a *bird* with small *tits.* Person

Of Restricted Tittage, *eg.* Thirsty wine *gobshite* Jilly Goulden.

port and starboard scran spanners *n. naval.* Knife and fork.

portion *n.* A large but non-specific quantity of *the other*, of the sort that Max Miller might talk about having. See also *one, a length, a bit. 'I'd give her a portion, and no mistake.'*

Portsmouth Harbour *euph.* The arrival of an attractive female and her ugly friends, in the style of a sleek ocean liner coming into port surrounded by a flotilla of tugboats.

Portuguese breakfast *n.* A hearty bowlfull to start the day. A watery, clotted *shit* that resembles the sort of thing they'd probably eat over there.

Portuguese man o' war *1. n.* Name given to a buoyant jelly-fish, *Physalia atlantica,* characterised by the presence of one or more large air-sacs, by means of which it drifts about on the surface of the ocean. *2. n.* Swimming shorts so inflated with poisonous *carbon dibaxide* that they float above the surface of the pool, causing alarm to fellow swimmers.

posharean *n. medic.* In obstetrics, a Caesarean section performed for no other reason than to keep the mother's *twat* nice and tight.

posh wank *n.* A *mess*-free masturbatory manoeuvre undertaken whilst wearing a *jubber ray.*

post-it over the webcam, put a *v.* To take an elementary precaution when surfing the web, in order to prevent other internet users from inadvertently seeing you grappling with your *joystick.*

postman's arse *n. medic.* Condition caused by chronic chaffing of the *bum cheeks* and thus characterised by a painful red ring around the *tea towel holder* which afflicts those whose working day involves much walking and sweating.

potato fat *n.* The starchy gloop that issues from a gentleman's *spuds* when he mashes them a bit. *Spunk, tattie watta, spud juice.*

pot brown *v.* To sink a long *pink* into the *herbert pocket.*

potch *v. Wales.* To partake of an extra-marital affair in the valleys. *'See that Jones the song? Well he's been potching for years, isn't it, Look you, boyo, bach?'*

potholer *n.* An adventurous *mud child,* one end of which is connected to your *chuff* whilst the other has made its way round the U-bend, where its head pokes out through the meniscus in the trap, like a small, blind Loch Ness Monster. Also known as a *bumbilical.*

Pot Noodle horn *n. Brewer's droop.* A *cock like a wet noodle.*

pot pink *v.* To moor the *skin boat* in *cod cove.*

Potsdamer Platz *1. n. prop.* Area of no-man's land between dour, communist east and capitalist fun-loving west Berlin. *2. n.* The area of *no-man's land* between a lady's dour, communist *arse* and capitalist fun-loving *minge.* The *butfer, carse, tinter, taint, notcher, snarse, biffin bridge, Humber Bridge, niftkin's bridge etc. Checkpoint Charlie.*

potter's wheel *1. n.* A thick, convoluted *blurtch,* sagging under its own weight such that it resembles a trouser-suited *joskin*'s attempt to throw a clay pot on the *Generation Game* in about 1975. *2 n.* Situation where a man carefully attempts to nurture a relationship with a lady over a period of time, only to ruin all his hard work by *copping a feel* too early. The *baker's impatience.*

pottyfingers *n.* An inarticulate person who only shows up their lack of vocabulary by resorting to bad language when texting or writing emails, *eg.* Giles Coren.

potty-mouth *n.* US. A sweary *cunt.*

potty slot *n.* The *bum crack, bottom line.*

pouch *n.* An ageing, saggy *mott* that hangs between the legs like a sporran.

pound the pork *v.* Of *pinksmiths*, to pummel a hot *pork sword* into shape. *Pound the pudding.*

pouring Pot Noodle *adj.* Producing an unappetizing, runny *poo*, though not quite unappetizing and runny enough to be described as Cup-a-Soup.

power ballad *n.* An *Elvis killer* of such colossal girth that, as it is passed, the victim raises his clenched fist into the air and pulls a face which calls to mind that of the lead singer of Boston during the chorus of *More than a Feeling.* A *Meatloaf's daughter.*

power cake *n.* A turbo-charged *cupcake* which is unleashed in front of an electric fan.

powerwank *n.* A brisk, efficient *tug* slotted into a busy work schedule. Often performed by politicians, captains of industry and de Vere Hotels bar staff on a fag break.

pox *n.* Venereal disease, specifically syphilis. *Cock rot, clap.*

prairie dogging *v.* Of an *arse*, to have a stool poking in and out like an inquisitive gopher checking to see if the coast is clear. A moving *turtle's head.*

prairie wind 1. *n.* 2005 album by warblesome country rocker Neil Young; a moving song cycle of dreams, memories, family ties and the passage of time, if you will. 2. *n.* A gently sulphurous zephyr that softly rustles the *arse cress* as it wafts across the barren *flies' graveyard.*

pram face *n.* A famous woman, perhaps a pop star or TV presenter, whose face would more suitably adorn a young mother pushing a pram around a council estate, for example misunderstood *Celebrity Big Brother* multiculturalist Jo O'Meara.

pram fat *n.* *Plum sauce, heir gel, baby gravy.*

pramland 1. *n.* A shop on Hull's Holderness Road that sells baby paraphenalia. 2. *n.* Hull's David Lister School, whose pupils are allegedly amongst *1*'s biggest customers.

pranny *n.* Fool, *arsehole, twat.* A form of insult popular amongst The Troggs pop group during recording sessions in the 1960s. Also *prannet.*

prat 1. *n.* The *buttocks* of the *fundament* of the *arse.* 2. *n.* A *pranny, fuckwit, arsehole.* A doltish sort.

prawn *n.* A girl with a fit body, but an ugly face. From the edible crustacean, where the body is tasty, but the head is thrown away. A *bobfoc.*

prawn crackers *n.* The crispy tissues found beneath the bed. *Popshottadoms.*

prawn penknife *n.* A more diminutive version of a *pork sword*, possibly incorporating a small tool for removing stones from seahorses' hooves.

prawn sandwich 1. *n.* Delicacy as famously served in the Directors' Boxes at Old Trafford. 2. *n.* A lady being *roasted* by a pair of poorly-endowed professional footballers.

prebound *n.* Realising your current relationship is doomed, the act of beginning another one before finishing your old one, the better to facilitate a smooth changeover of services.

Precious McKenzie *n*. A small, but nonetheless very powerful, erection, capable of cleaning and jerking many times its own bodyweight. Named after the small, but nonetheless very powerful, Commonwealth Games gold medal-winning weightlifter of the 1970s.

pre-cum *n*. Substance often referred to in the letters pages of *jazz mags* but rarely mentioned elsewhere. Certainly not on *You and Yours* on Radio 4. *Perseverance soup, dew on the lily, ball glaze.*

pre-emptive strike *n*. The act of emptying one's *shot pouch* a couple of hours before going into action so as to make the ensuing battle last a bit longer.

predator's face *n*. A somewhat unsettling vagina, which you would nevertheless not mind swinging a stout length of *wood* into.

preek *n. medic.* That fluid which is secreted from the *bishop's mitre* before *spoffage*, to lubricate the *gut stick*. *Ball glaze, tatty watter.* A contraction of *pre-cum*.

prefer one's peas minted *euph*. To be a *pastry chef*. Alluding to one who *fumbles spuds*.

pregnot *adj*. Of a lady, to look like she's *up the duff* when she is, in fact, just *big-boned*. Particularly the stomach bone. *Gregnant.*

prehab *n*. That extended period of being *heavily refreshed* which typically precedes a stopover in the Priory.

premature pinch *n*. The snipping off of an unsmoked *bum cigar* when disturbed in the act, by an important telephone call for example, or a fucking Jehovah's Witness knocking on the fucking door.

prem de la crème *n. Fr.* One who is *up and over like a pan of milk.*

prepare for the wurst *exclam*. A romantic imprecation uttered to a lady by a gentleman just before he *slams in the lamb*.

prepare yesterday's lunch *v*. To go for a *shit*.

present from Margate, a *euph*. Any inanimate object which is introduced into the *back passage*. From the famous medical case of an unfortunate gentleman who was admitted to hospital with a pepperpot stuck up his *arse*, presumably following an incident involving falling backwards whilst dressed in a loose-fitting dressing gown. The medical record apparently stated: "On removal, the object was found to be inscribed with the words ' A Present from Margate'."

pressed ham *n*. The effect achieved by pushing one's naked *buttocks* onto the photocopier at the office Christmas party.

pressing matter *n*. An urgent *tom tit*. 'No time to open the new parliamentary session today, I'm afraid, Lord Chancellor. I've got a pressing matter to attend to. By the way, you haven't seen this week's Autotrader anywhere, have you?'

press the devil's doorbell *v*. To *flick the bean*.

presuptual agreement *n*. Legally-binding drinking itinerary agreed at the beginning of an evening, *eg*. "Right, so we start at the red Lion, go on to the White Horse and finish at the Miner's Arms before having a magnificent Ruby Murray at the Curry Capital." As is the case with its ante-matrimonial contract counterpart, a presuptual agreement typically ends in a vicious fight and a costly court appearance.

prick *1. n.* A penis. *2. n.* A *twat, fuckwit,* fool. *3. n.* A life-threatening finger injury often suffered by fairy tale princesses. *4. n.* A small doctor with a hypodermic syringe on a seaside postcard.

prick-stick *n.* A white DIY glue in a handy tubular dispenser used solely to stick the pages of an *art pamphlet* together. *Man mastic.*

prick tease *n.* A woman who goads one's *knob* by calling it names.

priest's hole *1. n.* A cramped hiding place, usually behind the fireplace or under the floor in a large 17th century house, where fugitive Catholic clergymen could be concealed from the authorities. *2. n.* A choirboy's *nipsy.* *3. n.* A *minge* that's a tight squeeze. A *paper cut, pinhole, mouse's ear.*

pudcast *n.* A spot of *Frankie Vaughan* downloaded onto a video iPod.

primarni *n.* The sort of extremely cheap off-the-peg/floor clothing that makes no bones about its lowly origins. *'What do you think of my new suit? It's primani. Only cost one ninety-nine.'*

pringle *1. n.* Yet another word for one who sniffs bicycle seats. A *snufty, snurglar, barumpher.* *2. v.* To reach the point, when drinking, when one knows, realises and accepts that one is going to continue drinking until becoming unconscious. From the famous eponymous saddle-shaped crisp advertising slogan, *viz.* "Once you pop, you just can't stop". *'We're on air in five minutes. Where's Moira?' 'I saw her in the bar at lunchtime, but she was already pringling then. Best see if you can find Huw instead, he's only had a couple.'*

Pringle piss, have a *v.* To go for your inaugural first *wee* of the night when out on the ale, thus opening the floodgates to a lavatory visit every five minutes. From the previously mentioned ad tagline for the popular crisps which come in a cylindrical cardboard bag. To *break the seal.*

prison pussy *n.* The *anus, mud pussy.*

prison vision *n. medic.* A condition brought on by prolonged abstinence from female company, which causes the sufferer to lower his standards considerably, finding almost any woman attractive. *Porridge goggles, Camp X-ray specs. 'When I came out after 27 years of predominantly solitary confinement, I was suffering from terrible prison vision. Shortly after my release, I remember being entertained by Her Majesty the Queen at Buckingham Palace, and getting a bit of a chirp-on when her mum bent over to pat a corgi. Truly, incarceration is a terrible thing.'* (from *The Long Walk to Freedom* by Nelson Mandela).

private fur *n.* A lady's *secret squirrel.*

privates *1. n.* Inoffensive unisex term for genitalia invented by the Women's Institute in 1904. At the opposite end of the rudeness scale to *fuckstick, hairy bollocks* and *cunt.* *2. n.* A double entendre enabling *Carry On* scriptwriters to confuse low-ranking soldiers with their *meat and two veg.*

probe and drogue *n. RAF.* Repeated attempts, whilst drunk, to achieve penetration. Named after the mechanism used for in-flight refueling.

probo *n.* One who makes a very comfortable living from vagrancy. A professional *Harold Ramp* with a mobile phone and a Rolls Royce parked round the corner, of the sort only ever encountered by the puce-faced letter-writers in the *Daily Mail.*

procrasturbation *1. n.* The act of repeated, and often pleasureless *self-love* brought on by the need to stave off more weighty tasks. *'For heaven's sake, Lester, stop procrasturbating and get your tax return filled in.'* *2. n.* The situation whereby a man is keen to partake in an *act of personal pleasure*, but is nevertheless entirely unable to decide which *bongo flick* or *grumble mag* to use for inspiration.

prodworthy *1. adj.* Of a fortunate young lady, deemed suitable for sexual relations by a man. *2. n. prop.* Ironic surname of the feminist Councillor played by June Whitfield in the film *Carry On Girls*.

profanigram *n.* The sort of selection of consonants and vowels which it would be nice to see Rachel Riley pull out during the letters round of *Countdown, eg.* Ssipflasp, rowneyeb *etc.*

professional outdoorsman *n.* A Ray Mears-type who drinks metal polish. A *Harold Ramp.*

Professor Pissflaps *n. prop.* An epithet given to a female who thinks she is more intelligent than the average bloke, *eg.* Any *bird* who turns up on *Newsnight Late Review. 'Alright, Professor Pissflaps, you've had your say. Let some fucker else get a word in edgeways.'* (David Dimbleby to Germaine Greer, *BBC Question Time,* March 2002).

Professor Plum *1. n.* The purple-bodied player in a game of *Cluedo. 2. n.* The purple-headed player in a variety of bedroom games.

proles' royce *n.* A stretch limousine with a screeching gaggle of drunken teenage girls hanging out of the window.

prolog *1. n.* The *turtle's head. 2. n.* A small *Sir Douglas* which is strategically expelled, thus allowing the passage of its much more serious and significant big brother in the near future.

promance *n.* The sort of semi-regular relationship enjoyed with a specific *lady of the night.*

promise to oneself, on a *euph.* Of a gentleman, to be anticipating a spot of *rhythmic relaxation. 'Where are you off to, Otis? I thought we were going badger baiting.' 'Sorry lads, but I'm on a promise to myself.'*

promosexual *n.* One who is unnecessarily forward in promoting the fact that *he knows what's in his flowerbeds.* Characterized by an unwelcome excess of exaggeratedly camp behavior. One who is forever banging on about being *good with colours.*

proof of purchase *n.* The sort of expensive, showy jewellery and expensive, showy vehicles bought for nubile blonde *pieces* by professional footballers.

prostitrout *n.* A good time girl who needs a bloody good wash.

protein shake *1. n.* Thickly-textured sports drink, freshly-prepared to help young men build muscle mass, and thus *2. n.* Gloopy *splod*, made from *plums* and thus rich in *vitamin S.*

pro track *n. rhym. slang.* Skydiver slang for the *arsehole.* Named after some sort of helmet-mounted audible warning parachutist's altimeter thing which, it says here, can be set to bleep at any height between 0 feet and 10,000 feet. From pro-track dytter = shitter. *'It's terrible. I accidentally set the warning beeps to go off at 0 feet and broke my arms, legs, neck, back, pelvis, ribs and skull. I'm stuck in this full body cast for the next year at least, the doctor says. I even* *have to get the district nurse in twice a day to wipe me pro track. But on the plus side, I did raise eight pounds for the donkey sanctuary.'*

Proud Mary 1. *n.* A large Mississippi river boat. 2. *n.* A lady's pronounced pubic mound. The *mons veneris, grassy knoll.* 3. *n.* A *bird's bits* that *keep on burnin'.* A *clapped-up clapping fish.*

prune juice 1. *n.* Anal seepage. 2. *n. Mabel syrup.*

prunetang *n.* A lady of considerably advanced years who has, by some unearthly means or other, managed to remain a bit of a looker, *eg.* Catherine Deneuve, Ginger Spice, Margaret Beckett. A *gilf.* A witty corruption of *poontang,* an American word for *blart.*

pruning the roses *euph.* To have *hairache.* Once used by the late Brian Clough as an excuse for non-attendance at Nottingham Forest matches in the 1980s/90s.

psychedelic yodelling *n.* Vocal projection of a *rainbow* out your *gob.*

PTSD *abbrev. medic.* Partial Tug Stress Disorder. The mental confusion suffered by a gentleman whose wife unexpectedly arrives home from the shops ten minutes early, prematurely terminating his act of *self delight.*

pubcast *n.* An endlessly-repeated, dull, *pile of wank* story overheard by the unfortunate people who find themselves sitting near a public house bore as he regales each of his mates in turn with the same tale as they filter into the bar on a Friday night.

pube dude *n.* Schoolboy phrase used to describe the kid in the playground who had a hairy chest and 4 o'clock shadow by the age of twelve. *'Oi, Venables. Stop*

drawing on that desk at once or I'll send you to the headmaster's office, you annoying little pube dude.'

pube farmer *n.* An unemployed person. A *doley.*

pube in an afro, looking for a *sim.* A crude variation on "looking for a needle in a haystack". Also, *looking for a baw hair in an afro (Scot).*

pube lunch *n.* A tasty *bacon sandwich* with a token garnish of *gorilla salad,* served all day in a friendly atmosphere. *Cunch, fish dinner.*

pubic library *n.* An array of *flesh books* kept on top of a wardrobe for easy reference.

pubiquity *n.* The uncanny ability of stray strands of *gorilla salad* to turn up anywhere and everywhere, *eg.* On a bar of soap, between one's teeth, in the back of one's throat in the middle of the night, in McDonald's burgers, McDonald's chicken nuggets, McDonald's thick shakes *etc.*

public hair *n.* The *smurf beard* appearing on each side of an unshaven *bird's* bikini bottom. Also *Jimmy Edwards, Noddy Holders, thighbrows.*

pub scarecrow *n.* The inhabitant of one's boozer who has the uncanny ability to frighten away the *birds.*

pub singer *n.* A solo performer, grunting and yodelling in a cubicle whilst *laying a cable.*

pub terrier *n.* A breed of small, yappy, unpredictable, aggressive though not necessarily dangerous, man whose presence makes one feel oddly uneasy. Found in most public houses in Britain.

PUD/pud *acronym.* Post Urinal Drip. A *wet penny in the pocket.*

pud 1. *n.* The *willy.* That which was

always *pulled* by Ivor Biggun (aka Doc Cox of *That's Life* rude vegetable fame), in his *Wanking Song*. 2. *n.* An economically-drawn three-line graffito of the male genitalia.

pudding burner *n.* Slatternly lady who frequents pubs on a Sunday lunchtime when she should really be at home cooking a hearty traditional meal for her husband.

puddle, dropped in a *euph.* The state of a *bongo periodical* which has been subject to heavy and/or prolonged use. *'Christ. I wouldn't have lent you my Razzle if I'd have known it would come back in this state, George.' 'Yeah, I know. Sorry. I dropped it in a puddle. Of spunk.'*

puddle jumper *n.* A *fruit feeler, spud fumbler.*

pudendum *n.* Genital area. From Latin pudes = meat pie & dendum = two potatoes.

pudoku *n.* Any number puzzle that can be successfully completed on the toilet by a man in the time it takes him to *lay a cable.* About an hour-and-a-half, then.

pud-whapper *n. US. Wanker*, jerkwad, an obnoxious person.

puff 1. *v.* To exhale cigarette smoke. 2. *n. prop.* Magic dragon that lived by the sea. 3. *n.* A consumer *of fancy cakes.*

puff fluff *n.* An insufficiently-malodorous *dropped hat*, which calls the *farter's* sexual orientation into question. A *gaseous gay, botter burp.*

pugwash *n. Aus.* Cleaning of the teeth using *tapioca toothpaste* and a *naughty paintbrush.* A *blow job.*

puh-seh *n. US.* A *grumble flick* vagina. Something that a more-or-less tumescent *meat vid* thespian seems generally keen to stick his *hampton* up.

puke *v.* To spew, *yoff, shout soup.*

pull 1. *v.* To *tap*, pick up members of the opposite sex. *'I pulled last night.'* 2. *n.* A spot of *self improvement. 'I didn't pull, so I went home, watched the free ten minutes of the Fantasy Channel and had a bit of a pull.'*

pull a pint on the piss pump *v.* To pour oneself a 5ml *hand shandy.*

pullaby *n.* Something which, when accompanied by a rhythmical rocking motion, soon brings on a state of contented slumber.

pull a muscle *v.* To *relax in a gentleman's way* so much that you give yourself a limp.

pull a train *v.* To take turns at *stirring the porridge*, to participate in a *gang bang.*

pulled the ripcord *euph.* Descriptive of a once svelte lady who has sadly ballooned like an inflatable raft and turned into a *bed breaker.*

pulletariat *n.* That class of society principally engaged in *monomanual labour.* The plebian social stratum that lives alone and watches *sockumentaries* whilst awaiting news of gainful employment. *Doleys, pube farmers.*

pullfilment *n.* The tired yet satisfied feeling a chap has after spending an evening perusing *seed catalogues* or watching *socktator sports.*

pulling power *n.* The strength of one's *fanny magnetism.*

pull off 1. *v.* To manoeuvre a car away from the kerb. 2. *v.* To drag a drunken friend away from a fight in which he has the upper hand, usually whilst shouting "It's not worth it" or "Leave it, he's had enough". 3. *v.* To masturbate. *'I picked up a hitchhiker in and she offered to pull me off in my cab. I was so dis-*

gusted that I pulled over, strangled her and rolled her up in some carpet. Then I pulled myself off.'

pull out and pray *n.* A method of contraception that is also a test of faith. Birth control as used by people with dozens of children. *Vatican roulette.*

pull programme *n.* A *jazz magazine* or *boob brochure.*

pullseye *exclam.* Humorous ejaculation spoken by a fellow who has just successfully reduced his *bird's* field of vision by a factor of fifty percent.

pull the Pope's cap off *v.* To *bash the Bishop, box the Jesuit.*

pull the turkey's neck *v. Choke the chicken.* See *throttle the turkey.*

pull up to the bumper *v.* To *do* Grace Jones *up the shitter,* but only after she's asked you nicely.

pull your pud *1. v.* To *wank. 2. v.* To drag a dessert along in some sort of trailer.

pullympics *n.* Televised female sporting events that leave a certain type of male viewer in a somewhat more exhausted state than the participants, *eg.* Beach volleyball, ladies' tennis, nude mud wrestling on the Playboy channel.

PUMA/puma *acronym.* Pants Up My Arse. A specific reference to *cleftal* discomfort. *Hungry arse.*

pummel horse *n.* In a public house, that worn-out, leathery woman who is nevertheless accommodating to any of the regulars who fancy swinging their leg over her in return for a bag of Nobby's Nuts.

pump *v.* To *fart, poot, pass wind, shoot bunnies, drop a rose petal.*

pump action mottgun *n.* An advanced, rapid-fire development of the *mutton musket. twelve bore popshotgun.*

pumper's lump *n. medic.* The condition of enhanced right forearm muscle due to excessive *wanking. Arnie's arms, hairy pieceps.*

pumping up the tyres *v.* Involuntary movement of the leg during the *vinegar strokes. Elvis's leg, Elvis tremble.*

pump room *1. n.* In a spa town, such as Harrogate, Bath or Leamington, a place where invalids and murder mystery authors used to go in order to take the waters. *2. n.* Any designated area for the controlled release of noxious, sulphurous gases. The water closet. *'Excuse me, your holiness, I need to pop over to the pump room.'*

pump up the jam *v.* To take a *cranberry dip.* To *stir the paint.*

punami *n.* In a bar, a tidal wave of binge-drinking *flange* out on a *slag night.* From punani + tsunami.

punani *n.* A lady's bits and bobs.

punani granny *n.* A significantly older woman who is none the less still worth *one.* A *gilf, lulu.*

punch above one's weight *1. v.* In boxing, to come out on top in a bout with a superior fighter. *2. v.* Of a gentleman, to succesfully *woo* a young lady whom he might ordinarily consider to be out of his class, *eg.* Les Dennis *pulling* Amanda Holden, anyone at all *pulling* Charlotte Church, Shane MacGowan *pulling* anyone at all. To *curl one in.*

punch its head in *v.* What a gentleman does to his *gentleman* when *relaxing in a gentleman's way.*

punch the clown *v.* To make *custard* shoot out the top of *Charlie Cairoli's hat.* To *wank.*

punch the Spaniard *v.* To perform an act of *personal pollution.* To attempt to "knock Juan out".

punch up the whiskers *n*. A *knee trembler* or similar romantic encounter in a train lavatory, taxi queue, Radio 5 lift or Building Society doorway.

punish *v*. To put one's ladyfriend *to the sword* in an enthusiastic manner. To administer a few strokes of the *old walking stick* to a *bird* who wants it really.

punk cock *n*. A *hampton* adorned with multifarious piercings. A *knob* which is upsettingly bejewelled with chains, rings and pop rivets.

punks *rhym. slang*. Breasts. From punk rockers = knockers. '*Gonorrhoea was powerless to resist. His eyes burned into hers like topazzes. His strong arms enfolded her softly yielding body as she felt herself being swept away in a solar wind of passion. Before she had a chance to protest, he had whipped off her tit pants and started mucking about with her punks.*' (from *The Lady and the Powdered Egg Salesman* by Barbara Cartland).

punt from the Cambridge end *v*. To *stick your pole into the mud*, like they do in the Fens.

puppies *n*. *Bubbies*. Affectionate euphemism for *thru'penny bits*. Also *two puppies fighting in a bag*.

puppies' noses *n*. Little cold, wet nipples.

purple-headed womb broom *n*. See *purple-headed yoghurt warrior*.

purple-headed yoghurt warrior *n*. See *purple-headed womb broom*.

purple helmet 1. *n. Pink Darth Vader*'s headgear, *bobby's helmet, German helmet, Roman helmet, bell end*. 2. *n*. Any member of the former Rover Aerobatic display team.

purple pearler *n*. An extendable icing tool for decorating pink blancmanges.

purse *n*. A *snapper*

push gas *v*. To *poot, let rip*.

push her guts in *v*. To have sex with a lady. '*Oh Joan Hunter Dunn / With your strong legs in shorts / Your boyish good looks / Your excelling at sports / Your long golden hair / Your ruby red lips / Let me push in your guts / Twixt the council dump skips.*' (*Joan Hunter Dunn* by John Betjeman).

pushing a wet mattress up a spiral staircase, like *sim*. Phrase descriptive of the effort which has to be expended when trying to constipate a relationship with an unresponsive woman.

pushing sauce *v*. The stage of coitus immediately after the *vinegar strokes*, ie. When the *yoghurt truck* has *crashed* and is in the act of *tipping out its filthy concrete*. Ejaculation. '*Bond and Fanny Akimbo made love on the silken sheets of the mini-sub's bed. Suddenly, the videophone crackled into life and the face of M appeared, seated at his familiar Whitehall desk. 'Ah, there you are 007. We've had reports that Blofeld is planning to blow up China with a big ray gun,' he said excitedly. 'I'm afraid I have my hands rather full at the moment, Sir,' replied Bond, raising a quizzical eyebrow. 'Call me back in about 10 minutes after I've pushed me sauce and zuffled me charlie.*'' (from *Goldtops and Goldfingers* by Ian Fleming).

push the envelope 1. *v*. In test pilot circles, to test the aeronautical capabilities of a prototype aircraft. 2. *n*. In *pant shitting* circles, to *shit* one's *grundies*.

push through *n*. the consequence of buying "Economy Brand" *bumwad*. "*Would you care for another scone, Father Brown*', *asked Lady Chelmshurst*. '*Bless you, but thank you no,*' *replied the small priest, blinking owlishly and proffering a smelly digit towards his hostess's nose. 'I've just been to lay a cable and I fear I had a push through.*'" (from *Father Brown Points the Finger* by GK Chesterton).

pussy 1. *n*. Of erstwhile British TV sitcoms set in quiet, overstaffed department stores, a much-stroked pet cat frequently referred to by Mrs Slocombe. 2. *n*. Molly Sugden's *cunt*.

pussycat trolls *n*. A group of unattractive females.

pussy pelmet *n*. A short mini skirt, a *greyhound skirt*.

pussy poof *n*. A *todger dodger*, a *three wheeler*, a *tennis fan*. A lady who is *fond of walking holidays* in preference to having a penis pushed up her vagina.

put some fur around it *exclam*. A fellow's plaintive plea for help whilst attempting some sort of congress with his missus following a night *on the medicine*.

put the baby to sleep *v*. To administer the rocking action which is often required to get a restless *baby's arm* to settle down at night. Or at lunchtime. Or halfway through the afternoon, and again twice before tea-time for that matter.

put one's mind to other things *euph*. To *give it six nowt* on one's *old walking stick*. To masturbate. '*Once settled in my cell, and in some comfort, I put my mind to other things. Into a sock.*' (from *Borstal Boy* by Brendan Behan).

put the handbrake on *v*. To *hide your pride* during an act of *personal pollution* when rudely interrupted by an unwanted visitor, *eg*. Your mum, your granny, Noel Edmonds with a Gotcha! Oscar, the police, *etc*.

put the red lights on *v. naval*. To have a silent *wank* in bed so as not to disturb one's wife. Also *silent running, American beauty*. See *outrigger*.

putting from the rough *v*. Golfing equivalent of *bowling from the pavilion end*.

putting toothpaste back in the tube *sim*. Descriptive of the difficulties encountered when attempting sexual congress whilst less than fully tumescent. *Thumbing in a slacky, playing snooker with string, pushing a marshmallow in a moneybox.*

put to the sword *v*. To make love to. '*From the Charing Cross Theatre, where I saw Mr Herbert give his Death of Icarus, to tea with the French Ambassador, and thence home to bed whereupon I put Mrs Pepys to the sword before settling down to sleep.*' (from *The Diary of Samuel Pepys*).

putz *n*. A Yiddish *prick. Schlong*.

PWILF/pwilf *acronym*. An alluringly expectant young lady. Pregnant Woman I'd Like to Fuck.

pygmies' cocks *n*. Erect nipples. '*Did you see Sharron Davies on Olympic Grandstand? She had jockeys like pygmies' cocks.*'

pyjama glue *n*. A handy starch-based adhesive, particularly useful for bonding and stiffening cotton fabrics. Also good for sticking together the pages of *tit catalogues*, the wife's eyelids *etc*. *Prick-stick*.

pyroclastic flow *n*. In curryology, an explosive outburst in which dust, rock, lager, vindaloo and hot, sulphurous gas are ejected from one's *crinkly crater* at high temperature and speed.

pyroflatulate *v.* To light one's *farts*. See also *afterburner, blue streak*.

pyropastie *n.* Excrement wrapped in newspaper, then set alight on next door's doorstep in the hope that the occupant will stamp it out.

Pythagoras piss *n.* Ancient Greek act of trigonometrical urination performed such that one's forehead is propped against the lavatory wall, and one's rigid body consequently forms the hypotenuse of a right-angled triangle.

Pythonesque *1. adj.* Of humour, in the distinctive surrealist style of the groundbreaking programme *Monty Python's Flying Circus. 2. adj.* Of a gentleman's *parts, fucking* massive.

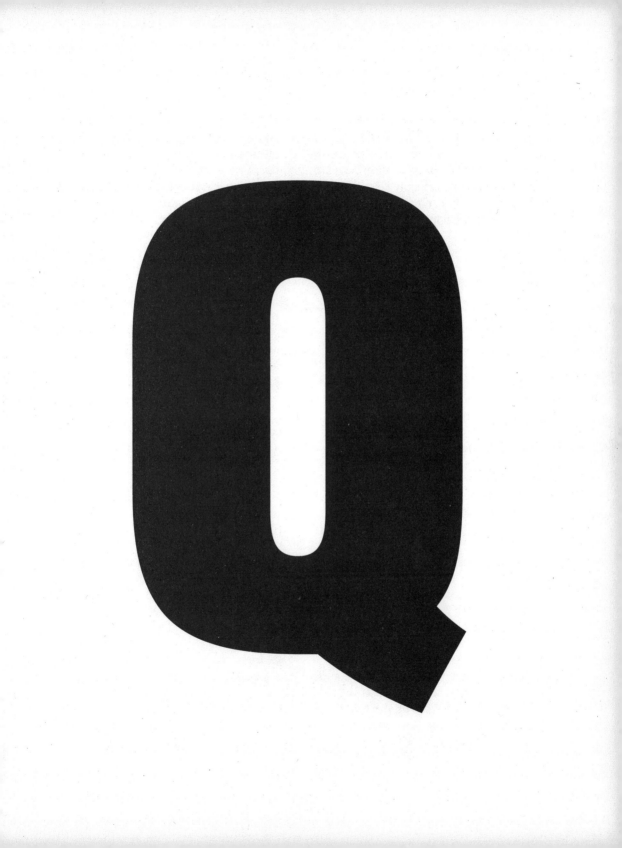

Q-tits *1. n. Fun bags* that are not what they appear to be, *ie.* Ones that have been artificially enhanced by the use of padded *tit pants,* leading to disappointment after *unwrapping the meat.* Derived from Q-ship, a term used to describe warships disguised as civilian vessels in 20th century naval warfare, so actually the opposite meaning if you think about it. *2. n. Knockers* that blow the wax out of your ears.

quack *n. onomat.* A sudden sound emanating from one's *bills* when one *steps on a frog.*

quackamole *n.* A smooth, greenish paste occasionally produced after an over-ambitious clearance of the *nether throat.* Not suitable for dipping nachos into.

quacker *n.* Poetic epithet for a lady's *garden of delight.*

quail *n.* A tasty young *bird* who's game for anything.

Quaker, to bury a *v.* To *lay a cable.* *'Do come in, Mr D'Arcy. Miss Bennet has just nipped upstairs to bury a Quaker. Would you care to wait in the drawing room until she has wiped her arse?'* (from *Pride and Prejudice,* by Jane Austen).

quakers *n. Oats.*

qualifications *n.* Breasts, *first impressions, competitive advantages. 'Admittedly her CV looks a bit thin, and her interview responses were somewhat lacklustre, but she has some excellent qualifications.'*

quality control *n.* The release of a small amount of *fart* to see how bad it is before releasing the rest. *Tasting the wine.*

quandong *1. n. Aus.* A difficult *lay,* a hard, as opposed to an easy, woman. One who wears armour-plated *knickers.*

2. n. A prostitute, *hooker, ho'.*

quantitative easing *1. n.* In economics, increasing a country's money supply by printing a pre-determined quantity of new money, which is then used by the government to buy debts off itself, or something. So that's all clear, then. *2. n.* Emptying one's *Simon Cowells* of a substantial build-up of toxic *feeshus. 3. n.* Discharging a pair of heavily-overloaded *bollocks* following a prolonged period of celibacy. *'Are you still in there, Sir Cliff? You're due in the Royal Box in less than thirty seconds to sing Congratulations to the Centre Court crowd.' 'I'll be with you in a moment, Sue. I'm just doing a spot of quantitative easing.'*

quantum wank *n.* An act of *personal pollution* performed whilst mentally re-living past sexual failures and "trying to right what once went wrong".

quarter pounder *1. n.* An unacceptably thin woman. *2. n.* An unacceptably fat *shit.*

quattro formaggio *1. n.* A pizza which has been topped with four different cheeses. *2. n.* A woman who has been topped with four different *knobcheeses.* A *plasterer's radio.*

quaynte *n.* Chaucerian *placket.*

quaz *n.* An ugly half-human *wanker,* a *bell end* ringer. Abbreviation of Quasimodo.

Quebec Bravos *n.* Metropolitan Police phonetic radio code. QBs = Quality Breasts, used by bored *scuffers* on Saturday night city centre duty. *'Calling all units, calling all units. Quebec Bravos in the High Street. Any units wish to assist? Over.'*

queef *n. Can.* A *Lawley kazoo,* a *hat dropped forward,* a *flap raspberry.* Also *kweef.*

queen *n*. A person who is raving *good with colours.*

Queen Amidala's lipstick *n. Chod bin* seat *skidmark* named after its resemblance to the *Phantom Menace* character's bizarrely-applied *gob* make-up.

Queen Mum's smile *n*. A *pan smile.* The staining on the lavatory carpet created by years of *pissing like an American pilot*

Queensway *n*. A regular mammoth rectal stock clearance where "everything must go". *Next sale.*

queer *1. adj. pre-1960.* Odd, peculiar. *2. n. post-1960.* A *spud fumbler 3. adj. post-1960. Colwyn Bay.*

queerdo *n*. A strange homosexualist, *eg.* Pete "Dead or Alive" Burns.

quiche *1. n. Taint, notcher, barse,* whatever. *2. n . Puff's pizza.*

quick, Carruthers, the net! We've found one! *exclam*. Humorous riposte to a *rectal retort.*

quick game of cup and ball *n*. The actions of a fellow getting into a *monkey bath, ie.* Lowering his *clockweights* slowly into the scalding water and then suddenly whipping them out again in the style of a Victorian child playing the repetitive nineteenth century parlour game.

quickie *n*. A swift bout of intercourse that one often fancies in the same way that one fancies a cup of tea. A hurried one. *'Oh, it's half time. Do you fancy a quickie, love?' 'Er... go on, then. But stick the kettle on first.'*

quick lick and a spit *1. n*. An effective personal hygiene procedure performed in the handbasin. A *gentleman's wash* or *vicar's bath. 2. n*. A somewhat rushed *Boris Johnson. 'Oh, alright then. But I'm reading the Shipping Forecast in ten minutes, so it'll just have to be a quick lick and a spit.'*

quick word from our sponsors, and now a *exclam*. A cheeky preface to an *arse jingle.*

quiff *n*. A bad smell emanating from an unwashed *quim.*

quigley *n*. A hairy *minge*. From the *biffer*-like moustache of film actor Tom Selleck in the film *Quigley Down Under.*

quim *n*. Refined word for the *mapatasi* such as a gentleman might use at a hay clarse cocktail party. From the Welsh Cwm = Valley beneath the 13 amp fuse wire.

quimbecile *n*. A stupid fellow who is also a *cunt, eg.* "Lord" Jeffrey Archer.

quimble *n*. A tremor of excitement in a *bird's snatch*. A *fanny gallop*. From quim + tremble.

quimbledon *euph*. Any ladies' sporting event watched by gentlemen who are paying precious little attention to the scores. *'Where's me socks, love? Maria Sharapova's playing Serena at Quimbledon.'*

quim bling *n*. Ladies' genital jewellery. *Mufflinks, curtain rings.*

quimby *n*. The middle person in a *threesome*, the filling in a sex sandwich. See also *lucky Pierre.*

quim chin *n. Muff mouth, cunty chops.* A bearded fellow. *'Did you see Noel Edmonds on telly last night? What a stupid fucking quim chin.'* (Ludovic Kennedy on *Did You See?* BBC2, 1983).

quim de la quim *n. Tussage* of the highest order. *'Well, that's the end of the evening dress section, and I think it's safe to say that the judges here at the Royal Albert Hall certainly have their work* *cut out tonight, because this year's contestants really are the quim de la quim. Now it's time for my favourite round, when we see them once again in their swimsuits, and I don't know about the viewers at home, but my cock's already got a bit of a twitch on and the girls haven't even come out yet.'* (Michael Aspel, presenting the *Miss World Show*, BBC1, 1974).

quiminals *n.* Prison lesbians. *Queen bees.*

quim pro quo *n. Lat.* An ancient Roman *blarter* system where goods and services are exchanged for *gash. Hairy cheque book.*

quimle *v. onomat.* To eat *hairy pie.*

Quimper *1. n. prop. Fr.* Town in Western France best known as the ancient capital of the Bretons, whoever they were. *2. n. onomat.* The barely audible moan made at the moment of first contact between a chap's *pork sword* and his ladyfriend's *landing gear.*

quimple *n.* One of them chin dimples that looks quite like a *fanny.* As sported by Martin Kemp, Kirk Douglas and Katie Melua. From Quite like a fanny + Dimple.

quim reaper *n.* A fellow who harvests more than his fair share of *meat harps.*

quimpotent *adj.* Descriptive of a frigid lady who is unable to reach the required level of sexual arousal required by a gentleman.

quims on rims *n.* Female cyclists; the hapless prey of the *snurglar.*

quim strings *n.* Imaginary internal female organs, resembling *Coronation Street* Deirdre's neck, that tighten in stress-ful situations. *'Bob Cratchit raised his glass. 'To Mr Scrooge, the founder of the feast', he said cheerily. 'Ha! Founder of the feast indeed,' screeched his wife. 'Why, I'll no sooner drink a toast to him that I would the devil himself, the mean-hearted, penny-pinching, tight-fisted old...' 'Now, now, Sara,' interrupted Bob. 'Don't go snapping your quim strings. It's Christmas day, and we shall drink to Mr Scrooge.''* (from *A Christmas Carol* by Charles Dickens).

quimwedge *v.* To *do it* with a lady.

quince *1. n. Aus.* A mincing *queen. 2. n.* Something that owls and pussycats eat with a runcible spoon.

quite happy to wait in the fudge queue *euph. Good with colours.* Said of a chap *with a penchant for craft fairs.*

quoasis *n.* Humorous epithet which can be applied to any popular music combo whose new songs sound exactly the same as their previous oeuvre.

quoit *n. Ring, hoop, rusty sheriff's badge, balloon knot, tea towel holder.* That which gets *tossed* on a ship.

quornography *1. n.* Softcore vegetarian pornography, *ie.* No *meat. 2. n.* Any photographic or video imagery where the principal female subject is gaining pleasure from using a *fanny hammer*, that is to say a "meat substitute".

quumf *v.* To sit in waiting outside a public library and take the opportunity to sniff ladies' bicycle seats as soon as possible after their owner has dismounted and gone inside. To *barumph, snurgle, moomph, scrunge.*

qwank *n.* A quick *wank.* Derivation unknown.

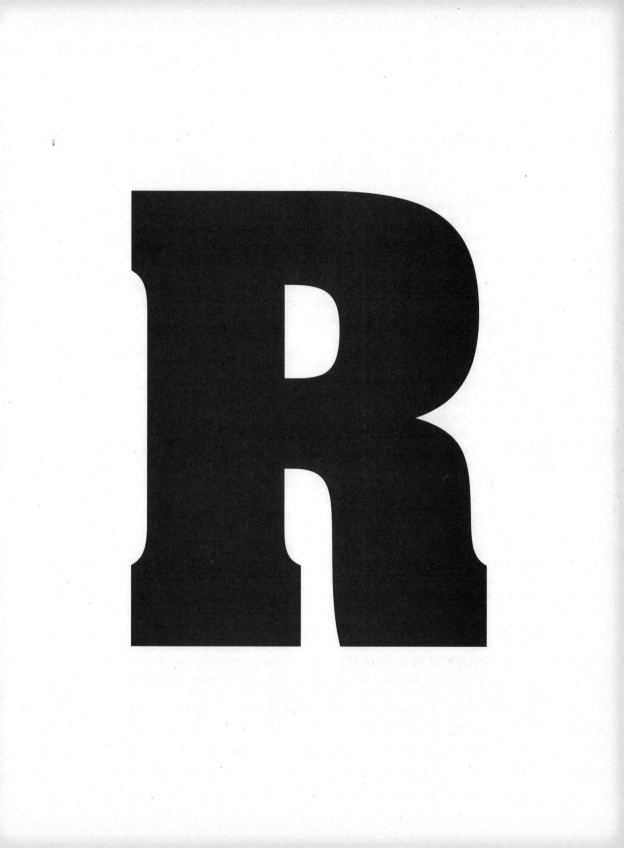

rabbit *n*. Her indoors, *giving it this*. Major cause of *GBH of the ear-hole*.

rabbit pie *n*. The *faff*.

rabbit's chops, arse like a *sim*. Descriptive of the unsettling twitching of the *blood orange* when one is in imminent need of an *Eartha*.

rabbit's nose, twitching like a *sim*. Descriptive of the behaviour of one's *gammon ring* following a particularly spicy *Pete Murray*.

rabbit's tail *n*. The split second flash of white cotton gusset caught in one's peripheral vision when a lady crosses her legs at the other side of a waiting room.

rabid dog, fanny like a *sim*. A *clown's pie, cappuccino twat, fish drowner*.

race snails *v*. Of a gentleman and former Conventry City manager, to drive very slowly close to the kerb in order to ask directions from a prostitute after becoming lost in a red light district.

racing dog's bollocks on a frosty morning *sim*. Descriptive of the state of one's eyes the morning after a heavy night *on the turps, eg*. Hungover dead chef Keith Floyd. *Eyes like sheep's cunts*.

rack *n*. Female mammarial display, collectively the *tits, funbags*. 'She's got a lovely rack on her. Very well presented. And nips like a fighter pilot's thumbs.'

rackattack *exclam*. Secret gentlemen-only phrase that can used to surreptitiously alert one's companions to an approaching feast of *eye magnets*. 'You join us here at the Munich Geschwimmgesch plashenpond as the contestants line up for the Ladies' Olympic 200m breast stroke final...Fuck me, rackattack!'

radar trap *n*. A hairy *fadge*, named after the popular speed enforcement devices of the sort often wielded by an over-zeal-ous *tithead* ensconced in the greenery, *ie*. "A cunt behind a bush".

Radcliffe *n*. A car that at first sight looks like a good runner, but ends up completely *fucked* at the side of the road after about fifteen miles.

Radcliffe, do a *1. v*. To fail to finish a pint. *2. v*. To give up three quarters of the way through a pub crawl, fall in a gutter, and have a bit of a cry.

radge *1. v*. To become furious, to lose one's *blob*. *2. n*. A furious episode that a person "takes" or "throws". *'This little bairn puked on us, so I took a fuckin' radge.'* (Mother Teresa of Calcutta). *3. n. adj*. In a state of *radge*.

radgey *n*. One who is predisposed to taking or throwing *radges*.

radio rental *rhym. slang. Radgy, hatstand*, mental, *Mabel*.

RAF *abbrev*. Rough As Fuck. Particularly ugly or unattractive.

RAFCAM/rafcam *acronym*. Rough As Fuck, Common As Muck.

rag and bone man *n*. One who doesn't mind getting a *barber's pole* now and again.

rag doll *n*. A tasty-looking *tart* that is temporarily *off the menu*.

ragman's coat *n*. A *turkey's wattle*, a *raggy blart*, a *pound of liver*, a *club sandwich*. An untidily-presented vagina.

ragman's trumpet *n*. A capacious *fanny. Big Daddy's sleeping bag*.

ragtop *1. n*. A convertible motor car. *2. n*. An uncircumcised *charlie, aardvark's nose*.

rag week *1. n*. Seven days during which students get *pissed* and behave like *cunts* in the name of charity. *2. n*. Time of the month when the *flags are out. Blob week*.

railbird 1. *n*. In poker, a non-participatory spectator at a game. 2. *n*. In a pub or club, a *heavily-refreshed* young lady who gives the impression that she has had a drink from every one of the optics on the rail behind the bar.

railway sleeper *n*. The largest, firmest and most angular *Thora* known to mankind, which makes a *dead otter* look like a minor *follow through*.

rainbow yawn *n*. *Puke*, a *technicolour laugh*, *pavement pizza*, a *sung rainbow*.

raindance *n*. The Native American-style rhythmical stamping moves made by the feet of one with a full *beer sack* as he tries to get his keys in the front door following a night *on the pop*.

rainman *n*. A woman with phenomenal mental capacity, who can commit to memory every single male misdemeanor committed throughout the duration of a relationship. These are then regurgitated *ad nauseam* during arguments or for guilt trip purposes, emotional blackmail *etc*.

rainwater washdown *n*. A resourceful fellow's *al fresco* means of using any water which is available to him on his way back from a night out to rinse away unwanted perfume, make-up marks or *blip* from his person, prior to entering the house and encountering his eagle-eyed/nosed girlfriend/wife. During the more clement months, in the absence of convenient precipitation, morning dew or damp leaves can be successfully utilised to achieve a similar end.

raised manhole cover *n*. A particularly pronounced *front bottom*. A big *camel's foot* that could take your exhaust off.

raise 'n' gaze *n*. Charming male quirk.

In the newsagents, the unavoidable and instinctive act of lifting one's eyes and checking out the top shelf *jazz periodicals*. *Action Man Eagle-eyes*.

raisin *n*. The *corn dot, freckle*.

raisin bag *n*. The *nut sack, clackerbag, hairy pod purse, John Wayne's hairy saddlebags*.

raisin factory *euph*. An old people's home. From the fact that senior citizens are left there to dry out and wrinkle before being shipped out in a small box.

rake the cage out *v*. To *build a log cabin*, give birth to a *Richard*.

Ralph *onomat*. To vomit. Also *call Huey*.

Rambo'd *adj*. So *pissed* that one believes that one can take on any amount of people in the car park and win.

ram job *n*. Vatican-approved, conventional heterosexual sex, as opposed to a *blow job, hand job, Hawaiian muscle fuck* or *Boston pancake*. A *knob job*.

rammadanny *n*. An enforced monthly *Jacky Danny* fast.

ram raiding on a scooter *adj*. Descriptive of a less than attractive young lady. '*She was a worthy woman, yette sore ugglie, with a face lyke shede been rammeraidynge onn a scooter.*' (from *The Medical Receptionist's Tale* by Geoffrey Chaucer).

ram shackled *adj*. Engaged in the act of *botting*.

RAM sleep *n. abbrev*. The phase prior to deep sleep. Rapid Arm Movement.

Rancor's arms *n*. A collection of large, leathery *digestive transits* resembling the monster from *Return of the Jedi*.

randy *n*. Cowboy version of *horny*.

range is in use, the *euph. milit*. Army term denoting the fact that red (danger) flags are flying and thus a particular firing area cannot presently be entered, used by women when they've *got mice. Arsenal are at home, Aunt Irma is visiting, the tomato boat has docked etc.*

Rangoon ring *n. medic.* Curry-induced blistering of the *nipsy.* A *Wigan rosette, Japanese flag, Johnny Cash, Hawaiian sunrise.*

rantallion *n. 18thC.* One whose *shot pouch* is longer than the barrel of his *fouling piece.*

rapier wit *n. rhym. slang. 'That Jimmy Carr is a rapier wit.'*

rascal wrapper *n. French letter, blob, rubber johnny, cheesepipe clingfilm.*

raspberries in syrup *sim.* The consistency of *shit* after a night *on the hoy.* The kind that makes you pull a face like Kenneth Williams going "Ooh, Matron!"

raspberry *rhym. slang.* Break wind. From raspberry tart = fart. *'Did you just drop a raspberry?' 'Yes. And when I bent down to pick it up, I farted and it fucking stinks.'*

raspberry pavlova *n.* Reams of unflushed, blood-stained *bumwad* left floating in the *pan* by the missus when she is *dropping clots.*

Rasputin *n.* An unkempt vaginal or anal beard of which it is a shame how it carries on.

rat *n.* A lady's *bodily treasure.* The *parts of shame. 'Excreta was powerless to resist. His eyes burned into hers like sequins. His strong arms enfolded her tender body as she felt herself being swept away in an Aurora Borealis of passion. Then he said the words her heart had ached to hear for so long. 'Giz a quick shot on your rat, love. I want to catch last orders.''* (from *The Lady and the Disgraced Former Manchester United and Northern Ireland Footballer* by Barbara Cartland).

rat arsed *adj. Shit-faced.*

rat boy slim *n.* A youthful fellow, using his high-tech MP3 mobile phone to play a mash-up of his favourite clownstep songs at full volume in order to entertain his fellow commuters.

rat catcher's bait box *n.* An unpleasant tasting *fanny.* A *nine volter, crabby patty.*

rather have dinner round Suggs's place, I'd *exclam.* Rhetorical apophthegm delivered in response to someone who suggests you do something, the prospect of which is less than inviting. From the unedifying prospect of the table full of fish finger sandwiches which appears to be on the menu every night round the ex-Madness novelty singer's place. *'Oh look. Jimmy Carr's on QI again. Shall we watch?' 'I'd rather have dinner round Suggs's place. Pass me the sledgehammer, dear, my Basildon Bond and a stamp. I'm going to put the screen through and send Stephen Fry the bill.'*

rat killer *n.* A foul *turd* capable of exterminating any pipe-dwelling rodent within a mile of the S-bend.

rat nav *n.* A fellow's inbuilt propensity, when intoxicated, to scan his immediate locale for *fanny. 'Don't mind me, pal. I'm on the rat nav at the moment, looking for the best rat in this here barn.'*

rat's back *n.* A light brown, nicely-curved *muff.*

rat's cocks! *exclam.* Expression of extreme disappointment. Drat, confound it, curses, *etc.* "My God!" the boatswain cried. 'What has happened to the ship?' 'The Pequod has been stove in by a Leviathan, a Great White

Whale!' replied the helmsman, scarce able to comprehend the enormity of his own words. 'Rat's cocks,' yelled Ahab. 'That's fucking torn it!'' (from *Moby Dick* by Herman Melville).

rat's nose *n.* An inquisitive bit of *poo* poking out of the *nipsy* to see if the coast's clear. *'FX: DOOR OPENS, BUCKET CLANKS. Mrs Mopp: There you go, Mr Handley. Your smallest room's as clean as a chinaman's chopsticks. Tommy Handley: Thank Christ for that, Mrs Mopp. I've been stood out here three quarters of a fucking hour with the rat's nose. FX: RUNNING FOOTSTEPS, DOOR OPENS AND CLOSES, ZIP, FOGHORN, SOUND OF LARGE SHIT HITTING WATER. Orchestra: Signature tune to finish.'* (Script of *It's That Man Again*, broadcast on the BBC Home Service, March 1942).

rat stance *n.* Characteristic, hunched standing position adopted by a fellow who is having a spot of *hand to gland combat* in a shower. *'So there I was in the rat stance, I'd got to the jester's shoes and she walked in on the vinegar strokes. Nothing could stop me by then.'*

rattle and hum *1. n.* Title of a 1987 documentary about Bonio and his pop group. *2. n.* A loud and obnoxious-smelling visit to the *cackatorium* when, if it is the weekend and you have had a heavy night and a curry, you may find yourself singing *Sunday Bloody Sunday.*

Ravi Shankar *rhym. slang.* A gentleman who plays a small, pink sitar.

Ray Mears trying to start a fire, going at it like *sim.* Descriptive of a very energetic and vigorous session of tugging and rubbing at one's *twig*, which is reminiscent

of the tubby TV nettle-chomper attempting to instigate an *al fresco* conflagration without using matches. *'Oi, mind me bloody banjo string there love. You're going at it like Ray Mears trying to start a fire.'*

razz *v.* To *hoy up, puke.*

Razzle *n. prop.* An unpretentious, no-nonsense *jazz mag.* In its own words "The magazine that makes your cock go big".

Razzle dazzle *1. n.* Porn glare. *2. n.* Temporary blindness caused by a particularly nasty *growler shot* in a *self help book.*

Razzle stack *n.* The fondly-remembered, and deeply erotic tabeau in the said *art pamphlet,* featuring six vertically-arranged *quims.* Now sadly banned due to the regular near-suffocation of the lowermost participant.

Razzlet *n.* A slightly overweight, not too bright female, whose only hope of escaping her humdrum existence is to appear in cheap 'n' cheerful *bongo mags.*

reach around *n.* In *botting,* pouring your partner a *hand shandy* whilst *ram shackled.*

reading Cosmo *euph.* Of a lady, to be absorbed in one of her regular *monthly periodicals.* To be *dropping clots, up on blocks, on her rags etc. 'Fancy a quickie, babe?' 'Nah. I'm reading Cosmo this week,'* or indeed *'I'm getting worried, love. Cosmo hasn't been delivered yet. It's nearly a fortnight late.'*

Reading Hoover *n.* Foot used to clean the carpet by grinding in the dirt until it vanishes. Named after the houseproud Berkshire town. *'Oh no, I've knocked the ashtray over.' 'No problem, love. I'll use the Reading Hoover on it.'*

reading the Financial Times *n*. Performing *cumulonimbus* on a particularly large, loose-lipped, pink *clopper*.

reading the paper *v*. To examine one's used toilet tissue to catch up on the latest news of one's anal health. To peruse the *rusty bulletin*.

readybrek glow *n*. The fuzzy, red outline surrounding everyone on a 6th generation copy of a *stick vid*. *Porn fuzz*.

readybrek turd *n*. A *night watchman* that has been residing in the bottom of the *pan* for some time and has, consequently, acquired a ruddy aura not unlike the hot breakfast treat's trademark glow as seen on adverts in the last century. A *rusting copper pipe*.

Ready, Steady, Wank *n*. A game of skill based on the popular, similarly-named cookery show. The competitor has just half an hour and the most unpromising of materials (a month-old copy of *Chat*, *Murder She Wrote* on the telly *etc*.) to *crack one out*.

reality wank *n*. A *toss* over someone one could *poke* in real life, therefore making it better and more realistic. Likely subjects include one's girlfriend, the local *bike* or Sonya off *EastEnders*.

rear admiral *n*. A sailor who prefers to navigate the *Windward passage*.

rear goggles *n*. Notably unreliable mechanism whereby one fondly imagines the front elevation of a woman merely by assessing her rearward appearance.

rear gunner *n*. In aviation terms, a marksman who shoots one of his own side by firing his *lamb cannon* into their *bomb bay*.

rearotica *n*. *Seed catalogues* for *uphill gardeners*.

rear tits *n*. The fleshy parts of the body that hang over the *titpant lashing straps* of ladies with *nice personalities*. *Gwats*.

receiver of swollen goods *n*. Someone involved in a nefarious transaction with a *bum bandit*.

reconnaissance chip *n*. When making proper chips, the brave, lone pioneer that enters the pan on his own to test whether the fat is hot enough.

rectal barometer *n*. The miraculous sensor that is situated in the anal tract and identifies whether the chamber is loaded with gaseous or solid matter, enabling the operator to decide whether or not to risk an *air biscuit*. The sensitive surfaces of the *rectal barometer* are prone to malfunction, giving erroneous readings uner certain circumstances, *eg*. When swamped with curry and lager.

rectal retort *n*. A witty *fart*.

rectoplasm *n*. A message from the other side which makes everybody's hair stand on end. Something that comes out of your *bum* which is so scary it makes you *shit* yourself. A *McArthur Park*.

rectospect *n*. The realisation that, with hindsight, something was a bit *arse*.

red alert *exclam*. Discreet *sotto voce* warning exchanged between males, advising each other to tread carefully around the lady of the house/office due to her having *women's things*. Also *code red*.

red chef's hat *n*. A penis which has been polished within an inch of its life.

red ring *n*. Inflammation of the *chocolate starfish* as a result of being *skittered*. See *Japanese flag*.

red sock, arse hanging out like a *sim. medic*. Descriptive of a full rectal prolapse. Such as one caused by a deliciously fatal plate of Curry Hell, the hottest curry in the world. Exclusively available at the Curry Capital, Bigg Market, Newcastle upon Tyne, the only restaurant to receive the coveted 5 Prolapses award in the *Viz Good Curry Guide.*

red tee, play off the *1. v.* To be good with colours. *2. v.* To *put a long one into the hole* when the green has *fallen to the communists.*

red tie *n.* To finish oneself off with a *sausage sandwich* after having had enough of the *cranberry dip.*

red wings *n.* Dubious honour bestowed upon one who eats *haddock pastie* during *rag week.*

reef 'n' beef *adj.* Of a lady, *half rice half chips.* '*Marie-Antoinette was powerless to resist. The Scarlet Pimpernel's eyes burned into hers like sapphires. His muscular arms enfolded her body as she felt herself being swept away in a tai fung of passion. Suddenly, there was a knock at the door. "Oh no, it's the maid," he said. "If she discovers us together, we'll be undone." "Never mind," said the Queen. "I'm reef'n' beef. Let her in and I'll do her when I've finished with you."*' (from *The Lady and the Man and the Other Lady* by Barbara Cartland).

reedle *v.* To *piss* through an awkward opening or inconvenient gap, *eg.* Between the flaps of a tent, out of a partially opened Velux window, through Esther Rantzen's letterbox.

refecate *v.* To fill one's bowels by eating *crap.* '*The missus has had me on a veggie diet all week, so I'm just popping along to Maccy D's to refecate.*'

referee's coin, cock like a *sim.* A reference to a well-worn *tool* which has been subject to an inordiate amount of *tossing* over the years, *eg.* The one belonging to

that tramp who hides in a rhododendron bush in Heaton Park, Newcastle-upon-Tyne. Or the one belonging to Jonathan Ross, assuming they're not one and the same person.

refreshed *adj. Fucking mortal.*

refusal *1. n.* In show-jumping, when a horse approaches the fence but only briefly puts its nose over the bar instead of jumping. *2. n.* In *shitting,* when a reluctant *Sir Douglas* pokes its nose out of the *ringpiece* for a second before, despite Herculean efforts from the toiletee, returning back to the warmth and safety of the *dirt bakery.*

reggae like it used to be *n.* Masturbation. Wearing a bowler hat.

relaxed her fitness regime, she has *euph.* Of a svelte lady who has got married and evidently *found the key to the pie cupboard.* '*I see that Claire out of off of Steps has relaxed her fitness regime, then.*'

relax in a gentleman's way *v. euph.* To *interfere with oneself* down there. '*Scrooge pulled up his nightshirt, tucked it under his whiskery old chin and began relaxing in a gentleman's way, trying hard to conjure up a mental picture of Mrs Cratchit in the rik. Suddenly the room was filled with an eerie light, and there before him stood the second spirit, the spirit of Christmas Present.*' (from *A Christmas Carol* by Charles Dickens).

release the chocolate hostage *v.* To liberate *Richard the Third* after his incarceration in one's *chamber of horrors.*

release the handbrake *v.* To *drop a gut* into your hand and then present it into a friend's face for their olfactory delectation. To offer a *cupcake.*

release the hounds *n*. To empty one's *arse*.

remaster the back catalogue *1. v*. In the world of pop music, to re-release an artiste's old records with slightly different covers and the loudness turned up. *2. v*. To enjoy a romantic interlude up an old flame.

remould *n*. *Rubber, single finger Marigold glove, blob*.

rent boy's ringpiece, face like a *sim*. Descriptive of someone who looks like life has given them a regular, relentless and vigorous *shafting*. *'Ladies and gentlemen, our next guest needs no introduction from me. He's a musician, singer and songwriter and he's got a face like a rent boy's ringpiece. Let's have a big Alan Titchmarsh Show round of applause for Mr Mark E Smith!'*

re-offender *1. n*. In the world of probation officers and their clients, a little *shit* that keeps appearing over and over again. *2. n*. In the world of going to the toilet, a buoyantly recalcitrant *thirty-three-and-a-third* that re-surfaces repeatedly after flushing.

repeater Kay *n*. A man of low wit, who attempts to get laughs in the pub by lamely repeating comedy catchphrases, *eg*. "Garlic bread" *etc*.

rerack *1. v*. In snooker, pool or billiards, to use a triangular frame to re-arrange the balls on the table at the start of a game. *2. v*. To surgically improve a woman's *headlamps*. *'No way those bad boys are real, Detective Inspector. She's been reracked for sure.' 'You might be right, doctor. Anyway, let's cover them up and we'll get the husband in to see if he can positively identify her.'*

research a book *v*. To look at *Frankie*

Vaughan beamed in from the more *glittery* reaches of cyberspace.

reserve chute *1. n*. In the world of skydiving, a secondary canopy which can be deployed in the event that the first one fails to open properly. *2. euph*. The *arsehole*. *'Woman in hotel bed wearing a corset and bridal veil, and with a 'Just Married' suitcase on the floor: 'Sorry, love. I'm on me rags. You'll have to use the reserve 'chute.' Red-nosed man in a top hat who is removing his trousers: 'Geronimo!''* (postcard by Donald McGill from *Bamforth's Funny Seaside Chuckles Series*, circa 1936).

rest in piss *phr*. Heartfelt eulogium delivered by a *turps nudger* over the prostrate form of his slumbering companion.

restoration fund *1. n*. Appeal run by your local vicar who, despite the fact that the Church of England has an investment fund totalling several trillion pounds, has no money to fix a couple of tiles back on his roof. *2. n*. Whatever's left in your wallet after a night *on the pop*, which can be used the next day to buy aspirin, water, a fry-up, the hair of the dog or whatever else is required so you can rejoin the human race. *'I went out with a hundred quid, but there's only sixteen pee in the restoration fund.'*

retain water *v*. Of a *plumper*, to eat lots of cake.

retch *v*. To vomit, but with more noise and less *puke*.

retox *n*. The opposite of a detox, undergone by offshore workers after a two-week alcohol-free shift on the rigs. *'That trip was shit, Dave. I'm hitting the boozer for a retox.'*

retrosexual *n*. One who has sexual intercourse with someone from his or her past, *eg*. A former friend from school, college, prison, chapel of rest *etc*.

retro tug fodder *n*. A lady who, whilst decidedly ropey now, was an absolute *shit hot wank* in her younger days, *eg*. Debbie Harry, Kim Wilde, that Minogue piece on the *X Factor* who looks like she's fresh out of the burns unit.

return fire *n*. A cold, sniping splash of *chod bin* water that darts straight up one's *wrinkled penny* while *bombing China*. *Splashback*.

return serve *n*. The reappearance of a *turd* you thought you had seen the last of.

reveille *n*. An early morning *brass eye* fanfare delivered with military precision, that makes your company jump out of bed.

reverse cowgirl *n*. A *cowgirl* who has been bucked through 180 degrees, a sexual position much favoured by *meat vid* cinematographers as one can see it *going in*. A *fucking bronco*.

reverse Doagan *n*. *NZ*. A *chocolate hostage* released into the *chod bin* whilst sitting the wrong way round, leaving a breathtaking *skidmark vista* for the next unfortunate lady patron of the toilet.

reverse elephant *n*. What happens when one has *flown right past Dresden* without managing to locate a lavatory. A large *Thora* hanging out of one's *bomber aris*, creating the illusion when viewed from the rear of a pink-eared, brown-trunked pachyderm.

reverse peach *n*. A rearward elevation of a lady's *parts of shame*, such that they resemble a ripe and juicy, fuzzy pink fruit.

reverse rucksack *n*. A large *abdominal holdall*, used by the *lard of the manor* for storing all the pies.

reverse thrust *n*. The act of *getting off at Edge Hill*. The *interruptus* of one's *coitus*.

revision timetable *euph*. A student's carefully worked-out holiday roster of examination preparation which comprises sixteen hours per day of sleep, five hours per day of space invaders, and three hours per day of masturbation.

RFHTFH *abbrev*. Phrase applied to eastern European women, or a fat lass in a Sheffield bun shop. Rather Fuck Her Than Fight Her.

rhino horn *n*. A well-matted tarantula among *arse spiders*. Definitely not an aphrodisiac.

rhythm and blues *n*. Viagra-enhanced *art appreciation* for the mature gentleman.

rhythm mag *n*. *Jazz mag, scud book, art pamphlet*, one-handed reading material.

rhythm section *1. n*. In a pop group, the bass and drums. *2. n*. In a newsagent's, the shelf where they put the *jackage*. *3. n*. In a *jazz mag*, the mucky pictures of bare ladies as distinct from the textual padding.

rhythm stick *n*. The late Ian Dury's *cock*. The *sixth gear stick, joy stick, copper stick, giggle stick, blood stick*. *Slag bat*.

rib *n*. The missus, her indoors. From the children's fairy story *Adam and Eve*.

rib cushions *n*. *Dirty pillows*. Breasts.

Richard *rhym. slang*. A stool. From Richard the Third = turd. *'I've just given birth to a ten pound Richard. Ooh, my poor ringpiece!'*

Rich Tea quickie *n*. A sexual encounter which is reminiscent of the act of dipping one of the popular biscuits in one's tea, *ie*. A solitary dunk followed swiftly by a disappointing collapse.

Rick Stein's bin *n*. Derogatory phrase

implying that a lady's *bodily treasure* smells not unlike the celebrated fish-chef's dustbin. *'No offence, Cilla, but I'm going to have to call it a day. It's like Rick Stein's bin down here.'*

Rick Witter *n. rhym. slang.* The *crapper.* Named after the ex-singer of York-based Brit-pop underachievers Shed Seven, who now fronts Rick Witter & the Dukes. *'Where are Rick Witter & the Dukes? The gig was supposed to start half an hour ago.'* Keep your hair on. *'They're just getting changed in the Rick Witter.'*

riddle of the sphincter *n.* A mysterious *Bakewell tart* that could make your nose fall off.

ride *v.* That which one does to a *bike.*

rider's block *n.* To irretrievably lose *wood* half way through intercourse as a result of a sudden, unexplained nasty sexual image entering the mind, *eg.* Jack Duckworth doing *oral* on his wife Vera while a pot-trout-pout Ivy Tilsley *bobs* him with a *strap-on.*

ride the baloney pony *v. US.* To *wank.*

ride the clutch *1. v.* To teeter on the brink of the *vinegar strokes* in an effort to prolong the act of coitus. *2. v.* To maintain the hovering state between releasing the *pace car* and making *skidmarks* on one's underpants. To rein back the *turtle's head.* To *fight a rearguard action.*

ride the dirtbike *v.* To partake in a bit of *backdoor action.*

ride the great white knuckler *v.* To have *one o'er the thumb.*

ride the porcelain bus *v.* To be suffering from the *Engelberts.*

ride the waves *v.* To poke an amply proportioned lady. See also *moped.* *'It's not as bad as you might think, if you just slap the fat and ride the waves.'*

ridge paste *n.* The sweaty, *smegma pate* that collects under the *brim* of the *farmer's hat.*

riding sidesaddle *n.* Descriptive of the *mincing* trot much favoured by men who are *good with colours.* The kind of gait adopted by Mr Humphries when he was summoned by Captain Peacock.

riding the goose *n.* Vigorous, two-handed male masturbation technique. Often performed with the legs out-stretched up in the air, creating the illusion for a casual onlooker that the perpetrator is gripping onto an extremely short-necked goose like a jockey, whilst avoiding scuffing his shoes as his feathery steed gallops over rough ground. Also known as a *Bernie Clifton.*

rift valley *1. n.* In geography, a linear-shaped lowland between highlands or mountain ranges, often volcanic. *2. n. medic.* In *bumology,* the low-lying territory between the buttocks; the cleft of the *arse,* which occasionally erupts emitting clouds of sulphurous fumes.

right hand cream *n.* Hand and face moisturiser made from a special blend of *nut oils.*

rigid digit *n.* An erect penis, *bone, bonk on.*

rik, the *n.* That which a bare person is in. The *nuddy.*

Rigsby *n.* A no-handed urination of such vigorous release and force that the hands can be safely placed on the hips for its duration.

rim *1. n.* Circumference of the *anus. 2. v.* To *go around the world.* Looking for a shop selling extra strong mints.

rim job *n.* A bout of *bummilingus.*

rim shot *1. n.* That thing the drummer

does after David Letterman has read out a joke. *Bahdumb bahdish. 2. n.* When having a *pony and trap,* the deeply regrettable experience of inadvertently directing a stream of urine under the seat, but over the rim of the *chod bin,* soaking one's *hoggers.*

ring *1. n.* Hole, *jacksie, anus, brown eye, chocolate starfish. 2. n.* Confusingly, also the *fadge.*

ring bandit *n.* A *fruit feeler.*

ringbinder *1. n.* A notebook containing spring-loaded clamps for the purpose of holding loose sheets of paper. *2. n.* An exceptionally tenacious *arse baby* which necessitates repeated wiping before the *freckle* is even vaguely free of *bum chutney.* A *Marmite pot.*

ring bling *n. Arse jewellery.* Haemorrhoids, *Adrian Chiles, Emma Freuds.*

ring burner *n.* An exceptionally hot curry prepared for the entertainment of the waiters and kitchen staff in Indian restaurants.

ringcraft *1. n.* A generic term covering the multitude of techniques, moves and tactics associated with the ancient and noble art of boxing. *2. n.* A generic term covering the multitude of techniques, moves and tactics associated with the ancient and noble art of *giving someone one up the council gritter.*

ringlets *n.* A young lady's anal beard.

ring master *1. n.* The master of ceremonies at a circus. *2. n.* An expert *botter. 3. n.* A person who rarely breaks wind, from the fact that they are "in control of their Billy Smarts".

ringmaster's dog *euph.* Said of a sexually experimental and enthusiastic lady who shocks even the most seasoned lover with her willingness to perform strange and exotic acts, *ie.* One who "knows more tricks than a ringmaster's dog".

ring of death *1. n.* The light display which indicates to a pasty-faced teenage troglodyte that his XBox is beyond help. *2. n.* A really stinky *dirtbox.*

ringpeace *n.* The uneasy truce finally called between you and your sphincter after two hours of post-Madras nuclear fallout.

ringpiece *n.* A *Samantha Janus.*

ring pirate *n.* A renegade *rear admiral.*

ring rusty *1. adj.* Descriptive of an ageing pugilist who has not fought for quite some time. *'Prince Naseem Hamed, the ring-rusty boxer, was yesterday jailed for fifteen months by a judge at Sheffield Crown Court.'* (from the *Yorkshire Post,* May 13th 2006). *2. adj.* Descriptive of someone who has abstained from giving or taking it *up the back garden* for a while. *'Prince Naseem Hamed of E-wing is no longer ring-rusty, according to sources close to the former boxer's showering companions.'* (from the gossip column, *Wakefield Prison News,* May 16th 2006). *3. adj.* Descriptive of one who has gone through a prolonged period of constipation.

ringside seats, have *v.* To be *turtling* something rotten. To have a heavyweight *mole at the counter.*

rings of sat-on *n.* The bright red semi-circular marks left imprinted on a man's thighs and buttocks after a long and satisfying session of study in the *bog library.*

ringstinct *n.* A mysterious seventh sense that tells a *farter* to wait until he is safely ensconced on the *chod bin,* thus preventing *follow through* in his *scads.*

ring sting *n. medic. Soreness* of the *sev-*

enth planet.

ring stinger *n.* A *Ruby Murray* that induces *ring sting* and leaves one with an *arse* like *a Japanese flag.*

ring the bell *v. Pop the cork*, detonate the *fanny bomb.*

ring the waterboard *exclam.* A humorous announcement made following the birth of a particularly hefty *toilet baby. 'Oi love. You'd better ring the waterboard and tell them to get the big knives out at the shit farm to chop that one up.'*

ringtone *n.* A *fart.*

ring worm *n.* A *shirtlifter's Jimmy Wonkle.*

rinky dink 1. *n.* Stink, that unpleasant odour created by a *fyst, Richard the Third's BO.* 2. *adj.* Descriptive of the Pink Panther.

rinse the lettuce *v.* To wash the *beef curtains, in situ* as it were. Female equivalent of a *gentleman's wash.*

Rio *n.* A bald *cunt* with wavy lips, often seen in the "Readers' Wives" pages of *bongo mags,* or on the pitch at Old Trafford.

rip a grumpy *v.* To *snip off a length of dirty spine. 'Right, I'm off to rip a grumpy. Here's Daniel Corbett with the weather.'*

rip one out *v.* To fart slowly and painfully, in the style of a cowboy having an arrow pulled out of his shoulder.

rip out one's skeleton *v.* To attempt to remove your body's internal supporting framework by pulling repeatedly and viciously on the most visible *bone* about your person.

ripped out fireplace *n.* A *butcher's dustbin.*

ripped sofa *n.* A *badly-packed kebab.*

ripped to the tits *adj.* Inebriated using drink and drugs. Also *whipped to the tits.*

ripping up rags *sim.* Descriptive of the sound of a long drawn out *fart.*

rise from the dead *v.* To achieve a *bone on* by looking at erotic pictures of women who have since passed on, *eg.* Marilyn Monroe, Jayne Mansfield or Hattie Jacques, *etc.*

rising main *n.* In pubic plumbing, the *tatty watta* supply pipe usually fed in through the *flange.* The *main cable.*

Ritz squits *n. medic.* The unedifying, though impressively thorough, purging of the *Simon Cowells* which sometimes occurs following the over-enthusiastic consumption of foodstuffs one can't really afford. *'I knew I shouldn't of ate them swan canapes, Dr McKeith. They've give me terrible Ritz squits.'*

Rives Gaucher *n. rhym. slang. Fr.* French cockney rhyming slang for a *twat.* From left banker = wanker. *'Cette Monsieur Michael McIntyre, il est un homme tres humereux, n'est-ce pas?' 'Pas du tout. Moi, je pense que le vagin unamusant est un veritable Rives Gaucher de l'eau premier.'*

rivet dance *n.* The uncoordinated, awkward, fast motioned-jig associated with those who are desperately trying to avoid *dropping their guts* on the hallway carpet. A *Michael Shatley.*

riveting stick *rhym. slang. Dick.* From the jeweller's instrument.

R Kelly weather *n.* A chill in the air during the summer. When the temperature is "dipping into the teens". From the singer's alleged, though unproven, penchant for cooling meteorological conditions.

road apples *n.* Horse *shit.*

roadhead *n. US*. Hitch hiker's currency. An act of *horatio* performed in return for a lift.

roadkill *n*. A rather flat, dry, *hedgehog*.

roadkill ruby *n*. A curry containing meat of dubious provenance.

road less travelled, the *1. n*. Title of a poem by Robert Frost, which has been interpreted as a declaration of the importance of personal freedom. *2. euph*. The *back passage*. A tasteful and cultured turn of phrase which can usefully be employed whilst subtly suggesting to one's ladyfriend that she might like to *turn over a new leaf*.

road thrill *n*. An *art pamphlet* which has been discarded in a layby by a trucker.

road to Grimsby *n*. The *farse, tinter, carse etc, etc*. The bit between a lady's *front* and *back bottoms*. So called because there's always a whiff of fish and it's not far from a *shit-hole*.

roast *1. n*. What a normal bloke has for his Sunday lunch when his missus is at home. *2. n*. What a professional footballer has when his missus is away climbing Mount Kilimanjaro for charity, to pick a completely hypothetical example entirely at random.

roast chicken *n*. Any member of a one woman/two premiership footballers configuration who gets cold feet at the last minute.

roast ghost *n*. An *air buffet* that is not suitable for vegetarians.

roasting joint *n*. A club or institution frequented by Premiership footballers, where they can experience *real end to end stuff*.

robbing the date locker *n*. The burgling of *turds*.

Robert Plant *1. n*. prop. Erstwhile, big-choppered Brummie pop vocalist. *2. n*. An excessively large *lemon curd*. Named after the eponymous singer's 1982 single *Big Log*. *3. n*. A marathon day of heroic multiple self pollution. Named after the eponymous singer's 1990 single *29 Palms*.

Robin Cook's beard *n*. A sparsely-vegetated ginger *minge*. A *grated carrot*, a *council twat*.

robocrap *n*. The ominous feeling in the lower bowel which leaves a fellow in no doubt that he only has "twenty seconds to comply".

robot nipple *n*. The top of a battery.

rock around the cock *n*. For any number of reasons, a quantity of seaside confectionary strewn about the male genitals.

rock candy *n*. An effeminate, yet intimidating fellow. A *muscle Mary*.

rocket polisher *n*. An over-enthusiastic cleaning of the *pocket rocket* leading to detonation on the launchpad. And *spunk* everywhere.

rocket socket *n*. Vagina.

rocket strap *n*. The waist band of the *undercrackers* when used to tether the *old man* discreetly upwards to allow a be-*travel-fatted* fellow to alight decorously from the bus.

Rockfords *rhym. slang. Arse grapes, Nobbies, Emmas, Michaels, farmers, ceramics, Chalfonts*. From the TV series *The Rockford Piles*.

rock poodle *n*. A lightweight heavy metallurgist, complete with long shaggy hair and puffed-up leather jacket.

rocks *1. n*. Masses of hard, stony matter, esp. an extensive formation of such matter. *2. n*. Big, hairy *bollocks*. *3. n*. Those which one "gets off" whilst *on the job*.

Rocky press-ups *n*. The act of *wanking*

in the shower, pulling on one's genitalia with one hand whilst using the other one to lean against the wall for balance. The aquatic sinner ends up looking vaguely reminiscent of Mr Balboa doing one of his impressive one-armed, biceps-building exercises.

rod *n. Spam sceptre.*

Rod Hull's roof, as wet as *adj.* Descriptive of a sexually-excited lady; one who is *frothing like bottled Bass. 'Septicaemia was powerless to resist. His eyes burned into hers like 18-carrot diamond-cut Moissanites™. His muscular arms enfolded her body as she felt herself being swept away on an El Niño of passion. She could wait no longer. 'Take me now, Kendo,' she panted. 'Me cunt's as wet as Rod Hull's roof.''* (from *The Lady and the All-In Wrestler* by Barbara Cartland).

Rodin's stinker *euph.* Time spent in sombre introspection on the *crapper* the morning after a night *on the pop*. From one's spent, naked, head-resting-in-hands pose, which is reminiscent of the famous statue of Bruce Forsyth by the eponymous French sculptor (1840-1917).

Rodney *n. prop. rhym. slang.* Convoluted term for a *shite,* named after the mediocre Australian fast bowler Rodney Hogg, whose name rhymes with *log. 'Where've you been, Olivia?' 'In the dunny having a Rodney, Cliff.'*

Rod Stewart's disease *n. medic. Rabbit tods.* Named after the gravel-throated veteran crumpeteer's early band the Small Faeces.

rod the drains *v.* To *back scuttle.*

rod walloper *n.* One who *gives it six-nowt on the old walking stick.*

rodeo sex *n.* A borderline-illegal bedroom game where the couple adopt the *doggy position.* The gentleman then calls out an ex-girlfriend's name and sees how long he can stay on for. Also *bronco sex.*

rogan splosh *n.* An incredibly runny *shit,* accompanied by a fusilade of splattering *farts* the morning after a *roadkill ruby.*

roger *v.* To *fuck.* Often in the past tense. *'I gave her a jolly good rogering.'*

roger and out 1. *exclam.* In radio communications, something that *scuffers,* cabbies and airline pilots say at the end of their transmissions. 2. *euph.* The gentleman's act of leaving extremely preveniently following the successful conclusion of an act of intercourse. *'Honestly, darling. She didn't mean a thing to me. It was just roger and out, all twenty-three times.'*

roger ramjet *n.* A *botter.*

roid rage 1. *n.* Sudden attack of uncontrollable anger from a pumped-up bouncer when somebody's looked at him funny, or has tried to come in the club wearing the wrong sort of shoes. 2. *n.* The violent anger exhibited by a haemorrhoid sufferer whose bum grapes have just been twatted with a metal ruler, for example.

Roland Kirk 1. *n. prop.* A jazz musician (1936-1977) rightly lauded for his ability to get a tune out of two or more horns simultaneously, and thus 2. *euph.* A *jazz actress* rightly lauded for her ability to get a tune out of two or more *horns* simultaneously.

Rolf Harris eating a banana *sim.* Descriptive of the close-up intercourse scenes in a very blurred, 200th generation *scruff video.*

Rolfies *n.* The pseudo-Aboriginal gasps

and grunts produced when trying to pass an extremely large *didgeridoo*.

rolling down the hill *euph.* Of a *custard*, to make its way under its own steam down the guts towards the *chuff*. *'I'd open a window if I was you, your Holiness. Only I had Chicken Tonight and six pints of homebrew for tea yesterday, and I can feel one rolling down the hill.'*

rolling the dice *n. Feeding the ducks, spanking the monkey.*

rolling thunder *n.* An overlong *air buffet* served up whilst walking past a line of people, such as would be dropped by Her Majesty the Queen backstage at the Royal Variety Performance.

roll in the hay *n.* What everyone wanted to have with Julie Christie in *Far From The Madding Crowd*. And Donald Sutherland did with her in *Don't Look Back*.

roll mop *n.* A mature lady's rolled-up *mackerel flaps*.

roll of tarmac *n.* An enormous, thick, black, treacly, post-Guinness-session *digestive transit* that looks like it could be used to re-surface the driveway.

roll out the barrel *v.* To introduce your sizeable new girlfriend to your mates.

roll out the carpet *v.* To unpick the end of a fresh *bogroll* in order to impress a visitor.

roll out the red carpet *1. v.* When hosting a ceremonial event, to make someone feel very welcome. *2. v.* When *hosting the decorators*, to make someone feel very unwelcome.

rollover week *n.* When the *painters are in.*

roll the crevice *v.* To attempt to wipe one's *freckle* with the coarse cardboard tube after exhausting the supply of *bumwad.*

roly-poly *adj.* Tabloid prefix for any celebrity who's half a stone overweight. For example, *'Roly-poly actor Leonardo Di Caprio...'*

romance lake *n.* A pool of *banana yoghurt* left on the sheet following a torrid interlude of some sort.

romancing the bone *n.* An evening in alone with a meal, a bottle of wine and some soft music, followed by a top shelf *stick vid. Everything but the girl.*

Roman shower *n.* Term for the act favoured by *emetophiles, ie.* People who obtain sexual excitement by vomiting on one another. Really, they should just drop the fucking bomb.

romp *v.* To chase a woman in a corset round and round a bedroom about one-and-a-half times actual speed, lifting the knees very high and accompanied by "BOING!" noises when leaping onto the bed.

Ronaldo piss *n.* A *wazz* taken with the feet placed a yard apart in the style of the Manchester United/Portugal midfielder preparing to take a free kick. Usually by an inebriated fellow at a pub urinal or building society doorway.

Ronnie's cue *euph.* The gift of *spambidexterity*, that is to say the ability to *line up a long pink* with either your left or right hand.

Ronson *rhym. slang.* Arse. From Ronson lighter = shiter.

Roobarb and Custard moment *n.* A complete failure to *pull* where, in the style of the popular wobbly teatime animation, "the birds all laughed".

rook's nest *n.* An exceptionally untidy *faff. 'Cor! Look at her. I bet she's got a* *minge like a rook's nest - all shit and sticks.'*

room clearer *n*. Of flatulent emissions, a *fart* which registers one notch higher than *breaking company* on the sphincter scale.

Rooneyed *adj*. Descriptive of one demonstrating an advanced case of sunburn, in the fashion of the scouse footballing wunderkind Wayne. *'Bugger the sunscreen, let's just get Rooneyed.'*

Rooney ramble *n*. A gentle stroll through a red light district.

Rooney's boot *euph*. An item that is meant to offer protection when worn whilst *shooting* but which fails at an inopportune moment with catastrophic results. *'Frankly, son, you were a mistake. Every time I look into your smiling little upturned face I rue the day I bought them Rooney's boots from the vender in the pub bogs.'*

Rooney's charisma *n*. That mysterious and indefinable quality which allows a fat, potato-ugly, prematurely-balding prostitute visitor to secure a *top shelf* bit of *cabbage* for himself.

rooster *n*. A lady's *nether-wattle. Half a pound of liver.*

rooster tail *1. n*. In the world of Grand Prix motor racing, the characteristic plume of water which arcs up behind a Formula 1 car which is speeding around a waterlogged track. *2. n*. In the world of stomach upsets, a particularly spectacular, and wet, bout of the *Brads*.

root *v*. To make love to.

root beer *n*. *Aus. Spooge.*

rope on a soap *n*. Someone else's *clockspring* embedded on your bar of Imperial Leather.

rope the pony *v*. To *gallop the lizard.*

ropey tit wank *n*. A less-than-satisfactory *diddy ride* off a *fenchested bird*. *'Fancy a ropey tit wank, Pete?' 'No thanks, Kate. I'm just off out to buy some crack and a Jag.'*

rorschaching *n*. Idly examining your postwipe *bum wad* to see if the *shite* smudge reminds you of anything.

Rory Delap *n*. The act of throwing one's *balls* into the *box* from a great distance, named after the Stoke City and Ireland right back Rory "The Human Sling" Delap.

Roseberry Topping *1. n*. Frequently climbed hill offering unrivalled vistas over the magical petrochemical wonderland that is Middlesbrough. *2. n*. Put bluntly, the appearance of a chap's *bald man's hat* following a rampant session of *hide the sausage* whilst *Arsenal are playing at home.*

rose-tinted testicles *n*. Those items through which one looks back fondly on all previous sexual encounters when trapped in a long-term relationship.

roshambo *n*. Light-hearted game apparently played by members of the Royal Marines, Parachute Regiment *etc.*, when they are competing for women, booze or sundry otherwise worthless items that somehow acquire value after a night out *on the piss*. The rules, such as they are, are as follows; Player 1 kicks Player 2 squarely in the balls. If Player 2 does not collapse in agony, he may kick Player 1 in the balls. The last man standing is the winner.

rotoplooker *n*. *US*. Penis, *chopper.*

rotters *n*. Unpleasant looking *lungs*. The sort of saggy *tits* with *kneeshooter nips* normally encountered during amateur-style entertainment in the furthest reaches of the satellite television channel menu. *Nasty bags.*

roughage *n.* Unkempt pubic foliage. High-fibre *holefood.* A portion of *gorilla salad* that counts towards your five-a-day.

rough as a three quid handjob *sim.* Used in reference to something or somebody unpleasantly coarse. Popular *tit* model Jordan could accurately be described as being *rough as a three quid handjob,* for example. And often is.

roughing up the suspect *v.* What a vice squad copper tells his superiors he's doing when he's caught *polishing* his *bobby's helmet* in the seized porn store room.

round at Freddie's *adj.* To be *nicely poised, good with colours, light on one's feet. 'That Duncan Norvelle - he's married with three kids, you know.' 'Never. I thought he was round at Freddie's.' 'No. That's just an act.'*

roundhead *n.* A *pink Darth Vader* after the surgical removal of his *Kojak's rollneck,* a *yiddled whanger.*

round the houses *1. rhym. slang.* A cockney fellow's trousers. *'Have you seen my round the houses, love? I need them to go for a piece of chalk down the frog and toad to the rub-a-dub for a kitchen sink and a kids from fame of horse and carts with my dinner plates.' 'Aren't they in the Bobby Moore with your student grants, electric shocks and love really hurts? I'm sure I put them there after I Clarence the cross-eyed lionned them this four-minute warning.' 2. n.* Prostitutes' argot for all-over erotic stimulation. *'How much for a spot of round the houses in a skip, love?' 'Fifteen quid, Lord Archer. Or ten if I don't have to touch your disgusting spotty back.'*

round up the tadpoles *v.* To *wank, bash the bishop.*

rover's return *1. n.* Name of the fictional public house where every single resident of Coronation Street goes drinking three or four times a day. *2. n.* The act of stepping on a freshly-laid *dog's egg* on the way back from the pub, and dragging it home on the sole of your shoe.

rowlocks *n.* British comedy staples. *'These contrivances on my boat serve as fulcrums for my oars.' 'Rowlocks.' 'No, it's true I tell you.'*

row the boat *v.* A dual *tug* boat, multiple *wanking.* Nautical variation on the *downhill skiing* position.

royal decrees *n. Movements* passed whilst sat on the *throne.*

Royal Enfield *euph.* A *ride* that goes through her life in a constant state of arousal, leaving small pools of lubricant wherever she settles, in the style of the erstwhile British motorbike of the 1950s and 1960s, whose various flanges were renowned for their lack of oil-retaining properties.

royal flush *n.* When a previous visitor to the *spam fritter* has flushed the bowl with, it would seem, a child's watering can, ensuring that the aftermath of their colonic extrusions remains all over the shop, and you have to clean up the mess lest any subsequent visitors think that the culprit was you. *Scraping one for the team.*

Royal Marine *n.* A *fanny* with a buzz cut.

Royal premiere *n.* The act of menstruation, *ie. Rolling out the red carpet.*

Roy Castle's kettle *n.* The use of a choked down *nipsy* in order to use a forcible *Exchange & Mart* to "scratch" an itchy *ringpiece*. A *Dutch cornet*.

Roy Castle's last blow *n*. A frankly unimpressive *trouser trumpet* that sounds like it's feeling very sorry for itself.

Roy Walker moment *n*. A satisfying but morally dubious sexual encounter, *eg*. With a friend's wife or a woman old enough to be one's mother. Or a friend's mother. From the *Catchphrase* personality-vacuum's TV catchphrase "it's good, but it's not right".

rub-a-tug shop *n*. Brothel, bordello, house of ill repute. Massage parlour supplying a rub down and a *tug off*.

rubber beer *n*. Booze bought with a return ticket. A pint one hasn't seen the last of. *Jesus beer, comeback Special Brew*.

rubber gash *n*. The sailor's favourite. A plastic *fanny* which the manufacturers claim is "better than the real thing". At £8.99, that's got to be the bargain of the century.

rubber Johnny *n*. A *blob*, contraceptive, *a jubber ray*. Also *rubber, trojan, dunky*.

rubber kebab *n*. An item of fast food with a high coefficient of restitution which bounces back from the stomach onto the pavement or taxi driver's head.

rubber's rag *n*. A rigid piece of once-absorbent fabric kept conveniently close to a bachelor's computer workstation.

rubbie burns *n*. *Scots*. Chaffing of the *bell end* as a result of *going commando*. Originates in Scotland, where all men typically suffer from the affliction due to the scratchiness of their harsh, woolen kilts, which wear away their *wee heids* whilst they are roaming in the gloaming.

rubiks *rhym. slang*. *Gorilla salad, fusewire*. From Rubik cubic hair = pubic hair.

Ruby Murray *rhym. slang*. A *cuzza*.

Ruby Tuesday 1. *n*. Rolling Stones song which was the 19th best-selling record of 1967. 2. *n*. The day the missus goes *up on blocks*. Especially if it's a Tuesday.

rucksack *n*. A badly-adjusted underpant or thong, hitched up a lady's back. With a tin mug and a frying pan hanging off it.

rudimentary *n*. A late night TV *wanking* opportunity, thinly-disguised as a factual programme, *eg*. A behind-the-scenes looks at the worlds of lap-dancing, the US hardcore porn industry or *tits* and *fannies*. Also *masturmentary, sockumentary*. '*Are you coming up to bed?*' '*In a minute, dear. I'm just watching a rudimentary. Do you know where there's any tissues?*'

ruffle my lettuce *euph*. What a polite Canadian woman says when she is going to take a *Chinese singing lesson*. '*If you would excuse me for a moment, gentlemen, I'm just going to ruffle my lettuce. In fact, fuck it. Whilst I'm on the shitter I may as well snip off a length of dirty spine too.*'

rug hugger *n*. Male version of a *fag hag*. A straight man who seeks out the company of women who enjoy the mastication of carpet *on the bus to Hebden Bridge*.

rug munchers *n*. *Fanny noshers*.

ruined *adj*. A very attractive woman whose sex appeal has nonetheless been almost entirely nullified by her association with an unsuitable gentleman. '*Christ, that Billie Piper's a horny chimpoid.*' '*Yeah, but that ginger twat Chris Evans has been there. That's ruined her for me.*'

rumble strips 1. *n*. A "cool" indular pop

beat combo from Tavistock in Devon. *2. n.* The raised sections of bumps at the edges of the carriageway which are supposed to draw long distance lorry drivers' attention to the fact that they have fallen asleep at the wheel. *3. n.* The convoluted ripples of adipose tissue on girls with *big bones* who are crammed into cheap, one-size-fits-all leggings, and are often to be seen congregating around Great Yarmouth market's famous chip stalls.

rummage *n.* A jumble sale-style act of *self-delight* indulged in by a dirty lady.

rump gully *n.* Viewed from *biffin bridge*, the gradually sloping valley beyond *kak canyon*.

Rumpleforeskin *n.* Penis, *John Thomas, junior.*

rumpo *n. Rumpy pumpy.*

Rumpole suntan *n.* An alcoholic red face as modelled by the late *Rumpole of the Bailey* actor Leo McKern.

rump ranger *n.* A *brokeback mountaineer.* One who takes a lively interest in *rusty sheriff's badges.*

rumpy pumpy *n.* Lightweight sexual shenanigans, slightly more erotic than *how's your father.* US equivalent *hoochie-coochie.*

running behind *euph.* Polite excuse which can be given when one is unable to stop and chat with a friend or colleague as a result of an overdue appointment *dropping a load of semi-viscid kids off at the pool.* 'Film actor, director, grand old man of the British stage, tonight, Sir John Geilgud, this is your life.' 'Sorry Eamonn, can't stop. I'm running late.'

runs, the *1. n.* What English cricketers get when they face fast bowlers. *2. n.* What English cricketers don't get when they face fast bowlers.

run the taps *v.* To take a *leak* following a spot of *bumfoolery.* From the practice of letting the taps run in a house with rusty pipes, in order to let out any unpleasant brown residue which may be present in the water.

runway, taxiing down the *n.* The sensation experienced as you cross the last six feet towards the *crapper,* as your long-delayed stinky *passenger* slips into the *departure lounge* and makes a *break for the border.*

rushin' roulette *n.* A suicidally-dangerous game whereby a gentleman attempts to *knock one off* when there is a fairly good chance that his wife may walk in on him.

Rusholme roulette *n. Farting* in the full knowledge that there is a one in six chance of *shitting* one's *kex.* Named after Rusholme, the district of Manchester famed for its curry houses.

russet gusset *n. Skidmarks* or *dangleberrian* deposits on the *shreddies. Marmite stripe,* the *starting grid at Brands Hatch.*

Russian wedding ring *n.* Three different shades of gold. Found on close inspection of the missus's *tea towel holder* after she's had a good curry-night *crap.*

Russian yawn *n.* A *thirty-four-and-a-halfer,* a *cannonball.* A self-service *suck-off.*

rusting copper pipe *n.* A *night watchman.* One of them stubborn *arse sausages* that sit in the *pan,* refusing to be flushed away, and giving off a Readybrek-style brown aurora into the water.

Rustler's relish *n.* The kind of *man mayonnaise* typically guzzled down by the type of chap who *knows what's in his* *flowerbeds*. Named after the slightly less appetising condiment provided in a squeezable sachet for consumers of the eponymous microwavable burger.

rusty Brillo pad *n*. The pubular portions of a natural redhead. For other synonyms for ginger pubes, see also *brandy snap, fubes, fire down below, grated carrot, Noddy Holder's sideburns, orangina, orang utan salad* and *Robin Cook's beard*. *'Blimey, Rula. It's like a rusty Brillo pad down here.'*

rusty door bolt *n*. A compacted *shit* that is extremely difficult to force out of the *nipsy*. *'What's up, Whitney?'* *'Come in here and see if you can't get this rusty door bolt out my ass, Bobby.'*

rusty scone cutter *n*. A very unhygienic dough-shaping implement. The *arse-hole*.

rusty sheriff's badge *n*. Ride south along *biffin bridge* from *John Wayne's hairy saddlebags* and there it lies, right in the middle of *kak canyon*. Just before you reach *rump gully*. The *anus*.

rusty trumpet, play the *v*. To perform *horatio* very shortly after receiving a *rear admiral's* attention.

rusty water *n*. Liquid *feeshus* which is *pissed* out of the *arse*.

rusty zip *n*. An improperly-wiped buttock cleft, where the *shite* has been spread about and then left to dry out. *Robert Smith's mouth*.

rut 1. *v*. To *tup*. In the style of a deer or billy goat. 2. *n*. Any single member from the pop band the Ruts, *eg*. John "Segs" Jennings or Gary Barnacle.

sack artist *n*. A womaniser, gigolo, *fanny rat, fanny hopper, crumpeteer*.

sack nav *n*. Relying on the inbuilt *fanny-homing* instincts of one's overladen *hairy conkers* in order to negotiate one's way around a dancefloor in search of *mackerel* whilst r*at-arsed*.

sack race *n*. A *milk race*.

sacofricosis *n. medic*. A mental condition, the main symptom of which is the desire to cut a hole in one's pocket to facilitate *self-pollution* in public places. *'We've get your test results back, Mr Ross OBE, and it's bad news. You've got advanced sacofricosis.' 'Oh, cwumbs!'*

saddlebags *1. n*. Labia, *piss flaps*. *2. n*. Scrotum. *3. n*. Leathery receptacles on bicycles where testicles are stored.

safety dance *1. n*. Song by Men Without Hats that reached some position or other in the charts in a particular year in the previous century. *2. n*. The rhythmical *buttocky* shuffle performed whilst trying to find a position on the toilet seat that guarantees a smooth, efficient, smear-free and non-hazardous passage of one's *digestive transit*.

saga lager *1. n*. Sherry or mild, depending on gender. *2. n*. Geriatric *piss*. *'I'd visit my granny more often if it wasn't for the smell of saga lager.'*

saga louts *n*. Packs of tea-fuelled pensioners travelling by coach who lay waste to garden centres and stately home gift shops.

sailor's ale *n*. The thick, salty, tangy beverage drunk by *sea bent* mariners whilst on long voyages. *'Adrift upon a glassy sea / No wind upon our sail / We pulled the boatswain's trousers off / And drank his sailor's ale'* (from *The Rime of the Ancient Mariner* by Samuel

Taylor Coleridge).

sailor's shot sock, fuller than a *sim*. Descriptive of when something is filled to bursting, *eg*. A post-Christmas bin-liner, the 4.24pm Newcastle to Prudhoe train, Tom Jones's skin, Cliff Richard's *saddlebags*.

salad bar at Butlins, quieter than the *sim*. Descriptive of a very, very quiet place indeed.

salad days *n*. Descriptive of the *lettuce-licking* past times of a woman who is now back chomping sausages like a good 'un.

salad dodger *n*. A contumelious epithet for a *fat bastard*. One who, at a buffet, sidesteps the lettuce and celery and heads straight for the pork pies. *"Contrarywise', continued Tweedledee, 'if it was so, it might be; and if it were so, it would be; but as it isn't, it ain't. That's logic'. 'That's not logic, that's bollocks, you salad dodger."* (from *Through The Looking Glass* by Lewis Carroll).

salami slapper *n*. He who tolls upon his own *bell end*. A *wanker*.

Salem slot *n*. A *fanny* that is as frightening as a reasonably frightening 1970s TV mini-series starring David Soul.

Salford snail *n*. Common species of mollusc (*Helix aspersalford*) that leaves a distinctive trail of thin horizontal lines scratched into the doors of 4x4s in inner city areas. Evidence of *Salford snail* activity is often found in the vicinity of groups of hooded *scratters*.

Sally bumps *n. Peanuts* in the process of being *smuggled*. Prominent nipples. From the *chapel hat pegs* constantly visible through the clothing of *Coronation Street* character Sally Webster.

Sally Gunnell *n. prop*. A motor trade

term to describe a used car, *ie.* "It's not much to look at but it's a fucking good runner".

salmon *1. rhym. slang.* Sexual excitement. From salmon on prawn = the horn. *'I saw Pam Anderson's video on the internet last night. It didn't half give me the salmon, I can tell you.'* *2. rhym. slang.* HMP. Tobacco. From salmon and trout = snout. *"Ere, you don't half give me the salmon, Lord Archer. Fancy giving me a blow job for an ounce of salmon?"*

salmon canyon *n.* Piscatorial pass leading to *tuna town.*

salmon handcuffs *n. Pink handcuffs.* Invisible restraints that keep a gentleman from seeing any of his friends. The metaphorical restraints with which a *pussy- whipped* gentlemen is shackled. *"This is quite rum do, Jeeves', I exclaimed. 'I've met Piggy for cocktails every Friday for ten years. Where the pip can he be?' 'If I may be so bold,' intoned Jeeves in that way of his, 'he has recently taken up with a soubrette from a London show, and I fear she has slapped the salmon handcuffs on the poor cunt."* (from *What the Fuck, Jeeves?* by PG Wodehouse).

salmon's head *n.* A hatless *one-eyed zipper fish* as viewed from underneath.

saloon doors *n.* A pair of well-used, swinging *fanny flaps* that one's *cock* swaggers into, only to be thrown out three minutes later after a bit of frantic banging. Wild West-style *beef curtains.*

salsa dip *n.* A splash about in the *crimson waves.*

salt *n.* 1960s Mod term for a *bird.*

salt and pepper *n.* Horrible little *tits* where the nipple area is larger and more protruding than the rest of the breast, giving them the appearance of the silver-capped condiment shakers found in cafes.

Samantha *rhym. slang.* A *ringpiece.* From Samantha Janus.

Samantha foxhole *n. arch.* A bucolic repository for relaxation-themed literature.

Sam Plank *rhym. slang. Stoke-on-Trent.* An act of *self abuse* named after the popular Radio Stoke disc jockey. *'Did you manage to pull last night?' 'No. I went home for a Pot Noodle and a Sam Plank.'*

Sam Spoon's rhythm pole *n.* A male *member,* generously equipped with *Alberts, cock rings,* bolts, chains and what-have-you, such that the ensemble provides a musical accompaniment during intercourse or *rub-and-tuggage.* From the apparent aural similarity to the sound made by the be-belled "rhythm pole" played by erstwhile Bonzo Dog Doodah Band percussionist Sam Spoons. See also *the full Roger McGuinn.* *'Ooh, Evan. I didn't realise you had a Sam Spoon's rhythm pole.'*

Samurai *n.* A fearsome, ceremonial *pork sword.*

sandies *n. rhym. slang.* Pubic lice *(Phthirus pubis).* Named after the famous 1930s Scottish international midfielder Sandy McNabs = crabs.

sand hole *n.* Of crowded beaches, the hole caused by sunbathing on one's stomach in order to conceal a *Jake.*

S and M *n. Rub-a-tug shop* parlance for sado-masochism. *Mr Whippy, fladge and padge.*

Sandy Lyles *rhym. slang.* Haemorrhoids.

Sangatte, do a *v.* Of married men, to make

a *bid for the tunnel* in the middle of the night, almost certainly only to be turned back by the wife.

sanitised *adj.* Descriptive of the trouble-free view of the world induced by quaffing vast quantities of Spanish lager.

Santa's beard *n.* A festively voluminous example of *jelly jewellery* festooning a lady's chin.

Santa's sack on Boxing Day, like *sim.* Something that is exceedingly empty. 'Look, Mr Davro, we're going to have to cancel half the dates on your tour. The theatres are going to be like Santa's sack on Boxing Day.'

Santa stuck up the chimney *exclam.* A reference to *blobstopper* removal problems, often as a consequence of drunken intercourse.

Santorum *n.* Amongst people who are *nicely poised*, the frothy mix of lubricant and faecal matter that is sometimes the by product of their saucy carryings-on. Amusingly named after the anti-gay US senator Rick Santorum. *Sexcrement, shum, toffee yoghurt.*

Sarah Jessica Porker *n.* A *bird* who wears all the right clothes from all the right labels, but not necessarily in the right sizes.

sarlacc pit *n.* A particularly angry-looking, frightening, voracious yet dry *minge*. Named after that big pink thing with all them teeth which was in that hole in the ground out of off of *Return of the Jedi* (1983).

sarson's nose *adj.* The condition of the *old fella*, post *vinegar strokes*, after leaving a *salty dressing* on the *pink lettuce salad*.

Satan's banquet *n.* An unlikely sounding variation on the *devil's kiss*, whereby a saucy lady delivers a still-warm baguette from her *dirt bakery* into the waiting mouth of a *poovert* friend underneath, by way of a kinky treat.

Satan's piano, noises like *sim.* Descriptive of a prolonged eighty-eight note chromatic scale played on his *nipsy* by an unaccompanied virtuoso ensconced in the *sweet wrapper*. *'Bloody hell, Simon. I've just walked past the Rick Witter that Amanda's in and her arse is making noises like Satan's piano."*

sat chav *n.* When you are lost in a strange town, a surly feral youth from whom you are forced to ask directions, in the full and certain knowledge that he will send you in entirely the wrong direction and then have a good laugh about it with his *scratter* mates as soon as you have driven away.

Satchmo *n.* The technique of skillfully cupping your hand over the bell of your *muck trumpet* in order to elicit a more muted, jazz-infused timbre whilst *sounding the charge*. Named after Louis "Satchmo" Armstrong (1901-1971), whose charismatic, improvised approach to tonality and phrasing revolutionised the world of *farting*.

satiscraptory *adj.* Decriptive of something of a poor, but adequate standard, *eg*. BBC local radio, the Edge's guitar playing, McDonald's food.

sat-nav *1. n.* An in-car electronic device which allows reps to find their way to cheap hotels and massage parlours whilst avoiding areas of traffic congestion. *2. n.* An in-head device which allows *bladdered* gentlemen to find their way home on a Saturday night whilst they are unconscious with the drink.

sat'n'aving *phr.* Amusing way of declaring

one's toilet activity to a curious interlocutor. *'Hey Tom! Tom! What you doing in there?' 'Not much dear, just sat'n'aving a dump.'*

Saturday night beaver *n.* Dancefloor fauna and, you would imagine, the title of a *grumble film* or two.

Saul Hudson, I'm just going for a *exclam.* A means of explaining that you are going to take a *Chinese singing lesson*. From the real name of the straggly-barnetted, top-titfered Guns'n'Roses plank spanker Slash.

sauce 1. *n.* Booze, usually when taken in large quantities. *'That Keith Chegwin didn't half hit the sauce, you know.'* 2. *v.* To seduce. 3. *n.* Cheek. *'He asked to borrow me motor, and then said could I bring it round and make sure the tank was full. What a fucking sauce!'*

saucepan tit *n.* A breast with an outline sadly reminiscent of a saucepan hanging by its handle. A *sock-full-o-beans*.

saucy 1. *adj.* Of British seaside postcards; featuring busty young ladies, fat old ladies, hen-pecked husbands, frigid spinsters, honeymooning couples, nudist camps, people sticking their *cocks* through fences and getting them bitten by a goose *etc.* 2. *exclam.* Barbara Windsor's inevitable response to a sexual overture, whether intended or accidental.

sausage and doughnut situation *n.* Heterosexual intercourse. *'I did NOT engage in a sausage and doughnut situation with that woman. Miss Lewinsky. She merely sucked me off a bit and stuck my cigar up her cludge. Then I dropped my yop on her frock.'* (President Bill Clinton giving evidence to Special Prosecutor Kenneth Starr).

sausage casserole *n.* The insertion of more than one porky *banger* into a lady's *hotpot* for a warming winter treat. A *top hat*.

sausage derby *n.* A duel fought with a pair of *pork swords*.

sausage fat *n. Jitler.*

sausage grappler *n.* A *salami slapper*.

sausage jockey *n.* Any small Irish man who sits on a sausage and then bounces up and down. A *sausage rider*.

sausage kennel *n.* The *rear quarters* of a *good listener*.

sausage pizza *n.* The closest thing to a *sausage sandwich* that *Miss Lincolnshire* is able to provide. A *diddy ride* on a lady with *stits*.

sausage pot *n.* A lady's privates.

sausage sandwich *n.* A juicy *salami frotted* between two pink *baps*, the end result of which is a *pearl necklace. Dutch.*

sausages under the grill, have *v.* To be in imminent need of the lavatory for a sit down visit. To *have the turtle's head;* to be *touching cloth. 'Mr Burrell regrets that he will not be able to accede to your request that he re-attend the hearing, your honour, as he informs me that he has sausages under the grill.'*

sausage supper *n.* Female equivalent of a *fish supper*. A *nosh* on a *cock* sticking out of a pile of mashed potato.

sausage wallet *n.* A wallet for putting sausages in. A *fanny*.

SBD *abbrev.* Of *farts* and *farting*, Silent But Deadly. A subtle release of fatally-pungent *botty gas*.

SBJ *abbrev. medic.* Doctor's notes terminology for a senior citizen or *coffin dodger, low flying angel, estate agent's dream*. Still Breathing, Just.

SBV *abbrev.* Of *farts* and *farting*, Silent

'Up betimes, and much perturbed to find a veritable piece of sixty grit alongside me in the fart sack. Resolved never again to mix the port and the stout.' ~ *The Diary of Samuel Pepys.*

But Violent. *Minging fizzle* from the *fart fissure.*

scads *n. Kicksies, dunghampers, thunderbags.*

scaffolder's laptop *n.* A fruit machine.

scallywagon *n.* A boxy white van with blacked-out square windows, the preferred mode of transport for guests of Her Majesty.

Scania scotch *n.* Dark yellow, pungent spirit found in old lemonade bottles at the side of motorways and A-roads, having been discarded there by the hitch-hiker-murdering HGV drivers who distil it in their kidneys. Also known as *wagon wine* or *trucker's Tizer.*

scared stiff *adj.* Aroused whilst watching a horror movie, for example by Drew Barrymore's jumper arangement in *Scream.*

scare the cat *n.* To produce a startlingly loud *trouser cough.*

scarlet emperor *n.* A red, rather bruised, male reproductive organ after an extended session of *self-help.*

scat n. Form of *shite*-fixated *grumble* particularly popular amongst our saucy Germanic cousins.

scatman *1. n.* A jazz singer who improvises nonsense Bill and Ben-style lyrics because they've forgotten the proper words, *eg.* Sammy Davis Jnr., Cleo Laine. *2. n.* A teutonic *poo-game enthusiast.*

scheissberg *n.* A titanic *floater*, a full 90% of which lies hidden below the waterline.

schizophrenic face *n.* Of a lady, to have stunningly beautiful eyes, but a nose like Ricky Tomlinson's.

schlong *n. Yiddish.* A large *putz.* A *schlonger.* A *kosher dill.*

schlong shed *n.* Condom, *stopcock, stiffy*

stocking.

schmeckie *n.* Opposite of a *schlong.*

scholar's bonus *n.* A rare, but cherished glimpse of a short-skirted young lady's intimate nethergarments as she pedals past in a cycle-heavy city such as Oxford or Cambridge. *Rabbit's tail.*

schoolboy error *n. Shooting one's load* far too early whilst *on the job.* Premature ejaculation.

school dinner *1. n.* A foul, brown mess, served in a large white bowl, the smell of which makes you heave. *2. n.* A toilet full of *shit.*

school play curtain, fanny like a *sim.* A lady's *part* that has so many flaps and folds that it obstructs and frustrates one's progress. From the familiar childhood experience of fumbling about behind a large curtain trying to make your way onto the stage to deliver your lines during a school play. A *labiarinth, hampton maze.*

school run *1. n.* The act of dropping one's kids off at the school at the same time every morning. *2. n.* The act of *dropping one's kids off at the pool* at the same time every morning.

Schrodinger's twat *n.* Unsettling, paradoxical thought experiment regarding the as-yet undisclosed genital areas of a potential sexual partner who - prior to being subject to a more intimate inspection - exists in a state of ontological uncertainty, *viz.* They may be credibly regarded as, simultaneously a) a female person with a suspiciously prominent Adam's apple and big hands, and b) an unusually plausible male transvestite. At a suitable point in the evening, a surreptitious manual investigation may be performed in order to "collapse the waveform", thereby sending the rest of the night and history down one of two radically divergent paths.

Schwarzenegger *n.* A lady's *tinter*, so-named because it lies "between her ARse and her fanNY".

scissor bone *n.* The nipsular guillotine which chops one's *logs* into manageable lengths. The *cigar cutter*.

scissor sack *n. medic.* A non-fatal genital injury in men caused by sitting down awkwardly in overly tight trousers. A *gentleman's discomfort, torsion of the testes.*

scissor sisters *n. Tennis fans bumping fur.*

scissors, paper, stone *1. n.* A traditional playground game. *2. n.* The hand motion used by German porn stars in *fisting* movies, *ie.* First two fingers, then four, then the full monty. *'Get out of the pool and we'll have a game of scissors, paper, stone.'*

scissorwork *n.* Hot *quim*-to-*quim lezbo* action.

scleg *n.* The sweat-prone yet sensitive area of skin between a fellow's *haggis* and his leg. Not to be confused with the *barse*. From scrotbag + leg. Also *bluck leg.*

scobie *n.* The low-level urinal at the end of the row, used by children, midgets and Dwight York. From Scobie Breasley, the diminutive jockey of the 1960s and 70s.

scooberty *n.* That period of adolescence when the male voice oscillates wildly and unpredictably between *basso profundo* and *soprano*, and thus resembles that of a popular, cheaply-animated caretaker-hunting cartoon Great Dane.

scoobysnack *n. Oral sex* involving a dog

and a very tall sandwich.

scooter *n.* A two-stroke *arse.*

scoots *n. medic.* An affliction characterised by morbid frequency and fluidity of faecal evacuations. The *Brads, Engelberts.*

score from a set piece *v.* To *pull* a *bird* who is a friend of a friend, or one on a blind date, *etc.*

score from open play *v.* To *pull* a *bird* one has never met before by simply bumping into her in a pub, club, chippie, funeral parlour, *etc.* and chatting her up.

scosser *n.* A *wanker* from north of the border. A clever elision of the words Scotch + tosser.

Scotch egg *1. n.* Party foodstuff of absolute last resort. *2. n.* A *turd* which has rolled out of the trouser leg of a *Harold Ramp* who hails from north of the border.

scotchguard shite *n.* A *Brad* which, no matter how messy it feels on exit, leaves one's *brown eye* miraculously unsullied. Named after the 3M product sold to countless paranoid housewives by surly soft furnishing salesmen.

Scotch pancake *n.* A pool of *spew.* A *pavement pizza.*

Scotsman's lounge *1. n.* An historic pub in Cockburn Street, Edinburgh. *2. n.* The gutter. *'That's my 20th pint of the day. I'm just off for a lie down in the Scotsman's lounge.'*

Scottish bedwarmer *n.* A *fart*, anal announcement.

Scottish breakfast *n.* Two paracetamols.

Scottish play *1. euph.* Shakespearean drama (*Macbeth* or *Hamlet* or something), the title of which cannot be spoken by superstitious *chickenshit* actors in case ill fortune befalls them. *2. n.*

Anal sex with an otherwise respectable partner.

Scottish salad *n*. The only vegetables that are ever spotted on a plate north of Carlisle, that is to say chips and beans.

Scottish sunshine *n*. Rain.

scouse *v*. To misappropriate opportunistically. *'I say, what a poor show. I left my dressing room unlocked for five minutes and when I came back my gold and diamond cigarette holder had been scoused.' (Terry-Thomas, Liverpool Magistrates Court, 1960).*

scouse dreadlocks *euph*. Any haircut longer than a grade 0 all over. See *geordie curls*.

SFZ *abbrev*. The Southern Frigid Zone; everything south of a lady's belt which is a no-go area. Named after the similarly chilly geographical region located between the Antarctic Circle and the South Pole.

scouse honour *exclam*. Merseyside-based variation of Baden-Powell's famous oath of youthful trustworthiness. *'Yeah, no worries. I'll look after the till, mate. Scouse honour.'*

scouser's cashpoint *n*. A fruit machine.

scouser's digit *n*. *medic*. Affliction, particularly common in the north west of England, preventing the sufferer from keeping his fingers out of the till.

scouser's fingers *sim*. Descriptive of an unkempt *clunge*. *'Jesus, woman. Your clout's as sticky as a scouser's fingers.' 'I know. But to be fair, I only came in to have my root canal done.'*

scouser's key *n*. A crowbar, hammer, half a brick or anything used to open someone else's back door.

scouser's laptop *n*. A pizza.

scouser's library *n*. A job centre.

scouse slippers *n*. Prison-issue white training shoes.

scouse tax *n*. A cheeky charge levied out of one's pockets by lovably light-fingered Liverpudlians when shopping on Merseyside.

scout movement *n*. A wholesome act of defecation performed in the great outdoors. A *brown owl* or *bear grill*.

scout's salute *n*. The act of inserting three digits into a lady's *beaver*, whilst reciting the following oath: "On my honour, I promise that I will do my best to do my duty to God and to the Queen, to help other people, and to keep the Scout Law."

scran *1. n*. That bit of a fellow's anatomy which falls between his *hairy swingers* and his clackervalve. The *barse, tintis, notcher, stinker's bridge*. The *perineum*. *2. n*. Dinner, *snap*.

scrank *n*. An inadvertent scrape of the *clockweights* or *clackerbag* which turns, as sure is eggs is eggs, into an act of *personal pollution*. Typically occurs when watching television during the day, alone.

scranus *n*. The fucking *barse* again.

Scrapheap Challenge *1. n*. Channel 4 programme where teams compete to construct contraptions from scrap metal. *2. n*. The prospect of having to perform *cumulonimbus* on a *bird* who is *up on blocks*. So called because of the general messyness, metallic taste and all-pervading odour of dirty blood.

scrapyard dog, going at it it like *sim*. Phrase evocative of a newly-acquired ladyfriend administering a *chewy* in the romantic surroundings of a vandalised playground or other bit of hastily-discovered abandoned wasteland.

scratch *v. Liverpud*. Of a scouse fellow, to sign on. *'I can't fix your roof Thursday. I'm scratching.'*

scratcher *n*. Bed, *fart sack, wanking chariot*.

scratosphere *n*. Extra-urban region surrounding a town that is populated by *scratters*.

scratter *n*. A person of limited finances, education and breeding, *eg*. 8 Ace. Also *ronker, pog, ned*.

scrattitude *n*. The cocky self-confidence that members of the lower orders display by stepping off the kerb and causing traffic to slow down or stop while they take their time casually sauntering across the road. Literally the attitude of a *scratter*.

screamer *n*. A raving *good listener*.

screamin' eagles *n*. *Stick vid* cinematography term for a scene where a man feeds his *cock* to two or more open-mouthed women who are on their knees, like a parent bird feeding a big purple worm to its hungry chicks. *Baby birding, passing the mic*.

screaming monkey *n*. A bit of female genitalia. Probably the bit which looks the most like a screaming monkey.

scree *1. n. coll*. Shale-like nuggets of *shit*. Approximately the size of a marrowfat pea.

screw *v*. To have sex piggy-style, rotating clockwise due to a corkscrew-shaped *cock*.

screwnicorn *n*. A mythical and somewhat magical sex act whereby a lesbian puts a *strap-on dildo* on her forehead and goes at her partner like a bull at a gate.

scrincter *n*. The bit between the scrotum and the sphincter. The *tintis, scran*.

script for a jester's tear *1. n*. Title track of a 1983 album by progressive rock band Marillion. *2. n*. The unnecessary plot-establishing footage that is routinely fast-forwarded through by the impatient viewers of adult-oriented cinematographic productions who are only really interested in seeing it going *up, in, out and off. Expresso bongo, foreporn*.

scrobbing *n. onomat*. The sound made by a dog when licking its own genitalia.

scrogg *1. v*. To partake in in an act of penetrative sexual intercourse up a lady. To *fuck*. *2. n*. An act of penetrative sexual intercourse partaken up a lady. A *fuck*.

scrogglings *1. n*. Olde English term for the small, irrelevant apples left on the tree after the main scrumpy crop has been harvested. *2. n. Spunk bubbles*.

scrolling the ipod *n*. Manually setting the missus's *playlist*. A more modern version of *finding Radio Luxembourg* for the gent with a delicate touch.

scrotal recoil *n*. Involuntary retraction of the *clockweights* into the body in harsh winter climes, when swimming in cold water or when watching Neil Kinnock's "We're alright! We're alright!" speech at Labour's 1992 Sheffield election rally.

scrote *1. n. Knacker, bollock brain*. A versatile testicular term of abuse. *2. n*. Someone who fails to fit *Country Life*'s preferred readership demographic profile.

scrote couture *n*. Clothing worn by the economically inactive denizens of the urban underclass. *Armani and Navy*.

scrotee *1. n*. The sort of feeble, adolescent beard which appears to be composed principally of spare *nadbag* fluff. *2. n*. The clump of pretentious, tufted jazz hair growing off the lower slopes of one's *chicken skin handbag*. From scrotum + goatee.

scrote rack *n.* Any civic amenity to which track-suited, baseball-hat-wearing ne'er-do-wells flock, in the style of the crows who congregate on the climbing frame in Alfred Hitchcock's *The Birds*, *eg.* Bus shelters, playgrounds, war memorials *etc.*

scrotinise *v.* Of a female friend, to carefully and expertly examine a chap's *clockweights.*

scrotorbike *n.* One of them small motorcycles that *chasbos* use to ride round on the pavements of our less salubrious housing estates.

scrotum pole *n.* Old Red Indian erection at the foot of which lie *John Wayne's hairy saddlebags*, and around which *Madam Palm and her five sisters* do ritual dances to precipitate *jizzle.*

scrotum ticklers *n.* The huge comedy moustaches favoured by the acutely-observed *fruit feelers* who used to populate the cartoons illustrating Richard Littlejohn's columns in *The Sun.*

scrub *n.* An exfoliant facial treatment bestowed upon the *nosher* of a *stubbly bush.*

scrubber *n. Slapper*, vulgar woman, *dollymop.*

scrubbery *n.* Any place where groups of young ladies tend to gather, *eg.* By the tills in a 24-hour garage, round a night bus driver, on a shopping precinct bench, outside an off-licence, in an abortion clinic waiting room *etc.*

scrubbing the cook *n. milit. US. Bashing the bishop, cuffing the suspect, knocking off Patton's tin hat.*

scruburb *n.* A less than desirable area to live.

scruff *n.* Pornography, *muck, grumble.*

"Look what I've got', said William breathlessly , as he emptied the contents of his jumper at the Outlaws' feet. 'It's a load of scruff. Jumble found it under a hedge." (from *William's Milk Race* by Richmal Crompton).

Scruggs style *1. n.* In the world of banjo musicianship, a popular approach to bluegrass playing popularised by Earl Scruggs, which gets impressive results from frenetic picking with the thumb, index and middle fingers. *2. n.* In the world of *invisible banjo playing*, to place one's thumb on a lady's *clematis* and one's index and middle fingers up her *blurtch* and *chuff* respectively, before trying to get a tune out of her. *3. n.* A lady *practising her fingerwork, perfecting her licks.*

scrumping *1. n. US.* Having sex. *2. n. UK.* Stealing apples.

scruncher *n.* One who stores his discarded vestments in his *floordrobe,*

scrunchies *1. n.* Of *slappettes*, the colourful elasticated hairbands captured by rival teenage *slappers* in battle. *2. n.* Excess batter in a chip shop. *Scraps.*

scrunger *n.* Another name for one of those bike seat sniffers found lurking around the cycle racks of convents and women's drop-in centres. A *garboon, snufty, snurglar, nurfer.*

scrunion *n. Aus. medic.* The wrinkly scrotal remnant immediately preceding the perineum. From scrotum + onion.

scrunt *n. coll. Blart, flange, gusset.* A group of attractive women. *'Suddenly, at the age of 25, the Prince was cast as the world's most eligible bachelor. On a Royal tour of New Zealand in 1973, he found himself having to batter off top-end scrunt with a shitty stick.'* (from

HRH The Prince of Wales by Jim-Bob Dimbleby).

scrut *n*. Hardcore *oyster grumble* that would satisfy the curiosity of even the most ardent amateur gynaecologist. *Close up pink*.

scruttock *n*. The area of skin 'twixt *scrot* and *bot*. The *barse, tintis*.

scuffer *n*. A *cozzer*, a *rozzer*, a *tit-head*, a *filth*. *'Look out, it's the scuffers!'*

scuffing *n*. Hands-free *self abuse* technique, which involves rubbing one's *cock* against the mattress until the job is done. Presumably the hands are then brought back into service in order to clean up the mess.

scuff it *1. v*. In football, to lose concentration at the critical moment, leading to a disappointing shot. *2. v*. In *fucking*, to lose concentration at the critical moment, leading to a disappointing *shot*. *To suffer a lack of composure in front of the goal*.

scufflink *n*. The resulting mess when, whilst wiping your *balloon knot* at the conclusion of a particularly stercoraceous *digestive transit*, the wrist of your shirt inadvertently comes into contact with the *Marmite pot*.

scumbag *n*. The ultimate term of abuse known to British tabloid journalists.

scumble *1. n*. A *shit*, heavily-dated paint effect inflicted on the participants of TV room makeover programmes. *2. n*. A language spoken exclusively by *Harold Ramps*. From Scottish + mumble.

scumbrella *n*. Any item pressed into service to keep the rain off a poor person, in lieu of a genuine umbrella, *eg*. A Greggs carrier bag.

scum-dog millionaire *n*. Contumelious epithet applied to any female "celeb-rity" who somehow manages to amass a seven-figure fortune despite displaying no evidence that she possesses any talent whatsoever.

scummertime *n*. The start of the school holidays when a flood of teenage *ronkers* descends upon a town's unwitting shoppers.

scummy mummy *n*. The opposite of a *yummy mummy*. A coarsely plebeian materfamilias, if you will.

scumper *n*. Someone who lays sheets of bog roll on the seat of a public toilet so as his *arse* does not touch the same place as someone else's *arse* has touched. The late *Carry On* star Kenneth Williams was known to *scump*.

scum shovel *n*. Any form of public transport used extensively by the underprivileged, *eg*. The no.11 Torry to Northfield bus in Aberdeen.

scumwad *n*. *US*. The ultimate term of abuse known to American tabloid journalists.

scungies *n*. Disreputable *scads*. *'What's the matter, Carol?' 'While I was onstage, performing a medley of my hits including China in Your Hand, some dirty bastards have been in the dressing room and wanked on my scungies.'*

scuns *n*. *Scads*.

scunt *n*. Like a *scosser*, but even worse.

scutter *n*. *Slut, shag bag, scrubber, slapper*. A lady of easy virtue.

scuttle *1. v*. To *sink the pink*, or *brown*, esp. in a hurried fashion from behind. *2. n*. A swift, frantic act of intercourse. Or something to keep the coal in.

scuttler *n*. A fellow who, for whatever reason, will not *piss* alongside another at a urinal, but instead scuttles off into a cubicle, usually locking the door too.

sea bent *adj.* Descriptive of a matelot whose sexual tastes have been re-oriented due to a prolonged period of enforced maritime abstinence. Of otherwise heterosexual sailors, tempted to have a *ride on the other ferry* whilst at sea. *'Kiss me Hardy, I'm feeling distinctly sea bent.'*

sea biscuit 1. *n.* Legendary (not literally) US racehorse, recently immortalised (not literally) in a *shit* (literally) film. 2. *n.* Nautical equivalent of an *air biscuit*, delivered whilst in an over-relaxing bath. 3. *n.* A *turd* floating in the *briny*. *'Observant Admiral (Who has, through his extended telescope, spotted trouble in store for the heroic Channel swimmer half way through his heroic natation of "La Manche" 'twixt Dover and Calais, and resolves to vouchsafe this important information "post-haste" to the natatorial half-man half-fish by hailing him at the top of his not inconsiderable voice): 'Look out, Captain Webb. There's a sea biscuit on the top of the next wave.' Captain Webb (With a big turd stuck in his mouth): 'Too late.'* (cartoon by Sir John Tenniel in *Punch*, 1875).

seafood splatter *n.* The inevitable consequence of a night spent eating a big silver tray full of prawns, mussels, squid *etc.*

seafood taco *n.* A lady's *clout* that smells like a fishmonger's hands and could lead to an upset stomach.

seagulling 1. *n.* The mischievous act of dropping *jizz* onto a passer by from a height, *eg.* A tree, a roof or a Status Quo hotel room balcony. Could lead to *Graham Norton's hair.* 2. *n.* Amongst the *dogging* community, spattering the windscreen of a vehicle with *spongle*, in the manner of a passing kittiwake with loose *Camillas.*

seagulls' wellies *n.* Maritime used *blobs.* *'How was your swim, David?' 'Awful. I was only in the water ten minutes and I swallowed a turd and three seagulls' wellies. I'm going to write to the council.'*

seahorse *n.* A man doing a woman's job, *eg.* Arranging flowers, designing dresses, pushing a baby about in a pram. From the comedy fish the hippocampus, the male of which species carries its wife's young about like some sort of *puff.*

Sealink salsa *n.* Cross-Channel ferry passenger vomit. *'Careful on your way to the bar, your majesty. There's Sealink salsa all over the fucking shop.'*

seal of Hades *n.* The boundary between our world and the *devil's kitchen.* The *ringpiece.*

sea monster *n. Swamp donkey, hippocrocapig.*

seaside shithouse, fuller than a *sim.* Descriptive of something that is replete to bursting point. *'Take that bin bag out will you, Your Highness. It's fuller than a seaside shithouse.'*

season cliff hanger 1. *n. US.* In TV drama series, a final show which ends just at the exciting part, encouraging viewers to watch the next series. 2. *n.* A large *shit* which cuts off at the exciting part causing one to wait for what feels like an eternity to get the ending.

seaweed *n.* The fishy mixture of girl hair and *fanny batter* that needs to be extricated from the plughole every once in a while.

secaturds *n. medic.* The muscles surrounding the *nipsy* that provide the power to operate the *turtle guillotine.*

second handrex *n.* The somewhat unlikely

use of someone else's pre-*spangled* tissue for the purpose of cleaning up your own manly emissions, in the absence of anything else to hand, *eg.* Tea towel, sock, living room curtains, dog's ears *etc.*

second post *n.* A supplementary delivery of *anal parcels* which takes one by surprise half way through the morning.

second sitting *1. n.* An immediate, unavoidable return visit to the *shitter* after wiping and washing. *2. n.* One of those times when the first gush of feculence smells so foul - and fills the bowl to such an alarming depth - that one is forced to flush before continuing, perhaps following a delicious meal at Heston Blumenthal's Fat Duck restaurant.

secret lemonade drinker *n.* A *good listener.*

secret smile *n.* A *cunt.*

security check *1. n.* Rounds made last thing at night to assure oneself that the front and back doors are definitely locked. *2. n.* Last thing at night grope of the missus to check that her *front* and *back doors* are definitely locked.

sediment *n.* The *totty crud* that remains unsyphoned at chucking out time in a night club. *Floor sweepings.*

see a friend to the coast *euph. Drop the kids off at the pool.*

seed *n.* That which was scattered on the stoney croft by Onan, and great was the wrath of the Lord.

seed catalogue *n.* A *flesh mag* for *onanists.*

seedless grapes *n.* Post-vasectomy *knackers.* As swallowed by women whilst languorously reclining on *chaises longues.*

seeing to *n.* Sexual servicing, a "jolly good" one of which is often said to have been given to a woman by a man. And vice versa, occasionally.

see to Uncle Albert *euph.* To *knock one out.* A phrase made popular by the character Ken Barlow in old episodes of *Coronation Street. 'Ken (on phone): What's that Dierdre? There's a big order to fill at the factory and you've got to work late...? I see. And after that, there's an emergency council meeting at Weatherfield Town Hall...? (sigh) No, don't worry about me, love. I'll just grab a hotpot at the Rovers, then go home and see to Uncle Albert.'*

see you next Tuesday *sort of acronym.* Ingeniously offensive parting pleasantry allowing you the satisfaction of calling someone a *cunt* to their face without them knowing it.

self-catering *n.* See *self discipline.*

self-cleaning oven *1. n.* In the world of kitchen appliances, a cooker which does not in any sense whatsoever clean itself. *2. n.* The *cludge* of a female *ejaculatrix.*

self contact sport *n.* The exercise regimen of choice for the armchair athlete who lives alone.

self discipline *n.* Character-building regime engendered in the armed forces and public schools. *Masturbation, self improvement, self harm.*

self help manual *n.* An item of literature that aids *relaxation.* An *art pamphlet*, a *flesh mag*, a *bachelor's newsletter.*

self indulgent *adj.* Prone to treating *junior* to a brisk *rub down* from time to time.

selling Buicks *n. US.* Vomiting. From the similarity of the sounds made by a *chunderer* to the cries of the Buick street vendors of Detroit, *viz.* "Buick! Buick!"

semen *n. Aphrodite's Araldite, joy gloy,*

gunk, spunk, goo.

semen-olina *n. Spunk* of an especially lumpy nature.

sement *n.* Quick-drying, gloopy substance used for binding *hardcore. Sement* has to be mixed vigorously for a couple of minutes before it is applied. The main constituent of *cumcrete. Jazz glue.*

Shanghai finish *1. n.* In the world of darts, triple twenty; twenty; double top. *'I'll never forget the Shanghai finish I got at the Lakeside Country Club, Frimley Green.' 2. n.* In the world of romance, *arse; fanny; double top (tits). 'I'll never forget the Shanghai finish I got off that slapper in a layby near the Forth Road Bridge.'*

semi *1. n.* A *lazy lob on*, a *dobber*, a half-erect penis. *2. n.* A house joined to one other house. See *semi-detached.*

semi-demi-on *n.* A *quarter-on, half a lob on.* The first stirrings of *dobberdom.*

semi-detatched *1. adj.* Of a house, completely attached to another house. *2. n.* A partial tumescence of the *giggle stick* which arises of its own accord and for no particular reason whilst one is daydreaming.

seminal *adj.* A highbrow, intellectual way of referring to something as being *wank.*

semi-on *n.* A partially-tumescent *membrum virile. Half a teacake*, a *dobber.*

send a sausage to the seaside *euph. Sink a few U boats.*

senorita beater *n.* Any Spanish lager, such as San Miguel *etc. Pedro's piss.*

separate-us apparatus *n.* A *condom, stiffy stocking. 'Did you remember to bring the separate-us apparatus?' 'Oh, Rat's cocks! I didn't. Perhaps we'd better just play the bagpipes tonight.'*

serpent socket *n.* That hole into which the *one-eyed trouser snake* is plugged.

serpent's tongue *n.* A forked *piss* caused by a *jazz egg* blocking the *hog's eye. Twin jets. 'Jesus! You've pissed on the floor again.' 'Sorry, love, only I had the serpent's tongue this morning.'*

serve and volley *1. n.* A dynamic form of tennis whereby, having served, a player makes his way directly to the net in order to despatch his return shot. *2. n.* When a drinker, having consumed an elegant sufficiency of alcohol, finds himself unable to take any more on board and immediately throws up on the spot. *'Terrific serve and volley there from Amy Winehouse. That shot went straight back into the glass.'*

serving *n.* A single sitting's worth of *bumwad. 'I say Lizzie matey peeps, next time you're a-goin' down the Spar, get me a new roll of shit tickets will you? There's only enough left in here for a couple of servings, innit.' 'Right you are, Philip.'*

serving it up *v.* Of a gentlemen, to be *having it off* with, or *slipping a length* to, a lady. *'Throughout the early eighties, Prince Charles was plagued by persistent rumours that Major James Hewitt was serving it up to Princess Diana.'* (from *Charles the Biography* by Little Jimmy Dimbleby).

Seth Armstrong in a SARS mask *sim.* An erotically-alluring description of a vaginally-hirsute lady wearing thong underpants.

set on fire and put out with a shovel, looks like she's been *sim.* Light-hearted expression which can be used to gently broach the subject of an *eight-pinter's* appearance. *'I don't fancy yours much,* *mate. She looks like she's been set on fire and put out with a shovel.'* (Dr Rowan Williams, the Archbishop of Canterbury, whilst officiating at the wedding of His Royal Highness the Prince of Wales and Camilla Parker-Bowels in the function room of the Travelodge, Windsor, on 9th April 2005).

setting the video *v.* Sexual position, in which the lady is on her knees and elbows, with her *arse* in the air, tutting exasperatedly.

seven pint stunner *n.* A *bird* whose inner beauty only struggles to the surface after one has quaffed the best part of a gallon of *Nelson Mandela.*

seven stepper *n.* An extended *Exchange & Mart* which, as its name suggests, lasts for a good few paces as one saunters down the street. A length-specific *string of pearls, duckwalk.*

seven/ten split *1. n.* In ten-pin bowling, a *pair of skittles* so far apart that hitting them both with a single shot is almost impossible. *2. n.* A really wide *fanny* that can only be taken on whilst wearing special shoes.

seventy-one-er *n.* A *sixty-niner*, but with two fingers up the lady's *bonus tunnel* for good measure.

sex *1. n. It, the other, dirties. 2. v.* To pump someone full of semen. *'Babe, I'm gonna sex you up.'* (*Sex You Up* song lyric, George Michael). *3. n.* A lady's *mingepiece. 'I want your sex.'* (*I Want Your Sex* song lyric, George Michael).

sex act *1. n.* Versatile, vague tabloid term used to describe and denigrate specifically non-specific acts or *shenanigans* which have been "performed". Usually prefixed "vile", "lewd" or "sordid". *2. n.* Vile, lewd and sordid acts performed on

a stage at Club Baghdad, Barcelona, to pluck an example out of thin air.

sexcrement *n. medic.* The foul mix of bodily fluids that is passed through the *nipsy* after several sessions of *backdoor love. Santorum.*

sex fruit *n.* A baby.

sexile *n.* A forlorn, lonely fellow in a bar, constantly checking his watch and desperately trying to make a half last all evening because his flatmate is *getting his end away.*

sex wee *1. n.* An ejaculation of *spongle.* *2. n.* The *spongle* that is ejaculated.

sexual athlete's foot *n. medic. Happyrash.*

SFW *1. abbrev.* Internet reassurance that the content being linked to is Safe For Work. *2. abbrev.* Internet reassurance that the content being linked to is not safe for work. Suitable For Wanking.

Shabba *1. n. rhym. slang.* Multiple acts of masturbation. From the name of the famous *puddlejumperphobic* Jamaican dancehall artiste Shabba Rultipleactso fmasturbation. *2. n. exclam.* Shouted catchphrase of *shit-for-brains* former BBC Radio 6Music faux-cockney *cunt-bubble* George Lamb and his band of clueless *fart catchers*, which was repeated *ad fucking nauseam* throughout his dismal, unlistenable programme during the half-hour gaps between records.

shackled *adj.* The condition of a man searching the house for *arse paper* with his trousers and underpants round his ankles.

shackles, arse like a bag of *sim. naut.* Charming maritime expression used to describe the rear end of a lady who has successfully *dodged* a significant quantity of *salad, ie.* Whose *back porch* is reminiscent of half a hundredweight of lumps of steel in a sack. *'Isn't that Vanessa Feltz putting her shopping in her car? Christ on a bike, she's got an arse like a bag of shackles.'*

Shadsworth six-seater *n*. An ambulance, named after the delightful area of Blackburn, where trips home after a night out are customarily taken in just such a conveyance.

shaft *1. v.* To *shag, screw. 2. n.* The mast on the *skin boat. 3. n. prop.* A black private dick that's a sex machine to all the chicks in town. Damn right.

shafterburn *n*. Painful friction-induced scorching of the *skinclad tube* caused by excessively *relaxing in a gentleman's way.*

shag *1. v.* To copulate, to *fuck.* A once shocking term, now lame enough to be used by "right on" vicars and CBeebies presenters. *2. n.* A sexual encounter, a *screw. 3. n. US.* 1950s dance craze. *4. n.* Type of sea bird. *5. n.* Tobacco. *6. n.* Something to do with piles on carpets.

shag bag *n*. Loose woman, *a bike.*

shag dust *n. Fuck powder.* Make-up.

shag factory *n*. Joint which is heaving with *blit, knickerville, blart city.*

shaggability *n*. Measurement of how *prodworthy* a person is on an arbitrary, non-scientific scale.

shaggable *adj*. Worth a *one.*

shagged out *adj*. Exhausted, *jiggered, buggered, zonked, fucked.*

shaggin' wagon *n*. A *passion wagon*, a *fuck truck*, a *spambulance.*

shagging a bike *sim*. To describe sex with an extremely thin woman. *'These supermodels, nice faces, some of 'em, but get 'em in the fart sack and it's like shagging a bike. I would imagine.'*

shagging a waterbed *sim*. To describe sex with an extremely fat woman. *Slapping the fat and riding the waves.*

shaggis *n*. A Scotsman's bloated, blotchy scrotum.

shag lag *n*. Mild temporal disorientation brought on by an excess of sexual shenanigans.

shag monster *n*. A not necessarily ugly woman who has a voracious appetite for something to do with carpets or pipe tobacco. A *nymphomentalist.*

shagnasty *n*. A *shag monster* who is also extremely ugly.

shag pile *n*. The small heap of *Richards* typically left on a gentleman's mattress after he has *kicked* a particularly relaxed sexual partner's *back doors in.* *'Cor, that bird Dave was with on Friday was a bit pished, wasn't she?' 'Yeah. He said she let him do her up the council, but the dirty cow left him with a shag pile.'*

shag slab *n*. The *altar of lurve*, bed, *passion pit, cock block, fart sack, scratcher.*

shag tags *n*. Love bites, *hickies, suckers.*

shake a tit *v*. To defecate spooneristically.

shake hands with the French *v*. To push one's finger through the *bumwad* when wiping the *freckle.* To *breach the hull, push through.* From the similarity to the moment when the two bore drills met in the Channel Tunnel and the English bloke forced his hand through the thin divide to shake the hand of his Gallic counterpart. *'Did you wash your hands before kneading that dough, Nigella?' 'Erm, no, Charles. But it's okay, it's not as if I've shaken hands with the French today.'*

shake hands with the mayor *1. v.* To greet the leading alderman in one's borough, perhaps whilst he is judging a sandcastle, snowman or large vegetable competition in a municipal park. Like they do. 2. *v.* To interfere with your own *bits and bobs*, whilst paying scant regard to the medically-documented risks that you run, *viz.* Going blind, insane, hairy-handed, bald and/or short.

shake hands with the wife's best friend *v.* To perform an act of *self-pollution*.

shake hands with the Wookie *v.* Of those men blessed with eight-foot-long hairy *cocks* that make growling noises, to *wank*.

shake shifter *n.* The first pint of the day. *'Good morning and welcome aboard flight BA 103 from Oslo. The captain's had a shake shifter, so we'll shortly be proceeding to the runway to commence our take-off.'*

shake the bishop's hand *v.* To have a *piss*, as opposed to sticking your hand through a hole in the lavatory wall *and wanking* him off.

shake the lettuce *v.* Of females, to *pee* and give the *beef curtains* a quick tumble dry afterwards.

shake the snake *v.* Male equivalent of *shake the lettuce*, the object being to dislodge any *forget-me-nots* before returning the *schlong* to the *shreddies*.

shaking hands with the unemployed *n.* Having *one off the wrist*.

shaking like a shitting dog *sim.* A bad attack of the DTs after a night on the *sauce*.

shaking like a flatpack wardrobe *sim.* Descriptive of the female equivalent of the *vinegar strokes*.

shampoo *n.* A pretend *shit*. A toilet break taken for the sole purpose of avoiding an unpleasant task. *'Where's Dave?*

I thought I told him to take the bins out.' 'I think he's gone to the bogs for a shampoo.'

shampoo the rug *v.* To lose one's *population paste* on a *mapatasi*. Perhaps when *getting off at Edge Hill.*

sham-rock *n.* Descriptive of a man who, despite talking the talk, couldn't knock the head off a half of shandy. *'Today's Birthdays: Jean Picard, French astronomer, 1620; Ernest Hemingway, Nobel Prize-winning American author, 1899; Isaac Stern, Ukrainian violin virtuoso, 1920; Ross Kemp, balding sham-rock Fruit & Fibre ad actor, 1964.'*

Shamu *n.* An overly-acrobatic *dreadnought* that splashes the spectating testicles. From the performing whale of the same name that lives simultaneously in Florida, California and Texas. And occasionally tucks into its handlers.

shandy andy *n.* A *jizzmop*.

shandydextrous *adj.* To be blessed with the ability to give one's *monkey* an equally vicious *spanking* with either hand.

shandygram *n.* A luridly-worded SMS message, typically texted to a female acquaintance with the left hand after one has taken onboard a plethora of love potion. In 2004, the *News of the World* published several *shandygrams*, purported to have been sent to Channel 5 pig-*wanker* Rebecca Loos by simpleton billionaire free kick merchant David Beckham.

shandy sunbed *n.* A bench in a park or a precinct. The *tramp grill*.

shandy tan *n.* The ruddy-red complexion sported by *Harold Ramps* after spending too long asleep on the *shandy sunbed*.

shandy tickler *n.* One who has foolishly

decided to masturbate whilst drunk.

Shanks Bay *n*. The habitat of the toilet duck. A natural harbour, flowing into the *China Sea*, which is noted for its high concentrations of effluent.

shanny *1. n.* A type of fish, specifically the smooth blenny. *2. n.* Appropriately enough, a depilated vagina. From shaved + fanny.

shark *v*. To go on the *pull*, using aggressive, sly or cunning tactics.

shark's fin *n*. The profile of a neighbour's *beetle bonnet* viewed through a tight bikini bottom whilst sunbathing on the beach. *Pigeon's chest.*

shark's mouth *n*. A somewhat unsettling term for a gentleman's urinal.

shark's nose *n*. A lady's *clematis* when it is in an advanced state of arousal, to the extent that it would scare away all but the bravest *muffdivers*.

sharks sniffing, have the *euph.* Of a lady, to be afflicted with her monthly uncleanliness. *"My darling, at last we are alone,' murmured Heathcliff, as he took Cathy in his arms. 'I cannot wait a moment longer. I must have you now.' 'Sorry, love, I've got the sharks sniffing,' she replied.'* (from *Wuthering Heights* by Tracey Bronte).

shark week *n*. That quarter of each month when there is blood in the water. Also *rag week, blob week, rollover week, gipsy week, blow job week* and *cricket week.*

Sharon sixteen stone *n*. A *bird* who crosses her legs when she isn't wearing any knickers and you still can't see anything. See also *J-lower.*

shart *v*. To pass wind with an unexpected non-gaseous component. To *follow through.*

shat nav *n*. The use of cutting-edge automotive GPS technology in order to locate a fast food restaurant where one can *go for a McShit.*

shat on from a height *v*. To be badly exploited, humiliated, let down.

shatin underwear *n*. The amusingly-soiled *undercrackers* found up back alleys, in shop doorways and stuffed through building society letterboxes on Sunday mornings.

shatkins *n*. Rapid, astonishingly-effective diet based on the somewhat controversial theory that the most effective way to lose weight is to acquire a bacterial stomach infection by the intake of meat only, especially 2am burger bar fayre. *'Good grief, you've lost weight since yesterday.' 'Yes, six stones. I've been on the shatkins diet.'*

shat trick *n*. The professional goal of the salaried worker, ie. Three *Mr Browns* in one working day.

shave a horse *v*. To have a *piss, take a leak, turn your bike around.*

shaven haven *n*. A bald *monkey's forehead, John Craven.*

Shearer's Island *n*. That increasingly isolated patch of hair on the front of a balding gentleman's head. Named after balding former footballer Alan who, if you look, has a distinctly desolate-looking doormat of hair on the front of his head. Viewers of the recent *South Bank Show* about Dusty Springfield will agree that Neil Tennant out of the Pet Shop Boys now has one of the most impressive *Shearer's Islands* in modern day Britain.

she-bass *n*. The fishy, female equivalent of *he-dam.*

she could shit on my chest and slap it

with a cricket bat *exclam*. A romantic young man's declaration of his deep, undying love for the new girl in his life. *'Did my heart love 'till now? Forswear its sight. For I never saw true beauty 'till this night. 'Tis Juliet, and if she's not my true love I wouldst eat my hat. She could shit on my chest and slap it with a cricket bat.'* (from *Romeo and Juliet* by William Shakespeare).

shed *n*. A large, promiscuous woman. Somewhere to stick *tools* and keep the lawnmower.

shedded *adj*. Trousered, cattled.

sheep dog trials *rhym. slang*. *Carpet tiles*.

sheep's heart on a Vim tin *sim. Scot*. Descriptive of a *hard on* to be proud of.

sheep sitting *adj*. *On the blob, dropping clots*.

sheep's twats *n. medic*. The appearance of the eyes in the morning after a night on the sauce. Or, for that matter, the appearance of the eyes in the afternoon after a morning on the sauce. Also *eyes like sheep's cunts, piss holes in the snow. 'Christ, Judy. You can't go on looking like that. You've got sheep's twats.'*

sheet music *n*. Aeolian emanations from beneath the covers as two lovers semi-consciously serenade each other with their *wind sections*. Usually performed at the break of day following a night *on the pop*.

sheezer *n*. A woman who exhibits a disproportionate number of male traits in her everyday behaviour, *eg*. Drinking beer, watching football, excessive masturbation, shagging *birds*.

Sheffield hammer *n*. A rolled-up newspaper used to hammer nails into bits of wood, which can be unrolled before the *scuffers* arrive.

she-gulling *n*. The popular post-coital act whereby the lady scoops the *man fat* from out her *blurtch* and flings it back into her paramour's face.

Sheila's wheels *n*. The *clockweights* of a trans-gendered Antipodean *trolley dolly*.

shejaculate *n*. The *love relish* that some women supposedly fire from their *fur burgers* when they suffer an organism.

shelling *n*. Yet another supremely unlikely-sounding homosexual practice, most probably cooked up in the fevered imagination of a popular tabloid columnist, which involves the removal of a snail from its shell and the insertion of said evicted mollusc into a *puddle jumper's nipsy* in order that he can savour the wriggling sensation. If they do do it, they ought to be bloody well ashamed of themselves.

she may be up on blocks but the boot's always open *phr*. Offensively sexist suggestion made by a boorish male to his *blue-balled* mate whose *tart* is *on her rags*.

shenis *n*. What you need in order to make the most of a *mangina*.

Sherman *rhym. slang*. A *tug*. From Sherman tank = wank.

sherry monocle *n*. Upper class equivalent of *beer goggles*.

she's a bit bang! knock knock *exclam*. Humorous phrase used to describe a lady with a substantial *bow frontage*. Descriptive of a woman caller whose *generous provisions* inevitably make contact with the door before her knuckles do.

Shetland *n*. A tiny *turd*. From the fact that it is, like the miniature horses famously drawn by the late Norman Thelwell, a small *pony*.

Shetland fudge *n*. Stiff, caramel-coloured *feeshus*, which comes in a Tartan tin and makes an ideal gift for an elderly relative.

Shetland pony's cock, sticks out like a *sim*. Useful expression descriptive of something which is conspicuously obvious. From the fact that the *blood sausages* of the popular miniature horses are noticeably sizeable in comparison to their diminutive stature. *'It's no good, Johnny. We're going to have to lose the syrup. It sticks out like a Shetland pony's cock under the studio lights.'*

Shetland rabbit, hung like a *sim*. To have a *cock* like that of Bobby Davro. Also *hung like a Chinese mouse, hung like the Rt Hon Jack Straw MP.*

she-tox *n*. A period when a married gentleman's spouse is away, during which he cleanses his system of her wholesome influences. A welcome relapse into bachelorhood ways of drinking, *wanking* and curry-eating himself daft. A *total wifeout*.

shift *v*. To *bang, poke, screw*.

shifting furniture *euph*. To produce a loud, scraping *horse & cart* which sounds like people moving heavy objects around in the flat upstairs. *'Eat your lunch at the Curry Capital, Bigg Market, Newcastle upon Tyne and I, the late Lord Abdul Latif of Harpole, personally guarantee that you'll be shifting furniture by teatime.'*

shift, put in a *v*. To have sexual intercourse with a partner when one can't really be *arsed*. *'What's up, George? Why the long face?' 'Oh, it's me and the missus's 34th wedding anniversary.*

She'll be expecting me to go home and put in a shift tonight.'

shims *n*. Ladyboys, flippers.

Shipman, to do a *v*. From Harold Shipman. To *inject* a lady much older than oneself. *Granny banging, biddy fiddling.*

shirt fly *n*. A "yes man". One who is always up the gaffer's *arse*. A *fart-sucker*, a *brown noser*, a *Penfold*.

shirtful *n*. A well-stocked *rack*. *'My, what a shirtful. You've got the job.' 'Thankyou Mr Berlusconi.'*

shirt lifter *n*. A tall man employed in a clothing shop to place stock on high shelves.

shirtlifter's arms *n*. Any pub frequented by *style conscious* gentlemen.

shirt potatoes *n*. Tits, melons, top bollocks, fat rascals, milky swingers.

shirt potato salad *n*. A healthy, tossed mixture of *chest spuds* and *man mayonnaise*. A disarranged *solicitor's tie*.

shirt raiser *n*. A mighty zephyr from the *brass eye*. An enormous *Bakewell*.

shirt turnips *n*. Small, yet upwardly-perky breasts. *Chest swedes*.

shit 1. *v*. To *shit*, defecate, *sink the Bismarck, build a log cabin, crimp one off, light a bum cigar*. 2. *n*. Crap, excrement, stools, assorted faecal matter. 3. *n*. Git, sod, get, a *shitty* person, usually "little". 4. *adj*. Crap, useless. *'Shit weather for this time of year, eh, vicar?'* 5. *exclam*. Oh dear.

shit a brick 1. *interj*. Exclamation of surprise. 2. *v*. To be scared, to *papper* one's *trolleys*.

shit, all the *phr*. The full range of extra condiments, seasonings, and what-have-you added to a comestible item purchased from a 2am *kebabulance* by a *wankered* fellow. From the scene in the Bravo Channel's hard-hitting *Booze Britain* documentary series, in which an incoherent *Friday foal* in Hartlepool or Doncaster or somewhere was asked whether he wanted sauce or onions on his purchase and replied: "Oh aye, all the shit", whilst losing his balance and falling sideways into the wall of the burger van.

shitarette *n*. The first cigarette of the day, which wakes up your bowels. A *player's number two, arse fuse*.

shit bit *n*. What American comedy writers call that *yoff*-inducing little moral homily, expository sermon or hortatory discourse they are contractually obliged to include towards the end of each script.

shitboy *n*. *Northumb*. Term of abuse for one engaged in menial employment. *'How, shitboy! Big Mac and chips!'*

shitch *n*. An annoying itch which is so far up your *bottle* that the only way to scratch it is to pass a *Thora* down past it.

shitcloud *n*. A common meteorological phenomenon involving a silent movement of wind and a strong smell of bad eggs.

shitcom *n*. A lamentable situation comedy, such as that thing with Boycie out off of *Only Fools and Horses*.

shit diamonds *v*. The end result when one is desperate for a *number two*, but is nevertheless denied access to the *chod bin*, so that one's *feeshus* get packed tightly into the *bomb-bay*. *'Hurry up in there, your Holiness. I'm shitting diamonds out here.'*

shite *n. & v.* See *shit*.

shite alight *n*. A doorstep incendiary *Thora* used as an offensive-smelling weapon against one's neighbour's slippers.

shit-eating grin *n*. Exaggerated, smug, self-satisifed smile as worn by the likes of Noel Edmonds.

shitebulb *n*. A thoroughly disapppointing source of luminescence of the sort greatly prized by world-saving types for their eco-friendly properties. *'Have you noticed, love? I've put a shitebulb in at the top of the cellar steps.' 'Who said that? Aargh, I've fell down the stairs and broken my neck.' 'Who said that?'*

shitegeist *n*. Collective consciousness or shared feeling that the world is *crap*.

shite house 1. *n*. A poorly-constructed abode. 2. *n*. A well-constructed brick lavatory building with a door which is prone to oscillate percussively when the wind blows. 3. *n*. The smallest room.

shiter *n*. *Arse, kak cannon*. That which *shites*.

shit-faced *n*. *Arseholed*, intoxicated, *wankered*.

shit-for-brains *n*. One who is intellectually challenged. A *joskin, fuckwit, dolt*.

shit house *n*. See *shite house*.

shit house shin pad *n*. *nav*. A concealed *grumble mag* wrapped around a sailor's leg under his sock as he makes his way to the HMS Ark Royal *crappers* for a *wank*.

shitingale *n*. One who breaks into song whilst *dropping a length of dirty spine*, usually in order to shield his audience from the slightly less tuneful sounds being produced by his *turtle guillotine*.

shititch *n*. *medic*. *Brass eye* irritation suffered by one who has exited the *cludgy* without wiping properly. An attack of *arse wasps* or *wire spiders*. From shit + itch. *'Mr Glitter, will you please stand still while we take aim?' 'Sorry mate,* *only I had a dodgy plate of Tai Hea Ngam Chua for my final meal and then when I went off to drop me shopping there was no paper in the crapper. I've got terrible shititch here, I tell you.'*

shit kiss *n*. A small, star-shaped brown mark left on the chin of a none-too-fussy *cumulonimbulist*.

shit limpet *n*. A lady who is hopelessly devoted to her loutish *cunt* of a boyfriend, despite regular beatings and his constant infidelity.

shit locker *n. Arse, bomb bay, chamber of horrors.*

shit machine *n*. A dog. *'I fired three shots, and moments later the hellish, glowing beast, whatever it was, lay dead in the Grimpen Mire. If I had hesitated for a second, or had my aim been less than true, it would most certainly have killed Sir Henry where he stood, as Stapleton had intended. 'My God, Holmes,' I expostulated breathlessly. 'What on earth is it?' The great detective stepped forward and examined the foul creature's still-luminous form through his eyeglass. 'A simple trick, Watson,' he announced presently. 'It is merely a large shit machine which has been coated with phosphorus.''* (from *The Shit Machine of the Baskervilles* by Arthur Conan-Doyle).

shitmus test *n*. Like a litmus test, only instead of indicator paper in a laboratory there's *arse paper* in a lavatory, and instead of an acid/base there's an *anus* that might have let *something slip* whilst *stepping on a duck*. *'Crikey, I think there was something in that. I'd better go and take a shitmus test.'*

shit on a shingle *euph. US. milit*. Chipped beef on toast, whatever chipped beef is.

shit on your own doorstep *euph. Foul the nest, eg. Shag* one's mother-in-law whilst totally *pissed. Piss on your chips, fart on your Weetabix.*

shitpot 1. *n*. A flushing, porcelain receptacle for one's *feeshus*, typically found in the bathroom. 2. *n*. A contumelious epithet applied to an idiot or person of restricted intellectual capacity. *Fuckwit.* 3. *n*. The *back body* or *wrong'un*. *'Tell you what, love. Just for a change I'll do you up the shitpot tonight.'*

shit pump *n*. The television. *'I'm off to bed, love. Don't forget to turn the shit pump off when you come up.'*

shits, the *n*. Of *smallroom dancing*, those up-tempo *trots* which include the *Tijuana cha-cha*, the *sour apple quickstep* and the *Aztec two-step*.

shit scrape *n. Arse wipe*, bathroom tissue.

shit shadow *n*. A noisome *guff* smell that sticks tenaciously to a fellow like Bud Flanagan used to stick to Chesney Allen. A *velcro fart.*

shit-smuggler's rucksack *sim*. The *ne plus ultra* of halitosis. *'Fuck me, what have you been eating, Your Majesty?' 'I don't know what you mean, Lord St. John.' 'Your breath smells like a shit-smuggler's rucksack, ma'am.'*

shitsophrenia *n. medic*. The condition where the sufferer alternates between having wild *squirts* and normal bowel movements.

shit splitter *n*. A g-string worn so tight on the lady's *heave-ho* as to fillet the *brown trout* in the unlikely event that she *follows through* on a *cheese cracker.*

shit stabber *n*. A stylish *pork swordsman*.

shitstopper *n*. An unexpectedly large

household bill, derived from the practice of reading the mail whilst on the toilet. *'And now we move onto the case of Mr Jack Trubshaw of St Neots, who last winter received a right shitstopper from British Gas, even though his central heating is oil-fired.'* (Nicky Campbell, *Watchdog*, BBC TV).

shitter 1. *n.* Anus, *kakpipe, council gritter.* 2. *n.* A sit down lavatory, the *pan.*

shitterati *n. coll.* Collective term for the heroic figures of the age who turn up on programmes such as *I'm a Celebrity, Get me Out of Here, Britain's Worst Celebrity Drivers' Pets from Hell, etc.* The kind of people who would happily fuck a pig if it were to get their face on TV, *eg.* Bubble off *Big Brother*, the coughing major off *Who Wants to be a Millionaire*, The Hamiltons, Jeremy Spake *etc.*

shitter chatter *n.* Long-winded anal babble emitted when a *shit* is expected.

shitter's ridge *n.* The *scranus etc.*

shit tickets *n. Bumwad, arsewipes, turd tokens, brown shield stamps.*

shit tie 1. *n.* The rather unsavoury end result of a spot of vigorous *back door work* followed by a *diddy ride* to finish. 2. *n.* The sort of studiedly-eccentric, garish neckwear typically worn by Jon Snow when he's presenting the news on Channel 4.

shitting glass *n.* A morning-after *crap* that feels like half your torso is being stripped away from the inside.

shitting through a sponge *n.* A novel toilet ability gained after a night eating delicious curries at the Curry Capital.

shit trigger *n.* The first cigarette of the day, which has the effect of pulling the pin out of the *chod grenade. 'I Love Phillip Morris king size. It's not just because they're clean and fresh tasting. It's not just because their mellow taste gives me mouth and throat comfort and freedom from cigarette cough. And it's not just because they have a great shit trigger action and give me all day smoking enjoyment. I love them because they're the mildest high tar cigarette on the market.'* (*I Love Philip Morris* advertisement featuring Lucille Ball, 1953).

shitty shitty gang bang *n.* A particularly messy *arsefest.*

shitty stick *n.* A stick, covered in *shit*, used by men with powerful cars and expensive aftershave to stave off advancing *scrunt.*

shituation *n.* A bad situation. *'Hello Houston, we've got a shituation here.'* (Commander James Lovell, speaking from Apollo 13 when the main turd valve short-circuited during the Trans-Lunar Injection Phase of the troubled Moon mission, filling the Command Module with weightless *bangers and mash*).

shitwreck *n.* The broken-up remnants of a scuttled *dreadnought*, lying in deep water by the S-bend.

shit-wrecked *adj.* Laid waste by a terrible *arse*-related mishap at the moment when everything seemed to be plain sailing.

shit your pants *v.* To *drop a brick, cake your kecks, papper your trolleys.*

shniffle-piffler *n.* Somebody else who sniffs lady's bicycle seats.

shocked hippo, fanny like a *sim.* Descriptive of a generously-proportioned *Rick Stein's dustbin.*

shocker *n.* A Mr Spock-style hand gesture which alludes to the practice of wedging one's middle and index fingers in a lady's *front bottom* whilst simultaneously interpolating one's pinkie into her *back bottom*. See also *two in the pink, one in the stink; the old shocker.*

shock to the cistern *euph.* An uncomfortably large *copper bolt* that challenges the swallowing capabilities of the average *chod bin.*

shoebox special *n.* A magnificent *Thora*, exhibiting a length and girth of which one is so proud that one feels tempted to fish it out of the *bum sink*, put it in a shoebox and take it to work to show it off to one's colleagues.

shoe bun *n.* A profiterole of *hound cable*, a *barker's egg custard tart. 'This is one small step for a man, one giant leap for...Fuck me, I've just stepped in a shoe bun.'*

shoelace view *n.* A gentleman's surreptitious glimpse of a *bird's* gusset gained whilst pretending to tie his shoelaces.

shooting boots on, to get one's *1. v.* Football commentator's phrase, to describe the actions of a player who has excelled in the "kicking the ball at the goal" part of the game. *'Rooney's certainly got his shooting boots on for Manchester United today, Gary.' 2. v.* Phrase describing the bizarre contortions a gentleman's feet go through in the moments leading up to a *pop shot. 'Rooney's certainly got his shooting boots on up that raddled old prostitute today, Gary.'*

shooting bunnies *n.* Polite euphemism for *letting rip*. Passing wind, *blowing off*. Also *killing the Easter bunny.*

shooting jam *adj.* Menstruating, *on the blob, dropping clots, up on blocks.*

shooting times *n. Self help literature, DIY mags, bachelors' newsletters.* Bongular magazines.

shooting wax darts *n.* Unpleasantly evocative phrase describing a chap *blowing the tanks* following a long period of abstinence. *'Okay, whatever you want Cliff, but don't finish in my mouth. After this long it could be dangerous, you'll be shooting wax darts.'*

shoot in your boot *euph.* To be so sexually excited as to ejaculate into one's footwear.

shoot putty at the moon *v.* To *go off.*

shoot your load/bolt/wad/stack *v.* To ejaculate, *lose your mess, discharge the mutton musket.*

shopkeeper *n.* A sudden, movement of *stoolage* into the *bomb bay*, that occurs completely unexpectedly. Named after the fez-wearing fancy dress shopkeeper in *Mr Benn*, who would habitually appear in a similar unnerving manner.

shopping *n.* The underpant aftermath of *follow through. 'Did I detect a twin tone there, your Honour?' 'I'm afraid so. Court adjourned for fifteen minutes whilst I check my trolleys for shopping.'*

shop round the corner *v.* To be *good with colours.*

shortage *n. coll.* Collective term for a group of vertically challenged persons.

short arms inspection *n. milit.* Armed services slang for an *under the bridge* medical examination, specifically looking for evidence of *cock rot.*

short-changed *adj.* Descriptive of the situation that obtains when a video clip one has downloaded stops just short of the *money shot*, so you have to phone Barclaycard and get them to cancel the transaction.

Short Stirling *n.* A perfect visit to the *chod bin*, which consists of a smooth sit-down, efficient opening of the *bomb-bay doors* and release of *payload*, and which concludes with the *drawing of an ace*, the whole operation taking place in the blink of an eye. Named after the famous British four-engined heavy bomber which saw service in the Second World War, dropping excrement onto Germany without getting its undercarriage all dirty.

shot from the starter's gun *euph.* A *cock up the arse*. See *jockey's starting position*.

shotgun fart *n.* A sudden ballistic *poot* which peppers pellets of *crapnel* into the toilet bowl or underpants.

should've gone to Specsavers *exclam.* Amusing apophthegm said of a mate who has inexplicably chosen to *cop off* with a *right boiler*. *'Charles Philip Arthur George, will you take Camilla Rosemary to be your wife? Will you love her, comfort her, honour and protect her, and, forsaking all others, be faithful to her as long as you both shall live? You may lift the veil ... Jesus Christ. If you don't mind me saying so, your royal highness, you should've gone to Specsavers.'*

shoving paper down a Greek toilet *n.* Attempting to sort out a problem, but only succeeding in making things a whole lot worse. *'I cannot help making the observation that complaints about the Government's policy over Iraq would be more acceptable from those who had opposed this reckless excursion in the first place. My right honourable friend's answers, however, give an impression that is not borne out by events on the ground. The United Nations calculates that 3,000 Iraqi civilians are being killed every month. In those circumstances, how long is the Prime Minister prepared to continue pursuing his current policy of forcible occupation, which is merely shoving paper down a Greek toilet?'* (Sir Mingice Campbell MP, quoted in *Hansard,* June 8th 2007).

show job *1. n.* The making of theatrically appreciative noises by a gentleman who is the recipient of a particularly artless act of oral *horatio*. *2. n.* The sort of transparently fake *nosh* typically performed in front of a roaring fire and filmed from behind a lace curtain in one of them glossy, softcore *spam vids* they show on the Sci-fi Channel late at night, where a *bird* moves her head up and down in front of a bloke whilst he pulls a face like he's just shut his *knackers* in the car door.

showroom finish *n.* The effect of rubbing your *naughty polish* into a ladyfriend's *bodywork* and then buffing her *headlamps* till they gleam.

shoulder boulders *n.* Big breasts, *gazungas*.

shown the ropes *1. phr.* In the world of office work, of a new employee on their first day, having had the location of the kettle, teabags, cups, sugar and spoons pointed out to them. *2. phr.* In the world of factory work, of a new employee on their first day, having been stripped naked, secured across an inspection pit using a broom handle and duct tape, and then had axle grease and sump oil smeared across their testicles. *3. phr.* In the world of romance, of a new sexual partner, having had their face and/or body ejaculated upon, but not their back.

show off *v.* Of a woman, to exhibit the

hystrionic symptoms of pre-menstrual tension.

shpaddiel *n*. Long-winded comedy anecdotage from David Baddiel which results in a death-like silence.

shramp *v*. To enjoy the incredibly common hobby of sniffing ladies' recently-vacated bicycle seats. To *quumf, snudge, snurgle, snuftify*.

shreddies *n*. *Undercrackers, kecks, trolleys, scads, scuns*.

Shrek *n*. A large, shaven-headed man with bad teeth and protruding ears found on low-brow, daytime moron-bating programmes such as *Trisha* and the *Jeremy Kyle Show*.

shrimp *v*. To suck someone's toes for perverted sexual gratification.

shrink-wrapped gammon *n*. A lady who wears clothing several sizes too small for her *lovely personality*.

shrivel me timbers *exclam*. Pirate-like phrase used by a fellow looking down at his *shrunken treasure* when getting out of a cold shower, cold bath, unheated swimming pool *etc*.

shrunken treasure *1. n*. Reduced circumstances in the *family jewels* brought about by chilly weather or immersion. *Shrinky-dinkage*. *2. n*. A *laptop, midget gem* or *cock puppet*.

shtup *v*. *Yiddish*. To have sex, *fuck, bang*.

shuffling the deck *n*. *Winding the clock, sorting out the boys, nipping and rolling*. The act of manually relieving testicular torsion or *Betty Swallocks*.

shum *n*. That mixture of excrement and ejaculate which is a by-product of certain practices which are frowned upon by readers of the *Daily Mail. Santorum*. From shit + cum.

shunt *v*. To *shtup*.

shushes *n*. One's early morning preparations for the day ahead. A *shag*, a shave, a *shit*, a shower and a shampoo. *'His Holiness will be out to canonise you in a moment, Mother Teresa. He's just finishing off his shushes.'*

shuttle cock *n*. One who *explodes* on re-entry. Or occasionally *goes off* a few seconds after lift-off.

shwank *n*. A multi-task-enabled showering experience.

Siamese quims *n*. Scissor sisters. *Lezzas* who are constantly *bumping fur. Carpet bumpers*.

sicasso *n*. A colourful bit of pavement art in which can be seen figurative elements of diced carrots, peanuts and crisps. An example of late night abstract expressionism reminiscent of the action paintings of Jackson Pollock.

side winders *n*. *Spaniel's ears* which appear to be gravitating towards the oxters. *Pit fillers*.

sideburns *n*. The marks left on multi-storey car park walls by women who should either get power steering or trade down to a *witch's broom*.

sidepipe *n*. A semi-erect *cock* visible down one leg of a tight pair of trousers, as sported by *rock poodles* and gentlemen in tightly-packed London Underground carriages.

sidesaddle *1. n*. A demure horse-riding style preferred by ladies so as not to snap their *virgin strings* before their wedding night. *2. n*. Non-conventional *porcelain pony*-riding style favoured by the more capaciously-buttocked defecator.

sidewinder *1. n*. Some sort of snake that is often seen in nature documentaries, scuttling across the desert sand like a scaly brace and bit. *2. n.* Missile used by the Americans to shoot British reporters. *3. n.* The elevation of one's left or right buttock in order to facilitate the surreptitious release of a *Judi Dench*. A *one cheek sneak*.

siesta with a Fiesta *n.* That relaxing afternoon interlude of *art pamphlet* perusal typically snatched by a married gentleman whilst his wife is paying a visit to the hairdresser. A *siesta with a Fiesta* is usually brought to an abrupt conclusion when the sound of the front door rudely rouses the siestee from his slumbers, and he finds that he has nodded off on the sofa with his trousers round his ankles and his *wanking spanner* glued to his forehead.

shot at the title *n.* A do-or-die chance to have a go on a *bird's snatch*.

sign no dockets, tip the load and *euph.* Of a gentleman, to deposit his *filthy concrete* in a place where he wouldn't want anyone to find out about, *eg.* Up the *clopper* of a lady who his mates might regard as falling short of their rigorous quality control standards. From the habit of cheeky HGV drivers who, in order to avoid tedious form-filling and ridiculous red tape, prefer to empty skipfuls of rubble, asbestos, toxic clinical waste, dead hitch-hikers *etc.*, in remote lay-bys and under picturesque country hedgerows.

Signora Romero *n.* An apparently beautiful woman who, on closer inspection, is sporting a moustache under her makeup. From the natty facial hair visible in close-ups of Cesar Romero's Joker in the 1960s *Batman* TV series.

sign the visitor's book *v.* To leave a note of appreciation at the bottom of another's *skidpan*. *Sign the guest book.*

Sigourney Weaver *rhym. slang. Beaver.*

silencer *n.* A *pap-baffle*.

silent movie, watch a *1. v.* To enjoy the slapstick, dialogue-free antics of Buster Keaton, Harold Lloyd, Fatty Arbuckle and friends. *2. v.* To anxiously thrash one's genitals within an inch of their lives whilst watching a *grumble vid* with the sound muted so as not to disturb the wife asleep upstairs.

silicone strap *n.* The strap of a shoulder or handbag which pulls tightly in between the *baps*, enhancing their size and profile without the need for costly cosmetic surgery. A *tit splitter*.

silicone valley *n.* The cleavage 'twixt adjoining *bazongers*. The *Bristol Channel*.

silly mid on *1. n.* Cricket fielding position, on the leg-side forward of the batsman's wicket and very near to the batsman. *2. n.* A *lazy lob* or *plod*; a half-cocked *stonk-on* which is too big to hide, yet too soft to be of any practical use.

silly string *1. n.* A light-hearted novelty *shit* that squirts out of one's *aeros-hole* in a rapid and erratic manner. Breaks the ice at parties. Occasionally incorporating small solid lumps, when it is known as a *bicycle chain*. *2. n.* Sticky substance light-heartedly sprayed in the face of an actress in a slapstick *art film*. Kept in a cannister that requires vigorous shaking.

silver sandwich *n.* A group sex session involving liberal-minded senior citizens.

Simon Cowells *rhym. slang. Bowels, ie.* Things that can be irritable and are usually full of *shit*.

Sindy's dildo *n.* A particularly underendowed endowment, that is to say a risibly small penis. *'I seen that Keith*

Chegwin nude quiz show last night. Fuck me, I thought I had a small cock, but Cheggers's was like Sindy's dildo.' (HRH Prince Charles, addressing the Royal Institution of British Architects, Mansion House 2002).

sine trousers *phr. leg. Lat.* Archaic legal terminology. When a judge wishes to retire to his chambers in order to consider the evidence prior to sentencing in a case involving pornography, he is said to *'adjourn sine trousers'*.

sing a rainbow *v.* To *shout soup*.

sing at St. Pauls *v.* To perform *cumulonimbus* on a woman with a *bucket fanny*.

Singer *n.* Sexual athlete, he or she who goes *at it* like a sewing machine.

singing for your supper *n.* Of a *bog ostrich*, making those vocal noises from which a spectator could safely infer that he is shortly going to be reunited with his tea.

singing ginger *n. Scot.* Glaswegian slang for any beverage containing alcohol. *'An' gie me a bottle o' yer cheapest singing ginger, Jimmy.'*

singing into the mic *sim. Horatio* performed in the style of a *slag night* karaoke star.

singlie rosettes *n.* The discarded *jizzmops* that adorn the floors of unattached men's rooms. *Poppadoms, wanker's crisps, porn crackers.*

sing sweet violets *v.* Airy version of *building a log cabin*, to *take a dump*.

sink a few U boats *v.* To drop a few *depth charges*.

sink plunger *n.* A *tug* administered by an inexperienced woman where she appears to be attempting to snap your *banjo* and pull your *fiveskin* over your *clock-weights;* the action she would use when unblocking a plughole. Opposite of a *squid wank*.

sink the Bismarck *v.* To launch one *fucking* enormous dreadnought, deposit a *U blocker.*

sink the sausage *v.* To get one's *leg over.*

sin lumps *n. Jubblies, kahunas, shirt potatoes, boobs, sweater fruit, knockers, cab man's rests, baps, funbags, bumpies, neddies, chichis, mambas, dirty pillows, chebs, charlies, diddies, doos, cajooblies, jugs, bubbies, zeps, bazongers, headlamps, whammies, norks, bangers, dumplings, hogans, thrupennies, assets, churns, whammers, yoinkahs, begonias, mumbas, pink pillows, top bollocks, melons, oomlaaters, nellies, choozies, chubblies, chumbawumbas, blimps, charms, baby's dinners, fun cushions, paps, bojangles, garbonzas, airbags, Gert Stonkers, puppies, Bristols.* That'll be *tits*, then.

siphon the python *v.* To take a *Chinese singing lesson, see a man about a dog.* To go for a *gypsy's kiss.*

sip that off a spoon, you could *exclam. medic.* Expression used in the medical profession to describe the more fluviatile *digestive transits* of a patient. *'How is the Mrs Rantzen in bed five coming along, doctor?' 'It's hard to tell really, sister. One day you could bolt the door with her shits, the next day you could sip them off a spoon.'*

Sir Anthony *rhym. slang.* A proper *charlie*. From Sir Anthony Blunt = cunt.

Sir Cliff's neck *n.* The bit of taut, elongated *scrotum* just above the bit that's got your *knackers* in.

Sir Douglas *rhym. slang. Shit.* From Sir Douglas Turd.

SISO/siso 1. *acronym*. A gentleman who suffers from premature ejaculation. A *two-push Charlie*. From Straight In Straight Out. 2. *acronym*. Allowances claim protocol for members of the European Parliament. Sign In, Sod Off.

site box 1. *n*. In the construction industry, a filthy, dented, cold and rattly receptacle that everybody is allowed to chuck their tools in at the end of the day. 2. *n*. In a public house, a resident female with a filthy, dented, cold and rattly *box* that everybody is allowed to chuck their *tools* in at the end of the night. A *shed*.

sit on a mortar *v*. To suffer the catastrophic consequences of a *dirty bomb* detonation. *'Unfortunately my dear Mrs Bennet, Mr D'Arcy had some dodgy prawn chimichongas for lunch and has sat on a mortar; thus he will not be able to attend tea.'* (from *Pride and Sensibility* by Jane Austen).

sit on job *n*. Term used in the construction industry referring to the hanging out of a contract. *'You want it finished for the 2012 Olympics Opening Ceremony? Up your bollocks, this is a sit on job, mate. We'll get eight more turkeys out of this one, don't you worry.'*

sitting on an elephant *adj*. To be highly *burbulent*, to have *brewed a massive one up*.

sitting on the stove *euph*. Of a lady, to have been *scuttled* from behind so hard and so often that she develops twin circular red glowing patches at the back and top of her thighs, as if she has been resting her *arse* on the two front rings of the cooker hob.

sitting on your balls, it's like *sim*. Descriptive of the unpleasant and distinctly sickening feeling experienced when watching the fake jollity and camaraderie between the hosts of BBC's Breakfast Programme.

six-back *n*. The not-overly-attractive rolls of lard on the backs of fat grannies. *Back tits*.

six nowt *euph*. Descriptive of something performed on the *old walking stick* with gusto and enthusiasm.

six-pack grip *n*. See *tenpin*.

six point niner *n*. A *sixty-niner* which is interrupted by a period, *viz*. "6.9".

sixteen valve *n*. A stunner, a corking *bird*.

sixth gear *n*. *Wanking*, especially in a parked car. See *stick shifter*.

sixtitty-nine *n*. A sort of splendid lesbian version of *looping-the-loop* which somehow involves four knockers.

sixty grit 1. *n*. The coarsest grade of sandpaper available. 2. *n*. The coarsest grade of woman available. *'Up betimes, and much perturbed to find a veritable piece of sixty grit alongside me in the fart sack. Resolved never again to mix the port and the stout.'* (from *The Diary of Samuel Pepys*).

sixty-eight *n*. Oral sex undertaken on the understanding that the favour will be returned. *''Ere, give us a sixty-eight and I'll owe you one.'*

sixty-nine *n*. *Soixante-neuf, loop the loop*. Also *sixty-niner*.

size aero *euph*. The opposite of size zero. The dress size of a lady who has a tendency towards over-indulgence in the popular, eponymous bubble-filled chocolate confection.

size ten *euph*. How girls of sizes fourteen to eighteen describe themselves prior to going on a blind date.

skanky panky *n*. Scoring with a member

of the lower orders.

skeet *1. v. US.* To shoot clay pigeons. *2. v.* To *shoot your load.* To come off at the *Billy Mill roundabout.*

skeeze *v. US.* To *shag, shtup.*

Skeggie donkey *euph.* A *bint* who'll let anyone get their *leg over* for a quid. And has all flies round her arse.

skelpit erse *sim. Scot.* Descriptive of a face that looks like a *smacked arse.*

skiddy fiddler *n.* One with an unhealthy interest in soiled undergarments. *'Today's birthdays: 1804 - Alan Clark, pioneering telescope manufacturer; 1841 - Oliver Wendell Holmes Jr., US Supreme Court Justice; 1859 - Kenneth Grahame, author of Wind in the Willows; 1943 - Lynn Redgrave, eminent film and stage actress; 1964 - Mark Oaten MP, skiddy fiddler.'*

skid marks *n.* Severe *russet gusset, pebble dashing* of the *undercrackers,* the *turtle's brylcreem.*

skidmata *n.* The miraculous brown wounds which manifest themselves on the fingertips of one who is a martyr to thin *bumwad.* Also *taxi driver's tan, mechanic's fingernails, Linda Bellingham's fingertips..*

skiing position *n. Wanking* two men off at the same time while wearing only a h*elmet, goggles and thick mittens. Crane operating.*

ski jump *n.* That challenging first *slash* of the day when one has woken up *piss proud.*

skimmed milk *1. n.* Horribly thin and weedy dairy produce that invariably spoils a perfectly good cup of tea. *2. n. Baby gravy* with all the goodness taken out. *Decaff spaff* that would also, to be fair, spoil a cuppa.

skin boat *n.* Penis. *'I think I'll sail the old skin boat to tuna town.'*

skin chimney *n.* A flue that requires regular sweeping with a *womb broom.*

skin-clad tube *n.* A *live sausage,* a *girlometer.*

skin flick *n.* A tame *fuck feature,* blue movie, *mamba matinee.*

skin flute *n.* A *fleshy flugelhorn, bed flute, pink oboe.*

skin grafts *n.* Somewhat unimpressive *tits.*

skinternet *n.* Ceefax, teletext. From skint + internet.

skinny latte *n.* The thin, watery fluid typically released at the climax of a chap's third *glad-handing* of the day when he is *working from home.*

skipper *1. n.* A lady's elusive *clematis, love button, wail switch.* See *bald man in a boat. 2. v. naut.* In naval parlance, to wipe one's *arse* on a slice of bacon prior to presenting it to the captain in a sandwich.

skipper's tablecloth *n.* Several sheets of *bumwad* laid carefully across a *self indulgent* chap's stomach and legs in order to contain and absorb any spillages which may occur whilst he is *tossing* in his bunk.

skippy *n.* A promiscuous male who jumps about from *bush* to *bush.* A *fanny hopper.*

skips without a rope, he *euph.* Descriptive of a man who has *yet to find the right girl.*

skirt *n. coll. Fanny, blart, toosh, talent. 'I've got a pink ticket tonight. Let's get down the bar and pick up a bit of skirt.'*

skirt lifter *n.* The female equivalent of a *shirt lifter.* A *carpet muncher,* a *lezza,*

Victorian photographer.

skit *v.* To *shit* diarrhoea.

skittered *adj.* Afflicted with the *skitters.*

skitters, the *n.* The *shits,* the *squirts,* the *Earthas, Alex Wurtz.*

skittling *n. Dining at the Y* during *rag week.* From the popular fruit-flavoured confectionery catchphrase, *ie.* "Taste the rainbow".

skittuin *n.* The product of the *skitters,* especially in dogs; *canine paint stripper,* puddles of brown acidic gunge on the carpet.

Skoda going over a cattle grid, like a *sim.* Phrase used to describe the throes of female ecstasy. *Shaking like a flat-pack wardrobe. 'After some hours tramping across the remote glens beyond Cairnsmore of Fleet, I found myself hungry and tired at the door of a herd's cottage set in a nook beside a waterfall. The door swung open as I knocked, and stepping inside the lowly dwelling I was surprised to see the householder, a dour, elderly shepherd, up to his apricots in his wife. He was banging away like a steam-hammer as I entered, and, oblivious to my presence, the lady of the house was shaking like a Skoda going over a cattle grid.'* (from *The Sixty-Nine Steps* by John Buchan).

skull buggery *n. Pugwashing, salami-sucking.* Also *skull-fucking.*

skunk stripe *n.* The characteristic white residue left by dried-up *bum sweat* in a pair of ladies' black *grundies.*

skyagra *n.* A quick flick through the satellite TV channels before bedtime, made by a middle-aged gentleman in search of something to boost his flagging sex-drive.

slabberdash *v.* In fighting or romance, to slap one's opponent or lover upon the side of the face with a semi-erect penis. To *chap.*

slack mabbut *n.* A *hippo's mouth,* a *beef Wellington.*

slacktivity *n.* Swinging the lead in the workplace, *eg.* Idly rating the women who walk past, stealing stationery, masturbating in the toilets.

sladger *n.* A west country term for a lady's *minge.* A *Cornish fanny, konz.*

slag *1. n.* A woman of little virtue, *slapper. 2. n.* Waste material from a mine. *3. n.* Term of abuse (pronounced "*slaaaaaag*") applied liberally to male criminals and other assorted *toe rags* in *The Sweeney.*

slag off *v.* To deprecate verbally.

slagazine *n.* Ladies' periodical that does not make too many intellectual demands on its readership, *eg. Take a Break, Chat, Hello, OK, Spare Rib etc.*

slagbait *n.* Aftershave.

slag bat *n.* A crude term for the *blood stick.*

slaggle *n. coll.* Collective noun for a group of young ladies who are generous with their affections. From slag + gaggle.

slag hammer *n.* A *tool* a gentleman uses for *banging twats* rather than nails.

slag heap *n.* A run-down pub or nightclub in any northern town.

slag night *n.* High-spirited female binge drinking excursion in a town centre. A *hen night.* Also *slag do.*

slag pellets *n.* Small tablets used by women to ward away unwanted pests. The *Benny Hill.*

slag stamp *n.* A tattoo applied to the small of a *salad dodger's* back in the mistaken belief that it will draw attention away from her enormous *arse.*

slagtime *n.* Type of music that gets every

lass in the place up on the dancefloor. Popular *slagtime* numbers include Gloria Gaynor's *I Will Survive*, Whigfield's *Saturday Night and So Fuckin' What* by the Anti-Nowhere League.

slag wellies *n*. Knee-high boots.

slam dumping *n*. A light-hearted jape whereby the prankster *shits* in the cistern rather than the bowl. *Top decking, slam dunking, top loading.*

slam hound *n. US. Slapper, slut.*

slam in the lamb *v*. Bayonet manoeuvre involving the *mutton musket*.

slam on the brakes *v*. To stop wiping one's *arse* for some reason, *such as t*he house burning down, with the full knowledge that the process is incomplete, resulting in *skid marks* or *russet gusset.*

slam spunk *v*. To have *it off.*

slap and tickle *n*. A sex act, a bit like *rumpy pumpy*, whereby a man wearing a dress shirt and sock suspenders chases an excited lady round a bed before catching her, playfully slapping her *buttocks*, tickling her ribs and *fucking* her up the *cunt* with his *cock*. A *romp.*

slap and trickle *n*. A perfunctory, routine act of *self abuse* that elicits only a half-hearted return on one's *wristy investment*, possibly as a result of the four *wanks* one has had in the previous couple of hours. A low budget *money shot.*

slaphead *n*. A *chrome dome*, a *baaldie.*

slaphood *n*. A *slapper's* prime of life.

slapper *n*. A dirty woman. She who has been around a bit. From the Yiddish "schlepper" meaning "I don't fancy yours much".

slapperazzi *n. coll.* The humorous youths who use their mobile telephones to make amusing films of their friends committing acts of grievous bodily harm on innocent bystanders. *Happy slappers.*

slapper trapper *n*. A man who, lacking the wherewithal to trap a *fox*, settles for hunting *swamp hogs* instead. A *pig-sticker.*

slappertite *n*. A hunger for loose women. *'Do you fancy a fuck, Bill?' 'No thanks, Hillary. I don't want to ruin my slappertite.'*

slappette *n*. A betracksuited, *hickied*, bubblegum-chewing, *scrunchie*-wearing fledgling *slattern.*

slapster *n*. One afflicted by male pattern baldness, alopecia or mange.

slapstick *n*. A light-hearted, comical *wank*, accompanied by frantic piano music.

slap the monkey *v*. To *chimp oneself* till one is *blue in the arse*. To do a *Mary Chipperfield.*

slash *n*. A *piss, wee wee, number one.*

slash and burn *1. n.* Impressively-efficient third world deforestation technique. *2. n.* A painful symptom of the *pox* and the *clap.*

slash palace *1. n.* Public lavatory. *2. n.* The home of the top-hatted guitarist out of Guns 'n' Roses.

slash point *n*. Sheltered area in a town centre which affords privacy for the purpose of depositing urine. *'Hang on lads, I've just got to nip to the slash point before I flood me Calvins.'*

slate layer's nailbag *sim*. Descriptive of very saggy or battered *labia.*

slats *1. n.* Ribs. *'I'm gonna rattle her slats with me womb broom.' 2. Aus. Beef curtains. 'I'm gonna part her slats with me womb broom.'*

Slaven Bilic *rhym. slang.* Spillage, specifically the emptying of a couple of *nutsworth* onto a game young lady's face. Named after the anvil-faced Croatian footballer.

sledge *n.* A bloke who is constantly *pulled* by *dogs*.

sledging 1. *n.* Unsporting cricket match repartee designed to put batsmen off their stroke. 2. *n. Aus.* Consenting impolite *rumpy pumpy*. Acts of intercourse during which one or both parties abuse each other with colourful profanities. Foul-mouthed pillow talk. *'August 6th. To the BBC for a recording of Call My Bluff with Frank (Muir), Ian (Ogilvy), Angharad (Rhys), Hannah (Gordon) and Joyce (Grenfell). Joyce afterwards invited me to take tea in her room at the Savoy. One thing led to another and we ended up sledging into the early hours. Gracious, what a potty-mouth she can be.'* (from *Fiddling in the Foliage*, the memoirs of Arthur Marshall).

sleep in a tent *v.* To have a large penis. *'Fancy coming back to my place? You'll not be disappointed. I sleep in a tent.'*

sleeping beast *n.* Flaccid *cock, marshmallowed main pipe.* A *dead budgie.*

sleeping cat *n. A brown beast slumbering contentedly in the U-bend.*

sleeping fruit bat *n.* A vagina with *flaps* which are so big and leathery it appears that the lady has a mammal of the genus *Pteropus* napping between her legs. A *resting pterodactyl.*

sleeping head to toe *n.* Of two *women in comfortable shoes*, to take off their comfortable shoes and get into bed to perform an act of mutual gratification. *Lesbotic sardines. 'I bet there is plenty of sleeping head to toe going on in Style Prison tonight, Home Secretary.'*

sleeping policeman 1. *n.* A hump in the road, designed to slow down traffic and remove exhaust pipes from sports cars. 2. *n.* An officer of Her Majesty's Constabulary in his pyjamas with his eyes shut. 3. *n.* An *angry* penis, tucked up behind the belt in order to conceal it from family or friends. A *Kilroy.*

sleeping pull *n.* When a fellow is unable to sleep, he may have one or two of these to help him nod off.

sleep vaulting *n.* Gentleman's nocturnal discomfort, which involves him growing a massive *tent pole* whilst asleep, only for it to jam into the sheet when he tries to turn over, thus startling him into pained wakefulness. A *motorcycle kickstand* complication.

sleep with *v.* To *fuck* someone, for example up against the side of a bus shelter.

slice *n.* A portion of *hairy pie*. A vagina.

slice of cheesecake *n.* A *plate* of *horatio*. *'Belgravia was powerless to resist. His eyes burned into hers like caborundums. His strong arms enfolded her tender body as she felt herself being swept away in an Aurora Australis of passion. Eagerly she fell to her knees, pulled down his scuds and helped herself to a slice of cheesecake.'* (from *The Lady and the Darts Player* by Barbara Cartland).

Slimbridge, dawn chorus at *sim.* The cacophonous symphony of hooting, quacking, honking and whistling which emanates from a lavatory cubicle occupied by a person *paying in installments* for a particularly virulent and delicious *slip-up* feed. From the aural similarity to the early morning sounds heard at the late Sir Peter Scott's famous duck zoo.

slime *v. Aus.* To ejaculate, *chuck one's muck*. To reach *Lake Wendouree*. *'Have* *you slimed yet Rolf?'*

slip a length *1. v.* To *give a good seeing-to to someone. 'I'd slip her a length any day of the week.'* 2. *v.* In the world of *saucy* seaside postcards, a conversational misunderstanding involving a landlady with a tenant who works at a linoleum factory.

slip her a crippler *v.* A few notches up from *slip her a length*, to *shtup* someone so hard they can't walk.

slippers, shit in his *v.* To *do the dirty* with a good friend's missus. *'Are you going to poke me then, Eric? I'm absolutely gagging for it.' 'No, I can't Patti. It just wouldn't be cricket to shit in George's slippers like that.'*

slippery as a butcher's cock *sim.* Untrustworthy, sly. From the well known fact that all butchers take carnal advantage of the meat in the back room before selling it. That's why you should always cook it thoroughly.

slit *n. Blit, fanny, vertical bacon sandwich.* See *slot.*

slobberchops *n.* The thin film of translucent *blip* secreted from the *bacon sandwich* that forms a crust in a *bird's dunghampers* after intercourse. *'How dare you accuse me of knocking one out whilst you were on holiday, that's the remnants of your slobber-chops, you cheeky cow.'*

slob's oven *sim.* Descriptive of an overused and undercleaned *fanny.* With black, carbonized chips lying round the bottom of it. One that would benefit from a good scrubbing with Mr Muscle and a wire brush.

slo-mo-sexual *n.* A *bongo vid* viewer who fast forwards through the foreplay before pausing at the crucial moment and inch-ing through the *money shot* frame by frame.

sloom *n. medic.* The lubricating secretion of the lady's Bartholin's glands. *Blip, moip, chin varnish.*

slop dodger *n.* A prudish or frigid lady who for some reason objects to getting her face *bespunkled* by a gentleman.

slop on *n.* A state of female sexual arousal. A *wide on.*

sloppy seconds *n.* To *stir the porridge.* To stick one's *naughty paintbrush* into a *billposter's bucket* filled with another chap's *population paste.*

slot *n. Slit.*

slot garnish *n.* A frilly bit of nothing which looks nice, but is quickly pushed to one side so one can tuck into the *meaty main course.* Any ladies' *farting crackers* bought from the Ann Summers shop.

slot machine *n.* A battery-powered neck massager, shaped like a big nobbly *cock.* A fruity vibrator.

slow puncture *euph.* One of those days when one seems to be constantly losing gas. *'I don't know what was in that fifteen pints of Younger's Scotch Bitter I had last night, but I seem to have a slow puncture today.'*

slug *n.* A woman who simultaneously combines the twin qualities of sluttishness and ugliness, *eg.* That fucking nightmare off of *Wife Swap* again.

slug and lettuce *1. n.* Name of a chain of hilarious pubs where, you might think, it would be a good idea to avoid the salads. 2. *n.* The post-sexual congress state of a chap's *pocket rocket* wilting inside a woman's *man mayonnaise*-filled *cabbage.*

slug on a brillo pad *sim.* Poetic description of the result of *relaxing* rather too often and violently in a *gentleman's way*. *'I tell you what, Natasha, I'm going to have to cancel my wank channel subscription. My cock looked like a slug on a brillo pad this morning.' 'Thanks, Dermot. And now over to Everton Fox with the weather.'*

sluice the caboose *v.* To use the shower head to direct a high pressure jet of water up between one's buttocks in order to remove accumulated pubes, *winnits*, badger hair and other miscellaneous anal flotsam, jetsam, detritus and effluvium.

slumberlumber *n. Morning wood.* A timber kickstand for one's wrinkly, pink-wheeled hairy motorcycle. *Dawn horn.*

slut *n.* A woman who doesn't wash her nets often enough and has the milk bottle on the breakfast table.

slut hut *n.* An inner city pub.

slutton *n.* A cross between a *slut* and a *slattern.* Which are both the same thing, if you think about it. *'Where are you going dressed like that, you dirty slutton?' 'Westminster Abbey. I'm going to get married to Prince Andrew.'*

slybrarianship *n.* A chap's discreet stewardship of his *grumble* stash.

smackanory *n.* The heart-rending tale of woe with which heroin addicts routinely regale passers-by in the hope of relieving them of their small change.

smackdonalds *n.* A residence in a less than salubrious *scruburb* where money is deposited in one window and pharmaceuticals are dispensed at another.

smacket *n.* A drug addict's multi-pocketed coat worn when skulking round shops.

smack generator *n.* A retailer of second hand electrical goods which is used by thieves to convert stolen goods into cash to spend at *smackdonalds*.

smackhead special *n.* A nourishing bus station cafe feast, consisting of pie, chips, peas, two slices of buttered toast and a pot of tea, all for £1.25.

smack oneself about *v.* To *relax in a gentleman's way.*

smackpool illuminations *n.* Extremely premature and gaudy Christmas lights found adorning houses in the country's less exclusive locales.

smacksuit *n.* A set of market-bought athletic clothes of the sort favoured by youngsters on Britain's more vibrant estates.

smack tokens *n.* Items of electronic equipment, *eg.* Car radios, laptop computers, videos *etc.*, with the plugs cut off.

small fanny footprint, he's got a *euph.* Said of an altruistic chap who does his bit to ensure there are more women available for his fellow men by electing to *travel on the other bus.*

smank *n.* An act of self pleasurement which unaccountably involves hitting your own penis and testicles. From smack + wank.

smart fart *n.* A targeted act of flatulence that only affects its intended victim.

smashing pumpkins 1. *n.* US popular musical combo of some sort. 2. *n.* Lady's secondary sexual characteristics.

smear campaign 1. *n.* A series of verbal or written attacks deliberately intended to defame or discredit someone. 2. *n.* What happens inadvertently when one has the *turtle's head. Fudging the issue. 'Oh come on, just answer the question, Mr Howard. In your capacity as Home Secretary, did you or did you not threaten to over-rule the head of the Prisons*

Service Derek Lewis? Yes or no.' 'I'm not going to answer that, Jeremy, but what I will say is this - if I don't pot the brown soon I'm going to embark on a smear campaign.'

smear test 1. *n. medic.* Medical procedure which detects precancerous cells in the cervix. 2. *n.* Toilet procedure to determine if one has got all the *shit* off one's *nick*.

smear test pizzas *n.* Budget supermarket pizza on which the toppings have been kept to a minimum for reasons of economy.

smedgie *n. Can.* An hilarious practical joke whereby a lady's *bills* are vigorously yanked up her *clopper*. From smeesh + wedgie.

smeesh 1. *n. Can.* Female reproductive *farmyard area*. The *snapper*. 2. *n. Can.* A collective noun for ladies. *Blart, tussage, cabbage.* 3. *n. pej. Can.* A doltish fellow. A *fuckwit*.

smeesh hawk *n. Can.* A *clout* with the *gorilla salad* shaved into a mohican.

smeg 1. *n.* Pungent *knob cheese.* 2. *n. prop.* Amusingly-named Swedish manufacturer of white goods. 3. *n.* A substitute for *fuck* overused in *Red Dwarf*.

smeg cup *n.* The cupped hand traditionally used by *wankers* as a receptacle to catch their *muck* when *pulling the Pope's cap off* in a standing position. A *wanker's chalice, poly grail*.

smegma dome *n.* A baby *bell end*, with a waxy, red skin. The *lid, Dutch strawberry*.

smegma *n. Smeg.*

smeg peg *n.* An unwashed penis, with a gamey aroma redolent of cheese, *spunk* and stale *blip*.

smelling mistake *n.* Emitting an unpleas-

ant miasma and/or a comical sound from one's *fundament* at a time when one would be best advised to grit one's teeth and hang on for dear life in an attempt to keep it in, *eg.* At a funeral, whilst exchanging one's wedding vows, when being chased through a spaceship by an alien, whilst hiding in Rachel Riley's wardrobe at Yorkshire TV *etc.*

smellmet *n.* A smelly *helmet*. From smelly + helmet.

smellody *n.* A *botty bugle* solo of a particularly musical timbre.

smells like a Beach Boy's bird's fanny *sim.* Found wanting in matters of personal freshness. From the lyrics to the song *California Girls*, *viz.* "Those Southern girls with the way they talk, they knock me out when I'm down there".

smell the toffee, wake up and *exclam.* Useful phrase which a married man can use when a *breakfast maker* has failed to rouse his missus from her slumbers.

smig *n. W. Yorks.* A person of *shit* quality from Huddersfield.

sminge *n.* The act of inserting a sugar-free mint into a *minge* for freshness. For the male alternative, see *smint shuffle*.

smint shuffle *n.* The practice whereby a gentlemen allows a small breath-freshening mint to dissolve under his *fiveskin* in order to make his *herman gelmet* cool and tingly in preparation for a subsequent *wank*. The technique can also be used by the more considerate *noshee* prior to receiving a *nosh* to mask the aroma of *hedam* and thus make the experience slightly less vile for his *noshatrix*.

Smithfield porter's cap *n.* A *clopper* deprived of its necessary monthly launder.

SMOG/smog *acronym*. Suck Me Off Gob. A lady's mouth which appears capable of drawing a golfball through 200 yards of garden hose, *eg*. Angelina Jolie, Sophie Marceau or any Brazilian *bird* one cares to mention.

smoke *n*. A *chewie*, a *nosh*. A *blow job*. *'Excuse me, Miss Taylforth, this is a no-smoking taxi.'*

smoke a gadgee *v*. To take a few drags on a *pink cheroot*. Though not in a public place.

smoke out the mole *v*. To induce a reluctant *feeshus* by means of lighting up a cigarette.

smoke the bald man *v*. To light up a *salami cigarette*.

smoke the white owl *v*. To commit an act of *horatio*.

smoking bangers *sim*. Descriptive of a woman with a lovely personality, *ie*. A *bird* who looks as though she's been sparking up fireworks.

smoo *n*. *Aus*. A *minge*, a *sportsman's gap*.

smoot *n*. *medic*. A *bird's* private area. *'The babysitter wanted me to go to bed after Big Brother, so I gave her a right kick up the smoot, mum.'*

smuggling a brownie *v*. To have the *turtle's head*. *'He seemed quite anxious to get away, officer. I suspect he was smuggling a brownie.'*

smurfing *v*. *Blue surfing*. Trawling the information superhighway on the look-out for pictures of *tits, bums, fannies, the lot*.

smush piece *n*. The *faff*. A lady's *front bottom*, a *clopper*.

smut *n*. Mild *jazz*. *Porn lite* that would make a maiden aunt purse her lips like a dog's *ringpiece*.

snag your jeans on a nail *v*. To emit a high-pitched, rasping *ringtone*.

snail's doorstep *n*. A *clapping fish* that is as *wet as an otter's pocket*.

snail trail *n*. *Smoo juice* in a lassie's well-worn *scuns*.

snake *v*. To *fuck, poke, bang, futter*.

snake charmer *n*. A girl who has an uplifting effect on your *pant python*, such that it rises up and sways about in her face.

snakeskin *1. n*. The clothing sloughed off in one piece and found at the bottom of the bed after a night *on the piss*. *2. n*. The dried, flaky layer that tends to form overnight on the stomach of an unhygienic male who nods off after commiting an act of *self-pollution*.

snake spit *n*. The clear fluid that precedes the *jizz bolt*. *Pre cum, perseverance soup, ball glaze, preek*.

snap and tickle *n*. Of an *earthing cable*, the phenomenon of it touching the bottom of the *chod bin* before snapping off at the *clackervalve*, and then striking the back of the *chicken skin handbag* as it falls.

snap, crackle, plop *onomat*. The sound made in the bowl during a particularly satisfying session of *parking one's breakfast*.

snapdragon *n*. A normally agreeable female who under certain circumstances, *such as* when *up on blocks* or full of *tart fuel*, becomes a vicious, fire-breathing monster.

snapped candles *sim*. Descriptive of one's legs after a night *on the lash*, when one is wearing one's *wobbly boots*.

snapper *1. n*. North-east colloquialism for a thin fellow. *2. n. milit*. Royal Naval slang for one who is *nicely poised*. *3. n*. A lady's *bodily treasure*.

snap the key off in the lock *v.* To suffer an unsatisfying *shit*. *'Good dump, dear?' 'Sadly not, my petal. I'm afraid I've snapped the key off in the lock. I'll have this pine cone in all night now.'*

snart *n.* To sneeze and *fart* at exactly the same moment, resulting in *nose jizz* on the face or *rabbit tods* in the *bills*. Or both.

snatch *n.* *Quim*, vagina, *liver sock.*

snatch 22 *n.* An aesthetically unconventional woman who would, paradoxically, require so much beer to *fuck* that you couldn't *get it up* anyway.

snatch fence *n.* An invisible, *cock*-proof barricade erected down the centre of a matrimonial bed following a domestic argument. A *gash barrier.*

snatchlings *n.* Up-and-coming *talent.*

snatchment area *n.* The geographical radius from which a drinking establishment draws its female clientele.

Snatchmo *n.* A *fanny* with lips strong enough to play *Basin Street Blues* on an E-flat trumpet.

snatch mouse *n.* A tampon, *cotton pony*, *Prince Charlie*, *chuftie plug.*

snatch patch *n.* A feminine hygiene product. A *fanny nanny.*

snatchphrase *n.* A particularly successful chat-up line.

snatch quack *n. medic.* One who has the sexy, enviable job of examining malfunctioning *minges*. A *box doc, fanny mechanic.* A gynaecologist.

snatch rats *n.* Ladies' sanitary products. *Jampaxes, jam rags, etc.*

snatchwork quilt *n.* An impressive display of pornographic images arrayed across the duvet prior to indulging in a *five knuckle shuffle.*

snatch worms *n.* Tiny pieces of tightly-rolled bog paper that lurk in the labial folds, normally only discovered during particularly expert *cumulonimbus* which dislodges them from their hidey-holes.

sneaky Hitler *n.* The surreptitious slipping of one's index finger under one's nose in order to savour the aroma of one's ladyfriend's *blip.*

sneaky Kiki *n.* A clump of pubular follicles protruding above the trouser line. A reference to the sexually-provocative French frog who used to climb up a ladder and poke her head over the garden wall in *Hector's House*. A *hairy Kilroy.*

snedge 1. *n.* Snow. 2. *n.* Jism.

snedger *n.* *Snufty, snurglar, snudger, quumfer.* Another name for a smeller of ladies' bicycle seats.

sniffers' row *n.* In a strip club, the seats that are closest to the stage.

sniff the air, kiddies. there's vitamins *exclam.* A Wildean apophthegm uttered by the purveyor of a particularly pungent *poot.*

sniff the cork *v.* To check one's finger the morning after going *knuckle deep* up the missus's *bonus tunnel*, to determine whether your hand needs a proper wash with soap or whether a quick wipe on her flannel will suffice.

sniggerette *n.* A drug addict's *tab* containing a quantity of *happy baccy*. A *spliff.*

sniping *n.* Accidentally shooting a jet of *slash* through the gap between the rim of the *chod bin* and the underside of the seat and onto your *kex* whilst sat down having a *tom tit*. A *Wee-Harvey Oswald, rim shot.*

snipper reflex *n. medic.* The counterproductive and inexplicable urge to cut a *cable* before it is fully *laid*, usually resulting in an *arse like a Marmite pot.*

snippit valve *n*. The *anal sphincter*. The *nipsy*.

snitches *n*. *Two aspirins on an ironing board, stits, fried eggs.*

snob sick *n*. Vomit with plenty of canapes and Chardonnay in it outside a wine bar.

snobtoss *n*. An act of cultured *self-pollution* committed whilst watching a sophisticated, subtitled movie on Film Four.

snog *v*. To *swap spit, tongue wrestle, play tonsil hockey.*

snogging water *n*. A male grooming lotion that smells like *Joan Collins's knickers. Fanny-magnetic* aftershave, such as Hi Karate, Brut 33 or Old Spice.

snood 1. *n*. Some sort of peculiar scarfy-balaclava-cum-hat sort of contrivance. 2. *v*. To surreptitiously sniff the saddles in a ladies' bicycle shed. To *snuft, snudge, shramp, quumf, scrunge, pringle, snerge, snedge, snaffle, snarze, snerk, snerdle, shniffle-piffle, nurf, moomph, barumph, garboon, poon, snarf, snurdle* or *snurge.*

snoodling *n*. An unlikely-sounding sexual practice reputedly favoured by gents who are *good with colours*, whereby one of them pulls his *fiveskin* over the *herman gelmet* of his chum. Also *docking*, a *clash of heads.*

snookered behind the red *adj*. Unable to *sink the pink* due to the time of month, and faced with a *difficult brown.*

Snoopies *n*. *Spaniel's ears, Ghandi's flip-flops.*

snoregasm *n*. The culmination of a *wet dream.*

snorkeller's lunch *n*. A wet fish dish which is a particular favourite amongst *muff divers.*

snorkelling *n*. The holding of a gentleman's *nollies* in a lady's mouth whilst she applies a repetitive stroke to his *favourite member.*

snorker *n*. A *sausage, poky banger, Cumberland.*

snot *n*. The perineum of the lady. Because "it's not" *etc. etc.*

snotty hammock *n*. The gusset area of a *bird's* intimate apparel at the end of a long day. A *toddler's sleeve.*

snoutcasts *n*. Those poor unfortunates who are forced to huddle in pub, factory and office doorways to enjoy their *cancer sticks. Fag lepers.*

snout pout *n*. That haughty uptilt of the nose favoured by *pedigree ratters* with ideas somewhat above their stations, *eg*. Posh Spice, Candice who used to be *in Corrie.*

snowball *v*. To blow *salami cigarette* smoke back into the tobacconist's mouth.

snowdrifts *n*. The extra *fanny lips* that larger ladies have, which are crisp and white due to the fact that they never receive any sunlight.

snowdropper *n*. Underwear fetishist who steals to sniff, usually from washing lines. A *knicker bandit.*

snowman, do a *v*. To exit the water closet having completed a *Camillas*-emptying movement of such magnitude that one feels as if one is "walking in the air".

snudge *v*. To sniff a lady's bicycle seat after she leaves it chained to the railings. *To moomph.*

snuffling for truffles *sim*. Descriptive of a loud and somewhat messy performance of *cumulonimbus*. From the act's resemblance to the phenomenon of a large, wet-nosed pig rooting through the topsoil looking for a pungent, yet valuable actinomycete. Though presumably without a large mob of excitable French peasants watching. *Darth vulva.*

snufty *n.* One who *snudges.* A *garboon.*

snurge *v.* To *snudge, snurgle, barumph.*

snurglar *n. Quumfer, snudger,* bicycle *snufty.*

snurglar's delight *n.* A velocipede which offers double the *quumfing* opportunities for an enterprising *snufty, shnifflepiffler* or *shramper.* A tandem.

snurgle *v.* To *snuft, snudge, shramp, quumf, scrunge, pringle, snerge, snedge, snaffle, snarze, snerk, snerdle, shnifflepiffle, nurf, moomph, barumph, garboon, poon, snarf, snurdle* or *snurge.* To sniff the recently-vacated bicycle seats of young ladies, a hobby that seems to be named more often than it is performed.

soap dropper *n.* One who is *good with colours.* One who is *light on his feet.* From the prison shower etiquette where, like a Georgian lady dropping her handkerchief in the park to attract the attention of a suitor, a big, hairy *nick-bent* psychopath with an erection drops the soap in the showers to woo a prospective companion. A *botter.*

so solid poo *n.* An extremely troublesome *dump* which feels like passing a handgun wrapped in a sock.

soap-on-a-roper *n.* One who prefers not to bend down in communal showers.

soapy carpenter *n.* A man who is *good with colours.* From the fact that he "lathers at the sight of wood".

soapy tit wank *n.* A *sausage sandwich* served in the bath or shower. *'Take two bottles into the shower? Not me. I just go in there with me bird and she gives me a soapy tit wank.'*

sob stopper *n.* A small present of little value which is acquired on the way home by a thoughtful man who has drunk too much and stayed out too late, in the hope of stopping his missus turning the fucking waterworks on. Examples include cheap chocolates bought from all night garages and bunches of flowers stolen from cemeteries and railings.

social hand grenade *n.* A married man who comes out *on the pop* so infrequently that when he does he is a major liability to those around him.

social netwanker *n.* An opportunist who befriends an attractive female colleague via a web-based online community not because he is interested in receiving a constant stream of pithy updates about her life, but in order to *relax in a gentleman's way* over her scantily-clad holiday snaps.

social sticks *n.* Crutches that are only used when the bearer is going for a medical, signing on, cashing his giros *etc.* See also *dole pole.*

sockbreaker *n.* A *strum* of such vim and vigour that the weft of one's chosen *jitler* receptacle is eroded.

sock full of sand *euph.* A *heavy dick.*

sock jock *n.* One who likes to ride the *baloney pony* harnessed with a trusty item of hosiery.

sock method *n.* To *roll the dice* into a sock in the absence of anything else to *roll the dice* into. See *crunchie.*

sock starch *n.* Easily whipped-up paste which has been used by generations of males to convert their hosiery into *bachelor's boomerangs, midget's surfboards, Wombles' toboggans etc.*

sock sucker *n.* A prudish woman who insists on one donning a *dunky* before deigning to *nosh* on one's *slag hammer.* A *French puritan.*

socktator sport *n*. Any game played by scantily-clad and copiously-perspiring young ladies which is broadcast to a rhythmically appreciative male audience. Also *pullympics, quimbledon fortnight.*

socktits *n*. Very long, saggily pendulous *chichis. Spaniel's ears.*

sockumentary *n*. A *masturmentary, rudimentary, palmorama.* A TV programme best enjoyed whilst wearing an odd number of socks.

sod *n*. A loose piece of turf in an *uphill garden.*

sodom eyes *n*. The look of love that one gives the missus at bedtime to let her know that there is more than a cuddle on the cards.

sofa spud *n*. *US.* An enthusiastic televisual autodidact. An American equivalent to the British *couch potato.*

soft on, have a *v*. To be confronted by a less-than-exciting amorous prospect.

soggy moggy *n*. A romantic epithet to describe the *back to front* of a lady who has reached a sufficient state of arousal so that it will *go in* without too much fuss. A *slop on.*

soixante-neuf *n*. Top-to-tail *horatio-cumulonimbus.* French for *sixty-nine. Loop the loop.*

soldier's toecap *n*. A very shiny, rounded thing that a Sergeant Major likes to be able to see his face in. A *bell end* which has been polished with a generous portion of spit and *guardsman's gloss.*

solicitor's office *n*. Something a gentleman enters in a spirit of optimism, only to leave a short time later screwed, shafted and penniless.

solicitor's tie *n*. *Fr*. A *pearl necklace.* Costing £160 an hour plus disbursements.

solid air *1. n*. 1980s album by John Martyn when he had two legs and was still alive. *2. n*. A *backdraft* resulting in *trouser shittage.*

someone let him in *exclam*. An amusing remark which can be used immediately after an audible *rectal report* has been filed. See also *more tea vicar; speak on, sweet lips that never told a lie.*

someone's tinkered with Herbie *exclam*. A witty riposte one delivers when one *backfires* unexpectedly. From the lines delivered in *The Love Bug* after the baddy has sabotaged the eponymous VW beetle, causing its engine to cough and splutter. See also someone *let him in; more tea vicar?*

something to bite on *n*. After a prolonged bout of diarrhoea, the first green shoot of recovery; something vaguely solid that you take as a sign that you might be getting better. '*May 7th 1867. Lake Victoria. After eleven days of the ague, at last something to bite on! However, prudence dictates that I should forfend from coughing or sneezing for several days yet.*' (from *The Diary of David Livingstone*).

something to go on *1. phr*. What the police require in order to pursue an enquiry into a crime which has been committed, *eg*. Reliable forensic evidence which points to the perpetrator, a reliable eye-witness account linking a suspect with the crime scene, a local roller-skating simpleton who can be fitted up. *2. n*. Onanistic fodder. '*Come on, love. Just a quick flash, that's all I'm asking for. Only I've got a wank window this afternoon and I could do with something to go on.*'

somewhere to park the Harley *euph*. A particularly massive *arse.* From the fact that the buttock cleft on just such an outsized posterior would be the ideal place to lodge the front wheel of a 700lb 1340 Softail Fatboy motorcycle in order to prevent it falling over.

sonic bog lock *n.* The random assortment of whistles, coughs, hums and throat clearings that are made by the patron of a public *crapper* cubicle with no lock on the door.

SO19 officer *euph.* Any overly eager gentleman who, whilst in a state of excitement, prematurely pumps several rounds from his *mutton musket.* Into an innocent *Brazilian.*

sooker *n. Scots.* A tit.

Sooty and Sweep moment *n.* The act of a female who indulges in an act of one-handed *self delight*, attempting to *bring herself off* in record time by means of the rapid movement of all four fingers and her thumb. Dedicated to the memory of famed Yorkshire entertainer Harry Corbett who could, through sheer manual dexterity, make his eponymous glove puppets clap their hands and nod their heads simultaneously.

Sooty and Sweep's frying pan *n.* Capacious women's genitalia.

Sooty's arse *n.* Something furry that Matthew Corbett and his dad could both fit their hands up.

soporiflick *n.* Late night *strumming* technique employed by members of the fairer sex to stave off insomnia. A feminine equivalent of the *sleeping pull* beloved of bachelors the world over.

Soprendos *n.* A series of gentle *farts* which precede a *Thora.* From the catchphrase of Victoria Wood's formerly-obese magical faux-Spaniard ex-husband: "Piff, paff, poof".

soreskin *n.* A sore *foreskin.*

sounds like a problem with your SCART socket *exclam.* An amusing phrase used by techie types to mark the audible release of a *gravy*-soaked *air biscuit, eg.* When their companion accidentally *follows through* in the doorway of Maplins whilst waiting for the bus to Gateshead. From scat + fart.

sound the charge *v.* In a row of engaged toilet cubicles where shyness prevents any and all occupants from performing their foul ablutions, to blow the first *botty bugle* blast. *'I was sat in there ages until someone sounded the charge.'*

soup but no croutons *adj. medic.* Descriptive of a low *springle count, spoogeless spaff. Firing blanks, derren.*

soup cooler *n.* A lipless *fart* that has the characteristics of a gourmet gently and silently blowing across a bowl of piping hot lobster bisque in a posh restaurant.

sour apple quickstep *n.* Another diarrhoea dance. The *Tijuana cha-cha. 'Your wife is taking rather a long time in the powder room'. 'Yes, I'm afraid she's dancing the sour apple quickstep tonight.'*

sour mash *n.* A particularly soft morning *shit,* usually sponsored by Jack Daniels or Jim Beam.

south Cluanie *euph. RAF. Scots.* Put crudely, the *back passage.* From mountain rescue terminology, referring to the north and south Cluanie ridges in the north of Scotland where, apparently, attempting to scale the south ridge is regarded as going "up the wrong 'un".

south col *n.* Mountain climber's euphemism for a lady's *front bottom.*

southern sideburns *n. Thighbrows.*

South London tapas *n.* The result of adding pork scratchings, peanuts and Mini

Cheddars to an open packet of crisps, in order to gourmandise the consumption of the said snacks into a sociable, European-style, epicurean experience. *'Fancy a drink, Tel?' 'Yeah, pint of Nelson please, Dave. Oh, and get some South London tapas while you're at the bar, will you? Cheese and onion.'*

southmouth *n*. The *snatch, fadge, quim.*

Southport *1. n.* The *arsehole. 'Fancy a trip to Southport tonight, love?' 'Yeah, alright then.' 2. n.* Lancashire town at the mouth of the Ribble Estuary. *'Fancy a trip to Southport tonight, love?' 'Eurgh! Certainly not. Don't be disgusting.'*

Southwark sellotape *n*. Police crime scene cordon tape. Named after the peace-loving London borough where it is a somewhat ubiquitous item of street furniture. *Balham bunting, Hackney bunting.*

SOW/sow *1. acronym.* Sexy Older Woman. A lady one wouldn't ask to leave the bed, despite her advanced years, *eg.* Honor Blackman, Nanette Newman, Geri Halliwell. *2. n.* One notch up from "cow" on the female insult scale.

space docking *n. Pooing* into a ladyfriend's *furry hoop.* They should bring back National Service. Or hanging.

space hoppers and seafood *euph.* Big, bouncy *bollocks* teamed with a little, prawn-like *cock.*

spacers *n.* A pair of breasts which, though large in size, exhibit no cleavage due to their distance apart. *East-westers.*

space shuttle *n.* A *shit* that has a tendency to break up on entry into the *bog bowl.* A *Columbia, six million dollar man.*

SPAD *acronym.* Signal Passed At Danger. To drive your *Interclitty 125* at full pelt into the *tunnel,* despite seeing the red warning signs at the entrance. To stick

your *cock* into *Billy Connolly's beard.*

spaddel *n. Spooge, spoff, spaff, spangle, gunk, jitler.*

spadework *n.* The hard graft that must be undertaken before planting one's *seed* in the *ladygarden. Frigmarole, choreplay.*

spadger *n. Aus.* Vagina.

spaff *1. v.* To *spoff* or *spod. 'No, no, no, Gunther! Be professional, spaff on the chest, not in the pussy.'* (from an unidentified grumble flick, circa 1980). *2. n. Splid, splunt, sploffer, sprankle.*

spam alley *n.* The target zone for *spam javelin* throwers.

spambidextrous *adj.* Able to *beat one's truncheon meat* with either *wanking spanner.*

spambulance *n. Shaggin' wagon, fuck truck, stick transit.*

spam butterfly *n.* A finger-assisted *close-up pink* shot in a *bongo mag.* A *peel.*

spam castanets *n.* Percussive *scallops,* a *clapping fish.*

spam danglers *n.* The sloppy, protruding inner flaps of a lady's *hooter.* Generously-proportioned *bacon strips, gammon goalposts.*

spam dunk *n.* The act of gently ushering a lady's head southwards, so that she may enjoy a short *reformed meat* snack.

spam fritters *n.* Labia. *Dangly ham,* especially when served in *batter.*

spam javelin *n.* An 8-foot long *cock* with a sharpened end.

spam monkey *n.* An ape that is partial to indulging itself with *luncheon meat.*

spamogram *n.* Stylised pictographic representation, or hieroglyph, of a disembodied set of male genitalia, usually seen scrawled on toilet walls, bus shelters, religious textbooks and the backs of photographs of washing machines posted to disc jockey Mike Read. A *three-line pud*.

spamouflage *n*. Copies of *Time, The Economist, London Review of Books etc*., picked off the lower shelves of newsagents in an effort to give the impression that one's copy of *Hot 'n' Horny* was merely an ironic afterthought. *Palmouflage*.

spampon *n*. A ball of absorbent *shitscrape* inserted under a chap's *fiveskin* during his *unclean times*. *'Did awaken late in the night and, unable to get back to my slumbers, did decide to perform an act of personal delight upon my turgid membrum virile. Thus resolv'd, I betook myself off to the earth closet with a tallow candle, my looking spectacles and the latest copy of Enrazzlement. I had been ensconced in there fully five minutes, vouchsafing it half a dozen to nothing on my aged knobkerrie over the most comely centrefold, and was at the praxiomatic point of discharging my foul seed when Jane banged on the earth closet door to tell me of a great fire that hadst been seen in the City. I was forced quickly to fashion myself a series of small spherules of vellum, or spampons, which I did insinuate round the brim of my farmer's hat to prevent any of my base spendings from leaking therefrom. By and by Jane did come and tell me that she heard that above 300 houses had been burned down in the night by the fire we saw, and that it is now burning down all Fish Street, by London Bridge. There was nothing to do, so I went and had another wank.'* (from *The Diary of Samuel Pepys*, September 2nd 1666).

spam purse *n*. A particularly unsightly *snapper*, usually found in the nether regions of women with *lovely personalities*.

spam sceptre *n*. The ceremonial rod that sits atop the *crown jewels*.

spamurai *n*. A fellow who waves his *pork sword* around somewhat over-melodramatically whilst *turning Japanese*.

spandrels *n*. *Men overboard, croutons, tiger nuts*. General vaginal detritus.

spangle *1. n*. A sticky, unpleasant mouthful that is most often spat out. *2. n*. Old English-flavour *spunk*.

spangle bangle *n*. A hair band kept close to her bed by a keen *fellatrix*, in order to keep her *barnet* out of her eyes as she performs *horatio*.

spangle dangle *n*. A lady's intimate jewellery item, hanging off her pierced *pygmy's thumb*, popular amongst actresses in *self help* films.

spaniel's ears *n*. Sagging, flat *thruppenny bits. Snoopies, Fred Bassets*.

Spanish archer *n*. The push, the "El Bow". *'She caught me in bed with her sister and her mum, and she gave me the old Spanish archer. Tchoh! Women, eh?'*

Spanish cravat *n*. A *pearl necklace*. Also *Dutch cravat, Chinese bow tie*.

Spanish plumbers *n*. Ill-tailored trousers, from their tendency to pinch the base of the urethra and thus "always leave it dripping".

spank banks *n*. A mental reference library of erotic imagery, which can be consulted when *spanking the monkey*. Also *mammary banks*.

spankerchief *n*. A tissue, or square of fabric for mopping up post-*monkey-spanking banana yoghurt*.

spanking *n*. A form of corporal punishment still practised in *rub-a-tug shops*. See *Mr Whippy, fladge and padge*.

spankrupt *adj.* Descriptive of a gentleman who, upon *advancing the manly meat*, finds himself bereft of inspiration.

spank the monkey *v.* To *bash the bishop, burp the worm*.

spank the plank 1. *v.* To play the electrical guitar in a "pop" beat combo. 2. *v.* To *toss* oneself off.

spanky hanky *n. Jit gel rag, wank sock.* Anything used for clearing up *gunk* after a *tug.* A *spankerchief*.

spanner 1. *n.* Not the sharpest tool in the shed; a right *fuckwit.* 2. *n.* Top *stoat*, one who "tightens one's nuts" A *monkey wench*.

spare *n.* In a *meat market*, that *flap* which is not yet sold.

spare elbow skin *n. John Wayne's hairy saddlebags, chicken skin handbag.* The scrotal sac.

spare room offence *n.* Any minor misdemeanor that upsets a wife or girlfriend, *eg.* Coming home drunk, forgetting her birthday, *fucking* her sister *etc.*

sparrowfart *n.* Early morning.

sparrowfuck *n.* A rapid act of *congress* between a man and a woman, reminiscent of the 1-second *spunk up* of the common house sparrow, *Spuggius domesticus*, or Boris Becker.

spasbo *n.* In modern youth slang, one who has picked up an anti-social behaviour order for a really *wank* reason, such as swearing in the street, dropping litter or having sex with a horse.

spasm chasm *n. Spam alley.*

spastard *n.* A politically incorrect term for one who exhibits the qualities of both a spastic and a *bastard*.

spatchelor *n.* A single fellow who results

to *floor-scraping* tactics in order to pick up the crusty bits of *sediment* off the dance floor at chucking out time.

spat out toffee, face like a *sim.* Descriptive of a lady with a physiognomy somewhat reminiscent of an *exotic dancer's clitoris*.

spawning *v.* The saucy act of masturbating in a public swimming pool.

speak duck *v.* To communicate with pond-dwelling avians in a Dr Doolittle style whilst lowering yourself into the bath. To squeeze out an *apple tart* just as your *nipsy* touches the surface of the water, thus creating a noise that only a mallard would understand.

speaking clock *n.* A fellow afflicted with premature *spoffage.* A *two-push Charlie*. From the fact that he "never gets past the third *stroke*".

speak on, sweet lips that never told a lie *exclam.* Poetic riposte which can be delivered to humorous effect after a *frog* has been audibly *stepped on*. See also *someone's tinkered with Herbie; keep shouting Sir, we'll find you*.

speak up caller, you're through *exclam. Speak up Brown, you're through.*

speak Welsh *v. Shout soup, blow chunks, yoff, sing a rainbow.*

spearmint wino *n.* A *heavily refreshed* gentleman of no fixed abode who insists on undressing and gyrating in the street.

spear the bearded clam *v.* to perform a trick involving a *spam javelin* and an hirsute bivalve.

spear the blow hole *v.* To have sex with a *BWR*.

specrackular *adj.* Of a *rack*, spectacular. *'Gosh, your worship. That new bicycle rack outside the Council offices is abso-*

lutely specrackular. As are your knockers.'

speech! *exclam.* Humorous riposte to a clearing of the *nether throat* that rattles the wine glasses on the table.

speed bump bird *n.* A sexually-alluring young lady walking along the pavement who causes male drivers to slow down dramatically, as if approaching a traffic calming measure, when in fact they are merely interested in having a good old ogle at her *tits/arse*.

speed dating *1. n.* Something people probably do in bloody Richard Curtis films or them fucking Bridget Jones books. *2. n.* The use of the fast forward button whilst watching a *Baywatch* DVD in order to find a suitable lady with which one can enjoy a brief yet torrid relationship. *3. n.* The act of looking out of a train or bus window into the bedroom windows of passing houses in the hope of seeing a nice pair of *milkers*.

speed hump *n.* The existing boyfriend of a girl that you fancy. From the fact that "it doesn't stop you, it just slows you down".

speeding ticket *1. n.* Expensive piece of ephemera resulting from a minor motoring misdemeanour. *2. n.* A small *tod* which nevertheless entails a lot of paperwork. A *shit of a thousand wipes*.

speed of shite, the *n.* Amusingly rhetorical expression implying that an object is travelling very slowly. *'Hello, is that the Gas Board? My boiler's not working and there's a very strong smell of gas in the house.' 'Don't worry, madam. We'll send somebody round at the speed of shite.'*

speedophile *n.* A suspicious-looking man in a swimming pool who does a lot of watching but very little swimming.

spelky fence *sim.* A *John Craven* that is in the early, stubbly stages of pubular regrowth. A *cuntry file. 'It was like running my hand across a spelky fence.'*

spend a pound in pennies *v.* To play the *tuppenny waterfall,* to *shit the jackpot.* To suffer a *fall of old shoes from the loft.*

spend one's money before one gets to the shop *euph.* Of an over-eager gentleman, to *spongle* his *spaff* before the *glebe end* has entered the *faff.* To suffer the enjoyable, time-saving affliction of premature ejaculation.

spend tuppence in ha'pennies and farthings *v.* To pass loose stools, have diarrhoea. To release a *flock of pigeons.*

spenk *n.* The final, limited issue of semen when one achieves one's *personal best.* The spendings generated by a pair of *knackers* that have been *wanked flat,* possibly during the Olympic Beach Volleyball competition. From spent + spunk.

spent fuel rod *1. n.* A bar of depleted uranium following its removal from a nuclear reactor. *2. n.* A sadly-depleted and flaccid *giggle stick* following its removal from a *clunge.*

sperm *n. medic.* How doctors refer to *spunk, gism.*

sperm bank *n.* A chap's personal account, in which he invests before a night out, cutting back his reckless spending for several days so that he can *blow it all* on a pretty lady.

sperm burper *n.* A sensible lady who isn't afraid to guzzle *spadge.*

sperm curdler *1. n.* A Victorian kitchen utensil made from copper. *2. n.* A satanically *fugly woman, eg.* Olive off *On* *the Buses*, the late Kathy Staff, Tracey Emin.

sperminator *n*. Lady who is the subject of a mental image summoned by a gentleman to delay his delivery of *man milk* when a dead puppy isn't having the desired effect, *eg*. Sofa-bound wobbler Judy Finnegan, Dodd-alike art nun Sister Wendy or alarming pasta ad parliamentarian Ann Widdecombe MP.

spermint *n*. Diabolical flavour of tooth whitener, usually dispensed from a pink tube. With all blue veins up the side. And a big pair of hairy *bollocks* hanging down underneath.

spermit 1. *n*. The licence given by one's partner that it is okay to do without supplementary latex prophylaxis during bouts of *penetrative affection*. 2. *n*. A particularly unsuccessful Muppet character which, inexplicably, never really caught on.

sperm noodle *n*. An airing cupboard-dried sleeping bag which has previously been used by a sexually-overactive male who has inadvertantly impregnated it with a quantity of *dream topping*. Best avoided by ovulating, damp females.

sperm perm *n*. Tonsorial style achieved by the application of three squirts of glutinous *heir gel* from a cylindrical container.

sperm wail *n*. A low grunting noise emitted at the moment one's *moby dick spouts*. An ejaculatory ejaculation. See *spuphemism*.

sperm worm *n*. The penis.

spew 1. *v*. To vomit, *park a tiger*, be sick. 2. *n*. The sick itself. *'Mum. This soup tastes like fucking tramp's spew.'*

sphinny *n*. The *nipsy*. *'I think we should stop, Rod. Me sphinny isn't what it used to be.'*

Spice island *n*. *Stinkhole Bay, Dilberry Creek*. A foul-smelling archipelago favoured by sailors on their *trips around the world*. The *arsehole*.

spicy duck *n*. An *Exchange & Mart* that sounds like Donald Duck throwing up, and probably presages a swift trip to Primark to buy some clean *underkecks*.

spiddle *n*. A term for the *piss* a lady takes after intercourse. A mixture of *spunk* and *widdle*.

Spiderman wank *n*. Of a gentleman, an act of *self-pollution* undertaken whilst wearing a pair of lady's *bills* on the head, such that the *gusset* is directly over the nose, leaving eyeholes in the place normally filled by legs. A *musk mask*.

Spiderman, do a *v*. To *spunk up* into one's hand, then attempt to remove it by *flicking ropes* against the wall.

spiders' legs *n*. Of *muffs*, rogue pubic hairs which protrude beyond the knicker line, the hairs of a *pant moustache*.

spill one's beans on the worktop *v*. To *ice* a lady's *buns*. To *lob ropes*.

spill the beenys *v*. Of a bachelor television watcher, to experience the inevitable *yop-dropping* climax to a session of viewing Channel 4's *Property Ladder* programme, hosted by the magnificently-fronted Sarah Beeny.

spill the Brasso *v*. To *drop one's yop, donate to the church fund*. To ejaculate whilst *polishing the coal scuttle*. *'What's all this mess on the carpet?' 'Sorry mum, I spilled the Brasso. What's good for getting spunk out of tufted Wilton?'*

spin cycle *n*. The final, frenzied stages of a *gentleman's act of relaxation*, when the floor starts to vibrate and nearby crockery starts to rattle and fall off shelves *etc.* A *wanker's vinegar strokes.*

spinnaker stiffy *n.* A majestic *erectivitation* sadly achieved too late to serve any useful purpose, for example after the wife has come back from the shops. Named after the tower built in Portsmouth to mark the new Millennium, which was opened in 2005.

spinner *1. n.* Member of that semi-religious, polo-neck wearing folk band without whom no variety programme in the 1970s was complete. *2. n.* A petite lady who can be spun on one's *cock* like the propellor on a beany hat. A *throwabout*, a *cock puppet.*

spinning plates *n.* An old-fashioned novelty act in which the performer attempts to keep both of a lady volunteer's nipples erect at the same time.

spirit level arse *n.* A little bubble of *fart* that lodges between the *arse cheeks* and acts as an indicator of one's inclination.

spirit levelled *adj.* In the ultimate state of *refreshment.* As *refreshed as a fucking newt.*

spiss *n.* The mixture of sperm and urine produced during a post-coital wee-wee. *Spiddle. 'That was a truly beautiful lovemaking experience, darling. Now keep toot for the scuffers while I have a spiss in Bradford & Bingley's doorway.'*

spit *v.* What fussy or frigid women do instead of *swallowing.*

spit a nut *v.* To *gamble and lose.* To *follow through*, to *shoot the breeze.*

spit her rag out *v.* Of a lady during *cricket week*, to uncontrollably eject her *jammy dodger* onto the floor whilst undergoing a spontaneous and unnecessary bout of *showing off.* Also *pop a knocker.*

spit roast *n.* Someone simultaneously skewered at both ends by *pork swords.* A *sausage jockey* who plays a *pink oboe* whilst still *in the saddle.* Something like that, anyway. A *corn on the cob.*

spitwank *n.* A lazy or prudish lady's *horatio* avoidance technique; specifically a saliva-assisted *J Arthur* masquerading as a *blow job.* Normally experienced when the man has recently spent time shifting a heavy filing cabinet up or down a fire escape, imbibed several pints of export strength lager or *EastEnders* is about to start.

spla water *n.* Semen, *gunk.*

splash 'n' dash *1. n.* In motor racing, the act of heading to the pits for a quick fill when short on fuel within the last few laps of the race. *2. n.* In *dumping*, to head to the *crapper* when *touching cloth* whilst late for an important engagement. *'Where's Huw? He's on air in forty-five seconds.' 'Don't worry. He's just gone for a splash'n'dash.' 3. n.* A *squat 'n' squirt.*

splashback *1. n.* An area of tiles behind a sink. *2. n.* Unfortunate tidal effect of a *depth charge* or *belly flopper* within the pan, resulting in splashing of the *arse* and *barse.*

splash barrier *n.* Any *ad hoc*, improvised contrivance employed by a lavatory user, usually made from *bog roll*, constructed in order to counteract the uncomfortable sensation of *splashback* when taking a *dump.*

splashdeck *1. n.* A bit of a canoe, probably. *2. n.* The tastefully tattooed portion of a *grumble flick* actress's back that provides a convenient target at which her male co-star may aim his *spod* during the *money shot. Arse antlers.*

splash diet *n.* A weight loss programe

that involves the shedding of pounds of unsightly excrement. A *dump*. *'I can't do these jeans up again. I'd best just go on a splash diet. See you in ten minutes.'*

splashdown *n. milit.* Official Parachute Regiment terminology for a *wetting of one's bed* after a mammoth drinking session.

splash me boots *v.* To have a *piss*, take a *leak*.

splash the pot *1. v.* More poker terminology. To throw one's chips down in a disorderly fashion. *2. v.* To *drop the kids off at the pool* in a disorderly fashion.

splat *n. medic.* *Bollock batter, fetch.*

splay *v. US.* To draw back the *beef curtains* and make a grand entrance.

splice *v.* British version of *splay.*

splifty-fifty *phr. Lancs.* Amongst drug addicts in the red rose county, the correct ratio of ordinary tobacco to specially-cultivated herbs in one of their hand-rolled organic cigarettes.

splinge *n.* A particularly lubricious *kipper mitten.* A *bag of slugs.*

split a kipper *v.* To *part the whiskers*, to *have it off.*

splitarse *n.* An offensive, sexist term for a *bird.* *'Birthdays: TV and film actor Tom Selleck, 57. Olympic Gold medalist diver Greg Louganis, 43. Splitarse boffin Germaine Greer, 64.'* (from *The Times*, Jan 29th 2003).

split bag of mince *n.* A *gutted rabbit*, a *butcher's dustbin*, a *stamped bat.*

splitter cable *1. n.* An adaptor from Maplins for plugging two television sets into a single chipped satellite decoder. *2. n.* A *Thora Hird* which is so humungous that it rents one's *Jap's flag* in twain.

split the beard *v.* To *part the whiskers*, again. After 20 minutes or so. And a fag.

split the winnings *euph.* To halt the *laying of a cable* halfway through. *'And after four days without movement Job took up his toilet and great was his relief. But even as he released his burden there came a voice and it was the Lord. And the Lord spake in a loud voice saying Come unto Me Job. And Job replied saying Oh God, what is it this time, for I have only just sat down. And great was the wrath of the Lord. And He commanded Job to split the winnings and come now unto Him. And great was Job's discomfort.'* (from *The Book of Job*).

splod *1. n. Sprag, spoff. 2. v.* To *sprag, spoff.*

splodge *v.* To masturbate semen over a glossy magazine.

splodgenessabounds *1. n.* Lightweight British punk band, fronted by Max Splodge (real name Maxwell Splodgeworth), whose sole 1980 hit unwittingly provided the title for evergreen BBC3 shitcom *Two Pints of Lager and a Packet of Crisps. 2. n.* A massive ejaculation covering everyone and everything in the vicinity with *Harry Monk.*

splosh *1. n.* Money. *2. n.* Britain's leading periodical for those interested in genito-spaghetti pursuits.

spluff *1. v.* To *spunk up.* *'She took her bra off and I spluffed in my pants.' 2. n. Spunk.* *'Nice tits, Mother Superior. By the way, is there anywhere I can put these pants? They're full off spluff.'*

splurry *n. Fizzy gravy.* Diarrhoea.

splutterbeans *n.* The *Eartha Kitts.*

Spock *v.* To make a "V" with one's fingers and boldy go where no man has gone before, *ie.* Two up the *twat* and two up the *arse.*

'And after four days without movement Job took up his toilet and great was his relief. But even as he released his burden there came a voice and it was the Lord. And the Lord spake in a loud voice saying Come unto Me Job. And Job replied saying Oh God, what is it this time, for I have only just sat down. And great was the wrath of the Lord. And He commanded Job to split the winnings and come now unto Him. And great was Job's discomfort.' ~ The Book of Job.

spocks *n.* Socks that have been used as a ejaculation receptacle or post-*bust off* clean-up device. From spodge, spadge, spoodge, spaff, spangle, spingle, spongle, *etc.* + socks.

spod *n.* See *spooge.*

spof *n. Spod.*

spoilers *1. n.* Aerodynamic wing modifications that prevent Citroen Saxos from flying into the sky when being driven up and down in Burger King car parks. *2. n Buttocks, mudflaps.*

spoilsports bra *n.* An item of intimate apparel used by women who unaccountably wish to suppress the natural movement of their *bangers.*

spondle *n. Spooge, spluff, spangle, jitler, knob toffee.*

sponge *1. n.* In a *puddle jumping* couple, the one who has feathers stuck in his teeth. *2. n. prop.* A silent character played by Colin Bean in *Dad's Army.*

Spongebob's nose *n.* A distinctly unimpressive, yellow *cock.*

spooge *n. US. Spoff.*

spooge scrooge *n.* A *trojan*, condom, *rubber policeman.*

spooge stick *n. Gut stick, fuck rod, slag bat.* The penis.

spoot *n. Scot.* A word for *spunk.* Usage limited to Campbeltown on the Mull of Kintyre. If you went into the pub in Machrihanish and said the beer tasted like spoot, they wouldn't know what you were talking about.

sporran catalogue *n.* A *grot mag.* Specialising in ladies with snap-shut, shaggy grey *snatches, eg. Hoots Mon Only.*

sport relief *1. n.* Marathon charity event at the end of which one feels compelled to make a £15 donation to the cause. *2.* *n.* Trampy marathon *self abuse* session at the end of which one feels compelled to make a 15ml donation to the pages of West Bromwich's most dispiriting daily newspaper.

sports bag *n.* A handy *cottaging* accessory in which one partner stands to conceal his feet and avoid detection by lavatory attendants or *scuffers* looking under the door. See *bagging.*

sports model *n.* A woman who has had her *tubes* tied and thus provides worry-free sexual fun for caddish males.

spouse *1. n.* One's marital partner. *2. n.* Her *fanny.*

sprag *1. n. Spoff, splod. 2. v.* To *spoff, splod.*

spraint *n.* Otter *shit.* Now there's a word that's going to come in useful.

spray the pine *v.* To go for a good *sit-down visit* which could endanger the ecosphere.

spread bet *1. n.* In the world of gambling, a bet whereby the eventual payout is dependent upon the accuracy of the wager rather than a simple "yes/no" outcome, whatever that means. For more details, have a look at Wikipedia, which is where this definition was ham-fistedly precised from. *2. n.* The perspicacious act of proceeding simultaneously with two or more concurrent courtships, thereby increasing the mathematical odds that at least one of your ladyfriends will "spread".

spreader *n.* A variation on a *moonie*, whereby the buttocks are manually pulled apart to reveal the *freckle.*

spreadsheet *n.* Shiny, crinkly toilet paper found in public lavatories which only succeeds in smearing the *shit* around one's *arse* like a plasterer's float.

sprew *n. Spongle, jitler, spragg. Spunk.*

spring a coil *v.* To *lay a cable, drop a copper bolt, build a log cabin, grow a tail, drop your fudge, pinch a loaf, crimp one off, drop the shopping, drown a copper, give birth to a dead otter, light a bum cigar, park your breakfast* or *drop off a length of dirty spine. 'Anyone seen the new Viz kicking about anywhere? I'm off to spring a coil.'*

spring clean *n.* A gentleman's first morning visit to the *crapper* after a night on the *lash*, where he has a *dump* and a *slash*, blows his nose, picks the sleep from his eyes and generally begins the miraculous process of coming back to life.

spring onion roots *n.* An elderly *tart's* unruly *gorilla salad.* The *welcome mat* of a lady of advanced years.

sprogdrop *n. medic.* Pregnancy. A state of *up-the-duffness*, expecting a *lawn monkey.*

sprouts *n.* Children.

spud fumbler *n.* A *puddle jumper. 'Today's birthdays: Antoni Gaudi, Catalan biomorphic architect, 1852; Alexei Alexeyevich Abrikosov, Nobel Prize-winning Russian physicist, 1928; George Michael, drug-driving spud fumbler, 1963.'*

spud, to *v.* To deliberately mess up a job interview in order not to jeopardize one's benefits. Named after the character in *Trainspotting.*

spuds deep *adj. Up to the maker's nameplate.*

spuffer *n.* An extremely localised Tyne Dock colloquialism describing male ejaculate.

spuffing dust *n.* The plight of a gentleman who is experiencing a *jizzbolt* drought, following a 6-hour *wanking* marathon.

spuncle *n.* A sperm donor. From spondle + uncle.

spunctual *adj.* Of a gentleman *grumble thespian.* To be able to *spoff* on cue or to a pre-arranged schedule.

spuncture *n.* An incidence of latex failure at a critical moment whilst using a *jubber ray.* A leak in a *beef wellington*, a bursted *blob.*

spunk *1. n.* Semen, *seed. 2. n.* Spirit, pluck. *3. n. Aus.* A good-looking man, dish, hunk. *4. n.* Tinder made from fungus. *5. v.* To ejizzulate, to *spooge*, esp. vertically.

spunk-curdling *adj.* Descriptive of a woman who can induce an instantaneous *derection* at a hundred paces. *'Deaths; Andrea Dworkin, spunk-curdling American feminist writer, 58.'*

spunk double *n.* Ersatz *man milk*, fake semen. Any substance used on a pornographic film set when the lead actor has already *jizzed* his *balls* as *flat as a bat's wings*, eg. Yakult, wallpaper paste, Tippex, egg nog, Scott's emulsion, No More Nails, salad cream, toothpaste.

spunk-drunk *adj.* Delirious nature brought on by over-consumption of *root beer.*

spunk dustbin *n.* A *spooge bucket, box of assorted creams.* An exceptionally accommodating young lady, who has a *twat like a billposter's bucket.*

spunk gurning *n.* The delightful faces a *grumble flick* actress pulls as she excitedly anticipates the *tipping* of the romantic lead's *cement* onto her face.

spunk juggler *n.* An *onanist* on a unicycle.

spunkled *adj.* Besprinkled with *spunk.*

spunkling *adj.* Sparkling or glistening as a result of being *spunkled*, eg. Gillian

Taylforth's chin, the hat of a commissionaire at a hotel where Status Quo have booked a room with a balcony.

spunk mail *n*. The lifelong postal monsoon of unsolicited pornographic brochures and catalogues received as a result of foolishly buying a Linzie-Dawn McKenzie video from an ad in the back of the *Sunday Mirror* twelve years ago.

spunk rat *n*. A good looking bloke, as described by females.

spunk run *n*. *RN*. On Her Majesty's warships, the 2-inch gap down the side of a sailor's bunk where he stows *pop-up books*, soiled *grundies* and tissues on which he has *blown his nose*.

spunk shuffle *n*. The walk adopted by one's girlfriend to stop the *congregation* leaving the *cathedral* before she reaches the *bog*.

spunky wrench *n*. A *wanking spanner* or *cunt scratcher*. A gentleman's hand.

spuphemism *n*. A humorous *sperm wail*. A jolly shout upon *spoffage, eg*. "There she blows!" "Tim-berrrrr!" or "Yabba Dabba Dooooo!"

Spurlock, Morgan 1. *n. prop*. Controversial US documentary film maker. 2. *n*. Any source of erotic stimulus, such as a *bongo mag, grumble flick* or *left-handed website*, which results in a fellow's *hampton* becoming *supersized*.

Spurt Reynolds *n*. Pet name for the tearful *bald man* who sits on the *hairy beanbags*.

spurtual reality *n*. The act of pausing a *skin flick* before *lobbing ropes* onto the TV screen, in order to create the impression that you are involved in the action; a feeling that, one would imagine, very quickly gives way to a vivid sense of self-loathing, not to mention an urgent need

to clean a load of *jitler* off the telly before the missus comes in.

spurt your curd *v*. To spread your *spunk*, to *squirt* others with your pluck and spirit.

squack *onomat*. The sound of a male ejaculation.

squaddie's delight *n*. A woman in the armed forces who is not *on the bus to Hebden Bridge*. A heterosexual Army, Navy or Air Force lady.

squaddie's mattress *n. milit*. Army version of the naval *matelot's mattress*. A lady who *spreads* for soldiers, especially round the back of Cheeks nightclub, Aldershot.

squaddie's sleeping bag *n*. A well-used and crusty *haddock pastie*. '*Joan Hunter-Dunn was nothing like the bird in the poem, you know Michael. I licked her out once behind a skip in Camberley and she had a blurtch like a squaddie's sleeping bag, I can tell you*.' (Sir John Betjeman on *Parkinson*, BBC TV, 1975).

squashed spuggy/spoggy/sparrow *n*. An elderly lady's vagina. *Granny's oysters*.

squat 'n' squirt *n*. A manoeuvre often performed up dark alleys by ladies returning from the pub, and filmed by *wanking* CCTV operators. A *splash 'n' dash*.

squatter *n*. An annoying little *turd* that takes up residence in one's *arse* and refuses to leave, unless threatened by Bermondsey Dave.

squatter's rights *n*. The unwritten rule that, when a man takes a newspaper into the *stink hut* to do some *bum rubbish*, not even the might of the British legal establishment can move him until he's finished. '*Winston, please do hurry up darling. Black Rod is waiting and His*

Majesty has terrible cramps.' 'I have the News of the World, a cigar, and am about to drop a second H-bomb. So you can fuck off and tell them I've got squatter's rights.'

squeak the breeze *v. US.* To *fart, talk German, pass wind.*

squeaky toy *n.* A *fart* which sounds, and indeed occasionally smells, not unlike the popular, shrill noise-producing dog amuser.

squeeze the fig *v.* When needing a *tom tit* in a public place, to keep one's *nipsy* firmly clenched to prevent the *turtle's head* poking out.

squeeze the lemon *v.* Of women, to urinate. Possibly onto a pancake.

squeezing the cheese *v. Sausage stretching.*

squench *1. n.* A moist *fart* which feels like one has *gambled and lost. 2. n.* A character in Dickens's *The Old Curiosity Shop* who suffered a *fall of soot* during Little Nell's funeral.

squibble *n.* The second in a triumvirate of gentleman's *popshots*, the first of which is a squirt and the third of which is a dribble.

squidge *n.* A vagina with a *wide on.*

squid legs *n.* The thin, rubbery tentacles found floating on the water after a bath night session of *making nylon.*

squid marks *n.* Fishy *skids* in a lady's *fairy hammock.*

squid wank *n.* The kind of *toss* received from a lady inexperienced in the provision of such things. Derived from the distinctive cuttlefish-like movement of the hand. A *tail of the unexpected, scuttlefish.*

squinternet *1. n.* The eye-damagingly microscopic web pages to be found on the screen of a mobile telephone. *2. n.* The somewhat larger internet pages to be found on a full-size computer, which are nonetheless just as deleterious to the viewer's visual faculties.

squirrel covers *n.* A lady's *dunghampers.*

squirter's alley *n. medic.* The *bodily treasure.*

squirting like a badly laid paving slab *sim. medic. Shitting* through the *eye of a needle, pissing rusty water* out of one's *arse*, in the style of an *affpuddle*, as defined in the *Meaning of Liff.*

squirts *n. medic.* In proctology, a series of fiery eruptions from the *chamber of horrors* resulting in a pyroclastic flow from the *farting fissure.* A condition also known as the *skitters*, the *Earthas*, the *Engelberts.*

squirty dirt *n. Medic.* Faeces of an extremely low viscosity. *'Come to the Curry Capital, Bigg Market, Newcastle upon Tyne - for a curry you won't forget in a hurry.'*

squirt your dirty water pistol *v.* To *tip your filthy concrete, drop your yoghurt, lose your mess. 'Aw, bloody hell. Who's been squirting their dirty water pistol into me knicker drawer?'*

squishpot *n. US.* The area right below the *devil's doorbell.*

squits *n. medic.* Dangerous wet *farts*, constantly bordering on the *follow through.* Junior *squirts.*

squiz *n.* Having a *shit* whilst doing a puzzle in a tabloid newspaper. *'Just pull the nose up to the docking tower, will you number two? I'm off to the bogs for a squiz.'*

STA *abbrev. Grumble* industry code denoting the job prospects of a starlet with less than conventional good looks.

Straight To Anal.

stab in the dark *n*. The act of attempting to slip one up the wife's *wrong 'un* while she's asleep. Please see *striking north* for legal implications.

St. Bernard's chin *sim*. Descriptive of a *muff* that has had lots of *ropes lobbed* at it. A heavily *bespunkled mingepiece*. Also *bloodhound's jowls*.

St. George *v*. To lance one's old dragon from behind. To take part in a *dog's marriage*.

St. Ivel *n*. An imperial measurement of beer, equal to two and a half quarts or five eigths of a gallon. Five pints. *'Mr Barratt appeared unsteady on his feet as he got out of the car. I asked him if he had been drinking and he replied 'Not really. I've only had a St. Ivel.''*

stabbin' cabin *n*. A secondary residence kept for the sole purpose of quick extra-marital encounters, *eg*. A discreet flat in Belgravia, a small cottage in the Cotswolds, or a 12-foot caravan on the cliffs at Scarborough.

stabbing the cat *n*. *Self discipline*. From the motion of knifing an invisible feline on one's lap. Similar to *feeding the ducks*, but with the emphasis on the downward stroke.

stack blow *n*. A gentleman's *organism*.

stacked *adj*. Overstocked *rack* in the *snork* department. *'I fell in love with my wife at first sight. She is particularly well stacked.'*

stackwhacker *n*. A friend or colleague who possesses a phenomenally large and well-kept collection of *jazz periodicals*. *'Today's birthdays: Lewis Caroll, English author, 1832; Elmore James, American blues musician, 1918; Frank Skinner, Brummie stackwhacker, 1957.'*

stagecoach *n*. A cramped, filthy ride which leaves you in need of a wash. Also *riding shotgun*.

staining in *n*. Having a quiet night at home, watching DVDs and leaving blotches on the living room upholstery.

stalactits *n*. Hanging breasts of the long, thin variety.

stalagshites *n*. Naturally-occurring, upward-pointing turdiferous deposits which form in porcelain basins.

stale bait *n*. A *bit of stuff* that's gone slightly past its "best before" date.

stalk *n*. Erection, *stiffy*. A *third leg, middle stump*. *'Excuse me, if I look like a tripod. I just can't seem to get rid of this stalk. Anyway, let's carry on. Ashes to ashes, dust to dust.'*

stalk fever *n. medic*. Condition affecting men on *big cock day*.

stall shy *1. adj*. An equestrian figure of speech referring to a racehorse that doesn't want to go into its box. *2. n*. A public lavatory figure of speech descriptive of a fellow's inability to make eye contact with the man who has just emerged from the next cubicle, after spending the last five minutes being forced to listen to what sounded like a Sumo wrestler giving birth to several catering-sized black puddings through a loud-hailer. Also *bogshy*. *3. adj. medic*. The psychological condition that renders borderline *scuttlers* unable to micturate in public lavatories unless there is vacant stall between them and the next micturater. *Stage fright*.

stamped bat *euph*. One of the most horrific kinds of *ladypart* imaginable; a *bodily treasure* that resembles nothing so much as a flying rodent that has been subjected to a heavy shoeing. A *snatch* that not even Ozzy Osbourne would consider eating. *'Nostalgia was powerless to resist. His eyes bored into hers like zirconium-coated drill bits. His muscular arms enfolded her body as she felt herself being whisked away on a souffle of passion. Gently he lowered her bloomers, and a thrill of forbidden excitement shot through her loins as she felt his hot Latin breath beginning to creep down her crab ladder towards her altar of Venus. But it was not to be. 'Bloody Nora,' shouted Sextus Empiricus from between her legs. 'I'm not licking that out. It looks like a fucking stamped bat.''* (from *The Lady and the 2nd Century Pyrrhonic Skepticist Philosopher* by Barbara Cartland).

stamp on the toothpaste *v.* To ejaculate in an over-excitable manner.

standard eight *1. n.* More-or-less obsolete double-run home movie format which involved opening the side of the camera half-way through the exposure of the film in order to turn the spool over, thus ensuring that the mid-point of any domestic cine presentation in the early 1970s was characterised by flashing psychedelic orange lights. This was followed shortly by the splice, where the two twenty-five foot lengths of longitudinally split 16mm film had been joined together at the processing laboratory, snapping in the projector and the image on the screen melting before one's very eyes like something out of *The War Game* and a bout of swearing whilst your dad tried to re-thread the film through the white-hot gate with his fingers. *2. n.* Crapulent 1950s small family automobile, particularly suitable for the sort of small family that didn't require any boot

space or a car that would climb any sort of gradient, and hence *3. n.* A gentleman equipped with a small, underpowered *trouser engine* which is inclined to conk out mid-journey.

standby on *n. Half a teacake.* A penis in a state of semi-tumescence ready to leap into action if required.

stand on *n.* A *bone on*, a *stalk*.

standing on the fireman's hose *sim.* At the conclusion of the evening's fourth or fifth bout of *Jesuit boxing*, a complete failure to release *jaff*. An *air horn.*

standing ovation *1. n.* Mark of respect given to a *digestive transit* which is so impressive that one has to get to one's feet and have a good look at it. *2. n.* Characteristic posture taken up by someone attempting to lay a particularly recalcitrant *dog's egg.* Half standing up and hammering the knees in agony.

stand lunch *v.* To provide an *air buffet* which stops everyone in the room feeling hungry any more.

stanky *n.* The glaze that is left on the *shaft* of the *choad* after a bout of *kipper splitting.* May be *zuffled* on curtains or wiped on a *stankychief.*

starboard bow *n. RN.* The *arse.*

starch pill *n.* A Viagra tablet, a *bluey.*

starfish trooper *n.* An *arsetronaut.*

starfucked *adj.* The loss of credibility suffered by a product as a result of its endorsement by a *shit* celebrity. Walkers crisps, Benecol margerine and Homebase DIY have all been *starfucked.*

stargazer *n.* A gentleman's *pork sword* with a pronounced upwards curve, allowing the *hog's eye* to scan the heavens.

staring at the last After Eight *euph.* Whilst *scuttling* one's significant other *doggie-style*, looking down at her puckered *gazoo* with a longing which is tempered by the knowledge that to indulge yourself would be to commit a social *faux pas* on a par with snaffling the last wafer thin minty slice in the tray. *'Pray, what is troubling you back there, Mr Brown?' 'Nothing at all, your majesty. I was just staring at the last After Eight.'*

staring at the sun *n*. An act which is apt to make one go blind. *'Oi, Gerald. What are you doing under your coat?' 'I'm just staring at the sun into my popcorn bucket, dear.'*

starter button *n*. The *clematis*, the *wail switch*. The *clit*.

starter leads *n*. Suspenders, *giggle bands*.

starting line at Brands Hatch *1. sim*. Descriptive of severely *be-skidmarked undercrackers*. Guaranteed to cause embarrassment the first time they are handed to one's newly-wedded bride for washing. *2. sim*. The *skid pan* of a student house or dysentery hospital *chod bin*.

starting pisstol *n*. During a sit down lavatory visit, the initial wee which heralds the start of a really big *shit*.

start the horn mower *v*. To perform the particularly vicious upstroke often demonstrated by the inexperienced female *masturbatrix*.

star trek *n*. Any sexual encounter where one would be going (boldly or otherwise) where no man has gone before, *eg. Getting tops and fingers* off Ann Widdecombe or doing Richard Littlejohn up the *shitter*.

Star Wars door *sim*. In *backdoor work*, descriptive of the manner in which the *death star* closes after the *pink Darth Vader* is removed. See *hoob*.

stash dash *n*. The sprint from front room window to *grumble* collection once the front gate is securely fastened behind the wife as she pops out for a pint of milk.

state of the art *n. rhym. slang*. An act of rectal flatulation. A *broken heart*. *'Jesus! Is that your state of the art, Dot? I thought it was the bleeding Noggin the Nog.'*

stauner *n. Scot*. A dour, granite-hard *bone on*. An *Old man of Hoy*.

stay in the shallow end *exclam*. A request made by a female to an inexperienced *fanny nosher*.

steak drapes *n. Gammon goalposts, beef curtains*.

steakwich *n*. The external genitalia of a lady of a certain age which resembles a traditional British pub snack.

steal mill *n*. Any place where industrious *neds* exchange purloined goods for money and/or drugs.

stealth bomber *n*. A subtle *leg lifter*. A mystery *benefactor*, phantom raspberry blower. An anonymous, gaseous altruist.

stealth bummer *n*. An undercover, hard-to-detect *puddle-jumper* who flies under the *gaydar*.

stealth moose *n*. An *LRF*.

stealth shit *n*. An act of public lavatory defecation performed surreptitiously, that is to say under the *covering fire* of some sort of masking sound, *eg*. A toilet flush, somebody washing their hands vigorously or heavy breathing from Chuck Berry in an adjoining cubicle.

stealth sites *n*. Football, car and DIY websites which can be quickly clicked on after *desktop dusting* in order to fool the more IT-literate missus.

steamroller effect *n*. Last resort of one who discovers that there is no *arse* *paper* left whilst suffering from severe post-curry *ring sting* in the *crapper*. The gentle rolling of the cool cardboard tube backwards and forwards across the anal cheeks to afford soothing, albeit temporary, relief.

steg *n*. A woman resembling a ferocious, spiny, squat, prehistoric dinosaur. Abbrev. of stegosaurus.

stellabate *adj*. Chaste, as a consequence of imbibing excessive quantities of *wifebeater*. *Stellabacy* is a situation neatly summed up in the phrase "The spirit is willing but the flesh is weak because the export strength lager is strong".

stellacetamol *n*. A large amount of continental lager, the consumption of which anaesthetises the drinker, protecting him from any sensation of pain when falling through plate glass windows, being hit by cars or toppling off scaffolding.

stellacide, commit *v*. To purposely down an excessive quantity of *Nelson Mandela* in order that one's sorrows choke on their own vomit.

stellanoia *n*. The state of aggressive paranoia which one attains shortly after imbibing one's tenth pint of *wifebeater*.

stella performance *euph*. A comprehensive act of spousal abuse.

stellaporter *n*. A futuristic form of instantaneous transportation which warps the time/space continuum, leaving one outside the front door mere moments after leaving the pub. Often with a wet trouser leg, a shoe full of *piss* and a half-eaten kebab.

stellarisation *n*. Process by which a man is rendered unable to father children. *'Sorry love, I can't do it. I've been stellarised, see.'*

stellavision *n*. Premium strength, kaleidoscopic *beer goggles*.

stellify *1*. *n*. Title of Ian Brown's latest two verses and a half-arsed chorus masquerading as a complete song. *2*. *v*. To imbibe a reassuringly excessive quantity of a certain Belgian beer.

stelloquence *n*. Term descriptive of a mightily *refreshed* late night kebab shop customer's witty, free-flowing banter and the fluent, well-informed discourse with which he regales his fellow prospective catmeat snack purchasers.

stemmer *n*. A *chewie* in which the dirty lady is able to swallow the whole shebang. A *deep throat*.

stench trench *n*. The *ha'penny*.

Stephen Hawking's treadmill *sim*. Descriptive of something or someone of little use, *eg*. "Personal transport revolution" the Sinclair C5.

step on a duck *v*. To create a quack, *fart*. *'Pardon me, Ladies and Gentlemen. Do not adjust your wireless set, Mrs Simpson just stepped on a duck.'* (from The Abdication Broadcast of Edward VIII, 1937).

step on a frog *v*. To *step on a duck*.

step on a rake *v*. To attain a particularly speedy erection.

step on one's dick *v*. To make a mistake or blunder. *'It is with deep regret that I am today leaving the office of Home Secretary, in which capacity it has been my great honour to serve in this administration for the past 16 months. It is a job with an exceptionally wide brief, encompassing as it does many serious issues, not least of which is the treatment of foreign national prisoners who have completed their sentences – a matter for which I have taken overall responsibility and on which I* *have staked my reputation. The Prime Minister, as is his right and responsibility, has made the judgement that I have stepped on my dick, and therefore my continued occupation of my current position is likely to stand in the way of the continued reforms which remain necessary. I am therefore being relieved of my cabinet post with immediate effect, and returning to the back benches.'* (Rt Hon Charles Clarke MP, statement to the House of Commons, reported in *Hansard*, May 5th 2006).

Steptoe & Son *n*. A drab and depressing sexual position, whereby a solitary, clapped out old nag kneels on the bed, proffering her knackered back end up to her old man, who slowly and disgruntledly *bangs* her whilst gurning and muttering under his breath. And then stops to shovel her steaming dung into a bucket.

Steptoe's face *n*. A saggy non-too-fussy set of *flackets*. ie. "They will take in any old rag or bone".

Steve *n*. A Scotsman who *shops around the corner*, eg. Jimmy Somerville. From Steve McQueen.

Steven and the twins *euph*. A fellow's *meat and two veg*, often referred to by Ian Beale in *EastEnders*. The *Kennedys*.

Steve Wright *n. rhym. slang*. A *shite* with a contingent of turdy-hangers on. *'I'm just off for a Steve Wright in the afternoon.'*

Stevie Wonders, the *n. medic*. The involuntary wobbling of the head that one exhibits when desperately trying to stay awake, *eg*. A student in a Friday afternoon lecture or a lorry driver on the M6. From the erratic head movements of the Motown star. *'The trial of the Millennium*

Dome Jewel Robbers was held up today after Judge Michael Coombe was spotted having a severe attack of the Stevie Wonders during the defence council's summing up.' (Nicholas Witchell, *BBC News*, November 2003). *2. n*. The act of rocking one's head from side to side whilst negotiating a particularly large and recalcitrant *turtle's head*, usually after several pints of Irish stout.

St George *n*. The act of *lancing your old dragon* from behind.

stick at 15 *v*. From the pontoon playing gambit, to settle for a low quality score; thus to go for the first half decent bit of *blart* who shows interest in a night club. See also *go ugly early*.

sticklebrick *n*. A particularly difficult and uncomfortable *tod*. A *pine cone*.

stickman *n*. A *fanny hopper*, a *skippy*.

stick shifter *n. Wanker*.

sticky belly flap cock *n*. Post *curd-spurting* condition enjoyed by *monkey spankers*.

sticky keys *1. n*. Some sort of annoying computer function on the Windows operating system which is activated by pressing the shift key five times, apparently. *'I was just messing about on the computer and I turned on sticky keys by accident.' 2. n*. The inevitable result of an overenthusiastic and poorly-aimed session of *one-handed web-surfing*. *'I was just messing about on the computer and I got sticky keys by accident. And spunk all over the mousemat and screen. And printer.'*

sticky toffee pudding *n*. A thick, dense *Thora* that adheres to everything it touches, particularly one's *arse cress*.

sticky wicket *n*. A well used *crease* with all the bounce *fucked* out of it. A *box of* *assorted creams.*

stiff drink *n.* A warming tot of *vitamin S* quaffed by females and *puddle jumpers*. A *drink on a stick.*

stiff enough for the wife *adj.* Descriptive of something which, while not optimal, is adequate for the job at hand. *'Is that plaster dry yet, Dave?' 'No mate, but I reckon it's stiff enough for the wife. Let's sling the wallpaper up and we can piss off down the pub early.'*

stifficult *adj.* Awkward as a consequence of unwanted tumescence in the generative member. *'Fuck me, look at the knockers on that stripper. By the way, Dave, it's your round.' 'I can't just now, Bob. It's a bit stifficult.' 'Why are you frantically looking for change in your trouser pockets, then?'*

spooch *n. Spooge, spodge, spadge, splang etc. Jism.*

stiff *n.* A corpse. *'Come on jerkwad, let's plant the motherfucking stiff and get out of here.' 'Very well, vicar. I'll tell the organist to miss out the last two verses of the Funeral March.'*

stiff lock *n.* A *piss-proud spooge stick.*

stiffy *n.* A *stalk.*

stiffy stocking *n. Rascal wrapper, cheesepipe clingfilm, Spurt Reynolds's sickbag.*

stig *n.* One who is a little bit *council*. One who is *common as shite*. A dump dweller. *'Birthdays: JK Galbraith, economist, 95. Arthur Schlessinger, historian, 86. Mario Puzo, author, 83. Sarah Ferguson, Royal stig, 44.' (The Times,* Oct 15th 2003).

Stig of the dumps *n.* A turbo-charged *bum cigar* that whips round the U-bend faster than the eponymous, anonymous, white-suited *Top Gear* racing driver and registered trademark.

stigor mortis *n. medic.* Torpid condition affecting jobseekers, students and men who work from home, whereby they are regularly rendered completely immobile watching repeats of *Top Gear* on Dave all afternoon.

stillborn dachshund, cock like a *sim.* A deeply unpleasant simile used when describing a *membrum virile* which maintains impressive length, weight and girth, even whilst it is on the slack.

still fighting *adj.* Of a curry or spicy meal, to display the same or greater aggression on the way out as it did when it went in. *'Are you all right in there, love?' 'No. It's that chilli I had last night. It's still fighting.'*

stilt on *n.* A long, thin, cheesy erection.

stilton muffle *n.* A pungent and unwashed *fish mitten*. A particularly stenchsome *trench.*

stiltons *n. Lady dumplings* which don't get see a great deal of sunlight, and as a result are usually very white and covered with prominent blue veins.

Sting wank *n.* A post-pub act of *self-pollution* which, as a result of the amount of alcohol one has consumed, becomes a turgid marathon lasting many hours. From the former Police frontman's notoriously fruitless attempts to *go off* up his missus.

stink 1. *n.* The distinctive odour of well-matured *knob cheese*, eggy *air biscuits*, a *Stilton muffle* etc. 2. *v.* To emit such a smell, to *ming*. 3. *n.* A fuss. 4. *n. Aus.* A scrap, fight, *pagga.*

stinking bishop *n.* The miasmatic result of poor *fiveskin* husbandry, that is to say, *smegma*. Also *brimula, foreskinzola, Fred Leicester, fromunder, helmetdale,* *knacker barrel, Hamish blue, he-dam, Lymeswold, knob stilton, bell end brie, trollop snack* and *willydelphia*.

stink sponge *n.* A chair or bus seat which someone has just *dropped a gut* into.

stinky finger *n.* Having ate up the *captain's pie* without a knife and fork. *Stinky pinky*.

stinky Mervin *n.* The *Finsbury bridge, biffin bridge, barse, carse, taint, notcher, etc.*

stinky rooster *n.* A rousing report that wakes up the farmer as well as the rest of the household.

stir the stew *1. v.* To *arrange the orchestra, wind the clock, nip and roll, sort out the boys, tune the banjo, pop the mouse back in the house.* To rearrange the trouser furniture. *2. v.* To perform the anal sex.

stir the tanks *v.* To have a *wank* without ejaculating. From the routine procedure on the ill-fated Apollo 13 which inadvertently led to an explosion. See *almosturbate*.

Stirling *rhym. slang.* A *wank*. From Stirling Moss = toss.

stirring the porridge *n.* Having *sloppy seconds*, dipping one's *naughty brush* into a *billposter's bucket*.

stits *n.* Small *tits, bee stings, Dutch Alps*.

stoat *n.* In the world of pant nature, the natural prey of the *one-eyed trouser snake*.

Stobart *n.* An articulated *turd* that jackknifes in the pan.

Stobby doorbell *n.* A handful of gravel directed at the window of an upper floor residence to alert the occupants as to one's presence below. Used extensively in the salubrious Stobwells district of Dundee.

Stockholm syndrome *1. n.* Recognised psychological response whereby, after being held prisoner for a considerable period of time, captives begin to identify with their abductors. *2. n.* Situation that can occur after a prolonged bout of constipation, when one's *chocolate hostages* start to sympathise with the *Simon Cowells* where they are being held, and begin to actively wish to stay in captivity.

Stockport overcoat *n.* A thick coating of glitter spray which, when combined with a boob tube and miniskirt, keeps the young ladies of the Cheshire town snug and toasty on the bitterest of winter evenings. A *Bigg Market duffle coat, Whitley Bay parka*.

Stoke chamois leather *n.* An orbital sander, used to remove grafitti from the boarded-up windows which are commonplace in the popular Potteries *shit hole*.

stonads *n.* Testicles which have fossilized due to under-use. *'A lifelong celibate, Sir Isaac got the idea for his popular Newton's Cradle executive toy when his stonads banged together as he was sitting down under an apple tree to invent gravity.'* (from *Connections* by James Burke).

stone *n.* The reason a *sponge* has got feathers stuck in his teeth.

stone cold stunner *1. n.* A wrestling move, actually a variation on the ace cutter, made popular by redneck grapple fave "Stone Cold" Steve Austin. *2. n.* An actress in a vintage black and white movie who manages to give one the *horn* despite the fact that she is almost certainly six feet under. See *rise from* *the dead.*

stone of contentment *n.* The excess 14lbs avoirdupois rapidly acquired by a bloke when he moves in with his ladyfriend and starts spending a significant proportion of his spare time sitting on his *arse* watching repeats of *Coronation Street.*

stoner's grocer *n.* An all-night petrol station selling family-sized chocolate bars and biscuits to narcotics enthusiasts at unsociable hours.

stones *n. arch.* Olde Worlde *balls. Bollocks, knackers.*

stonker *n.* Erection, *hard on, stiffy.*

stool box *n.* Coarse epithet for a *bird's shit hopper. 'Look at the stool box on that, your honour. It's like a violin case.'*

stop at Boots *v.* Phrase expressing optimism about the outcome of a romantic interlude. *'You going to get in Tracey's knickers tonight, then Steve?' 'Well, I'm stopping at Boots, put it that way'.*

store defective *n.* A retail store *fuckard.*

storming Batista's palace *euph.* An unexpectedly bloody episode of *falling to the communists.* Named after the events of March 13th 1957, when a group of revolutionary students attacked the Havana stronghold of Cuban dictator Fulgencio Batista, whilst his missus was *dropping clots.*

stout trout *n.* The impressively charcoal-hued *Eartha* that transpires following an eighteen-hour sampling of dark ales and burgundy pie.

stoutzheimers *n. medic.* Condition suffered by drinkers in Irish theme pubs, where the bar staff completely forget about waiting customers whilst half way through pulling their pint of Guinness, and wander off to serve someone else.

stradivarious *adj.* Descriptive of the sundry miscellaneous techniques that may be employed by anyone having a good old *fiddle.*

straightening your hat *n.* Raking one's kex out the crack of one's *arse.*

straighten your tie, let me *exclam.* Phrase used by a woman who is offering to give a man an erection in the *trouser department.* Or just possibly suggesting that she is about to re-arrange his neckwear.

strain the potatoes *v.* To *strain your greens.*

strain your greens *v.* To have a *piss.*

strange *n.* Any woman whom one has not had *carnival knowledge* of. An antidote to a *groundhog lay. 'I know she's minging compared to the girlfriend, but you can't beat a bit of strange, can you?'*

stranger, the *n.* The act of sitting on one's hand until it falls asleep before a bout of *bishop rage,* giving the feeling of a *hand job* from someone else.

strangle Kojak *v.* To *make the bald man cry,* to *peel the carrot.*

stranks *n.* The delightful "fridge magnet bunch of grapes"-style *shit* clusters one finds plastered to the porcelain in public convenience *chod bins.*

strapadictomy *n.* Routine operation to strap on a *dildo.*

strawberry Sunday *n.* Of a gentleman, the point when he is so desperate for a *scuttle* that he no longer cares that *rag week* is not yet over.

stray spray *n.* Wayward urination caused by cheese-based occlusion of the *snake's eye. Twin jets.*

stray steaks *n.* Outsized flappage. *Beef curtains* of Brobdingnabian proportions.

streaker *1. n.* One who removes their

clothes and runs about at sporting events whilst the BBC pretend they are not there, *eg.* That witless *twat* from Liverpool. *2. n.* A *Richard the Third*, slightly smaller than a *U-blocker* and with a slightly pasty consistency, which leaves behind a brown streak as it scuds around the *pan* on being flushed away. A *brown arrow.*

streetmate *1. n.* Lighthearted TV dating show featuring *wankbank* favourites Fearne Cotton and Holly Willoughby. *2. n.* An act of wobbly-legged coitus performed in an alley up against a wheelie bin. A *fork lift truck,* the *chinook position, a flying buttress.*

Stretch Armstrong *n.* One gifted with the ability to eat *gorilla salad* whilst simultaneously *finding Radio Luxembourg.* Also *Superman.*

stretched quimosine *1. n.* An extremely elongated *fanny* that has taken plenty of people for a ride. *2. n.* One of those ridiculous American cars, well stocked with wine, nibbles and plenty of *gash,* that are typically seen failing to negotiate corners in British town centres on Friday nights.

strike a damp match *1. v.* To stimulate oneself against an unwitting stranger in a crowd, *eg.* On a tube train, in a queue to see the Pope lying in state. To *frotter. 2. v.* To attempt to have a *wank* with a *soft on.*

strike oil *v.* When doing a *duty* on the lavatory, to eject a *feeshus* with such force that its impact causes a vertical spout of water which hits one squarely in the *jotter.*

strike up the colliery band *euph.* To produce a protracted *trouser cough* from your *brass eye.*

strike while the iron's hot *v.* To have an opportunistic *Barclay's* as a result of spotting something completely *wankworthy* when out and about, *eg.* In the bus station toilets after spotting a *cracker* on the number 38, or in a department store toilet after encountering a really sexy mannequin in the lingerie department.

striking north *n.* Light-hearted violation of Section 74 of the Sexual Offences Act 2003. Missing the target and taking the missus unawares, thus initiating an inadvertent game of *Bronco.*

string *n.* Wood, tumescence. *'Quick, everybody, Gunther's got string. Fluffer off set, please and roll camera.'*

stringbean *n.* A long, thin, probably green, penis that gets left at the side of your plate.

string of pearls *n.* A series of tiny *botty burps* released in quick succession whilst walking. *Air croutons.*

stripper's clit, face like a *adj.* Of a woman, having a *charming personality.*

stripy laugh *n.* A *parked tiger,* a *Welsh monologue.*

stroke mag *n.* An item of top shelf literature, *art pamphlet, gentleman's interest magazine.*

stroke of midnight *n.* A free *one off the wrist,* courtesy of the Adult Channel. A *discount wank.*

stroker *1. n.* A *wanker, ie.* One who masturbates, *eg.* Jonathan Ross. *2. n.* A *wanker, ie.* One who is a *twat, eg.* Jim Davidson.

stroker's cough *n.* The retching gag reflex of a lucky lady who has bitten off more than she can chew.

stroke the dog through the letterbox *euph.* To slide one's hand down the front of a lady's knickers.

Stromboweli *n.* Somewhat contrived alternative to *Vesuviarse*, describing a fumerole that ejects bursts of hot gas and high velocity debris on a regular basis.

strong favourite *n.* A *fart* that can be forced out as hard as you want with no risk of *following through*, because you have just been and went for a huge *shit*. From the fact that you know for certain that you are not going to *gamble and lose*. A *banker.*

strop 1. *n.* A sort of leather thing that old fashioned barbers use to sharpen their razors. 2. *n.* A lady's, usually period-propelled temper tantrum. A *wobbly,* a *wendy.* 3. *n.* That which a bachelor has in order to *relax* whilst reading a *newsletter* or watching a *masturmentary.*

strop sign *n.* A sometimes subtle indication that one's female partner *has the painters in.* If missed, a *strop sign* can lead to painful repercussions. *'Did you get any last night?' 'Nah. When I got back from the pub I went straight through a strop sign and had to sleep in the spare room with a bag of frozen peas on my bollocks.'*

struggle nugget *n.* A troublesome *duty* that only comes out after putting up a fight.

strum *v.* A relaxed *tug* on the *one-string banjo.*

strumpet *n. arch.* Olde Worlde *Brass.* Also *strombone.*

strumping *v.* Predatory behaviour by a *bird,* the female equivalent of *sharking.*

strum the hairy harp *v.* Of a disgusting lady, to essay a few arpeggios on her *upside down piano.* To *shuffle the Kit-Kat,* gus*set type.*

student garden *n.* An uncared-for *fritter.* A scrubby area of *cunt turf.* With a fridge in it.

student knob *n. medic.* A *cock* that has been *wanked* black and blue.

stuffing a marshmallow in a piggy bank *v.* Of those unfortunate situations involving *brewer's droop,* to attempt to force one's *loose sausage meat* into the *slot.*

stump nest *n.* Another name for a fellow's pubulent outcroppings. The *stump bed.*

stunt cock *n.* In a *bongo vid,* when the leading thespian is unable to sustain *wood* or provide a *money shot*; cue the *stunt cock,* a fat ugly cameraman with a *concrete donkey* on a *hair trigger.*

stuntman's knee, face like a *sim.* A light-hearted, affectionate putdown for a lady with a *lovely personality.*

stuntman's tyre *sim.* Descriptive of the state of the *council gritter* after spicy food, *ie.* Like a tyre that has been doused in petrol and set on fire ready for a daredevil to jump through.

sty at night, the *n.* The last pickings of *salad dodging swamp hogs* hanging round the *swill* van outside a nightclub after the *two am bin rake.*

style conscious *adj.* A euphemistic term describing a fellow who is *good with colours. Stylish. 'Has your youngest lad married yet, Maureen? He was very style conscious, as I recall.' 'No he hasn't. Well, he's not really found the right girl yet, you see. And he's very busy, too, of course. He runs a company manufacturing poppers, gimp masks and butt plugs.'*

sub-prime wine *n.* Late vintage alcoholic refreshment for the more economically challenged, *eg.* White Lightning, *spesh,* Wilko window polish. Also *credit crunch* *punch, prol-seco.*

subtitles *euph.* A triumvirate of *big-boned* ladies walking in a line abreast. From the Teletext page familiar to those who are hard of hearing, *viz.* 888.

subway *n.* The well-proportioned, meaty result of a mammoth session on the *porcelain throne*, boasting the same dimensions of one of the larger offerings from the eponymous, well-known sandwich emporium.

succubus *n.* A phantom night-time *cocksucker* once thought to be responsible for *nocturnal emissions.*

suckers *n. Shag tags.*

suck face *v.* US. To kiss. *'Git a goddamn move on an' finish your mother fuckin' popcorn, you sonofabitch. I wanna suck some face.'*

suckhole *n.* In radio studios, one who is employed to scream with laughter at everything Russell Brand or Chris Moyles says. A *brown noser, toady, arselick, sycophant, fart catcher.*

suckhole's dilemma *n.* Of a *shirt fly*, to be in a situation where they don't know whose *arse* to lick first, *eg.* A salesman in a room full of purchasing managers, or Ben Elton in a palace full of Royals.

sucking a tramp's cock, like *sim.* Descriptive of the consumption of something which is unpleasant, or which leaves a foul taste in the mouth, *eg.* Netto budget fishcakes or Ricky Tomlinson's penis.

suck off *v.* To perform *horatio*, to do a *chewie*, give some *head.*

suck the poison out *v.* Of a young lady, to perform an altruistic act of *horatio* on a man who is suffering from a life-threatening erection. *'She clasped his neck, and for the first time Bertram learnt what an impassioned woman's kisses were like upon the lips of one whom she loved with all her heart and soul, as Tess loved him. 'There - now are you convinced of my true feelings?' she asked, flushed, and wiping her eyes. 'I'm still not sure, love,' he replied, undoing his zip and withdrawing eight quivering inches of pink steel. 'But I might believe you if you suck the poison out of this bastard.''* (from *Tess of the d'Urbervilles'* by Thomas Hardy).

sudoku wank *n.* Something that takes about ten minutes, gives you a brief feeling of satisfaction when you complete it, but leaves you wondering why you bothered.

sugar-free spongle *n.* The ejaculate of a vasectomised male. *Australian gravy.*

sugared almond *n.* The *clematis.*

sugar puff *n.* A diabetic.

sugarpuffs, mouth full of *euph.* A description of dentition that leaves something to be desired, cosmetically speaking. *Queen mum's teeth, English teeth.*

sugar walls *n.* Sheena Easton's *slice* sides.

suitcase handle, gusset like a *sim.* Descriptive of the petrified state of a dirty *bird*'s crusty 3-week-old knickers.

summer assessments *n.* The first day in the year when ladies deem it opportune to leave their jumpers at home and venture forth wearing tight tops and loose blouses, so that gentlemen can review their *qualifications. 'Take the table outside the pub, lads, and don your examiners' sunglasses for the summer assessments.'*

summoning Moira *n.* The desperate act of frantically conjuring up a mental picture of cadaverous newsreader Moira Stewart in order to suppress a potentially embarrassing *diamond cutter* just before getting off the bus.

summoning Parcelforce *n.* The act of going for a *gypsy's kiss*, *tom tit* or a *Sherman tank*, or any other activity that leaves you incapable of getting to your front door in the three nanoseconds it takes for a Royal Mail Delivery operative to tickle your door with a hummingbird feather and ram a card through the letterbox saying "Sorry we missed you".

sump *n. medic.* The part between the *front* and *back bottoms* on a lady. The *manifold*, the *rocker box*, the *fire break*, the *kerb*. The *tinter*.

sunblest loaf *n.* A festivalgoer's *shite* deposited in a bread bag, thus avoiding the long walk to the toilets.

sunburnt ginger, arse like a *sim.* Descriptive of one's *ringpiece* following a particularly piquant Indian repast. The reddest possible thing in the world.

sundance *n.* The fairer member of a *lesbidaceous* couple. From Butch and Sundance.

Sunday joint without the string on *euph.* A *clunge* which has far too much flabby gristle, collapsed fat and stubbly skin going on.

Sunderland's trophy cabinet, a fanny like *sim.* A large, empty void, based on the fact that the eponymous, notoriously unsuccessful football team owns a large, empty trophy cabinet shaped like a *vagina*. A simile which can be varied, depending on one's footballing allegiances and/or geographical prejudices.

sunnies *n. Aus.* Tits, baps.

superbeero *n.* The *alter ego* of an otherwise mild-mannered chap, revealed in all its glory after fifteen pints of *dizzyade*.

Powers include *shitting* himself, dashing into a phonebox to *piss* all over the floor, being sick down his shirt and the ability to fall off buildings in a single bound.

superfuzz bigmuff: deluxe edition *1. n.* 1992 re-issue of the classic album by Seattle grunge combo Mudhoney. *2. n.* A dead hairy *fanny*. A *biffer, Judith*. *'That's a superfuzz bigmuff: deluxe edition you've got there, your worship, look you. Isn't it.'*

Superman *n.* Name given to the occasional consequences of a chap *tipping his filthy concrete* onto the bedsheet so that it adheres to his partner's back when she gets up in the morning to go for a *shit* and make his breakfast, thus mimicking the style of the erstwhile comic book superhero's cape.

supermarket smack *n.* Special Brew.

super trouper *n.* A person who desperately needs to urinate, yet overcomes the urge by means of superior mental strength. From the lyric of the eponymous Abba song, *viz.* "Smiling, having fun / Feeling like a number one."

surfboard *1. n.* A flat-chested female, *Miss Lincolnshire*. *2. n. Aus.* A piece of equipment used by women to *catch the waves* when the *red flag is flying*. A *fanny nanny* for a heavy *aunt Flo*.

surfing the crimson wave *n. Riding the menstrual cycle.*

surf 'n' turf *1. n.* The act of orally probing a lady's *rusty sheriff's badge* during an act of *cumulonimbus*. *2. n.* An 1980s-style meal served at a Berni Inn, consisting of a fish and steak combo that tasted like one was orally probing a lady's *rusty sheriff's badge* during an act of *cumulonimbus*.

supreme champion *1. n.* That pedigree

dog which has been raised on a diet of fillet steak and patty de fwa grar that gets paid thousands of pounds to sit by a big silver cup and advertise tinned kangaroo bollocks for a couple of weeks after it wins Cruft's. 2. *n*. Offensive, sexist terminology describing the *best in show* out of a group of *hounds*.

surbrowned sound *n*. A burst of window-rattling noise from one's *sub-woofer*.

surprise, sur-fucking-prise! *exclam*. Remark made at a depressingly predictable event, *eg*. England losing on penalties.

survivor *n*. A buoyant *stool* which resists all attempts to *send it to the beach*.

SWAB/swab *acronym*. Young ladies who respond to a gentleman's attempts at wooing with monosyllabic disinterest. Single Word Answer Bitches.

Swaffham *v*. Of a lady, to practise the gentle art of cramming both a gentleman friend's *clockweights* in her mouth at the same time. Named after the town in Norfolk, where all the womenfolk, without exception, are experts in this procedure.

swaffling *n*. The act of a chap putting his flaccid member against a famous building, *eg*. The Berlin Wall, Buckingham Palace, the Taj Mahal *etc*., taking a photo of it and displaying said snap on the internet. A popular pastime in the Netherlands, apparently, where they still have to make their own entertainment.

SWAG/swag *1. n*. What is written on the sack in which a traditional, stripy-jerseyed burglar places candelabras and silver trays. 2. *acronym*. A well-manicured chap who always seems to have a female hanger-on, but who never seems to have a girlfriend. One who, it might

be suspected, *throws a light dart*. Secret Will And Grace.

swagman's hat *n. medic*. Condition of the *anus* when infested with numerous *tagnuts*. '*Holmes surveyed the water closet cubicle before announcing, 'The game is afoot, Watson, and our quarry has a bandy-legged gait.' 'How the devil do you know that, man?' I exclaimed. 'Elementary. The Izal toilet paper means he will almost certainly have a ringpiece like a swagman's hat.''* (from *The Red-Ringed League* by Sir Arthur Conan-Doyle).

swallow *v*. What proper women do.

swallow the bear *v*. To perform *cumulonimbus* on a lady with a right old *biffer* on her.

swallow the oysters *exclam*. A phrase of friendly encouragement to a *nosher* who is being a little too fussy about eating all her *porridge* up.

swamp *v. milit*. To *piss*, urinate.

swamp donkey *n*. Female who is not overly endowed with physical beauty. A *tug boat, boiler, sea monster, steg*.

swan *1. n*. Big posh duck that can break a man's arm with one flap of its wing. 2. *n*. The wife of a *pavilion end bowler*, whom he marries in order to mask his true sexual orientation. So-called because she's a *queen's bird*. The *beard* in a *lavender marriage*. 3. *n*. Style of *wanking* that can break a chap's arm.

swan shag *1. n*. The, presumably treasonable, practice of copulating with one of Her Majesty's favourite waterfowl. 2. *n*. The last, dying sexual act of a doomed relationship. 3. *n*. A romantic dalliance with a *bird* so beefy it could result in a fractured humerus.

swank *1. v*. To walk into a room like

one was walking onto a yacht. *2. n.* A secretive *five knuckle shuffle* utilizing minimal wrist action which is enjoyed whilst lying next to one's sleeping partner. Normally practised following the rejection of drunken sexual advances. An *American beauty.*

swan strangler *n.* Stretchy piece of plastic which throttles large waterbirds. Can also be used to secure several cans of *wifebeater* together at once. A term coined on Armando Iannucci's *Charm Offensive* programme on the Home Service.

swap spit *v.* To *suck face.*

sweatermeat *n.* Phrase used to alert friends to the presence of a nice pair of *tits.* Usually accompanied by clockface directional information. *'Sweatermeat at 3 o'clock.'*

sweater puppets *n. Fondleberries.* Particularly animated breasts that keep a fellow entertained. *Milky swingers.*

sweats *rhym. slang.* An affectionate term for people of Caledonian extraction. From sweaty socks = jocks.

sweaty bullets *n.* Low calibre *slugs* that appear in a fellow's *grundies* whilst he is undertaking strenuous physical exercise, such as moving a filing cabinet up a fire escape or throwing twenty car batteries into a high skip.

sweaty Morph *n.* A *mudchild,* a *turd.*

swedge *n.* That piece of folded bogroll which a sweating *pie shifter* wedges in his *potty slot* in order to stop his *farting clappers* rubbing together. A *manpon, botcap, toffee rizla. 'Substantial Andrex swedge worn by Bad Manners frontman Buster Bloodvessel (Douglas Trendle) whilst performing Just a Feeling in a deep-sea diver's suit on Top of the*

Pops c. May 1981. Complete with certificate of authenticity. Estimate £3000 - £4000.' (extract from Christie's Rock Memorabilia Auction Catalogue, August 2004).

Swedish *n. Greek.*

Sweeney! *exclam.* A humorous utterance shouted out in the style of Flying Squad DI Jack Regan by a man who is *kicking a lady's back doors in.*

sweep's brush *n.* A *Judith.*

sweep the yard *v.* To loudly scratch one's pubic area making a sound like brushing paving slabs with a hard-bristled broom.

sweetbreads *n.* The testicular component of the *family jewels.* The *clockweights,* the *plums,* the *knackers.*

sweetcorn itch *n.* An itchy ringpiece as a result of insufficient wiping. *IRS.*

sweet FA *acronym.* Sweet Fanny Adams, *fuck all,* absolutely nothing. Nowt.

sweet tits *n.* Affectionate male term of endearment for females. *'Goodnight, goodnight! Parting is such sweet sorrow / That I shall say goodnight until it be morrow, sweet tits.'* (from *Romeo and Juliet* by William Shakespeare).

sweet wrapper *n. rhym. slang.* The lavatory bowl or, indeed, the cubicle wherein it is typically situate.

swift *n.* A bit like a *swallow,* only faster. So fast, in fact, that there isn't the option to spit.

swill out the trough *v.* Female equivalent of *cleaning inside the farmer's hat.*

swim against the tide *v.* To take a *dip* whilst the *red flag* is flying. *To surf the crimson wave.*

swine flu *n. medic.* Mild nausea and cold sweats experienced upon waking up in bed with a right *pig.*

swing both ways *v.* To be a *switch hitter.*

swingers 1. *n*. Sinister, grim-looking couples who have uninhibited sex in suburban houses with other sinister, grim-looking couples. 2. *n*. Clockweights, knackers, pods, gourds. 3. *n*. Big bangers.

swinging grimp *n*. A tiny ball of *poo* hanging like grim death onto the tip of an *arse* hair. Named after the Playstation Network game *Pixel Junk Eden*, in which players control a plip-like "grimp", which tarzans on an *arse* hair from flower to flower in a pyschedelic garden.

swirly *n*. Bullies' lavatory game whereby the victim's head is pushed into the *crapper* and the flush pulled. *'I say you chaps, look out! Campbell and Milburn are in the bogs and they've just given Clare Short a swirly.'*

Swiss *adj*. Completely useless. *'Did you see England playing Germany? They were completely fucking Swiss.'*

Swiss army wife *n*. Rare and amazing lady who can work, bring up the kids, cook, hoover, open beer bottles and polish her husband's *family jewels* all at the same time.

Swiss finger *n*. An erect *todger* with a pink iced topping, upon withdrawal from a lady on the eve of a week's *visit from the painters*, or in the 24 hours following their departure. From the similarity to the doughy confection of the same name to be found in the window of all Ainsley's branches.

Swiss kiss *n*. A *post-horatio spangle*-flavoured snog.

Swiss movement *n*. A *chod* dropped in the *pan* with almost nazi-like precision by a person with disciplined and regular bowel habits.

Swiss wank account *n*. An optimistic fellow's untraceable email account, created solely for the purpose of registering with *left-handed websites*.

switchcraft *n*. The magical ability of a woman to make incredible amounts of cash disappear into thin air whilst out shopping.

switch hitter *n*. *US*. Person who *bats with both hands*; a bisexual, a *happy shopper*. One who approaches the *oyster* and *snail buffet* with a broad plate.

switching to manual *n*. Solo completion of a bout of sexual activity due to the missus falling asleep before you've finished.

swive *v*. 17thC. Fuck. *'Swiving hell. I've had to take six chops at the King's neck and I've still not got his swiving head off.'*

swope *n*. The hairstyle affected by balding men whereby strands of hair on one side of the head are grown long and swept over the dome, giving the impression of a full head of hair, *eg*. Robert Robinson, Bobby Charlton, Desmond Morris.

sword heavy *adj*. Of a party or other social gathering, suffering from an evident plethora of male attendees, and consequently a marked dearth of *tussage*. *'I reckon I'm going to stop going to the Masons, Chief Constable. The meetings are a bit too sword heavy.'*

swordsman's shelf *n*. The conveniently-placed ledge, normally used for one's washing requisites, located in the corner of a hotel shower and upon which one's ladyfriend can place one foot or, in extreme cases, one knee, thus encouraging unfettered access to her *bodily treasure* during the sort of bouts of sexual intercourse which are normally encountered only when on holiday.

'Thoughtful gestures such as night-time chocolates, fluffy towelling robes and a swordsman's shelf make this hotel a winner with honeymooners.' (Kuoni Winter Sun brochure, 2007/8).

sword swallower *n*. A circus *fellatrix*.

swotty totty *n*. The sort of female television personalities who can do simple mental arithmetic, play a bit of piano or look things up in a dictionary, *eg*. Carol Vorderman, Myleene Klass, Susie Dent *etc*.

Syd 'n' Eddies *euph*. A pair of asymmetrical *knockers*, with one noticeably larger than the other. A frankly unsatisfactory and distinctly unamusing combination. *'Have you seen today's Daily Star? Kelly Brook's got her Syd 'n' Eddies out on the middle pages.'*

syllojism *n*. A logical argument about *wanking* that begins: "All men are human".

syrup *n*. Hairpiece. From syrup of fig = Irish jig. *"Q: 'Just look at this, 007.' Bond: 'What is it, Q? Looks like an ordinary syrup to me.' Q: 'Yes, but one tug on the chinstrap and it turns into a miniature helicopter.' Bond: 'Hmm! Hair raising!'' (From Never Say Never Again, 1983).*

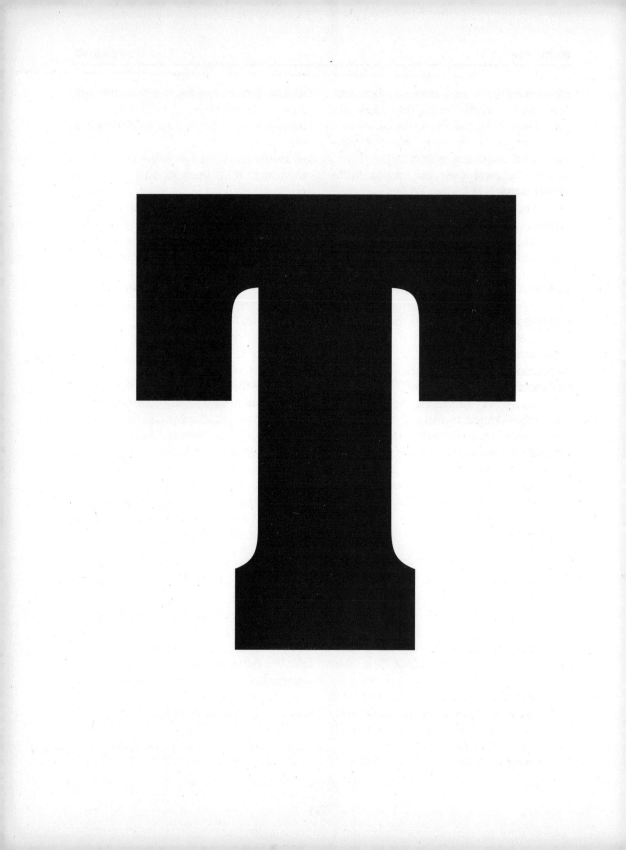

tabby afro *n.* A collection of different-coloured *pubes* found blocking the plughole of the bath in a shared flat.

tacho break *n.* A lorry driver's four-and-a-half-hourly respite interval, during which he pulls over and has a hitch-hiker-strangling fantasy-fuelled *wank* in his cab, before *shedding his load*. *'I just come through the centre of Birmingham and after seeing all that blart I had to stop at Keele Services for a tacho break and a KFC.'*

tackle *n.* What you hold onto when you go *fly fishing*.

tacklebags *n.* Underpants, *bills, scads, scuns, dunghampers*.

tackleshack *n. Tacklebags.*

taco tickler *n.* A *gusset typist*.

tactical chunder *n.* Student *refreshment* technique. A deliberate *technicolour yawn* performed to make a bit of extra beer room in the stomach, or to delay the arrival of a *helicopter attack*.

tadger *n.* A thing that tadges. Also *todger*, so it presumably todges as well.

tadpole net *n. Blob, rubber johnny, cheesepipe clingfilm.*

tadpole yoghurt *n. Gentleman's relish, man mayonnaise*, dressing for a *sausage sandwich*.

tagnuts *n. Toffee strings, winnets, clinkers, dangleberries, bead curtains. Rectal hangers on, arse cress Tarzans.*

tail *1. n. arch.* That which wags when it sees a pretty lady. The *veiny bang stick. 2. n. Fluff, totty, skirt, talent. 3. n.* Your *bum.*

tail ender *n.* A small dollop of *doings* that one must wait for after the main stool has been expelled, the finial on a *log cabin* roof. *Geetle.*

tail gunner *n.* A *style-conscious* fellow.

tailpipe *1. n.* The exhaust of a motor car. *2. n. US. Corybungo.*

tail sap *n.* Any sticky secretion from a man's *stem.*

tail shot *n.* A *change of heart.*

tail wind *n.* A *southern breeze* tending to push one forward.

taint *n. Niftkin's bridge.* Because "'tain't your arse and 'tain't your fanny".

take a packed lunch *v.* To take one's girlfriend on holiday to avoid all the *fucking about* and loss of drinking time that goes with finding a suitable female at one's destination. *'I went to Ibiza last year and wasted the first day and a half sorting myself out with some tart to bang. I'm going to Agya Napa this year, and I'm taking a packed lunch.'*

take an air dump *v.* To *let rip, blow off.*

take Captain Picard to warp speed *v.* To *make the bald man cry.* To *strangle Kojak, pull Paul Daniels' head off.*

take communion *v.* To kneel before the altar and partake of a portion of *haddock pie* during *rag week. Fish on Friday.*

take Herman to the circus *euph.* To engage in an *act of personal delight.*

take one in the company's time *v.* Whilst at work, to hold in a *number two* until one's unpaid break is over, thus ensuring that one gets paid the full hourly rate for having a *shit.*

takeout *n.* A professional escort, whose door-to-door sexual services are ordered from a menu over the phone.

take the cat to the vet *euph.* To knock off work early. See *let the dog out, fire the one o'clock gun.*

take the crust off *v.* Nautical term describing the precautionary pre-disembarkation *wank* taken by trawlermen before they are reunited with their ladyfriends.

Take the edge off.

take the edge off *v.* To *relax in a gentleman's way* in order to prolong a putative *scuttle* with one's partner. To *put a wank in the bank*. '*Got a big night with the missus planned. I'd better go and take the edge off first.*'

take the goalie off the pitch *v.* To withdraw protection in a positive effort to conceive a *turf chimp*.

taking the steps at Goodge Street *euph.* A lonely, last resort act of *self pollution*, only embarked upon to *get the boys out of the tube* in extreme circumstances. From the lonely, last resort means of exiting the eponymous London Underground station, which entails a life-sapping trudge up 136 steps.

talent *n. coll. Crumpet, bush,* attractive females. *Scrunt.*

talent scout *n.* A designated member of a group who looks round the pub door to check that the *blart* inside is worth pushing one's way to the bar for.

talk broken biscuits *v.* To speak in a somewhat unintelligible manner whilst *heavily refreshed*. '*BBC1, 11.35; This Week. The programme that brings you the big political stories of the last seven days. Join Andrew Neil, Michael Portillo and Diane Abbott as, fresh out of the BBC bar, they talk broken biscuits about the top topics in Westminster and the wider world.*'

talk German *v.* To *fart, blow off,* puff on an imaginary *bum cigar*.

talk on the great white telephone *v.* To be sick in the lavatory. *Drive the porcelain bus.*

talk to the boss *exclam.* A married man's response to his wife's request for some of his hard-earned cash to fritter away on luxuries. An instruction to perform an act of *horatio*. '*It's no good, love. I'm going to have to go shopping. We're right out of baby food and the twins need new shoes.*' '*It's not up to me, you'd better talk to the boss.*'

talk to the judge *n.* To *suck a copper's truncheon* by way of avoiding a speeding ticket. '*I know I was doing 75 in a 30 zone, officer, but is there any way we can work this out? Perhaps if I spoke to the judge behind that skip?*' '*I'm not sure that's going to make any difference, sir.*'

tallywhacker 1. *n.* 18thC. Penis, *old man.* 2. *n.* A not-overly-attractive young lady with whom a bloke has *carnival relations* merely in order to increase his "tally" of sexual partners.

tammy dodger *n.* A gentleman forced to go to the pub, chippy, video shop, church, round the world balloon attempt *etc.*, to avoid his *blob-stropping* missus.

tammy huff *n.* A monthly feminine mood swing. A *rag rage* or *blob strop.*

tamnesia *n.* Male short term memory failure; accidentally forgetting that it is your partner's *cricket week*. Symptoms include being hit in the face with a pan and getting stabbed with a bread knife.

tampon 1. *n.* A small, highly-sophisticated implant which enables women to play tennis. 2. *n.* An injury-prone footballer, from the fact that he is "one week in, three weeks out", *eg.* Darren "Sicknote" Anderton, who didn't play for Spurs, Birmingham and England.

tam rag *n. Jampax.*

tamtrum *n.* A monthly exhibition of petulance. From Latin tampus = fanny rags & trum = hissy fit. A *blobstrop,* a *tammy huff, showing off.*

Tamworth *n.* Perjorative term for a ginger person, named after them pigs which have ginger bristles and funny-looking eyes.

tandem *n.* A *bike* of such prodigious sexual appetites that she would happily take two men at once.

tandoori whisper *n.* A silent, yet exquisitely rancid, burst of *wind* following an Indian meal.

tango butter *n. Fanny slobber, sloom.*

tank *v.* To *scuttle, roger.*

tank driver's hat *n.* A particularly hairy *fanny* with flaps that fasten under your chin. A *biffer, bear trapper's hat, deerstalker.*

tanked up *1. adj.* Usefully drunk, sufficient to fight or drive a car very fast. *2. adj. milit.* To be sufficiently equipped with tanks.

tank slapper *1. n.* An exciting incident that happens to a motorcyclist shortly prior to a thrilling ride in an ambulance. *2. n.* An ugly biker's moll.

tanorexia *n. medic.* Psychological disorder common in footballers' wives types who, despite daily *cancer shop* sessions, still believe they are pasty when in fact they have the skin tone of an Oompah-Loompah.

tantric shit *n.* An extremely prolonged visit to the porcelain *chod bin*, where one sits for four hours, *humming.*

tap in *n.* Any drinking venue where *pulling* presents little or no difficulty.

tap off *v.* To successfully *tap up.*

tapioca tash *n.* Facial ornamentation, popular amongst *stick vid* starlets.

tapioca toothpaste *n.* Dental gel for a *trouser leg trombonist*, just the thing when *brushing the au pair's teeth.*

tapping on the high hat *v.* Rhythmic, per-cussive *jazz* masturbation.

tapping out *1. n.* In American wrestling, the point at which a combatant can't take any more and concedes that he has lost his bout. *2. n.* During a bout of *horatio*, the point at which the *noshee* can't take any more and *loses his mess.*

tapping the ash *n.* Refers to the vigorous shaking and pulling apart of the buttocks in an attempt to force out the troublesome *turd* that ends a *shitting* session, but refuses to drop into the *pan*. Akin to tapping the end of a cigarette in order to encourage the ash to drop. *'Are you going to be long in the crapper, Archbishop?' 'Shouldn't be long now, your Majesty, I'm just tapping the ash.'*

TAPS/taps *acronym. medic.* Technical term used by doctors on medical notes, Thick As Pig Shit.

tap up *1. v.* Of football managers, to make an illegal approach to a player who is signed to another team. *2. v.* Of Football Association officials, to chat up and attempt to instigate a sexual liaison with a typist in a lift at FA headquarters in Soho Square.

Tara's tits *euph.* Nothing. Fuck all. From the notorious It-Girl Tara Palmer-Tomkinson's distinct lack of *bikini filler. 'We have spent three months searching the secret bunkers and military bases of Iraq in search of chemical warheads and weapons of mass destruction, but thus far I must report to the Security Council that we have come up with Tara's tits.'* (Dr Hans Blix's report, 27th Jan 2003).

Tarantino hangover *n.* The kind of hangover whereby one's memory behaves in the style of *Pulp Fiction*; one's recollections of the night before appear in a seemingly random order and one has to wait until one has seen all of them to finally understand what happened.

tar baby *1. n.* A sticky, black trap that nearly proved the undoing of Brer Rabbit in the *Uncle Remus* stories. *2. n.* A sticky, black *crap* that proves the undoing of anyone who has spent a night quaffing Guinness. Leads to an intractable combination of an *arse like a Marmite pot* and *buoys from the black stuff*.

Tarbucks *n.* A set of *tits* so impressive that the viewer involuntarily shouts "ho-ho!" in the manner of the cheeky, gap-toothed scouser comedian and golf enthusiast Jimmy.

Tardis fanny *n.* A deceptively spacious *snatch*. Opening the saloon doors to find a disappointing *cathedral* when one was expecting a *priest's hole*.

tarmacing *n.* Like preparing a *Boston pancake*, but instead of your buttocks, you use a 14-ton Aveling & Porter steamroller to flatten your *turds* across your missus's *knockers*.

tarmac round the garage *sim.* Descriptive of a slightly grubby *path to the back door*, making *rear entry* an unpleasant prospect.

tarrantless *adj.* Even less talented than Chris Tarrant, *eg.* Steve Penk, Eamonn Holmes, that arsehole mate of Robbie Williams's who used to do *You've Been Framed* for a few weeks before they got Harry Hill in.

tart *n.* Slapper, dolly bird, a nice bit of *cheesecake*.

tart farmer *n.* A *pimp, flapmonger, fanny magnate*.

tart fuel *n.* Any alcoholic drink consumed by young women which gets them going. *Knicker oil.* 'She's very light on tart fuel. She'll go all the way to Cockfosters on three bottles of Hooch.'

tart ink *n.* That which is used to draw a more attractive face onto a plain woman. Make-up, *fuck dust*.

tart's window box, a *sim.* What one smells like when one has too much aftershave on. *Joan Collin's knickers*.

tart-throb *n.* A low grade hunk who is unaccountably alluring to ladies from the lower echelons, *eg.* Peter Andre, Robson Green.

Tarzan cord *n.* The narrow lace which attaches *Kojak's roll-neck* to the *bobby's helmet*. The *guy rope*, the *banjo, Darth Vader's chinstrap*.

tash *n.* Any one of a wide variety of vaginal topiary arrangements, ranging from Robert Mugabe to Nietzsche.

tassel *n.* Innocent schoolboy term for the penis. *Winkle, willie, winkie-woo, slag hammer*.

taste the rainbow *v.* To have a little taste of everything from the "All You Can Eat" *pant buffet*.

ta tas *n. Noinkers, jubblies, cajooblies, jugs, bubbies, charms*.

Tatchell satchel *n.* A man-bag.

'taters *n. Nads, balls, bollocks.* The testicles. Contraction of potatoes. *'We Englishmen are conscious of our status / Which is why the beastly foreigners all hate us / But it's always seemed to me / that it's simply jealousy / 'Cos they're envious of the size of English 'taters.'* (From *The Stately Genitals of England* by Noel Coward).

tatties *n.* Testicles, *love spuds*.

tat twat *n.* A snobbish term used to describe a member of the pond-level social class often to be seen swimming round car boot sales and *Car Booty* on daytime BBC1. *Scratter, ronker.*

tatty watta *n. Nat. Am.* Red Indian word for *spud juice*, semen. Literally "potato water".

tawdry Hepburn *n.* A fine-boned, porcelain-skinned beauty who, on closer inspection, is revealed to be cheaply-constructed and of poor quality.

taxi *v.* To *come* late. Or never at all.

taxi driver's clutch *euph.* An overly-eager *fellatrix.* *'Fuck me, Dave. I brought that fucking howler who works in the fishmongers home the other night and she went down like a taxi driver's clutch.'*

taxi driver's minute *n.* Any period of time which is longer than half an hour.

taxi driver's tan *1. n.* An area of sunburn on the right index finger caused by hooking it on the top of the cab whilst driving along. *2. n.* A similar effect caused by *breaching the hull.* A *filter tip, mechanic's nails.*

taxi for Brown *exclam.* A witty riposte to an *anal retort,* such as what Dorothy Parker or Oscar Wilde might have said after they *dropped their guts.*

taxi floor, dirtier than a *sim.* Sexually compliant. *'Phwooar! Have you seen that new tart with the massive tits they've got doing the weather on the local news? Bet she's dirtier than a taxi floor, her.' 'Thank-you, Archbishop. Tomorrow's Thought for the Day will be from the Chief Rabbi, Dr Jonathan Sachs.'*

taxi greyhound *n.* One who bolts out of a cab door like a whippet, leaving his mates to pay the fare.

taxi tiger *n.* A desperate last-chance lunger on the way home.

Taylback *n.* A traffic jam caused by an ill-timed act of *horatio.*

Taylforth *1. n.* A disastrous *blowjob* in a car. *2. n. medic.* A severe attack of pancreatitis which can only be relieved by being *sucked off* in a layby.

Taz *1. n. prop.* A hairy cartoon beast that dribbles, found in the Antipodes. *2. n.* A hairy *grotter* that dribbles, found in ladies' *dunghampers.*

TBS *abbrev.* Toxic Bott Syndrome. Severe noxious emissions or *brewer's farts. Burning bad powder.*

TCM *1. abbrev. medic.* Turd Cutting Muscle, *crimper, cigar cutter,* anal sphincter. The *nipsy, secaturds. 2. abbrev.* A Two Cock Mouth. *A Wallace.*

TCP *abbrev.* A sterilizing morning routine that can lead to a certain amount of stinging, *viz.* Tea, Ciggy, Poo.

TCS *abbrev.* Traction Control System. When *farting* following a bellyfull of *dizzyade* and/or curry, the precise control of the *nipsy* required to allow one to *squeak one out* without producing any *wheelspin,* thus preventing *laying rubber* in the *banana hammock.*

teabagged by the dentist, like being *sim.* Describes the experience of finding yourself in a situation over which you have little or no control, and are unable to do anything about the grim outcome, *eg.* Having to use your hand when there is no bog roll, having to smell other people's *Exchange & Marts* in a crowded lift, going for a "friendly chat" with your bank manager. *'I was just getting ready for Prime Minister's Questions when Norma found some of Edwina's pubes in my toothbrush. There was nothing I could do. It felt like being teabagged by the dentist.'* (from *Me and my Big Grey Cock - The Memoirs of a Prime Minister* by John Major).

teabagging *n.* Making a strong brew with *Fussell's Milk* and two lumps. A last-resort sexual practice whereby the man lowers his *pods* into the lady's mouth.

tea chicken *n.* Game played by severely hungover flatmates, whereby they sit immobile waiting for the first one to bottle it and offer to put the kettle on.

teaching William a lesson *n. Punishing Percy, pulling the Pope's cap off. "What's all this banging and groaning?' bellowed Mr Wilkins as he burst into the dorm. 'Please, Sir,' piped-up Venables. 'It was Darbishire teaching Jennings a lesson."* (from *Jennings and the Mysterious Body Hairs* by Anthony Buckeridge).

tea cosy *n.* A place to hide one's *spout* whilst thinking about the true object of one's affections. *'Deaths: Lady Diana Spencer, shopping enthusiast, landmines campaigner and Prince's tea cosy, 36.'*

tea fairy *n.* Term used to describe a rather poor drinker. *'Come on, George, you big tea fairy. One drink won't hurt you.'*

tea pot *1. n.* A male from the Larry Grayson school of posturing. *'You know that bloke at number thirty-three? Well I was talking to Edna in the butchers and, well, not to put too fine a point on it, let's just say he's a bit of a teapot, I'll put it no stronger than that.' 2. n. Self harm* position. One hand pulling at the spout and the index finger of the other hand stuck up the nipsy to stimulate the *walnut.* Superficially resembles the "I'm a little teapot" nursery rhyme dance, though with distinctly less innocent overtones.

teapot shuffle *n.* Descriptive of the pose adopted by internet-fuelled *self-polluters, ie. Pulling themselves off* with the left hand, whilst the right arm is extend-ed to faciltate control of the mouse.

teapot sucker *n.* A *bottom shelf drinker,* a teetotaller.

tear in a coalman's jacket *sim.* A large, raggy *blart.*

tear off a piece *v. US.* To have sex. *Tear one off.*

tearful wank *n.* A light-hearted taunt directed at a newly heartbroken male colleague. It involves sticking the bottom lip out, and doing a masturbating gesture with one hand and a "boo hoo" gesture with the other.

tearing cloth *n.* The frankly alarming stage which immediately succeeds *touching cloth.*

tea strainer *n.* A bowel movement that is forcibly withheld during teabreak so that one can have a *tom tit* and get paid for the pleasure. *Time and a turd, taking one on the company's time.*

tea towel holder *n. Anus, ringpiece, freckle.* From the 1950s plastic "finger poke" cat's *arse*-style kitchen accessory. Also *old-fashioned fifties tea towel holder.*

teat-seeking missile *n.* A man who fails to maintain proper eye contact when talking to women.

techie's perks *n.* Whilst fixing a mate's PC, taking the opportunity to search his hard-drive for photographs of his missus in highly compromising positions. *''Ere, John. What's that pic of our Angie with a dildo up her Gary doing on your mobile phone?' 'Techie's perks, mate.'*

technical area *1. n.* In football, the designated space that a manager, other coaching personnel and team substitutes occupy during the course of a match. *2. n.* The *fruit bowl. 'Now look here, officer. You've got this all wrong. I was just taking the opportunity to re-arrange* *my technical area whilst the cinema lights were down.' 'Save it for the judge, Gerald.'* 3. *n.* The missus's *bits and pieces.* Not to be confused with her *dugout,* unless you want to be *on the bench* for the rest of the season.

technicolour yawn *n.* A *yoff.*

Tecwens *n. medic.* An attack of pathetic fake coughing that one effects at work the day before one throws a sickie. From the *Who Wants to be a Millionaire* coughing *knacker* Tecwen Whittock. *'The lads are playing Locomotiv Moscow tomorrow, live on Sky, only the kick off's at two in the afternoon. Cough! Cough! Ooh, dear. I can feel a touch of the Tecwens coming on.'*

ted *n.* The *Teddington.*

Teddington *rhym. slang.* The Penis. From the *Magpie* studio address Teddington Lock = corn on the cob.

teddy's leg *n.* State of stool expulsion somewhere beyond the *turtle's head*, but prior to *touching sock.* Point midway through *smoking a bum cigar. Bungle's finger.*

tee off *v.* To *wank* and/or *fart.* Not necessarily at the same time.

Tees duck *n.* Sky rat, *shitehawk.* A seagull.

teeter meter *n.* Calibration scale assessing the attractiveness of women based on how far from sober one would have to be to *slip them a length. eg.* Kylie Minogue would be 0 on the teeter meter, whereas Gail Tilsley off *Coronation Street* would be 15 pints of Stella with whisky chasers.

Tegel airport *1. n.* Berlin's busiest air transport hub, famous for having two hexagonal terminal buildings. *2. n.* Overexcited planespotter terminology for a lady's twin nether openings.

teggat *n.* A short-necked *turtle's head* which is unable to *touch cloth*, and retreats back into the *bomb bay.* A *Hoskins.*

telescoping *n.* Looking squarely into the end of a stiff *stalk*, waiting to get a proper eyeful. *'Admiral Fellatio Nelson lost his eye quite early in his naval career, following a telescoping accident below decks on HMS Dolphin.'*

temazepalm *n. medic.* Hand-induced insomnia relief.

tenapause *n.* The stage in a woman's life-cycle when she loses the ability to control her bladder effectively.

TENFOLD/tenfold *abbrev. RAF.* A young lady who is blessed with smashing *eye magnets* whilst, somewhat off-puttingly, being cursed with the crumpled face of a 1970s northern club comedian. Tits Extremely Nice. Face Of Les Dawson.

ten gallon twat *n.* A *fanny* like a bucket.

ten of clubs *euph.* A *chod* which is so messy that it requires a whole roll of *bumwad* to clean up the *crime scene.* The diametric opposite of *drawing an ace.*

ten minutes' peace and quiet *n.* An offensive term used by sexist men to describe getting a *chewie* off their *bit of fluff. 'Mr Campbell-Bannerman: Yes, Mrs Pankhurst, I agree that the introduction of universal suffrage is a worthy political objective, and I shall endeavour to include it in the King's speech at the beginning of the next parliamentary session...but only if you give me ten minutes peace and quiet. Mrs Pankhurst: Glub! Glub!'.* (Cartoon in *Punch* by Bernard Partridge, 1905).

Tennants association *n.* A group of widely-travelled *Terence Stamps* enjoying a well-earned noggin of their favourite tipple on the *tramp grill.*

Tennants poetry *n.* A moving sonnet of threats and expletives, usually *scumbled* by a dishevelled Scotsman while leaning forwards.

Tennants tan *n.* The reddish-purple glow that an ardent lager connoisseur acquires after years of wandering from bar to bar in a *pissed-up* frenzy of unquenchable thirst. Also *tramp's tan.*

tenner lady *1. n.* A female who is *pissed* after just ten quid's worth of *sauce. 2. n.* A cheap, incontinent *prossie. 'Excuse me, are there any tenner ladies in the area? I fancy a cheap, sordid poke with a tart who is the very antithesis of my own, fragrant missus who has full control of her bladder.' 'There's one over there by that skip, Lord Archer.'*

tennis elbow *n. medic.* A condition of the right arm caused by repeated games of *singles. 'Ooh, that's a nasty case of tennis elbow you've got there, Tim. And Andy.'*

tennis fan *n.* A woman who takes the *other bus* to Wimbledon. A *lady golfer.*

tenpin *v.* To place digits simultaneously in the *tea towel holder* and the *fish mitten.* From the grip used in ten pin bowling. To *spock.*

ten pint princess *n.* A *donner.*

ten points to Gryffindor *n.* Another witty riposte which can be delivered upon hearing a *botty burp.*

Tenpole Tudor *n.* A *slapper, ie.* One who has had "the *swords* of a thousand men".

ten-to-two shuffle *n.* A perfunctory dance that *pissed up* gentlemen engage in with the *floor sweepings* at the end of a long

and unspectacular evening *on the pull. 'Any luck last night?' 'No. Ended up doing the ten-to-two shuffle with some dental receptionist. She gave me a bit of duck sausage and got the last bus home.'*

tent pole *n. Stiffy*, erect penis, especially in bed. A *trouser tent, morning glory, dawn horn, dusk tusk.*

ten pounds of shit in a five pound bag *euph.* Useful phrase which can be used when referring to either a deceptively-powerful motor car or a *generously-boned* woman who has shoehorned herself into a dress which is several sizes too small for her. *'How do I look, Andrew?' 'Like ten pounds of shit in a five pound bag, Sarah. But we've got to get going. The Archbishop of Canterbury is waiting.'*

tequila sunrise *n.* The awe-inspiring visual effect produced when a man's bright yellow urine flows into the *pan* where the previous (female) occupant has *blobbed.*

Terence Stamp *n. prop. rhym. slang.* A gentleman of the road.

terminal five *1. n.* The *landing strip* on a very large woman. Named after the biggest runway in the UK, which is at Heathrow Airport. *2. n.* A completely blocked system in which nothing moves. *'Pass me the Senokot tin, love. I haven't been able to park my breakfast from four days ago yet, or indeed any meal since. I've become the human equivalent of Heathrow Airport's terminal five on opening day. Only with turds instead of suitcases.'*

terminate the call *v.* To cut short a *Lionel Bart* for fear of *following through.* To *reverse the charge.*

terra firmer *n.* Following several days of

post-curry *squits*, a return to somewhat more solid bowel movements. *'Ah-haar, me hearties! 'Tis good to be back on terra firmer at last.'*

terrorist's backpack, ticking like a *sim*. Of a woman with a very loud biological clock. *'I'd steer clear of her if I was you, mate. She's ticking like a terrorist's backpack.'*

Terry Funk *1. n. prop.* A popular Discotheque personality in the Midlands, circa 1970. *2. rhym. slang.* Marijuana cigarettes, from Terry Funk = skunk. *3. rhym. slang. Spooge*, from Terry Funk = spunk. *'Waiter. There's some Terry Funk in my soup'. 'Yes, Mr Winner. That's because the chef, the entire kitchen and serving staff, and indeed the rest of the customers have masturbated into it.'*

Terry Waite *v.* To lock an item firmly to an immovable object, such as a radiator. *'Will your new bike be alright left out in the street?' 'Don't worry. I've Terry Waited it to a lamppost.'*

Terry Waite's allotment *sim.* Descriptive of a badly-overgrown *ladygarden*. *'Marriette was powerless to resist. His eyes burned into hers like emeralds. His muscular arms enfolded her body as she felt herself being swept away in a monsoon of passion. 'Bloody hell! You've got a twat like Terry Waite's allotment!' he cried, as he pulled out the waistband of her bloomers and peered inside.'* (from *The Peasant Girl and the First World War Soldier* by Barbara Cartland).

Tesco bags full of piss, tits like two *sim.* A delightful turn of phrase that wouldn't have sounded out of place being enunciated in the cut-glass tones of Sir Noel Coward. Breasts that hang like saucepans.

tescosterone *n.* Hormone which causes aggressive behaviour in males who are forced to queue up behind a long queue of lottery-ticket-buying OAPs just in order to buy themselves a packet of fucking fags.

Tesco finish *n.* In pornographic cinematography, the sort of *pop shot* where the over-enthusiastic gentleman actor vigorously attempts to squeeze every last drop of *spaff* out of his *gut stick*. From the all-conquering town centre-fucking supermarket's well-known advertising slogan; "Because every little helps".

tescosexual *n.* A man whose incidence of sexual activity peaks during his wife's trips to the shops.

test card wank *n.* A *tug* one has, not because one is feeling particularly *fruity*, but simply because there is nothing else to do. A *loose end away*.

test cricket shit *euph.* A particularly troublesome *turd* which is played out over many sessions and involves multiple trips to the crease, halts for tea and follow-ons. See *test match*.

testing the Fray Bentos *n.* The unfortunate experience of *breaching the hull* whilst wiping, resulting in a finger end which is covered in gravy. From the eerie similarity to the act of pushing a digit through the pastry on one of them pies in a tin.

test match *n.* An extremely long sit-down sojourn in the lavatory, which to the subject feels like it is taking five days to achieve any sort of conclusive result. So-named due to the similarity to the cricket competitions, *viz.* Long, silent periods of intense concentration broken by occasional grunts, cracks and thuds, irregularly interspersed with splatters that sound not unlike bursts of applause.

test ride *n*. In the executive world, the act of taking the *office bike round the block* before deciding whether or not to dump one's missus for her.

Tewkesbury doorstep, wetter than a *sim*. A no-longer-topical description of a lady who is suffering a flash flood *down south*. *'I tell you what, Geoff, she can't have had it for a while. Her fanny was wetter than a Tewkesbury doorstep.'*

textbook dog *n*. The recognition of an absolutely perfect *doggy-style* position seen in everyday situations, *eg*. A secretary crawling on the floor to find a contact lens.

TFFA *abbrev*. Initials never used as a catchphrase by erstwhile syrup-topped Radio 2 disc geriatric Jimmy Young. Thanks For Fuck All.

Thames trout *n*. A fishy-smelling, rainbow-coloured, *spawn*-filled object with its tickling days now long behind it, typically found floating near one of London's major sewerage outlets. A spent *jubber*. A British variation on the American *Coney Island whitefish*.

Thames whale *n*. A large *turd* which appears in the *pan* without any explanation, and which is reluctant to return to the sea.

thanks for that, now can you please throw something? *exclam. interrog*. Another one of those phrases that can be employed to humorous effect after someone has *dropped* a high decibel *spare part*. From the risible satellite television programme *Most Haunted*, when Yvette Fielding and her crew pretend to see ghosts, hear unexplained thumps and groans *etc*., prior to the *chubster* makeup girl and the baldy *twat* camera-man getting scared, punched scratched or possessed.

thanksgiving dinner *n*. An act of *oral affection* performed on a *big bird* who has *got the painters in. Dinner at the Y* with extra ketchup. *Cranberry dip*.

thatched cottage *n. arch*. A delightfully picturesque half-timbered *cunt* with roses round the *pissflaps*, which would make a good jigsaw puzzle or tea tray. Also *thatched mottage*.

thatch hatch *n*. A chocolate-boxy *box*.

thatch 22 *n*. Sexual dilemma faced by a gentleman considering committing *cumulonimbus* on a lady with an horrendous *clown's pie*.

that fart had back-up *exclam*. Phrase uttered as a plea of mitigation shortly after inadvertently *buttering one's cheeks, drawing mud from the well, dropping one's revels, preparing a portion of duck soup, failing one's driving test, suffering a fall of soot* or being the victim of a *jacksydent. 'Jesus Christ, Margot! Do you mind?' 'Sorry, Rudolph. I was just trying to sneak it out during the grand jete, but that fart had back-up.'*

that one came with a prize *exclam*. Polite phrase acknowledging that an *air biscuit* has been accompanied by a *malteser* or two. *'That one came with a prize, Judy. You run through the star signs while I nip into Fred the weather man's dressing room to scouse a pair of clean grundies.'*

that one jumped the queue *exclam*. Humorous phrase which can be used when one has inadvertently *dropped* an item of *shopping* whilst *stepping on a duck* in polite company.

that's a clear round for David Broome!

exclam. Uttered when someone breaks wind. From the commentaries on TV showjumping back in the 1970s, when the horses always seemed to *step on a duck* after clearing the last fence.

that one's got a skin on it *exclam.* Humorous riposte following the release of a *fart* that has been *stewing* a little too long in the *back boiler*. From the similarity to a milky coffee that has been left too long in the cup.

that's numberwang! *exclam.* From the famous Mitchell & Webb (or possibly Armstrong & Miller) gameshow sketch, a phrase that can be pressed into service for cheap comic effect following a resounding *bottom burp*.

that's working, now try your lights *1. exclam.* Phrase shouted by a motor mechanic following the successful testing of a car's horn. *2. exclam.* Phrase shouted following the successful floating of an *air biscuit*. Also *sew a button on that; catch that one and paint it blue; good health;, pin a tail on that* and *you should put that on eBay..*

that would be lovely - milk and two sugars please *exclam.* Light-hearted witticism uttered when someone nearby *steps on a duck*. See *yes you did - you invaded Poland.*

that would cure bacon *n.* A throwaway quip uttered when a pal emits a particularly potent mole of intestinal *carbon dibaxide*.

Theakston's *rhym. slang.* The rear *fundament.* From Theakston's bitter = Gary Glitter. *'Jesus love, no offence, but your breath stinks. Tell you what, I'll do you up the Theakston's tonight, eh?'*

the killer is in this very room *exclam.* A light-hearted remark used to cover one's embarrassment after *stepping on a duck* in public. Usually followed by an incredulous gasp from the assembled company.

Thelonious *rhym. slang.* Semen. Named after the jazz pianist Thelonious Spunk.

the other *n. It*, the old *how's your father.*

there's a fog out in the channel, Cap'n *exclam.* Witty maritime riposte following a *nautical chart* of a particularly deep and sonorous timbre.

there's an app for that *sim.* One of those humorous idiomatic apophthegms that can be usefully employed following a loudly *dropped gut.*

there we are then *exclam. acronym.* A covert way of calling another person a *twat.* See also *see you next Tuesday, can't understand new technology.*

there will be blood *1. n.* Title of an Oscar-seeking epic film starring Daniel Day-Lewis. *2. exclam.* Statement made as one pushes one's chair back from the table following a particularly stodgy Christmas dinner, in reference to the inevitable *arse*-ripping *yule log*-based activities which will ensue on Boxing Day.

the Salvation Army are tuning up *exclam.* Another one of those humorous idiomatic apophthegms that can be usefully employed following a loudly *dropped gut.*

thesbian *n.* A *grumble flick* actress who does *girl on girl* professionally, but is not a *tennis fan* in real life.

the third place *n. Splaystation 2.* The *arse.*

they're firing Sir, they're firing! *exclam.* A humorous riposte to a *rumpet voluntary.* See also *well struck Sir.*

thick as a ghurka's foreskin *sim.*

Descriptive of someone who is as *thick as a Welshman's cock.*

thickening up *adj.* To be in the early stages of erectile tumescence. The penile equivalent to that moment when you're stirring a pan of Bisto on the hob and it suddenly starts to look and behave a bit like gravy. *Getting a bit of blood in it.* '*You'll have to excuse me sitting down whilst I read this next disgusting continental hardcore scan magazine, Mrs Whitehouse, only I'm definitely thickening up in spite of myself.*' '*Feel free, Lord Longford. I'm as horrified as you at these explicit photographs of depraved behaviour, yet I am ashamed to admit that I'm dripping like a fucked fridge.*'

thick repeater *n.* A large bore semi-automatic, single barrel *mutton musket.*

thick spunk *n.* Extremely fertile, high motility *spaff. Jitler* that requires factor 40 contraception. '*I've got eight brothers and six sisters thanks to Pop's thick spunk. Gee whiz, his sperm count is so high, I'll bet mom has to chew before swallowing.*' (Little Jimmy Osmond interviewed in *Look In*, 1972).

thigh ticklers *n. Bugger's grips, face fannies, sideboards.* '*Ooh, Dr Rhodes Boyson. What a magnificent set of thigh ticklers.*' '*Thank-you, Your Majesty.*'

thighbrows *n.* A profusion of bikini overspill. *Loose baccy.*

think of the money shot *n.* In *bongo videography*, the less than enthusiastic expression on the lead actress's face as Ron Jeremy, Bill Margold or Ben Dover, or possibly all three, empty their *pods* into it.

think outside the box *1. v.* Yet another meaningless corporate buzzword expres-

sion commonly used by the sort of desperate utter *arseholes* who appear on programmes like *The Apprentice. 2. v.* The actions of a thoughtful gentleman in bed, *ie.* One who doesn't immediately focus his attentions on his ladyfriend's *cludge*, but considerately mashes her *tits* for a couple of minutes first.

thine *n.* The seamless blending of a lady's thighs into her spine without any intervening buttocks, as featured on such scrawny, *arse*less scarecrows as Posh Spice, Kate Moss and that Trinny out of Trinny and Susannah. From thigh + spine.

thin lizzy *n.* An undercracker *skidmark.* From the verse in that group's song *Dancing in the Moonlight (It's caught me in its spotlight)* which goes "I should have took that last bus home / But I asked you for a dance / Now we go steady to the pictures / I always get chocolate stains on my pants."

third leg *1. n.* Cricketing position between mid-off and gully. *2. n.* The *middle stump.*

third up, the *euph.* Building site terminology for a mistake. From the fact that in the construction industry there are three "ups", *ie.* Muck up, tea up and fuck up.

third way, the *1. n.* Tony Blair's way of combining traditional socialist and conservative policies. *2. n.* Anal sex.

thirty-four-and-a-halfer *n.* A hermit blessed with the miraculous ability to perform *horatio* upon himself. A *human cannonballer.*

Thora bird *n.* A *nana Kournikova.*

Thora Hird *1. n. prop.* Pelican-throated actress of stairlift testimonial fame, no longer alive at time of going to press. *2. rhym. slang.* A *turd.*

Thorntons, little bit of *sim*. Euphemism used when attempting to talk the wife into a bit of *backdoor action*. From the famous gift toffee manufacturer's advertising slogan, *ie*. "Skilled in the ways of the chocolatier". *'Roll over, love. I fancy a little bit of Thorntons tonight.'*

thousand island dressing *n*. The sauce which coats one's *naughty spoon* after tossing the *gorilla salad* when *cranberry dip* is on the menu.

thousand mile service *euph*. A woman's *unclean time*, when she is *up on blocks*. An *oil and filter change*.

thrap *v*. To masturbate furiously, to give it *six nowt* on the *Right Honourable Member for Pantchester*. Also *thrape, fap fap fap*.

three bells in a row *1. n*. A disappointingly low fruity payout. *2. n*. Finding all three urinals in a public lavatory unoccupied, thus allowing one the luxury of a comfortably relaxed *gypsy's kiss*.

three card trick *rhym slang. Prick. 'She got her jazz bands round me three card trick and started giving it six nowt.'*

three cocks to the cunt *euph. Con gusto*. Doing anything to the extreme, *eg*. Driving at 180mph down a country lane, drinking vodka in pint glasses, driving at 180mph down a country lane whilst drinking vodka in pint glasses. *'Ferdinand Hiller remembered Sterndale Bennett's piano playing as "perfect in mechanism, and, while remarkable for an extraordinary delicacy of nuance in the quieter passages of the Mendelssohn Barcarolle, full of soul and fire in the finale, which he always played three cocks to the cunt".'* (Cecil Gaybody, writing in *Classic FM* Magazine).

three coiler *n*. A canine *turd*, the curled and crimped result of not having walked the dog, usually found on a carpet.

three day event *n*. A swift half after work on Friday, which lasts all weekend until you return to the office on Monday morning, much to the chagrin of the wife.

three dick gob *n*. A capacious mouth. *'The next record is You're So Vain by Carly Simon, the lady with the three dick gob. And it's for Terry, who is seven today. Lots of love from mummy, daddy, nana and granpa Johnson and nana Robins.'* (Ed "Stewpot" Stewart, *Radio 1 Junior Choice*, 1974).

three-fag omelette *n*. For a non-smoker, the satisfying yet unfamiliar pattie of phlegm coughed up the morning after having drunk enough to *ponce* a few fags off a mate at about ten past eleven.

three for a bob *rhym. slang*. The *corn on the cob*, the *Teddington Lock*.

three inch soilpipe, fanny like a *sim*. Charming plumber-speak to describe the genital accoutrements of a lady whose *bodily treasure* is at the other end of the tightness scale from a *mouse's ear*.

three-legged race *n*. When *fuckstruck*, to stumble up the stairs with a *bone on*.

three mile island *n*. An extremely noxious rectal meltdown with a half-life of about ten minutes. A *Smellafield*.

three piece suite *n*. That which has to be plumped up and rearranged on a regular basis to ensure seated comfort. The *Meat and two veg, wedding tackle*. The male *undercarriage*.

three quarters of half a soft on *euph*. When a chap's cock has almost got a bit of a lazy lob on, but not quite. *'Sasparilla was powerless to resist. His eyes burnt into hers like lab-grown cristinites. His* *strong arms enfolded her softly yielding body as she felt herself being swept away on a vertically-oriented, rotating atmospheric vortex of passion. 'Take me, Figaro! Take me now!' she gasped. 'Sorry, love,' replied Doctor Fernando. 'I just had one off the wrist over the bra pages of me mam's Freeman's catalogue, so I won't even be able to manage three quarters of half a soft on for at least another twenty minutes.'* (from *The Gypsy Ballerina Princess and the Tree Surgeon* by Barbara Cartland).

three wheeler *rhym. slang. Dyke, lesbian.* From three wheeled trike, which is a popular means of transport for *women in comfortable shoes.*

thripe *n.* The so-called "three-stroke method" of wiping one's *arse*, as recommended by parsimonious parents, factory overseers, orphanage managers *etc.* That is to say, "one back, one forward, and one to polish."

throatmanship *n.* The noble art of gagless *horatio*, as practised by the late actress Linda Lovelace. Also *throatsmanship.*

throbbin' hood *coll. Notts.* A sore *five-skin.* A *Little John* that as been excessively "made merry on".

throb on *n.* A *wide on, slop on.*

throbservation *n.* When a fellow notices a particularly attractive lady, and consequently experiences an involuntary palpitation amongst his *wedding vegetables.*

throne *n.* The Queen's *crapper.*

throne bone *n.* The throbbing *bonk on* that sometimes pops up temptingly whilst a young man is *dropping a length of dirty spine.*

throne room *n.* The Queen's *shit palace.*

throng *adj.* Descriptive of a fashionably skimpy item of intimate apparel being worn by someone who really should have known better, *eg.* Women with nice personalities or oldies. From thong + wrong. *'Did you see what Bob's bird was wearing when she bent over?' 'Aye Joe, that's just throng, that.'*

throttle pit *n. Aus.* The *dunny.* Toilet.

throttle the turkey *v.* To masturbate in Norfolk. *'I just throttled the turkey and it was boodiful, really boodiful.'*

througher *n.* A 24-hour drinking session. A *Leo Sayer, MGM.*

throw *v.* To *barf, hoy, chuck.*

throwabout *n.* A petite woman who can be easily and casually "thrown about" from one position to another during sex. A *laptop.*

throwing a Woodbine up Northumberland Street *sim. NE.* Unsatisfying sex with a *bucket-fannied* individual. Also *throwing a sausage up Briggate* (Leeds), *chucking a fag down Parliament Street* (Nottingham). *'Why man, it was like throwin' a Woodbine up Northumberland Street.'*

throw meat at the problem *v.* Of a couple whose relationship is on the rocks, to engage in an act of penetrative romance.

throw one's cap into the hangar *v. milit.* To have sex with a lady endowed with a *poacher's pocket.* From the naval act of throwing a rating's hat into the bowels of a through-deck cruiser. Also *throwing a kitbag in a dry dock.*

throw out the garbage *v.* To flush out one's *spooge pipe.*

throw the meat dart at the brown bullseye *v.* To *bott*, hopefully not whilst Tony Green stands next to you, saying: "Okay, take your time. Nice and easy, nice and easy. Settle in now. You've got all the time in the world."

throw the towel in *1. v.* Of a boxing trainer, to concede defeat when his fighter is getting his *fucking* head kicked in. *2. v.* To give up trying to have a *poke* because the missus has got *the painters and decorators in. 3. v.* Of a lady, to casually insert a *mouse*.

throw your bollocks at the clock *exclam.* An exclamation of total exasperation. *'We've been talking about the future of power sharing in Northern Ireland for five weeks now, and they still won't sit in the same bloody room. It's enough to make you want to throw your bollocks at the clock.'* (Senator George Mitchell, Report on the Northern Ireland Peace Process).

thru'penny bits *1. rhym. slang.* Tits. *2. rhym. slang.* The *shits*.

thruster *n. medic.* A muscle, somewhere in the neck or jaw, the tensing of which forces out stubborn *shits* and *farts*.

thumb a ride on the rocket *adj.* To *take Captain Picard to warp speed.*

thumb bumming *v. Touching last night's tea.*

thumbing in a slacky *v.* The first act of an optimistic bout of lovemaking for which the gentleman's spirit is willing, but his flesh is weak. *Pushing a marshmallow into a moneybox.*

thumbrise *n.* The time of day at which a fellow in a loving relationship is allowed out of the house by his other half, to go for a quick drink with his mates.

thumbset *n.* The time by which he has to be back in the house with his *pink handcuffs* on.

thumper *1. n.* A big, pounding erection, a *stalk*, a *stiffy. 2. n.* In the Walt Disney film *Bambi*, the annoying rabbit who, if the extracts shown every fucking week on *Screen Test* were anything to go by, spent the entire movie encouraging the lead character to walk out onto a frozen pond.

thumpology *n.* The resolution of disputes by recourse to physical argument. *Closing time counselling, chin music.*

thunder bags *n.* Underpants, *trolleys.*

thunderbirds *n.* Women of ample proportions. *Barge arses, size aeros.*

thunder box *n. arch.* Lavatory, *shitter.* Also *thunder bowl.*

thunderbox shuffle *1. n.* A song by Skiffle king Lonnie Donnegan that reached no. 3 in 1960. *2. n.* The *arse* dance performed whilst sitting on the *chod bin* trying to *get* the *pit bull out of the kennel.*

thundercrack *n.* The kind of *fart* that requires one to check one's *kex* for *bullets.* A *squench.*

thunder mug *n.* Chamber pot, *guzunda.*

thunderslash *n.* A splendidly loud urination delivered *con gusto* directly into the water of the pot. A *dad's piss*, a *round of applause*, a *standing ovation.*

Tibetan blackbird *n.* How an ornithologist would refer to a massive *shit.* From the said bird's Latin name, *viz. Turdus maximus. 'Where are you off to, Chris? We're on air in thirty seconds.' 'Sorry Kate. I'm off to the khazi to free a Tibetan blackbird.'*

tickets for the away end *n. Anal sex. 'Arsenal are at home. So I might try and get tickets for the away end.'*

ticket to tottieville *euph.* See *token for the cockwash, pink ticket.*

tickle Fat Ed *v.* Of a fellow, to *pleasure himself* in a leisurely, almost lackadaisical manner. As one would do on a chaise-longue in a gazebo, or in a blazer and straw boater whilst drifting in a punt.

ticklers *n*. Corrugated condoms, amusing *French letters* which are ribbed for your pleasure.

tickle tackle *n*. *Anteater's nose, cock collar, lace curtains*. The *fiveskin* or a *charlie* so equipped.

tickle the baby *v*. To engage in a spot of sexual intercourse with a pregnant ladyfriend. *'What was the milkman doing upstairs?' 'Nothing love. He was just tickling the baby.'*

tickle the pickle *v*. See *jerkin' the gherkin*.

tickle your pip *v*. To be aroused sexually by Leslie Philips or Terry-Thomas.

tickling the scampi *v*. A means of getting *fish fingers*. Feminine *monkey spanking*.

tickling the turtle's nose *n*. A wipe which gets the *turtle's autograph* on the paper, but which doesn't, in any meaningful sense, get the job done.

tied by the brown rope *adj*. To be confined to the *chod bin* by an intractable *Brad*.

tiffin *n*. An afternoon *fuck* up the *cunt* off Sid James in a pith helmet.

tiffter *n*. An unwanted erection, *Jake*.

tiger's back *n*. The decorative striped effect left in the *pan* after a particularly sticky *Meatloaf's daughter* has *gone to the beach*.

tighter than airport security *sim*. Description of a frigid *bird;* one who "refuses to take any liquids on board".

tighter than a teenage wanker's curtains *sim*. Descriptive of something which is very secure. *'And as the Queen's car-riage glides majestically up to the steps of the Palace of Westminster, security is, of course, tighter than a teenage wanker's curtains.'* (David Dimbleby, commentating on the State Opening of Parliament, 2007).

tightie *n*. *Scot. medic.* The feeling of discomfort experienced when attempting to peel back the *fiveskin* due to it being stuck to the *helmet* with *cheese*. Possibly something to do with the humid atmosphere found inside a kilt.

Tijuana bible *n*. A *jazz mag*.

Tijuana cha-cha *n*. The *trots*. See *sour apple quickstep, Mexican screamers*.

tile hanger's nailbags *sim*. Sagging, lumpy *charlies*. *'She had tits like a tile hanger's nailbags.'*

timber merchant *1. n*. Typically the man in a town who has the fewest complete fingers remaining on his hands. *2. n*. A person who *gives you wood*. *'That Claire in accounts, she's a right timber merchant she is.'* *3. n*. A reliable male *grumble* thespian, a *woodsman*.

time and a turd *n*. The art of having a *tom tit* at work whilst being paid overtime by an unwitting employer. *Taking one in the company's time*, an *I'm allright cack, time and a turd*.

timebomb fuse *n*. A length of string emanating from a lady's *bodily treasure*, from which a trained expert can infer that a violent, explosive outburst is imminent. Also known as a *party popper, mouse's tail*.

time dream *n*. Lazy Sunday evening television watcher's pleasant reverie enjoyed whilst broken-pot-obsessed show *Time Team* is on. The dozing, sofa-bound viewer allows his mind to wander, specifically to pondering which of the comely, fresh-faced, trench-dwelling young female archaeology students he would most like to discover his own fossilised *bone*, before rubbing the soil off it with her thumb.

Time Team, do a *1. v.* To reinstate a casual sexual relationship with an ex-girlfriend. To *open up a second trench*. *2. n.* The regulars in your local pub to whom you invariably find yourself talking, even though you hate them. Much like watching the television show of the same name, the experience is strangely depressing and you're not entirely sure why you started doing it in the first place. It's even more profoundly dispiriting when you realise that you are a member of their *time teams* too.

time to water the cactus *euph.* Women's things. From the fact that a lazy man often uses his wife or girlfriend's *thousand mile service* interval as a reminder to perform his regular monthly chores. Also *time to to pay the rent, time to worm the cat, time to feed the ducks*.

Tim Henman *n.* A *penis* which promises great things but fails to achieve anything even vaguely resembling hardness, *ie.* It doesn't even get to the *semi* stage.

Timmy twostroke *n.* A gentleman blessed with the enviable ability to *blow his stack* after a couple of *cock stabs*. A *two-push Charlie*.

tincture *n.* An alcoholic drink taken for medicinal purposes, perhaps at breakfast time or during an early morning walk back from Boozebuster.

tin, it does what it says on the *1. exclam.* Advertising slogan for a popular range of DIY timber treatments. *2. exclam.* A humorous remark made by a man to a lady who is about to *polish his wood*

whilst he lies back and observes.

tinker's curse *n.* An involuntary and highly ill-timed erection that takes the gloss off social occasions. *'Do you, Charles Philip Arthur George, take Diana Frances...oops, sorry about that. I've got the tinker's curse.'* (Dr Robert Runcie, the Marriage of Prince Charles and Lady Di, 1981).

tinker time *1. n.* On *Scrapheap Challenge*, the extra hour allotted to the teams on the morning after the build, when they are allowed to make minor adjustments to their deathtraptions. *2. n.* Sunday afternoon televisual interlude enjoyed by bachelors when Lisa Rogers is on the screen.

tinkle on the ivories *1. v.* To play the piano, usually in a *half-arsed* sort of way, the opposite of going at it *three cocks to the cunt*. You could never accuse Count Basie of *tinkling on the ivories*, for example, whereas it describes Richard *fucking* Clayderman's insipid noodlings to a tee. *2. v.* To participate in a particular sort of *watersport*. To take a *gypsy's* in a ladyfriend's *north and south*. Or on your piano keyboard.

tinny mallet *n.* A perfectly normal bloke, who turns into an utter, utter annoying *cunt* after a couple of cans. A *halfpint Harry* or *two pot screamer*.

tin of Vim with an apple on top *sim.* A fictitious penis measurement.

tinter *1. n.* High class *totty*, top class *talent*. *'That Mick Hucknall's a jammy get. A face like his and he still gets all the top tinter.'* *2. n.* A lady's *barse*, because "'tin't 'er arse and 'tin't 'er fanny". The *taint*.

tipping the teapot *n.* Situation which occurs when, owing to a fully or semierectivated state, a fellow is unable to aim his *tassel* at the toilet bowl for a *slash* and must therefore bend his whole body to attain the required angle of incidence.

tipping the velvet *n*. Of TV companies, the practice of promising *full-nutted* viewers explicit *lesbo cumulonimbus* in order to boost ratings.

tipple *n*. The very tip of the nipple.

tip-toe through the two lips *euph*. Of a lady, to gently strum her *invisible ukulele*.

tip-toe tottie *n*. The various *wank pamphlets* adorning the top shelves of *Grumbelows*, which would thwart shorter men such as Ronnie Corbett, "diddy" David Hamilton and wee Jimmy Krankie when he grows up.

tip-toe trap *n*. A public house lavatory which abstains from the operation of a regular cleaning regime, thus requiring the user to stand on tip-toes to avoid unpleasantness.

Tipton barbershop *n*. The harmonious chorus made up from the combined sirens of two police cars, an ambulance and a fire engine, all racing towards another "domestic incident" in the boisterous Black Country town of the same name. Usually heard at three in the morning, and typically followed by an hour-long *son et lumiere* courtesy of the West Midlands Police helicopter.

Tipton uppercut *n*. A knee in the *bollocks*.

TIPTOP/tiptop *acronym*. A transexual who has yet to go the whole way and is still mid-way through the gender re-alignment process. Tits In Place, Tackle Op Pending. A *bobby dazzler*.

tip your concrete *v*. A sophisticated term for ejaculation when *cough your filthy yoghurt* seems inappropriately coarse. *'If you could just go into the booth and tip your concrete into this receptacle, Mr Elton.'*

tisnae *n*. A scotch lassie's perineum. The *McSnarse*.

tisn'ts *n*. Very small, practically non-existent breasts. *Knockers* that barely merit the description *tits*.

tissent *n*. The *taint, tinter, tintis*.

tissue chrysanthemum *n*. Once dry, the shape of any piece of *bumwad* in which one has *caught the lads* at the culmination of a *ride on the great white knuckler. Prawn cracker, wanker's poppadom*.

Titanic *n*. A lass who *goes down* first time out. An *Ikea bulb*.

titan punkvag *n*. One of them downward-pointing mohawks that you occasionally get between a woman's legs.

tit fairies *n*. Mythical visitors who magically transform the wife's *fried eggs* into *TNTs* during and after *sprogdrop*. Not that she'll let you on them for the next ten years.

tit for tat *n*. Barter system by which a gentleman pays for a prostitute's services on another continent using fake Western designer goods, *eg*. A pair of Oaklie sunglasses or some nice Serjio Armani jeans.

tit for brains *n*. A woman who makes up for her lack of intellectual capacity with a surfeit of *chesty substances*. *'Today's birthdays: George Best, thirsty Northern Irish footballer, 1946; Dale Winton, orange television also-ran, 1955, Morrissey, daffodil-arsed miserablist, 1959; Katie Price, tit for brains Grattan Celebrity Mum of the Year and*

Face of Foxy Bingo, 1978.'

tit for twat *n*. The act of fondling a woman's breast in the vain hope of getting her sufficiently aroused to permit one to have a shot on her *blurtch*.

titilate *v*. To excite with bosoms.

tit kitten *n*. A diminutive lady who compensates up for her small stature by having superior *leisure facilities*. A *midget gem*.

tit leech 1. *n*. A baby. *'Births: Fforbes Hhamilton. 23rd November, at The Portland Hospital. To the Hon Hector and Julia (nee Ffyffe-Lewethwaite-Ffyffe), a 6lb 4oz tit leech, Tarquin Hector Sebastapol, brother for Semolina. Deo Gracias.'* (*The Times*, Dec 2nd 2001). 2. *n*. A bloke who enjoys sucking on his wife's *jugs*.

tit man *n*. He who prefers *Bristols* to *arses* or *gams*.

titnotised *adj*. To be involuntarily mesmerised by a smashing pair of *churns*. *Nipnotised*.

tit nystagmus *n*. *medic*. Ophthalmological condition in red-blooded males, characterised by the involuntary rhythmic oscillation of the eyeballs from side to side whilst cycling or driving in summertime, due to the presence of scantily-clad *blart* on either side of the thoroughfare.

tit pants *n*. A bra.

tit pizzas *n*. Big, round, mottled, crusty aereolae. With garlic bread for starters.

tit rank *n*. A *bunny rub* administered between a right pair of *rotters*.

tits 1. *n*. Breasts, *knockers*. *'What a pair of tits.'* 2. *n*. Foolish or derisory people. *'What a bunch of tits.'* 3. *n*. Nerves. *'Christ, that Justin Lee Collins gets on my tits.'*

tits first, I ain't a tart *exclam*. A phrase heard in the back seat of a Ford Cortina in Bristol in the 1970s.

tit-shaped eyes *euph*. A grown-up version of square eyes; a consequence of watching too much porn. *'Jonathan, you've been sat looking at that computer all night. Honestly, you'll end up with tit-shaped eyes, you will.'*

tits on a fish *n*. Descriptive of a supremely useless thing. *'Did you see (insert name of striker currently having a run of bad form) play on Saturday? He was about as much use as tits on a fish.'*

tits out for the lads, get your *exclam*. A compliment proffered by a large group of aggressively drunken men to any female above the age of puberty.

tit scrap *n*. The fighting motion of the breasts of a very *big-boned* council estate woman who chooses not to wear *tit pants* as she walks to Netto, Boozebuster or bingo.

tits in her handbag, she's got her *euph*. An amusing reference to a lady who has failed to attain a sufficiently impressive level of mammary development. *'I don't fancy that Tara Palmer-Tomkinson much, Dalai Llama. She's got her tits in her handbag, her.'*

tit splitter *n*. A lady's fashion bag worn diagonally across the torso such that it bisects the *headlamps*.

tit tap *n*. *medic*. A nipple. *'Camera three. Forget about the crazy paving, zoom in on her tip taps, quick.'* (Director's instruction, *Ground Force*, BBC TV).

titti politti *n*. *Ital*. The policy of Silvio Berlusconi's Forza Italia party regarding the recruitment of its female parliamentary representatives.

tittlish *adj*. Prone to laughing at ladies' secondary sexual characteristics for no apparent reason.

tittoo *n*. A small piece of body art found in the breastular region. A *tit* tattoo.

tittybollocks *n*. *medic*. Women's breasts which are no bigger than a man's testicles.

titty fuck *n*. A *sausage sandwich*, a *diddy ride*.

titty mustard *n*. *Daddy's sauce*.

tit up *v*. To get one's *tops* off a *bird*. 'The Man Who Titted Up the Lord Mayor's Mother During the Loyal Toast'. (Cartoon in *Punch* by HM Bateman, 1926).

tit wank *n*. A *soapy tit wank*, without the soap.

titwicks *n*. *medic*. Ladies' nipples. 'When it comes to feeding baby, breast really is best. Mother's milk contains the perfect balance of nutrients that your child needs, and although the titwicks may be painful for the first few days, feeding quickly becomes a relaxing and bonding time for both.'

tit window *n*. When engaged in a serious conversation with a lady, that split second when her attention is momentarily diverted elsewhere and you have a chance to take a *sneaky peek* at her *rib cushions*. 'When the doctor told me the outlook was bleak, I looked her straight in the eye and asked her how long I had left. It was at that moment that the phone rang and I knew I had my tit window.'

TNTs *abbrev*. Two Nifty Tits.

toad in the hole *n*. An ugly bloke accompanied by an absolute stunner, *eg*. Rod Stewart and whichever blonde *piece* is letting him *on her nest* this week.

toast a bum crumpet *v*. To *fart*. 'Houston, we have a problem. We're down to our last two hours of oxygen and Fred has just toasted one hell of a bum crumpet.' (Mission Control TX log. Transmission from Jim Lovell, Commander, Apollo 13).

toasted cheese sandwich, like a *sim*. Phrase used to describe a woman's *kitten purse* that hasn't seen any saucy action for an inordinately long time, if at all. 'Right then. Would you shag Ann Widdecombe for a grand?' 'I don't think it'd be possible. It would be like trying to pull apart a toasted cheese sandwich.'

toaster *n*. A crumb-filled vagina with two slots and a spring mechanism that you have to fish your *cock* out of with a wooden spoon.

toaster sex *euph*. Polite expression describing *backdoor action*. From the fact that, like a slice of bread, "the longer you leave it in, the browner it gets". Also known as *the third way* or *bum craft*.

toast to the Queen *n*. A *fart* that scores highly in all three categories; volume, longevity and stench. Often followed by a round of applause.

Toblerone tunnel *n*. The gap, triangular in cross section, between the tops of a slender woman's thighs and her *skin gusset*, into which the popular confection would slide neatly.

tockley *n*. *Aus*. The *gut stick*. 'Ooyah! I've caught me tockley in me zip.'

toddlers *n*. Collar bone decorations of the sort worn by *Miss Lincolnshire*. *Dutch Alps*, *stits*.

todger *n*. That which todges. The penis. Also *tadger*, *tockley*, *tool*. 'Ooyah! I've caught me todger in me zip.'

todger dodger *n*. One who leaps out of the way of an on-coming *male genital*. A lesbian.

to do list *1. n.* In the workplace, a schedule or agenda of jobs yet to be completed. *2. n.* The mental list of workplace *tussage* that a sexually-frustrated office employee would like to *do,* all things being equal.

toffee apple *n.* The glans of the *gut stick* after it's been dipped in something hot and sticky.

toffee Rizla *n.* An absorbent pad of toilet paper worn in the *arse cleft* of a *double sucker* to absorb moisture and guard against *buttering* of the *cheeks*. A *man-pon, swedge.*

toffee strings *n.* See *bead curtains.*

toffee yoghurt *n.* That semi-viscous mixture of mingled bodily fluids which, one fondly imagines, dribbles down the backs of *puddle jumpers'* legs after they have successfully completed one of their randy romps. *Santorum, shum, sexcrement.*

togging *n.* Indulging in promiscuous, semi-public sex with middle-aged Radio 2 listeners in the car parks of Dobbies, National Trust properties and farm shops.

toggle and two *euph. Nav.* A jolly Jack Tar's *meat and two veg.*

toilet dick *n.* A hand-held, nozzle-ended dispenser used by gentlemen to clear *pebble-dashing* from the lavatory pan. Also known as the *yellow toilet brush* or *piss chisel*

toilet duck *n.* An untimely and probably unwanted erection which manifests whilst one is sitting on the *pot*. Named after the well known brand of *chod bin* cleaner which boasts of "reaching under the rim".

toilet snails *n.* Cryptozoological molluscs that slither around the *bog pan* in student houses, leaving brown *skidmarks* that no-one claims responsibility for.

toilet stilt *n.* A particularly long and rigid *stool* which stands on one end and clears the water surface by at least three inches. A *bowl vault.*

toilet suicide *n.* A loud explosion followed by a low groan from a lavatory cubicle.

token for the cockwash *n.* A romantic gift bestowed upon a lady by a man, (*eg.* Flowers, chocolates, bottle of *screwtop*) in the hope that it will get him *a bit. 'I'm just nipping down the off licence to get a token for the cockwash.'*

Tokyo optician *sim.* A light-hearted term of abuse for a *slapper, ie.* One who has seen her fair share of *Japs' eyes.*

toley *n. Scots.* A *shite* or *jobby. 'Och the noo, Eric. I just dropped a braw toley in your shoe.'*

tolly ring *n. medic.* Condition prevalent amongst employees in the printing industry, the chief symptom of which is soreness in the anal area. So-called because sufferers believe that inhalation of the aromatic hydrocarbon solvent toluene, which is used as a cleaning agent in their workplace, is what causes their *farts* to burn their nipsies. *'I'm sorry, Mr Caxton. You'll have to finish typesetting the 1475 edition of Recuyell of the Historyes of Troye yourself. I'm off home to put some ointment on me tolly ring.'*

tom *1. n.* Prostitute. *2. v.* To carry out prostitution. *'Are you tomming it?' 3. rhym. slang.* Tomfoolery = joolery.

tomahawk *n.* A little penis. From the smaller version of the "Chopper", the very popular 1970s Raleigh bicycle, which was named after a big *cock.*

tomato boat has docked, the *euph.* Phrase used to put hubbie off his stroke when

Arsenal are playing at home.

tomb raider *n.* A gentleman whose preference in ladies lies at the more mature end of the scale. A *granny fucker, biddy fiddler.*

Tom Daley *euph.* A medal-winning expulsion of *biosolids* that gracefully enters the water without a hint of a splash, even though it has the weight of a sixteen-year-old boy.

tomfuckery *n.* Light-hearted dealings with a *lady of the night*. *'I don't know what you're getting so cross about, darling. It was just a spot of drunken tomfuckery on a lads' trip to Amsterdam.'*

Tom Hank *rhym. slang.* A *Jonathan Ross.*

Tom Kite *n. rhym. slang.* A *shite*. *'And the tension's really building up at the eighteenth hole here at Barnsley International Golf Course. Tiger Woods is lining up the birdie shot that could see him awarded the magnificent onyx and pewter trophy of the inaugural South Yorkshire Golf Championship. And... oh no. He's trod in a big pile of Tom Kite. Aw, fucking hell, the poor cunt. It's one of them orange, blancmangey ones and it's gone right over the top of his shoe.'*

Tommy Cooper, to do a *v.* To die on the big stage in mid-performance. To lose *wood*, just like that. *'Sorry, love, we'll have to stop. I've done a Tommy Cooper.'*

Tommy's out *n.* A light-hearted party game where one of the guests secretly lays a cable in the house and shouts "Tommy's Out", whereupon everyone else tries to find it. *'To Aldeborough for the weekend, guest of Benjamin (Britten). What a hoot. Simply everyone was there including Larry (Olivier), Ivor (Novello), Terrence (Rattigan) and Alfie (Bass). Charades in the orangery, then after supper we played a game of Tommy's Out which ended at three in the morning when Kit (Hassall) found a dead otter in the piano stool, courtesy of Johnny (Gielgud).'* (From *The Diary of Noel Coward).*

Tommy squeaker *n.* A small, high-pitched *Daimler Dart* released unwittingly when lifting something heavy, such as a manhole cover or Dame Margot Fonteyn.

toms *rhym. slang.* The *splatters*. From tom tits = squits. *'Please excuse Peaches Honeyblossom from games today as she's got the toms something rotten. Yours sincerely, Sir B Geldof (dad).'*

Tom Thumb's arsehole, a fanny like *sim.* The kind of *twat* one would imagine Emily Bishop off *Coronation Street* to have. A *mouse's ear.*

tom tom 1. *n. prop.* A popular satellite navigation system used by motorists. 2. *n.* Simultaneously *exorcising one's morning demon* whilst dropping a *copper bolt*. From *tom tit* and *Tommy tank.*

tongue and groove 1. *n.* Basic carpentry technique. 2. *n.* Basic *carpet-munchery* technique.

tongue fu *n.* An over-zealous act of *cumulonimbus* which leaves the victim feeling like her *gammon flaps* have just gone five rounds with Jackie Chan.

tongue job *n.* A lick, as opposed to a *blow job.*

tongue punchbag *n.* A *bald man in a boat*, a *clematis.*

tongue shui *n.* The ancient, mystical art of knowing the best place to stick your tongue to get the best flow of energy through your missus's *snatch.*

tongue wrestling *n. Tonsil hockey.*

tonight Matthew *euph.* A plain, ugly or

indeed plain ugly, girl seen at the start of a drinking session, who returns later, magically transformed by one's *beer goggles* into a gorgeous celebrity lookalike.

tonk *v. onomat.* To *fuck, poke, shtup.*

tonsil hockey *n. Snogging, spit swapping.*

Tony Martin *n.* The act of *giving it* to someone from behind with both barrels. A double *back scuttle.*

tookus *n. Totty, scrunt.*

tool *n.* Penis, *manhood.* All the *DIY* enthusiast needs, along with his *wanking spanners* and a couple of suitably-sized *nuts*, to perform a spot of *DIY.*

toosh *n. Totty, blart. 'There's not enough toosh on this oil rig.'*

toot *v.* A child and vicar-friendly term for a *parp.*

toot meat *n.* Penis. From the fictional musical sweet of a similar name. *Bed flute, meat flute, pink oboe.*

TOOTS/toots *acronym.* The toppest sort of *top bollocks* available. Derived from the fact that they could be termed Ten Out Of Tens.

toot toot *1. n.* Risqué BBC parlance for vagina. *2. onomat.* The noise made by the *spunk trumpet* during a *blow job.* *3. n.* That part of Denise Lasalle with which one would be well advised not to mess.

tooth coming through, have a *euph.* To be suffering from *IRS.* To have a *wire spider,* a *sweetcorn itch, pine cone.* To have a very itchy *ringpiece.*

tooth fairy *n.* A promiscuous person of either gender or persuasion. Because, like the eponymous nocturnal dental philanthropist, they have seen more than their fair share of bedrooms.

toothless gibbon *n.* A *clapping fish.*

toothless sea lion *sim.* A smelly and unkempt *minge. 'I don't think I'll see her again, Cilla. She had a fanny like a toothless sea lion.'*

top banana *exclam.* Give that man a coconut, whacko-the-diddle-oh. Jolly good.

top bollocks *n.* Breasts, *jubblies.*

top bottom *n.* The mouth.

top bum *n.* A woman's embonpoint and decolletage.

top deck *v.* Of a house guest, to defecate in one's host's cistern, rather than, more conventionally, in the toilet, for comic effect. *"I say, Jeeves, he was a bit of a rum cove, what? Did you see him pass the port from left to right?' 'Indeed I did, Sir,' replied the sage retainer. 'I took the liberty of top decking the servants' bathroom before leaving."* (from *Heil Hitler, Jeeves!* by PG Wodehouse).

top dog *n.* An unattractive woman in a workplace whom one fancies simply because all the others are even worse. The least unattractive of a set of unattractive ladies. Default *blart, best in show.*

top dressing *n.* A term used in the catering industry for an *air crouton* dropped next to a table by a disgruntled waiter.

top hat *n.* The implausible achievement of a lady with three blokes up her *wizard's sleeve.* After a highly erotic dish of the same name in the restaurant on the Stenna Ferry, consisting of three pork sausages in mashed potato sitting in a Yorkshire pudding.

topless hand shandy *1. n.* A lemonade and beer drink, pulled from a pump by a barmaid naked from the waist up. *2. n.* A squirt of something fizzy pulled from a *love pump* by a masseuse who is naked from the waist up. *Topless relief.*

'We Englishmen are conscious of our status / Which is why the beastly foreigners all hate us / But it's always seemed to me / that it's simply jealousy / 'Cos they're envious of the size of English 'taters.'~ *The Stately Genitals of England* by Noel Coward.

£15 ono.

topless relief *n.* The cheapest item on the menu in a *toss parlour.*

toploader *n.* A shared marijuana joint, in which the roller has generously over-filled his own half in order to get himself more *monged* than his sharee.

top of a coconut *n.* Descriptive of a *Hitler tash* which has been neglected.

tops and fingers *adj.* Scale on which sexual achievement is measured by teen-age males. See also *cloth tit. 'Get far last night?' 'Not bad. I got my tops and two fingers.'*

top shelf tornado *n.* A purchaser of *bliff mags,* who rushes into the shop, selects his quarry in the blink of an eye, swiftly secretes it within the covers of a daily newspaper and heads for the till with remarkable haste.

top stealth *n.* The alternative approach of entering a newsagents, grabbing your desired *bongo mag,* paying and leaving with such cunning that no-one bats an eyelid.

tornado alley *1. n.* The area of the USA in which twisters are most frequent, encom-passing the lowland areas of Mississippi, Ohio and the lower Missouri River val-leys. *2. n.* The low-lying region between the *council gritter* and the *love spuds,* in which unusually fierce spiralling winds run wild. The *taint, tintis, notcher, barse etc.*

torpaedo *n.* A public swimming pool patron who, suspiciously, heads straight for the shallow end with all frothy bub-bles coming off his feet.

toss *1. v.* To *wank,* usually "oneself off". *2. n.* A Noel Coward-style act of casual *self-delight. 3. v.* To flip pancakes through 180° during cooking.

tossanova *n.* Any gentleman that is cele-brated for his prowess at wrist-intensive, bachelor-orientated pursuits.

tossed salad *n.* US. Anal sex between male prisoners. *'More tossed salad, Lord Archer?' 'No thanks, Mr Big, I'm com-pletely stuffed.'*

Tosser del Mar *1. n.* prop. Principal town on the Spanish Costa Brava. *2. n.* A discreet underwater *wank* at a topless beach, rendered undetectable thanks to the laws of refraction and Mediterranean murk.

tosser's twitch *n.* Nervous affliction suf-fered by *wankers* during periods of absti-nence.

tossing the caber *v.* Having *one off the wrist* with a massive length of *wood.*

toss parlour *n.* A *rub-a-tug shop.*

tosspitality *n.* The thoughtful facilities provided for hotel guests who wish to *relax in a gentlemanly manner, eg. Grumble* channels on the telly, box of tissues on the bedside table, curtains *etc.*

toss pot *1. n.* a jar for keeping *toss* in. *2. n.* A person held in low esteem, a *fuck-wit.*

tosstalgia *v.* The act of *smacking oneself about* whilst fondly remembering a for-mer ladyfriend.

total eclipse of the blart *n.* Whilst eyeing up some *fit* piece of *tussage* across the pub/street/nunnery, the phenomenon of having some vast, planet-sized *salad dodger* slowly drift into your line of sight, completely obscuring the object of your scrutiny.

TOTM pole *n.* A gentleman's *love length,* a *fanny mouse* or any other more or less cylindrical object which enters a woman's *teepee* during *rag week.* From

Time Of The Month.

Tottle *n*. A bath-time *air biscuit*. From the joke with the punchline "But, Sir I distinctly heard you say, 'What about a water bottle, Tottle?'". An *Edward Woodward*.

totty *n. coll.* Girls, *fanny*. '*Hey, this car's a fanny magnet. Since I bought it I've been beating off the totty with a shitty stick.*'

touch *v*. To *fondle*, usually "up", esp. with a paintbrush.

touch and go *euph*. The phenomenon of premature ejaculation, the unfortunate affliction whereby the sufferer can barely *stick it in* before shooting his *population paste*. '*HAMLET: What a piece of work is man! How noble in reason! How infinite in faculties! And yet, dear Rosencrantz, with narry a pregnant pause my accursed spongle did spray. Hardly did I tarry within dear Ophelia's sweet clout. ROSENCRANTZ: Verily, my Lord, her ladyship did lament that your congress was an ephemeral joy; a fleeting pleasure, fading afore 'twouldst be prehended. HAMLET: Aye, 'tis true. It was touch and go alright.*' (from *Macbeth* by William Shakespeare).

touch base 1. *v*. Nonsensical corporate *twat* buzzword. 2. *v*. To make a spatial awareness misjudgement whilst wiping one's *teatowel holder* following a *tom tit*, sometimes resulting in a *taxi driver's tan* or, in extreme cases, *beef palm*. A *masonic handshake*.

touching cloth *adj*. That stooling stage immediately after *turtle's head* when the *Sir Douglas* establishes contact with the *trolleys*. '*Is there a bog round here mate? I'm touching cloth.*'

touching socks *adj*. The stage by which

time it is too late to look for a toilet, but time to look for a trouser shop.

touching the void 1. *n*. The unsettling sensation of wearing a dressing gown without any clothes on underneath. Also a successful film about falling down a hill. 2. *n*. A lady's act of filthy self pollution.

touch last night's tea *v*. To insert a digit into the *ringpiece* of someone with loose morals.

touch on *n*. The first vague stirrings of a *panhandle*, caused by something like the swimwear pages of the Grattan catalogue, or the problem pages of a tabloid newspaper. A *twitch on*.

touching ball 1. *n*. In snooker, a situation where one ball is touching another, allowing the participant to shoot in any direction without a penalty. 2. *n*. In pornography, exactly the same. *Newton's cradle*.

Tourette's juice *n*. Freshly-squeezed orange juice, of the sort that is so bitter it makes the drinker twitch and swear involuntarily.

tourist's touchpool 1. *n*. In a marine wildlife complex, the much-visited but rarely-cleaned, crab-infested section which smells of fish and where members of the public can dip their hands in. 2. *n*. A filthy *slut's clout*.

towbar *n*. A bulbous *turtle's head*. With a 12 volt output.

towel hook *n*. A *hard on* that's strong enough to support the weight of a damp bath towel.

tow oneself round the cabin *v. naut*. To indulge in a bout of vigorous *self abuse*.

Toxteth airshow *n*. A low-level aeronautical spectacular performed by police helicopters chasing scouse *twockers*, drug traffickers and other sundry ne'er-do-wells. A *Moss Side airshow*.

TPTs *abbrev. Tara Palmer-Tomkinsons*. See *Braille tits. stits, tisn'ts*.

tracer fire *n*. Type of food that passes through the alimentary canal entirely unscathed (*eg*. Sweetcorn), and shows up the next day in the toilet as good as new.

tractor pull *1. n*. A sophisticated entertainment enjoyed by inbred redneck Americans whereby a large block of concrete is dragged along some mud by a piece of souped-up farm machinery. *2. n*. A romantic Italian lovemaking technique whereby the gentleman sticks his *charlie* up his *bird's shitter* whilst he has his *pods* stuffed up her *clopper*.

tradesmen's entrance *n*. The *back passage*.

trade spit *v*. To osculate.

traff *1. v*. To *fart, let off. 2. v*. To stifle a *fart*, and sort of swallow it back up one's bottom. '*I was sat next to this cracking bird on the train all the way from Doncaster to Manchester. I must've traffed eighty or ninety times.*'

traffic calming measure *n*. A *turd* in the road that could take your exhaust off. A *Radcliffe's sleeper*.

train horn *n*. A lady's party trick in which she *drops a gut*, and *drops her hat forwards* in quick succession, creating a tuneless, two-toned blast. Also known as a *Robson and Jerome*.

trampagne *n*. A homeless person's celebratory beverage, laid down for special occasions, *eg*. White Lightning, Red Label Thunderbird, Mr Muscle Drain Foamer. '*Break out the trampagne, boys. I've found an Embassy with ten left on it.*'

trampanzee *n*. A foliage-dwelling *Harold Ramp* sitting amongst the bushes in the park, *wanking* furiously and throwing his *shit* at passers-by.

trampari *n*. A turpentine substitute aperitif taken as an appetiser before a bin-rifling buffet.

tramp duty *n*. A guilt-based tax levied on one who passes a *Harry Ramp* on a regular basis.

tramp eating a kebab *sim*. An enthusiastic performance of *cumulonimbus*. The male equivalent of a *dog eating hot chips*.

tramp grill *n*. Any city centre area where *Harry Ramps* gather in the summer to soak up the sun. The *shandy sunbed*.

trampitheatre *n*. The arena chosen by a cohort of drunken gentlemen of the road to drink white cider, shout incoherent abuse at one another and engage in *mortal combat*. Especially applies to circular public spaces, such as the central areas of road underpasses, *eg*. The St James Barton Roundabout in Bristol (*aka* The Bear Pit).

trampoline *n*. Any petroleum-based beverage of the type preferred by *gentlemen of the road. Trampari, trampagne, tramp's treacle*.

trampon *n*. A *dangermouse* that's been left in the *trap* long after it should have been taken out.

tramp's aftershave *n*. The manly and sexy aroma which wafts out of a pub at eight o'clock in the morning, and drives the bag ladies wild.

tramp's decanter *n*. A used soft drinks bottle into which neat spirits can be poured so that a drinker can get discreetly *refreshed* in an inappropriate or otherwise awkward situation without undue risk of detection. A *coach driver's flask*.

tramp's oyster *n*. A *hockled*-up *sheckle* on the pavement; a salty *al fresco* delicacy blessed with very few, if any, aphrodisiac properties. Also *tramp's breakfast, docker's omelette, greb, greeny, prairie oyster, gold watch, Dutch pikelet* or *Old Leigh oyster*.

tramp sauce *n*. The rancid, sticky substance painted over the tongue and on the corners of the mouth by elves whilst one is asleep following a night *on the piss*.

tramp's breakfast *n*. A *docker's omelette*. A pavement *greb, prairie oyster*.

tramps' humidors *n*. The fag-bins outside drinking establishments which provide *paraffins* with their daily supply of fine smoking requisites.

tramp stamp *n*. Any tattoo on a slatternly *bird's* body, usually around the base of the spine or on the left *qualification*. A *tittoo*.

tramp's delight *n*. Low cost cider.

tramp's housewarming *n*. The act of *pissing* oneself.

tramp's hat *n*. A large, shapeless, sweaty and discoloured *clopper*. With knitted pubes. A *shell hole, John Merrick's cap*.

tramp's jackpot *n*. A perfectly-intact discarded cigarette.

tramp's mate *n*. Someone who looks like they probably stink, *eg*. Jim Royle, Jocky Wilson, Tracey Emin.

tramp's tan *n*. The healthy, ruddy complexion achieved by spending a lot of time in the fresh air. Drinking metal polish. *Shandy sunburn*.

tramp steamer *1. n*. A ship which doesn't have any fixed schedule or published ports of call. *2. n*. A refreshingly *al fresco*

dreadnought left for us all to enjoy by a cheery *Harold Ramp*.

tramp's tiara *n*. A bobble hat.

tramps' treacle *n*. *Supermarket smack*. Special Brew.

tramps' truffles *n*. Discarded chips.

trampton *n*. An area frequented by those of no fixed abode where they consume copious amounts of *trampagne* and watch the world go by, generously sharing their profanities with members of the public.

trampy tea *n*. Unsavoury beverage made by someone who, despite having filthy, scabby fingers, insists on squeezing the teabag against the spoon with their thumb. Into your fucking tea.

tramputee *n*. A *Terence Stamp* who has become separated from his can of *treacle*.

tramp Vegas *n*. telephone booths, vending machines and parking meters that are regularly checked for rejected coins by *gentlemen of the road*.

tranny *1. n*. An old fashioned radio. *2. n*. Transvestite, transparency or transit van, *eg*. A fetish photographer might say *'Shit. I left that tranny of the tranny in the back of the tranny.'*

tranny wreck *n*. A real woman who has no real concept of how to put on make-up, and therefore effects the look of a man in a dress who has no real concept of how to put on make-up, *eg*. Ruth Kelly MP before her "style makeover".

transalvite *n*. Peculiar term for a transvestite used by your grandad, who is not sure how to pronounce the word correctly as there weren't any around while he was busy winning two world wars. Mind you, he had a few close shaves in the brothels out east after the last lot, he can tell you.

transferred phallus *euph.* Adapted from the well known legal term "transferred malice", whereby a person receives a blow which is intended for another person. *Transferred phallus* is where a woman receives a *scuttling* which is likewise intended for another, *eg.* When her husband *gives her one* whilst fondly imagining he is *banging* Kylie Minogue.

transformer *n.* One who, on *coming out*, transforms instantaneously into a being that lives up to every homosexual stereotype, *eg.* Purchasing tight T-shirts, adopting a mincing gait, drinking G&T and constantly going on about Judy Garland.

Transit of Venus *1. n.* Small spot crossing the face of the Sun behind thick clouds once every 150 years. *2. n.* A mobile boudoir, *ie.* A van containing a heavily-stained mattress and the smell of *spunk*. A *shagging wagon, fuck truck, lust bus, spambulance.*

trap *n.* A toilet cubicle in a line of toilet cubicles.

trapped in the Himalayas *adj.* To be midway through a *tit wank*.

trap pirouette *n.* The light-footed, on-a-sixpence-style 180 degrees twirl performed when a fellow walks into an empty public lavatory cubicle only to find that it has been the subject of a *dirty protest*, been *pebbledashed* with *arse-gravy* or is full of *bangers and mash*.

travel fat *n.* Unwanted *stalk* which sprouts on public transport. A *purple-headed gristle thistle* germinated by sitting on a seat located directly over the axles of a corporation omnibus. Also *travel fat, traveller's marrow, diesel dick, routemaster, Varney teacake.*

travel iron *1. n.* A small, hard thing that puts creases in one's trousers on holiday. *2. n.* A small, hard thing that puts creases in one's trousers on a bus.

Travelling Wilberries *1. n.* Short-lived pensioner supergroup. *2. n.* Time-served *clagnuts*.

trawlerman's wellie, fanny like a *sim.* Descriptive of a commodious *snapper*. With the eye-stinging smell of dead kipper.

trawler's bilge *n.* Festering *moip*, stagnant *blip*.

traxedo *n.* Elegant evening wear sported by the *scratting* classes on a night out, consisting of a fake designer tracksuit purchased from a market stall.

treacle *1. n.* Term of affection used solely by Pete Beale in *EastEnders*. *2. rhym. slang.* An *air biscuit*. From treacle tart = Bakewell tart.

treading air *n.* Sitting on the *crapper* for an indefinite period, pushing tiny pockets of gas from one's *arse*.

treading bacon *n.* Depressing state of affairs whereby a chap has failed to bring his lady to a sufficient state of erotic rapture. *'I'm getting cramp in my hand here, Cleopatra. Can I just call it a day and go to sleep, love?' 'Aye, go on then, Mark Anthony. You've been at it for half an hour and you're still treading bacon.'*

treading water *n.* Light *strumming* on the *banjo* in order to keep one's interest up during the dull plot bits in a *grumble flick*. Maintaining a *satiscraptory* level of *wood*. *'You're under arrest, Mr Herman.' 'But officer, I wasn't wanking, I was just treading water.'*

tread on a frog *v.* A wetter sounding version of *step on a duck*.

treasure trail *n.* The female equivalent of

the *crab ladder*. The hairy line of fluff that joins the navel to what's buried down below.

tree log *n*. A *chocolate shark* whose snout is in the water before its tail leaves one's *arse*; a *Cuban bum cigar*, a *bridger*, *earthing cable, bottom log*.

tree monkey *n*. A *hand on heart*.

tremble trigger *n*. The male *G-spot*, lurking up the *chocolate starfish*, just behind the *doughnut*. *'How about there, Edward?' 'That's it, Sophie, bit higher. Yes, that's me tremble trigger alright.'*

trenchmates *n*. Multiple comrades who have had *carnival knowledge* of the same *bird*, whether simultaneously or otherwise.

treseme *n*. A lower-class *lady of the night, ie*. One who is, like the eponymous TV-advertised shampoo, "professional but affordable".

triage *n*. Mental process of a chap entering a nightclub, whereby he mentally sorts the attending *flap* into three groups; those that deserve attention immediately, those who can wait until after a few pints and those who are beyond help.

tribe tribe tribe tribe *exclam*. Peer-pressurised chant which is shouted at a drinking companion who is imbibing a mind-bending lager against his better judgement. From adventurer Bruce Parry's *Tribe* programme, during which he gets administered with poisonous frogs' anal bum juice and what-have-you.

trick *n*. Customer in a *rub-a-tug shop*, a *Hillman Hunter*, a *gonk, a John*.

trick or treat *n*. A *tree monkey* that could easily *drop a log*. A possible *follow through*.

triffid, the *n*. Bizarre and frankly point-less sexual act whereby a fellow presses the tip of his *referee's whistle* against his partner's forehead, then pinches the *fiveskin* between his finger and thumb whilst pulling back gently, causing a slight vacuum. Done correctly, this apparently leaves a lovebite-type circle on his victim's skin, as if they have been in a fight with a carnivorous tulip.

trifucta *n. Aus*. A *three root* weekend, with three different *Sheilas*.

triggernobetry *n*. The ability to produce instant ejaculation in a man by prodding his prostrate gland with the finger, practised by pros, nurses and Countess of Wessexes.

trilogy *n*. Also known as *brown Star Wars*. A *turd* of such epic proportions it has to be released in three instalments. The first can stand on its own as a complete adventure. The second links to the first, but has a dark, inconclusive feel generating an air of foreboding and leaving itself wide open for an unknown ending. The final chapter has drama, excitement and moments where you think all is lost. A grand battle is waged where good overcomes evil and peace is restored in your *arse*.

trim *n*. Tidy *bush, talent, totty*.

tripe hound *n*. A *fugly dog*.

tripe stick *1. n*. Evil-smelling piece of chewable gristle which keeps a faithful dog's mouth occupied. *2. n*. A pet food treat.

triple crown *1. n*. The Holy Grail of Rugby Union players; to win matches against the other three home nations. *2. n*. The Holy Grail of Rugby Union players; to *shout soup, piss* and *shit* oneself in the back of a taxi.

triple jump *1. n*. A soft playground sport

as practised by grinning sometime God-botherer Jonathan Edwards. 2. *n*. To *have* all three available *holes* in one session.

triple point shite *n*. A far-from-sublime *feeshus* in the *Camillas* that exists simultaneously in the three known states of matter, *viz*. Gas, solid and liquid.

Trisha fodder *n. coll*. Those *Essex tartan*-clad inhabitants of *nillionaires' row* whose personal tragedies and woes are meat and drink to the producers of plebeian daytime TV talk shows.

Trisha porn *n*. Cheaply-produced *grumble vids* where thick, single mothers get "seduced" and *fucked* by the likes of Ben Dover and Marcus Allen.

Trisha trash *n*. The kind of human vermin that appear on mid-morning riff-raff debates. British *caravan trash*.

Tristram hand shandy *1. n*. An amusing, yet rambling and ultimately inconclusive, *wank*, named after the book by Laurence Sterne which nobody has ever finished, and what's more anybody who tells you they have is a liar. A *cock and balls story*. *2. n*. An act of *personal pollution* performed by the brother of James Herriott's boss on *All Creatures Great and Small*, probably when he was supposed to be sticking his arm up a cow's *arse* in a barn or drinking a cup of tea and eating a slice of cake whilst Tricky-Woo *pissed* on his shoe or something.

trogg *n*. A simpleton, or *fuckwit*. See also *pranny*.

Trojan *n. US*. An American brand of warlike, Greek *French letters*. A brand name which brings to mind the story of the Trojan horse is, if you think about it for a moment, a strange one for a condom manufacturer to have chosen.

Trojan arse *n*. A toilet bowl invasion that takes one by surprise in the middle of the night and sends one back to bed in a state of sleepy bemusement. A somnambulodefecation.

trolley bag *n*. A *fugly* stewardess working for a budget airline. The opposite of one of them *trolley dollies* off of the Virgin Airlines advert.

trolley dash *n*. Of a punter, to chase a prostitute who has stolen his trousers down a back alley, wearing his underpants, shoes and socks.

trolley dolly *1. n*. An air hostess. *2. n*. A *ladyboy, shim, bobby dazzler, tiptop*.

trolleys *1. n.* Kecks *2. n*. Underkecks.

trolleytubby *n*. An overweight airline stewardess, usually found working in the first class cabin because she's too wide to fit down the economy aisle.

trollop *n*. See *trull*.

trollop snack *n*. *Helmet cheese, foreskinzola*.

tromboning *v*. A thoroughly impractical sex act in which a woman or *Colwyn Bay* man *rims* his pal's *brass eye* whilst simultaneously reaching round the front to give it some elbow on his *horn*, the action being akin to playing a trombone. A *George Jism*.

troop the colour *v*. To leave a *skidmark* down the right or left hand side of the pan as a result of sitting side-saddle on the *crapper*, like the Queen on parade.

trots, the *n*. The rapid foot movement required to convey a diarrhoea sufferer to the lavatory urgently. See also *Tijuana cha-cha, sour apple quickstep, Turkish two-step*.

trouble Tripitaka *v*. To have *one off the wrist*. From the popular, badly-dubbed-into-English, Chinese kids' serial of the late 1970s, where the androgynous monk regularly used to *punish the monkey* when he got out of order.

trough out *v.* To *lick out* your missus like a pig looking for truffles.

trouser arouser *n.* A *fit* lass, good looking *bird.*

trouser bandit *n.* Slightly more polite version of *turd burglar.* A *puddle jumper* who steals trousers.

trouser browser *n.* In a lap-dancing establishment, public park or cinema specialising in continental "art" films, a gentleman engrossed in an increasingly agitated search for loose change in his pockets.

trouser chuff *n.* A Cornish seagull that lives in some trousers.

trouser cough *n.* A clearing of the nether throat.

trouser department 1. *n.* Section of a department store dealing with men's legwear. 2. *n.* Area of the department store in which middle-aged men experience problems.

trousered 1. *adj.* To be wearing trousers. 2. *adj. Wasted, arseholed, wankered, shit faced.*

trouser engine *n.* Gentleman's machinery which, when sufficiently fuelled with beer, can be cranked into life and will thenceforth run by itself with a vigorous repetitive action until its *nuts* work loose.

trouser folder *n.* A person who, one would imagine, would have to carefully fold their clothes after taking them off before they could indulge in sexual intercourse, *eg.* Sven Goran Ericsson, Simon Cowell, Bruce Forsyth.

trouser jazz *n.* A session of different-sounding blasts on the *bum trumpet* released in quick succession.

trouser leg trombonist *n.* Popular female musician who plays in the same ensemble as the *skin flautist* and *pink oboe* virtuoso.

trouser Mauser *n.* A small rapid firing *porridge gun.* A *pump action mottgun, mutton musket.*

trouser rain *n.* A small downpour in the *keg* region leading to a few damp patches in the south. A *wet penny in the pocket.*

trouser rake *n.* A stiffer version of the *trouser snake.* Often pops up and hits women in the face when stood on.

trouser rouser *n.* A *brass eye*-opener. A *Bronx cheer.*

trouser snake *n. One-eyed pant python.*

trouser tent *n.* Embarrassing portable erection made from canvas or other trouser material, with a zip up one side, supported by a rigid *wood shaft.* If occurring whilst seated this can easily be concealed with one's bowler hat.

trouser tits *n.* A large pair of prominent *testicles. Man marbles. 'I tell you what, Colin. My trouser tits battered her chin.'*

trouser trout *n.* Something one tickles in one's *trolleys* before taking it out and banging its head against a rock.

trouser trumpet 1. *n.* A be-bop solo blown on the *botty bugle.* 2. *n.* The E-flat *anus.*

trouser truncheon *n.* The stiff *pole* a bobby takes out in the back of his van on a Saturday night. A *turned-on copper's torch.*

trout *v.* To *pull. 'I was out trouting last night. Ended up with a right old five-to-twoer. Had to chew me own arm off this morning.'*

trout jelly *n.* Artificial sexual lubricant. *I can't believe it's not batter, Grandma's little helper, granny batter.*

trout's mouth *n.* The *down there part* of a genuine 18-year-old piece. The real deal.

trucker's mate *n.* Someone who looks like he could be a sex case, *eg.* Roy off *Coronation Street.*

trucker's Tizer *n.* Brownish-yellow liquid, thought by many to be the urine of long-distance lorry drivers, often spotted in plastic bottles reposing on the hard shoulders of motorways, disguised as pop.

truffle hunting *v.* Taking a *trip around the world. Rimming.*

truffleshuffle *n.* The characteristic gait of one who has *split the winnings.*

trull *n.* 19thC. A prostitute, a *hoo-er.* With fat *tits* but not many teeth, as stabbed up by Jack the Ripper in Old London Town.

trump *v.* To *fart* or *pass wind* in a chair-shaking way.

trumpeter's lips *n.* The involuntary pursing of the *tea towel holder* at moments of extreme fear. *'Any man who tells you he is not afraid to go into battle is either a fool or a liar. It is the fear that makes him fight. I personally had the trumpeter's lips throughout the North African campaign.'* (from *The Memoirs of Field Marshal Montgomery*).

truncheon *n.* A solid, one piece *turd* which, if grasped, firmly could be used to stun a miscreant.

truncheon voucher *n.* A *ticket to the policeman's ball.* A constabulary bribe, a *cop tip.*

trunk *n.* A large *knob* which squirts water over Johnny Morris.

try a little Freddie *v.* To indulge in a spot of light *bummery*, out of curiosity more than anything. *'After Lancing, Evelyn Waugh went up to Oxford, where he read History at Hertford College. During his three years there, he neglected his formal studies and threw himself into a vigorous social scene populated by artists, actors, poets and aesthetes. He later recalled: "Moving in such artistic circles in those heady, hedonistic days between the wars, one was inevitably tempted to try a little Freddie from time to time. I tried it at least twice, but found it most disagreeable as it tended to make my nipsy feel sore."'* (from *Waugh and Peas - The Novelist and his Allotment Produce* by Michael Holroyd and Alan Titchmarsh, Macmillan Books).

trying to get the last pickled onion from the jar *euph.* Deep *gusset typing* whilst biting the tongue.

try on the comedy beard *v.* To perform *cumulonimbus*, impersonate Stalin.

tubby chaser *n.* A man who thinks *thunderbirds* are go. Also a woman who prefers her *beefcake* to be a *salad dodger.*

TUBER/tuber *1. acronym. medic.* Doctor's shorthand written on the notes of good-looking female patients. Totally Unnecessary Breast Examination Required. *2. acronym.* Descriptive of certain aesthetically-upsetting breeds of dog, such as the Basenji, Beagle, Elkhound, Fox Terrier, Chow Chow and Bichon Frise. Tail Up, Brown Eye Revealed. *'Have you met my pedigree tuber, Portnoy Fauntleroy of Ballykissangel? Oh he likes you, look. He's just ejaculated down your leg.'*

tubesteak *n. Beef bayonet on the bone.*

tube strike *n.* That time of the month.

TUBFUF/tubfuf *acronym.* Thumb Up

Bum, Finger Up Fanny. All business.

tufty club *n.* A *vertical bacon sandwich* surrounded by scraggy outcrops of *gorilla salad*. Named after the 1960s/70s schools road safety campaign fronted by a threadbare squirrel which was animated in a sub-Ray Harryhausen style repeatedly nearly stepping out in front of motor vehicles.

tug *v.* To *pull*, as in a *pud*. A light-hearted *wank. 'Dinner's ready, Sidney!' 'Down in a minute, dear. I'm just having a little tug.'*

tug boat *n.* A woman of plain appearance and compact, muscular build. A *swamp donkey.*

tuggernaut *n.* A lorry driver *shedding his load* in his cab at Barton Park Services on the A1.

tug of love *n. Pulling your string,* and putting your heart into it.

tug of phwoar *n.* A spontaneous and urgent *one off the wrist* brought on by a particularly *horny* sight, *eg.* An attractive *bird*, the bra adverts on Underground escalators.

tug of raw *n.* The tenth *Barclay's* of the day for the gentleman who is *working from home.* A *blood wank.*

tug of war *1. n.* A notably hard and tiring act of *self pollution* undertaken whilst *heavily refreshed.* A *J Arthur* which requires a lot of willpower to bring to a *satiscraptory* solution. *2. n.* A jobseeker or student's eighth *ham shank* of the day, enjoyed at about ten in the morning.

tugpusher *n.* Of schools, workplaces and police stations, the individual who has taken on the responsibility for distributing hardcore *art pamphlets* amongst his colleagues. A *pornbroker*, a *grumblemonger.*

tug pamphlet *n.* A *jazz magazine.*

tugs aft *exclam. marit.* An apposite response to the sound of a *Lionel Bart.* From the Merchant Navy practice whereby tugboats sound their foghorns when approaching the aft of a ship, which is usually acknowledged by the ship's mate announcing "tugs aft" over the tannoy. Which is a trade name, so it should be written with a capital letter, but fuck that. And here's some more, portakabin, biro and hoover.

tug typing *n.* The ability to watch *grumble* on one's *jerk station* screen whilst simultaneously *glazing the knuckle*, without once averting the eyes down to one's turgid *old man*, even when it erupts a torrent of *hot fish yoghurt* onto the keyboard.

tugwax *n. Spongle, spadge, jitler.*

tumblepube *n.* A fur ball of *clock springs* and other discarded pubic foliage which wafts around when the *bog* door opens.

tummy banana *n.* A *gut stick.*

tummy Tetris *n.* The strange, yet not unpleasant, sensation whereby one's unborn *change of hearts* slot together satisfyingly in one's alimentary canal, before disappearing with an amusing noise.

tummy truncheon *n. Sixth gear stick, porridge gun*, penis.

tump *n. Welsh.* The *beetle bonnet*, the *monkey's forehead.*

tumwiper *n.* Any unfashionable item of clothing received as a gift from a well-meaning relative or friend that is immediately relegated to the function of wiping *spoof* off one's stomach after *self help.* A *jazz rag.*

tuna taco *n.* A hot dish, not requiring cutlery, served when *dining at the Y.* If eaten with a side order of *cranberry dip*, it could lead to *Mexican lipstick*.

tuna town *n*. The female genitalia, *Billingsgate box*.

tup *1. v.* To have sex, *fuck*. *2. v.* Of sheep-to-sheep shagging, red hot *horny* ram on ewe action.

tuppence licker *n*. A *lesbo, bean flicker, carpet muncher, pelt lapper*.

tuppenny all-off *1. n.* A cheap, no-nonsense haircut popular amongst national servicemen in the 1960s. *2. n.* A no-nonsense *fannicure*. A *Brazilian*.

tuppie *n. Scot*. A Dundonian term for a lady's *fluffit*. *'There's nae a kitten, moose or puppy / Ha'f sae soft as ma wife's tuppie.'* (from *The Song O' the Dundee Growler* by Robbie Burns).

turbo shit *n*. The high-speed *dump* required to fool a ladyfriend into thinking you had only went for a *gypsy's kiss*. A *greyhound's egg*.

turbot for tea *exclam*. Announcement that the *fish supper* is served. *'Never mind that tug, Sidney. It's turbot for tea.'*

turd *n*. A cylindrical unit of *shit*, longer than a *tod*. A link of *feeshus*.

turdberg *n*. A feculant shipping hazard of such deceptively gigantic proportions that ninety percent of its bulk typically remains underwater. A *growler*.

turd burglar *n*. Stealthy thief who forces entry into the rear of a person's premises via the inside of the *chocolate drainpipe*.

turd clippers *n. US*. Buttocks.

turd degree burns *n. medic*. Post-curry *shitting* injuries. *'A man was taken to hospital last night after being found unconscious on the pavement outside a curry restaurant in Newcastle upon Tyne. He was suffering from shock, alcohol poisoning and had turd degree burns covering 90% of his anus. A spokesman for the restaurant said 'Come to the Curry Capital, Bigg Market, Newcastle upon Tyne.''* (BBC News 24).

turd eagle *n. Aus*. A large *blowfly*. A *dunny budgie, poobottle*.

turder *n*. The begetter of a *feeshus*.

turd eye *n*. The mystical sixth sense that usually, though not always, enables a pedestrian to avoid tripping over a length of *canine cable*.

turd fairies *n*. Mythological creatures that are thought to be the cause of the mysterious *ghost shit* phenomenon, *ie*. Those stools of which there are no trace when one turns round to admire them in the *pan*.

turdigo *n. medic*. Psychological condition, *viz*. In the *shitehouse*, the inability to look down at, or indeed to do anything about, the enormous *skidmarks* you've just left on the *pan*, which you then leave to the unalloyed delight of the next user.

turdis *n*. One of them detached, modern, portable, space-age-looking public conveniences that could well be a phonebox or small internet cafe. A *turd tardis*.

turdmoil *n*. A state of extreme perturbation, confusion, commotion, agitation or tummult occasioned by being in desperate need of a lavatory.

turdsearch *n*. The desperate hunt for reading material one embarks upon when *Mr Brown is at the window*.

turdulence *n*. The area of dirty air affected by a particularly foulsome *trouser trumpet*, usually dispensed by a man walking in front of one in a tightly-packed shopping establishment, *eg*. The make-up section at John Lewis.

turfer's knee, wetter than a *sim.* Descriptive of a lady's *clunge* in a state of preternatural excitement. A phrase that can be usefully employed when referring to a *fish drowner* that is *frothing like bottled Bass* or, indeed, *dripping like a fucked fridge.*

turf out *1. n.* An anal spring clean. A well needed *tom tit. Next sale, Queensway.* *2. v.* To excrete.

Turin shroud *1. n.* Famous medieval sheet with Mick Fleetwood's face painted on it. *2. n.* A piece of lavatory tissue draped tastefully over a floating *log* that will not flush away.

turistas *n. Turkish two-step.*

turk *v.* To take someone or something up the *council. 'Sit down please, Lord Archer.' 'If it's all the same with you, Governor, I'd rather stand. I've just been turked in the showers by Jonathan King.'*

turkey *n.* The *cracker* you think you've pulled whilst drunk at the office Christmas party who turns out to be a rough old *bird* who only gets *stuffed* once a year.

turkey moss *n.* Serious *fluff* on a *bird's bodily treasure. Gorilla salad.*

turkey-neck *n.* That which is *throttled* in Norfolk.

turkey twizzler *1. n.* Unappetizing helix of nondescript brown matter of mysterious and sinister provenance, served to schoolchildren in lieu of real food. *2. n.* A thin, spiralling *turd* which retains its corkscrew shape even after it has been dropped into the *pan.*

turkey's wattle *n.* A *ragman's coat*, a *club sandwich.*

Turkish *1. n.* Heterosexual *back door work*, whilst wearing curly slippers. *Irish. 2. rhym. slang.* An excrement. From Turkish delight = shite. *'What's the matter, Eric?' 'Jocky Wilson done a Turkish in me shoe. Again.'*

Turkish bath *n.* A *Glasgow shower.*

Turkish dagger *n.* A curved *Thora.* With a jewel-encrusted handle that one wouldn't, frankly, fancy holding in one's teeth.

Turkish revenge *n.* A *stab* up the *arse.*

Turkish rinse *n.* A quickfire bathing technique popular amongst *soap-dodgers*, consisting of a rudimentary scrub of one's armpits, gusset and *giggle stick.*

Turkish shower *n.* A *Glasgow shower.*

Turkish slippers *n.* The *jester's shoes.*

Turkish tumbleweed *n.* Kebab boxes, bits of uneaten salad and other cosmoplitan post-pub detritus blowing about the high street at 2am.

Turkish two-step *n. Smallroom dance* not dissimilar to the *sour apple quick step, Tijuana cha-cha,* or *Aztec twostep.* The *skitterbug.*

turned-out trouser pocket, arsehole like a *sim.* A dropped *clacker valve*, resulting from either an excess of *Turkish,* or a red hot Indian.

turn Japanese *v.* To make like a *Chinese helicopter pilot*, gripping his *joystick* for grim life and concentrating on keeping his *chopper* up.

turn your bike round *v.* To go to the lavatory. *'Excuse me, I'm just going to turn my bike round. Have you got any arse paper?'*

turpsichord *n.* A public house pianoforte, as played by rubber-fingered drunks.

turps nudger *n.* A *top shelf drinker.* *'Have you seen that bloke who reads the local news? Jesus, what a fucking* *turps nudger.'*

turquoise *n.* A lady who allows the *dog in the bathtub*. One who doesn't object to being *turked* up the *bonus tunnel*.

turtle *1. n.* A passive sexual partner, *ie.* "Get her on her back and she's fucked". *2. n. coll.* Blit, fanny, fluff, talent. Birds. *3. n.* One of the least sexy *bum games* a flatulent couple can play in the bedroom, the winner being the last one to poke their head out from under the duvet.

turtleberries *n. Winnets, dangleberries, Payne's Poppets.*

turtle bungee *n.* The dangerous sport of releasing and retracting *turds* by clever use of the sphincter muscles just before they *touch cloth. Prairie dogging, gophering.*

turtle guillotine *n.* The *nipsy, cigar cutter, clackervalve.*

turtle power *n.* The unstoppable superhero-like strength exhibited by a determined *chod* as it tries to overcome the tightly-clenched *nipsy.*

turtle recall *v.* The brief retraction of the *turtle's head* whilst en route to the *thunderbox.*

turtle's breath *n.* The very final warning *fart* before the turtle pokes its head out to *autograph the gusset.*

turtle's den *n.* The *bomb bay, dirt kitchen.*

turtle's head *n.* The initial protrusion of a stool though the *tea towel holder*, the point at which contracts are exchanged for the building of a *log cabin. Touching cloth, the monkey's toe.*

turtle soup *1. n.* Politically incorrect testudinoid delicacy served as a starter in certain, high-end Oriental restaurants. *2. n.* A very runny reminder of a meal in a low-end Oriental restaurant. *'Four score and seven years ago our fathers brought forth on this continent, a new nation, conceived in Liberty, and dedicated to the proposition that all men are created ... I'm sorry, does anyone know where the bogs are? I've got the turtle soup.'* (text of address by Abraham Lincoln, Gettysburg, Pennsylvania, November 19th 1863).

turtle's tail *n.* The last bit of *Gladys* to drop out of the *back bottom* at the pleasingly relaxed end of a sit-down toilet visit that began somewhat more urgently.

tush *n. US. Bum* (but not a tramp), *ass* (but not a donkey).

tussage *n. Talent*, female *buffage, blart, totty.*

tutu *n.* A tissue paper bib placed around the base of the tumescent generative member to catch any *ropes* which get *lobbed* whilst masturbating. Named after the famous Anglican Archbishop of Cape Town who popularised this practice.

TV *1. abbrev.* A television. *2. abbrev.* A *tranny.*

TWABs/twabs *acronym. Scots.* Scrotal condition which principally affects oil workers who find themselves stranded on the rig beyond their usual fortnight working period due to bad weather. Three Week Away Baws.

twactor *n.* A tragedian of dubious thespolographical accomplishments, such as Robson Green, any Kemp or that lanky *gimp* off the BT broadband adverts who's like a poor quality Martin Clunes, if that's not tautology.

twanger *n. Whanger.*

twangers *n. onomat.* Generic term for ladies' undercrackers, but more specifically those worn by dirty *scutters*. Named after the sound the gusset makes as it leaves the crotch when pulled hastily down from either side. *'And Lady Diana Spencer looks resplendent as she walks down the aisle, keeping up the age old traditions. She's wearing an old 18th century tiara, a magnificent new wedding dress, a diamond necklace borrowed from her friend the Duchess of Argyll, and a pair of blue twangers.'* (Sir Alastair Burnett, Royal Wedding commentary, ITN, 1981).

twang the wire *v.* To pluck out a *jazz rhythm* on the *one-stringed banjo*.

twankunt *n.* Descriptive of someone who is not just a *twat*, but also a *wanker* and a *cunt* to boot. *'Today's birthdays: Sandro Botticelli, Italian painter of the Florentine school, 1445; Augustus Pugin, Gothic revivalist architect, 1812; Nick Griffin, twankunt, 1959.'*

twastard *n.* A person who is not only a *twat*, but also a *bastard*. From twat + bastard. *'Today's birthdays: Sandro Botticelli, Italian painter of the Florentine school, 1445; Augustus Pugin, Gothic revivalist architect, 1812; Nick Griffin, twastard, 1959.'*

twaste *n.* The taste of a *twat*. From twat + taste, one would imagine. *'Come on, eat it all up.' 'I don't like the twaste.'*

twat 1. *n.* A *minge*. 2. *n.* Stupid person. 3. *v.* To hit, beat up. 4. *v.* Past participle of the verb "to twitter". *'I just twat my followers and told them I was stuck in a lift.'*

twatalogue *n.* A magazine of pornotholgical interest. An *art pamphlet*.

twat burger *euph.* A polite euphemism for an *act of oral affection* performed upon a woman's *bodily treasure*. Hopefully without too much ketchup on it.

twat burglar *n.* A man, presumably wearing a mask and stripy jersey, who steals another bloke's missus.

twaterpillars *n.* Female version of *willipedes. Cloppular crabs, mechanical dandruff.*

twatful 1. *n.* A good *seeing to* in the sexual sense. *'Just 8 pints tonight, lads. Got to get home to give the rib a twatful.'* 2. *n.* An imperial measure of *spangle*, equal to 2 *nutsworths* or *one tenth* of an *Almond. 'Sister Amoeba was powerless to resist. His eyes burned into hers like a sort of stone. His papal arms enfolded her body as she felt herself being swept away in some sort of weather system of passion. Then he lifted his cassock and gave her a twatful.'* (From *The Mother Superior and the Holy Father*, by Barbara Cartland).

twat hour *n.* The times of day, typically around 8.30 am and 3.30 pm, when every road near any school in Britain is brought to a halt by large numbers of parents attempting to reverse their enormous off-road vehicles into 8-foot parking spaces. *'Sorry I'm so late. I hit twat hour just as I turned onto St Paul's Road, Cambridge. I was stuck outside Sancton Wood School for two hours while some fuckwit drove her VW Touareg backwards and forwards 635 times without turning the steering wheel in the hope that it might somehow magic the thing into the fucking space.'*

twat mag *n. Bongo periodical.*

twatmosphere *n.* The unpleasant feeling that develops in a room the moment a *twat* walks in.

twatter *n.* In-your-face workplace version of the popular, pointless internet microblogging service, whereby you are unable to avoid the *twat* sat three seats away loudly announcing to everyone in the room absolutely everything they've done since leaving the office the night before.

twatmates *n.* Gentlemen who have both had a portion of the same *haddock pastie*, eg. Bryan Ferry & Mick Jagger, Michael Jackson & Nicholas Cage, and Sir Donald Campbell & Claude Greengrass off *Heartbeat*. No, it's true. Look it up. *Custard cousins.*

twat nappy *n.* See *clot mop.*

twat nav *n.* Motoring terminology; the wife with a road atlas.

twat of nine tales *n.* The fellow office worker who always has a story that whips whatever it is that you are talking about.

twatois *n.* The sort of fake Jamaican dialect favoured by middle class youths wishing to enhance their street credibility. *Jafaican.*

twat pamphlet *1. n.* A *grumble book* or *flesh mag* purchased by people who aspire to having a *wank*, eg. *Razzle, Knave, Splosh etc. 2. n.* An aspirational lifestyle magazine read by *wankers*, eg. *Dazed & Confused, Wonderland™, Wallpaper.*

twatplates *n.* Car registration plates where the numbers have been re-spaced or mutilated in order to make them spell out something that they don't from a distance, *eg.* Those on a Fiat Punto where the owner has placed a black screw at the bottom of the two 1s in P11 NTO.

twat rats *n. Cunt mice* for ladies with a heavier flow of *fanny jam*. Industrial strength *dangermice.*

twat rattler *n.* A *plastic cock*, a vibrator, *neck massager, bob.*

twatriot *n.* Someone who waved a Union Jack and shouted "Come on Tim", between every point whilst Tim "Spoilt Bastard" Henman got thrashed at Wimbledon every fucking year between 1994 and 2007. Also, to be found wearing a plastic Union Jack hat and singing *Land of Hope and Glory* at the Last Night of the Proms.

twat seats *n.* The back two rows on the upper tier of a double-decker bus or an EasyJet flight from Newcastle to Alicante, reserved for cap-headed *scratters* who wish to cycle through their ringtones, engage in foul-mouthed, shouted debates and/or light-hearted vandalism and otherwise *act the cunt.*

twatslapping *n.* The untraceable slapping noise generated *below the stairs* when a man and a lady are doing *thingy*. A *Blair's ovation.*

twatters *n.* Smashing *churns*. The sort that Nell Gwynn would have sported. *Fat rascals.*

twattoo *n.* A badly-conceived, situated, designed and/or executed piece of body art, eg. The word "Brooklyn" written above someone's *arsecrack* in Ye Olde English capital letters.

twatwrapper *n.* A multi-pocketed garment of the sort worn by the sex cases who stand at the end of railway platforms spotting trains. An anorak.

tweedle *1. n. rhym. slang.* Male ejaculate, *jitler* or *Thelonious*. From Tweedledum = cum. *2. n. rhym. slang.* Urine, *wazz* or *piss*. From Tweedledee = wee.

tweezerpleaser *n.* A two-fingered *wank*. A *Harvey Smith, snapping the chick's neck.*

twentieth century fox *n.* A *milf.*

twenty-eighth of Mayhem *n.* The day marking the start of *rag week. Ruby Tuesday.*

twenty-five yard screamer *1. n.* Some sort of long range kick in an association football match. *2. n.* A former ladyfriend whose only means of social interaction with you seems to involve yelling your sexual shortcomings at you from a distance whilst full of *bitch piss*.

twenty-four sheeter *1. n.* Printing terminology for one of those large billboard posters you find at railway stations. *2. n.* A woman whose attractiveness is inversely proportional to a viewer's proximity to her. An *LRF* - from the fact that, like *1.*, she is attractive from three platforms away, but covered in spots close up. *3. n.* A *Marmite pot*.

twernt *n.* The *tinter*.

twhat *n.* Piece of self-consciously eccentric millinery sported by the sort of *cuntish* oik who thinks that such headgear marks them out as being someone special and wacky. Pete Doherty wears a *twhat*.

twice off the same hard *1. n.* Of a gentleman, the once-in-a-lifetime phenomenon of achieving two orgasms from the same erectivation with no intervening *downtime*, and thus *2. euph.* Any once-in-a-lifetime phenomenon. *'And what is there to look forward to in the night sky next year? Well of course, the big story is the return of Halley's Comet which is only visible every 76 years. So it's a real twice off the same hard for most astronomers.'* (Patrick Moore, *The Sky at Night*, 1985).

twig & giggle berries *n.* The *fruitbowl*, the *meat and two veg*.

twiglet factory *n.* A heaving dancefloor populated by sweaty-*arsed* women wearing G-strings or thongs.

twink *n.* A *fart* so potent that it makes the hairs on your *arse* curl. Named after the home perm solution of the 1970s.

twinkie *1. n. US.* Turd, *chocolate log.* *2. n.* An apprentice *mudhole plumber*.

twin peaks *1. n. prop.* An experimental television series of the early 1990s created by David Lynch. *2. n.* Smashing *tits* like Audrey's in the series. *Dunce's hats, sweatermeat*.

twins, the *n.* A fine pair of *milky swingers* that could prevent a fellow getting a good night's sleep for months on end.

twin SUs *1. n.* Type of *tit*-shaped carburettors fitted to British Leyland automobiles. *2. n.* The *assets* of a well-endowed lady. Also *Strombergs*. *'Phwooar! That's a nice pair of twin SUs, your Highness.'*

twin tone *n.* A *fart* which suddenly and ominously drops in pitch, indicating something other than *marsh gas* may have been expelled. A *follow through, squench, Doppler shit*.

twin tub *n.* Back, then frontal penetration.

twirly *n.* An affectionate term used by omnibus drivers to describe senior citizens who attempt to use their free passes before 9.00am. ie, They are "too early" and have to be rudely thrown off the bus.

twist *1. rhym. slang. US.* Girl. From twist and twirl. *2. n.* Of *carpet munching* relationships, the *carpet*, as opposed to the *muncher*. A passive *lesbo*. *3. v.* From the pontoon playing gambit, to risk losing a scoring hand in the hope of getting a better one; thus to turn down the advances of a half decent lady in the hope that one will later *cop off* with something better.

twister *n. US.* Pervert, a *nonce*.

twist on nineteen *1. v.* In the world of blackjack - which seems to be a bit like pontoon, but played for money instead of matches - to foolishly risk busting your hand by asking the dealer to turn over another card. To gamble when the odds are stacked against you. *2. v.* In the world of flatulence, to *fart* recklessly whilst *touching cloth*. '*Open a window, love. I've had three Guinnesses and a prawn egg foo yung but I'm gonna twist on nineteen. By the way, is there a twenty-four hour Tesco round here that sells underpants?*'

twitcher *n.* A *bird watcher, ie.* One who light-heartedly takes photographs of his female colleagues on his mobile phone in the full knowledge that he will later *wank his knackers flat* at home whilst viewing the snaps. So-called because of the involuntary twitches his *knob* makes whilst he's taking the pictures.

twitcher's chin *n.* A very scruffy, chronically untrimmed lady's *front bottom* which resembles the unkempt lower mandible of bino-toting grumpy TV ornithologist and former funnyman Bill Oddie.

twitching Buddah *n.* A short, fat, excitable erection.

twitching wurzel *n.* An early morning visitor to a corner shop or supermarket, getting in his daily supply of cut-price apple-based beverage before most people have thought about sparking up the kettle for their first cup of tea.

twitter *n.* A lady's perineum, that area of the anatomy between the *twat* and the *shitter. Duffy's bridge, biffin bridge, tinter, taint.*

Twix lips *n.* A *front bottom* version of *hungry arse. Knicker sausages.*

two a.m. grab bag *n.* In a night club, the ropey assortment of frankly second-rate *tussage* which is all that is left to choose from at chucking out time. The *floor sweepings, bin rake*, sediment.

two aspirins on an ironing board *sim.* Descriptive of the bosoms of the slimmer-figured lady. Flat *stits, fried eggs, lung warts, TPTs.*

two bagger *n.* Someone so ugly that two bags are required in order to go *quim wedging* with them; one over their head and one over yours, just in case theirs falls off.

two bob billionaire *n.* A young man in an £80 shirt who still lives with his mum and dad.

twoc *v.* Take Without Owner's Consent. To borrow someone's car, not in order to steal it, but merely to drive it through Dixon's window and set it on fire. Also *twock.*

two can Van Damme *n.* In the pub, the jumped-up little *shit* that starts acting like the hardest man on the planet after a couple of drinks. *Tinny mallet.*

twocker *n.* A cheeky rapscallion who *twocks*. A loveable rogue, a lively urchin or rapscallion.

two flush push *n.* An obstinate *digestive transit* which requires a second pull on the *bog* handle before it will set off for the seaside.

two nut shuffle *n.* Action of a man *going commando*, gently manoeuvring his his hips from side to side so that his *clockweights* rock between his thighs, giving him a pleasant, swinging sensation. Normally practised whilst leaning on a counter of some sort; awaiting medicines, dry cleaning, a pint *etc.*

two page charlie *n.* The literary equivalent of a *two push charlie*. An overexcited *one-handed reader* who foolishly doesn't take the opportunity to peruse his new *art pamphlet* in a leisurely manner before *squirting his curd*.

two pee peace *n*. A relaxing toilet break taken at work, which lasts so long that there is time to *piss* twice.

two-piece jigsaw puzzle, easier than *sim*. Said of a lady who is particularly accommodating. *'I tell you, that bird I was with last night was a right little raver. She was easier than a two-piece jigsaw puzzle.' 'Did you get any, then?' 'Not as such, no.'*

two-pot bechamel *n*. A thick, white *bollock sauce* produced by heating up one's *two-pots* without serving. *'The wedding was pucka, but straight after the honeymoon I had to spend a month away filming. By the time I saw Jools again, I was gasping to dish up a portion of the old two-pot bechamel.'* (from *Mockney Rebel*, the autobiography of Jamie Oliver).

two pot screamer *n*. *Aus*. Someone who cannot hold their beer. A more reserved British equivalent would be *halfpint Harry*.

two puppies fighting in a bag *n*. Large, mobile and unrestrained breasts, like what Twickenham streaker Erica Roe had.

two ring circus *n*. The greatest show on earth. *Over the shoulder boulder holder*, a bra.

twoskin *n*. Half a *fourskin*.

two stroke poke *n*. Similar to a *one pump chump*, only twice as sexually satisfying for his lucky missus. A *two push Charlie*.

two up *n*. A *twos up*, a *threesome* with two gentlemen and a lady.

two wombles looking over a balcony *sim*. Descriptive of *NGTs*.

twunt *n*. Useful, satisfying yet inoffensive combination of two very rude words which can safely be spoken in the primmest and properest company.

Tyne Bridge *adj*. Descriptive of the position adopted by a dog trying to lay a particularly tenacious *egg*.

tyre *n*. *medic*. Swollen condition of the *fiveskin* caused by over-zealous *relaxation*. *'Did you get your internet sorted out, Clive?' 'Yes, I got it connected yesterday, and I've already got a tyre.'*

U-boat *n*. A *Richard III* lodged in the U-bend of the *crapper*, enforcing a naval blockade against enemy *shitting*.

U-bend straightener *n*. A mighty powerful *depth charge*. A *rat killer* of such impressive length and tensile strength that it could push the kinks out of the *chod bin* pipework. See also *neckbreaker*.

UB40 winks *n*. A mid-afternoon nap taken after a hard morning at the telly face.

U-blocker *n*. A titanic *dreadnought* so big it causes a *jobbie* jam in the foul drainage system. The Moby Dick of *brown trouts, a plumber's bonus*.

udders *n*. Breasts with absolutely no erotic qualities whatsoever.

udderpants *n*. A utility brassiere in which function is more important than form.

udder scudder *n*. An agricultural-grade *sausage sandwich*.

UDI *abbrev*. Unidentified Drinking Injury. Inexplicable damage sustained during a *bender* of which the victim has no recollection. A mystery *binjury*.

ugly as a Thai stripper's scrotum *sim*. Graphic metaphor, descriptive of that moment when something which seems to be going along swimmingly suddenly takes a distinctly unpleasant turn. *'Senna's lap looked perfect until he ran wide into the Tamburello Curve, when things turned as ugly as a Thai stripper's scrotum.'*

ugly bus *n*. A vehicle that mysteriously turns up after one has had eight pints on a Friday night and takes all the ugly women home, leaving the pub full of beautiful ladies.

ugly duckling *n*. A long, protracted *Exchange & Mart* which is launched mid-walk, where the benefactor "walks with a quack and a waddle and a quack".

ugly lights *n*. A revealing illumination apparatus which is switched on in pubs at chucking out time.

ugly taxi *n*. The vehicle which mysteriously delivers an unattractive *bird* into one's *fart sack* on a Saturday morning.

Ulrikas *n*. A pair of *kahoomas* that look smashing in clothing, but pitifully saggy when released on a beach. *Metatarsal breakers*.

ummfriend *n*. A *fuck buddy*. From the commonly-heard introduction at parties: "Hi, Gillian. Have you met Kate? She's my ... ummm ... friend."

unblocking the sink *sim*. A vigorous and impatient *wank*, presumably using both hands. *Starting the hornmower*.

Uncle Albert's beard *n*. *Jelly jewellery*.

Uncle Doug *rhym. slang. Self abuse*. From Uncle Doug = tug. *'I'm just off for an Uncle Doug, but if there's anything you need, just ask one of the stewardesses.'*

Uncle Fester *n*. A *goolie*-ish *bald-headed man* from the *old Adam* family, who occasionally rises up and puts the *willies* up your missus.

uncork the brown champagne *v*. On the morning after a night of strong ale and spicy foodstuffs, to bring in the *pace car*, thus unleashing a frothy torrent of foul, effervescent liquid.

undefuckable *adj*. *Bust*, damaged beyond repair. *'Oh, and there goes Barricello's engine on the warm-up lap. He'll head straight for the pit lane, but that looks pretty undefuckable. It's certainly the end to his Portuguese Grand Prix, Martin.'* (Murray Walker, commentating as Frentzen's front left wheel came off on the final corner, Belgian Grand Prix 1999).

underbeard *n.* Minge.

undercarriage *n.* Genitals, usually male. *The fruit bowl, family jewels, pudendas.*

underchunders *n. Trolleys, tacklebags.*

undercoat *n.* A soft drink ordered to accompany the first pint of a long session which prepares the stomach's surface for the later layers of alcoholic emulsion. Also *George Best undercoat, Winehouse lining paper, Keith Floyd's primer.*

undercover cop *1. n.* A plain clothes detective. *2. n.* A crafty spot of *DIY* under the bedsheets whilst the missus is in the ensuite. *3. n.* A trivial, opportunistic sexual assault committed on a crowded bus or underground train.

undercrackers *n. Underchunders.*

underdaks *n. Undercrackers.*

underkecks *n. Underdaks.*

under one's wing, take someone *v.* To perform a spot of *bagpiping.* To essay a *Hawaiian muscle fuck.*

under starter's orders *adj.* Suffering from that uncomfortable rising pressure in the lower gastric tract that signals the onset of *arse labour.* *'Christ, nan, hurry up and get out of there before I papper me trolleys, will you? I'm under starter's orders here.'*

undertaker, play the *v.* To bury a *stiff.* *'Was it okay meeting up with your ex-wife?' 'Yeah, not bad. She let me play the undertaker, anyway.'*

undertaker's privileges *n.* Acts of carnality performed by a *corpse packager* on his recently-deceased clients. Funeral director's perks. *'Wanted. Hard-working young man to train as Mortuary Attendant in a busy London hospital. Must have 4 GCSEs at grade C or above. 35 hours per week, occasional weekends. Starting salary £10,000 plus clothing allowance & undertaker's privileges.'*

under thunder *n.* Ominous rumbles from the bowels of Hell.

under the bridge *1. n.* Dwelling place of easily-dissuaded billygoat-gruff-eating trolls. *2. n. Down below.* You know, where your *unmentionables* are.

underworld *n.* A post-binge *poo* that is about 90% lager. Because it is, like the title to the eponymous group's 1996 hit record, "Born Slippy".

unexpected item in bagging area *1. exclam.* Announcement made by one who has unexpectedly found a portion of *shepherd's pie* in his *dunghampers* after *blowing off.* So named after the subtly-coded tannoy announcement which is made to alert supermarket security staff to the presence of a suspected shoplifter at one of the self-service tills. *2. exclam.* The irritated vociferation of a ladyfriend when you inadvertently attempt to *pot the brown. 3. exclam.* Shout of a chap who has just, using only the sense of touch, inadvertently identified a *Bobby dazzler.*

unisexual *1. adj.* Descriptive of one who is *self-sufficient* as long as he doesn't break his right wrist. *2. n.* A chap who lives the *good life.*

unit *1. n.* The genitals, usually male, esp. the *veiny bang stick. Pud. 2. n. Bird*, an individual piece of *talent.*

unleash the dobermans *v.* After a night on the Guinness, to let loose with a particularly savage and uncontrollable outburst of *black and tan* from the *back gate.* Let out the *boys from the black stuff.*

unless I could piss petrol *phr.* A humorous codicil to the commonly-used vituperative exclamation "I'd not piss on him if he was on fire," which can be used to rich comic effect, *viz. 'That Bono's a tosser. I'd not piss on him if he was on fire...unless I could piss petrol.'*

unload *v*. To drop a *depth charge* or launch an *air biscuit*. To empty one's *hatchback* of *shopping*.

unmentionables *n*. Roman Catholic word which enables mother-in-laws to mention genitals or underwear. *'Sweet Jesus mother of Mary, stop playing with your unmentionables, will you, and have another slice of cake.'*

unmown crease 1. *n*. An unprepared cricket pitch. 2. *n*. A particularly hirsute clopper. *Terry Waite's allotment*, a *biffer, Judith etc*.

unpleasantless *n*. The triangular tuft of hair that inexplicably sprouts under the lower lip of certain men. The *moip mop. 'How was your date last night? Do you think you'll see him again?' 'I don't think so. He sounded lush over the phone, but when he showed up in person, there was some unpleasantness.'*

unstipation *n*. Medical condition of the *back body* which necessitates trips to the *shitter* every five minutes or so. Usually caused by a heavy night on the beer and curry. *'I went to the doctor and said, "Have you got anything for unstipation?" He said yes, have this fucking bucket.'* (Routine by Bernard Stone-Age-Manning, Neanderthal stand-up comedian, 500,000 BC).

untidy sock drawer *n*. A *ripped sofa, badly-packed kebab, ragman's coat.*

unwrap the meat *v*. To *let the twins out*. Of Lord Owen, to get *his tits out for the Liberal Democrats*.

up and over like a pan of milk *euph*. Descriptive of a gentleman who is so good at sex that he can ejaculate before he's even got his pants off.

up and twichin' *adj*. The point at which the gentleman is ready to engage in the courses of love.

upchuck *v*. To *laugh at the carpet*.

upgrade *v*. To go to the *chod bin* for a *number one*, but decide to take the opportunity to have a *number two* whilst one is there. And a *wank*, time permitting.

upgrade a fart *v*. To go for a *shit. 'I would love to stand here chatting all day, Your Majesty, but I really must go and upgrade a fart.'*

uphill gardener *n*. He who sows his *seed* on the *backyard allotment*. A pusher of a *cheesy wheelbarrow* up the *lavender* path. A *crafty butcher*.

uphill wanking *n*. Masturbating over somewhat challenging *whack fodder*, for example a knitting pattern or a birthday card from one's granny.

up on blocks *adj*. Of a woman. A monthly *MOTT* failure due to a recurring leak under the *beetle bonnet*.

up periscope *n*. Bathtime game for up to one person. *Polishing the lighthouse, waxing the dolphin, making nylon.*

upstairs *n*. The *rack, top bollocks, top bum. 'What's she got upstairs?' 'Two knockers.'*

up the Beeston ginnel, one *n*. The act of *making love* up the *wrong 'un*, from the name of a narrow, malodorous passage in the environs of the notorious Leeds *shit hole. 'Tamoshanta was powerless to resist. His eyes burnt into hers like agates. His muscular arms enfolded her body as she felt herself being swept away* *on a dustpan of passion. 'I'm sorry, Your Grace, but you'll have to give me one up the Beeston ginnel this morning as I am up on blocks at present."* (from *The Milkmaid and the Bishop* by Barbara Cartland).

up the duff *adj. medic.* Up the pasture, in the pudding club.

up the gable end, do someone *v.* To *do it* up the *back passage*, if you will.

up the Jimmy Savile, to take a lady *v.* To indulge in a session of *back door work.* So called because of the warbling "eeurgh!-eeurgh!-eeurgh! now then! now then!" noises made by the lucky recipient.

up the pasture *adj. medic.* Up the poke, up the duff.

up the poke *adj.medic.* Up the stick, up the pasture.

up the stick *adj. medic.* In the club, up the poke.

up the Tregenna, take the missus *v.* To *poke* one's good lady up the *coal hole.* A phrase coined with reference to Merthyr's poshest restaurant, where the South Wales man-about-town takes his wife for birthdays or anniversaries. To have a *once a year special.*

up to the apricots *adj.* Up to the back wheels, up to the maker's nameplate.

up to the back wheels *adj.* Up to the apricots, up to the buffers.

up to the buffers *adj.* Up to the bumper, up to the cannon wheels.

up to the bumper *adj.* Up to the cannon wheels, up to the eggs.

up to the cannon wheels *adj.* Up to the eggs, up to the buffers.

up to the eggs *adj.* Up to the maker's nameplate, up to the back wheels.

up to the maker's nameplate *adv.* An engineering term for being *conkers deep.* Also *up to the boilermaker's nameplate.*

up to the wrist, go for the elbow *phr.* A more imaginative alternative to "in for a penny, in for a pound," which is much in use amongst farm vets, gynaecologists and customs officers.

up to your nuts in guts *adj. Aus.* In a *sausage and doughnut situation*, to throw oneself fully into one's work.

up to your pots *adj.* Amazingly enough, not to be *up to the apricots, wheels, buffers, bumper, cannon wheels, eggs or maker's name plate*, but to be *ripped to the tits* on drink. *Pissed, wankered, shitfaced, arseholed, refreshed.*

up, in, out and off *phr.* Comprehensive plot synopsis essential to all *grumble flicks.*

Urals, the *n.* Vague and tenuous British film comedy euphemism for the testicles. See also *the Balkans, Balearics.*

Uranus *1. n.* A large planet with brown rings around it. With a big smelly *shit* coming out a hairy hole in the middle of it. Sadly, these days it usually pronounced "Ur-arn-us" to save the blushes of Patrick Moore. *2. n. Urarse.*

urban cockerel *n.* A loud, rasping reveille emitted from under the duvet around sunrise, with enough volume to wake everyone in the street. A *dawn chorus.*

urban vibe *euph.* Term used by Kirsty Allsop on Channel Four's *Location, Location, Location* to describe an area steeped in stabbings, drugs and all manner of violent crime. *'Yeah, the Bransholme Estate certainly has quite an urban vibe, and at just eight pounds, this four-bedroom semi represents a great way to get your foot on the hous-*

ing ladder. Ooh, Phil. I think I've been shot.'

Uri *rhym. slang.* Premium Belgian lager. From cutlery-*fucking* man of mystery Uri Geller = Stella. Also *Nelson Mandela.*

Uri Geller smeller *n.* After one has dropped a major-league *nine inch nail* in the *pan*, the foulsome miasma that emanates from the smallest room and spreads round the house, bending spoons and stopping clocks as it goes.

urineapple chunks *n.* The fruit-like yellow cubes that nestle around the plughole of a *shark's mouth. Kola cubes.*

urine shroud *n.* A cotton or nylon arte-fact, clearly showing the miraculous crusty image of a *bearded clam. ie, A* pair of discarded *scads* found sunny side up on a lady's bedroom floor.

UTAH FD *1. acronym.* The people who come to the rescue when the Osmonds catch *ahad. 2. acronym.* An accommo-dating one-night-stand ladyfriend. Up The Arse Hole First Date.

UTBNB *abbrev.* Up The Bum, No Babies. A reliable, yet malodorous contraceptive device. Opposite of an IUD.

utility wank *n.* A masturbatory act car-ried out prior to a train journey, exam, Presidential Investiture *etc.*, purely to preclude the possibility of an unwanted erection taking place later. *'Tony, are you doing a speech at Lady Di's funeral tomorrow? If so, you'd best have a util-ity wank in the morning just in case you get a bone-on from the excitement.' 'Don't worry, Cherie. I'll be stood behind a lectern, and if I start getting a heavy dick I'll do what I do at PMQs and look over at Margaret Beckett.'*

vadge *n*. A *fadge*. A *fanny*.

VAG *acronym*. The Volkswagen Audi Group.

vagging out *n*. Of a young lady, the act of relaxing at the beach with legs akimbo whilst wearing a bikini, affording any less reconstructed males who happen to be passing a smashing view of their lunch.

vaggie *n*. An uncomfortable front-tuck for a lady. A vaginal *wedgie*, a *smedgie*, *vedgie*. '*A major diplomatic row errupted today after the Australian Premier gave the Queen a vaggie when she was attending the State Opening of Parliament in Melbourne.*'

vagilant *adj*. On the sharp-eyed look out for *cunker*.

vagimite *n*. Unpleasant-tasting yeast derivative, most commonly sampled *down under*.

vagimix *n*. Noisy electrical appliance which makes life easier for housewives. Usually has three speeds and is perfect for whipping up a light and frothy *batter*. A *fanny hammer, bob, neck massager*.

vagina decliner *n*. The male equivalent of a *todger dodger*. A *beaver leaver*, a *pie-shy guy*.

vaginosaur *n*. A rather mature actress in a *meat flick*.

vagitarian *n*. He who only eats *hairy pie, fur burgers,* and *vertical bacon sandwiches*. Plus the occasional *fish supper*. An inveterate *diner at the Y.*

vagitation *n*. Agitation of the *meat flower*. *Bean flicking, invisible banjo playing, gusset typing,* female masturbation.

vajayjay *n*. A *John Craven*. That which is *vajazzled*.

vajazzle *v*. To gaudily decorate Jennifer Love Hewitt's *vajayjay* by pasting a selection of Swarovski crystals onto it.

vajillion *n*. In mathematics, an unspecified but very high number, specifically referring to an innumerable multitude of *fannies*. '*Having now spent a time in excess of thirty years as the capital's leading gynaecologist, I have built up the London Surgical Home for Women into one of Europe's most pre-eminent establishments specialising in the treatment of feminine complaints. Indeed, it is scarcely an exaggeration to say that during my medical career, I have successfully treated countless ladies and performed medical procedures on a vajillion twats.*' (Preface to *On the Curability of Certain Forms of Insanity, Catalepsy and Hysteria in Females*, by Dr Isaac Baker Brown, 1866).

Valentine's day mascara *n*. *Eyelid glue.*

Valentine's day porridge *n*. *Semen-o-lina, spaff, spangle, snedge, gunk, liquid pearls.*

valley of decision *1. n*. A literary work penned by late 19th century author Edith Wharton; the story of a man who is forced to choose between two conflicting loyalties during an Italian revolution. *2. n*. The story of a man forced to choose between two conflicting loyalties during a romantic episode, *ie*. The *nipsy* or the *minge*.

vampire *n*. A *big-boned bird* who forces her fat *arse* into tight jeans, because "she obviously can't see herself in the mirror".

Van Gogh's beard *euph*. The illusion of ginger facial hair achieved by a man who has performed an act of *cumulonimbus* on a woman who *has the Post Impressionist painters in*. Named after the Dutch artist Vincent Van Gogh

(1853-1890), who painted a famous self-portrait in 1897 shortly after *licking out* his neighbour Madame Ginoux, who was *up on blocks* at the time.

vandal grease *1. n.* Substance used to deter Liverpudlians from climbing onto the tops of public buildings. *2. n.* Substance used by *botters* to lubricate their bottoms so that they can be *botted* by other *botters*.

vangina *n.* A *twat* in a white Transit who cuts you up at the roundabout.

van Halen *n.* A solo on the *one-string guitar*, either administered by oneself or an assistant, which involves "both hands on the neck". From the trademark "tapping" style of playing favoured by eponymous *rock poodle* plank spanker Eddie.

vanilla *n. US.* A term used by sadomasochists to refer to normal, respectable people, *eg.* Doctors, lawyers, *etc.* who do not share their foul perversion. Also *civilians*, *muggles*.

vanilla strip *n.* The *tinter*, the *carse*, the *taint*. A lady's perineum, named after the vanilla strip which, in a tub of Neapolitan ice cream, is found precisely between the pink and the brown.

varnished eel, stiff as a *sim.* Figure of speech which can be usefully employed when describing a long, hard thing. Such as a penis. *'I'm as disgusted, sickened, horrified and revolted by this live sex show as you are, Mrs Whitehouse. I'd walk out of the theatre too; however, I can't stand up as my nob's as stiff as a varnished eel.'*

varnish the cane *v.* To give the old *walking stick* a one-handed waxing. To *oil the bat*.

varse *n.* That strip of skin between a lady's *fanny* and her *shitter*, also variously referred to as the *taint, tinter, twernt, carse, biffon, Humber Bridge etc.*

VAT *1. abbrev.* Any *blurtch* which has been so adorned as to materially increase its appeal, *eg.* By the addition of some form of pubic topiary or a piece of erotic ironmongery in the *clematis*. Value Added Twat. *2. abbrev.* Female mammary glands which have been surgically enhanced, and are thus worth between fifteen and twenty percent more than they were originally. Value Added Tits.

Vatican roulette *n. Pull out and pray*. A method of contraception practised by *left-footers* with very large families.

V-bone steak *n.* A sumptuous, meaty meal, eaten off a *hairy plate*.

vedgie *n.* A vaginal *wedgie*. Also known as *splitting the twix*.

vein strainer *n.* A *hog's-eye*-popping *diamond cutter* of potentially life-threatening proportions, which could quite easily place intolerable demands on one's circulatory system. *Pink steel* that looks like it's in danger of going off like that bloke's head in *Scanners*.

veiny bang stick *n.* The *slag hammer*.

velcro arse *n. medic.* Descriptive of the condition of the *bum cheeks* after a long, hot day.

velcro triangle *n. Minge, mott, mapatasi*.

Velma *n.* The act of deliberately or accidentally shooting *jitler* into one's *bird's* eyes, reproducing the disorientating effects suffered by Velma from *Scooby Doo* each time she lost her glasses. *Spunkblindness. St. Valentine's Day mascara, Gabrielle, King Harold*.

venetian bind *n.* An awkward situation in which a gentleman finds himself when there isn't a curtain available to wipe his *cock* on.

Venezuela *euph*. A malodorous and dishevelled *minge*. From the line in the popular cartoon film *Avatar*, where Colonel Quaritch says: "Venezuela, that was some mean bush".

Venus *n*. A tiny *porky banger*, such as the one belonging to creepy former Lord High Chancellor and Secretary of State for Justice the Rt. Hon. Jack Straw MP. And Bobby Davro. From the fact that, like the popular planet, it is rarely visible to the naked eye and women tend to point at it and laugh. A *gnomon*.

Venus pie trap *n*. A fat lass who lies in ambush for Greggs delivery drivers.

verandah *phr*. The best joke in the film *The Three Amigos*. *'We could take a walk and you could kiss me on the verandah' 'That's OK... lips will be fine.'*

verandah over the toyshop *n. Aus*. An *ocker's* lovingly-nurtured beergut. A *one-pack, party seven, Foster's child*.

verminillionaire *n*. A lottery winner who doesn't deserve it, has a criminal record as long as your arm and spends all the money on helicopters and Ferraris. Mind you, the ones who say it won't change their lives are even worse. Bastards.

versnatche *n*. A designer *cunt*.

vertical bacon sandwich *n*. That which is clearly visible in *hamburger shots*. Also *vertical smile, vertical taco, club sandwich, haddock pastie*.

vertical eyebrow *n*. A *bush* that has been trimmed to within a quarter of an inch of its life. A *Pires's chin*.

vesser *n*. A silent *fart, SBD*.

vestal virgin *n*. A person who has never worn a vest before.

vesta vespa *n*. The two-stroke engine-like noise one's *anus* makes the morning after eating a box of the foul, dried curry substitute. Accompanied by a puff of blue smoke.

vestosterone *n*. Middle-aged male hormone caused by drinking in the afternoon during summer, an excess of which leads to the wearing of sleeveless singlets and sudden bursts of manly violence.

Vesuviarse *n*. A mighty eruption of sulphurous lava from your *fumerole* the morning after a hot curry. Named after Mount Vesuviarse, which erupted on August 24th A.D.79, burying the town of Pompeii under a superincumbent mass of hot diarrhoea. Also *Cackatoa, Stromboweli*.

vet's bin *n*. A grim old *clout*. Like a *butcher's dustbin*, but much more highly-qualified.

V festival *1. n*. An annual musical concert of some sort featuring electrically amplified guitars, which is no doubt very popular with the young people. *2. n*. A club or party which is notable for the unusually high number of nubile females in attendance. *3. n*. A lesbian *orgy*. A gathering of sweaty *twats* lip-synching.

vibration white fanny *n. medic*. A *plastic-coccupational* hazard. Semi-numbed condition of a *bird's farmyard area*, typically resulting from prolonged use of heavy duty *snatch plant*.

vibration white finger *1. n*. A medical condition which commonly affects miners and people who use powerful drilling machinery. *2. n*. Condition commonly suffered by teenage boys.

vicar's bath *n*. An emergency Sunday morning wash; face, testicles and under each arm.

vicar's calling card *n*. Sticking the *organ*

up the *reredos*. A *sting in the tail*. *Bumming*.

vicar's piss *n*. Any particularly weak beer.

Victorian photographer *n*. Any *cunning linguist* who performs under the skirts of a lady.

video cripple *n*. One who can normally walk perfectly well, but loses this ability when returning a video to the shop and has to park right outside, even if it's a double yellow line or they are restricting traffic. Similar to a *cashpoint cripple*.

video ref, go to the *v*. Humorous, rugby-based expression meaning to check the back of one's shorts following a particularly violent *back pass*, when one is unsure whether one has *touched down* or not.

viewrinal *n*. A stand-up lavatory at a club or night spot frequented by unusually well-groomed young men. Sometimes with a *water sports* enthusiast reclining in the trough, so they say. Mind you, anyone would look well-groomed next to someone who'd been lying down getting *pissed* on in a pub bog.

Vince *1. n. rhym. slang*. An excreta. From the name of Parker-out-of-*Thunderbirds* lookalike Lib Dem MP Vince Cable = *Auntie Mabel*. *2. n. rhym. slang*. The contraceptive pill. From the name of 1970s Happy Shopper Andy Williams Vince Hill = *the Benny Hill*.

vindaluminous *adj*. Descriptive of a glowing *teatowel holder* whose proprietor has over-indulged in the culinary delights of the Orient, and which can be seen glowing in the dark as he gropes his way towards the bathroom for the tenth time of the night.

Vin Diesel *1. n. prop*. Gravel-voiced, bald actor who always wears sunglasses. *2. n*. Happy Shopper wine costing less than £2, and which leaves one gravel-voiced, bald and wearing sunglasses. *Screwtop*.

vidiot *n*. A translucent, spotty youth who spends most of his time cooped up in his bedroom kidding himself he's in the magical land of Zelda and not Basingstoke.

Viennetta *n*. A rich and satisfying multi-layered toilet pudding, consisting of several alternating layers of *turd* and *bumwad*. *Bangers and mash*.

vinegar Joe *n*. The *stick vid* actor responsible for causing *porn trauma*.

vinegar string *n*. The *banjo*.

vinegar strokes *n*. Of males *on the job*, the final climactic stages of intercourse or masturbation. From the similar facial expression associated with sipping non-brewed condiment. *'Would you believe it? The phone rang just as I was getting onto the vinegar strokes. I nearly ran into the car in front.'*

vinegar tits *n*. The sort of miserable, sour-faced woman that looks, one might unfairly judge, like her *lils* would deliver neat Sarson's into the mouth of any unfortunate suckling infant, *eg*. Her off *Emmerdale* with the Jimmy Cricket hat.

viper's tongue *sim*. A figure of speech, or trope, illustrative of the bifurcated stream of micturant which issues from a urethral *meatus* which is partially occluded by post-coital *sponglement*, fossilised *smegma* or a piece of sweetcorn. *Twin jets*.

virgin oil *n*. The facial grease secreted by *scoobescent* teenagers.

virgin poo *n*. The first *turd* laid at work after the cleaning lady has scrubbed the rim.

visit from aunt Flo *euph. Having the painters in. Sheep sitting, dropping clots.*

visiting day at Preston Prison *euph.* An assortment of rough-looking women, inexpicably dressed as if going to a discotheque at ten-thirty on a Monday morning.

visit the V&A *v.* To spend a leisurely time exploring two of the more interesting exhibits *down south.*

vital organs *euph.* Breasts. *'We've got a female, mid twenties, been in an RTA. Irregular heartbeat, her breathing's erratic and shallow, she's semi-conscious with a weak radial pulse, but her vital organs are looking good.'*

vitamin P *n.* The luminescent lime green *wazz* produced after one has consumed high dose multivitamins.

vitamin S *n.* A naturally-occurring substance which men insist is very good for women when taken orally in 5ml doses. *Michael Winner's dietary supplement.*

vixen *n.* Wily *bird*, a young temptress, a foxy *chick, nymph, eg.* Stevie Nicks in about 1978.

Viz moment *n.* Time taken out of a busy day to *snap off a length of dirty spine* whilst perusing your favourite humorous magazine. Or *Viz*, for that matter.

vogue *1. n.* A briefly-fashionable pose-striking dance made popular by Madonna. *2. v.* To strike an artistic pose prior to *dropping one's guts* in order to amuse friends or charm young ladies into bed.

voice of Winehouse, face of shitehouse *n.* A cumbersome bit of terminology describing a local pub karaoke queen who, despite having a fair voice on her, has a *face like a sack of broken bells.*

void the warranty *v.* To perform a sexual act with one's partner that is clearly at odds with the maker's intentions. *'Aw go on, Sophie. Let me void the warranty.' 'Go on, then. But make it quick, will you? I'm reading the news at six.'*

vol au vent *n.* A light, savoury snack served as an appetiser before the main, sit-down event. A posh *air biscuit*. From the French meaning "a flight in the wind".

Volvo, drop a *v.* To do a *poo* that keeps its headlamps on during daylight hours and has very poor aerodynamics, but would score 5 stars in the Euro/NCAP crash tests.

vommunition *n.* Anything eaten to line the stomach before a drinking session. *'Giz some of them scratchings, mate. I need some vommunition.'*

voodoo butter *n.* The raw material of *squid marks. Ghee.*

vote for Tony Blair *v.* To rush enthusiastically into the cubicle expecting big things, only to get a pathetic little *fart.* To be constipated.

vowel and towel *n.* The daily pleasure of relieving one's internal tensions whilst watching quiz-show lexatrix Rachel Riley going about her business.

VPL *abbrev.* Visible Panty Line. A dead giveaway that a *bird* is wearing *Alans*, and therefore frigid.

Vulcan bomb doors *sim. RAF.* Huge, gaping *piss flaps*, making the *hairy pie* resemble the underside of the eponymous delta-winged bomber making a low pass over the runway at Port Stanley.

vulvo *n.* A solidly-built *fanny* which is unlikely to set your *heirbags* off, but could nevertheless withstand an offset frontal impact at 40mph and come out reasonably unscathed.

vulvuzela *n.* A *fanny fart* that sounds like kick-off in a South African football match.

vurp *n.* A burp which brings up a small but foul-tasting quantity of stomach contents which is small enough to be gulped straight back down again. A *broat, Bob's full mouth.*

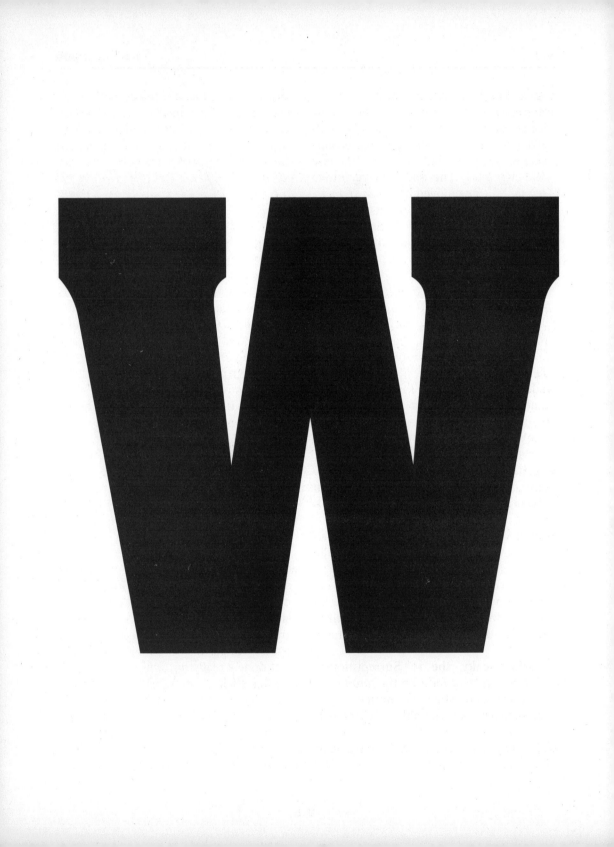

wab *n.* The *bald-headed hermit*.

wacaday *1. n.* A morning television show for children, broadcast between the mid-80s and the early 90s, starring hyperactive, bespectacled *arsehole* Timmy Mallett. *2. n.* The sad and repetitive sexual routine enjoyed by a single male.

wad *1. n.* The large sum of money which Harry "Loadsamoney" Enfield waved around after he started getting advertising work. *2. n.* That featured in a *money shot*. A small package of *hot fish yoghurt* flying out the end of a *mutton musket*. A *jizzbolt*.

wad chomper *n.* A lady who is anxious to please. One who enjoys a portion of *man pop* and sees no reason to spit it out. A *swallower*.

wade in *1. v.* To *move in for the kill* immediately prior to pulling a *bird*. *2. v.* To walk towards the centre of a *pagga*, with one's arms above one's head in order to join the fun.

wag bag *n.* A middle-aged woman who, despite her advancing years, elects to dress like the wife of a famous footballer.

Wagon Wheel *1. n.* A sickly, cream-filled confection. *2. n.* A large *cock*. From the 1980s advertising slogan for *1*. "You've got to grin to get it in".

wags to witches *euph.* The change in women from being attractive to *minging* over decades. Or overnight after a *piss up*.

Waikiki sneaky, the *n.* Surreptitiously slipping your *old fella* up the *wrong 'un* when you think she won't notice.

wail switch *n.* An excitable lady's *clematis*. *The devil's doorbell*.

waist height delight *n.* A fun-size lady, ideal for vertical *horatio* or enthusiastic

cowboy. A *laptop*, a *throwabout*.

wait for the wings, to *v.* To eagerly anticipate the demise of an elderly loved one to fund the purchase of luxury items in their memory. '*Sadly, my granny is very ill at the moment. I'm just waiting for the wings, then I'm going to get some 8 by 18-inch Wolfrace Spirit alloys for my Saxo. And a big exhaust pipe.*'

waiting for the red cheque to clear *euph.* Of a married man, to endure the monthly four to five day period of sexual limbo which occurs whilst *Aunt Flo is visiting* his wife's *below stairs areas*.

wake the wife *v.* Of a sleeping gent, who has enjoyed a surfeit of brown beer and spicy comestibles, to *let the cat out of the bag* in the middle of the night. To somnolently light a *Dutch oven*.

wake up with Jake up *v.* To have a *dawn horn, morning glory, motorcycle kickstand*. To *pitch a tent*.

walk in the country *n.* Taking a gentle stroll with the index and middle fingers through, in and around a woman's *ladygarden*. A pubic ramble.

walking condom *n.* Descriptive of a breed of young male who is up to no good in a baggy tracksuit with a hood. An *asbo*.

walking on the Moon *1. n.* The feeling one experiences after depositing a particularly weighty *Thora*, similar to that encountered by astronauts in one-sixth gravity. *2. n.* Autobiographical song written by Sting out of the Police after he'd just done a really big *shit*.

walking stick *1. n.* Long piece of nobbly wood wielded by senior citizens on buses. *2. n.* That old object upon which a fellow gives it *six nowt* whilst *relaxing in a gentleman's way*.

walking tripod *sim.* A well-endowed male,

donkey-rigged individual. When admiring *buffage,* a sexist lady might offensively remark *'Look at the third leg on that. He's a walking fucking tripod.'*

walking wounded *n. milit.* Women who go out on the pull despite the fact that they are *bleeding from a shotgun wound.* *'I wouldn't bother buying her a drink, Geordie. She's walking wounded.' 'So? She's got a mooth, hasn't she?'*

walkman shit *n.* Pairs of dead AA or AAA batteries found on bus seats and in other public places.

walk the line *v.* To go for a *Johnny Cash. 'Watch runways three, four, five and seven will you? I'm off to walk the line.'*

walk the plank *1. rhym. slang.* To masturbate. Whilst a jeering monocular unidexter jabs a cutlass in your *arse. 2. v.* To avoid *splashback* at a urinal when doing a high-pressure *gypsy's kiss* by standing three or four feet back, and avancing slowly towards the *shark's mouth* as the flow recedes.

Wallace *rhym. slang.* To vomit. From Wallace & Gromit. *'Ashley's Wallaced all over my new carpet.'*

wall of death *1. n. Attack of the helicopters. 2. n. Last hot dog in the tin.*

wallop *n. Cookin'.* Any beer bought by a hearty *twat* with a beard who calls the barman Landlord or Squire.

walnut *1. n.* The leaky washer in an old man's *waterworks.* The prostrate gland, *doughnut. 2. n.* Those annoying, little bits of feculant that "walnut" come off. *Tagnuts, dangleberries.*

walnut manoeuvre *n.* The legendary method by which good looking nurses are trained to poke one's prostrate in order to obtain an instant *Thelonious* sample.

walnut whip *1. rhym. slang.* A minor operation which removes the *cream,* but leaves the *nuts* intact. The *snip. 2. n.* A firm, cone-shaped stool that has been hollowed out and filled with a sickly cream-like substance, usually whilst a couple is exploring *the third way.*

walrus fold *n.* On a young lady with a *lovely personality,* that unsightly bulge of blubber that protrudes forwards further than her *headlamps* when she is seated.

walrus, the *n.* Another unlikely sounding, probably illegal, and certainly immoral sexual act whereby a fellow gets his ladyfriend to swallow his *mess* before karate chopping her on both sides of the neck, causing "tusks" of *jitler* to run out of her nostrils in a style reminiscent of the popular moustachioed underwater dog. *'Reader, I married him. A quiet wedding we had: he and I, the parson and clerk, were alone present. On the way back from church, I've gave Mr Rochester a nosh in the back of the carriage and he done the walrus on me.'* (from *Jane Eyre Does Milcote* by Charlotte Bronte).

Walter Raleigh *n. prop.* The selfless act of a true gentleman, *viz.* Following coitus, laying his discarded *underkegs* on the wet patch for his lady to sleep on without undue discomfort. Named in honour of the erstwhile naval hero (1552-1618), who famously laid his cloak across a puddle of *spunk* so that Queen Elizabeth I wouldn't get any of it on her shoes.

wancunian *1. n.* A *wanker* from Manchester. A *manker. 2. adj.* Descriptive of a *wanker* from Manchester.

wanderlust *n.* Masturbating whilst walking around the house, typically in order to combine the performance of mundane household chores with a nice *hand shandy. Wanderlust* can also be practised on its own, in the style of a heavy metal band lead guitar solo, accompanied by appropriate facial expressions.

wand waver *n. Flasher*, sexual exhibitionist.

wang *n. Wab.*

wangst *n.* Post-masturbatory anguish. A *wank hangover.*

wanic *n.* The state of perturbation that occurs when a wife or girlfriend returns home unexpectedly just as one is reaching the *vinegar strokes* in front of one's favourite *scud mags*. A *wank panic, jazz funk.*

wank 1. *n.* A bout of *self help.* '*If you have a wank every day you'll go blind.*' 2. *n.* Rubbish. '*Don't talk wank.*' 3. *v.* To masturbate. '*Well my brother wanks all the time and he's gone blind.*'

wankache day *n.* A special day which a fellow spends gripping a *panhandle* whilst *tossing hot batter* towards the ceiling.

wankaid *n.* Any item pressed into service by a gentleman (or dirty lady) to be used as an accessory during *relaxation, eg.* Fingerless gloves, bag of carrots, Bodyshop peppermint foot lotion, big pink electric neck massager with all veins up the side and a bit sticking out the side to go up your arse *etc.*

wank against time *n.* An anxious, *Tarzan cord*-chafing act of *self harm* indulged in during Television X's ten-minute freeview, in the hope of *dropping one's yop* before it becomes necessary to phone in one's credit card details to the topless *scrubber* on the screen.

wankarium *n.* A box room containing a chair, a computer and a sock drawer.

wankathon *n.* A single man's right arm excercise endurance test. Days of frenzied *self abuse* heralded by the arrival of a large brown envelope with a Dutch postmark. Often ends with a dehydrated and disorientated *self-harmer* being wrapped in a large sheet of tin foil and wheeled to an ambulance on a drip.

wank chaser *n.* The act of topping off any activity with a swift *one off the wrist.* '*Pardon me, your Lordship. I'm just off to the bog for a shite with a wank chaser.*'

wank clamp *n.* A hand, *spunky wrench.*

wank crank *n. medic.* Elbow.

wanker 1. *n.* One who practises a secret vice. 2. *n.* A fellow road user, a motorist at whom one waves.

wanker butter *n.* Salty, off-white spread usually eaten on cracker biscuits or toast at public schools. '*I say, Brown,*' cries *Flashman, catching Tom by the collar as he passes the older lad's study door. 'These crumpets are dry, you cursed young skulk. You know perfectly well that I always have my fags put wanker butter on my crumpets, don't you?' But alas, before poor Tom can answer, he has been dragged into Flashey's dorm to get his cheeks roasted in front of the fire by every chap in the Remove.*' (from *Tom Brown's Schooldays* by Thomas Hughes).

wankerchief *n.* A *spanky hanky, jizz sock, toss rag, j-cloth.*

wankered *adj.* See *blitzed.*

wanker's badge *n.* A moustache. From the fact that most people sporting moustaches tend also to be *wankers, eg.* Steve Wright, Des Lynam, Anne Robinson. '*Short back and sides, is it Sir? Not too much off the top and tapering at the* neck? And would you like me to trim your wanker's badge?'

wanker's block *n.* A complete absence of imagination or inspiration when trying to stimulate a reaction in the *trouser department*. Often occurs when one has the *horn* but is too *pissed* to think of anything rude.

wanker's cocoa *n.* A late night *tug* that induces a restful night's sleep. *Temazepalm*.

wanker's colic *n. medic.* Of seasoned factory/warehouse workers, a humorous diagnosis of the cause of hiccups or burps in their younger colleagues.

wanker's crisps *n.* Brittle, ready-salted tissues found under any healthy gentleman's bed. *Porn crackers*.

wanker's genie *n.* The irresistible force that resides inside one's *magic lamp* and regularly summons one to release it via a quick *magic buff*.

wanker's hankie *sim.* Descriptive of something very brittle. *'Come along to the Curry Capital, where the food is hot, the beer is cold and the popadoms are as brittle as a wanker's hankie.'* (Press release from the late Abdul Latif, Lord of Harpole).

wanker's rickets *n.* The wobbling movements of the legs caused by orgasmic weakening of the knees.

wanker's tache *n. medic.* The vertical line of hair between the navel and the top of the *pubes*. Develops as a consequence of masturbation, along with spots, hairy palms, shortsightedness, insanity and stunted growth. The *crab ladder*.

wanker's tan *n.* Ghostly pallor effected by young men who spend far too much time alone in their rooms with the curtains shut. *'I've just got Need for Speed ProStreet for Christmas, so I'll be spending the next few months working on my wanker's tan.'*

wankety blank *n.* The state of mental blockage during attempted masturbation when one's *mammary banks* are in the red. *Wanker's block*.

wank handle *n. medic.* In sex, a male erection of the penile shaft and glans. A turgid *crank*.

wank hangover *n.* Post *self abuse* self-loathing. *Wangst* which can only be assuaged by the hair of the dog.

wank hat *n.* The *titfer*-like remains on a chap's *helmet* after leaving his *nob turban* on for too long.

wank holiday 1. *n.* An exhausting day off work spent masturbating. 2. *n.* Contrariwise, a period of self-imposed abstention from *bishop-bashing*, brought on through guilt and/or severe cramp.

wankier mâché *n.* The malleable sculptural compound produced when an onanist's *love glue* mixes with his cleaning-up apparatus. *Bedroom popadoms* - also known as *wankerchiefs, porn crackers* or *wanker's crisps* - as well as *monks' trunks, crunchies* and *midget's surfboards*, are made of *wankier mâché*.

wanking and banking *n.* What most males use the internet for.

wanking chariot *n.* A single bed.

wanking ears *n.* Descriptive of the bat-like, heightened sensitivity of hearing achieved by a fellow indulging in a bit of *self discipline*, allowing him to detect the faint sound of his wife's / girlfriend's / parents' key entering the lock two floors below. *'September 2nd, 1666, Morning. Up betimes, and finding the house deserted, was minded to settle down with a hose for a brief strum over* *the corsetry pages of Mr Grattan's esti-mable catalogue. However, Mrs Pepys return'd unexpectly, and, had it not been for my wanking ears, would surely have discovered me in a most compromising situation. Afternoon. London burned down.'* (from *The Diary of Samuel Pepys*).

wanking jacket *n*. Dressing gown.

wanking Jap, grin like a *sim*. To smile broadly in the style of a *spamurai war-rior*. To *turn Japanese*.

wanking parlour *n*. Brothel, house of ill repute; any club popular with *gonks*. A *toss parlour, rub-a-tug shop*.

wanking spanners *n. Spunky wrenches, cunt scratchers, dick skinners.*

wanking studs *n. medic*. Warts on the hands or fingers.

wanking with sand, like *sim*. A reference to an act of penetrative afection per-formed up a particularly dry and barren lady's *foofoo*. *'Christ, my roundhead is sore. Her clunge was so dry it was like wanking with sand.'*

wank into her pant drawer, I'd *exclam*. A charming tribute to an attractive public figure. *'Springwatch? I couldn't give a tuppenny fuck about hedgehogs. Mind you, that Kate Humble, I'd wank into her pant drawer anytime. And now over to Daniel Corbett for tomorrow's weather.'*

wankish *adj*. Slightly useless. *Mouse, Swiss. 'That Eamonn Holmes is a bit wankish, isn't he.'*

wank jockey *n*. A chap who takes control of the arm which is providing him with *manual relief, eg*. While its owner is fast asleep.

wanklash *n. medic*. Debilitating lower back injury commonly suffered by young men who have over-reached themselves whilst *actively seeking work*. A *slipped dick.*

wank it dry *v*. To ossessively persevere with something long after it is clear that there is no more benefit to be gained, *eg*. Mohammed Al Fayed going on about his conspiracy theory, the *Daily Express* going on about Mohammed Al Fayed's conspiracy theory, BBC News 24 news-paper reviewers mentioning the head-lines on the front of the *Daily Express*. *'Christ, not Norman Collier doing his broken microphone routine again. He wanked that dry thirty years ago on the Wheeltappers' and Shunters' Social Club.'*

wankle 1. *n*. A type of rotary engine. 2. *n. medic*. The wrist. From wank + ankle.

wank lyrical *v*. To praise someone or something so enthusiastically that an observer may gain the impression that the speaker is about to *knock one off* over them or it, *eg*. Football pundit Clive Tildsley when talking about Manchester United or John Terry.

wank-me-downs *n. Bongo mags* inherited from an elder brother or friend. Also *one-hand-me-downs. Pubic hairlooms.*

wank or bank *n*. The quandary faced by a gentleman who must decide whether to *knock himself about a bit* or conserve his fluids until his ladyfriend's next visit when he can *make a deposit.*

wank out a bollock *v*. To masturbate furi-ously until a *spud* is loosened.

wank outsider *n*. A chap who prefers the hedgerow to the bedroom as a location for a *five knuckle shuffle.* An *al fresco onanist.*

wank pie *n*. Something third rate, *eg*. Any programme with Jimmy Carr in it.

wankquiliser *n.* A self-administered, stress-relieving bedtime *knockout yop*. A *knuckle nightcap, pullaby, sleeping pull*.

wank robber *n.* Onanistically speaking, a parent who, returning home unexpectedly early, robs their teenage son of his *money shot*.

wankroll, put her on the *exclam.* Phrase used by a businessman when deciding to employ a pulchritudinous young female, despite the fact that her CV may not be quite as impressive as those of certain other candidates. *'Let's cut the bollocks, darling, you're a lightweight, you're a quitter, you're a schmoozer and you're a bullshitter. And let me tell you this, I don't like lightweights, I don't like quitters and I don't like bullshitters. But when I saw you bending over to open the filing cabinet I thought Alan, do yourself a favour. Put her on the wankroll. Michelle, you're hired.'*

wankrupt *adj.* Descriptive of one who has *spent his wad* and has an empty *pod purse*.

wank seance *n.* Whilst *pulling one's pud*, the eerie feeling that one is being watched disapprovingly by dead relatives. Also *Doris Strokes*.

wank slacks *n.* Type of dirty tracksuit trousers, designed to afford the wearer easy and unencumbered manual access to his *fruit bowl* at short notice. Worn by students, jobseekers and other people who find themselves spending a lot of time lounging round the house. *'Have you seen my smart trousers, Jane? I've got an interview this afternoon.' 'They're in the wash, Jonathan. Why don't you just put your wank slacks on? Your legs will be behind your desk, and everybody will be looking at Madonna anyway.'*

wanksmith *n.* An enthusiastic or workmanlike *onanist*.

wank sock *n.* Cylindrical cloth item tied to a bedpost, designed to indicate when wind conditions are suitable for *monkey spanking*.

wank stain *n. Bum scrape, piss flap, dip shit, toss pot*. General purpose insult. *'Oi, I said a Crunchie McFlurry, you fucking wank stain.'*

wankster's paradise *euph.* A situation or period in a man's life, for the duration of which all barriers to repeated acts of *self-pollution* are removed, *eg.* Solitary confinement, attending university, being trapped in a lift for a Bank Holiday weekend, accidentally getting locked overnight in a porn warehouse or a career in journalism. *'Ever since my wife was hospitalised / 'bin livin' in wankster's paradise.'*

wankstop *n. medic.* The flange that prevents the *wanking spanner* disengaging from the end of the *shaft* when revving your *single cylinder engine*. The *brim* of the *herman gelmet*. The *sulcus*.

wank tanks *n. Balls, nads, knackers*.

wank Tardis *n.* A blue portable lavatory of the sort frequented by builders during their teabreaks.

wankticipation *n.* Feeling of hollow, mounting excitement experienced by a man sitting in front of his computer with his trousers round his ankles and his *pink mouse* in his hand, whilst he waits for his *cyber scud* to download.

wanktique *n.* An ancient *rhythm pamphlet*, such as a dog-eared 1978 *Whitehouse* found behind some tins of paint in your late grandfather's garage.

wankton *n.* A unicellular life-form that

inhabits the shallow waters of the bath after a session of *dolphin waxing. Dutch jellyfish, nylon squid, frigspawn.*

wankupuncture *n.* Ancient, tried-and-tested alternative therapy self-administered by ailing gentlemen. The belief that the symptoms of an illness can be ameliorated, if not cured completely, by a quick *hand shandy.* The *placebone effect.*

wank window *n.* An opportune moment during which a crafty gentleman can enjoy a swift bout of *relaxation. 'A woman tells her husband she is just popping to the shops to get a pint of milk and a loaf of bread. The shops are 4 miles away and her husand knows that his wife's car travels at an average speed of 22 mph. He also knows that his wife will spend ten minutes selecting each of the items from the shelves of the supermarket and a further twelfth of her total journey time queuing at the till. For how long is the man's wank window open?'* (Associated Examining Board GCE Applied Mathematics paper, Summer 1986).

wank xerox *1.n.* One who *knocks one out* repeatedly throughout the day, only to find the quality diminishes as his *toner* runs out. *2. n.* Masturbating over and over again to the same *jazz mag. Groundhog wanking.*

wanky *adj.* Self-indulgent, pretentious, *eg. Newsnight Late Review.*

wankydextrous *n.* Blessed with the gift of being able to manually pleasure a gentleman using either hand with equal facility. *'Have you met my granny, your Holiness? She's wankydextrous you know.'*

wannocks *n.* The area of no-man's land between the *nuts* or the *fadge,* and the *ringpiece.* The *biffin bridge, notcher, barse, taint, tintis, twitter, scranus.*

wanquility *n.* The all-too-brief post-*toss* period of serenity experienced immediately before the loathing, self-hatred, *wangst* and shame set in.

wanxious *adj.* Anxious for a *wank.* Derivation unknown.

wapp off *v.* To masturbate furiously over a two-inch pornographic image on your phone, which has cost you several pounds. One of the many benefits of third generation mobile communications technology.

wap-waps *n. medic.* A lady's mammary glands. *'Now, Mrs Johnson, if you'll just get your wap-waps out, I'll start the examination.'*

warm Norman *n.* A *hotplate, Cleveland steamer.*

warm up the choirboys' breakfast *n.* Of a vicar, to *relax in a gentleman's way.*

warning George and Gracie *n.* To emit a long, drawn-out *basso profundo Bakewell tart* that resembles plangent whalesong and hence could have been used to warn the two humpback cetaceans, George and Gracie, about the whaling vessel they were about to encounter in the film *Star Trek IV.*

war paint *n.* Of *birds* getting ready to go out at night, their make-up. *Fuck dust.*

warren *n.* Generic term for one not blessed with attractive features. From "Warren ugly bastard".

warthog whammies *n.* Fantastic *chudle-ighs* on an ugly woman. *Hefferlumps.*

wartime searchlights *n.* Descriptive of the amusingly dis-collimated vision of one who is in an advanced *state of refreshment,* whose eyes appear to be independently raking the heavens for incoming Heinkel bombers. *'Look out everyone, Ronnie's got his wartime searchlights on.'*

Warwick Passage fayre *n*. Ugly, rough or slatternly women. A reference to the alley next to the Old Bailey where the wives and girlfriends of the accused traditionally await access to the public galleries of the courtroom, saying "My fella never done nothing, bless", and other lies.

washing machine doors *n*. Swirling, export strength *beer goggles*.

Washington refill *n*. The type of night-time urination carried out in a rush in order to return to the warmth of one's bed as soon as possible. From the speedy nature of petrol station customers in Washington DC and surrounding districts during their 2002 Beltway sniper shenanigans.

wash the cosh *v*. To polish the *love truncheon, oil the bat*.

wasping *n*. Cruising well-known *dogging* hotspots around one's locale with a ready-made excuse to hand in case of unwelcome constabulary interest, *viz*. "But I'd just stopped to let a wasp out of the car, officer, honest."

waste *n*. An attractive feature on an otherwise unattractive individual. *'Jesus. Have you seen the chebs on that Kerry Catona, your grace?' 'I know, Archbishop. What a fucking waste.'*

waste the morning *v*. To *relax in a gentleman's way*. *'I wasted the lot of the morning and then felt guilty all afternoon.'* (from *Tony Benn's Diaries*, Sunday March 18th 2007).

watching Trisha *euph*. Of a female lady taking time off work, lying in bed furi-ously *flicking her bean*. *'What did you do while you were off sick?' 'Well, there's not really a lot you can do when you've got the swine flu. Mainly I just stayed in and watched Trisha.'*

water babies *1*. *n*. Aquatic fairies featured in the Victorian novel by Charles Kingsley. *2*. *n*. Floating clumps of semi-congealed *merry monk* in the bath, toilet, *Sunday Times* restaurant critic's drinking glass *etc*. *Frigspawn*.

watering can wazz *n*. The uncontrollable multi-directional *gypsy's kiss* taken after a bout of *horizontal jogging* or a *five knuckle shuffle*.

water music, play Handel's *v*. To swish one's *tallywhacker* around whilst doing a *number one*, in order to create melodious sounds from the water, porcelain, toilet seat, adjacent carpet and pile of old copies of *Viz* which you are about to put on eBay. Best performed whilst *heavily refreshed* at 2.30 am.

water puppies *n*. Term used by swimming pool lifeguards to draw each other's attention to a large pair of *milky swingers* bobbing playfully up and down whilst their owner does the backstroke.

water sports *n*. *Recreational Chinese singing*. European way of expressing romantic feelings for another person by *pissing* onto their face, *etc*.

Watney houston *n*. A *discount diva* who, after downing a few pints, will tunelessly belt out pompous tear-jerking anthems over the jukebox. A bit like Whitney Houston, if you believe what you read in the papers.

waving a sausage in the Albert Hall *n*. Sticking one's *cock* in a *fanny* that can seat five thousand people and the London Symphony Orchestra.

wax one's slats *v.* Of a woman, to *play the invisible banjo* until her *blip tap* begins to drip.

wax the bonnet *v.* To *spoff* over a *bird's* bodywork, then lean over and polish it in until the desired shine is achieved.

wax the dolphin *v.* To *polish the lighthouse.*

wazoo *n. Jacksie, anus.*

wazz *v.* Variously to *piss*, to *puke*, to *wank.* 'Who's *wazzed* on the bathroom floor?' Erm...'It might be me, mum. What sense of wazz are you using?'

wazzed *adj. Pissed* on, *puked* on and *wanked* off. And *pissed up*, come to think of it. 'Ollie, you're completely wazzed.'

wazzock *n.* Mild northern insult for a great, useless, spawny-eyed, parrot-faced person.

weakender *1. n.* One who frequently calls in sick on a Monday and/or a Friday. *2. n.* Any punchline-free sketch - that is to say any sketch at all - on Radio 4's erstwhile topical comedy show *Weekending.*

wear a Twyfords collar *v.* To *drive the porcelain bus*, to *shout soup*, to *yoff*, call Ralph on the great white telephone.

Wearside vines *n.* Exposed outcrop of *Annabels* which looks for all the world like an attractive bunch of Gamay grapes, glistening on a sun-kissed slope.

wear the beard *1. v.* To perform *cunning linguistics* on a woman. *To impersonate Stalin. 2. v.* Of *bean flickologists*, to be the *stone.* 'You can tell which one of them two wears the beard.'

weathered on *1. adj.* Of North Sea offshore workers, to be unexpectedly stranded on an oil rig due to poor meteorological conditions and have nothing to do but sit about and *wank*, and thus *2. adj.* Descriptive of the dejected mien of a man whose missus has *fallen to the communists.*

we 'avin' 'em or no? *exclam. Corn. dial.* Poetic prelude to the West Country act of love.

webbed tits *n. Frankentits* of elderly Hollywood actresses with a highly-stressed membrane between, caused by the sheer weight of *blimplants.*

webcamouflage *n.* The use of cheaply-available photo editing software to "clean up" low resolution internet-sourced images of rough women, thus making them suitable fodder for *relaxation.* Using the technique, superficial blemishes such as spots, scars, wrinkles, varicose veins, stretchmarks, bruises, boils, herpes and prison tattoos *etc.* become difficult, if not impossible, to detect. Especially if the perpetrator's eyesight isn't very good. And it won't be, all things considered.

wedding milk *n. Spingle, spangle, spint, spongle, spadge, spedge, spidge, spodge, spudge, etc. Spunk.*

wedding tackle *n.* The male genitalia. Also *wedding furniture, wedding vegetables.*

wedge *v.* To pull another's *bills* up the crack of their *arse.*

wedgie *n.* Nickname of politician Anthony Wedgwood Benn, who's *bills* are always getting pulled right up the crack of his arse.

wedgie, atomic *n.* The act of pulling someone's *bills* up the *crack* of their *arse* with a dockyard crane, whilst their shoes are bolted to the floor.

wed zeppelin *n.* A former *looker* who, once she has got married, lets herself go and fills up with hydrogen. And then explodes in a ball of flame at Lakehurst Naval Air Station, New Jersey, killing 36 of the people on board her.

wee heid rules the big heid *phr. Scot.* Descriptive of the moment when a gentleman, usually wearing *beer goggles*, decides that sexual intercourse with the woman he has just met and whose name he does not know is the correct course of action.

wee-hole surgery *n.* Do-it-yourself medical experiments carried out by bored bachelors, involving the insertion of foreign objects into the urethra. *'Is there a man doctor I can see please, nurse? Only it's a bit delicate. I was doing a bit of wee-hole surgery and I've got a propelling pencil lead stuck in my hog's eye.' 'I'll just see if there's anyone available, Mr Brown. It is Mr Brown, isn't it? The former publisher?'*

weekend flat in Brighton, to have a *v.* Of a gentleman, to be a *good listener* on a part-time basis. Likewise of a woman, to be an occasional *consumer of tufted wilton*. To be *half rice half chips*.

weenie *n. US.* Penis. Also *wienie, wiener.*

weenie waggler *n.* A *wand waver.*

weenis *n.* A minuscule *veiny bang stick*, such as those sported by jockeys, Channel swimmers, Arctic explorers and former Lord High Chancellor and Secretary of State for Justices.

weeze *v.* To experience a genital *organism* without producing any bodily fluid. To fire the *air pistol.*

weft *n.* Lady's *pubes*, which are all lying in one direction after she has been wearing particularly tight briefs. *Twat nap.*

weggy *adj.* Of a flatulent emission, to be wet and eggy. From wet + eggy. *'Open the window, Buzz. that's a weggy one.'*

weigh anchor *v.* To drop an immensely large *turd*, being careful not to break the porcelain.

weighing up the poos and cons *v.* The process by which a public lavatory visitor must compare the lamentable states of the various adjoining *shit-pots* available before deciding which one to patronise with his *arse*'s custom.

we just lost the moon *exclam.* Phrase used by Tom Hanks in the film *Apollo 13*, which can also be used to great effect in everyday life when something goes drastically wrong and you are unable to reach your objective but have to go through the motions nevertheless. For example, when a fellow is having to *bang* his *pissed* wife at her instigation and he knows that there's no way on God's earth that his *taddies* are going for a swim tonight.

welcome to Monkton Manor m'lady *exclam.* Useful phrase which can be usefully employed by a gentleman at the moment of ejaculation in order to maintain a composed and dignified facial expression.

welder's bench, face like a *sim.* An ugly woman. Also *blind cobbler's thumb, burglar's dog, box of frogs, sack of chisels, bag of spanners.*

welder's shoelaces, fanny like a *sim.* Evocative phrase which is descriptive of the state of a particularly unkempt *lady-garden*. From the visual similarity to the said artisan's footwear fastening appurtenances, which have typically been frazzled and re-tied many times. *'Sorry pet, but I'm going to call it a day. You've got a fanny like a welder's shoelaces. It's like bobbing for apples in a bucket of* *pipecleaners down here.'*

well fair state *n*. The state of drunkenness only achievable for many on Giro day.

well man clinic *n*. The *smallest room*, *water closet* or *shite house*. From the fact that it is the only health check a real man ever needs. A *squaddie's medical*.

well-presented *adj*. Of a large-breasted lady, wearing a low-cut top and, for example, riding a bike with low handle-bars, so that she is leaning forwards as she pedals, thus giving a delightful pros-pect to any gentleman aproaching from the opposite direction. *'Whilst driving into work this morning, there was a very pretty lady cycling towards me. She was so well-presented that I mounted the pavement. With all Benny Hill music playing and that. And now over to Daniel Corbett for tomorrow's weather.'*

well struck Sir! *exclam*. An amusing remark which can be used immediate-ly after someone has hit *a corker* for six with their *arse*. Also *what's that, Sweep?*

well thumbed *adj*. Much consulted or handled, *eg*. The state of Will Self's Thesaurus and (reference to Ulrika Jonsson removed on legal advice).

welly top *sim*. A term used to describe the larger *billy goat's mouth*. A *yawn-ing donkey*. *'That (reference to Ulrika Jonsson removed on legal advice) must have a fluffit like a welly top.'*

welly tubbies *n*. Small, fat lasses squeezed into *slag wellies*, and out *on the lash*. So-called due to their similarity to the children's TV characters, in both their appearance and limited vocabulary.

Welsh *n*. Masturbation while listening to a male voice choir.

Welsh letter *n*. Same as a *French letter*, but with a leak.

Welshman's cock *sim*. Descriptive of someone who is short and thick, *eg*. Dennis Wise.

Welsh mist *n*. A particularly dense and clammy *fart* which hovers around ankle level and chills the bones.

Welsh salad, go for a *v*. To urinate, go for a *leak*. From the Welsh national vegetable, the pea.

Welsh shot *n*. The knocking back of the contents of a *smeg cup*. A *Dutch oyster*.

wenchmarking *n*. The practice amongst gentlemen of comparing the carnal per-formance of their repective ladyfriends.

Wendy *n*. An uncomfortable front tuck for a lady. A vaginal *wedgie*, a *vaggie*, *vedgie*.

Wendy's melt *1. n. US*. A sandwich served at the popular eponymous fast-food res-taurant, consisting of two prime strips of beef, bacon strips, cheese and mayon-naise in between. *2. n*. A *ladyburger*.

werecow *n*. A nice, pleasant woman who mysteriously transforms into a right *fucking cow* once a month.

we're gonna need a bigger boat *exclam*. From the famous scene in the fish-based film *Jaws*. A witty apophthegm follow-ing the release of an ominous-sounding double-bass-like *Bakewell tart*, which implies that the *benefactor* is liable to an imminent attack from a *great brown shark* which could well leave him ripped in two and bleeding profusely below the waterline.

we're over Dresden *exclam*. Phrase used by someone who is about to open his *bomb-bay doors* in advance of a *heavy drop*, in the certain knowledge that expe-diency must over-ride any ethical consid-erations.

west country trim *n*. Yokel alternative to a *Brazilian* or *Hollywood wax* which is situated somewhere between a *landing strip* and *Terry Waite's allotment* on the feminine intimate grooming spectrum. A rudimentary trim of the *spider's legs* sticking out the sides of the large pants using the wallpaper scissors, before trotting off to the local barn dance. *Luton airport*.

western grip *n*. Manner of *wanking* in which the *cock* is held as a rodeo rider holds onto his steer, *ie*. With the fingers of one hand on top, the thumb underneath and the other hand waving a hat behind his head.

West Kent Hunt *rhym. slang*. A lady's *bodily treasure*. Famously mispronounced as "cunt" by *West Kent Hunt*-like disc jockey Nicky Campbell on two separate occasions during the same breakfast programme on Radio 5Live.

wet as an otter's pocket *sim*. Descriptive of the moistness of an object, *eg*. A face flannel, a raincoat, a *frothing gash*.

wet cress, eat *v*. During an act of man-on-lady, or indeed lady-on-lady, oral-type sex, to munch on a bit of exceptionally moist *gorilla salad*.

wet dream *n*. A night-time reverie which leads to *milmed jim-jams*. Can be avoided either by having a cold bath or a right good *pull* into a sock before retiring.

Wetherspoon's run *n*. A trip to one's nearest Wetherspoon's pub for the sole purpose of *laying a cable* in one of their spotlessly-clean, luxury cubicles, thus avoiding the *shit/puke/spunk*-covered seats of the average drinking house *bogs*. *'Watch me pint lads, me taxi's here. I'm just off on a Wetherspoon's run.'*

wet Hurst *n*. A *Wolstenholme*. The final bit of *piss* which waits until the *cock* is safely back in the trousers before dribbling out causing a *wet penny in the pocket*. From the commentary describing Geoff Hurst's final goal in the 1966 World Cup final. "They think it's all over... it is now".

wetmare *n*. A dream that is both wet and a nightmare. A *wet scream*.

wet one *1. n*. A pre-moistened cleaning tissue. *2. n*. An untrustworthy *fart*, possibly a *twin tone* that would require the use of *1*. A pre-moistened *Bakewell tart*.

wet penny in your pocket *n*. A circular *piss*-stain on the trouser frontage, caused by insufficient shaking of the *wang*.

wet season *n*. That time of the month when the *crimson tide* comes in. *Blow job week*.

wet scream *n*. A nocturnal erotic reverie in which the *vinegar strokes* are marred by the dawning realisation that one's sexual partner is one's mother/granny/ Janet Street-Porter *etc*.

wetsuit *1. n*. In sub-aquatic pursuits, a protective rubber garment worn whilst one plumbs the murky depths. *2. n*. In *sub-bridge* pursuits, a protective rubber garment worn whilst one sticks one's *cock* up a *clunge*.

wet the baby's head *v*. To have intercourse with a woman who has a *bun in the oven*. To *tickle the baby*. *'And so it was that Mary and Joseph came to an inn in Bethlehem. And Mary was heavy with child and the innkeeper spake unto them saying, Behold, there is no room at the inn. And Joseph replied unto him saying, Yea, we have travelled from Nazareth, and my wife is heavy with child, and I have great need to wet* *the baby's head. And he gave unto the innkeeper a wink. And lo the wink was cheeky.'* (from *Matthew*).

wet your whistle *1. v.* To pop into the pub for a drink in order to stop your hands shaking. *v.* When *dropping the kids off at the pool*, to suffer an unexpected splash of water up your *nipsy*.

whackademy award *n.* Any of the various accolades which are conferred upon the makers of *bongo flicks* in recognition of excellence in a particular field, *eg.* The Palms d'Or. *Toscars*.

whacknicolour *n.* The luridly-alluring, garishly-hued inks with which *seed catalogues* are printed.

whack off *v.* To pleasure oneself manually, for example onto a *TV's ass*.

whackpot *n.* A windfall of *grumble* that unexpectedly comes the way of a lucky gentleman. *'I tell you what, I really hit the whackpot when I got the job of clearing the effects of the late poet and lifelong jazz enthusiast Philip Larkin from his house.'*

whacksmith *n.* A workmanlike masturbator who seems intent on beating his *pork sword* into a *ploughshare*. *'Birthdays: Tom Wolfe, journalist and author; 74, Jonathan Ross, TV & radio presenter, film reviewer, interviewer, whacksmith, 48.'* (from *The Times*, March 2nd 2007).

whalesong *n.* A melodic, though slightly eerie, sequence of whines, squeaks, clicks and whistles that emanate from a toilet cubicle.

whaletail *1. n.* A laughable aerodynamic feature favoured by the smaller-penissed car driver. *2. n.* The unsightly effect produced when a lady in ill-fitting jeans's *throng* rides up her *arse crack*.

whammers *n.* Bazoomas, Gert Stonkers, big tits.

whanger *n.* An extremely large *wang*.

what's that, Skippy? The miners are in trouble? *exclam.* Witty interjection following a voluble *horse and cart*.

what's that, Sweep? *exclam. interrog.* Amusing rhetorical expression which can be used to fill the silence following a high-pitched, wavering *Bakewell tart*. From the catchphrase of late Yorkshire-based Sooty puppeteer Harry Corbett when responding to his mute star's comedy dog sidekick's squeaky interlocutions. Also *someone's tinkered with Herbie; more tea vicar?*

wheek *v. Scot.* To remove *jobbies* from an aeroplane toilet.

wheelie bint *n.* A woman so ugly that she only gets taken out once a week. In the dark. By dustmen.

whidgey *n. Front bottom.*

whiffhanger *n.* A *dropped gut* so pungent that it clings to your *duds*. A *velcro fart*.

whiff of lavender *n.* Of a marriage, the suspicion of a *beardsome* bride. *'I don't know about Edward. There's a distinct whiff of lavender about that marriage if you ask me, Phil.'*

whiff of the cat's breath *n.* A *fanny fart* or *queef*. A fishy gust from the wife's *whiskers*.

whinge drinker *n.* An overly-*refreshed* patron of licensed premises who insists upon sharing his problems - be they marital, financial, professional or whatever - with any of his fellow drinkers who are unfortunate enough to inadvertantly make eye contact with hm.

whip round, to have a *v.* To r*elax in a gentleman's way* into a coachdriver's hat.

whirling pits *n.* Attack of the *helicopters, wall of death.*

whirly wheel challenger *n.* Something which drops to the ground unexpectedly, *eg.* A small nugget of excrement which hits the landing carpet when you are shuffling across to the *bogroll* cupboard.

whisker biscuit *n.* A *fur burger.*

whisker pot *n. Fanny, minge, whidgey.*

whistle down the Y-fronts *v.* To *fart,* pass wind.

whistling gorilla *n.* An inviting and voluptuous *toothless gibbon.*

whistling in the dark *n. Muff diving,* eating *hairy pie.*

white arrow angels *n.* Van-driving messengers who bring catalogue goods to those ill-equipped to afford them.

whitecastleassitis *n. medic.* Alimentary canal condition afflicting up to 90% of the US population, caused by consumption of that country's most infamous small burgers, six at a time, steamed and lavished with onions. *Whitecastleassitis* is principally symptomised by the passage of stools which are indistinguishable from the said burgers - affectionately known as *belly bombers* - in both appearance and odour.

white knuckle ride *n.* A solo thrill which makes your eyes bulge and lasts about three minutes. *One off the wrist.*

white lightnin' Hopkins *n.* An *al fresco* beverage enthusiast who is wont to sing about his woes to the world in general. Also *blind drunk Lemon Jefferson.*

white mouse *n.* Tampon. A *cotton mouse, fanny mouse, chuftie plug, jampax.*

white-out! *exclam.* When two large, pale breasts are exposed.

white pointers *n.* Extremely impressive *tits* found inhabiting a wet T-shirt.

Whitesnake, going for a *n.* The act of sloping off to indulge in a bit of *one-handed worm-burping.* From the lyrics to the famous song by the erstwhile Middlesbrough-based poodle rockers, *viz.* "Here I go again on my own / Going down the only road I've ever known".

whitewash the hall *v.* To *spoff* up a lady's *cunt.* A far more fulfilling job than *painting the ceiling.*

whitewater wristing *v.* To rapidly paddle the *skin boat.* To *pull your pud,* masturbate.

white wee-wee *n.* Planet Skaro Dalek term for semen.

white witch *1. n.* A believer in - and practitioner of - magic who uses her evil powers for good. *2. n.* A dirty *slapper* who doesn't mind getting covered in *spunk.* A willing *plasterer's radio, cock mess monster* or *quattro formaggio.*

Whitney dressed as Britney *n.* Descriptive of a lady who's done a few miles, and is gamely attempting to turn the clock back. *Mutton dressed as lamb.*

Whitfield tan *n.* The blue and red tartan effect often seen on the legs of residents of Dundee's premier housing development, achieved by the simple expedient of sitting in front of a two-bar electric fire. *The Whitfield tan* is a look which is always in fashion amongst those who choose to opt out of the work ratrace.

whiztits *n.* Unusually conicular breasts. Named after the seldom-loved children's television show which featured a crudely-animated magic cone with the voice of balding confabulist Paul Daniels. *Dunce's hats.*

whoof *v.* To *fart* at a burglar.

whoof whoof! *1. exclam.* Term of approval directed at passing *talent.* '*Whoof*

whoof! Give that dog a bone.' 2. *exclam.* Term of disapproval aimed at passing women who haven't made the effort to look attractive.

whoops a gaysy *n.* Of a gentleman, slipping over in an effeminate manner whilst emitting an unexpectedly girly whimper.

whoopsy *n.* A *piss* or *shit*, usually done by a cat in Frank Spencer's beret.

whore d'oeuvres *n.* The unnecessary appetizers before the main course at a massage parlour, *ie.* The massage.

whoredrobe *n.* the special place where, in a bloke's opinion, his girlfriend keeps her best outfits.

whore from Fife *n. derrog.* A term of abuse that incorporates the two insults of being a whore and of coming from Fife. *'Hey, you've just taken my last fag, you whore from Fife.'*

whore frost *n.* A *good time girl's* sudden change of attitude once the *dirty deed* is done.

whoreganisation *n.* Of a commercial traveller, the practice of sorting out the order of his evening's entertainment using the contact ads section of the *Daily Sport* and a highlighter pen. Perhaps whilst sitting in a Vauxhall Vectra outside a Little Chef situated just off the A1 north of Newcastle upon Tyne.

whoregasm *n.* The unconvincing, appreciative noises made by a *lady of the night* to persuade her customer that he is getting his money's worth, despite sensory evidence to the contrary.

whore licks *n.* Malty bedtime drink for a gentleman or lady, consisting of either warm *spongle* or a *furry cup* of *kitten tears.*

whoremark *n.* A small tattoo on a lady's lower back, aping the classy style originally adopted by porn actresses. A *tramp stamp* or *slag tag.*

whore's bath *n.* An act of personal hygiene practised by ladies of the lower orders; a brief, yet fulsome handwash of the *undercarriage* often performed at a sink. *Rinsing the lettuce.*

whore's brass *n.* The shiny Lizzie Duke *tack* found decorating women in southern pubs. *Bingo clink.*

whoreshoes *n.* Fashionable pink stilettos. *Fuck me shoes.*

whoresome *adj.* Heaving with easy *blart.* *'Hey lads, it's going to be a great night. I've heard this place is whoresome.'*

whorienteering *n.* The time-honoured bachelor's habit of following his genital compass and journeying to the exotic far east in search of *pros.*

whorism *n.* The horizon-broadening practice of travelling the world to experience different and exotic cultures via the medium of going with prostitutes.

whorist *n.* A person who is prepared to trek to far-flung destinations in order to expand his cultural *whorizens.*

who's the daddy? *exclam. interrog.* Another one of those phrases which can be shouted after one has *dropped* a noisily noisome *gut.*

why, are you hungry? *exclam.* Humorous riposte to someone who asks if one has *farted.*

whybrows *n.* The bizarre tonsorial result of a lady armed with a pair of tweezers and an eyebrow pencil, *eg.* Theresa Gorman.

wick *1. n.* Penis. See *dip your wick.* *2. n.* Nerves, *tit ends.* *'I wish that Tim Westwood would fuck off. He really gets on my fucking wick.'*

wicked pisser *n. US.* A good egg or a

good show, top notch person or experience. As in *'Thank you very much for your kindness and generosity. You really have been the most wicked pissers. My name's Bing Crosby. Goodnight.'*

wicker basket *n.* A matted and tangled *bush* in which the previous night's *clacker lacquer* has been allowed to dry out.

widdle *1. n.* Childish term for a *wee wee*. *2. v.* To do some *wee wee*.

wide on *n.* Female equivalent of a *hard on, a slop on*.

widow wanky *n.* The first despondent, but necessary, *act of self violation* indulged in after the wife or girlfriend has left for good.

widow's memories *n.* Penis-shaped sausages, cucumbers *etc.* Indeed, anything vaguely cylindrical in a supermarket which is fingered nostalgically by old ladies.

widower's tears *n.* The involuntary dribble of *spunk* from the end of a long-disused *cock.*

widower's tickle *n.* The short burst of pleasure a man experiences when he flushes whilst in a sitting position and his *three piece suite* is caught in the spray. A thrill of almost Netto cheapness.

wifebeater *1. n.* An unnecessarily strong lager. *Wreck the hoose juice. 2. n.* US. A string vest or singlet, usually worn with a pair of shorts.

wifectomy *n.* An extremely painful divorce. One invariably experiences an *OPE* during the operation.

wife saver *n.* The new 4% Stella, as opposed to full-strength *wifebeater.*

wife's radar *n.* A lady's bat-like ability to detect the merest rustle of a *jazz mag* from a hundred yards.

wifestyle *n.* The expensive and excessive level of comfort in which one must keep one's good lady, in order to ensure regular and unencumbered access to her *quim* and *charlies.*

wifetamer *n.* An impressive *weapon* that affords one the respect of one's spouse, like a whip and chair would on a lion in a circus. A *cuntbuster.*

Wigan rosette *n.* The state of the *freckle* after a particularly fierce *all nighter*. A *Johnny Cash.*

wil *n.* A lady's *snarse, tinter, taint, carse,* whatever. Her perineum. So-called because it is situated "between the *Gary* and the *Mott*".

WILF/wilf *acronym.* Term used when referring to the sexier *chavettes*, office cleaners, burger van girls *etc.*, which one encounters in the course of one's daily round. Wilkinson's shopper I'd Like to Fuck.

Wilfrid *n.* The spontaneous retraction of the prepuce, exposing the *bellend.* Named after the character whose domed head pokes out the top of his pullover in *The Bash Street Kids.*

Wilkinson, to do a *v.* To perform a defecation in a hovering, squatting position over a *pissy*-seated pub *bog*. From the pose's similarity to the hands-clasped, sticky-out-*arsed* stance struck by rugby star Jonny before he makes a kick and goes off injured.

willets *n.* A type of *jugs.*

willie *n.* A ten-foot penis that has to be cut with a rake. *John Thomas, Percy the pork swordsman*, he who gives *Gert Stonkers* a *pearl necklace*. The *tassel*, the *Peter*, the *charlie*. Also *willy.*

willie and the hand jive *n.* Rhythmic,

throbbing cork-popping combo who perform the *Bologna bop* among other dances.

willie-metres *n.* Any flattering unit of measurement that enhances the teller's side of the story, *eg.* Any sweating bloke on *Booze Britain* recounting the quantity of drink he has thrown down his neck on a particular evening will invariably measure that amount in *willie-metres*; likewise any correspondent stating the length of his *cock* in a letter to a *jazz mag. Dog inches. 'Mr. Speaker - the Chancellor's fiscal forecast seems so extraordinary that one has to conclude that he is now running the country's economy in willie-metres.'*

willie welly *n. French letter, French safe, English overcoat.*

willie woofter *rhym. slang. Fruit feeler, spud fumbler.*

willipedes *n.* Genital arthropods. *Mechanical dandruff.*

willnots *n. Tagnuts, dangleberries.* Toffee entwined in the *kak canyon* undergrowth which simply "will not" come off. *Walnuts.*

will o' the nipse *n. A visible state of the art.* For example, one released whilst bending over in the shower in a cold house.

willydelphia *n.* Soft, spreadable *knob cheese.* Often to be found on your *crackers.*

willy mid-on *n.* Amusing cricketer's term for a *semi,* such as like what might make it uncomfortably cramped in one's box. *'I say Aggers, the batsman's Holding the umpire's Dickie. If I'm not much mistaken he's getting a willy mid-on.'*

Wilmslow panzer *n.* A large 4-wheel-drive vehicle which is designed to operate in the harshest of terrain and to protect its occupants from the most inclement conditions, but which only ever gets used to drive the hundred yards from a 4-bedroom house on a Balfour-Beatty estate to a Montessori fucking primary school. The north-west equivalent of a *Chelsea tractor.*

Wilton to Stilton, prefer *v.* To be a woman suffering from *lesbicious* tendencies; specifically to be keener on *munching carpet* than chomping down on a savoury mouthful of *blue-veined cheese. 'Sorry pal, you're wasting your time. I prefer Wilton to Stilton.' 'Never mind. I'll just sit over here and watch instead, then.'*

Wimbornes *rhym. slang.* Haemorrhoids. From the Dorset village of Wimborne St. Garsegrapes.

wimp wiper *n.* In an office or workplace environment, one who takes his/her own toilet tissue in rather than use the rough industrial type.

wind break *1. n.* Series of wooden poles held together with striped canvas which is arranged to prevent gentle winds, gusty sea breezes, horizontal Arctic sleet and what-have-you spoiling the enjoyment of beach-bound British holidaymakers. *2. n.* Intermission during a business meeting or similar which allows the attendees to leave the room in order to *drop their guts,* having politely refrained from doing so thus far. *'Well, ladies and gentlemen, I think we'll adjourn there for a fifteen minute wind break. When we re-convene, Mr Burrell will begin his evidence.'*

windchimes *n.* Gravitationally-challenged breasts which sway gently in the morning breeze, occasionally clanging together in a restful and melodic manner.

wind farm *n. milit.* A barracks full of vigorously *farting* squaddies.

wind in the pillows 1. *n.* Unlikely-sounding bedtime practice, involving a squatting gentleman and his very accommodating prostrate ladyfriend. 2. *n.* A laterally-diffused *Dutch oven.*

wind jammer *n.* A *style-conscious* man.

wind off the top of the iceberg *n.* A chilling *blast* that marks the impending arrival of something far bigger, more serious, and capable of ripping its way through your hull without any warning.

window cleaner's pocket *n.* A large, sad, damp, dishevelled *fadge.*

window of opportunity *n.* The short period of time after someone has admitted *dropping a gut,* during which it is safe for others to do likewise, safe in the knowledge that the earlier confessor will take the rap.

window of plopportunity *n.* That brief period of time in the digestive process when a *turd* comes out just lovely.

window shopping *v.* Of a lady, to go out on the town and give blokes the impression that she is interested when she actually has no intention of opening her *purse.*

wind sketch *n.* The masterpiece that's left in the *apple catchers* when a fine *fartist* inadvertently *follows through.* *'Lot 356. Scotch Jim (fl. 1990-2006). A fine wind sketch on purple Y-fronts gusset by this much sought-after morbidly-overweight office furniture delivery man. This particular work was created whilst single-handedly manoeuvring a loaded filing cabinet up a narrow Middlesbrough fire escape on a very hot day. A fine sepia image which exhibits mild vignetting,* *approx. 65mm x 72mm. Est. £3500-£4000.'*

windsock *n.* A particularly low-hanging *fiveskin.* An *anteater's nose, lace curtains.*

wind that shakes the barley 1. *n.* Title of a controversial Ken Loach film depicting the history of the English Black & Tans in Ireland in the early part of the century, and the formation of the IRA. 2. *n.* An *air biscuit* so strong that it blows all one's *arse cress* in the same direction, creating the appearance of a dark Irish wheat field in one's *cleft.*

windy pops *n. Bunny-shooting bullets, chuffs, anal announcements.*

wind your watch *euph.* To commit a disgusting act of *self delight* upon one's generative member. From the similarity of a *relaxing gentleman's* hand movements to the characteristic rapid wrist flicks and rotations which must be performed in order to prime the mainspring of an automatic timepiece. *'What were you doing in there?' 'I was just winding my watch, love.' 'But your watch is at the mender.' 'I know. I meant having a wank.'* (*Bamforth's Seaside Chuckles* postcard, by Donald McGill, 1933).

wine flu *n. medic.* Virulent disease which leaves its victim suffering from a headache, stomach upset, fever, night sweats, vomiting, diarrhoea, dizzyness and a bright red nose.

wingspan *n.* A measure of manual spreadability in *meat mag* models posing for *spam butterfly* shots. *'Have you seen Irene from Walsall in Readers' Wives? What a fugly cow.' 'Yeah, but she's quite a peeler. Just look at the wingspan she's achieved.'*

winking *n.* When preparing to *hack off a*

lump, the uncomfortable feeling of the *anus* twitching whilst still undoing the belt. The *point of no return.*

winking the Jap's eye *n.* An emergency cutting-short of an act of micturition. Curtailing a *slash.*

winking walnut *n. Brown eye, chocolate starfish.*

winkle picking *1. v. medic.* Anal sex with one afflicted with piles. *2. v.* Ancient seafarer's practice acheived using special pointed shoes.

winky *1. n.* A tiny *cock. 2. adj.* Having a tendency to wink a lot.

winkybag *1. n.* A tiny scrotum. *2. n.* An ugly old woman with a tendency to wink a lot.

winky wanky *n.* Whilst watching *The Weakest Link*, timing an act of masturbation to perfection such that you are able to pretend to have *shot your bolt* in Anne Robinson's eye. For whatever reason.

winner *n.* Unit in which *spunk* is traditionally measured in the catering industry. *'Boil 1 small tablespoon of sago in very little water till clear. Dissolve a teaspoonful of meat or vegetable extract in a cup of boiling water. Strain the cooked sago into the made broth. Season to taste, and lastly, if a red-faced cunt is coming to dine, stir in a winner of gentleman's spendings.'* (from *Household Management* by Mrs Beeton).

winner corner *n.* Secluded quarter of a restaurant kitchen, where staff members may retire in order to discreetly prepare *perseverance soup* for their less popular customers.

winnered *adj. Wanked dry.* Term used to describe the *clockweights* of kitchen staff following a sudden rush on *chef's special sauce.*

Winner's sauce *n.* That which, in the catering industry, is added to the recipe wherever the *Sunday Times* food critic eats. *Spunk.*

Winner takes all *1. n.* Erstwhile TV quiz programme featuring scouser comic Jimmy Tarbuck. *2. n.* Game played in restaurant kitchens whereby everyone (including head chefs, sous-chefs, waiters, bar staff and the other customers) perform acts of onanistic *self-delight* into a red-faced columnist's soup.

Winner widow *n.* The disgruntled wife of a cordon bleu chef whose sexual energies have been entirely redirected into the production of *special sauce* for the consumption of the popular film director and fat *cunt.*

winnet *n. Kling on, dag, dangleberry, willnot, brown room hanger on.* Also *winnit.*

winnet picker *n.* Someone of arguably lower social standing than a *jizz mopper. 'I only got three A's and a B at A-Level, so I'm working as a winnet picker.'*

winnie *n.* A lesbian, she who licks the *honey pot.*

winnit *n.* See *winnet.*

winosaur *n.* A lady of advanced years who enjoys a drink or two.

Winslet twins *n.* A nice proper pair of buoyant breasts as sported by *Titanic* actress Kate.

wintercourse *n.* Frosty sex, the kind had with a lady who doesn't approve of that kind of carry on. One would imagine Margot and Jerry out of *The Good Life* and the Queen and Prince Philip engage in *wintercourse. Grumpy pumpy.*

win the chocolate lottery *v.* To receive a particularly large *milkman's bonus.*

win the speedboat *v.* Having already secured a dead-cert *bang* whilst out *on the pull,* to go for - and miraculously get the go-ahead from - a much better option. From the closing round on TV quiz-show *Bullseye,* where the contestants could gamble their safe sixty-pounds winnings on scoring a hundred-and-one with six darts or fewer and thus win a mystery prize, which was invariably revealed as a speedboat full of fat-titted, bikini-clad blonde *birds* when they lost. Or a trailer tent if they won.

wipe your feet *v.* To vigorously *beskid* a lavatory *pan.* "*I is the only nice and jumbly giant in Giant Country! I is the Big Friendly Giant!' 'I don't care who you are,' replied Sophie. 'I'm not using that crapper. It looks like you've wiped your feet in there, you mucky old cunt.*" (from *The BFFG* by Roald Dahl).

wiping the hard drive *euph.* In the interests of prolonging an impending bout of *carnival pleasure,* the process of *clearing the pipes* in order to *take the edge off* one's ardour. Restoring one's *mammary banks* to their factory settings.

wire spiders *n.* The hairs around the *chocolate starfish* that come to life when you are in a meeting or in the checkout queue at Asda. *Arse wasps.*

Wirral peninsula 1. *n.* The area of land which falls between Chester and Liverpool. 2. *n.* Them bits of skin that separate *cunts* and *arseholes.* The *taint, notcher, carse, snarse, biffin bridge, Humber Bridge, tinter etc.*

witch doctor's necklace, mouth like a *sim.* A description of a particularly unimpressive set of pearly whites. See also *teeth like a crossword, English teeth, mouth full of sugarpuffs, Queen Mum's teeth* and *pan of burnt chips.*

witch doctor's rattle *n.* Descriptive of a woman with a *nice personality.* A *monk's pin-up.*

witch's cave *n.* A *wizard's sleeve, clown's pocket, wall of death.* An enormous *fadge.* '*Soldier, soldier, would you marry me / For you are so strong and brave / Oh no, sweet maid, I cannot marry you / 'Cos your twat's like a witch's cave*' (Traditional folk song).

witch's lips *n.* The cold kiss of a porcelain toilet bowl on one's *bell end* occasionally felt whilst *dropping off the shopping.*

witch's tit, flat as a *sim.* In the retail world, a reference to a period of slow sales. '*How's the C5 doing, Sir Clive?' 'Terrible. Business has been flast as a witch's tit for - ooh, let me see now - the last twenty-two years.*'

witch's trick *n.* The phenomenon of a *back beauty, backstabber* or *golden deceiver* who appears stunning from behind, only to reveal herself as looking like Grotbags off *Emu's World* from the front.

witch wagon *n.* Elongated white, left-hand-drive vehicle designed to shunt drunk harpies of limited vocal and cerebral capacity to and from, to pick a destination at random, The Black Sheep, Croydon CR0 1NA on a Saturday night. A stretch limo. '*Will you be having pissed up sex in the back of the witch wagon? Only we charge an extra fiver for the hire of a special sheet to keep spunk and vomit off the velour seats.*'

withdrawal symptoms *n.* *Spangle* on the stomach, *iced buns, iPod earphones, jelly jewellery* and other assorted evidence of *aerial jackrobatics.*

with one's cock out, do something *v.* To perform a task or action badly. '*My right* *honorable friend would have us believe that he can increase government spending in the health service whilst at the same time delivering tax cuts across the board. Well I'm afraid he must have written this budget with his cock out, because I can tell him that the figures simply do not add up.'*

witten *n*. See *winnet*.

Wittgenstein, do a *v*. Yet another classical piano-based term for a specific act of *self pollution*. To perform a few *five finger exercises* with the left hand on one's short, pink *upright*, possibly in front of a large audience in the Royal Albert Hall. Named after the unidextrous Austrian concert pianist Paul Wittgenstein (1887-1961), who lost his right arm in WWI, but nevertheless continued his musical career using his remaining limb to play a number of specially-commissioned works. And it always felt like someone else was doing it.

wizard's sleeve *n*. A *witch's cave*. A particularly capacious *sausage wallet*. *'I can't feel a bloody thing, Mother Teresa. You must have a fanny like a wizard's sleeve.'*

wizards' hats *n*. *Dunces' hats, motorway cones.*

WKR *abbrev.* Any male caught drinking WKD after the age of fourteen.

WLD *abbrev.* Weapon of Lass Destruction. An *ICBM* that would not leave a woman standing, a *cuntbuster*.

WOAT/woat *acronym.* A light-hearted term for a woman at a football, rugby or cricket match. Waste Of A Ticket.

wobbly boots *adj.* Uncontrollable alcoholic footwear. *Seven pint boots* worn when you've got *legs like snapped candles*.

wobbly landing *n*. Trying, when drunk, to manoeuvre your under-inflated *zipper Zeppelin* safely through your wife's *hangar doors.*

Wogan *n*. An impressively large *gut stick*, possibly *half a teacake*, poorly disguised by tight-fitting trousers, which causes middle-aged ladies to gasp. From Sir Terry's notoriously semi-priapismic *Points of View* appearance on October 14th 2007.

wolfbagging *v*. To have sex with a wolf inside a large bag.

wolf bait *n*. An unusually meaty, pungent *fart*, similar to the smell encountered when opening a tin of Butcher's Tripe Mix. A *fyst*.

wolf bite *n*. A really painful *arsehole*, eg. After a curry. *'Would you care to ride with us to Wenlock Edge, Captain Tremaine?' she asked. The Captain winced. 'I regret I must decline your kind offer, Mrs Dugdale,' he replied. 'I lately partook of a monstrous vindaloo with the Lord of Harpole, and I still have a wolf bite upon my postillion.'* (from *Middlemarch*, by George Eliot).

wolf pussy *n*. A nasty, exceptionally hairy *growler* that looks like it could inflict serious damage if provoked. *'Girl, you ain't coming no muthafucking way near me with that goddam muthafucking wolf pussy of yours and mess up my muthafucking dick, bitch. Shiiit.'* (Eddie Murphy in *Nutty Professor II The Klumps*).

woman in comfortable shoes *n*. A *tennis fan*, a *lady golfer*. A *bird* who is *fond of walking holidays*.

women's things *n. medic. Flangina.*

wombies *n. Tits*, breasts, *baps*.

womb service *n*. What a randy woman may request of her *fuck buddy* at 1am when she is alone and feeling a tad *peckerish*.

womb strudel *n*. An un-savoury *strawberry* dessert baked once a month in a *hairy pie-dish*.

womfer *n*. The female equivalent of a *barse*. *Chinrest* used to avoid cramp at a *hairy pie* tasting.

womit *n*. Dribbly sick.

wonderwank *n*. An act of *self abuse* carried out without the use of visual stimulation. Named after the pop singer Stevie Wonder.

Wonder woman *n*. A lady with a *lovely personality*. A *boot* that only a blind man could fancy.

wongle *v*. To rive one's *passion cosh* up and down one's wife's *arse* in an attempt to wake her up for a *poke*.

wonk 1. *n*. A political researcher. Usually a young man with glasses and a *wanker's tan*. 2. *n*. A desperate and ultimately unsatisfying act of *self help* with multiple interruptions. *'Bless me Father for I have sinned.' 'Do you mind coming back in about ten minutes, my son? I'm half way through a wonk in here.'*

woo *n*. A *wee* that unexpectedly and unilaterally makes the decision that a *poo* has to follow it. From, not surprisingly, wee + poo.

wood *n*. Erectification of the peniculastical appendulation.

woodburner *n*. An enthusiastic *masturbatrix* who gives it *six nowt* whilst *playing fives* on a fellow's *walking stick* to such an extent as to cause a certain amount of charring to his *wood*. A woman who goes at it *like Ray Mears starting a fire*.

woodpecker *n*. A woman who performs rapid, hands-free *horatio*. From the movement of the *bird's* head as she hammers your *trunk*.

woodpecker, the *n*. The bizarre act of a woman *bobbing* her husband up the *cigar cutter* with a *dildo* that is strapped to her forehead. An impractical-sounding heterosexual variation on the fabled *screwnicorn*, which involves similar equipment, only used by a couple of *lezzers*.

woodsman *n*. In the *Frankie Vaughan* industry, an actor who almost certainly will not be able to act, but who can be relied upon to get venous blood to flow into his *corpora cavernosa* just before the director shouts "Action".

woodwind *n*. Open air *tuggery-pokery* of the *pink oboe*.

woody *n*. What a young American surfer dude takes to the beach.

woodwrecker *n*. An inopportune thought that comes unbidden into a fellow's mind at a vital moment whilst entertaining a young lady, causing a catastrophic *felling of timber*, eg. A train accident, a full nappy, the missus's face *etc*.

wookie hole 1. *n*. Uninspiring tourist attraction consisting of a hole in the ground and a gift shop. 2. *n*. A particularly hairy *Mary Hinge*. A *biffer*, a *Judith*.

wool *n*. coll. US. Fluff, blart, fanny, totty.

woolly bird *n*. Aus. A sheep.

woolly wardrobe *n*. A bulky, cavernous receptacle in the bedroom where gentlemen stuff their *roll neck sweaters*.

Woolworths *n*. A plain *bird* that will not impress your mates, but who will do absolutely anything you can think of, though not to a particularly high standard.

work a split shift *v*. Of a lovable, lucky,

cheeky chappie, to have two *ladyfriends* on the go at the same time.

working from home *euph.* Spending the day *relaxing in a gentleman's way*. *Jerking from home*.

working in the Tamworth gang *euph.* Descriptive of a homosexual. From a legendary troupe of railway track labourers whose camaraderie reputedly progressed beyond banter and cups of tea.

working on a dream *1. n.* Title of a chart-topping album by Bruce Springsteen and the E-Street Band. *2. n.* A ferocious early-morning *hand shandy*, essayed whilst desperately trying to recapture the essential details of what was going on in one's reverie just moments earlier.

working on my guns *euph.* Indulging in a gruelling, epic bout of *self improvement*, which will leave the arms aching.

world cup Willy *n.* Regular sexual intercourse with the missus, *ie.* Once every four years.

world of leather *n.* The *parts* of an aged lady. *Granny's oysters, grandma's Wolseley*.

wormhole *1. n.* A *cludge* into which a lucky gent could only fit the slenderest of *custard cannons*. A *mouse's ear* or *paper cut*. *Bugner's eye*. *2. n.* An inexplicable highway-based space/time phenomenon, whereby a taxi driver takes a sharp turn-off from a supposedly straightforward route, and takes a short cut which inevitably ends up trebling the distance travelled and hence the fare.

worm's belt, tighter than a *sim.* Descriptive of a particularly unaccommodating *snatch*, a *butler's cuff, mouse's ear, mole's eye*. 'DUCHESS OF BERWICK: *My dear Lord Plymdale. I really do not understand why you associate with Mrs Erlynne. She is such a tiresome conversationalist. LORD PLYMDALE: Conversation is, I find, a somewhat over-rated virtue, your ladyship. Besides which, Mrs Erlynne kindly vouchsafed me tops and fingers in Lord Darlington's gazebo last night and believe you me, her twat's tighter than a worm's belt.'* (from *Lady Windermere's Fanny* by Oscar Wilde).

worth an empty *adj.* *W Yorks.* An expression of heartfelt appreciation for the charms of a young lady which is apparently common parlance in Bradford.

worth a squirt *adj.* Sexually desirable. *Prodworthy*.

worzel gusset *n.* The *fairy hammock* of a girl with a *minge like a rook's nest*, with all bits of straw and twigs sticking out the sides and probably a robin or a cuckoo living in it.

WOT *acronym.* An aesthetically-challenged person who nevertheless sports a fine pair of *eye magnets* on their chest, for example Liz MacDonald off *Coronation Street* or Kerry Catona off the Iceland adverts. *Waste Of Tits*.

wounded soldier's walk *n.* The trip a gentleman makes to the bathroom after completing a messy act of *relaxation* when he has nothing to hand with which to clean up the resultant mess. From the fact that cupping a few teaspoonsful of rapidly-cooling *spuffer* to his belly causes him to assume a hunched posture which is very reminiscent of a shot infantryman clutching his injured stomach as he hobbles off the battlefield.

wozny *n.* *Scots/Ir.* A *bird's* perineum or taint, from the fact that "if it wozny there, you'd be in the shit". The *tinter, carse, Humber bridge, Niftkin's bridge,* *tisnae, snarse etc.*

WRAC *1. abbrev. milit.* The Women's Royal Army Corps. *2. abbrev. milit.* Coarse squaddies' argot for Weekly Ration of Army Cunt. *'Good news lads. The WRAC's arrived. Bagsy fog up.'* (General Bernard Montgomery addressing his troops on the eve of the battle of El Alamein, North Africa, October 29th 1942).

wrestling Sergeant Brown *euph.* Struggling to force out a particularly recalcitrant *pop.* From the film *Bear Man*, in which the protagonist describes a fight between two bears thusly: "Crikey, what a horrible mess. It looks like someone's been wrestling Sergeant Brown."

wring the rattlesnake *v. Siphon the python.* To *piss, strain the greens.*

wrinkled penny *n. US.* The *ringpiece, balloon knot, tea towel holder, nipsy.*

wrist flick *n.* A *grumble vid*, a *stick film.*

wristicuffs *n.* A bout of *knocking oneself about a bit. Boxing the Jesuit.*

writer's cock *n.* The excuse used by authors caught looking at illegal *grumble* whilst *researching a book. Writer's cock* can be so bad that some of the books being researched take many years to be completed, if they ever appear at all.

write the letter 'M' *v.* To inscribe the thirteenth letter of the alphabet in *arse* sweat on the toilet seat whilst having a *Queensway.*

wrongbow *n.* White cider. A tangy, refreshing apple-based alternative to *trampagne, supermarket smack* or metal polish.

wrong 'un *n.* The *coal hole.* To quote Roy Walker, "it's good, but it's not right."

wuilty *adj.* Descriptive of the sense of shame a fellow experiences when he inadvertently bumps into a lady over the thought of whom he has *knocked himself about a bit* earlier that very day. *'Did you catch Jonathan Ross interviewing that stripper who's married to Marilyn Manson the other night? He didn't half have a wuilty expression on his face.'*

wu-wu *1. n.* Childish name for a *fufu* or *toot-toot. 2. n.* The noise a train makes.

wuffle dust *1. n.* Magical compound utilised by erstwhile aphasic bear Sooty and his handler, who spoke not unlike Norris off *Coronation Street. 2. n.* The somewhat less-than-magical faecal matter that, in terms of collateral damage, falls somewhere between a crisp, clean *treacle* and a catastrophic *shart.* A junior *follow through.*

wuffle nuts *n.* The fruits of the *dangleberry* tree.

Wurzel *1. n. prop.* A member of the English rock supergroup of the 1970s. *2. n.* An embarrassingly small penis. An *acorn*, a *Jack Straw.*

wurzel quimmage *n.* A dense, unkempt and rain-forest-like *hairport* of *gorilla salad.* A *crow's nest.* Named after the badly-stuffed scarecrow character played by Dr Who, who had a series of novelty hits about tractors and cider in the 1970s.

WYSINWYG/wysinwyg *1. acronym.* What You See Is Not What You Get. Computer-talk for flirting on the internet with a pert bit of blonde, A-level *fluff* who turns out to be a 58-year-old *sex case* panel beater masturbating in his mum's spare room. *2. n.* Welsh for helicopter.

X-flow, rough as a cold *sim.* A mechanic's term when referring to an aesthetically unconventional female. Named after Ford's notoriously noisy pushrod engine of the 1970s. *'No, but seriously though, fuck me, she's as rough as a cold X-flow.'* (Dr Rowan Williams, the Archbishop of Canterbury, addressing the reception following the wedding of His Royal Highness the Prince of Wales and Camilla Parker-Bowels, in the cafe of the Wacky Warehouse, Bracknell on 9th April 2005).

X-piles *n.* Mysterious, unidentified throbbing objects from *Uranus*. That's pronounced "your anus", by the way.

X-ray specs *n.* Cheap, cardboard spectacles, available only by mail order from the back of pubescent boys' comics, which enable the wearer to see through women's clothing. A more expensive version, which is available from the back of the *Lancet*, is used to diagnose fractures in hospital Accident & Emergency departments.

XX *adj.* Special video certificate awarded to pornographic films of poor sound and picture quality.

XXX *adj.* Special video certificate awarded to pornographic films of exceptionally poor sound and picture quality.

xylophone *1. n.* Like a piano, but you twat it with little sticks. *2. v.* To move along a line of naked women who are all bending down, and spank their bottoms - which are of varying sizes - with one's penis. To play a tune on women's buttocks. From the Greek xylo = wood & phonnicus = to be hit tunefully by a fat astronomer at a Royal Variety Performance.

yabba dabbas *n*. In stone age cartoon intercourse, the climactic stages of coitus which immediately precede the *doooooooos*. The *vinegar strokes*.

yachting *n*. The stirring sight of a dog in full sail, tacking its way across the living room carpet, attempting to remove the *barnacles* from its *keel*.

yaffle the yoghurt cannon *v*. To *nosh* voraciously.

yak *1*. *n*. Big hairy animal of untidy appearance. *2*. *n*. A big hairy *eskimo's glove* of untidy appearance. A feminist's *beaver*, a *minge* with a *pant moustache*.

yambag *n*. The wrinkled retainer in which the *gourds* are kept.

yang *n*. US. A *wang*.

yank *1*. *n*. An inhabitant of the northern states of America. *2*. *n*. A "one-man-band"-type device with which an American sex case attaches his penis to his ankle in order to *pull himself off* whilst walking about.

yank fuel *n*. Onanistic *fodder*. Frankie Vaughan. *'Mam, where did you put me yank fuel when you tidied me bedroom?'*

yank off *v*. To *relax* vigorously *in a gentleman's way*.

yank the plank *v*. To *tug* one's *wood*, whilst running the risk of getting a hand full of splinters.

yarbles *n*. Testicles. *'He's lost his yarbles.'*

yard *1*. *n*. *arch*. Olde Worlde Penis. *2*. *n*. Confusingly, the *ladygarden* too.

yardbrush *n*. A bristly *fanny* one could sweep out the garage with.

yard high club *n*. The exclusive group of sexual adventurers who have made love in the lavatory of a static caravan.

yard on *n*. An extra large *hard on* achieved when particularly aroused, although probably still smaller than 3 feet. A *faint on*.

Yaris fanny *euph*. A lady's *bodily treasure* which is, like the eponymous Toyota vehicle, "bigsmall". Something you think is going to be like a *mouse's ear* which ends up being like the Albert Hall. A *twat* where you can fold down the seats and get your week's shopping, an Old English Sheepdog and four sets of skis in.

Yarmouth clam *n*. Similar to a *Viennese oyster*, only performed by a malodorous woman from the Norfolk seaside town.

Yasser *abbrev*. US. Erection. From "Yasser Crack-a-fat". A lame and pointless pun on the name of the late tea-towel-titfered Palestinian Ringo Starr lookalike.

yawnography *n*. Dull, uninspiring *grumble* of the sort shown on the telly, where they don't let you *see it going in* or anything.

Y-bone steak *n*. Female opposite of a *tube steak*. The *beef curtains*.

Y-box *n*. Much more fun than an X-box, and only costs the price of a bunch of flowers from the 24-hour garage.

yearn *n*. A lengthy, wistful session on the *casserole pot*, awaiting the arrival of a *religious relic*. A bout of constipation. *'Derek's been a while in the gents.' 'Aye, he's having a yearn. His wife told me he's not been for a week.'*

yellow arrows display *n*. In a busy male public lavatory with a bank of urinals, the precisely co-ordinated positional exchange of *slashers*. As the first phalanx of blokes finish their *wees* and move out of the way, waiting men move smoothly into their vacated spaces with all the practised elegance of a Red Arrows air display.

yellow-fronted brown-backs *n*. *Nether garments* which are in need of a good wash. *'Eeh, we had a smashing night at the Arena. Tom Jones come on for his encore and did Delilah, and your nan got so excited she threw her yellow-fronted brown-backs up on the stage.'*

yellow party *n*. A specialist German club night at which, instead of dancing, the participants *piss* on each other around their handbags.

yellowstone *n*. The morning-after effect of a powerful *Ruby Murray* on one's digestive system. Named after the famous American National Park tourist attraction where, every so often, a brimstone-smelling gush of scalding liquid shoots out uncontrollably from a muddy, bubbling hole.

yellow toilet brush *euph*. The use of a skilfully-controlled stream of high-pressure *wazz* to clean the *Bisto skids* off the sides of the *gravy bowl*.

yes you did - you invaded Poland *exclam*. Another bit of post-flatulatorial drollery. See also *that would be lovely - milk and two sugars please* and *you'll need to give her a little more throttle sir*.

yeti's welly *n*. A voluminous *fadge*, a *donkey's yawn, a hippo's mouth*.

yinyang 1. *n*. *US*. Arse, bum. 2. *n*. *US*. *Fuckwit, jerkwad, asswipe, dicksplash*.

yitney *n*. One who is *yitten*.

yitten *adj*. Scared of something very tame, *eg*. David Milliband when he went into that school hall in Israel or somewhere and the PA system crackled and he *shat* himself.

yobble *v*. To *shit* somewhere other than a toilet, usually for the amusement of oth-

ers. *eg*. Onto a cow from a tree.

Yoda's ears *n*. *Piss flaps* which conjure up the image of the erstwhile wisdom-filled mystical *Star Wars* Jedi Master, who spoke with the same voice as Fozzie Bear off *The Muppets*.

yodel *v*. To vomit, to *sing a rainbow*.

yodel in the canyon/valley *v*. To *growl* at a very *capacious badger* whilst wearing a small hat with a shaving brush stuck in it.

yoffy's finger *euph*. *Touching cloth*. From the 1970s children's show *Fingerbobs*. "Yoffy lifts a finger / and a mouse is there / puts his hands together / and a seagull takes the air / Yoffy lifts a finger / And a scampi darts about / Yoffy bends another / and a tortoise head peeps out".

yoinkahs *n*. A pair of *twin peaks* that cause a volcanic eruption in your *under-krakatoas*.

Yoko *n*. A *bird* who accompanies her boyfriend everywhere, *eg*. Down the pub with mates, fishing, recording sessions for the *Let It Be* album, the *fucking* lot.

yongles *n*. *US*. *Clockweights*, testicles.

yoni *n*. Ancient Hindu female genitals, *twat*.

yonks! *exclam*. Popular speech balloon reaction to finding a tenner on a cartoon pavement.

yoo poos, you lose *exclam*. A mordant aphorism uttered to one returning from a lengthy trip to the *khazi*, only to find that the final glass of wine or share of spliff has been consumed in their absence.

york *onomat*. To vomit, *call Huey*.

Yorkie bar *n*. A *puddle jumper, botter* or *gaylord*. From the popular chocolate confection advertising slogan. "It's not for girls".

Yorkshire caviar *n.* A refined delicacy enjoyed by sophisticated gourmands from the world's finest tri-ridingous county. Mushy peas. See also *Geordie hummus.*

Yorkshire flamingo *n.* A tired-looking, malnourished, pink-faced *bird* who, due to the sorry state of her shabby surroundings (*eg.* The Frontier Club, Batley), appears exotic and alluring to the untrained eye.

you can't piss in the sink when it's full of teabags *phr. Yorks.* Confucious-like profound aphorism much used by denizens of the South Riding Shangri-La of Barnsley. '*Well, Geoffrey, he's pitched the ball up well wide of off-stump, and the batsman's nicked it to short leg.*' '*Aye. That was woeful batting, that, especially on a turning wicket. But England need three hundred and six off the next four balls and, as we say in Fitzwilliam, you can't piss in the sink when it's full of teabags.*'

you could shove him/her in a flute and still hear the tune *phr.* Phrase which could be used to describe Peter Crouch, Amy Winehouse or any other ludicrously skinny person. '*Radcliffe on the starting line there, waiting for the signal to go. And there's not an ounce of excess flesh on her, is there Brendan.*' '*That's right, Steve. You could shove her in a flute and still hear the tune.*'

you'll have to buy that now, you've ripped it *exclam.* Humorous phrase which can be used to great effect after someone has *let rip* in a particularly rip-roaring manner. See *you're only supposed to blow the bloody doors off.*

you'll need to give her a little more throttle sir *exclam.* See also *that would be lovely - milk and two sugars please* and *yes you did - you invaded Poland.*

you milk? *interrog.* A phrase used by far-eastern prostitutes to ascertain whether or not their client has *dropped his yop.*

you still have two wishes left! *exclam. hum.* Amusing phrase which can be used to lighten a ladyfriend's rancorous mien after you have used your *magic wand* to cover her face with *jizz*, for example.

You're only supposed to blow the bloody doors off *exclam.* Post-flatus repartee. See *you should put that on Ebay.*

you should put that on Ebay *exclam.* Something to say after somebody *drops a gut.* Also *if that's not out I'm not playing; can I quote you on that?; fall out the officers; thanks for that, now can you please throw something?; is that Ziggy?; a bit more choke and she would have started; a confident appeal by the Australians there; an excellent theory, Dr Watson; anybody injured?; don't tear it, I'll take the whole piece; how much?; keep shouting sir, we'll find you; more tea vicar?; someone let him in; someone's tinkered with Herbie; speak on, sweet lips that never told a lie; speak up caller, you're through; taxi for Brown; that's working, now try your lights; well struck sir!; what's that, Sweep?; you'll have to buy that now, you've ripped it; sew a button on that; catch that one and paint it blue; good health!; pin a tail on that; there goes the elephant; my, that duck's got bad breath* and many, many more.

yo-yo knickers *n.* A *bike*, loose woman; she whose knickers are up and down faster than Richard Branson's hot air balloons.

yule log *n*. The smoking centrepiece of festivities on December 26th. A monster *feeshus* with all the trimmings. And a robin sat on top of it.

yule tide *n*. The alarming, rising water level in a *crapper* that is occluded with a *Boxing Day log*.

yummy mummy *1. n*. A middle-aged woman worthy of a good *seeing to*, eg. Helen Mirren. *2. n*. A young mother with a fantastic *arse* pushing a buggy. *3. n*. On a cannibal menu, either a delicious, well-cooked mother, or jerky made from an Egyptian pharaoh.

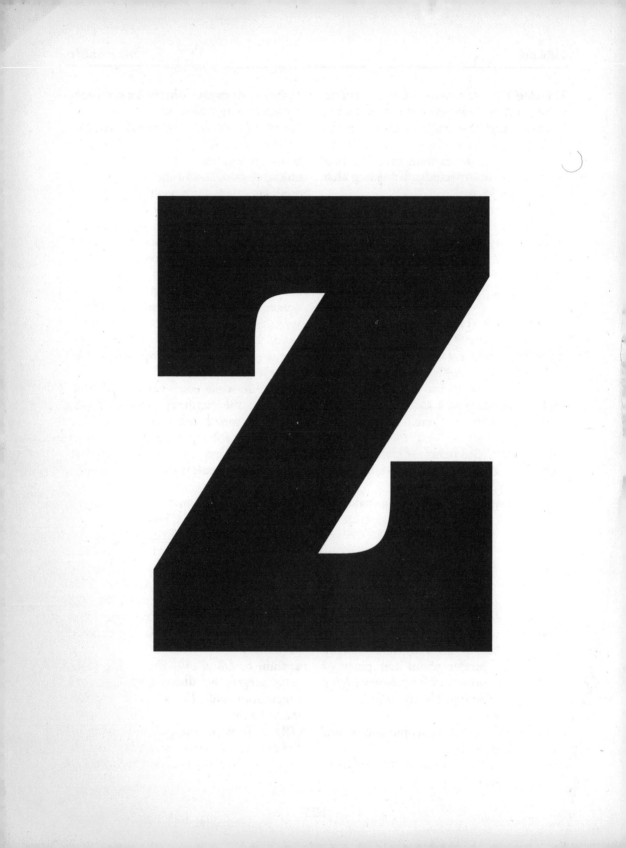

Zebedee 1. n. At school, a face, complete with "Julius Pringles"-type moustache, drawn onto the glans with a biro in order to amuse one's classmates or pupils. 2. n. A tea-time erection that springs up unexpectedly, signalling that it is "time for bed".

zeps abbrev. Zeppelins. Large, hydrogen-filled, flammable meat balloons. Hindenburgs, blimplants. See also dead heat in a Zeppelin race.

zerotica n. Wanking material of the lowest imaginable potency, eg. A thermal underwear catalogue, a picture of a nuns' hockey team, a stamp or the letters page in the People's Friend.

zig-a-zig ahhhh! onomat. arch. To have a bloody good one off the wrist whilst watching a Spice Girls video.

zilch n. Fuck all, jack shit.

Zinzanbrook rhym. slang. NZ. Short for fuck.

zipper fish n. The penis, or trouser trout.

zipper sniffer n. A keen penis enthusiast of either gender.

zipper Zeppelin n. Shiny, cigar-shaped craft which occasionally explodes at its moorings. 'Watch it! Watch it! Oh get out of the way of my zipper Zeppelin! Too late! Oh, the humanity! Oh, the humanity! Let me get you a tissue, your Majesty.'

zip snip n. An unintentional circumcision and/or vasectomy operation performed using the flies of one's trousers. Usually carried out under about ten pints of general anaesthetic. 'Don't worry about that, love. I've had the zip snip.'

zit n. A pluke.

Z-list n. Mental list of people you would like to sleep with.

Zoes n. Balls, clockweights, gonads, testicles. From the Strictly Dance Fever presenter Zoe Bollocks.

zonked adj. Pissed, wankered, wazzed. Trousered.

zoob n. Penis.

zook n. A prostitute, a ho'.

zookkake n. A quite possibly made up sexual practice whereby ten Japanese men wearing noh masks take turns to wank onto an otter's face. It's a good job Johnny Morris never lived to see this.

zorba 1. rhym. slang. To have a Chinese singing lesson. From Zorba the Greek = leak. 2. v. To have sex in the Grecian style. 'Oscar Fingal O'Flahertie Wilde, you are charged with zorba-ing a load of jockeys.'

Zorro v. To wield one's tumescent manhood as the fictional masked bandit would his rapier, and with a skilful flick of the wrist lob ropes benevolently over a lucky slattern in a zig-zag fashion. 'Please don't spaff over my face, Harry. We're meeting your nan in twenty minutes.' 'Fine, pop your tits out and I'll Zorro them instead, Chelsy.'

Zorro mask n. A Saturday morning disguise worn by the wife of a big drinker. Nature's make-up.

zounds n. arch. God's wounds. 17th century swear word banned by Act of Parliament in 1651, but okay now if used in moderation. Also g*dzooks, fuckanory.

zucchini n. US. Cock. Something stuck into burgers by disgruntled fast food preparation staff. Dill, the man mayonnaise bottle.

zuffle v. To wipe one's charlie clean on the curtains after having a bang, usually in a posh bird's house, ie. One that has curtains. *To fly the flag.*

zuffle bag *n.* A dirty woman whose soft furnishings show evidence of substantial previous *zuffling.*

zuffle coat *n.* The topmost item of clothing in the pile on a bed at a party. Used by a male guest to clean the *sloom* off his *three card trick* after a furtive *poke.*

zylophone *n.* Incorrect spelling of *xylophone.*

ZZ bottom *n.* An exceptionally long-haired *muff,* from the resemblance to the unsightly, unkempt beards sported by members of the Texan blues rock band ZZ Top. But not the drummer.

ZZ tops and fingers *n.* The act of *firkyfoodling* one's missus whilst she's asleep.

ZZZ tops and fingers *n.* The act of *firkyfoodling* one's missus whilst she's in a coma.

ACKNOWLEDGMENTS

Sir Roger Mellie OBE would like to thank the following people, without whom this book would not have been possible: Caroline Addy, Russell Blackman, Alex Collier, Chris Donald, Simon Donald, the proprietors of The Framley Examiner, Richard Herring and all the Viz readers who have so selflessly sent in contributions.

Roger's Profanisaurus is updated every five weeks in *Viz* Comic.

Submit your own favourite obscenities to *profanisaurus@viz.co.uk*

www.viz.co.uk